Best Practices in School Psychology-II

Best Practices in School Psychology-II

Edited by

Alex Thomas
Port Clinton City Schools
Port Clinton, Ohio

Jeff Grimes
Iowa Department of Public Instruction
Des Moines, Iowa

The National Association of School Psychologists
Washington, DC

First Printing: 1990

Published by The National Association of School Psychologists
Washington, DC

ISBN 0-932955-11-8

Printed in the United States of America

Acknowledgments

Best Practices in School Psychology–II has been an ambitious undertaking and we acknowledge the valuable work of Lawrence Moran, Judy Fulwider, and Ellen Coppeler for their diligent copyediting, typesetting, and proofing. We are also grateful to Cathy Telzrow, Tom Fagan, and Sharon Petty for sheparding this three year project through the various phases requiring association support.

A particular note of appreciation is extended to Dennis Rectenwald (Superintendent of the Port Clinton City Schools) and to Frank Vance (Chief of Iowa Bureau of Special Education) for fostering a professional environment supportive of the editorial involvement necessary for this book's completion. As a district school psychologist (Alex Thomas) and as a state consultant (Jeff Grimes), we appreciate the professional environment that Dennis and Frank have fostered.

Our goal in this undertaking has been to provide a resource for practitioner school psychologists, particularly those who must daily address a variety of issues and whose professional practice would be enhanced by the availability of broad based information on a variety of professional topics.

We would like to thank the cadré of school psychologists who provided excellent suggestions in chapter reviews. They were:

E. M. Bard
Susan G. Barnes
Pamela Beeman-Rabut
Jo Kay Boyle
Rhonda Broadwater
Emily Brown-de Cabezudo
Andrea Canter
Sandra L. Carpenter
Robert J. Cattoche
John Correll
Beth Deemer
Stewart Ehly
Patricia A. Ellis
David Stephen Engelstad
Gary Etcheson
Dianne E. Friedman
Richard G. Games
Darla R. Griffin
Rachel Gundersen
George M. Harper
Virginia Smith Harvey
Craig Hoadley
Steven Iverson
Joe Jackson
Theresa Hubbell Jozwiak
Laural Kilpatrick
David J. Kisilewski
Rick Klawiter
Kay E. Konz
Bea Ager Koontz

Damon Lamb
Hans Langner
Naomi Lennox
Kathie Lodholz
Beverly MacMahon
Teresa McCarthy
Christopher McHugh
Kathleen McNamara
Jacqueline Morgan
Barbara Pildis
Dennis P. Pinciotti
Sheila M. Pottebaum
Gay Rosenthal
Marilynn L. Russ
Julie Schendel
M. Carol Sensor
Janet Werner Shelver
Frank Smith
Robert O. Smith
Gary Stanton
Charlene Talkington
Dennis Urso
Deborah D. Waddell
Israel Wahrman
Jacalyn Wright Weissenburger
Darleen Welsh
Linda Williamson
Bonnie Winslow
Dan Wright
Jean Yamada

We fervently hope that the material in this book will assist you in enhancing the school and life success of the children with whom you work.

Alex Thomas
Jeff Grimes

From NASP Publications Policy Handbook

The content of this document reflects the ideas and positions of the authors. The responsibility lies solely with the authors and does not necessarily reflect the position or ideas of the National Association of School Psychologists.

Contents

Appendices

1

Best Practices in the Academic Assessment of Secondary-Age Students

Kit Gerken
The University of Iowa

OVERVIEW

Many students in need of special services are not identified until they are adolescents and they have likely endured repeated and painful school failure by the time they reach junior high or high school. Many have repeated one or more grades, and the gap between their actual achievement and grade expectancy level seems to widen as they progress through high school.

The major need of the secondary-age student who is having academic problems is an improved assessment and intervention process. Sabatino, Goh, and Jenson (1982) stated that assessment, as well as other specialized services at the secondary level, represent a serious challenge to the profession of school psychology. In 1990, that challenge is still there. Neither the national reform movements that apply to education in general nor the current popular and controversial reform movements that are touted by special educators and school psychologists (regular education initiative [REI], curriculum-based assessment [CBA], curriculum-based measurement [CBM]) have dealt with implementation at the secondary level in a satisfactory way (Chalfant, 1989; Orlich, 1989; Shinn, Tindall, & Stein, 1988).

The regular education initiative recommends adapting the regular classroom to make it possible for handicapped students to learn in that environment. Schumaker and Deshler (1988) believe

there are three significant barriers to implementing REI strategies in the secondary schools: (a) the large gap between the skill level of students and the academic requirements in secondary classrooms; (b) the intensive instruction needed to ameliorate skill and strategy deficits; and (c) the structural limitations inherent in secondary schools. It is unlikely that REI can work at any level unless practitioners and consumers become more directly involved.

The same thing is true of CBA and CBM. CBA and CBM have received acknowledgment as appropriate alternative assessment methods. CBA is usually identified as an informal procedure used to determine the instructional needs of students from their performance within their own classroom materials (Gickling & Thompson, 1985), whereas CBM is a measurement system, considered to have its roots in the University of Minnesota Institute for Research of Learning Disabilities (Deno, 1985, 1986), that consists of very specific curriculum-based measures identified in the areas of reading, written expression, spelling, and math.

CBA and CBM are not new approaches to assessment and CBM in particular can be misused just as blatantly as the old approaches. Two chapters in this volume deal directly with CBA and CBM and contain specific information regarding appropriate uses. However, it must be pointed out here that the CBA and CBM movement contains few references to implementation at the secondary level and few attempts to include in the movement regular educators, specialists in the areas of reading, written expression, and mathematics, or the consumers.

Current initiatives have failed to provide the improved assessment and intervention process that is needed. The causes of academic failure must be considered and an early identification process must be put in place. Students experience academic failure because of (a) factors within the student such as overall ability, motivation, study skills, school attendance, and behavioral or social deficits; (b) factors within the instructional environment, such as the curriculum and teaching methods and materials; (c) factors within the interpersonal environment, such as interaction with family members, peers, and teachers; (d) factors within the student's physical environment, such as physical and health care, space; and (e) interactions among the above factors. However, the attempt to distinguish among the primary sources of school failure needs to be the second step in the assessment process. First we must identify the students at risk for school failure.

Hypothetical Case Study in Problem Identification at the Secondary Level

Sue was 16 years old and was referred for assessment during the summer after ninth grade. She had failed English during the last semester of ninth grade and received *D*s in two other subject areas during the ninth grade. Although she was of average intellectual ability, she had always struggled with academic tasks.

Sue had been referred to a school psychologist and a pediatrician when she was 8 years old and in the third grade. The pediatrician indicated that she had an attention deficit disorder and perhaps should be given Ritalin. The school psychologist administered the WISC-R (except for the Arithmetic and Object Assembly subtests), WRAT, Bender Gestalt, and Draw-A-Person. The psychological report consisted of one short narrative paragraph and a listing of scores. The narrative

report indicated that Sue was a cooperative, friendly, active, impulsive child who would not qualify for any special program. It was suggested that it might be beneficial for her to repeat third grade. The repetition of third grade and tutoring were the only interventions that were tried.

Each year at conference time her parents met with classroom teachers and everyone expressed concern about her progress. By the time Sue had completed ninth grade, both she and her parents had many concerns about her academic progress and the parents were also concerned about her loud talking, acting without thinking, poor concentration and attention, immaturity, and nervousness. Sue also expressed concern about her ability to make friends and her relationship with her parents. She had stayed away from home overnight without permission on at least two occasions during the summer she was referred.

Sue was in good health when seen by the psychologist, had missed few school days over the years, and was reported by her classroom teachers to be well-behaved. Narrative comments on Sue's progress over the years indicated that she continued to be easily distracted and needed guidance to stay on task and complete in-class work and homework.

Sue's grades from seventh grade on, and the results of standardized achievement tests, indicated that without additional assessment and intervention she was at risk for continued school failure.

CBA procedures were employed to determine the nature of her difficulties with the academic materials with which she was currently working. Sue was asked to read and answer questions from her U.S. history textbook, and a piece of fiction she had read in language arts. She was also asked to read and answer problems from her mathematics textbook. Sue listened to the examiner read from the history textbook and answered questions. Her rate of reading was satisfactory for her grade level. She handled literal comprehension questions well (100%). She did not do as well in responding to inferential questions (0%). She read with expression and made very few errors in decoding. When she worked on a page of problems randomly selected from the material she had covered in the last few weeks of introductory algebra, she was unable to recall the procedure necessary to complete the more complex problems of each type. Sue could grasp the basic concept, but had difficulty expanding the concept to accommodate more complex problems (25% correct, all of which involved single digits in basic computation).

Additional interviewing with Sue revealed that she did not have good study habits. She was often disorganized and lost her homework after it was completed. Often she failed to ask for help in class even when she did not understand an assignment. A staffing held with Sue and her parents, classroom teachers, guidance counselor, and school psychologist was successful at pinpointing her strengths and weaknesses in each class. This information, combined with the curriculum-specific data, allowed for the establishment of a successful intervention program. Sue was held responsible for making sure she understood all assignments and completed all work undertaken. The classroom teachers helped her to focus her work toward achieving improved organization. The social studies and language arts teachers provided more opportunities for her to improve her inferential thinking. Sue's language arts teacher also provided her with supplementary materials for aiding her development of good study skills. For math, Sue chose to change to a less rigorous class and began to experience success working with the basic concepts she had not mastered sufficiently to apply to algebra.

"Traditional" assessment had been conducted with Sue when she was 8 years old and had failed to produce any effective intervention; her problems had persisted. Use of the CBA approach, in combination with consultation with teachers and awareness of Sue's experiences in her family environment, gave direction to curricular planning that afforded Sue long-overdue success in her schoolwork.

This case study should serve to demonstrate that in order to improve academic assessment at the secondary level, we need to conduct comprehensive assessment that involves students, their parents/guardians, and regular and special educational personnel who are committed to serve at-risk students. We need to accommodate, respect, and value individual differences.

BASIC CONSIDERATIONS

Professional Preparation

Few psychologists have been trained to direct or conduct academic assessment at the secondary level. The minimum training requirements are an understanding of the secondary school environment, basic measurement theory, learning theory, child and adolescent development, and the theories underlying skill development in reading, writing, spelling, and arithmetic, as well as demonstrated application of this knowledge during coursework and field experiences. Nagle and Medway (1982) stated that the psychologist serving the high school student must be cognizant of the nature of the student, dimensions of the secondary school environment, characteristics of the local community, and the joint interaction of these variables.

Psychologists who work with secondary-age students need to be interested in these students and knowledgeable about the interests and needs of adolescents. They also need to be aware of the factors that influence the learning environment in the secondary school, not just physical, social, and environmental influences, but also the influence of the teachers' expectations and the students' characteristics on achievement.

A need assessment — school by school, classroom by classroom — should be conducted in order to determine the interest and support of classroom teachers, support personnel, and administrators for improving academic assessment and intervention for secondary students. Secondary teachers often feel overworked and harried, unable to give individual attention to students. To be effective in meeting the needs of secondary students with academic problems, the school psychologist must first be effective in determining ways to "fit" improved assessment into the already existing culture of the school rather than assuming that one can change the culture.

BEST PRACTICES

Screening and Diagnosis

Improvement in screening and diagnostic assessment of academic problems is essential. Halpern and Benz (1987) indicate that four curriculum areas appear to accommodate the needs of all secondary age students: (a) basic knowledge and skills; (b) academic knowledge and skills; (c) vocational knowledge and skills; and (d) independent living knowledge and skills.

Sabatino, Goh, and Jenson (1982) categorize these areas as (a) academic, (b) vocational, (c) social, and (d) personal. A thorough assessment and intervention plan for a secondary age-student must begin with screening for problems in each of these areas and then focus on the area or areas of greatest need. (Vocational and social/personality assessment are covered in other chapters of this book.)

Lieberman (1981) suggests that we need to focus on the age of the student, grade, years of instruction with minimal results, motivation, conformity needs, severity of deficit, and nature of school performance pressures. We cannot afford to wait for referral of secondary students if we hope to effect positive changes. Thus, the traditional assessment model that begins with referral is incomplete. A screening and prereferral system must be put in place for secondary-age students.

Shepard (1989) states that current diagnostic assessments appear to be of no direct benefit to students, because they are mainly aimed at the question of eligibility and have no immediate implications for instruction. In addition, misidentification has occurred frequently resulting in the provision of no services or inappropriate services for students. Algozzine and Ysseldyke (1986) and Shepard and Smith (1983) report that

numerous professionals administer countless tests even though half the time the placement decision is made on the basis of educational need rather than on an insight about an underlying handicap. Major professional efforts have centered on correcting the problems by attempting to develop better tests, test batteries, or test-taking procedures. Numerous instruments have been developed in the 1980s to assess academic skills, but many have the same problems as the instruments they were intended to replace. We need to focus on our assessment and stop the endless search for the ideal assessment instrument.

Screening. In an attempt to design a method for identifying students who have failed to master the basic skills and thus will fail their high school competency tests, Smith, Stuck, and Johnson (1982) examined already existing data in the cumulative folders of students to determine how well they predicted the subsequent failure. Although the prediction results in their studies were not perfect, they were encouraging and useful. They found that the variables that discriminated between the two groups of students were available at the eighth-grade level and earlier. The variables that could be of practical use were average school attendance, teachers' ratings, and the results of prior group tests, all of which were routinely collected and available in the students' cumulative folders.

Stone, Cundick, and Swanson (1988) found that using group achievement data and setting the cutoff at the fifth percentile level would identify, almost exclusively, children who had been classified as special education students through the traditional refer, test, and place process. They reported that if such group testing had been used for identifying this particular set of students, between 400 and 600 hours of school psychologist and classroom teacher time could have been spared. They proposed a four-step screening process:

1. Use group standardized test data to form an initial roster of students.

2. Set a district-level percentile cutoff and include all children scoring below that percentile.
3. Have parents and teachers of identified students meet to plan intervention or determine if additional information is needed.
4. Those scoring above the cutoff could still be referred, tested, and placed by an individualized assessment process.

Stevens and Pihl (1987) propose that elementary school teachers can accurately discriminate students who are at risk for failure in high school. They developed a Grade Six Screening Form that asks questions about the student's previous learning in school and asks the teacher to indicate whether a student is likely to cope well with school the next year.

Sabatino, Goh, and Jenson (1982) also argue that a secondary school screening system should be built around existing school records. A systematic review of these records should identify students who are failing one or more academic subjects, display long-standing academic difficulties, exhibit higher frequencies of unusual behavior, have high rates of absenteeism or truancy, and have received low scores on group achievement and/or learning aptitude measures. The initial review would result in a large pool of students who appear to be at risk for academic problems.

Figure 1 presents a model for assessing the academic skills of secondary students that is based on the work of Sabatino, Goh, and Jenson (1982), Stevens and Pihl (1987), and the present author's experiences with other models. The model presented recognizes the need to check the study skills and the vocational goals and skills of secondary students as part to the academic assessment process. However, these two areas are covered elsewhere in the text.

Diagnosis. The screening process should define the problem area, but additional assessment is necessary in order to pinpoint the strengths and weaknesses in the area and the possible reasons for problems.

Norm-referenced tests, criterion-referenced tests, and informal measures all may be used as part of the assessment process. In fact, some norm-referenced tests also are criterion-referenced tests and can be used to compare a student's performance to the objectives being assessed as well as to the norm group. Informal measures include a wide variety of procedures, such as observation, interviews, error pattern analyses, checklists, self-report inventories, and informal task analysis materials. Commercially available informal tests are more correctly labeled criterion-referenced tests, because they focus on how well a student can perform on the particular materials and objectives in that test, which may or may not be similar to the student's classroom materials.

Numerous individual achievement tests have been developed or revised in the 1980s. Five instruments that appear to add a new dimension to the assessment of adolescents who are experiencing academic difficulties are the Basic Achievement Skills Individual Screener (BASIS), the Kaufman Test of Educational Achievement (KTEA), the Sequential Assessment of Mathematics Inventories (SAMI), the Brigance Diagnostic Inventory of Essential Skills (BDIES), and the Diagnostic Achievement Test for Adolescents (DATA). The BASIS and KTEA have been well standardized and can serve as efficient screening tests. The KTEA also provides information on conducting error analysis. The SAMI was initially developed as an informal math inventory and may still be most useful as such; however, the standardization population is not representative of the current U.S. population and some subtests have low reliability coefficients. The Brigance Inventory is useful in planning and evaluating instruction for adolescents who are functioning below average, but it cannot be used as a norm-referenced test; evidence of interrater reliability or alternate form reliability is needed even for its continued use as a criterion-referenced instrument.

The Diagnostic Achievement Test for Adolescents (DATA) (1986) is an individually administered, norm-referenced test

A. The Screening Process
1. Review standardized group test data. Screening team develops cutoff scores. The files of any student whose scores are below this will be reviewed.
2. Review grade reports. The files of any student failing one or more subjects will be reviewed.
3. Check attendance records. Screening team determines standards for excessive absences. The files of any student demonstrating excessive absences will be reviewed.
4. Develop a brief rating form for sixth-grade teachers to complete that indicates identified students' current academic and behavioral adjustment and projected adjustment to junior high.
5. Develop a checklist summary sheet that can be completed for all students identified during the screening process. These questions need to be answered on the checklist.
   a. Is there concern about academic skills or problems in specific content areas?
   b. Are there descriptive samples of behavior and work samples available?
   c. What is known about school-related variables?
   e. What, if any, intervention efforts have been attempted?
6. Ask for current information from teachers and parents about the students who were identified during the screening process.

B. The Diagnostic Process
1. Determine academic expectations.
   a. Review district/school/teacher goals in the academic or content area.
   b. Review textbook objectives, content, reading level, etc.
   c. Review specific classroom requirements.
2. Carry out assessment
   a. Observation: parents, teachers, psychologists.
   b. Interview: classroom teacher or psychologist.
   c. Curriculum-based assessment: classroom teacher, special teacher, or psychologist.
   d. Informal analysis of responses — error pattern analysis.
   e. Standardized diagnostic assessment (if needed).
   f. Check readability level of informal inventory and curriculum materials available.
3. Check skill levels in the academic or content area.
   a. Word recognition (sight vocabulary, phonetic analysis, structural analysis, word meaning).
   b. Reading comprehension (literal, interpretive, critical, and words in context).
   c. Mathematics (integration of mathematical knowledge, problem solving, communication, reasoning, mathematical concepts, mathematical procedures, mathematical disposition).
   d. Written expression (mechanics, usage, ideation).
   e. Spelling and handwriting.
   f. Science (vocabulary, problem solving).
   g. Social studies (vocabulary, graphic aids).
4. Check study skills
   a. Organization.
   b. Book use.
   c. References.
   d. Study habits.
      (1) Outlines.
      (2) Study techniques.
      (3) Adjustment of reading rate.
5. Check vocational goals and skills.
   a. Interest.
   b. Aptitude.
   c. Opportunities.

C. The Intervention Process
1. Describe present level of performance.
2. Set goals/priorities.
3. Provide guidelines for remediation.
4. Evaluate effectiveness.

FIGURE 1. Academic assessment of secondary-age students.

that requires minimal reading from a student and has simplified directions. It has nine subtests covering reading, writing, and math, as well as science, social studies, and reference skills. The manual reports evidence of adequate reliability and validity, but technical adequacy has not been substantiated with research over time.

The publishers' manuals for the Woodcock Reading Mastery Tests–Revised (1987), the KeyMath–Revised (1988), the Woodcock–Johnson Psycho-Educational Battery–Revised (WJ-R) (1989), and the Peabody Individual Achievement Test–Revised (PIAT-R) (1989) report normative samples for each of these tests that are generally representative of the 1980 U.S. student population in respect to grade in school, geographic region, gender, race or ethnic group, and parents' educational level. However, the minority populations did not always match the U.S. Census figures for all demographic variables. Evidence of reliability and validity is presented in each manual and these new instruments seem to be sensitive to current priorities and trends in assessment. However, it is necessary to look at the specific subtests in order to determine whether these instruments can identify specific academic strengths and weaknesses of secondary students. Split-half internal consistency reliability coefficients appear to be adequate. However, only the PIAT-R provides test–retest reliability information (on small groups of selected children). The KeyMath-R provides alternate-form reliability information that appears to be adequate for the total test but quite variable for individual subtests.

If subtests do not have adequate test–retest reliability, they cannot be used to plan interventions. This is true at any level, but especially important at the secondary level. Screening should have already identified the broad area of concern. The specific area of concern must now be pinpointed.

If the screening process has indicated a student has an academic problem, the diagnostic process steps outlined in Figure 1 need to be implemented. A decision must be made as to what techniques will be used

to collect data and who will collect the data. School psychologists, other support personnel, and classroom teachers need to work together to determine what information each will gather. The secondary classroom teacher will usually be better prepared to do curriculum-based assessment in a content area than the school psychologist. But the school psychologist may have a better understanding of the psychology of learning and can serve as a consultant in both the assessment and intervention phases.

Reading

Often the training of content area teachers at the secondary level does not include the teaching of reading because it is assumed that students can read by the time they enter seventh grade, yet these teachers are finding increasing numbers of students who are significantly behind in their reading abilities.

School psychologists need to assist the teachers in determining if students have the skills necessary to succeed in a particular content area, such as understanding and using parts of textbooks, interpreting maps, tables, charts, graphs, diagrams, knowing specialized vocabulary, using reference materials, recognizing special symbols, formulas, and abbreviations.

How can we assess the reading difficulties of secondary students and how can we help these students? Valencia and Pearson (1987) note that the tests used to measure reading achievement do not reflect recent advances in the understanding of the reading process and that the best possible assessment of reading occurs when teachers observe and interact with students as they read authentic texts for general purposes. Shapiro and Derr (1987) and Good and Salvia (1988) found substantial variability in the match between widely used reading achievement tests and reading curricula, indicating the inappropriateness of administering a single standardized reading test or subtest to a student regardless of his or her specific curriculum.

Houck (1983) suggests that the following information be gathered as baseline data when assessing an adolescent's reading difficulties: (a) a profile of previous assessment data; (b) records from previous remedial efforts; (c) perceived and self-reported attitudes toward reading; (d) current reading performance and habits; (e) current reading opportunities and demands; and (f) the environmental response to the presenting reading deficit.

If the screening process has indicated that a student has a problem in reading, the specific reading skills assessed in the latest group achievement test should be reviewed. Were there problems with word analysis skills, comprehension, or vocabulary? If the level of reading skills appears adequate on these tests, one should assess the student in her or his own content area textbook or materials and not waste time with administering individual reading tests. If the reading levels were problematic, the types of errors need to be analyzed to determine the focus of any additional reading assessment.

Informal reading inventories (IRIs). The assessment of the reading skills of secondary students can be done thoroughly only if one uses an informal reading inventory based on the student's content area materials.

The following are general guidelines for preparing and administering IRIs at the secondary level:

1. Obtain the textbooks that are used in the school.
2. Select 100- to 200-word passages from the beginning, middle, and end of the texts.
3. Determine the readability level of the passages. (A readability formula can be applied as a rough approximation of level of difficulty of the reading material. There are computer programs available that analyze a text sample to quickly obtain a readability level. The *School Utilities* [1982] readability program is designed for the user to select from six different readability methods.
4. Prepare 6–10 comprehension questions for each selection. The questions should assess different levels of comprehension (factual, inferential, vocabulary, evaluative, etc.).
5. Have the student read the passages silently. (The secondary student is seldom expected to read orally.)
6. Check oral reading in order to record decoding errors.
7. Read some passages to the student in order to check listening comprehension.
8. Record any oral reading errors (there are several recording systems that can be used to record errors).
9. Analyze oral reading errors.
10. Ask the student to answer questions at the end of each passage (note who read the passage and how it was read).
11. Record the comprehension errors.
12. Analyze the type of questions to distinguish those answered correctly from those answered incorrectly.

Swaby's (1984) guidelines for establishing an instructional reading level could be adapted in the secondary setting.

1. Independent reading level: The student scores 98% or above on word recognition, 90% or above on comprehension.
2. Instructional reading level: The student scores 90–97% on word recognition. 70–89% on comprehension.
3. Frustration reading level: The student scores 89% or below on word recognition, 50% or below on comprehension.

For students who score at the frustration level in any of their textbooks, adaptations need to be made in the classroom. The school psychologist who asks students to read orally needs to determine how well they are using phonic information, syntactic information, and semantic information during reading and how well they monitor and correct their errors in reading. Analysis of miscues will help determine what kind of intervention is needed in reading. Hansell (1982) stresses the importance of the informal diagnosis of content area reading skills and differentiating between students who need to learn to read and those who need to read to learn.

Pikulski and Shanahan (1982) and Farr and Carey (1986) provide critical reviews of the use of IRIs. Farr and Carey suggest that several problems limit their use: the criteria for evaluating IRI performance are subjective and arbitrary; selecting passages from a graded reading will not accurately guarantee a progressing range of reading difficulty; the examiner needs to have considerable knowledge about reading in order to record errors and make judgments about a student's performance; IRIs are not as useful at the upper grade levels as they are at the lower grade levels because of differences in reading materials (background information takes on greater importance, and oral and silent reading appear to be less similar at the upper grade levels).

Pikulski and Shanahan (1982) propose the following: (a) Published IRIs should provide information about alternate-form and test–retest reliability; (b) selections for IRIs should be chosen carefully because of the variability within reading texts; (c) published IRIs should be used only if they are similar in the content and skill demands in the students' classroom; (d) traditional criteria for establishing independent, instructional, and frustration levels of reading should be used until research results suggest adopting some other criteria; (e) errors or miscues should be analyzed qualitatively and quantitatively; and (f) qualitative analysis of oral reading errors or miscues should focus on the deviations from text that take place at or very near a student's instructional level.

The Advanced Reading Inventory (1981) and the Burns/Roe Informal Reading Inventory, Third Edition (1989) are examples of informal instruments that may be useful in the secondary setting. However, consumers will have to determine if these tests match the content and skill demands in the secondary classroom and can aid in setting up intervention.

Word recognition. When measured, word recognition should be assessed in a way that enhances instruction. A majority of reading tests contain word recognition subtests, but just as there are numerous theories and methods of teaching word recognition, there are numerous testing methods also. Farr and Carey (1986) suggest that if a student can read satisfactorily at a particular level that would require word recognition skills such as phonetic and structural analyses, then it is not necessary to assess those skills; instead one should assess word meaning and comprehension. Knowledge of the meaning of words is considered by many to be the most important of the word recognition skills. Word recognition skills should be assessed in as much context as possible. Do not use nonsense words to determine the word recognition skills of adolescents. Any word recognition test should be considered just a sample of the many word recognition behaviors that could be tested. The test should be of adequate length to assure stable results.

Howell and Morehead (1987) provide a format for evaluating decoding, adapted here for assessing the secondary-age student (Table 1).

Comprehension. Most reading professionals agree that the purpose of reading is comprehension, but they do not agree about how to assess it. There are six common approaches to measuring comprehension: (a) asking questions requiring either recall or recognition answers; (b) having students paraphrase; (c) having students retell a story exactly as heard; (d) having students fill in missing words (cloze technique); (e) having students select the correct word to complete a sentence (mazes); and (f) presenting an original sentence and asking the student to paraphrase the sentence to check for meaning (sentence verification).

In summarizing and contrasting these techniques, Howell and Morehead (1987) indicate that there is no simple best procedure for assessing comprehension and that one needs to use more than one method across texts of various styles. If the results of survey tests indicate that comprehension is a problem, comprehension within the students own materials should be assessed. Is the student having comprehension problems because of a

TABLE 1
Assessment of Word Recognition Skills

Known Information	Probable Causes	Assessment	Intervention
Oral reading is slow but accurate	Lack of practice in reading quickly	Ask student to reread passage	If rate increases work on improving rate
	Poor use of passage content	Same as above	Same as above
	Poor use of phonics; speed would increase errors	Analyze decoding errors	Teach the use of skills emphasizing rate
Oral reading is inaccurate	Not reading for accuracy	Tell student the purpose for reading and have student reread passage	Emphasize reading for accuracy
	Poor use of context	Check the use of text	Emphasize accuracy; teach higher-level strategies
	Learned error patterns	Categorize decoding errors by strategy	Correct the error patterns
	Poor use of decoding	Categorize decoding errors by content	Teach the use of skills within passage reading

Note. Adapted from *Curriculum-based Evaluation for Special and Remedial Education* by K. W. Howell and M. K. Morehead, 1987. Columbus, OH: Merrill.

deficit in background knowledge, decoding skills, vocabulary, language syntax, or comprehension strategies? Howell and Morehead provide very specific guidelines for determining the cause of the problem and for intervention.

Mathematics

The curriculum and evaluation standards being prepared by a working group of the Commission on Standards for School Mathematics (1989) contain many specific guidelines for determining what students know and think about mathematics. The standards emphasize aspects of assessment and program evaluation that depart from current practice and include the following points:

1. Assessment is integral to teaching.
2. Assessment focuses on a broad range

of mathematical tasks and a holistic view of mathematics.
3. Assessment includes problem situations involving the application of a number of mathematical ideas.
4. Assessment applies a variety of techniques, including written, oral, and demonstration formats.
5. Calculators, computers, and manipulatives are appropriate for use in assessment.
6. Program evaluation includes systematic collection of information on outcomes, curriculum, and instruction.
7. Standardized achievement tests are used as only one of many indicators of program outcomes.

The student assessment focuses on integration of mathematical knowledge, problem solving, communication, reasoning, mathematical concepts, mathematical procedures, and mathematical dispositions. Each area is described and examples of appropriate assessment techniques are given for grades K–12.

If the screening process has indicated that a student has a problem in mathematics, the steps outlined in Figure 1 under the diagnostic process need to be carried out: determination of academic expectations in mathematics, observations, interviews, curriculum-based assessment, and informal analysis of responses. The results of the most recent group achievement test would give a general idea of a student's functional level in mathematics. An individually administered mathematics test should be given only if there is a technically adequate one available that assesses the important components of mathematics that this student is expected to master. Numerous tests have been developed as diagnostic math tests, but few provide enough information regarding strengths and weaknesses to plan intervention.

The KeyMath–Revised (1988) emphasizes current priorities and trends especially in the application subtests, which include Estimation, Interpreting Data, and Problem Solving. These three areas reflect the national commitment to functional mathematics (Commission on Standards for School Mathematics, 1989). However, these subtests do not appear to have adequate alternate-form reliability coefficients to justify using them. The concurrent validity evidence provided for KeyMath–R indicates that it is only moderately correlated with CTBS and ITBS math scores. What is needed is evidence that it is related to classroom performance in mathematics.

Informal assessment in mathematics ranges from interviews to diagnostic tests and inventories. Guidelines for conducting a diagnostic mathematics interview are provided by Bartel (1986), Reisman and Kaufman (1980), and Schoen (1979). The main purpose of the interview is to determine, in a relaxed atmosphere, how a student solves problems in mathematics and how she or he feels about mathematics. Reisman (1982) also provides specific guidelines for developing diagnostic math

tests. General guidelines include these steps:

1. Decide the purpose of the test.
2. Choose the specific content to be assessed (based on the student's curriculum).
3. Determine the appropriate level of learning for the individuals.
4. Use a hierarchical chart to determine the desired behaviors for each skill area.
5. Write the actual items.
6. Make sure there are several items for each skill area.
7. Make sure sentence structure and reading level are appropriate for the students being assessed.
8. Interview the student regarding errors.

Several examples of informal math inventories or checklists are available (Choate et al., 1987; Evans, Evans, & Mercer, 1986; Howell & Morehead, 1987; Kerr, Nelson, & Lambert, 1987; Zigmond, Vallecorsa, & Silverman, 1983). These could be adapted to fit the mathematics being taught in the secondary classroom. Rees and Barr (1984) provide a thorough informal diagnostic assessment in mathematics. Reisman and Kaufman's (1980) Screening Checklist covers Grades K–12. Marquis (1988) has developed a specific test to assess common mistakes in algebra.

The need for teaching and testing computational estimation has been emphasized in the 1980s (Benton, 1986; Schoen, Blume, & Hoover, in press; and Usiskin, 1986). The 1986 and earlier NAEP results indicated a need to teach and test for problem-solving skills also. Malone, Douglas, Kissane, and Mortlock (1980) provide guidelines for assessing problem solving, and Schoen and Oehmke (1980) developed the Iowa Problem Solving Project Test, which can be used to assess individuals or classes.

Computer-based testing programs in mathematics could be developed that would assess more quickly with precision and offer more diagnostic information than our current assessment approaches. Rohau (1986) reviews some of the available diagnostic programs, such as the Mathematics Error Analysis Series, and makes suggestions for changes that will make such programs useful for students at all ability levels. Blume and Schoen (1988) found that computer programming experience had a positive effect on mathematical problem solving, not in terms of number of correct responses but in the approach to solving problems.

Written Expression

The components of written expression can be divided into many areas but they are usually thought of as handwriting, spelling, mechanics, usage, and ideation. It is generally accepted that there is a hierarchy of written expression and that expression of ideas through writing is the last of the skill areas acquired by students. The minimal competencies to be desired are that students be able to write legibly and express their thoughts in writing well enough for others to understand them.

If concern about any aspect of written expression is noted during the screening process, the steps outlined in Figure 1 need to be carried out. It is necessary for the psychologist to know (a) what writing skills have already been introduced to the student, (b) which skills are appropriate for the student's grade placement, (c) the requirements of the writing tasks the student has failed, (d) the intervention programs and techniques available to the student, and (e) the student's desire to perform writing tasks.

During the 1980s there has been an increase in the availability of standardized tests or subtests of written expression, and if these instruments are technically adequate and contain content and methods of assessment that fit the students' needs, one of these instruments should be used to follow up the screening of written expression.

The Woodcock–Johnson Psycho-Educational Battery-Revised (WJ-R) and the Peabody Individual Achievement Test-Revised (PIAT-R), both of which were published in 1989, have added new written language tests, recognizing the importance of assessing writing. Both require a direct sample of a student's writing skills but both have technical and practical problems.

The norms for the Written Expression subtest of the PIAT-R are different from the norms for other subtests: grade-based stanines for Level I and Level II and developmental scaled scores for Level II. Since secondary students would be given Level II of the subtest, the present discussion will focus on the technical adequacy of Level II. Median interrater reliability is only .58 and test–retest reliability was reported at .63 for the total sample of 168 students. The manual provides cautions about scoring and interpretation. No validity evidence was provided for the Written Expression subtest. The WJ-R measures all areas of written expression if the Supplementary Battery is administered. Internal consistency reliability coefficients were calculated for all tests except Handwriting and Writing Fluency. The reliabilities for Writing Samples appear adequate for secondary-age students (.80's and .90's). Test-retest reliabilities on Writing Fluency do not appear adequate (.60's and .70's) for secondary students. A recent study by Mather (1989) reports low to modest correlations between two WJ writing tests (Dictation and Proofing), two WJ-R writing tests (Writing Fluency and Writing Samples), and various other measures of writing, namely the Test of Written Language, the Picture Story Language Test, and the MAT6 Writing Test of the Metropolitan Achievement Tests. Mather suggests that the two new tests on the WJ-R that require several small samples of writing should be considered as alternatives to the single-sample approach to writing assessment. It is clear that further research is needed before any of these tests are used to plan intervention in written expression.

Informal assessment. Informal tests and inventories, and such techniques as observation, error pattern analysis, and task analysis, are necessary to assess written expression. The most important aspect of the informal assessment of written expression is the gathering of writing samples of the referred student along with the writing samples of average students for comparison. Each component of written expression can be analyzed through writing samples. There are many examples and guidelines available for developing informal inventories and checklists (Choate et al., 1987; Cramer, 1982; Evans, Evans, & Mercer, 1983; Goodman, Casciato, & Price, 1987; Hammill, 1987; Howell & Morehead, 1987; Moran, 1987; Zigmund et al., 1983).

One example of a thorough informal diagnostic test is the Diagnostic Evaluation of Writing Skills (DEWS) by Weiner (1980). Weiner suggests asking the student to write an autobiography, allowing 30 minutes for writing and 15 minutes for revision. The DEWS contains 41 criteria for six categories of writing skills: (a) graphic (visual features), (b) orthographic (spelling), (c) phonologic (sound components), (d) syntactic (grammatical), (e) semantic (meaning), and (f) self-monitoring skills.

Poteet (1980) has also developed an informal technique for analyzing samples of students' written work. The evaluator places a check mark in the columns that best describe the student's achievement in the first three components of written expression: penmanship, spelling, and grammar. A column designated *TA* is for those skills or characteristics that are too advanced or not appropriate for consideration at this time. An *A* column is for those skills that are adequately used in the sample; a column labeled *I* is for those skills that need to be introduced to improve the quality of writing; and the last column, labeled *R*, is for those skills that need remediation or review. The evaluator fills in the blanks on a checklist for the fourth component, Ideation. Poteet (1980) suggests that after the student has completed the writing task, he or she should read aloud what was written, and the evaluator should note any discrepancies between the oral and written sample. This will help the evaluator decipher misspelled and unrecognized errors. Following that, the evaluator should begin a careful and critical analysis of the written sample, using the checklist to check each component. Poteet (1980)

provides a detailed explanation of each component and suggestions for analyzing the component. Simple curriculum-based measures of written expression have been developed at the University of Minnesota Institute for Research on Learning Disabilities and are described in the chapter on CBM.

The major controversies regarding tests of written expression center around whether direct or indirect measures of writing skills should be used, and what scoring methods should be used to analyze direct samples of writing. There seems to be more or less consensus that direct assessment and analytic scoring should be used to pinpoint strengths and weaknesses in writing skills.

Teacher and peer evaluations, as well as self-evaluations, of writing can help students acquire evaluative skills and improve their writing ability.

Science and Social Studies

If there is concern about academic achievement in science or social studies, the same steps outlined in Figure 1 should be carried out. Emphasis should be placed on determining skills in reading, vocabulary, problem solving, using graphic aids, and assessing study habits.

SUMMARY

Standardized achievement test batteries are administered frequently during a normal K–12 public school experience, yet many teachers, administrators, parents, and students have no clear idea why the tests are being administered other than to report the scores. In one in-depth study of a school system, Carey (1985) was unable to find one teacher who used test results for any curricular or instructional purpose. Farr and Carey (1986) report that although teachers are encouraged to use informal techniques to assess students, there is a paucity of research on how often this kind of assessment takes place, how reliable or valid it is, and what use is made of the results. We still don't have an assessment process in place that identifies and addresses the needs of students at risk for school failure. We need to develop, implement, and evaluate the best possible assessment and intervention process and ensure that students succeed in learning basic skills in the elementary grades. By the time students are in the secondary schools, we need to focus on what they can do and tailor our expectations to the realistic needs of the student. We cannot cure the academic problems of all the students, but we can improve the assessment process by using already existing data, gathering additional data to provide a link between assessment and intervention, and making sure that both assessment and intervention are functional.

REFERENCES

Algozzine, B., & Ysseldyke, J. E. (1986). The future of the LD field: Screening field: Screening and diagnosis. *Journal of Learning Disabilities, 19*(7), 394-398.

Bartel, N. (1986). Problems in mathematics achievement. In D. D. Hammill & N. R. Bartel (Eds.), *Teaching students with learning and behavior problems*. Boston: Allyn and Bacon.

Benton, S. E. (1986). A summary of research on teaching and learning estimation. In H. L. Schoen & M. J. Zweng (Eds.), *Estimation and mental computation* (pp. 239-248). Reston, VA: National Council of Teachers of Mathematics.

Blume, G. W., & Schoen, H. L. (1988). Mathematical problem-solving performance of eighth-grade programmers and non-programmers. *Journal for Research in Mathematics Education, 19*(2), 142-156.

Carey, R. F. (1985). *Program evaluation as ethnographic research*. Providence: Department of Education.

Chalfant, J. (1989). Learning disabilities: Policy issues and promising approaches. *American Psychologists, 44*(2), 387-391.

Choate, J. S., Bennett, T. Z., Enright, B. E., Miller, L. J., Poteet, J. A., & Rakes, T. A. (1987). *Assessing and programming basic curriculum skills*. Newton, MA: Allyn & Bacon.

Commission on Standards for School Mathematics. (1989, March). *Curriculum and evaluation standards for school mathematics*. Prepared by the Working Groups of the Commission on Standards for School Mathematics of the National Council of Teachers of Mathematics.

Cramer, R. L. (1982). Informal approaches to evaluating children's writing. In J. J. Pikulski & T. Shanahan (Eds.), *Approaches to the informal evaluation of reading* (pp. 80-93). Newark, DE: International Reading Association.

Deno, S. (1985). Curriculum-based measurement: The emerging alternative. *Exceptional Children, 52*, 219-232.

Deno, S. (1986). Formative evaluation of individual student programs: A new role for school psychologists. *School Psychology Review, 15*, 358-374.

Evans, S. S., Evans, W. H., & Mercer, C. D. (1983). *Assessment for instruction*. Boston: Allyn & Bacon.

Farr, R., & Carey, R. F. (1986). *Reading. What can be measured?* (2nd ed.). Newark, DE: International Reading Association.

Gickling, E., & Thompson, V. (1985). A personal view of curriculum-based assessment. *Exceptional Children, 52*, 205-218.

Good, R. H., & Salvia, J. S. (1988). Curriculum bias in published norm-referenced reading tests: Demonstrable effects. *School Psychology Review, 17*(1), 51-60.

Goodman, L., Casciato, D., & Price, M. (1987). LD students' writing: Analyzing errors. *Academic Therapy, 22*(5), 453-461.

Halpern, A. S., & Benz, M. R. (1987). A statewide examination of secondary special education for students with mild disabilities. Implications for the high school curriculum. *Exceptional Children, 54*(2), 122-129.

Hammill, D. D. (1987). *Assessing the abilities and instructional needs of students*. Austin, TX: Pro-Ed.

Hansell, T. S. (1982). Informal diagnoses of content area reading skills. In J. J. Pikulski & T. Shanahan (Eds.), *Approaches to the informal evaluation of reading* (pp. 63-79). Newark, DE: International Reading Association.

Houck, C. (1983). The reading disabled adolescent: An examination of significant factors influencing program success. *Reading Improvement, 20*(1), 28-36.

Howell, K. W., & Morehead, M. K. (1987). *Curriculum-based evaluation for special and remedial education*. Columbus, OH: Merrill.

Kerr, M. M., Nelson, C. M., & Lambert, D. L. (1987). *Helping adolescents with learning and behavior problems*. Columbus, OH: Merrill.

Lieberman, L. L. (1981). The LD adolescent . . . When do you stop? *Journal of Learning Disabilities, 14*(7), 425-426.

Malone, J. A., Douglas, G. A., Kissane, B. V., & Mortlock, R. S. (1980). Measuring problem-solving ability. In S. Krulik & R. E. Roys (Eds.), *Problem solving in school mathematics* (pp. 204–215). Reston, VA: National Council of Teachers of Mathematics.

Marquis, J. (1988). Common mistakes in algebra. In A. F. Coxford & A. P. Shulte (Eds.), *The ideas of algebra* (pp. 204–205). Reston, VA: National Council of Teachers of Mathematics.

Mather, N. (1989). Comparison of the new and existing Woodcock-Johnson writing tests to other writing measures. *Learning Disabilities Focus*, 4(2), 84–95.

Moran, M. R. (1987). Individualized objectives for writing instruction. *Topics in Language Disorders*, 7(4), 42–54.

Nagle, R. J., & Medway, F. J. (Guest Eds.). (1982). Psychological services in the high school. *School Psychology Review*, 11(4), 357–432.

Orlich, D. C. (1989). Education reforms: Mistakes, misconceptions, miscues. *Phi Delta Kappan*, 70(7), 512–517.

Pikulski, J. J., & Shanahan, T. (1982). Informal reading inventories: A critical analysis. In J. J. Pikulski & T. Shanahan (Eds.), *Approaches to the informal evaluation of reading* (pp. 94–116). Newark, DE: International Reading Association.

Poteet, J. A. (1980). Informal assessment of written expression. *Learning Disabilities Quarterly*, 3, 88–98.

Rees, R., & Barr, G. (1984). *Diagnosis and prescription in the classroom: Some common math problems*. London: Harper & Row.

Reisman, F. K. (1982). *A guide to the diagnostic teaching of arithmetic* (3rd ed.). Columbus, OH: Merrill.

Reisman, F. K., & Kauffman, S. H. (1980). *Teaching mathematics to children with special needs*. Columbus, OH: Merrill.

Rohau, R. N. (1986). Mathematical diagnosis with the micro computer: Tapping a wealth of potential. *Mathematics Teacher*, 79(3), 205–208.

Sabatino, D. A., Goh, D. S., & Jenson, G. (1982). Special education programs for the handicapped adolescent. *School Psychology Review*, 11(4), 377–383.

Schoen, H. L. (1979). Using the individual interview to assess mathematics learning. *Arithmetic Teacher*, 27(3), 34–37.

Schoen, H. L., Blume, G., & Hoover, H. D. (in press). Outcomes and processes on estimation test items in different formats. *Journal for Research in Mathematics Education*.

Schoen, H. L., & Oehmke, T. (1980). A new approach to the measurement of problem-solving skills. In S. Krulik & R. E. Reys (Eds.), *Problem solving in school mathematics* (pp. 216–227). Reston, VA: National Council of Teachers of Mathematics.

School Utilities (Vol. 2). (1982). St. Paul: Minnesota Educational Computing Consortium.

Schumaker, J. B., & Deshler, D. D. (1988). Implementing the Regular Education Initiative in secondary schools: A different ball game. *Journal of Learning Disabilities*, 21(1), 36–42.

Shapiro, E. S., & Derr, T. F. (1987). An examination of overlap between reading curricula and standardized achievement tests. *Journal of Special Education*, 21(2), 59–67.

Shepard, L. A. (1989). Identification of mild handicaps. In R. L. Linn (Ed.), *Educational measurement* (3rd ed.; pp. 545–572). New York: Macmillan for the American Council on Education.

Shepard, L. A., & Smith, M. L. (1983). An evaluation of the identification of learning disabled students in Colorado. *Learning Disability Quarterly*, 6, 115–127.

Shinn, M. R., Tindal, G. A., & Stein, S. (1988). Curriculum-based measurement and the identification of mildly handicapped students: A research review. *Professional School Psychology*, 3(1), 69–85.

Smith, M., Stuck, G. B., & Johnston, D. R. (1982). The identification of students likely to fail the North Carolina competency tests. *Educational and Psychological Measurement*, 42(1), 95–104.

Stevens, R., & Pihl, R. O. (1987). Seventh-grade students at risk for school failure. *Adolescence*, 22(86), 333–345.

Stone, B., Cundick, B. P., & Swanson, D. (1988). Special education screening system: Group achievement test. *Exceptional Children*, 55(1), 71–75.

Swaby, B. E. (1984). *Teaching and learning reading: A pragmatic approach*. Boston: Little Brown.

Usiskin, Z. (1986). Reasons for estimating. In H. L. Schoen & M. J. Zweng (Eds.), *Estimation and mental computation* (pp. 1–15). Reston, VA: National Council of Teachers of Mathematics.

Valencia, S., & Pearson, P. D. (1987). Reading assessment: Time for a change. *Reading Teacher*, 40(8), 726–732.

Weiner, E. S. (1980). Diagnostic evaluation of writing skills. *Journal of Learning Disabilities*, 13(1), 43–48.

Zigmond, N., Vallecorsa, A., & Silverman, R. (1983). *Assessment for instructional planning in special education*. Englewood Cliffs, NJ: Prentice-Hall.

ANNOTATED BIBLIOGRAPHY

Choate, J. S., Bennett, T. Z., Enright, B. E., Miller, L. J., Poteet, J. A., & Rakes, T. A. (1987). *Assessing and programming basic curriculum skills.* Boston: Allyn and Bacon.
This book provides a very comprehensive curriculum analysis of the basic subject areas, as well as study and content area skills. The appendices contain skill objectives and sample test items for all the areas. It is intended for teachers, prospective teachers, and educational diagnosticians.

Commission on Standards for School Mathematics. (1989, March). *Curriculum and evaluation standards for school mathematics.* National Council of Teachers of Mathematics.
Fourteen evaluation standards are presented focusing on student assessment, general assessment, and program evaluation. Each standard is explained and examples of ways to evaluate are given.

Farr, R. & Carey, R. F. (1986). *Reading: What can be measured?* (2nd ed.). Newark, DE: International Reading.
This is a comprehensive monograph that organizes and describes the research literature related to reading measurement. It should be of value to educators, psychologists, reading researchers, test developers, school administrators, and policymakers.

Howell, K. W., & Morehead, M. K. (1987). *Curriculum-based evaluation for special and remedial education.* Columbus: Merrill.
This text integrates the basic concepts and issues in assessing handicapped children, provides a format for deciding what to teach, and gives techniques for measuring daily progress. There are very useful flow charts, checklists, and examples of other informal techniques to measure academic skills.

Kerr, M. M., Nelson, C. M., & Lambert, D. L. (1987). *Helping adolescents with learning and behavior problems.* Columbus: Merrill.
Current practices and research findings are presented in a practical way. Academic and nonacademic assessment and planning are presented, as well as strategy chapters that tell you how to intervene on special problems and how to teach important skills to adolescents.

2

Best Practices in Adaptive Behavior

Daniel J. Reschly
Iowa State University

Adaptive behavior has become increasingly prominent in consideration of best professional practices over the past 15 years. The following topics will be discussed in this chapter: (a) Conception and definition of adaptive behavior; (b) Legal requirements and professional association guidelines; (c) Domains of adaptive behavior; (d) Assessment issues such as choices among approaches, critique of existing instruments, and judicious selection of assessment procedures; (e) Use of adaptive behavior in eligibility determination; and (f) Use of adaptive behavior in interventions with at risk and handicapped students.

In the 1970's, adaptive behavior was considered primarily in the context of mental retardation (MR) eligibility determination and, to a lesser extent, in programming for students with MR. In the 1980's, adaptive behavior is increasingly seen as essential for two broad purposes: (a) A mandatory component of multifactored assessments with all handicapped students; and (b) A critical area for interventions with many students that might be classified as at risk or handicapped. Indeed, it appears that increased success in resolution of adaptive behavior deficits in educational settings may reduce the use of pull out and other kinds of interventions that separate handicapped or at risk students from regular classroom activities.

OVERVIEW

Confusion about the meaning and use of adaptive behavior can be clarified through careful delineation of conception, definition, and professional association recommendations.

The Adaptive Behavior Construct

Prior work on social competence (Reschly, 1987–88) was significantly influenced by Greenspan's (1979) model, a comprehensive scheme of personal competence that had four broad domains: physical, cognitive, social, and emotional (see Figure 1). Social competence was further subdivided (Gresham & Reschly, 1988) into the subdomains of adaptive behavior and social skills (see Figure 2). The figure serves to emphasize the overlap between adaptive behavior and social skills, between social and emotional competence, and between social and cognitive competence. The overlap among domains and subdomains suggests that certain cognitive competencies are fundamental to adaptive behavior just as certain emotional or affective qualities (e.g., motivation and appropriate attitudes) are essential to other social skills or adaptive behaviors. Recognition of the overlap between adaptive behavior and other domains of competence sets the stage for later consideration of appropriate domains of adaptive behavior and for the analysis of content on instruments.

Although there are many definitions of adaptive behavior, the most influential current definition appeared in Grossman (1983); " . . . the effectiveness or degree with which the individual meets the standards of personal independence and social responsibility . . ." (p. 1). The concepts of personal independence and social responsibility were used earlier by Doll (1941, 1953) to describe social competence, the critical first criterion in his definition of mental deficiency. The construct to which adaptive behavior refers is not new.

The American Association on Mental Retardation (AAMR) definition of adaptive behavior (Grossman, 1983) includes two additional critical assumptions. First it is assumed that adaptive behavior is developmental, meaning simply that expectations vary with the age of the individual. The developmental nature of adaptive behavior is recognized in the AAMR *Classification in Mental Retardation* through the development of different criteria for adaptive behavior competencies at three broad age groupings; preschool, school-age, and adult. During the preschool period the primary criteria are sensory motor skills development, communication skills including speech and language, self-help skills such as dressing, eating, and toileting, and socialization including interacting appropriately with others. During the school age years, denoted by AAMR as childhood and early adolescence, the most important criteria are use of basic academic skills in practical situations, use of reasoning and judgment in coping effectively with the environment, and the acquisition of social skills such as participation in group activities and establishing and maintaining satisfactory interpersonal relationships. In late adolescence and adulthood the principal criteria for adaptive behavior are independent functioning in the community and vocational responsibilities including economic self-support. Competencies from earlier ages are included in the criteria for later ages.

The second essential consideration in the AAMR conception of adaptive behavior is environmental/cultural context. Environments and cultures vary with respect to expectations for children and adults as well as the kinds of opportunities provided for, or demands placed on, individuals.

Although there is increasing consensus on a basic definition of adaptive behavior, there is still considerable debate over application of the concepts of personal independence and social responsibility, especially at the school age period, roughly ages 5–17. The major issue is the inclusion of practical cognitive skills, later called functional academic skills. The degree to which the cognitive skills that

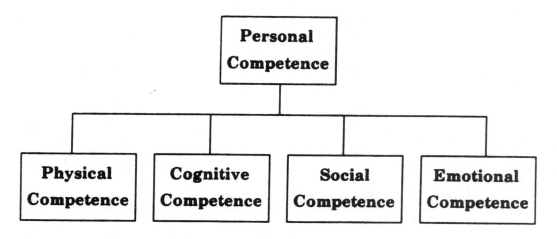

FIGURE 1. A model of human competence (Greenspan, 1979).

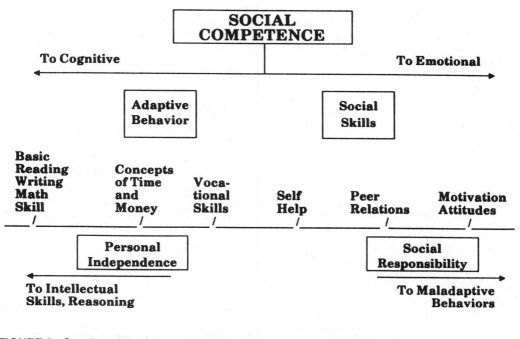

FIGURE 2. Overlap of social competence with emotional competence and cognitive competence.

underlie adaptive behaviors are included in the conception of adaptive behavior and are reflected in the measurement operations has vast implications for assessment method, setting(s) examined, observers or respondents, and classification/placement decisions.

Developmental task theory was used earlier to explain the inclusion of underlying cognitive skills in the conception of adaptive behavior (Reschly, 1982, 1987–88). Expectations for the acquisition of literacy skills and adequate academic performance are common to all sociocultural groups in the United States (Bickel, Bond, & Carter, 1981). Inclusion of underlying cognitive competencies in adaptive behavior is consistent with the AAMR notions of developmental level and environmental/cultural context.

Many examples of adaptive behaviors with underlying cognitive skills could be cited. Handling money and very basic skills as an earner and consumer are nearly universally recognized as essential to personal independence. Competent per-

formance of these skills has underlying cognitive components such as computation skills and knowledge of money values. If these cognitive components are ignored in conception and measurement, inaccurate decisions about adaptive behavior will result, affecting eligibility determination and program planning.

Legal Requirements and Professional Association Guidelines

Legal requirements and professional association guidelines over the past 15 years have exerted enormous influence on the use of adaptive behavior information. Adaptive behavior was prominent in the analysis of placement bias issues in both the *Larry P. v. Riles* (1979) and the *Marshall v. Georgia* (1984) trials. Although both trials reached markedly different conclusions (Reschly, Kicklighter, & McKee, 1988) the essential view of the court was unmistakable; adaptive behavior must be assessed as part of MR classification and placement. Furthermore, the Marshall court required the adoption of the *AAMR Classification in Mental Retardation* (Grossman, 1983) conception and criteria for both general intellectual functioning and adaptive behavior.

Further legal influences on use of adaptive behavior come from the federal regulations concerning implementation of the Education of the Handicapped Act, where the term "adaptive behavior" appears three times, most prominently as a component of MR. Most state special education rules include adaptive behavior as part of MR classification criteria as well as an important component of a multifactored evaluation. Although much more could be said about legal requirements, these critical points are inescapable: (a) Adaptive behavior deficits must be established as part of eligibility determination with students with MR; (b) The AAMR classification in MR is the most authoritative source. If state rules are silent on a specific issue or if they contradict AAMR, the AAMR guidelines will probably be adopted in a legal proceeding; and (c) Adaptive behavior is a component of the multifactored assessment.

There are two professional associations that have commented extensively on adaptive behavior in recent years, the AAMR (Grossman, 1983), and the Council for Exceptional Children–Mental Retardation Division (CEC-MR). Readers concerned about the use of adaptive behavior in determination of eligibility or in educational programming for students with MR are urged to consult basic sources describing AAMR and CEC-MR policies.

The most authoritative source, AAMR, provides a conceptual definition of adaptive behavior as well as criteria that vary depending on the age of the individual (Grossman, 1983). There is much that is not discussed by AAMR including domains of adaptive behavior, how adaptive behavior ought to be measured, and criteria to determine deficits in adaptive behavior. The latter point is often misunderstood. AAMR does *not* suggest, let alone specify, a cut-off score or a discrepancy determi-

nation method to guide decisions on whether or not a deficit exists in adaptive behavior.

The CEC-MR policy statements on adaptive behavior (Polloway, 1985; Zucker & Polloway, 1987) provide little additional specificity. CEC-MR recognizes that adaptive behavior should be assessed, both *in school* and *out of school*, but suggests that that *in school* measurement of adaptive behavior should be given more weight if there are differences between levels of performance across the two settings. AAMR is silent on the issue of setting. The legal requirements and professional association guidelines are useful, but much is left unspecified.

BASIC CONSIDERATIONS

Adaptive behavior is used in two general kinds of decisions with students. The first, and most prominent to date, is the MR classification/placement whereby we determine the eligibility of a student for a classification such as MR, describe strengths and weaknesses and develop general goals for programming, and recommend the kind of placement option that seems most appropriate to carry out the individualized educational program. Adaptive behavior should be included, prominently, in the decision about eligibility *and* in the decisions about the development of IEP general goals and the selection of a placement option. The second kind of decision relates more specifically to instructional programming or intervention design, a significant consideration for all at risk or handicapped students. Here we need to identify specific objectives within general adaptive behavior goals, conduct functional analyses, develop and implement interventions, monitor progress, and provide for generalization/maintenance of those skills. Both kinds of decisions are improved through better understanding of the domains of adaptive behavior, the measurement choices, and decision making strategies.

Domains of Adaptive Behavior

The exact number and names for adaptive behavior domains are arbitrary. Based on a thorough review of the literature and examination of available instruments, four adaptive behavior domains were suggested in a monograph distributed widely now in two states (Reschly, 1987–1988). The four domains described below are most useful for MR eligibility determination, development of general goals for interventions, and selection of placement options.

Independent functioning. Competencies dealing with personal independence constitute the most widely accepted component of adaptive behavior. Independent functioning virtually always includes a broad range of items varying from basic toileting, feeding, and dressing skills to considerably more complex competencies such as traveling independently within the community, consumer skills, use of complex communication devices, acceptable use of leisure time, and degree of need for supervision.

Social functioning. Nearly all adaptive behavior scales include items regarding interpersonal relationships and what are sometimes referred to as social skills (Gresham, this volume; Gresham & Elliott, 1987). Some of the key competencies in this domain included appropriate attention to other persons, acceptable orientation and posturing, acceptable efforts to communicate, sharing appropriately, expressing feelings in an acceptable fashion, forming friendships, recognition of the needs and feelings of others, avoidance of obnoxious behaviors and situational appropriateness of social behaviors.

Functional academic competencies. Adaptive behavior conceptions and instruments vary on the degree to which functional academic competencies are included; some ignore this area, while others emphasize these competencies. The AAMR criteria for adaptive behavior during the school age years, as well as the criteria for the adult years, include the application and use of academic skills in daily life activities. The domain of functional academic competencies refers to basic, fundamental literacy skills, knowledge of concepts of time and number and other cognitive competencies essential to personal independence and social responsibility. This domain does not include esoteric intellectual competencies that, although desirable, are not essential to competent functioning in every day settings.

Functional academic skills are different from performance on standardized achievement tests. Two criteria are suggested for determining whether or not a particular skill meets the criteria for the functional academic domain: (a) Does nearly everyone of a particular age master the skill? and (b) Is the skill essential for adequate *current* personal independence and social responsibility?

Vocational/occupational competencies. The competencies associated with the vocational and occupational domain become increasingly important at higher age and grade levels, particularly for IEP development and instructional planning. The vocational and occupational domain includes at least three subdomains: (a) Knowledge about careers and work; (b) Appropriate attitudes and values concerning careers and work; and (c) Specific skills required for successful job performance.

Nearly all adaptive behavior instruments provide content on the four domains described above. These four domains are particularly useful for decision making about MR eligibility, the determination of general goals for programs, and for the selection of placement options. Further discussion of these applications is provided in later sections.

Purposes of Assessment and Criteria for Instruments

Determination of purpose for assessment, i.e., the specification of the questions to be answered through gathering information, is critical to all areas of assessment including adaptive behavior. The two major purposes for assessment for which adaptive behavior information is most often used are classification/placement and program planning intervention. Different kinds of instruments are needed for these two major purposes.

Classification/placement. The classification/placement purpose typically involves four major decisions: (a) Determination of eligibility for classification as handicapped; (b) Determination of discrepancies from average levels of performance; (c) Determination of general strengths and weaknesses that are then translated into programming goals; and (d) Selection of a placement option. Norm-referenced instruments are typically most appropriate for classification/placement decisions. Criteria for selection of norm-referenced adaptive behavior instruments are the following: (a) Appropriate item content; (b) Items provide a **representative** sample of behaviors from all important domains; (c) Adequate norms; (d) Appropriate derived scores; (e) Reliability; (f) Validity; and (g) Feasibility. Extensive discussion of these criteria and evaluation of a number of adaptive behavior instruments was provided in Reschly (1987-1988).

Program planning/interventions. The second major purpose, requiring criterion referenced information, involves identification of specific skills that are then: (a) Translated into intervention objectives; (b) Used to monitor progress after interventions are implemented; and (c) Applied to the evaluation of outcomes. Criteria for criterion-referenced adaptive behavior instruments include: (a) Appropriate item content (note similarity to norm-referenced instruments); (b) *Thorough* coverage of all important skills in the critical domains of behavior (note dissimilarity to norm-referenced instruments); (c) Hierarchy and sequence of skills; (d) Skills related specifically to objectives; (e) Objectives related to interventions; and (f) Feasibility.

Careful delineation of purpose for assessment in terms of the question(s) to be answered with the information gathered is critical to good assessment, in adaptive behavior as well as in other areas.

Determination of whether or not the major decision is classification/placement or program planning/intervention has vast implications for the selection of an adaptive behavior measure. Different criteria are necessary to judge the adequacy of norm-referenced and criterion-referenced adaptive behavior measures.

Decisions in Adaptive Behavior Assessment

Purpose and target population. A critical feature of best practices in the assessment of adaptive behavior, in addition to specification of purpose, is careful matching of the choice of adaptive behavior instrument to the nature of the target population. Adaptive behavior instruments tend to be more or less appropriate for specific populations. Some adaptive behavior instruments, e.g., the Balthazar Scales, were designed for severely and profoundly MR students. In contrast, certain other adaptive behavior scales were designed primarily for mildly handicapped to normal functioning populations. Use of the Balthazar Scales with students functioning in the mild range of MR would, in all likelihood, provide virtually no useful information on relevant skills. Most of the skills in the Balthazar Scale would be far below the social competence levels of school-age children and youth with mild MR. In contrast, use of the Scales of Independent Behavior (SIB) would provide very little information in the assessment of adaptive behavior with a young, severely or profoundly MR student. Most of the items on the SIB would be considerably above the typical level of functioning of profoundly handicapped persons. Target population characteristics are a critical feature of choice of adaptive behavior procedures.

Setting. A second critical decision in choice of an adaptive behavior approach for school-age children and youth is determination of setting(s). In the first edition of *Best Practices* I strongly emphasized the importance of assessing adaptive behavior in two settings, *in school* and *out of school*. The rationale for assessment of adaptive behavior *in school* is that mastery of literacy skills is the key developmental task for persons between the ages of 5 and 17 and the expectation for acquisition of educational competencies is common to most if not all major sociocultural groups in the United States. The assessment of *in school* adaptive behavior should emphasize collection and consideration of a broad variety of information including a variety of indices of achievement, classroom coping skills, interpersonal or social skills, and maladaptive behaviors. This information can be collected through a variety of methods including teacher interview, review of cumulative records, examination of samples of classroom work, classroom observations, formal tests, and informal measures.

The assessment of adaptive behavior should not be restricted to the school setting. *Out of school* adaptive behavior should be assessed because a variety of nonacademic competencies are also developed between the ages of 5 and 17 and demonstrated in home, neighborhood, and community settings. The expectations for and opportunities to develop these nonacademic competencies may vary among different contexts. Furthermore, these nonacademic competencies may be very important to critical program objectives regarding attainment of competencies in several domains of adaptive behavior such as independent functioning, social functioning, and vocational/occupational functioning. The assessment of *out of school* adaptive behavior should focus on areas such as peer relations, family relationships, degree of independence, responsibilities assumed, and economic or vocational activities. A variety of methods of collecting this information can be applied including structured interviews with parents, informal interviews with students, and observation.

The use of adaptive behavior information from both *in school* and *out of school* settings is probably more widely accepted today than when the first edition of *Best Practices* was published. It is important that both settings be considered and that information from both be incorporated in making critical decisions, a topic discussed in a later section.

Method. Another critical consideration in the assessment of adaptive behavior is determination of method to gather information. George Batsche recently pointed out that there were four (and only four) methods to gather information: Testing, interview, reviewing records, and observation. Each of these methods should be considered as decisions are made about how to assess adaptive behavior. Several of these approaches are used in the currently available standardized adaptive behavior measures. Use of additional methods to gather adaptive behavior information is especially important when adaptive behavior information from different sources or settings is contradictory.

Sources/respondent. There are four plausible sources of adaptive behavior information: (a) Parent; (b) Teacher; (c) Child or adult; and (d) Peers. The most commonly used method is third-party respondent using either the teacher or the parent. Some critical issues in the use of third-party respondents include the knowledge base of the respondent, subtle response biases that affect the respondent's reporting of information, and the degree to which the respondent is encouraged or even required to guess about adaptive behavior competencies that have not been observed. Adaptive behavior assessments using third-party respondents with a vested interest in a particular outcome or respondents that have not had opportunities to observe the behaviors in question have relatively limited value.

Adaptive Behavior Instruments and Domains

Substantial improvement in the quality of available adaptive behavior instruments has occurred since the preparation of this chapter for the prior edition of *Best Practices*. Three instruments published in late 1984 provide considerably better information on adaptive behavior for the classification/placement and, to a limited extent, for program planning/intervention purposes. Each of these instruments will be briefly reviewed with tables provided matching various scores from these instruments to the four adaptive behavior domains specified earlier in this chapter. The full references and publishers for a number of adaptive behavior instruments are provided in Table 1.

NABC/CTAB. The Comprehensive Test of Adaptive Behavior (CTAB) and a brief version, the Normative Adaptive Behavior Checklist (NABC), assess adaptive behavior over the ages of birth to 21 across six domains using a checklist format. The NABC, like brief versions of other instruments, should be used cautiously, perhaps limited to general screening for possible adaptive behavior difficulties. None of the subtest scores on the NABC should be interpreted. The CTAB provides a checklist format with approximately 500 items organized into six subtests and 24 item groupings. The CTAB can be administered to or completed independently by a parent, teacher, or both. The CTAB is fairly efficient and inexpensive due to the checklist format. It can be used for classification/placement and, to a significant extent, program planning/intervention purposes. The CTAB provides outstanding objectivity of items, excellent reliability, solid validity, and adequate norms. Among adaptive behavior instruments, the CTAB provides the best available measure of the domain of functional academics. The CTAB may not have sufficient ceiling to provide an adequate measure for older mildly handicapped students (above age 14).

SIB. The Scales of Independent Behavior (SIB) provides assessment of adaptive behavior over the ages of birth to adult through a 226-item scale administered via highly structured interview. The respondent can be the parent, teacher, or both. The item content is organized into four adaptive behavior subtests with fourteen item groupings. An optional problem behavior domain with three subtests and eight item groupings is also provided. The SIB provides excellent content validity, a useful problem behaviors domain, adequate norms, excel-

lent reliability, excellent validity, and, with the highly structured interview format, can be administered by trained paraprofessional personnel. The SIB provides excellent information for classification/placement decisions, but relatively little useful information for program planning/intervention.

Vineland Scales. The Vineland Adaptive Behavior Scales (VABS) consist of two independent sets of items and three administration procedures. Most prominent of these instruments, the VABS-Survey (VABS-S) and the VABS-Expanded (VABS-E) are administered through a semi-structured interview with the parent requiring considerable skill on the part of the interviewer. None of the items are to be read verbatim to the respondent, but quite specific information must be gleaned from a general discussion of skills in a particular domain or behaviors in a specific setting. The VABS-S consists of 297 items covering the ages of birth to 19, organized into four subtests and 11 item groupings. A maladaptive behavior section is provided. The VABS-S appears to have excellent content, outstanding norms, a variety of appropriate derived scores, mediocre reliability, adequate validity, but requires considerable expenditure in terms of the costs associated with gathering the information due to the semi-structured interview format. The VABS-S provides good information for classification/placement decisions.

The VABS-E has the same organization as the VABS-S, but with 577 items. The VABS-E is designed for program planning/intervention, but fails to meet some of the critical features for such instruments. Although the content validity of the VABS-E is excellent, and the information provides a solid basis for determining more specific skill deficiencies in weak areas, critical features of instruments for program planning/intervention are missing, e.g., the tie between items and intervention objectives, the relationship between objectives and interventions, and a clearly specified hierarchy and sequence of skills. The VABS-E is very time consuming. The VABS-E can be utilized best as

TABLE 1
[1]Recently Published Adaptive Behavior Measures

A.   [2]*Normative Adaptive Behavior Checklist (NABC)* and *Comprehensive Test of Adaptive Behavior (CTAB)* by Gary Adams, published in 1984 by Charles E. Merrill (Merrill was purchased by Psychological Corporation in March, 1986). Order from Psychological Corporation, 555 Academic Court, San Antonio, TX 78204. (800) 228-0752.

B.   [2]*Scales of Independent Behavior* by Robert H. Bruininks, Richard W. Woodcock, Richard F. Weatherman, and Bradley K. Hill, published in 1984 by DLM Teaching Resources, One DLM Park, Allen, TX 75002. (800) 527-4747.

C.   [2]*Vineland Adaptive Behavior Scales* by Sara S. Sparrow, David A. Balla, and Domenic V. Cicchetti, published in 1984 by American Guidance Service, Publishers' Building, P.O. Box 99, Circle Pines, MN 55014. (800) 328-2560.

D.   *AAMD Adaptive Behavior Scale School Edition,* revised and standardized in 1981 by Nadine Lambert and Myra Windmiller, distributed by Publishers Test Service, 2500 Garden Road, Monterey, CA 93940. (800) 538-9547.

E.   *Adaptive Behavior Inventory for Children* by Jane Mercer and June Lewis, published in 1978 by the Psychological Corporation, 555 Academic Court, San Antonio, TX 78204. (800) 228-0752.

F.   *Social Behavior Assessment* by T. M. Stephens, published in 1981 by Cedars Press, P.O. Box 29351, Columbus, OH 43229. (614) 846-2849/

G.   *Balthazar Scales of Adaptive Behavior for the Profoundly and Severely Retarded Sections I and II.* Published in 1973 by Consulting Psychologists Press, P.O. Box 60070, Palo Alto, CA 94306.

H.   *Social Skills Rating Systems* by Frank Gresham and Steve Elliott, published in 1989 by American Guidance Service, Publishers' Building, P.O. Box 99, Circle Pines, MN 55014. (800) 328-2560.

I.   *Walker-McConnell Scale of Social Competence and School Adjustment* by Hill Walker and Scott McConnell, published in 1988 by PRO-ED, 8700 Shoal Creek Blvd., Austin, TX 78758. (512) 451-3246.

[1]Listing of an inventory does not constitute endorsement of technical adequacy or usefulness.
[2]Reviewed briefly in this chapter.

a means to further assess any weak areas identified on the VABS-S.

The VABS-Classroom (VABS-C) is a 244-item checklist covering the ages of 3 to 12, organized around four subtests. There is no maladaptive behavior domain. The major problem with the VABS-C is questionable content validity; teachers are required to rate domestic tasks that have never been observed. The norms appear to be too tough and the reliability is mediocre. The author of the test manual for the VABS-C should be complimented for the development of excellent derived scores and outstanding interpretive aids. Although the VABS-C is very efficient, the questionable content validity makes use of the instrument in making significant decisions questionable.

The subtest content of these recently published, technically adequate adaptive behavior scales is matched with the four domains of adaptive behavior in Table 2. Generally, several quite adequate subtests scores are available for each of the adaptive behavior domains.

Other instruments. A number of other adaptive behavior instruments were reviewed extensively in Reschly (1987-1988). Each of these instruments has significant limitations regarding technical adequacy, e.g., norms, content validity, or

TABLE 2
Measures of Adaptive Behavior Domains

Instrument	Subtest	[1]Single or Mixed	Score Quality
Independent Functioning (IF) Measures			
CTAB	Self Help	Single (IF)	Adequate
CTAB	Home Living	Single (IF)	Adequate
CTAB	Independent Living	Mixed (IF, FA, VO)	Adequate
NABC	Self Help	Single (IF)	Poor
NABC	Home Living	Single (IF)	Poor
NABC	Independent Living	Mixed (IF, FA, VO)	Poor
SIB	Personal Living	Single (IF)	Adequate
SIB	Community Living	Mixed (IF, FA, VO)	Adequate
VABS-C	Daily Living	Mixed (IF, FA)	Adequate
VABS-E	Daily Living	Mixed (IF, FA)	Adequate
VABS-S	Daily Living	Mixed (IF, FA)	Adequate
Social Functioning (SF) Measures			
CTAB	Social Skills	Single (SF)	Adequate
NABC	Social Skills	Single (SF)	Poor
SIB	Social Interaction and Communication	Mixed (SF, FA)	Adequate
VABS-C	Socialization	Single (SF)	Adequate
VABS-E	Socialization	Single (SF)	Adequate
VABS-S	Socialization	Single (SF)	Adequate
Functional Academics (FA) Measures			
CTAB	Independent Living	Mixed (FA, IF, VO)	Adequate
CTAB	Language & Academic	Single (FA)	Adequate
NABC	Independent Living	Mixed (FA, IF, VO)	Poor
NABC	Language & Academic	Single (FA)	Poor
SIB	Social Interaction and Communication	Mixed (FA, SF)	Adequate
SIB	Community Living	Mixed (FA, IF, VO)	Adequate
VABS-C	Communication	Single (FA)	Adequate
VABS-C	Daily Living	Mixed (FA, IF)	Adequate
VABS-E	Communication	Single (FA)	Adequate
VABS-E	Daily Living	Mixed (FA, IF)	Adequate
VABS-S	Communication	Single (FA)	Adequate
VABS-S	Daily Living	Mixed (FA, IF)	Adequate
Vocational and Occupational (VO) Measures			
CTAB	Independent Living	Mixed (VO, IF, FA)	Adequate
NABC	Independent Living	Mixed (VO, IF, FA)	Poor
SIB	Community Living	Mixed (VO, IF, FA)	Adequate

KEY: CTAB — Comprehensive Test of Adaptive Behavior; NABC — Normative Adaptive Behavior Checklist; SIB — Scales of Independent Behavior; VABS — Vineland Adaptive Behavior Scales; VABS-E — Vineland Expanded; VABS-C — Vineland Classroom; VABS-S — Vineland Survey; IF — Independent Functioning; SF — Social Functioning; FA — Functional Academics; VO — Vocational and Occupational.

[1]Single means that virtually all of the content of the subtest is from one domain. Mixed means that the content of the subtest reflects two or more domains.

criterion related validity. These instruments are not reviewed here due to space limitations.

BEST PRACTICES

1. *The best possible match between the explicitly stated purpose for assessment of adaptive behavior, the nature of the student, and adaptive behavior assessment approach (method, setting, and source) should be developed.* (Discussed in prior sections).

2. *Discrepancies in adaptive behavior results arising from the application of different methods, settings, and sources should be resolved using the convergent validity principle (Gresham, 1985).*

Discrepancies in the apparent level of adaptive behavior between results obtained from different sources (parent vs teacher), different settings (*in-school* vs *out of school*), or different methods (third party respondent vs. observation) have been reported frequently. Generally, the results are in the same direction, e.g., the results from parents may be higher than results from teachers, but both are considerably below average. Further investigation of large discrepancies is mandatory. One way to further investigate the large differences is to apply additional methods for assessing adaptive behavior or to consider other sources of information. Observation or direct testing of students over relevant skills are good methods to resolve discrepancies between third party respondents, one or both of whom may have limited information or unintentional response biases. Application of the convergent validity principle involves careful examination of the consistency of the information across different sources, settings, and methods of assessing adaptive behavior.

3. *The determination of a deficit in one or more adaptive behavior domains is mandatory in classification of students with mental retardation. Determination of the size of the discrepancy to constitute a deficit must be based on judgment, buttressed by logic and evidence.*

There are no numerical guidelines suggested by any professional association concerning the size of an adaptive behavior discrepancy to constitute a deficit. The major authoritative professional organization in this area, AAMR, suggests the use of clinical judgment, which should, of course, be substantiated by logic and evidence. The logic and evidence to support the conclusion that an adaptive behavior deficit exists should be stated explicitly. Obviously, the level of performance should be well below average, but it does not have to be as low or lower than the performance on the dimension of general intellectual functioning.

4. *A profile of adaptive behavior, intellect, and age should be used in choice of placement option for students with mild mental retardation.*

Generally, part-time special education or resource options should be used with students who are young, have moderate discrepancies, overall performance near classification cut-off points, and deficits in single domains of adaptive behavior or deficits restricted primarily to a single setting such as the schools. Immediate placement of a student with mild MR from a regular classroom to a self-contained special class is an enormous and usually unnecessary change. A less drastic option such as part-time special education using resource or similar models is more appropriate for initial placement for most students with mild MR. Consideration of the profile in Table 3 will assist in choice of placement option.

5. *Adaptive behavior, including classroom coping skills, should be screened, and, where indicated, assessed thoroughly in all prereferral interventions and in all multifactored evaluations for at risk and handicapped students.*

Classroom social behaviors exert considerable influence on achievement, popularity with peers, and acceptability to teachers. Several measurement procedures are available to assess peer acceptance, appropriateness of social behaviors, task persistence, attention, and so on (See Stephens referenced in Table 2, Gresham,

TABLE 3
Use of Intellect, Adaptive Behavior, and Age in Choice of Placement Option

Parttime Resource	Variable	Self-Contained Special Class
Younger	AGE	Older
Moderate	DISCREPANCY	Large
Close to	CUT OFF	Far Below
Single Domain	COMPREHENSIVENESS	Most Domains
One Setting	SETTING	All Settings

this volume, and Reschly 1987–1988). A number of successful interventions with these skills are available and, combined with academic interventions, can substantially improve overall classroom performance.

6. *Explicitly stated general goals and specific intervention objectives should be developed whenever adaptive behavior deficits are identified.*

Consider this reasoning: If the student's deficit in adaptive behavior is of sufficient magnitude and importance to justify the classification of mental retardation, then the individualized educational program needs to reflect one or more general goals in adaptive behavior with appropriate intervention objectives. Furthermore, classroom coping skills with all students exhibiting learning or behavior problems need to be examined and, where appropriate, interventions implemented. These interventions may significantly improve academic performance and thereby prevent or reduce the degree of separation needed from regular education.

7. *Adaptive behavior should be the central issue in all triennial reevaluations with students with mental retardation (Reschly, 1988).*

Adaptive behavior should be a central theme in the programming for all students classified as MR. Progress in the attainment of social competencies should be carefully monitored and, if necessary,

significant changes made in programs in order to ensure the acquisition of essential social competencies.

Students functioning at the severe and profound levels of mental retardation need frequent assessment and continuous monitoring of the acquisition of adaptive behavior competencies. Adaptive behavior instruments should take precedence over measures of general intellectual functioning in classification decision making and in triennial reevaluations. The rationale, briefly stated, is as follows. There are typically few if any questions regarding whether the general intellectual functioning of severely and profoundly retarded students is significantly subaverage. Readministration of IQ tests provides little or no information useful to any decision, either classification/placement or program planning/intervention. In contrast, adaptive behavior information is useful for: (a) Determining level of mental retardation; (b) Identifying specific skills mastered and not mastered; (c) Determination of intervention objectives; (d) Monitoring implementation of interventions; (e) Assessing progress; and (f) Evaluating outcomes. Adaptive behavior scales with both norm and criterion-referenced characteristics such as the CTAB or the VABS-E should be used extensively with severely and profoundly retarded students.

8. *The most recent revisions of technically adequate, standardized adaptive*

behavior instruments should be used as part of the assessment of adaptive behavior.

The recently published standardized adaptive behavior scales, particularly the CTAB, VABS, and SIB, meet the usual standards for technical adequacy. Other sources of information, data collection methods, and alternative settings should be examined at least informally, and commented on explicitly, in decisions about adaptive behavior. Inconsistent results should be investigated further.

SUMMARY

Adaptive behavior is an essential component of assessment and interventions for handicapped and at risk students. Conception of adaptive behavior and assessment practices that reflect considered judgment of sources of information, settings, and methods of collecting data are crucial to best professional practices. Use of information from standardized adaptive behavior instruments is necessary in most instances. Interpretation of adaptive behavior information from different assessment methods and sources needs to follow best practices principles. Most important, this information must be applied in the design, implementation, monitoring, and evaluation of interventions.

REFERENCES

Bickel, W. E., Bond, L., & Carter, A. (1981). Educational priorities among urban black populations. *Journal of Negro Education, 50*, 3-8.

Doll, E. A. (1941). The essentials of an inclusive concept of mental deficiency. *American Journal of Mental Deficiency, 46*, 214-219.

Doll, E. A. (1953). *Measurement of social competence.* Circle Pines, MN: American Guidance Service.

Greenspan, S. (1979). Social intelligence in the retarded. In N. R. Ellis (Ed.), *Handbook of mental deficiency, psychological theory and research*, 2nd ed., Hillsdale, NJ: Lawrence Erlbaum.

Gresham, F. M., & Reschly, D. J. (1988). Issues in the conceptualization, classification, and assessment of social skills in the mildly handicapped. In T. R. Kratochwill (Ed.), *Advances in School Psychology (Vol. VI)* (pp. 203-247). Hillsdale, NJ: Lawrence Erlbaum, Inc.

Grossman, H. J. (Ed.). (1983). *Classification in mental retardation.* Washington, DC: American Association on Mental Deficiency.

Gresham, F. (1985). Behavior disorder assessment: Conceptual, definitional, and practical considerations. *School Psychology Review, 14*, 495-509.

Gresham, F. M., & Elliott, S. N. (1987). The relationship between adaptive behavior and social skills: Issues in definition and assessment. *Journal of Special Education, 21*, 167-181.

Larry P. v. Riles. (1979, 1984, 1986). 343 F. Supp. 1306 (N. D. Cal. 1972) (preliminary injunction). aff'd 502 F. 2d 963 (9th cir. 1974); 495 F. Supp. 926 (N. D. Cal. 1979) (decision on merits) aff'd (9th cir. no. 90-427 Jan. 23, 1984). Order modifying judgment, C-71-2270 RFP, September 25, 1986.

Marshall et al. v. Georgia. (1984, 1985). U. S. District Court for the Southern District of Georgia, CV482-233, June 28, 1984; Affirmed (11th Cir. No. 84-8771, October 19, 1985). (Appealed as NAACP v. Georgia).

Polloway, E. A. (1985). Identification and placement in mild mental retardation programs: Recommendations for professional practice. *Education and Training of the Mentally Retarded, 20*, 218-221.

Reschly, D. J. (1987-1988). *Adaptive Behavior.* Tallahassee, FL: Florida Department of Education, Bureau of Education for Exceptional Students. A revision of a similar monograph prepared for the Minnesota Department of Education in 1987.

Reschly, D. J. (1988). Assessment issues, placement litigation, and the future of mild mental retardation classification and programming. *Education and Training of the Mentally Retarded, 23*, 285-301.

Reschly, D. J., Kicklighter, R. H., & McKee, P. (1988a). Recent placement litigation Part II, Minority EMR overrepresentation: Comparison of *Larry P.* (1979, 1984, 1986) with *Marshall* (1984, 1985) and *S-1* (1986). *School Psychology Review, 17*, 20-36.

Reschly, D. J., Kicklighter, R. H. & McKee, P. (1988b). Recent placement litigation Part III: Analysis of differences in *Larry P. Marshall*, and *S-1* and implications for future practices. *School Psychology Review, 17*, 37-48.

Zucker, S. H., & Polloway, E. A. (1987). Issues in identification and assessment in mental retardation. *Education and Training in Mental Retardation, 22*, 69-76.

ANNOTATED BIBLIOGRAPHY

Edgerton, R. B. (Ed.). (1984). *Lives in process: Mentally retarded adults in a large city*. Washington, DC: American Association on Mental Deficiency.
Provides extensive, insightful accounts of the adaptive behavior problems experienced by young adults with mild mental retardation. These findings have considerable importance for adaptive behavior conception, assessment, and interventions.

Grossman, H. J. (Ed.). (1983). *Classification in mental retardation*. Washington, DC: American Association on Mental Deficiency.
This is the most authoritative source on the construct of adaptive behavior and on conceptions of mental retardation. This is essential reading for school psychologists involved with mental retardation classification/placement decisions.

Journal of Special Education, 1987, *21*(1).
The entire special issue, co-edited by Patti L. Harrison and Randy W. Kamphaus, was devoted to adaptive behavior. An excellent array of articles was provided.

McGrew K., & Bruininks, R. (1989). The factor structure of adaptive behavior. *School Psychology Review*, *18*, 64–81.
An excellent article summarizing research on the structure of adaptive behavior.

Meyers, C. E., Nihira, K., & Zetlin, A. (1979). The measurement of adaptive behavior. In N. R. Ellis (Ed.), *Handbook of mental deficiency, psychological theory and research*, (2nd ed.). Hillsdale, NJ: Lawrence Erlbaum.
This is a comprehensive, scholarly treatment of the theory and research pertaining to adaptive behavior measurement.

Reschly, D. J. (1982). Assessing mild mental retardation: The influence of adaptive behavior, sociocultural status and prospects for nonbiased assessment. In C. Reynolds & T. Gutkin (Eds.), *The handbook of school psychology*. New York: Wiley Interscience.
This chapter includes further discussion of the placement bias litigation as well as commentary on adaptive behavior theory, research, and measurement.

Reschly, D. J. (1987–1988). *Adaptive behavior*. Tallahassee, FL: Florida Department of Education, Bureau of Education for Exceptional Students. A revision of a similar monograph prepared for the Minnesota Department of Education in 1987.
This monograph provides thorough treatment of adaptive behavior conception, domains, legal regulations, professional association guidelines, critical reviews of instruments, and decision making strategies.

Reschly, D. J. (1988). Assessment issues, placement litigation, and the future of mild mental retardation classification and programming. *Education and Training of the Mental Retarded*, *23*, 285–301.
Based on an address at the CEC-MR 25th anniversary symposium, this article explores greater use of adaptive behavior and the possible elimination of IQ in MR classification.

3

Best Practices in the Administration and Supervision of School Psychological Services

Ronda C. Talley
Jefferson County (Kentucky) Public Schools

OVERVIEW

Leadership is key to the advancement of any profession. School psychology is no exception. While the generation of a knowledge base and language are fundamental to the development of a profession, active implementation and evaluation of program initiatives by leaders in the field transform knowledge into reality, language into understanding.

At no other time in history has there been greater opportunity for the infusion of appropriate and meaningful psychological services into schools. Drucker (1989) dramatically noted: "Today we are in the early stages of a social and technological revolution that should drastically and irrevocably change the meaning of education and the art of teaching in our society." In addition, a myriad of reports on the state of education (*A Nation At Risk*, 1983; *Time for Results*, 1986) suggest that change will be the by-word of educational reform in the 1900s and beyond. In this climate, leaders in the profession of school psychology face the critical task of riding reform efforts while administering and supervising effective programs which will assist students, parents, teachers, and administrators to competently and confidently advance into the 21st century.

The purpose of this chapter is to provide guidelines for school psychology leaders who will be charged with the task of translating theory into real-world school psychological services (SPS) programs which meet the needs of our changing schools and society. The chapter will focus on (a) distinctions between school psychological services administration and supervision, (b) program administration issues, (c) program and staff supervision issues, and (d) characteristics of effective, "best practices" programs directed by innovative leaders.

BASIC CONSIDERATIONS

Limited research is available regarding the supervision of school psychological services programs (Disenhouse, 1987; Ross-Reynolds & Grimes, 1981). Since professionals within the field have called for increased attention to this neglected area of school psychological services functioning (Curtis & Zins, 1986; Murphy, 1981), this section will define basic terms relevant to the administration and supervision of SPS before addressing issues related to program organization and staff supervision.

Program Administration

Program administration forms the over-all umbrella term under which all activities of the SPS director may be subsumed. It involves all the complex and myriad functions of a manager, who works with and through others to accomplish objectives of both the organization and its members (Conger & Kanungo, 1988), while including duties specific to program development and staff supervision. Program administration can be conceptualized as encompassing three interrelated areas: (a) organizational leadership and direction, (b) long range planning and policy-making, and (c) technical management (Orlosky, McCleary, Shapiro, & Webb, 1984). Specific activities of the SPS director which represent this umbrella area include, but are not limited to, program innovation (Baldridge & Deal, 1975; Baldridge & Deal, 1983; Zaltman, Florio, & Sikorski, 1977), strategic marketing (Illback, 1988), continuing professional development for staff (Gerken, 1981; Robinson, 1981), program evaluation and research (Maher, 1979; Phillips, 1982), and resource allocation (Montana & Charnov, 1987; Riggs, 1985). As a whole, program administration constitutes a complex, diverse area of professional functioning which requires the leadership and vision of a politically astute and technically knowledgeable school psychologist program supervisor.

In all these areas, the SPS administrator must be aware that communication and appropriate interpersonal relationships, both within and outside the SPS unit, form the key to effective leadership. However, it is not enough for the SPS director to seek strategic placement in key information networks; similar positions within a variety of communication networks should be sought for all interested staff psychologists. For instance, organizational leadership and direction may be provided by securing positions for the SPS director and school psychologists on key district committees, thus enhancing visibility of the unit while providing a means by which other district staff may become familiar with school psychologists and the range of expertise they may bring to many pressing issues. Likewise, filling seats on professional organization and community boards or in local government, while time consuming, enhances school psychologists' access to persons with decision making power and influence. Securing affiliation of school psychologists

with the local organization which represents school administrators may also prove to be an effective means for developing avenues to advocate for program needs.

In the area of long range planning and policy-making, communication also plays an important role. Developing long range plans and policies provides the SPS director with both an internal and external communication challenge. First, the director must facilitate the work of staff to formulate written plans which represent a congruence of thought by many unique individuals who come to the district from school psychology programs with a variety of philosophical orientations. While this is being accomplished, the director must assure that administrators higher in the organizational chain are kept informed and educated regarding how professional standards, best practices, district reform efforts, and staff philosophy will impact long range plans for development of the SPS unit. The degree of trust which is present between the SPS director and the next higher administrator as well as the levels of power, influence, and security which both administrators enjoy may have a significant impact on the acceptance of planning and policy-making initiatives.

In the area of technical management, SPS directors must be able to communicate district policy and rules in an equitable manner to all staff. When dealing with SPS staff, interpersonal effectiveness is key. The director should generously reward and reinforce desired behavior, while providing incentives and support to those who need skill enhancement in one or more areas. In order to accomplish this, the director should establish clear communication lines between and among staff and be consistent when discussing the same issue with different staff. Often, development of a SPS program policies and procedures manual is helpful. Relatedly, distinctions between friendships and work relationships may prove useful.

Administrative supervision. Administrative supervision refers to a subset of program administration which deals with the procedural direction of individual staff members. Also termed managerial supervision (Hart, 1982), administrative supervision involves assisting staff to follow institutional rules or policies that help the organization function more efficiently. Recording staff attendance, approving professional leave, and overseeing payroll are all examples of administrative supervision. With this form of supervision, technical knowledge of the field is not mandatory, therefore, in many districts, administrative supervision of SPS staff is provided by a non-psychologist administrator. This issue, also addressed by Simonsen (1987), will be discussed further in the section on organization of the SPS unit.

Clinical supervision. The topic of clinical supervision has been explored in a variety of fields (Cherniss, 1984). Within school psychology, Knoff (1986) indicated that clinical supervision is:

> an intensive, hierarchical, interpersonally-focused relationship involving a supervisor who oversees the development of a supervisee's professional knowledge, skill, confidence, objectivity, and interpersonal interactions on behalf of or with a specified client for the purpose of facilitating and/or improving competence and effective service delivery and promoting accountability in the field. (p. 529)

He further noted five related goals of supervision:

> (a) to develop a supervisory system, process, and/or style that encourages supervisees to seek and respond to supervision; (b) to evaluate, formatively and/or summatively, supervisees . . . to determine their current developmental levels and professional strengths and weaknesses; (c) to enhance supervisees' growth in necessary, identified areas such that their provision of services and job and self-satisfaction improves; (d) to provide training such that supervisees can develop their own supervision skills; and (e) to monitor the welfare of clients serviced by supervisees. (pp. 529–530)

Procedures specific to the clinical supervision process have been outlined in detail by Goldhammer, Anderson, and Krajewski (1980) and Valett (1963). Other experts have applied this form of supervision in educational settings, but, interestingly, have kept the term "clinical supervision."

Within educational frameworks, clinical supervision is outlined as a five step process. In the first step, content/task analysis, the supervisor and staff member engage in content analysis of the job by identifying and prioritizing tasks, then specifying how well each task needs to be done. In diagnosis, the second step, the staff member's abilities and performance are measured against the written job expectancies. To do this, the supervisor observes the psychologist in action and records specific data, identifying what is done well and noting areas of concern. Next comes prescription, where the supervisor determines areas which need attention and writes objectives, considering the psychologist's previous experiences, personality, and relationship patterns. Objectives are rank ordered and one is selected as top priority. In addition, the types of help the supervisor will provide are specified.

In the fourth step, an instructional conference is held. At this time, the supervisor provides positive feedback, elicits the staff psychologist's ideas, and offers suggestions and assistance. Lastly, after the psychologist has had the opportunity to meet the objectives established, a formal evaluation conference may be held. During the conference, the supervisor offers positive feedback for meeting goals and, for persons who do not meet their goals, explores areas of difficulty, sets new strategies and time lines, and discusses possible outcomes. While this form of clinical supervision is currently in vogue, it represents only one of many variations which is currently being applied in education settings.

As noted earlier, clinical supervision and administrative supervision form permeable, interrelated subsets under the general umbrella of program administration. This relationship is depicted in Figure 1. Clinical supervision differs from administrative supervision in that clinical supervision requires the supervisor to

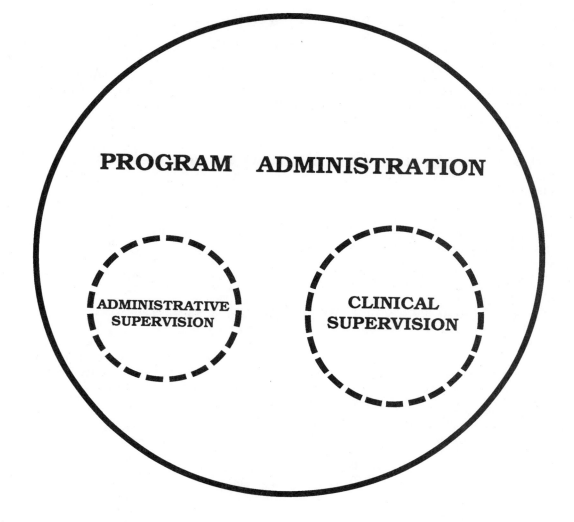

FIGURE 1. Interrelated components of the SPS administrative/supervisory process.

possess technical knowledge of the field and to conduct direct observations, joint planning meetings, and constructive feedback sessions with individual staff members. While administrative supervision is aimed at helping the staff member function as part of an organization, clinical supervision is concerned with developing the staff member as an interpersonally effective clinician (Hart, 1982).

Because of the lack of differentiation between these supervisory dimensions, many school administrators have difficulty understanding the need to have SPS programs supervised and directed by a school psychologist. Generic administrators tend to view administrative supervision as the dominant supervisory function and ignore the need for the content foundation which is required to be effective in both clinical supervision and SPS program administration. Often, school psychologists have expressed distress regarding this lack of understanding. As school psychologists better articulate differences among program administration, administrative supervision, and clinical supervision, increased understanding by our educational peers may result.

School Psychological Services (SPS) Program Unit

The American Psychological Association (APA) *Specialty Guidelines for the Delivery of Services by School Psychologists* (1981) defines a SPS unit as "the functional unit through which school psychological services are provided" (p. 672). It further states that the unit:

1. provides SPS to individuals or to a school system, district, agency, corporation, or consortium,
2. operates as part of the administrative organizational unit or as an independent professional service,
3. employs at least one professional (doctoral) school psychologist who provides SPS services within a multidisciplinary context, with supporting psychological services staff, if any,
4. may consist of doctoral psychologists who offer SPS on a contractual basis.

Concurrently, the National Association of School Psychologists (NASP), in its *Standards for the Provision of School Psychological Services* (1984), states simply that "where two or more school psychologists are employed, a coordinated system of SPS is in effect within that unit" (p. 29).

School Psychological Services Director

In providing guidance regarding the position of SPS program director, the APA *Specialty Guidelines* indicate that "wherever a SPS unit exists, a professional [doctoral] school psychologist is responsible for planning, directing, and reviewing the provision of SPS" (p. 674).

In contrast, the NASP *Standards* define a supervising school psychologist as "a professional psychologist who has met all requirements for credentialing, has completed three years of successful supervised experience as a school psychologist, and who has been designated by an employing agency as a supervisor responsible for SPS in the agency" (p. 24). Under this definition, it is not required that the SPS director hold a doctoral degree.

Since many small districts may employ only one school psychologist and may not have access to a full-time doctoral school psychologist, within the context of this chapter, the designation "SPS director" will be applied to the certified school psychologist who serves as head of the SPS unit.

BEST PRACTICES IN ADMINISTRATION AND SUPERVISION

Best practices in the administration and supervision of school psychological services are influenced by many program administration variables, such as professional practice standards for staff supervision, unit direction, and work with interns and practicum students. With these guidelines, it is essential to work within an organizational context to position the SPS unit; develop its mission, philosophy, and goal statements; and assign staff in such a manner as to address system demands while advancing the field toward compliance with professional standards. The next section is offered to assist beginning SPS administrators in their initial efforts to assimilate professional standards related to program administration and supervision.

Program Administration

Professional practice standards. Several critical professional documents offer direction on the organization and supervision of school psychological services. These include the APA *Specialty Guidelines for the Delivery of Services by School Psychologists* (1981) and *Accreditation Handbook* (1986) and the NASP *Principles for Professional Ethics* (1984), *Standards for the Provision of School Psychological Services* (1984), *Standards for Training and Field Placement Programs in School Psychology* (1986), and *Standards for Credentialing of School Psychologists* (1986). In addition, the Council of Directors of School Psychology Training Programs' *Guidelines for Meeting Internship Criteria in School Psychology* (1983) also provides information relevant to supervision of the internship experience. Key points pertaining to program development standards are presented next.

SPS unit structure. In addition to supervisory standards, the APA *Specialty Guidelines* also provide a clear outline for the composition of the formulation of an SPS unit. The program is to be structured to facilitate effective, economical service delivery which is responsive to the needs of the school population. Its organization and lines of responsibility are to be described in written form, along with a statement of unit objectives and the scope of services. Procedural guidelines for the delivery of SPS are also to be developed and distributed to various groups, including district officials, for review and agreement; revision is to be conducted annually. Documentation regarding the delivery of SPS is to be maintained. In addition, the unit must have a record retention and disposition policy and a system to protect the confidentiality of their records.

To facilitate a comparison of the APA and NASP standards regarding unit structure, refer to Table 1.

Staff supervision. The APA *Specialty Guidelines* indicate that "the professional school psychologist supervises no more than the equivalent of 15 full-time specialists in school psychology and/or other school psychological personnel" (p. 673) and provides no less than 1 hour per week of direct face-to-face supervision for each staff member. However, when a district does not have a full-time professional school psychologist to direct the SPS unit, the standards state that the district should hire one on a part-time contractual basis to assume all responsibilities of the unit director. The guidelines further note that if the professional school psychologist has "insufficient time to carry out full responsibility for coordinating or directing the unit, a specialist in school psychology is designated as director or coordinator of the SPS and is supervised by a professional school psychologist employed on a part-time basis, for a minimum of 2 hours per week" (p. 674).

NASP, in its *Standards for the Provision of School Psychological Services*, specifies that "employing agencies assure that an effective program of supervision and evaluation of SPS exists" (p. 26).

Based on these standards, it appears that APA and NASP agree on the intensive, minimum amount of time needed for individualized clinical supervision. According to the APA formula, a SPS director with 15 staff members would spend over two full days per week providing supervision, 38% of the director's available time in a 40 hour work week. Using NASP's guidelines, the director would clock a minimum of 10 hours weekly, or 25% of the available time, in clinical supervision with SPS staff. To a practicing SPS unit director, these figures represent a substantial investment to assure program quality and develop staff skills.

It is interesting to note that while the APA Guidelines emphasize the supervision of non-doctoral school psychologists, they also mention that all SPS staff should receive face-to-face supervision. The NASP *Standards for Credentialing* stress face-to-face supervision only during the first three years of practice with primarily peer supervision thereafter, while the NASP *Standards for the Provision of School Psychological Services* indicate that "supervision should be available to all school psychologists to an extent sufficient to ensure the provision of effective and accountable services" (p. 26). The reality of practice is that the SPS director will, in all likelihood, be required by the school district to evaluate all staff on a yearly basis; more frequent supervisory sessions, however, are not only promulgated in professional practice standards, but are also suggested to enhance the professional development of staff, build morale, and ensure program accountability.

A summary of standards relevant to staff supervision is presented in Table 2.

Interns and practicum students. As noted in Table 2, NASP *Standards* indicate that the SPS unit director, as defined previously, assumes principal responsibility for interns and provides direct super-

TABLE 1
Professional Standards for SPS Program Structure

APA	NASP
1. headed by doctoral school psychologist	1. headed by designated supervising school psychologist
2. facilitates effective, economical, responsive service delivery	2. offers effective, comprehensive, responsive services
3. one school psychologist may constitute an SPS unit	3. 2 or more school psychologists constitute an SPS unit
4. required documents:	4. required documents
a. organization and lines of responsibility	
.b. unit objectives, goals, and scope of services	
c. procedural guidelines, including referral system; to be reviewed/revised annually	
d. service delivery accountability/evaluation	
e. policy of records retention/disposal	e. no written requirement
f. confidentiality system	f. no written requirement

vision two hours weekly to no more than two interns at a time. The supervisor should have at least one year of district experience. This position is also consistent with NASP's *Standards for Training and Field Placement Programs in School Psychology.* In contrast, the primary responsibility for supervision of the SPS practicum student rests with faculty from the sending university.

Standards related to the supervision of interns and practicum students are outlined in Table 3.

After professional standards pertaining to administration and supervision are understood, the SPS director may give attention to organizational positioning of the program and the impact this has on staff's ability to deliver services. Because of the related nature of organizational positioning of the SPS program and potential service options, the SPS director may consider what organizational configuration could potentially best facilitate the mission and goals of the unit, then work to secure any changes which are needed. To assist in this comparison, the following section outlines a representative number of service delivery models and discusses advantages and disadvantages of each.

Placement within the Organizational Context

The issue of placement of a SPS unit within the open system of a school district has been debated by professionals in the field for many years (Cutts, 1955; Gray, 1963; Magary, 1967). More recently, Jackson (1986), Jackson and Pryzwansky (1987), and Franklin (1989) have offered views on this topic. Since it is the structure and organization of a unit that provides a foundation for functioning (Maher, Illback, & Zins, 1984), unit placement within the district's organizational pattern becomes of paramount importance. Even so, no notable research regarding how organizational placement impacts effective service delivery has been conducted (Curtis & Zins, 1986; Sandoval, 1986). In reality, the specific alignment of an SPS unit has great impact on the articulation of its mission and the sanction that mission receives from the larger organization. Therefore, in this section, five models for the delivery of SPS will be presented along with advantages and disadvantages of each. Four of the within-district models are depicted in Figure 2, while a fifth model, that of regional service delivery, represents an outside-district model and will be discussed separately.

TABLE 2

Professional Standards for the Supervision of School Psychological Services Staff

Source	Supervision Amount/Hours	Supervisor Credentials	Supervision Activities	Supervisor Responsibilities	Supervisees	Supervisor: Supervisee Ratio
APA *Specialty Guidelines for the Delivery of Services by School Psychologists* Guideline 1.1–1.3	A minimum of one hour/week of face-to-face supervision for all staff Amount and nature of supervisio is specified in writing If unit not directed by Professional School Psychologist, designated coordinator (specialist in school psychology) must be supervised by a Professional School Psychologist for a minimum of 2 hrs./wk.	Professional School Psychologist (i.e., has a doctoral degree from a regionally accredited university or professional school psychology program) or, if unavailable, by specialist in school psychology supervised by a Professional School Psychologist	Coordinates activities of school psychological service unit with other professionals; reviews & discusses intervention strategies, plans, and outcomes; maintains comprehensive view of school procedures & special concerns; discusses discrepancies among views of supervisor, supervisee, and other school faculty	Assumes professional responsibility & accountability for services provided Plans, directs, & reviews provision of school psychological services Recruits qualified staff, justifies appropriate ratios of school psychological services staff to users, directs training & research, maintains high level of ethical & Professional practice, ensures staff members function only in areas of competency	All non-doctoral school psychological services staff members	1:15
NASP *Standards for the Provision of School Psychological Services* Section 3.2: Professional Evaluation, Supervision, & Development Section 4.6.2-5 Continuing Professional Development	To an extent sufficient to ensure the provision of effective & accountable services Individual face-to-face supervision for a minimum of one hour per week or equivalent	A professional psychologist who has met all the NASP requirements for credentialing, completed 3 yrs. of successful supervised experience, & been designated by employing agency as supervisor responsible for school psychological services	Overall development, implementation, & professional supervision of school psycholoigical service program Articulates those programs to others in the employing agency & to the agency's constituent groups Shares professional responsibility and accountability for services provided		School psychologists, for the first three years of full-time employment; afterwards, peer supervision if other supervision is not available School psychologists with complex or difficult cases of when expanding services into new areas	1:10

(Table 2, continued)

Source	Supervision Amount/Hours	Supervisor Credentials	Supervision Activities	Supervisor Responsibilities	Supervisees	Supervisor: Supervisee Ratio
NASP *Principles for Professional Ethics* Section III, G, 2				Provides experiences to further professional development of staff, appropriate working conditions, fair & timely evaluation, & constructive consultation		

Note: From "School Psychology Supervision" by B. Doll, 1989, paper presented at the convention of the National Association for School Psychologists. Adapted by permission.

TABLE 3

Professional Standards for Supervision of School Psychology Interns and Practicum Students

Source	Supervision Amount/Hours	Supervisor Credentials	Supervision Activities	Supervisor Responsibilities	Evaluation of Experiences	Supervisor: Supervisee Ratio
APA Accreditation Handbook Section VII Practicum & Internship Training	75 hrs. of formally scheduled supervision for 400 hrs. of practicum	Practicum training coordinated by active faculty member of adjunct professor associated with the practicum	Access to Professional School Psychologists who will serve as appropriate role models			
a) Practicum b) Internship	2 hrs/wk. of formal, scheduled, intensive individual supervision of high quality & ample quantity	Professional School Psychologist with licensure/certification in the state in which they work. Recognition or distinction within professional associations or possession of an ABPP diploma in the appropriate specialty field. Should themselves have completed an internship in the appropriate specialty		Maintain integrity & quality of the training program	Interns actively involved in evaluating their own experience, including the quality of supervision & Instruction received. Training program evaluates its own effectiveness in achieving goals with interns. Interns kept informed of their progress by means of clearly identified evaluative sessions	Two interns in each setting
NASP Standards for the Provision of School Psychological Services Section 3.2: Professional Evaluation, Supervision, & Development		Credentialed school psychologist meeting requirements of supervising school psychologist with at least one year of experience at the employing agency				1:2

(Table 3, continued)

Source	Supervision Amount/Hours	Supervisor Credentials	Supervision Activities	Supervisor Responsibilities	Evaluation of Experiences	Supervisor: Supervisee Ratio
NASP *Standards for Training & Field Placement Programs in School Psychology* 6.5 Practica Experiences 6.7 Internship Experiences	Field-based internship supervisors provide direct supervision 2 hrs./wk. University-based supervisors maintain an on-going relationship and provide at least one contact per semester	Field-based internship supervisors hold a valid credential as a school psychologist for that portion of the internship that is in a school setting Any portion of the internship that is in a non-school setting requires supervision by an appropriately credentialed psychologist		Practica experience occurs under conditions of supervision appropriate to the specific training objectives of the program Internship experience occurs under conditions of appropriate supervision	Internship experience is systematically evaluated in a manner consistent with specific training objectives	Field-based internship supervisors: 1:2 University internship supervisors: 1:12
NASP *Principles for Professional Ethics, I* Section III, G, 2 re: Interns			Reviews & evaluates assessment results, conferences, counseling strategies, & documents	Assures the profession that training in the field is supervised adequately		
Council of Directors of School Psychology Training Programs *Guidelines for Meeting Internship Criteria in School Psychology*		Professional School Psychologist (i.e., has a doctoral degree from a regionally accredited university or professional school psychology program)				

Note: From "School Psychology Supervision" by B. Doll, 1989, paper presented at the convention of the National Association for School Psychologists. Adapted by permission.

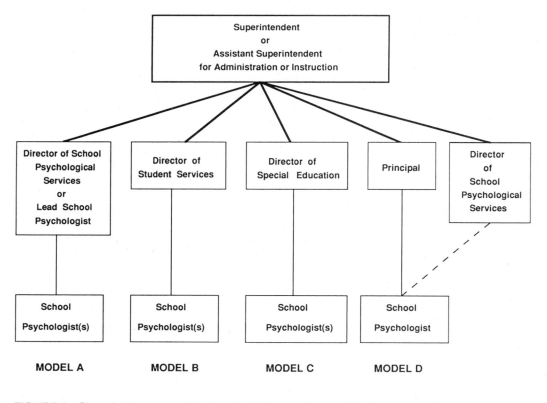

FIGURE 2. Organizational models for the delivery of school psychological services.

Model A: School psychology as a separate department. In many systems, a free-standing SPS program commands the visibility and autonomy needed to offer services to a wide range of students. Within this structure, the SPS director typically reports to an assistant superintendent for school administration or curriculum. Free of the encumbrances often associated with the special education label, unit staff offer a comprehensive range of services with the support of an appropriately credentialed school psychology unit director. Under this arrangement, APA and NASP professional standards are more easily followed than with some other organizational patterns since conflicting service requests can be directly negotiated between the SPS director and the assistant superintendent, thus bypassing bureaucratic layers.

Model B: School psychology within student services. Another model for SPS delivery is found within student, or pupil personnel, services. In this model, SPS staff report directly to the Director of Student Services, who may or may not be a school psychologist. School social workers, school guidance counselors, and school health personnel may also provide services from the student services department. Advantages of this model include the fact that school psychologists may be viewed as service providers for all students (depending on departmental philosophy), collaborative opportunities with other service providers may be available, and at least some independence from special education dictates is available. Disadvantages include the lack of assurance of school psychology leadership and program administration, as previously defined, as well as appropriate clinical supervision.

Model C: School psychology within special education. A third and commonplace model for the delivery of SPS is placement within the special education department. Typically, school psychology is still highly associated with special education since the gate-keeping assessment function provided by our profession forms the cornerstone to funding in that field. Unfortunately, in some districts, school psychologists whose salaries are paid from EHA Part B funds are allowed to work only with handicapped students (Driscoll, 1984), a misinterpretation of federal requirements.

School psychologists who find their programs housed within special education departments must educate non-psychologist directors regarding professional standards, practice guidelines, and the wide array of services which, if given sanction, may be provided to assist students throughout the district. Varied and creative services may still be provided by the school psychologist who is placed in this organizational pattern, however, individual persistence in overcoming the special education administrators' lack of knowledge regarding SPS delivery, plus the lack of a clear SPS advocate, such as a unit director, will need to be addressed. One way to tackle this potential organizational dilemma is to advocate for a school psychologist to be appointed to direct the SPS program, thus assuring a clear voice for psychological services.

Model D: Building-based school psychology. Districts that employ sufficiently large numbers of school psychologists may base SPS staff in school buildings. In some instances, the school psychologist may be assigned to serve only that school or a special program within the building. In other cases, the school psychologist is based at one school, but serves several schools or programs.

If the school psychologist is assigned to one school or program, supervision is provided by the building principal or special program director. When the school psychologist serves several schools or programs, but operates from one location, supervision is primarily provided by the principal at the home school with input from principals of other locations served. With this pattern, indirect supervision may be offered by an SPS director, who may also have input into performance evaluations.

School-based school psychologists are close to the needs of the students they serve. An on-site office allows immediate access to faculty and students. However, program direction may be diffused, staff may be requested to perform a myriad of unrelated activities, isolation from school psychology colleagues may occur (Smith, 1987), and appropriate clinical supervision may not be available. The school-based school psychologist would need to take measures to assure that SPS were clearly focused and directed to those in need.

Regional service delivery. Many rural school districts that would not otherwise have access to SPS do so through a regional service delivery structure. In this model, school psychologists are employed by a cooperative or regional service center that provides a wide range of services, including those for low incidence populations, to small or geographically separate school districts.

This arrangement promotes cost efficiency, improves service variety by skilled specialists, and facilitates staff retention (Benson, 1985). In addition, the likelihood of appropriate supervision and collegial interchange is greater in a cooperative than it would be if the school psychologist were a sole practitioner employed by one district. Given the number of districts with which a school psychologist might work, opportunities to influence change might also be greater. However, this arrangement also affords the chance for misunderstanding of the school psychologist's role and function. Once again, the individual practitioner's advocacy for the appropriate delivery of a wide range of SPS becomes essential.

Summary. As stated earlier, there is no one best model for the delivery of school psychological services. Each model, whether within-district or outside, offers distinct advantages and disadvantages.

Curtis and Zins (1986) noted that the organization of services should be driven by identification of the client. Other factors, such as leadership, supervision, communication, focus, and funding have been highlighted. However, regardless of model, it is the individual school psychologist's responsibility to adhere to professional standards while providing meaningful services within the organizational framework established.

Internal Program Organization

· Once an SPS program is placed within the organizational structure, it becomes the SPS unit director's job to develop the program's internal framework. This involves an infinite number of activities related to (a) organizational structure, such as development of a program mission statement, philosophy, policies, and development of programs/services; (b) organizational processes, such as conducting an organizational needs assessment, including "customer satisfaction" measures, planning, evaluating, communicating information, and making educational/staff development decisions; and (c) organizational behavior, such as defining roles, responsibilities, and relationships (Maher, Illback, & Zins, 1984).

The SPS unit director must demonstrate leadership in and knowledge of a wide variety of areas in a short period of time, taking a three-dimensional "picture" of the program from the perspectives of both service recipients (teachers, students, administrators, parents, community members) and service providers (SPS and supporting staff). Once the picture has developed, the SPS director should work with staff to formulate a long-range plan with short-term objectives and actions which will lead to or continue the delivery of SPS which meet professional standards, address consumers' needs, and provide satisfaction to the school psychologist service providers. In our developing field of school psychology, both strategic marketing and planned change form necessary ingredients for the development of a long-range plan designed to produce effective, comprehensive SPS delivery (Illback, 1988).

Internal organizational structure: Mission, philosophy, and policy. No single activity takes on greater importance in SPS program development than does the generation of a mission statement. This short, simple notation forms the heart of the unit and drives all facets of program administration, including program philosophy, long-range planning, policies, procedures, and funding priorities. The SPS director, in working with staff to develop the mission statement, may wish to challenge them to clarify the beliefs which undergird their views of appropriate service delivery.

After the mission statement has been developed and agreed on by the SPS staff, then statements of philosophy or beliefs regarding service delivery in the district can be listed and refined. The further development of policies, then procedures, will fall from this effort. After the completion of this process, the new documents can be disseminated to all relevant publics. In addition, they may form the basis for delineating individual staff goals and objectives.

Organizational processes: Program development. After generation of the mission statement, philosophy, policies, and procedures which are fundamental to the SPS unit, program development activities may be undertaken by the entire staff or a subset of interested members. Generally speaking, it is wise to include all persons who wish to participate so that ownership may be increased, broad perspectives may be reflected, and individual as well as organizational development may occur. If staff is large, several groups could work on the activity and meet to share ideas.

The major task within the area of program development is twofold. First, current program status must be established. Second, based on the program's mission and philosophy along with the status check data, long range plans for change must be developed. Long range goals should address the difference between *what is* and *what is desired*.

Following this, short-term objectives, responsible parties, and evaluation criteria must be specified and progress must be periodically reviewed. Both program accountability and staff evaluation activities should provide key data regarding the unit's effectiveness in accomplishing its objectives and goals.

Organizational behavior: Roles, responsibilities, and relationships. To be successful in program development, SPS staff must be sensitive to their roles and responsibilities within the organization, and the relationships which are needed in order to facilitate change. All seasoned SPS directors know that just because a change is "right" or "desired" doesn't mean it will happen. The politics of organizational change within educational systems, reviewed elsewhere by Harrington (1985) and Henning-Stout and Conoley (1988), must be addressed if fundamental change is viewed as necessary by the SPS staff. Bridges with key groups and individuals within and outside the system, based on shared interests and common goals, must be built and fortified over time. Holloway & Brager (1989), addressing the politics of supervision within human services, note that "the more extensive one's network, the greater the potential for obtaining support with respect to . . . organizational initiative" (p. 50).

Staff Supervision

A noted earlier, staff supervision forms a subset of program administration. Staff supervision may be of a strictly administrative nature, or may take the form of clinical supervision. Since staff supervision forms a critical portion of the SPS director's duties, information on appropriate supervision practices is treated in the next section.

Line supervision of school psychologists. School psychologists, as members of a highly trained group, wish to be evaluated according to the standards of their profession. The SPS director knows that staff wish to receive recognition as valued contributors and to be accorded with dignity and autonomy within the bounds of professional practice and district guidelines. Therefore, evaluation procedures which are employed with line staff must be individualized, yet similarly structured for all staff (Bittel, 1985).

One means by which successful staff evaluation can occur is by using the technique of management by objectives. Within this framework, which can be used with either administrative or clinical supervision, the director works with each staff member at the beginning of the year to define specific, measurable objectives, assign responsibilities, develop performance standards, and appraise performance (Montana & Charnov, 1987). Routine objectives as well as innovation objectives and improvement objectives can be addressed with each school psychologist, thus providing system-sanctioned opportunities for professional growth through role expansion or special projects. In addition, clinical supervision issues can be addressed. Periodically throughout the year, the director and staff member may meet to review progress, and at the end of the school year, evaluation data are available for inclusion in program evaluation data or district personnel files.

Peer supervision among school psychologists. School psychologists who possess advanced skills in select areas may be found within a staff or in a neighboring district or cooperative. These individuals, with advanced training and/or experience, provide the practitioner with yet another means for securing appropriate supervision. In such instances, the school psychologist may be paired with another psychologist by the SPS director or may voluntarily seek association with another staff member. The purpose of the relationship is to provide the school psychologist with new information, instruction, modeling, guided practice, role play, and feedback regarding the acquisition of new skills or the further development of existing skills.

Peer supervision is beneficial for several reasons. First, it offers a relatively less skilled staff member (in that area) the opportunity to learn new skills under controlled conditions. Second, it provides a relatively more skilled staff member the opportunity for further learning through teaching while offering recognition of their expertise. Third, it allows a more varied role for both participants: the learner is increasing his/her repertoire of school psychology practice while the teacher is learning the supervisory process and receiving feedback from the SPS director.

Self-supervision by school psychologists. In a sense, all school psychologists are supervisors, that is, we are each ultimately responsible for our own professional growth and development. The concept of self-supervision has recently begun to be addressed in the professional literature of school psychology. Although this form of supervision can be employed by any school psychologist, it may be particularly useful to the sole SPS practitioner employed by a small district who needs to formulate a plan which will assist in his/her acquisition, evaluation, and enhancement of skills. Self-supervision offers one means by which this may occur.

The concept of self-supervision embodies self-evaluation combined with the formulation of a plan for improvement. It is defined as "a self-directed and formal process to promote the delivery of quality educational services" (Fleming, Fleming, Oksman, & Roach, 1984, p. 323). With this model, the responsibility for recognizing the need for professional growth rests solidly with the school psychology practitioner. First, the supervisee selects high priority areas of job functioning to be targeted (*focusing*). Next, the supervisee specifies the resources and methods needed to analyze current job performance, collects data (*monitoring*), and completes data analysis procedures (*appraising*). In step 4, *reacting*, the supervisee decides what changes in practice are needed, if any, and outlines a professional development plan.

Professional development activities selected by the supervisee to meet identified practice needs may be numerous. They may include supervision through the use of a supervisory pool, that is, selecting one or more supervisors from a group of professionals with specific skills which the

psychologist wishes to obtain (Strein, 1982). Other activities to address self-supervisory findings may take the form of university course work, NASP self-study programs, topical readings, or other types of self-managed professional development (Rosenfield, 1981). Of key importance to the self-supervision concept is the individualized nature of the needs assessment, instructional design, and evaluation, along with the motivation of the supervisee to assume responsibility for continuing professional growth.

Contractual supervision. Since SPS directors cannot be all-knowing in every area related to psychological practice (despite the fact that their staff sometimes think they should be), there are times when it may be desirable for SPS staff members to receive supervision on a contractual basis from a psychologist outside the system (Bowser, 1981; Yanowitz, 1981). This may take several forms. In some instances, the SPS director may arrange for contractual supervision for one or more staff members in specific topical areas or for limited periods of time at district expense. On other occasions, a staff member may wish additional supervision for professional development purposes and privately arrange for services. Additionally, the APA specialty guidelines state that if a unit is not directed by a doctoral psychologist, the designated coordinator must receive a minimum of 2 hours a week of supervision by a doctoral school psychologist; in this event, contractual supervision may provide an option for meeting the professional standard.

When securing contractual supervision, the practitioner would be wise to closely examine the proposed supervisor's training, experience, and credentials. Meet with the potential supervisor and specify in detail the supervisory needs. Discuss the ability and availability of the potential supervisor to meet those needs. Together, formulate a supervisory "action plan" and determine your degree of comfort with it before formalizing the relationship. Talk to others who have received supervision from the person. Don't be afraid to ask questions. And, finally, be sure to discuss fees associated with the provision of supervision.

Supervision of interns and practicum students. The school psychology administrator is also responsible for establishing contacts with local universities which will allow for interns and practicum students to have appropriate professional practice opportunities. Since this issue is dealt with more extensively in another chapter (see Internship Supervision), it will not be addressed in depth within this chapter. However, it should be noted that internship and practicum experiences should be formulated and arranged from very structured and supervised to almost totally independent (Alessi, Lascurettes-Alessi, & Leys, 1981).

In terms of administrative assignment, the SPS director should be sure that doctoral program interns are supervised by a doctoral-level psychologist. The reasons for this are multiple. First, both the American Psychological Association and the Council of Directors of School Psychology Training programs indicate that supervisors should possess the doctoral degree. Second, since many state boards of psychology require doctoral internship supervision prior to according psychologists candidacy to sit for the psychology licensing examination for private practice, offering doctoral-level supervision meets this mandate. Third, the provision of doctoral-level supervision affords modeling opportunities to the doctoral intern by one who has received a similar degree of formal university training, thus providing a good match within the organizational hierarchy.

Staff psychologists who are ready to assume supervisory duties or who have been successful in previously providing the service to others would be good candidates for an expanded role which would include supervision. Since practicum students and interns receive their closest supervision during this period of professional growth, time should be allocated to the assigned supervisor for preparation, observation, analysis, and feedback sessions. The supervision of interns and practicum students provides school psychological services staff with an opportunity for professional growth and an appreciation of the difficulty and nuances of the supervisory role. In this event, the SPS director's role then transforms into one of metasupervisor; the director supervises the staff member's performance as supervisor in addition to providing feedback on his/her other activities.

Supervision of support staff. One of the most neglected areas of program administration is the supervision of SPS support staff. Within an SPS unit, any number of secretaries, records clerks, word processing specialists, and paraprofessionals may serve to do the basic work of answering the telephone, taking messages, and routing calls; typing reports, letters, and memos; preparing presentation handouts and overheads; scheduling appointments; retrieving and filing student records, due process forms, and other paperwork; ordering and cataloging test kits and protocols; entering data and generating reports in a data-based management system; conducting parent interviews; and a myriad of other tasks which are essential to the functioning of the unit. All support staff must be evaluated according to their individual job functioning and personal goals.

While procedures for the evaluation of support staff will vary across districts, the SPS director should ensure that timely, specific, and individualized feedback is given to each support staff member on a regular basis. One way of accomplishing this is to meet with each person at the start of the school year to review their board-approved job description, discuss any variances needed to accurately reflect the functioning of the individual, and set behaviorally-specific personal goals to enhance the unit's operations. At that time, an evaluation schedule should also be established. The agreements made would form the basis of a "contract" between the SPS director and support staff member, and may be written and signed by both parties. Some administrators may prefer to conduct the conference and conclude with an oral understanding, however, caution should be exercised in this event since if disagreements occur regarding performance standards, there will be no verification of the oral contract.

SUMMARY

There is no one best way to administer and supervise a school psychological service unit. Quality program administration, including clinical and administrative supervision of staff, depends on a host of variables related to the organizational context as well as to the philosophical orientation, interpersonal posture, and technical preparedness of the supervisor and staff members.

While both APA and NASP have developed standards for the delivery of SPS in today's schools, it will take the dedication, strength, and perseverance of leaders in the field to ensure that these standards are translated into reality. Directing an SPS unit can often be a lonely task; hard decisions often involve risk and require courage. But, as Kanter (1989) states, "the years ahead will be best of all . . . for those who learn to balance dreams and discipline" (p. 18).

The challenge that remains for SPS program directors, who control the flow of school psychological services throughout the nation, is to continue to advocate within the educational system for comprehensive SPS for all students. We can do this by providing vision, integrity, strength, and skill in the way we represent SPS throughout the school system and community; by rewarding the tremendous commitment which our staff bring to their roles; and by working on a daily basis to give the best of our talent, creativity, and energy to our staff and, ultimately, to the children we all seek to serve. We must have an insatiable desire to lead school psychology into the 21st century.

REFERENCES

Alessi, G. J., Lascurettes-Alessi, K. J., & Leys, W. L. (1981). Internships in school psychology: Supervision issues. *School Psychology Review, 10*, 461-469.

American Psychological Association. (1981). Specialty guidelines for the delivery of services by school psychologists. *American Psychologist, 36*, 670-681.

American Psychological Association. (1986). *Accreditation handbook.* Washington, DC: Author.

Baldridge, J. V., & Deal, T. E. (1975). *Managing change in educational organizations.* Berkeley: McCutchan.

Baldridge, J. V., & Deal, T. E. (1983). The basics of change in educational organizations. In J. V. Baldridge & T. Deal (Eds.), *The dynamics of organizational change in education* (pp. 1-11). Berkeley: McCutchan.

Benson, A. J. (1985). School psychology service configurations: A regional approach. *School Psychology Review, 14*, 421-428.

Bittel, L. R. (1985). *What every supervisor should know* (5th ed.). New York: McGraw-Hill.

Bowser, P. B. (1981). On school psychology supervision. *School Psychology Review, 10*, 452-454.

Cherniss, C. (1984, August). *The supervisory process in context.* Paper presented at the meeting of the American Psychological Association, Toronto.

Conger, J. R., & Kanungo, R. N. (1980). Introduction: Problems and prospects in understanding charismatic leadership. In J. R. Conger, R. N. Kanungo, & Associates (Eds.), *Charismatic leadership: The elusive factor in organizational effectiveness* (pp. 1-11). San Francisco: Jossey-Bass.

Council of Directors of School Psychology Training Programs. (1983, February). Guidelines for meeting internship criteria in school psychology. *1989 Directory of internships for doctoral students in school psychology.* University Park, PA: Joint Committee on Internships for the Council of Directors of School Psychology Programs.

Curtis, M. J., & Zins, J. E. (1986). The organization and structuring of psychological services within educational settings. In S. N. Elliott & J. C. Witt (Eds.), *The delivery of psychological services in schools: Concepts, processes, and issues.* Hillsdale, NJ: Lawrence Erlbaum.

Cutts, N. E. (Ed.). (1955). *School psychologists at mid-century.* Washington, DC: American Psychological Association.

Disenhouse, H. A. (1987). The supervisor as practitioner. In J. Grimes & D. Happe (Eds.), *Best practices in the supervision of school psychological services* (pp. 127-138). Des Moines, IA: Iowa Department of Education.

Doll, B. (1989, March). *Supervision of school psychologists.* Paper presented at the meeting of the National Association of School Psychologists, Boston.

Driscoll, D. W. (1984). Improving the coordination of special and regular education. In C. A. Maher, R. J. Illback, & J. E. Zins (Eds.), *Organizational psychology in the schools* (pp. 121-142). Springfield, IL: Charles C Thomas.

Drucker, P. F. (1989, May). How schools must change. *Psychology Today*, pp. 18-20.

Fleming, D. C., Fleming, E. R., Oksman, P. F., & Roach, K. S. (1984). An approach to self-supervision for school practitioners. In C. A. Maher, R. J. Illback, & J. E. Zins (Eds.), *Organizational psychology in the schools* (pp. 323-344). Springfield, IL: Charles C Thomas.

Franklin, M. R. (1989, February). Field-based supervision offers many benefits. *Communiqué, 17*, pp. 16, 21.

Gerken, K. C. (1981). The paraprofessional and the school psychologist: Can this be an effective team? *School Psychology Review, 10*, 470-479.

Goldhammer, R., Anderson, R. H., & Krajewski, R. J. (1980). Clinical supervision (2nd ed.). New York: Holt, Rinehart, & Winston.

Gray, S. W. (1963). *The psychologist in the schools.* New York: Holt, Rinehart, & Winston.

Harrington, R. G. (1985). Best practices in facilitating organizational change in the schools. In A. Thomas & J. Grimes (Eds.), *Best practices in school psychology* (pp. 193-206). Kent, OH: National Association of School Psychologists.

Hart, G. M. (1982). *The process of clinical supervision.* Baltimore: University Park Press.

Henning-Stout, M., & Conoley, J. C. (1988). Influencing program change at the district level. In J. L. Graden, J. E. Zins, & M. J. Curtis (Eds.), *Alternative educational delivery systems: Enhancing instructional options for all students* (pp. 471-490). Washington, DC: National Association of School Psychologists.

Holloway, S., & Brager, G. (1989). *Supervising in the human services: The politics of practice.* New York: Free Press.

Illback, R. J. (1988). Improving school psychology services through strategic marketing and planned change. In J. L. Graden, J. E. Zins, & M. J. Curtis (Eds.), *Alternative educational delivery systems: Enhancing instructional options for all students* (pp. 457-469). Washington, DC: National Association of School Psychologists.

Jackson, J. H. (1986, August). *Administration and supervision of school psychological services.* Paper presented at the meeting of the American Psychological Association, Washington, DC.

Jackson, J. H., & Pryzwansky, W. B. (1987). An audit-evaluation of a school psychological services unit utilizing professional standards: An example. *Professional School Psychology, 2*, 125-134.

Kanter, R. M. (1989). *When giants learn to dance: Mastering the challenge of strategy, management, and careers in the 1990s.* New York: Simon and Schuster.

Knoff, H. M. (1986). Supervision in school psychology: The forgotten or future path to effective services? *School Psychology Review, 15*, 529-545.

Magary, J. F. (Ed.). (1967). *School psychological services: In theory and practice, a handbook.* Englewood Cliffs, NJ: Prentice-Hall.

Maher, C. A., Illback, R. J., & Zins, J. E. (1984). Applying organizational psychology in schools: Perspectives and framework. In C. A. Maher, R. J. Illback, & J. E. Zins (Eds.), *Organizational psychology in the schools* (pp. 5-20). Springfield, IL: Charles C Thomas.

Maher, C. A. (1979). Guidelines for planning and evaluating school psychology service delivery systems. *Journal of School Psychology, 17*, 203-212.

Montana, P., & Charnov, B. (1987). *Management.* New York: Barron's.

Murphy, J. P. (1981). Roles, functions and competencies of supervisors for school psychologists. *School Psychology Review, 10*, 417-424.

National Association of School Psychologists. (1984). *Professional conduct manual: Principles for professional ethics and standards for the provision of school psychological services.* Washington, DC: Author.

National Association of School Psychologists. (1986). *Standards: Training programs, field placement programs, and credentialing standards.* Washington, DC: Author.

National Commission on Excellence in Education. (1983). *A nation at risk: The imperative for educational reform.* Washington, DC: U.S. Government Printing Office.

National Governors' Association. (1986). *Time for results: The governors' 1991 report on education.* Washington, DC: Author.

Orlosky, D. E., McCleary, L. E., Shapiro, A., & Webb, L. D. (1984). *Educational administration today.* Columbus, OH: Charles E. Merrill.

Phillips, B. N. (1982). Reading and evaluating research in school psychology. In C. R. Reynolds & T. B. Gutkin (Eds.), *The handbook of school psychology* (pp. 24–47). New York: John Wiley.

Riggs, J. L. (1985). *The productive supervisor.* Englewood Cliffs, NJ: Prentice-Hall.

Robinson, G. A. (1981). Supervisor effectiveness: Perceptions of a first year psychologist. *School Psychology Review, 10,* 458–460.

Rosenfield, S. (1981). Self-managed professional development. *School Psychology Review, 10,* 487–493.

Ross-Reynolds, G., & Grimes, J. (Eds.). (1981). Supervision: School psychology services. *School Psychology Review, 10*(4).

Sandoval, J. (1986). Models of school psychological service delivery. In S. N. Elliott & J. C. Witt (Eds.), *The delivery of psychological services in schools: Concepts, processes, and issues.* Hillsdale, NJ: Lawrence Erlbaum.

Simonsen, J. B. (1987). Operations of a staff without a designated supervisor. In J. Grimes & D. Happe (Eds.), *Best practices in the supervision of school psychological services* (pp. 107–112). Des Moines, IA: Iowa Department of Education.

Smith, E. (1987). Individualized growth of professionals. In J. Grimes & D. Happe (Eds.), *Best practices in the supervision of school psychological services* (pp. 37–46). Des Moines, IA: Iowa Department of Education.

Strein, W. (1982, August). *Applying the supervisory pool concept to supervision in school psychology.* Paper presented at the meeting of the American Psychological Association, Washington, DC. (ERIC Document Reproduction Service No. ED 227 418)

Valett, R. E. (1963). *The practice of school psychology: Professional problems.* New York: Wiley and Sons.

Yanowitz, B. (1981). I want a supervisor. *School Psychology Review, 10,* 455–457.

Zaltman, G., Florio, D., & Sikorski, L. (1977). *Dynamic educational change: Models, strategies, tactics, and management.* New York: Free Press.

ANNOTATED BIBLIOGRAPHY

Deep, S., & Sussman, L. (1988). *The manager's book of lists.* Glenshaw, PA: S. D. D. Publishers.

Deep and Sussman present structured techniques to assist managers in dealing with tasks every leader must address. Issues discussed include communicating successfully, delivering powerful presentations, writing for results, providing assertive supervision, managing for quality results, running effective meetings, managing conflict productively, conducting successful interviews, finding more time, and achieving personal success. This book would be especially useful for the beginning administrator.

Grimes, J., & Happe, D. (Eds.). (1987). *Best practices in the supervision of school psychological services.* Des Moines, IA: Iowa Department of Education.

In this book published by the Iowa Department of Education, Grimes and Happe have collected the only set of writings exclusively about the supervision of school psychological services found outside the 1981 *School Psychology Review* special issue on the topic. Chapters address such topics as program research, continuing professional development, personnel evaluation, recruitment, conflict resolution, communication, staff morale, and staff orientation.

Roberts, W. (1985). *Leadership secrets of Attila the Hun.* New York: Warner.

In this short, readable book, Roberts uses the example of Attila the Hun to demonstrate principles of a great leader. Qualities and characterists of leaders, staffs, and programs are presented in an engaging, illustrative manner. Lessons presented are easily applied to the leadership of school psychology programs.

Ross-Reynolds, G., & Grimes, J. (Eds.). (1981). Supervision: School psychology services. *School Psychology Review, 10*(4).

This special issue of the *School Psychology Review* contains the first published set of writings in the field to address the supervision of school psychological services. Viewpoints on the topic are presented in a series of articles authored by both academicians and practitioners.

ACKNOWLEDGMENT

The author wishes to acknowledge the devoted, professional School Psychological Services staff of the Jefferson County Public Schools, the contribution they each made to the growth and development of the author, and their dedication to the delivery of quality, comprehensive services to the children and youth in their charge.

4

Best Practices in Adopting a Prevention Program

A. Dirk Hightower
University of Rochester

Deborah Johnson
California State Department of Mental Health

William G. Haffey
Monroe Board of Cooperative Educational Services #1
Rochester, New York

OVERVIEW

Prevention in this chapter means secondary and primary prevention; tertiary prevention is referred to as *treatment*. The essence of secondary prevention is the early identification of problems during their earliest stages and intervention before the problems become severe. By identifying problems in their initial stages, interventions are designed to shorten their duration and minimize the intensity, thus reducing the prevalence of disorders. Frequently, children are targets of secondary prevention because of their psychological malleability and flexibility. The younger the child, the less likely problems will be entrenched and the more favorable the prognosis.

Defining primary prevention has proven to be difficult. Indeed, a consensus among authors has not been reached (Hightower & Braden, in press). However, primary prevention efforts universally seek to change the incidence of new cases by intervening proactively, i.e., *before* disorders occur. For example: (a) Competencies may be increased through education; (b) training may be provided to help people develop coping strategies to short-circuit negative effects of stressful life events and crisis; (c) environments may be modified to reduce, or counteract, harmful circumstances; or (d) support systems may be developed more fully. Whole populations or groups considered to be "at risk," rather than individuals, are targets for such interventions. Primary prevention efforts do *not* attempt to reduce existing problems; rather they call for proactive preemptive efforts to prevent problems from occurring.

In support of prevention programs, Bloom (1985) states that "if we insist on waiting until all direct treatment needs are met before allocating resources to prevention, we will doom our profession to continuation of the hopeless downward spiral in which we now find ourselves." While school psychology traditionally has not been in the forefront of working with prevention programs, the field's current movement supports and enables school psychologists to become more proactive in providing for a better educational system for our children. Realistically, school psychologists will have to divert some time, money, and energy from direct services, such as assessment and special education, toward working with school systems implementing prevention programs. This involves risk taking, time, energy, role changes, and patience. But, it can be done.

The paradigm shift from treatment to prevention is a small, yet a logical, change for many school psychologists. Whereas many treatment and prevention technologies are, at times, surprisingly similar, conceptual and philosophical distinctions between treatment and prevention are important. In essence, treatment and prevention differ primarily in terms of the *time* of intervention in relation to the period of onset of difficulties and the *target* of such interventions. Treatment serves individuals experiencing problems, whereas prevention deals with the population of interest. The ever present need for more school psychology services, the continuing shortage of school psychologists, and the relatively small gains made in *treating* various learning problems, behavioral conditions, or mental disorders, all point to the need for further adoption of effective prevention programs.

BASIC CONSIDERATIONS

For the purpose of this chapter, it is assumed that the school psychologist has identified a potential prevention program to adopt. If more information is needed regarding well-documented and available prevention programs for children of all ages and for adults, the reader is referred to the annotated bibliography, the abridged prevention bibliography, the list of prevention clearinghouses, and the list of journals that routinely feature prevention, which are provided at the end of this chapter.

BEST PRACTICES IN ADOPTING A PREVENTION PROGRAM

This chapter considers concrete ways that have been found useful in introducing and conducting school-based prevention programs. The first section focuses on determining if a school is ready to implement a prevention program and introducing such programs into the school.

The second section focuses on issues of implementation, including program size, staffing, needed building support, training, and developing realistic goals and objectives.

The third section provides suggestions for maintenance of prevention programs and for quality control. The latter two processes rest on successful system analysis and program introduction.

System Analysis and Prevention Program Introduction

Identifying needs. In any plan for change, the school psychologist must have a clear understanding of system needs and how a prevention program might meet those needs. The school psychologist must understand the school system — a step that may require investigation *before* a prevention program can be proposed.

Prevention programs, like all applied endeavors, must have relevance for, and address the needs of, those who are involved. For school-based prevention programs, this means the needs of the community, the central administration, the principal, the teachers, and students must be addressed. But, until a system's gatekeepers perceive a need, prevention programs cannot start, much less succeed.

How is need identified? One way is to conduct a formal needs assessment. The hazards of such global needs assessments are that they (a) may identify more needs than can be addressed and (b) they may raise expectations unrealistically. If the resources or programs to address the identified needs are unavailable, then the relative good and harm resulting from global assessments should be weighted.

An alternative to formal needs assessment is to follow one's "sense of the obvious," which is then confirmed by convergence across sources. To do this means the school psychologist must spend considerable time in open discussion and active listening with building staff to identify sources of repeated frustration. For example, a colleague who was doing many individual psychoeducational assessments followed by teacher conferences observed that many elementary students had poor peer relationships and that teachers were aware of and especially concerned about these children. At almost the same time a high school teacher commented, "Kids these days don't even have enough interpersonal skills to work together on a half hour chemistry lab." In a research project it was noted that many young elementary school children believed it was against the rules to help other children with their work. In their words: "It's cheating!" These observations reflected a convergent message from independent sources and confirmed an obvious need: Many children lack important peer social skills.

Delineation of a school's needs offers a framework for developing a hierarchy of concerns, identifying the most important ones, and selecting from those needs the ones that fit the *expertise* and *interest* of the school psychologist. Other relevant questions in this early exploration process include the following: Will staff require training within the selected "need" area? Which interventions have been tried in the past? How can the largest number of students be reached? Across which grades are there common needs?

Addressing such issues effectively through a prevention program will usually require major shifts in the thinking of school personnel. One fundamental shift is for the teaching staff and the school psychologist to move away from automatically addressing only problems and to move towards issues of health and the development of competencies. For a discussion of this needed change, as well as other resistances and excuses likely to be encountered, the reader is referred to Hightower & Braden (in press).

Prevention program review. Once a program of interest and relevance has been identified, but not necessarily selected, as much information as possible should be obtained. Attending program workshops, visiting schools that have implemented the program, communicating with school personnel who have implemented similar programs, and reading relevant journal articles and research

reports are all important aspects of the initial review process. The goal of such inquiry is to find out as much as possible about a program and to conceptualize how it may best be adapted to a specific need in a specific school *before* it is recommended for adoption. Time spent in the above activities will significantly improve the chances of successful program implementation and maintenance.

Introduction of the system. Once the above steps are well under way, the process of introducing the prevention program into the system begins. For school psychologists who (a) have worked for years in the same system, (b) have a good understanding of a school's governance and decision-making processes, and (c) are knowledgeable about the system's entry and negotiation procedures, the following section may be familiar. This section is written primarily for those who are new to the field, who come from an outside agency and are not familiar with the school system's way of operating, or who would like a review of practices and procedures appropriate for prevention program adoption.

Each system should be approached at its "safest" point. Identifying this safest point means that each system should be analyzed, or in clinical terms "diagnosed" in terms of its functional structures and processes (see Schein, 1969). Gatekeepers, allegiances, managerial styles, and communication pathways exemplify some areas of diagnostic importance. System analysis, though often complex and time consuming, is always necessary. Whatever one's conceptual orientation, the diagnostic process remains surprisingly similar. The point to keep in mind is that an essential first step *before* approaching a system with a new idea is to find out as much as one can about the system, i.e., a social history.

Talk to anyone who knows about the system; retired principals or teachers, for example, are often informative sources. Read documents about the system's lineage, strengths and weaknesses, key leaders, and power structures. Helpful documents in this process include minutes of board meetings, policy and procedure handbooks, superintendent's or director's "state of the school" or annual reports, and *budgets*, which are available for most public schools. As an example, one school psychologist, who works regularly in different schools, reads the school board minutes religiously. As a result, she often knows more about what is happening within her school district than the principals!

Remember everything, or better yet, record your impressions, because human memories are limited. Look for convergence. As a general rule, if something appears *once*, remember it; if it appears *twice* from different sources, recognize it is likely to be true and important; and if it appears *three* times from different sources, it is almost certain to be true and important.

In absence of prior contacts with informed inside sources, starting with the highest levels of administration is one way to enter a system. But it may also be a very dangerous place to start. Dangerous because top administrators have the power to quash an idea immediately, or, worse yet, they may like an idea and proceed to push the program down the throats of those below them without consideration. In many school systems middle management, that is, school principals, supervisors, or directors of pupil personnel, may be the best place to make an initial contact for several reasons. Although middle managers typically cannot give definitive approval to new proposals, they are often influential gatekeepers and decision shapers. In addition, middle managers are also familiar with the system's administrative concerns, style, and jargon, which means they can provide useful cues about the best ways to proceed. For example, in talks with a principal about a new primary prevention program designed to teach third graders assertiveness, communication, relaxation, and problem-solving skills, it became clear that use of the word *assertiveness* made him squirm. During the discussion the principal remarked that the superintendent's focus for the year was to develop students' "coping

skills." On the basis of this visit, the initially named Assertiveness Training Program was retitled the Classroom Coping Skills Program. In that form it was eagerly adopted by the school district. Equally important is the fact that if middle managers like a prevention program they have the power to support it from within the system. Such support is a necessary but not a sufficient condition for adopting a prevention program.

Although it is often a good idea to begin discussions about new programs with middle managers, eventually others must be involved. A carefully conducted organizational assessment can often provide useful cues about when and how to take those next steps. Answers to the following questions may help in making good decisions about when and how to proceed:

- How do others perceive the principal? The superintendent?
- How and by whom are decisions made?
- Who are the real leaders? Who follows whose lead?
- How does communication take place within the system?
- Who are the "thinkers"? The "doers"?

In assessing a school system, it is helpful to diagram a school's de facto power structure, how the system actually operates. Power can either support success or facilitate failure. Three examples follow. Figure 1 depicts one common school structure. The school board and superintendent are at the top; the rest of the system falls neatly in line below them. In reality, however, not all schools function in this prescribed manner. Indeed, there are often important differences between how a school system's structure appears on paper and its de facto power structure. Identifying these differences can be very helpful in getting new programs started.

Figure 2 depicts a system with considerable potential for program implementation. In this model there are open lines of communication among teachers, principal, psychologist, and pupil personnel director. However, with this or any other structure, negotiations must involve

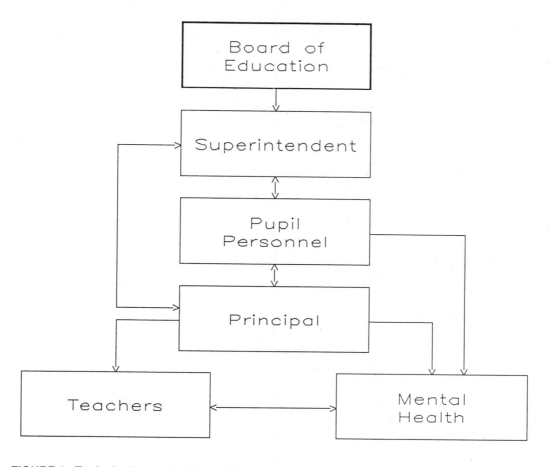

FIGURE 1. Typical school district organization.

such school staff as will implement or be involved with the new prevention program. Although facilitated by this structure, whenever possible a school psychologist should use a bottom-up mode of communication, that is, have the approval and input of the teachers, principal, and supervisor *before* a proposed prevention program is taken to the superintendent.

Figure 3 depicts a structure that differs sharply from the system presented in Figure 2. It represents a divided system. The two teacher groups often bypass the prescribed structure and deal directly with the Board of Education, which apportions only superficial power to the central administration. The psychologist easily can be caught between the teacher groups, trusted by neither and rendered powerless. Such a system, concerned as it is with internal power struggles, is typically not ready for any new programs.

In summary, system analysis is needed to establish (a) that a prevention program is potentially feasible and how best to proceed; or (b) that a system is not ready for the introduction of change. In our experience the entry process works best if the school psychologist keeps three considerations in mind: (a) School systems do not always function as one might infer from their tables of organization. Knowing how a system actually functions helps the school psychologist proceed in ways that can best advance program objectives. (b) Getting a new program started requires considerable time and respect for district procedures. Patience,

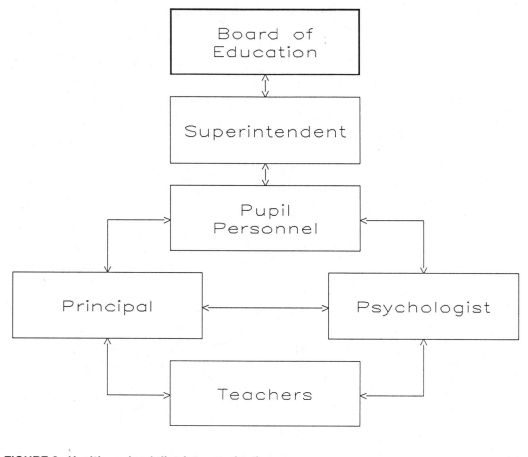

FIGURE 2. Healthy school district organization.

sensitivity, and persistence are necessary for the long run. (c) It is prudent to develop solid support from those who will be conducting the program, as well as the system's middle managers.

In many ways the process of introducing a prevention program into a school is like introducing any other program. We have found "professional small talk" and the initial presentation, however, to be of particular importance in introducing prevention programs.

Professional small talk. In many situations, before a prevention program is introduced, the first order of business is "professional small talk" (PST). A goal of PST is to develop a professional relationship between the school psychol-

ogist and relevant school personnel that is characterized by trust, respect, good communication, and understanding. The development of such a strong professional relationship enhances the likelihood that a prevention program or even a pilot program can be started. Because prevention is an abstraction to many, the more specific the program description and its objectives, the more likely a program will be understood and attempted. On the other hand, if the working relationship between the school psychologist and school staff is weak or poor, the best prevention program does not have a chance of getting started. The point is that the time invested in establishing effective working relationships with school personnel can contribute importantly through-

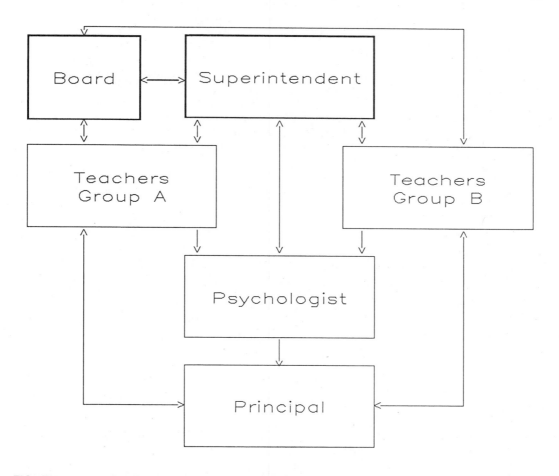

FIGURE 3. Unhealthy school district organization.

out the adoption processes of a prevention program.

Initial presentation. After the needs assessment, program selection, system analysis, and entry processes are well under way, an initial program presentation is made. This is an important step, which, when properly taken, can set a positive tone for the entire program. The two main goals of such a meeting are to provide information about the program and to answer questions. Some guidelines that have been found useful in making such presentations follow.

It is important to anticipate what types of information are likely to be relevant to the host and to address those points. These concerns typically center around the program's rationale, target group(s), procedures, and concrete goals and objectives. One approach to identify other salient information to present is to brainstorm a list of potential questions with those who will be involved in the presentation and to develop clear answers to all such questions. This type of initial test can be fleshed out further by consulting with people who know the system well and by soliciting other concerns from them.

The following are examples of questions that are frequently posed at meetings introducing new prevention programs.

- How will the new prevention program interfere with ongoing programs or curricula?

- Does this prevention program duplicate Ms. X's efforts?
- How will the program's effectiveness be assessed?
- Have others run similar programs? What did they find?
- Who will pay for this program?
- Who will be hired and what will be their credentials? Can we use Ms. G from our staff?
- What does the teachers' union think about this program?
- Who should parents call if they have a question?
- Why implement this program now?

These questions are representative, not exhaustive. The key point to stress is that concerns should be anticipated to the greatest extent possible before starting. Also, essential consumer information should be provided, and false turns should be minimized. If unanticipated questions arise for which clear answers are not available, it is best to indicate that you will find out the answer and get back to the concerned individual than it is to make up an answer.

Another suggestion for the initial presentation is to limit the opening program statement to 10–15 minutes, and then say something like "Let me stop here and answer your questions." This will enable the audience to clarify points they have missed, raise questions, and identify matters that may need more in-depth coverage.

It is not safe to assume that what is said during a presentation will be remembered *accurately*. Before making a presentation, a brief, two-page, written proposal should be developed. Typically, a one-page proposal is too short and more than two pages is too long. The clearly written proposal, in simple and straightforward prose, should answer the program's basic questions: Why Who will be doing What with Whom, When.

The proposal should include a catchy nonjargon program name appropriate to the host school. For example, "Wings," "Special Friends," "Growth Center," "Project Try," "Primary Intervention Project (PIP)," and "Primary Project," are all adaptations of "Primary Mental Health Project." The latter title, though descriptive, may include potentially negative associations. Given that a program's name is used more often than anything else associated with the program, it can help to choose a name with a positive connotation. Naming a program also expedites the transfer of program ownership.

Other points to include in the brief written description are succinct statements of (a) the program background and rationale, including brief references to past relevant research; (b) the program's central goals and objectives stated in concrete and specific terms; (c) a program description, including its basic structures and activities; (d) a listing of responsibilities of relevant program and school staff. An appendix can include drafts of letters and permission forms for parents, sample curriculum materials, a reading list, and a budget. This does not necessarily mean that all audiences should receive all of the above documents; each audience should receive only a set of documents pertinent to it. Unless the written materials will be referred to in the verbal presentation, documents should be handed out *after* the presentation is concluded, so that attention can be focused on the presentation.

We have also found it helpful to assume that the host *might* have useful notions about how best to proceed with a program. That assumption orients one to the following questions: "From your perspective, what would you suggest as to the best way to proceed from here?" or "What next steps need to be taken?" Such questions put school staff in an active participant role and enhance their sense of project ownership. School people can respond to such queries in several directions: (a) "I'll take it and run with it" or (b) "You need to do X, Y, and Z." The confidence you place in your system analysis often structures how best to proceed. For example, before a meeting of the present authors with a known and trusted pupil personnel director about implementing a prevention program, it was assumed that he would take the proposal to the superintendent. Instead, he commented on that strategy approximately as follows:

> "I can take it to the chief, but then I would have to defend it. If you mail it to him, he will seek my advice and approval, which I have no problem giving. I think that's the way to go this time because I've been asking for a lot of things lately."

His suggestion was followed and the scenario unfolded as he predicted.

Another guiding principle is to recognize that systems move slowly and that due process and realistic time lines must be respected. After an initial presentation, several months lead time may be needed before a preventive program can actually start.

We have found it helpful to describe evaluation components of a program as *part* of the program from the beginning. At times, however, there are points of conflict between evaluation and service components. In such instances, evaluation ideals may need to be modified to respect pressing service needs. In most cases, however, a compromise can be worked out that addresses both sets of concerns satisfactorily. Also, we typically avoid using the term *research*. In an applied setting we find the term *program evaluation* to be better received.

Finally, before the initial program presentation meeting ends, action steps to be taken next should be specified and a set of "contracts" (Cowen, 1985) about the responsibilities of all concerned parties should be established. In other words, it should be clear who will be doing what by when in order for the program to proceed smoothly.

The above guidelines are practical rules for an initial presentation, and an important step in the overall implementation process for a prevention program. Although it helps to think through these matters carefully before making the initial presentation, professional skill, wisdom, and sensitivity need to supplement these basics. Other pertinent program implementation processes are considered later in this chapter.

Summary of diagnostic and introductory steps. The essential processes during the early stages of implementing a new prevention program are reviewed in Table 1. In sum, the ultimate goal of these steps is to maximize the likelihood of successful program implementation by paying close attention to a system's characteristic ways of functioning, due process, procedures, and human sensitivities.

Implementing a Prevention Program

Although the diagnostic, implementation, and maintenance processes associated with prevention programs are considered in separate sections of this chapter, these processes often overlap. Clearly, good system analysis will advance the introduction and implementation of a program, and effective implementation, in turn, facilitates program maintenance. In essence, however, all these processes are intended to advance the same goal: to develop a successful, durable prevention program. Some frequently asked questions about prevention programs' implementation processes are discussed next.

How big should the initial program be? It is better to start small when implementing a prevention program. The main reason is that most schools have had little experience with such programs. The paradigmatic shift in thinking required to provide services to students *before* serious problems are evidenced takes time. Although school personnel may endorse the idea of prevention as an abstraction, concerns may develop, for example, when services are to be provided to a relatively healthy Nathan before a "problem-ridden" William. Starting small, that is, targeting a single grade in one school instead of four grades in six schools, allows for careful program scrutiny and a focus on quality control. Smaller implementations permit the school psychologist(s) a chance to address thoughtfully the inevitable "brush fires" associated with new programs and to give all parties involved the attention needed. Also, a successful pilot program can provide a solid foundation on which

TABLE 1
Introductory Steps and Processes of Implementing a Prevention Program

1. Understand the needs of the school.
   a. Formal needs assessment, and/or
   b. A "keen sense of the obvious."

2. Choose a well-documented validated program that meets the school's needs.

3. Conduct a system analysis observing:
   a. Communication and interaction pattern.
   b. Leadership and decision-making styles.
   c. Staffs' conceptual and motivational strengths.
   d. The system's power structure.

4. Develop internal allies who can assist in all stages of program development.

5. Allow enough time for the program to be understood.

the school psychologist can build effectively in future years. Starting small costs less, leaves more room to address mistakes, reduces administrative worries, provides valuable experience to program implementers, and provides a basis on which to decide whether the program merits more widespread dissemination.

Who should be involved in a prevention project? It is important for the school psychologist to determine, as much as possible, who will participate in and who will staff a prevention program. The best school-based prevention programs available will fail if the wrong persons are involved. The persons who enhance the chances of success include those who (a) have a good understanding of school systems and their general operating procedures; (b) demonstrate good interpersonal skills with students, faculty, and administrators; (c) understand the prevention program; (d) are motivated to learn and receive training in the skills needed to implement the prevention program; and, most importantly, (e) *want* to be involved.

If school faculty are involved in a prevention program, "wanting to be involved" may be the only variable over which a school psychologist will have control. Frequently, those faculty members who volunteer to participate embody the characteristics described

above. The process of self-selection needs to be respected, which also means that faculty should *not* be forced to participate by powerful figures, such as principals. In fact, forcing faculty to participate usually creates ill will and inspires program sabotage.

When attempting to hire staff for a prevention program, it is not always easy to find personnel with the attributes listed above, but they do exist. Most institutions have specific policies and procedures for hiring and these need to be consulted. In addition, asking trusted faculty or colleagues for referrals is one good method. Over the years, we have found word-of-mouth to be more productive than newspaper ads in finding good staff. Depending upon the strength of the various collective bargaining units, seniority may be an issue. If so, asking experienced staff with desirable virtues to apply for the prevention program position may be a solution. In general, it is better to have a certain flexibility in hiring.

Once applicants are identified, several independent interviews are recommended to finalize the selection process. For example, to find nonprofessionals to work individually with primary grade children as "special friends," four separate interviews have been the standard: one with the project coordinator, a second with the school principal, a third with a teacher, and the fourth with a school mental health professional. When there is consensus from different perspectives regarding the appropriateness of an individual, there is rarely dissatisfaction and the prevention program thrives. Using this process has been very successful, but at times months have passed and many persons have been interviewed before the right person was found. However, when there is a lack of consensus among interviewers, difficulties can develop. In sum, the time spent to recruit excellent staff, even if it seems excessive, is time well spent.

Communicate to whom, when? Communication regarding a prevention program should be planned, ongoing, and systemic. Plans should include appropriate communication to each level of the school's hierarchy. For example, school boards, superintendents, and other district administrators are typically interested in the program's general goals, efficacy, fiscal costs, school district liabilities, and responsibilities. These groups typically want the "big picture." They need yearly updates of the program's activities and accomplishments. Indeed more frequent updates are recommended during a program's first 2–3 years.

As much information as possible about a prevention program should be communicated to the principal. A principal's routine communications involve parents, teachers, district administrators, and the superintendent. As strategic gatekeepers, principals can enhance a program's support and success or increase the likelihood of foul-ups and failure. Program updates for the principal should occur at least weekly for new programs and monthly for more seasoned ones. Those implementing a prevention program need to communicate with their principal often enough to generate enthusiasm and support for their prevention program during budget crunches and brush fires. The more a principal perceives a prevention program as a necessary part of the school's continuum of services, the more likely the program will endure.

Teachers also need to know the basics of most school-based prevention pro-grams. If they are not directly involved in implementing a prevention program, *their* students may be. Although teachers are directly responsible for only their respective classrooms, a loss of their support can jeopardize preventive services not only in that teacher's classroom, but also in the rest of the school. Accordingly, weekly and sometimes daily communication with teachers is advisable. Communicating with teachers is no less important than similar processes with the principal, but it may be of lower priority when competing demands limit available time.

Parents are intimately involved in some, but not all, prevention programs. However, parents should be informed about all programs by mail and/or phone. At times parental permission will be required, so a letter sent home describing the program and asking for permission will be built into the program. If prevention programs are part of a formally adopted curriculum, parent permission for a child to participate may not be needed. Even so, good communication about the prevention program is needed. Parents can advocate for a prevention program, but only if they are informed about it. In our 40+ collective years of experience with prevention programs, parents have *never* sabotaged an effective prevention program, *if* they have understood it. Hence, feedback to parents is needed at the time a program starts and while it is in progress.

Reporting prevention program elements in school and community newspapers, by way of letters home from the principal, and on local radio shows usually enhances community understanding and support. And since a fundamental goal of many prevention programs is to enhance support from families, peers, the school, and the community, adequate information to these constituents increases the chances that these processes will be carried out, and that program support, acceptance, and success will result.

How important are support networks for prevention practitioners? It is helpful, if not critical, to develop and maintain support networks among prevention practitioners both within and across programs. Support networks are defined here as groups, the smallest group being two people, who are able to support (i.e., encourage, inspire, assist, reassure, and strengthen) each other in the face of the day-to-day operations and occasional brush fires, and during more formidable complications. Support networks that reflect these capabilities do not happen by chance; they take time and effort to develop.

Program support can be facilitated by planning and scheduling regular meetings. Meetings can be (a) formal, with participants sitting around a table and following an agenda; (b) informal, for example, in the hall or faculty room over a hot or cold liquid refreshment; or (c) via the telephone with someone who is experiencing or has experienced a similar situation. For those starting a program, it is recommended that formal meetings occur at least weekly, and it should be recognized that at times daily meetings might be needed. Informal and telephone contacts should occur as needed, but may also be scheduled as routines necessitate. Time spent over cups of tea or coffee may seem like a luxury in a hectic schedule, but in reality it may be some of the most valuable time spent in building and maintaining support. It takes time to be supportive and to receive support, so it is necessary to plan for such time accordingly.

Timeliness is an important dimension that needs to be designed into a support network. For some "hassles" or "significant complications," almost instantaneous responses will be needed. The more critical an issue is *perceived*, the quicker the need for a response. For example, if someone is supposed to be available to answer questions or facilitate problem solving, but no one answers the phone, perceived support could easily be zero. In this case the "support network" may actually have a negative impact. In most cases prevention programs' "emergencies" do not require immediate responses but do require timely responses. In sum, tardy responses produce insecurity and anger; timely responses build support and trust.

How important are consultation and problem-solving skills in implementing prevention programs? Consultation and problem-solving skills are key to building strong prevention programs, as well as support networks. The saying, "Give me a fish and I eat for a day, teach me to fish and I eat for a lifetime," accentuates the philosophy needed. Most school personnel would rather be guided over rough spots than told how to accomplish certain tasks. A goal should be to develop a "we" versus a "they" orientation so the responsibility for the success or failure of a prevention program is not localized in a few (i.e., primarily the program school psychologist) but rather generalized across many: the school staff, parents, and the community. In addition, and almost paradoxically, the greater an individual's sense of responsibility, accomplishment, and control, which are processes accelerated by good consultation, the greater the perceived support from others.

How important is training? Quality training enhances the likelihood that a prevention program will succeed. When various program participants know *how*, *when*, and *why* they are supposed to do various tasks, they feel empowered.

Good training articulates needed materials and for whom a program is most appropriate. It also clarifies what program elements are (a) *necessary* for successful program implementation, (b) *likely to improve* the chances of realizing the program's goals, and (c) *open to modification* without detrimental outcomes. Adoption of a successful prevention program is not easy and requires careful attention to training those involved.

As much as possible, prevention program training should be relevant and fun. If training is boring or irrelevant, school staff will find excuses for not attending or for leaving early. It is important to keep training meetings as short and as task-oriented as possible. Even though school staff may be experts in providing instructional materials to others, they may not be experts in prevention programs. In fact, the more concrete and specific the training, the more effective it is likely to be. Good general teaching principals apply here: first *tell*, then *show*, and finally *let the trainees practice* what needs to be done before they return to their particular schools.

Prevention training should accentuate the positive. Prevention trainers should look for and mention first that which has been accomplished best, no matter how difficult it is to find. Following the positive, assistance can be given as to what might be done better. Well-timed constructive criticism is a difficult diplomatic process that taxes consultation skills to their maximum.

Prevention program trainers must also be flexible and sensitive to important issues. Issues that may interfere with learning about how to conduct a prevention program may, at times, intrude and have to be addressed. An example of such a pressing issue might be a recent school board resolution limiting school personnel salaries. Like children with life stressors, school personnel may need to deal with vital matters before learning new material. On occasion, it is better to provide time for such discussions in order that productive time can be spent in prevention training.

A pleasant atmosphere can also help make a more conducive learning environment. Training is usually enhanced by comfortable rooms and refreshments.

How should prevention programs be integrated into schools? To whatever extent possible, prevention programs should be integrated into existing school structures and processes. For example, one structural component of the Primary Mental Health Project (PMHP) is early detection and screening to identify children who show early signs of school adjustment problems. Instead of having a separate screening process just for PMHP, many schools have incorporated PMHP screening into their existing kindergarten screening process. Both time and efficiency are maximized. The point to stress is that it can help, while reviewing a prevention program, to focus on how and where the program will fit into the totality of existing programs and services.

Should those adopting a "successful" prevention program evaluate their efforts/ *Every* prevention program should incorporate an evaluation component (see McConnell, Chapter 24, "Best Practices in Evaluating Educational Programs"). Because adoption of a prevention program is at best difficult, both formative and summative evaluations are needed to determine if a program has been successful, if program goals have been attained, and where improvements might be made.

How can a prevention program be funded? Prevention programs are rarely, if ever, mandated by those who govern schools. Developing funding sources for such programs is an important issue. Although seeking fiscal support from school boards is an obvious place to start, that does not always work initially. Recently, state departments of education and mental health have released requests for proposals (RFPs) for various types of prevention programs. In general, state agency applications for program support tend to be much shorter, less involved, and time-consuming than federal agency grants. Buzz words from states to look for include "Youth At Risk," "Drug and Alcohol Education," "FOCUS on Youth," "Primary Intervention Projects," and other, similar titles. If such RFPs are not available, state school psychological associations and NASP members are well advised to advocate for such resources.

The private sector should also be considered. Private foundations, the United Way, community volunteer organizations, and for-profit corporations frequently look for ways to demonstrate community interest and involvement. Prevention programs that address important community needs have a good chance of being funded, at least on a start-up basis.

Prevention Program Maintenance

Maintaining a prevention program depends upon many processes used to initiate and implement such a program.

Assuming a program has been *successfully* introduced and implemented, primary goals are to foster (a) system ownership and (b) program integrity and program efficacy.

System ownership. Fostering system ownership requires (a) planning from the outset, (b) establishment of support and information networks, (c) integration of the program into the curricular structure, and (d) securing of school district commitment.

1. Plan from the beginning. Thoughtful planning to facilitate program maintenance should start when the program starts. Even if it proves relatively easy to get a school district to implement a prevention program on a short-term pilot basis, getting a district to maintain a prevention program beyond the initial funding period, past the tenure of the person who starts the program, and over an extended period of time is more difficult. For example, in one prevention project, the project school psychologist did not attend to how the project could be maintained until the final year of support. Only during the final year did the school psychologist approach the district superintendent, who knew relatively little about the program, to request that project funds be incorporated in the district's budget for the following year. The project was discontinued.

Establishing system ownership of prevention programs takes time. It takes time for a program to become assimilated by the school staff and to be incorporated into the school system. To accomplish this goal there are no simple, "how to" recipes available. There are, however, some guiding principles based upon observations of successfully maintained prevention programs.

2. Support and information networks. Support networks are built from information networks. As mentioned earlier in the chapter, the less teachers, principals, district administrators, and school boards know about a prevention program, the less they perceive the program to be theirs and the less likely that program will continue.

Establishing formal, ongoing communication channels helps program continuity. In one school, for example, the school psychologist strategically requested, and was allowed to review a prevention program with the school board each February, which also happened to be budget month. His presentation is now a standard part of the school board's February meeting. With little effort, this "institutionalized" progress report can continue after he leaves. Such reports help to keep concerned parties informed and to maintain program support.

Another formal communication channel is a program operations handbook. Such a handbook can be structured and standardized following a specific format, or it can be informal and non-standardized. An informal handbook can start with a three-ring notebook in which all relevant program memos, letters to parents, minutes of meetings, and copies of presentations to PTAs, school boards, and so forth are placed. Not only is such a notebook/handbook a valuable resource for those currently involved with the program, but it can be even more valuable to those who are beginning with the project and know little of the program's history.

Program support is also built upon relationships — relationships with positions as well as with people. Key project positions or roles, for example, project coordinator, often transcend incumbency. While it is obvious that each person brings specific strengths and weaknesses to a position, essential program functions and relationships must continue when incumbency in a position changes. This means knowledge of important program relationships and functions must be communicated clearly to those who become responsible for a position. Written job descriptions detailing functional responsibilities help, but planned briefings by significant others are also indispensable. Although the departure of a key person cannot always be foreseen, the codification of basic program information is the best insurance that a program will survive inevitable personnel changes.

3. Integration of the prevention program into the school's curricular structure. To be maintained in schools, a prevention program will eventually need to be integrated into the totality of school services, as well as the school's philosophies and policies. Prevention programs isolated from the rest of a school's program are likely to have relatively brief histories. Ideally, a prevention program should address some of the more broadly accepted goals of education, the school district, and the school in which it is implemented, for example, improving classroom behavior and maximizing students' learning. Prevention programs considered to be frills or fads are more likely to be eliminated from school budgets and the school.

4. School district commitment. Essential to the maintenance of a prevention program is getting school and district administration to allocate sufficient professional time for completing the program's responsibilities. Because school districts have limited resources, they must allocate those resources according to their policy priorities. Staff time is the most costly of all expenses. So, if a school allocates staff time to a prevention program, one essential element of program maintenance has been established.

Once again, one obvious way to get support for a program is to ask for it. Although this may suffice as a short-term solution, more is needed for the long term. For continued support, prevention programs need to show concretely what they are preventing and/or what skills they are promoting or enhancing. The formative and summative evaluations suggested previously must address these issues. Nothing breeds support and program maintenance like documented success.

Short-term is defined here as less than 5 years. One critical issue in program maintenance is developing *a realistic time perspective* (Sarason, 1986). Because many prevention programs cannot realistically claim that there will be immediate and dramatic results, reasonable and achievable short-term expectations should be proposed.

Program integrity and program efficacy. Once realistic timelines have been established, both formative and summative program evaluations must assess how well the program adoption matches the model and how well the adoption has met its goals. Programs frequently stray from their original model, which can be associated with less than expected results and disappointing outcomes. Therefore, prevention programs need to be monitored to ensure that essential program elements are being implemented faithfully. If they are not, modifications will need to be made. Similarly, if implementation of a program accurately reflects the original model, but the program does not meet its goals, then modification or termination of the program should be considered. Over time, nothing will hurt prevention program adoption and maintenance more than the continuation of inert, ineffective, or harmful programs.

None of the above is intended to suggest that a program should be rigid or inflexible; quite the opposite is true. A program as initially implemented may not fully generalize to a different school environment, or it may operate very successfully for a number of years and then become less successful. Prevention practitioners must recognize that all systems change. Systems experience internal and external pressures that require flexibility and alterations. Prevention program implementers must be sensitive to the need for change and plan for it by repeatedly assessing the efficacy of specific program elements and the overall results and by-products of the prevention program.

SUMMARY

Many of the processes involved in adopting a prevention program are similar to those involved in adopting any program. One important difference, however, is the change required in thinking about how best to approach a problem. In schools there is a tradition of working with the most seriously impaired first. School psychology has only recently begun to recognize the significant limitations of this tradition. Many schools and school psychologists, however, continue to focus on casualties of the system. Hence, for many school personnel a paradigm shift (Kuhn, 1970) in thinking is required. Although we know that systems respond slowly to change, we also know that small changes in one part of a system can catalyze change throughout the system.

Another important difference in our thinking when adopting prevention programs is a new sense of appropriate "time." It takes time to "prevent" something or to know if something has been prevented. Our society wants immediate results. Schools are no different. For most prevention programs, immediate positive results are rarely possible. Although changing school professionals' expectations as to what should occur by when — that is, the "magic bullet" syndrome — will not be easy to accomplish; doing so is a major responsibility of those implementing a prevention program.

Finally, most prevention programs available are still in their infancy. Few have been validated across different settings, populations, or time. These realities dictate that restrained optimism should be used when introducing and implementing a program. It also suggests strongly the need for adequate program evaluation strategies to be part of every prevention program. Practitioners need to be innovative, yet not so foolish or naive to maintain programs or practices that produce questionable results or that simply do not work.

ACKNOWLEDGMENTS

We gratefully acknowledge the assistance of Emory L. Cowen, Raymond P. Lorion, Arlene Spinell, and four anonymous reviewers for their comments on earlier drafts of this chapter.

REFERENCES

Bloom, B. L. (1985). Psychiatric epidemiology and prevention: The possibilities. In R. L. Hough, P. A. Gongla, V. B. Brown, & S. E. Goldstein (Eds.), *New possibilities in prevention*. Los Angeles, CA: Neuropsychiatric Institute.

Cowen, E. L. (1985). Two little magic words. *Professional Psychology, 16*, 181-190.

Hightower, A. D., & Braden, J. (in press). Prevention. In T. R. Kratochwill & R. Morris (Eds.), *Practice of therapy with children: A textbook of methods* (2nd ed.). New York: Pergamon.

Kuhn, T. S. (1970). *The structure of scientific revolutions* (2nd ed.). Chicago: University of Chicago Press.

Sarason, S. B. (1986, August). *And what is in the public interest?* Paper presented at the American Psychological Association annual convention, Washington, DC.

Schein, E. H. (1969). *Process consultation: Its role in organizational development.* Reading, MA: Addison-Wesley.

ANNOTATED BIBLIOGRAPHY

Felner, R. D., Jason, L. A., Moritsugu, J. N., & Farber, S. S. (Eds.). (1983). *Preventive psychology: Theory, research, and practice*. New York: Pergamon. A text that defines and describes the basic elements of prevention and reviews major topical areas in prevention.

Joffe, J. M., Albee, G. N., & Kelly, L. D. (Eds.). (1984). *Readings in primary prevention of psychopathology*. Hanover, NH: University Press of New England. Provides a representative sample of papers published by the Vermont Conference on the Primary Prevention of Psychopathology and an overview of the field of primary prevention. Topics include factors that affect incidence, stress and stress reduction, increasing competence and coping skills, improving self-esteem, and fostering support systems and networks.

Lorion, R. P. (1989). *Protecting the children: Strategies for optimizing social and emotional development*. New York, NY: Haworth. Summarizes 10 preventive intervention strategies used successfully with children. Target groups for the various programs range from preschool through adolescents.

Price, R. H., Cowen, E. L., Lorion, R. P., & Ramos-McKay, J. (Eds.). (1988). *Fourteen ounces of prevention: A casebook for practitioners*. Washington, DC: American Psychological Association. Reviews 14 prevention programs judged to be exemplary and replicable. Early childhood, children and youth, and adult programs are discussed. Information needed to make the programs work is provided.

Rickel, A. U., & Allen, L. (1987). *Preventing maladjustment from infancy through adolescence*. Newbury Park, CA: Sage.

Describes representative preventive intervention approaches used with children at risk for maladjustment. It examines various risk factors and then intervention programs that deal with those risk factors.

PREVENTION BIBLIOGRAPHY

Albee, G. W., & Joffe, J. M. (Eds.). (1977). *The primary prevention of psychopathology: The issues.* Hanover, NH: University Press of New England.

Cowen, E. L. (1973). Social and community interventions. In P. Mussen & M. Rosenzweig (Eds.), *Annual Review of Psychology, 24,* 423-472.

Cowen, E. L. (1982). The special number: A compleat roadmap. In E. L. Cowen (Ed.), *Research in primary prevention in mental health. American Journal of Community Psychology, 10,* 239-250.

Cowen, E. L. (1984). A general structural model for primary prevention program development in mental health. *Personnel and Guidance Journal, 62,* 485-490.

Cowen, E. L., & Hightower, A. D. (in press). The Primary Mental Health Project: Alternative approaches in school-based prevention interventions. In T. B. Gutkin & C. R. Reynolds (Eds.), *The handbook of school psychology* (2nd ed.). New York: Wiley.

Kelly, J. G., & Hess, R. E. (Eds.). (1987). *The ecology of prevention: Illustrating mental health consultation.* New York: Haworth.

Kessler, M., & Goldston, S. E. (Eds.). (1986). *A decade of progress in primary prevention.* Hanover, NH: University Press of New England.

Lorion, R. P., & Lounsbury, J. (1982). Conceptual and methodological considerations in evaluating preventive interventions. In W. R. Task & G. Stahler (Eds.), *Innovative approaches to mental health evaluation* (pp. 24-57). New York: Academic.

Prevention Task Panel Report. (1978). *Task Panel reports submitted to the President's Commission on Mental Health* (Vol. 4; pp. 1822-1863). Washington, DC: U.S. Government Printing Office, Stock No. 040-000-00393-2.

Price, R. H., & Smith, S. S. (1985). *A guide to evaluating prevention programs in mental health.* Rockville, MD: National Institute of Mental Health.

Roberts, M. C., & Peterson, L. (Eds.). (1984). *Prevention of problems in childhood: Psychological research and applications.* New York: Wiley.

Sarason, S. B. (1971). *The culture of the school and the problem of change.* Boston: Allyn & Bacon.

Shaw, M. C., & Goodyear, R. K. (Eds.). (1984). *Primary prevention in the schools. Personnel and Guidance Journal, 62,* 443-495.

Strayhorn, J. M. (1988). *The competent child: An approach to psychotherapy and preventive mental health.* New York: Guilford.

Zins, J., & Forman, S. G. (Eds.). (1988). Mini-series on primary prevention: From theory to practice. *School Psychology Review, 17*(4).

CLEARINGHOUSES FOR MATERIAL ON PREVENTION

VCPPP Prevention Training Clearinghouse
Department of Psychology
University of Vermont
Burlington, VT 05405
(802) 656-4069

Ontario Prevention Clearinghouse
984 Bay Street, Suite 603
Ontario M5S 2A5
Canada
(416) 928-1838

JOURNALS THAT FEATURE PREVENTION

American Journal of Community Psychology
Plenum Publishing Corporation
233 Spring Street
New York, NY 10013

Prevention in Human Services
Haworth Press, Inc.
28 East 22nd Street
New York, NY 10010

Journal of Community Psychology
Clinical Psychology Publishing Company
4 Conant Square
Brandon, VT 05733

The Journal of Preventive Psychiatry
Mary Ann Liebert, Inc.
1651 Third Avenue
New York, NY 10128

The Journal of Primary Prevention
Human Sciences Press
72 Fifth Avenue
New York, NY 10011

The Journal of Public Health Policy
Milton Terris, M.D., Editor
208 Meadowood Drive
South Burlington, VT 05403

5

Best Practices in Assessment and Intervention with Persons Who Have Severe/Profound Handicaps

David P. Wacker
Mark W. Steege
Wendy K. Berg
The University of Iowa

OVERVIEW

Students who are labeled severely handicapped constitute a diverse population that demonstrates wide ranges in behavior. Within a single classroom, the range of students may include students who have severe motoric and sensory limitations, others make few responses and appear to be socially unresponsive, and still others are gainfully employed students who actively participate in most daily living tasks. Assessment and intervention practices must vary accordingly, and for this reason we have selected three distinct case examples that represent modal referrals we have received and illustrate different approaches to assessment and intervention. For each example, we borrow heavily from Powers and Handleman (1984) and Browder and Snell (1988), who have provided more comprehensive descriptions of many of the techniques we discuss.

A second area of diversity is the change in educational practices that have occurred during the last 10 years. The goals of instruction are frequently referenced to behaviors displayed by nonhandicapped peers and to expectations for behavior found in the community (i.e., chronological-age-appropriate and community-referenced instruction). These changes in the goals of instruction are accompanied by corresponding changes in the setting of instruction and in the objectives established for individual students. In some school programs, the majority of instruction occurs in community settings or in integrated programs within the school.

The expectations for individual students vary, depending on the skills they have previously acquired and the expectations of the setting in which they will demonstrate those skills. Unilateral decisions about what constitutes adequate skills cannot be determined in a priori fashion. Instead, decisions should be based on a more refined determination of how the students can participate best in an activity within a given setting, not on whether they can participate at some minimal level. This is sometimes referred to as partial participation, and a major goal of assessment is to identify conditions that maximize student participation.

Thus, the services provided by the school psychologist are determined as much by the activity the student is being taught and where the student is being trained as by the strengths and weaknesses of the student. Global measures of skills, although useful for placement, frequently have limited relevance to ongoing instruction. For this reason, we devote more discussion to ongoing instruction than to placement.

The three cases are described in Table 1. The first example, Doug, was a typical

TABLE 1
Case Descriptions and Assessment Approach

Student	Description	Referral issue	Assessment approach
1. Doug	A 3-year-old with multiple handicaps; new to district; no previous information	Most appropriate placement; adaptive skills; general functioning level	Intellectual and adaptive behavior assessment[a]
2. Frank	A 10-year-old; diagnosed as profoundly mentally retarded; engages in severe self-injurious behavior	Decrease self-injurious behavior; increase active participation in adaptive activities	Functional analysis of behavior[b]
3. Lisa	A 14-year-old; diagnosed as severely mentally retarded; displays few independent motoric behaviors, but has adequate active range of motion	Increase partial participation in adaptive activities	1. Reinforcer preferences 2. Analysis of stimulus control[c]

[a]Based on Browder and Snell (1988) and Salvia and Ysseldyke (1988).

[b]Based on Iwata, Dorsey, Slifer, Baumen, and Richman (1982) and Durand and Carr (1985).

[c]Based on Wacker, Berg, Wiggins, Muldoon, and Cavanaugh (1985) and Steege, Wacker, and McMahon (1987).

referral that entailed the initial question of his overall level of functioning. The issue for Frank and Lisa was to increase their participation in instruction. Both students were currently enrolled in school programs, so placement was not a question. Frank displayed excessive behavior that limited his participation, whereas Lisa displayed a lack of behavior that limited hers.

BASIC CONSIDERATIONS

Purposes of Initial Assessment

In all cases, the involvement of parents and teachers in the assessment process is critical, as they can provide valuable information regarding the history of the student, previous approaches to assessment and treatment, and the current goals for the student. Given that a number of approaches to assessment are possible, we recommend that the first step be to determine, in operational terms, the purpose of the assessment from the perspectives of the teacher, parent, and other staff.

We view initial assessment as the first step of intervention and begin assessment by first identifying the goals of instruction for a student through interviews and direct observation. The data obtained through direct observation constitute the beginning of intervention and are used to guide or modify further intervention. Given that the first assessment session is also the first intervention session, it is critical to identify the specific purposes of assessment from the beginning of the assessment process. In Table 2, using the case example of Frank, we identify purposes of initial assessment and the information obtained from assessment.

A descriptive approach is used to obtain information on current occurrence of behavior or to identify individual strengths and weaknesses. For Frank, an observation of behavior might provide useful information on the extent of the problematic behavior and on progress in other educational activities (is the behavior interfering with progress?). If Frank engaged in mild forms of stereotypic behavior (e.g., hand waving), the major

TABLE 2
Purposes and Outcomes of Initial Assessment for Frank
(Target Behavior: Self-Injurious Behavior)

Type	Procedure	Outcome
Descriptive	Observe frequency, intensity, and duration of behavior; observe interactions with teacher or peers; evaluabe progress on task.	Document occurrence and ongoing performance.
Predictive	Compare to other individuals.	Document severity and need for intervention.
Prescriptive	Evaluate performance under specific antecedent and consequence conditions.	Document reason for occurrence and maintaining variables.

issue might have been whether hand waving interfered with learning, and a descriptive assessment would be helpful. A common approach is to develop a task analysis of desired performance, to observe the student attempting to complete the task, and to determine if the student's hand waving interferes with task completion. This type of descriptive assessment is useful for identifying training needs on specific tasks, but it is not particularly relevant for Frank.

A predictive assessment is used to make predictions about student performance, given identified strengths and weaknesses. In most cases, a predictive evaluation is conducted to identify current levels of global functioning and to predict the type of placement that is most reasonable for a student. In other cases, predictive assessment is used to determine the status or diagnostic label of a student. In almost all cases, predictive assessment is conducted by comparing performance against a norm group and determining if the behavior or performance of a student is what would be expected. For Frank, a predictive assessment is unneeded, but it would be a reasonable first step for Doug.

A prescriptive assessment attempts to identify the conditions that serve to guide and maintain behavior; it is used to prescribe treatment approaches for an individual student. An assessment approach is considered to be prescriptive when the results of assessment are directly related to intervention. For Frank, a prescriptive assessment might evaluate both task demands (high and low demands on occurrence of self-injury) and consequences of self-injury (attention versus escape). Prescriptive assessments are based on hypotheses regarding what maintains behavior and they usually involve direct observation of behavior under specific conditions. If, for example, the hypothesis for Frank (based on parent and teacher interviews) was that Frank's self-injurious behavior was maintained by attention, then observations of Frank would be conducted when he received attention and when he did not receive attention in response to self-injurious behavior. The results of observation would either confirm or negate the initial hypothesis and would provide a basis for treatment (e.g., using attention for adaptive behavior and withholding attention for self-injurious behavior).

BEST PRACTICES

Diagnostic Assessment

If the primary reason for assessment is diagnosis and placement, then the use of standardized tests of intelligence and development and of adaptive behavior are necessary. The overriding issue in conducting intellectual, developmental, and adaptive behavior assessments is to provide the parent and classroom teacher with information that can be used to develop instructional programs. The validity of these assessments should be considered in light of two considerations: first, whether the test items provide for an adequate sample of the student's knowledge and skills (which test should be administered?); second, whether the method of assessment allows the student the opportunity to most effectively and efficiently demonstrate his or her knowledge and skills (how can the test be administered best?).

Assessment of intellectual functioning (predictive). When a student such as Doug has severe skills deficiencies and multiple sensory and motor handicaps, determining a specific level of intellectual functioning is often impossible. Thus, disabilities and certain behaviors frequently limit the use of standardized, norm-referenced measures of intelligence, and definitive conclusions should be avoided. Instead, ranges of ability should be reported under specific testing conditions ("On this administration of this test . . ."). Developmental assessments of students with severe, multiple handicaps can provide alternative data and frequently can be completed through interviews. This approach assumes that the sequence of development of nonhandicapped and handicapped children is similar and that certain basic skills are prerequisite to more advanced skills. If the results of the two types of assessment provide comparable information, greater confidence in the validity of assessment is possible.

There are a variety of standardized, norm-referenced tests of intelligence and of development (Salvia & Ysseldyke, 1988; Sattler, 1988) that can be used to evaluate the cognitive functioning of a student with severe, multiple handicaps (e.g., Bayley Scales of Children's Abilities, Test of Nonverbal Intelligence, Hiskey-Nebraska Test of Learning Aptitude). The choice of instrument is dependent upon several factors, including the chronological age of the student, the student's mode of communication (e.g., verbal vs. nonverbal), and the student's motor and visual–spatial capabilities. Thus, although the Stanford-Binet Intelligence Scale might be an appropriate instrument for a 12-year-old child who has verbal communication skills, and who has the visual and motor abilities to discriminate between and to manipulate test stimuli, the Peabody Picture Vocabulary Test–Revised would be more appropriate for a 3-year-old child who is nonverbal and appears to have adequate hearing and vision, but whose motor skills are limited to reaching and pointing to pictures of objects. Selection of the test to use is dependent on the skills of the student, and no test always provides comprehensive information or is always appropriate for use with children who have multiple disabilities.

Assessment of adaptive behavior (descriptive). Of the standardized assessment procedures available to the school psychologist, those measuring adaptive behavior skills provide the most educationally relevant information. Most adaptive behavior scales are designed to identify the student's individual strengths and weaknesses across several domains, including self-help, community living, recreation–leisure, motor, communication, academic, and vocational. Both norm-referenced (e.g., AAMD Adaptive Behavior Scales, Scales of Independent Behavior, Vineland Adaptive Behavior Scales) and criterion-referenced (e.g., Pyramid Scales) adaptive behavior scales are available. The former are most useful in identifying global intraindividual strengths and weaknesses and in making decisions regarding diagnosis and placement, whereas the latter are used to compare, student performance against a predetermined criterion and to identify educational goals and objectives.

Conducting diagnostic assessments. Prior to conducting standardized evaluations (intellectual or developmental) with a child who evidences severe, multiple handicaps, the following factors should be sequentially reviewed. First, the child's sensory, motor, physiologic, attentional, and behavioral strengths and needs should be determined through review of records and consultation with parents and multidisciplinary team members. The purpose of this consultation is to identify methods for eliminating or reducing the effects of interfering disabilities and behaviors on valid test administration. For example, if it were determined through consultation that Doug is nonverbal, nonambulatory, and easily fatigued, but has adequate vision and hearing and can manipulate objects with both hands when provided with a particular type of postural support, assessment would be conducted in short testing sessions when Doug is properly supported. Finally, in consultation with the speech pathologist, one needs to determine Doug's most functional means of communication (e.g., language board with light beam indicator, head stick pointer, or eye gaze; computerized communication system with voice synthesizer). These issues concern how best to maximize Doug's performance during assessment and also to determine which tests might be applicable for Doug.

The assessment for diagnosis and placement with persons such as Doug might begin with the administration of the Stanford-Binet Intelligence Scale: Fourth Edition. If the subject does not respond appropriately to the test items, the administration of the Peabody Picture Vocabulary Test–Revised might be considered if he has a pointing response or makes choices. In most cases, the administration of a developmental test (such as the Developmental Profile II), with parents as informants, is useful to determine the global level of functioning and to confirm the results of intellectual assessment. In cases such as Doug's, adaptive behavior skills might be measured by interviewing parents and teachers using the Vineland Adaptive Behavior Scales. Thus, at the completion of assessment, three independent pieces of assessment data (intellectual, developmental, and adaptive behavior) are available to provide an indication of the level of overall functioning across a variety of tasks and activities.

Behavioral Assessment (Prescriptive)

Behavioral assessments are conducted for two interrelated purposes: (a) to provide clear, unambiguous definitions of behavior, and (b) to establish the conditions guiding and maintaining behavior. Behavior is always defined in a specific context, which is composed of both antecedents (cue, prompts, and directions) and consequences to behavior.

Defining and measuring behavior. Behavioral definitions describe the specific behavior the student exhibits in such a way that two or more individuals can agree that the target behavior has occurred. The focus of a behavioral definition is on the behavior displayed by a student and on the moment when the student displays this behavior, but not on the presumed causes or intent of the behavior. To illustrate, compare the following two statements about a student's behavior:

Definition 1: When given educational tasks, Frank frequently puts the finger of his right hand in his eye.

Definition 2: Frank frequently engages in self-stimulatory behaviors in class.

The first definition more clearly defines the behavior; the second definition focuses on the presumed reason for eye gouging.

Behavior can be measured (observed) in terms of topography, intensity, latency, duration, frequency, and accuracy, but usually in terms of frequency or duration. Frequency, how often the target behavior occurs, involves the use of event or interval recording. Since in event recording, the observer counts how often the target behavior occurs, the behavior must be a discrete event with a clear beginning and end (e.g., Frank striking himself in the head with a closed fist). With interval recording, the observer notes the occurrence or nonoccurrence of a target behavior during prespecified intervals of time (e.g., behavior is recorded as occurring or not occurring every 6 s, 10 s, or 1 min for a specified period of time).

Duration recording measures the time that elapses from the onset of the response until the response ends. Unlike repetitive, discrete behaviors, which can be measured by event recording, behaviors most appropriate for duration recording can be broadly considered as measures of persistence. The duration of a student's eye gouging, for example, could be recorded with a stop watch. In most cases, this requires defining a certain interval of time (e.g., 5 s) that separates the occurrence of one behavior from the next.

The selection of event, interval, or duration recording is based on the occurrence of behavior and the purposes of instruction. Event recording is most useful for high-frequency behaviors that are discrete. Interval recording is most useful for high-frequency behaviors that are not discrete or when multiple behaviors are occurring. Duration recording is preferred when the time spent in a behavior or activity is important or when low-frequency responses persist for extended time periods.

Functional analysis of behavior. Once the target behavior is defined, and a measurement system is selected, there is a need to identify the conditions producing and maintaining behavior. The best approach is to conduct a functional analysis of behavior (Iwata, Dorsey, Slifer, Bauman, & Richman, 1982). A functional analysis of behavior involves systematic examination of the relative influence of antecedent and consequence variables on the occurrences of a specific target behavior.

To evaluate Frank's behavior, two different approaches, both based on a functional analysis of behavior, can be attempted. The first type of assessment is direct observation of Frank's behaviors in a variety of analogue conditions. The primary objective in conducting assessments in analogue conditions is to provide maximal control over the assessment procedure. For example, observations of Frank's behavior under several 10-min analogue conditions that vary with respect to the type and amount of different sources of positive and negative reinforcement might be conducted. Table 3 depicts the analogue assessment conditions, the

school psychologist's response, and potential controlling variables.

The assessment involves recording the occurrence and nonoccurrence of Frank's self-injurious (hand-biting) and appropriate (task-directed) behaviors using a 6-s interval recording system. By repeating each of these conditions at least twice, and by comparing the rates of self-injury across conditions, the maintaining conditions of Frank's self-injury may become apparent. With Frank, assume that self-injury was observed during 75% of the intervals during the demand condition (i.e., the psychologist makes instructional demands) and occurred only rarely during all other conditions. These data suggest that Frank's self-injury is maintained primarily by negative reinforcement (i.e., escape from demanding activities). Thus, when demands for performance are placed on Frank, he typically responds by engaging in hand biting, which, in turn, leads to a termination of the activity.

To validate the results of the analogue assessment, the school psychologist might next conduct a series of observations of Frank's behavior in the classroom. In this type of assessment, the school psychologist interviews the classroom teacher and identifies specific classroom activities that are representative of Frank's daily routine (e.g., vocational skills, domestic skills, community living training sessions). Table 4 depicts the classroom observation conditions.

Throughout these conditions, the school psychologist records the occurrence and nonoccurrence of Frank's self-injurious and appropriate behaviors. The results of 3 days of assessment across conditions are consistent with the data obtained from the analogue assessment. Thus, the results of the classroom assessment confirm those obtained through the analogue assessment. By combining these two methods of assessment, the school psychologist has been able to identify likely maintaining conditions of self-injury that are confirmed subsequently in the classroom.

TABLE 3
Behavioral Assessment Protocols for Assessment of
Self-Injurious Behavior (SIB) Using an Analogue Approach

Condition	School psychologist's response	Activity	Contingency
Alone — no task	None	None	None
Alone — with task	None	Recreation — leisure task	None
Demand	Psychologist presents instructional demands; ignores appropriate behavior	Training in educational task	Psychologist provides brief time-out from task contingent upon SIB
Social attention	Psychologist in room; ignores appropriate behavior	Recreation — leisure task	Psychologist provides social attention ("Don't do that; you'll hurt yourself") contingent upon SIB
Tangible	Psychologist in room; ignores appropriate behavior	None	Psychologist presents preferred toys, objects, etc., contingent upon SIB

Note. Protocols based on Iwata, Dorsey, Slifer, Bauman, and Ridman (1982).

TABLE 4
Assessment of Self-Injurious Behavior Using a Classroom Observation Approach

Time	Activity/ instructional domain	Condition	Average frequency of occurrence of SIB (3 days)
9:00–9:20	Vocational training (janitorial tasks)	Demand	40
9:30–9:45	Toileting	Alone — no activity	2
9:45–10:00	Recreation — leisure	Alone — with activity	5
10:00–10:30	Community living (folding laundry)	Demand	60
10:30–10:45	Break with peers	Social attention	3

Reinforcer identification. For students such as Lisa, who demonstrate a lack of behavior, the best approach is to identify a reinforcer by observing behavior under different consequence conditions. To identify reinforcers, systematically vary the consequences across sessions for behaviors already displayed (at least occasionally) by the student. For example, assume that the only response observed for Lisa is that she sometimes raises her right arm to her face when positioned in her wheelchair. Now assume that, to begin the assessment, three 15-min baseline sessions are conducted to determine the frequency of this behavior, the results being 9, 8, and 7 times. To begin to assess reinforcer preferences, hand raising is reinforced with two distinct potential reinforcers, which are alternated across sessions. The two most likely reinforcers, selected from parent and teacher reports, are social attention and drinks of juice. During the fourth session (following the three baseline sessions), social attention is provided by the teacher. Each time Lisa raises her arm, she receives 10 s of attention. During the fifth session, a small sip of juice is provided for the behavior. All subsequent sessions (5 with attention, 5 with juice) are counterbalanced or randomized between the two potential reinforcers. Finally, assume that the observed occurrences demonstrate that juice functions as the reinforcer (she raised her arm an average of 17 times), but that attention has no effect (she raised her arm an average of 8 times, the same as baseline). In this case, juice is a defined reinforcer for Lisa because it has resulted in an increase in her motor response over that observed for baseline, and because it has resulted in higher frequencies of behavior than the alternative consequence. The teacher can now use this information to reinforce Lisa's participation in more functional activities and can use a similar procedure to define other reinforcers.

Antecedent assessment. A similar approach can be used to identify antecedents that control responding. Assume that one goal for Lisa is to participate more actively during mealtime, one objective being to drink independently from a cup. In view of the consequence assessment, juice is used for drinking, but Lisa continues to ignore the cup in front of her and to require complete assistance to drink. In this case, an assessment of different antecedent cues might be conducted as follows: (a) The cup is placed in front of Lisa, and she is told, "Take a drink"; or (b) Lisa's hand is guided to the cup, and she is told, "Take a drink." By recording how often she attempts to reach for the cup under each of these antecedent conditions, the examiner can identify which antecedent condition most often produces approximations of the desired response.

Instructional Planning

As discussed previously, the primary purpose of initial assessment is to provide guidance for ongoing instruction. Once the initial assessment is completed, it is possible to begin instruction immediately, because the results of assessment constitute the first phase of intervention. The following examples of intervention with Lisa and Frank show how the assessment data can be translated directly into ongoing instruction.

Use of stimulus control procedures with Lisa. The goal for Lisa is to independently raise a glass, and a reinforcer (juice) and an antecedent (placing hand on glass) have been identified. The next step in instructional planning is to determine the antecedent conditions that will normally be available to guide responding. In this case, the reinforcer is naturally available, but the antecedent of physically guiding her hand is not desirable. To identify more natural antecedents, one can observe people performing the target task in criterion environments. Surveying these environments allows the examiner to identify not only the relevant stimuli within those environments, but also the variations (size of cups) in stimuli that are likely to occur across settings (school, home, and restaurants).

Once the naturally occurring, or desired, stimuli are identified, two approaches to instruction are most reasonable: (a) programming common stimuli, and (b) teaching sufficient exemplars (Stokes & Baer, 1977). Programming common stimuli means ensuring that the stimuli used to train behavior match the stimuli that will normally be available to guide performance in the criterion environments. In the case of Lisa, because the assessment of antecedent conditions has indicated that Lisa attempts to pick up the cup only when she is given physical prompting, training is designed to transfer stimulus control from physical prompts to the sight of the cup on a table at mealtime. This is accomplished by pairing the effective antecedent cue (physical prompt) with the desired antecedent cue (sight of glass). The effective antecedent cue is faded gradually as the student begins to respond to the more desired, visual cue by providing more limited physical contact, providing contact only intermittently, or delaying the physical contact for increasingly longer periods of time after presenting the verbal cue.

With sufficient exemplars, training is provided with many examples of cups, or criterion environments, to increase the likelihood that the student will respond correctly in the presence of stimuli not included in training (other cups or settings). In the case of Lisa, possible variations of her drinking task would include using containers that varied as to shape, size, and material in different settings (school, home, and restaurant). Training would be provided on examples that sampled each of these dimensions of containers and settings. Otherwise, the student might be able to drink only in very restricted situations. For example, if the only cup used during training is red, Lisa may learn to pick up only red cups. If the color is varied, the likelihood of Lisa selectively responding to the irrelevant dimension of color is systematically decreased.

In general, programming common stimuli is used to establish control over behavior from one set of antecedent stimuli to other, more desired stimuli, and

training with sufficient exemplars is carried out to promote generalization across variations in the desired stimuli. Assessment provides necessary information regarding how to begin training with either of these procedures by identifying effective stimuli and those that normally guide behavior.

Use of consequence procedures with Frank. The results of the functional analysis demonstrated that Frank's self-injurious behavior was maintained by negative reinforcement. Thus, when Frank was provided with a demanding or non-preferred task, he would gouge his eyes, which resulted in temporary escape from the task. Given these findings, three intervention strategies are possible, any of which may be perceived as most acceptable to the IEP team and parents. Of importance here is that the assessment data be used to develop treatment plans, thus providing guidance for instructional planning.

The three treatments that are appropriate for Frank are: (a) providing him with only nondemanding or preferred tasks, which requires a complete restructuring of his education program and the development of a plan to reintroduce more demanding tasks; (b) providing him with brief "work breaks" contingent on appropriate behavior (rather than for self-injurious behavior) and denying escape for self-injurious behavior; or (c) teaching him to sign "stop" or "break" to indicate that he wants a brief break, and provide escape for this appropriate, communicative response. Each of these intervention plans is based directly on the results of assessment, and the outcomes of intervention will ultimately confirm the validity of the assessment data.

Evaluating Ongoing Progress

Once intervention is initiated, there is a need to develop an ongoing evaluation plan that teachers and parents can use to monitor the progress of the student. In most cases, the plan will involve direct observation of student performance, because the purpose of intervention is to teach specific skills under specific conditions. Thus, the use of more generic assessments, such as developmental assessments for evaluating student improvement, is not typically recommended, because these generic measures are not sensitive to gains in specific behaviors. In other words, evaluation of ongoing progress requires a measurement of achievement and not of ability. If an ability assessment is conducted, the student may demonstrate no progress or very minimal progress simply because changes in overall ability have not occurred. Conversely, direct observation may demonstrate substantial improvement in specific behaviors under specific conditions.

For Frank, the method of ongoing evaluation entails event recording of both self-injurious and adaptive responding during demand conditions. By means of the same observation system described for initial assessment, it is possible to show whether, over time, Frank is engaging in substantially fewer instances of self-injurious behavior and more instances of appropriate task responding. The optimal approach is to show Frank's teacher how to collect the observation data; the school psychologist's role being to conduct intermittent probes. During these intermittent probes, the reliability (interrater agreement) of the ongoing assessment can be evaluated by comparing the observation data collected by each observer. For each observation, both the teacher and the school psychologist indicate on the recording form whether Frank engaged in self-injurious behavior, appropriate task behavior, or neither response (e.g., off task). At the end of the observation session, each recorded response is scored as an agreement (the teacher and school psychologist agreed that the same responses occurred), a disagreement, or a nonoccurrence (neither behavior occurred). Overall reliability is calculated by dividing agreements by agreements plus disagreements. If, for example, 50 responses occurred during a 30-min training interval, and the teacher and school psychologist agreed on 40 of these responses, then interrater reliability is 80%.

For Lisa, the primary measure of progress is her completion of the steps on a task analysis for drinking from a cup under specific antecedent conditions. A similar procedure is used to document progress, except that steps of the task analysis replace intervals or frequencies of behavior. If drinking from a cup requires 10 steps, the teacher and school psychologist might score each step of the task analysis as "+" (appropriate response) or "0" (no response). For more detailed information, each step might be scored by type of antecedent cue used (verbal instruction, verbal instruction plus physical guidance, etc.). If both the teacher and the school psychologist score Lisa's performance at the same time, again during intermittent probes, the interrater reliability is computed by dividing the number of agreements on each task step by agreements plus disagreements. If they have agreed on 9 of the steps, interrater agreement is 90%.

Ongoing evaluation provides direct data on student progress. If the assessment data are valid, and an effective treatment is developed that is based on the results of assessment, improvement in behavior should occur. Conducting reliability probes provides teachers with information regarding the consistency of instruction and of equal importance, demonstrates the ongoing commitment of the psychologist. Once initial assessment is completed, and a training plan is developed, an evaluation plan should be developed that specifies when follow-up observations will be conducted and what data will be collected during follow-up.

SUMMARY

Most commonly, school psychologists have their first contact with students who are severely handicapped when they conduct some type of assessment. It is critical that the primary purpose of assessment be identified and discussed with the parents and IEP team. Assessment can be conducted to describe current functioning, to predict future functioning, or to prescribe intervention plans. Each type of assessment approach leads to different assessment strategies and outcomes. The approach selected should be based on the reason for referral, previous assessment results, and ultimately on the instructional goals for the student.

Assessment and intervention of students diagnosed as severely handicapped might be best conceptualized as constituting a continuum, ranging from initial assessment that prepares for direct intervention, to ongoing evaluation of intervention that leads to either documentation of improvement or to changes in the intervention plan. Even when placement is the major outcome, assessment and intervention are both driven by the educational goals developed for the student and by hypotheses developed about the student's responding in certain conditions. The initial assessment results serve to confirm or disconfirm these hypotheses. If confirmed, intervention is initiated that serves to further substantiate original hypotheses or to modify initial conclusions. If disconfirmed, further assessment may be needed. In either case, assessment is the first step of intervention. Ultimately, the outcomes of intervention provide the final analysis of assessment. When evaluation of student progress is the major reason for assessment, it is essential to establish whether the primary purpose is to determine placement within a particular program or to improve performance. Ability measures are useful for documenting the need for a particular placement, but not for measuring progress. When progress is the major issue, direct observation of performance on identified tasks is needed to better reflect the student's achievement.

REFERENCES

Browder, D., & Snell, M. (1988). Assessment of individuals with severe handicaps. In E. Shapiro & T. Kratochwill (Eds.), *Behavioral assessment in schools: Conceptual foundations and practical applications* (pp. 121-159). New York: Guilford.

Durand, V., & Carr, E. (1985). Self-Injurious behavior: Motivating conditions and guidelines for treatment. *School Psychology Review, 14*(2), 171-176.

Iwata, B., Dorsey, M., Slifer, K., Bauman, K., & Richman, G. (1982). Toward a functional analysis of self-injury. *Analysis and Intervention in Developmental Disabilities, 2,* 3-20.

Powers, M., & Handleman, J. (1984). *Behavioral assessment of severe developmental disabilities.* Rockville, MD: Aspen.

Salvia, J., & Ysseldyke, J. (1988). *Assessment in special and remedial education* (4th ed.). Boston: Houghton Mifflin.

Sattler, J. M. (1988). *Assessment of children* (3rd ed.). San Diego: Jerome M. Sattler.

Steege, M., Wacker, D., & McMahon, C. (1987). Evaluation of the effectiveness and efficiency of two stimulus prompt strategies with severely handicapped students. *Journal of Applied Behavior Analysis, 20,* 293-299.

Wacker, D., Berg, W., Wiggins, B., Muldoon, M., & Cavanaugh, J. (1985). Evaluation of reinforcer preferences for profoundly handicapped students. *Journal of Applied Behavior Analysis, 18,* 173-178.

ANNOTATED BIBLIOGRAPHY

Powers, M., & Handleman, J. (1984). *Behavioral assessment of severe developmental disabilities.* Rockville, MD: Aspen.
This book provides a comprehensive, multidimensional review of methods of conducting behavioral assessments for individuals with severe developmental disabilities. The authors devote the majority of the book to discussing what can be accomplished with assessment rather than identifying the limitations of various assessment approaches.

Rusch, F., Rose, T., & Greenwood, C. (1988). *Introduction to behavior analysis in special education.* Englewood Cliffs, NJ: Prentice Hall.
This book describes an alliance between special education and applied behavior analysis, reviews the practical and conceptual issues relative to behavior assessment and intervention with special education populations, and describes the application of behavior analysis to adaptive and maladaptive behaviors. The chapter describing the use of single-case designs to evaluate student progress is very useful.

Salvia, J., & Ysseldyke, J. (1988). *Assessment in special and remedial education* (4th ed.). Boston: Houghton Mifflin.
This text offers an introduction to psychoeducational assessment in special and remedial education. The authors focus on basic considerations in conducting psychoeducational assessment and provide the reader with useful information about specific intelligence and adaptive behavior tests that are frequently used in the assessment of students with severe, multiple handicaps.

Sattler, J. M. (1988). *Assessment of children* (3rd ed.). San Diego: Jerome M. Sattler.
This text focuses on the assessment of children from birth through 18 years of age and offers a comprehensive review of the latest in clinical and psychoeducational research. Of particular interest to readers might be chapters addressing the assessment of adaptive behavior, assessment of mental retardation, and assessment of behavior by interview and observational methods.

Shapiro, E., & Kratochwill, T. (Eds.). (1988). *Behavioral assessment in schools: Conceptual foundations and practical applications.* New York: Guilford.
This text offers a thorough review of the conceptual issues related to conducting behavioral assessments of a variety of target behaviors that constitute many of the types of referrals presented to school psychologists. The chapter by D. Browder and M. Snell, "Assessment of Individuals With Severe Handicaps," is particularly relevant.

6

Best Practices in the Assessment of Bilingual Children

Richard A. Figueroa
University of California, Davis

OVERVIEW

Between 15% and 20% of the K–12 student population in the United States come from homes where another language is spoken. For Hispanics alone, the U.S. Census Bureau estimates that by the year 2020 as much as 37% of the total population in this country could be Hispanic (high estimate; U.S. Bureau of the Census, 1986). The question of best practices with bilingual pupils is not really a minority issue. For many school psychologists, particularly in large urban areas, the matter is and will continue to be a major professional problem.

The present study reviews the historical and contemporary issues relevant to the testing of bilingual populations. A critique and review of practices in the measurement of intelligence with bilingual children is also presented.

The Historical and Contemporary Literature

Though the testing literature on minorities prior to the 1950s has been criticized on technical grounds, it is interesting that even the most cited reviews on this matter (e.g., Peal & Lambert, 1962) fail by ignoring the effects of "bilingualism on the pre-1950 literature, Figueroa (in press) reaches several conclusions: (a) Tests in English degenerate in unknown degrees into tests of English language proficiency as perennially manifested by the low verbal/high nonverbal

(and occasionally high math) scores of every language-minority group studied in the United States; (b) although internal indices of reliability are insensitive to language background, external indices of validity are not so unequivocally pure; (c) the impact of a language other than English on verbal test scores seems longitudinally unerasable; and (d) the politics of the primacy of English have usually tainted the putatively scientific findings of studies even to the point of ignoring what the data show or imply. The legacy of this history manifests itself most clearly in our present state of ignorance about how to assess children who come from non-English-speaking homes. Best practices for this population entail a great deal of knowledge about what should *not* be done, some indicators of what might be done, and an extensive degree of hypothesizing (e.g., Figueroa, Sandoval, & Merino, 1984; Martinez, 1985; Esquivel, 1985).

BASIC CONSIDERATIONS

There are at least four main parameters that define the terrain on which best practices must be situated: the regulatory context, the nature of bilingualism, schooling of bilingual pupils, and test bias.

The Regulatory Context

The preeminent directive from the courts (*Diana v. Board of Education*, 1970; *Jose P. v. Amback*, 1979) in respect to the assessment of linguistic minorities has been to test in English (L2) and in the primary language (L1). This principle has become the sole direct reference to meeting the assessment needs of linguistic minorities in Public Law 94-142, state laws and regulations, and the *Professional Conduct Manual* (Standard 3.5.3.3.) of the National Association of School Psychologists (1984). The broadness of this directive, coupled with the fact that diagnostic tests in L1 for bilingual pupils in the United States are virtually nonexistent, makes this directive both hollow and the potential source of malpractice (i.e., translating tests). *Diana* assuaged the matter by also permitting nonverbal tests of intelligence to be used instead of verbal ones. Though a salutary solution given the relative insensitivity of nonverbal IQ means to socioeconomic status (SES) and language background, there is a down side of this accommodation, as will be discussed later.

The strongest regulatory statement ever set forth on testing bilinguals exists in Chapter 13 of the latest *Standards for Educational and Psychological Testing* (American Educational Research Association, American Psychological Association, American Council on Measurement, 1985). That chapter, "Testing Linguistic Minorities," surpasses everything that has ever been published as a regulation, or a law, or a court decision on this matter. In fact, its principal flaw is that it virtually proscribes or censures existing testing practices, technology, and training.

Chapter 13 includes seven standards and an outstanding introduction. The essence of the entire chapter can be summarized in the following propositions: (a) For a bilingual, any test that relies on English becomes confounded since in unknown degrees it becomes an English test; (b) Bilingualism is a complex phenomenon involving all aspects of literacy, communication, and social functions; (c) Mental processing in the weaker language may be slower, less efficient, and less effective; (d) Language *background*, not just language proficiency, must be taken into account in every facet of assessment such as test development, selection, administration, and interpretation; (e)

Tests developed without accounting for language differences are limited in their validity and on how they can be interpreted; (f) Psychometric properties do not translate from one language to another and hence translations do not work; (g) Measuring proficiency in L1 and L2 "may be necessary" to design instructional programs; (h) Proficiency in English should be determined along *several* dimensions; (i) The ability to speak English in naturalistic situations may not predict the ability to learn academic material in English; (j) Assessment of nonnative speakers of English will take extra time (more tests and observations); (k) Particularities of cultural background can lower test performance; (l) Special training for bilingual communication in testing may be profitable and beneficial; and (m) tests must be proven to be equivalent if they are formulated in L1 and L2.

Nature of Bilingualism

Psychologists working in the K–12 system need, above all, a working knowledge of two aspects of bilingualism: The factors that mediate the acquisition of English, and the measurement of language proficiency. The former is discussed in this section.

One of the primary reasons why language-minority children are referred for special education testing is their slow acquisition, or perceived nonacquisition, of English. Such a finding about a student whose sibling is reported to have learned English much more quickly can take on a great deal of urgency. But, assuming that tests in L1 and L2 are available, even bilingual testing of such children becomes problematic if low scores (in L1 and L2) result and the psychologist does not weight them against the factors now known to affect the learning of a second language: the length of time (2 years) to acquire basic interpersonal communicative skills (BICS) (Cummins, 1984); the length of time (5–6 years) to acquire language that can support academic learning (cognitive academic language proficiency, CALP) (Cummins, 1984); access to English-speaking peers; personality traits such as extroversion and motivation; chronological age; L1 development; societal attitudes toward L1; intelligence; and the multiple interactions among these (Ruiz, 1988). The entire undertaking is made all the more complex by the fact that for many children as L2 develops, L1 regresses, often giving psychometric profiles on language-robust tests (in L1 and L2) that indicate they are deficient in both languages. The *alingual child* is a misleading diagnostic category among uninformed clinicians; "alinguals" are artifacts devoid of any empirical standing.

The more that the complex phenomena subsumed under the term *bilingualism* are understood, the clearer it should become to school psychologists that valid assessment for these pupils defies simpleminded assessment strategies such as administration of English-normed tests and then supposedly comparable L1-normed tests.

Schooling of Bilingual Pupils

There is ample evidence that bilingualism and underachievement have always gone hand in hand in our country. For language groups whose geographical isolation or whose geographical proximity to the country of the primary language guaranteed maintenance of the primary language, underachievement has been shown to be a longitudinal phenomenon. Native Americans and Hispanics are the preeminent examples in this regard. However, the historical record does indicate that even for present-day, high-achieving language–minority students (most notably Asian-Americans), early generations confronted the same academic problems in U.S. schools. What is most often ignored about the latter groups is the tenacity with which they provided primary language instruction to their children in "foreign language schools" (Bell, 1935) concurrently with English-immersion public schooling. Then as now, this form of bilingual schooling was denounced as contrary to American patriotism, an impediment to the acqui-

sition of English, and the cause of underachievement (Symonds, 1924).

The debate about bilingual education has been going on for a very long time. Ironically, the empirical data have tended not to support the commonsense notion that English-only study is the best vehicle for instruction. Most school psychologists and most of the literature on school psychology have ignored the debate on bilingual education. Yet, for the majority of bilingual pupils in the United States (Hispanics) the bilingual controversy is at the heart of a pattern of underachievement spanning over a century.

Assuming that the majority of the empirical literature supports the notion that instruction in the primary language is the most efficient and effective way for educating bilingual children (Willig, 1985; U.S. General Accounting Office, 1987; Ramirez, Wolfson, Talmage, & Merino, 1986), what are school psychologists to do if emotionally their belief systems are on the side of English-only? At present, data would suggest that school psychology has not been an agent for change with respect to the primary language instructional needs of bilingual children assessed for special education (Ortiz & Yates, 1987; Rueda, Cardoza, Mercer, & Carpenter, 1984).

Test Bias and Nonbiased Assessment

In the last two editions of his highly influential textbook on assessing children, Sattler (1982, 1988) has consistently asserted that for bilinguals bias in tests does not exist and that, if some precautions are observed (Sattler, 1988, p. 586), the tests are all right as they are. This is simply not true. The historical and contemporary literature is not unequivocal on this matter (Figueroa, in press). Furthermore, appropriately designed studies on this question have yet to be done with bilinguals. Until the language proficiency factor, together with all the caveats in Chapter 13 of the *Standards* are taken into account, our knowledge about test bias and bilingualism will remain incomplete. The same applies to nonbiased assessment.

BEST PRACTICES

There is a lot that school psychologists *can* do to assess bilingual pupils. Most of their conclusions, however, will rely on professional judgment rather than a test outcome or a profile of scores. In fact, the preeminent recommendation of this chapter is that until such time as our knowledge about tests and bilinguals improves, the psychologist should operate from the position that, at best, tests measure the low end of bilingual students' potential (Ruiz, 1986). Assessment takes longer for bilingual than for monolingual children and relies more on observation and judgment.

Assessment of Instructional Programs

In 1982, the National Academy of Sciences examined the phenomenon of ethnic overrepresentation in special education (Heller, Holtzman, & Messick, 1982). The report of Heller, et al. is flawed in not fully appreciating the special issues that pertain to linguistic minorities. However, one recommendation has unique potential for changing existing testing practices with bilingual students. The Academy suggested that assessment be conducted in two stages: first the instructional program, and then the pupil. For language-minority children, this in many ways is a major recognition that the path to special education is not just an outcome of processing problems but also a consequence of their educational experiences — those provided and those not provided. Four major criteria by which to evaluate instructional programs are offered in the report. For the bilingual child these would include the following: (a) determine that the curriculum is effective with bilingual pupils on the basis of objective evidence including test scores, or grades, or research, or publisher's data; (b) determine that the curriculum is effectively implemented by the teacher as shown by the performance of other bilinguals, the quality of the instruction in L1 and L2, the comprehensibility of the teaching, and the degree of student participation; (c) determine that, in fact,

the student has really failed to learn; and (d) determine that modifications of the program were tried, that they were documented, and that they were reasonably comprehensive.

For a school psychologist working with bilinguals these are powerful directives. They are also problematic. Data collected by two federally funded handicapped minority research institutes in Texas (Garcia, 1985; Ortiz & Polyzoi, 1986; Wilkinson & Ortiz, 1986; Swedo, 1987; Ortiz & Yates, 1987) and California (Rueda et al., 1984) indicate that Hispanic pupils, *prior* to being referred to special education, had seldom had their regular programs modified, that only 20% had had any primary language support in the regular program, and that their grades were similar to those of their peers.

If the National Academy recommendation to first assess the instructional program has merit, and if bilingual children do perform better when their primary language needs are met (Willig, 1985; United States General Accounting Office, 1987), school psychology may have to take an unpopular position on bilingual instruction.

Assessment of Culture

The *empirical* literature on how culture should be used in psychoeducational assessment has yet to appear. Ironically, the profession functions as if this knowledge and technology exist. School psychologists are routinely required to make diagnostic determinations about handicapping conditions without consideration of the possible effect of culture or disadvantage (e.g., Regulations for 94-142: 121a.5[b][9]).

In this author's opinion, examination of a student's *culture* serves three functions in assessment. First, it serves to describe the child's experiential world outside of school and in school. This requires more than one home visit and more than one interaction with the instructional program as it is objectively presented and as it is perceived and interpreted by the student. The former may be aided by a working knowledge of the larger culture of the child (e.g., the "typical" Filipino family's hierarchical authority relationships, child-rearing practices, religious values, reinforcers–punishments, perceptions of educators, dependence–independence, etc.), but it is most affected by an acquired understanding of the experiential culture of a child's family. This is not really anthropology. It is more like ethnography (Saville-Troike, 1982): interacting, observing, and describing from a nonjudgmental perspective the internal dynamics of a *family* (such as the type of teaching, parenting, or mediation in the home), its relationships with the larger society, and its impact on the child. Ethnographic studies of linguistic minorities are providing some of the most robust knowledge on the needs of bilingual children (Heath, 1986; Valdes, 1986). Their results and methodology offer a rich source of skills and knowledge for school psychology on how to describe the culture of a child.

The second function that consideration of a child's culture serves in assessment is to contextualize all scores and behavioral indicators. This is a very old idea that has been suggested for use in testing bilinguals since the 1920s and that has found contemporary expression in authors as diverse as Arthur Jensen and Jane Mercer. It is essentially looking for the norm for a given bilingual student. It is an attempt to explain present performance. In its simplest terms, it boils down to a statement such as: "This FSIQ of 73 is a severe underestimation of what this child can do. She has been exposed to English for only 15 months, and has lived in a very densely populated community of Hmong families in this rural community; this student's ability is substantially higher than test results indicate. Cultural differences mask her potential." Clearly this is a judgment call. Because of the extended experience of school psychologists with "objective" tests, "subjective" or "judgmental" data may be equated with error. There is no reason to assume that, in regard to bilinguals, a judgment call will contain more error than a psychometric test.

Third, drawing on the student's culture can be used to "remediate." Some language-minority families are so intent on having their children learn English that they will demand an English immersion program and occasionally try speaking only English at home. Neither technique guarantees better or faster acquisition of English. In fact, data suggested quite the opposite (Ramirez et al., 1986). Using the primary language at home and school is a powerful "remedial" tool.

Of course, there are family-culture (experiential-culture) *situations* that may require direct intervention and change. This applies to environmental health risks, to circumstances that endanger the child and, as Feuerstein (1979) noted, to homes where pathology or illness have paralyzed the parents' role as mediators.

Assessment of Language

There are at least two reasons for measuring language proficiency: to determine the language in which testing and instruction should be done, and to determine whether poor linguistic skills are consistent with other indicators of a possible handicap. Regretably, there are no reliable empirical data to suggest how to do either.

These caveats notwithstanding, there are three techniques for assessing language proficiency: surveys, tests, and observations. The first can be as simple as a two-page census to determine what languages are used at home and in the neighborhood, and by whom and how much they are used, or as complicated as a census of a child's daily bilingual language use patterns.

The second technique, tests, are generally recognized as failing to capture the pragmatic, contextual, and spontaneous uses of language in bilingual pupils, besides being riddled with construct and psychometric problems (Merino & Spencer, 1983). The *Standards for Educational and Psychological Testing* recommend that at least two tests of language proficiency be given in order to lessen the problem. A critical difficulty with the psychometric approach in assessing bilingualism is that for large language groups, bilingual children's command of language can be exceedingly dynamic, fluctuating between proficiency and loss over time, depending on migration, availability and quality of media in L1, and segregation. For small language groups, normed tests of English language proficiency and primary language proficiency are either inappropriate or nonexistent. For the present, the use of tests with bilinguals may well constitute the most flawed procedure because it is deceptive in its appearance of objectivity.

The third procedure, observation, requires training in L2 acquisition and competency in the child's L1. The technique includes dialogues with the child in L1 and L2, interviews with teachers, parents, and peers on the child's formal (school) and informal communicative competence, and observations of the child's involvement in games that entail sociodramatic play (Ruiz, 1986).

In our present state of knowledge, bilingual children should be given wide latitude in how they evolve linguistically. Extensive and even extreme periods of silence, slow learning & English, loss of the primary language, articulation "problems," and so forth, can all be explained by causes other than a disability. The safest approach is to use surveys, tests, *and* observations. However, the most useful and informative, at present, is observation. Whether one uses the safest or the most useful approach, a school psychologist, once again, must contend with the fact that it is going to be a judgment call.

Assessment of Intelligence

Table 1 presents this author's three categories of practices in the measurement of bilinguals' intelligence: five practices considered to be not valid, four that are problematic, and finally three that show promise.

1. *Not valid: Using translations.* The current *Standards* on testing virtually bans this procedure. Many practicing school psychologists know that a translated test is a mystery test whose scores defy interpretation. It has been observed,

however, that many practitioners note these problems in their case reports and then proceed to "gain useful information" from such tests (Esquivel, 1985). This is one instance when confession does not absolve. Using a Cambodian translation of the PPVT, in all instances, fails to inform about individual Cambodian children's "receptive language" or "verbal intelligence."

Clearly, verbally loaded tests are the most prone to producing dissimilar, invalid hybrids when translated into another language. Nonverbal tests are not as vulnerable. However, the manner in which their instructions are translated merits substantial similar concern (Cummins, 1984). If the grammar and vocabulary in the translated instructions of a nonverbal test are not readily understood by the majority of children at the lower end of the age distribution for that test, then the same negative, uncontrolled impact of a translation may be produced as for a verbal test.

2. *Not valid: Administering tests only in L2.* Children with little or no English proficiency have seldom been studied in regard to their performance on English tests of mental abilities. The results would make little sense unless one wanted to see how the test results essentially vary according to English proficiency, a fairly unenlightening and perhaps wasteful procedure. The same children, however, have been and continue to be routinely tested in English because of suspected handicaps. More than any other malpractice, this has caused the greatest misdiagnoses and misplacements of bilinguals in special education (Rueda et al., 1984).

Not so obvious, but just as injurious, is the tendency to test only in English when the child may be bilingual or of limited English proficiency. Jensen's (1973, 1974) research has clearly shown that a Spanish-language background *alone* is sufficient to lower English test scores. But there are no empirical data to guide professional practice on *when* a bilingual child can be tested exclusively in English. Historical and contemporary data on the imprint of bilingualism on English test scores do

TABLE 1
Practices in Measuring the Intelligence of Bilingual Children

Considered Not Valid	Considered Problematic	Considered Promising
1. Using translations	6. Adjusting the IQ	11. Using non-verbal IQs
2. Administering tests only in L2	7. Using adaptive behavior	12. Applying test-teach-test paradigm
3. Using poorly trained interpreters	8. Using criterion testing	13. Using theoretical frameworks
4. Substituting achievement test scores	9. Using "properly" trained interpreters	
5. Doing nothing	10. Using foreign-normed tests	

seem to suggest that the effects of L1 seem unerasable (Figueroa, in press). However, this may not mean that an English-dominant child can be easily or properly tested with L1 tests (*assuming* these are appropriate and available).

3. *Not valid: Using poorly trained interpreters.* In many settings, when a child with limited English proficiency is referred for testing, it is not unusual for the psychologist or speech clinician to ask the bilingual secretary to help out in the assessment. The psychologist, the interpreter, and the child then proceed to unsystematically compound error upon error. The clinician gives the question in English; the interpreter translates extemporaneously to the child; the child responds; the interpreter translates back to the psychologist. Every once in a while the child asks a question and the interpreter and child engage in a complicated verbal exchange that in translation takes only one-tenth as long to express and explain. Much is lost in translation.

A poorly trained interpreter with an English-speaking psychologist is a travesty. In many ways, rolling dice would be preferable to using scores derived from this practice. Standardization, validity, scoring, and interpretation may all be compromised.

4. *Not valid: Substitution of achievement test scores.* For many language-minority students, a classical achievement profile emerges: lower scores on subjects in which a command of complex English structures are a prerequisite, and higher scores where math and memory skills are called for (Figueroa, in press). Substituting achievement scores may not resolve many of the problems encountered by bilinguals with verbal IQs. For some bilingual groups, this sort of substitution may even be more detrimental. For example, Hispanic children's grades and achievement scores are often much lower than those of Anglo pupils. In the case of achievement tests, their scores have been reported to be 0.84 (reading) and 0.70 (math) standard deviation units below those of Anglo children (Figueroa & Sassenrath, 1989). Compare this with the 0.33 difference, standard deviation units, between Anglos and Hispanics on the WISC-R nonverbal IQ (Mercer, 1979) and it becomes clear why substituting grades for the latter is potentially more hazardous for Hispanic pupils.

5. *Not valid: Doing nothing.* When Hispanic children repeatedly fail to make academic progress in spite of various attempts to remediate their problems through program changes (i.e., linguistically appropriate instruction, remedial programs, small-group instruction, etc.), those children, like their Anglo peers, should be referred for psychological

assessment. Because of the litigation surrounding minority IQ testing, many teachers, particularly bilingual teachers, have often been reluctant to consider this option. Similarly, many psychologists have been reticent about evaluating Hispanic children whenever language and cultural factors require special assessment procedures. In California, some school districts routinely stopped any such assessments because of misunderstandings surrounding the *Diana* case. Others thought that if language and culture were pertinent, a 2-year waiting period was necessary to insure sufficient acculturation and English language development. If a Hispanic child is failing in school, psychological assessment and special education placement should not be foreclosed because of considerations of language, culture, or the history of test litigation.

6. *Problematic: Adjusting the IQ.* In the 1930s, researchers noted that proficiency in Spanish ("bilingualism") directly and negatively affected English IQ scores (Mitchell, 1937; Mahakian, 1939). Since then, many suggestions have been made about "correcting" or "adjusting" the IQs of bilinguals (Mitchell, 1937). Holland (1960) recommended using a "language barrier" score to estimate a bilingual child's potential. *Language barrier* was defined as the difference between scores from a straight English-only administration and the scores derived from either repeating the question in Spanish or accepting the responses in Spanish or English. Jensen (1973) cited Weyl's (1969) procedure (100 x nonverbal/verbal standard scores) for adjusting Hispanic children's IQs in order to control verbal/nonverbal ability score discrepancies. One of the most well known adjustments of IQ, not solely applicable for Hispanics, is the Altitude Quotient described by Sattler in his classic text, *Assessment of Children's Intelligence* (Sattler, 1974). The most controversial procedure developed for adjusting IQ is Mercer's (1979) *Estimated Learning Potential* (ELP). The beginnings of ELP can be traced to Mercer's 1972 study, in which she documented how Wechsler Intelligence Scale

for Children (WISC) IQs varied depending on the number of Anglocentric, middle-class characteristics extant in a Chicano child's background. The more Anglo the background, the higher the IQ. In the system of multicultural pluralistic assessment (SOMPA), Mercer (1979) generates ELP by comparing a child's IQ to those of children from a similar "sociocultural space."

Like all other versions of adjustment of IQ, ELP has failed to demonstrate that it provides a better, more robust, and more valid measure of minority children's intelligence (Figueroa & Sassenrath, 1989). For bilingual pupils, it is this author's opinion that should psychometric testing survive, something like ELP (except more relevant to linguistic and cultural differences) may yet be necessary.

7. *Problematic: Using adaptive behavior.* When adaptive behavior (AB) was resurrected in 1961 (Heber, 1961), its definition included the notion of "*culturally* imposed demands of personal and social responsibility" [emphasis added] (p. 61). But every subsequent effort at operationalizing AB has essentially ignored this very promising idea. Even Mercer's Mexico City-normed version of the *Adaptive Behavior Inventory for Children* (ABIC) (Direccion General de Educacion Especial, 1982) eschews the possibility of cultural and ethnocentric ways of becoming socially self-sufficient, and ignores the literature on this specific topic (Diaz-Guerrero, 1982; Kagan, 1986). The empirical data on AB and its use with bilingual populations are essentially incomplete. There are no studies that systematically control for, or consider the impact of, language proficiencies. The few studies that have included "Hispanics" or "American Indians" do suggest that sensitivity to language background is manifested (Figueroa, 1987) and that some measures of AB may be inappropriate for some bilingual populations (Kazimour & Reschly, 1981) or may have norms that do not generalize across geographical settings (Scott, Mastenbrook, Fisher, & Gridley, 1982). Also, Hispanic parents significantly differ from Anglo teachers'

judgments about their children's adaptive behavior (Keller, 1988).

8. *Problematic: Using criterion-referenced tests.* One of the most popular solutions to the IQ controversy has been to substitute criteron-referenced tests (CRTs). The procedure is deceptively simple. Instructional objectives that specify the learning task and the predetermined level of mastery necessary for inferring that learning has occurred are produced for individual children and substituted for normed tests. But a properly written CRT, one that is based on the needs and builds on the prior learning of a pupil, is a difficult accomplishment. It is a blueprint that assumes expertise quite unlike what most educators or testers possess. This is particularly true for bilingual children for whom variables such as culture, language, prior learning, motivation, affect, and so forth, have to be considered both in isolation and interaction.

The use of a linguistically appropriate commercial CRT, such as the Brigance in Spanish, may be particularly susceptible to biasing factors. For example, most bilingual children who attend bilingual education classes do not really receive much primary language instruction. With the Spanish Brigance, a psychologist can determine the academic functioning of a student but not *why* it may be low. Furthermore, recommendations about future expected growth may be useless if the bilingual program entails minimal L1 academic support.

A test like the Brigance can be useful if there is evidence that the L1 academic instruction is commensurate with the instructional objectives and grade equivalents in the test. It also can prove valuable if the items in the test are used to determine baseline behaviors, teach to new levels of mastery, and then estimate the child's zone of proximal development (Day, 1983). Indeed, CRTs may offer an excellent opportunity of psychologists to measure intelligence directly within the academic learning process.

9. *Problematic: Using properly trained interpreters.* Even after the psychological

professions come to grips with the demographics of large language groups in the United States and begin to require bilinguality for professionals providing diagnostic (and therapeutic) services to bilingual children, properly trained interpreters will have to be used in the assessment of bilingual children from small language groups. As already noted, the empirical literature offers no real guidelines on how to train and use an interpreter. Little, if anything, is known about the validity of measuring a bilingual child's intelligence when an interpreter is used.

Unvalidated models for training interpreters to do psychological assessments do exist (Langdon, 1986). For the present, psychologists who must work with an interpreter should be guided by the following working principle: What would appear genuinely reasonable to Judge Peckham if I had to defend my belief that my interpreter was properly trained? In this context it would seem advisable to overtrain. These other principles may also be worth considering.

(1) It should be recognized that the language used in testing is highly decontextualized. One or two repetitions of isolated items, examples, or instructions are usually allowed, and after that the student is on his own. Phonetic accuracy, in effect, is paramount. So is accuracy in comprehending what a student says in her/his primary, dialectal language.

(2) Interpreting is a cognitively demanding task. The best-educated native speaker is in all likelihood the best candidate to serve as an interpreter.

(3) During testing, an interpreter should never have to translate any part of the test being administered. Interpreters should only be used when there is a valid, normed translation of the test or when there are age-appropriate, written instructions for a nonverbal test.

(4) There should be no problems in ad-

ministering a test. The interpreter should know how to administer the test. The seating arrangements should be predetermined. And the pattern of communication(s) (who can talk to whom and when) should be set up before testing.

(5) New considerations should be given to due process and record-keeping provisions during interpreting. Parents should be asked to give their permission for using interpreters. Audio tapes of the testing session should be kept so as to score the pupil's responses with the interpreter after the testing session(s).

10. *Problematic: Using foreign-normed tests.* Intelligence tests that are developed and normed in other countries are often used in the United States. The most widely used come form Mexico and Latin America (e.g., the Mexico City WISC-R, K-ABC, and PPVT; the Bateria Woodcock Psicoeducativa en Espanol normed in Puerto Rico, Spain, Mexico, Peru, and Costa Rica). After several years of using these with Hispanic children in California, this author considers such tests extremely problematic. The conditions under which they can be used in this country with some degree of confidence occur very infrequently. With the Mexico City normed tests, for example, only *recently* arrived pupils from the Mexico City public schools can be tested. Once a child begins public schooling in the United States under the usual conditions of English immersion, Spanish language proficiency begins to decline. The Mexico City WISC-R becomes progressively more and more inappropriate. With other tests such as the Bateria Woodcock, it is not known when and with what Hispanic children it can be used, since the norming sample is so heterogeneous and so undefined.

Foreign-normed tests are often used in conjunction with the English versions of these tests. The mistake is often made of thinking that these are comparable tests. At present, this is a gratuitous assumption. Certainly even if the contents were "comparable," the comparability of the English and Spanish norming samples (SES, curricula, etc.) is suspect.

There is yet a further problem. Using foreign and U.S. tests that are similar so as to do bilingual testing assumes that the test takers are bilingual in the manner that the tests are "bilingual." Valid bilingual testing requires that the tests be developed and normed on U.S. bilingual children (with full consideration of the many possible variant proficiencies in their home language and in English, as well as the various dialects and nationalities). Using tests normed on monolingual populations in two countries cannot produce results.

11. *Promising: Nonverbal tests.* This is the ancient solution that has been applied in testing virtually every linguistic minority since the 1920s. The major virtue of these tests is that they yield high group mean scores for most linguistic minorities. There are five reasons why this is to be regarded only as a promising procedure. (a) These tests are often not good predictors of academic achievement, and (b) data now suggest that for Hispanic pupils, they have especially poor predictive power when Spanish is the language of the home (Figueroa, in press). This type of predictive hypersensitivity to language background is not what one would expect from nonverbal IQs. Substantially more research is needed on this matter.

12. *Promising: Using a test–teach–test paradigm.* The Russian psychologist Vygotzky proposed as part of a social-interaction theory of intelligence the concept of "zone of proximal development" (ZPD) as an index of cognitive ability. The ZPD refers to the hypothetical distance between what children can do by themselves on a first try at a mental task and what they can subsequently do after training. The greater the improvement of performance with training, or the greater the distance between pretest and posttest, the wider the ZPD. A wide ZPD would indicate high ability. At the other extreme, inability to do a task before and after training would indicate low ability, or a narrow ZPD. Drawing on several sources

on ZPD, Day (1983) presented seven possible operational definitions of ZPD:

> (a) how much a child benefits from a particular training intervention; (b) how explicit training must be to raise performance to a certain level; (c) how well the child maintains trained skills; (d) how much additional training is needed to get a child to maintain; (e) how well a child transfers spontaneously; (g) how easily the child transfers with assistance; (h) how quickly the child acquires a skill over different problem types. (p. 159)

The most well known technique for doing what is essentially an assessment of the ZPD is Feuerstein's (1979) Learning Potential Assessment Device (LPAD), a test–teach–test technique involving non-verbal mental tasks (such as those in the Raven Progressive Matrices) and short-term memory learning problems. Unfortunately, LPAD includes an interpretive framework that is as complex as psycho-analysis. Though the technique has been used in Latin America, there are no substantive empirical data on its effectiveness with any U.S. populations that vary in L1 and L2 measured proficiencies.

13. *Promising: Using theoretical frameworks.* Working from theory (e.g., Piagetian) or from theoretical constructs (Sternberg, 1982) such as speed of processing, knowledge base, learning strategies, metacognition, and executive control makes high demands on the intelligence of the tester. The "theory" must be thoroughly understood and its ideographic application must be learned during supervised, long-term internship. Piagetian theory has never gotten very far in school psychology assessment. The Sternberg research program is much newer and its fate the discipline of school psychology remains unknown.

In this author's judgment, theoretical models for assessing bilingual populations offer a great deal of promise. First of all, they will require observation of a bilingual child's functioning in many settings and over an extended period of time. In addition, the psychologist will quite likely have to *look* for intelligence in various contexts and will have to design situations for eliciting learning, measuring zones of proximal development, plan home- and school-based interventions, and interact with children intensely and personally. This method of measuring intelligence is more congruent with the challenge posed by the U.S. bilingual student. There are, of course, caveats. How will the school psychologists learn and use theories in a heuristic manner? How is such assessment to be done in L1? Would such a paradigm lead to even greater problems in special education misdiagnoses?

ASSESSING THE SCHOOL PSYCHOLOGIST

From an economic (Rueda, 1988) and a professional (Mehan, Hertweck & Meihls, 1986) perspective, the functioning of school psychologists in school-based assessments is suspect and warrants some form of self-redefinition. The problems documented with bilingual pupils (Rueda et al, 1984; Ortiz & Yates, 1987) further suggest that the technology available to school psychologists may be seriously flawed for this segment of the school-age population. If knowledge and judgment may come to play a critical role in the assessment of bilinguals, it may well be that an M.A.-level preparation may not be sufficient for the job, and that further training for school psychologists may be necessary.

REFERENCES

American Educational Research Association, American Psychological Association, American Council on Measurement. (1985). *Standards for educational and psychological tests.* Washington, DC: American Psychological Association.

Bell, R. (1935). *Public school education of second-generation Japanese in California.* Stanford: Stanford University Press.

Cummins, J. (1984). *Bilingual special education: issues in assessment and pedagogy.* San Diego: College-Hill.

Day, J. D. (1983). The zone of proximal development. In M. Pressley & J. R. Levin (Eds.), *Cognitive strategy research: Psychological foundations* (pp. 155–176). New York: Springer-Verlag.

Diana v. Board of Education, No. C-70-37 RFT (N.D. Cal. 1970).

Diaz-Guerrero, R. (1982). *Psicologia del Mexicano.* Mexico City: Editorial Trillas.

Direccion General de Educacion Especial. (1982). SOMPA: Sistema de evaluacion multicultural y pluralistico, manual de calificacion. Mexico, DF: Author.

Esquivel, G. (1985). Best practices in the assessment of limited English proficient and bilingual children. In A. Thomas & J. Grimes (Eds.), *Best practices in school psychology* (pp. 113-123). Kent, OH: National Association of School Psychologists.

Feuerstein, R. (1979). *The dynamic assessment of retarded performers.* Baltimore: University Park Press.

Figueroa, R. A. (1987). *Special education assessment of Hispanic pupils in California: Looking ahead to the 1990s.* Sacramento: California State Department of Education, Office of Special Education.

Figueroa, R. A. (in press). Linguistic minority pupils and school psychology: Tests, knowledge-base and regulations. *Exceptional Children.*

Figueroa, R. A., Sandoval, J., & Merino, B. (1984). School psychology and limited-English-proficient children: New competencies. *Journal of School Psychology, 22,* 131-144.

Figueroa, R. A., & Sassenrath, J. M. (1989). A longitudinal study of the predictive validity of SOMPA. *Psychology in the Schools, 26,* 5-19.

Garcia, S. B. (1985, Fall). Characteristics of limited English proficient Hispanic students served in programs for the learning disabled: Implications for policy, practice and research (Part 1). *Bilingual Special Education Newsletter,* pp. 1-5.

Heath, S. B. (1986). Sociocultural contexts of language development. In Bilingual Education Office, California State Department of Education (Eds.), *Beyond language: Social & cultural factors in schooling language minority students.* Los Angeles: California State University, Evaluation, Dissemination and Assessment Center.

Heber, R. (1961). A manual on terminology and classification in mental retardation. *American Journal on Mental Deficiency* (Monography Supplement).

Heller, K. A., Holtzman, W. H., & Messick, S. (1982). *Placing children in special education: A strategy for equity.* Washington, DC: National Academy Press.

Holland, W. (1960). Language barrier as an educational problem of Spanish-speaking children. *Exceptional Children, 27,* 42-50.

Jensen, A. R. (1973). *Educability and group differences.* New York: Harper & Row.

Jensen, A. R. (1974). How biased are culture-loaded tests? *Genetic Psychology Monographs, 90,* 185-244.

Jose P. v. Amback. (1979). C-270. United States District Court, Eastern District of New York.

Kagan, S. (1986). Cooperative learning and sociocultural factors in schooling. In Bilingual Education Office, California State Department of Education (Eds.), *Beyond language: Social and cultural factors in schooling language minority students.* Los Angeles: California State University, Evaluation, Dissemination and Assessment Center.

Kazimour, K., & Reschly, D. (1981). Investigation of the norms and concurrent validity for the Adaptive Behavior Inventory for Children (ABIC). *American Journal of Mental Deficiency, 85*(5), 512-520.

Keller, H. (1988). Children's adaptive behaviors: Measure and source generalizability. *Journal of Psychoeducational Assessment, 6,* 371-389.

Langdon, H. (196). *The interpreter/translator in a school setting.* Unpublished manuscript, University of California at Davis, Division of Education.

Mahakian, C. (1939). Measuring the intelligence and reading capacity of Spanish-speaking children. *Elementary School Journal, 39*(10), 760-768.

Martinez, M. A. (1985). Toward a bilingual school psychology model. *Educational Psychologist, 20,* 143-152.

Mehan, H., Hertweck, H., & Meihls, J. L. (1986). *Handicapping the handicapped.* Palo Alto, CA: Stanford University Press.

Mercer, J. R. (1972, September). IQ: The lethal label. *Psychology Today,* pp. 44-47, 95-97.

Mercer, J. R. (1979). *The System of Multicultural Pluralistic Assessment: Technical manual.* New York: Psychological Corporation.

Merino, B. J., & Spencer, M. (1983). The comparability of English and Spanish versions of oral language proficiency instruments. *NABE Journal, 7,* 1-31.

Mitchell, A. J. (1937). The effect of bilingualism on the measurement of intelligence. *Elementary School Journal, 38,* 29-37.

National Association of School Psychologists. (1984). *Professional conduct manual.* Stratford, CT: NASP Publications Office.

Ortiz, A. A., & Polyzoi, E. (1986). *Characteristics of limited English proficient Hispanic students served in programs for the learning disabled: Implications for policy and practice* (Report No. ED 267597). Austin: University of Texas. (ERIC Document Reproduction Service)

Ortiz, A. A., & Yates, J. R., (1987). *Characteristics of learning disabled, mentally retarded, and speech-language handicapped Hispanic students at initial evaluation and re-evaluation.* Unpublished manuscript, University of Texas, Austin.

Peal, E., & Lambert, W. E. (1962). The relation of bilingualism to intelligence. *Psychological Monographs: General and Applied, 76,* 1-23.

Ramirez, J. D., Wolfson, R., Talmage, G. K., & Merino, B. (1986). *First year report: Longitudinal study of immersion programs for language minority children* (submitted to U.S. Department of Education, Washington, DC). Mountain View, CA: SRA Associates.

Rueda, R. (1988). *Eligibility criteria for special education for Spanish/English speaking pupils in California.* Unpublished manuscript, University of California at Davis, Department of Education, Special Education Demonstration Project.

Rueda, R., Cardoza, D., Mercer, J. R., & Carpenter, L. (1984). *An examination of special education decision making with Hispanic first-time referrals in large urban school districts.* Los Alamitos, CA: Southwest Regional Lab.

Ruiz, N. T. (1986). *Language for learning in a bilingual special education classroom.* Unpublished doctoral dissertation, Stanford University.

Ruiz, N. T. (1988). *The nature of bilingualism: Implications for special education* (Crosscultural Special Education Series, Vol. 2). Sacramento: California State Department of Education, Special Education Division; Program, Curriculum, and Training Unit.

Sattler, J. M. (1974). *Assessment of children's intelligence.* Boston: Allyn & Bacon.

Sattler, J. M. (1982). *Assessment of children's intelligence and special abilities* (2nd ed.). Boston: Allyn & Bacon.

Sattler, J. M. (1988). *Assessment of children* (3rd ed.). San Diego: Sattler.

Saville-Troike, M. (1982). *The ethnography of communication.* Baltimore, MD: University Park Press.

Scott, L., Mastenbrook, J., Fisher, A., & Gridley, G. (1982). Adaptive behavior inventory for children: the need for local norms. *Journal of School Psychology, 20,* 39-44.

Sternberg, R. J. (Ed.). (1982). *Handbook of human intelligence.* New York: Cambridge University Press.

Swedo, J. (1987, Fall). Effective teaching strategies for handicapped limited English proficient students. *Bilingual Special Education Newsletter,* pp. 1-5.

Symonds, P. M. (1924). The effect of attendance at Chinese language schools on ability with the English language. *Journal of Applied Psychology, 8,* 411-423.

U.S. Bureau of the Census. (1986). *Current population reports, Series P-25, No. 995, "Projections of the Hispanic population: 1983 to 2080."* Washington, DC: U.S. Government Printing Office.

U.S. General Accounting Office (1987). Briefing report to the Chairman, Committee on Education and Labor, House of Representatives. *Bilingual education: A new look at the research evidence.* Washington, DC: U.S. Government Printing Office.

Valdes, G. (1986, April). *Individual background factors related to the schooling of language minority students.* Paper presented at the University of California Conference of the Schooling of Minority Students, Berkeley.

Weyl, N. (1969). Some comparative performance indexes of American ethnic minorities. *Mankind Quarterly, 9,* 106-128.

Wilkinson, C. Y., & Ortiz, A. A. (1986). *Characteristics of limited English proficient and English proficient learning disabled Hispanic students at initial assessment and at reevaluation.* Austin: University of Texas, Handicapped Minority Research Institute on Language Proficiency.

Willig, A. C. (1985). A meta-analysis of selected studies on the effectiveness of bilingual education. *Review of Educational Research, 55,* 269-317.

ANNOTATED BIBLIOGRAPHY

Hakuta, K. (1986). *Mirror of language: The debate on bilingualism.* New York: Basic Books.
This is an objective overview of the historical and contemporary issues on bilingualism and bilingual education. The critical topics for psychologists include intelligence testing, cognitive processing, and instructional programs for bilingual children. The book is an excellent introduction to the very complex psychological set of factors involved in "bilingualism."

Bilingual Education Office, California State Department of Education. (1986). *Beyond language: Social and cultural factors in schooling language minority students.* Los Angeles: Evaluation, Dissemination and Assessment Center, California State University, Los Angeles.
This is one of the best texts on the cultural and sociocultural contexts in schooling bilingual pupils. Heath's chapter on "Sociocultural Contexts of Language Development" is a must for anyone working with bilingual children for the purposes of assessment and diagnosis. The various chapters broaden the notion of "culture" to include not just what the child brings but also what the school culturally presents.

Mehan, H., Hertweck, H., & Meihls, J. L. (1986). *Handicapping the handicapped.* Palo Alto, CA: Stanford University Press.

Special education, from an anthropologist's perspective, does not function like a rational, decision-making process. It is an irrational, bartered, political game. The role of school psychology, as gleaned from this longitudinal study, comes across as being biased and arbitrary. This is a sobering and painful invitation to re-examine what P.L. 94-142 has done to the profession.

Figueroa, R. A., Fradd, S. H., & Correa, V. I. (Eds.). (1989). Meeting the multicultural needs of Hispanic students in special education (Special issue). *Exceptional Children, 56.*

This special issue of *Exceptional Children* presents the most recent and comprehensive knowledge-base in the emerging discipline called Bilingual Special Education. Of particular interest to psychologists will be the research-based principles for the appropriate instruction of Hispanic pupils with learning problems. Ruiz's paper, though a bit wordy, is an excellent resource in this area.

Whitaker, H. A. (Ed.). (1989). Bilingualism [Special Issue]. *Brain and language, 36.*

Durgunoglu, A. Y. & Roediger III, H. L. (1987). Test differences in accessing bilingual memory. *Journal of Memory and Language, 26,* 377-391.

Paivio, A., Clark, J. M., & Lambert, W. E. (1988). Bilingual dual-coding theory and semantic repetition effects on recall. *Journal of Experimental Psychology: Learning, Memory and Cognition, 14,* 163-172.

Dornic, S. (1979). Information processing in bilinguals: Some selected issues. *Psychological Research, 40,* 329-348. Though most of the research on psychological tests report that there is no bias when testing bilinguals, the experimental literature on bilingualism reports that there may be qualitative differences in how bilinguals think. These references offer a rich source of diagnostic information for assessing children with two language systems, and for reconsidering the role of tests in such an endeavor.

7

Best Practices in the Assessment of Competence in Preschool-Age Children

Kathleen D. Paget
University of South Carolina

OVERVIEW

Grownups love figures. When you tell them that you have made a new friend, they never ask you any questions about essential matters. They never say "What does his voice sound like? What games does he love best? Does he collect butterflies?" Instead, they demand? "How old is he? How many brothers has he? How much does he weigh?" Only from these figures do they think they have learned anything about him.

— Antoine de Saint-Exupery,
The Little Prince

The passage above illustrates two limitations inherent in question-asking as an assessment strategy. First, the competencies displayed by a child often are a direct function of the questions asked and the tasks presented. Second, the questions may lead only to quantifiable responses if we are not aware of the need to require qualitative responses as well. Whether assessing social, cognitive, language, or motor functioning, we must remain open to the possibility that the questions and tasks we present to a young child may not be making contact with the child's understanding of the world.

In this chapter, best practices are conceptualized as an expansion in our scope of assessment activities beyond a test-based, question-asking format in an individual assessment setting. As asserted by Dunst and McWilliam (1988), certain behaviors may not be manifested when attempts are made to elicit them during testing if there is no *adaptive* reason for the child to manifest the behavior. Careful observation of children's abilities as they occur naturally and interviews with caregivers are key to making contact with a young child's understanding of the world. Thus, when we move beyond a "testing mindset," we see that preschool assessment is much more than the mechanics of testing.

The issues and challenges associated with the assessment of young children's competencies have had a longstanding history of discussion in the literature. The stigma of labeling, the limitations of prediction, and the validity of test results with young children are well-known topics to professionals involved in providing services to preschool-age children and their families. With the passage of the Education of Handicapped Act Amendments of 1986 (Public Law 99-457) and the resultant increases in services to young children, these salient issues are resurfacing and are in need of discussion in the context of current realities. The purpose of this chapter is to discuss best practices associated with the assessment of competencies in children 3-5 years of age. These best practices guide correct implementation of the new law and represent the intent or spirit behind it. Assessment is conceptualized in this chapter as a *process* of ongoing insight into how children think, interact, and behave developmentally (Almy & Genishi, 1979). The term *assessment* is used synonymously with *intervention planning* so as to reflect the ongoing, reciprocal, and mutable nature of the process. The range of abilities within a broad spectrum of areas (i.e., cognitive, adaptive–social, language) are conceptualized as *competencies* to emphasize an appropriately balanced focus on strengths and limitations. The reader is encouraged to supplement this chapter with the chapters in this volume on preschool social skills (Elliott) and preschool intervention (Barnett) and readings from the bibliography, because these references provide detailed explanation of implementation issues.

Bandura's (1978) reciprocal influence model has been proposed elsewhere as an appropriate framework to guide assessment practices for young children (Paget, 1985; Paget & Nagle, 1986; Reynolds, Gutkin, Elliott, & Witt, 1984) and is adopted for use in this chapter. Essentially, this ecological model emphasizes the reciprocal interplay among adult and child characteristics, behavior, and environmental phenomena and the situational specificity of young children's behavior and skill development; and it directs assessors to gather information about a child in all of the settings relevant to that child. Such a model is imperative as a guide for assessing preschool children because of time- and setting-sensitive variability in their behavior and the emergent nature of skills manifested by such children. The model also underscores the need to adopt an indirect service model to preschool services (Conoley & Gutkin, 1986; Paget, 1985), thus promoting consultation with teachers and parents as an ongoing assessment activity.

With an ecological, reciprocal influence framework as a backdrop, the chapter is divided into two major sections. The first section is focused on basic considerations in delivering preschool services, which form the basis for best practices discussed in the second section. Best practices are organized with respect to the major ecologies in which assessment should occur. Thus, relevant subsections include (a) the individualized assessment setting and issues relative to preparation, rapport, instrumentation, young children's development and behavior, and

interactive strategies; (b) assessment in naturally occurring contexts in the child's life (i.e., the preschool classroom and family); and (c) the use of play as an assessment medium.

BASIC CONSIDERATIONS IN PRESCHOOL ASSESSMENT

Considerations related to service delivery to children below the age of 6 years, at the most basic level, are dependent on the most recent legal influences from Public Law 99-457 (The Education of the Handicapped Act Amendments of 1986).

The Preschool Grant Program of the law is a downward extension of Public Law 94-142 in that it mandates a free and appropriate public education for children 3–5 years of age. The language of the recent law is similar to that of its predecessor, with provisions for least restrictive environment (LRE), multidisciplinary and nondiscriminatory assessment, parent involvement, and due process procedures. Many interpretive issues remain, including operational definitions of the terms *appropriate* and *least restrictive*.

There are several important differences in the language of the two laws. First, under PL 99-457, the documentation and count of children required by the federal government from the states does not have to be by diagnostic category for this age group, thus allowing states to serve 3- through 5-year-olds without labeling them. Second, expenses for parental instruction are written into the new law as allowable costs to reflect the vital importance of family influences on young children. Finally, the new law is more explicit in its support of variations in length of day and service model (i.e., home-based, center-based, combinations thereof), and local education agencies are encouraged to contract with appropriate nonpublic preschool programs to provide a range of services.

Although children between birth and 2 years of age are not a major focus of this discussion, it is useful to review briefly some basic information pertaining to the new law's application to this age group. The Early Intervention Program for Infants and Toddlers with Handicaps and their Families is a new discretionary program for the development and implementation of statewide, comprehensive, coordinated, multidisciplinary, interagency programs for early intervention services. The Early Intervention Program is directed to the needs of children, from birth to their third birthday, who need early intervention because (a) they are experiencing developmental delays in one or more areas of functioning (i.e., cognitive, physical, language and speech, psychosocial, or self-help skills); (b) they have a physical or mental condition that has a high probability of resulting in delay (e.g., Down Syndrome, cerebral palsy); or (c) they are at risk medically or environmentally for substantial developmental delays if early intervention is not provided. Critical to implementation of this part of the legislation is the definition of the term *developmentally delayed* adopted at the state level. Because the Early Intervention Program is a new amendment, many of its provisions describe new services. These new services include development of Individualized Family Service Plans (IFSPs), case management, and services to promote smooth transitions between programs.

It is clear that an expansion of skills is necessary for successful functioning by school psychologists in delivering services to very young children. To this end, training programs are augmenting their didactic and field-based offerings, practitioners are seeking opportunities in continuing professional development, and researchers are developing new assessment/intervention procedures and investigating the validity of currently used strategies. Danielson (1989) summarizes the various areas in which skills must be expanded as (a) learning new instruments, (b) evaluating standardized instruments that are currently available, (c) learning to adapt standardized instruments when necessary, (d) improving knowledge of child development, (e) increasing our willingness to observe rather than test, and (f) learning to work effectively with a team. In addition to these skills, learning to interact comfortably with normally developing young children, individually and in groups; learning the behavioral manifestations of risk factors and handicapping conditions; and understanding current theories supporting family involvement are essential to our knowledge and experiential base at the preschool level.

BEST PRACTICES IN PRESCHOOL ASSESSMENT

Even brief perusal of the basic considerations discussed above underscores the necessity of adopting an ecological framework for the delivery of preschool services. Whereas our assessment activities, in the form of individualized testing sessions, have been the mainstay of psychological services to school-age children and adolescents, such a situation is untenable at the preschool level. Beyond basic considerations, best practices demand an expansion of our skills in (a) the use of play as an assessment strategy; (b) classroom observation/assessment/ (c) teacher consultation; and (d) family involvement and support to a level at least commensurate with our often-practiced skills in administering the WISC-R. The next section of this chapter represents a modest beginning in a long-term process of learning the instrumentation available to us for expanding our skills. Presentation of this information carries with it the underlying message that in broadening the age range for which we are accountable, we must also intensify the seriousness with which we apply tenets of ecological psychology to school psychology.

The Individualized Assessment Setting

It goes without saying that in an ecological framework the individualized assessment setting is one of several contexts in which assessment should take place. By definition, the situation is limited by the demand characteristics of a particular room or rooms, the individualized nature of interactions, the developmental characteristics of the child, and

TABLE 1
Preparation for Individualized Assessment

LEARN the limitations of the room

LEARN physical limitations of the child

DRESS comfortably

PAY ATTENTION to impressions made on the child

BE PREPARED to adapt to the child

BE READY to move around/play

ADAPT the surroundings to the child's needs

ARRANGE playlike surroundings/childlike atmosphere

REMOVE possible distractions

PROVIDE materials designed for preschoolers

BE PREPARED to rearrange format of the test materials to "test limits"

OBSERVE interactions with significant others

LEARN about toys suitable for specific age groups

the requirements set by the particular questions asked and tasks presented. As Scarr (1981) states, "Whenever one measures a child's [cognitive] functioning, one is also measuring cooperation, attention, persistence, ability to sit still, and social responsiveness to an assessment situation" (p. 1161). This statement is especially appropriate to the assessment of preschool-age children, who display wide variability in experiences and behavior. Thus, although opportunities abound for gathering useful information about a child's functioning in an individualized context, the conclusions drawn are limited by features of the situation.

Detailed discussion of issues relative to preparing for an individual assessment with a preschool child and establishing and maintaining rapport is presented in Paget (in press). A general overview of the essential considerations with respect to these topics is presented in Table 1 and Table 2. Although many of these considerations pertain as well to the assessment of school-age children, a glance at Tables 1 and 2 reveals that using play and playful interactions, getting down on the floor to move around the room, and observing interactions with significant others are especially important components of the assessment of young children. In addition, careful observation of behaviors and the use of nonverbal interactive strategies are essential with young children who may be less skilled verbally than their school-age counterparts.

Instrumentation. The potential for misuse of tests for preschool children is substantial because of the potential variability across settings and time, the possibility of longer-term negative consequences of labeling, and the overdiagnosing of children with mild handicaps (Hobbs, 1975). Because of these concerns, recent discourse and research underscore the need for a multisource, multimethod approach to assessment, establishing a test-based approach as one of several strategies necessary to the individual assessment process (Anastasi, 1988; Neisworth & Bagnato, 1986, 1988; Paget & Nagle, 1986). Norm-, criterion-, and curriculum-referenced tests are the most frequently used instruments. Because of an emphasis on functional assessment tied to intervention planning, curriculum-referenced instruments are increasing in popularity (Bagnato & Neisworth, 1981; Bagnato, Neisworth, & Munson, 1989;

TABLE 2
Establishing and Maintaining Rapport

BE relaxed and enthusiastic

PLAY with the child; supplement test materials with games, toys, etc.

BE flexible

USE humor

AVOID being too formal or distant

STRIKE a balance between formality and informality

AVOID "baby talk"

USE a vocabulary understandable to the child

ALLOW time for informal observation of play behaviors

REASSURE the child about the testing experience

AVOID repetitive/stereotyped praise

USE nonverbal techniques for less verbal children

INCORPORATE play into assessment

WATCH for fatigue and signs of dependency

USE naturally-occurring distractions to understand child's abilities and preferences (e.g., how easily he or she is redirected, how he or she plays with a distracting toy, and language used while playing)

Neisworth & Bagnato, 1986, 1988) as important supplements to more traditional norm-referenced instruments. Bracken (1987) analyzed the technical adequacy of selected instruments standardized on preschool populations and concluded that for children below the age of 4 years (or functioning developmentally below that age) many tests lack sample practice items and are "limited in floor, item gradient, and reliability" (p. 325). Bandura's reciprocal influence model provides a framework for understanding these concerns by emphasizing how the behavioral and personal characteristics brought to an assessment situation by adult examiners and caregivers and young children affect quantified outcomes and the traditional interpretations of psychometric adequacy (Paget & Nagle, 1986).

An important issue relative to instrumentation for preschool-age children is the separation of some instruments, especially those that are criterion- and curriculum-referenced (e.g., the LAP, Battelle) into separate areas (i.e., do-

mains) of functioning. Many popular preschool instruments are described as "multiple-domain" tests, measuring skills in the areas of adaptive–social, cognitive, and language. The assumption that each domain represents a separate factor is contradicted by the principle that development is integrated and organized, with considerable overlap existing among areas of functioning (Kagan, 1984; MacMann & Barnett, 1984; Poth & Barnett, 1988). Thus, we must bear in mind that the realities of young children's development and functioning place limitations on the factorial validity of instruments.

Interpretation of test data for preschool children must account for differences in children's learning opportunities and their experiences with structured tasks similar to the test items. A distinction between functional and specific skills (Ulrey & Rogers, 1982) is of vital importance because developmental delays on tests may result from inexperience and would be interpreted more appropriately as functional rather than specific deficits.

Conversely, when two children have had similar experiences, delayed developmental skills may suggest different rates of growth and, in some cases, specific deficits. Correct interpretation of test-based information incorporates the experiential and cultural background of each child assessed. One strategy for accomplishing this is to *supplement* (not substitute) standardized assessment with nonstandardized presentation of tasks using materials with which the child is already familiar (Paget, 1989c). Professionals must consider previous preschool experience and prior exposure to tasks while attempting to discover (a) how the child responds to novel test items, (b) whether the child learns tasks quickly or slowly, and (c) the degree of structure required. From asking these questions it soon becomes clear how essential the examiner's flexibility and ingenuity are to the usefulness of testing procedures.

Developmental principles. Assessment of preschool children must also take into consideration the important psychological differences in thinking, motivation, and experiences between preschool children and those who are of school age. Testing procedures and knowledge of school-age children do not necessarily extrapolate downward to preschoolers, because age-related cognitive and emotional factors influence test administration and interpretation (Paget & Nagle, 1986). Thus, behaviors that might indicate a learning deficit or behavioral deviance if observed in a school-age child, might be normal and expected for the younger child. Piagetian theory and recent studies of preschool cognition provide a framework for understanding cognitive and behavioral differences between preschoolers and school-age children with respect to preoperational thinking, behavioral characteristics, language skills, and rapid growth of preschool-age children. An essential guiding principle is that within the age range of 3-6 years there is considerable variability with respect to developmental norms and expectations. A normally developing child who is 4 years 11 months of age is not only qualitatively

different from a child of 6 years but also different from a child who is 4 years 1 month old. Thus, we must avoid pitfalls associated with categorizing children below the age of 6 years simply as preschoolers without due consideration to the developmental principles pertinent to their specific age group. In addition, we must apply these principles both to their chronological *and* developmental age levels across various aspects of functioning.

Interactive strategies. The individual assessment situation with a preschool child affords the examiner an opportunity to use interpersonal interactions as a medium to link assessment and intervention. By doing so, the examiner becomes an important part of the child's environment. Variously termed testing the limits, "adaptive-process" assessment (Bagnato & Neisworth, 1981), dynamic assessment (Lidz, 1983), and using a test–teach–test approach (Ysseldyke & Mirkin, 1982), the goals of such a method are to identify instructional strategies that maximize success and are relevant to classroom teaching. As a supplement rather than a substitute for norm- and criterion-referenced instruments, this interventionist approach begins where the child fails, in an attempt to uncover the problem-solving strategies or styles of response that account for those failures (Lidz, 1983). Examiners may also alter their interactive styles to assess the child's social responses to frustration, playfulness, humor, and so forth.

Whereas several practical proposals in this respect are being advanced (Bagnato et al., 1989), other ideas are at the theoretical stage of formulation. Barnett (1984) suggests adapting Vygotsky's (1978) notion of zone of proximal or potential development, which posits that "what children can do with the assistance of others might be . . . more indicative of their mental development than what they can do alone" (p. 85). Lidz (1983) suggests adapting Feuerstein's (1979) learning potential assessment device (LPAD), which is based on the concept that the direct cause of cognitive deficiencies in children is faulty adult–child mediated learning experiences. Whether formulated at functional or theoretical levels, interventionist assessment strategies hold potential for assisting in the direct translation of assessment results into mechanisms that optimize preschool children's learning experiences.

In addition to interactions between the examiner and the child, interactive patterns between the child and caregivers should be observed, and the caregivers should be involved actively in the assessment process. The examiner may wish to observe (a) spontaneous, interactive play with a variety of materials, (b) instruction in a task the child is able to do, (c) instruction in a task the child has been unable to do, (d) interactions between a caregiver and the child, and (e) interactions between caregivers if more than one caregiver is present. Questions that may be of interest include how the caregiver structures the activity and how the caregiver responds to the successes and failures of the child. In addition, much can be learned from watching interactions between the child and her or his siblings.

Assessment in Natural Contexts

Because of the limitations inherent in any individualized assessment situation, information gathered from observing a young child's interactions in home and classroom environments is very important. Although the effects of physical and environmental differences between settings have been part of educational lore for some time, in recent years the systematic study of these variables has increased, particularly in the fields of ecological and environmental psychology (Gump, 1975; Smith & Connolly, 1980). Consequently, we are coming to view each setting as a unique ecosystem in which variables such as arrangement of space and materials, group size and composition, competencies of adults and children, and activities all interact reciprocally with young children's behavior (Rogers-Warren, 1982). Dunst and McWilliam (1988) argue cogently for assessment in natural contexts by stating, "If context plays an important role in

affecting behavior, then the assessment of given types of forms of interactive behaviors is best performed within the particular context in which the probability of evoking behavior is the highest" (p. 168).

Dunst and McWilliam (1988) further suggest there are five questions that should be posed when conducting an assessment in a child's natural environment, whether at home or school: (a) What competencies are manifested during routine events? (b) How does the child respond to a variation in the routine (e.g., adult does not respond to a request)? (c) How does the child respond to new materials introduced into the routine? (d) How does the child respond to the introduction of a second adult or second child into a child–person play episode? (e) Do the child's behaviors change with a change in the setting? These questions provide opportunities for information concerning naturally occurring behaviors and variations resulting from the introduction of novel items, changed expectations, and changes in the interpersonal and physical context.

The preschool classroom setting. The assessment of preschool children's behavior in their classrooms is the focus of much current research interest and activity (Carta, Sainato, & Greenwood, 1988; Dunst, McWilliam, & Holbert, 1986). Because these classrooms are the site of intervention activities, thorough knowledge of them contributes to a functional link between assessment results and intervention planning. Evidence demonstrates that preschool classroom environments and the manner in which they are managed can have significant effects on the behavior and cognitive development of both handicapped and nonhandicapped children (Bailey, Harms, & Clifford, 1983; Twardosz, 1984).

Several assessment instruments have been developed to quantify children's behaviors in the classroom and the various components of preschool environments. Among these, several focus on a child's involvement or engagement. These are the Planned Activity Check (PLA-Check) (Risley & Cataldo, 1974), Caregiver Assessment of Child Engagement (CACE) (McWilliam & Galant, 1984), and the Daily Engagement Rating Scale (DERS) (McWilliam, Galant, & Dunst, 1984). PLA-Check determines, for the number of persons present for a given activity, the percentage of children who are engaged and which materials, activities, people, or schedules generate the greatest amount of interest and participation. In contrast to the PLA-Check, which measures group levels of engagement, the CACE and DERS measure engagement levels for individual children. Both are rating scales that permit an assessment of different degrees of engagement. Two types (attentional and active) and three categories (adults, peers, and materials) of engagement are measured on each scale. The CACE measures engagement levels for specific classroom activities, and the DERS provides a daily measure of engagement for all classroom activities taken together.

The Early Childhood Environment Rating Scale (ECERS) (Harms & Clifford, 1980) is designed to provide an overall picture of preschool settings, including the manner in which materials, space, child-level activities, scheduling, and adult supervision are organized and used. The Classroom Observation Instrument (COI) (Stallings, 1975), the Infant/Toddler Learning Project Observation System (ITLP) (Rogers-Warren, Santos-Colond, Warren, & Hasselbring, 1984), and the Preschool Assessment of the Classroom Environment Scale (PACE) (Dunst, McWilliam, & Holbert, 1986) all measure dimensions of classroom environments that contribute to learning (e.g., organization, instructional methods, child–caregiver interactions). Accompanying the PACE is a form for the preschool classroom teacher to self-evaluate aspects of the classroom that he/she believes need to be changed.

In addition to the above instruments, Charlesworth (1979) described the importance of focusing on intelligent behavior, not in a test setting, but rather as it is observed in everyday situations. He developed a method called PROBA (Problem Behavior Analysis), by which problem-solving behavior can be observed in the ongoing activities of children. Essentially, the procedure reveals "(a) features of everyday living that are problematic; (b) who or what was responsible for these features; and (c) how the individual responded to them" (p. 215). This instrument exemplifies the application of functional analysis of behavior in the assessment of cognitively mediated behaviors.

Carta, Greenwood, and Atwater (1985) developed the Ecobehavioral System for Complex Assessment of Preschool Environments (ESCAPE). Ecobehavioral assessment strategies and research on teacher effectiveness are used with this instrument to (a) quantify teachers' and students' behaviors and relate them to academic gain, and (b) measure simultaneously with behavioral occurrences the situational factors surrounding those behaviors.

With the proliferation of instruments such as those mentioned above, the need arises to determine their psychometric adequacy. We lack standardized norms to serve as guidelines for making judgments about the influence of environmental factors on the cognitive growth of young children, although work in this respect is progressing (Carta, Sainato, Greenwood, 1988).

The family context. Despite the extensive evidence that the family is the primary influence on a preschool child's development (Bronfenbrenner, 1979), thorough assessment of families as systems has often been overlooked or done "on the run" (Karpel & Strauss, 1983, p. 2). This situation is changing with the increased emphasis on parent and family involvement mandated by PL 99-457, although a comprehensive evaluation is a large undertaking for any single professional, which points to the need for multidisciplinary interactions when conducting an assessment. Fortunately, instruments are being developed to assist in the conduct of interviews with family members and naturalistic observations within and outside the home (Carlson, in press; Dunst, Trivette, & Deal, 1988; Carlson & Grotevant, 1986; Paget, 1987).

At the center of this discussion is the message that professionals working in preschool programs, especially psychologists and social workers, need to be versed in family systems theory and the growing literature on family strengths and needs (Bailey & Simeonsson, 1988; Dunst et al., 1988; Turnbull & Turnbull, 1986). Examples of instruments designed to measure family strengths, needs, and resources are the Family Needs Scale, the Family Functioning Style Scale, and the Family Resource Scale (described in Dunst, Trivette, & Deal, 1988), the Parent Needs Inventory (Fewell, Meyer, & Schell, 1981), and the Personal Projects Scale (Little, 1983). In addition, assessment of parents' preferences with regard to the *specific* ways they wish to be involved with their child's education plan is essential (Bloch, 1988; Maple, 1977; Turnbull & Turnbull, 1986). Careful evaluation of "where the family is" in its own developmental life cycle and its adaptation to a special needs child can have significant implications for determining the goals of parental involvement.

To conclude this section on assessment in natural contexts, it is appropriate to discuss particularly innovative and useful instruments that provide opportunity to collect information from both the home and the classroom. The Parent/Professional Preschool Performance Profile (The five P's) (Bloch, 1988) facilitates *shared assessment* between parents and teachers with respect to their perceptions of a young child's functioning. From simultaneous but separate ratings twice a year of the child's observed performance, goals for the child are selected. According to Bloch (1988), differences in ratings are identified, and a lack of consensus often provokes dialogue. Comparisons may be drawn of the child's performance at home and school, and caregivers from each setting may determine the most appropriate strategies for implementing the child's education plan. The System to Plan Early Childhood Services (SPECS; Bagnato & Neisworth, in press) is a team decision-making model that synchronizes, or links, assessment information with intervention goals. SPECS relies upon structured clinical judgment data from several team members and parents to guide program decision making. School psychologists are in a unique position to facilitate the administration of these instruments, which operationalize the letter and spirit of Public Law 99-457 and exemplify best practices in preschool assessment.

Children's Play as an Assessment Strategy

Because play follows a regular developmental sequence from infancy through childhood and pervades young children's behavioral patterns across contexts, it makes sense to use play behavior as a medium for assessing young children's competencies. Observations of play behaviors and classification of these behaviors according to levels described in the literature can yield important information regarding a child's level of cognitive functioning. These observations can be done in an individualized assessment situation, in a classroom, or in the home.

Theories of play behavior are being operationalized, and play assessment scales are being developed, for use with infants and preschool children with various types of handicapping conditions. The instruments themselves are at various stages in their own development; some are being used solely for research purposes and others are available for practical use. In addition, the instruments vary with respect to the dimensions of play assessed, the degree of structure imposed on the observations, whether the play materials are specified, and the instruments' appropriateness for handicapped or nonhandicapped children.

Jeffrey and McConkey (1976) developed an observation scheme for measuring the frequency, duration, and diversity of children's imaginative doll play with specified materials, and Chappell and Johnson (1976) described a procedure by which children are presented with 12 specified objects and both the unprompted and verbally cued responses are recorded. Howes (1980) describes the Peer Play Scale, which is a rating scale of five levels of peer play (parallel, parallel with mutual regard, simple social play, reciprocal and complementary action, and reciprocal social play), and Westby (1980) incorporates structured observation *and* parent or teacher reporting into the Symbolic Play Scale Checklist.

Nicholich (1977) described levels of symbolic maturity through the analysis of pretend play and its correspondence to Piagetian stages of development, with a Manual for Analyzing Free Play (McCune-Nicolich, 1980), which explains a procedure for assessment of free play with specified toys, scoring criteria, and videotape analysis. Gowen and Schoen (1984) prepared a method for evaluating play in an unstructured free play situation that categorizes and evaluates play by using content, signifiers, and modes of representational analysis; and Lunzer (1958) developed a scale that measures the complexity of play and emphasizes adaptiveness, the use of materials, and integration of materials.

Two additional tests used with children who have handicapping conditions are available only in experimental editions from the authors. Bromwich, Fust, Khokha, and Walden (1981) developed the Play Assessment Checklist for Infants to supplement widely used infant development scales. The test requires a specific set of toys and the infant (or preschooler who is functioning at a low level) is videotaped while interacting with them. Fewell (1984) developed the Play Assessment Scale, which is built around a sequence of play behaviors and produces a play age. Children are given opportunities to play with various sets of toys, and their play is scored with the scale. This scale also includes procedures for eliciting and scoring play at higher levels than the spontaneous play used in the measurement of play age.

The above description of instruments attests to the recognition that play behaviors of young children are an important focus of our assessment activities. A state-of-the-art analysis of the instruments suggests they vary greatly along dimensions such as functionality, reliability, and theoretical soundness. Nevertheless, they hold much promise. In addition, curricula and instructional materials are being developed for using play as a vehicle for intervention programming. The interested reader is referred to Fewell and Kaminski (1988) for additional information about these materials.

SUMMARY

Best practice with respect to the assessment of preschool children requires special attention to issues and challenges that are unique to this age group. Among these issues are the variability in young children's exposure to structured learning situations and their experience with assessment measures, rapid developmental changes, and the potential for wide behavioral variability across settings. Competent administration and interpretation of tests is one phase of a multiphase process involving additional assessment of competencies as they are manifested in the child's natural environment. The application of developmental principles, use of testing-the-limits procedures, observation of play behaviors, and involvement of the family are essential to accurate understanding of a preschool child's functioning. In addition, best practice involves continuous vigilance to current research as it confirms or disconfirms the utility of certain approaches and strategies. School psychologists who strive to be competent assessors of preschool children must stay abreast of current developments, be adaptable, and understand the ethical constraints of their own skill development. As one of numerous professions committed to improvement in our services to preschool children and their families, school psychology is witnessing an exciting decade.

AUTHOR NOTE

Portions of this chapter also appear in K. D. Paget, Assessment of Intellectual Competence in Preschool Children: Conceptual Issues and Challenges. In R. W. Kamphaus and C. R. Reynolds (Eds.), *Handbook of Psychological and Educational Assessment of Children.* New York: Guilford.

REFERENCES

Almy, M., & Genishi, C. (1979). *Ways of studying children* (ref. ed.) New York: Teachers College Press.

Anastasi, A. (1988). *Psychological testing* (6th ed.). New York: Macmillan.

Bagnato, S., & Neisworth, J. (1981). *Linking developmental assessment and curricula.* Rockville, MD: Aspen Systems.

Bagnato, S. J., & Neisworth, J. (in press). *System to plan early children services.* Circle Pines. MN: American Guidance Service.

Bagnato, S. J., Neisworth, J., & Munson, S. M. (1989). *Linking developmental assessment and early intervention: Curriculum-based prescriptions* (2nd ed.), Rockville, MD: Aspen Systems.

Bailey, D., & Simeonsson, R. (1988). Home-based early interventions. In S. L. Odom & M. B. Karnes (Ed.), *Early intervention for infants and children with handicaps.* Baltimore: Paul Brookes.

Bailey, D. B., Harms, T., & Clifford, R. M. (1983). Matching changes in preschool environments to desired changes in child behavior. *Journal of the Division for Early Childhood, 1,* 61-68.

Bandura, A. (1978). The self system in reciprocal determinism. *American Psychologist, 33,* 344-358.

Barnett, D. W. (1984). An organizational approach to preschool services: Psychological screening, assessment, and intervention. In C. Maher, R. Illback, & J. Zins (Eds.), *Organizational psychology in the schools: A handbook for practitioners.* Springfield, IL: Thomas.

Bloch, J. (1988). Shared assessment: Another approach to the parental link. *Communicator* (The Division for Early Childhood), *15.*

Bracken, B. A. (1987). Limitations of preschool instruments and standards for minimal levels of technical adequacy. *Journal of Psychoeducational Assessment, 4,* 313-326.

Bromwich, R. M., Fust, S., Khokha, E., & Walden, M. (1981). *Play Assessment Checklist for Infants Manual.* Unpublished document. Northridge, CA: California State University.

Bronfenbrenner, U. (1979). *The ecology of human development: Experiments by nature and design.* Cambridge, MA: Harvard University Press.

Carlson, C. I. (in press). Assessing the family context. In C. R. Reynolds & R. W. Kamphaus (Eds.), *Handbook of psychological and educational assessment of children* (Vol. 2). New York: Guilford.

Carlson, C. I., & Grotevant, H. (1986). A comparative review of family rating scales: Guidelines for clinicians and researchers. *Journal of Family Psychology, 1,* 23-47.

Carta, J. J., Greenwood, C. R., & Atwater, J. B. (1985). *ESCAPE: Ecobehavioral system for complex assessment of preschool environments.* Kansas City, KS: University of Kansas, Bureau of Child Research, Juniper Gardens Children's Project.

Chappell, G. E., & Johnson, G. A. (1976). Evaluation of cognitive behavior in the young nonverbal child. *Language, Speech, and Hearing Services in Schools, 7,* 17-27.

Charlesworth, W. R. (1979). An ethological approach to studying intelligence. *Human Development, 22,* 212-216.

Conoley, J. C., & Gutkin, T. B. (1986). School psychology: A reconceptualization of service delivery realities. In S. N. Elliott & J. C. Witt (Eds.), *The delivery of psychological services in schools* (pp. 393-424). Hillsdale, NJ: Erlbaum.

Danielson, E. (1989). Expanding skills: Preparing to assess infants and preschoolers. *Preschool Interests, 4,* 1-9.

Dunst, C. J., & McWilliam, R. A. (1988). Cognitive assessment of multiply handicapped young children. In T. Wachs & R. Sheehan (Eds.), *Assessment of young developmentally disabled children* (pp. 213-238). New York: Plenum.

Dunst, C. J., McWilliam, R. A., & Holbert K. (1986). Assessment of preschool classroom environments. *Diagnostique, 11,* 212-232.

Fewell, R. R. (1984). Assessment of preschool handicapped children. *Educational Psychologist, 19,* 172-179.

Fewell, R., & Kaminski, R. (1988). Play skills development and instruction for young children with handicaps. In S. L. Odom & M. B. Karnes (Eds.), *Early intervention for infants and children with handicaps.* Baltimore: Paul Brookes.

Fewell, R., Meyer, D. J., & Schell, G. (1981). *Parent Needs Inventory.* Unpublished manuscript, University of Washington, Seattle.

Gowen, J., & Schoen, D. (1984). *Levels of child object play.* Unpublished coding scheme manuscript. Chapel Hill, NC: Carolina Institute of Research on Early Education of the Handicapped, Frank Porter Graham Child Development Center.

Gump, P. (1975). Ecological psychology and children. In M. Hetherington (Ed.), *Review of research in child development* (Vol. 5). Chicago: University of Chicago Press.

Harms, T., & Clifford R. (1980). *Early childhood environment rating scale.* New York: Teachers College Press.

Hobbs, N. (1975). *The classification of children.* New York: Jossey-Bass.

Howes, C. (1980). Peer play scale as an index of complexity of peer interaction. *Developmental Psychology, 16,* 371–372.

Jeffrey, D. M., & McConkey, R. (1976). An observation scheme for recording children's imaginative doll play. *Journal of Child Psychology and Psychiatry, 17,* 189–197.

Kagan, J. (1984). *The nature of the child.* New York: Basic Books.

Karpel, M., & Strauss, E. (1983). *Family evaluation.* New York: Gardner.

Lidz, C. S. (1983). Dynamic assessment and the preschool child. *Journal of Psychoeducational Assessment, 1,* 59–72.

Little, B. R. (1983). Personal projects: A rationale and method for investigation. *Environment and Behavior, 19,* 273–309.

Lunzer, E. A. (1958). A scale of the organization of behavior for use in the study of play. *Educational Review, 11,* 205–217.

MacMann, G. M., & Barnett, D. W. (1984). An analysis of the construct validity of two measures of adaptive behavior. *Journal of Psychoeducational Assessment.*

Maple, F. (1977). *Shared decision making.* Beverly Hills, CA: Sage.

Neisworth, J. T., & Bagnato, S. J. (1986). Curriculum-based developmental assessment: Congruence of testing and teaching. *School Psychology Review, 15,* 180–199.

Neisworth, J. T., & Bagnato, S. J. (1988). Assessment in early childhood special education. In S. L. Odom & M. B. Karnes (Eds.), *Early intervention for infants and children with handicaps.* Baltimore: Paul Brooks.

Nicolich, L. (1977). Beyond sensorimotor intelligence: Assessment of symbolic maturity through analysis of pretend play. *Merrill–Palmer Quarterly, 23,* 89–101.

Paget, K. D. (1985). Preschool services in the schools: Issues and implications. *Special Services in the Schools, 2,* 3–25.

Paget, K. D. (1987). Systemic family assessment: Concepts and strategies for school psychologists. *School Psychology Review, 16,* 429–442.

Paget, K. D. (in press). The individual assessment situation: Basic considerations for preschool children. In B. A. Bracken (Ed.), *The psychoeducational assessment of preschool children* (rev. ed.). Boston: Allyn & Bacon.

Paget, K. D. (1989b). Assessment of intellectual competence in preschool children: Conceptual issues and challenges. In R. W. Kamphaus and C. R. Reynolds (Eds.), *Handbook of psychological and educational assessment of children.* New York: Guilford.

Paget, K. D. (1989c). Assessment of cognitive skills in the preschool child. In D. B. Bailey & M. Wolery (Eds.), *Assessing infants and preschoolers with handicaps* (pp. 275–300). Columbus, OH: Merrill.

Paget, K. D., & Nagle, R. J. (1986). A conceptual model of preschool assessment. *School Psychology Review, 15,* 154–165.

Poth, R., & Barnett, D. W. (1988). Establishing the limits of interpretive confidence: A validity study of two preschool developmental scales. *School Psychology Review, 17,* 322–330.

Reynolds, C. R., Gutkin, T. B., Elliott, S. N., & Witt, J. C. (1984). *School psychology: Essentials of theory and practice.* New York: Wiley.

Risley, T. H., & Cataldo, M. F. (1974). *Evaluation of planned activities: The PLA/Check measure of classroom participation.* Unpublished manual. Lawrence, KS: Center for Applied Behavior Analysis.

Rogers-Warren, A. K. (1982). Behavior ecology in classrooms for young, handicapped children. *Topics in Early Childhood Special Education, 2,* 21–32.

Rogers-Warren, A. K., Santos-Colond, J., Warren, S. F., & Hasselbring, T. S. (1984, December). *Strategies and issues in quantifying early intervention.* Paper presented at the National Center for Clinical Infant Programs Conference.

Scarr, S. (1981). Testing for children: Assessment and the many determinants of intellectual competence. *American Psychologist, 36,* 1159–1168.

Smith, P. K., & Connolly, K. J. (1980). *The ecology of preschool behavior.* Cambridge, England: Cambridge University Press.

Stallings, J. A. (1975). Implementation and child effects of teaching practices in follow through classrooms. *Monographs of the Society for Research in Child Development 40*(7–8, Serial No. 163).

Turnbull, A. P., & Turnbull, H. R. (1986). *Families, professionals, and exceptionality: A special partnership.* Columbus, OH: Merrill.

Twardosz, S. (1984). Environmental organization: The physical, social, and programmatic context of behavior. In M. Hersen, R. Eisler, & P. Miller (Eds.), *Progress in behavior modification* (Vol. 18; pp. 123-161). New York: Academic.

Ulrey, G., & Rogers, S. J. (1982). *Psychological assessment of handicapped infants and young children.* New York: Thieme & Stratton.

Westby, C. E. (1980). Assessment of cognitive and language abilities through play. *Language, Speech and Hearing Services in Schools, 11,* 154-168.

Ysseldyke, J. E., & Mirkin, P. K. (1982). The use of assessment information to plan instructional interventions: A review of the research. In C. R. Reynolds & T. B. Gutkin (Eds.), *The Handbook of school psychology* (pp. 395-409). New York: John Wiley & Sons.

ANNOTATED BIBLIOGRAPHY

Bailey, D. B., & Wolery, M. (1989). *Assessing infants and preschoolers with handicaps.* Columbus, OH: Merrill.

This book provides current information on the assessment of infants and preschoolers with handicaps. It focuses on assessment for the purpose of instructional or intervention program planning. Three major sections cover (a) fundamental issues and considerations in assessment, (b) specialized assessment issues, and (c) assessment in the context of key developmental domains (cognitive, motor, communication, social, play, and self-care).

Bracken, B. A. (Ed.). (in press). *The psychoeducational assessment of preschool children.* Boston: Allyn & Bacon.

This book includes contributions from writers in the area of preschool assessment. Included are chapters addressing basic considerations for assessment, and assessment in the key domains of functioning, family assessment, and linking assessment with intervention design.

Bagnato, S. J., Neisworth, J. T., & Munson, S. M. (1989). *Linking developmental assessment and early intervention: Curriculum-based prescriptions (2nd rev. ed.).* Rockville, MD: Aspen Systems.

This book provides practical information about "linking" assessment information with curricula for young special needs children. Numerous strategies and curricula are presented, and case studies illustrate pertinent issues. Assessment as a multidisciplinary process is emphasized, with a discussion of instruments designed to measure congruence of perceptions among professionals and between professionals and family members.

Simeonsson, R. (1986). *Psychological and developmental assessment of special children.* Boston: Allyn and Bacon.

This book provides comprehensive coverage of assessment procedures appropriate for children whose assessment needs may require unique or modified stimulus materials, response options, administrative procedures, or test content. Emphasis is placed on the purpose, philosophy, and process of assessment, as well as assessment instruments and strategies. Assessment is viewed as a multidisciplinary process involving the child's family and various professional disciplines.

School Psychology Review, 15(2) (1986). Miniseries on preschool assessment.

This miniseries provides coverage of conceptual issues and practical strategies pertinent to the assessment of preschool children. An ecological model is presented to guide assessment activities, and the articles reflect emphases on family assessment, curriculum-based developmental assessment, cognitive and social–emotional assessment, and the role of neuropsychology in the comprehensive assessment of young children.

8

Best Practices in Assisting the Learning-Disabled College and College-Bound Student

Dorothy D. Miles
University of Hartford

OVERVIEW

There has been a dramatic increase in the need for services for learning-disabled students in postsecondary institutions during the last decade. The number of college freshmen who have learning disabilities has increased tenfold since 1978, according to a report issued by HEATH Resource Center (1986). Many factors have contributed to this growth. Historically, the growth was given impetus by Section 504 of the Rehabilitation Act of 1973, which required colleges receiving federal funds to furnish programs and services to the handicapped (Marion & Iovacchini, 1983). Concurrently, improved identification and support services to learning-disabled students in elementary and secondary schools were producing more graduates who expected an education that included support services. Finally, personnel in postsecondary institutions began finding that such students could succeed in college when they received appropriate support (HEATH Resource Center, 1987).

In the Ninth Annual Report to Congress (U.S. Department of Education, 1987), it was noted that almost 50,000 learning-disabled students graduated from high school in 1985. In growing numbers, these students are entering colleges that are increasingly eager to accept them. The colleges are now facing the challenge of providing appropriate services for this population.

Fagan (1989) has predicted that school psychology services will expand during the next decade to include adult populations in nontraditional settings such as junior colleges and four-year institutions of higher education. This expansion has already begun. He further envisioned role and function shifts for school psychologists in the direction of consultation and interventions (Fagan, 1989). Reschly (1988) has called for role and function changes with more emphasis on curriculum-based assessment, problem-solving consultation, designing behavioral and academic interventions, and promoting academic survival skills.

The transition from secondary school to college is difficult for many students, but it can be particularly difficult for even the brightest learning-disabled student (Dexter, 1982). The school psychologist working at the secondary level can be the catalyst for easing the transition by early identification, program planning, counseling, and consultation for those secondary students with college potential.

Training programs for personnel working with learning-disabled adults are sparse (National Joint Committee on Learning Disabilities, 1985; Shaw, Norlander, & McGuire, 1987). Despite the growth of the college learning-disabled population, few school psychologists are being prepared to work specifically with learning-disabled adults in universities and other settings (Levinson, 1986). However, most of the college learning disability services are those that are generally included in school psychology services.

Levinson identified these areas as identification/assessment, academic advisement/counseling, career/vocational counseling, staff development/consultation, individual counseling, peer support groups, parent groups, and research (Levinson, 1986). Other competencies desired for learning disability college personnel are instructional competency and management/leadership skills (Shaw et al., 1987). Although typically there is little in the school psychology training programs that is aimed at working with learning-disabled adults, it would seem that the school psychologist has sufficient training to work with adults in the postsecondary setting.

BASIC CONSIDERATIONS

Most school psychologists are familiar with Public Law 94-142, signed in 1975, which guarantees the right to a free and appropriate public education to all handicapped children between the ages of 3 and 21 years. The specific rights of the learning-disabled student who chooses to enter college, however, are delineated by Section 504 of the Rehabilitation Act of 1973 (PL 93-112), which states that

> No otherwise qualified handicapped individual in the United States shall, solely by reason of his handicap, be excluded from participation in, be denied the benefits of, or be subjected to discrimination under any program or activity receiving Federal financial assistance.

The term *qualified handicapped individual* has been interpreted to mean a person who, with auxiliary aid or reasonable program modification, can meet the academic requirements the institution considers necessary to its program (Brinckerhoff, 1985; Mangrum & Strichart, 1988).

The law prohibits discrimination against students because of a handicap. It states that the institution

> may not apply limitations upon the number or proportion of handicapped persons who may be admitted . . . [or] make use of any test or criterion for

admission that has a disproportionate adverse effect on handicapped persons . . . [it] shall assure itself that . . . [admission] test results accurately reflect the applicant's aptitude or achievement level or whatever other factor the test purports to measure, rather than reflecting the applicant's impaired sensory, manual, or speaking skills . . . [and] may not make preadmission inquiry as to whether an applicant for admission is a handicapped person but, after admission, may make inquiries on a confidential basis as to handicaps that may require accommodation. (PL 93-112, Subpart E, Section 84.42, 1973)

Although the institution is not required to make adjustments that would result in lower academic standards or alter the essence of a program, it is required to make reasonable accommodations (Brinckerhoff, 1985). Specific modifications listed in PL 93-112, Subpart E, Section 84.44, are "changes in the length of time permitted for the completion of degree requirements, substitutions of specific courses required for the completion of degree requirements, and adaptation of the manner in which specific courses are conducted" — as well as use of tape recorders in the classrooms. Section 84.44 also requires that one must ensure that the results of the evaluation represent the students' achievement in the course, rather than reflecting the students' impaired sensory, manual, or speaking skills.

BEST PRACTICES

Best Practices in Assisting the College-Bound Learning-Disabled Student

Early identification and program planning for the secondary school learning-disabled student who has potential for college is optimal (Norlander, 1987; Shaw, Byron, Norlander, McGuire, & Anderson, 1988). Development of a comprehensive high school program should be geared to the academic background needed for college, with cooperation between regular and special education teachers (Norlander, 1987; Seidenburg, 1987; Shaw et al., 1988; Siperstein, 1988). Course waivers should be given only on the basis of valid diagnostic data, with consideration for the effect of the waiver on postsecondary achievement (Norlander, 1987; Shaw et al., 1988).

Development of learning strategies should be incorporated into the academic plan (Seidenburg, 1987; Siperstein, 1988). College students will be better prepared for success if they have already mastered some basic learning strategies such as time management, use of a word processor, some memory and notetaking techniques, and have learned to work independently. Waiting until college to acquire these strategies is too late for most students, because they get caught up in the demands of the curriculum and have little time to learn strategies (Dalke & Schmitt, 1987).

By the time the learning-disabled students leave high school, they should have a thorough understanding of individual strengths and weaknesses and how the disability impinges on learning.

Many learning-disabled students have difficulty taking tests. Both Scholastic Aptitude Tests (SAT) and American College Testing (ACT) offer special accommodations such as extended time, cassettes, readers, large type, flexible test dates, separate test rooms, individualized supervision, and assistance with marking, depending on the diagnosed handicap. Arrangement for these special considerations must be made well in advance. Reports sent to colleges on the achieved scores usually note a nonstandard administration. The test services listed in the Resource section can be contacted for detailed information.

Locating colleges with appropriate resources, securing college admission, and developing a written individual college plan is a strategy recommended by Seidenburg (1987) and by Siperstein (1988). Recently, the state of Connecticut mandated that an Individual Transition Plan (ITP), which includes goals, services needed, projected timelines, and parties responsible, be written for each handicapped student who is graduating from the public school system (Act Concerning, 1987).

A simple psychoeducational form may be used to summarize cogent student data in order to facilitate decision making about the possibility of college (Figure 1).

Characteristics Important for Success in College

Mangrum and Strichart (1988), with the help of others, compiled a list of what college personnel in learning disabilities programs look for during an interview with a prospective student who is learning-disabled.

1. Thinking ability characteristic of college students.
2. An understanding of basic concepts in English, math, and the social and physical sciences.
3. Motivation to succeed in college.
4. Evidence that productive use was made of the high school years.
5. An understanding and acceptance of one's learning disability.
6. Understanding of one's academic strengths and weaknesses.
7. Understanding of how one learns.
8. Emotional maturity and stability.
9. An inquiring and questioning mind.
10. Willingness to self-advocate.
11. Awareness of the consequences of inappropriate behavior.
12. Awareness of one's underachievement in college prerequisite skills.
13. Self-sufficiency.

Comparing the characteristics of the learning-disabled college-bound student with this list of characteristics will aid in assessing the likelihood of college success.

Assisting with the College Search

Although a college is not permitted to reject a student because of a handicap if the student meets the established admissions criteria, services offered by the colleges vary. An important element in the decision-making process for the college-bound student is matching the student, the college, and the support program (McGuire & Shaw, 1987). It is particularly

Student Name   Date of Birth

COGNITIVE ASSESSMENT

Test	Date	

Comments:

ACADEMIC ASSESSMENT

Reading	Math	Other

Strengths   Weaknesses

Motivation:

COLLEGE BOARD SCORES

Test	Date	Scores	Adaptations

SUPPORT SERVICES DURING JUNIOR/SENIOR YEAR OF HIGH SCHOOL:

FIGURE 1. Psychoeducational profile for the college-bound learning-disabled student.

Name of College

College Interviewer

Telephone:

Average Board Scores of Students:

Average Class Size or Range from Smallest to Largest:

SPECIAL SERVICES FOR LEARNING DISABLED STUDENTS

Name of Director

Telephone

____ Diagnostic Testing

____ Academic Advising

____ Subject-area tutoring
(List subjects)

_____

_____

_____

____ Strategies tutoring

____ Professional tutoring

____ Peer tutoring

____ Charge for tutoring

Amount of time per week for tutoring: _____

Additional notes on general admission requirements:

____ Readers

____ Note Takers

____ Tape Recording of lectures

____ Untimed tests

____ Special scheduling

____ Separate classes

____ Reduced course load

____ Counseling

____ Peer support groups

____ More time to finish degree

____ Other _____

Admission requirements for LD support program:

FIGURE 2. College and college support services profile.

important that students with learning disabilities look carefully into possible postsecondary settings that appear to have the services or programs that meet their needs (Michael, 1987). There are published lists of colleges that offer special assistance to students with learning disabilities. For a partial listing, see the Resource section. A comparison of colleges and their services may be facilitated by the use of a checklist of the services offered, which can be filled out by the student (Figure 2).

After some tentative choices are made, the student should visit the colleges. If necessary, some role-playing techniques will prepare the student for a college interview.

Colleges are prohibited from soliciting information about handicaps, but the student is free to declare the handicap and to inquire about services. It is usually in the student's best interest to do so, and to visit the person or persons who are responsible for providing the services to learning-disabled students. The student should be prepared to state the type of service needed, and to provide a copy of recent psychoeducational reports that include a psychoeducational assessment, a high school transcript of grades and any other information, such as recent IEPs, that may prove helpful. If the Psychoeducational Profile in Figure 1 is used, the student may submit this for consideration as an unofficial record.

Students who are accepted into a postsecondary institution should be encouraged to take advantage of any special summer or transitional programs offered by the college. Most postsecondary institutions at least offer summer courses. Learning-disabled students can benefit from taking a summer course prior to fall matriculation; they can then become familiar with the campus and services and experience a college level course. An added advantage is that they may earn some credits toward graduation and feel more comfortable about taking a reduced course load in the fall semester.

Best Practices in Assisting the Learning-Disabled Student at the College Level

At college, many students are reluctant to declare their learning disabilities unless they are in academic difficulty and feel that they are in a crisis situation. At that time they may self-identify and demand immediate services that they previously have avoided and that are not necessarily appropriate for their needs. This crisis situation may be avoided by working with students prior to matriculation to reinforce understanding of their individual strengths and weaknesses and to make recommendations for self-advocacy, for a program of study, and for program modification and counseling. With input from the student, an academic plan can be developed as well as an appropriate means of communication with faculty.

Identification and assessment. The criteria to use for identification of learning disabilities at the college level probably will be a combination of standardized test scores and qualitative data such as in-terviews, observations, and review of past records. Some students will have extensive psychoeducational reports but others will never have had assessment, diagnosis, or treatment.

A problem unique to assessment at the college level is the scarcity of appropriate standardized diagnostic instruments for this age population (National Joint Committee on Learning Disabilities, 1985). For the upper age levels academic achievement measures often have few or no test items or appropriate norm groups.

If a team approach to assessment is used, it is important that the student be considered a vital member of the team. It may be possible for the school psychologist to form a professional network within the college community even if the only assessment being done is by the school psychologist. Faculty in education, special education, counseling, and psychology have expertise that may be especially valuable, as do personnel involved in college learning or tutoring centers. Qualified graduate students may offer assistance in testing or tutoring while they are gaining valuable experience in their discipline.

When an assessment is requested, a review of the records available on the student and an interview with the student is usually the first step in determining whether a formal assessment is warranted. Often included in the records from the high schools is valuable information regarding standardized test scores or teachers' comments. At the least, high school grades and SAT or ACT scores should be available in the students' records and can be used as preliminary data. Knowles and Knowles (1983) used ACT data combined with high school grades and a reading test to predict learning disability in entering college freshmen with 84% accuracy. Bennett, Rock, and Chan (1987), however, found that verbal-math discrepancies on the SAT were not good indicators of college learning disabilities.

During an interview with the student, the school psychologist can gather preliminary data about the student's oral ex-

Name:

Date:

DOB:

1. Standardized tests

	Test Name	Score	Date		Test Name	Score	Date
RDG or VER				Math			
IQ				SP/WL			
				Other			

Academic & Learning Strengths   Academic & Learning Deficits

Recommendations

Effective learning strategies to be used by student:

Modifications needed for effective teaching:

I agree to carry out the above recommendations to the best of my ability. Information on strengths and weaknesses and modifications will be communicated to professors.

_____   _____
Student   U. of H. Representative

Figure 3. Screening, assessment, and recommendations.

pression, motivation, and perspective on the problems encountered. In contrast with practice with the public school age population, parents are not contacted unless the student gives express permission. The school psychologist may wish to use a simple one-page form (Figure 3) to summarize preliminary screening data and to facilitate identification of missing data.

If further assessment is needed, the school psychologist may begin with some curriculum-based assessment. Simply asking the student to read from a college text and noting errors is a good place to start an assessment. An analysis of the reading level of the student's textbook often reveals that it is far above the student's level of reading achievement. If the text reading level is too difficult for the student, texts with parallel information but easier reading levels may be available. An analysis of math errors from a recent test is a means of identifying areas of weakness that can be targeted for remediation in math.

In any assessment situation, the school psychologist must make a choice between expediency and precision. In a majority of cases, the history, an assessment of cognitive abilities, and a measurement of the academic areas of strength and of weakness, together with some curriculum-based assessment and an analysis of motivation and of knowledge of study skills will provide the necessary information to proceed with the important next step of communication and intervention.

When interpreting intelligence test results, it should be remembered that cognitive strengths and deficits are only one type of information and they do not guarantee success or failure in college. Vogel (1986) cautioned against using minimum IQ scores as cutoff scores. Although the Verbal IQs of learning-disabled college students tend to be higher than the Performance IQs, this may be a result of selection and education. The relative strengths and deficits reflected in the verbal-performance scores and the grouped subtest scores within each scale can be revealing (Vogel, 1987). In a review

of several studies, Vogel reported the mean scaled scores on the Digit Span and the Arithmetic subtests were consistently the two lowest and the ACID (Arithmetic, Coding, Information, and Digit Span) category was the next to lowest (Vogel, 1986).

Assessment of academic achievement is complicated by the scarcity of adequate standardized tests for measuring academic skills of adults. Few achievement tests have adult norms. A measure of rate is useful in all areas of assessment, since many learning-disabled students process at a slow rate. When administering the academic skills tests, it is recommended that they be given as timed tests. If the student is not finished within the given time, the place may be marked and the student be permitted to continue. Two scores are then computed — both timed and untimed. If a student does significantly better taking untimed tests, it is important information in considering a recommendation of untimed testing as a modification for the student. An error analysis is recommended for any academic achievement skills that are measured. A list of selected standardized tests with adult norms is included in Table 1.

Behavioral observation in the classroom is not as efficacious as it is in the elementary level classrooms but if the student is well motivated, self-recording may prove quite useful in focusing on behavioral issues.

Program modifications. After information is gathered and analyzed, the most important step of communication begins with the student. A review of behaviors, past performance, and test performance can help the student identify and understand strengths and weaknesses. From that data, a program of modifications appropriate for the student and the college faculty can be planned. Some modifications that have been particularly beneficial are extended time or alternate test administration, reduction in course load, and strategies tutoring.

McGuire and O'Donnell (1989) suggested that faculty and student support service personnel can collaborate to help

TABLE 1
Selected Standardized Tests with Adult Norms

Name of Test	Author	Comments
Cognitive Abilities		
Slosson (SIT)	Slosson, 1971	Sometimes used as IQ screening test
Stanford Binet IV	Thornkike, Hagen & Sattler, 1985	Very new, little historical data
Test of Nonverbal Intelligence (TONI)	Brown, Sherbenou, & Dollar, 1982	Language-free intelligence
Wechsler Adult Intelligence Scale	Wechsler, 1955	Most widely used measure; Verbal, Perf, subtests
Woodcock-Johnson Tests of Cognitive Ability	Woodcock, 1978	Revised with new subtests in 1987.
Academic Achievement		
Reading		
Nelson-Denny Reading Test	Brown, Bennett, & Hanna, 1981	Reading comprehension, Vocabulary and Rate norms for junior and 4-year college
Stanford Diagnostic Reading Test–1984	Karlsen & Gardner, 1985	May be group-administered; norms thru Grade 13
Stanford Test of Academic Skills (TASK)	Gardner, Callis, Merwin, & Rudman, 1983	Reading comprehension and vocabulary; norms thru Grade 13
Woodcock-Johnson Tests of Achievement	Woodcock, 1978	Adult norms
Woodcock Reading Mastery Tests–Revised	Woodcock, 1987	Adult norms; diagnostic subtests
Mathematics		
Orleans–Hanna Algebra Prognosis Test	Hanna & Orleans, 1982	Norms are based on four reference groups depending on prior amount of math
Stanford Test of Academic Skills (TASK)	Gardner, Callis, Merwin, & Rudman	Ample problems but only one overall score
Woodcock–Johnson Tests of Achievement	Woodcock, 1978	Adult norms but few problems
Written Language		
Test of Written Language (TOWL)	Hammil & Larsen, 1983	Ceiling age for norm group is 18–11
Spelling		
Test of Written Language–2 (TOWL)	Hammill & Larsen, 1983	One of the subtests of the TOWL-2

(Table 1, continued)

Name of Test	Author	Comments
(Academic Achievement — Spelling, continued)		
Wide Range Achievement Test–Revised, Level II (WRAT-R, II)	Kastak & Wilkinson, 1984	Adult norms
Woodcock-Johnson Tests of Achievement	Woodcock, 1978	Adult norms
Language Usage/Grammar		
Stanford Test of Academic Skills (TASK)	Garwin, Callis, Merwin, & Rudman, 1983	Grade 13 norms
Test of Written Language-2 (TOWL)	Hammill & Larsen, 1983	One of the subtests of the TOWL-2
Woodcock-Johnson Tests of Achievement	Woodcock, 1978	Adult norms
Auditory Language		
Test of Adolescent Language-2, Revised (TOAL-2)	Hammill, Brown, Larsen, & Wiederholt	To age 18
Woodcock-Johnson Tests of Cognitive Ability	Woodcock, 1978	Adult norms
Foreign Language		
Modern Language Aptitude Test (MLAT)	Carroll & Sapon, 1965	Aptitude for foreign language
Other		
Bloomer Learning Test (BLT)	Bloomer, 1978	Information processing
Learning and Study Strategies Inventory (LASSI)	Weinstein, Schulte, & Palmer, 1987	Study strategies
Raven Advanced Progressive Matrices	Raven, Court, & Raven, 1979	Nonverbal reasoning
Survey of Study Habits and Attitudes (SSHA)	Brown & Holtzman, 1984	Study skills and attitudes

learning-disabled students to achieve. They emphasized three areas of weakness in learning-disabled students: (a) organizational strategies, which faculty can address by using detailed course syllabi, class handouts, and coordination with support services staff; (b) note-taking skills, which can be complemented by the use of a tape recorder, class handouts, or a class outline; and (c) test-taking skills, which can be improved by instruction in test-taking strategies or modifications such as extended time or oral testing. They also pointed out that many faculty members are not familiar with learning disabilities and may have misconceptions about these handicaps.

To increase faculty understanding of learning disabilities, the school psychologist may offer inservice training or individual faculty consultations. Minner and Prater (1984) found that college faculty viewed the learning-disabled student with favorable academic and social traits much less positively than the nonlabeled student with mediocre grades and social traits. They feel that workshops or 'training programs for faculty can lead to increased knowledge and improved attitudes toward learning disabilities.

Frequently, the school psychologist will serve as a consultant with individual faculty members. Some target areas for which consultation may be most appropriate are those identified by Lundeberg and Svien (1983) as areas of greatest concern for the college faculty: (a) the apprehension that learning-disabled students will be placed in classes in which essential tasks are in the areas of their disability, placing the burden of classroom modification and evaluation on the instructor; (b) the need for the documentation of students' learning disabilities by a qualified source so that unmotivated students can be distinguished from the learning-disabled; and (c) the need for further information in understanding, recognizing, and making modifications for the learning-disabled. The school psychologist is likely to find many faculty members who are relieved that there is a resource available to address these concerns.

Although self-advocacy is important for the learning-disabled student, communicating directly with faculty can be an intimidating experience for a college student. A joint conference involving the student, faculty member(s), and school psychologist can be a mutual learning experience. The school psychologist may also use a written form (Figure 4), with student permission, to facilitate communication. Using the written form also verifies that the learning disability is legitimate and the strengths and weaknesses as well as recommendations for modifications have been communicated to faculty.

Because administrators furnish impetus and provide the budgetary support needed for the support services, it is important to keep them informed about the handicap and how the support services are meeting the legal and ethical obligations of the institution toward the students.

Counseling with college students. College students with learning disabilities have to deal with many stresses, only some of which are academic, so they may have need for extensive counseling. Counseling techniques vary depending upon the philosophy of the school psychologist, and may include individual or group counseling. The issues most common to learning-disabled students other than academic matters are passivity, poor self-concept, poor social skills, attentional deficits, and lack of motivation (Lerner, 1989). Peer support groups may be especially helpful for attacking most of these issues as the group provides social interaction and support. Poor self-concept and motivation will be likely to improve as the student experiences success (possibly with strategies tutoring or tutoring in the academic areas, and with modeling of appropriate social skills to improve social interaction). Attentional deficits are difficult to remediate but some strategies are helpful, such as sitting at the front of the classroom away from distractions and establishing eye contact with the instructor.

Working with the student to achieve self-understanding and independence is extremely important. Many students already identified as learning-disabled have received services throughout the public school years and have developed a dependency that becomes deleterious at the college level. Self-regulated or independent learning is a major goal for all students. Another important skill for the student to learn is self-advocacy. Although the school psychologist is often the first advocate for students with learning disabilities, the goal is self-advocacy and independent learning.

SUMMARY

Growing numbers of students who are learning-disabled are entering two- and four-year colleges and universities. The school psychologist who works with learning-disabled students at the high

Date _____

To: Professor _____

From: Student _____

I have been identified as having the following disability/disabilities:

_____
_____

My areas of strength include:

_____
_____
_____

My weaker areas include:

_____
_____
_____

To equalize my chances of success in the classroom I would benefit from the following accommodations:

_____
_____
_____

Note to the Professor
From: Dot Miles, College of Basic Studies Director of Student Services

This data sheet has been prepared through consultation with me. This information should be considered confidential. The accommodations as listed above are among those identified in Section 504 of the National Rehabilitation Act of 1973 which deals with non-discrimination of disabled students in postsecondary settings. You and the student may want to negotiate the options that will be best for both of you in meeting the accommodations. Learning + (243-4312) is an excellent resource for students taking tests untimed and/or having tests read. Please contact me (243-4018) if you have any additional questions or concerns regarding this student. Thank you for your consideration of this student's special needs.

_____   _____   _____
Dot Miles   Date   Student

Figure 4. Data sheet for faculty. *Note.* **From** *Unlocking Potential: College and Other Choices for Learning Disabled People — A Step-by-Step Guide.* **(Sullivan, C., Disability Sheet, p. 120) by B. Scheiber and J. Talpers, 1982, Bethesda, MD: Adler & Adler. Copyright 1985, 1987 by Barbara Scheiber and Jeanne Talpers. Adapted by permission.**

school level can be a valuable resource in a number of areas, including identifying which students have the potential to succeed in college, planning an appropriate academic program, assisting the student in choosing an appropriate college, and in helping the student prepare for college entrance. Some students at the college level have not been classified as learning-disabled but are also in need of diagnostic, counseling, and academic support services. A problem unique to assessment at the college level is the dearth of appropriate standardized achievement testing instruments for this age population. Colleges are turning more frequently to school psychologists and other specialists to furnish these support services.

The rights of learning-disabled students attending college are guaranteed by Section 504 of the Rehabilitation Act of 1973 (PL 93-112), which assures them access to support services that 'must be provided by the postsecondary institution to which they are admitted.

The problems most frequently encountered in work with college learning-disabled students are the student's desire to hide the handicap rather than to advocate for services, a learned dependency that hampers the active pursuit of studies, and the student's lack of awareness of strengths, weaknesses, appropriate strategies, and services. The school psychologist will often serve as the first advocate of the student but the long-term goal for the student is self-advocacy and independent learning.

Other problems encountered will be lack of faculty understanding of learning disabilities and of the academic modifications necessary to ensure the student's success. Consultation with faculty can provide them with information and understanding regarding the handicap, the law, the student, and the appropriate modifications. Some faculty training can be done through faculty workshops.

Benefits to both colleges and learning-disabled students are accruing as these students are successfully completing college programs. The school psychologist can be the focal point of this process and an important resource for the student and the institution. As greater numbers of learning-disabled students are choosing college as an option, the school psychologists in the secondary and postsecondary settings are finding new demands for their services.

REFERENCES

Act Concerning Individual Transition Plans for Students Requiring Special Education. (1987). State of Connecticut (P.A. 87-324).

Bennett, R. E., Rock, D. A., & Chan, K. L. (1987). SAT verbal-math discrepancies: Accurate indicators of college learning disability? *Journal of Learning Disabilities, 3,* 189-192.

Brinckerhoff, L. (1985). Accommodations for college students with learning disabilities: The law and its implementation. In J. Gartner (Ed.), *Tomorrow is another day* (pp. 89-95). Columbus, OH: AHSSPPE.

Dalke, C., & Schmitt, S. (1987). Meeting the transition needs of college-bound students with learning disabilities. *Journal of Learning Disabilities, 20,* 176-180.

Dexter, B. L. (1982). Helping learning disabled students prepare for college. *Journal of Learning Disabilities, 15,* 344-346.

Fagan, T. K. (1989). NASP at thirty: A natural extension? *School Psychology Review, 18,* 215-216.

HEATH Resource Center. (1986). Learning disability update. *Information from HEATH,* May, p. 3.

HEATH Resource Center. (1987). Learning disabled adults in postsecondary education. *Information from HEATH.*

Knowles, B. S., & Knowles, P. S. (1983). A model for identifying learning disabilities in college-bound students. *Journal of Learning Disabilities, 16,* 39-42.

Lerner, J. W. (1989). *Learning disabilities* (5th ed.). Boston: Houghton Mifflin.

Levinson, E. M. (1986). School psychology and college disabled students: Training and service possibilities. *Psychology in the Schools, 23,* 295-302.

Lundeberg, M., & Svien, K. (1988). Developing faculty understanding of college students with learning disabilities. *Journal of Learning Disabilities, 21,* 299-306.

Mangrum, C. T., & Strichart, S. S. (1988). *College and the learning disabled student* (2nd ed.). Philadelphia: Harcourt Brace Jovanovich.

Marion, P. B., & Iovacchini, E. V. (1983). Services for handicapped students in higher education: An analysis of national trends. *Journal of College Student Personnel, 14*(2), 131-138.

McGuire, J. M., & O'Donnell, J. M. (1989). Helping learning-disabled students to achieve: Collaboration between the faculty and support services. *College Teaching, 37,* 29-32.

McGuire, J. M., & Shaw, S. F. (1987). A decision-making process for the college-bound student: Matching learner, institution, and support program. *Learning Disability Quarterly, 10,* 106-111.

Michael, R. J. (1987). Evaluating the college of choice. *Academic Therapy, 22,* 485-488.

Minner, S., & Prater, G. (1984). College teachers' expectations of LD students. *Academic Therapy, 20,* 225-229.

National Joint Committee on Learning Disabilities. (1985). *Adults with learning disabilities: A call to action.* Baltimore: Orton Dyslexia Society.

Norlander, K. A. (1987, October). *Transition from high school to college for students with learning disabilities: Issues and solutions.* Paper presented at the statewide conference on The High School-College Connection: Preparing Disabled Students for Postsecondary Education, New Britain, CT.

Rehabilitation Act of 1973, §504 (PL 93-112), as amended, 29 U.S.C. §794.

Reschly, D. J. (1988) Special education reform: School psychology revolution. *School Psychology Review, 17,* 459-475.

Seidenberg, P. L. (1987). The unrealized potential: College preparation for secondary learning disabled students. *Learning Disability News, 2,* 1-2.

Shaw, S. F., Byron, J., Norlander, K. A., McGuire, J. M., & Anderson, P. (1988). Preparing learning disabled students for college. *Issues in College Learning Centers,* Vol. 6. (ERIC Document Reproduction Service No. ED 285 316)

Shaw, S. F., Norlander, K. A., McGuire, J. M. (1987). Training leadership personnel for learning disability college programs. *Teacher Education and Special Education, 10,* 108-112.

Siperstein, G. N. (1988). Students with learning disabilities in college: The need for a programmatic approach to critical transitions. *Journal of Learning Disabilities, 21,* 431-436.

U.S. Department of Education. (1987). *Ninth annual report to Congress on the implementation of the Education of the Handicapped Act.* Washington, DC: U.S. Department of Education.

Vogel, S. A. (1986). Levels and patterns of intellectual functioning among LD college students: Clinical and educational implications. *Journal of Learning Disabilities, 19,* 71-79.

Vogel, S. A. (1987). Eligibility and identification considerations in postsecondary education: A new but old dilemma. In S. Vaughn & C. S. Bos (Eds.), *Research in learning disabilities: Issues and future directions.* Boston: Little, Brown.

ANNOTATED BIBLIOGRAPHY

Garnett, K., & LaPorta, S. (1984). *Dispelling the myths: College students & learning disabilities.* New York: Hunter College.
This small booklet is an excellent educational resource for communicating about LD to college faculty. It covers, in 21 pages, what LD is and is not, with focus on how the college-level LD student is identified and how the student can learn. It ends with a section on how the college professor can help.

Jarrow, J., Baker, B., Hartman, R., Harris, R., Lesh, K., Redden, M., & Smithson, S. (1986). *How to choose a college: Guide for the student with a disability* (Cooperative Agreement No. G0084C3501). Washington, DC: American Council on Education.
This is a good resource for the student contemplating college. It was developed by the Higher Education and the Handicapped (HEATH) Resource Center, One Dupont Circle, Suite 670, Washington, DC 20036-1193 and by the Association on Handicapped Student Service Programs in Postsecondary Education (AHSSPPE), PO Box 21192, Columbus, OH 43221.

Mangrum, C. T., & Strichart, S. S. (1988). *College and the learning disabled student.* Orlando, FL: Grune & Stratton.
This book is an excellent source for anyone working with the college LD population. It covers the gamut from a discussion of the history of the disability to the response of the colleges to the problem and the impact of federal laws on the universities and the students. Other areas covered are diagnostic testing, program planning and advisement, tutoring and remediation, counseling, and college selection. There are four appendices listing college LD programs and other resource guides.

Scheiber, B., & Talpers, J. (1987). *Unlocking potential.* Maryland: Adler & Adler.
This guide is written in easy-to-understand terms and may be particularly useful as an educational resource for the LD student. It also contains many practical suggestions and guides for choosing a program and for procedures and interventions for the student.

Vogel, S. A. (1985). Learning disabled college students: Identification, assessment, and outcomes. In D. D. Duane & C. K. Leong (Eds.), *Understanding Learning Difficulties* (pp. 179-203). New York: Plenum Press.
This excellent chapter covers the definition of disabilities in adults, issues involved in identifying LD college students, and suggestions for assessment, goal setting, and monitoring.

ADDITIONAL RESOURCES

Organizations listed may help in various ways from information service to support groups. For written resources or guides, check with the organization for current prices.

Academic Preparation for College: What Students Need to Know and Be Able to Do. The College Board. College Board Publications, Dept. A35, Box 886, New York, NY 10101.

ACT Assessment Special Testing Guide. ACT Test Administration, Box 168, Iowa City, IA 52243.

Association of Learning Disabled Adults (ALDA), PO Box 9722, Friendship Station, Washington, DC 20016.

Association on Handicapped Student Service Programs in Postsecondary Education (AHSSPPE), PO Box 21192, Columbus, OH 43221. Telephone: (614) 488-4972.

Association for Children and Adults with Learning Disabilities (ACLD), 4165 Liberty Road, Pittsburgh, PA 15234. Telephone: (415) 351-1212.

Council for Exceptional Children (CEC), 1920 Association Dr., Reston, VA 22091. Telephone: (703) 620-3660.

Foundation for Children with Learning Disabilities (FCLD), 99 Park Ave., New York, NY 10016. Telephone: (212) 687-7211.

HEATH Resource Center, The National Clearinghouse on Postsecondary Education for Handicapped Individuals, One Dupont Circle, Suite 670, Washington, DC 30026. Telephone: (202) 939-9320.

Liscio, M. (Ed.). *Guide to Colleges for Learning Disabled Students.* (1984). Academic Press, 6277 Sea Harbor Drive, Orlando, FL 32821.

Mangrum II, C., & Strichart, S. (Eds.). *Peterson's Guide to Colleges with Programs for Learning Disabled Students.* Peterson's Guides, PO Box 2123, Princeton, NJ 38540.

McGuire, J., & Shaw, L. *McGuire-Shaw Postsecondary Guide and Manual for Learning Disabled Students.* (LDC 4). Special Education Center Publications, University of Connecticut, U-64, 249 Glenbrook Rd., Storrs, CT 06268

National Center on Postsecondary Transition for Students with Learning Disabilities. Provides information and assistance to secondary and postsecondary professionals regarding implementation and development of support services for college students with learning disabilities. The service is free. The 24-hour hotline number is (203) 486-4036.

National Directory of Four Year Colleges, Two Year Colleges and Post High School Training Programs for Young People with Learning Disabilities, Partners in Publishing, Box 50347, Tulsa, OK 74150.

Orton Dyslexia Society, Inc., 724 York Rd., Baltimore, MD 21204. Telephone: (301) 296-0232.

Straughn II, C., & Colby, M. (Eds.). (1985). *Lovejoy's College Guide for the Learning Disabled.* Simon and Schuster, 1230 Avenue of Americas, New York, NY 10020.

Recording for the Blind, 20 Roszel Rd., Princeton, NJ 08540. Telephone: (609) 452-0606. Eligible perceptually handicapped may order textbooks on tape.

SAT (Scholastic Aptitude Test). *Information for Counselors and Admissions Officers.* Admissions Testing Program, Services for Handicapped Students, Institutional Services, Box 592, Princeton, NJ 08541.

SAT (Scholastic Aptitude Test). *Information for Students with Special Needs.* Admissions Testing Program, Services for Handicapped Students, Institutional Services, Box 592, Princeton, NJ 08541.

Skyer & Skyer. (1986). *What Do You Do After High School?* Skyer Consultation Center, Inc., PO Box 121, Rockaway Park, NY 11694.

Vocational Rehabilitation Office. Call your local office. This office can sometimes help with evaluation and placement.

9

Practices in ...ting with Promotion ...etention Decisions

Margaret M. Dawson
Exeter (New Hampshire)
Public Schools

Mary Ann Rafoth
Indiana University of Pennsylvania

Karen Carey
University of Cincinnati

OVERVIEW

Consider the following scenarios: (a) a preschool teacher tells the parents of a four-year old boy with a birthday just before the school cut-off date that they may want to have him spend another year in preschool before facing the demands of public kindergarten; (b) it is recommended to parents of a first grader that their daughter be retained in first grade because she's slow picking up reading and appears "younger" than her classmates; (c) a teacher recommends that a boy in her class repeat fifth grade because, while he appears bright and capable of doing the work, he has done very little in class and has handed in virtually no homework assignments; (d) a group of eighth grade teachers draw up a list of students they feel have not mastered the academic skills necessary to proceed to high school. Many of the students have already repeated one year in school; most are boys from lower socioeconomic classes who have been placed in the lower tracks since early in elementary school; and (e) a high school sophomore with frequent absences from school is forced to repeat 10th grade because she has failed to accumulate sufficient credits to enter the 11th grade.

Every year, approximately 2.3 million American students are held back in school, many under circumstances similar to those described above. Frequently,

school psychologists are involved in making retention decisions. While it is a common educational practice, a survey of the literature will show that student retention, for the most part, is of questionable educational benefit and may have deleterious effects on achievement, self-concept, and school drop-out rates. This chapter provides the school psychologist a brief review of the research on student retention as well as a discussion of the issues involved when schools make retention decisions. The concluding section will address the role school psychologists may play in making retention decisions and will suggest alternatives to retention that may better meet the needs of students experiencing school failure.

Of the many professionals involved either in developing district-wide retention policies or in making retention decisions about individual students, the school psychologist is uniquely qualified to act as a consultant in generating alternatives. School psychologists should help to evaluate the reasons for school failure, plan appropriate instructional programs for the following year whether or not the child is retained, and act as consultants to parents faced with retention decisions. Best practices regarding nonpromotion center around a thorough understanding of the research and careful consideration of the needs of the individual student.

BASIC CONSIDERATIONS

Retention or nonpromotion is the practice of requiring a child to repeat a particular grade or requiring a child of appropriate chronological age to delay entry to kindergarten or first grade. With the introduction of graded schools in the 19th century, retention emerged as a response to the problem of students unprepared for the academic demands of the next grade. While concern about possible negative effects of retention has been expressed since the 1930s, the practice continues to be widespread. In fact, retention remains a common educational practice although little research exists to validate its effectiveness (Holmes & Matthews, 1984; Medway & Rose, 1986). While these reviewers and others (e.g., Jackson, 1975) have concluded that much of the research is flawed or of poor quality, the use of statistical techniques such as meta-analysis and causal modeling can help overcome the weaknesses of individual studies and help establish more definitive relationships between retention and later achievement and social growth.

Kindergarten and Elementary Level

Children are often recommended for retention at the kindergarten level because they have failed to acquire basic readiness skills. Sometimes these determinations are made because of poor performance on a readiness test administered before entry into kindergarten or at the end of the year. Failure to display skills in the classroom coupled with low achievement scores is often the reason a child is suggested as a retention candidate after completing a year of kindergarten. Some children enter kindergarten with little exposure to academics, the school routine, or prerequisite skills such as letter and number recognition typically taught in most preschool settings. Children from home backgrounds where such exposure is limited may find themselves candidates for delayed entry into kindergarten or retention.

Delayed entry or retention at the kindergarten level also occurs because some children are judged to be "developmentally immature." These children seem to be slightly delayed in social, motor, and/or readiness skills and in need of a year to grow or mature neurologically and therefore catch up with their peers. Likewise, children who are physically small or relatively young compared to their peers (because of cut-off dates for school entry) are often candidates for delayed entry or retention. Many parents and teachers believe that the extra year will allow the child to compete more effectively with peers the following year.

While initially, late birth-date children who are retained or held out of school for a year may do better than those enrolled in first grade at the prescribed age, longitudinal studies show that initial achievement gains do not hold up over time. For instance, Miller and Norris (1967) divided first graders into three groups based on age at school entrance. They found significant differences between young, middle, and old first graders on three of six readiness measures. At the end of four years, however, the average achievement of the young group did not differ significantly from the average achievement of the middle group.

Many schools have adopted transitional or developmental programs for those children "not ready for first grade." However, these programs appear to be no more effective than retention (Matthews, 1977; Talmadge, 1981). Zinski (1983) found no significant differences between children attending a transitional program between kindergarten and first grade at the end of first grade and children who repeated first grade. Gredler (1984) reviewed seven studies investigating the effects of transition room placement and concluded that "research indicates that transition room children either do not perform as well or are at most equal in achievement levels to transition room-eligible children placed in regular classrooms."

Perhaps the most comprehensive review of the effects of retention was conducted by Holmes and Matthews (1984). They conducted a meta-analysis on 44 studies, calculating 575 effect sizes to determine the effects of retention on a variety of factors, such as achievement, personal adjustment, self-concept, etc. The authors defined effect size as "the difference between the mean of the retained group and the mean of the promoted group, divided by the standard deviation of the promoted group." Meta-analysis has become a popular way to aggregate a large number of studies investigating a common research question.

All studies selected by Holmes and Matthews compared a group of retained students with a group of promoted students. Thirty-three of the studies investigated achievement effects. These studies yielded an overall effect size of -.37, indicating that retained students scored significantly lower than promoted students on achievement measures. When the authors analyzed the data by the grade level in which the retention took place (grades 1-6), they again found negative effects at all grade levels. This calls into question the commonly held belief that the earlier a student is retained the greater the likelihood that retention will produce positive effects.

While proponents of retention maintain that promoting children when they are not ready can have a harmful effect on personal adjustment, the bulk of the research does not support this contention. In addition to achievement effects, Holmes and Matthews (1984) also calculated effect sizes on personal adjustment measures taken from 21 studies. They found negative effects for social adjustment, emotional adjustment, and behavior, as well as self-concept.

Many studies have found that students' attitudes toward retention are negative. Byrnes and Yamamoto (1984) found that children who are retained recognize the change as failure and feel ashamed. In their study children rated retention behind only blindness and parental death as most stressful experiences. Smith and Shepard (in press) reported that clinical interviews with retained students indicate that these students saw their retention as "flunking" and as punishment. In this same study,

parents of retained kindergarteners reported that their children experienced teasing and adjustment problems because of their nonpromotion. Johnson (1981) argued that children who have failed in school show characteristics of learned helplessness. Students in his study were likely to attribute failure to themselves and to deny responsibility for success.

Secondary Level

At the secondary level (i.e., middle school, junior high school, and high school) students are most often retained for two reasons: (a) a lack of sufficient credits to be promoted to the next grade level or to graduate from high school, or (b) a failure to pass mandated minimum competency exams.

Through the sixth grade, retention rates tend to decrease with each year. However, when students reach the seventh grade retention rates rise and continue to increase in subsequent years (Medway & Rose, 1986). Generally the increase in retention rates is due to students' inability to meet the school district's standards for promotion or to obtain sufficient credits to graduate from high school. Often these students have failing grades, higher absentee rates than their promoted peers, have been retained in the early elementary grades, and have higher rates of discipline incidents (i.e., suspensions) (Fleming & Zafirau, 1982). Alternative education is often not provided to these students, and for many, life outside of school becomes more rewarding.

Perhaps prompted by employers' doubts about the meaning of a high school diploma and society's current attitudes toward perceived deficiencies in the American educational system, many states now require students to pass minimal competency exams in order to receive a high school diploma. However, many students are unable to pass these tests due to poor reading skills and/or academic performance, and retention becomes the "intervention" of choice. Once retained, remediation often does not occur during the student's retained year, and the student makes little, if any, gains in academic performance (Purkeson & Whitfield, 1981).

Many school policy makers believe that retaining students unable to pass minimum competency tests will motivate those students to improve skills and complete the necessary requirements for graduation. However, students are often not motivated by retention and once a student has experienced retention, he/she often equates the practice with failure, views him/herself as a failure and thus, drops out of school (Thompson, 1980). It appears that higher standards and competency testing do not improve the academic performance of students most at risk for school failure. Instead, these actions may result in an increase in the number of students retained and dropping out of school (Hamilton, 1986).

Research on retention at the secondary level has generally examined the relationship between grade retention, attendance, suspension, and self-concept, with an emphasis on the correlation between retention and drop-out rates (Rumberger, 1986; Wehlage & Rutter, 1986).

Retention rates at the high school level have been found to be related to attendance and suspension rates (Fleming & Zafirau, 1982). Generally, students who are failing do not attend school on a regular basis. In addition, students who have been retained prior to the secondary level are less likely to attend school on a regular basis in junior and senior high school. Additionally, regardless of the grade in which retention occurs, secondary students who have been retained often exhibit low self-esteem. General conclusions drawn from many studies suggest that retention correlates negatively with students' self-concept, peer acceptance, and personal adjustment.

The majority of research on retention at the secondary level has focused on the relationship between retention and dropping out of school. This relationship may be explained by two competing hypotheses: (a) repeating a grade may increase the risk of dropping out, or (b) poor achievement may account for both retention and dropping out.

In many early studies undertaken to analyze the relationship between retention and dropping out of school, the achievement variable was not controlled. However, in a number of more recent studies (e.g., Grissom & Shepard, in press), the achievement variable was adjusted in order to focus only on the relationship between retention and dropping out. It has been found that the drop-out rate of overage students (retainees) is appreciably higher than the dropout rate of regularly promoted students when reading achievement scores are equivalent for the two groups. Even in high socioeconomic school districts where students are less likely to leave school, a significant increase in drop-out rates has been found for retained students.

Do Some Children Benefit from Retention?

Sandoval and Hughes (1981) found that children who make academic and social-emotional gains after repeating first grade lack serious academic deficits in the year prior to retention, have strong self-esteem and social skills, and showed signs of difficulty in school because of lack of exposure to material (e.g., because of high absenteeism, illness, or frequent family moves) rather than low ability. In a five year follow-up, Sandoval (1987) found that these same factors predicted success in the upper grade. However, Smith and Shepard (1989) make two points about this study: (a) since relatively high achievement and high self-concept prior to retention correlated with positive outcomes, this implies that the most successful retainees are those who need it the least, and (b) even the most successful retainees are no better than promoted controls on a variety of outcome measures at the end of first grade.

At times, retention is employed in an attempt to postpone or supplant special education. However, there is little evidence to support the use of retention in this way (Carstens, 1985; Chandler, 1984; Lieberman, 1980).

Cross (1984) found that the most important factors governing a teacher's decision to recommend retention were: failure to complete a primer designated by the school district, general immaturity, and anticipated resistance from the child's parents. The author found that there were no differences in the reading achievement test scores of recommended and nonrecommended children and none of these factors has been shown to be useful predictors of successful retention.

Some researchers have believed it possible to predict which students benefit from retention and have encouraged schools to develop decision-making procedures to aid in selecting likely candidates (Lieberman, 1980; Light, 1977). Others have rejected such a process. Smith and Shepard (1987) conclude from their own research and their review of the literature, "Although some small percentage of those retained may be helped, the evidence indicates that educators are simply unable to predict accurately which individuals these will be."

BEST PRACTICES

School psychologists' involvement with retention practices can occur on several levels. It can range all the way from participating in making retention decisions about individual students, to influencing school or district-wide retention policies, to lobbying for change on a state level through the collective efforts of a state school psychology association. An important effort at each of these levels should be to promote the use of alternatives to retention which will be more effective in remediating the skill deficits of students.

Individual Retention Decisions

School psychologists can be important participants when decisions are made about retaining students in their schools. They should help evaluate the reasons for school failure by looking at the child's school or developmental history, the effectiveness of the instruction they have received, and the remediation strat-egies or programs available to them. They should help plan an appropriate instructional program for the following year, whether or not the student is retained. And they should act as consultants both to parents and to school personnel to help them make retention decisions.

Two case discussions may help illustrate the part the school psychologist can play in making decisions.

In the first case, a child whose first grade teacher recommended retention was referred by her parents to the school psychologist for testing to rule out the possibility of a learning disability. The teacher reported that she was having trouble getting beyond the primer level in reading, her attention span seemed somewhat short, she had some difficulty completing her work independently, and she also seemed to be exhibiting some "immature behaviors" such as fidgeting in her seat and putting her fingers in her mouth. The child, an attractive, petite girl, was assessed as having average intelligence with achievement commensurate with her ability.

The school psychologist met with the child's teacher and parents. She reviewed the test results and then led a discussion about retention. She summarized the research on retention, stressing that there is little evidence that it helps over the long-term. She indicated that initially students who are retained in first grade show some improvement over similar students that are not retained, but that these gains tend to disappear by third grade. She noted that the child's teacher was trying to make the best decision for the child as she could precisely because she was worried about the child's progress in the coming year, thereby lending support to the teacher without necessarily espousing her recommendation. The school psychologist reported that while some children do seem to benefit from retention, at present educators lack the ability reliably to predict just which children will benefit. Therefore, she stressed, it will be important that the child's parents feel comfortable with whatever decision they make since undoubtedly the child will sense her parents' comfort or discomfort with the decision. This statement was emphatically echoed by the child's teacher. The decision was left in the parents' hands. The mother later reported to the school psychologist that she had decided not to retain her daughter. She indicated that as a child she had matured at a young age and she was worried that the same would happen to her daughter. She was concerned about the effect of early maturation, particularly if her daughter was already a year older than most of her classmates. While this parent decided to have her child continue on to second grade, she wanted to be sure her child would be able to get supplemental reading services and that her teachers would continue to monitor her progress in reading.

In a second example, a school psychologist became involved in the case of a kindergartener being considered for retention. In this case, the school psychologist led a team discussion, first questioning why retention was being considered. The classroom teacher pointed out that the child had spent most of the year in kindergarten with an undetected hearing loss and hence it was unclear how much the student had been able to benefit from instruction. The school psychologist then referred to the section of the NASP Position Statement on Student Retention which delineates when retention is less likely to be harmful. She went down the list: Does this student lack serious academic skill deficits? Does the student have positive self-esteem and good social skills? Has the student had difficulty in school because of lack of opportunity for instruction? The group decided that the answer to these questions was yes, and hence this youngster might benefit from retention.

Most parents and educators are unaware of the research on retention. The school psychologist should be willing to share this research to help schools and parents make informed decisions. This information should not be imparted in a dogmatic manner or in a way that impairs working relationships with colleagues and parents. In some cases, this may mean recognizing that schools will make decisions to retain children when the school psychologist feels it is not in the best interest of these children. Especially in these cases, it will be important for the school psychologist to participate in developing a specific plan of action whereby the student's skill deficits can be remediated. School psychologists are encouraged to gather follow-up data on children who have been retained and children of comparable achievement levels who are not retained to help their school districts better understand the outcomes of retention decisions.

School District/System Level

School psychologists' participation at a school district or system level can take many forms. As within their own schools, they can publicize the research on retention to help guide the development of informed policies. They can also serve an evaluative role, using district-wide data to assess outcomes of retention decisions. And they can monitor progress of students to ensure that problems are identified and addressed early, *before* retention becomes a consideration.

School psychologists can also promote the development of effective alternatives to retention at all grade levels, from preschool through high school. These can include both developing programmatic interventions which address the needs of failing students and expanding the capabilities of classroom teachers to meet the needs of students at different skill levels.

Programmatic interventions may include developing screening programs to identify children at risk for school failure and ensure early access to programs already available in the school or community, such as Head Start, Chapter I services, and remedial programs. It may also include developing intervention programs such as after-school tutoring or summer school courses. At the secondary level, school psychologists should encourage the development of "re-entry" programs for dropouts and alternative education programs such as ones that combine teaching basic skills with job training.

The instructional technology that enables classroom teachers to meet the needs of students of different skill levels is already available, but in many cases, teachers do not have access to that technology. School psychologists can assist their school districts in learning about this technology and arranging for in-service programs to bring this information into the classroom. Approaches such as mastery learning, adaptive education, team teaching, cooperative learning, peer tutoring, and curriculum-based assessment are all methods that have been shown to produce academic gains of students of all achievement levels (See Graden, Zins, & Curtis, 1988, for further discussion of these approaches). To be taught and implemented effectively, school districts must make a commitment to providing sufficient in-service training. School psychologists are often effective lobbyists for such continuing professional development. In making arguments for such training, school psychologists should help school administrators recognize the economic benefits of reducing retention rates. The National Education Association recently estimated that the average per pupil cost in this country is $4509 per year (*NEA Today*, May 1989). If a school district, for instance, retains 30 students annually, adding one year to these students' school careers will cost districts in excess of $135,000 each year. There is no doubt that quality training for teachers can be obtained at a far lesser cost.

State Education Agencies

As advocated for children, school psychologists can often be most effective when they move beyond the realm of their own schools and school districts to work at a state level to effect change. The discrepancy between what is known about retention and what is practiced is great enough to warrant action at a higher level. While a school psychologist acting alone cannot influence state policies and practices, through the efforts of a state school psychology association, change can be effected.

School psychology associations are encouraged to share the research on retention with their state education agencies and with other professional education associations (such as state principals' and superintendents' groups). They are also encouraged to use the lobbying efforts available to them to influence legislation, including funding for alternative service delivery and legislation that affects policy, such as decreasing the rigidity of minimal competency requirements. Associations are encouraged to make use of the NASP Position Statement on Student Retention and the Supporting Paper (Rafoth, Dawson, & Carey, 1988) in these efforts.

SUMMARY

While the research on retention is voluminous and much of it is flawed, most recent reviewers have concluded that there are no clear benefits to retaining students and the practice can have deleterious effects on student achievement, self-concept, and attitudes, and can increase the likelihood of dropping out of school. Although it is possible that a small percentage of students retained may benefit, it is impossible to predict which students those will be. Transition rooms prior to first grade are no more effective than retention, and whatever initial benefits may be derived from retention after kindergarten or first grade appear to be washed out by the end of third or fourth grade.

School psychologists should assist in making retention decisions about individual students and should promote effective alternatives to retention. Working to change school practices in the area of retention will require sharing the research decisions at the local level, and lobbying at the state level to promote changes in policy 'and to advocate for alternative service delivery systems which more effectively meet the needs of students experiencing school failure.

REFERENCES

Anderson v. Banks. 520 F. Supp. 472 (S.D. Ga. 1981).

Byrnes, D., & Yamamoto, K. (1984). Grade repetition: Views of parents, teachers, and principals. Logan, UT: Utah State School of Education.

Carstens, A. (1985). Retention and social promotion for the exceptional child. *School Psychology Review, 14*, 48-63.

Chandler, H. N. (1984). Retention: Edspeak for flunk. *Journal of Learning Disabilities, 17*, 60-62.

Cross, R. (1984). Teacher decision making on student retention. Paper presented at the Annual Meeting of the American Educational Research Association (New Orleans, LA). (ERIC Document Reproduction Service No. ED 252 930)

Debra P. v. Turlington. 644 F.2d 397 (5th Cir. 1981).

Fleming, M., & Zafirau, J. (1982). Grading issues in a desegregated system. Paper presented at the Annual Meeting of the American Educational Research Association (New York, NY). (ERIC Document Reproduction Service No. ED 215 051)

Graden, J. L., Zins, J. E., & Curtis, M. J. (1988). *Alternative educational delivery systems: Enhancing instructional options for all students.* Washington, DC: National Association of School Psychologists.

Gredler, G. (1984). Transition classes: A viable alternative for the at-risk child? *Psychology in the Schools, 21*, 463-470.

Grissom, J. B., & Shepard, L. A. (in press). Repeating and dropping out of school. In L. A. Shepard & M. L. Smith (Eds.), *Flunking grade: Research and policy on retention.* New York: Falmer Press.

Hamilton, S. F. (1986). Raising standards and reducing dropout rates. *Teacher's College Record, 87*, 410-429.

Holmes, C. T., & Matthews, K. M. (1984). The effects of non-promotion on elementary and junior high school pupils: A meta-analysis. *Review of Educational Research, 45*, 225-236.

Howe, H., & Edelman, M. W. (1985). *Barriers to excellence: Our children at risk.* Boston: National Coalition of Advocates for Students.

Jackson, G. B. (1975). The research evidence on the effects of grade retention. *Review of Educational Research, 45*, 613-635.

Johnson, D. S. (1981). Naturally acquired learned helplessness: The relationship of school failure to achievement, behavior, attributions, and self-concept. *Journal of Educational Psychology, 73*, 174-180.

Lieberman, L. M. (1980). A decision-making model for in-grade retention (nonpromotion). *Journal of Learning Disabilities, 13*, 268-272.

Light, H. W. (1977). *Light's Retention Scale.* San Rafael, CA: Academic Therapy.

Mathews, H. W. (1977). The effect of transition education, a year of readiness, and beginning reading instruction between kindergarten and first grade. Unpublished doctoral dissertation. St. Louis University.

Medway, F. J., & Rose, J. S. (1986). Grade retention. In T. R. Kratochwill (Ed.), *Advances in school psychology, Vol. I.* Hillsdale, NJ: Lawrence Erlbaum.

Miller, W. D., & Norris, R. C. (1967). Entrance age and school success. *Journal of School Psychology, 6*, 47-59.

Purkerson, R., & Whitfield, E. (1981). Failure syndrome: Stress for middle school children. Washington, DC: National Institute for Education. (ERIC Document Reproduction Service No. ED 207 680)

Rafoth, M. A., Dawson, P., & Carey, K. (December, 1988). Supporting paper on Retention Position Statement, NASP *Communique.*

Rumberger, R. W. (1987). High school dropouts: A review of issues and evidence. *Review of Educational Research, 57*, 101-121.

Sandoval, J. (1987). *A five year follow-up of children repeating the first grade.* Paper presented at the 19th Annual Convention of the National Association of School Psychologists (New Orleans, LA).

Sandoval, J., & Hughes, P. G. (1981). *Success in non-promoted first grade children. Final Report.* Davis, CA: University of California. (ERIC Document Reproduction Service No. ED 212 371).

Smith, M. L., & Shepard, L. A. (1989). Flunking grades: A recapitulation. In L. A. Shepard & M. L. Smith (Eds.), *Flunking grades: Research and policies on retention.* New York: Falmer Press.

Smith, M. L., & Shepard, L. A. (October, 1987). What doesn't work: Explaining policies of retention in the early grades. *Phi Delta Kappan*, 129-134.

Talmadge, S. J. (1981). Descriptive and predictive relationships among family environments, cognitive characteristics, behavioral ratings, transition room placement, and early reading achievement. Unpublished doctoral dissertation, University of Oregon.

Wehlage, G. G., & Rutter, R. A. (1986). Dropping out: How much do schools contribute to the problem? *Teacher's College Record, 87*, 374-392.

Zinski, J. P. (1983). *A study of the effects of a pre-first grade transitional class as compared with first grade retention on reading achievement.* (ERIC Document Reproduction Service No. ED 248 459)

ANNOTATED BIBLIOGRAPHY

Carstens, A. (1985). Retention and social promotion for the exceptional child. *School Psychology Review, 14,* 48–63.
This article reviews the theoretical and empirical support for retention, with particular focus on the exceptional learner. The assumptions and goals of retention are reviewed from several theoretical perspectives: Gesellian, behavior analysis, cognitive developmental, and mastery learning. The author concludes there is a lack of empirical support for retention, nor is there basis for retention on theoretical grounds. Exceptional children, including slow learners, learning disabled students, and students described as "immature" do not appear to benefit from retention, and the author urges schools to apply interventions that attempt to remediate specific skill deficits.

Gredler, G. (1984). Transition classes: A viable alternative for the at-risk child? *Psychology in the Schools, 21,* 463–470.
Gredler defines the transition room concept (the practice of providing an "extra year" between kindergarten and first grade) and reviews the research on the effectiveness of transition programs. He concludes that transition rooms are no more effective than retention following first grade in producing achievement gains, nor are they better than placement in regular first grade classrooms. Children who are placed in first grade classes with individualized instruction make significantly greater progress than comparable children placed in transition classes.

Holmes, C. T., & Matthews, K. M. (1984). The effects of non-promotion on elementary and junior high school pupils: A meta-analysis. *Review of Educational Research, 45,* 225–236.
This study employed meta-analysis to integrate the findings of 44 studies investigating the effects of retention on elementary/junior high students. Results found consistently negative effects of retention on achievement, personal adjustment, and attitude toward school. The authors conclude, "Those who continue to retain pupils at grade level do so despite cumulative research evidence showing that the potential for negative effects consistently outweighs positive outcomes."

Medway, F. J., & Rose, J. S. (1986). Grade retention. In T. R. Kratochwill (Ed.), *Advances in school psychology, Vol. I.* Hillsdale, NJ: Lawrence Erlbaum.
This chapter on grade retention places the practice within the context of the educational reform movement, discusses promotion policies, estimates retention rates, reviews the research, considers legal implications of retention, and attempts to identify the best candidates for retention. It concludes with a discussion of the role of the school psychologist in making retention decisions.

Smith, M. L., & Shepard, L. A. (1989). *Flunking grade: Research and policies on retention.* New York: Falmer Press.
Smith and Shepard edit this volume which provides a comprehensive review of the literature as well as discussion of their own research addressing policy and practice in student retention. Particularly noteworthy is their discussion of the relationship between retention and school dropout in which they demonstrate that students of comparable achievement levels are more likely to drop out of school if they have been retained than if they have been promoted. The book concludes with recommendations for alternatives to retention.

10

Best Practices in Behavioral Consultation

Thomas R. Kratochwill
Stephen N. Elliott
Pamela Carrington Rotto
University of Wisconsin–Madison

OVERVIEW

Consultation has become a major approach for providing psychoeducational services to children and youths in schools. Surveys of school psychologists (e.g., Meacham & Peckam, 1978; Smith, 1984) have found that consultation is a high priority for practicing school psychologists who wish to expand their services in this area. Three major models of consultation that are used most frequently include mental health consultation, organizational development consultation, and behavioral consultation. Although differences exist among these models, all emphasize an increase in the problem-solving expertise of the consultee within a triadic relationship (consultant-consultee–child). The behavioral model of consultation has emerged as an alternative to traditional service delivery approaches in applied settings (Reschly, 1988). Although the role of consultation is not new to school psychologists, the recent increases in use have been accompanied by a corresponding need for formalized training of school psychologists in behavioral consultation. Training programs increasingly are teaching school psychologists to perform as behavioral consultants with teachers whose students experience academic, behavioral, and social problems. Behavioral consultation also has been linked to major prevention programs (Kratochwill, Sheridan, & Van-Someren, 1988).

Behavioral consultation traditionally is affiliated with behavior modification and the intervention techniques from this theoretical school (Kazdin, 1989; Sulzer-Azaroff & Mayer, 1977). With this approach, school psychologists apply behavioral principles and techniques in developing classroom intervention programs and use behavior methodologies to evaluate the effectiveness of services (see Bergan, 1987). Several identifiable features are associated uniquely with behavioral consultation: (a) indirect service delivery, (b) problem-solving focus, and (c) development of a collegial relationship.

The most widely recognized feature of behavioral consultation is its *indirect service* delivery approach (Bergan & Kratochwill, 1990). Services are delivered by a consultant (school psychologist) to a consultee (teacher or parent) who, in turn, provides services to a child in the school or community setting. The indirect approach to service delivery generally is regarded as a distinct advantage of behavioral consultation, since it allows the psychologist to impact many more children than could be served by a direct service approach.

Behavioral consultation involves a collaborative relationship in which the consultant is viewed as a facilitator. Emphasis is placed on the collaborative *problem solving process* which occurs during a series of interviews and related assessment activities. Throughout this process, the psychologist's role is to elicit a description of the problem, assist in analyzing the problem, devise a plan for intervention, and monitor the program once implemented. The teacher's or parent's role is to describe clearly the problem, work with the child to implement the intervention program, observe progress, periodically evaluate the plan's effectiveness, and supervise the child's actions.

The development of a *collegial relationship* is essential to effective consultation. The personal characteristics and professional competencies of both the psychologist and parent/teacher influence the consultation relationship and outcome. Reviews of the literature in this area by Conoley and Conoley (1982) indicate the importance of the consultant's interpersonal skills. For example, characteristics such as acceptance through nonjudgmental statements, openness, nondefensiveness, and flexibility positively affect the interaction between consultant and consultee. The interested reader is referred to a more thorough discussion of these skills in books by Conoley and Conoley (1982) and Parsons and Meyers (1984).

BASIC CONSIDERATIONS

Behavioral consultation has two important goals: (a) to provide methods for changing a child's learning or behavior problem and, (b) to improve a consultee's skills so he/she can prevent or at least respond effectively to future problems or similar problems in other children. Given these goals, behavioral consultation can be both a proactive and a reactive service. Research reports and experiences indicate that behavioral consultation often has changed children's problem behaviors successfully (Gresham & Kendell, 1987). However, the more proactive goal of influencing a teacher's or parent's ability to handle future problems has not been observed consistently. The accomplishment of these goals requires teachers to

participate in a general process for analyzing problems that results in an effective plan to resolve the problem. Successful behavioral consultants must demonstrate expertise in both coordinating and facilitating the problem solving process and in behavior change methods. While competence in problem identification, applied behavior analysis, and behavior plan implementation are necessary conditions of behavioral consultation, they are not sufficient to facilitate effective consultative interactions. Integration of positive interpersonal skills and understanding with technical expertise are equally important to maximize consultant-consultee effectiveness. In the remainder of this section, we examine the basic components of problem solving in behavioral consultation, specific consultant-consultee relationship variables which influence the consultation process, and issues pertaining to training behavioral consultants.

The Structure and Process of Behavioral Consultation

Behavioral consultation has been conceptualized as a series of stages that structure and focus the problem solving interaction between a consultant and consultee. Bergan (1977) developed a heuristic four-stage framework for behavioral consultation that begins with *problem identification* and *problem analysis*, progresses to *plan implementation*, and concludes with *plan evaluation*.

Problem identification is the initial and perhaps most critical stage of consultation because it results in the design and implementation of an effective plan. During the problem identification interview, the consultant and consultee focus on describing and operationally defining the child's behaviors which are of concern to the parent/teacher. In behavior consultation a "problem" is a relative concept that is operationalized when the parent/teacher reports a significant discrepancy between the child's current level of performance and the desired level of performance. The determination of whether a significant discrepancy exists is not examined initially; however, once the current and desired levels of performance are defined objectively, this significant discrepancy becomes the focus. This approach to problem identification is based on the assumption that problems are the result of unsuccessful or discrepant interactions between persons (e.g., child and teacher, child and parent). Thus, the psychologist and parent/teacher first analyze the target problem within the context of the child and his/her interactions with the environment. When baseline data support the existence of the specific problem behavior, the psychologist and parent/teacher begin to jointly identify factors that might lead to behavior change and problem resolution.

Problem analysis, the second major stage of behavior consultation, focuses on the variables and conditions that are hypothesized to influence the child's behavior. Problem analysis is a natural extension of the problem identification stage, in that it essentially begins with the target behavior of concern and focuses on establishing functional relationships between it and the antecedent or consequent events. Questions about who, what, where, when, and under what conditions or contingencies are all relevant, and generally facilitate a better understanding of the problem behavior. In many cases, the problem analysis stage will require the psychologist to collect additional data about the child's target behavior. Thus, problem analysis may enhance refinement and consequently, redefinition of the target problem and the factor(s) which influence it.

Plan implementation follows the problem analysis stage and has dual objectives of (a) selecting an appropriate intervention and (b) implementing the intervention. Procedural details are essential at this stage, such as assigning individuals to various roles, gathering and preparing specific materials, or training individuals to implement the plan. The selection of interventions traditionally seems to have been based on the reported or assumed effectiveness of a particular method. Many consumers and providers of psychological services, however, are demanding that interventions also be acceptable (i.e., time efficient, least restrictive, fair and/or low risk to the target child) (Elliott, 1988a, 1988b). Likewise, interest in interventions that are consistent with the teacher's/parent's child management philosophy and compatible with existing resources and skills of the individual delivering the intervention also have gained recent consumer interest and empirical support (Witt & Martens, 1988). Thus, the design and selection of appropriate interventions during behavioral consultation is based on behavioral principles of human functioning and requires attention to issues of intervention acceptability, intervention effectiveness, and consultee skills and resources. Plan implementation also involves discussing and actually carrying out the selected intervention. This substage may consume several weeks and is characterized by interactions between the parent/teacher and child. These interactions may occur through brief contacts in which the psychologist monitors intervention integrity and side effects (Gresham, 1989), and possibly brainstorms with the parent/teacher ways to revise the plan and its use. The school psychologist's role also may involve observations to monitor child and consultee behaviors or training sessions to enhance the skills of the individual who is executing the treatment plan.

Plan evaluation is the final stage of consultation. The objectives of this stage are to establish an empirical basis for interpreting outcomes of the intervention for the targeted problem and to provide a forum for evaluating plan effectiveness. Single-subject designs and direct observations, which largely have been adopted as the methodology for applied behavioral psychology, provide the primary means for evaluating change in the child's behavior. When the reported discrepancy between the child's behavior and desired level of functioning is reduced significantly or eliminated, and the treatment is acceptable to both the teacher/parent and child, the consultant and consultee decide whether consultation should be terminated. Rigorous outcome criteria include maintenance of the desired behavior over time and generalization across multiple settings and conditions. In theory, a consultative case is not concluded until the discrepancy between the child's existing and desired behavior is reduced substantively and the plan is acceptable. Therefore, it often is necessary to recycle through previous stages of consultation and to re-evaluate refined or newly implemented interventions.

In summary, behavioral consultation is a model for delivering psychoeducational assessment and intervention services to children via teachers or parents through a series of interviews. A heuristic problem-solving framework and behavioral principles provide structure for collecting information and affecting behavior change. Although the problem-solving structure is sequential and overt, it should not be interpreted as inflexible or irreversible. The activities of consultants and consultees are multifaceted, involving at least interviews, observational assessments, treatment of the target behavior, and evaluation of the intervention. Such activities generally require several collaborative interactions between the consultant and consultee, as well as ongoing consultee and client interactions.

Consultant–Consultee Relationship

The interpersonal relationship between a psychologist and parent/teacher is assumed to play a major role in the use and effectiveness of behavioral consultation. Thus, as with psychotherapy, issues of trust, genuineness, and openness have been deemed important qualities for both consultants and consultees (Martin, 1978). These human qualities are magnified in a consultative model of service delivery due to the predominance of an interview mode of information sharing. The dynamics of communication, both talking and listening, are the medium through which psychologists display their attitudes about parents and teachers. Personal characteristics, professional competencies, and behavioral principles of reinforcement and modeling all are important elements in establishing and maintaining constructive and professional interactions.

Sensitivity to issues of importance to parents and teachers also contributes to the development of a positive consulting relationship. Variables commonly examined in treatment acceptability research (Elliott, 1988a; Witt & Elliott, 1985) and dimensions of helping emphasized by empowerment theorists (Dunst & Trivette, 1988; Witt & Martens, 1988) provide a list of issues consistent with a behavioral perspective and relevant to the enhancement of relationships with parents and teachers. Specifically, treatment acceptability researchers repeatedly have found that administration/management time and fairness of the treatment are important themes virtually to all teachers, and nonaversive approaches to intervention are valued highly by most teachers. Work by empowerment theorists applied to consultation suggests that (a) help is more likely to be perceived positively if it is offered proactively, (b) competence within teachers is best promoted by building upon their existing child management strengths rather than remediating deficits, and (c) use of existing resources in the school environment is preferred over the intervention or purchase of new resources (Witt & Martens, 1988). Thus, it is concluded that effective behavioral consultants (a) overtly communicate awareness of these issues that are central to parents'/teachers' daily functioning and (b) act cooperatively in accordance with design interventions. Such consultative actions enhance entry and overcome many potential sources of resistance.

In closing this section, it is appropriate to remember that "once the door to the classroom is closed, there is little that any of the educational specialists can do to insure the occurrence of any event that the teacher does not want to occur . . ." (Gutkin & Curtis, 1981, pp. 220-221). Hence, the interpersonal or therapeutic relationship skills of a psychologist are as important to the delivery of behavioral consultation as knowledge of assessment and intervention methods.

Training

There is growing interest in training practitioners as behavioral consultants. Despite growing enthusiasm over the potential impact of consultation, relatively little has been written about the actual training of school psychologists as consultants. Moreover, literature reviews in this area have indicated that researchers often do not specify the skills or criteria to which consultants are to adhere to (e.g., Gallessich, McDermott-Long, & Jennings, 1986). Basically, there are three major formats that can be used for establishing competencies in consultation, and these vary considerably in their empirical support. These three domains include individual competency-based training, workshop training, and self-instructional training formats. Each of these are reviewed briefly to provide a basis for consideration of how consultation skills might be obtained.

Individual competency-based training is essentially a format that identifies specific objectives within each phase of behavioral consultation to maximize psychologist success at identifying, analyzing, and evaluating a problem and related intervention. Approaches or techniques that have been developed to train consultants typically have used conventional formats to facilitate the didactic instruction of discrete verbalization skills and use of standardized interview protocols. Competency-based training materials have been developed by Kratochwill and his associates which consist of a training package utilized by individual consultants (typically graduate students in school psychology programs) to promote development of specific skills associated with each of the interviews in behavioral consultation. This package typically includes reading materials (Kratochwill & Bergan, 1990) videotaped models, simulated role-play situations, group discussions, self-monitoring, and performance-based feedback. Generally, empirical work in this area suggests that students can be trained quite effectively

through these opportunities for guided practice and immediate feedback. It is beyond the scope of this chapter to review research in this area and interested readers are referred to Bergan and Kratochwill (1990) for further information. Training in this competency-based format may be expensive and time consuming and typically requires a period of many months to implement. Therefore, this approach may be most useful in graduate training programs that have a low faculty-to-student ratio and resources to handle this type of training commitment.

A second method for training consultation strategies consists of workshops of varying lengths and formats. This training approach typically is used at many professional conferences at the state and national levels. Nevertheless, there is little empirical work to verify the acquisition of effective consultation skills from participation in training workshops. In a recent project McDougall, Reschly, and Corkery (1988) evaluated the effectiveness of a one-day inservice workshop that focused on behavioral consultation. In the project, 16 school psychologists submitted audiotapes depicting prereferral interviews and the audiotapes were analyzed through the Consultation Analysis Record. Although the authors found that overall, each of six problem identification interview objectives increased, few of these increases were significant. The results obtained by McDougall and associates emphasize the need for broad-based training in objectives rather than discrete verbal segments. The shortcomings of this study basically are that only the problem identification interview was examined and individual client outcome data were not presented. More systematic research focused on a broader range of consultation outcomes is desirable.

Finally, self-instructional approaches are often implicit in professional training. In this regard, we know of no specific research that has focused on an evaluation of self-instruction approaches in behavioral consultation training. Indeed, the format for this training probably would be some demonstration of baseline skills and then subsequent analysis of the consultation process following reading of materials such as the individual guide prepared by Kratochwill and Bergan (1990). Research in this area is a high priority in view of the need to evaluate training models that are more reflective of the usual practices outside university-based training programs. Indeed, it is likely that most practicing professionals would use an approach based on self-instructional tactics. Best practices in this area would suggest that the training module needs to include a number of opportunities for self-monitoring, feedback, and practice in conducting the interviews effectively.

BEST PRACTICES IN THE DELIVERY OF BEHAVIORAL CONSULTATION

As noted in the previous sections of the chapter, behavioral consultation consists of a series of stages or phases that are used to implement the process of consultation. These stages include problem identification, problem analysis, plan implementation, and plan evaluation. Each of these steps, with the exception of plan implementation, involves a formal interview resulting in specific objectives. Best practices in behavioral consultation suggest that psychologists adhere to specific objectives and activities with each phase. The major components for each of these phases are outlined next.

Problem Identification

Problem identification is achieved through an interview where the primary objectives are to specify the goals, assess the problem, and implement certain procedures. Behavioral consultation can involve a developmental or problem-centered focus. In developmental consultation the consultant establishes general, subordinate, and performance objectives. Usually these are obtained over a long period of time and in several series of interviews. In contrast, problem-centered consultation involves specification of problems that are specific and relate to one primary target behavior. Relative to

the developmental consultation process, problem-centered consultation is more time-limited.

Whether the nature of consultation is developmental or problem-centered, the psychologist needs to achieve clear specification of target problems. Typically, this process involves generating precise descriptions of the student's behavior, carefully analyzing the conditions under which the target problems occur, and establishing some indication of the level of persistence or strength of the target problems. Another important objective is establishing an assessment technique. Together, the teacher and/or parent and psychologist agree on the type or kind of measure to be used, what will be recorded, and how this process will be implemented. Finally, certain procedural objectives must be met during the problem identification phase. One of the first objectives involves establishing times, dates, and formats for subsequent interviews and contacts with the teacher or parent to examine procedural aspects of the consultation process. For example, the psychologist may agree to contact the teacher/parent weekly or biweekly to determine whether data are being gathered properly, or if any unique barriers have occurred. Witt and Elliott (1983) outlined nine components that facilitate the problem identification interview. These components were written as objectives and briefly are described as follows:

1. *Explanation of problem definition purposes.* The parent or teacher should be told what is to be accomplished during the interview and why problem identification is important. (Example statement: "I would like to talk with you a few minutes about John and his behaviors that bother you most. We will need to assess his behaviors, when and how often they occur, and what factors in your classroom [or home] influence them.")

2. *Identification and selection of target behaviors.* The parent or teacher should be asked to focus attention on the problematic aspects of a student's difficulties. (Example statement: "Please describe exactly what John is doing that

has caused you concern.") When individuals identify multiple problems, it is necessary to determine which to address. (Example statement: "Which of these concerns is most pressing to you now?")

3. *Identification of problem frequency, duration, and intensity.* After a target behavior has been defined, it is helpful to assess its basic characteristics: How often does it occur (frequency), how long does it last (duration), and how strong is it (intensity)? (Example statements: "How many times did John cry last week?" "How long does each crying session last?" "Does he cry loud enough for everyone in the room to hear him?"). To interpret descriptions of frequency, duration, and intensity, the parent or teacher may be asked to compare the target child's behavior with that of other children. In addition, a psychologist should have knowledge of normative expectations to which the child's behavior can be compared.

4. *Identification of the conditions under which the target behavior occurs.* The assessment of environmental factors that occur in conjunction with a target behavior is essential in understanding the problem. (Example statement: "How do you and the class react to John's crying?") Use of a simple model of behavior, such as the ABC model, can help unravel many problems. This model construes behavior (B) to be a function of antecedent (A) and/or consequent (C) events. Thus, once a behavior has been identified, a consultant looks at events that chronologically precede and follow it.

6. *Identification of the required level of performance.* Obtaining a description of the behavior required of a student is as important as obtaining a description of the student's problem behavior. (Example statement: "What would you consider to be an acceptable frequency for this out-of-seat behavior?") Once a desired or expected level of performance is identified, it serves as a goal.

7. *Identification of behavioral assessment procedures.* All interventions require some assessment or recording of behavior. Thus, a consultant should help a teacher or parent decide what, how, when, and where behavior will be recorded and who will do the recording.

8. *Identification of consultee effectiveness.* Given that one major goal of behavioral consultation is to enable a consultee to solve his or her own problems in the future, it may be necessary to teach or model problem-solving skills and enhance the consultee's confidence in his/her ability to solve problems. The goal obviously is for the consultant to be helpful to the consultee. To accomplish this, Witt and Martens (1988) advocate an empowerment, rather than an advice giving, philosophy of service for consultants. An empowerment philosophy assumes consultees basically are skilled individuals who can become more capable of solving their own problems by knowing what resources are available and how to gain access to them (Dunst & Trivette, 1988). One can determine the consultee's potential effectiveness by asking about how similar problems have been handled in the past, assessing what methods the consultee already has used to remediate the target problem, and judging whether the consultee is self-reliant or dependent on others for reinforcement (Meyers, Liddell, & Lyons, 1977).

9. *Summary of the interview.* The final step in the problem identification stage should include a summary of the important points discussed and a review of the problem definition. This summary should include a statement of the specific target behavior(s) or clarification of any further assessment necessary to refine the target behavior(s).

Specific objectives that are associated with the consultation problem identification interview are presented in Table 1. These objectives are general objectives that need to be established in the consultation interview, but typically correspond to features of the Consultation Analysis Record (see Bergan & Kratochwill, 1990).

Problem Analysis

After baseline data are collected on

TABLE 1
Problem Identification Interview

Behavior Specificaton

Definition: The consultant should elicit behavioral descriptions of client functioning. Focus is on specific behaviors of the child in terms that can be understood by an independent behavior. Provide as many examples of the behavior problem as possible (e.g., What does Cathy do?).

a. Specify behavior:

b. Specify examples of the problem behavior:

c. Which behavior causes the most difficulty? (i.e., prioritize the problems from most to least severe):

Behavior Setting

Definition: A precise description of the settings in which the problem behaviors occur (e.g., Where does John do this?).

a. Specify examples of where the behavior occurs:

b. Specify priorities (i.e., Which setting is causing the most difficulty?):

Identify Antecedents

Definition: Events which precede the child's behavior. Provide information regarding what happens immediately before the problem behavior occurs (e.g., What happens right before Kristy hits other children?).

Sequential Conditions Analysis

Definition: Situational events occurring when the behavior occurs. Environmental conditions in operation when the problem behavior occurs. For example, time of day or day of week when the problem behavior typically occurs. Sequential conditions are also defined as the pattern or trend of antecedent and/or consequent conditions across a series of occasions (e.g., What is happening when the behavior occurs?).

Identify Consequent Conditions

Definition: Events which occur immediately following the client behavior (e.g., What hapens after the problem behavior has occurred?).

Behavior Strength

Definition: Indicate how often (frequency) or how long (duration) the behavior occurs. Behavior strength refers to the level or incidence of the behavior that is to be focused on. The question format used for each particular behavior strength will depend upon the specific type of behavior problem (e.g., How often does Shelly have tantrums? or How long do Brett's tantrums last?).

a. Frequency of behavior:

b. Duration of behavior:

(Table 1, continued)

Tentative Definition of *Goal* — Question

Definition: Appropriate or acceptable level of the behavior (e.g., How frequently could Matthew leave his seat without causing problems?).

Assets Questions

Definition: Strengths, abilities, or other positive features of the child (e.g., What does Steve do well?).

Approach to Teaching or *Existing Procedures*

Definition: Procedures or rules in force which are external to the child and to the behavior (e.g., How long are Sue and other students doing seat work problems?).

Data Collection Procedures

Definition: Specify the target responses to record. This recording should include the kind of measure, what is to be recorded, and how to record. Specific details of data recording should be emphasized.

Date to Begin Data Collection

Definition: Procedural details of when to begin collecting baseline data.

---

the target behavior, the psychologist and teacher/parent meet to decide jointly on factors that might lead to some resolution of the problem. In this regard, the consultation process will focus on student, parent/teacher, and general environmental variables that may be of relevance.

The problem analysis interview includes five major steps: (a) choosing analysis procedures, (b) determining the conditions and/or skills analysis, (c) developing plan strategies, (d) developing plan tactics, and (e) establishing procedures to evaluate performance during implementation of any treatment program. Within the context of these phases, the psychologist might first analyze the factors that lead to potential solution of the problem and then develop a plan to solve the problem.

The psychologist focuses on conditions that facilitate attainment of the mutually agreed upon goals. Generally, the following steps are necessary:

1. specifying whether the goal of treatment is to increase, decrease, or maintain behavior,

2. identifying setting events and antecedent/consequential conditions associated with behavior,

3. determining what current conditions affect the behavior by comparing the existing situation to related research findings, and

4. identifying conditions not currently associated with the behavior, but which nonetheless could influence solving the problem.

Through mutual problem-solving efforts, the psychologist and teacher/parent must analyze the kinds of child skills necessary to achieve the goals of consultation during the problem analysis phase. This process includes analyzing skills that the child does not possess, and can include both academic and social performance. Basically, the psychologist must work with the teacher/parent (and child if possible), to identify psychological and educational principles that relate to attaining the goals of consultation. It is beyond the scope of this chapter to outline these procedures in great detail. Rather, the reader is referred to a number of sources that can be useful to analyze overt behavioral and cognitive features that relate to instructional and social functioning (e.g., Kazdin, 1989; Kratochwill & Morris, in press).

The outcome of successful problem analysis is a plan to put into effect during the treatment implementation process. Development of this intervention includes first specifying broad strategies that can be used to achieve the mutually agreed upon goals. The plan strategies typically specify *sources of action* to be implemented. Secondly, plan tactics are used to guide implementation of the strategy and outline principles to be applied during the intervention. For example, if reinforcement strategies are to be used, the person responsible for carrying out the plan and the conditions under which they will occur should be specified. During this phase psychologists also should assess treatment acceptability prior to its implementation. A number of scales have been developed for assessment of pretreatment acceptability and readers are encouraged to consult this material (Elliott, 1988b; Witt & Elliott, 1985). Attachment A to this chapter includes copies of several scales that can be used in the assessment of treatment acceptability.

Finally, during problem analysis the psychologist and teacher/parent must establish performance and assessment objectives that will be used during plan implementation. Typically this procedure follows from a conditions analysis and involves specification of an assessment procedure previously used during baseline. For example, when plan implementation involves skill development, some agreed upon format for collection of data on performances related to the final objectives achieved is necessary.

Table 2 provides an example of the general objectives that should be met during the problem analysis interview. These objectives generally involve validating the problem, analyzing the problem and related variables, designing the plan, and developing the procedural goals.

Plan Implementation

The third stage in behavioral consultation involves implementing the treatment plan. Some initial activities are necessary during the plan implementation process and involve ensuring that the intervention is likely to succeed. In this regard, the psychologist should maximize the probability that the intervention plan is put into effect by the teacher/parent and/or child during this part of the consultation process. This step will require collaborative decisions regarding role assignments, material assembly, and skill development, as needed during the process. Although there is no formal interview during the plan implementation phase, it is the responsibility of the psychologist to monitor the implementation of the intervention and work with the teacher/parent to revise procedures during plan implementation, if it is determined necessary. It also may be desirable for the consultant to observe the child and/or teacher or parent to monitor behaviors and determine the need for subsequent revisions in the plan.

During plan implementation the three major tasks that must be accomplished include skill development, monitoring the implementation process, and plan revision. Typically, the psychologist must determine whether the teacher/parent has the skills to carry out the plan. If skill development is required, the consultee must be offered some type of training or guidance.

A second task is to monitor data to determine if assessment is occurring as intended. Consultee records usually are examined to assess child outcome. This process usually will indicate to the school psychologist when data are being gathered, how the performance of the child is being assessed, and what behaviors are being observed. It also may help the psychologist determine whether the plan is actually proceeding as designed. If little progress is observed then it is advisable for the school psychologist to meet with the teacher/parent and revise the plan accordingly.

TABLE 2
Problem Analysis Interview

Strength of Behavior

Definition: Question or statement regarding behaviors, specific to the baseline data collected (e.g., It looks like Karen refused to do the assigned work except on Tuesday.).

Antecedent, Consequent, and Sequential Conditions

a. *Antcedent:* Events which precede the child's behavior. Information regarding what happens immediately preceding the problem behavior (e.g., Did you notice anything in particular that happened just *before* . . .).

b. *Consequent:* Events which occur immediately following the child's behavior (e.g., What happened *after* Mary . . .).

c. *Sequential:* Situational events or environmental conditions in operation when the problem behavior occurs. Pattern or trend of conditions across occurrences such as day of week, time of day, etc. (e.g., What was happening *when* Jimmy . . .).

Interpretation of Behavior

Definition: Consultant elicits the consultee's perception regarding the purpose or function of the behavior (e.g., Why do you think Justin is so disrespectful?).

Establishing a Plan

Definition: Consultant and consultee establish plan strategies and specific targets that might be used in treatment implementation. Consultant may ask for or provide strategies (e.g., What could be done to change the setting in which Charles gets into fights? — OR — We need to try something different. What could be done before Ron makes the abusive remarks?).

Continuation of Recording Procedure

Definition: Establish recording procedures to be used in treatment plan implementation.

Monitoring plan implementation generally occurs in two ways. First, the child's behavior is monitored on an ongoing basis by the teacher/parent. This monitoring is a continuation from the problem identification and problem analysis phases of consultation. A second type of monitoring activity involves an evaluation of the strategies that are associated with the plan implementation itself. It is essential for the school psychologist and teacher/parent to ensure that the plan agreed upon is being carried out as designed. The psychologist may choose to monitor plan implementation and integrity by discussing the intervention plan with the teacher or parent. A second procedure that can be used to complement this strategy is to actually observe the plan in operation. It is acknowledged that various individuals might serve in the role of treatment implementors. Nevertheless, it is very likely that the psychologist will use a variety of procedures to facilitate plan implementation that are compatible with resources and responsibilities in the school or setting.

Finally, changes should be made in the plan when necessary. If the child's behavior is not changing in the desired direction plan revision should occur. Generally, this outcome will require that the psychologist and teacher/parent return again to the problem analysis phase to further analyze variables such as the setting, intrapersonal child characteristics, or skill deficits. Likewise, it may be necessary to return to the problem identification stage if it is determined that the nature of the problem has changed.

Plan Evaluation

Plan evaluation is implemented through a formal plan evaluation interview and typically is undertaken to determine whether the goals of consultation have been obtained. The process of evaluation includes assessment of goal attainment, plan effectiveness, and implementation planning.

The first major step in plan evaluation is to decide whether or not the actual goals previously agreed upon have been obtained. This decision is determined through discussion with the consultee and observation of the client's behavior. The process of evaluating goal attainment first was initiated during problem identification where the objectives and procedures for measuring mastery were specified. The data that have been gathered since the problem identification phase should provide some evidence as to whether there is congruence between objectives and the problem solution. Basically, this step occurs on the basis of the data collected, but additional strategies might be invoked as well, such as social validation criteria. That is, the school psychologist will want to know whether the child reached some clinically established level of change and whether the intervention program brought the child's performance within a range of acceptable behavior as compared to normal or typical peers. Determination of the congruence between behavior and objectives generally leads the psychologist to conclude that no progress was obtained, some progress was made, or the actual goal was obtained.

The mechanism for evaluating plan effectiveness can occur through one of several clinical assessment and design strategies that have been used frequently in applied behavior analysis or single-case research. In this regard, a variety of clinical experimental procedures might be implemented to facilitate decisions regarding progress in the consultation process. Again, it is beyond the scope of this chapter to outline these in great detail. Instead, the interested reader is referred to a primary source where these designs are reviewed (e.g., Barlow, Hayes, & Nelson, 1984). The recommended strategies basically involve case study design or a simple time-series design which includes an A/B format.

Once it has been determined that the problem has been solved, post implementation planning occurs to help ensure that the particular problem does not occur again. There are some alternatives available for the psychologist and teacher/parent in designing post implementation plans. One strategy is to leave the plan in effect. Typically, however, a plan that is put into effect will need to be modified (another alternative) to facilitate maintenance of behavior over time. There is considerable evidence in the behavioral literature that specific tactics are needed to facilitate maintenance and generalization of behavior and this must be accomplished during this phase of consultation. Generalization may occur naturally, but more likely, it will need to be programmed. Several factors have been identified that have a bearing on the generalization of skills (Haring, 1988; White et al., 1988). Table 3 from White et al. (1988) lists the strategies for facilitating generalization along with a definition and example. The table is based on the seminal work of Stokes and Baer (1977) and can serve as a useful guideline for behavioral consultants.

Another major objective that should occur during the plan evaluation interview is discussion of post implementation recording. Generally, this procedure refers to the process of continuing record keeping activities to determine whether the problem occurs in the future. Usually, the school psychologist and teacher/parent select periodic measures that are convenient to use and may maintain specific features of the original plan to facilitate this data collection process. Best practices also suggest that the psychologist consider conducting post-plan implementation acceptability assessment as well. These procedures can be implemented informally or more formally with

TABLE 3
Strategies for Facilitating Generalization

Strategy	Definition	Example
Train & Hope	Providing simple instruction and then "hoping" that generalization will occur. Actually the *absence* of any special strategy	Three preschool boys who were blind and severely or profoundly retarded were taught to reach for noise-making toys always presented at the midline. None of the boys generalized to objects presented on the right or left.
Setting Training in the Natural Setting	Training is conducted directly in at least one type of setting in which the skill will be used. Generalization is then probed in other non-training settings.	The social interaction skills of several individuals with severe handicaps were trained in the classroom and courtyard during class breaks.
Sequential Modification	Training is provided in one setting, and generalization is probed in other settings. If necessary, training is conducted sequentially in more and more settings until generalization to all desired settings is observed.[1]	One girl with moderate handicaps needed articulation training in 3 settings before generalization to all remaining situations of interest; a second girl only required training in two situations before generalizing.
Consequences Introduce to Natural Maintaining Contingencies	Ensuring that the learner experiences the natural consequences of a behavior by: (1) teaching a functional skill which is likely to be reinforced outside instruction; (2) training to a level of proficiency that makes the skill truly useful; (3) making sure the learner actually does experience the natural consequence; and/or (4) teaching the learner to solicit or recruit reinforcement outside instruction.	Three teens who were multiply handicapped and severely retarded were taught to use symbols & pictures to request objects. Generalization was encouraged by using objects which would be regularly encountered outside instruction, making sure the boys always carried their communication boards, and that someone would always be present to provide any requested items.
Use Indiscriminable Contingencies	If natural consequences cannot be expected to encourage and maintain generalization, artificial consequences or schedules of natural consequences might be used. However, it is best if the learner cannot determine precisely when those consequences will be available, and so must behave as if they always are.	Two behavior disordered and five normal preschool children always generalized their interaction and study better when verbal praise by the teacher was provided after progressively greater delays, rather than immediately following each behavior.
Train to Generalize	The learner is only reinforced for performing some generalized instance of the target skill. Performing a previously reinforced version of the response is no longer reinforced.	Four youths with severe retardation were taught to name specific items. Contingencies were then altered so they were only reinforced if they named *untrained* items. After 3 sessions, all youths generalized well to untrained items.

(Table 3, continued)

Strategy	Definition	Example
Antecedents		
Program Common Stimuli	Selecting a salient, but not necessarily task-related, stimulus from the situation to which generalization is desired, and including that stimulus in the training program.	Stokes & Baer (1977) report a case in which an individual with severe retardation was taught exercise skills to facilitate integration in a physical education class. Music was played during the PE class, so music was also introduced into the individual's training sessions to make the two situations more similar.
Sufficient Exemplars	A strategy similar to Sequential Modification, involving sequential addition of stimuli to the training program until generalization to all related stimuli occurs.[2]	An adolescent with severe handicaps was taught to name objects, and probed with other objects from the same class. Some objects required only a single exemplar to produce generalized naming, while other objects required 5 exemplars before generalization occurred.
Multiple Exemplars	Several examples of the stimulus class to which generalization is desired are trained at the same time.	Three adults with profound mental retardation were trained in three types of exercise. Generalization occurred to a group exercise program and to two untrained exercises.
General Case Programming	The universe to which generalization is desired is analyzed and representative examples of positive stimuli (stimuli in the presence of which the skill should be used), negative stimuli (stimuli in the presence of which the skill should not be used), and irrelevant stimuli (stimuli which should not effect skill use, but might inappropriately do so) are selected for training.	Six young men with moderate or severe retardation were trained on three vending machines which reflected the range of machine-types found in the community. Good generalization was obtained to 10 untrained machines in the community.
Other		
Train Loosely	Settings, cues, prompts, materials, response definition, and other features of the training situation are purposely varied to avoid a ritual, highly structured, invariate program which might inhibit generalization.	Mothers were taught to vary the type of stimuli and reinforcers they used in working with their children's motor skills. All children learned their skills quickly and generalized well to another setting.
Mediate Generalization	Teaching a secondary behavior or strategy which will help an individual remember or figure out how and when to generalize, or which will dispel the differences between the training and generalization situations.	Five adolescents with moderate or severe mental retardation were taught to self-instruct task completion using a picture sequence. They then used the self-instruction skill to generalize task completion of a new task with a new picture sequence.

(*Table 3, continued*)

[1]Stokes and Baer (1977 described this strategy as training in one situation and, if that fails to produce generalization, training in all remaining situations of interest. The more literally "sequential" nature of the procedure as described above seems better suited for describing current application of the strategy.

[2]Stokes & Baer used this label to describe the successive introduction of new stimuli or settings, but separating the two variations seemed more advisable for the current study (see note 2, above).

[Source: White et al. (1978). Review and analysis of strategies for generalization. In N. R. Haring (Ed.), *Generalization for students with severe handicaps: Strategies and solutions* (pp. 15–51). Seattle: University of Washington. Reproduced by permission.]

acceptability instrumentation (Elliott, 1988b).

Finally, the teacher/parent should notify the school psychologist of any recurrence of the problem behaviors that might be indicated. These usually can be brought to the psychologist's attention and specific tactics will be set up to establish a system to analyze the problems. Table 4 provides an overview of the general objectives that are to be obtained in the plan evaluation interview.

WRITING BEHAVIORAL CONSULTATION CASE REPORTS

At various times during the course of behavioral consultation, the consultant may wish to formally communicate the results of the intervention program to the involved parent and/or teacher. Indeed, it is the ethical and professional responsibility of the consultant to ensure that information concerning an intervention is communicated in a valid, clear, and concise manner. Although a variety of traditional report formats exist (see Gelfand & Hartmann, 1984; Grimes, 1983; Martin, 1972; Ownby, 1987; for overviews), the present format provides a conceptual scheme for reporting interventions that are compatible with best practices in consultation. The consultant, however, is advised to modify this format to accommodate personal preferences and meet specific institutional needs and standards.

The present report format represents an outline for describing the activities of an entire consultation program (see Table 5). If reporting information prior to completion of the plan, only parts of this report would be appropriate. General characteristics of the behavioral consultation report include (a) Background Information, (b) Problem Definition, (c) Intervention Plan, (d) Plan Evaluation, and (e) Summary and Recommendations.

The section on *Background Information* includes demographic information describing the child and details regarding the setting in which the problem occurs. For example, the child's name, date of birth, age, gender, school, parents, address, telephone and teacher should be specified. The consultant also should include a description of the family, siblings, socioeconomic status, peers, teacher, and any other ecological features that are relevant to the case.

Many alternative ways exist to define a problematic situation. For example, problem behaviors may be described at various levels of specificity. Alternatively, a problem situation can be conceptualized in terms of reducing negative behaviors or increasing positive behaviors. The purpose of the *Problem Definition* is to provide a description and rationale for the problem as it was defined by the school psychologist (i.e., consultant) and teacher/parent during consultation. Information from the problem identification interview will be especially relevant. More specifically, details regarding the referral problem, target behavior(s), desired outcome behavior(s), critical setting or situations for change, and a preliminary functional analysis should be included.

Discussion of the initial referral issue should indicate the referral source and a description of the problem. The consultant also should note that consent for participation was obtained from the child's parents. An operational definition of the

TABLE 4
Plan Evaluation Interview

Goal Attainment

Definition: Determine specifically if the goals of consultation have been attained. Question treatment outcome (e.g., How did things go?).

Plan Effectiveness

Definition: Determine the effectiveness of the plan for the specific child. Was the specific plan effective in producing behavior change? What was the internal validity of the plan? (e.g., Would you say that the contract procedure was responsible for reducing John's profane language?)

External Validity of Plan

Definition: Determines the effectiveness of the plan for another child who has a similar problem (e.g., Do you think this plan would have worked with another student?).

Post-Implementation Planning

Definition: Decision is made regarding the advisability of leaving the plan in effect, removing the plan, or constructing a new plan. Selecting a post-treatment alternative may occur (e.g., Do you want to leave the point system in effect for another week to see if Bob's progress continues?).

Plan Modification

Definition: Establish new plan strategies to increase plan effectiveness. Consultant may suggest a change or question the need for change (e.g., How could we change the reinforcement procedure to make the plan more effective?).

Procedures to Facilitate Generalization and Maintenance

Definition: Procedures to encourage continued progress. Goal is to encourage generalization to other settings, or maintain behavior over a long period of time (e.g., What *procedures* can be implemented to be sure that Sally continues to finish her homework?).

Follow-Up Assessment

Definition: Discussion regarding follow-up recording procedures to monitor the behavior over time (e.g., Now that we have success in the program for George, how can we *monitor* his progress in the future?).

---

problem as agreed upon by the school psychologist and teacher/parent should be described in terms of deficits, excesses, frequency, intensity, and duration. Specification of the target behavior(s) and a statement regarding desired outcome behavior(s) also should be included. In addition, the consultant should discuss the critical setting where the child's behavior was expected to change and provide a detailed description of the situations necessary for such a change.

Finally, a preliminary functional analysis should compare the antecedents and consequences surrounding the problem behavior to those necessary for attainment of the desired behavior. This discussion should be based on assessment procedures such as interview, direct observation, and/or standardized tests. Hence, the consultant integrates the baseline data, observational data, and

TABLE 5
Outline for Writing a Behavioral Consultation Case Report

I. Background Information
   A. Demographic Information on the Child
   B. Ecological Context of the Problem

II. Problem Definition
   A. Referral Problem
   B. Target Behaviors
   C. Desired Outcome Behaviors
   D. Critical Setting/Situations for Change
   E. Preliminary Functional Analysis

III. Problem Analysis
   A. Description of Assessment or Data Recording Procedures
   B. Rationale for Use of Data Collection Procedures
   C. Presentation and Discussion of Data

IV. Intervention Plan
   A. Basic Design
   B. Contingencies
   C. Criterion for Contingencies
   D. Acceptability of Intervention to Teacher/Parent and Child
   E. Personnel Involved in Intervention Implementation
   F. Setting and Time
   G. Resources
   H. Procedures for Promoting New Behaviors
   I. Procedures for Increasing Existing Behaviors
   J. Procedures for Reducing Interfering Problem Behaviors
   K. Procedures for Facilitating Generalization
   L. Treatment Integrity Checks

V. Plan Evaluation
   A. Change in Behavior via Direct Observation
   B. Change in Teacher/Parent Performance Ratings
   C. Mainstreamed Peer Comparison
   D. Outcome Interview with Significant Adults
   E. Intervention Side Effects

VI. Summary and Recommendations
   A. Summary of Results Obtained
   B. Discussion of Effectiveness
   C. Suggestions for Increasing Program Effectiveness
   D. Suggestions for Future Follow-up

problem identification and analysis interviews to analyze the discrepancy between the existing behavior and desired behavior. A sample of each observational data sheet used during the case should be included in the report.

A description of any intervention programs or procedures implemented during the process of consultation should be included in the section entitled *Intervention Plan*. The consultant should characterize the basic design of the plan according to variables such as the (a) time needed for implementation, (b) contingencies, (c) criterion for delivery of contingencies, (d) setting and time, and

(e) resources or materials. In addition, the consultant should specify clearly the procedures used for promoting new behaviors, increasing existing behaviors, and/or reducing interfering problem behaviors. A rationale describing why the particular intervention procedure(s) are relevant to the target problem is essential. In some cases, a treatment "package" consisting of many specific techniques (e.g., feedback, reinforcement, modeling) may be used. Identification of the individuals who are responsible for implementing the plan and a discussion of the degree to which the plan is acceptable to the teacher/parent and child also should be included. Finally, it is desirable to document the strategies used to facilitate generalization and to verify that the intervention plan was implemented as intended.

This list is intended to serve as a resource and should be considered carefully. The consultant must determine the variables most pertinent to the specific case; thus, it may be necessary to generate additional dimensions that adequately describe the intervention. Likewise, some of the intervention variables listed may not apply to all cases. It may be helpful to use headings or an outline format similar to that in Table 5 to facilitate notetaking during consultation interviews and post-treatment preparation of a clear and concise report.

A complete description of the *Intervention Evaluation Plan* should be provided, including methods used to evaluate the specific treatment components and to document changes in the child's behavior. Especially relevant will be data from the plan evaluation interview. The school psychologist should present the results of the program in the context of the data collected over the duration of the program and during the generalization or follow-up phases. For example, direct observations and ratings of the child's performance may provide documentation of intervention outcome. In addition, the consultant may evaluate the performance of a mainstreamed peer for comparison before and after the plan is initiated. At least one figure should be used to portray

the data collected, and the school psychologist should acknowledge any unique features of the data (e.g., absence, program not followed) or challenges that may have occurred. The consultant should also provide details regarding any side effects which may have resulted from the intervention plan.

The *Summary and Recommendations* should begin with a brief overview of the results obtained and a rationale for program effectiveness or failure. The consultant also should include suggestions for increasing the effectiveness of the program. Recommendations may provide suggestions for (a) future follow-up, (b) enhancing maintenance/generalization, and (c) subsequent intervention plans. These suggestions should identify the involved socialization agents (e.g., parents, teachers, peers) and relevant materials that may be useful for the child or treatment personnel in future work.

SUMMARY AND CONCLUSIONS

Behavioral consultation is a four stage problem-solving approach that uses applied behavior analysis as the basis for problem identification, analysis, intervention, and evaluation. The major features of behavioral consultation include its indirect service delivery approach, problem-solving activity, and collegial relationship.

Behavioral consultation has two principle goals. The first goal is to produce change in the child's behavior indirectly through collaborative problem solving between a consultant (school psychologist) and consultee (teacher/parent). A second, yet equally important goal of behavioral consultation is to provide knowledge and skills that facilitate teacher/parent effectiveness with similar problems in the future.

Behavioral consultation generally is recognized as a series of four stages that are used to implement the process of consultation (Bergan, 1977). These include problem identification, problem analysis, plan implementation, and plan evaluation. Each of these steps, with the exception of plan implementation, is accompanied by a formal interview process and specific objectives.

Research and practice in behavioral consultation have expanded rapidly. Recent interest in consultative methods as they impact the delivery of psychological services in the schools has resulted in increased attention to this area in the literature. This growing enthusiasm over the potential benefits of behavioral consultation is apparent in the numerous articles on the topic published recently in both the psychological and educational literature (Pryzwansky, 1986). As school psychologists have become interested in the integration of behavioral consultation with daily activities in the schools, questions regarding the process and outcome of consultation have surfaced. Studies have examined the application of behavioral principles in consultation to achieve changes in behavior and have compared the effectiveness of behavioral consultation to other forms of service delivery.

Research documenting the effectiveness of behavioral consultation has been organized around four areas of investigation: (a) outcome research, (b) process research, (c) practitioner research, and (d) training research (Gresham & Kendell, 1987). Research addressing outcomes of behavioral consultation document its effectiveness in remediating academic and behavior problems manifested by children and youths in school settings (Bergan & Tombari, 1976; Conoley & Conoley, 1982). Likewise, these same studies suggest that changes result in the teacher's and parent's behavior, knowledge, attitudes, and perceptions. Although behavioral consultation typically is directed toward a single client, it also has been applied successfully with groups (Bergan, 1977).

Typically, much of the process research has focused on problem identification, since the consultant's ability to elicit a clear description of the problem in behavioral terms has been identified as the best predictor of plan implementation and problem solution (Bergan & Tombari, 1975, 1976). Studies in this area also have focused on comparing behavioral consultation effectiveness with other forms of service delivery (Medway, 1979). To date,

it remains difficult to draw conclusions from the studies addressing variables associated with the process of consultation due to limitations in scope, theoretical base, and research methodology (Gresham & Kendell, 1987).

Studies on practitioner utilization have suggested that school-based consultation is a preferred activity for school psychologists (Gutkin & Curtis, 1982; Meacham & Peckam, 1978). Likewise, teachers and administrators view consultation as an essential aspect of school psychological services (Curtis & Zins, 1981). However, many practitioners identify limitations in actually implementing consultation due to time constraints and lack of consultee commitment (Gresham & Kendell, 1987).

Relatively little has been written about training school psychologists as consultants. Literature reviews (e.g., Gallessich, McDermott-Long, & Jennings, 1986) have indicated limitations in this area due to the absence of specific skills or mastery criteria to be used for teaching consultation. The training of behavioral consultants traditionally has emphasized basic competency as specified by the behavioral consultation model (Kratochwill & Bergan, 1978; Kratochwill & Van-Someren, 1985). Likewise, the effectiveness of behavioral consultants typically has been evaluated in terms of cognitive knowledge and verbalization skills associated with predefined objectives (Brown, Kratochwill, & Bergan, 1982; Kratochwill, VanSomeren, & Sheridan, 1989).

Three major approaches used for establishing competency in behavioral consultation include training through individualized, workshop, and self-instructional formats. Consultation verbalization skills, attainment of behavioral objectives, and child behavior change are all essential to the success of behavioral consultation. Factors such as entry issues, professional role definition, and consultant–consultee relationship development are all areas in need of further elaboration and refinement.

Overall, behavioral consultation in the schools is a rapidly growing area in need of further research. Future studies must utilize more sophisticated designs and measurement strategies that effectively evaluate variables in consultation. Careful scrutiny of behavioral consultation will impact its future use as an alternative to traditional assessment and intervention practices in educational settings and may result in an increased emphasis on the development of formalized training in school psychology programs. In turn, these developments would contribute to the practice of school psychology and positively impact the children and teachers and parents receiving these psychological and educational services.

ACKNOWLEDGMENTS

Preparation of this manuscript was supported in part through grants to the authors from the U.S. Department of Education, Office of Special Education and Rehabilitative Services. The contents of the manuscript reflect those of the authors and do not imply an endorsement by the U.S. Department of Education.

REFERENCES

Barlow, D. H., Hayes, S. C., & Nelson, R. O. (1984). *The scientist–practitioner: Research accountability in clinical educational settings.* New York: Pergamon Press.

Bergan, J. R. (1977). *Behavioral consultation.* Columbus, OH: Charles E. Merrill.

Bergan, J. R., & Kratochwill, T. R. (1990). *Behavioral consultation and therapy.* New York: Plenum Press.

Bergan, J. R., & Tombari, M. L. (1975). The analysis of verbal interactions occurring during consultation. *Journal of School Psychology, 14,* 3-14.

Bergan, J. R., & Tombari, M. L. (1976). Consultant skill and efficiency and the implementation and outcome of consultation. *Journal of School Psychology, 14,* 3-14.

Brown, D. K., Kratochwill, T. R., & Bergan, J. R. (1982). Training interview skills for problem identification: An analogue study. *Behavioral Assessment, 4,* 63-73.

Conoley, J. C., & Conoley, C. W. (1982). *School consultation: A guide to practice and training.* New York: Pergamon Press.

Dunst, C. J., & Trivette, C. M. (1988). Helping, helplessness, and harm. In J. C. Witt, S. N. Elliott, & F. M. Gresham (Eds.), *The handbook of behavior therapy in education* (pp. 343-376). New York: Plenum.

Elliott, S. N. (1988a). Acceptability of behavioral treatments: A review of variables that influence treatment selection. *Professional Psychology: Research and Practice, 19,* 68-80.

Elliott, S. N. (1988b). Acceptability of behavioral treatment in educational settings. In J. C. Witt, S. N. Elliott, & F. M. Gresham (Eds.), *The handbook of behavior therapy in education* (pp. 121-150). New York: Plenum Publishers.

Gallessich, J., McDermott-Long, K., & Jennings, S. (1986). Training of mental health consultants. In F. B. Mannino, E. J. Trickett, M. F. Shore, M. G. Kidder, & G. Levin (Eds.), *Handbook of mental health consultation* (pp. 279-317). Washington, DC: National Institute of Mental Health.

Gelfand, D. M., & Hartmann, D. P. (1984). *Child behavior analysis and therapy* (2nd ed.). New York: Pergamon.

Gresham, F. M. (1989). Assessment of treatment integrity in school consultation and prereferral intervention. *School Psychology Review, 18,* 37-50.

Gresham, F. M., & Kendell, G. K. (1987). School consultation research: Methodological critique and future research directions. *School Psychology Review, 16,* 306-316.

Grimes, J. (Ed.) (1983), *Communicating psychological information in writing.* Des Moines, IA: Department of Public Instruction.

Gutkin, T., & Curtis, M. (1982). School-based consultation: Theory and techniques. In C. R. Reynolds & T. B. Gutkin (Eds.), *The handbook of school psychology* (pp. 796-828). New York: Wiley.

Haring, N. G. (1988). A technology for generalization. In N. G. Haring (Ed.), *Generalization for students with severe handicaps: Strategies and solutions* (pp. 5-11). Seattle: University of Washington Press.

Kazdin, A. E. (1982). *Single-case research designs: Methods for clinical and applied settings.* New York: Oxford University Press.

Kazdin, A. E. (1989). *Behavior modification in applied settings* (Revised ed.). Homewood, IL: The Dorsey Press.

Kratochwill, T. R., & Bergan, J. R. (1978). Training school psychologists: Some perspectives on a competency-based behavioral consultation model. *Professional Psychology, 9,* 71-82.

Kratochwill, T. R., & Bergan, J. R. (in press). *Behavioral consultation in applied settings: An individual guide.* New York: Plenum Press.

Kratochwill, T. R., & VanSomeren, K. R. (1985). Barriers to treatment success in behavioral consultation: Current limitations and future directions. *Journal of School Psychology, 23,* 225-239.

Kratochwill, T. R., VanSomeren, K., & Sheridan, S. (1989). Training behavioral consultants: A competency-based model to teach interview skills. *Professional School Psychology, 4*, 41-58.

Kratochwill, T. R., & Morris, R. J. (Eds.). (in press). *The practice of child therapy* (2nd ed.). New York: Pergamon Press.

Kratochwill, T. R., Sheridan, S. M., & VanSomeren, K. R. (1988). Research in behavioral consultation: Current status and future directions. In J. F. West (Ed.), *School consultation: Interdisciplinary perspectives on theory, research, training, and practice* (pp. 77-102). Austin, TX: The Association of Educational and Psychological Consultants.

Martin, R. P. (1978). Expert and referent power: A framework for understanding and maximizing consultation effectiveness. *Journal of School Psychology, 16*, 49-55.

Martin, W. T. (1972). *Writing psychological reports.* Springfield, IL: Charles C Thomas.

McDougall, L. M., Reschly, D. J., & Corkery, J. M. (1988). Changes in referral interviews with teachers after behavioral consultation training. *Journal of School Psychology, 26*, 225-232.

Meacham, M. L., & Peckam, P. D. (1978). School psychologists at three-quarters century: Congruence between training, practice, preferred role and competence. *Journal of School Psychology, 16*, 195-206.

Medway, F. J. (1979). How effective is school consultation? A review of recent research. *Journal of School Psychology, 17*, 275-282.

Meyers, V., Liddell, A., & Lyons, M. (1977). Behavioral interviews. In A. R. Ciminero, K. S. Calhoun, & H. E. Adams (Eds.), *Handbook of behavioral assessment* (pp. 117-152). New York: John Wiley.

Ownby, R. L. (1987). *Psychological reports: A guide to report writing in professional psychology.* Brandon, VT: Clinical Psychological Publishing Company.

Parsons, R., & Meyers, J. (1984). *Developing consultation skills.* San Francisco: Jossey-Bass.

Pryzwansky, W. (1966). Indirect service delivery: Considerations for future research in consultation. *School Psychology Review, 15*, 239-243.

Reschly, D. K. (1988). Special education reform: School psychology revolution. *School Psychology Review, 17*, 465-481.

Smith, D. (1984). Practicing school psychologists: Their characteristics, activities, and populations served. *Professional Psychology, 15*, 798-810.

Stokes, T. F., & Baer, D. B. (1977). An implicit technology of generalization. *Journal of Applied Behavior Analysis, 10*, 349-367.

White, O. R., Liberty, K. A., Haring, N. G., Billingsley, F. F., Boer, M., Barrage, Connors, R., Forman, R., Fedorchak, G., Leber, B. D., Liberty-Layin, S., Miller, S., Opalski, Phifer, C., & Sessoms, I. (1988). Review and analysis of strategies for generalization. In N. G. Haring (Ed.), *Generalization for students with severe handicaps: Strategies and solutions* (pp. 15-51). Seattle: University of Washington Press.

Witt, J. C., & Elliott, S. N. (1983). Assessment in behavioral consultation: The initial interview. *School Psychology Review, 12*, 42-49.

Witt, J. C., & Elliott, S. N. (1985). Acceptability of classroom intervention strategies. In T. R. Kratochwill (Ed.), *Advances in school psychology* (Vol. IV, pp. 251-288). Hillsdale, NJ: Lawrence Erlbaum Associates, Inc.

Witt, J. C., & Martens, B. K. (1988). Problems with problem-solving consultation: A re-analysis of assumptions, methods, and goals. *School Psychology Review, 17*, 211-226.

ANNOTATED BIBLIOGRAPHY

Barlow, D. H. Hayes, S. C., & Nelson, R. O. (1984). *The scientist-practitioner: Research and accountability in clinical and educational settings.* New York: Pergamon Press.
This text outlines specific assessment and measurement strategies that can be used in consultation. The text is especially useful in outlining research designs and case study techniques that can be helpful during the treatment implementation and treatment monitoring phase of behavioral consultation.

Bergan, J. R., & Kratochwill, T. R. (1990). *Behavioral consultation and therapy.* New York: Plenum Press.
This book provides an extensive overview of behavioral consultation research and practice. The text provides detailed information for researchers and practitioners in the conduct of behavioral consultation. The text is accompanied by a companion self-instructional guide (see Kratochwill & Bergan in press).

Kazdin, A. E. (1989). *Behavior modification in applied settings* (revised edition). Homewood, IL: The Dorsey Press.
This text presents an overview of behavior modification techniques in applied settings. It is extremely useful in consultation in that it includes material directly relevant to implementing treatments in applied settings.

Kratochwill, T. R., & Bergan, J. R. (in press). *Behavioral consultation in applied settings: An individual guide.* New York: Plenum Press.
This book is a practitioner guidebook devoted to behavioral consultation in applied settings. It details the problem identification, problem analysis, treatment implementation, and treatment evaluation phases of behavioral consultation. Specific formats for interviews are provided within the text.

ATTACHMENT A
The Children's Intervention Rating Profile[a]

	I agree				I do not agree
1. The method used to deal with the behavior problem was fair.	+	+	+	+	+
2. This child's teacher was too harsh on him.	+	+	+	+	+
3. The method used to deal with the behavior may cause problems with this child's friends.	+	+	+	+	+
4. There are better ways to handle this child's problem than the one described here.	+	+	+	+	+
5. The method used by this teacher would be a good one to use with other children.	+	+	+	+	+
6. I like the method used for this child's behavior problem.	+	+	+	+	+
7. I think that the method used for this problem would help this child do better in school.	+	+	+	+	+

[a]Developed by Witt and Elliott (1983).

ATTACHMENT B
Treatment Evaluation Inventory Short Form (TEI–SF)

Please complete the items listed below by placing a checkmark on the line next to each question that best indicates how you feel about the treatment. Please read the items very carefully because a checkmark accidentally placed on one space rather than another may not represent the meaning you intended.

	Strongly Disagree	Disagree	Neutral	Agree	Strongly Agree
1. I find this treatment to be an acceptable way of dealing with the child's problem behavior.	_____	_____	_____	_____	_____
2. I would be willing to use this procedure if I had to change the child's problem behavior.	_____	_____	_____	_____	_____
3. I believe that it would be acceptable to use this treatment without children's consent	_____	_____	_____	_____	_____
4. I like the procedures used in this treatment.	_____	_____	_____	_____	_____
5. I believe this treatment is likely to be effective.	_____	_____	_____	_____	_____
6. I believe the child will experience discomfort during the treatment.	_____	_____	_____	_____	_____
7. I believe this treatment is likely to result in permanent improvement.	_____	_____	_____	_____	_____
8. I believe it would be acceptable to use this treatment with individuals who cannot choose treatments for themselves.	_____	_____	_____	_____	_____
9. Overall, I have a positive reaction to this treatment.	_____	_____	_____	_____	_____

11

Best Practices in Building-Level Public Relations

Carol Kelly
Jefferson County (Colorado) Schools

OVERVIEW

Ongoing public relations efforts at the building level are an integral, vital part of the school psychologist's role. This chapter provides the practitioner with ideas and information necessary for starting or improving building-level public relations efforts. The need for public relations activities, explanation of fundamental concepts, a planning process, suggested building-level activities, and skills for working with the media are discussed.

The purpose of public relations for school psychologists is to build understanding and goodwill between us and our various audiences. For us to continue to support children, we must let parents, fellow educators, and community members know what we are doing and what we can do.

Public image is a major factor in determining the role we play and the services we provide. In 1952 Edward Bernays, the father of public relations, pointed out that educational improvement efforts were dependent upon a better public understanding of our schools. Pollster George Gallup (1982) stated that one of the biggest challenges educators faced was to let people know about the quality programs being carried out in the schools.

Confidence in public education is eroding and the competition for public funds is fierce. District budget allocations are under close public scrutiny. Services that decisionmakers know the least about are most often the first to go. Any position that is not solidified is in jeopardy.

If school psychologists were to go about doing their jobs in an exceptional manner, but without letting other people know about it, our days in the schools would be numbered. As long as there are parents, board members, business people, legislators, and others who do not understand our goals, skills and competencies, public relations efforts are necessary. We must work to convince others of our value in fostering children's academic success.

Public support leads to quality school psychology services. When lines of communication are open between us and our local school communities, we are better able to ascertain local needs and issues, and improve services to children accordingly.

Attitudes about school psychologists are determined at the local building level. Public relations efforts at the district, state, or national level serve to reinforce attitudes that have been generated by school psychologists in the buildings they serve.

By establishing strong relationships with our various publics at the local level, school psychologists become perceived as a proactive force contributing to the overall quality of education. School psychologists must design communications plans specific to their individual assignments. No one can do this for us.

Definition

The National School Public Relations Association (1982) offered the following definition. "Public relations is a planned and systematic two-way process of communication between an educational organization and its internal and external publics. It is a plan of action to encourage public involvement and to earn public understanding and support" (p. 2).

John Wherry (1988), executive director of the National School Public Relations Association, stated that the term was synonymous with the "practice of social responsibility," or doing the right thing in the public interest. He summed up public relations this way: "Do an effective job and let people know about the successes and challenges."

Public relations begins with quality school psychology services. It is not a cover-up or substitute for excellence. Communications efforts cannot convince anyone for very long that a good job is being done if it is not.

BASIC CONSIDERATIONS

To implement a successful public relations effort, the school psychologist needs commitment along with understanding of some fundamental concepts. This section covers identification of key publics, communication techniques, and issues management.

Identifying Key Publics

Instead of the general public, it is useful to think of specific audiences with whom relationships should be improved. The most effective message and approach can best be determined by considering the needs and interests of individual groups.

Internal publics are those that reside within the school family: professionals and support staff including teachers, students, administrators, secretaries, substitutes, custodians, board members, aides, and student teachers.

According to public relations veterans, the initial step in starting a public relations program is to "start internal." Community members listen to and trust information that comes directly from people within the school.

By involving and communicating with internal publics, school psychologists build a foundation that will lead to more successful external projects. Audiences within the school family can lend invaluable support to public relations efforts; they can just as easily undermine them. Credibility is established when strong relationships are maintained through positive personal interaction with those you directly serve.

External audiences are groups who are outside the school, or have a more indirect association with the building. These include parents, community agencies, churches, civic organizations, senior citizens, the business community, and realtors. Most external public relations efforts focus on parents.

Though parents are a critical group, educators need to keep in mind that nearly three-fourths of U.S. households have no children in school and that there are fewer school-age children than senior citizens. These voters and taxpayers are increasingly interested in the cost associated with maintaining quality education.

Communication efforts with external audiences will usually result in a more positive attitude toward support services in the schools. An informed public is more likely to support schools than not to support them (Kindred, Bagin, & Gallagher, 1984).

Mass versus Interpersonal Communication

Channels of communication should vary according to the intended audience. Mass communication techniques are useful for imparting information, making people aware of a specific situation, or reinforcing attitudes. Examples include newsletters, public service announcements, radio and television coverage, slide shows, films, posters, and brochures.

Too often, school personnel rely

exclusively on such sources. These strategies do little, however, to influence people's opinions or change behavior.

Interpersonal communication involves face-to-face interaction between two people and is more effective for influencing attitudes than mass media approaches. For persuasion to take place, two-way person-to-person communication must exist. Studies show that people who acquire their information about the schools directly from board members and school employees tend to support the schools more than people who get their information from other sources (Kindred, et al., 1984).

When people think about planning a vacation to a new place, they tend to rely more on a trusted neighbor's opinion than a glossy travel brochure. We generally have more confidence in people with whom a relationship has been established.

Examples of situations that involve interpersonal communication include staffings, back-to-school nights, parent conferences, staff meeting presentations, and telephone calls. Other opportunities for establishing interpersonal communications include church groups, beauty salons, bridge clubs, grocery stores, golf courses, and athletic clubs. Familiarize yourself with key community organizations and meeting places.

When using interpersonal communication, be cognizant of both your personal communication style and that of the receiver. This will help you come up with the best plan to get your intended message across. Keep in mind, for example, whether the receiver seems to be an authoritarian administration, a withdrawn parent, a controlling teacher, or an understanding school board member who looks to others to solve problems cooperatively. Does the person have a hidden agenda or anger that must be diffused? Be sensitive to cultural and socioeconomic differences.

Finally, keep in mind that positive public relationships are formed through a low-key, educational approach. Essential elements include authenticity, credibility, and trust. People develop confidence in you when you demonstrate

expertise in your field and display understanding of viewpoints different from your own.

Issues Management

Issues management is a key emerging trend in public relations. Public relations can be defined in terms of "generic PR" that is put into place for basic support, or "issues management PR." To ensure success, school psychologists must be aware of their publics and keep up with their thinking. Services can then be readjusted to coincide with shifting public interests. Planning from the issues, rather than being managed by them, allows school psychologists to take more control over the provision of services; it requires a proactive stance and awareness of relevant community problems and trends.

To find out what the issues are, scan publications that are read in the school community, maintain links with parent groups, visit the faculty lounge, and read periodicals such as *Education Week* and the *Kappan.* Look for concerns that you can do something about, and that will make you more effective at the building level.

Each year the National School Public Relations Association publishes the ten top educational issues, many of which have direct relation to school psychology services. Some of the issues identified have been parenting skills, the dropout rate, at-risk students, childhood stress, teacher burnout, child care, AIDS, and educational restructuring.

With an issues management orientation, your public relations program would be designed around needs and problems specific to your community. Projects could include offering a parenting class, chairing a drop-out prevention committee, working with the principal to improve staff morale, or helping to organize an after-school daycare program. Other efforts could include providing information on homework completion, school discipline, or improving motivation. Dealing constructively with local needs will result in a positive attitude from the staff and community and help build support for services to children.

BEST PRACTICES IN BUILDING-LEVEL PUBLIC RELATIONS

This section outlines a public relations planning process, presents suggested activities to communicate to various audiences, and offers tips for working with the media.

Getting Started

School psychologists will find a four-step process useful for devising an effective building-level public relations program. A planned approach will be more efficient than implementing ideas from someone else's list or, worse, responding to difficult crisis situations such as a proposal to reduce support staff.

The likelihood of developing workable, effective plans is increased when the school psychologist involves others in the process. Consult with colleagues who are well respected in their school communities, with your school principals, and with your supervisor.

Step 1. The first step consists of an *analysis* of the present situation. What groups are you already reaching out to and what are current perceptions? It is likely that you already are promoting school psychology in many ways.

Identify all the audiences you likely are reaching through your current efforts. Consider why communication with these groups is important and the effectiveness of present efforts. List additional audiences with whom you would like to communicate. Decide what they need to know, what their current perceptions are, and what you would like them to be.

A helpful tool in this beginning step is a "communications grid" (Figure 1). List target audiences across the top of a page. Write ongoing activities down the left side. Check all groups that are reached by each activity. For example, a regular article in the school's newsletter may reach parents, teachers, administrators, and support staff. Consider each school individually.

The grid will help you take inventory

of current activities and reveal where special efforts are needed. Think of audiences that may be uninformed about how school psychology contributes to education or those that may have negative preconceived attitudes toward the profession.

Find ways to determine directly the perceptions, priorities, and concerns that others have about school psychology services. Talk to opinion leaders in your school community. Listen to what teachers, parents, and administrators have to say.

A brief needs assessment can help the practitioner make appropriate decisions. Many schools conduct annual student and/or community surveys. Request that questions about psychological services be included. What perceptions do students, school personnel, and community members have? Are others aware of the broad range of services you provide? What are major concerns? Your public relations program can be tied to results of the needs assessment and your goals of service.

Before designing specific plans, find out all you can about your school community. For example, how many residents have children in school? What is the average income level? What are employment patterns? How many mothers work? What is the education background of parents?

Step 2. Once this information is gathered, school psychologists are ready for the next step, *planning* communication activities. Determine which audiences should be targeted and what messages need to be shared to help you reach your goals. Communications objectives may be to impart knowledge, improve perceptions and attitudes, or change behaviors. Goals may be to secure the hiring of additional psychologists, to gain a better reputation, or to get more cooperation from teachers. Think about your desired future versus your predicted future.

Set time lines, consider available resources, and ascertain any costs associated with your plans. It may be possible to coordinate your activities with public relations plans that your building, district, or state association is already implement-

Activity	Audience	Students	Teachers	Support Staff	Administrators	Parents	Senior Citizens	Non-parents
School Newsletter Column			x	x	x	x		
Faculty In-service			x		x			
Parenting Class						x		
PTA Book Shelf Project						x		
Student Council Sponsor*		x	x	x	x	x	x	x

*Student council sponsors community food drive, aide appreciation day, and adopt-a-grandparent program.

FIGURE 1. Sample communications grid.

ing. Other valuable resources may include your school principal, the district's media center, or the audio visual department.

You may benefit from expertise and materials that your district public relations officer can provide. Find out how this person can help you with your efforts.

It probably is not realistic to develop a plan that meets all areas of need. Each year, focus efforts on audiences most critical to your support. Set measurable objectives.

Consider a "marketing" approach. Identify audiences you want to reach and develop messages that emphasize how school psychology services meet their needs. Tell how school psychologists help teachers, make administrators' jobs easier, or help parents raise children. When messages appeal to the receiver's needs, they will be listened to with more interest.

Determine what strategies and communication channels will most likely help meet objectives for each target audience. Think of which channels your audiences believe and use.

Develop an organized plan about how you can best communicate your needs and services. Involve others in maintaining and improving support for children. Nothing proactive happens without communication.

Step 3. The next step is *implementation*, carrying out plans to get the intended message across. Good ideas need a support strategy. The most effective plans will use both mass and interpersonal communication techniques. Repeating a message through a variety of sources will strengthen what you are saying and make it better understood by your audiences.

Step 4. Finally, public relations efforts need to be *evaluated*. You can do this by looking at your original objectives and determining the success level of these activities. Identify modifications that need to be made in the future. From this analysis, activities can be maintained, deleted, added, or modified.

Many methods can be used for obtaining feedback, both positive and negative. By listening carefully, you will gain an accurate picture of the effectiveness of your efforts. For most accurate information, use a variety of sources.

A formal scientific system usually will not be necessary to get reliable feedback. Informally evaluate the success of your plans by using the following questions as guidelines: Do students bring friends in to your office or refer classmates in need? Do parents express appreciation of your services? Do they give your name to friends whose children may be having trouble in school? Do people make comments about useful articles you write in the school newsletter? Did the community strongly oppose a district proposal to reduce psychological services? Are you invited to make presentations in your community? Keep a scrapbook of any written feedback you receive and copies of any news clippings.

Attend to negative reactions and look for ways to address them in new plans. Encourage those that have criticisms to brainstorm alternatives with you.

This four-step cycle can be repeated each school year. When efforts have been evaluated, it is time to go back to Step 1. Reevaluate and modify plans on a continuing basis.

A Menu of Suggested Ideas

What follows are activities designed to build positive relationships with parents, administrators, teachers, support staff, students, and the local community. Though organized around selected audiences, much overlap exists. For example, an activity listed under the parent section may also reach teachers and administrators. These activities will be most successful when they are coordinated into your overall plan.

Parents

- Make yourself visible. Circulate at school functions such as back-to-school nights, open houses, special events, and social activities.
- Distribute handouts on common areas of interest such as self-esteem, study skills, and stress. Use NASP *Communique* parent handouts.
- Project a professional image: Use business and appointment cards, hang diplomas and awards, and dress in a professional manner.
- Make regular phone calls to parents of children on your caseload. Commend them for their efforts and their children's accomplishments.
- Be sensitive to the fact that nonnative parents may not understand everything you are saying. Speak slowly and learn about cultural norms of diverse community groups.
- Work toward home–school cooperation and actively involve parents in your service delivery.
- Write a regular school newsletter column.
- Maintain a flexible schedule for meetings with parents who are unable to come in during school hours. Include fathers and step-parents.
- Make a home visit when parents cannot or will not come to the school.
- Return phone calls promptly, the same day whenever possible.
- Establish a liaison with your parent-teacher organizations.
- Welcome opportunities to talk to parent groups. They are always interested in hearing about topics such as self-esteem, motivation, childhood stress, and parent–child communication. Do not wait to be invited.
- Offer a parenting class.
- Work with the PTA to develop a parent shelf in the school library. Write book reviews in the school newsletter.
- Communicate in simple language. You will not build confidence when people cannot understand you. Avoid jargon in reports and in face-to-face meetings.

Teachers

- Greet teachers and other staff members by name each day.
- Eat lunch in the staff lounge. Vary your lunch period to socialize with a larger number of staff.
- Introduce yourself at a beginning of the year faculty meeting. In new assignments, let the staff know how best to use your services.
- Involve teachers in any plans relating to your services with students.
- Give presentations to the faculty. Consider topics such as self-esteem, teacher stress, classroom management, and parent conferences.
- During School Psychology Week, bring refreshments to the lounge with a sign saying "Help me celebrate School Psychology Week."
- Hold regular open office hours.
- Volunteer to serve on building committees. Consider public relations or a school improvement group.
- Be a part of the school family. Attend faculty meetings and school social functions.

Students

- Maintain quality services and positive, caring, day-to-day relationships. Community opinions largely reflect student comments about school.
- Make presentations about your services to students.
- Sponsor a student group such a student council, honor society, or running club.
- Help develop and participate in student recognition programs.
- Send congratulatory notes or "happy grams."
- Continue to develop your knowledge and your skills by attending classes, taking workshops, and consulting with colleagues.
- Make positive referrals to the principal when students have been successful.
- Greet students by name around the building and in the halls. Walk through the cafeteria from time to time.

- Attend special events such as plays, field trips, assemblies, and award presentations.
- Consider alternative settings for sessions with students. Take a walk, sit on the swings, shoot baskets, or meet for lunch.
- Take students out to lunch when they have accomplished a major goal. Let them invite classmates.

School Community

- Become a visible, indispensable resource. Let community members know what the problems and issues are that children face and how your services help.
- Patronize local businesses, including those run by students' parents.
- Know the facts about your schools and district: board members, demographics, dropout rates, board policies, test scores, district strengths and weaknesses.
- Nominate individuals for district, state, or national recognitions. Consider a NASP Certificate of Appreciation.
- Write letters to the editor, guest opinions, or editorials about community issues for the local newspaper.
- Become involved in community activities such as church groups, sports programs, or service groups.
- Integrate school psychology activities and information into American Education Week events.
- Arrange media or newspaper coverage of special projects or events.
- Work with other service providers to sponsor a Saturday family workshop with a selection of speakers on various topics of interest to the community.

Administrators

- Establish a positive working relationship with your schools' leaders. Find out their interests, strengths, and leadership styles.
- Keep administrators abreast of your activities.

- Hold regular "lunch bunch" meetings with at-risk students along with your principal.
- Work with your principal in mutual areas of concern such as school climate, parent relations, reducing dropouts, and staff morale.
- Do not set yourself up for failure. Underpromise and overdeliver. Meet deadlines early and anticipate school needs.

Support Staff

- Keep in mind that the best-known people in the school are usually the nonprofessionals: bus drivers, custodians, and secretaries. They are most likely to live in the school neighborhood.
- Secretaries talk to more people in a month than most people do is a year; they are the "voice" of your school. Develop good relationships.
- Offer a behavior management in-service for teacher aides.
- Participate in appreciation days and events for support staff members.
- Recognize any special efforts.

Working with the Media

One way to improve communications with the community and foster a supportive attitude for school psychology is through the local news media. This is one of the primary ways parents and people without children find out about the school. The first step in establishing a relationship with the local media is finding out who covers educational news in your community. Call local newspaper, television, or radio stations directly for this information.

Your district public relations office can ease media relations for you. They may provide contacts, write news releases, or arrange for media coverage of events.

The media can help with building-level public relations efforts in many ways. They can send reporters to cover programs such as divorce groups, drug prevention assemblies, or social skills units. News sources can provide advance publicity about upcoming events such as parenting classes or talks to the PTA. Academic success, learning difficulties, stress, depression, discipline, and other issues that school psychologists address make for interesting feature story topics.

What is news? Good publicity depends on knowing what makes good news. You are the best judge of what should be of interest to the community. Send in news releases when you attend a convention, initiate a new program or service, make a presentation, receive a special award or grant, or are elected to a position in your professional association.

A key concept in story ideas is *timeliness*. Think of stories that are related to the time of year. Summer vacation activities, holiday pressures, children's fears (Halloween), adapting to a new school at the beginning of the school years, and junior high adjustment are a few examples. Do not forget to tie into national events and trends such as at-risk students, the divorce rate, and the latchkey children. Let people know what school psychologists are doing to counter these trends.

News releases. The most common way of letting the media know about upcoming events is by sending a news release. You will be more likely to get a favorable response if you adhere to the following guidelines.

- Send the release on a preprinted masthead. Use school stationery or a district news release form.
- Releases should be typewritten, double- or triple-spaced on standard-sized paper. Type only on one side and keep the release to one or two pages.
- Use the "inverted pyramid" style. Include the who, what, when, where, and how in the first paragraph. Following this quick summary of major facts, include information in descending order of importance. This allows editors to cut from the bottom of the story without having to rewrite it.
- Keep your message brief and concise. Omit needless words. Use the active voice.

- Indent paragraphs. Include no more than two to three sentences in each. Longer paragraphs lose readers.
- Use wide margins. This allows room for editing the release.
- Use first and last names: "Dr. Bill Armer received the award," not "Armer" or "Dr. Armer."
- Write releases in the third person, avoiding use of first-person references such as "we," "our," and "your."
- Eliminate jargon and write out any acronyms.
- For best readability, write at or below the ninth grade level. Fewer than 10 words out of 100 should have more than three syllables.
- Sentences should be short. The average length for best readability is no more than 19 words.
- Include a fact sheet about your school and/or school psychology.
- Send out releases 10 days to 2 weeks prior to any event. Mail them to a specific person.
- Designate the end of the release with "# # #" centered. Then clearly indicate the name of a person to contact for further information along with home and work phone numbers. Reporters often work day and evening hours.
- If you are not comfortable writing a full-fledged release, use a simple form. Figure 2 offers an example.

When your release is used, send a note of appreciation. Even if you follow all of the guidelines, your news may not be covered. Papers and news broadcasts have limited space and competition is keen. Try again.

Tips for Public Speaking and Interviews

School psychologists are often asked to make presentations to teachers, parents, or the school board. Occasionally practitioners are called upon by television, radio, or newspaper reporters to comment on a local issue or a crisis situation. The following suggestions are offered to help you present yourself as an effective and credible information source.

- Enroll in a public speaking course or group like Toastmasters to hone your skills.
- Consider factors relating to your audience such as education level, ethnic diversity, age, and income level.
- When asked to make a presentation, offer knowledge that will be of interest to your audience. A talk on school psychology, per se, will usually not be of much concern.
- Know your topic. Always take time to thoroughly prepare. Avoid on-the-spot interviews.
- Anticipate information your source will want to know. If possible, find out what questions will be asked. Prepare an organized information sheet.
- Even in a crisis situation, ask if you can call back in half an hour so that you can gather your thoughts and information. Outline the course of action being taken.
- Be honest. Admit problems and state what is being done to address them.
- Do say "I don't know," rather than bluff your way through a response. Offer to find the information.
- Maintain eye contact with your audience/interviewer.
- Do not speculate or answer "What if?" questions.
- Pause when collecting your thoughts. No "uh's" or "ah's." Pauses can be edited from recorded interviews.
- Eliminate buzz words, jargon, accusations, and negative comments.
- Respond with positive, complete quotable statements. Prepare 30-second quotes before the interview.
- Do not say "No comment" or "Off the record." Give a valid reason for declining to comment, such as maintaining confidentiality. If you do not want to hear or read about it, do not say it.
- Smile. Be excited about your topic. Use a warm and caring tone. Vary the rate and pitch of your speech. Keep your hands at your side. Gesture to emphasize points, but do not overdo.
- Learn the technique of "bridging": taking the conversation from where the interviewer may try to direct it to where you want it to go.

READ ALL ABOUT US!

Ust this form to notify local media or your district public relations office about interesting programs, projects, or awards, involving students, staff, or the community. Include as much detailed information as possible. Attach any flyers or other information about the event. Submit 2-3 weeks before the event.

_____   _____

School or Department   Date

1. Who: (People involved, title, grades) _____

_____

2. What: (Describe project, program award) _____

_____

3. Where: (Place and address) _____

_____

4. When: (Date and time) _____

5. Why and How: _____

_____

6. Points of Special Interest: _____

_____

_____

Contact Person: _____

Work phone: _____   Home phone: _____

FIGURE 2. Sample News Release Form. (Form courtesy of Jefferson County Schools, Colorado Communications Services)

- Tape yourself, both when you practice and when you present.
- Present yourself as a credible source. Do not wear clothes that might distract from your message.
- Recognize what is remembered in any presentation or conversation: appearance, 55%; voice, 38%; and content, 7%.

SUMMARY

Establishing strong relationships with audiences within the school community is essential. Attitudes that parents, community members, and educators hold about school psychological services are determined at the local building level. Planned communication creates understanding and support of the assistance our profession provides to children. The delivery of quality services to students is a prerequisite for successful public relations efforts.

A development and implementation cycle should be an ongoing part of the school psychologist's yearly routine. As a first step, current efforts are examined and information about the local school community is gathered. Next, priority audiences are determined along with the information each group needs to know. After planning and executing programs, practitioners find strategies to secure feedback and evaluate the effectiveness of their efforts.

Every school psychologist must attend to public relations activities at the building level. The profession will only be able to continue to meet children's needs to the extent that we build confidence in the services we provide.

REFERENCES

Bagin, D. (1972). *School communications ideas that work.* Woodstown, NJ: Communicaid, Inc.

Bagin, D. (1985). *Evaluating your school PR investment.* Arlington, VA: National School Public Relations Association.

Bernays, E. (1952). *Public relations.* Norman, OK: University of Oklahoma Press.

Gallop, G. (1982, December). Address to Glassboro State College Chapter of Phi Delta Kappa, Glassboro, NJ.

National School Public Relations Association. (1972). *Evaluation instruments for educational public relations programs.* Arlington, VA: Author.

National School Public Relations Association. (1982). *Participant workbook: School communication workshop, building level.* Arlington, VA: Author.

National School Public Relations Association. (1986). *Planning your school PR investment.* Arlington, VA: Author.

Wherry, J. (1988, July). *Ten top for 1988–1989 and what to do about them.* Paper presented at the National School Public Relations Association National Seminar, New Orleans.

ANNOTATED BIBLIOGRAPHY

Davis, R. (1986). *School public relations: The complete book.* Arlington, VA: National School Public Relations Association.
This practical "how to" text covers latest developments in effective building-level public relations programs.

Kindred, L. W., Bagin, D., & Gallagher, D. R. (1984). *The school and community relations.* Englewood Cliffs, NJ: Prentice-Hall.
In addition to providing expanded explanations of essential public relations concepts, this authoritative textbook offers worthwhile sections on oral presentations, radio and television basics, and preparing printed material.

National School Public Relations Association. (1980). *Basic School PR Kit.* Arlington, VA: Author.
The kit is designed to provide practical help for those starting a building-level public relations program. Guides are included in essential areas: *Involving all your publics, Building level PR programs, Internal Communication, PR for special programs, Working with the media,* and *Survey, feedback.*

Prus, J. S. (1987). *Public information/public relations: A sourcebook of projects for school psychology associations.* Washington, DC: National Association of School Psychologists.
Projects initiated by several state associations are described. Includes sections on product distribution, media coverage, and names and addresses of school psychologists willing to serve as resources.

12

Best Practices in Communicating with Parents

Bruce F. Jensen
Northern Trails Area Education Agency
Clear Lake, Iowa

Margaret L. Potter
Moorhead State University

OVERVIEW

Perhaps no aspect of the school psychologist's responsibilities is more important than communication with parents. If accomplished in an effective manner, good communication may lead to a productive collaboration on behalf of the child. On the other hand, if communication is poorly accomplished, obstacles may be erected that will stand in the way of an effective home–school relationship. Furthermore, poor communication on the part of the school psychologist may result in parental misunderstandings that affect a parent's perception of a child's motivations and behavior and that may even influence the interactions and relationship that the parents have with their child.

The recognition of the importance of skilled, sensitive communication of information between professionals and parents and recognition of barriers to effective communication is not new (Sarason, 1959). However, this topic has received increased attention since the passage of the Education for All Handicapped Children Act of 1975 (Public Law 94-142) and its emphasis on the role of parents in educational decision making. PL 94-142 affirms the "partnership" of parents and school in contrast to the previous model of the school as the final authority in special education programming decisions (Hoff, Fenton, Yoshida, & Kaufman, 1978). The Education of the Handicapped Act Amendments of 1986 (PL 99-457) adds even more emphasis to the role of the family in the education of children who are handicapped. (See the chapter by Barnett in this volume.) Furthermore, it is part of the ethical standards of the profession of school psychology to communicate openly and effectively with parents (see Appendix II, NASP Principles for Professional Ethics).

There have been numerous excellent books, chapters, and articles on parent/professional communication published in recent years (e.g., Dunst, Trivette, & Deal, 1988; Kroth, 1985; Seligman, 1979; Teglasi, 1985). The basic principles that appear across authors, and that underlie this chapter as well, are a commitment to genuine interpersonal respect and a commitment to helping parents be truly knowledgeable and effective partners in their children's education.

The communication of information from school psychologist to parents is much more than the reporting of data at a staffing. While that data sharing is often a key event, it occurs within a much larger communications context. If that larger context is ignored, there is little likelihood of truly effective communication.

While the basic principles of good

communication remain consistent across situations, the way these principles are applied may vary according to the needs of the particular parents involved. This chapter addresses communication considerations for a number of different types of parents. The categories used are not exhaustive nor mutually exclusive; information in each may be relevant in other cases as well.

BASIC CONSIDERATIONS

The relationship between the school psychologist and the parents should be one of collaboration and common problem solving. This relationship cannot exist without mutual respect and without a shared knowledge base. There must be an information flow not only from the psychologist and other school personnel to the parents, but also from the parents to the professionals. In many cases, it is the school psychologist who controls this information flow in both directions. Not only do school psychologists and other professionals control the nature and content of the information presented by them to parents, but by their attitudes and the information they elicit from parents, they influence the amount and type of information contributed by the parents. Effective melding of information from both parents and professionals should result in a perception of the student and the student's problems that neither party could have arrived at separately.

School psychologists need to engage in some reflection and self-examination in order to be certain of their own feelings about the proper involvement of parents in the educational process. It is helpful for psychologists to take the perspective of a parent and contemplate the expectations, roles, and communication that would be desired if the psychologist were engaged in an interaction with the school as a parent. Such a "walking in the shoes" perspective should help provide a sensitivity and respect for parents that is fundamental to good communication.

We recognize that many times professionals are dealing directly with only one of a child's parents. The term *parents* is used as best practices are described because best practice is to communicate directly with both parents whenever possible. The involvement of nontraditional family structures and working parents often makes it difficult to communicate directly with both parents; however, as Sarason (1959) pointed out, one should never assume that both parents have the same conception of a problem. Communicating directly with both parents not only reduces the chances of miscommunication, but also involves them personally in the problem-solving process, increasing the investment of both parents in working toward effective interventions.

BEST PRACTICES

Parents New to Special Education

For parents who have never had any contact with the special education system, the language, procedures, and concepts can be overwhelming. Just as we recommend presenting new information to students in a variety of ways to increase understanding, we should not expect all parents to understand information presented in only one way, with only one presentation, and in large quantities.

If the goal of communication is understanding, not only do we have a responsibility to communicate with parents the information specifically relevant to their children, but we must also educate them in the background information that makes understanding specific information possible. Hoff et al. (1978) argued that informed consent in placement and programming decisions is unlikely solely on the basis of parents' participation in a team staffing. Parents must understand the process as well as the content involved in reaching decisions about their children's programs.

When parents have been involved with school staff from the time concerns are first raised about a student's progress, and have been involved throughout the prereferral intervention process, they will have a basis upon which to build understanding if the case moves into the formal special education referral and assessment system, with all of its due process procedures and technical jargon. These parents already will have a sense of the staff involved and the nature of the concerns and can devote more attention to understanding the more sophisticated aspects of referral, assessment, and decision making.

Along with verbal explanations of special education procedures and jargon, written materials addressing these areas should be made available to parents early on in any situation that may lead to the parents' being asked to make a decision involving special education identification or programming. An informational packet might include such items as (a) a glossary of terms; (b) names of support staff and their role descriptions; (c) discussions of due process rights and responsibilities, protection in evaluation procedures, and least restrictive environment principles; (d) sample copies of forms that may be used by the school with an explanation of the purpose of each form; (e) a description of special and regular education services options; (f) a summary of the state's and other district's qualification criteria for service in various disability areas; and (g) a list of resources, such as books available in the local library or through a bookstore and a list of addresses for parent groups and informational services (ARC, ACLD, Closer Look, advocacy groups, etc.).

Familiarity with at least one person within the school will increase the chances that parents will feel comfortable enough to ask questions to clarify areas they do not understand. That contact person should be viewed by team members as a valuable link with the parents, and use should be made of that link by other team members. Additionally, the use of a parent advocate is sometimes helpful for parents new to the special education system. The advocate should have information and skills that will help the parents more completely understand and participate in conferences and staffings. Along with people specifically trained as parents' advocates, this role may be filled by another parent more experienced in special

education rules and procedures, or by a friend or community person who is able to provide support and an additional perspective.

It should be made clear to the parents that parents often do not understand everything the first time around, that questions and requests for repetition of information are encouraged and expected at any time. These kinds of statements to parents should be accompanied by genuine encouragement of questions, and follow-ups to verify understanding and to answer further questions. For example, before leaving a staffing, the parents might be asked to summarize in their own words their understanding of what took place in the meeting. Also, the school contact person should give the parents a telephone call a day or two after a staffing to see if there are any further questions or concerns. This follow-up is especially useful when one parent has had to relay information to the other parent.

Parents of a student newly identified as handicapped are having to deal not only with all of the factual information presented to them, they are dealing with the emotional impact of having a child identified as handicapped. While the inclination of the psychologist may be to temper the "bad news" with euphemisms and assurances that "it is not as bad as it seems," this often only makes the psychologist feel better while doing the parents a disservice. Parents usually would rather have information about their child presented in a clear, honest, and straightforward, yet tactful, manner (Murray, 1985; Teglasi, 1985). Often a diagnosis of a handicap just confirms suspicions they had already had, and it may actually be a relief to be able to put a name to the problem. Even in cases in which the diagnosis is not unexpected, dealing with the emotional impact of the key information presented may preclude understanding of any further information in a single meeting. Thus, it is important to periodically check for understanding and to assume that information probably will need to be repeated. Tape recording of staffings for parents is one way to help them deal with all of the information presented.

Information presented to parents should always be put in context with an emphasis not on the data, but on what the data mean. The relationship of data collected to other information about the child and to expectations for the child is what is important. Data presented without such a context are meaningless. Particular care must be taken if numbers are reported because it is numbers that often are remembered, not the explanation of the numbers. To a parent, a change of IQ from 102 to 99 may be viewed as a significant loss in spite of assurances to the contrary from the school psychologist.

Some parents find it very difficult to acknowledge or accept the suggestion that their child is experiencing difficulties. In these cases, it is important to talk about the specific behaviors the child is exhibiting rather than too quickly discussing diagnostic categories. Parents for whom denial is an issue are more likely to accept a description of what the child is doing rather than what the child "is" in a categorical sense.

Skeptical parents usually are more willing to accept the fact that their child has a problem if the psychologist's opinion is based upon an explanation of behavior that is data-based rather than highly inferential. Overt behavior should be emphasized. Frequency counts and graphs that depict the problematic behavior, especially in relation to behavior of other students in the school (local norms) are often helpful and convincing. Data that have been gathered across situations by several different observers or assessors lend further credibility to conclusions. This is especially true if the data gatherers include people the parents trust and, most importantly, the parents themselves. Information from interviews with the parents and from behavior rating scales completed by the parents may be extremely useful in this regard. Encouraging the parents to observe in the child's classes and to compile data at home not only may serve as a source of further assessment data, but may provide the parents with an important perspective on their child's academic and emotional/behavioral skills. Involving the parents in the assessment process helps them become invested in the process and in the conclusions that are reached.

By virtue of the title "psychologist" the school psychologist may be the most intimidating person on the team to the parent. Parents may perceive the psychologist to be examining not only their child, but also themselves as parents (Melton, 1984). A clear explanation of the role and function of a school psychologist may help put parents more at ease and thus make them more receptive to the information presented by the psychologist.

Experienced Parents

Parents who have had previous experience in dealing with the school psychologist and the special education system are often ready to function as full partners and collaborators. It is important for the psychologist to acknowledge and make use of the knowledge that experienced parents have. The psychologist also should determine if the parents have an accurate understanding of their child's present situation. A brief review of the educational history of the student, basic procedures, and jargon tends to serve as a good introduction to subsequent meetings once an ongoing relationship has been established.

There are invariably changes and new information that need to be shared with experienced parents. As schools look at new practices or innovations in programming, the school psychologist can play a role in involving parents and in helping them to prepare for these changes. Experienced parents must be kept informed of changes in rules and procedures and how such changes might affect their child. This sharing of information fits into the school psychologist's larger responsibility of continuing to educate the parents concerning the needs of their child and the resources and community systems that are available to them. This education is a part of empowering parents so that they increasingly can assume an advocacy and case management role on behalf of their child.

It is important for all parents to learn to help direct and manage their children's programs. As a family moves from one school district to another, as the educators who work with the student change, and as a student, especially an adolescent handicapped student, reaches the transition point between school and community services, the parents remain the constant factor that provides continuity for their child. The school psychologist through periodic and ongoing communication with parents can help them acquire the skills, attitudes, and information that will help them fulfill this case manager role.

School psychologists who "give away knowledge" and share responsibility actually enhance their influence with parents by developing a collaborative and even collegial relationship. Parents who are involved in such a process become less dependent upon the school and other institutions and develop skills and understandings that transfer to a variety of settings and across time. This is the process that Dunst et al. (1988) refer to as "empowerment."

Another opportunity that can be provided to experienced parents is that of becoming involved with parents new to the special education system. Not only does this provide them the opportunity to share knowledge and to be part of a mutual support system, but it may result in the increased self-understanding that often occurs when helping others deal with shared concerns.

Passive Parents

While communicating with passive parents seldom raises overt issues for the school psychologist, PL 94-142 and the procedures that have been developed for its enactment make the assumption that a child's parents are essential participants in the planning of a child's program. Therefore, the school psychologist has an obligation to involve parents in the discussion of their child's situation. While the assumption can be made that parents ought to be active discussants and participants, the variety of communication styles and behaviors among parents implies that it should not be assumed that the passive behavior represents a lack of interest in the child or antipathy toward the school. Parents may evidence passive behavior because of their own interpersonal style, or because of anxiety, depression, or cultural factors.

Some specific techniques that can be helpful in involving passive parents include (a) asking direct questions for information that only the parents may possess; (b) asking open-ended questions or soliciting parents' opinions, such as "What are some of the things that you have noticed at home that might be similar to the school behavior we have been describing?"; (c) asking for a history of events or developmental information from the parents' perspective; and (d) "checking out" what has been discussed with the parents by asking their reactions to the information that has been presented. For parents who seem intimidated by meeting with school personnel, meetings with a limited number of professionals, informal contacts on the telephone, or conferences held at the parents' home may help them feel more secure.

Assertive Parents

The school psychologist should attempt to view working with assertive parents as a positive opportunity to work with parents who have energy and commitment. Psychologists need to be confident in the contributions that they can make and respond in a frank and candid manner. This confidence is fostered by adequate preparation. The school psychologist who has carefully reviewed the case, is well organized, and is well prepared for the parent conference is better able to deal with assertive parents.

Assertive parents need to be welcomed as persons who are *for* the student, not *against* the school or the professionals. Public Law 94-142 anticipates that parents should be actively involved collaborators on behalf of their children. Assertive parents are simply implementing the process and exercising their rights in the way the system intended. It is important to accept their contributions and welcome their involvement. To do otherwise runs the risk of turning assertive parents into angry parents.

Angry Parents

When the school psychologist encounters angry parents, it is important to maintain composure and to listen carefully in an attempt to understand the source of the parents' anger. Indeed, there are many possible situations and events that may lead to hurt feelings, frustration, or misunderstandings and consequent anger. Although the school psychologist should not be expected to withstand threatening or verbally abusive behavior, there is an obligation to listen to the parents and to determine if there are legitimate concerns that need to be addressed. Even if the dissatisfactions do not seem to the school staff to be legitimate concerns, the fact that the parents perceive them as such must be respected.

Wise use of the school psychologist's counseling and communication skills may play an important role in reducing anger and tension. Reframing, problem clarification, and perception checking ("So, what you are saying is . . .") are techniques that can be productive in dealing with the anger and in de-escalating tension. On the other hand, defensiveness, anger, or rejection of the parents' concerns will only serve to escalate tensions. Maintaining composure and a professional moderation in responding are essential to helping parents regain their composure and reciprocate with moderation.

An example of reframing is to see parents' anger as an expression of genuine parental concern and involvement in their child's life. Although parents' anger may not always be directly attributable to the actual educational situation at hand, if it can be genuinely reframed as an expression of concern, and acknowledged to the parents and team as such, it can serve to reinforce the idea that the welfare of the student is the common concern of all involved.

Clarifying the nature of any grievances is an important step in dealing with angry parents. However, it is seldom productive to engage in an item-by-item recounting of all the past actions and reactions that have led to the present situation. Such a proceeding will often lead to a series of accusations, recriminations, and rebuttals that tends to intensify negative feelings and harden the positions of the participants while neglecting consideration of the needs of the student. Instead, the school psychologist should help the parents, and other school staff, focus on the present situation and the possible courses of action. The emphasis cannot be on whether the parents "win" or the school "wins," but on how the parents and educators can work together so that the student wins.

One approach that may help defuse an anger-filled situation is to ask the parents to describe their own remedy to the present circumstances in specific terms. The parents are asked to suggest what they would want done if they could "write their own ticket" for solving the problem. It is surprising how often educators can agree, sometimes with modifications, to such parental suggestions. The value of this method is two-fold. First, it communicates to parents a willingness to consider their ideas seriously. Second, this approach helps identify areas of consensus. It becomes easier to work on more controversial issues once it has been discovered that the parents and school can agree on some basic solutions. The parties then may begin to see themselves as collaborators who can work out solutions for the good of the student.

If the disagreement is over intervention approaches, the parents may be asked what they would accept as evidence that satisfactory progress or changes had occurred. This technique focuses on an agreed-upon accounting of results rather than a discussion of methods or means. Typically, a discussion of methods can proceed with greater flexibility and give-and-take once the parties understand that their goals are agreed upon.

Handicapped Parents

Just as students have varying ability levels, parents, too, have varying levels of cognitive and physical abilities. Some of these parents may have considerable experience with special education services and social service agencies themselves. Not only should this experience and expertise be acknowledged, but the parents' perceptions and attitudes toward such services should be explored to avoid misconceptions of the school's services and to address concerns the parents may have about the provision of services. It also may be necessary to help handicapped parents differentiate between their own handicap and experiences and their child's needs. For example, "We are now able to provide many more services to hearing-impaired students than we could when you were in school. We would like to work closely with you in developing a program for Susie that will allow her to experience success here in her home school. What suggestions do you have?"

If a parent's handicap might interfere with communication between the school and the parent, this should be discussed with the parent to find ways of minimizing such interference. This may mean providing an interpreter for conferences with hearing-impaired parents, tape recording meetings and information for visually impaired parents (in addition to providing them with written reports), or holding staffings in a location more readily accessible to a physically handicapped parent, such as a public library or the parents' home.

Some handicaps, such as poor reading skills or low general cognitive abilities, are not always readily apparent. Unless you have evidence that a parent is a good reader, strong reading skills should not be assumed. Important written material should always be reviewed verbally as a matter of routine. This, of course, should never be done in a manner that could be interpreted as condescending. Rather than reading a form to a parent, the staff person sitting next to the parent might hold the form so the parent can read along and say, "Before we ask you to sign this,

let me review it with you and the team so everyone is aware of what has actually been put into writing."

For low-ability parents, information should be presented concisely without long sentences and unnecessary elaborations, although analogies and concrete examples may be helpful (Teglasi, 1985). Key points should be addressed simply and the parents' understanding should be checked periodically. Frequent contacts of shorter duration and with limited agendas may help avoid confusion and frustration. This does not mean that shortcuts can be taken in reviewing rights, procedures, evaluation results, or service options. If anything, we have an even greater responsibility in assuring informed parental participation and informed consent when working with low-ability parents. Other parents or a local parent advocacy group may be particularly helpful in guiding a low-ability parent through the special education maze.

Finally, when working with handicapped parents, staff people need to examine their own level of comfort with, and stereotypes of, adults who are handicapped. Staff people should be careful to avoid the tendency to temper information about a student's difficulties and needs just because the student's parent is also handicapped.

Information should be presented just as honestly and tactfully to a parent who is handicapped as it is to a parent who is not handicapped. Their handicap generally is relevant only insofar as accommodations may be necessary to allow them to exercise their rights and fulfill their responsibilities as parents.

Mobile Parents

Parents are often the primary link between an old school and a new school. Thus, it is important for parents of a student who is changing schools to understand their child's needs and the services provided in generic and descriptive terms rather than in categorical terms, since disability and service labels may vary from district to district as well as from state to state. The particular type of services provided students even may vary within a district.

If parents inform the school in advance that they will be moving, exchange of information forms can be signed and communication initiated between the schools. Not only will this advance work expedite receipt of services in the new school, it also allows the schools to work with the parents in translating the terms and jargon from one school into the language of the other school. If this advance work is not possible, it is useful to supply an extra set of relevant forms and reports to the parents to hand-carry to the new school. Since school records are often slow in following students, parents who move frequently should be assisted in setting up a complete, organized file of their children's records to be shared with each new school. Reports and forms from the school should be written as generically and descriptively as possible to maximize the parents' understanding and minimize the degree to which they have to explain to the new school the actions of the previous school. A written summary of assessment results, services provided, and behavioral descriptions of successful and unsuccessful interventions can be useful both for the parents and for the new school. All written materials should clearly indicate the name and address of an appropriate contact person.

While the value of consistency in educational programming should be strongly emphasized, especially in the case of families that move frequently, this must be done in a manner which stresses the benefits for the student, but avoids criticism of the parents' lifestyle. Brainstorming with parents about ways of reducing the negative effects of moving is one way of discussing alternatives while still showing respect for the parents' input, values, and life circumstances.

Culturally Different Parents

Culturally different parents are those with a different cultural background than that of the school staff with whom they are communicating. This cultural background may reflect differences in socio-economic status within the same race (e.g., low income), as well as racial or ethnic differences.

Cross-cultural communication is a very complex topic to which justice cannot be done in this chapter. Rather, some general guidelines will be proposed that are consistent with this chapter's orientation of having genuine respect for parents and a genuine desire to share knowledge with parents and to work with them for the betterment of their child. For more comprehensive information about working with culturally different children and families, see the chapter on bilingual assessment in this volume, the chapter by Esquivel (1985) in *Best Practices I*, Argulewicz (1987), and relevant chapters in Anastasi (1988) and Sattler (1988).

Perhaps the most basic principle in working with culturally different families is to know as much as possible about their culture. Simply the fact that a sincere effort is being made to understand the parents' perspective and world view can go a long way in establishing rapport and trust. It is helpful to discuss cultural differences with parents, conveying a desire to avoid actions or statements that may be interpreted as disrespectful, but acknowledging that such actions or statements may inadvertently occur.

When working with any child it is important for support team members to ask parents if the information they have gathered about the child is consistent with the parents' perceptions. This is especially vital in the case of a culturally different child, since behavior patterns seen as inappropriate or unusual may actually be quite appropriate within that culture.

Some key areas that may vary from culture to culture and that are important to consider when sharing information with parents include perceptions of handicaps, educational values, individualism versus a community orientation, the relationship of the culture to the majority system — assimilation versus ethnic identity, appropriate behavior toward authority figures, interpretation of behavior according to a normative standard or to a personal standard, and the role of the school versus the role of the family.

In communicating assessment information to culturally different parents, the school psychologist needs to have a clear understanding of the issues related to assessment of culturally different students. A technical discussion of these issues usually is unnecessary, but the psychologist needs to put the assessment results in context with appropriate interpretations. The psychologist also must be able to respond knowledgeably to parents' concerns about the appropriateness of the assessment methods used with their child. The reader is referred to the sources listed above, particularly Anastasi (1988) and Sattler (1988) for discussions in this area.

Non-English-Speaking Parents

In addition to the cultural factors listed above, the mechanics of communication are a significant issue when the school psychologist is not fluent in the same language as the parents. Especially in these cases, the basic principle of *informed* consent must be continually kept in mind. The fact that it is difficult to communicate with a parent does not reduce that parent's right in regard to due process principles, nor does it reduce the school psychologist's ethical commitment to involve the parents as fully as possible in the educational decision-making process. Rather, it often means working a little harder, being more creative in finding ways of communicating with the parents, and thinking more seriously about the essence and purposes of the communication.

Often, the language barrier is dealt with through the use of an interpreter. Several points should be kept in mind when using interpreters. The interpreter should have a clear understanding of the issue, concepts, and processes involved. Ideally, the interpreter would have training and experience in interpreting in special education and regular education parent–school conferences. The knowledge and understanding of the interpreter is a key factor, since all information is filtered through that person. Not only may important aspects of the information shared not be readily translatable into another language, but underlying concepts also may be foreign to the parents and thus not easily understood.

The temptation to use the student or a sibling as an interpreter should be resisted, since to do so may well have a negative impact on the openness and accuracy of communication. Having a child within the family serve as interpreter may place a strain on family relationships (Sattler, 1988).

If interpreters are necessary, they should be used for informal contacts with parents as well as parent–school conferences. Because of the difficulties of communication, non-English parents or parents with limited-English-speaking skills often do not have the contacts with the school that other parents have and that we have recommended in other sections in this chapter. Yet, with parents with whom communication is difficult more frequent, informal contacts may help significantly in building the trust, rapport, and knowledge that can lead to understanding and cooperative efforts on behalf of the student. The involvement of a person trusted by the parents, such as a social services worker, the family's sponsor (in the case of new immigrants), or the family's religious leader may also help facilitate communication and rapport.

The use of an interpreter or the use of the parents' primary language by staff people should be seriously considered even in the case of parents who do speak some English. Although their English may be good enough to be able to carry on a social conversation, it may not be strong enough to adequately deal with the complexities of formal referral–assessment–qualification–intervention procedures.

Finally, if an interpreter is used, the school psychologist should always remember that it is the parents who are being spoken to, not the interpreter. Thus, it is the parents, not the interpreter, whom the school psychologist should be looking at when speaking.

Often resources that can be helpful when working with non-English-speaking parents or parents with limited-English-speaking skills are overlooked by the school. For example, the Minnesota Department of Education publishes pamphlets in several languages explaining special education terms and procedures. Social service agencies that sponsor and work with recent immigrants, local ethnic groups, and local universities can be helpful in locating interpreters even for parents who speak an uncommon language.

Noncustodial Parents

Although many of the issues that surface in the context of dealing with noncustodial parents can also be evidenced within intact families when parents disagree or have inadequate spousal communication, dealing with noncustodial parents does require an extra measure of sensitivity and a willingness to accommodate and overcome some special logistical problems. Although matters of child custody are governed by the statutes of the various states, noncustodial parents usually have the right to be informed about and to participate in discussions and decisions affecting the welfare of their children, except in the rare circumstance where the court has terminated parental rights (General Assembly of Iowa, 1988).

With this framework in mind, it becomes necessary to establish policies and procedures that address the educational agency's method of communicating with custodial, joint-custodial, and noncustodial parents. The procedures should specify what the responsibilities and limitations are in the area of involving joint-custodial and noncustodial parents and how communication is to be accomplished, recognizing that individual circumstances will vary widely and necessitate flexibility in the procedures. These procedures should be discussed with the parents with the aim of encouraging active participation of both parents in the educational decisions for their child.

Depending on the nature of their relationship, efforts to involve both parents may be more or less successful and beneficial for the student. The best chance for success occurs when the school staff maintains a firm focus on educationally relevant issues and on the common concern for the child. The orientation should be one of dealing with present issues and collaborative problem solving. A further emphasis should be on the increased likelihood of success of interventions if there is consistent support and follow-up from both parents.

SUMMARY

Successful communication of information to parents involves not only the application of professional skills but the willingness to view parents as full-fledged partners in the education of their child. A relationship with parents that fosters common problem solving and planning has the best opportunity for success.

School psychologists need to be clear about their own attitudes toward parents and about the role that parents should play in a student's educational program. Good communication exists in the context of good relationships. The school psychologist should demonstrate a genuine respect for the contributions of parents and proactively attempt to involve parents in the communication and planning process. Agency procedures and conference formats need to be designed in ways that promote parental participation and empowerment.

Parents approach a meeting with school personnel from a variety of perspectives and backgrounds. The psychologist must be sensitive to the unique needs that parents bring to a communication setting and be responsive to those needs. The school psychologist who attempts to understand and appreciate the perspective of individual parents will have taken the crucial first step toward effectively communicating in a way that will build rapport, trust, and the desired collaborative relationship.

REFERENCES

Anastasi, A. (1988). *Psychological testing* (6th ed.). New York: Macmillan.

Argulewicz, E. N. (1987). School psychology in bicultural settings: Implications for service delivery. In S. N. Elliott & J. C. Witt (Eds.), *The delivery of psychological services in schools: Concepts, processes, and issues.* Hillsdale, NJ: Erlbaum.

Dunst, C., Trivette, C., & Deal, A. (1988). *Enabling and empowering families: Principles and guidelines for practice.* Cambridge, MA; Brookline.

Esquivel, G. (1985). Best practices in the assessment of limited English proficient and bilingual children. In A. Thomas & J. Grimes (Eds.), *Best practices in school psychology.* Washington, DC: National Association of School Psychologists.

General Assembly of Iowa. (1988). *Code of Iowa 1989* (Vol. 3). Des Moines: Legislative Service Bureau, General Assembly of Iowa.

Hoff, M. K., Fenton, K. S., Yoshida, R. K., & Kaufman, M. J. (1978). Notice and consent: The school's responsibility to inform parents. *Journal of School Psychology, 16,* 265-273.

Kroth, R. L. (1985). *Communication with parents of exceptional children* (2nd ed.). Denver: Love.

Melton, D. (1984). *Promises to keep: A handbook for parents.* New York: Franklin Watts.

Murray, J. N. (1985). Best practices in working with families of handicapped children. In A. Thomas & J. Grimes (Eds.), *Best practices in school psychology.* Washington, DC: National Association of School Psychologists.

Sarason, S. (1959). *Psychological problems in mental deficiency* (3rd ed.). New York: Harper.

Sattler, J. M. (1988). *Assessment of children* (3rd ed.). San Diego: Author.

Seligman, M. (1979). *Strategies for helping parents of exceptional children: A guide for teachers.* New York: Free Press.

Teglasi, H. (1985). Best practices in interpreting psychological assessment data to parents. In A. Thomas & J. Grimes (Eds.), *Best practices in school psychology.* Washington, DC: National Association of School Psychologists.

ANNOTATED BIBLIOGRAPHY

Kroth, R. L. (1985). *Communicating with parents of exceptional children* (2nd ed.). Denver: Love.
Seligman, M. (1979). *Strategies for helping parents of exceptional children: A guide for teachers.* New York: Free Press.
Both of these books provide comprehensive discussions of issues and techniques related to communication between professionals and the parents of exceptional children. Examples of materials and case studies are included.

Markel, G. P. (1985). *Parents are to be seen and heard: Assertiveness in educational planning for handicapped children.* Ann Arbor, MI: Greenbaum and Markel.
This workbook provides exercises for instructing parents in how to become collaborators with educators and to be fully participating members of the staffing team. Many of the exercises might be usefully reviewed by professionals.

Wise, P. S. (1986). *Better parent conferences: A manual for school psychologists.* Washington, DC: National Association of School Psychologists.
Along with giving readers the opportunity to review their own conferencing skills, this manual provides practical suggestions for skill improvement.

Best Practices in Conducting Reevaluations

Jane Ross-Reynolds
Nicholls State University

OVERVIEW

Reevaluations, particularly the 3-year variety, have been the ugly stepsisters, the perennial bridesmaid in the family of evaluations performed by school psychologists. This statement is an arbitrary, unnecessary, and worse, a sexist characterization, you say. Well, I say, what little research is available has validated the existence of a negative opinion of reevaluations among practitioners (Elliott, Piersel, & Galvin, 1983). Besides, was this the first chapter you eagerly turned to in the new *Best Practices Manual?*

Why should this be so? Perhaps reevaluations are held in such low esteem because of their mandatory nature. The Rules and Regulations implementing Public Law 94-142 require a reevaluation at least every 3 years (USDHEW, 1977). Reevaluations may have been assigned a lower priority because kids in programs are being served and helped, we believe; top or first priority should be those not yet identified. Certainly in the early days of PL 94-142, there was a priority placed upon identification. Finally, the same survey that revealed such negative opinions of reevaluations also documented that the most widespread practices included a repetition of an initial test battery that was intended merely to validate the initial entry or eligibility requirements with little consideration of, and virtually no impact on, the individual's educational program (Elliott, Piersel, & Galvin, 1983; Hartshorne & Hoyt, 1985).

There is no evidence that conditions have changed substantially in the interim, although at least one state has incorporated a consideration of the student's progress and the adequacy of the student's program in the rules and regulations governing the conduct of reevaluations (Louisiana State Department of Education, 1985a).

For many psychologists, however, the 3-year reevaluation continues to be indistinguishable from the initial evaluation in both purpose (to determine classification and placement eligibility) and procedure (giving a routine test battery). Perhaps how we *feel* about reevaluations has something to do with how we *do* reevaluations. This chapter will propose some alternatives in the ways school psychologists can conceptualize and conduct reevaluations. These alternatives will focus on evaluating students' progress and program effectiveness rather than routine retesting (Ross-Reynolds, 1983).

BASIC CONSIDERATIONS

Best practices in reevaluations require changing both the purposes and procedures of reevaluations. The following points form the basis of a rationale for changing our approach to reevaluations. First, as Reschly has advocated for several years in discussions of bias assessment, evaluations that do not result in effective interventions should be regarded at best as useless and unfair and at worst as biased. The paramount concern in this approach is with the social and educational consequences of the procedure to the child (Reschly, 1981). In other words, it does not matter how many tests and sociocultural procedures you use, if effective interventions for the child are not the outcome, your evaluation should be regarded as biased and discriminatory. The message, then, is that the quality of our work must ultimately be judged by the effects it produces, not by the elegance of our psychometrics or our terminology. Reevaluations that document effective programs or at least a concern for the effectiveness of programs, therefore, are crucial in operationalizing nondiscriminatory assessment. While litigation based on the overrepresentation of minority students in special education classes appears to have abated, it has not vanished (Reschly, 1988a).

The individual education plan (IEP) is a contract between the school system and the parents (and the pupil) (Gallagher, 1972). A second reason for conducting reevaluations that focus on program effectiveness is the need to review the contract to make sure that what was promised has been delivered. Effective reevaluations are necessary to "insure that special education placement does not become a dead-end for the child" (Hartshorne & Hoyt, 1985, p. 212). Furthermore, the efficacy of special education programs continues to be debated (Reschly, 1988b). Reevaluations that focus on pupils' progress and on program effectiveness provide valuable data on efficacy pro and con.

Third, school districts are required to evaluate the effectiveness of their programs (Friedman, 1982). Often these evaluations and data-gathering activities are conducted quite apart from 3-year reevaluations and annual reviews. School psychologists can offer their skills and training in measurement and evaluation, particularly in smaller districts, to avoid needless duplication of effort and time taken from instruction. The data collected for 3-year reevaluations and annual reviews could be aggregated and utilized in district reports (Deno, 1986). Jones

(1979) advocated a combination of single-subject and group designs to evaluate the overall effectiveness of a program.

Fourth, nothing in the Federal Rules and Regulations for PL 94-142 requires that a routine battery of standardized tests be administered (Hartshorne & Hoyt, 1985; Safer & Hobbs, 1980). As a matter of fact, the requirements of protection in evaluation procedures refers to the *appropriateness* of the procedures selected. The inappropriate use of standardized tests (using tests normed exclusively on nonhandicapped populations or tests whose content does not reflect the content of the instruction received) in a reevaluation can possibly violate these regulations.

Finally, school psychologists are adding important voices to the chorus in the educational measurement literature that evaluation means more than testing (Salvia & Ysseldyke, 1988). Tests are but one means of gathering data. Evaluation requires the use of a variety of data collection and measurement procedures for the purpose of making a judgment or a decision. The challenge for the school psychologist is the selection or development of the most appropriate procedures to collect the most meaningful data. In reevaluations, it is suggested, the most meaningful data concern pupil progress and program effectiveness.

BEST PRACTICES

Best practices in conducting reevaluation will reflect the application of the following concepts: (a) there is a need to evaluate the IEP as a curriculum; (b) approaches associated with educational curriculum and program evaluation can be profitably applied to reevaluations; and (c) best practices will involve the use of a variety of measurement techniques. The IEP and associated evaluation requirements in the law can be viewed as integrated components in the development, implementation, and evaluation of an alternative curriculum for a handicapped child based upon the classic approach to curriculum design articulated by Ralph Tyler (1950). According to Tyler's *Basic Principles of Curriculum and Instruction* these components are designed to answer the following questions:

1. WHY? Why is there a need for this educational program?

2. WHAT? What are the objectives of the program? What will the program accomplish?

3. HOW? How will the program function to meet its objectives?

4. HOW WILL YOU KNOW? What kinds of information should be gathered so that you know whether the program is functioning to meet the objectives for the identified needs?

The initial evaluation is designed to answer the first question. The IEP document responds to the second and third questions. The annual review and 3-year reevaluation requirements address the question of how you will know.

Concepts borrowed from the literature on program evaluation (Payne, 1982) can also be applied to best practices in reevaluations. Therefore, it is proposed that the general objectives of reevaluations are both summative and formative. The summative aspect of reevaluations deals with determining the overall outcomes of the program. In order to be comprehensive, the summative evaluation should include both process evaluation (Was the program implemented according to its stated intentions?) and product evaluation (Did the program effect a change in the desired direction?). The formative aspect of reevaluations, on the other hand, has to do with feedback for program improvement. The primary goal of the formative evaluation is to specify recommendations for the modification of the program and services for the individual child.

The overall objectives of 3-year reevaluations using summative, formative, process, and product concepts may thus be stated as follows:

1. To determine whether the student's program was implemented as intended and needed.

2. To determine how much progress the student has made in the last three years.

3. To determine whether the student's program (including classification and placement) is appropriate.

4. To determine what changes need to be recommended.

A detailed outline based upon each of these objectives is provided in Table 1. This outline suggests some questions and procedures to guide the conduct of 3-year reevaluation. The questions are also useful in structuring the written evaluation report, as can be seen in a sample report in Table 2.

Many of the procedures advocated here are already being utilized by school psychologists in their reevaluations. Elliott, Piersel, and Galvin (1983) calculated the percentage of psychologists in their survey who reported undertaking the following activities in reevaluation cases: classroom observations (52.5%), parent contact (50%), teacher contact (45%), review of student's records (45%), team staffing (35%), and student interview (20%). Thus, it appears that school psychologists will not need to develop new skills or procedures in order to adopt this model. They only need alter the use they make of the procedures to include a consideration of the pupil's progress and program effectiveness in addition to a determination of continued eligibility for services.

There are reevaluations other than the mandatory triennial. As a matter of fact, the rules and regulations require that an evaluation be conducted "every three years or more frequently if conditions warrant or if the child's parent or teacher requests an evaluation" (USDHEW, 1977). Reevaluations may especially be requested by school personnel if a student is presenting a discipline problem. They may be automatic in some states after certain disciplinary actions such as exclusion, suspension, or recommended expulsion. Reevaluations of infants and preschoolers are triggered by changes in chronological age. It is suggested that the framework presented above can be useful for these

TABLE 1
Outline of Reevaluation Questions and Procedures

Questions to Address	Procedures
Objective 1: To determine whether the student's program was implemented as intended and needed.	
What were the relevant results of previous evaluations?	Review previous evaluation reports with emphasis on the most recent.

What was the basis for the recommended classification? What recommendations were made in that report?
  Academic
  Social
  Self-help
  Communication
  Vocational
  Motor
  Medical
	Review test scores, observations, interview data, and evaluation recommendations particularly for related services.

What have been the student's placement goals, objectives, and related services?	Review the student's IEP goals and objectives, placement, and related services. Supplement information in records with interview. Include summaries of reports of related services.
Were there any recommended, intended, or requested related services or objectives that have not been implemented?	Review file; interview teacher, parent, student.
Has the student received the appropriate follow-up (regular physicals, medication checks, vision and hearing screenings, counseling, or referral to other agencies)?	Review file; interview or send questionnaire to parent, school nurse, audiologist, physician, or other agencies.
What is an estimate of the degree to which the recommendations have been implemented and proposed services have been provided?	Summary determination of the match between recommendations, goals and objectives, and related services.
Have the student's goals and objectives been appropriate?	Determine whether student's goals and objectives have been sequential, appropriate, and consistent with the student's expected levels of achievement. Examine whether objectives have been included for maintenance and generalization of skills as well as for the acquisition of skills.
Have the methods and materials selected been appropriate?	Note if there has been a variety of methods and materials used and if these have been relevant and adaptable to the individual needs of the student.
Objective 2: To determine how much progress the student has made in the last three years.	
Has the student's progress been measured appropriately?	Review measurement procedures employed and performance standards set with current teacher. Review teacher records, graphs, and student work samples.

(Table 1, continued)

Questions to Address	Procedures
What changes have the interventions effected? Have there been any concurrent changes observed in addition to the specific outcomes of stated goals and objectives? Have the changes been in the desired direction?	Use behavioral assessment measures, curriculum-based measures, and norm-referenced measures, observations, and interviews with teacher, parent, and student.
What is an estimate of the amount of progress that the student has made?	Summary comparison of current performance levels with entry level or baseline measures. Take into account unreliability of measures and regression toward the mean.
What is an estimate of the overall effectiveness of the program?	Data compiled and compared with input from the other members of the multidisciplinary team. Areas of convergence are sought. Areas of divergence should receive attention in the formative part of the evaluation to consider recommendations for program change.

Objective 3: To determine whether the student's classification and placement are appropriate.

Does the student continue to require special education services? Are the student's classification and current placement option appropriate?	Consider exit criteria, need for a less restrictive environment; social validation of outcomes. Consider whether it is necessary for the student to meet the current criteria established for initial classification/placement. If not, compare current performance against criteria established for continuation of classification/placement.

Objective 4: To determine what changes need to be recommended in the student's program.

Are there any curricular areas that need to be added or terminated, such as academic, survival, self-help, social, or vocational areas? Are there any related services that need to be added or terminated, such as speech, occupational or physical therapy, and counseling?	Consider the age and developmental level of the student, the long-range goals for the student, and the student's expected levels of achievement. Lower expectations only when student experiences unreasonable levels of continuing failure. Removing all failure experiences is unrealistic.
What modifications in materials or instructional techniques can be recommended?	Determine modifiable administrative, teacher, and student variables. May utilize, observation, work samples, interviews, checklists, rating scales, and questionnaires.
What baseline measures should be obtained to evaluate outcomes in the future?	Consider using curriculum-based measurement procedures and behavioral assessment techniques, as well as published criterion-referenced and norm-referenced measures.

types of reevaluations. Certain questions can be emphasized and others deleted. Reevaluations initiated by disciplinary action particularly benefit from a consideration of the educational program that the student is receiving. Modifications of existing programs can often be tried as intervention alternatives to placement changes and exclusion.

The major problem encountered in conducting reevaluations by the proposed model is, of course, the lack of, or the inadequacy of, the measures obtained in the previous evaluation. Individual published norm-referenced tests can be used in a reevaluation in a summative vein to assess overall gain, but care should be taken to utilize the same tests as those previously used. This would be an example of use of the pre–post test design to evaluate change. The use of published tests administered in a reevaluation in this manner would be considered better than current standard practice in that at least progress would be assessed. However, given the problems identified with this design, the use of published norm-referenced tests would not be best practice (Marston, 1989). The major inadequacies of standardized published tests for this purpose are that they have been designed to measure individual differences rather than be sensitive to pupils' growth, and the content of the test may not match the instruction the child has received (Marston, 1989). Nevertheless for practitioners who currently feel restricted by state rules or regulations governing reevaluations, evolutionary steps toward change can be made by interpreting the results of standardized testing in a summative manner. For example, the evaluation report could refer to the results obtained 3 years previously and the amount of change observed in the scores.

In interpreting differences in test scores to estimate the amount of progress a student has made, the psychologist should keep in mind the unreliability of the pretest and posttest measures, the likelihood of regression towards the mean, and the possibility that initial grade-equivalent scores were misinterpreted in respect to the appropriate instructional

level for the student. The entry measures or pretests were as subject to measurement error as the current, or posttest results. Therefore, the apparent amount of progress may not be "real" in the sense that it is within the band of error associated with the two measures. Also, regression toward the mean tells us that the improvement of low-performing persons can be expected to occur even in the absence of any intervention (Phye, 1979). Thus, it is important to qualify the statements one makes in estimating the amount of progress the student has made.

The issue of validity is confronted particularly with reference to the summative objective of determining the overall effectiveness of the program. *Validity* in program evaluation refers to the necessity not only of documenting that change has occurred, but also of ruling out alternative explanations for the observed change. Two frequently mentioned alternative explanations are history and maturation (Phye, 1979). *History* here means the events that have occurred in addition to the intervention treatment. *Maturation* means the systematic biological and psychological changes in the pupil that have occurred as a result of the passage of time. The proposed questions and procedures do not completely ignore the question of validity, but neither do they adequately address it. The present model primarily seeks to provide documentation that change has indeed been observed. One response to the validity question is to establish procedures for ongoing and more frequent evaluation activities. In addition to the 3-year reevaluation requirement, the law requires an annual review. If adequate ongoing data collection and monitoring procedures can be established, annual reviews as well as 3-year reevaluations will be more meaningful. Thus, establishing appropriate instructional objectives and the means of measuring the student's performance can be viewed as an important subject for consultation with the teacher during a 3-year reevaluation.

Another issue turns on the selection of the appropriate standards or criteria upon which to base judgments in estimating the overall effectiveness of a program. A judgment of effectiveness requires comparison to some standard. One standard might be the degree to which the program has moved the student towards the attainment of long-range goals. Another standard may be the degree to which the child's performance has been brought within accepted levels for peers. The selection of the appropriate peer group would obviously not be on the basis of age alone for exceptional children, but on a number of relevant characteristics such as developmental level, degree of impairment, or handicapping condition. A consideration of the needs of society might also enter here in terms of the degree of habilitation desired for its citizens. Another standard might be to compare the effectiveness of the program against the effectiveness of nonintervention.

An IEP as a curriculum must specify the long-range focus of the program (high school diploma, certificate, or self-help skills), content, materials, and methods. Three areas in which an IEP particularly needs to be evaluated as a curriculum for a handicapped student are the identification and formulation of objectives, the specification of the scope and sequence of the content of instruction, and the selection of teaching–learning strategies. The 3-year reevaluation is the appropriate time to consider whether a change in the focus of a program — from academic to vocational, for example — would be advisable. In identifying and specifying objectives, IEP curriculum designers basically have three options available to them. They can adopt the regular curriculum as to published materials, selecting, for example, a basal reading series. They can adopt a prepared alternative curriculum such as the *Separate Minimum Standards* (Louisiana State Department of Education, 1985b), or they can start from scratch. The important question, in the first two instances particularly, is where and how do the individual's needs deviate from what has been spelled out for others? Which objectives can be de-emphasized or eliminated? Which ones need repetition and review? These curric-

ulum decisions are often unavoidably made by the teacher alone.

It is also important to evaluate how well the curriculum has articulated a scope and sequence for the instructional content. One should take care that knowledge and skills are interrelated both vertically (prerequisite skills) and horizontally (relevance to the child and her or his environment) (Lewy, 1977). For example, one would be forced to consider whether a mildly mentally handicapped student needed to learn to recite phonics rules in order to read.

The formative aspect of reevaluations reflected in the proposed set of questions and procedures has to do with what needs to be done next and what needs to be changed in the child's educational program. The purpose is to provide feedback for program improvement. Curricular areas or related services may need to be modified, added, or terminated. There may be suggestions for changes in materials and instructional techniques. Instructional dimensions research is a type of formative evaluation research providing information that may be usefully applied here (Gersten & Hauser, 1984). The value of this research for reevaluations lies in identifying modifiable variables such as the degree of structure in the classroom, the allocation of academic time, the amount of academic-engaged time, the degree of student engagement during lessons, the nature of reinforcement and consequent conditions, mode of task presentation and mode of student response, scope and sequence of tasks, prerequisite skills, pace of presentation, amount of feedback and practice provided, number of cues and prompts provided, the criterion at which the child experiences success, and the nature of the stimuli that capture and maintain the student's attention. Assessing an individual's needs on each dimension provides useful feedback for the improvement of instruction. Instructional dimensions research is also an additional source of standards for a summative evaluation of the effectiveness of the instruction being provided.

Recent advances in curriculum-based measurement (CBM) have made available reliable, valid, and practical repeated measurements that can be used in individual time series designs for both summative and formative purposes (Deno, 1986; Shinn, 1989). The advantages of using CBM for reevaluations are many. First, as a frequent and ongoing measurement system, CBM provides for the continuity of evaluation through the development, implementation, and evaluation of the curriculum in the IEP. CBM is particularly suited to the Tyler approach to curriculum and evaluation. According to the Tyler rationale, "The process of evaluation is essentially the process of determining to what extent the educational objectives are actually being realized by the program of curriculum and instruction. In other words, the statement of objectives not only serves as the basis for the selection and organization of learning experiences, but the standard against which the program is assessed. To Tyler, then, evaluation is a process by which one matches initial expectations in the form of behavioral objectives with outcomes" (Kliebard, 1977, pp. 63–64).

CBM provides a superior alternative to the use of standardized published tests in a pre–post test design. Curriculum-based measures are more sensitive to specific objectives of a curriculum, are more content-valid, and provide a better match between test content and curriculum. Curriculum-based measures are also more sensitive to small amounts of growth over short periods of time (Marston, 1989). It is interesting that the technical adequacy of standardized tests is based on stability of measures, rather than sensitivity to change.

Criterion-referenced and norm-referenced curriculum-based measures provide reliable, valid, and cost-effective standards to judge the effectiveness of an individual education program. Curriculum-based measures can be criterion-referenced to assess the degree to which the student is attaining both long-term and short-term goals (Fuchs, 1989). Norm-referenced CBM assesses efficiently how much the performance of the student

differs from accepted levels for peers. As a result, CBM provides a defensible technology for determining local exit and maintenance criteria (Allen, 1989). Tindal (1989) has discussed the selection of the appropriate peer group for determining standards of performance:

> The appropriateness of the typical regular education student as a comparison standard may be questionable. The average student in regular education may represent a performance level far greater than that needed by the special education student to be successful in that environment. A more appropriate comparison may be the lowest-performing students in regular education who are nonetheless maintaining minimally successful levels. This group could be comprised of the lowest 50% of students in the regular education classroom, Chapter I students, or students in the lowest skill groups in the regular education classes. The performance levels of these students would then serve as an appropriate comparison group for evaluating special education. (p. 217)

Finally, Deno (1986) has pointed out the value of CBM for a problem-solving approach in special education and a consultation role for school psychologists. The adoption of a problem-solving approach involves conceptualizing the development of an IEP as a hypothesis-testing process. This perspective also eases the consultation relationship because no scapegoat (the child, the parents, the school psychologist, the special education teacher) needs to be identified when an IEP does not result in improved performance. Instead, CBM provides technically adequate data that can be readily communicated and seen as the results of the test of a hypothesis about intervention. A new intervention can then be formulated. Using CBM, school psychologists can become 'more actively engaged with special education teachers in designing and evaluating academic interventions, thereby also enhancing the consultative effectiveness of the psychologist (Goodwin & Hamilton, 1989).

Although CBM has been primarily utilized and elaborated for students in

TABLE 2
Sample Reevaluation Report

Name: Gena R.   Date of Birth: 10-19-74   Evaluation Date: 4/30/87

School: South Middle   Age: 12 years, 6 months   Grade: 6

Parents: Gene and Marie R.   Address: 926 Hollyhock

Reason for Referral

Gena was referred for a required 3-year reevaluation, since her last complete evaluation was dated 5/11/84. The purposes of this evaluation were:

1. to determine whether Gena's program was implemented as intended and needed;

2. to determine how much progress Gena has made in the last 3 years;

3. to determine whether Gena's program (including classification and placement) is appropriate; and

4. to determine what changes need to be recommended.

Evaluation Procedures

Review of IEP, analysis of work samples, review of standardized test results, curriculum-based measurement procedures, teacher interviews, student interview, parent interview, and classroom observation were the evaluation procedures employed.

Review of Program and Progress

Gena is currently in her fourth year of special education in a resource placement. She was first enrolled in special education at Reine Elementary in the third grade on the basis of Mild Mental Handicap classification. Grades 4–6 have been at South with no retention. IEP goals have been in the areas of reading, spelling, math, and enhancing self-concept. She has received the maximum amount of time allotted in the resource program. Gena has made consistent progress over the years, as noted in the IEP.

Current levels of classroom performance according to her IEP, her teachers, and work samples indicate that Gena is in the second semester of the third grade basal reader. Curriculum-based measurement procedures yielded results in the number of words read correctly per minute (CWPM) and the number of errors in randomly selected passages from previously covered material. Gena's median scores for each grade level of the basal reader were:

	CWPM	ERRORS
Third grade (3-1)	55	3
Second grade (2-1)	57	4
First grade (1-1)	77	2

Standardized test results (Woodcock–Johnson Psychoeducational Battery) yielded a grade-equivalent score of 3.9. These scores indicate that Gena is receiving her instruction at the appropriate level, although it should be noted that her level of performance is nearly 3 years below current grade placement. Gena's speed in reading is slow in comparison with average third graders. Interventions designed to increase speed should be included in her educational objectives. When Gena's current reading scores are compared with those of 3 years ago, it is apparent that she has made progress, although she remains at the same position relative to her peers.

Spelling is an area of strength for Gena. She is achieving 70–90% on the 6-week review and mastery tests in the low series of fifth-grade-level words. Standardized test results confirmed that Gena has made consistent progress in spelling over the last 3 years.

Math continues to be another area of difficulty for Gena. She obtained a grade-equivalent score of 3.6 on the Woodcock–Johnson. Unit tests indicated that she has mastery in the areas of addition, subtraction, some degree of proficiency in multiplication, but significant difficulty with division, fractions, decimals, time, and money.

(Table 2, continued)

Socially, Gena is quiet and generally does not have trouble with classmates. She is proud of her work in spelling, language, and art, but states that she has difficulty with math and reading. She also stated a dislike for P.E. In an interview, Gena also noted that her resource teacher had helped her in understanding concepts in the regular class. Gena has improved and benefited from the special education resource program. Gena knows that she needs the assistance and responds positively to the support. Her sixth-grade teachers have made significant adaptations for her special needs. If pushed too hard, however, Gena becomes frustrated, withdraws, and becomes stubborn. With material presented at her instructional level, she can make continued growth and progress.

Measures of intelligence and adaptive behavior were also obtained. On the Wechsler Intelligence Scale for Children–Revised, Gena scored in the borderline range on the Verbal section, in the mildly mentally handicapped range on the Performance section, and in the mildly mentally handicapped range on the Full Scale. Previous scores revealed the same pattern, with slightly higher scores. Given that she worked well during the test, I believe these scores are reliable and valid. Mrs. R., Gena's mother, was interviewed with the Alpern–Boll Developmental Profile as a measure of adaptive behavior. Gena is 2–3 years below age level expectations in physical, social, communication, and academic areas. Gena's mother expressed concern that Gena does not socialize much. She can skate, swim, and bike, but does not do this with others or go to parties, despite her mother's encouragement.

Conclusions and Recommendations

On the basis of the review of her placement and progress, I conclude that Gena has been appropriately placed in her special education program and has made adequate progress with the special assistance and support of her regular and special education teachers. She continues to be eligible on the basis of a mildly mentally handicapping condition. Current vision, hearing, and speech screening results are normal. No significant health, social, emotional, or cultural factors were indicated. Motor screening suggested a need for further evaluation for adapted physical education.

Gena's skills in reading and math will pose significant problems in subject matter courses in junior high. Consequently, I believe it is in the best interest of this student to receive increased special education programming at the junior high school. I believe a program at the resource level will not be adequate for her needs for personal and social growth as well as academic progress. Gena should also be guided in an exploration of vocational education options. Gena, her parents, and her teachers are pleased with her progress and performance in school. This recommendation is viewed as the most likely way to continue to assure this progress in the near future.

Grades 1–6, it is also applicable for reevaluations of preschool, secondary, and exceptional students such as the seriously emotionally disturbed (Neisworth & Bagnato, 1986). For secondary students, curriculum-based approaches can be helpful in assessing their ability to handle the reading requirements in the content areas, for example. Curriculum-based measures provide very useful information about the academic progress of emotionally disturbed and other exceptional students.

A sample of a written report of a 3-year reevaluation following the proposed model is provided in Table 2. This report de-emphasizes the testing and places greater importance on a review of the child's program and progress over the last 3 years. For the reader interested in a sample report utilizing CBM assessment procedures exclusively in a reevaluation, the case study by Goodwin and Hamilton (1989) offers an excellent example.

SUMMARY

The central message of this chapter is that reevaluations are important and meaningful professional activities for school psychologists. Traditional reevaluations involving the administration of a routine battery of tests can make a valuable contribution in terms of longitudinal data, particularly in tracking deterioration due to illness or genetic abnormality. In addition, reevaluations can play a pivotal role in the development of a data-based, problem-solving approach in special education and a consultative role for school psychologists. Reevaluations provide scheduled opportunities for testing the hypotheses proposed in the IEP and in the formative creation of alternatives. The requirement of a reevaluation can provide the psychologist with entry into a consultative relationship with special classes.

The IEP serves a variety of purposes, one of which is outlining a curriculum for an exceptional student; therefore, there is a need to evaluate the child's IEP as a curriculum to insure that the child is receiving the appropriate scope and sequence of skills and making adequate progress. The 3-year reevaluation provides a reasonable opportunity to review the student's IEP as a curriculum. Approaches that are associated with educational curriculum and program evaluation and involve the use of a variety of measurement techniques can be profitably applied to reevaluations. Utilizing a variety of procedures to collect meaningful data regarding a pupil's progress and program effectiveness can transform reevaluations into real evaluations.

REFERENCES

Allen, D. (1989). Using CBM to make periodic and annual review and exit decisions. In M. R. Shinn (Ed.), *Curriculum-based measurement and special services for children* (pp. 184-204). New York: Guilford.

Deno, S. D. (1986). Formative evaluation of individual student programs: A new role for school psychologists. *School Psychology Review, 15*(3), 358-374.

Elliott, S. N., Piersel, W. C., & Galvin, G. A. (1983). Psychological reevaluations: A survey of practices and perceptions of school psychologists. *Journal of School Psychology, 21*, 99-105.

Friedman, D. (1982). *The evaluation of special education instructional programs: A manual.* Des Moines, IA: Iowa Department of Public Instruction.

Fuchs, L. S. (1989). Evaluation solutions: Monitoring progress and revising intervention plans. In M. R. Shinn (Ed.), *Curriculum-based measurement and special services for children* (pp. 155-184). New York: Guilford.

Gallagher, J. (1972). The special education contract for mildly handicapped children. *Exceptional Children, 38*, 711-720.

Gersten, R., & Hauser, C. (1984). The case for impact evaluations in special education. *Remedial and special education, 5*(2), 16-24.

Goodwin, M. S., & Hamilton, D. (1989, March). *Using curriculum-based measurement in teacher consultation: A case study.* Paper presented at the meeting of the National Association of School Psychologists, Boston.

Hartshorne, T. S., & Hoyt, E. B. (1985). Best practices in conducting reevaluations. In J. Grimes & A. Thomas (Eds.), *Best practices in school psychology* (pp. 207-215). Kent, OH: National Association of School Psychologists.

Jones, R. R. (1979). Program evaluation design issues. *Behavioral assessment, 1*, 51-56.

Kliebard, H. M. (1977). The Tyler rationale. In A. Bellack & Kliebard (Eds.), *Curriculum and evaluation* (pp. 56-68). Berkeley, CA: McCutchan.

Lewy, A. (Ed.). (1977). *Handbook of curriculum evaluation.* Paris: UNESCO International Institute for Educational Planning.

Louisiana State Department of Education. (1985a). *Bulletin 1508.*

Louisiana State Department of Education. (1985b). *Separate minimum standards for students with mild/moderate handicaps.*

Marston, D. (1988). The effectiveness of special education: A time series analysis of reading performance in regular and special education. *Journal of Special Education, 21*, 13-26.

Marston, D. (1989). A curriculum-based measurement approach to assessing academic performance: What is it and why do it? In M. R. Shinn (Ed.), *Curriculum-based measurement and special services for children* (pp. 18-80). New York: Guilford.

Neisworth, J. T., & Bagnato, S. J. (1986). Curriculum-based developmental assessment: Congruence of testing and teaching. *School Psychology Review, 15*, 180-199.

Payne, D. A. (1982). Portrait of the school psychologist as a program evaluator. In C. R. Reynolds & T. B. Gutkin (Eds.), *The handbook of school psychology.* New York: Wiley.

Phye, G. D. (1979). School psychologists as consultants in the evaluation of learning and intervention outcomes. In G. D. Phye & D. J. Reschly (Eds.), *School psychology: Perspectives and issues.* New York: Academic.

Reschly, D. J. (1981). Psychological testing in educational classification and placement. *American Psychologist, 36*, 1094-1102.

Reschly, D. J. (1988a). Recent placement litigation, Part III. Analysis of differences in Larry P., Marshall, and S-1 and implications for future practices. *School Psychology Review, 17*, 39-50.

Reschly, D. J. (1988b). Special education reform: School psychology revolution. *School Psychology Review, 17,*(3), 459–476.

Ross-Reynolds, J. (1983). Three-year reevaluations: An alternative to the reevaluation–means–retest model. In J. Grimes (Ed.), *Communicating psychological information in writing.* Des Moines, IA: Iowa Department of Public Instruction.

Safer, N., & Hobbs, B. (1980). Developing, implementing, and evaluating individualized education programs. *School Psychology Review, 9,* 212–220.

Salvia, J., & Ysseldyke, J. E. (1988). *Assessment in special and remedial education* (4th ed.). Boston, Houghton Mifflin.

Shinn, M. R. (Ed.). (1989). *Curriculum-based measurement and special services for children.* New York: Guilford.

Tindal, R. (1989). Evaluating the effectiveness of educational programs at the systems level using curriculum-based measurement. In M. R. Shinn (Ed.), *Curriculum-based measurement and special services for children* (pp. 204–240). New York: Guilford.

Tyler, R. W. (1950). *Basic principles of curriculum and instruction.* Chicago: University of Chicago Press.

USDHEW. (1977). Education of handicapped children: Implementation of Part B of the Education of the Handicapped Act. *Federal Register, 42*(163), 42474–42518.

ANNOTATED BIBLIOGRAPHY

Allen, D. (1989). Using CBM to make periodic and annual review and exit decisions. In M. R. Shinn (Ed.), *Curriculum-based measurement and special services for children* (pp. 184–204). New York: Guilford.
Allen's chapter, while focusing primarily on the use of curriculum-based measurement for annual reviews, gives the "nuts and bolts" of the technical application of CBM procedures in reevaluation data gathering and decision making. Allen discusses the rationale and technology for exit and maintenance criteria by distinguishing between eligibility and need and the determination of benefit by the comparison between academic progress with and without special education intervention. Allen advocates surveying a student's performance in curriculum materials from present grade placement through successively lower grade levels back to first grade, if necessary, making a comparison of the slope of improvement before placement with the slope of improvement after, as well as comparisons with normative CBM data.

Rosenfield, S. (1987). *Instructional consultation.* Hillsdale, NJ: Erlbaum.
As school psychologists become more intimately involved with classroom-based consultation services, both in regular and special education, there is an increasing need for comprehensive texts synthesizing consultation with a solid knowledge base in instruction and effective teaching techniques. Rosenfield's text describes the practical components of instructional consultation: the use of effective teaching research, the culture and ecology of the instructional system, and the assumptions and processes of consultation. There are also sections on problem identification and analysis, instructional intervention planning and implementation, and the termination stage of the consultation relationship. A collaborative, data-based, problem-solving approach is emphasized in instructional consultation relationship.

Shinn, M. R. (Ed.). (1989). *Curriculum-based measurement and special services for children.* New York: Guilford.
Shinn's book, with contributions by Allen, Deno, Marston, Fuchs, and Tindal, is a timely presentation of the state of the art of curriculum-based measurement. Deno presents the concept of special education as problem solving and shows the value of curriculum-based measures for providing data that serve continually in decision making. Curriculum-based data also improve communication between school psychologists and special educators and thereby enhance the consultation role of the school psychologist.

14

Best Practices in Applied Research

Timothy Z. Keith
Virginia Polytechnic Institute and State University

Why bother with a chapter on research? Conventional wisdom is that school psychologists are not interested in conducting research and that many are antagonistic toward research. Yet my experiences in conducting workshops for NASP on research and writing about research for our practitioner-oriented journal, *School Psychology Review*, lead me to believe that the conventional wisdom may be conventional, but is not wise. I have talked with many school psychologists who are indeed interested in conducting research in applied settings, and to many more who want to do a better job of incorporating others' research into their daily practice. Both of these are appropriate research roles for school psychologists, among others.

For the purpose of this chapter, *research* is defined as activities designed to produce new scientific knowledge or to use that knowledge to improve school psychology practice. I see three hierarchical research roles for school psychologists.

1. All school psychologists should strive to be competent *consumers* of research. The types of people we serve, our methods and instruments, and our roles are constantly changing. At the same time there are always plenty of bandwagons tempting us to hop aboard. The best way to stay abreast of current developments while avoiding bandwagons is carefully reading research. Research tells us which good ideas really do work.

2. There is also a need for a smaller number of school psychologists to act as *distributors* (or synthesizers and disseminaters) of research. They may read research relevant to a topic of interest and summarize and draw conclusions from it for other interested groups, such as other psychologists or a board of education.

3. Some school psychologists are interested in performing the role we normally think of as research: *conducting* research of interest to themselves, their colleagues, or their employers.

The three roles are hierarchical: One needs to be an effective consumer of research in order to summarize and distribute it effectively, and one needs to be able to summarize research in order to be an effective conductor of research.

As an example, consider three hypothetical school psychologists interested in the effectiveness of study skills instruction. John, a research consumer, is interested in study skills instruction as an educational intervention for a low-achieving child. He reads research to find out if study skills instruction is generally effective in improving achievement, to find out what methods of instruction are available, and to find out whether some methods are generally more effective than others, or whether some methods are more effective with children similar to the one John is working with. Elaine, a research distributor, is asked by her superintendent to investigate whether it would be worthwhile to teach study skills to incoming high school students, and if so, what approach would be most effective. Finally, Carolyn conducts research comparing the achievement of students in her district who were taught study skills to that of students who were not.

BASIC CONSIDERATIONS

The Consumer of Research Findings

Although the findings of social science research are often contradictory, research is also the one way we have of putting aside our hopes and prejudices and testing whether an intervention works or a test measures what we think it measures. If we are to serve children well, our practice needs to be consistent with research findings. Yet research results are often contradictory, and much research is of poor quality and limited applicability. School psychologists thus need to evaluate the research they read in order to separate the good from the bad.

To evaluate research, one asks two essential questions: Did the research demonstrate anything? And is it applicable to my situation? The training needed to become a competent consumer of research is not extensive and is probably included in most specialist-level school psychology programs. Basic statistics, research, and measurement courses are needed, but they should be focused on a *conceptual* understanding at least as much as computation. Unfortunately, many such courses continue to be taught as if most students were going to be conducting research rather than reading and evaluating it; more attention is needed toward the *evaluation* and use of others' research. Single-case research methods also need more coverage; this is one research method that practitioners need to use, but its coverage is spotty. The primary resource needed by consumers of research is access to relevant journals.

The Distributor of Research Findings

Although all school psychologists should strive to incorporate research results into their practice, not all need to integrate and distribute research to others or conduct research; whether one wants to become a distributor or conductor of research should be a matter of choice and job description.

Distributors of research first need to be good consumers of research, and they additionally need experience in sifting through and integrating research findings, which may be rather diverse and inconsistent. Their formal training should also include at least basic courses in research, statistics, and measurement, but guided experience in integrating and summarizing research is probably at least as important. All doctoral and many specialist-level psychologists should have this level of training and at least some experience, at minimum when writing a thesis or dissertation.

Research distributors need access to a wider range of journals and other sources of research: conferences in which research is presented, the ERIC Document Reproduction Service, and Psychological Abstracts. Electronic databases can enhance greatly the effectiveness of research distributors by providing the ability to search a broad range of journals. Access to a university library is also extremely useful.

The Conductor of Research

It is well known that not all school psychologists are interested in conducting research, but this role should be — and often is — available to psychologists with the appropriate interest and training. Again, these roles are to be seen as hierarchical; one needs to be a competent distributor of research in order to be a good conductor of research, because the conclusions drawn from previous research should guide our own research efforts.

The formal training of those who plan to conduct research needs to be more extensive and should include a series of research and statistics courses. Nevertheless, most doctoral and some specialist-level psychologists have completed such coursework, so interest and experience tend to be more limiting. Probably the best training for this role is to assist someone else in several research projects or to conduct several research projects under supervision (in addition to a thesis). A graduate research assistantship or some sort of research apprenticeship can be extremely valuable.

The conductor of research needs access to the same resources as the distributor of research: research publications and a good library. In addition, most psychologists who conduct research need access to a computer with a *good* statistical analysis program.

BEST PRACTICES

Consumer of Research

Reading and evaluating research. Consumers of research read and evaluate research as a means of improving their practice. In order to perform this role one must, of course, have access to relevant research. Consumers must also be able to evaluate the research they read. Since research in the social sciences yields contradictory reports, an effort to find the research answer to a question of practice can be quite frustrating. I do not believe this inconsistency means that research cannot inform our practice. It does mean, however, that *evaluation* of the research is necessary.

Journals, the primary source of research, accept only a fraction of the articles that are submitted for publication, thus supposedly ensuring that the research they do publish is of high enough quality to deserve our trust. Nevertheless, much research, even published in good journals, is not good research: Research problems are poorly conceived or are trivial; samples are small and poorly selected; inappropriate statistics are used, and mistakes are made in calculating and reporting statistics; research designs are weak and do not rule out plausible alternative hypotheses; designs do not fit the purpose of the research or test the hypotheses the researcher wants to test. Even when research is well-conceived and well-conducted, there are problems of interpretation. Most researchers have been guilty of overblown conclusions that extend well beyond what might reasonably be concluded by the results, but more subtle problems are common as well. It is not unusual, for example, for a discussion to address a different issue than that addressed by the research. This problem is common when there is a mismatch between the intended purpose of the research and the research that is actually conducted. For all of these reasons, much research is of poor quality, and consumers of research need to evaluate carefully the research they do read.

Fortunately, one does not have to be a statistician to evaluate research. Instead, what is needed is a *conceptual* understanding of research methods and what those methods can tell you. What is the purpose of a representative sample? Of random assignment to groups? When is research experimental and when is it nonexperimental? What threats does a multiple-baseline design control? What does significance mean? What does ANOVA or multiple regression or factor analysis tell us? Being able to answer these conceptual questions will help one evaluate research much more than being able to calculate *t* tests by hand. One also needs to read research articles carefully — even skeptically.

Research evaluation focuses on a number of different aspects of the research, but there are three very important questions to consider. First, are the internal features of the research conducted well enough so that we can have confidence in the results? The consideration is generally referred to as the internal validity of the research (Campbell & Stanley, 1963), but it may also be thought of as the power of the research design (Keith, 1988). In other words, is the research design powerful enough that we can be confident that it was the treatment, and not something else, that caused the resulting change in behavior?

Second, how generalizable or applicable are the results? This consideration — external validity — focuses primarily on the subjects used in research and the treatments. Are the people used in the research study similar to those one might encounter during normal practice? Similarly, are the treatments used similar to what we might use in applied settings, or have they been drastically modified to fulfill the requirements of the experiment? There is often a trade-off in these two aspects of research. For example, a school-based study in which various classes were assigned differing amounts of homework would likely be less powerful (more threats to internal validity) than a lab-based experiment in which college freshmen were assigned randomly to groups and given different amounts of time to study nonsense words. On the other hand, we would probably feel more comfortable generalizing the results of the first study to a middle school student who does not complete his homework. The second study is more powerful but less generalizable.

Third, is the article written well enough so that readers can understand what was done and the implications of the results? It does not matter how technically sophisticated research is if the writing is unclear and confusing.

Although skepticism is necessary in evaluating research, it should not be carried to an extreme. Be warned: No research is perfect. Conducting research consists, in large part, of making decisions and compromises, and there are weaknesses in any piece of research. When we evaluate research we need to weigh its strengths and weaknesses and decide whether the results obtained are trustworthy; whether the treatment described really resulted in the behavioral change found. On evaluation we will find some research in which the weaknesses are insurmountable, and the results suspect; these studies can be ignored. The rest will fall along some continuum; we can apply those that are strong in all areas with more confidence than we can those with many weaknesses.

Table 1 includes a list of questions that may be useful in evaluating research articles. Various sources that may be useful in gaining a conceptual understanding of the issues involved in research are listed in the annotated bibliography.

For research that is well conducted and well described, the next problem is application. It is obviously easier to implement applied research than research that is highly theoretical. Intervention studies and psychometric research are often directly applicable to daily practice. But basic and theoretical research may also be quite applicable, especially if it helps us understand how or under what conditions a treatment (or intervention) may be useful. Basic research comparing the effectiveness of various mnemonic devices for different types of subjects might be quite applicable to a student with poor memory skills, for example. The connection is not as direct, but a good mix of applied and basic research may be very useful in understanding a problem.

Sources. The primary source of research reports is journals that are pertinent to school psychology. A useful list of such journals is presented in Reynolds, Gutkin, Elliott, and Witt (1984, Appendix G). Conferences, conference proceedings, and the ERIC Document Reproduction Service are other outlets for relevant research, but these manuscripts are generally not as carefully reviewed as are those submitted to journals, so consumers of research need to be even more critical than with journal articles. Research reviews and book chapters are another good source for both consumers and distributors of research. If well done, they provide a concise, objective summary of research knowledge in an area, and their reference lists also provide good listings of the original research. These sources may also provide a good conceptual introduction that will be useful when reading the original research. But like original research, the quality of reviews and chapters varies considerably; you should have some familiarity with at least some of the original research so that you can be sure that the writer did a competent job of summarizing it.

If most school psychologists are to be consumers, rather than conductors, of research, their concern when taking research courses should be for a conceptual understanding of research. I believe,

TABLE 1
Questions for Evaluating Research Articles

Is the purpose well defined?

Is the literature adequately summarized?

Does the introduction establish the need for the study?

Is the research design appropriate? Is it powerful enough that you can trust the results?

Does the research design fit the purpose?

What type of research design is used (experimental, quasi-experimental, nonexperimental, single-case, etc.)?

Does the analysis fit the design?

How was the sample collected? Is it representative? Is it large enough to allow a good statistical test?

Is there evidence to support the reliability and validity of any tests or questionnaires used?

Are the results presented consistent with the purpose, the design, and the analysis?

Does the discussion flow from the results? Is it consistent with the purpose of the study?

Are the conclusions consistent with the results, or do they go well beyond them?

Are the limitations of the research discussed?

What are the major strengths and weaknesses of the study?

Is the article well written?

Are the results of the study generalizable to your population? Are the treatments generalizable into interventions?

Is this research applicable to your work?

Note. These quesitons provide an overview of the characteristics that may be important in evaluating research articles. They will not all be equally applicable for all articles.

however, that there is one exception to this rule: All school psychologists should be able to develop rudimentary single-case research designs. I do not expect most school psychologists to conduct single-case research (although such research is more applicable to applied settings than are most types of research), but knowledge of such designs is useful because they can be used to evaluate the effectiveness of virtually *any intervention* — behavioral or otherwise.

Example. As a hypothetical example, consider a fifth-grade boy, Sam, who is having trouble keeping up with his peers, and is referred to a school psychologist. The teacher does not think Sam is a candidate for special education but does want assistance in helping him deal with what appears to be a relatively mild learning problem. Assessment and a review of records confirms the teacher's

suspicions; Sam has never been a star student, but he has never experienced serious problems before either, and he has never been referred previously. He appears to have slightly below average abilities and achievement in a generally high-achieving school. Assessment also suggests that Sam, his teacher, and his parents are all fairly motivated and would be willing to cooperate with some sort of intervention (remember this case is made up!).

The school psychologist has read several articles recently on the effects of homework, and it occurs to her that homework might provide the basis for a cooperative home–school intervention. A cursory review of research suggests that homework is effective for this age group, especially when it is commented on by the teacher and when current homework demands are small (e.g., Keith, 1987; Paschal, Weinstein, & Walberg, 1984).

Further investigation reveals that the teacher currently assigns little homework.

The psychologist begins conducting curriculum-based assessments in reading (e.g., Deno, 1986) and charting Sam's weekly quiz grades in math and spelling. In cooperation with the teacher and the parents she plans a homework intervention: The parents will provide a quiet place for Sam to study at a regular time each day; the teacher will eventually provide daily, individualized homework in at least two of the three areas being charted, and she will check the homework, comment on it, and provide feedback to the parents about Sam's homework accuracy on a daily basis. The parents, in turn, will provide reinforcement at home for homework that meets an agreed-upon, adjustable criterion of accuracy.

Because the psychologist wants to ensure that it is the intervention, rather than some other, uncontrolled factor that causes any subsequent change in Sam's achievement, she designs the intervention as a multiple-baseline design across school subjects. Homework in reading is introduced first, although performance in all three areas continues to be charted. If the intervention is effective, she might expect to see improvement in reading after a few weeks of the homework intervention while spelling and math grades stay at about the same level. Homework could next be introduced in spelling, and after progress is shown, in math. Of course, if the homework seems to have been effective in reading, the teacher and parents might be tempted immediately to begin homework in the other two areas, but they would need to be cautioned against jumping the gun. By conforming to the multiple-baseline plan, the psychologist can feel confident that it is the intervention, not something else, that is causing any change in Sam's behavior. This knowledge is important because it provides information that may be useful in future interventions with Sam and other students and because it ensures that Sam, his parents, and his teacher are not completing all of this additional work for no purpose. This approach has the added benefit of introducing the intervention gradually and of providing data that may be used to make needed changes in the intervention. The approach is not a sophisticated single-case design, but it would provide evidence of the effectiveness — or lack of effectiveness — of the intervention; it also illustrates the connections among research, assessment, intervention, and evaluation. It should also be noted that a wide range of outcome measures (behavioral and otherwise) are possible in single-case designs. For example, if we were interested in the teacher's impressions of Sam's preparation for class, we could assess this possible outcome using a simple rating scale. These daily ratings of preparedness in the three subjects would also fit well in the multiple-baseline design.

Improving skills. Most school psychologists have had all or most of the training necessary to become effective consumers of research; what they need is to improve and use the skills they have. The books and articles in the annotated bibliography may help refresh that training, and they approach research more from a conceptual than a numerical level. Consumers should also read research regularly and attend research presentations at conferences. We should be interested in the results of research but always approach it skeptically. As Reynolds reminded us, our attitude should be "In God we trust; all others must have data" (1982, p. 178).

Of course, if school psychologists are to be effective consumers of research, their employers must recognize this as a part of their jobs. In my experience, most employers are pleased when their psychologists try to base their practice on solid research, provided that the knowledge (a) does not cost a lot of extra money, and (b) is not used as a weapon with which the psychologists battle policies of the administration (as in, "Well, the research says this program the superintendent started up last month is not very effective"). As with any new role, it may be necessary to start this process through an investment of one's own time rather than the employer's; when you can show some payoff — as through effective interventions — your employer will be much more willing to recognize the value of the research consumer approach.

Distributors of Research

Integrating research. Distributors of research consolidate and integrate research findings in order to draw conclusions from that research and make recommendations based on those conclusions. In order to do so, distributors first need access to a body of research, and probably a wider access than do consumers of research. Distributors need to be able to define their research topic so that their review is neither too broad nor too narrow. I find it helpful to organize research topics as a group of overlapping circles. For example, if I were interested in the effects of cooperative learning strategies on learning-disabled (LD) students' math achievement, I would be most interested in research that directly addressed that question, and I would want to read and evaluate that body of research as comprehensively as possible. Thus, my central topic – the central circle in Figure 1 — is research addressing the effects of cooperative learning on LD students' math achievement. I would also be interested in several related topics, such as the effects of cooperative learning on other types of exceptional children's achievement, the effects of cooperative learning on normal children's math achievement, and other important aspects of math learning in LD children; these topics are represented by circles that overlap the central circle. Although each of these related topics is of interest, they are less central to the main topic of interest and therefore my reading of research in these areas would not need to be as comprehensive. Much of my information about these topics could even rely on review articles, if they have been well done, are comprehensive, and are recent. The next set of circles from the center might include such topics as the effects of cooperative learning strategies on other subject areas and the design of cooperative learning strategies; while these topics should be considered, they might receive only a cursory review. Thus, although my reading of the research should cover all important aspects of the problem, I would also spend less time on research that is less central to my research question.

Like consumers, distributors of research need to be able to evaluate the research they read. In fact, this skill is even more important for distributors because they need to cover the research more thoroughly and are therefore more likely to encounter contradictory research findings. Distributors need to weigh better research more heavily in making conclusions.

Probably the most difficult part of consolidating research is *integrating* diverse research findings. The least useful review of research is one that simply lists in separate paragraphs the findings of each research study. Instead, the goal of a research review should be to combine and integrate the various research findings in order to draw one or several conclusions (with appropriate caveats) from the research. One rule of thumb that may make this easier is to avoid making the *researchers* the subject of a sentence or a paragraph, but rather to focus on the *findings* of research and make most citations to researchers parenthetical. For example, I might write that "coursework appears to be an important influence on students' learning (Anderson, 1989), whether learning is measured by test scores (Smith, 1988) or by grades (Jones, 1979)." This sentence integrates the findings of three hypothetical studies. In contrast, I might have written: "Smith (1988), in a regression analysis of 867 high school students, found that the coursework taken by those students had a strong effect on their subsequent achievement test scores. Jones (1979) studied students in academic versus general high school tracts and found that . . ." and so on. The first method integrates the findings; the second method treats them separately.

The steps listed above as important in distributing research are identical to the steps involved in a literature review: Review an appropriate body of research, integrate the findings, and make conclusions. Distributors of research need to take

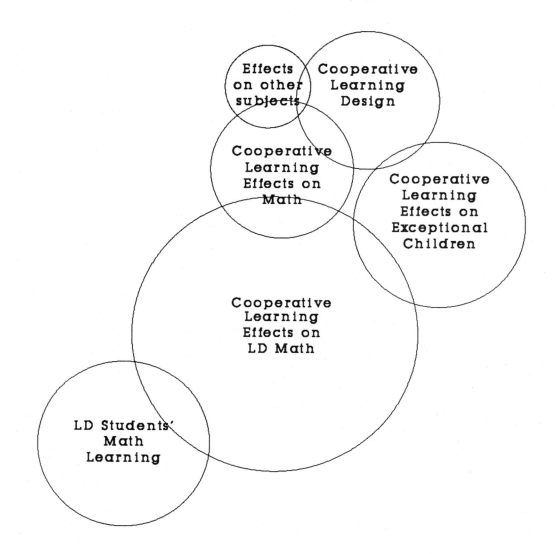

FIGURE 1. Topics included in a review of the effects of cooperative learning on LD students' math achievement. The farther the circle is from the center, the less extensive the review.

this process one step further, however. They are presumably conducting a research review because they wish to bring research findings to bear on some practical problem; they also are conducting the review to share with others. As a final step in such a review, a research distributor should be able to make recommendations for action based on the conclusions drawn from research.

Quantitative research synthesis, or meta-analysis, is becoming increasingly common and can be a valuable tool for research distributors. Even those who do not use the quantitative methods of meta-analysis can profit from a discussion of the considerations necessary for valid research synthesis (e.g., Light & Pillemer, 1984).

Scores. Research distributors need a wider access to journals and other sources of research than do most consumers. In addition to school psychology journals, distributors need access to educational psychology, special education, behavioral, and counseling and clinical psychology journals. University libraries and electronic data bases that can search many journals quickly for keywords of interest can be extremely useful resources for research distributors. Distributors also need access to other sources of research (conferences, ERIC, etc.) and they should be able to integrate basic, theoretically oriented research with applied research.

Improving skills. Psychologists interested in improving their research-distributing skills may also profit from the books and articles listed in this chapter's bibliography. They should also develop the practice of critically reviewing the research they read and should study research reviews written by others. One excellent way to practice reviewing research is to serve as a referee for articles submitted to journals. Most journal editors are eager to find colleagues who are willing to serve as occasional reviewers for research and review articles submitted for publication in their journals (and editors of school psychology journals are often especially eager to find *practitioners* willing to review articles). Most journals use anonymous reviewing (the reviewer does not know the identity of the author or other reviewers and vice versa) in order to insure honesty in reviews; courtesy should not be sacrificed as a result of anonymity. Serving as a reviewer provides practice and often feedback; most editors send each reviewer the comments of the other reviewers in addition to their own blinded letter to the author.

Without realizing it, most psychologists hear questions that are amenable to research review constantly, from parents, teachers, and administrators. Do you think young boys should wait an extra year before starting kindergarten? Should I give homework to second graders? Should we institute a cooperative learning program in the elementary schools? All of these questions address educational topics that have been the focus of research, and answering those questions

may be easier with a solid understanding of what research says about the effectiveness of the programs in question. Psychologists who wish to add the role of research distributor to their jobs can begin by volunteering to help provide answers to some of these questions or by volunteering to serve on policy-making committees. For example, districtwide policies on homework are becoming popular; a psychologist serving as a research distributor could provide valuable information to a policy-making committee on the effects of homework on student learning.

Conductors of Research

Designing and conducting research. Conductors of research first need to be competent consumers and distributors of research. Beyond that, they of course need to be competent in research design and analysis. Arguably, they also need another, often overlooked skill: They should be able to transform vague questions of practice and policy into general research questions. In my experience, the most common mistake made by inexperienced researchers is that they tend to focus immediately on the details of a study (the sample, the statistics to be used); a common mistake made by experienced researchers is that they have vague or poorly defined research questions. The missing step in both cases is to go beyond the vague questions that led to an interest in the topic being studied and to derive general, testable research questions. Do you wonder what can be done to best educate disadvantaged youth, or whether low-achieving first graders should be retained? These vague questions of policy can be phrased as research questions in a variety of ways, each of which would lead a slightly different research design. I find it helpful to force myself to phrase these vague questions as questions of ten words or less, usually in the form of does x affect (or improve, or influence) y? Does retention in grade improve later achievement? Does an academic curriculum affect disadvantaged students' future economic success? Once the general question has been phrased, conducting research is simply a matter of making choices (how do we define *disadvantaged*?) and compromises (should we use a small, but intensively interviewed local sample, or a larger regional sample with less information per person?). With practice, you will find research questions popping up everywhere — as a result of normal conversations, articles in journals, newspaper stories and editorials, and other unlikely sources (for example, the seed for my question about educating disadvantaged youth was planted by an article in *Reader's Digest*).

Conductors of research also need competence in a variety of research designs in order to ensure that the design chosen indeed tests the research question asked. *Expertise* in research design is not necessarily needed if you are willing to collaborate or seek the advice of someone with that expertise, but a broad understanding of research design is needed. In particular, competence is needed in research methods that are appropriate in applied settings but may not be stressed in a typical graduate program: quasi-experimental, single-case, and nonexperimental designs and psychometric methods.

Similarly, conductors of research need a general, broad competence in analysis, in order to ensure that the method of analysis is compatible with the research design and the research question. For any sort of statistical analysis one needs access to a good statistics computer program. There are multitudes of programs available for personal computers, ranging from simple to complex and from cheap to expensive. Psychologists who choose their own program rather than using one that someone else has chosen need to make sure that the program calculates the statistics wanted and calculates them accurately; the first requirement is easier to fulfill than the second. One option is to use one of the major programs derived from mainframe statistics packages (e.g., SAS or SPSS). These programs are widely used and regularly updated, and so one may have confidence that any errors will be quickly spotted and remedied. Unfortunately, these packages also tend to be the more expensive and largest programs available. Fortunately, there are many less expensive programs, but care is needed in choosing a program that is accurate and easy to use. Reviews are one source of help in choosing a program, and are becoming more commonplace in professional journals and computer magazines. Beyond reviews, one needs to look for a program that computes the statistics wanted, is easy to use, is widely used, and is regularly revised. Statistical programs are increasingly becoming required purchases in statistics classes and are often available at a considerable discount through such classes; the opportunity to purchase a good program at a low cost may be an extra benefit for anyone planning to take a new or refresher research class.

Conductors of research also need competence in communicating the findings of research orally and in writing. Nothing spoils a good piece of research faster than a report of that research that is poorly written, vague, or full of jargon.

Improving skills and becoming a research conductor. Many psychologists have the knowledge necessary to conduct research, and most have, or could easily have, access to data that would be useful for research purposes. School psychologists are awash in data (test scores, ratings, observations), much of which would be ideal for research purposes with a little prior planning. What is generally missing is *practice* doing research; even school psychologists who have completed a thesis or dissertation often do not feel comfortable with the process of doing research. If this assessment is correct, what psychologists - those with the requisite skills — need is to work with, or even serve as apprentices to, others who are actively conducting research.

Probably the easiest way to develop a research apprenticeship is to contact faculty in school psychology or related areas at a local university. Most faculty at universities with graduate programs are expected to carry on a program of research as a part of their jobs; most would welcome help in data collection, analysis, writing, and the other tasks of research, especially if you can provide a source of data and are interested in answering research questions that are of interest to them. Another option is to work with others at a local level who are doing research. For those interested in serving as an apprentice, proximity is important in order to experience all aspects of research; for those with research experience who are looking more for collaboration, proximity may not be as important. With computers and electronic mail (even with regular mail), long-distance collaboration is quite possible and increasingly common.

The best way to assume the role of conductor as a part of your job description is essentially the same as for a research distributor: Volunteer to find the answer to a research question that evolves from a problem facing your school system (or mental health center, etc.). If your research will answer a question of interest to your employer, not cost a lot of money, and not interfere with your other responsibilities, you will probably be welcome to conduct it. It may take a commitment of your own time in the beginning, but if you can prove your worth as a research conductor, your employer will begin to see this role as a part of your job.

SUMMARY

All school psychologists should be involved in research, although there is little need for most actually to conduct research. All psychologists need to be effective consumers of research; they should be able to read critically research that has implications for their practice and incorporate the findings of that research into their practice. A smaller number of psychologists are needed to serve as research distributors: They summarize the findings of research and convey those findings to their colleagues and employers. A still smaller number may be interested in actually conducting research: They should be able to design and conduct studies that answer research questions of interest to themselves and their employers. It is not particularly difficult to serve in any of these roles; the hardest part is getting started.

ACKNOWLEDGMENTS

I am grateful to Jeff Braden and Christy Novak for their helpful comments on earlier drafts of this chapter.

REFERENCES

Barlow, D. E., & Hersen, M. (1984). *Single case experimental designs: Strategies for studying behavior change* (2nd ed.). New York: Pergamon.

Campbell, D. T., & Stanley, J. C. (1963). *Experimental and quasi-experimental designs for research.* Chicago: Rand McNally.

Deno, S. L. (1986). Formative evaluation of individual student programs: A new role for school psychologists. *School Psychology Review, 15,* 358–374.

Huck, S. W., Cormier, W. H., & Bounds, W. G., Jr. (1974). *Reading statistics and research.* New York: Harper & Row.

Keith, T. Z. (1987). Children and homework. In A. Thomas & J. Grimes (Eds.), *Children's needs: Psychological perspectives* (pp. 275–282). Washington, DC: NASP.

Keith, T. Z. (1988). Research methods in school psychology: An overview. *School Psychology Review, 17,* 508–526.

Kerlinger, F. N. (1979). *Behavioral research: A conceptual approach.* New York: Holt, Rinehart & Winston.

Kerlinger, F. N. (1986). *Foundations of behavioral research* (3rd ed.). New York: Holt, Rinehart & Winston.

Light, R. J., & Pillemer, D. B. (1984). *Summing up: The science of reviewing research.* Cambridge, MA: Harvard University Press.

Paschal, R. A., Weinstein, T., & Walberg, H. J. (1984). The effects of homework on learning: A quantitative synthesis. *Journal of Educational Research, 78,* 97–104.

Phillips, B. N. (1982). Reading and evaluating research in school psychology. In C. R. Reynolds & T. B. Gutkin (Eds.), *The handbook of school psychology* (pp. 24–47). New York: Wiley.

Reynolds, C. R. (1982). The problem of bias in psychological assessment. In C. R. Reynolds & T. B. Gutkin (Eds.), *The handbook of school psychology* (pp. 178–208). New York: Wiley.

Reynolds, C. R., Gutkin, T. B., Elliott, S. N., & Witt, J. C. (1984). *School psychology: Essentials of theory and practice.* New York: Wiley.

ANNOTATED BIBLIOGRAPHY

Barlow, D. E., & Hersen, M. (1984). *Single case experimental designs: Strategies for studying behavior change* (2nd ed.). New York: Pergamon.
This comprehensive book is probably the single most important reference for single-case research methods.

Huck, S. W., Cormier, W. H., & Bounds, W. G., Jr. (1974). *Reading statistics and research.* New York: Harper and Row.
This fine book is intended primarily for people who want to read and understand the research of others (here called research conductors and distributors). It presents statistics and research designs from a conceptual standpoint and, although dated in places, does a nice job of demystifying research. It also contains a nice introductory chapter on single-case research.

Keith, T. Z. (1988). Research methods in school psychology: An overview. *School Psychology Review, 17,* 508-526.

This article provides a conceptual overview of diverse research methods used in school psychology, with a particular emphasis on understanding the power of different methods for inferring that a research treatment produces an outcome.

Kerlinger, F. N. (1986). *Foundations of behavioral research* (3rd ed.). New York: Holt, Rinehart, & Winston.
Kerlinger's book is probably the best single book on research; his is primarily a conceptual, theoretical approach, although he does not shy away from numbers. Despite some unevenness of coverage (single-case designs are not discussed; the presentation of LISREL is overly enthusiastic), this is a very thorough book. For an even less numerical approach, try Kerlinger, F. N. (1979). *Behavioral research: A conceptual approach.*

Phillips. B. N. (1982). Reading and evaluating research in school psychology. In C. R. Reynolds & T. B. Gutkin (Eds.), *The handbook of school psychology* (pp. 24-47). New York: Wiley.
Phillips presents a variety of issues pertinent to research in school psychology, written primarily for consumers and distributors.

15

Best Practices in Considering Cultural Factors

Ena Vazquez Nuttall
Northeastern University

Brunilda De Leon
Holyoke (Massachusetts) Schools

Mercedes Valle
East Orange (New Jersey) Schools

OVERVIEW

On Monday morning Susan Smith, a school psychologist, is planning her work agenda for the week. Examining the list of referrals, she realizes that the types of problems to be solved are different from those she faced 10 years ago. She must find a way of assessing LiChieh, a Chinese high school student who is not making progress in English, even though her achievement in math is exceptional. Ms. Smith must serve several new Spanish-speaking children who need to be tested first for language dominance and then, depending on their knowledge of English, sent out to be tested or assessed internally for psychoeducational problems. Participation in a committee to study the causes of the high dropout and pregnancy rates of minority children at her school will also take her time during the week. How is she going to handle these new clients and concerns?

This chapter is designed to help school psychologists like Ms. Smith deal effectively with the cultural factors that increasingly impinge on the practice of school psychology. Serving culturally different children has become part of the role of most school psychologists throughout the country. In 1980, minority children constituted 27% of the population. It is predicted that shortly after the turn of the century 1 of every 3 U.S. citizens will be nonwhite. In each of the 25 largest schools in the country, minority students (Black, Hispanic, Asian) constitute the majority of the student body. The number of Hispanics increased by 60% between 1970 and 1980. Also, high rates of migration from South and Central America, the Caribbean, and Asia add to these totals (Staff, 1987).

In addition to growing in numbers, some minority groups are also experiencing increased dropout rates. A *Time* magazine article (Bowen, 1988) reports that in seven cities with high proportions of minority students, dropout rates ranged from 30% to 46%. Teenage pregnancy is also a problem. Births to teenagers from all groups constituted 14% of all births in 1983. However, Blacks, who are only 15% of the teenage population, delivered half of the babies born. The implications of these figures are serious when one considers that about 20% of teenage mothers give birth to low-birth-weight babies who tend to be less healthy and later to develop more learning problems than their normal counterparts. This problem is compounded by the fact that teenage mothers also tend to give birth to children who become teenage mothers themselves. Half of teenage mothers drop out of school and never return.

While minority children possess characteristics that place them more at risk than majority children, they lack personnel of their own ethnic and linguistic background to serve their needs. Minority professionals are underrepresented in the fields of regular education, special education, and school psychology (Baca & Chinn, 1982; Vazquez Nuttall, 1987). Thus majority school psychologists need training to deal appropriately with their needs.

In order to help school psychologists serve minority children competently, this chapter will provide answers to the following questions: What are important concepts that school psychologists should use when serving culturally different children? What attitudes do school psychologists need in order to work with minority children? What kinds of knowledge should school psychologists possess? What strategies can they implement?

BASIC CONSIDERATIONS

Certain key concepts need to be understood by those serving minority children. The first of these concepts is *culture*, which is defined by Linton (1945) as "the configuration of learned behavior and results of behavior whose components and elements are shared by members of a particular society" (p. 32).

A related but narrower concept is *ethnicity*, which includes "patterns of values, social customs, perceptions, behavioral roles, language usage, and social interaction shared by group members" (Rotheram & Phinney, 1986, p. 11). Many people think the term *race* has the same meaning as the term *ethnicity*. However, racey is essentially a biological term that refers to a system by which both plants and animals are classified into categories according to specific physical and structural characteristics (Atkinson, Morten, & Sue, 1989). Anthropologists conceptualize race as consisting of three basic types — Caucasoid, Mongoloid, and Negroid — but the usefulness of this classification is questionable, since differences within types are larger than those between. The case of a Vietnamese refugee is a good example to illustrate these basic concepts: this person is racially Mongoloid, of Asian culture, and of Vietnamese ethnicity.

Minority group is another central concept to master. In the context of the present chapter it is appropriate to use a definition that stresses the element of oppression (Atkinson et al., 1989) such as Wirth's (1945): "a group of people who because of physical and cultural characteristics, are singled out from others in the society in which they live for differential and unequal treatment, and who therefore regard themselves as objects of collective discrimination" (p. 347).

Another extremely useful term to understand when serving minorities is *acculturation.* The term has been defined by Redfield, Linton, & Herskovits (1936) as "those phenomena which result when groups having different cultures come into first hand contact with subsequent changes in the original cultural patterns of either or both groups. The results of acculturation are either acceptance, adaptation, or rejection" (p. 150).

In order to understand acculturation at the individual level, Atkinson et al. (1989) have proposed a model of identity development that explains how minority persons respond to the dominant culture, in five stages.

1. Stage 1. Conformity: In this stage individuals dislike themselves, and members of their own group, and discriminate against other minority groups. However, they admire members of the dominant group.

2. Stage 2. Dissonance: Individuals experience conflict between depreciating and appreciating themselves and their own group. They are torn between the views held by majority society against other minority groups and their own feelings of shared experience. They also feel ambivalent about members of the majority culture.

3. Stage 3. Resistance and Immersion: Individuals begin to appreciate themselves and their own group. They experience conflict between their own feelings

of empathy for other minority groups and their own ethnocentric feelings. Dislike for the majority group emerges.

4. Stage 4. Introspection: Individuals question the basis for liking themselves and members of their own group. They are concerned with the ethnocentric basis for judging other minorities and the dominant group.

5. Stage 5. Synergetic articulation and awareness: Individuals appreciate themselves, members of their own group, and members of different ethnic groups. They begin to appreciate selected aspects of the majority culture.

School psychologists need to learn how to apply the stages of identity development to their practice. In schools with sufficient personnel, knowing the stage that has been reached by a client may help determine who should be seeing the client. When clients are at Stage 1 or 5, they are more accepting of a professional from a dominant culture. On the other hand, minority families in Stage 3 may demand that only a member of their own group deliver services to their children.

Before ending this section, it is important to inform school psychologists that using terms such as *culturally deprived,* and culturally disadvantaged or language disadvantaged hurts the feelings of many minority group members. They feel insulted and demeaned by these terms. Everyone has a culture and knowing a language other than English should be considered an asset. Terms such as *educationally* or *economically disadvantaged* are more appropriate. Cultural differences of children and families should be respected and celebrated, not perceived as deficits.

BEST PRACTICES IN CONSIDERING CULTURAL FACTORS

Professionals serving culturally different clients need to develop competencies in three areas: attitudes, knowledge, and behavior. Sue and his associates (Sue et al., 1982) developed a series of cross-cultural counseling competencies to guide

the provision of effective services for minorities. The work to be presented in this section was inspired by the ideas of this group.

Attitudes

School psychologists need to explore their own cultural backgrounds. Many school psychologists fail to realize that their social and cultural backgrounds affect the way they perform their roles. To better serve minorities, school psychologists need to be aware of themselves and their ethnic roots. Questions such as: "Who am I? What is my ethnic family background? What values do I hold highly? What values do I reject?" need to be asked and considered. If a psychologist comes from a family of recent migration and from a cultural group whose values are close to the minority child's values, acceptance and understanding of the child are more likely to come easily. However, the psychologist who comes from a family that is totally assimilated may have difficulty comprehending the situation of the culturally different child if the child's values differ markedly from those of the majority culture.

School psychologists need to be aware of their attitudes toward children and families from different ethnic groups. School psychologists should reflect on their attitudes toward culturally different children. Questions to ask in this area are: What stereotypes do I hold about families and children of different ethnic groups? What positive or negative experiences have I had with members of this particular ethnic group? What are my expectations regarding the intellectual ability and career expectations of these children? Do I stereotype these children? Do I think all Black children are of low intellectual functioning or that all Asian adolescents should become laundry or restaurant workers?

School psychologists should respect and feel comfortable with children and families of different ethnic groups if they are to serve them effectively. It is recommended (Nuttall & Walton, 1988; Casuso, 1978) that school psychologists develop sensitivity and comfort working with different ethnic groups by doing some of the following things: (a) If needed, learn the language of the particular ethnic group you are serving or at least learn a few key words that will facilitate the establishment of rapport; (b) take courses in cross-cultural issues in school psychology; (c) if possible, visit the countries from which the children have come; (d) visit their homes, eat their native foods, and live in their community in direct contact with the native institutions and cultural practices; (e) read fiction and nonfiction about the different ethnic groups; (f) accompany a minority family to the welfare office, local hospital, or housing authority and experience first-hand the way they are treated; (g) if you are not bilingual, try to ask for directions in a part of town where no one speaks English so that you can experience the frustration of not being able to communicate your needs; and (h) if you work with low-income families, try to live for a week on the salary of a single parent with a handicapped child.

Knowledge and Behavior

When serving minority and majority children whose cultures the school psychologist does not know, it is important for the school psychologist to learn about them. In this section, we present a brief overview of the four major minority groups in the United States: Asians, Hispanics, Native Americans, and Blacks. Although there are many differences within each of these groups, elements shared by members of each group as a whole will be presented. Use of these concepts should be accompanied by careful evaluation of the particular child and family. This evaluation should include, if relevant and appropriate, information about their geographical origin, birthplace of family members, generation in this country, level of education both in the country of origin and in the United States, and the child's linguistic and academic history. Eliciting the information suggested above is more appropriate for recent immigrants, established immi-

grants with strong family ties, and traditional members of these groups (Ho, 1987). School psychologists should consider that all children partake of mainstream and ethnic cultures, but also develop their own personal one. Stereotyping of any ethnic group, majority or minority, should be avoided.

Hispanic Americans

Hispanics constitute the second-largest minority group in the United States, and it is predicted that they will be the largest by the year 2000. Census Bureau figures report an estimated 12 million Hispanics broken down into the following categories: Mexican-Americans, 7.2 million; Puerto Ricans, 1.8 million; and 3 million Spanish, including Central and South Americans, Cubans, and persons from other Spanish origin countries (U.S. Bureau of the Census, 1980).

Most Hispanics are Catholic. However, they practice their religion in different ways. Mexicans are especially devoted to the Virgin of Guadalupe, the patron saint of Mexico (Martinez, 1988). Puerto Ricans and Cubans tend to mix their Spanish Catholic medical and religious practices with African and other belief systems. The most common are santeria and espiritismo. Santeria combines the beliefs of Yorubans (Africans from South Nigeria) with espiritismo, a belief system that posits an invisible world that is populated by spirits and that surrounds the visible world. Espiritismo is a form of mental health care in which espiritistas (mediums) pay attention to the client's problems and explain them in terms of psychosomatic theory or espiritismo (e.g., a person is depressed because a tired spirit is attached to his or her soul). Then they prescribe remedies such as saying prayers to different saints or using water to clean the soul of evil spirits. Some psychologists have worked conjointly with espiritistas to help families solve mental health problems (Ramos-McKay, Comas-Diaz, & Rivera, 1988).

Conceptions of time as well as of spirituality differ between mainstream U.S. culture and Hispanic culture. Hall

(1976) categorizes use of time in two ways: polychronic and monochronic time. In polychronic time many activities happen at once, and stress is placed upon completion of activities rather than adherence to preset schedules. Timelines for activities are flexible and people tend not to be worried about being on time. In monochronic time, single events happen one at a time and activities are tightly scheduled. Most Hispanics, especially recent immigrants, tend to follow a polychronic time orientation. Parents tend to be late for appointments and have difficulty understanding that meetings with teachers occur on a very tight schedule. Mainstream school psychologists interpret their tardiness as a measure of lack of interest or as a discourtesy.

According to Triandis (1987), cultures differ about whether they pay most attention to what people do or who people are. Collectivist cultures tend to emphasize who a person is and almost always assume that in-group members in authority do the right thing, while out-group authorities are viewed with suspicion. Individualist cultures are more likely to focus on behavior and hence question people's actions. In collectivist cultures there are more differentiations among persons based on age, sex, religion, language, race, tribe, or status. People are more sensitive to the views of others and conform to in-group norms more consistently than in individualistic cultures. The fact that Latin America includes some of the most collectivist cultures, while the United States is among the most individualistic, presents challenges to school staff.

Communication between Hispanics and mainstream Anglos is sometimes difficult. To communicate effectively three factors should be considered: use of space, degree of self-disclosure, and eye contact. Hispanics tend to prefer shorter distances between participants during social interaction and interpret longer distances as coldness. Thus Hispanic parents may feel that majority group school psychologists are uncaring because they keep a relatively longer distance. However, appropriate space is affected by sex, and thus male school psychologists should keep distance when working with Hispanic mothers.

Hispanics are less self-disclosing than mainstream Anglos and do not tend to speak directly about issues. The school psychologist has to learn to infer from the context and should avoid asking direct questions, especially at the beginning of the relationship. Although Hispanics tend to use direct eye contact, children are taught to show respect when being reprimanded by looking down. This practice tends to create problems with mainstream teachers who expect the children to look at them in the eye when they are reprimanded.

Family and social structure. Hispanics tend to feel strong ties to both the nuclear and the extended family. Grandparents, aunts, uncles, cousins, nieces, and nephews tend to keep close contact with each other. Hispanic children tend to use both their mother's and their father's last names. Thus, a Hispanic child might write her name Ana Garcia Perez if Garcia is the father's surname and Perez is the mother's. School staff who do not realize this arrangement and call the children by the mother's surname create confusion.

The roles of the sexes in Spanish cultures tend to be more differentiated than in U.S. culture. Men tend to perform certain roles such as earning money, protecting the family, and making major decisions. Women are expected to deal with childrearing and home maintenance. However, some of these roles are changing and Hispanic males, especially educated ones, are becoming more democratic, sharing more of the family decisions with their wives. Many women are working outside the home and demanding more rights and power (Vazquez-Nuttall, Romero, & De Leon, 1987). Notwithstanding the progress made, male school psychologists are urged to visit Hispanic families with a female colleague or to wait until the father is home, because protective Hispanic males may question their intentions.

The compadrazgo (godparent relationship) plays an important role in many Hispanic families and results from the

Catholic ritual of baptism; a male and female compadre participate in the baptism of a child. Later, compadres act like surrogate parents, helping to solve child and school problems.

Rearing of Hispanic children emphasizes dependence on family, and respect and obedience to adults. Girls are required to take responsibility in the home, but the boys are left on their own (Vazquez-Nuttall & Romero-Garcia, 1989). Playing with relatives and loyalty to siblings is emphasized. Collaboration with siblings is encouraged. Children are urged to do well in school to make their parents and extended family proud. They are often walked down to school in the morning and picked up in the afternoon. This is in contrast to the practice of mainstream parents, who encourage their children to go off to school on their own, take initiative, and achieve for their own satisfaction (McGill & Pearce, 1982).

School issues. Because Hispanic children have been in our schools longer and constitute substantial numbers, there are more bilingual education programs, assessment devices, and special education services geared to meet their needs than for other limited English-speaking groups (Vazquez-Nuttall, Goldman, & Landurand, 1983). However, provision of these services has not come without controversy, especially over the use of bilingual education. Two of the greatest sources of controversy are the time the children take to learn English and in what language to start teaching reading. Two concepts introduced by Cummins (1984) are crucial in understanding this debate. One of them is *basic interpersonal communicative skills* (BICS) which is defined as the manifestation of language proficiency in everyday communicative behavior. The second is *cognitive academic language proficiency* (CALP), which is defined as the manipulation of language in decontextualized academic situations. According to Cummins, children need at least 6 years to become proficient at the CALP level, and they do better when they start reading in their native language. However, most school systems transfer these children into regular classes as soon as they are at the BICS level and usually start teaching reading in English.

Asian Americans

The term *Asians* or *Asian and Pacific Americans* (APAs) describes a conglomeration of ethnic groups that originated in the Asian and Pacific Basin. The 1980 Census included the following groups among APAs: Chinese, Filipino, Asian Indian, Japanese, Korean, Vietnamese, Guamanian, Hawaiian, Samoan, and "other." Asians vary within and across groups in language, education, and social class (Chan & Kitano, 1986).

Most Asian cultures have been influenced by the doctrines and philosophies of Buddhism, Confucianism, and Taoism. Confucian thought centers around the concept of harmony, which is seen as the key to existence. Individuals strive to maintain harmony with themselves, others, and nature as well as time. The preservation of the social order is deemed important, each individual occupying and acting out the specific roles assigned. Asian culture demands filial piety, which is unquestioned loyalty and obedience to parents, and concern for and understanding of their needs and wishes (Chan, 1986).

Family and social relationships emphasize subordination and interdependence. Individuals perceive themselves as members of their families and of the larger social structure. Cooperation, dependence, obligation, and reciprocity are essential elements of social interaction (Chan, 1986).

Disclosure of feelings is not as open and free in Asian as in U.S. culture. The manner and content of communication depends on factors such as age, sex, education, occupation, social status, family background, marital status, and whether one has children or not. These factors influence who will bow lowest, initiate conversation, change subjects, speak more softly or loudly, look away first when eyes meet or be most accommodating (Shon & Ja, 1982). Situations in which these behavioral guidelines are unknown, such as school meetings, cause a great deal of anxiety. Because Asians cherish harmony, direct confrontation is avoided as much as possible. Thus, much communication is indirect and involves talking around the point.

Family and social structure. Southeast Asian families tend to be large (Tran, 1982) and to include the extended family. In addition to the nuclear family, the household may include grandparents, cousins, aunts, and uncles who participate in childrearing. Indochinese children are socialized to show deference to their parents and their elders (Chinn & Plata, 1986).

Men are considered the principal breadwinners and heads of households. The traditional role of the mother is to be the nurturant caretaker of both her husband and their children. She is clearly the devoted, nurturant parental figure who feeds the children, takes care of them when they are sick, and helps them with homework. Within traditional families, sons are more valued than daughters. The eldest son is the most important child, receiving better treatment and more respect but also shouldering more responsibility (Shon & Ja, 1982).

Asians' names are written in opposite order from U.S. names. The first name is the family name; the last is the given name. Asians usually use the given name for identification (Wei, 1983).

Children are inculcated early with a sense of moral obligation and loyalty to the family. Behaviors that maintain and enhance the family are considered valuable. When disciplining, parents appeal to a child's sense of obligation to others. Children's behavior reflects on the family. If a child behaves well in school or outside the family, pride and honor increase. However, if the child is disobedient, is disrespectful, or shirks responsibility, the whole family is shamed and dishonored and the child is severely punished (Morrow, 1987).

School issues. Morrow (1987) recommends that school staff serving Asian families should (a) review the parents' background, including their educational level, country and city of origin, and length of time in this country; (b) learn their cultural values; (c) help parents develop trust in the school and its staff; (d) recognize the family's "face-saving" needs, especially when dealing with a handicapped child (Asians view handicaps as punishment for moral transgressions of parents or ancestors, or as the work of evil spirits); (e) know that Southeast Asians want schools to be demanding and instill discipline and teachers to be respected and in control; and (f) understand that treatment of illness differs. Some Vietnamese groups use "cupping," which consists of dipping a piece of cotton in alcohol, lighting it inside an empty cup, and quickly putting the cup on the back of the child. This practice will leave marks and may be confused by mainstream staff with child abuse (Wei, 1983).

Native Americans

The 1980 U.S. Census indicates that the total population of Native Americans and Alaskan Natives is 1.8 million, including more than 400 tribes. Many Native Americans are traditional, live in rural areas or reservations, and know a limited amount of English. Many others live in urban areas and have assimilated to the lifestyles of mainstream society while maintaining little contact with their Indian heritage (Ho, 1987).

Most Native American tribes believe in a supreme force and in harmony between human beings and nature (Everett, Proctor, & Cartnell, 1989). They believe that all growing things and animals have souls and spirits, and should be treated as humanely as possible. To attain maturity, some must learn to live a life that is believed to contain both good and evil, maintaining a high degree of self-control, patience, and a sense of humor (Lewis & Ho, 1989; Edwards & Edwards, 1989).

Native Americans have a time orientation that emphasizes the present and is based on natural phenomena such as morning, day, night, months in terms of moons, and years in terms of seasons or winters (Tracks, 1973).

Native Americans believe in working together and helping each other. Interaction among group members is based on honesty, modesty, and respect for self and others. They are taught to value their own and others' right to make choices without interference (Ho, 1987). Manipulation, coercion, and control over others or over nature are contradictory to most Native American cultural values (Edwards & Edwards, 1989; Everett et al., 1989).

Native American children are encouraged to participate in group activities in which cooperative behavior, collaterality, and respect for each individual are encouraged. These qualities are in conflict with the dominant Anglo culture's emphasis on individuality and competition. Thus, Native American children in public schools are likely to be referred to school psychologists because they are perceived by teachers as lacking in motivation and interest in schoolwork, when in reality they may just be reluctant to compete with peers (Ho, 1987; Johnson & Ramirez, 1987).

The relationship between the individual and the tribal group is complex (Ho, 1987; Everett et al., 1989). For most tribes, the individual's rights and place in the universe are highly valued. Individuals are given the freedom to make their own decisions. At the same time, there is a strong sense of group cohesiveness, and decisions are ideally reached through consensus (Everett et al., 1989; Ho, 1987; Lewis & Ho, 1989).

Some of the most important communication patterns of traditional Native Americans can be summarized as follows: (a) As children, they are not encouraged to verbalize their needs; (b) glorification of self is not promoted; (c) interrupting a conversation is considered to be rude; (d) use of indirect communication through tales, stories, paintings, or other symbolic representations is preferred; (e) silence is customary practice and must take place before meaningful conversation begins; (f) interactional styles are collateral and manipulation of social interaction is rarely used; (g) a complex set of rules determines intragroup (i.e., marital, parent/child, spouse/in-laws, etc.) communication styles, sequence, and place (for example, elders in the family must be greeted and talked to first); and (h) social norms regarding touching and eye contact are changing (for example, Native Americans view a firm handshake as aggressive and direct eye contact as disrespectful).

Historically, Native American family systems have been extended networks that include several households, providing a close-knit family structure. The family structure is an active kinship system that includes parents, children, uncles, aunts, grandparents, cousins, and other members of the extended family network. The extended family and the clan have responsibility to and for one another and function as social units in which the welfare of each member is shared by all (Everett et al., 1989; Ho, 1987; Edwards & Edwards, 1989). Roles and responsibilities are clearly defined among family and tribal members.

Authority figures for Native Americans are not necessarily biological parents or members of the family. Often the real authority figure is that person who is identified and highly visible to the tribe, such as a medicine man or woman, a community leader, or an elder within the tribe. Interventions on behalf of Native American children will be significantly influenced by authority figures and leaders. Therefore, efforts to learn who the leaders are and if possible to engage them in the helping process are highly recommended (Everett, 1989; Edwards & Edwards, 1989).

Children occupy a central position in their family and tribe because "they represent the renewal and preservation of life" (Everett et al., 1989). Children are taught and disciplined by many caretakers and they enjoy the warmth and support of many people. Children are considered to be unique and they are believed to be born with power, ability, and the right to make decisions and choices. In contrast to the practices of mainstream U.S. society, Native American children are allowed to develop freely without major concerns about achieving developmental milestones. Parents have the attitude that a child will do things when he or she is ready (Everett et al., 1989). Such child-rearing practices may at times be interpreted by others as permissive or negligent.

Children are encouraged to engage in activities in which cooperation, sharing, self-control, patience, and tolerance are practiced. Children are not taught to feel guilt, because parents believe they have no control over others or their own environment (Ho, 1987). When children "misbehave" they are either ignored or, when necessary, corrected quietly and verbally (Everett et al., 1989). Traditional parent–child interaction is often determined by sex role; parents being responsible for children of their own sex (Ho, 1987).

Because of different expectations about developmental milestones, Native American parents may have difficulty understanding the school's concerns regarding academic, learning, and emotional problems. Language barriers also bring confusion and misunderstanding to the Native American parent. For example, in some Native American languages there is no word that means *retarded* or *developmentally disabled*. Therefore, trying to explain children's problems to Native American parents may require a great deal of time (Edwards & Edwards, 1989). In addition, a child's problem or disease may be seen as a phenomenon of the supernatural world and full of moral implications (Everett et al., 1989).

School issues. In order to serve Native Americans more effectively, the psychologist must be aware of the following issues: (a) Parent involvement must include information and training about due process and procedural safeguards; (b) excessive questioning and discussion of concerns may be intimidating; (c) the needs of the family or clan should be a high priority; (d) their natural support and healing systems must be acknowledged; (e) acceptance of service providers may take time since they may be considered outsiders who must undergo some rite of passage to gain access to the community; (f) Native Americans may be more comfortable if psychologists share some information about themselves and their families; (g) feelings of guilt should not be imposed; (h) short-term goals often help Native Americans see that something of worth is being accomplished; (i) because of the belief in individuality, it is considered inappropriate to discuss the problems of members of their family; (j) group intervention should be a natural and effective medium since Native Americans value collaboration; (k) school projects, and groups to develop awareness of community resources and to develop talents, skills, and leadership are effective ways of working with Native Americans.

Because of the close-knit family structure, when there is a problem, the extended family will be the first point of contact. A religious leader or the tribal community elders will be contacted next. If all this fails, the family may seek help from outside mainstream mental health service providers (Ho, 1987; Edwards & Edwards, 1989).

Blacks

Blacks make up approximately 11% of the U.S. population. Until recent decades, the majority of Blacks lived in the South, but between 1940 and 1970 over 1.5 million migrated to the North and the West Coast in search of job opportunities (Moore, Hines, & Boyd-Franklin, 1982). Over 81% of the Black population lives in urban areas. Black families have come to the United States from many different countries, but the largest group of Blacks are those of African origin whose ancestors were brought to the Americas as slaves. Blacks are a highly diversified group with different values, geographic origins, levels of acculturation, socioeconomic status, religion, and cultural background.

The two major philosophical principles that guide Black families are the survival of the tribe and the oneness of being (Boykin, 1983; Nobles, 1973, 1974). These guidelines are primarily reflected in principles such as unity, cooperative effort, and mutual responsibility, reinforced by a deep sense of the family or kinship. Boykin (1983) explains that the belief system of Afro-American culture is manifested in nine major dimensions: spirituality, harmony, movement, verve, affect, communalism, expressive individualism, orality, and social time perspective. Religion is important for Black families (Nobles, 1972).

Traditional African philosophy has two dimensions of time: past and present; time is elastic and determined by the connection between important events, place, changes of seasons, and environment. However, many assimilated Blacks follow the mainstream culture's concept of time, with its adherence to tight schedules. Nevertheless, a flexible concept of time is likely to be found among some Blacks, particularly low-income families (Nobles, 1972; Boykin, 1983).

Group activities that encourage cohesiveness and corporate and communal experiences are preferred by most traditional Blacks, particularly young people. Blacks, particularly young children, enjoy activities in which spontaneous verbal expression, sharing, physical closeness, and movement and dance are involved (Boykin, 1983).

Because of cultural values and despite the extremely difficult conditions of most Blacks in the United States, the family, kinship, and extended family networks remain the most important social units. Although individuals are encouraged to step forward and to establish and achieve personal goals, their identity as individuals is most likely to be tied to their roles as members of their family and community. Individual versus group dilemmas involve a blending of communality with expressive individuality. Therefore, one achieves individual identity through exercising duties to the collective in a personal manner (Nobles, 1972, 1974; Boykin, 1983).

Interaction and communication among Blacks tend to be characterized by direct and spontaneous expression of feelings and emotions and involves physical closeness and touching. Subjective and passionate interpretations of others' actions are not out of the ordinary among Blacks (Boykin, 1983).

Family and social structure. Black families are likely to have more flexibility of male and female roles in child rearing and household responsibility than mainstream families (Nobles, 1974; Jackson, 1976). Role flexibility can be a strength that can be mobilized in times of crisis, such as divorce, separation, illness, hospitalization, or death of a family member. A variety of parenting arrangements, for example, are likely to be found among Black families (Moore Hines, & Boyd-Franklin, 1982). When fathers are minimally involved or not living in the home, it is not uncommon to find role models for a child within the extended family. Because of the practice of informal adoption of children by members of the extended family, an aunt or grandparent may share the responsibility for childcare.

Regardless of income, Black fathers are likely to demand and to receive recognition as heads of households from their wives and children. In the case of female-headed households, or when fathers are minimally involved or not living in the home, authority and leadership roles, again, are flexible and shared among mothers, members of the nuclear family, or the extended family network. Authority, child-rearing, and household responsibilities are often shared by parents and older siblings (Jackson, 1976; Moore Hines & Boyd-Franklin, 1982). This practice can cause confusion about division of responsibility.

Because Black families believe that children belong to the collective union, children are likely to receive love, support, and advice from many significant people. Black children are taught to value themselves and others. Child rearing emphasizes respect for human beings, ability to examine both verbal and nonverbal cues from the environment, pride, self-reliance, personal and group loyalties, and effective strategies to cope with prejudice and oppression (Boykin, 1983).

Socialization places a strong emphasis on interpersonal relationships. Conformity in the classroom and in the school is of top priority for many Black parents. Parents impart information about teacher-peer-pupil interactions, socially complex situations, and cross-sex relationships (Shade, 1982). Black children are prepared to take on appropriate sex and age roles, which historically have been flexible and interchangeable. They are also prepared to take on the racial role, which by social and political definition is one marked by resistance, suspicion, and caution (Nobles, 1974).

School issues. Academic and emotional problems of children are a major concern for most Black parents. However, differences in culture, socialization, and learning styles, as well as differences in teachers' expectations, create many misconceptions and conflicts that bring Blacks to the attention of the school staff. When they first come to school, for example, Black children are expected to conform to traditional classroom norms while suppressing some of the behaviors characteristic of their more active and oral style (Boykin, 1983).

Because of differences in child rearing, Black children often come to school lacking cognitive skills demanded by the school curriculum (Boykin, 1983) but with a high degree of social intelligence. They are penalized because of their initial disadvantage in specific skills.

Owing to their many negative experiences with mainstream culture, Black families tend to be mistrustful of agencies and rely primarily on family for emotional and financial support. Younger Blacks tend to be more mistrustful of whites than older Blacks who have years of experience with racial discrimination and have learned to evaluate and respond to people on an individual basis (Miller, 1988).

Black parents place great value on education and respond well if they perceive school personnel as sensitive, supportive, and interested in the welfare of their children. Building rapport may take some time, but once established, the psychologist will be trusted and seen by Blacks as a person with authority and power to help them (Jackson, 1976).

Awareness of the cultural values and school expectations of Black families that are in conflict with those of school personnel will help ameliorate problems.

In some Black communities, for example, abilities expressed in streetwise behaviors, playground sports, and sexuality and by doing domestic and child-rearing chores, supplementing family income, and taking on other adult roles at an early age are considered to be adaptive responses to reality (Moore Hines & Boyd-Franklin, 1982).

A summary of the different family- and school-related values of Blacks and the three other minority groups discussed previously is presented in Table 1.

General Recommendations

In this section general professional strategies needed by school psychologists to serve minority children and their families effectively are presented.

1. *School psychologists should take an active, flexible, problem-solving approach when helping minority clients.* School psychologists cannot expect to deal with low-income minority families in the same way that they deal with their suburban middle-class counterparts. These families have to deal with basic problems of survival before they deal with problems of schooling. Helping the family find housing, learn English, get medical treatment, find a job, or secure welfare benefits are the types of services they need.

2. *School psychologists should be advocates for minority children.* Minority children are frequently the objects of prejudice and discrimination. Many school systems are reluctant to provide the services they need or lack the resources and knowledge to do it properly. School psychologists need to advocate for the needs of minority children at the local, state, and national level.

3. *School psychologists who have special skills in dealing with minority children should act as consultants and in-service training providers for school staff.* School psychologists can help teachers understand cultural differences and how they affect a child's performance in the classroom. The staff of the National Clearinghouse for Bilingual Education

TABLE 1
Comparison of Hispanic, Asian, Black, Native American, and Mainstream U.S. Values

Mainstream U.S.	Hispanic	Asian	Black	Native American
Nuclear-family-oriented	Extended-family-oriented	Extended-family-oriented	Nuclear- and extended-family-oriented	Extended family and large network units; clan, tribe
Individualistic	Family comes before the individual	Family central focus	Expressive individuality tied to family and community	Belief in rights of individual as well as others
Children socialized to be independent and competitive	Children taught to be obedient, cooperative, and dependent	Children taught to be obedient, cooperative, and dependent	Children taught dependence on family and community	Children are encouraged to be independent, to make decisions
Competition is valued	Cooperation is valued	Cooperation is valued	Loyalty to family and network	Cooperation is valued
Time is valuable; events are tightly scheduled	Time is flexible; events are not tightly scheduled	Time is "elastic," can be stretched or contracted	Most have mainstream time concept; some have flexible time concept	Spatial'temporal concept of time; present-oriented
Direct eye contact	Children lower their eyes when reprimanded	Lack of eye contact in deference to authority	Physical touching and verbal expression of emotions	Limited eye contact and physical touching
Direct ways of dealing with issues	Indirect ways of dealing with issues	Indirect, subtle response	Direct and spontaneous expression of feelings	Indirect; no interruptions, use of silence
Likelihood parents to value education	For low-income families, daily survival is more important than education	Parents value education	parents respond well if school demonstrates interest	Parents are influenced by staff sensitive to their values and needs
Tendency to use and trust outside agencies	Use family and religious personnel, then outside agencies	Agencies are last resort — usually when problem is extremely serious	Takes time to develop trust, but if staff is sensitive, they will listen	Extended family first; then outside agencies as last resort

Note. This table reflects the ideas of the authors and of the other sources cited in the text.

(Staff, 1989) recommend that teachers (a) provide opportunities for minority students to share information about their culture during social studies, geography, and other classes; (b) encourage minority students to interact with majority-group students, especially in classes in which language is not needed, such as art and gym; (c) pronounce the children's names correctly; (d) pair new students with "buddies" from the same language and cultural background who have been in this country longer; (e) pose questions in class related to instruction to check if the students are learning; (f) use nonverbal gestures to supplement instruction; (g) write out class assignments and important instructions as well as presenting them orally.

Information about festivities, religious holidays, medical practices, and cultural patterns likely to affect a student's behavior in school should be conveyed to school staff. To communicate acceptance and understanding to children and parents of minority groups, it is good to put up bilingual signs welcoming them to the school and indicating the location of the principal's office. Pictures of their heroes or heroines, maps, and cultural artifacts are also important ways of demonstrating care and respect.

4. *School psychologists need to help minority parents to learn about U.S. mainstream culture and school programs, especially those for the handicapped.* Schools reflect the political and social systems of their countries. Children who migrate may come from systems markedly different from those in the United States. Parents need to be introduced to the different school personnel, the curriculum, and the services offered, in particular special education services. If the parents are not bilingual, the services of an interpreter will need to be secured.

5. *School psychologists should help the community and mainstream parents to welcome parents and children from minority groups.* Community groups play an important role in the adjustment of minorities. All across the nation racial incidents are reported such as beatings of minority children or the burning of homes or churches of minority members. These incidents make minority members feel generally unaccepted and unrespected. Positive forces such as church groups, parent associations, and agencies set up specifically to serve minorities can be marshaled by school psychologists. Organizing meetings of these groups to discuss how they can best help, or how to integrate services, is a role the school psychologist can play. School fairs in which members of different groups give information about their countries, display cultural artifacts, and cook ethnic foods are an excellent opportunity for parents and children to develop awareness and respect for other cultures.

SUMMARY

Children from culturally different homes constitute a substantial proportion of schoolchildren nationwide and in many large cities the majority. School psychologists need to develop appropriate attitudes, knowledge, and behaviors to cope with this challenge. This chapter discusses some basic anthropological concepts necessary to understand cross-cultural issues. It also introduces the reader to the cultural values and family patterns of four minority groups: Asians, Hispanics, blacks, and Native Americans. Ways in which their cultural background affect school behaviors are highlighted. Readers are urged not to stereotype cultural minorities or to perceive differences as deficits. Children's cultural diversity should be celebrated and perceived as an opportunity to develop new ways of serving children.

REFERENCES

Atkinson, D. R., Morten, G., & Sue, D. W. (Eds.). (1989). *Counseling American minorities*. Dubuque, IA: W. C. Brown.

Baca, L., & Chinn, P. (1982). Coming to grips with cultural diversity. *Exceptional Education Quarterly, 2*(4), 33-45.

Bowen, E. (1988, February). Getting tough. *Time*, pp. 52-58.

Boykin, A. W. (1983). The academic performance of Afro-American children. In J. T. Spence (Ed.), *Achievement and achievement motives* (pp. 321-369). San Francisco: Freeman.

Casuso, V. (1978). Working with families of preschool handicapped children in Spanish-speaking communities. In P. L. Trohanis (Ed.), *Early education in Spanish-speaking communities* (pp. 17-27). New York: Walker.

Chan, S. (1986). Parents of exceptional Asian children. In M. K. Kitano & P. C. Chinn (Eds.), *Exceptional Asian children and youth* (pp. 36-54). Reston, VA: Council for Exceptional Children.

Chan, K. S., & Kitano, M. K. (1986). Demographic characteristics of exceptional Asian students. In M. K. Kitano & P. C. Chinn (Eds.), *Exceptional Asian children and youth* (pp. 1-12). Reston, VA: Council for Exceptional Children.

Chinn, P. C., & Plata, M. (1980). Perspectives and educational implications of Southeast Asian students. In M. K. Kitano & P. C. Chinn (Eds.), *Exceptional Asian children and youth* (pp. 12-29). Reston, VA: Council for Exceptional Children.

Cummins, J. (1984). *Bilingualism and special education: Issues in assessment and pedagogy*. San Diego, CA: College-Hill.

Edwards, E. D., & Edwards, M. E. (1989). American Indians: Working with individuals and groups. In D. R. Atkinson, G. Morten, & D. W. Sue (Eds.), *Counseling American minorities* (pp. 72-84). Dubuque, IA: W. C. Brown.

Everett, F., Proctor, N., & Cartnell, B. (1989). Providing psychological services to American Indian children and families. In D. R. Atkinson, G. Morten, & D. W. Sue (Eds.), *Counseling American minorities* (pp. 53-71). Dubuque, IA: W. C. Brown.

Hall, E. T. (1976). *Beyond culture.* New York: Anchor/ Doubleday.

Ho, M. K. (1987). *Family therapy with minorities.* Newbury Park, CA: Sage.

Jackson, G. G. (1976, August). The African genesis of the Black perspective in helping. *Professional Psychology*, 292-308.

Johnson, M. J., & Ramirez, B. A. (Eds.). (1987). *American Indian exceptional children and youth.* Reston, VA: Council for Exceptional Children.

Lewis, R. G., & Ho, M. K. (1989). Social work with Native Americans. In D. R. Atkinson, G. Morten, & D. W. Sue (Eds.), *Counseling of American minorities* (pp. 85-92). Dubuque, IA: W. C. Brown.

Linton, R. (1945). *The cultural background of personality.* New York: Appleton.

Martinez, C. (1988). Mexican Americans. In L. Comas-Diaz & E. E. H. Griffith (Eds.), *Clinical guidelines in cross-cultural mental health* (pp. 182-204). New York: Wiley.

McGill, D., & Pearce, J. K. (1982). British families. In M. McGoldrick, J. Pearce, & J. Giordano (Eds.), *Ethnicity and family therapy* (pp. 457-483). New York: Guilford.

Miller, F. S. (1988). Network structure support: Its relationship to the psychosocial development of Black families. *Journal of Black Psychology, 15*(1), 17-39.

Moore Hines, P., & Boyd-Franklin, N. (1982). Black families. In M. McGoldrick, J. K. Pearce, & J. Giordano (Eds.), *Ethnicity and family therapy* (pp. 84-108). New York: Guilford.

Morrow, R. D. (1987, November). Cultural differences — be aware. *Academic Therapy*, 143-149.

Nobles, W. W. (1972). African philosophy: Foundations for Black psychology. In R. Jones (Ed.), *Black psychology* (pp. 18-31). New York: Harper & Row.

Nobles, W. W. (1974). Africanity: Its role in Black families. *Black Scholar, 5*(9), 10-17.

Nuttall, E. V. (1987). Survey of current practices in the psychological assessment of LEP children. *Journal of School Psychology, 25*, 53-61.

Nuttall, E. V., Goldman, P., & Landurand, P. (1983). *A study of mainstreamed limited English proficient handicapped students in Bilingual Education.* Newton, MA: Vazquez Nuttall Associates.

Nuttall, E. V., & Romero-Garcia, I. (1989). From home to school: Puerto Rican girls learn to be students in the United States. In C. T. Garcia Coll & M. L. Mattei (Eds.), *The psychosocial development of Puerto Rican women* (pp. 62-84). New York: Praeger.

Nuttall, E. V., Romero, I., & De Leon, B. (1987). Perceptions of femininity among Hispanic women: A review of the literature. In H. Amaro & S. Russo (Eds.), Special issue on Hispanic women. *Women's Quarterly Journal, 2*, 409-425.

Nuttall, E. V., & Walton, J. (1988). *The assessment of culturally different preschoolers.* Paper presented at the National Association of School Psychologists, Chicago.

Ramos-McKay, J., Comas-Diaz, L., & Rivera, L. (1988). Puerto Ricans. In L. Comas-Diaz & E. E. H. Griffith (Eds.), *Clinical guidelines in cross-cultural mental health* (pp. 204-233). New York: Wiley.

Redfield, R., Linton, R., & Herskovits, M. (1936). Memorandum on the study of acculturation. *American Anthropologist, 38*, 149-152.

Rotheram, M. J., & Phinney, J. S. (1980). Ethnic behavior patterns as an aspect of identity. In J. S. Phinney & M. J. Rotheram (Eds.), *Children's ethnic socialization* (pp. 180-201). Newbury Park, CA: Sage.

Shade, B. J. (1982). Afro-American cognitive style: A variable in school success? *Review of Educational Research, 52*, 219-244.

Shon, S. P., & Ja, D. Y. (1982). Asian families. In M. Goldrick, J. K. Pearce, & J. Giordano (Eds.), *Ethnicity and family therapy* (pp. 208-229). New York: Guilford.

Staff (1987, No. 9). Minority issues in special education: A portrait of the future. *News Digest,* pp. 1-7.

Staff (1989, No. 3). Educating refugees: Understanding the basics. *Forum: National Clearinghouse for Bilingual Education,* p. 1.

Sue, D. W., Bernier, J. E., Durran, A., Feinberg, L., Pedersen, P., Smith, E., & Vazquez-Nuttall, E. (1982). Cross-cultural counseling competencies. *Counseling Psychologist, 10*(2), 45-52.

Tracks, J. (1973). Native American non-interference. *Social Work, 18*, 30-34.

Tran, X. (1982). *The factors building Indochinese parents participation in school activities.* San Diego, CA: San Diego State University, California Institute for Cultural Pluralism. (ERIC Document Reproduction Service No. ED 245 018)

Triandis, H. (1987). Some major dimensions of cultural variation in client populations. In P. Pedersen (Ed.), *Handbook of cross-cultural counseling and therapy* (pp. 21-29). New York: Praeger.

U.S. Bureau of the Census. (1980). *Estimates of the population of the United States by age, race, and sex* (Series p-25, no. 870). Washington, DC: Government Printing Office.

Wei, T. D. D. (1983). The Vietnamese refugee child: Understanding cultural differences. In D. R. Omark & J. G. Erickson (Eds.), *The bilingual exceptional child* (pp. 197-213). San Diego, CA: College-Hill.

Wirth, L. (1945). The problems of minority groups. In R. Linton (Ed.), *The science of man in the world crisis*. New York: Columbia University Press.

ANNOTATED BIBLIOGRAPHY

Atkinson, D. R., Morten, G., & Sue, D. W. (Eds.). (1989). *Counseling American minorities*. Dubuque, IA: W. C. Brown.
Edited book containing the following parts: 1. Why a cross-cultural perspective. 2. The American Indian client. 3. The Asian American client. 4. The Black client. 5. The Latino client. 6. Implications for minority groups/cross-cultural counseling. Contains an Appendix entitled "A position paper: Cross-cultural counseling competencies."

Johnson, M. J., & Ramirez, B. R. (Eds.). (1988). *American Indian exceptional children and youth*. Reston, VA: Council for Exceptional Children.
Edited book focused on Native American exceptional children containing the following sections: 1. Parent and family involvement. 2. Language and curriculum development. 3. Personnel preparation. 4. Public policy.

Kitano, M. K., & Chinn, P. (Eds.). (1986). *Exceptional Asian children and youth*. Reston, VA: Council for Exceptional Children.
Edited book focused on Asian children and youth. Contains the following chapters: 1. Demographic characteristics of exceptional Asian students. 2. Perspectives and educational implications of Southeast Asian students. 3. Psychoeducational assessment of Asian students. 4. Parents of exceptional students. 5. Gifted and talented Asian children. 6. Curriculum development for exceptional Chinese children of limited-English-proficiency.

McGoldrick, M., Pearce, J. K., & Giordano, J. (Eds.). (1982). *Ethnicity and family therapy*. New York: Guilford.
Edited book containing the following sections: 1. Conceptual overview. 2. The paradigms. 3. Special Issues. The book describes families from 18 ethnic groups, including Native Americans, black, West Indian, Mexican, Puerto Rican, Cuban, Asian, French Canadian, German, Greek, Iranian, Irish, Italian, Jewish, Polish, Portuguese, Norwegian, and British.

Phinney, J. S., & Rotheram, M. J. (Eds.). (1987). *Children's ethnic socialization: Pluralism and development*. Newbury Park, CA: Sage.
Edited book containing the following parts: 1. Ethnicity and the young child: Awareness, attitudes, and self-identification. 2. Minority status and the child. 3. Later childhood and adolescence: Ethnic identity and ethnic group patterns. 4. The study of ethnicity: Emerging themes and implications. This volume focuses on black and Hispanic cultures.

16

Best Practices in Coordinating Multidisciplinary Teams

E. Scott Huebner
Western Illinois University
Barbara M. Hahn
Great River Area Education Agency #16
Burlington, Iowa

OVERVIEW

The purpose of this chapter is to discuss school-based multidisciplinary teams (MDTs). Given that as many as 57,000 children have been diagnosed and placed in special education programs for the first time in one year (Zill, 1985), it may be conservatively estimated that school psychologists in the United States have devoted at least 57,000 work hours to participation in MDTs. It should thus be apparent that serving on MDTs is an important and time consuming function of school psychologists.

Maher and Yoshida (1985) argue cogently that MDTs can provide useful vehicles for the delivery of a wide variety of educational services at the individual (e.g., individual pupil or teacher), group (e.g., resource room), and organizational (e.g., school, school district) levels in school settings. MDTs have been used in limited ways in school settings to date, however. Their major functions have been: (a) assessment of children with suspected handicapping conditions, (b) development of IEPs for children placed in special education, and (c) periodic review of the progress of children placed in special education (Maher & Yoshida, 1985). Thus, this chapter will be aimed primarily at improving MDT functioning in these contexts.

BASIC CONSIDERATIONS

Origin of School-Based MDTs

Public Law 94-142 mandated that MDTs make decisions concerning eligibility and programming for special education students. The rationale for the team approach was based upon the notion that "two heads are better than one." That is, representatives from multiple disciplines working together can make better decisions than individuals working alone. The law thus limited the influence of any single profession by requiring input from a variety of professionals as well as parents. One intent of the team approach was to provide a safeguard against decision-making errors by individuals, particularly those related to bias in the assessment of minority children (Kaiser & Woodman, 1985; Pfeiffer & Heffernan, 1984). Additionally, the MDT approach was expected to guarantee greater adherence to due process and to promote enhanced educational services (Pfeiffer & Heffernan, 1984).

Research on MDT Outcomes

In general, research in social psychology and business management supports the effectiveness of team decision-making. Team decisions have been reported to be superior to those made by individuals

(Hare, 1982), especially when the decisions are complex and require different, but complementary skills (Taylor, Berry, & Block, 1958). Under conditions of high complexity, teams generate more novel and creative solutions to problems (Napier, 1968).

Research on the decision-making capabilities of school-based MDTs has been sparse, however, In one study, Vautour (1976) presented the Rucker-Gable Educational Placement Scale (Rucker & Gable, 1973) to 127 professional educators from 20 MDTs. Working alone, the educators were asked to select one of seven placement options ranging from regular class placement to placements outside of regular public schools (e.g., residential treatment) for 30 fictitious handicapped children. Vautour then had the individuals repeat this decision-making task as part of an MDT. The results indicated that MDTs were more accurate in their decision-making than individuals, based upon a comparison with the placement selections of 35 university experts. The results also indicated that team decisions were more reliable (i.e., less variable) than individual decisions.

Pfeiffer and Naglieri (1983) presented two fictitious psychological reports to 86 professionals from 22 teams. One psychological report described a mentally retarded child, while the other described an emotionally disabled child. The educators were asked to select the most appropriate educational placement from one of the seven options on the Rucker-Gable on two occasions — independently and as members of MDTs. The results also showed that the MDTs displayed less variability in placement recommendations than individuals operating alone. Pfeiffer (1982) obtained comparable findings using similar methodology with a sample of educators from Puerto Rico. In both studies, the results indicated negligible differences in mean placement scores between the individual and MDT ratings.

These studies offer some very tentative support for the notion that MDTs produce more reliable placement decisions than individuals acting alone. However, further research is needed to document the utility and effectiveness of MDTs, particularly when confronted with decisions other than placement decisions, such as diagnostic decisions, prognostic decisions, and decisions related to the selection of specific behavioral objectives and associated intervention methods.

Research on MDT Processes

Researchers have also investigated the *processes* involved in team decision-making. The available literature suggests that a variety of process problems have plagued placement MDTs. First, MDTs are not composed of members who all contribute equally to the decision-making process. Assessment personnel, especially school psychologists and special education teachers, often contribute the most to diagnostic decision-making, which constitutes the vast majority of time used in MDT meetings (Ysseldyke, 1983), while regular class teachers and parents frequently contribute very little to such decisions (Ysseldyke, Algozzine, & Mitchell, 1982). Ysseldyke (1983) reported that regular classroom teachers seldom offered suggestions about educational goals or methods, even though they probably have the most knowledge about the child's skills and classroom curriculum and methods. Unfortunately, the extent of participation by members is highly related to their reported degree of satisfaction with the team experience and decision (Yoshida, Fenton, Maxwell, & Kaufmann, 1978).

Second, Ysseldyke (1983) pointed out that a disproportionately small amount of meeting time is spent by members discussing interventions for the student. In actuality, the majority of time is spent describing a child's problems and presenting formal psychoeducational test data and observations.

Pfeiffer and Heffernan (1984) noted three additional difficulties that are frequently associated with MDTs: (a) unsystematic approaches to collecting and analyzing assessment information, (b) use of unstructured, unsystematic decision-making processes, and (c) lack of interdisciplinary collaboration and trust. The latter difficulty includes concerns such as territoriality among members, dominance by one member or a small group of members, and lack of clarity regarding team roles and goals.

The development of a team into an effective problem-solving unit thus often presents many potential difficulties. Teams do not *automatically* demonstrate greater effectiveness than individuals. Without training in team process skills, some teams are no more effective than individuals or nominal (non-interacting) groups (Campbell, 1968). Team membership may yield feelings of dissatisfaction and discouragement. Team members and leaders must display particular skills in order to contribute to an effective, satisfying team experience (Maher & Yoshida, 1985). Thus, a systematic program of ongoing team building and evaluation activities will likely be necessary to maintain effective team functioning.

BEST PRACTICES

Leadership

The coordination of MDTs requires effective leadership skills. Although any member can perform such functions, we would argue that the school psychologist is uniquely suited to this role for several reasons. First, school psychologists are broadly trained in education, psychology, and related fields. As a result of such broad training, they should be most able to integrate and synthesize the multiple disciplinary perspectives represented by the various team members. Second, school psychologists have been shown to perform many boundary spanning functions (Illback & Maher, 1984), that is, serving as liaisons among various school and non-school systems (e.g., families, community agencies). Taken together with the documented high levels of activity and influence that school psychologists display in MDT meetings (Gilliam & Coleman, 1981; Knoff, 1983), school psychologists already appear to play a major role in MDT functioning. Thus, school psychologists

appear to be logical candidates to assume the leadership of many MDTs.

While school psychologists may already serve as MDT leaders in some areas, particularly rural areas (Huebner & Wise, 1988), they do not in others. It should be underscored that support for this role should always be obtained from school administrators (e.g., principal). Organizational changes, such as any of the MDT development and evaluation activities described herein, should be attempted only with the endorsement of those with the legitimate authority to sanction such changes.

Three leadership styles are often described in the literature. Authoritarian leaders dominate the group through dictating decision-making processes and outcomes. Communication generally flows in one direction, in the form of mandates from the leader to followers. In contrast, laissez-faire leaders provide negligible leadership, demonstrating a passive approach to decision-making, avoiding decision-making as much as possible. Democratic leaders allow input from all group members in the determination of goals and decision-making. Communication flows in all directions so that each participant shares power in decision-making. Democratic procedures are generally recommended for most MDT activities because persons have a higher probability of implementing decisions that they have helped make rather than decisions others have made for them (Cooper & Wood, 1974; Maher & Yoshida, 1985).

Coordinating an effective democratic problem-solving team requires the leader to accomplish several team tasks. The major tasks facing the MDT are to develop methods for (a) facilitating effective communication, (b) clarifying roles, (c) setting goals, (d) solving problems, (e) developing collaboration of effort, (f) ensuring follow-through and completion of tasks, and (g) conducting product and process evaluations (Dyer, 1987). In the following section, we will discuss specific skills and strategies needed to accomplish each of these tasks.

Facilitating Effective Communication

A characteristic of effective teams that underlies all others involves the development of a climate of trust and open communication among *all* team members. Prior to effective problem-solving and decision-making activities, team members must feel free to communicate openly with one another — expressing positive and negative feelings toward the various tasks and issues that confront the team. Without such a climate of trust and openness, subsequent efforts at goal setting, problem-solving, and evaluation will be impaired.

Team leaders must display effective communication skills that encourage open discussion among team members. The foremost role of the leader is thus to model open communication skills. As the leader expresses feelings and ideas openly and honestly, others may more readily contribute their ideas and feelings in a manner that promotes cohesion and effective team functioning. To elicit similar behavior from all members, leaders should encourage the expression of all points of view. Skillful use of specific communication skills; such as active listening, perception checking, summarizing, and providing feedback is essential to such goals. Anderlini (1983) provides training materials to teach communication skills relevant to coordinating MDTs.

MDT leaders must also perform communication skills that relate to task and maintenance functions. Task functions involve the completion of work tasks and maintenance functions involve the development of satisfying interpersonal relationships. Arends and Arends (1977) include the following task functions in a listing of communication skills that leaders and other members need to use to carry out effective group work.

1. *Initiating:* Proposing tasks or goals, defining a group problem, suggesting a procedure for solving a problem, suggesting other ideas for consideration.

2. *Information or opinion-seeking:* Requesting facts on the problem, seeking relevant information, asking for suggestions and ideas.

3. *Information or opinion giving:* Offering facts, providing relevant information, stating a belief, giving suggestions or ideas.

4. *Clarifying or elaborating:* Interpreting or reflecting ideas or suggestions, clearing up confusion indicating alternatives and issues before the group, giving examples.

5. *Summarizing:* Pulling related ideas together, restating suggestions after the group has discussed them.

6. *Consensus testing:* Sending up "trial balloons" to see if the group is nearing conclusion, or agreement has been reached. (p. 53)

Arends and Arends (1977) also describe the following maintenance functions:

1. *Encouraging:* Being friendly, warm, and responsive to others; accepting others and their contribution; listening; showing regard for others by giving them opportunity and recognition.

2. *Expressing group feelings:* Sensing feeling, mood, relationships within the group; sharing one's own feelings with other members.

3. *Harmonizing:* Attempting to reconcile disagreements, reducing tension through "pouring oil on troubled waters," getting people to explore their differences.

4. *Compromising:* Offering to compromise one's own position, ideas, and status; admitting error; disciplining oneself to maintain the group.

5. *Gatekeeping:* Seeing that others have a chance to speak; keeping the discussion a group discussion rather than a one-, two-, or three-way conversation.

6. *Setting standards:* Expressing standards that will help the group to achieve, applying standards in evaluating group functioning and production. (p. 54)

To be most effective, team leaders must seek a balance between task and maintenance functions (Schmuck & Runkel, 1985).

Clarifying Roles

Clarifying the roles of various team members is also a team function that is a critical prerequisite to other team activities. This entails answering the question, "Who is responsible for what activities?" Responsibilities for such roles (e.g., leader coordinates decision-making activities using consensus approach, teacher presents analyses of previous intervention efforts and outcomes) should be delineated and agreed upon prior to MDT formation. In some situations, written policy statements outlining responsibilities may be developed cooperatively by team members with the support of relevant administrators (see Kabler & Carlton [1982] for an example). If the agreed upon responsibilities can be determined prior to MDT activities, this may ameliorate turf disputes as well as reduce role ambiguity, both of which may lead to decreased participation by team members. Since membership on placement MDTs is unstable (i.e., some roles, such as parents and teacher, are filled by different persons for each case), role expectations should be addressed and clarified before starting problem-solving activities. Specifically, team members may profit from explaining the rationale for MDTs and expected behaviors to new members (e.g., encouraging parents to actively participate in decision-making processes) and eliciting feedback from them at the beginning of the initial meeting. In this manner, all participants can share in the process of role definition and negotiation.

Setting Goals

Goal setting is an important component of effective team meetings. Goals for MDT meetings are needed to focus and organize subsequent activities, establish reasonable time limits for activities, and allow for the evaluation of the effectiveness of meetings.

This task requires setting goals that are clear and mutually agreed upon. The participants must resolve such issues as "Should this meeting address both diagnostic and intervention decisions?" The effective leader will ensure that goals for each meeting are established by the team

prior to the advent of problem-solving and decision-making activities.

The team leader may use agenda setting procedures (Schmuck & Runkel, 1985) to set a reasonable number of goals for team meetings. It is our experience that many MDT meetings have produced limited effectiveness by attempting to accomplish too many activities in too short of a time period. For example, teams often attempt to present multidisciplinary assessment data, discuss parental reactions, determine eligibility and placement, and develop an IEP for a handicapped child in a one-hour meeting. In contrast to setting aside a predetermined amount of time for all MDT meetings, the coordination of more effective meetings might be achieved by developing individualized meeting plans, including the flexible selection of agenda items and timelines according to the needs of *each* situation.

Facilitating Effective Problem-Solving and Decision-Making

The major function of the MDT is to solve problems, i.e., develop workable programs to meet children's special needs. The effective team leader will use systematic approaches to draw upon all the resources of the various team members to elicit creative ideas to educate children more effectively. The use of the term systematic in this context cannot be overemphasized. Many MDTs utilize problem-solving and decision-making strategies that are unsystematic and do not reflect *team* decisions. For example, many MDTs place almost exclusive responsibility for decisions on one member. Others attempt to include everyone, but without a systematic means to do so effectively. Also, many MDT meetings deteriorate into adversarial relationships between parents and school personnel because of an apparent lack of mechanisms to facilitate truly conjoint decision-making. Using systematic strategies, including a problem-solving "roadmap" such as the one described below, should increase democratic decision-making in MDTs.

Effective problem-solving necessitates a sound data base. Prior to making decisions, team members must collect relevant and comprehensive data. Team members must thus have a clear idea about what assessment questions are to be addressed, what methods are most appropriate to address the questions, and who should collect what information. This demands that the data, which are collected and presented, are appropriate to the various decisions at hand. Many teams may thus have to collect data directly relevant to interventions (vs. classification) if effective intervention programs are to be developed (Ysseldyke, 1983). Comprehensive and appropriate individual data collection procedures are discussed in many publications, including Salvia and Ysseldyke (1988) and Sattler (1988). Following the assessment process, the following problem-solving steps should be addressed.

1. *Defining the problem*. In this step, the MDT members evaluate the assessment data to define the specific educational needs of the child that have not been met by the child's program (Kabler & Genshaft, 1983). The team must agree on the specific strengths and weaknesses of the child, and whether or not a problem exists that must be addressed through intervention. Plas (1981) underscores the importance of assessing and acknowledging student and system *strengths* as well as deficits in order to facilitate later problem-solving efforts. For example, knowing that a student is particularly capable and interested in sports may lead to the identification of a powerful reinforcer in a behavior modification program. Similarly, recognizing the influence of a child's grandparent on the family system may lead to inclusion of the grandparent on an MDT. To facilitate effective problem definition, problems should be stated in behavioral (observable, measurable) terms to ensure that everyone is discussing the same concerns. For example, rather than discussing a child's hyperactivity, we recommend using specific behavioral descriptors (e.g., high frequencies of speaking without raising his hand, leaving his seat without permission, and failure to complete assignments).

Once agreement on the problem(s) has been obtained, objectives for the child should be set. Objectives, also defined in behavioral terms, should provide direction for subsequent problem-solving activities. Helmer (1966) provides a method for selecting objectives when agreement is particularly difficult to obtain. The method involves four major steps. First, all participants write objectives they believe are appropriate for the child. These are combined and tabulated by the leader into a single list of those most frequently mentioned. Second, all participants prioritize the objectives, writing a "1" beside the objective they believe is most important, a "2" beside the objective they believe is the next most important, etc. The leader then tabulates the ratings and presents a verbal report of the findings. Third, all participants again prioritize the objectives. Those who differ from the majority are asked to state their reasons. Fourth, all participants prioritize the objectives again and a final rating is calculated. This method seems particularly useful for resolving conflicts with large groups composed of members from different disciplines and perspectives, such as MDTs.

2. *Generating Alternative Solutions*. In this stage, the MDT leader facilitates the discussion of alternative solution strategies to meet the identified needs of the student. Brainstorming is one method used at this stage in many problem-solving situations. Brainstorming requires that all participants be encouraged to contribute ideas. Initially, suggestions are not evaluated, but rather are accepted and recorded without discussion in an effort to generate as many solutions as possible.

After a sufficient number of ideas has been offered, participants are encouraged to provide a rationale for their suggestions. During this process, the use of effective communication skills (e.g., active listening, summarizing) by the leader and other members can be especially helpful in ensuring that all participants understand the various proposals.

Other more structured methods of problem-solving include social judgment analysis (Hammond, Rohrbaugh, Mumower, & Adelman, 1977), the Nominal Group Technique (Delbecq, Van De Ven, & Gustafson, 1975) and the Decision Analytic Model (Maher, 1981). Kaiser and Woodman (1985) discuss each of these methods in detail and argue that the Nominal Group Technique is particularly suited to groups that experience difficulties related to individual dominance, personality clashes, or group think. The Nominal Group Technique, which is very similar to Helmer's (1966) aforementioned problem-solving method, is described in detail in Delbecq et al. (1973).

Throughout this process, special attention should be paid to increasing the involvement of parents and regular class teachers in MDT functions. Turnbull and Leonard (1981) provide useful suggestions for increasing the involvement of parents, which seem equally applicable to teachers. Specifically, Turnbull and Leonard recommend that leaders: (a) direct questions to the parents, (b) clarify questions and disagreements, (c) explain technical information in jargon-free language; and (d) reinforce parents for their participation. The involvement of teachers in particular has been increased by having an elected regular class teacher serve as a regular MDT member (Pfeiffer, 1980). Not only did this strategy increase the satisfaction and involvement of regular class teachers, but it also improved the practicality of intervention recommendations, which should increase the likelihood of intervention implementation and success.

We would underscore the need to involve teachers and parents in discussion from the very beginning of the meetings, rather than following presentation of other team members' assessment findings and/or intervention recommendations. For example, parents can be asked to: (a) share any concerns they have about their child, (b) provide information about the child's behavior at home, and (c) offer feedback regarding professionals' judgments of their child's unique strengths and

weaknesses and educational needs — as these topics are discussed.

Next, the leader can begin the process of selecting one or more of the proposed strategies to achieve a particular student objective. Again, we recommend the use of a democratic decision-making process (e.g., consensus) in which each member is provided with the opportunity to share in the decision-making. Gordon (1974) and Hare (1983) described detailed procedures for achieving consensus among group members. Arends and Arends (1977) underscored that consensual decision-making requires "solution shaping" rather than "people shaping." That is, team members who dislike a proposal should indicate how the *solution* could be changed to become more acceptable. Thus, team members may spend less time trying to change each others' attitudes and more time developing creative intervention strategies for children. At this time, MDT members should openly express reservations to ensure that the various strategies are thoroughly critiqued. In this manner, those charged with implementing the strategies are more likely to influence and feel ownership for the decision and thus implement the selected strategies.

It is important to note that the same procedures can be used by an MDT to evaluate and solve team process and outcome problems (e.g., role ambiguity, interpersonal tensions). These techniques can be used to examine issues that inhibit effective team functioning and to generate solutions to resolve such problems.

Finally, although democratic decision-making procedures have been shown to increase MDT team members' satisfaction (DeWitt, 1982), they are often time-consuming. Given the many tasks that must be accomplished during typical MDT meetings, effective time management skills (e.g., see Maher, 1981) must be employed. In general, MDT meetings can be conducted most efficiently when reasonable agendas and associated timelines have been established and adhered to. One inefficient use of time we have frequently observed in MDTs involves inadequate methods of organization and presentation of assessment information. Many members' presentations include unnecessary detail, lack a focus or central theme, and fail to summarize findings in a coherent manner. If team members can be taught a more organized and efficient means of presenting data, then more time can be spent on subsequent problem-solving activities. Batsche's (1983) referral oriented consultative assessment report writing model, in which communication is organized according to specific referral questions, can be adapted easily to provide a viable format for presenting information orally in MDT meetings.

Developing Collaboration of Effort

Throughout MDT activities, efforts must be directed toward achieving truly collaborative interactions among team members. The goals are for all participants to acknowledge their resources and limitations, share resources, and recognize mutual gains (Tyler, Pargament, & Gatz, 1983). This means that members must view the problem-solving and implementation processes as involving shared responsibility so that team members don't expect that responsibility for a particular problem area will always be delegated to one team member or particular discipline. Such a cooperative approach "should increase involvement, ensure more meaningful and carefully thought out decisions, and increase the probability of successful execution of recommendations" (Pfeiffer & Heffernan, 1984, p. 297).

In order to set the stage for such cooperative interactions, the aforementioned team objectives must be reached. For example, the MDT team leader and participants should have successfully established a climate of trust and openness, set mutually agreed upon goals, utilized democratic decision-making procedures when appropriate, etc. If these objectives have not been met, team cooperation will be impeded. Perhaps the most important contribution the leader can make to elicit collaboration is to model an appreciation for the multiple, often conflicting disciplinary perspectives represented on the typical MDT. This often

requires a willingness to suspend judgment based on disciplinary loyalties and to acknowledge the contributions of another disciplinary perspective. Plas (1981) points out the utility of an ecological psychology perspective to achieve such synthesis and to increase commitment to carry out the intervention plans.

Ensuring Follow-through and Completion of Tasks

To maximize the probability of implementation, the primary role of the team leader throughout the problem-solving process is to coordinate activities and information sharing. While team leaders may offer intervention suggestions, they should not play the role of the expert and try to coerce adoption of their viewpoint through any means. The goal is to elicit mutually agreed upon strategies, primarily from those who will be directly responsible for implementing intervention efforts. Encouraging implementers to play an active role in decision-making should increase the likelihood that the strategies will actually be carried out.

Once interventions have been agreed upon, it is recommended that they be recorded in written form (Yoshida, Fenton, Maxwell, & Kaufman, 1978). At the same time, the assignment of individual responsibilities, timelines, and review dates should also be determined and recorded. MDT members should be required to sign the intervention document to increase commitment to carry out the plans. Team members who are not directly involved in implementation efforts can provide continuous consulting support to implementers. For example, Pfeiffer (1980) suggests that MDT members could assume parent advocacy roles to help provide follow-up support based on the most appropriate match between parent needs and available team members.

After the written intervention plan has been developed, one person may be designated as the team monitor who will be responsible for coordinating and reviewing the implementation of the plan (Ohio Department of Education, 1985). The role of team monitor can be rotated among team members, encouraging shared responsibility for the evaluation of implementation efforts.

It seems appropriate to note here that the formulation of a comprehensive intervention program can seldom be accomplished in one MDT meeting. Subgroups may need to be created to work out the details of various components of the plan. However, particular attention should be paid to *sharing* responsibilities for program development and implementation. Too often, MDTs rely solely on classroom teachers without providing adequate support and resources (Pfeiffer, 1981).

Conducting Evaluations

The last phase of the MDT process includes formative and summative evaluations of the intervention program. Such program evaluation procedures have been discussed extensively elsewhere, including Maher and Yoshida (1985).

MDTs should also conduct periodic reviews of their own functioning. The collection of data for evaluation purposes can be achieved in several ways. First, the leader can develop checklists or brief questionnaires that allow the participants to provide feedback regarding the effectiveness of the leader, the team, and/or team processes. Dyer (1987) provides examples of questionnaires that could be modified easily to be appropriate for school MDTs. Second, outside observers can be brought in to observe team functioning and provide feedback concerning team processes. Third, videotapes of team meetings can be made. Team members can subsequently replay the tape and critique their interactions. Of course, this method requires a leader and members who are comfortable enough to honestly and skillfully evaluate one another in a positive manner.

When evaluation data suggest that a team is not functioning as effectively as desired, then members must determine how to address the problems. Prior to implementing team building efforts, the MDT must first decide who will lead the efforts; i.e., the leader or an external consultant. Shonk (1982) recommends that an external consultant be used when the following conditions are met.

1. When the leader's style of management is a major contributor to the team's problems.

2. When there are major conflicts or relationship problems that require an impartial third party facilitator.

3. When non-productive patterns of behavior and team norms have been reinforced over a long period of time and are therefore hard to change and often not challenged by the work group (1982, p. 31).

Again, Dyer (1987) provides an excellent sourcebook for team development activities. As noted previously, the team can apply the problem-solving and decision-making processes described in the preceding pages to influence its own processes and desired outcomes.

SUMMARY

School psychologists perform many of their functions as leaders or members of MDTs. For example, since the advent of PL 94-142, school psychologists have conducted assessments and made special education placement decisions as part of mandated MDTs. School psychologists likely perform many other functions through MDTs.

The efficacy of MDTs has been questioned, however (Yoshida, 1983). A brief review of the literature reveals numerous problems that have plagued school-based placement MDTs. These problems include unequal participation and satisfaction among team members, unsystematic assessment procedures, lack of interdisciplinary collaboration and trust, use of unsystematic decision-making processes, and insufficient time devoted to developing intervention plans.

The use of teams can be supported by research in social psychology and business management. Such research shows that decisions made by groups are often superior, particularly when the decisions are complex and require different, but complementary skills (Taylor,

Berry, & Block, 1958). However, without training in team process skills, teams may be no more effective than individuals (Campbell, 1968). Teams do not automatically demonstrate greater efficacy compared to individuals, but rather members must put into practice particular skills to be effective. Unfortunately, little attention has been paid to preparing school psychologists and other pupil personnel specialists to function as MDT leaders and/or members (Courtnage & Smith-Davis, 1987; Smith, Woods, & Grimes, 1988). In order to function effectively, MDT members would thus likely benefit from preservice and inservice training in team process skills such as those described in this chapter. Structured training materials, such as those developed by Anderlini (1983) may provide a useful starting point for interested trainers. With adequate training, participants should be able to improve MDT effectiveness and increase the likelihood that the promises of multidisciplinary collaboration can be fulfilled.

REFERENCES

Abelson, M. A., & Woodman, R. W. (1983). Review of research on team effectiveness: Implications for teams in schools. *School Psychology Review, 12,* 125-136.

Anderlini, L. S. (1983). An inservice program for improving team participation in educational decision making. *School Psychology Review, 12,* 160-167.

Arends, R. E., & Arends, J. H. (1977). *Systems change strategies in educational settings.* New York: Human Sciences Press.

Batsche, G. M. (1983). The referral oriented consultative assessment report writing model. In J. Grimes (Ed.), *Communicating psychological information in writing* (pp. 27-43). Des Moines, IA: Iowa Department of Public Instruction.

Campbell, J. P. (1968). Individual versus group problem solving in an industrial sample. *Journal of Applied Psychology, 52,* 205-210.

Cooper, M. R., & Wood, M. T. (1974). Effects of member participation and commitment in group decision making on influence, satisfaction, and decision riskiness. *Journal of Applied Psychology, 59,* 127-134.

Courtnage, L., & Smith-Davis, J. (1987). Interdisciplinary team training: A national survey of special education teacher training programs. *Exceptional Children, 53,* 456-458.

Delbecq, A. L., Van de Ven, A. H., & Gustafson, D. H. (1975). *Group techniques for program planning.* Glenview, IL: Scott Foresman & Co.

DeWitt, J. (1982). *Participation and satisfaction on multidisciplinary teams.* Unpublished Master's thesis, The Ohio State University.

Dyer, W. G. (1987). *Team building: Issues and alternatives* (2nd ed.). Reading, MA: Addison-Wesley Publishing Co.

Gilliam, J. E., & Coleman, M. C. (1981). Who influences IEP committee decisions? *Exceptional Children, 47,* 642-644.

Gordon, T. (1974). *Teacher effectiveness training.* New York: Peter H. Wyden.

Hammond, K. R., Rohrbaugh, J., Mumower, J., & Adelman, L. (1977). Social judgment theory: Applications in policy information. In M. F. Kaplan & S. Schwartz (Eds.), *Human judgment and decision processes in applied settings.* New York: Academic Press.

Huebner, E. S., & Wise, P. S. (1988). [A survey of Illinois school psychologists' networking activities, job satisfaction, and professional needs]. Unpublished raw data.

Hare, A. (1983). *Creativity in small groups.* Beverly Hills, CA: Sage Publications.

Helmer, O. (1966). *The delphi method for systematizing judgments about the future.* Los Angeles, CA: Institute of Government and Public Affairs.

Illback, R. J., & Maher, C. A. (1984). The school psychologist as an organizational boundary role professional. *Journal of School Psychology, 22,* 63-72.

Kabler, M., & Carlton, G. (1982). Education's exceptional students: A comprehensive team approach. *Theory into Practice, 21,* 88-96.

Kabler, M. L., & Genshaft, J. L. (1983). Structuring decision-making in multidisciplinary teams. *School Psychology Review, 12,* 150-159.

Kaiser, S. M., & Woodman, R. W. (1985). Multidisciplinary teams and group decision-making techniques: Possible solutions to decision-making problems. *School Psychology Review, 14,* 457-470.

Knoff, H. M. (1983). Investigating disproportionate influences and status in multidisciplinary child study teams. *Exceptional Children, 49,* 367-369.

Maher, C. A. (1981). Decision analysis: An approach for multidisciplinary teams in planning special service programs. *Journal of School Psychology, 19,* 340-349.

Maher, C. A., & Yoshida, R. K. (1985). Multidisciplinary teams in the schools: Current status and future possibilities. In T. R. Kratochwill (Ed.), *Advances in school psychology* (Vol. IV), (pp. 13-44). Hillsdale, NJ: Lawrence Erlbaum.

Napier, H. E. (1968). Individual vs. group learning: Note on two task variables. *Psychological Reports, 23,* 757-758.

Ohio Department of Education. (1985). *Intervention assistance teams.* Columbus, OH: Author.

Pfeiffer, S. I. (1980). The school-based interprofessional team: Recurring problems and some possible solutions. *Journal of School Psychology, 18,* 388-393.

Pfeiffer, S. I., & Heffernan, L. (1984). Improving multidisciplinary team functions. In C. A. Maher, R. J. Illback, & J. E. Zins (Eds.), *Organizational psychology in the schools: A handbook for professionals* (pp. 283-301). Springfield, IL: Charles C Thomas.

Pfeiffer, S. I., & Naglieri, J. (1983). An investigation of multidisciplinary team decision-making. *Journal of Learning Disabilities, 16,* 588-590.

Plas, J. (1981). The psychologist in the school community: A liaison role. *School Psychology Review, 10,* 72-81.

Rucker, C. N., & Gable, R. K. (1973). *Rucker-Gable Educational Programming Scale.* Storrs, CT: Rucker-Gable Associates.

Salvia, J., & Ysseldyke, J. E. (1988). *Assessment in special and remedial education* (4th ed.). Boston: Houghton Mifflin Co.

Sattler, J. M. (1988). *Assessment of children* (3rd ed.). San Diego, CA: Jerome M. Sattler, Publisher.

Schmuck, R. A., & Runkel, P. J. (1985). *The handbook of organizational development in schools* (3rd ed.). Prospect Heights, IL: Waveland Press.

Shonk, J. H. (1982). *Working in teams: A practical manual for improving work groups.* New York: Amacon Co.

Smith, C. R., Wood, F. H., & Grimes, J. H. (1988). Issues in the identification and placement of behaviorally disordered students. In M. C. Wang, M. C. Reynolds, & H. J. Walberg (Eds.), *Handbook of special education: Research and Practice* (Vol. 2), (pp. 95-124). New York: Pergamon Press.

Taylor, D. W., Berry, P. C., Block, C. H. (1958). Does group participation when using brainstorming techniques facilitate or inhibit creative thinking? *Administrative Science Quarterly, 3,* 23-47.

Turnbull, A. P., & Leonard, J. (1981). Parent involvement in special education: Emerging advocacy roles. *School Psychology Review, 10,* 37-44.

Tyler, F. B., Pargament, K. I., & Gatz, M. (1983). The resource collaborator role: A model for interactions involving psychologists. *American Psychologist, 387,* 388-397.

Vautour, J. A. (1976). A study of placement decisions for exceptional children determined by child study teams and individuals. (Doctoral dissertation, University of Connecticut). *Dissertation Abstracts International, 36,* 6007A.

Yoshida, R. K., Fenton, K. S., Maxwell, J. P., Kaufman, M. J. (1978). Group decision-making in the planning team process: Myth or reality? *Journal of School Psychology, 16,* 178-183.

Ysseldyke, J. E. (1983). Current practices in making psychoeducational decisions about learning disabled students. *Journal of Learning Disabilities, 16,* 226-233.

Ysseldyke, J. E., Algozzine, B., & Mitchell, J. (1982). Special education team decision-making: An analysis of current practice. *Personnel and Guidance Journal, 60,* 308-313.

ANNOTATED BIBLIOGRAPHY

Dyer, W. G. (1987). *Team building: Issues and alternatives,* (2nd ed.). Reading, MA: Addison-Wesley Publishing Company.
This book presents an overview of the basic concepts and methods related to team building from an organizational psychology perspective. A section on applications includes chapters on resolving team conflicts, revitalizing complacent teams, and overcoming unhealthy agreement. The book includes numerous evaluation questionnaires that could be adapted for school contexts.

Maher, C. A., & Pfeiffer, S. I. (Eds.). (1983). Multidisciplinary teams in the schools: Perspectives, practices, and possibilities. [Special issue]. *School Psychology Review, 12,* 2.
This special issue presents nine articles on school-based MDTs. Several articles describe practical approaches for training school psychologists and others to coordinate MDT activities. Several articles also suggest innovative uses of MDTs in school settings.

Maher, C. A., & Yoshida, R. K. (1985). Multidisciplinary teams in the schools: Current status and future possibilities. In T. R. Kratochwill (Ed.), *Advances in school psychology* (Vol. IV), (pp. 13-44). Hillsdale, NJ: Lawrence Erlbaum.
This chapter explores expanded uses for MDTs at the individual, group, and organizational levels from a systems perspective. Specific guidelines for planning and evaluating MDTs are provided.

Pfeiffer, S. I., & Heffernan, L. (1984). Improving multidisciplinary team functions. In C. A. Maher, R. J. Illback, & J. E. Zins (Eds.), *Organizational psychology in the schools: A handbook for professionals* (pp. 283–301). Springfield, IL: Charles C Thomas.

This chapter provides a concise overview of the research on problems involved in implementing school-based MDTs. Excellent suggestions for improving the identified difficulties are offered subsequently.

Schmuck, R. A., & Runkel, P. J. (1985). *The handbook of organizational development in schools* (3rd ed.). Prospect Heights, IL: Waveland Press.

This book includes sections on improving group communication, problem-solving, and evaluation skills. Numerous activities are included to demonstrate relevant skills and issues in group processes.

17

Best Practices in Counseling Senior High School Students

Marcia B. Shaffer
Steuben-Allegany Board of Cooperative Educational Services
Bath, New York

OVERVIEW

The passage of Public Law 94-142 has thrust school psychologists into counseling, some of them ill prepared for it. This is not the first time in the brief history of school psychology that practitioners have had to teach themselves a skill, nor will it be the last. The problem may be most extreme for those in rural areas, who do not have access to advanced university courses. I recommend, beyond the words of this chapter, reading of the books in the annotated bibliography, attending traveling workshops when they are held within tolerable driving distance, and never missing state and national conventions, where even the most casual conversations may enhance one's knowledge.

In 1956, the Division of Counseling Psychology, American Psychological Association, adopted this definition of counseling: "to help individuals toward overcoming obstacles to their personal growth, wherever these may be encountered, and toward achieving optimum development of their personal resources." To the school psychologist who is struggling, by force of Phase 1 individual educational plans (IEPs), with the idiosyncrasies of middle and high school students, this high-minded definition may sound like the stuff of dreams; but it is well to keep in mind that our fundamental purpose *is* lofty. It should be remembered, also, that counseling is not lecturing; it is not moralizing. Others can take care of those matters. The counselor's role is more neutral and often more advocative.

The line between counseling and psychotherapy is a delicate and sometimes ambiguous one. In the context of this chapter, it is of consequence because some states do not permit school psychologists to practice psychotherapy, just as school physicians are not permitted to prescribe medication. One may assume that counseling has less breadth and depth than psychotherapy, and focuses more on specific situational problems. That is an oversimplification, but it will suffice for the circumstances in which most school psychologists find themselves.

For many years, school psychologists spent minimal amounts of time with senior high school students, particularly in counseling relationships. There were several reasons for this, some of which occur even in these days of widespread counseling.

1. High school teachers see large numbers of students each day, are unlikely to know individuals well, and may miss any but the most egregious of problems. This means that a major source of referrals to school psychologists is not operating at full capacity.

2. High schools offer more guidance services than do elementary schools, and

therefore the need for psychological services is decreased. It may also be that guidance counselors do not wish to share concerns with school psychologists.

3. Perhaps the most encompassing reason why school psychologists confine their work to elementary schools is the belief, prevalent among educators, that if the problems of small children are solved, there will be no problem children in the upper grades. Therefore, efforts concentrated on primary grades are often felt by school administrators to be more valuable than work with older students.

However, even if the problems of small school children are smoothed out, new problems occur to *different* children at later stages of growth. Accidents happen — a child may suffer neurological damage in a car crash; illness may result in impairment of vision or hearing. Family circumstances may change; parents may die or be divorced. Currently, drugs, including alcohol, may so attract youngsters as to disrupt their entire lives.

Perhaps most important, at least in terms of the number of difficulties engendered, is human development itself. It is not one steady trip along the road to maturity; human growth inherently goes through periods of tumult. Sometimes a child takes one step forward and two steps back. School psychologists often hear parents say, "He did so well until he got to seventh grade"; or "She never acted like this until she started middle school." Perfectly capable, well-behaved youngsters may suddenly fail or become truant or who knows what else, in the regressive period of preadolescence (Redl). We do not arrange school structures and schedules suitably for this developmental stage, so natural struggles are exacerbated. Likewise, midadolescence is chaotic (Stone & Church, 1968). Most young people are convinced that they should be in control of their own lives, but are vague about the responsibility involved. Society adds to their confusion. Laws permit them to assume such "adult" function as driving, smoking, and drinking alcoholic beverages at different ages in different states. The teen years are an uneasy, intense time of life. The very vehemence of the adolescent's love and loyalty causes personal and social upheaval.

The Age and the Obstacles

It is true that there are real obstacles to the counseling of adolescents. These should be taken into account when deciding whether to counsel, when setting goals, and when contemplating one's success or lack of it.

First, the emotional nature of adolescence: In addition to being in turmoil, the teenager is, by nature, egocentric; the world is viewed in terms of what people and events mean to himself or herself. Anxiety and depression are not necessarily evidence of psychopathology; a degree of these feelings tends to be "normal." Adolescents' emotions are extreme: They typically exaggerate love and hate, anger and passion.

Adolescents are prone to be uncommunicative with adults. This quality varies with the "stage." Specialists in human development divide the years from 12 to 20 into early, middle, and late adolescence. These groups do not react to counseling in the same way. Research (Mills, 1985) has shown that early adolescents (12–14) respond to the questions put in counseling with the greatest amount of information about themselves. Midadolescents (15–16) tell least. Late adolescents (17–18) fall in the middle in respect to self-disclosure. Other relevant findings are that (a) scholastic underachievers are inhibited in expressing emotions, (b) same-sex peer groups enhance students' willingness to reveal their feelings, and (c) homogeneous groups show more interpersonal communication than heterogeneous groups. Among themes set by the counselor, studies have indicated that less intimate subjects, e.g., hobbies and music, brought the most verbal response; happy and unhappy moments, which are thought to be highly intimate subjects, the least.

Adolescents are even more likely than adults to misperceive their own roles and others' behavior. Those who work with teenagers may visualize, from their client's description, a monstrous father who punishes with ferocity, only to meet a mild-mannered man who wishes he could talk with his son; or a mother limned as totally self-sacrificing may turn out to be a self-centered seductress with little concern for her offspring. It is important, while sympathizing with the teenager's plight, to keep in mind the intensity and distortions of the age.

Adolescents may be unaware of problems in their own lives, and may not agree even when the problems are pointed out to them. They may feel no motivation to change. Motivation to change, and a history of positive accomplishments, are felt by some authorities to be essential to success in counseling. Considering the counselees usually assigned to a school psychologist, one can only laugh at those requirements. The school psychologist is likely to be sent, or to attract, the most troublesome, the most defiant, and the least self-confident students in any school. So it is not unusual to start with two strikes against you — but occasionally to succeed even against those odds.

Although counselors working with adolescents sometimes feel that their efforts are futile, they tend to persist. Many practitioners in seeking to provide services that are appropriate and effective with this difficult population are convinced that group counseling, for example, improves overall performance of underachieving students. Many believe that adolescents' fears and feelings of isolation (of potential runaways, in particular) are allayed by simply having a friendly relationship with an adult. And so on. In general, there is insufficient evidence on the efficacy of counseling either to disdain it or to tout its results with any certainty; but for those deeply engaged in it, the exigencies of development offer ample reason to continue.

BASIC CONSIDERATIONS

Who Should Counsel?

Forty years ago there were two kinds of school psychologists. One group consisted of teachers who had taken enough courses to become "testers"; the others were clinical psychologists, schooled in therapeutic techniques and eager to use them. The latter group brought counseling to schools. Currently, with changes in training, one cannot assume that counseling courses and practica have been included in a school psychologist's preparation for practice.

Some seasoned school psychologists feel very strongly that it is necessary to have undergone in-depth training to do counseling. They vigorously support academically based knowledge and supervised practical experience in both individual and group counseling, which they feel require quite disparate skills. The most strictly ethical also believe that certain personal characteristics are requisite for the school psychologist who counsels, including, but not limited to, pervasive empathy, trustworthiness, and tolerance of obscene language and unusual lifestyles.

All of us subscribe to the ethical principle that school psychologists should do only what they have been trained to do. But over the past quarter century they have been forced by lack of training resources and the needs of their school populations to learn much on their own. Consequently, it is difficult to be dogmatic about what constitute adequate qualifications for counseling, and how to acquire them. It is one of the questions on which professional organizations could and should provide guidelines.

It has become fashionable to suggest counseling in cases of school failure, and many school staff members seem to feel that counseling is helpful, no matter who does it. It is highly improbable that very young children or retarded children, for instance, benefit much from counseling unless it is done by trained professionals; and perhaps not even then. But that possibility appears to elude members of CSES (Committees on Special Education; these committees have different names in different states), who are imbued with faith in the process. School psychologists may want to attempt to monitor who does what with children within their purview along the line of counseling.

Philosophies

A description of best practices in counseling must include consideration of theoretical structures. One can administer a test adequately without knowing fundamental principles of test construction, or sit on a CSE without knowing every detail of one's state regulations. But counseling does not permit any similar limitations. It is possible to "wing it" for a session or two by simply being a kind person, genuinely interested in adolescents. For longer than that, one should have a philosophy, a technique, a purpose, even though they may rest on an abstraction. One's philosophy serves as a basis for responses in counseling sessions.

Each of two of the books in the annotated bibliography (Thompson & Rudolph, 1983; Prout & Brown, 1983) explicates some of the more popular schools of therapy, which they translate into useful intellectual tools for the school psychologist. The following list does not cover every detail; it is intended only to give the barest identification of each of the several philosophies.

1. *Adlerian approaches* rest on the belief that all behavior is purposive and goal-directed. Behavior has social meaning; everyone seeks to belong.

2. *Behavioral approaches* are rooted in learning theory concepts developed through experimental psychology, as are behavior modification techniques. Behaviorists believe that maladaptive as well as adaptive behavior is learned and may be modified through the application of learning principles, most often those dealing with reward and punishment. They focus on specific overt behavior rather than on internal causes.

3. *Logotherapy*, advocated by Victor Frankl, focuses on the will to find meaning in life. Meaning, if lost, can be restored by doing a (good) deed; experiencing a value; or by suffering.

4. *Person-centered approaches*, based on the work of Carl Rogers, are espoused by those who believe that people naturally strive toward self-fulfillment. It is from this approach that the writer derived her admonition to "listen."

5. *Rational-emotive therapy*, to most people synonymous with the name of Albert Ellis, can be traced to Stoic philosophers, who believed in changing feelings by changing thinking. The major purpose is to assist clients in ridding themselves of emotional disturbance by ridding themselves of distorted ideas.

6. *Reality therapy*, brainchild of William Glasser, has been popular in schools. In fact, it was begun in a school for "female incorrigibles." It involves the assumption of responsibility for one's own behavior, and teaches improved ways of fulfilling needs.

7. *Transactional analysis*, whose best known adherent is Eric Berne, considers various components of the personality, namely the parent, the child and the adult. It is the basis of a popular book entitled *I'm OK, You're OK*, by Thomas Harris (1969).

If counseling is the most recent expansion of your role as a school psychologist, read about any of these theories that appeal to you. It is not necessary to choose only one. Eclecticism is acceptable. The American Heritage Dictionary defines it as "choosing what appears to be the best from diverse sources."

School psychologists who do not wish to commit themselves to a philosophy, who feel uncomfortable without structure, or who wish to deal with emotions generally rather than personally may prefer to use commercially-prepared techniques sometimes referred to as "affective education." There are card games and board games, and detailed approaches to a variety of social situations. Almost any catalog of psychological or guidance materials will provide information about such programs.

Finally, one possible choice of counseling methods in which the school psychologist may be involved is peer counseling. It is not necessary that the counselor-peer be an A student or even a model of decorum. Indeed, special students and underachievers have been found to be successful with younger pupils, and to improve their own behavior and grades into the bargain. Although their chief contribution is sympathetic ears, they may offer friendship as well. The school psychologist may prefer to write a syllabus for training peer counselors, but commercial plans are available, one of which is listed below in the annotated bibliography.

Referrals

Once school psychologists have made it known that they will offer counseling, referrals come from predictable sources. On occasion, teachers see emotional distress and report it. More often, they mention annoying or, by their standards, immoral behavior. Administrators may also send adolescents to school psychologists — for example, the high school sophomore who had confiscated the entire treasure of a school club; part of his punishment was to "see Mrs. Shaffer." Parents may ask for assistance. The ambiance of a school at a given time may suggest the need for counseling, especially of groups. Current laws and regulations regarding the handicapped have added a new dimension to the school psychologist's responsibilities for counseling.

The most interesting and often the most numerous are self-referrals. They arrive by a number of routes, usually in desperation. Some have friends who have found the school psychologist helpful. Others have read about psychologists in popular magazines. Still others have heard the school psychologist speak to a health class. School psychologists who make themselves known to a portion of the student body are almost certain to find clients knocking at their doors.

Rarely, students refer themselves as a hoax, to see what the "shrink" is all about. The hoax tends to backfire, the jokesters discovering that, after all, they have some concerns to discuss.

Although it is not a unanimous conviction among school psychologists, there are those who believe that some referrals should not be accepted. Hagborg (1988) questioned whether students in counseling under duress, for example, by dint of

Phase I IEPs or as punishment (above), should be counseled at all. Not only are they prey to the vicissitudes of adolescence and their own special problems; they may be actively resistant, in which case counseling is almost fated to be unsuccessful. I have reduced the incidence of this difficulty by telling such students that counseling is required by someone in authority over both of us, and that it is necessary to give it a try. I then indicate that the student will be expected to attend four weekly meetings with me. After that, if the student wishes to discontinue counseling, I will explain to the administration that the effort has been made.

In my opinion, severely disturbed young people, such as the psychotic or the drug-dependent, cannot competently be handled in a school setting. The school is an unsuitable site for the plumbing of emotional depths that severe disturbances require. Students cannot tear their souls apart during one period and sit calmly in science class the next. It is well to remember that schools are not mental health clinics, but places to dispense learning.

With the decision that the school cannot provide an analyst's couch, is one's duty done? Not in the opinion of most "old hands." Students suffering from severe emotional distress should, if possible, be routed to an appropriate social agency or individual therapist. It may take time to persuade the student and his or her parents that treatment outside the school is advisable, and to help them find a satisfactory therapeutic situation. Even when that task is accomplished, the school psychologist should maintain communication with the agency and make provision for the student's educational programming.

When and where to "refer out" is not as clear-cut as the discussion above may imply. Who is "severely disturbed," for example, is a question that plagues school psychologists, especially those who have had no training in abnormal psychology, and no experience with any but "normal" children. Committees on special education, composed chiefly of educators, are not very helpful in making such decisions.

In areas where competent child psychiatrists are available, they offer the most propitious referral for the psychotic, the addicted, and the extremely socially maladjusted. Such cases may also be referred to clinical psychologists, but a medical person is preferable to ensure that physical causes are eliminated and medication can be given if needed. Family problems may be taken to mental health clinics, social agencies, or persons in the private practice of family therapy. The key to the decision is to have investigated the resources in your community, so that you know what is in fact available.

It is desirable, according to ethical practice, to recommend at least three resources. For those who work in remote areas, even one agency or individual may not exist. In such instances, the school psychologist may need to proceed alone with the support of the best-qualified practitioners to be found. And wherever one labors, it is important to consider such alternatives to counseling as changes in classroom management, changes of teachers, behavior modification, and other techniques of altering behavior that can be carried out with the aid of school personnel.

ETHICAL DECISIONS

It has been suggested elsewhere (Shaffer, 1982) that there is personal or family information to which school psychologists should not be privy. School files of any sort are, in a legal showdown, not really secret. Families deserve protection of their privacy. As an extension of that reasoning, school personnel are not equipped to cope with the intricacies of family problems. There are counselors who disagree with this separation of school and family. They deal with marital relationships, family finances, and a myriad of interfamilial conflicts. While this writer prefers to refer out in instances of family distress, the question remains moot, to be decided by each school psychologist according to his or her own conscience.

Whether counseling is by group or individual, is voluntary or forced, the question of parental involvement arises. Students who refer themselves often request that their parents not be told. The most widely held school of thought appears to be that unless parents are informed, students cannot be accepted for counseling. Some states require signed parental permission. Those who espouse this opinion often spend a few sessions trying to convince the students that they should assume the responsibility of advising their parents. Another course of action is to offer to talk with the parents on a student's behalf. Still another is to decide upon an age at which students can be regarded as "adult," say 15 or 16, and can act on their own behalf.

Much of what a student tells a school psychologist can be kept confidential between them. The student must be forewarned, however, that revelations regarding such unlawful or potentially harmful acts as drug use, the sale of drugs, or acts of violence will be reported to legal authorities.

Official codes of ethics (Ethical Principles of Psychologists, 1981; Professional Conduct Manual, 1985) make broad statements regarding confidentiality. Actual situations tend to be more complicated. Young people who have dredged up enough trust to present themselves voluntarily are already troubled by the approach of adulthood, the outcropping of unfamiliar impulses, the remnants of childish feelings, and, usually, the perceived perfidy of the adults with whom thy are acquainted. Some 16-year-olds, after all, are emancipated minors, or parents, or, in some localities, felons. Should one disregard their privacy? As for the law, where, on a continuum of consequential crimes, does one place the information that a kid illegally purchased a six-pack of beer and drank two cans on the way to school? Conflict about confidentiality is a recurrent problem for the school psychologist who works with adolescents, conflict between the rules that school administrators expect one to uphold, and the advocacy of adolescents.

BEST PRACTICES

In Individual Counseling

If one believes in working with individuals; if a theory of counseling has been decided upon; if the significant ethical questions have been answered satisfactorily; if students are banging at the door — what next?

First, consider when each individual student will be seen. Study hall periods are agreeable to school staff; if that time is otherwise inconvenient, vary the time from week to week, so that the same class is not missed regularly. No teacher will then feel put out except the one who thinks that psychologists are crazy anyway. It is important to be obliging but not obsequious. The students in counseling will gain as much from 45 minutes with the school psychologist as from 45 minutes in any class.

Now the student has arrived in the psychologist's office. No matter what theory is espoused, from Rogers to Freud, the first step in counseling is the same: LISTEN! Listening cannot be overemphasized. Even if it were the only response ever given, respectful attention would be helpful. It also assures that the school psychologist does not leap into action before problems are made clear.

One should ask a few straightforward questions, touching on such topics as with whom the student lives; sex and age of siblings; sources of family income; school achievement. This mundane information is necessary to complete one's grasp of the situation. In addition, it will serve to bring talkative or hysterical clients to a halt and help them to regain control, or induce shy clients to talk.

Once one has listened, various paths are open. One may focus on the students' relationships to the school environment; on their goals and how their behavior affects their achievement; on what alternative behavior is possible. Alternatives are in fact important in the philosophies of many school psychologist counselors. It is perfectly safe for the psychologist to lead the discussion, but wise not to be too rigid in controlling it. Given a little leeway and some tolerant encouragement, almost all adolescents will reveal their major problems in almost any context, eventually.

Techniques of counseling can be enhanced by the imagination of the counselor. The counselee may be assigned tasks that alleviate some aspect of the problem, such as "try walking away when your sister screams at you; let me know, next week, what happens." Students can be asked to pretend that they are a psychologist dealing with their parents; or some informal *psychodrama* can be used. Many adolescents, as we have said, are uncomfortable in talking with adults, so it may be useful to rehearse encounters with parents or teachers, as "Mr. Pauling, I'm sorry that my book report is late," etc.

Like many school psychologists of clinical background, I was trained in the years when Carl Rogers was king in the world of psychotherapy. I do not ordinarily set goals for individuals; the student uses me for his purposes. I tend to follow the student's lead at the expense of orderly procedures. I hear the same stories over and over, because I believe in the value of catharsis. In other aspects of counseling, I am probably more directive than most of my colleagues. Because so many troubled young persons have no clear standards by which to live, I risk telling them my own values and standards. They are under no obligation to believe or act as I do, but they may be saved from excessive trial and error behavior in an emotional vacuum and a hostile world. Other school psychologists who work with teenagers will have developed procedures congruent with their theoretical biases.

For deciding when counseling of individual students should be terminated, at least temporarily, two criteria are useful. If appointments are frequently broken, it is most likely a sign that the student's interest in the counseling relationship is ebbing and often that the problems are diminishing. It is true that broken appointments may have other meanings, such as a conflict in transference or an evasion of dilemmas. The healthy refusal to keep appointments has an open quality that distinguishes it from the unhealthy: "I like you, Mrs. S., but I'd rather play volleyball."

The other criterion is a relinquishment of egocentricity. When students begin to show concern about the counselor ("Is your cold better?" "How is your husband?") before launching into an account of their own experiences, it is a sign that they are emerging from themselves, beginning to mature. Counseling may not be terminated immediately, but its intensity will start to wane.

Special Cases

Kids who want to run away from home and those who threaten suicide may involve a school psychologist in unexpected crises. How to respond may be a very personal matter. At the risk of incurring the wrath of those who believe that the social distance between the psychologist and the client should be as great as possible, I venture to say what I do: Any student among my counselees who seems to be at risk for leaving home or committing suicide has my home phone number. Calling me at home at any time is allowed. A potential runaway is not told to stay at home. He or she is asked not to leave until there is somewhere to go; to tell me where he or she will be (shades of confidentiality!); and to phone me at intervals, or tell me where to call.

To the possibly suicidal student, in addition to my phone number, I give orders like "wash your hair (or grease your car, or some other everyday chore) and come to see me in the morning." The idea is to give such students something specific to do and to anticipate, to keep them in contact with the real world; and to assure them of being a valuable person whom I, personally, do not wish to lose.

For the student so enmeshed in trouble and so dejected that suicide seems like the only way out, I recommend what one colleague, who also recommends it, calls a "suicide watch." This is exactly what it sounds like: monitoring the student so that there is no opportunity for attempts at self-destruction. Parents may be recruited to help, as may other concerned school personnel. It is not necessary to pursue the student constantly. The "watch" may be as simple as phone calls at hourly intervals.

There are at present plain and fancy plans for what to do, on a whole-school basis, to prevent suicides and what to do if they occur. These plans usually involve complicated, tear-jerking procedures to comfort the bereaved and help them deal with the fact of death. I do not believe that such plans get to the heart of the matter. What is important is to hear the distress call of the beleaguered student, to find out what factors are so burdensome, so dreadful, that death looks better than life, and to walk with him or her through the darkest hours. That may be involvement more deep than is "professional," but it is preferable to a lost young soul.

No more than a dozen students, in 30 years, have called me at home. I have not, to the present, had a suicide among my clientele; and I have guided a number of young people home.

Group Counseling

There are school psychologists who feel that individual counseling is not suitable for high school students, that its verbal demands may be discomfiting for the counselee and frustrating for the school psychologist. Adolescents of this view may opt for group counseling.

School psychologists offer a number of reasons for choosing group over individual counseling, not the least of which is that the psychologist's time is limited. Some rely on research data that indicate that adolescents respond more readily in a group than alone with a counselor. Others see the formation of groups as a way to get to the root of conditions that may trouble a school staff, such as defiance or truancy, or to deal with social problems of the times, such as drug use or teenage suicide. Assembling a group is also an excellent way to learn the mores of a community or of a school gang.

There are groups that are highly structured as to topics. In the belief that adolescents are troubled chiefly by social/moral questions, some schools set up what may most accurately be described as group discussions, inviting specified students to participate. Conversation is stimulated by showing a filmstrip about a contemporary issue, for example, relationships with authority, or peer pressure.

One writer who currently exerts considerable influence on group work with young people is Lawrence Kohlberg (1981). Kohlberg's ideas have to do with what he calls "moral reasoning." Put briefly, he presents a method of values clarification as it occurs and matures in groups, moving from egocentric, divisive opinions to decisions that take into account the good of the group. The counselor acts as facilitator, not searching for one correct answer, but eliciting alternatives.

Carl Rogers's nondirective, client-centered approach works with groups as well as individuals. Students' most personal attitudes surface quite rapidly in an atmosphere that is not rigidly controlled by a leader. The interactions among group members are gradually divulged, defined, and discussed. Counseling can home in on the aspects of their lives that really distress the students. The disadvantage of this arrangement is that it is difficult to keep the group in line. Conversations are likely to go off on tangents; the leader may be left out of the discourse entirely. A school psychologist who cannot bear disorder should shun group techniques that permit students to choose their own routes to self-discovery.

Hagborg (1988) has learned from bitter experience the tumult that can arise from groups of adolescents who do not wish to change their lives, discuss their emotions, or have any truck with the school psychologist. He advises the use of game-like procedures to keep group members interested and in a semblance of control. He has devised ingenious ways to spend counseling sessions, of which the following are examples:

Draw-a-family. Goal: To understand group member similarities and differences. Students are requested to draw a family portrait including all family members engaged in their favorite activity. Once drawings are done, each student describes his drawings. The counselor assists students in uncovering similarities and differences.

Courtroom drama. Goal: To improve relationships with authority. Students are asked to listen to actual disciplinary reports from their school. One student serves as the prosecutor and another as defense attorney. After the lawyers present their cases, the remaining group members serve as a jury. The jury must select one of several possible options: no punishment (case dismissed), after-school detention, or suspension. After the jury has decided, the counselor reads out the school administrator's actual decision.

A few practical matters should be considered before one plunges into group counseling:

1. Groups seem more manageable if the number of sessions is established at the initial session.

2. An administrator can usually find a place for a group to meet. Time for meeting may be more troublesome. One solution that is not too offensive to teachers is a staggered schedule (e.g., Feb. 10, period 1; Feb. 17, period 2; Feb. 24, period 3, and so on.) Every administrator and teacher in the building should have a copy of the schedule.

3. In spite of what textbooks may say, if the counselees are at all antisocial, *six* is the maximum number a counselor can endure without danger of breakdown.

4. It is absolutely essential to announce a few rules at the outset. Minimally, no physical assault on another person should be permitted, nor property destroyed. Rules should be set on the basis of the psychologist's intimate self-knowledge and consideration of the behavior that he or she can tolerate.

5. Offering individual counseling to group members, on request, adds to the efficacy of the group process.

6. Even nondirective leaders sometimes need to take control of the group. Socially maladjusted adolescents, in particular, tend to have no standards of behavior or belief. The school psychologist may have to suggest what is "good" behavior or a decent attitude, simply be-

cause no such thoughts occur to the group. A whole generation of high school kids in Williamsville, New York, said, "We don't say 'nigger' in here," almost catechistically, thanks to the unyielding ways of their school psychologist.

7. The loyalty that may be engendered among group members will surprise the novice group leader. It is one of the signs that a group is maturing.

8. Be aware of the likelihood that counselees will need a buffer between themselves and adults. This is true for individual counselees, too, but there is a more conspicuous, public quality to the interference that must be run for group members.

9. Set simple goals. For several years the writer worked with groups of acting-out students of average ability and both sexes, for whom there was only one aim: to keep them from being invited out of high school before they were graduated. The success rate was 80%.

10. Counseling is said to be most effective with clients who have mild rather than severe problems. Yet it is the latter whom school psychologists are most likely to see. It is appropriate to have dreams of mayhem regarding those who take only the mild problems.

In Conclusion

Schools have changed in the past 30 years. A wider variety of courses and "tracks" offers suitable programs for many students and decreases the number who are academically misplaced. Social agencies come into schools to help the socially befuddled. PL 94-142 and its corollary "spin-offs" have resulted in the prevention of some problems that accrue to high school students. No matter how altered the school environment, however, the course of life itself and the pressure of social change will leave a few troubled teenagers confronting the school psychologist in search of succor.

When they arrive, bear in mind a few homespun guidelines, some of which have already been mentioned here, but are important enough to be repeated.

1. No drastic changes will occur in the lives of students who are counseled. Be satisfied with achievable goals, germane to their school careers.

2. Not only words are significant in counseling; so are body movements and arrangements of furniture. For example: (a) As little as possible should separate counselor and counselee. It is better to have the student sit around the corner of a desk than to have the desk between counselor and student. Barriers make the counselor look inaccessible and/or scared. (b) Preferably, the student should be between the counselor and the office door, so that the former does not feel trapped. (c) Leaning away from the student may indicate a negative reaction; on the other hand, leaning too far toward the student can be equally distressing. (I recently saw a counselor — not a school psychologist — lean so far forward that he seemed to be pushing the student into the wall.) Strike a happy medium.

3. There are some personal qualities of the school psychologist that contribute to the success of counseling: *dependability*, which means, for example, being where one has promised to be, and informing students if it is necessary to break an appointment; *honesty*, which may extend to reacting with anger to patently stupid or destructive behavior; *empathy*, which is the ability to pretend to be someone other than oneself.

4. When the school psychologist acts as a liaison between students and adults, each side must know that he will not plead for a relinquishment of penalties, nor promise perfection thereafter. What will be done is to explain extenuating circumstances and to try to arrange a really fair deal.

5. Never forget for a moment that the purpose of counseling is to support emotional and social maturation. The school psychologist is neither an evangelist nor a scout leader. He is not there to convert students to a particular moral viewpoint, but to help them live fulfilling lives according to their own standards.

6. Remember that each counselee, although not always lovable, is an impor-

tant person worthy of respect. Finally, LISTEN!

SUMMARY

Middle school and high school students may encounter problems in the very process of growing up. Counseling should be available to them.

Students may be referred by teachers, administrators, or parents; self-referrals are frequent. Severely disturbed students should be sent to an outside agency or therapist, and the school psychologist should maintain contact.

Potential runaways and suicides may confront the school psychologist on an emergency basis. Methods for dealing with these problems are idiosyncratic, and should be planned ahead of time. Confidentiality is an equivocal ethical problem, with parent involvement a major issue.

School psychologists who counsel should be dependable, honest, and empathic. Ideally, they should have training in theories of counseling plus supervised experience. Any preferred counseling theory may be adopted: listening is always the vital ingredient.

Groups in counseling vary from highly structured to client-directed. Even the latter need a few limits, for example, no physical attacks allowed. It is important to settle practical matters such as time and place of meetings and number of sessions before counseling begins. Try to adapt to the wishes of teachers and administrators.

To facilitate positive change in students, and to preserve the morale of the school psychologist, simple, achievable goals should be set. It is unrealistic to expect radical personal changes as a result of either group or individual counseling, but if aims are sensibly planned, counseling is rewarding to both the student(s) and the school psychologist.

REFERENCES

Ethical Principles of Psychologists. (1981). *American Psychologist, 36*(6), 633-638.

Hagborg, W. (1988, November). *Group counseling with emotionally handicapped early adolescents.* Paper presented at the annual conference of the New York Association of School Psychologists, Lake George, New York.

Harris, T. (1969). *I'm OK, You're OK.* New York: Harper and Row.

Kohlberg, L. (1981). *Essays in moral development: (Vol. 1). The philosophy of moral development.* New York: Harper and Row.

Mills, M. C. (1985). Adolescents' reactions to counseling interviews. *Adolescence, 20,* 83-95.

National Association of School Psychologists. (1985). *Professional conduct manual.* Kent, OH: Author.

Prasse, D. (1989, March). *Privacy, confidentiality and minors: The public school arena.* Paper presented at the National Association of School Psychologists, Boston.

Shaffer, M. (1969). Group counseling in a senior high school. *The School Counselor,* 22-25.

Shaffer, M. (1982). Helping children cope with parental problems. In J. Grimes (Ed.), *Psychological approaches to problems of children and adolescents* (pp. 43-45). Des Moines, IA: Iowa Department of Public Instruction.

Stone, L. J., & Church, J. (1968). *Childhood and adolescence* (2nd ed.). New York: Random House.

Redl, F. Pre-adolescents: What Makes Them Tick? Source unknown.

ANNOTATED BIBLIOGRAPHY

Claiborn, C. D., & Strong, S. R. (1982). Group counseling in the schools. In C. R. Reynolds & T. B. Gutkin (Ed.), *The handbook of school psychology* (pp. 530-553). New York: Wiley.
The style is academic and the reader must translate ideas into practical procedures, but the chapter provides an excellent overview of theories of group counseling.

Fine, M. (1982). Issues in adolescent counseling. *School Psychology Review, 11*(4), 391-398.
This useful article reflects Fine's considerable experience with children and families and his theoretical orientation in working with them.

Myrick, R., & Erney, T. (1985). *Youth helping youth: A handbook for training peer facilitators.* Minneapolis, MN: Educational Media Corporation.
Myrick, R., & Erney, T. (1984). *Caring and sharing: Becoming a peer facilitator.* Minneapolis, MN: Educational Media Corporation.

These books serve the purpose of preparing high school students to be group discussion leaders, big brothers/sisters and/or tutors. Book 1 is the teacher's manual. Book 2 is the text for students. They provide a course that can appropriately be taught by a school psychologist, each session being explained in detail.

Prout, T., & Brown, D. (1983). *Counseling and psychotherapy with children and adolescents.* Tampa, FL: Mariner Publishing Company.

Brown and Prout have collected chapters on several theories of counseling and psychotherapy, each including the theoretical basis, the usefulness of the techniques with either individuals or groups, and even classroom applications. An unusual section is a chapter on counseling of handicapped children. An extensive bibliography accompanies each chapter.

Sandoval, J. (Ed.). (1988). *Crisis counseling, intervention, and prevention in the schools.* Hillsdale, NJ: Erlbaum.

Highly practical, this volume addresses such situations as school-related crises, which include, among others, school entry and change of schools; maltreatment of children; children with handicapped parents; moving; peer conflicts; and adolescent parenthood. It is a valuable addition to the books kept close at hand for use in crises in one's own practice.

Thompson, C. L., & Rudolph, L. B. (1983). *Counseling children.* Monterey, CA: Brooks/Cole.

This is an exceptionally informative volume dealing with (a) several theories of counseling, their advantages, and disadvantages; and (b) step-by-step suggestions for responding to common problems of students. There are excellent reference lists.

18

Best Practices in Crisis Intervention

Scott Poland and Gayle Pitcher
Cypress-Fairbanks (Texas) Public Schools

OVERVIEW

Crisis intervention skills for school psychologists are becoming indispensable as the numbers of crises in our schools spiral upward. At present all schools are at risk for crises — even "successful" schools in prominent neighborhoods (Jay, 1989).

Although few of us feel completely prepared to face and manage shootings, kidnappings, emotionally out-of-control staff members, or assaults on teachers, the simple reality is that most of will face just such challenges. Government figures for 1985 documented 450,000 violent crimes in our nation's schools and colleges. Assaults accounted for most of the incidents, followed by robbery and rape (Mayfield, 1986). Keen (1989) noted that three million children are attacked at school each year and that weapons were used in 70,000 assaults. A 50% increase has been cited in the number of attacks on teachers form 1973 to 1985, and youth homicide has doubled in the last 20 years (Envoy, 1988). Memmot and Stone (1989) report that one child is killed every day in accidental shootings and 10 more are injured.

In addition to violent crime and accidental shootings, child and adolescent suicide has similarly evidenced dramatic increases. It is difficult to get accurate figures on the incidence of teen suicide, but recent governmental figures indicate that approximately 5,000 young people in the 15- to 24-year-old age group commit suicide each year, whereas only 200 young people under the age of 14 commit suicide. The incidence of teenage suicide appears to have tripled since 1955 and doubled since 1970 according to Vidal (1986). Leder (1987) cited suicide as the second leading cause of death for teenagers. Several researchers have commented on the percentage of high school students who have made suicide attempts. A range of 8.4% to 13.0% was found by Harkavy-Friedman, Asnis, Boe, and DiFiore (1987), Smith and Crawford (1986), and Ross (1985). Gordon (1985) has estimated that 1,000 teens attempt suicide each day. Friend (1988) summarized a study of 11,419 eighth and tenth graders that found that 34% of those surveyed had seriously thought about suicide and 14% had actually attempted suicide. Pfeffer (1986) has addressed the question of what the incidence will be in the year 2000. An increase of 94% is predicted in the 15- to 19-year-old category.

Several years ago the department of psychological services of the Cypress-Fairbanks Public Schools received a phone call from a superintendent requesting that psychologists be sent to the site of an in-school shooting. Precisely what had happened, who was in charge, or how exactly we might improve the situation was completely undetermined. Nothing could have prepared us for what we found:

Television news teams roamed the halls, large numbers of frightened students were unaccounted for, telephone lines were clogged with frantic calls from parents, teachers were rattled from the near hysteria, and administrators felt ill-equipped to manage the barrage of problems that fell upon them in the course of a fleeting moment. It was generally felt that a psychologist ought to know what to do with an incident that carries with it such emotionality. Those of us who approached the scene, however, felt the same sense of helplessness, anxiety, and confusion.

Since administrators frequently see school psychologists as the experts in this area and since we may be the only school personnel trained in the management of strong emotions and preventive program planning, it is logical that the responsibility for crisis intervention fall squarely on us. Our profession, however, has been slow to prepare us to fill such a role or to be proactive in establishing and organizing crisis intervention activities in the schools (Smead, 1985).

This chapter will outline a practical model for crisis intervention in the schools that will enable school systems to organize and respond effectively in the face of a crisis. The role of the school psychologist ranges from that of manager to trainer to program planner. The overall model first establishes competent reaction to crises, then presses on to establish competent prevention of crisis. It is our intent to pass along the information we have accumulated in nearly a decade of research and management of school crises (Pitcher & Poland, in press).

BASIC CONSIDERATIONS

Probably the most pronounced characteristic of a crisis in the schools is the intense emotional upset or "disequilibrium" experienced by the system. Much as in personal crises, staff members experience feelings of helplessness, denial, inadequacy, and confusion. If the crisis is not resolved, depression or burnout, physical symptoms, and disorganization of functional working relationships occur. It

is for this reason that school psychologists are frequently seen as the most appropriate personnel to intervene and support staff in crises.

In inexperienced or unprepared districts, however, psychologists are typically summoned at the least advantageous moment. Traditionally, crises have been regarded as unfolding in four stages: First, there is an initial rise in tension due to the crisis event. Second, in the face of the continued impact of the stressing event, there is a lack of success in the usual problem-solving techniques. During the third stage other problem-solving resources are mobilized, and, following failure of these, tension mounts to the breaking point during the fourth and final phase of severe emotional disorganization (Caplan, 1964). All too often school psychologists are called during the last portion of the third or fourth phase. It is of necessity, then, that we develop the arsenal of skills required to restore emotional organization at this time.

There is, however, a second and very significant aspect of crisis in the schools that we must prepare ourselves and our profession to embrace. During and just subsequent to crisis there is a reduced defensiveness or increased openness on the part of the system, again paralleling personal crisis. Crisis has been frequently recognized as a time of potential danger as well as potential opportunity (Wilhelm, 1967; Lidell & Scott, 1968; Slaikeu, 1984). If our profession is able to manage the danger, that is manage the immediate crisis and quickly return the system to normal functioning, then there exists a tremendous opportunity to stimulate long-term systemic change. Once seen as effective and credible, the psychologist has infinitely more opportunity to move the system in the direction of prevention. Thus, the general intent of our approach is actually two-fold: (a) To establish crisis management procedures that support effective coping/management behavior during extreme emotional states (which will return the system to normal functioning as quickly as possible), and (b) To introduce crisis prevention activities that will reduce the probability that the crisis will recur.

As in public health, our concept of prevention can take three forms: primary, secondary, and tertiary prevention (Bloom, 1977; Caplan, 1964). Primary prevention includes activities that prevent crises from occurring altogether, secondary prevention includes activities that arrest potential crises from escalating, and tertiary prevention aims to repair damage from the occurrence of a crisis (i.e., crisis management). By way of illustration, then, primary prevention might be educating elementary school teachers about custody laws and establishing school policies and procedures to regulate authorized removal of children from the school. Effective implementation of such safeguards would constitute secondary prevention, and competent management of a crisis in which a child has been removed from school by an unauthorized person would be tertiary prevention.

School psychologists who have been trained in organizational and community intervention will quickly recognize primary and secondary prevention as the mainstay of most systems-level intervention (Danish and D'Augelli, 1980; Rappaport, 1977; Reiff, 1975). However, school administrators usually are infinitely more amenable to primary or secondary activities once they have found themselves face to face with the tertiary prevention problems of managing a crisis. In reality, therefore, school psychologists are frequently faced with the somewhat illogical approach of beginning to intervene at the tertiary level of crisis management, and only later focusing on primary and secondary activities. Enter the tremendous opportunity for school psychologists in crisis intervention.

Administrative personnel who have managed an intense crisis are far more motivated to avoid having to do so again. Frequently this phenomenon occurs at the highest levels of administration and the school board. These officials are scrutinized by the entire community for making the right decisions under pressure. The question rises from parents, children, the media, and faculty: What's being done? Districts that can answer this question most convincingly and reassuringly are the ones that have planned activities and procedures along all three avenues of prevention, as stressed by the present model.

BEST PRACTICES

Developing a District Program for Crisis Intervention

Nelson and Slaikeu (1984) pointed out that crisis intervention needs to be included in the job descriptions of school personnel such as administrators, counselors, and school psychologists. Guetzloe (1988) emphasized that educational associations are recognizing that more needs to be done in preparing schools to deal with a crisis. Guetzloe pointed out that California in 1982 mandated that schools be safe and stressed the following points: (a) Teachers and administrators should be trained in crime prevention and safety procedures. (b) School security engineers should approve of school construction, and schools have a responsibility to keep students safe.

Historically attempts to prevent a crisis from occurring at school have concentrated on evacuation procedures such as fire and natural disaster drills. The incidence of violence in our schools and society indicates that we have to prepare for violent behavior. As one teacher put it, "We have to be prepared for violent intrusion from an outsider or violent behavior on the part of a member of our school."

An examination of a number of school district procedures on crisis intervention is enlightening. Most procedures address chain of command issues such as when to call the superintendent or security and whether to evacuate the building in the event of a bomb threat. These organizational issues are certainly important, but a crisis team that can provide a range of services is needed.

There is little information about exactly how crisis teams are organized.

Ruof and Harris (1988) described three options in setting up a crisis team:

1. An inside model that includes only staff from one building on the crisis team.

2. An outside team composed of community mental health professionals or itinerant school personnel such as school psychologists and special education personnel.

3. A combined model utilizing building personnel and professionals who do not regularly work in the building.

Ruof and Harris pointed out that there are many advantages to the inside team format, because students know the team members and they are more immediately available. A disadvantage may be that a building may not have the necessary personnel or the personnel may not have crisis intervention skills. In contrast the outside model utilizes more trained personnel, but they do not know the students and must be called to the building. One outside crisis team reported to us that they were ready to assist in the aftermath of a student death but the principal did not call on them. Pelej and Scholzen (1987) and Schulman (1986) have cautioned against having the school system always call in outside experts when a crisis occurs. And Ruof and Harris cited two additional problems with this approach: There may not be enough itinerant school personnel to call on, and outside professionals may be too costly. However, Comstock (1985) stressed that outside mental health professionals are willing to assist at little or no cost if the school system will involve them in a meaningful way and listen to their recommendations. All in all the combined model is recommended by Ruof and Harris, because it utilizes personnel in the building who know the students and the expertise of itinerant school personnel or community mental health personnel.

The size of a particular school district and the availability of resources are important factors in developing a crisis team. It is recommended that small school districts use the combined model with emphasis on assistance from area and community mental health specialists. A large school district should utilize a combined model but will probably not need assistance from professionals outside the school system.

Selecting crisis team members is very important. Ruof and Harris (1988) recommend that membership on the crisis team be voluntary. Team members should not only be willing but should have attributes and skills that will enable them to perform well. The question of how many school personnel should be on a crisis team was discussed by Ruof and Harris, who recommended a minimum of two persons and preferably one team member for every hundred children. We recommend that teams be composed of four to eight members. A team approach is needed because no single person can do everything. Principals have commented that they could not be in the four or five places they need to be at the same time during a crisis.

Theoretical Model

Crisis team members need to be familiar with Caplan's (1964) model. Most people think of crisis intervention only as what is done in the immediate aftermath of a crisis. The most important issue is what can be done to prevent a crisis from happening. One principal who experienced a shooting at school feels very strongly that students must not keep a secret about life-threatening behavior. Many efforts have been directed towards improving and maintaining close communication between faculty and students. Too often students know about potential crisis events but keep the information to themselves.

It is not possible to specify all the *primary prevention* activities that a crisis team could be involved in. Examples are high schools that decide to do something about drunk driving by establishing a safe ride program and working to prevent teen suicide by establishing a school crisis helpline. On one occasion the students of a local teacher who had rehearsed a "secret signal" of danger with her class followed her cue and violence was averted when a gunman entered her class. The types of questions that crisis teams need to think about to prevent a crisis are:

1. What is worrisome about the school or the neighborhood?

2. Is there a potentially violent student or parent?

3. How could we notify students to stay away from windows or to evacuate the playground or the school quickly?

4. If we evacuate the school, where do we go?

5. What has worked or not worked to handle a crisis situation in the past?

6. Is all playground equipment safe?

7. Do school personnel know CPR and first aid? Who will summon medical assistance? What if the nurse is not available?

8. How can a teacher summon help from the office?

9. Does the school offer a gun safety program?

10. Is the school system prepared to deal with the media?

11. Have school staff been provided with information on how to deal with a violent person?

12. What communication systems are available to contact police and to inform the superintendent of schools?

Dillard (1989) made these additional recommendations for primary prevention:

1. Know how to call on mental health resources in your community.

2. Establish close cooperative relations between the school system and police and fire departments.

3. Be prepared to provide ongoing assistance to students, their parents, and school staff after a crisis. Group meetings held at school can convey factual information and dispel rumors.

Many issues concerning safety also need to be addressed in the curriculum. One of the most important involves educating students about gun safety. Ten children each day under the age of 18 are killed in handgun suicides, homicides, or accidents (Memmot, 1989). One school system that is educating its students about gun safety is Dade County in Florida. Doup (1989) reports that the program begins in the first grade and is modeled after drug prevention programs.

The *secondary level* of intervention in Caplan's (1964) model emphasizes responding quickly to minimize the chance of long-lasting effects to a crisis. School buildings may want to form medical emergency teams and rehearse their response to various situations. Control of students is also very important. Plans need to be developed to direct students to classrooms or out of the building without mass confusion. One high school crisis team has made evacuation arrangements with local churches near the high school campus; the team also has ready a "crisis box" with materials that would be needed in the event that the school needed to be evacuated. The school faculty must also be told promptly when a crisis occurs. Thought needs to be given to how to accomplish that. The faculty needs to process the crisis event and their feelings about it as soon as students have gone home. This meeting to process the event can also be used to plan for the next school day.

Contacting law enforcement personnel is also part of secondary intervention. Which law enforcement personnel will be called and what to expect when they arrive are important questions to be addressed. Parent contact is also very important. The parents of injured and upset children need to be contacted. Parents may simply appear at the school and they might be upset and make demands upon the school or they might have come to help out. One crisis team elected to involve parents in a positive way. They contacted parents who lived near the school and who were home during the day and made them a part of their crisis team. Communication to parents after a crisis is very important. It is important to clarify how this communication will take place and who will do it.

The emotional effects of a crisis must also be dealt with immediately in order to minimize long-lasting debilitating effects. This point is well illustrated by Sandall (1986), who not only discussed immediate steps taken in the aftermath of a school bombing in Cokeville, Wyoming, but contrasted actions taken there with those taken in Chowchilla, California, in the 1970s. A school bus full of children was kidnapped in Chowchilla and was sequestered in the desert for several days. The children escaped and were physically unhurt. Sandall reports that the Chowchilla school children were told to go home and forget about the incident, and it was felt that only a small percentage of them would suffer permanent psychological effects. A follow-up study 5 years later found 100% with psychological problems as a result of their experience. By way of contrast, Sandall describes the steps taken in Wyoming to provide opportunities for children and faculty to discuss their feelings. School was held the day after the bombing and all who could be released from the hospital were encouraged to attend. Sandall commented, in part, "Those children who verbalized most effectively and in the greatest quantity have managed recovery best" (1986, p. 2). Children who have witnessed a traumatic event commonly react, according to Pynoos and Eth (1986), by (a) reexperiencing the event mentally, (b) fearing that it will happen again, and (c) withdrawing from the outside environment and clinging to family members.

Schulman (1986) discussed immediate steps taken in Concord, New Hampshire, to deal with emotionality following the Challenger shuttle disaster that killed Christa McAuliffe, a teacher at the high school. Schulman emphasized that having a crisis team already in place was of great benefit. Students and teachers were provided many opportunities to express their emotions and given flexibility with regard to their schedule and movement around the building. Students had a number of choices. They could go to the gym and vent frustrations and anger through physical activity, they could go to the cafeteria to support and be supported by others, or they could go to the library, which was a quiet wake area.

Tertiary prevention involves the long-term follow-up of those affected by a crisis. Sandall (1986) stressed the need for tertiary intervention and pointed out that counseling was provided over the summer in Cokeville, Wyoming. Follow-up questionnaires are also recommended. School psychologists are in a position to provide follow-up and monitoring to those most affected by a crisis. If we cannot provide the long-term assistance ourselves, we can recommend that the family seek it privately. Anniversary dates of losses and crisis events are important.

Training Issues for Crisis Team Members

Team members need first of all to be able to recognize a crisis, which Jay (1989) pointed out is an event that is likely to (a) interrupt normal routine and escalate in intensity, (b) draw attention to the school and jeopardize the school's image, (c) interfere with student's and staff's ability to focus on learning. Smead (1985) discussed the importance of responding immediately to a potential crisis to minimize its effects. The crisis team should meet if at all possible even if the event does not seem to be of crisis proportions. What this immediate response should be was emphasized by Slaikeu (1984), who outlined the following principles of psychological first aid:

1. Make contact with the victim and give him/her permission to express thoughts and emotions.

2. Explore the problem in terms of the past, present, and future.

3. Identify possible solutions to assist victim.

4. Take definite actions to assist victim.

5. Provide follow-up assistance.

Psychological first-aid addresses immediate concerns and helps the victim sort out such needs as welfare, safety, shelter, and so forth. Ruof and Harris (1988) recommend that team members receive as much as 30 hours of training.

One District's Approach

The development and implementation of a district crisis intervention plan was assigned by the superintendent to psychological services. The following steps were taken:

1. The literature was surveyed and a few crisis plans from other school districts were located.

2. Principals were interviewed to get their input and to involve them in the process.

3. Directors of security, nursing, transportation, and public information were all interviewed.

4. A building crisis team approach was recommended with district personnel involved in a support role.

5. Building principals were designated as crisis coordinators and the media spokespersons. An in-service was provided to clarify their role.

6. Principals designated liaisons in the following areas: counseling, law enforcement, student, parent, campus and medical. These liaisons together with the principal formed the building crisis team. Training was provided to the various liaison roles.

7. Principals were provided with training on dealing with the media; emphasis was placed on being cooperative but also containing the media.

8. District transportation personnel received training.

9. A tip sheet for teachers and aides for dealing with a crisis was developed and presented at an in-service in every school building. Teachers were encouraged to make plans to deal with such behavior as tantrums, fights, running away, and medical emergencies. A worksheet to address these problems was provided.

10. A basic premise was emphasized that these steps were only a starting point and that the most important recommendation was for the building crisis teams to meet regularly and discuss their school.

11. Crisis intervention activities were publicized and shared with the community.

Crisis drills. The district had on paper an excellent crisis plan, but to make crisis intervention an integrated part of the school regimen more steps had to be taken. The superintendent authorized conducting crisis drills and gave the principals forewarning. A script for the initial crisis drill was written and various central administrators went to the scene to role-play the crisis. To minimize school disruption the crisis drill took place outside the school building. A sample crisis scenario appears below.

Incident:
A female student has been shot in the foot by a pistol in front of the school by the flagpole. The pistol, which she was carrying in her purse, discharged with students nearby. Your first notification of the incident is when several hysterical students rush into the office. The student has a younger brother who attends the same school. The superintendent's secretary will role-play the mother; please call her.

Task:
Please respond to this incident following the district crisis intervention procedures. District personnel are on the scene to role-play and ask questions. This is a *practice drill* and district personnel should be alerted; however, it is *not necessary* to notify agencies outside the district.

Verbal and written feedback were provided to the crisis team. The importance of a team effort was stressed, along with indications of prior planning. The first two drills were videotaped and were shown at the principals' meeting. Numerous drills have since been conducted, including even a surprise crisis drill at the central office. No one has complained about the crisis drills, and they serve the purpose of making crisis intervention a regular part of conducting school.

DEALING WITH DEATH

Stevenson (1986) pointed out that one of every 750 young persons will die each year. The most frequent causes of death for school-age children in order of magnitude are accidents, suicide, and homicides. School crisis team members need to be trained to assist in the aftermath of a death. Verification of a death is essential. A second or third verification needs to be accomplished before the death is announced. The principal is the logical person to direct the crisis team and to announce the death. Fitzgerald (1988) makes a number of recommendations in this area: (a) Announce the death over the intercom so that everyone gets the same information; then visit as many classrooms as possible, especially those most affected. (b) Provide opportunities for discussing emotions, going through the grief process, and funeral arrangements. (c) Send a letter home to parents that gives information about the death and how parents can help their children. (d) Counseling grief groups may need to be provided on an ongoing basis.

Educators often expect all children to react to a death in the same way, the typical expectation being that children should cry. Children should be given permission for a range of emotions. The child stating he doesn't care today may cry tomorrow. Crabb (1982) suggested the following classroom guidance activities to assist students: (a) unfinished sentence writing; (b) drawing a picture to express feelings; (c) using music to express thoughts and emotions.

Do not rush to remove desks and personal possessions of the deceased. Involve students in that process and encourage students to contact the family of the deceased in person or through cards and letters. It is recommended that a school psychologist follow the class schedule of the deceased. Stevenson

(1986) recommends minimizing religious platitudes or symbolism and advises that there is no correct response to a death. Physical contact may comfort some students. Students may be flooded with waves of emotions. Their individual life histories will influence their ability to cope with the death. Stevenson states that it is appropriate to just let students sit but not to leave them unsupervised. The most common reaction is shock as students try to grasp the finality of the loss. It is important that all school personnel model expression of emotion; curriculum concerns may have to be set aside.

Oates (1988) recommends a model to determine the expected degree of trauma following a death: The popularity of the person who has died and his or her length of time at a particular school are determinants. The circumstances of the death are also important. Suicide or murder result in more trauma than death by natural causes. A death that occurs at school also results in more trauma. These factors that address who, how, and where are very relevant to dealing with death.

Team members will need to be advocates for giving schoolchildren and staff the opportunity to express their emotions. This point is illustrated by the following comments of a teacher whose classroom had been bereaved.

> "I heard about the murder of R, a seven-year-old girl in my class, the night that she was killed. I went to school early the next morning. My principal was just moving her desk out of my room. The principal said that all of her possessions had been removed and that I should avoid talking about her murder and concentrate on academics. I was angry and so were my students; we all felt robbed of a chance to express our emotions and to say our farewells to her. One student asked if we couldn't at least let a balloon ascend to heaven in her memory. I allowed that and it helped her classmates."

Crabb (1982) emphasized that children's emotional problems after a disaster continue until help is provided. Children need to be provided the facts in age-appropriate terms, and rumors must be dispelled. Dillard (1989) recommended providing parents and children the opportunity to be together and share experiences after a tragedy. Dillard described meetings that were held over the summer following a shooting in Winnetka, Illinois. These meetings helped children achieve mastery over the shooting. Dillard stressed that a traumatic event is stored in active memory until mastered. Details fade from immediate memory when mastery occurs.

Developing A Suicide Intervention Program

Youth suicide has many implications for the schools. Legislation has passed in five states that addresses the role of the school in prevention. Most states are studying the problem of youth suicide. No national legislation has been passed, although a national conference was sponsored by the federal government in 1985. The question of the responsibility of the schools with regard to youth suicide is not a new one. Stekel, a social scientist, commented on an outbreak of youth suicide in Europe in the early 1900s: "The school is not responsible for the suicide of its pupils, but it also does not prevent these suicides. This is its only, but perhaps its greatest sin" (quoted in Peck, Farberow, & Litman, 1985, p. 158). Few schools are prepared to deal with youth suicide and very few policies and procedures have been written to clarify the role of school personnel (Harris & Crawford, 1987). Ross (1985) stressed that it is fear and not lack of concern that results in school administrators' reluctance to work on this problem. Few school administrators have received any formal training in suicide prevention. They hold many misperceptions about youth suicide and see it as a problem that happens elsewhere. School prevention programs began in California in the 1970s and have spread by a grassroots effort, each school reinventing the wheel (Ryerson, 1988). School psychologists are in a position to clarify the schools' role and write policies and procedures to work on this problem. Several writers have emphasized that intervention programs in the school are effective (Cantor, 1987; Ross, 1985; Ruof & Harris, 1988).

Case example. A high school English teacher read a theme that a ninth-grade girl had written that made many references to hopelessness and nonexistence. The teacher asked the girl to stay after school in order to directly inquire about how things were going for the student. The girl shared many family, school, and romance problems that were bothering her. The girl stated, "My life is hopeless and not worth living." The teacher told her that help was available and that the teacher cared. The teacher escorted her to the school counselor's office. The school counselor spent a lot of time establishing rapport with the student and gathering a careful case history.

The girl had attempted suicide 6 months previously by taking aspirin. She had become ill but told no one what she had done. Her aunt had committed suicide by carbon monoxide poisoning and she planned to utilize that method next time. She had carefully thought out when she could go into the garage without being detected and had imagined how others would react to her death. The school counselor called the school psychologist for assistance. The girl signed a no-suicide contract and was told that her parents would be called and that this was in her best interest and in accordance with school policy. She was told that many other students had been helped and that the school psychologist and counselor would solicit a supportive reaction from her parents.

The parents initially refused to come to school. When they did arrive, they were angry at their daughter for not telling them about her suicidal thoughts. A referral was made to a private practitioner who had experience working with suicidal teenagers. The parents were provided with specific suggestions about supervision and support of their daughter. A follow-up appointment was made at school with the student and the school counselor. The principal was informed of the situation and the referring teacher was complimented on her role. The girl was monitored closely over the next several years. She never attempted suicide again. Shortly before graduation she stopped in and thanked her English teacher for helping her. The student stressed that her life wasn't wonderful but she was glad to be alive.

Forces and factors in youth suicide. There are numerous forces and factors that school psychologists need to be aware of. These are outlined in detail by Poland (1989). A precipitating event may cause a young person to act on suicidal thoughts, the most common precipitating events being arguments with parents or with boyfriends or girlfriends, or the loss of a loved one (Eyeman, 1987; Porter, 1985). Shaffer (1988) stressed that discipline incidents and loss of face with peers are also factors.

Depression has long been considered the most important warning sign of suicide. Numerous researchers stress that depression in children does exist but does not account for all youth suicides. Adolescents with conduct disorders are also at risk of committing suicide (Eyeman, 1987; Shaffer, 1988).

Use of controlled substances is now known to play an important role in youth suicide. Substance abuse can cause a young person to lose contact with reality, increasing the chances of a suicide attempt. Alcohol and many other drugs are depressants, which only add to psychological problems. Davis, Sandoval, and Wilson (1988) suggest that substance abuse be added as a major warning sign of suicide.

Student runaways also may be at risk for suicide. Researchers have found that runaways attempt suicide approximately 20% of the time (Engleman, 1987; Fortinsky, 1987).

How children develop their concept of death is important. The young child may view death as something that is either reversible or only happens to the very old (Davis, 1985; Pfeffer, 1986). Adolescents may also have some misperceptions about the finality of death. Young children who talk about life-threatening risk-taking behavior need to understand the possible fatal consequences. School psychologists should inquire as to the beliefs that the suicidal young persons have about death. Youths who have spent lots of time imagining the reactions of others to their suicide may be at high risk of committing suicide (Davis, 1985).

Much of youngsters' suicidal behavior is attention-getting and manipulative. Barrett (1985) stressed that parents need to recognize such behavior means their children want something to change and parents should let themselves be manipulated until they get professional help.

Other factors that may greatly influence a particular child are the following: (a) suicidal statements or suicide attempts by a parent, (b) motion pictures that deal with suicide, (c) suicidal lyrics in songs, (d) news coverage that glamorizes or mysticizes a suicide.

There has been a dramatic change in the methods employed to commit suicide by young people. Females are increasingly committing suicide by using guns. Lester (1988) stressed the strong correlation between gun ownership and suicide and reported that guns are involved in approximately 60% of all suicides. School psychologists will be in a position to address availability of guns with young people and their parents. Many researchers have pointed out that reducing availability of the guns will reduce suicides.

There is no single factor or cause that explains youth suicide. Siebel and Murray (1988) have stressed that there may be as many as 28 factors or causes. School personnel need to be aware of these factors; if they are at all concerned about a particular student, they need to inquire further.

The school's role in suicide interventions. Every school system needs a written policy to clarify the school's role in suicide intervention. These procedures need to address the three levels of intervention outlined by Caplan (1964). Vidal (1986) stressed that help for a suicidal student is contingent on school personnel knowing the policy. The obligations of the school at a minimum are the following: (a) to detect suicidal students, (b) to assess the severity of their suicidal symptoms, (c) to notify parents, (d) to secure the needed mental health services and supervision for the student, and (e) follow-up at school.

Detection. All school personnel including bus drivers and aides need information on the warning signs of suicide as identified by the American Association of Suicidology (1977). These warning signs include the following verbal and behavioral clues: (a) suicide threats or statements (b) an attempt at suicide, (c) prolonged depression, (d) dramatic change of behavior or personality, and (e) making final arrangements. School personnel should be encouraged to reach out to help suicidal students and should follow district policy in referring students. School personnel *must not* keep a secret about suicidal behavior. They need to understand the situational nature of youth suicide and should clearly feel that they could save a life, as in the case example.

Assessment. Someone in every school system must be skilled at assessing the severity of a suicidal student's symptoms. The most logical personnel to do this are school psychologists. Preparation is required in advance to work through personal issues and perceived inadequacies in this area, and to investigate the various suicidal assessment scales. It may be advisable to rehearse with a colleague or even a drama student.

There is no single scale or set of questions that is recommended for use with a suicidal student. Davis et al. (1988) reviewed the available instruments and noted the following instruments as the most promising:

1. The Hilson Adolescent Profile, developed by Inwald, Brobst, and Morrissey (1987)

2. The Suicidal Ideation Questionnaire, developed by Reynolds (1987)

3. The Suicide Probability Scale, developed by Cull and Gill (1982)

Davis et al. cautioned that more validation needs to be done with all three instruments. But Hoff (1978) questioned the effectiveness of lethality assessment scales

and instead stressed communication and the establishment of rapport with the student. Barrett (1985) has emphasized the importance of carefully gathering information from the student to guide actions and pointed out the distinction between assessment and prediction, and McBrien (1983) has emphasized that practitioners must stay calm and ask a series of questions as if the student is planning a trip.

The need for direct inquiry into suicidal thoughts and plans is essential. The need for a careful case history and thorough inquiry into the suicidal plans and actions is outlined through sample questions by Poland (1989). A number of suicidal assessment scales classify students into the categories of low, medium, and high risk for suicide. School psychologists must be careful not to categorize a student as at low risk on the basis of their own need rather than information gathered from the student. No-suicide contracts help students take control over their suicidal impulses and reduce the anxiety of both the students and the school psychologist (McBrien, 1983). Contracts should not be used in isolation (Barrett, 1985). Students who refuse to sign a no-suicide contract should be supervised until parents can pick them up; hospitalization may be needed.

Parent Notification

Parents must be notified any time that it is believed that a child is suicidal. The question is not whether to call them but instead what to say to them. The goal of notifying parents is to safeguard the welfare of the student, but it also serves to protect the psychologist from liability.

Slenkovitch (1986) has stressed that schools should never take a suicide threat lightly. School districts and school employees have been sued for inadequate suicide prevention programs. Davidson (1985) and Henegar (1986) addressed the question of liability, stressing the importance of duty to care and foreseeability of the actions of a client and that the primary issue is negligence. Henegar commented in part: "A negligence theory in a suicide case is not generally a claim that one caused the suicide but rather that one did not take reasonable steps to prevent it" (1986, p. 14). Henegar made several recommendations that have implications for school psychologists treating suicidal students: (a) increase supervision of the student, (b) limit access to self-destructive instruments, (c) obtain psychological treatment.

Once their parents have been notified, most suicidal students are relieved that their parents now know what has been on their mind. Parents' reactions may range from extreme cooperation to extreme denial and anger at the school. A common initial reaction of parents is hurt that their child is thinking of suicide. Johnson and Maile (1987) recommend that parents do the following: (a) Be patient, show love, and seek out the help their child needs; (b) take threats and gestures seriously; (c) keep communication open and get help with no strings attached.

The challenge to the school psychologist is to notify parents in a way that elicits their support and to convince the parents to obtain the needed services for their child. Stanton and Stanton (1987) stressed the point of finding parental strengths and empowering the parents with the belief that their child can be helped. However, it is advisable to document notification of parents and to have two school personnel present at the conference during which parents are notified. A resistant parent should be asked to sign a form acknowledging that they have been notified of their child's suicidal state. Parents who refuse to follow through on a recommendation for treatment services in the community must be told that it is neglectful not to get treatment for a suicidal child and that school personnel will call the child welfare department. A resistant parent might forbid the school psychologist to talk with their child. Some states, such as Texas, have passed legislation that allows psychologists to provide services to a suicidal minor without the parents' permission.

Working with suicidal students causes anxiety. Brown and Schroff (1986) rec-ommended that school psychologists take care of themselves by getting the opinion and support of others and processing feelings and by recognizing that no one can assume the responsibility for the life of an individual who is threatening suicide.

Community services. School psychologists should not accept the primary responsibility of treating a suicidal student. They need to be familiar with community resources to assist suicidal students and should establish a cooperative relationship between the school, the parents, and the community mental health provider, so that maximum support is provided to the student. However, they need to continue to provide support and monitoring at school even though the student is receiving community services.

Postvention. Schools are not usually prepared to deal with the aftermath of a suicide. Experts have emphasized that a series of planned steps must be accomplished to minimize the chances of a second suicide and to help students and faculty deal with their grief (Kneisel & Richards, 1988; Lamb & Dunne-Maxim, 1987). Policies designed to meet these needs must be in place prior to a suicide. Numerous writers have emphasized that suicides must be acknowledged and talked about (Biblarz, 1988; Ryerson, 1988). Normal procedures in the event of a death should be followed with an emphasis on avoiding a dramatic, romantic, or mystic treatment of the suicide. The task facing most school survivors is resolution of grief. Homeroom discussions should provide an opportunity for students to express their grief. Individual and group counseling needs to be provided at school (Coleman, 1987). Lamartine (1985) pointed out that the suicide of a student increases the probability 300% that a second suicide will occur. School psychologists need to identify other students who are at risk of committing suicide and provide assistance to them. Everyone at school needs to know the warning signs of suicide and to feel empowered to prevent further suicides. The following additional recommendations are suggested after a student suicide has occurred.

1. The suicide should be acknowledged and school activities should continue.

2. The faculty should be assisted first, then students.

3. The family of the suicide victim should be contacted to express condolences and to request the funeral be during non-school hours.

4. Memorials to the student who committed suicide should be downplayed.

5. Media coverage of the suicide should avoid front page coverage and should downplay simplistic explanations and avoid details of the method employed. Prevention information and community resources available should be included.

Curriculum issues. Curriculum approaches to suicide prevention fall into two categories. The first approach emphasizes a positive school climate, affirms life, and promotes life skills, especially problem solving, for the students (Sowers, 1987). All professionals agree with the importance of this approach. The second approach involves directly talking in the classroom about suicide as a mental health problem (California State Department of Education, 1987): Classroom presentations stress the warning signs, befriending skills, intervention by friends, and the situational nature of suicide. Also included are the relationship between suicide and use of controlled substances and the community services available to help a suicidal youth.

There is debate about whether the curriculum approach is to be recommended. Shaffer (1988) called for a moratorium on such curriculum presentations and noted that they were developed because the schools felt a need to do something. Smith (1988), commenting on Shaffer's research, noted that most students who participated in curriculum programs viewed them positively. The central point of controversy seems to be the contention that curriculum presentations somehow plant the idea of suicide. This premise is at the basis of Schafly's (1985) objections. A very logical question arises: Can teenagers translate information presented to them into life-saving behavior. Numerous evaluators have said yes to this question.

The question of whether parental permission should be obtained before a student participates in a curriculum presentation has been raised as well as the relevance of the Hatch Amendment (Davis et al., 1988; Schafly, 1985). Florida requires parents' permission, for example; California does not. A very unfortunate consequence of the curriculum debate is that many school districts have misinterpreted the debate to mean that professionals do not agree that schools need to prepare and take systematic steps to prevent youth suicide. This is not the case. There is no debate about the basic role of the school in detecting and assisting suicidal youth. School psychologists should be involved in determining the need for curriculum presentations in their district and selecting materials if presentations are to be provided to students.

SUMMARY

There has been an increase in the number of crisis events that affect the schools. School psychologists are the logical personnel to respond. It is important that school psychologists respond on these occasions to help all concerned and to broaden the role of school psychology. The initial intervention of school psychologists tends to be at the secondary or tertiary level. Among other interventions, it is important that they advocate for opportunities for those who experience a crisis to express their emotions. In addition, the focus of future practice by school psychologists needs to be on primary prevention activities in the schools.

REFERENCES

American Association of Suicidology. (1977). *Suicide and how to prevent it.* West Point, PA: Merck, Sharp, and Dome.

Barrett, T. (1985). *Youth in crisis: Seeing solutions of self-destructive behavior.* Longmont, CO: Sopris West.

Biblarz, D. (1988, April). Not in my school: Entry issues: In S. Perlin (Chair), *Tackling the tough issues in school based suicide awareness programs.* Symposium conducted at the meeting of the American Association of Suicidology, Washington, DC.

Bloom, B. L. (1977). *Community mental health: A general introduction.* Monterey, CA: Brooks/Cole.

Brown, S., & Schroff, B. (1986). Taking care of ourselves. *Network News, 4,* 5-6.

California State Department of Education. (1987). *Suicide prevention program for the California public schools.* Sacramento: Author.

Cantor, P. (1987, November). Communication with students at risk. In A. McEvoy (Chair), *Suicide prevention and the schools.* Symposium sponsored by Learning Publications, Orlando, FL.

Caplan, G. (1964). *Principles of preventive psychiatry.* New York: Basic Books.

Coleman, L. (1987). *Suicide clusters.* Boston: Faber & Faber.

Comstock, B. (1985). Youth suicide cluster: A community response. *Newslink, 2*(2), 6.

Crabb, A. (1982, February). Children and environmental disasters: The counselor's responsibility. *Elementary School Guidance and Counseling,* pp. 228-231.

Cull, J., & Gill, W. (1982). *Suicide probability scale manual.* Los Angeles: Western Publishing Services.

Danish, S. J., & D'Augelli, A. R. (1980). Promoting competence and enhancing development through life development intervention. In L. A. Bond & J. C. Rosen (Eds.), *Competence and coping during adulthood.* Hanover, NH: University Press of New England.

Davidson, H. (1985). Legal issues. In N. Farberow, S. Altman, & A. Thorne (Eds.), *Report of the national conference on youth suicide* (pp. 297-303). Washington, DC: Youth Suicide National Center.

Davis, J. (1985). Suicidal crises in schools. *School Psychology Review, 14,* 313-324.

Davis, J., Sandoval. J., & Wilson, M. (1988). Strategies for the primary prevention of adolescent suicide. *School Psychology Review, 17,* 559-569.

Dillard, H. (1989). Winnetka: One year later. *Communique, 17*(8), 17-20.

Doup, L. (1989, June 16). Children and guns can be a dangerous combination. *Houston Chronicle,* p. 6e.

Engleman, R. (1987). Running away from home is a sign of suicidal bent. *Network News, 7,* 9.

Eyeman, J. (1987, March). Pre-conference workshop. *Suicide prevention in schools.* Symposium presented at the meeting of the National Association of School Psychologists, New Orleans.

Fitzgerald, H. (1988). Helping children when a classmate dies. *Communique, 16*(5), 19.

Fortinsky, R. (1987). U.S.M. study finds link between runaways and suicidal potential. *Network News, 7,* 9.

Friend, T. (1988, December 5). More teens are dying violently. *USA Today,* p. 1d.

Gordon, S. (1985). *When living hurts.* New York: Union of Hebrew Congregations.

Guetzloe, E. (1988). Suicide and depression: Special education's responsibility. *Teaching Exceptional Children, 20*(4), 24-29.

Harkavy-Friedman, J., Asnis, G., Boe, M., & DiFiore, J. (1987). Prevalence of specific suicidal behaviors in a high school sample. *American Journal of Psychiatry, 144,* 1203-1206.

Harris, M., & Crawford, R. (1987). *Youth suicide: The identification of effective concepts and practices in policies and procedures for Texas schools* (Monograph No. 3). Commerce: East Texas State University, Center for Policy Studies and Research.

Henegar, C. (1986). Suicides in the shelters: Liability in the runaway centers. *Network News, 4,* 4-7.

Hoff, L. (1978). *People in crisis: Understanding and helping.* Reading, MA: Addison-Wesley.

Inwald, R., Brobst, K., & Morrissey, R. (1987). *Hilson adolescent profile manual.* Kew Gardens, NJ: Hilson Research.

Jay, B. (1989, January). Managing a crisis in the schools. *National Association of Secondary School Principals Bulletin,* pp. 14-17.

Johnson, S., & Maile, L. (1987). *Suicide and the schools.* Springfield. IL: Thomas.

Keen, J. (1989, February 2). USA schools wrestle with kid violence. *USA Today,* p. 1a.

Keen, J., and Fiest, P. (1989, January 18). Are our kids safe while at school? *USA Today,* p. 1a.

Kniesel, D., & Richards, G. (1988). Crisis intervention after the suicide of a teacher. *Professional Psychology: Research and Practice, 19*(2), 165-169.

Lamartine, C. (1985). Suicide prevention in educational settings. In *After a suicide death* (pamphlet). Dayton, OH: Suicide Prevention Center.

Lamb, F., & Dunne-Maxim, K. (1987). Postvention in the schools: Policy and process. In E. Dunne, J. McIntosh, & K. Dunne-Maxim (Eds.), *Suicide and its aftermath* (pp. 245-263). New York: Norton.

Leder, M. (1987). *Dead serious: A book for teenagers about teenage suicide.* New York: Atheneum.

Lester, D. (1988). Research note: Gun control, gun ownership and suicide prevention. *Suicide and Life-Threatening Behavior, 18,* 176-181.

Lidell, H. G., and Scott, R. (1968). *The Greek–English lexicon.* Oxford: Clavendon.

Mayfield, M. (1986, December 8). Assaults top the list of classroom chaos. *USA Today,* p. 10a.

McBrien, J. (1983). Are you thinking of killing yourself?: Confronting students' suicidal thoughts. *School Counselor, 31*(1), 79-82.

McEvoy, A. (1988). Shocking violence in schools. *School Intervention Report, 1*(7), 1-3.

McGinnis, J. (1985). Suicide in America-moving up the public health agenda. *Suicide and Life-Threatening Behavior, 17,* 18-32.

Memmot, C., & Stone, A. (1989, June 15). Firearms and youngsters: Deadly, tragic mix. *USA Today,* p. 3a.

Nelson, E., Slaikeu, K. (1984). Crisis intervention in the schools. In K. Slaikeu (Eds.), *Crisis intervention: A handbook for practice and research* (pp. 247--263). Boston: Allyn and Bacon.

Oates, M. (1988, Fall). Responding to death in the schools, *Texas Association for Counselor Development Journal, 16*(2), 83-96.

Peck, M., Farberow, N., & Litman, R. (Eds.). (1985). *Youth suicide.* New York: Springer.

Pelej, J., & Scholzen, K. (1987). Postvention: A school's response to suicide. In R. Yufit (Ed.), *Proceedings of the Twentieth Annual Conference of the American Association of Suicidology* (pp. 387-390). San Francisco: American Association of Suicidology.

Pfeffer, C. (1986). *The suicidal child.* New York: Guilford.

Pitcher, G., & Poland, S. (in press). *Crisis intervention in the schools.* New York: Guilford.

Poland, S. (1989). *Suicide intervention in the schools.* New York: Guilford.

Porter, W. (1985). *Inservice and resource guide for children and adolescent suicide prevention.* Unpublished manuscript. Denver, CO: Cherry Creek Schools.

Pynoos, R., & Eth, S. (1986). Child psychiatrists describe children's reactions to disaster. *Communique, 15*(2), 3.

Rappaport, J. (1977). *Community psychology: Values, research, and action.* New York: Holt, Rinehart, & Winston.

Reiff, R. (1975). Of cabbages and kings. The 1974 Division 27 annual distinguished contributions to community mental health. *American Journal of Community Psychology, 3,* 185-196.

Reynolds, W. (1987). Suicidal ideation questionnaire. Odessa, FL: Psychological Assessment Resources.

Ross, C. (1985). Teaching children the facts of life and death: Suicide prevention in the schools. In M. Peck, N. Farberow, & R. Litman (Eds.), *Youth suicide* (pp. 147-169). New York: Springer.

Ruof, S., & Harris, J. (1988). How to select, train and supervise a crisis team. *Communique, 17*(4), 19.

Ryerson, D. (1988, April). The importance of school personnel and researchers collaborating. In K. Smith (Chair), *How do we know what we've done? Controversy in evaluation.* Symposium conducted at the Meeting of the American Association of Suicidology, Washington, DC.

Sandall, N. (1986). Early intervention in a disaster: The Cokeville hostage/bombing crisis. *Communique, 15*(2), 1-2.

Schafly, P. (1985). The school and youth suicide. In N. Farberow, S. Altman, & A. Thorne (Eds.), *Report of the National Conference on Youth Suicide* (pp. 269-275). Washington, DC: Youth Suicide National Center.

Schulman, N. (1986). A crisis intervention response to the shuttle disaster, *Newslink, 12*(3), 4.

Seibel, M., & Murray, J. (1988, March). Early prevention of adolescent suicide. *Educational Leadership,* pp. 45-51.

Shaffer, D. (1988, April). School research issues. In K. Smith (Chair), *How do we know what we've done? Controversy in evaluation.* Symposium conducted at the Meeting of the American Association of Suicidology, Washington, DC.

Shipman, F. (1987). *Crisis intervention: A handbook for practice and research.* Boston: Allyn and Bacon.

Slenkovitch, J. (1986, June). School districts can be sued for inadequate suicide prevention programs. *Schools' Advocate,* pp. 1-3.

Smead, V. (1985). Best practices in crisis intervention. In A. Thomas & J. Grimes (Eds.), *Best practices in school psychology* (pp. 401-415). Kent, OH: National Association of School Psychology.

Smith, K. (Chair). (1988, April). *How do we know what we've done? Controversy in evaluation.* Symposium conducted at the meeting of the American Association of Suicidology, Washington, DC.

Smith, K., & Crawford, S. (1986). Suicidal behavior among "normal" high school students. *Suicide and Life-Threatening Behavior, 16,* 313-325.

Sowers, J. (1987, November). Issues in curriculum and program development. In A. McEvoy (Chair), *Suicide prevention and the schools.* Symposium sponsored by Learning Publications, Orlando, FL.

Stanton, J., & Stanton, S. (1987). Family and system therapy of suicidal adolescents, *Family Therapy Today, 2*(11), 1-4.

Stevenson, R. (1986, December). How to handle death in the schools, *National Association of Secondary Principals Bulletin,* pp. 1-2.

Vidal, J. (1986, October). Establishing a suicidal prevention program. *National Association of Secondary School Principals Bulletin,* pp. 68-72.

Wilhelm, R., (1967). *The book of changes or I Ching.* Princeton, NJ: Princeton University Press.

ANNOTATED BIBLIOGRAPHY

California State Department of Education. (1987). *Suicide prevention program for the California public schools.* Sacramento: Author.
Provides the information needed to train school personnel to detect suicidal behavior. A lesson guide is provided that is appropriate to use in the curriculum for Grades 9-12, emphasizing warning signs of suicide, community resources, and intervention by friends.

Pitcher, G., & Poland, S. (in press). *Crisis intervention in the schools.* New York: Guilford.
The authors discuss both theoretical and practical aspects of managing crises in the schools. The role of the psychologist ranges from that of consultant to trainer to provider of direct services. Practical information regarding staff in-services, managing organizational crises directly, and stimulating intrasystemic change is presented. Special emphasis on moving the system in the direction of providing preventive services is emphasized.

Poland, S. (1989). *Suicide intervention in the schools.* New York: Guilford.
The role of the school is defined, and case examples provided step-by-step guidelines for setting up and maintaining a comprehensive program. Issues covered include the following: forces and factors in youth suicide, assessment, parent notification, liability, legislation, curriculum, and dealing with the media. Detailed procedures for intervention following crises.

19

Best Practices in Curriculum-Based Assessment

Sylvia Rosenfield
Temple University

Sally K. Kuralt
Hyde Park (New York) Central School District

Learners are often confused when they either "learn" something they already know or are "taught" something beyond their understanding . . .

Goodman and Burke, 1980, p. 32

OVERVIEW

Definition

Curriculum-based assessment (CBA) is a procedure that provides a window on student learning for instructional decision making. It has been defined most recently as "a system for determining the instructional needs of a student based upon the student's on-going performance within existing course content in order to deliver instruction as effectively and efficiently as possible" (Gickling, Shane, & Croskery, 1989, pp. 344–345). Since CBA comprises procedures that directly assess student performance within the classroom curriculum, it facilitates the alignment of instruction with student learning needs and enhances teachers' decision making.

Importance of CBA to Student Learning

As Tucker (1985) has said, there is nothing really new about CBA: "the basic idea is as old as education itself" (p. 199). A history of the term *CBA* has been provided by Coulter (1988), who traces the present use of the term to the title of Ed Gickling's presentation to Texas pupil appraisal personnel in 1977. However, the concepts involved in CBA relate to current models of effective instruction. While much of the effective instruction movement has focused on the presentation, monitoring, and feedback phases of instruction, the planning and diagnostic phases are equally important, perhaps particularly so for at-risk, low-achieving students (Gickling, 1989). It is widely accepted that lack of attention to entry-level skills of learners will lead to the failure of even the most effective teacher presentation, monitoring, and feedback techniques. CBA contributes essential information in the formative assessment and planning phases, as well as being a useful procedure for collecting monitoring data.

During the past decade, research has provided a growing body of information regarding the relationship between teachers' instructional decision making and students' gains in achievement (Fuchs, 1986; Porter & Brophy, 1988). Since instructional decision making and curriculum-based assessment are interdependent, CBA strategies and procedures facilitate the link between assessment and instruction. CBA provides a window on the learner that can be utilized by the teacher to make an "instructional match," i.e., to assist the teacher in providing on-going effective instruction. To be of greatest utility, the window of CBA must reflect what we know to be true about effective learning and teaching and thus frame instructional interventions that enhance learner outcomes.

Role of School Psychologists

School psychologists function as key personnel in schools with respect to educational assessment and decisions. Increasing awareness has developed that assessment data are used to make different types of decisions. Salvia and Ysseldyke (1981) have delineated five types of decisions: screening, placement, instructional planning, pupil evaluation, and program evaluation. The model of CBA being described here (see Shinn, Rosenfield, & Knutson, 1989, for a comparison of different types of CBA procedures) is most useful for instructional planning. Therefore, the concepts in this chapter are highly relevant for school psychologists who seek to provide services at the prereferral level through expanding their capacity to work with teachers in developing academic competence in students.

Much of the assessment expertise of school psychologists has developed around techniques and instruments designed to gather data to be used in making decisions other than those of instructional planning. However, despite the considerable evidence that documents the value of precisely knowing the entry-level skills of the learner as a grounding for instructional decision making, the importance of carefully determining entry level for individual students is not widely accepted in the schools (see, e.g., Wesson, King, & Deno, 1984). According to Fuchs (1986), even special educators "typically formulate decisions on student mastery of IEP goals on the basis of unsystematic observation rather than on the basis of systematic assessment . . . Although teachers express confidence in the accuracy of . . . judgments, their informal evaluations about objective mastery tend

to overrate student performance" (p. 6). School psychologists who are committed to consultation with teachers will make an essential contribution by communicating the importance of, and assisting teachers in, gathering and utilizing data for instructional planning.

In addition, school psychologists who are involved in classification and placement decisions also would benefit from understanding CBA's contribution to that role. An assumption that underlies the legal definition of learning disabilities, for example, is that the student has received adequate instruction. Messick (1984), in his review of the results of the National Research Council Panel, commissioned at the request of the Office of Civil Rights to examine overrepresentation of minority students in special education, also stated the finding that a disproportion of minority students in educable mentally retarded (EMR) classes is inequitable if children are unduly exposed to placement because they have received poor-quality regular instruction. School psychologists must be knowledgeable about the elements of effective instruction. One of the key components of adequate instruction is the planning stage, based on competent diagnosis of a student's entry level. It is important for school psychologists to be able to ascertain whether students are not benefiting from instruction because it is not at their instructional level. If CBA data are not available, it is difficult to judge the extent to which the student is failing to learn because of a student-centered problem or because instruction is not provided at a level appropriate for the student.

BASIC CONSIDERATIONS

CBA procedures require an understanding of the concepts of *curriculum* and *effective instructional design*.

The Role of Scope and Sequence

The most basic concept in CBA is that of the curriculum, which may be defined as a set of learning tasks "sequenced, calibrated, and organized to facilitate learning" (Howell & Morehead, 1987, p. 26). Where CBA departs from some other academic achievement techniques is that it is assumed that the scope and sequence of the school's curricula must be utilized in the process of assessing a student's instructional needs and progress. There is now a considerable empirical base that demonstrates that standardized achievement tests cannot serve this purpose, as they do not closely enough reflect the reality of the classroom in which the student and teacher interact (e.g., Shapiro & Derr, 1987; Shriner & Salvia, 1988).

The scope and sequence of the curriculum involves two levels. There is the scope and sequence of the syllabus or the curriculum guide used by the school or school district. This usually consists of a list of key concepts, skills, procedures, and objectives to be taught at each grade level, frequently with a recommended sequence, or order, in which they should be taught. Some models of CBA (e.g., Blankenship, 1985; Idol, Nevin, & Paolucci-Whitcomb, 1986; Howell & Morehead, 1987), sometimes called inventory or task analysis models of CBA, work from these lists of objectives to frame test items or probes that are used to indicate mastery of the objectives. When given prior to instruction, the test items, or probes, enable the teacher to place the student at the appropriate level for instruction. When given after instruction, they indicate how much mastery has been achieved.

There is, however, also the implemented scope and sequence, which results from the teacher's ongoing planning and use of materials. On a day-to-day basis, teachers set tasks within the larger, school curriculum scope and sequence. Porter (1989), in presenting data on "how much time is allocated, what topics are covered, for which students, and to what standards of achievement" (p. 13) in the implementation of the curriculum in elementary school mathematics, has demonstrated considerable diversity across classrooms. While this daily planning usually reflects the scope and sequence built into the curriculum materials, such as basal reading series or math workbooks utilized in the classroom, differences among individual teachers are considerable and not always in concert with good instructional principles (e.g., Porter, 1989).

On occasion, teachers may not have a clear understanding of how daily lessons relate to the larger set of objectives or understandings. It is sometimes difficult to work with such teachers to develop the CBA, as they are not clear about the specific skills, concepts, and knowledge that their daily lessons are organized to develop. For example, a fifth-grade teacher referred a youngster for a "math disability" on the basis of the student's inability to complete her math worksheets correctly. However, during the referral interview, it became apparent that the teacher's math curriculum consisted of a series of ditto sheets. Aside from these, the teacher did not have a clear conception of the skills or understandings that she wanted each of her students to master. The consultant developed a basic scope and sequence in math, and constructed a CBA for the student that pinpointed what she knew and what she did not know against this base. However, even with this information, the teacher had difficulty adjusting her teaching for the child because she was not working from a clearly articulated math curriculum.

School psychologists who wish to use CBA techniques will benefit from increasing their familiarity with curriculum outcomes, objectives, and materials in their districts. For the school psychologist unfamiliar with the basic concepts of school curriculum, Howell and Morehead (1987) provide a useful introduction. Talking with curriculum experts or knowledgeable teachers and principals is an excellent way to learn about the local curriculum practices. Reading teacher manuals and examining student materials, if these are not familiar, are also invaluable experiences, in preparing to develop CBA procedures. Attending staff development programs in the district intended for teachers on topics of curriculum and instruction is also valuable. School psychologists should consider utilizing any or all of these opportunities to become knowledgeable about the academic issues at the core of their local district.

Effective Instruction

The purpose of CBA is to plan and guide instruction in the most effective and efficient manner. This involves accurate and continuous assessment that takes minimal time away from instruction itself. It requires the school psychologist to be informed about the professional literature on learning and on effective teaching.

However, the research on effective instruction, combined with the importance of assessment in the curriculum used in the individual school setting, raises an interesting dilemma for school psychologists. The surge of activity in research has increasingly demonstrated that mastery of any subject or basic skill is dependent upon possession of certain prerequisite cognitive and metacognitive skills, strategies, and processes, and on learning particular content with understanding (e.g., Porter & Brophy, 1988). To be effective, for example, drill and practice must have functional meaning — must be based on conceptual understanding. However, all too often, children report that they think the purpose of a task is to complete work for the teacher or to finish the questions at the end of the chapter, no matter what the answer.

Moreover, the results of recent investigations of memory, comprehension, and problem solving increasingly suggest caution against conceptions of discrete skill hierarchies and ordered taxonomies of educational objectives (e.g., Cancelli, Bergan, & Jones, 1982; Wirtz, 1985). This ever-growing body of research has clearly placed the thinking skills, strategies, and processes that pervade school subjects and content areas at the core of effective instruction, and therefore, by definition, at the heart of the best practice of CBA. Although the importance of conducting CBA of student understanding and problem-solving processes has been recognized and discussed (e.g., Meyers & Kundert, 1988; Rosenfield, 1987), to date most models for CBA practice have generally focused on techniques for assessing discrete, ordered subskills, such as knowledge of phonics, and examining error patterns in memorized procedures, such as borrowing in subtraction.

The research-based need to frame cognitive considerations as central to effective instruction, before developing ways to assess them within the curriculum scope and sequence, necessitates extending and refocusing the perspective on curriculum development. It is not enough to simply assist teachers in making decisions about instruction from the current scope and sequence of the curriculum in place in the classroom. If the focus of this scope and sequence is on acquisition of isolated skills or rote factual recall only, it is also a responsibility of the school psychologist to facilitate expanded teacher understanding of the scope and sequence of cognitive considerations that research has indicated are central to academic achievement, and to assist teachers in curriculum-based assessment of these competencies as well. School psychologists who attempt to work in the classroom setting with teachers to facilitate academic progress of handicapped and at-risk students need a solid grounding in the effective instruction literature, including the focus on cognition.

BEST PRACTICES

Although the concepts of CBA are readily grasped, conducting the process requires a clear roadmap. This section will provide examples of best practices in different levels and content of curriculum. No matter what the content of the curriculum, the following questions constitute the basic paradigm at the heart of CBA and must always be addressed in instructional decision making.

1. What is the central understanding that the teacher wants the student to develop from this instructional task, activity, or unit? What concepts, strategies, skills, procedures, or knowledge does the teacher want the student to develop and acquire? CBA begins with a clear understanding of the scope and sequence

of the curriculum against which the student's performance can be assessed.

2. What, if any, discrepancy exists, between the outcomes the teacher has anticipated and those the student has achieved? After defining the goals, the student's performance in respect to the goals is assessed, preferably in the curriculum materials themselves, to determine the instructional match.

3. If an instructional mismatch exists, what prerequisite competencies (strategies, skills, concepts, knowledge) does the student need to attain in this experience? Which of them does the student have? Not have? Assessment proceeds to delineate the specific strategies, skills, concepts, and/or knowledge that are required.

4. As instruction is undertaken, does each task or experience match the student's entry skills and learning needs? Monitoring is ongoing and regularly done throughout the instructional process; progress is assessed, graphed, and used for instructional decision making at regular intervals.

5. Is the instruction presented so that the student is learning as efficiently as possible? Is maximum use made of instructional time? Performance is monitored to assess whether the student is engaged in the learning process.

Who Does the Assessment?

Given the instructional nature of the assessment, CBA most naturally should be done by the classroom teacher. However, when functioning as a consultant, the school psychologist can serve as a support person for the classroom teacher in this process. This contribution takes on many different aspects: establishing the importance of having this information for assessing the student's problem; assisting in preparing materials and/or developing assessment procedures; and working with the teacher to link the assessment information to classroom intervention. Some classroom teachers have difficulty finding time for, or lack interest in, this type of assessment, and the school psychologist

may need either to conduct the assessment or train other personnel to do so, especially when this type of assessment is alien to the school culture (Rosenfield & Rubinson, 1985).

Conducting Curriculum-Based Assessment

Fundamental to the learning process in all subject areas are student understanding of concepts; selection and implementation of strategies; application of an array of functional skills; and self-monitoring or metacognition. This framework facilitates the development of a unified and easily transferable assessment and instructional intervention process. Gickling (1989) has developed an integrative procedural CBA model for instructional decision-making that is based on the concept of instructional match. After teachers select the instructional objective, as well as the particular experience or task, this assessment process enables them to match the student's entry level with the task demands, and then plan for instruction based upon that information. This CBA procedural model has four basic steps that can be applied to any curricular task.

1. Assess the student's performance in a required curriculum task.

2. Interpret the learning situation by comparing student's entry level to the demands of the instructional task to determine how much variance exists.

3. Adjust the learning task so that it conforms to the appropriate instructional level and rate of the student.

4. Monitor performance and measure progress.

Applications

These steps provide a general guide. Examples of their application to reading and mathematics will be provided to clarify the process.

Reading. Reading is a problem-solving process in which the reader, through the use of the strategies of predicting, confirming, and integrating, interacts with the text to construct meaning. Use of such strategies is dependent upon information that comes from cues. The types of cues are: (a) semantic, based on the meaning of language; (b) syntactic, based on the structure and pattern of the written language; (c) phonographemic, based on letter–sound relationships; and (d) other context or picture cues.

Assess student performance. The assessment phase is begun by selecting passages from the reading material that the teacher will be using for instructing the student. Generally, in the early grades of elementary school this is defined by basal or literature-based reading series, anthologies, or selected trade books.

Next, the student's known, hesitant, and unknown responses are determined. Procedures that can be used to determine the level of difficulty of the passage include the informal reading inventory (IRI) and miscue analysis. An informal reading inventory can be constructed from a basal reading series (readers who seek further information on how to construct an IRI can consult Shapiro, 1989, Rosenfield, 1987, or reading teachers/consultants within their district); and the student's instructional level, that is, the point within the series where the student has the entry level skills to benefit from instruction, can be established. The assessment should include timing the number of words per minute read correctly, recording the words that yield known, hesitant, and unknown responses, and noting the student's reading behaviors.

In a second approach, the miscue analysis method, the student is placed in an appropriate level of literary or expository text. The record of the student's oral reading forms the basis for analysis of errors, defined as miscues that result in a loss of meaning, to determine what cueing strategies students are using or not using. Student miscues can then be tallied, analyzed for use in planning interventions, and summarized numerically for monitoring student progress through use of a mis-

cue recording checklist. Figure 1 shows a modification of such a checklist from the *Impressions* series (Booth, Booth, Pauli, & Phenix, 1986). For a complete discussion of the process of miscue analysis, the reader is referred to Clay's *Early Detection of Reading Difficulties* (1985).

There is often resistance in many school systems to placing students in below-grade-level materials, even if it is at the appropriate instructional level for the individual student. To accommodate to this reality, Gickling (1988) has developed the concept of the "workable passage," a process by which assessment of entry-level skills can be accomplished in available reading materials even when they are not initially matched appropriately to the student's entry level. The process involves assessing the difficulty level of the material for the student and the types of modifications necessary to enable the student to achieve success in the curriculum materials (see Gickling, 1989, for procedures).

In addition to gathering baseline data on rate and on known/unknown words, it is important to dialogue with the student to determine the degree of understanding of the text. Information is gathered with regard to prior knowledge about the concepts, content, and vocabulary in the passage; comprehension of the who, what, when, where, why, and how; and cognitive and metacognitive strategies used before, during, and after reading. Comprehension responses can be easily summarized, analyzed, and scored numerically through use of a checklist, such as the Comprehension Checklist found in the *Impressions* series (Booth et al., 1986).

Interpret the learning situation. Once the basic information is gathered, the planning phase continues with a comparison of the student's entry-level skills with the demands of the instructional task. A decision is made about how much variance exists between the task and the student's needs and skills. Where the task is not at the instructional level of the student (over 90% accuracy in connected text with 75% comprehension), it becomes

Miscue Recording Checklist

Type of Miscue	Miscues resulting in no loss of meaning ("home" for "house")	Miscues resulting in loss of meaning ("house" for "horse")
Substitution		
Omission		
Insertion		
Repetition		
Reversal		

Summary:
Total number of miscues _____   Cueing system used:
Miscues resulting in no loss of meaning _____   Syntactic _____
Miscues resulting in loss of meaning _____   Semantic _____
Correction attempts _____   Phonographemic _____

Comments: _____
_____
_____
_____

FIGURE 1. Modified miscue recording checklist. From *Impressions* by J. Booth, D. Booth, W. Pauli, and J. Phenix, 1986. Toronto: Holt, Rinehart, & Winston. Copyright 1986.

important to move to Step 3, and adjust the learning task for the student.

Adjust the learning task. The learning task is shaped to approximate the ratio of known to challenging items, either by dropping back to an earlier level in the scope and sequence of the reading series, by modification of the materials, or by further mediation of the text by the teacher. The rate of instruction may also need to be modified, so that new concepts and material are introduced with enough practice for the student to achieve not only accuracy, but automaticity of strategies and skills. Students differ on the

amount of repetition and practice required. Good instruction in reading involves utilizing effective and efficient instructional techniques to establish a purpose for reading; to access prior knowledge; to model prediction, confirmation, and integration; to develop contextual word accuracy and vocabulary; and to build fluency (see, e.g., Graden, Zins, & Curtis, 1988, Section 5; Palinscar, Ogle, Carr, & Ransom, 1985).

Monitor performance and measure accuracy. After the CBA assessment has established baseline and entry-level skills in reading, it is important to ensure that the student is engaged in a high level of on-task behavior. In addition, a system should be established to systematically monitor student progress. This can be accomplished on a short-term basis by using the CBA approach. For example, systematic and regular analysis of miscues and comprehension responses in texts at the student's instructional level provides an ongoing snapshot of student progress. Monitoring of long-term progress can be facilitated by the use of the CBM approach (see Shinn, 1990). However, it should be understood that CBM monitors progress toward a final curricular outcome; it is less useful for specific daily decision making than to sound the alarm that the student is not making adequate progress under current instructional conditions.

Mathematics. As the central focus of the school mathematics curriculum, problem solving is the "primary goal of all math instruction and an integral part of all mathematical activity;" it should not be considered "a distinct topic but a process that should permeate the entire program and provide the context in which concepts and skills can be learned" (National Council of Teachers of Mathematics, 1989, p. 2). Although current mathematics instruction in the classroom may not approximate this end closely enough (Porter, 1989), the CBA process should be founded on this research-based perspective. It is obviously not enough to have rote mastery of math rules and factual combinations, although many math curricula neither teach nor demand much more. Assisting the classroom teacher to understand the importance of the cognitive structures underlying the understanding of mathematics is a good example of "giving psychology away."

Assess student performance. Within the problem-solving framework, traditional CBA procedures in mathematics, such as error analysis of student work samples, can be extended or refocused to assess students' understanding of prerequisite concepts and known, imperfectly understood, and unknown operations, skills, and strategies, as well as rote algorithms and facts. This type of error

analysis, for example, asks questions such as: (a) Does lack of awareness of the repertoire of available strategies (such as making tables/graphs, finding a pattern, using physical models, guess and check, etc.) or inappropriate strategy selection underlie the student's implementation of the wrong operation? (b) Is this error the result of a misunderstood concept or the lack of a prerequisite one? (c) Does the student understand the steps of the problem-solving sequence?

Similarly, the cognitively based interview is designed to explore students' ability to understand concepts, use appropriate strategies, and define and solve problems. Before beginning the interview, CBA practitioners might ask themselves "What questions should I ask? What basic understanding should I question first? How might I incorporate the use of manipulative materials? How might I vary the task to gain a different perspective of the student's abilities" (Labinowicz, 1987, p. 23). Audiotaping such an interview permits valuable reflection on the interaction.

Problem-solving worksheets, such as the one in Figure 2 (located in the final section of each Teacher Edition of the Scott, Foresman and Company's *Invitation to Mathematics*, 1985, Grades 3–8), outlines questions that might be used to interview students while they are solving problems. In the case of older students such worksheets can be completed independently by the students as they work in the classroom. Later these sheets can be attached to referral work samples or used as a means of monitoring instructional interventions. Observing students' problem-solving behaviors, including the rate at which they work, provides additional useful information.

Interpret the learning situation. Once again the teacher now has information useful both for determining how much variance exists between the task and the student's prerequisite competencies and for matching the student's entry level with the demands of the math curriculum. If, for example, the problem deals with the Pythagorean Theorem and the student

Name		Problem-Solving Worksheet
READ	Understand the question	What are you asked to find? _____
	Identify needed data	What facts are given? _____
		(circle any facts that are not needed to solve the problem.)
PLAN	Analyze this action	Is computation needed? If yes, what operation(s)?
	Select strategies	Will other strategies help? Which ones? _____
SOLVE	Carry out the plan	Give an estimate of the answer. _____
		Find the answer. Show your work here.
	Try again, if needed	
ANSWER	Give a complete answer	Give this answer in a complete sentence. _____
LOOK BACK	Check for reasonableness	Did you answer the question? _____
		Did you use all needed data? _____
		Does your answer make sense? _____
	Check your computation	Is the answer close to your estimate? _____
		Did you compute correctly? _____

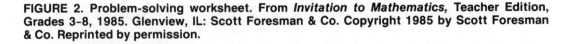

FIGURE 2. Problem-solving worksheet. From *Invitation to Mathematics*, Teacher Edition, Grades 3–8, 1985. Glenview, IL: Scott Foresman & Co. Copyright 1985 by Scott Foresman & Co. Reprinted by permission.

lacks understanding of squares and/or square roots, significant mismatch exists; or, similarly, if the problem calls for subtraction with renaming and the student lacks understanding of place value, it is essential to move to Step 3 and adjust the learning task for the student.

Adjust the learning task. As was the case in the reading example, information provided through the math CBA process enables teachers to make decisions that effectively modify student instruction. The instructional match can be improved by such strategies as modifying the task by constructing a variety of experiences or problems that build on knowns and that develop lacking or misunderstood prerequisite concepts and partly understood or unknown operations, strategies, or skills; by using a variety of materials and/or additional teacher mediation with the current task; or by selectively dropping back to an earlier level in the scope and sequence of the math series.

Monitor performance and measure progress. As noted earlier, the problem-solving worksheets can serve as an aid in monitoring student progress. Since math problem solving generally has two components — a thinking process and a solution or product, good evaluation and monitoring should consider both aspects. One such technique, suggested by Otis and Offerman (1988), uses a scoring system to evaluate the student's progress that includes characteristics of the student's solution: inappropriate strategy started, but problem not finished (1 point); inappropriate strategy, but showed some understanding of the problem (2 points); appropriate strategy but ignored a condition in the problem (3 points); appropriate strategy but incorrect answer due to a copying or computational error (4 points); and appropriate strategy and correct answer (5 points). This system, like miscue and comprehension recording checklists, permits quantification and graphic monitoring of the student's progress.

Commonly Asked Questions about CBA

Several recurrent questions are asked by professionals learning to use CBA. Although there has been an attempt to answer many of them in the course of this exposition, it might be helpful to address directly the most common ones.

1. *Can you do CBA in science or social studies; in preschool programs (or a vocational program, or any other type of program)?*

The key to this type of question is an understanding of the instructional process. In every instructional program, accessing the scope and sequence as well as the underlying conceptual foundation provides the key to developing the CBA procedures. It is important first to identify the goals, objectives, and understandings that the teacher intends for the student to learn. Once these are clearly established, an assessment process can be developed.

In every school subject area, concept formation is the content organizer of the instructional process. It forms the foundation for other thinking processes. Therefore, assessment of students' development of concepts essential for understanding an instructional task is an important focus for CBA. Assessment materials in social studies and science, for example, just as in reading and math, can thus be constructed. Neisworth and Bagnato (1986) have addressed some of the issues at the preschool level.

2. *In how many subjects should I do CBA?*

CBA is the diagnostic and planning stage of the effective instructional paradigm. It would be useful to have CBA used routinely by teachers. However, the school psychologist should ask in which curriculum areas a target student's progress is of concern and begin the CBA there.

3. *How can the school psychologist motivate the teacher to use CBA?*

This question takes us into the domain of consultation and is beyond the scope of this chapter. However, when the assessment information provided is relevant to the instructional process and relatively easy to obtain, teachers find the process useful and are motivated to use it.

Research Base

The research base underlying CBA is still in the developmental stage. Some research has been done to document the effectiveness of CBA techniques (e.g., Gickling et al., 1989). In the future it is likely that case studies will provide a more solid basis in helping us to understand and clarify the parameters of this assessment approach. Treating CBA in terms of a behavioral paradigm for research purposes appears to be a meaningful direction to develop an empirical base (Shinn et al., 1989).

SUMMARY

School psychologists who seek to provide services to teachers of students with academic problems need to know the effective learning paradigm and understand how instructional and learner characteristics interact. CBA is a process that facilitates the diagnostic and planning phases of instruction, enabling the teacher to determine relation of the entry level of the students to the demands of the academic task. It begins with clarity in knowing the scope and sequence of instructional objectives that form the curriculum of the classroom. Instructional tasks should have a clear purpose related to learner outcome. Where that is not clear to the teacher or student, the instructional process is often flawed. Once the curriculum goals and objectives have been established, the CBA process itself proceeds in four stages that can be applied to every curriculum: assessing the student's performance in the curriculum; interpreting the results of the assessment against the task itself; adjusting the task so that it is matched to the learner's entry level; and monitoring performance and measuring accuracy and mastery of the objectives over time.

REFERENCES

Blankenship, C. S. (1985). Using curriculum-based assessment data to make instructional decisions. *Exceptional Children, 52,* 233-238.

Booth, J., Booth, D., Pauli, W., & Phenix, J. (1986). *Impressions.* Toronto: Holt, Rinehart, & Winston.

Cancelli, A. A., Bergan, J. R., & Jones, S. (1982). Psychometric and instructional validation approaches in the hierarchical sequencing of learning tasks. *Journal of School Psychology, 20,* 232-243.

Clay, M. M. (1985). *The early detection of reading difficulties* (3rd ed.). Hong Kong: Heineman.

Coulter, W. A. (1988). *Curriculum-based assessment: What's in a name?* Unpublished paper. (A brief version was published in the *Communique,* November, 1988, p. 13.)

Fuchs, L. (1986). Monitoring progress among mildly handicapped pupils: Review of current practice and research. *Remedial and Special Education, 7,* 5-12.

Gickling, E. (1989, March). *Curriculum-based assessment: Much more than assessment.* Paper presented at Temple University, Philadelphia.

Gickling, E. E., Shane, R. L., & Croskery, K. M. (1989). Assuring math success for low-achieving high school students through curriculum-based assessment. *School Psychology Review, 18,* 344-355.

Goodman, Y., & Burke, C. L. (1980). *Reading strategies: Focus on comprehension.* New York: Holt, Rinehart & Winston.

Graden, J. L., Zins, J. E., & Curtis, M. J. (Eds.). (1988). *Alternative educational delivery systems: Enhancing instructional options for all students.* Washington, DC: NASP.

Howell, K. W., & Morehead, M. K. (1987). *Curriculum-based evaluation for special and remedial education.* Columbus, OH: Merrill.

Idol, L., Nevin, A., & Paolucci-Whitcomb, P. (1986). *Models of curriculum-based assessment.* Rockville, MD: Aspen.

Labinowicz, E. (1987, November). The interview method. *Arithmetic Teacher, 35*(8), 22-23.

Messick, S. (1984). Assessment in context: Appraising student performance in relation to instructional quality. *Educational Researcher, 13,* 3-8.

Meyers, J., & Kundert, D. (1988). Implementing process assessment. In J. L. Graden, J. E. Zins, & M. J. Curtis (Eds.), *Alternative educational delivery systems: Enhancing instructional options for all students* (pp. 173-197). Washington, DC: NASP.

National Council of Teachers of Mathematics. (1989). *Curriculum and evaluation standards for school mathematics.* Reston, VA: National Council of Teachers of Mathematics.

Neisworth, J. T., & Bagnato, S. J. (1986). Curriculum-based developmental assessment: Congruence of testing and teaching. *School Psychology Review, 15,* 180-199.

Otis, M. J., & Offerman, T. R. (1988, April). How do you evaluate problem solving? *Arithmetic Teacher, 35*(8), 49-51.

Palinscar, A. S., Ogle, D. S., Carr, E. G., & Ransom, K. (1985). *Teaching reading as thinking: Facilitator's manual.* Alexandria, VA: Association for Supervision and Curriculum Development.

Porter, A. C. (1989). A curriculum out of balance: The case of elementary school mathematics. *Educational Researcher, 18*(5), 9-15.

Porter, A. C., & Brophy, J. (1988). Synthesis of research on good teaching: Insights from the work of the Institute for Research on Teaching. *Educational Leadership, 45,* 74-85.

Rosenfield, S. (1987). *Instructional consultation.* Hillsdale, NJ: Erlbaum.

Rosenfield, S. (Producer). (1988). *CBA with Ed Gickling* [videotape]. Philadelphia, PA: Temple University School Psychology Program.

Rosenfield, S., & Rubinson, F. (1985). Introducing curriculum-based assessment through consultation. *Exceptional Children, 52,* 282-287.

Salvia, J., & Ysseldyke, J. E. (1981). *Assessment in special and remedial education* (2nd ed.)! Boston: Houghton Mifflin.

Scott, Foresman, & Co. (1985). *Invitation to mathematics, K–8.* Glenview, IL: Author.

Shapiro, E. S. (1989). *Direct assessment and intervention for academic skill problems.* New York: Guilford.

Shapiro, E. S., & Derr, T. F. (1987). An examination of overlap between reading curricula and standardized achievement tests. *Journal of Special Education, 21,* 59-67.

Shinn, M. R. (1990). Best practices in currirulum-based measurement. In A. Thomas & J. Grimes (Eds.), *Best practices in school psychology, II* (Chapter 20). Washington, CD: National Association of School Psychologysits.

Shinn, M. R., Rosenfield, S., & Knutson, N. (1989). Curriculum-based assessment: A comparison and integration of models. *School Psychology Review, 18* 299-316.

Shriner, J., & Salvia, J. (1988). Chronic noncorrespondence between elementary math curricula and arithmetic tests. *Exceptional Children, 55,* 240-248.

Tucker, J. (1985). Curriculum-based assessment: An introduction. *Exceptional Children, 52,* 199-204.

Wesson, C., King, R. P., & Deno, S. L. (1984). Direct and frequent measurement of student performance: If it's good for us, why don't we do it? *Learning Disability Quarterly, 7,* 45-48.

Wirtz, R. (1985). Some thoughts about mathematics and problem-solving. In A. L. Costa (Ed.), *Developing minds: A resource book for teaching thinking* (pp. 97-101). Alexandria, VA: Association for Supervision and Curriculum Development.

ANNOTATED BIBLIOGRAPHY

Idol, L., Nevin, A., & Paolucci-Whitcomb, P. (1986). *Models of curriculum-based assessment.* Rockville, MD: Aspen.
The first six chapters provide models of criterion-referenced CBA materials in a wide range of subjects, including reading, spelling, math, science, and study skills. The book also includes reprints of two articles from the 1985 issue of *Exceptional Children* on CBA and CBM.

Rosenfield, S. (Producer). (1988). *CBA with Ed Gickling.* Philadelphia, PA: Temple University School Psychology Program.
In this videotape, made for training purposes, Ed Gickling demonstrates how to conduct a reading CBA using the concept of the "workable passage." He also teaches a school psychologist how to build fluency in a reader.

Shapiro, E. (1989). *Direct assessment and intervention for academic skill problems.* New York: Guilford.
This book presents a behavioral approach to CBA, providing specific information on how to conduct reading and math assessments in the context of the curriculum.

Shinn, M. R., Rosenfield, S., & Knutson, N. (1989). Curriculum-based assessment: A comparison and integration of models. *School Psychology Review, 18,* 299-316.
This article provides a descriptive overview of four different models of CBA/CBM, and compares them on several dimensions, including primary decision-making purpose, relationship to instructional planning, and technical adequacy.

Tucker, J. (Ed.). (1985). Curriculum-based assessment [Special issue]. *Exceptional Children, 52*(3).
The issue contains articles on each of the different models of CBA/CBM and is one of the first and most comprehensive overviews of the topic.

20

Best Practices in Curriculum-Based Measurement

Mark R. Shinn
Victor Nolet
Nancy Knutson
University of Oregon

OVERVIEW

It is logical to expect that schools should be especially adept at meeting the needs of students with achievement difficulties. Based on the latest available data (1986–87), there are now more than 4,420,000 students receiving special education in the United States. Nearly two million of these students have severe academic deficiencies and are labeled learning disabled (U.S. Office of Education, 1988). Learning disabilities prevalence figures increased almost 3% from the previous year alone. When these data are combined with the substantial number of students who receive remedial basic skills services through Chapter 1 programs (another 4.5 million students), it is clear that we cannot claim to be successful at remediating students' achievement problems.

How do we explain this apparent lack of success? Cohen (1987) maintains that most teachers are effective but usually at the wrong things. He argues that much of our lack of success is not caused by ineffective teaching but by a misalignment of what teachers teach, what they intend to teach, and what they assess. If, as Cohen suggests, a misalignment between instruction and assessment is responsible for the large share of instructional problems, to whom can we turn to rectify this situation? In large part, school psychologists have been less involved in the assessment of academic performance than in other areas (e.g., learning aptitude, social behavior). For example, in a survey of school psychology practitioners and faculty trainers (Reschly, Genshaft, & Binder, 1987), only two achievement measures appeared in the top 10 most frequently administered devices or procedures. Practitioners are almost twice as likely to give either one of the *Wechsler* scales *and* the *Bender* than the most frequently given achievement measures. They are 50% more likely to administer the *Draw-A-Person*.

The achievement measures that are the most frequently administered, the *Wide Range Achievement Test* (WRAT) and the *Woodcock-Johnson Achievement Test*, were rated numbers 6 and 8 in frequency of use, respectively. Not only have these and similar published achievement measures been criticized for technical adequacy reasons, the kinds of data they provide are considered less than useful by teachers for instructional planning (Thurlow & Ysseldyke, 1982) or "largely irrelevant" for that purpose (Reschly et al., 1987). At best, these measures are suitable only for academic screening.

Regrettably, the responses of school psychology faculty trainers in the Reschly et al. survey are not optimistic for school psychologists' improvement in the assessment of academic performance. Faculty members included three achievement measures in their top 10 procedures for which they provided supervised practice. The WRAT was rated number 4 with 79% of faculty respondents reporting supervised training with that measure. The Woodcock-Johnson Achievement Test was rated ninth, and the Peabody Individual Achievement Test (PIAT) tenth with supervised training reported by 67% and 66% of faculty respectively.

Perhaps this limited (and we would say less than adequate) involvement of school psychologists in academic assessment is related to two hypotheses and their interaction. First, school psychologists place too much emphasis on assessment for special education eligibility determination; second, they delegate responsibility for assessment for instructional intervention purposes to teachers. Given that the published achievement measures typically used for determining eligibility are not useful for intervention planning (Howell, 1986), the status quo *may* be acceptable practice *if* school psychologists recognized the very limited role these data can play in making other decisions. Other resources (e.g., teachers) then should be, or currently are assumed to be, given responsibility to collect relevant data for intervention.

We are not convinced that school psychologists recognize the limitations of the academic data they collect, however. Further, we believe that it would be erroneous to assume that teachers currently are "capable" of conducting appropriate educational assessments. Teacher training programs are characterized by a complete absence of measurement training and teachers too often conduct assessments that may lead to erroneous decisions (Stiggins, 1988). Perhaps as important are teachers' perceptions that educational measurement is irrelevant to them (Gullickson, 1986).

Calls for Improved Educational Assessment Strategies

School psychologists are being inundated with calls to change their roles with respect to intervention planning from within the field (Bardon, 1988; Reschly, 1988; Ysseldyke & Christenson, 1988).

Most change initiators are espousing two themes. First, assessment must extend beyond testing of students alone; procedures also must be ecological and assess the students' instructional environment. This theme is exemplified in some of the change directions summarized by Bardon (1988, p. 565) including:

1. More attention must be given to what parents, teachers, and administrators need to know in order to help children learn and be managed in schools.
2. More attention must be given to instruction, school curriculum, and what actually takes place in classrooms and other learning environments.
3. Integration of children with special needs in regular educational settings requires environmental assessment as well as individual assessment.
4. A search for pathology is misplaced. The emphasis should be on educability.
5. Local norms and individualized tailoring of assessment to educational functioning are necessary.

An ecological perspective attends to the evaluation of three major components (and their interactions) of the instructional environment: (a) the quality of the curriculum in which a student is receiving instruction (e.g., sequencing, quality, and quantity of examples), (b) the quality of the methods with which the student is instructed (e.g., number of opportunities to respond, systematic correction procedures, guided drill-and-practice), and (c) the student's skills and motivation. Lentz and Shapiro (1986) have identified the importance of these domains and described in detail procedures for their measurement.

In addition to the theme of assessing the instructional ecology, change initiators have been consistent in communicating the importance of linking assessment to intervention so that better interventions can be developed. To link assessment to intervention, a radical shift in educational assessment tools is necessary. A thorough discussion of what this shift requires and its full rationale is beyond the scope of this chapter (see Marston, 1989; Shapiro, 1987 for more detail). Instead,

TABLE 1
A Comparison of School Psychologists' Prevailing and
Preferred Educational Assessment Practices

Prevailing	Preferred
1. Current assessment is constrained primarily to testing the child with published, norm-referenced achievement devices.	1. Assessment must be multi-method and assess student skill, motivation, instruction, and curriculum.
2. Relationship of the content of assessment to students' curricula is often unknown and may be too limited for accurate conclusions about student performance to be drawn.	2. Items for assessment must be drawn from the students' own curricula.
3. Many of the most frequently used tests have questionable or unknown reliability and validity.	3. Tests must be reliable and valid.
4. Most tests employ selection-type responses (e.g., pointing to, filling in the bubble).	4. Tests should use production-types responses (e.g., writing words, reading words) to facilitate error analysis to identify ineffective problem-solving strategies and skills.
5. Most tests are tied to national or regional norms.	5. Tests should be tied to local norms to operationalize expectations and facilitate decision making.
6. Instructional planning is based on an assumption that effective interventions can be identified by testing prior to instruction.	6. Effective instruction is identified from experimentation during the instructional process and documentation of effects.
7. Evaluation of interventions effects is characterized by subjective judgment and/or pre-post testing with published norm-referenced devices.	7. Evaluation of intervention effects is accomplished through frequent testing on material(s) from the curriculum.
8. Published achievement tests are insensitive to change.	8. Tests must be sensitive (i.e., capable of reflecting change in functioning when learning has occurred).
9. Most tests have only 1 form.	9. Tests must have multiple forms to facilitate continuous, frequent measurement for monitoring progress.
10. Expensive published tests are used for eligibility determination, administration.	10. Testing costs are reallocated to generate frequent measures of student outcomes.
11. Student performance is often summarized in inapproprite metrics ((e.g., grade-equivalents) at worst and metrics insensitive for assessing student improvement (e.g., percentiles). Most decisions are made on the basis of achievement "level."	11. Scores must be interpretable by parents and teachers when norm-referenced decisions are made (e.g., percentiles) and be sensitive to change (e.g., fluency). Most decisions are based on achievement change (slope of improvement).
12. Educational assessment is "atheoretical" and is undifferentiated by the kind of decision to be made.	12. Educational assessment must be model based and tied to specific decisions.

a summary comparison between prevailing and preferred educational assessment practices is presented in Table 1.

As is clear from the table, it is our perspective that little of what represents current educational assessment practice for school psychologists should be retained. At best, the too typical practice of administering published norm-referenced achievement tests is suitable only for gross screening. We are not alone in this opinion. Reschly (1988), for example, argues that effective assessments "will need to be useful in all stages of intervention, from problem definition to evaluation of outcomes. A poor or ineffective assessment procedure will be one which has little or no usefulness in interventions. Most of the current assessment in school psychology fails to meet these criteria" (p. 474).

CURRICULUM-BASED MEASUREMENT AS AN EMBODIMENT OF PREFERRED PRACTICES

Curriculum-Based Measurement (CBM) was designed with the goal of increasing attainment of the preferred educational assessment practices identified in Table 1. CBM is considered a type of curriculum-based assessment (CBA) in that it uses the general education curriculum as the basis for decision making. Currently, great confusion exists among school psychologists and special educators as to what CBA is and there is a predilection to treat CBA as a unified set of procedures. Unfortunately, accurate discrimination among the four or five prevalent models is lacking (Shinn, Rosenfield, & Knutson, 1989; Tindal, 1988).

Essential Features

CBM is a set of *standardized* and *specific* measurement procedures that can be used to quantify student performance in reading, spelling, mathematics computation, and written expression. It evolved out of an extensive program of research that was initiated at the University of Minnesota Institute for Learning Disabilities under the direction of Stanley L. Deno and Phyllis Mirkin. Their initial research has been translated effectively into field-based CBM applications that in turn have generated an extensive research base about implementation (Germann & Tindal, 1985; Marston & Magnusson, 1985, 1988; Shinn, 1988; Tindal, 1988).

The core CBM measures consist of the following:

1. In reading, students read aloud from basal readers for 1 minute. The number of words read correctly per minute constitutes the basic decision-making metric.

2. In spelling, students write words that are dictated at specified intervals (either 5, 7, or 10 seconds) for 2 minutes. The number of correct letters sequences and words spelled correctly are counted.

3. In written expression, students write a story for 3 minutes after being given a story starter (e.g., "Pretend you are playing on the playground and a spaceship lands. A little green person comes out and calls your name and ..."). The number of words written, spelled correctly, and/or correct word sequences are counted.

4. In mathematics, students write answers to computational problems via 2-minute probes. The number of correctly written digits is counted.

These measures have the advantage of being curriculum, peer, and individual referenced. *Curriculum referenced* refers to the fact that assessment materials are drawn from the local curriculum. This process assures content validity. CBM measures are *peer referenced* in that typically, local norms are collected to facilitate decision making. Most importantly, CBM is *individual referenced*. That is, the measures are designed so that a student's current rate of progress in the basic skill areas can be compared over time to her/his previous progress. These data can serve as a key indicator of intervention effectiveness. To facilitate the development of a peer-referenced and individually referenced data base, CBM measures are of short duration and low cost so that educators can collect large amounts of data in terms of numbers of subjects and/or frequency. Additionally, CBM has an advantage of a number of technical adequacy investigations documenting reliability and validity.

A CBM Decision-Making Model

As detailed in Table 1, current educational assessment practices are characterized as being "atheoretical" or devoid of a decision-making model. Testing too often is an end in and of itself and is undifferentiated with respect to what decision is being made. CBM on the other hand, is tied very closely to what has been

TABLE 2
CBM Problem-Solving Model Decisions, Measurement Activities, and Evaluation Activities

Problem-Solving Decision	Measurement Activities	Evaluation Activities	Specific Tasks
Problem Identification (Screening)	Observe and record student differences, if any, between actual and expected performance	Decide that a performance discrepancy exists	Peer-referenced assessment
Problem Certification (Eligibility determination)	Describe the differences between actual and expected performance in context of likelihood of general education resources solving the problem	Decide if discrepancies are important enough that special services may be required for problem resolution	Survey-Level Assessment and Evaluate General Education modifications
Exploring Alternative Solutions (IEP goal setting and intervention planning)	Determine probable performance improvements (goals) and costs associated with different interventions	Select the program reform (i.e., the intervention) to be tested	Write long-term goals(s), determine curriculum level, and necessary pre-skills that may be required for succes
Evaluating Solutions and Making Modifications (Progress Monitoring)	Monitor implementation and student performance change	Determine whether intervention is effective or should be modified	Collect progress monitoring data and compare with aimline
Problem Solution (Program Termination)	Observe and record student differences, if any, between actual and expected performance	Decide that existing discrepancies, if any, are not important and program may be terminated	Repeat peer-referenced assessment

Adapted from S. Deno (1989). Curriculum-Based Measurement and special education services: A fundamental and direct relationship. In M. R. Shinn (Ed.), *Curriculum-Based Measurement: Assessing special children* (pp. 1–17). New York: Guilford Press.

referred to as a problem-solving model (Deno, 1989). The five problem-solving steps in the CBM model are presented in Table 2.

Deno (1989) grounds the model on three fundamental assumptions. First, a problem is defined as any discrepancy between what is expected and what occurs. In the context of academic handicapping conditions, a problem exists when a student does not perform the academic behavior(s) that is expected of him/her. According to Deno (1989), handicaps are situational and may not be the student's "internal problem." For example, a problem can exist when a student's actual academic performance is typical but the teacher's expectations may be too high. The second assumption is that there is a subset of students whose discrepancies between what is expected and what is achieved are so significant that it may be unreasonable for them to achieve in general education unless their programs are modified. Currently, it remains a value judgment as to when the discrepancy is so severe that special services are warranted, despite repeated attempts to make it quantifiable using a battery of tests and regression formulas. The third fundamental assumption is that effective problem solving requires "that problem solvers generate many possible plans of action prior to attempting problem solution" (Deno, 1989, p. 11). Presently, we lack the assessment technology to say *with certainty* what instructional program will work with any student. Therefore, we need to treat all of our interventions as testable hypotheses that must be evaluated formatively. Individually validated interventions are maintained; invalidated hypotheses are discarded and/or modified.

Each of the problem-solving model decisions presented in Table 2 is associated with more familiar terms in special education decision-making jargon (e.g., Salvia & Ysseldyke, 1987). Problem-Identification and Problem-Certification decisions, for example, are related to the traditional processes of screening and eligibility determination, respectively. Exploring alternative solutions could be considered synonymous with instructional planning. With special education students, this process corresponds to the development of an individual education plan (IEP). Evaluating solutions relates to pupil progress monitoring while problem solution is analogous to program termination. We chose to use the problem-solving terminology to the greatest degree possible to reflect the radical changes necessary to improve the link of educational assessment to effective intervention.

Problem Identification. It is in the best interest of schools and students to ensure that extensive evaluation activities are employed only in those instances when an actual problem has been identified. Should a problem be identified, evaluation and intervention procedures that might involve considerable expense and time would be warranted. If no problem is identified, no further systematic efforts may be called for. The Problem-Identification step requires a decision about whether a particular student's performance on academically important tasks is sufficiently discrepant from the performance expectations to indicate the existence of a problem and to justify further assessment. The question asked, "Does a problem exist?" requires a yes/no response.

CBM Problem Identification differs from a traditional conception of screening and the two should not be confused. In prevailing interpretations, the purpose of screening is "child-find" activity. Students are tested on a *group* basis to spread them out along a distribution so that those

performing below a certain level may be identified and examined more closely. Almost all schools perform a number of activities that fit this definition. For example, all entering kindergarten students may point out the directions of arrows or letters for vision screening.

The CBM Problem-Identification process begins as the current system does, with a teacher perception of a problem. While teachers have been demonstrated to be highly *accurate* in identifying potential student achievement difficulties (Gerber & Semmel, 1984), they also have been shown to be susceptible to gender and ethnicity biases (Shinn, Tindal, & Spira, 1987). Therefore, CBM decision making is predicated on the essential value of *objectifying* initial teacher referrals in a consistent and meaningful way.

As identified in the measurement tasks and evaluation activities of Table 2, CBM Problem Identification uses *peer-referenced* procedures that compare an individual student's level of performance, measured on a repeated basis, to an expected level of performance. In contrast to prevailing practice where the expectation is derived from within-student ability-achievement discrepancies (e.g., IQ-achievement), with CBM, expectations are operationalized through the use of the achievement levels of "typical" same-grade peers on typical grade-level curriculum tasks. For a more detailed rationale, see Deno (1989), or Shinn (1988; 1989). An estimate of the magnitude of the difference between the student's actual and expected performance is obtained and decision making regarding the need for further assessment is made via a cutting score.

Use of CBM in this way allows decision making tied to the local general education curriculum. Student performance in this curriculim is referenced to the performance of a local norm group that is presumably maximally similar in acculturation (e.g., learning opportunities, background experiences) to the student in question. Specific CBM Problem-Identification procedures will be discussed later in the chapter.

Problem Certification. After a problem has been identified by quantifying a discrepancy between student performance and expectations (i.e., typical peer achievement), a decision often must be made as to whether it is *important* enough that resources beyond general education (e.g., Chapter I or special education) are required. This decision is not an easy one to make and, as everyone in education knows, is filled with great controversy. As mentioned earlier, this decision is one that is tied to *values* about what special services should be delivered to whom.

As detailed in Table 2, CBM best practice in program-certification measurement and evaluation activities typically should include two related processes: (a) documenting that alternative general education modifications are insufficient to produce substantive improvements in achievement, and (b) determining that a student's skills are so discrepant that it is unlikely that any general education modifications currently will produce the desired achievement outcomes. The former process requires that alternative general education interventions be tried and evaluated, an approach described generically (and perhaps, incorrectly) in the school psychology literature as "pre-referral intervention" (Graden, Christenson, & Bonstrom, 1985). Some schools that use CBM label the process Six-Week Assessment (SWAP) (Marston & Magnusson, 1988). Survey-Level assessment (Howell & Morehead, 1987) data are required where a student is tested in successively lower levels of the curriculum and is compared to the performance of lower grade-level students.

For a student to be certified for additional resources, it must be demonstrated that general education likely is incapable of making requisite changes in instruction so that the student can profit. This decision is based on the finding that a referred student's skills fall far outside the range of "reasonable" general education curriculum offerings. It also must be demonstrated that no obvious explanation(s) (e.g., sensory impairments) for the discrepancy can be found.

CBM provides one component of a decision-making system for certification; as with any achievement data alone, however, it does not provide sufficient information about other critical aspects of the problem for valid decision making. Best practice requires team decision making about individual students and that a variety of types of data that are related directly or indirectly to the student's educational program are considered. Ideally, when a multidisciplinary team makes the certification decision, it considers not only student achievement, but also data obtained using the ecological analyses of instructional environments and curricula identified earlier in the chapter, health, social, and family factors, and previous opportunities for adequate instruction.

Exploring Alternative Solutions. As presented earlier, CBM's problem-solving model ascribes to an intervention process as an iterative, experimental approach where initial student performance data are collected, intervention hypotheses are developed and implemented, the effects are evaluated continuously, and ineffective interventions are modified. As CBM problem-solving decision making is proposed in Table 2, measurement activities in Exploring Alternative Solutions involve determining probable performance improvements that are accomplished by setting goals, and determining the costs (i.e., resources required) for different interventions. Current performance data in the curriculum are required so that goal setting can be accomplished and potential interventions can be suggested based on an analysis of student skills within the curriculum. Evaluative activities include deciding what the specific goal(s) will be and what intervention will be implemented initially.

Goal setting corresponds to the writing of the long-term and short-term goals of the Individualized Educational Plan (IEP). Prevailing practices in writing IEP goals are problematic in several respects, including the use of target behaviors of questionable interest or social validity, and their limited utility for assessment of attainment (e.g., insensitivity, lack of measurement materials for frequent measurement). A related problem probably is the direct result of the first two: objectives tend to be either too broad and therefore unmeasurable or too specific to facilitate efficient (frequent, easily interpretable) progress monitoring. Use of CBM data to write and monitor IEPs can mitigate against these problems because they lead directly to explicit, measurable goals in the curriculum that can be evaluated frequently and efficiently.

Each CBM IEP objective is based on the format of traditional behavioral objectives, and consists of a *behavior* to be measured, *conditions* (timeline, measurement situation, and measurement material) for attainment, and *criterion* (the level of the behavior the student must attain) for success. A key feature of CBM is that the behavior "tested" remains consistent across the steps of the CBM problem-solving model. Therefore, the behavior component of the following sample reading IEP objective is "read aloud." The complete IEP objective would read as follows:

Conditions	"In 36 weeks, when given a randomly selected passage from level 3-1 of *The Scribner Reading Series*, Rachel
Behavior	will read aloud
Criterion	at a rate of 85 words per minute correct, with 6 or fewer errors."

A long-term goal (LTG) rather than a short-term goal (STG) approach is used to write CBM IEP objectives. The LTG and STG approaches differ primarily in the choice of measurement material that is used to measure student progress (For more detail, see Fuchs & Shinn, 1989). When a LTG is specified, measurement items are selected from an item pool that represents the domain of *all* items to be taught during the goal duration. Monitoring probes are created by randomly selecting subsets of items from this large pool and student progress is measured repeatedly on these probes.

The experimental nature of the CBM model becomes explicit during the second major activity of exploring solutions, intervention planning. The alternative solution is written into the IEP. At a conceptual level, there exists an infinite number of potential interventions that can be used with any student. Presumably, this number is reduced based on the interaction of what is expected to be needed to remediate the student's skill deficiencies and what resources (e.g., teacher time, materials) are available. An estimate is made of the probable success and costs of various interventions and the intervention hypothesized to be the balance between these two factors is selected.

Among the key tasks to be accomplished are determining: (a) a student's instructional placement, and (b) skills that must be taught for student success in the curriculum. The data gathered during Problem Identification and Problem Certification are integral to this process. Instructional-level decisions are made by applying decision rules as to what constitutes appropriate instructional-level performance to the scores earned by the student in Survey-Level assessment. If the student is in third grade, for example, the highest level of the reading curriculum that is read at 70–100 words correct may be selected as the instructional-level material (Deno, Mirkin, & Wesson, 1984).

It is assumed that effective remedial instruction is based on teaching the requisite skills for success in the curriculum and that the initial solution requires identification of what the student does and does not do correctly on curriculum tasks. Determining the essential skills that must be taught is accomplished by a task analysis requiring the development and testing of hypotheses regarding student errors. This process is labeled *Specific-Level assessment* (Howell & Morehead, 1987). It begins when the student's errors made during the entire previous assessment process are organized and analyzed systematically. Hypotheses about these errors are generated, measures are developed to test the hypotheses, new data are collected and analyzed and so on, until a set of statements regarding the student's performance in the task of interest can be generated.

Implementing Solutions. Exploring Alternative Solutions has been presented as a process of developing goals and selecting an initial intervention based on the presence or absence of student's skills in the curriculum that are *hypothesized* to solve the educational problem(s). Once an intervention has been selected, it must be implemented and its effectiveness evaluated. The success of the intervention can be appraised only in terms of the extent to which it solves the problem identified. In Table 2, the measurement activities of monitoring implementation and student performance changes are specified. Evaluation activities involve deciding whether the program is effective or needs modification.

The intervention must result in making the change in achievement specified by the LTG of the IEP, at the minimum, to be considered effective. When this change is not evident, an alternative solution must be selected, implemented, and evaluated. As noted earlier in Table 1, traditional measures of achievement are not sufficiently sensitive to growth to be useful in evaluating the success of instructional interventions. A published norm-referenced achievement test is analogous to a single photograph of a cloud formation. The photo provides no information about the direction of movement or the velocity of the clouds, nor is it possible to tell from the photo whether the clouds are thickening or dispersing. A single second photo taken at a later point in time (analogous to pre- post-testing), likely will capture an entirely different cloud formation. To know about multiple qualities of a particular cloud formation, numerous photos must be taken systematically over time and a reference point included against which the movement of the clouds can be compared. When viewed together, these photos allow an accurate description of the movement cloud formation. Student progress monitoring is analogous to the cloud example. CBM decision making incorporates the repeated photo-

graph approach. Testing occurs on a frequent (i.e., at least weekly) and repeated basis using probes that are developed from LTG curriculum specified in the IEP. In reading, for example, 1-minute probes are administered ideally twice per week. To facilitate decision making, results of the repeated probes are graphed so that data can be analyzed visually.

Problem Solution. It is important for educators to know when they have succeeded as well as when they have failed to solve a problem. Problem-Solution decisions are valuable in that they facilitate potential changes in level of remedial services consistent with the LRE and/or result in termination of these services. In current special education practice, we too infrequently return students to the mainstream or terminate services because problems are resolved. In large part, it is hypothesized that the state of affairs is due to a lack of appropriate decision-making and assessment technology. As noted earlier, published achievement tests are likely too insensitive, even on a 1-year, pre-post basis, for positive changes in improvement to be noted for individual students.

As presented in Table 2, the CBM model specifically identifies Problem Solution as a critical step in best practices decision making. Conceptually, it would seem logical that the conditions that resulted in the identification of the problem are reconstituted when a decision is to be made as to whether the problem is solved. Therefore the measurement and evaluation activities in Problem Solution are *identical* to those used in Problem Identification. The peer-referenced assessment is repeated and problems are considered solved when the discrepancy between the student who receives special services and typical achievement of peers is not considered to be significant. Because of the time efficiency of data collection, problem solution decisions can be made routinely as part of the periodic and annual review process, regardless of whether the team actually is considering terminating services (Allen, 1989).

BEST PRACTICES IN CBM IMPLEMENTATION

For best practices implementation of CBM, (Germann, 1987) identified several specific tasks that are critical. First, school personnel that are considering implementing CBM procedures must develop an overall implementation plan including timelines. This plan must be based on an analysis of: (a) *initial personnel resources*, and (b) *administrative support*. The number of personnel will dictate the degree of CBM implementation. With limited personnel (e.g., one school psychologist), change should be confined to the school level, initially, and likely one step of the problem-solving model. For more widespread implementation (e.g., across problem-solving steps and schools), Germann (1987) maintains the use of a *team* of support staff (e.g., school psychologists, special education lead teachers) who are knowledgeable and skilled in CBM is fundamental. This team works with smaller groups of school personnel regarding implementation procedures and the underlying philosophy of CBM problem solving (Marston & Magnusson, 1988) through intensive inservice training, regular workshops, and on-going support. The roles and responsibilities of the staff involved must be identified to ensure efficient coordination of implementation activities. The amount and level of administrative support also is important in deciding the degree of implementation. Unfortunately, administrative support is much like a "Catch-22;" support can only be garnered after program implementation and success. Without administrative support, it may be unlikely to implement a program successfully. Small CBM demonstration projects or activities (case studies of successful interventions, classroom or school local norms) are potential solutions to this dilemma.

After the analysis of initial resources, the scope of implementation must be specified, including how and when changes will be phased into the existing service-delivery model. Because of the widespread changes required to shift to a problem-solving model, districts often begin one step at a time. In these circumstances, a decision must be made as to which of the problem-solving steps (e.g., Exploring Solutions) will take priority and a sequence for full implementation must be made *prior* to initiating the change process. If the model cannot be implemented in its entirety, it is recommended that resources be devoted to the Exploring and Evaluating Solutions steps because they focus most directly on improving academic programs. Too often, schools start the change process at the Problem Identification and Problem Certification steps. While these steps can give a new project visibility, a school system runs the risk of only substituting one "child-find" activity for another and may not move to the other, more critical decision-making steps that may improve interventions more dramatically. The reader is referred to Shinn (1988, 1989) for more detail on this concern. Once the priorities for implementation are identified, specific procedures corresponding to the different steps must be developed. Written products including assessment materials and procedural manuals are most helpful.

A frequently raised question is the importance of local norms for implementation of CBM. CBM's cost and time efficiency means that local norms can be developed on a reasonable logistical basis for school systems. Norming materials are easy and inexpensive to assemble. For example, individual student packets containing measurement material for the different domains can be reproduced using a photo-copier or ditto machine. While the reading measure is individually administered, the math, spelling, and written expression can be administered to groups of students (e.g., an entire classroom) in approximately 20 minutes. Normative data typically are collected three times per year with equal intervals between testing periods.

An elaborate norming process is not required for successful CBM implementation, especially at the initial implementation level. The reader is referred to Shinn (1989) for issues and specific details in developing local norms. Three levels of normative data have been collected with increasing levels of resources and commitment required: (a) classroom, (b) building, and (c) district norms. The types of educational decisions that can be made vary with the level of norms collected. Classroom norming requires testing only 5 to 10 students per grade. These data may provide a general estimate of the level of achievement of the typical student in that particular classroom and can be used for initial individual Problem-Identification and Exploring and Evaluating Solutions decisions. School or district norms may require up to 15 to 20% of the students from each grade to be tested. These data are useful in all the CBM problem-solving steps.

Regardless of the level of local norming, two activities are critical. The first task involves creating the measurement net (i.e., selecting representative grade-level stimulus material for each grade in each academic area). In reading, for example, the reader in which average students are instructed for most of the year is specified for each grade. Students are tested typically on three passages for each norming period. The other critical task is determining a sampling plan. The strategies involved in determining the number of students, the specific selection process, varies depending on the level of norming (e.g., classroom, district). Once the measurement net is created and the sampling plan identified, data collectors are trained, data are collected, and then summarized.

Specific Problem-Identification and Problem-Validation Procedures

The CBM problem-solving model provides a general framework to structure decision making. However, variability exists in the ways school systems implement the model, particularly in the areas of Problem Identification and Problem Certification. Some districts combine the first two decision-making steps (Germann & Tindal, 1985) while others (Marston & Magnusson, 1988) treat them as separate, albeit related, decisions.

Combined-step process. The Pine County Total Special Education System (Germann & Tindal, 1985) combines Problem Identification and Problem Certification decisions into a single-step using a peer-referenced process as the specific task listed in Table 2. The Pine County Model consists of direct and repeated measurement of the student's current level of performance only on grade-level curriculum tasks. The referred student's performance is compared to that of typical grade-level students that are tested as part of school-district norming on the same material. A critical feature of this model is that CBM probes are administered daily over a period of 3 to 5 days. Use of repeated measures provides information about the variability of the student's performance as well as an estimate of the current trend of the student's learning in the material. A sample of the student's performance across 5 days of assessment in reading and spelling is presented in Table 3 and shown graphically in Figure 1.

The dark horizontal lines on the figure represent the median performance of district third graders for each academic area. For example in reading, the normative-level score is 110 words read correctly; in spelling, it is 68 correct letter sequences. The dotted lines represent the cutting scores that correspond to a –2.0 discrepancy score. Sara's performance in reading and spelling is represented by the data points in each category. As shown in the figure, Sara performed below the cutting score in reading, but above the cutting score in spelling. Therefore, she could be found eligible for special education services in reading only.

This information is used in making the eligibility decision as well as in later development of an educational plan if the student is found eligible for services. In most instances that a combined Problem-Identification/Certification decision-making process is used, schools employ a *discrepancy ratio* as the cutting score. This type of cutting score is calculated by dividing the highest score (most frequently the normative score) by the lowest score (most frequently the referred student's score). When the referred student's score is higher than the norma-

TABLE 3
Results of CBM Problem Identification for Sara

Academic Area	Day 1	Day 2	Day 3	Day 4	Day 5	Median
Reading						
Passage 1	33	16	32	26	29	
Passage 2	40	27	42	38	24	
Passage 3	38	33	30	24	27	
Daily Median	38	27	32	26	27	27
Spelling						
Daily Spelling List	55	45	56	53	49	53

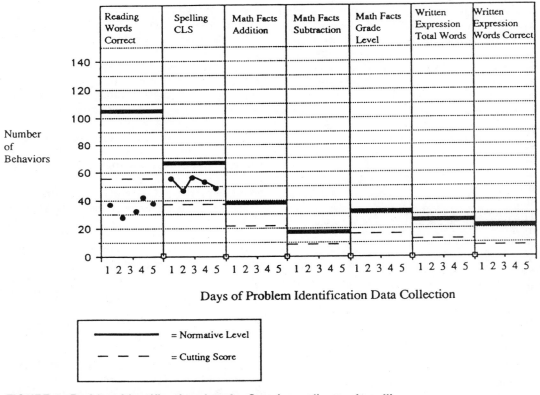

FIGURE 1. Problem Identification data for Sara in reading and spelling compared to school norms.

tive score, a positive (+) value is assigned to the resulting ratio; when the referred student's score is lower than the normative score, a negative (–) value is assigned. In Pine County, the discrepancy ratio must be equal to or greater than –2.0 for the multidisciplinary team to be able to find an elementary-aged student eligible for special education. In Figure 1, Sara's discrepancy score in reading is –4.1 (110/27).

Discrepancy scores are often very difficult for general education teachers and parents to understand easily and do not lend themselves well as a metric for making other kinds of decisions (Tindal, Shinn, & Germann, 1987). To alleviate interpretation and utility difficulties, it is recommended that percentile rank scores be used as cutting scores. In the example presented in Figure 1, the student's discrepancy score is equivalent to a percentile rank of 3. For example, special education eligibility could be considered when the student's performance on grade-level tasks falls below the 5th percentile. This criterion corresponds to the typical CBM performance level of students identified as eligible for special education using traditional measures (Shinn, Tindal, Spira, & Marston, 1987). The use of percentile ranks does require norms of a minimum of 100 students per grade level, however. Smaller school districts may have to aggregate students' scores across years to obtain norms of this size.

Procedures for separate Problem-Identification and Problem-Certification steps. When the Problem-Identification and Problem-Certification steps are separated, a more extensive decision-making process occurs than with the combined-step model exemplified by Pine County. The two steps have been operationalized in slightly different ways among various schools, varying mostly in the frequency of testing and the type of cutting score used. Four communalities among multi-step models are:

1. The referred student is tested in grade-level material and compared to grade-level peers as part of Problem Identification.

2. Students who perform significantly differently subsequently are tested using measurement materials sampled from progressively lower grade levels.

3. Percentile ranks derived from school-district norms constitute the cutting scores.

4. Data are collected regarding the types of errors made by the student on the CBM probes.

Problem-Identification procedures are identical to those of the combined decision-making process. Referred stu-

dents are tested on a repeated basis and their performance is compared to typical, same-grade peers. What may vary, however, is the normative sample to which the referred student is compared and the cutting score for decision making. The referred student may be compared to specific classroom norms under the premise that the least restrictive environment principle would require the student's performance to deviate significantly from that specific instructional environment. Presumably, students whose academic achievement does not differ significantly from typical performance levels in that environment may progress therein, if provided appropriate instruction. Alternatively, the referred student may be compared to the performance of peers at the school level. This approach may increase the consistency of Problem Identification decisions by diminishing the impact of potential classroom to classroom variability. However, this increase in consistency may come at a decreased cost in precision about the expectations of a specific classroom. In both classroom and school-based norm Problem Identification decisions, discrepancy scores are used as the decision-making metric.

The most consistent Problem-Identification model is to use school-district norms and percentile rank cutting scores. The use of school-district norms likely would mean that a problem identified as significant in one building would be identified similarly in another building (i.e., *reliability* in decision making would be achieved). However, this consistency could mean a loss as of the *validity* of the identified achievement expectations for a specific student with a specific teacher.

Once a problem is identified, decision making moves into the Problem Certification process. As detailed earlier, this step entails two major activities: (a) evaluating general education modifications, and (b) Survey-Level assessment. Evaluating general education solutions to presumed student learning problems involves implementation and examination of alternative interventions available in the student's classroom. The Six-Week Assessment Plan (SWAP) uses 30 school days past the referral date to evaluate a specific intervention(s) in the student's classroom. The SWAP can be coordinated by a school psychologist or a special education consulting teacher who oversees identification of the alternative intervention, data collection and organization, and decision making regarding program effectiveness. Some examples of alternative interventions include, changes in error-correction strategies, assistance through a Chapter 1 program, peer tutoring, placement in a lower-level reading group or additional review of material, etc. As with Evaluating Solutions, student progress is monitored continuously to evaluate the effectiveness of the alternative intervention. However, in SWAP, monitoring occurs on a more frequent basis (e.g., 3 to 5 times per week) and STG material (i.e., from current instruction) is used. Additionally, criterion for program success is set on a 2-week interval and a percentage growth basis. The increased measurement frequency and 2-week goal date allow for ineffective interventions to be identified and at least two alternatives implemented and evaluated during SWAP. As an experimental criterion, students have been expected to improve at a 15% growth rate per week. The results of a sample SWAP are displayed in Figure 2. After a baseline of 1 week in the current instructional program, the student's median performance is determined. Using this median, the short-term 1-week and 2-week goals are identified and plotted on a graph. These goals are translated into an expected rate of progress symbolized by the aim line in Figure 2. In this example, the first alternative intervention failed to produce the desired growth and was modified after two weeks. The second intervention was even less effective. Students whose alternative general education interventions are effective continue to be served in the general education classroom; consultative services may be provided as needed. Students who do not progress at an acceptable rate proceed through the Problem-Certification process.

As stated earlier, Survey-Level assessment is intended to determine that a student's skills in the curriculum are so discrepant that it is unlikely that any general education modifications currently will produce the desired achievement outcomes. During Survey-Level assessment, the referred student's behavior on the relevant CBM tasks is recorded first from their testing grade-level material that was part of Problem Identification. The student then is tested in progressively lower grade-level material(s) until a *normative score* is obtained. Multiple probes are used at each level and median scores are converted to percentile ranks. A sample Survey-Level assessment is presented in Table 4. During Survey-Level assessment, Sara read in successive levels of the curriculum until her performance was within the range of typical students. In this example, Sara read outside the range of typical third and second graders, but read first grade materials like typical first graders.

In contrast to Problem Identification, where evaluative decisions are based on the referred student's skills compared to the *level* of typical peers, Problem Certification takes normative variability into account. The *range* of scores typical (i.e., plus or minus one standard deviation from the mean) within a grade on curriculum tasks constitutes the basic decision-making criteria. These scores correspond to the range in which two of every three students in the general education classroom perform (i.e., the 16th to 84th percentile). A referred student's *normative score* is obtained when their level of performance in material sampled from a particular grade level falls between the 16th to 84th percentiles of that grade's typical students. Decision making is accomplished most easily through the use of a figure. The range of typical students reading scores in first- through sixth-grade level materials for the winter norming and the referred student's scores is presented in Figure 3.

As indicated in the figure, the student reads third- and second-grade material at levels that fall outside the range of typical students in those grades. The student reads first-grade material at a level of 55

FIGURE 2. Six Week Assessment Plan (SWAP) data for Sara in reading.

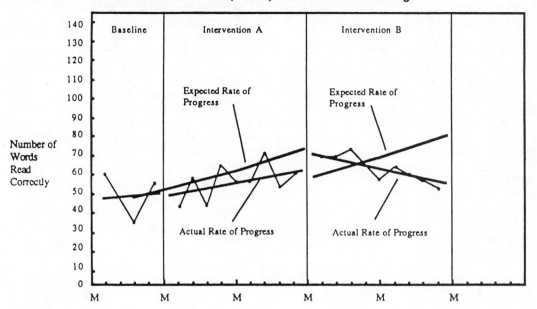

TABLE 4
Reading Survey-Level Assessment Data for Sara

Grade Level of Material	Passage	Words Read Correctly	Errors	Median
3		Available from Problem Identification		27
2	1	37	7	37
	2	39	10	
	3	35	8	
1	1	55	5	55
	2	33	7	
	3	70	4	

words correct, a score that falls between the 16th and 84th percentiles of scores of typical first-graders. It would be concluded that Sara read first-grade material like a typical first-grader. Decision making about special education eligibility is tied to percentile rank cut-off scores. Marston and Magnusson (1988) describe the results of one school district where students must earn scores below the 16th percentile on materials one grade-level below their grade-level placement to be considered eligible.

Specific Strategies for Exploring Alternative Solutions

Writing data-based CBM IEP objectives requires the use of the Survey-Level assessment data collected as part of Problem Certification. Procedurally, the measurement conditions (goal date and measurement material) are specified first, followed by selecting the criteria for success. Schools using CBM typically write IEP objectives to correspond to the time of annual review. The goal termination date for the objective is chosen to conform to the number of weeks in 1 school year from the time of the writing of the IEP (approximately 36 weeks for a 180-day school year). Measurement material is selected based on the expectation of "what level of the curriculum the student may be expected to be performing in 1 year, if the intervention is effective." Practically, a balance must be achieved between choosing material that is too difficult (broad domain) and choosing material that is too easy (narrow domain) because of the implications for valid decisions regarding student progress. For example, LRG measurement material that is too difficult may be insensitive to student improvement (for more detail, see Fuchs & Shinn, 1989).

A variety of methods can be used to select the measurement material in which the goal is written, including procedures with and without local norms. For example, as presented in Figure 3, results of Sara's Survey-Level reading assessment indicated that she reads first-grade material like a typical first-grader. If the multidisciplinary team expected 1-year's growth during the IEP period, she could be expected to perform like a typical second grader by the goal date. If this approach was used to write the IEP, Sara's goal would be written in second-grade reading material.

When local norms have not been available, other methods for determining IEP goals can be used. One method, instructional placement standards (Fuchs & Shinn, 1989), is based on the identification of the student's instructional-placement level in the curriculum and how much growth the multidisciplinary team determines to be desirable by the goal date. In reading, for example, instructional placement criteria is defined as the highest level in the curriculum in which students in grades 1 and 2 read 40–60 words per minute correctly with 4 or fewer errors, and students in grades 3 to 6 read 70–100 words per minute correctly with 6 or fewer errors (Fuchs, Fuchs, & Deno, 1982). Based on the Survey-Level assessment data in Table 4, the level of the curriculum in which Sara meets this

FIGURE 3. Survey-Level assessment data for Sara, a third grader, compared to the range of typical reading scores (between the 16th and 84th percentiles) in the regular education classroom during the Winter norming period for grades 1 to 6.

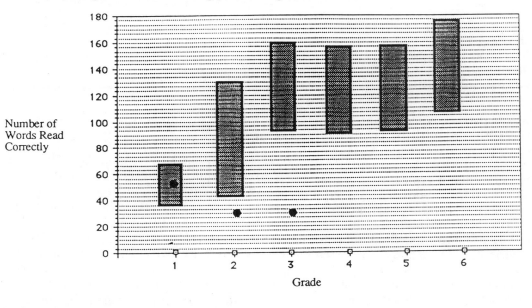

criteria is grade 1. After the student's instructional placement level has been determined, the team must decide how much growth in the curriculum is desired. For example, if the team agrees that Sara can attain 1-year's growth in the curriculum, level 2 would represent the goal material.

After LRG material is designated,the criterion for success must be specified. In large part, this decision relates to the "ambitiousness" of the goal (Fuchs & Fuchs, 1986). One way to determine the criterion of the objective is to index improvement to local norms. A benchmark in reading, for example, is that typical students show growth of 1 to 3 words per week in LRG material. An IEP criterion thus might set a standard that represents growth of 1 word correct per week (a less ambitious goal) or 3 words correct per week (a very ambitious goal) as the criterion for success. Because of the potential complexity of goal setting procedures, the reader is referred to Fuchs and Shinn (1989) for more detail on these procedures.

Specific instructional planning strategies. Planning initial interventions is tied to two major areas, the *what* to teach (instructional content) and the *how* to teach (instructional methods). CBM assessment procedures are useful only for initial ideas as to the former. The latter, the *how* to teach, must be determined only by evaluating the effects of different instructional strategies.

Initial assessment data obtained during the Problem-Certification process can be useful in generating ideas about what to teach. These ideas break down generally into two domains, Instructional Level (IL), the level of the curriculum in which the student should be placed, and essential missing preskills. IL can be determined by examining the Survey-Level assessment data and applying criterion for instructional placement. In reading for example, it has been recommended that fourth-grade students be placed in the highest level of the curriculum that they can read 70–100 words correctly with 4 or fewer errors (Deno,

Mirkin, & Wesson, 1984). Other criteria for instructional placement are identified in Deno and Mirkin (1977) and Shapiro and Lentz (1985).

Identifying essential curriculum skills that must be taught is accomplished by examining students' patterns of errors from Survey-Level assessment. Howell and Morehead (1987) suggest that it is useful to summarize these errors by organizing them systematically into three columns. In reading, for example, the stimulus words (i.e., the original text) misread by the student are listed in the first column. The third column indicates the error type(s). Tape-recording survey-level responses facilitates the error-analysis process. A sample listing follows:

Stimulus	Response	Error
hat	hate	cvc-e error
term	team	r-controlled vowel

This organizational strategy facilitates the identification of recurring error types. Hypotheses can be developed regarding potential missing skills and specialized probes to test these hypotheses can be constructed (see Howell & Morehead, 1987, for more detail), as part of Specific-Level Assessment. When no clear pattern of errors is discernible, additional narrowly focused probes (i.e., those that contain additional items identical to item that the student missed) may need to be developed. The probes may include lists of previously missed items presented in isolation. For example, a student might be presented with a list of words misread during the Survey-Level reading assessment and be asked to read each in isolation. Assessors also can use ready-made probes such as are found in some criterion-referenced assessment batteries (e.g., criterion-referenced tests such as the *Multiple Assessment Skills Inventory*) to save time in test construction. However, the ability to analyze test-curriculum overlap is critical in this process.

Specific Procedures for Evaluating Solutions

To evaluate the effectiveness of the solutions proposed for remediating the identified problem, CBM procedures are used to monitor student progress on a frequent basis (Deno, 1985). The same measures utilized in the other problem-solving steps in the CBM model are used to collect progress monitoring data. Typically, students are assessed once or twice weekly on CBM measures from the IEP goal domain. Measurement material for monitoring the student's progress consists of a large pool of probes that are constructed from the LRG material stated in the IEP. In reading, for example, passages selected randomly from the basal series that the student is expected to be reading in by the goal date are used. With the LTG approach, student progress is assessed in material that he/she is expected to be performing in by the goal date, not current instructional material. For example, Sara is expected to be performing in level 2 of the reading series in 1-year's time. Her progress in reading, therefore, would be assessed twice weekly for 1-minute intervals on passages selected from level 2.

Time-series analysis of student performance data is a critical component of the CBM progress monitoring system. Graphed student progress data provide a basis for determining whether and when to change a student's instructional program by comparing the student's *actual* progress (as represented by a trend line) toward a specific goal to their *expected* progress (as represented by the aimline). An instructional program is considered to be effective if it results in student progress which is equal to or greater than the expected rate stated as determined by the IEP goal. An ineffective program results in progress that is less than expected rate and therefore is modified. The rate of Sara's progress towards her IEP objective in reading is presented in Figure 4. By comparing Sara's actual rate of progress to the expected rate, it can be concluded that Sara is making adequate progress,

and that therefore the intervention plan is effective.

Two methods of evaluating data have been used by schools utilizing CBM for progress monitoring, treatment-oriented and goal-oriented (Fuchs, 1989). The latter has been used most frequently because analysis is consistent with a long-term progress monitoring paradigm and is easier to implement.

Specific Problem Solutions Procedures

Making decisions about whether a problem has been resolved or whether the intervention services are approximating more closely problem resolution is accomplished routinely and efficiently within CBM. As described generally earlier in the chapter, the assessment procedures involve comparing the student receiving special services with the expectations of other same-grade students in same grade curriculum through peer-referenced assessment. Testing is conducted once per grading period akin to informal periodic reviews. An annual review is conducted once per year as required by PL 94-142.

In most ways, the process is identical to Problem Identification assessment procedures. Instead of testing over a 3- to 5-day period, however, the student most frequently is tested on one occasion using repeated probes from the curriculum. The student's median score is compared to local norms at the classroom, school, or school-district level. Should the former two normative groups be used, the decision-making score is the discrepancy ratio. Should school-district norms be used, the decision-making score would be the percentile rank. With both types of scores, care should be taken in how they are represented since both are ordinal data. Changes in performance should not be subtracted one testing period from the other. In the case of Sara, her performance from her initial placement in the winter to the time of her first periodic review improved from the 3rd percentile to the 5th percentile.

Problems are considered solved when assessed student performance exceeds the criterion for certifying a problem

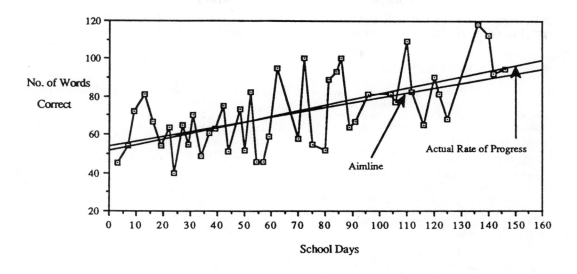

FIGURE 4. Sara's rate of progress towards her IEP objective in reading.

(Allen, 1989). For example, if the Problem Certification criterion is performance below the 10th percentile on materials one grade-level below grade placement and the student now earns a score at the 18th percentile, termination of services may be considered. The peer-referenced data should be used in combination with another important indicator of Problem Solution, the rate of progress towards attainment of the CBM IEP objective. Should the student be attaining or exceeded the rate of progress established in the IEP objective and be performing in the range of typical peers, a team may be more comfortable in reaching a Problem-Solution decision. Of course, this decision is a team-decision-making process.

An alternative CBM process for making Problem Solution decisions that is promising is using the normative performance levels of same-grade peers in the lowest general education grouping. Routinely, a student who is receiving services outside the general education classroom is tested and compared to the performance levels of students in the lowest group in the mainstream. When the student consistently earns scores in the range of these peers, the problem should be considered as being solved and a

termination of services deliberated. See Allen (1989) for more details on this process.

SUMMARY

Curriculum-Based Measurement (CBM) is a consistent and continuous measurement system that bases decision making on performance in local curriculum compared to local norms. In this chapter "best practices" in CBM has been portrayed as more than a measurement system, however, and as a commitment to a problem-solving model of resolving educational challenges. We believe that CBM meets the challenges put forward to contemporary school assessment; an ecological assessment strategy is linked to intervention and the improvement of educational outcomes. It is important to note that CBM procedures are not to be used in isolation from a problem-solving model. As is implied throughout this chapter, knowledge of curriculum content and sequence is integral. Further, CBM should be embedded as a cornerstone of the best practices in educational assessment identified by Lentz and Shapiro (1986). The CBM technology, while still in adolescence, has much to offer to school psychologists and other educators interested in educational improvement.

REFERENCES

Allen, D. (1989). Periodic and annual reviews and decisions to terminate special education services. In M. Shinn (Ed.), *Curriculum-based measurement: Assessing special children* (pp. 182-201). New York: Guilford.

Bardon, J. I. (1988). Alternative educational delivery approaches: Implications for school psychology. In J. L. Graden, J. E. Zins, & M. C. Curtis (Eds.), *Alternative educational delivery systems: Enhancing instructional options for all students* (pp. 563-571). Washington, DC: National Association of School Psychologists.

Cohen, S. A. (1987). Instructional alignment: Search for a magic bullet. *Educational Researcher, 16*, 16-20.

Deno, S. L. (1985). Curriculum-based measurement: The emerging alternative. *Exceptional Children, 52*, 219-232.

Deno, S. L. (1989). Curriculum-based measurement and alternative special education services: A fundamental and direct relationship. In M. Shinn (Ed.), *Curriculum-based measurement: Assessing special children* (pp. 1-17). New York: Guilford.

Deno, S. L., & Mirkin, P. (1977). *Data-based program modification: A manual.* Reston, VA: Council for Exceptional Children.

Deno, S. L., Mirkin, P., & Wesson, C. (1984). How to write effective data-based IEPs. *Teaching Exceptional Children, 16*, 99-104.

Fuchs, L. S. (1989). Evaluating solutions: Monitoring progress and revising intervention plans. In M. Shinn (Ed.), *Curriculum-based measurement: Assessing special children* (pp. 153-181). New York: Guilford.

Fuchs, L. S., & Fuchs, D. (1986). Effects of systematic formative evaluation: A meta-analysis. *Exceptional Children, 53*, 199-208.

Fuchs, L. S., Fuchs, D., & Deno, S. L. (1982). Reliability and validity of curriculum-based informal reading inventories. *Reading Research Quarterly, 18*, 6-26.

Fuchs, L. S., & Shinn, M. R. (1989). Writing CBM IEP Objectives. In M. Shinn (Ed.), *Curriculum-based measurement: Assessing special children* (pp. 130-152). New York: Guilford.

Gerber, M., & Semmel, M. (1984). Teacher as imperfect test: Reconceptualizing the referral process. *Educational Psychologist, 19*, 137-148.

Germann, G. (1987). *Administrative issues in implementation of curriculum-based measurement.* Minneapolis: Minneapolis Public Schools.

Germann, G., & Tindal, G. (1985). An application of curriculum-based assessment: The use of direct and repeated measurement. *Exceptional Children, 52*, 244-265.

Graden, J., Christenson, S., & Bonstrom, O. (1985). Implementing a prereferral intervention system: Part II: The data. *Exceptional Children, 51*, 487-496.

Gullickson, A. (1986). Teacher education and teacher-perceived needs in educational measurement and evaluation. *Journal of Educational Measurement, 23*, 347-354.

Howell, K. (1986). Direct assessment of academic performance. *School Psychology Review, 15*, 324-335.

Howell, K. W., & Morehead, M. K. (1987). *Curriculum-based evaluation for special and remedial education.* Columbus, OH: Merrill.

Lentz, F. E., & Shapiro, E. S. (1986). Functional assessment of the academic environment. *School Psychology Review, 15*, 346-357.

Marston, D. (1989). Curriculum-based measurement: What is it and why do it? In M. R. Shinn (Ed.), *Curriculum-based measurement: Assessing special children* (pp. 18-78). New York: Guilford.

Marston, D., & Magnusson, D. (1985). Implementing curriculum-based measurement in special and regular education settings. *Exceptional Children, 52*, 266-276.

Marston, D., & Magnusson, D. (1988). Curriculum-based assessment: District-level implementation. In J. Graden, J. Zins, & M. Curtis (Eds.), *Alternative educational delivery systems: Enhancing instructional options for all students* (pp. 137-172). Washington, DC: National Association of School Psychologists.

Reschly, D. (1988). Special education reform: School psychology revolution. *School Psychology Review, 17*, 459-475.

Reschly, D. J., Genshaft, J., & Binder, M. S. (1987). *The 1986 NASP survey: Comparison of practitioners, NASP leadership, and university faculty on key issues.* Washington, DC: National Association of School Psychologists.

Salvia, J., & Ysseldyke, J. E. (1987). *Assessment in special and remedial education* (4th ed.). Boston: Houghton-Mifflin.

Shapiro, E. S. (1987). Behavioral assessment of academic skills: Conceptual framework and overview. In E. S. Shapiro (Ed.), *Behavioral assessment in school psychology* (pp. 63–81). Hillsdale, NJ: Lawrence Erlbaum.

Shapiro, E. S., & Lentz, F. E. (1985). Assessing academic behavior. A behavioral approach. *School Psychology Review, 14*, 325–338.

Shinn, M. R. (1988). Development of curriculum-based local norms for use in special education decision making. *School Psychology Review, 17*, 61–80.

Shinn, M. R. (1989). Identifying and defining academic problems. In M. Shinn (Ed.), *Curriculum-based measurement: Assessing special children* (pp. 90–129). New York: Guilford.

Shinn, M.R., Rosenfield, S., & Knutson, N. (1989). Curriculum-based assessment: A comparison and integration of models. *School Psychology Review, 18*, 299–316.

Shinn, M. R., Tindal, G., & Spira, D. (1987a). Special education referrals as an index of teacher tolerance: Are teachers imperfect tests? *Exceptional Children, 54*, 32–40.

Shinn, M. R., Tindal, G., Spira, D., & Marston, D. (1987b). Practice of learning disabilities as social policy. *Learning Disability Quarterly, 10*, 17–28.

Stiggins, R. J. (1988). Revitalizing classroom assessment: The highest instructional priority. *Phi Delta Kappan, 69*, 369–372.

Thurlow, M., & Ysseldyke, J. E. (1982). Instructional planning: Information collected by school psychologists vs. information considered useful by teachers. *Journal of School Psychology, 20*, 3–10.

Tindal. G. (1988). Curriculum-based measurement. In J. L. Graden, J. E. Zins, & M. C. Curtis (Eds.), *Alternative educational delivery systems: Enhancing instructional options for all students* (pp. 111–136). Washington, DC: National Association of School Psychologists.

Tindal, G., Shinn, M. R., & Germann, G. (1987). The effect of different metrics on interpretation of change in program evaluation. *Remedial and Special Education, 8* 14–28.

United States Department of Education (1988). *Tenth annual report to Congress on implementation of PL 94-142*. Washington, DC: Author.

Ysseldyke, J. E., & Christenson, S. L. (1988). Linking assessment to intervention. In J. L. Graden, J. E. Zins, & M. C. Curtis (Eds.), *Alternative educational delivery systems: Enhancing instructional options for all students* (pp. 91–109). Washington, DC: National Association of School Psychologists.

ANNOTATED BIBLIOGRAPHY

Deno, S. L. (1986). Formative evaluation of individual programs: A new role for school psychologists. *School Psychology Review, 15*, 358–374.
In this article, problems associated with traditional assessment practices and functions of school psychologists are identified and a new role for school psychologists is proposed. The use of CBM formative evaluation is presented as a methodology that permits school psychologists to provide assessment information that is relevant in determining the effectiveness of educational interventions.

Fuchs, L. S. (1986). Monitoring progress among mildly handicapped pupils: Review of current practice and research. *Remedial and Special Education, 7*, 5–12.
A review of research is presented in this article on the use of formative evaluation to improve instructional programs for mildly handicapped students. Critical issues regarding this methodology for monitoring student progress discussed are: focus of measurement, frequency of measurement, data display, and data-utilization methods.

Germann, G. & Tindal, G. (1985). An application of curriculum-based assessment: The use of direct and repeated measurement. *Exceptional Children, 52*, 244–265.
This article reviews issues in the delivery of special education services and a description of the model used by the Pine County Special Education Cooperative is given. This model, based on CBM procedures, takes an integrated approach across special education decision making regarding academic and social behaviors of special education students.

Shinn, M. R. (Ed.). (1989). Curriculum-based measurement: Assessing special children. New York: Guilford Press.
This book contains contributions of the work of the core-group of researchers and school practitioners who developed and implemented CBM. Specific procedures for implementing CBM in school settings are detailed. General background information and conceptual issues surrounding the development and use of CBM as an alternative to traditional school psychology practice are discussed also.

21

Best Practices in Designing Preschool Interventions

David W. Barnett
John D. Hall
University of Cincinnati

After many years of relative neglect, educational services to young children and their families are now of critical significance due to the passage of PL 99-457. The success of the legislation depends on the adequacy of interventions. This chapter reviews major features of intervention design for preschool populations within the context of alternative service delivery.

OVERVIEW

One of the propositions of the NASP Position Statement on Early Intervention Services in the Schools (1987) is that service delivery should be provided to the greatest extent possible without unnecessary diagnostic labels. The characteristics of alternative services include the following concepts and strategies (Barnett & Paget, 1988). First, *normalization* is the guiding principle. Second, a range of service delivery alternatives usually is required in order to meet children's and parents' needs. These alternatives include center-based parent and child programs, and home-based programs for parents and/or children. Third, intervention decisions are based on (a) the analysis of the current situations of children and caregivers, and (b) functional objectives that are developmentally appropriate and that stem from mutual problem-solving and intervention-based assessments.

The Promise of Early Intervention

Perhaps counterintuitively, reviews of the effectiveness of early intervention are mixed. Basic intervention questions include the quality and magnitude of developmental changes that are possible given biological and environmental realities (Gallagher & Ramey, 1987). While summaries are difficult, three generalizations can be made.

First, substantial evidence exists for significant changes for many aspects of cognitive, personal, and social functioning in the developmental years. The trajectories of changes may be in positive or negative directions, and are not easily predicted for individual children. Second, there are biologically determined limits of change for individuals, but similarly, the limits cannot be easily established. Third, research in intervention design is currently undergoing rapid innovation. Without full consideration of intervention research, issues concerning the potential for developmental change cannot be adequately addressed.

The analysis of large scale efficacy studies. An important foundation for estimating the promise of early intervention is the outcomes associated with intervention programs such as Head Start, Abecedarian, and Hi/Scope (e.g., Gallagher & Ramey, 1987; Guralnick & Bennett, 1987; Schweinhart, Weikart, & Larner, 1986). While relative gains in cognitive functioning have been reported in some studies, children have experienced greater school success not necessarily revealed by higher achievement or aptitude scores, but by fewer referrals for special services and retentions, and by a greater likelihood of completing school. Furthermore, social gains have also been promising as revealed by fewer legal transgressions and teenage pregnancies. However, there are many difficulties in evaluating the outcomes associated with large scale intervention programs.

The importance of single case studies. Single case studies are important in early intervention programs for several reasons. First, handicapped and at-risk preschool children have diverse needs since they present a wide range of behavior and learning difficulties. This diversity necessitates at least some individual programming. Second, reviews of early intervention effectiveness reveal many gaps in research and "unknowns" concerning procedures commonly employed. Single case designs encompass needed methods for accountability in order to evaluate and to make necessary changes in interventions. Third, numerous effective interventions can be found in the literature for many learning/behavior problems. They provide an important context for decisions concerning intervention alternatives.

BASIC CONSIDERATIONS

For at-risk and handicapped children, there may be cumulative benefits of participating in sustained programs that must be weighed against cumulative risks for not intervening adequately. *Sustained* programs include early interventions, planned transitions to regular school programs, and continued support for children, parents, and teachers as needed. The foundations of intervention design based on alternative services (Barnett & Paget, 1988) include: (a) ecological problem-solving whereby adaptation, potential change agents, and needed resources across settings are evaluated; (b) behavioral assessments that result in strategies

for changing behaviors; and (c) a well-planned functional curriculum.

Consultation services to families and teachers are of critical importance. In contrast to traditional methods, assessments need to be more functional and related to caregivers' concerns and intervention plans, and curriculum-based measurement needs to assume a prominent role (Bagnato, Neisworth, Paget, & Kovaleski, in press).

BEST PRACTICES IN DESIGNING PRESCHOOL INTERVENTIONS

In this section, we address assessment practices related to designing interventions, considerations in prioritizing and selecting target behaviors (Barnett & Carey, in press), examples of interventions, and factors important in considering intervention outcomes.

Assessment for Intervention Design

Ecological/systems interviews. Ecological assessments provide the foundation for intervention decisions (Cantrell & Cantrell, 1985). Ecological principles stress that problems potentially can be resolved in a number of alternative ways that include modifying the problem behavior, altering or clarifying the expectations of persons encountering the problem behavior, or changing the situation. The techniques involve "mapping" social, family, and preschool networks and behaviors, and changes that occur (Hartman, 1978). An Eco-Map is depicted in Figure 1. Squares have been used to represent males while circles represent females. Relationships are depicted through different connecting lines (solid lines for good, dashed lines for tenuous, and Xs for conflicted or stressful relationships). Other symbols may be added. In the figure, a young boy (3) has a dysfunctional relationship with his young mother (17). The mother is working in a job that she enjoys (Job), and is dating a man (B) who has not yet established a relationship with the child. The child's primary caregiver is the grandmother (GMo); the grandfather (GFa) does not provide emo-

FIGURE 1. Eco-Map.

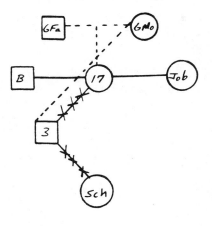

tional support or assistance. The child's behavior in the preschool (Sch) is characterized by frequent acting out behaviors that are also troublesome at home. Thus, initial consultations may include not only the mother, but also the grandmother and preschool personnel.

Waking Day interview. Whereas the eco-map focused on identifying key persons, settings, and relationships, the "Waking Day" interview (e.g., Wahler & Cormier, 1970) involves a detailed description of behaviors across settings used to help select and prioritize target behaviors and settings, and to possibly expand learning opportunities. In conducting the interview, the parent is asked to describe the child's typical day focusing on events, routines, and behavior from awakening until bedtime. Salient behaviors of greatest importance to the caregiver often emerge in the interview. Furthermore, it can be directed towards preschool routines and behaviors as well. Table 1 provides examples of questions.

Problem "solving" interviews. Parents and teachers have "expert" status concerning their observations, interactions, and knowledge regarding a child while professionals provide expertise and assist with the problem solving process (e.g., Curtis & Meyers, 1988). Problem solving interviews encompass two func-

tions: scanning the problem behavior and circumstance, and the indepth analysis of a problem situation (Peterson, 1968). They are used throughout the assessment-intervention process. Problem solving is characterized by the following steps: (a) problem definition and clarification; (b) solution generation and analysis; (c) mutually agreed upon assessment/intervention plans and roles; (d) trial periods for interventions; (e) evaluation; and (f) replanning as necessary. In practice, ecological and problem solving functions of interviews are often combined.

Direct observations. While interviews provide a means of identifying potential problematic settings, target behaviors, and likely change agents, reliable observations are necessary for the analysis of specific skills, interactions, and interventions. Two general strategies typically underlie the development of an observational assessment system.

First, preliminary observations are used to help determine target behavior selection. *Real-time* observations conducted in naturalistic environments enable the determination of characteristics of behaviors, interactions, and sequences of behaviors. They are useful for the development of structured observations. An example is depicted in Figure 2. The arrows indicate a judgment concerning

TABLE 1
"Waking Day" Interview

What is it like to be a parent of your child?
　　Waking up time?
　　Breakfast?
　　Dressing?
　　To school (bus behavior)?
　　After school?
　　Dinner time?
　　Bath time?
　　Bed time?

Other questions?
　　In the car?
　　Play? With siblings? Peers?
　　Discipline?
　　Chores?
　　Community (e.g., church, shopping)?
　　With visitors?

the overall adaptiveness of behavior (adaptive [↑] / maladaptive [↓]). The child's activity changes are recorded by time notations. For young children the technique provides a recording of the stream of behavior including: (a) peer relationships; (b) relationships with adults; (c) responses to learning tasks, demands, and rules; (d) antecedent and consequent events for specific behaviors; and (e) language samples.

Second, structured observations are conducted based on a focused integration of the problem identification and clarification stages, and through an analysis of relevant intervention research. Structured observations may include: (a) frequency measures of behaviors (hitting); (b) discrete skill sequences or categories of behaviors (e.g., social skills); (c) behaviors sampled within intervals of time (occurrences/nonoccurrences); (d) the duration (e.g., crying) or latency of a response (e.g., time before beginning a task); (e) interactions, antecedents, and consequences (e.g., compliance/noncompliance with parent/teacher commands); (f) peer comparisons, and (g) permanent products (e.g., work completion). Alessi and Kaye (1983) provide examples of observation formats.

Observations are used to help evaluate interventions. The evaluation includes both measures of treatment integrity discussed in a subsequent section and the effects of the intervention on target-related behaviors.

The use of other assessment techniques. Other developmental measures should be appraised for their contributions to the intervention process. The impact of traditional developmental scales and profiles on intervention plans has been untested. The outcomes frequently may be irrelevant and/or erroneous (e.g., Barnett, 1988; Macmann, Barnett, Sharpe, Lombard, & Belton-Kocher, in press).

Considerations in Target Behavior Selection

Typically, target behavior selection requires decisions between alternative behaviors, and questions about where, when, how, and with whom to intervene. In this section we present several broad considerations and several specific examples of strategies.

Determining physically dangerous behaviors. Evaluating the "dangerous-

FIGURE 2. Real-Time Observation.

Time	Behavior
8:45 a.m.	Child in block area engaged in block building with 2 peers (1 M, 1 Fe), [↑].
8:47	Teacher's aide enters area, states to the group: "When you finish playing, put the blocks on the shelf."
8:48	Teacher's aide leaves area, children continue to play [↑]. _____ states to M peer: "Give me that!" (pointing to peer's block). M peer does not comply. _____ walks over to M peer and takes block away [↓], then hits peer [↓]. Peer begins to cry. Child resumes play. Child throws block at Fe peer [↓].
8:52	She leaves area, goes to painting area where teacher's aide is present.
8:53	Teacher's aide returns to block area and states to M peer: "What happened?" M peer states: (pointing to child) "Hit me, took my block!" Teacher's aide states to _____: "Did you hit your friend and take his block?" Child states: "Yes, but he had one of my blocks." Teacher's aide asks child to apologize for taking block, child complies [↑]. Aide also asks _____ to place his blocks on shelf, child complies [↑]. Aide directs child to go to painting area.
8:58	_____leaves block area, goes to painting area [↑]. Child sits down at table, teacher present plus 3 peers (1 M, 2 Fe). Teacher states to child: "Would you like to paint?" _____ states: "Yes, paint a house." Child begins to paint [↑] . . .

ness" of behaviors and/or situations is an important initial step in many referrals. First, it may be necessary to determine risk status for children in abusive home situations and/or in cases of severe neglect. Second, it is important to assess potential outcomes and risk for other children (peers, siblings) and adults given a child referred for severe conduct disorders. Third, the need for health and injury-related interventions may be assessed (Mori & Peterson, 1986). Risks for children may be related to parental situations, motivation, skill, and stressors that influence parental monitoring and responding to child care needs.

Identifying behaviors that have damaging social and economic implications for parents. Intervention decisions must take into consideration the economic and social realities of parents. There are many facets to the issues. First, interventions may place increased demands on parents. For some parents, respite may be more important than exacting interventions. For working parents, initial consultations may focus on disruptive day care behaviors in prioritizing target behaviors. Interventions may

focus on parental needs such as, for example, improved "shopping behaviors" of children (Clark et al., 1977).

Second, another point of analysis is suggested by the concept of *insularity.* Mothers that are "cut-off from social contact," and who view the limited contacts that they do experience as "unsolicited" or aversive have been described by this term (Wahler, 1980, p. 208). Without the buffers of social supports and help, insularity may contribute to neglectful or coercive styles of parent–child interactions. Furthermore, "insular" mothers are at increased risk of treatment failure.

Establishing sequences of behavior change. Intervention design is based on a process of sequential rather than diagnostic decision making. Plans are made to expand positive behaviors and to reduce maladaptive behaviors. Assessment and intervention plans are evaluated periodically and changed when necessary.

Target behaviors may be selected because they are prerequisite to other behaviors. An example is that of *preattending skills.* Preattending skills encompass looking at the materials, listening to instructions, and sitting quietly during instruction. The skills can be successfully taught (Etzel, LeBlanc, Schilmoeller, & Stella, 1981).

Another strategy in determining sequences of behavior change is through the identification of *keystone* behaviors (or "response classes") (Wahler, 1975). Selecting a keystone behavior is important because of the increased potential for positive intervention outcomes and beneficial side effects. An example relevant to many preschool intervention decisions is noncompliance. Successful interventions for noncompliant children may lead to improved child care, social gains for children, and reduced risk for more serious conduct disorders (e.g., Patterson & Bank, 1986). Russo, Cataldo, and Cushing (1981) demonstrated improvements in compliance accompanied by decreases in maladaptive behaviors (e.g., crying, self-injury, and aggression) that were obtained without direct contingencies. Forehand and McMahon (1981) have developed an intervention package for noncompliant children and their parents.

Another promising strategy that serves as an example of sequential decision making is to assess behavior both in the current (i.e., special preschool classroom) and transition (i.e., integrated classroom) environments. Children who are successful in the transition setting (termed *index children*) are identified to help evaluate both child and teacher–child behaviors necessary for successful adaptation in the new setting. The procedure (referred to as "template matching") helps with the identification of probable transition settings, the selection of target behaviors, and interventions to help with transitions (e.g., Hoier, McConnell, & Pallay, 1987).

Planning for self-regulation and regulation by natural communities. A significant amount of behavior may be regulated by an individual's internal standards. Also, self-regulation is often necessary due to limitations of external procedures for managing certain behaviors. Therefore, planning for young children's development of self-regulation is critical to adaptation.

Self-mediated techniques can be incorporated into many intervention plans. Furthermore, well-functioning classrooms help regulate disruptive behavior in powerful ways, and many developmental skills including self-management may be taught directly and incidentally by peers and teachers.

Examples of Interventions for Common Preschool Target Behaviors

Examples of interventions were selected based on their potential for use by caregivers and their empirical support. Basic scientist–practitioner strategies are critical for ethical and professional practice (e.g., Barlow, Hayes, & Nelson, 1984). It is important to use established guidelines for interventions. Positive approaches should be used before aversive and/or restrictive interventions when possible. Aversive and restrictive procedures require special legal and ethical considerations. The rights of parents, children, and teachers need to be protected (see Rekers, 1984). The overall decision framework should be based on collaborative parent and teacher consultation.

The basics: Provision of learning experiences, differential attention, use of discipline/reprimands. *Positive learning experiences* should be a major point of analysis. Thus, the learning and mediational environments of families (e.g., Laosa & Sigel, 1982) and classrooms may be a point of broad-based intervention. Opportunities for incidental and direct teaching occur during dressing, meals, shopping, and serendipitous occasions in addition to planned instruction. The power of countless and often brief encounters may be greatly underestimated.

Furthermore, play behaviors can be explored through interviews and observations. Assessment/intervention may include (a) the active structuring and/or monitoring of experiences by caregivers that incorporate cognitive, language, affective, social, and motor learning; and (b) adult-child, child–peer interactions, and solitary play.

Differential or systematic attention consists of social reinforcement given to a child contingent on the display of desired behavior. Its effectiveness has been well-established across a variety of behaviors, settings, and change agents. Considerations include the use of public or private praise, and the use of back-up reinforcement. A variety of specific reinforcing verbalizations should be used that immediately follow the desired response. Modeling of appropriate responses may be important (Hall & Hall, 1980a).

Withdrawal of attention in a systematic fashion is referred to as *planned ignoring* or *extinction* (Hall & Hall, 1980b). Inappropriate behavior is often strengthened and maintained by attention. The adult should first inform the child of his/her inappropriate behavior and of plans to ignore the behavior. The procedures typically include the following steps: the adult (a) focuses attention away from the child, (b) exhibits a passive expression, (c) does not verbalize, and (d) withdraws from the immediate setting within 5 seconds. An increase in the undesirable behavior may occur initially, but will likely decrease over time. The intervention should be combined with social attention for appropriate behavior.

Reprimands are perhaps the most common strategy for behavior control. However, when used ineffectively, they are associated with intensifying maladaptive behaviors. Houton (1980) lists nine guides: (a) specify the inappropriate behavior, state why the behavior is inappropriate, and provide an example of an appropriate behavior; (b) use a firm tone; (c) use nonverbal expressions of disapproval; (d) deliver the reprimand within close proximity; (e) avoid ignoring inappropriate behavior; (f) use a more intrusive intervention with a dangerous behavior; (g) use social reinforcement for appropriate behaviors; (h) if necessary, follow reprimands with other acceptable behavioral strategies; and (i) maintain emotional control.

Noncompliance and behavior problems: Time-out, contingent observation, DRO, overcorrection. *Time-out* (from positive reinforcement) is a mild but effective form of punishment. Different procedures vary according to their range of restrictiveness and specific steps that are followed. Roberts, Hatzenbuehler, and Bean (1981) described a moderately restrictive procedure consisting of four steps. Upon exhibiting inappropriate behavior, the child is (a) informed of the consequence for the maladaptive behavior and is provided with an example of an appropriate behavior, (b) prompted to sit in a chair located in the corner for a 2-minute period, (c) instructed to remain in the chair until signaled to leave, and (d) allowed to leave time-out contingent upon the display of "quiet behavior" during the last 15 seconds of the period. If the child exhibits an emotional outburst during the final period, an additional 15 seconds is added until the contingency is finally met. If the chair is left without permission, the child is returned to the chair, the rule and contingencies are restated, and the timer is reset for 2 minutes. Other behavior is ignored during time-out.

Contingent observation ("sit and watch") may be useful for aggressive or other inappropriate play behaviors (Porterfield, Herbert-Jackson, & Risley, 1976). The procedure combines nonexclusionary time-out with incidental teaching. The following steps are used: (a) the child is provided with a brief description of the inappropriate behavior and an example of an appropriate behavior; (b) the child is removed to the periphery of the activity area and is instructed to briefly observe the appropriate behavior of other children (less than 1 minute); (c) the child is asked if she/he is ready to rejoin the group; and, depending on the child's response (verbal or nonverbal), (d) the child is allowed either to return to the activity; or (e) to continue to observe the group for an additional minute followed by the procedure in (c). Upon returning to play, the child receives positive reinforcement (i.e., praise) when exhibiting appropriate behavior. If outbursts continue, or if the play of others is disrupted, a more restrictive time-out may be used.

Differential reinforcement of other behavior (DRO) is an effective procedure for decreasing maladaptive behaviors. The technique requires reinforcement of all responses except the target behavior. Thus, reinforcement is administered if the child does not display the maladaptive behavior.

An example of the use of DRO with extreme rates of aggressive behavior is described. First, a critical 20 minute free play period was selected, divided into 1 minute time intervals (based on the interval between incidences of target behaviors). A timer was set at the beginning of each interval. The child was shown the timer, and was given the explanation that it was necessary to play "nicely" (through examples of acts) in order to earn a reinforcer. If an aggressive act was not exhibited during the interval, the child was reinforced with praise and a square of colored paper that represented a step on a "Path of Good Behavior" chart. At the end of the 20 minute interval, the child stapled the squares earned on the path. When the chart was filled (e.g., with 15 squares), he was allowed to select an activity reinforcer (e.g., riding a trike in the gym). The interval was gradually increased over time.

Overcorrection also is used effectively with some disruptive, destructive, or aggressive behaviors. As described here, the procedure combines restitution and positive practice. The restitution component requires the child to "restore" the environment to an improved condition. The positive practice component requires the child to display and practice a behavior incompatible to the target behavior. For example, Shapiro (1979) used the procedure with a child who was tearing books. The restitution component required the child to pick up the paper and clean the area. Physical prompts were used as necessary. Positive practice consisted of looking at books with an adult and turning pages on command without tearing them.

Social withdrawal and isolation: The "Classroom Manager"; peer and teacher mediated techniques. *The Classroom Manager* intervention involved placing socially withdrawn children into leadership positions (Sainato, Meheady, & Shook, 1986). The following rationale was given: "by placing withdrawn children in 'status' positions and making them the dispensers of preferred activities, their positive peer interactions would be increased and new friendships would be formed" (p. 188). The following steps were employed: (a) The teacher announced to the class that she had selected a new helper; (b) the child was given a large "manager" button to wear; (c) the role consisted of leading and/or directing preferred activities (e.g., feeding class pets); (d) the duties were reviewed each day with the child and class; (e) a picture board displaying the tasks was used to prompt the child with respect to responsibilities; (f) following a 10 day period, the teacher complimented the child on a "great job" and suggested that the class applaud the efforts.

Teacher and peer mediated techniques have been used widely to increase social interactions. Targets for interventions include direct teaching of functional social routines (e.g., turn taking), strategies for gaining access to play, communication skills, and toy play skills. Peer mediated strategies employ the use of another child to engage and maintain the socially withdrawn child in play through the use of behaviors such as organizing play (e.g., specifying a play role or activity), sharing (e.g., using a common object in play), and assisting (e.g., helping another) (Hendrickson, Strain, Tremblay, & Shores, 1982).

Teacher mediated techniques consist of verbal and physical prompts, and contingent praise (e.g., Fox, Shores, Lindeman, & Strain, 1986). Tarpley and Saudargas (1981) effectively used a procedure for a withdrawn child that required the teacher to: (a) openly participate with the child's peers, (b) conduct class discussions regarding the positive aspects of group activities, (c) make brief comments during the group activities related to the satisfaction and rewards of interactions with peers, (d) provide direct social reinforcement to the withdrawn child upon joining a group of peers, and (e) use planned ignoring when physical distance from other children was exhibited. Research is needed with respect to response maintenance and generalization effects. Furthermore, teacher mediated interventions should not increase teacher–target child interactions; this may have the effect of decreasing child–peer play (Hecimovic, Fox, Shores, & Strain, 1985). Other intervention examples include the use of modeling (Rao, Moely, & Lockman, 1987).

Language and preacademic skills: Incidental learning, the use of delay. *Incidental teaching* employs unstructured situations and brief positive interactions between children and adults to expand language (Hart & Risley, 1982). Attention is focused on the child's language productions, and elaboration is encouraged on the child–specified topic. The intervention requires a caregiver to respond to the child's initial requests (including nonverbal) or comments with: (a) attention, and/or social praise; (b) a request and/or encouragement for more information concerning the request and/or comment; and (c) a statement related to the request and/or comment that serves to expand the child's performance with respect to the initial request.

Brief time delays have also been used effectively to improve language. The focus is also on natural, functional, and frequent learning opportunities (e.g., snacks, dressing). The intervention calls for the adult to use a time delay as a cue for the child to emit a verbal response. The conditions are as follows: (a) the caregiver is in close proximity, is attending to the child, and does not vocalize; (b) visual prompts may be used; (c) the caregiver assumes an expectant look; (d) a 5 second delay guideline is used; and (e) the verbalization should be appropriate to the situation (Halle, Baer, & Spradlin, 1981). Delay may be used to encourage verbalizations for typically nonverbal requests (e.g., for juice, shoes tied). If language is not initiated, the teacher may model an appropriate response and wait for an imitation prior to fulfilling the request. *Delayed prompting* is a form of errorless learning that has been used successfully with young children with preacademic skill deficiencies (Bradley-Johnson, Sunderman, & Johnson, 1983).

Examples of interventions for self-regulation and regulation by natural communities. External means are used to teach self-regulation. Basic procedures include helping children with self-monitoring and evaluating behaviors. Kaplan, Kohfeldt, and Sturla (1974) developed a variety of self-recording forms for use with young children.

Self-instruction typically includes modeled verbalizations consisting of (a) questions about the task, (b) answers to the questions, (c) self-instructional guidelines, and (d) self-reinforcement. While promising, the results have also been difficult to replicate and need further development (Bornstein, 1985).

An example of a well researched *self-mediated* technique is that of "correspondence training." The intervention involves reinforcing a child for verbally planning to engage in a behavior and exhibiting (or accurately reporting) the response. The technique has been used with young language delayed/socially withdrawn children and has many other possible applications. An example of the intervention involved the following steps (Osnes, Guevremont, & Stokes, 1986): (a) Prior to free play, the child was asked what she/he planned to do. If the child verbally responded appropriately (e.g., "I'm going to talk to the kids a lot"), she/he was allowed to play. Prompts were used as necessary. (b) After free play, the child was provided with feedback concerning his/her behavior. (c) If a preestablished criterion was met, the child received social praise plus an activity pass. (d) If the criterion was not met, feedback was given, the contingencies for reward were reviewed, and the child returned to play. The criterion for performance may be established through baseline data and by peer comparisons. The activity pass resulted in the child selecting a reinforcer from a "Happy Sack" containing slips of paper with various brief but fun events.

Training parents in self-regulation skills may enhance the effectiveness of interventions when the parent is the primary change agent. Sanders and Glynn (1981) demonstrated the effectiveness of teaching parents self-management skills when intervening with disruptive child behavior. Parents were trained in goal setting, self-monitoring, and planning skills related to the performance of parenting skills across settings.

Preschool classrooms have considerable potential for teaching self-regulation and enhancing the generalizability of skill development (Stokes & Osnes, 1988). Thus, one of the first steps in preschool services is likely to be classroom and/or organizational consultation.

Children who exhibit difficulties with attention and/or task completion may benefit from *switching tasks* (Jacobson, Bushell, & Risley, 1969) whereby the completion of a task is required before activity changes. For example, upon leaving the first activity area, the child is required to stop at a centrally located table in the classroom and to complete a simple task (e.g., puzzle). An adult (i.e., parent volunteer) can help with task completion through prompts and modeling. Following completion of the task, the child may choose a different activity area. Activity passes may be used to monitor the activities selected. Rowbury, Baer, and Baer (1976) used token mediated access to play to promote task completion.

Factors Related to the Success of Interventions

Estimating the probable success of a range of interventions is critical to decision-making, and is based on many different factors. The concept of *acceptability* encompasses child, parent, and teacher judgments abut the appropriateness of interventions (Wolf, 1978). Interventions that are viewed as more acceptable have increased chances of engaging the caregivers and being carried out as planned. Collaborative planning may enhance the acceptance of plans, and is fundamental to intervention design. Many other strategies that are discussed in the chapter are intended to involve parents and teachers in the process, and to enhance motivation.

Another strategy related to acceptability is the evaluation of naturalistic interventions based on the analysis of evident styles of teaching and parenting (Barnett & Carey, in press). Naturally occurring parent and teacher interventions may be successful with modifications, guidance, and feedback. Alternatively, research-based interventions may be adapted based on the roles, routines, skills, and interests of caregivers.

Intervention success is also dependent upon the availability of resources. Teachers may need support, and siblings (James & Egel, 1986), extended family, and babysitters may be helpful in carrying out interventions.

Treatment integrity refers to whether or not an intervention was conducted as planned (e.g., Gresham, 1989). Since intervention outcomes are often crucial in subsequent planning, treatment integrity is of major significance, and, if not evaluated, intervention outcomes are questionable. Training, modeling, role playing, and guided practice enable a change agent to become competent in the intervention technique prior to actual use. Also, using a simple, standard protocol that identifies intervention steps may help with treatment integrity. For example, when conducting an intervention for noncompliance, the parent is asked to check whether or not the steps were carried out (Table 2). Success with interventions is likely to influence subsequent judgments about intervention acceptability.

Assessing the Side Effects of Interventions

Interventions may result in planned as well as unplanned outcomes for children, peers, families, teachers, and parents. Furthermore, the outcomes may be either helpful or harmful. Procedures for evaluating side effects involve measuring multiple behaviors, assessing outcomes for others in the social environment, and observing behaviors for extended time

TABLE 2
Treatment Integrity Protocol for Compliance Training

Compliance Training

Date: _____

Behavior: Noncompliance to Parental Requests

Directions: Please complete this protocol each time the intervention is used by making a check mark in the appropriate boxes.

STEPS	Yes	No
a) I provided _____ with a direct, single verbal command and allowed him 5 seconds to comply.		
b) _____ complied within 5 seconds of the command and I provided him with immediate reinforcement or _____ did not comply and I provided him with a verbal warning (e.g., "If you do not _____, you will have to sit in the chair in the corner").		
c) The warning was ineffective within 5 seconds and I made _____ go to time-out either by directing or placing him in the time-out chair.		
d) I required _____ to remain in the chair for 2 minutes (using a timer) and be quiet for the last 15 seconds of the 2 minute time-out period. If he was not quiet during the latter portion of the period, I added an additional 1 minute to the time-out period.		
e) Upon completion of time-out, _____ was returned to the task where I began again with step a or b.		

periods. Well-planned and successful interventions are likely to have beneficial side effects.

SUMMARY

Preschool intervention design was discussed within the context of alternative service delivery. The basic consideration is providing needed services to caregivers.

The foundations of intervention design are based on collaborative problem solving and empirically evaluated interventions. Because of the importance of criteria related to acceptability, examples were given of interventions that may be adapted to the teaching styles of many parents and teachers.

ACKNOWLEDGMENTS

Appreciation is extended to Rita Barnett, Ron Bramlett, Karen Carey, Nancy Hampel, Pam Honsa, and Randy Siler for their review of an earlier draft of the chapter.

REFERENCES

Alessi, G. J., & Kaye, J. H. (1983). *Behavior assessment for school psychologists.* Washington, DC: National Association of School Psychologists.

Bagnato, S. J., Neisworth, J. T., Paget, K. D., & Kovaleski, J. F. (in press). The developmental school psychologist: Professional profile of an emerging early childhood specialist. *Topics in Early Childhood Special Education, 7.*

Barlow, D. H., Hayes, S. C., & Nelson, R. O. (1984). *The scientist-practitioner: Research and accountability in clinical and educational settings.* New York: Pergamon.

Barnett, D. W. (1988). Professional judgment: A critical appraisal. *School Psychology Review, 17,* 658-672.

Barnett, D. W., & Carey, K. (in press). Intervention design for young children: Assessment concepts and procedures. In B. A. Bracken (Ed.), *The psychoeducational assessment of preschool children* (2nd ed.). New York: Grune & Stratton.

Barnett, D. W., & Paget, K. D. (1988). Alternative service delivery in preschool settings: Practical and conceptual foundations. In J. Graden, J. Zins, & M. Curtis (Eds.), *Alternative educational delivery* systems: *Enhancing instructional options for all students* (pp. 291-308). Washington, DC: National Association of School Psychologists.

Bornstein, P. H. (1985). Self-instructional training: A commentary and state-of-the-art. *Journal of Applied Behavior Analysis, 18,* 69-72.

Bradley-Johnson, S., Sunderman, P., & Johnson, M. C. (1983). Comparison of delayed prompting and fading for teaching preschoolers easily confused letters and numbers. *Journal of School Psychology, 21,* 327-335.

Cantrell, M. L., & Cantrell, R. P. (1985). Assessment of the natural environment. *Education and Treatment of Children, 8,* 275-295.

Clark, H. B., Greene, B. F., Macrae, J. W., McNees, M. P., Davis, J. L., & Risley, T. R. (1977). A parent advice package for family shopping trips: Development and evaluation. *Journal of Applied Behavior Analysis, 10,* 605-624.

Curtis, M. J., & Meyers, J. (1988). Consultation: A foundation for alternative services in the schools. In J. L. Graden, J. E. Zins, & M. J. Curtis (Eds.), *Alternative educational delivery systems: Enhancing instructional options for all students* (pp. 35-48). Washington, DC: National Association of School Psychologists.

Etzel, B. C., LeBlanc, J. M., Schilmoeller, K. J., & Stella, M. E. (1981). Stimulus control procedures in the education of young children. In S. W. Bijou & R. Ruiz (Eds.), *Behavior modification: Contribution to education* (pp. 3-37). Hillsdale, NJ: Erlbaum.

Forehand, R. L., & McMahon, R. J. (1981). *Helping the noncompliant child: A clinician's guide to parent training.* New York: Guilford.

Fox, J., Shores, R., Lindeman, D., & Strain, P. (1986). Maintaining social initiations of withdrawn handicapped and nonhandicapped preschoolers through a response-dependent fading tactic. *Journal of Abnormal Child Psychology, 14,* 387-396.

Gresham, F. M. (1989). Assessment of treatment integrity in school consultation/prereferral intervention. *School Psychology Review, 18,* 37-51.

Halle, J. W., Baer, D. M., & Spradlin, J. E. (1981). Teachers' generalized use of delay as a stimulus control procedure to increase language use in handicapped children. *Journal of Applied Behavior Analysis, 14,* 389-409.

Hall, R. V., & Hall, M. C. (1980a). *How to use systematic attention and approval.* Austin, TX: Pro-ed.

Hall, R. V., & Hall, M. C. (1980b). *How to use planned ignoring.* Austin, TX: Pro-ed.

Hart, B., & Risley, T. R. (1982). *How to use incidental teaching for elaborating language.* Austin, TX: Pro-ed.

Hartman, A. (1978, October). Diagrammatic assessment of family relationships. *Social Casework,* 465-476.

Hecimovic, A., Fox, J. J., Shores, R. E., & Strain, P. S. (1985). An analysis of developmentally integrated and segregated free play settings and the generalization of newly acquired social behaviors of socially withdrawn preschoolers. *Behavioral Assessment, 7,* 367-388.

Hendrickson, J. M., Strain, P. S., Tremblay, A., & Shores, R. E. (1982). Interactions of behaviorally handicapped children: Functional effects of peer social initiations. *Behavior Modification, 6,* 323-353.

Hoier, T. S., McConnell, S., & Pallay, A. G. (1987). Observational assessment for planning and evaluating educational transitions: An initial analysis of template matching. *Behavioral Assessment, 9,* 5-19.

Houten, R. V. (1980). *How to use reprimands.* Austin, TX: Pro-ed.

Jacobson, J. M., Bushell, D., & Risley, T. (1969). Switching requirements in a head start classroom. *Journal of Applied Behavior Analysis, 2,* 43-47.

James, S. D., & Egel, A. L. (1986). A direct prompting strategy for increasing reciprocal interactions between handicapped and nonhandicapped siblings. *Journal of Applied Behavior Analysis, 19,* 173-186.

Kaplan, P., Kohfeldt, J., & Sturla, K. (1974). *It's positively fun: Techniques for managing learning environments.* Denver, CO: Love.

Laosa, L. M., & Sigel, I. E. (1982). (Eds.). *Families as learning environments for children.* New York: Plenum.

Macmann, G. M., Barnett, D. W., Sharpe, M., Lombard, T. J., & Belton-Kocher, E. (in press). On the actuarial classification of children: Fundamental studies of classification agreement. *Journal of Special Education.*

Mori, L., & Peterson, L. (1986). Training preschoolers in safety skills to prevent inadvertent injury. *Journal of Clinical Child Psychology, 15,* 106-114.

Osnes, P. G., Guevremont, D. C., & Stokes, T. F. (1986). If I say I'll talk more, then I will: Correspondence training to increase peer-directed talk by socially withdrawn children. *Behavior Modification, 10,* 287-299.

Patterson, G. R., & Bank, L. (1986). Bootstrapping your way in the nomological thicket. *Behavioral Assessment, 8,* 49-73.

Peterson, D. R. (1968). *The clinical study of social behavior.* New York: Appleton-Century-Crofts.

Porterfield, J. K., Herbert-Jackson, E., & Risley, T. R. (1976). Contingent observation: An effective and acceptable procedure for reducing disruptive behavior of young children in a group setting. *Journal of Applied Behavior Analysis, 9,* 55–64.

Rao, N., Moely, B. E., & Lockman, J. J. (1987). Increasing social participation in preschool social isolates. *Journal of Clinical Child Psychology, 16,* 178–183.

Rekers, G. A. (1984). Ethical issues in child behavior assessment. In T. H. Ollendick & M. Hersen (Eds.), *Child behavior assessment: Principles and procedures* (pp. 244–262). New York: Pergamon.

Roberts, M. W., Hatzenbuehler, L. C., & Bean, A. W. (1981). The effects of differential attention and time out on child noncompliance. *Behavior Therapy, 12,* 93–99.

Rowbury, T. G., Baer, A. M., & Baer, D. M. (1976). Interactions between teacher guidance and contingent access to play in developing preacademic skills of deviant preschool children. *Journal of Applied Behavior Analysis, 9,* 85–104.

Russo, D. C., Cataldo, M. F., & Cushing, P. J. (1981). Compliance training and behavioral covariation in the treatment of multiple behavior problems. *Journal of Applied Behavior Analysis, 14,* 209–222.

Sainato, D. M., Maheady, L., & Shook, G. L. (1986). The effects of a classroom manager role on the social interaction patterns and social status of withdrawn kindergarten students. *Journal of Applied Behavior Analysis, 19,* 187–195.

Sanders, M. R., & Glynn, T. (1981). Training parents in behavioral self-management: An analysis of generalization and maintenance. *Journal of Applied Behavior Analysis, 14,* 223–237.

Schweinhart, L. J., Weikart, D. P., & Larner, M. B. (1986). Consequences of three preschool curriculum models through age 15. *Early Childhood Research Quarterly, 1,* 15–45.

Shapiro, E. S. (1979). Restitution and positive practice overcorrection in reducing aggressive-disruptive behaviors: A long-term follow-up. *Journal of Behavior Therapy and Experimental Psychiatry, 10,* 131–134.

Stokes, T. F., & Osnes, P. G. (1988). The developing applied technology of generalization and maintenance. In R. H. Horner, G. Dunlap, & R. L. Koegel (Eds.), *Generalization and maintenance: Life style changes in applied settings* (pp. 5–19). Baltimore: Brookes.

Tarpley, B. S., & Saudargas, R. A. (1981). An intervention for a withdrawn child based on teacher recorded levels of social interaction. *School Psychology Review, 10,* 409–412.

Wahler, R. G. (1975). Some structural aspects of deviant child behavior. *Journal of Applied Behavior Analysis, 8,* 27–42.

Wahler, R. G. (1980). The insular mother: Her problems in parent-child treatment. *Journal of Applied Behavior Analysis, 13,* 207–219.

Wahler, R. G., & Cormier, W. H. (1970). The ecological interview: A first step in out-patient child behavior therapy. *Journal of Behavior Therapy and Experimental Psychiatry, 1,* 279–289.

Wolf, M. M. (1978). Social validity: The case for subjective measurement or how applied behavior analysis is finding its heart. *Journal of Applied Behavior Analysis, 11,* 203–214.

ANNOTATED BIBLIOGRAPHY

Bricker, D. D. (1986). *Early education of at-risk and handicapped infants, toddlers, and preschool children.* Glenview, IL: Little, Brown.
Knowledge of best educational practices is necessary to intervention planning. Bricker takes a functional approach to curriculum to facilitate adaptability and independence.

Gallagher, J. J., & Ramey, C. T. (Eds.). (1987). *The malleability of children.* Baltimore: Brookes.
Leading researchers offer analyses of the concepts, empirical bases, and new directions in early intervention. Given the fundamental questions of altering children's developmental trajectories, it is important reading.

Guralnick, M. J., & Bennett, F. C. (Eds.). (1987). *The effectiveness of early intervention for at-risk and handicapped children.* Orlando, FL: Academic Press.
The strengths include frameworks for early intervention, and the focus on the future. Some chapters are organized by specific conditions (e.g., language and communication disorders, visual impairments).

Odom, S. L., & Karnes, M. B. (Eds). (1988). *Early intervention for infants & children with handicaps: An empirical base.* Baltimore: Brookes.
This is a forward-looking collection of chapters relevant to program planning for young children. Topics include language, preacademic, play skills, parental interactions, in addition to other areas addressed by leading researchers.

Paget, K. D. (1988). Early behavioral interventions: Grasping the complexities. In J. C. Witt, S. N. Elliott, & F. M. Gresham (Eds.), *Handbook of behavior therapy in education.* New York: Plenum.
This chapter provides an overview of early intervention research, conceptual frameworks and useful interventions.

22

Best Practices in Developing Accountability Procedures

Joseph E. Zins
University of Cincinnati

OVERVIEW

Being able to demonstrate that one's efforts were effective in resolving a problem can be one of the most rewarding and satisfying aspects of being a school psychologist. After all, most of us entered the profession out of a desire to help children and their families. For this reason, gathering data on the results of psychological services has become a routine matter for many school psychologists as they recognize that holding themselves accountable for the delivery of effective and efficient services is not an "elective" activity. Rather, providing services in an accountable manner is a responsibility that accompanies being a professional. Excuses such as "It's a nice idea, but I just don't have time," or "No one else in the schools is doing it," can no longer be tolerated. We simply do not have the option of ignoring the need to evaluate our services, as these activities increasingly are necessary for our survival as individual practitioners and as a profession.

It is encouraging to observe accountability routinely being discussed as an essential aspect of school psychological services. For example, Brown, Pryzwansky, and Schulte (1987) included a chapter on evaluation in their consultation book, as did Zins, Curtis, Graden, and Ponti (1988) in their book on intervention assistance programs, and several chapters in Elliott and Witt's (1986) text on the delivery of psychological services addressed this topic. Hopefully, these discussions reflect an increased recognition of the importance of the topic. Unfortunately, however, there have not been a large number of articles reporting data gathered by school psychologists published in the school psychology literature since the first edition of *Best Practices in School Psychology*. This fact arouses concern that the numbers not involved in accountability efforts may rise as feelings of job security increase in response to the growing shortage of school psychologists nationally (Fagan, 1988).

There are several purposes of this chapter. The overall goal is to help practitioners objectify and systematize their professional practices in a way that will enable them to provide needed services more effectively and efficiently. Thus, it is intended to increase interest among school psychologists in accountability efforts and, it is hoped, to stimulate related actions. A second objective is to provide specific, practical suggestions about how school psychologists can make accountability an integral component of their practice. Finally, sources of additional information are provided to facilitate efforts to obtain more in-depth knowledge of this area.

BASIC CONSIDERATIONS

The Need to Be Accountable

A basic assumption of the chapter is that research and practice can be integrated in a way that leads to better services. There are four primary, interrelated reasons for being accountable for our professional actions. Clearly, a major reason is to *benefit clients/systems and other consumers* of psychological services, particularly with respect to generalization and maintenance of treatment gains. In other words, accountability data can be obtained not only to evaluate consumer satisfaction, but also to determine the impact of services through the assessment of outcome variables. Therefore, data collection should be associated with improved services. While this goal is self-explanatory for the most part, it occasionally seems to be forgotten, as in the case of a practitioner becoming overly involved with the research design (and the potential of a case for publication) to the detriment of what might be best for the child. However, this is not a widespread problem as it is far more common to find too little attention being paid to designing interventions in such a way that they can be evaluated adequately.

A second goal is to *assist us in becoming better practitioners*. Evaluative information can be of great assistance in determining professional development needs, in charting progress toward one's goals, and in leading to more effective and efficient practices. We may find out, for instance, that we consistently develop the same two or three interventions, with little apparent regard to the presenting problem. Unless formal, systematic efforts are made to evaluate the process and outcomes of services, there is no way of determining whether our day-to-day practices are achieving their desired goals or of examining the durability of our efforts. Consequently, we run the risk of continually engaging in ineffective, inconsistent practices or in making systematic errors. With respect to this point, Barnett (1988) presented a thoughtful discussion of professional judgment issues that may have an impact on practice.

On a broader level, accountability data can be collected to obtain information that is useful in *improving the overall psychological services program*. Strengths, weaknesses, and areas in need of modification can be identified and then addressed on the basis of these data. For example, patterns in the use of services might suggest that more intensive efforts are needed to reach certain consumer groups who frequently do not make use of psychological services. Or we may learn that most of the time of the school psychology staff is spent in assessment and classification activities, and little of it is devoted to intervention design. From a programmatic perspective, either of these findings might suggest a need to alter the manner in which psychological services are provided to consumers. In the first instance, it may be necessary to develop a plan to reach out to additional consumer groups and to make services more accessible. The second problematic area might suggest a need for additional staff training or for a systems-level intervention that would expand the range of services provided.

There also are *potential benefits to the overall profession* that may accrue from accountability efforts. Evaluation of psychological services may be helpful in establishing a need to expand the numbers of school psychologists employed in school districts, may encourage states to require lower ratios of psychologists to students so that a broader range of services can be provided, or may enhance the image of the profession to consumers by demonstrating its effectiveness. Furthermore, specific treatments that are identified as particularly effective can be incorporated into school psychology training and practice. Cost-effectiveness data also become especially salient in economically difficult times. For instance, they might be used to address empirically the question of whether it is indeed more expensive for districts to make use of contractual services or to employ their own psychologists (Fagan, 1985). However, broad, general questions such as "Are school psychological services effective?" need to be recast as more focused and specific inquiries about particular services and issues.

More broadly speaking, given that school psychologists are skilled in accountability and program evaluation procedures, they also can be involved in the evaluation of various educational programs and thus helpful to schools in meeting the public's increasing demands for accountability in that domain (e.g., Maher & Bennett, 1984). While such activities clearly fall in the realm of school psychology practice, the present discussion is limited to school psychology services only.

From a different perspective, there also are possible negative results from *not* demonstrating accountability. School psychology services could be evaluated through procedures that are inappropriate (e.g., procedures designed for teacher evaluation) or that yield little information that is helpful in improving performance (Zins, 1981). Should personnel not familiar with school psychology practice primarily determine the target of an evaluation effort, there is a high risk that they unwittingly may focus on areas quite peripheral to or different from those that would be selected by the school psychologist. Examples include focusing on the number of psychoeducational evaluations completed or counseling sessions held, with seemingly little attention devoted to qualitative issues. Simple numbers may be important, but they tell only part of the story. Although it is clear that supervisors and administrators must be involved in establishing the accountability program, it is equally obvious that school psychologists must proactively assume integral roles in this activity.

Accountability: What is it?

The term *accountability* has been used to refer to a broad range of activities. Oftentimes, it refers to evaluation of the efforts of an individual practitioner, such as in assessing the outcome of a cognitive-behavioral intervention developed during counseling. Sometimes it refers to determining the efficacy of the entire psychological services program, that is, what might be called program evaluation. In this chapter, the term is defined broadly as an

evaluative effort designed to gather systematically information relevant to the performance assessment of school psychologists. It enables them to demonstrate the effectiveness of their services to others, and it provides an evaluation of how well they met their performance objectives. It is concerned with both quantitative and qualitative aspects of practice and addresses both individuals and groups. It particularly is useful in improving service delivery and in enhancing professional development. (Zins, 1984, p. 58)

Accountability efforts are *undertaken in a systematic, carefully planned manner.* Too often, accountability and program evaluation activities are developed as an afterthought when a program is well under way or are hurriedly conducted at the conclusion of a program. As an alternative, from a scientific validity as well as from a utility standpoint, it is highly desirable that such activities be undertaken on a proactive basis so that they are an integral, essential component of the psychological services program. Of course, it is essential that any program to be evaluated first have well-defined goals and target populations along with clear operational plans.

Accountability efforts should *address specific areas of practice* rather than more global, undefined aspects. As noted earlier, the question "Are psychological services effective?" is too vague and will not yield information useful for improvement of the services. Instead, more helpful information would be that "Ninety percent of the parents found the psychologist to be readily accessible for conferences" or that the Good Behavior Game was used with elementary school students experiencing conduct disorders and resulted in improved prosocial classroom behaviors 72% of the time. Such data-based information can be communicated to others more readily, and can be related directly to performance goals established at the outset.

Both *quantitative and qualitative types of information* help to answer questions about effectiveness. A reliance on one type to the exclusion of the other

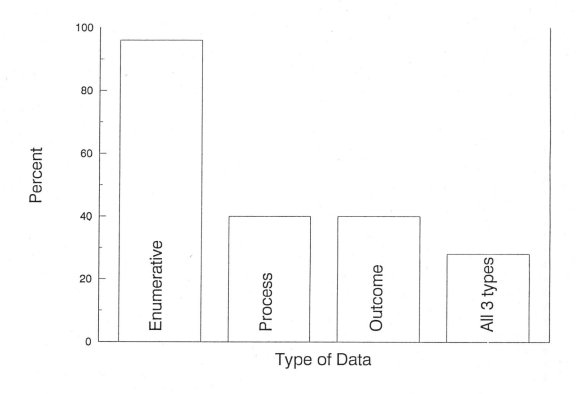

FIGURE 1. Percentages of Practitioners Collecting Various Types of Accountability Data.[a]

[a]Percentages include only the 60% of respondents who were collecting some type of accountability data.

can decrease the value of the information. Knowing that you spent 37% of your time consulting with teachers is important, but you also would want to know the specific outcomes of these sessions with regard to improvements in students' behavior and related to teachers' satisfaction with the service.

Finally, accountability data *must be useful, relevant, and applicable* to the realities of daily practice. To the extent that this information is used to inform decision makers and thereby improve services, it is useful. If data are gathered in a systematic, planned manner, if specific areas of practice are targeted, and if both quantitative and qualitative data are gathered, the chances are increased that the accountability effort will achieve desired results.

CURRENT PRACTICES

In recent years there have been several investigations of the efforts that school psychologists devote to accountability. A survey of presidents of each state school psychology organization conducted several years ago found that 40% of the respondents were unaware of accountability efforts in their states (Zins et al., 1982). This survey was followed by another one sent to state consultants or contact persons for school psychology that sought to determine whether accountability information was collected systematically on a state level (Guthrie, 1982). With a return rate of 68%, it was found that only seven states reported collecting accountability data. Similarly, in a national survey of individual school psychology practitioners who were members of the National Association of School Psychologists (NASP), Zins and Fairchild's (1986) respondents indicated that 18% of the states required that such information be collected.

Zins and Fairchild (1986) found that 60% of their individual respondents currently were collecting accountability data. The specific types of data they collected are shown in Figure 1 (complete definitions of these categories 'are included below in the Measures of Effectiveness section). A similar survey was conducted by Moore and Carlson (1988) in which a highly consistent number (53%) indicated that they were gathering accountability information. These authors also found that 65% of those collecting data indicated that the process was "imposed" on them by supervisors or administrators, and Zins and Fairchild found that 46% of their respondents' supervisors required it. Coincidently, similar numbers of school counselors and school psychologists engage in accountability activities (Fairchild & Zins, 1986).

DESCRIPTION OF BEST PRACTICES

Key Aspects of the Accountability Process

The need for engaging in accountability efforts should be clear by now; however, the method to do so may remain a problem. In this section, the discussion of best practices is organized according to the categories listed in Table 1.

Foci of analysis. In gathering accountability data, there are two logical foci or targets of analysis: the consumers of psychological services and the psychological services provided. Of course, an approach that addresses both is usually most desirable.

Consumers. There are many different consumers of psychological services, including individual students, teachers, and parents, groups of these persons, and even the entire school district. Data (feedback) can be collected from one, all, or some combination of these persons, and ideally a representative sample of consum-

ers should provide it. Webster-Stratton (1989), for example, did a systematic, session-by-session comparison of consumer (parent) satisfaction with three parent training programs for children with conduct disorders. Zins and Fairchild (1986) found that 56% of those collecting accountability data sought feedback from administrators, 48% from teachers, 22% from parents, 21% from ancillary staff, and 14% from students. In addition, school psychologists themselves may be recipients of supervision services, thereby becoming consumers.

Services provided. The services listed in Table 1 constitute the range of comprehensive services that all school psychologists should provide (NASP, 1984). As an illustration, we can evaluate the effectiveness of our assessment services (e.g., Are referrals for psychoeducational evaluation completed within a specified time period? Did they lead to specific interventions?). This list of services thus can be useful in developing an accountability plan as it may serve as a checklist by which practitioners can assess whether they indeed are delivering a full range of services. Similar to the situation with consumers, the ideal plan would simultaneously target several services for accountability efforts.

For accountability data to be representative and most valid, they should be obtained from several different consumer groups and in relation to various services, as our performance may vary among these groups and from service to service. A later section of the chapter discusses a process for determining specific target populations and services to address.

Measures of effectiveness. There are several types of accountability data that can be gathered and a wide variety of approaches that can be used. While these data can be described in various ways, in the present discussion they are classified according to the type of data collected: enumerative, process, and outcome (Fairchild, Zins, & Grimes, 1983). For examples of specific instruments that can be used to collect each of these types of data, see Zins et al. (1982).

TABLE 1
Accountability Foci and Measures of Effectiveness

Foci of Analysis	Measures of Effectiveness
Consumers	Enumerative
Students	
Teachers	Process
Administrators	Outcome
Parents	Single subject
Systems	Other examples
	Goal Attainment Scaling
Services Provided	Psychologist's Data Management System
Consultation	Peer review
Assessment	
Intervention	
Program planning and evaluation	
Research	
Supervision	

Enumerative. Enumerative data are those gathered by tallying the number of times various activities occurred or by computing the percentage of time involved in them. Examples include tabulating the number of consultation sessions held, the percentage of time spent traveling between schools or writing reports, the types of presenting problems referred, or the procedures selected for treatment of these problems (e.g., see Charlop, Parrish, Fenton, & Cataldo, 1987). From such information, we may learn that inordinate amounts of time are spent providing direct services to individual students with little devoted to prevention and competence-promotion or to systems-level issues.

Enumerative information frequently is gathered through a daily log such as the abbreviated example shown in Table 2. Many practitioners code services in various categories so that the data easily can be entered into and analyzed by a personal computer (e.g., PC-File, File Express, etc.). Monthly activity reports can then be provided to each school psychologist and their supervisor, and departmental reports can also be produced for larger districts. Among the various types of accountability data, enumerative data generally can be gathered at the least cost and therefore are commonly used. In the Zins and Fairchild (1986) study, of those involved in accountability efforts, 96% gathered this type.

A caveat about enumerative data is in order. It is *not* recommended that these data be used in a simplistic accounting fashion to determine that it costs x dollars to conduct a psychoeducational evaluation. Such calculations often are inappropriately used, for example, in making comparisons between the costs of school-based versus contractual services. These analyses usually do not take into account issues such as continuity and comprehensiveness of services, familiarity with the school organization, availability of follow-up services, quality of services, and so forth.

Process. Process data reveal how effectively an objective was attained, how the treatment activities were experienced or perceived, or how well services were provided; the focus is on qualitative rather than quantitative issues. In other words, this approach involves evaluating *how* something was done or experienced as opposed to *what* resulted (or was seen as resulting) from it.

One of the more common types of process data obtained is attitudinal information regarding the effectiveness of the psychologist's performance provided by consumers in response to such questions as the following: Is the psychologist knowledgeable about the behavior of individual students? Is he or she a good

TABLE 2
Psychologist's Daily Log of Requests for Assistance

Date Received	Student	Referral Source	Problem	Intervention	Follow-up

listener? Were you actively involved in developing specific recommendations regarding the presenting problem? Such information usually is obtained through questionnaires or rating scales, but individual and group interviews are other methods to gather it. As with enumerative data, this type is relatively easy to obtain. Although attitudinal data have limitations and the research on self-report measures in particular is equivocal (interested readers are referred to Howard [1980] and Barlow, Hayes, & Nelson [1984] for interesting discussions of this issue), such information potentially is quite useful and valid, and therefore serves as a popular accountability procedure. In the Zins and Fairchild (1986) study, 40% of respondents collected this type of accountability data. An example of a process instrument useful for assessing intervention assistance or prereferral intervention programs is shown in Table 3.

Outcome. Outcome or behavioral data, which usually are the most powerful, describe actual behavior changes such as those that occur in a child, in parents, in

an entire school system, and so forth. The focus may be on one or more aspects of the change including degree of goal attainment, related program effects, cause–effect relationships, or cost effectiveness (Illback, Zins, Maher, & Greenberg, in press). Somewhat unexpectedly, Zins and Fairchild (1986) found in their survey that 40% of those collecting accountability data obtained this type of information despite the difficulties inherent in gathering it. Several examples of outcome approaches follow.

Single-subject designs provide a very practical approach for studying important changes that take place in a student's behavior. As entire books have been written on this topic (e.g., Barlow & Hersen, 1984), only a brief summary of these procedures follows. Basically, single-case designs begin with the gathering of baseline data about the naturalistic occurrence of a particular behavior of an individual that has been identified as problematic, or a positive behavior that is low-frequency, until a stable trend is observed. A treatment that targets a single

TABLE 3
Intervention Assistance Process Rating Scales

The criteria listed below are important for establishing effective relationships with consultees and for efficient problem solving. Rate the degree to which each of the following scales reflect the interactions that occurred by circling the appropriate numbers.

1. Problems were defined in specific, observable terms.
   Specific   7   6   5   4   3   2   1   General

2. Data were used to define problems.
   Data-Based   7   6   5   4   3   2   1   No Data Collected

3. Open-ended, clarifying questions were used initially to obtain an overall picture of the problem situation.
   Open   7   6   5   4   3   2   1   Closed

4. Factors external to the child such as instructional techniques, peer influences, and classroom organization were examined in addition to internal factors as possibly contributing to the problem.
   External Factors Only   7   6   5   4   3   2   1   Internal Factors Only

5. The consultant and consultee explicitly agreed regarding the definition of the problem.
   Agreed   7   6   5   4   3   2   1   No Agreement

6. If more than one problem was identified as being a concern to the consultee, problems were prioritized to determine which should be addressed first.
   Prioritized   7   6   5   4   3   2   1   Not Prioritized

7. Multiple alternative strategies for resolving the problem were generated.
   Multiple Strategies   7   6   5   4   3   2   1   Single Strategy

8. Suggestions to resolve the problem were made in a noncoercive manner so that they did not require the consultee to change his or her behavior.
   Noncoercive   7   6   5   4   3   2   1   Coercive

9. Both the consultant and the consultee contributed to the identification and to the development of strategies for resolving the problem.
   Both Contributed   7   6   5   4   3   2   1   One Contributor

10. Responsibility for the child remained with the consultee.
    Consultee Responsible   7   6   5   4   3   2   1   Consultant Responsible

11. Specific plans were made to evaluate the effectiveness of the chosen intervention.
    Evaluation Planned   7   6   5   4   3   2   1   No Evaluation Plans

12. The relationship between consultant and consultee was collaborative; both participants respected the contributions and expertise of the other.
    Collaborative   7   6   5   4   3   2   1   Unequal

13. Active solicitation of consultee involvement was sought as a means of obtaining her or his commitment to supporting plans to enhance the child's education.
    Consultee Very Involved   7   6   5   4   3   2   1   Consultee Uninvolved

(Table 3 continued)

14. Good communication and interpersonal skills such as active listening (demonstrated both verbally and nonverbally) and expressions of empathy were used to convey a sense of caring and interest to the consultee.

    Active Listening/Empathic Statements   7   6   5   4   3   2   1   Low Interest Level

15. Paraphrasing and summarizing were used to demonstrate an understanding of what the consultee said and to keep the conference well directed and on target.

    Summarization/Clear Direction   7   6   5   4   3   2   1   Little Summarization/Direction

---

behavior is then introduced, and all other conditions are kept as constant as possible. Changes in the targeted behavior across various conditions are observed to determine whether the change can be controlled and maintained. In the simple design described (there are more complex variations), changes in the dependent variable then are attributed, usually with reservations, to the effects of the intervention (Barlow & Hersen, 1984).

A more complicated single-subject design that is very powerful as a means of demonstrating functional control over behavior in school settings is the multiple baseline design. In this technique, one or more behaviors of concern are identified and measured over time to establish baselines against which subsequent changes can be evaluated. Multiple baselines can be established across behaviors, settings, or students. When they are used across behaviors, a treatment is developed and implemented with one of the behaviors after the baselines have been established. As change is brought about in this behavior, the other behaviors remain in the baseline condition, usually with little or no change in them. Subsequently, the same intervention is applied to a second behavior and changes are observed. This procedure continues until all of the behaviors of concern have been subjected to the treatment. Changes in the targeted behavior then are attributed to the intervention, again usually with some reservations (Barlow & Hersen, 1984).

An outcome approach to performance evaluation that has been discussed frequently in the community mental health literature, but less in school psychology, is goal attainment scaling

(GAS) (Kiresuk & Lund, 1977; Kiresuk & Sherman, 1968). As noted in the first edition of this book, GAS is a systematic means of identifying the problems experienced by a student, assigning weights to those problems in terms of their importance or significance, estimating the goals or expected outcomes for each problem, and collecting follow-up information on results of interventions in each area. An attempt is made to predict outcomes or levels of goal attainment for each problem according to a five-goal scale. Points on the scale range from "much less than the expected level of outcome" to "much more than the expected level of outcome." The expected level focuses on what is *most likely* to occur rather than on what may be most desirable, and an emphasis is placed on making the goals as realistic as possible. This process has much "potential utility in school psychology as a help in establishing realistic goals for intervention plans and in determining the effectiveness of various procedures" (Zins, 1985, P. 499).

Another example of an outcome measurement process, which also includes substantial amounts of enumerative data, is the Psychologist's Data Management System (PDMS), developed by the Iowa Department of Public Instruction (Grimes & Ross-Reynolds, 1981) and illustrated in Table 4. Among the major components are (a) behavioral specification of the target behavior, (b) description of the procedures for measuring the behavior, (c) an indication of the direction of the intended behavior change, (d) level of baseline data, (e) desired criterion level, (f) specification of the intervention procedures, and (g) case review data. A coding system for most of these components facilitates entry of

TABLE 4
Psychologist's Data Management System

	Whose Behavior	Direction of Change	Entry Level	Criterion Level	Imple-mentor	Intervention Method	Case Review Date
Behavior —————— Measurement —————							—— —— Yr. Mo.
Behavior —————— Measurement —————							—— —— Yr. Mo.

Note: From Grimes and Ross-Reynolds (1981).Adapted by permission.

information into the PDMS. The procedure can be very helpful as a means of systematically developing, organizing, and monitoring intervention efforts. A computer program has been developed to facilitate data entry and analysis.

A large number of school psychologists are involved in various types of peer review or peer support groups (Claiborn, Stricker, & Bent, 1982; Zins, Ponti, & Murphy, in press; Zins, Wess, & Murphy, 1987). Although these groups can have a variety of goals, they often deal with quality assurance and professional development issues, both of which are relevant to accountability.

Peer review groups provide an opportunity for a small number of school psychologists to come together to discuss, review, and learn about professional issues of mutual concern. Often these discussions involve case presentations, reviews of professional practices, or presentations of new knowledge and techniques, but they may also include direct observations and feedback. While all of these learning formats have the potential to lead to improvements in professional practice, constructive feedback about one's practices from peers might be seen as the area most relevant to helping with accountability.

Developing a Practical Accountability System

Although it is quite probable that none of the currently available approaches will meet all of the unique needs that your situation demands, what is of primary importance is to identify an overall process that can most effectively address as many needs as possible. Accountability methods are available that can be adapted to most situations, thereby saving the time and energy required to start from scratch. Some items from the collection of instruments published by NASP (Zins et al., 1982) might be useful to persons seeking to develop an accountability system or to those who desire to modify their current procedures. However, we must remember that, given the vast number of potential accountability strategies and the various dimensions that could be addressed, not all possible aspects of practice can be addressed at once.

As with other organizational endeavors, efforts to develop and implement an accountability system begin with securing administrative sanction. Of course, it is essential that a thorough understanding of accountability and program evaluation be gained *before* approaching the administration so that the discussion with them can address specific issues related to adoption of these procedures and such questions as they might raise can be answered. Administrators might also have informational needs that must be considered in developing the accountability system. Furthermore, by means of collaborative work with supervisors and administrators, performance standards that are relevant and meaningful are more likely to be developed, and there is less risk of being subjected to inappropriate evaluation procedures.

As discussed earlier, many school psychologists have found it beneficial to work together within peer support groups (Zins et al., 1987). Not only can colleagues be helpful in performance appraisal activities, but they also can be collaborators in the development of accountability procedures. In districts with a number of school psychologists, one person might be placed in charge of accountability efforts and work cooperatively with the remainder of the staff to develop appropriate procedures that meet the needs of the individual psychologists and of the school district.

As should be clear by now, there are a variety of specific techniques that can be used to gather accountability data, each with its own strengths and limitations. These include strategies such as interviews, checklists and rating scales, self-report measures, self-monitoring, analogue studies, peer reviews, standardized academic tests, and direct observations (Kratochwill, 1982). To help in narrowing down this multitude of options, Fairchild et al. (1983) and Zins (1984, 1985) described the application of a systematic problem-solving process. The behavioral problem-solving steps of this process are interrelated and reciprocal in as much as what happens at one stage influences what occurs at subsequent points in the process. The discussion of these steps is based on Zins (1985).

Defining needs and clarifying the evaluation question. To be most useful, information to be gained from accountability procedures must result from carefully defined needs. The information requirements of district supervisory personnel and of the psychologists generally are similar, but it is important to ensure that all have their informational needs met. In addition to obtaining input from supervisors, examination of job descriptions is an additional way of clarifying and prioritizing activities to assess, and this process can provide a feedback loop to substantiate the job description. Identifying the specific goals of the performance evaluation is usually the most difficult and critical aspect of developing an effective accountability system, but unless this step is completed and accurate information is obtained, the next steps may be unsuccessful.

Generating alternative approaches. From the list of potential accountability targets in Table 1, specific areas on which to focus the evaluation process should be identified. In this step, a wide variety of alternative approaches to measuring these targets are developed through a brainstorming process. Since the major reason school psychologists do not engage in accountability efforts is that they are unfamiliar with these procedures (Zins & Fairchild, 1986), the list of accountability procedures referred to earlier (Zins et al., 1982) may be of particular assistance in generating alternatives. Also as suggested previously, peers can be helpful in identifying appropriate strategies. In fact, most practitioners will have to work collaboratively to develop their accountability programs, as such topics are not ordinarily covered in many university training programs (Zins & Fairchild, 1986).

Selecting an approach to meet local needs. From the list of alternatives generated in the previous step, specific procedures should be identified. Each potential approach has positive and negative characteristics that must be carefully weighed before making a decision on which to use. They may vary in regard to time required, associated expenses, personnel requirements, ease of administration, intrusiveness, and potential personal or interpersonal effects of implementing the plan. You are the best judge of your individual needs.

Implementation. As the accountability plan is implemented, there should be routine, periodic opportunities for review and feedback. It is crucial to ascertain whether the procedures are meeting the identified informational needs and whether implications for practice most likely will emerge. If difficulties in the implementation stage arise, it may be necessary to return to an earlier point in the problem-solving process to identify the source of the problems and to reformulate the accountability plan.

Examining the results of the evaluation. The data that result from the accountability procedures should be helpful in answering *specific* questions about the effectiveness of the psychological services program. Needed alterations in practice might be identified, or consumers might report overall satisfaction with current approaches. Or we may learn that a certain type of intervention was effective with specific types of students most of the time. In analyzing these data, we must remember that *we cannot be successful in every case. Our goal is to establish an overall winning percentage* (Grimes, 1983).

Disseminating evaluation results. The next step is to develop a strategy for disseminating the results of the evaluation, because "the time has come to stop telling consumers that school psychological services are important; the need to *demonstrate* their significance has arrived" (Zins, 1985, p. 105). The Zins and Fairchild (1986) survey found that of those who collected accountability data, 69% submitted a formal report to administrators and 27% made a presentation to the school board, but only 1% published the results in a teachers' or in a school newsletter. Additional discussion regarding utilization of the accountability data is contained below.

Meta-evaluation. Following the completion of the evaluation process, the entire sequence of events that took place should be reviewed. A determination is made regarding the effectiveness and efficiency of the evaluation process, and an assessment is conducted to determine whether each aspect was worthwhile in terms of the costs incurred and benefits derived. As a result, needed changes in the accountability plan can be identified for future efforts.

Utilizing and Communicating Evaluation Data

Accountability data are worthless and a waste of valuable professional time if they are not used properly (Zins, 1984). It is important to note that an individual practitioner or an entire psychological services program must be open and receptive to change if change is to occur. Among the common reasons that evaluation results are not utilized are that they (a) reached decision-makers after decisions had already been made, (b) addressed the wrong issues, or (c) were incomprehensible to all but the most sophisticated program evaluator (Sproul & Larkey, 1979). Further elaboration of all of these points is contained in Zins et al. (1988).

As has been emphasized repeatedly throughout this chapter, a major use of accountability information is to *improve services delivery*. The more specifically the information that is gathered pertains to related job functions, the more likely it will lead to improvements. Thus, as noted earlier, learning that "psychological services were judged to be at least moderately effective by 72% of the teachers," will not provide guidance about how to improve their efficacy in the future, or about the reasons why 28% of the teachers did not perceive them to be effective. Furthermore, public schools today are being charged with educating more and more diverse and discrete groups of students — children of limited English proficiency and of low socioeconomic status, the homeless, abused, deprived, and so forth — and school psychologists increasingly are becoming involved in programs directed toward them. As these students are identified and targeted for intervention, there is a wonderful opportunity as well as a fundamental professional obligation for school psychologists to evaluate these efforts and provide data to decision makers and the public.

Another way to use the information is to *expand the range of services offered.* Particularly when a new service such as curriculum-based assessment is being considered for introduction by a school district, it may be easier to convince administrators to implement it at least on a pilot basis if data are gathered regarding its strengths and weaknesses. Zins (1981) presented a practical case study in which he utilized accountability data to increase the quantity of services available as well as to improve those provided.

Convincing consumers or decision makers about the value and worth of psychological services is clearly important, particularly with escalating educational costs and the rise in the public's demand for all professionals to be more accountable. Therefore, *marketing efforts to publicize the psychological services program* also can be beneficial and can be directed toward informing consumers about the availability of services, of appropriate uses of them, and of their value. Too often, school psychologists' extensive skills are underutilized; marketing efforts can help to overcome this problem and lead to role expansion. Levant (1987) used such techniques to facilitate involvement in prevention-oriented parenting programs. Contemporary school psychologists can no longer continue spending the majority of their time administering IQ tests and writing related reports; too many students need to have us direct our expertise toward providing help in the classroom.

SUMMARY

Obtaining accountability data must become a routine but essential component of school psychological services if the profession and its practitioners are to be most effective in helping children. Ideally, school psychologists should become involved proactively in developing such procedures to maximize the usefulness of information gathered, but accountability programs must also be responsive to consumers' and decision makers' needs. Whether or not we recognize the importance of becoming so involved, the general public is expecting more and more accountability from schools and their staffs. Consequently, schools are under increasing pressure to answer these demands and school psychologists can help them to meet this challenge.

It is hoped that the information in this chapter is beneficial to those who wish to be more accountable in their practice and who desire to advance our understanding and knowledge of the field within the realities of daily practice. A primary goal of professional accountability is to integrate research and practice in a way that leads to provision of better services. Not only can we apply the results of others' research to our practice, but we also can use research methodologies to guide our professional functioning. As has been emphasized, such an approach can lead to improvement in the performance of individual practitioners, and it can also result in contributions to our collective knowledge so that children, their families, and school organizations can be better served.

The conclusion from the 1985 edition of this chapter remains pertinent today: "The slogan of the 1981 Olympia Conference on the Future of School Psychology was, 'School Psychology can make a difference in the future.' Through the effective implementation and use of accountability procedures, this motto can be expanded and practically realized: School psychologists can also *demonstrate* that they make a difference" (Zins, 1985, p. 501).

REFERENCES

Barlow, D. H., Hayes, S. C., & Nelson, R. O. (1984). *The scientist practitioner: Research in clinical and educational settings.* New York: Pergamon.

Barlow, D. H., & Hersen, M. (1984). *Single case experimental designs: Strategies for studying behavior change* (2nd ed.). New York: Pergamon.

Barnett, D. W. (1988). Professional judgment: A critical appraisal. *School Psychology Review, 17*(4), 658-672.

Brown, D., Pryzwansky, W. B., & Schulte, A. (1987). *Psychological consultation.* Boston: Allyn and Bacon.

Charlop, M., Parrish, J., Fenton, L., & Cataldo, M. (1987). Evaluation of hospital-based pediatric psychology services. *Journal of Pediatric Psychology, 12*, 485-503.

Claiborn, W. L., Stricker, G., & Bent, R. J. (Eds.). (1982). Peer review and quality assurance [Special issue]. *Professional Psychology, 13*(1).

Elliott, S. N., & Witt, J. C. (Eds.). (1986). *The delivery of psychological services in schools.* Hillsdale, NJ: Erlbaum.

Fagan, T. K. (1985). Cost effectiveness considerations in the delivery of school psychological services. *Rural Special Education Quarterly, 5*, 8-12.

Fagan, T. K. (1988). The historical improvement of the school psychology service ratio: Implications for future employment *School Psychology Review, 17*, 447-458.

Fairchild, T. N., & Zins, J. E. (1986). Accountability practices of school counselors: A national survey. *Journal of Counseling and Development, 65*, 196-199.

Fairchild, T. N., Zins, J. E., & Grimes, J. (1983). *Improving school psychology through accountability* (filmstrip and manual). Washington, DC: National Association of School Psychologists.

Grimes, J. (1983, February). *Improving school psychology through accountability.* Presentation at the Ohio Department of Education School Psychology Intern Conference, Columbus.

Grimes, J., & Ross-Reynolds, G. (1981). *Some thoughts on writing psychological interventions.* Unpublished manuscript, Iowa Department of Public Instruction.

Guthrie, P. (1982). *Survey of state consultants regarding accountability practices.* Unpublished report, Professional Standards and Employment Relations Committee, National Association of School Psychologists.

Howard, G. S. (1980). Response-shift bias: A problem in evaluating interventions with pre/post self-reports. *Evaluation Review, 4*, 93-106.

Kiresuk, T., & Lund, S. (1977). Goal attainment scaling: Research, evaluation, and utilization. In H. Schulberg & F. Baker (Eds.), *Program evaluation in the health fields* (Vol. 2, pp. 214-237). New York: Human Sciences.

Kiresuk, T., & Sherman, R. (1968). Goal attainment scaling: A general method for evaluating comprehensive community mental health programs. *Community Mental Health Journal, 4*, 443-453.

Kratochwill, T. R. (1982). Advances in behavioral assessment. In C. R. Reynolds & T. B. Gutkin (Eds.), *The handbook of school psychology* (pp. 314-350). New York: Wiley.

Illback, R. J., Zins, J. E., Maher, C. A., & Greenberg, R. (in press). An overview of principles and procedures of program planning and evaluation. In T. B. Gutkin & C. R. Reynolds (Eds.), *The handbook of school psychology* (2nd ed.). New York: Wiley.

Levant, R. F. (1987). The use of marketing techniques to facilitate acceptance of prevention programs: Case example. *Professional Psychology: Research and Practice, 18*, 640-642.

Maher, C. A., & Bennett, R. E. (1984). *Program planning and evaluation in special education.* Englewood Cliffs, NJ: Prentice-Hall.

Moore, C. M., & Carlson, D. L. (1988, April). *Accountability: Practices and issues.* Paper presented at the annual meeting of the National Association of School Psychologists, Chicago.

National Association of School Psychologists. (1984). *Standards for the provision of school psychological services.* Washington, DC: Author.

Sproul, L., & Larkey, P. (1979). Managerial behavior and evaluator effectiveness. In H. C. Schulberg & J. M. Jerrell (Eds.), *The evaluator and management* (pp. 89-104). Beverly Hills, CA: Sage.

Webster-Stratton, C. (1989). Systematic comparison of consumer satisfaction of three cost-effective parent training programs for conduct disordered children. *Behavior Therapy, 20*, 103-115.

Zins, J. E. (1981). Using data-based evaluation in developing school consultation services. In M. J. Curtis & J. E. Zins (Eds.), *The theory and practice of school consultation* (pp. 261-268). Springfield, IL: Thomas.

Zins, J. E. (1984). A scientific problem-solving approach to developing accountability systems for school psychologists. *Professional Psychology: Research and Practice, 15*, 56-66.

Zins, J. E. (1985). Best practices in accountability. In A. Thomas & J. Grimes (Eds.), *Best practices in school psychology* (pp. 493-503). Washington, DC: National Association of School Psychologists.

Zins, J. E., Curtis, M. J., Graden, J., & Ponti, C. R. (1988). *Helping students succeed in the regular classroom: A guide for developing intervention assistance programs.* San Francisco: Jossey-Bass.

Zins, J. E., & Fairchild, T. N. (1986). An investigation of the accountability practices of school psychologists. *Professional School Psychology, 1*(3), 193–204.

Zins, J. E., Grimes, J., Illback, R. J., Barnett, D. W., Ponti, C. R., McEvoy, M. L., & Wright, C. (1982). *Accountability for school psychologists: Developing trends.* Washington, DC: National Association of School Psychologists.

Zins, J. E., Ponti, C. R., & Murphy, J. J. (in press). Peer supervision for special services practitioners. *Special Services in the Schools.*

Zins, J. E., Wess, B. P., & Murphy, J. J. (1987, August). *Professional peer support groups: Current practices of school psychologists.* Paper presented at the annual meeting of the American Psychological Association, New York.

ANNOTATED BIBLIOGRAPHY

Barlow, D. H., Hayes, S. C., & Nelson, R. O. (1984). *The scientist practitioner: Research and accountability in clinical and educational settings.* Elmsford, NY: Pergamon.
Presents an excellent discussion of single-case methodology and describes the empirical means of obtaining objective data on treatment outcomes. Also included are precise descriptions of practical measures of behavior change that may be useful in schools.

Herman, J. L. (Ed.). (1988). *Program evaluation kit* (2nd ed.). Newbury Park, CA: Sage.
This nine-volume series presents a practical, detailed, step-by-step guide to conducting a program evaluation that takes the reader through the entire evaluation process from initial planning to program design to presentation. The evaluation process and a discussion of research design and statistics are presented in nontechnical language.

Illback, R. J., Zins, J. E., Maher, C. A., & Greenberg, R. (in press). An overview of principles and procedures of program planning and evaluation. In T. B. Gutkin & C. R. Reynolds (Eds.), *The handbook of school psychology* (2nd ed.). New York: Wiley.
Provides conceptual as well as practical discussions of principles and procedures of program planning and evaluation for school psychologists. The chapter emphasizes the relationship of planning and evaluation activities to organizational change, and also includes discussion of approaches to overcoming barriers and sources of resistance.

Maher, C. A., & Bennet, R. E. (1984). *Program planning and evaluation in special education.* Englewood Cliffs, NJ: Prentice-Hall.
This excellent book contains a comprehensive overview of how to evaluate a wide range of service programs for exceptional children. The practical methods and procedures described encourage a systematic, data-based approach to decision making for each program area. If you purchase only one book in this area, this should be it.

Zins, J. E., Fairchild, T. N., & Grimes, J. (1983). *Improving school psychology through accountability* (filmstrip and manual). Washington, DC: National Association of School Psychologists.
This multimedia package was developed to stimulate discussion about accountability and to provide direction for school psychologists regarding specific procedures. A resource booklet containing examples of accountability instruments is included. The materials are suitable for use in in-service training as well as for university classes.

23

Best Practices in Establishing an Independent Practice

Steven L. Rosenberg
Donald M. Wonderly
PSI Associates, Inc.

OVERVIEW

As an increasing number of school psychologists enter the private sector, the issue of independent practice — on either a full- or part-time basis — has become a topic of considerable debate. This change of focus has the potential for significantly expanding the role of school psychology, and enhancing the probability that practitioners may obtain enhanced status, as well as professional and financial rewards. Unfortunately, the possibility of serious legal, professional, ethical, and fiduciary problems is also associated with individual practice. Causes for the shift from the public sphere to private enterprise include the raising of educational standards for school psychological practice, modifications in state licensing laws, encouragement by professional organizations, and, most importantly, an increase in the number of situations calling for psychological intervention.

Many of these challenges present exciting opportunities. One of the most salient may be the opportunity for school psychologists to expand their professional role. Long attached only to conservative, publicly administered educational institutions, school psychologists have discovered that independent practice allows for professional role expansion far beyond what most school systems permit. Innovative programs, systemic interventions, and comprehensive psychological services can be part of an independent practice. Such opportunity allows for the provision of a service which should be at least as significant as traditional school-based models.

Service purchased from an independent practitioner represents a commodity obtained because it is desired rather than required. Such a shift from mandated programs (e.g., services received because of PL 94-142 regulations) to optional ones (e.g., services received because they are perceived by the consumer to be valuable) would be most significant to the field of school psychology. It would encourage members of the profession to function with more autonomy since they would be less dependent on institutional support. Expanding the role in this way could help school psychologists assume a status similar to that of older and more established disciplines, such as medicine and law.

The success of most commercial ventures depends in large part upon the skill and innovative talent of the operator. Unless very specific circumstances prevail, the provision of psychometric services only will rarely provide an adequate income. Such services are readily available from almost every independent practitioner and from virtually all schools at no charge. As every commercial enterprise operates within a competitive environment, few practitioners have the luxury to ignore such competitive forces. Successful entrepreneurs are most sensitive to these factors and continually modify their work product or delivery system to reflect — and to take advantage of – them.

Entry into independent practice demands skill and talent not usually called for in a public setting. Foremost among these is an entrepreneurial orientation. Would-be practitioners must be prepared to take full responsibility for their venture. They must be willing to risk considerable time and money. If the goal is the provision of a unique service, such psychologists must prepare to become business oriented. Either a new product, a new technique, or a new delivery system must be developed, or established methods and techniques must be applied to new populations. Entrepreneurship is more than simply starting another fee-for-service private practice. Such an approach is neither innovative nor experimental. In order for school psychology to expand and to stand on its own without the protection of an institutional umbrella, the principles of school psychology must be blended with essential elements of business practice. Finding new service and delivery models, as well as methods to reach the public in innovative ways, are the real challenges of independent practice.

A wide array of models that employ small business principles are available. The traditional fee-for-service approach, which is essentially a direct, face-to-face method of intervention, is perhaps the most common. It may be argued that issues of relevancy to other commercial operations (e.g., competition, marketing) do not apply to practitioners of the traditional fee-for-service approach. The widespread failure of these types of practice, however, should provide strong evidence that no independent practitioner is exempt from the forces which affect all businesses. Some psychologists may be more immune from these forces than others, but people who value their profession can not afford to ignore the basic considerations common to all commercial enterprises.

Other models have become popular during recent years, including contractual and consultancy paradigms. There are many varieties of each. Contractual services range from individual arrangements with schools or other institutions, to the provision of such services by a staff of school psychologists who are employed by "third party" agencies. Consultancies range from the provision of psychological services on an as-needed basis, to the presentation of workshops, seminars, and lectures on specific topics related to child development. Beyond these are forensic models (involving litigation, as in custody or parent care), vocational and employment evaluation models, and in some states, a medical model wherein the psychologist works with a hospital or similar public or private institution.

The prospect of an independent practice is obviously intriguing. "The positives are oh-so motivating. The entrepreneur answers only to himself. His income is limited only by his abilities and energies" (Pollan and Levine, 1989, p. 76). Furthermore, trendy offices and large incomes are often associated with psychologists working in private settings. Such idealistic images often overlook the many negative features of any independent business. Anxiety concerning financial and professional issues may cause stress that affects relationships with colleagues and family members. Long, unpredictable, and often uncompensated hours plague all business owners. The real or potential effects of financial loss can also be most damaging. These effects, combined with the loss of such benefits as health and life insurance, vacation allowances, personal leave time, and a regular paycheck, most of which are provided as benefits of institutional employment, can be discouraging.

BASIC CONSIDERATIONS

Financial Issues

School psychologists considering independent practice must be prepared to deal with a wide range of issues associated with the financial aspects of such activity. Consideration of fiduciary principles and factors may be anathema to practitioners who have worked only as publicly-employed school psychologists. Yet a host of financial issues must be squarely faced if an independent practice is to flourish. It is often assumed that all one needs to begin a practice is a professional license and a good supply of business cards. While these are necessary, they are far from sufficient if one intends to operate successfully. Cost/benefit analysis, capital preservation, overhead expenditure, hidden costs, and risk analysis are but a few of the initial issues to fully review and understand. If an independent practice utilizes a contractual model with the hiring of employees, the issues become even more complex. Payroll costs, benefit packages, legal and accounting fees, promotional and staff recruitment expenses all must be accounted for accurately. Such personnel issues as employee and client contracts, secretarial services and employment status must also be carefully reviewed.

Many school psychologists are hesitant to consider such economic concepts even in our free enterprise, open-market economy. To think of a return on investment is often viewed as somewhat distasteful and far from "professional." Regretfully, successful entrance into the world of independent practice demands a realistic view of the free enterprise system. The larger established professions have accepted the dual systems of public and private service without any implications of hierarchy. However, when a hierarchy is assumed, independent practitioners often hold higher status than do institutional providers. Within our own field, clinical and industrial psychologists working in private settings are considered the most prestigious members of the professional community.

Planning

A comprehensive business plan — preferably in written detail — must be established. The development of a plan provides an opportunity to formalize clearly and carefully what may have previously been merely a collection of amorphous aspirations. The business plan must be a rigorous description of how the new enterprise is to function and how it is to be supported.

A business plan should focus initially on anticipated income sources.

- Who shall be your clients (children, special clinical groups, schools, hospitals)?
- Why may your services be sought (convenience of location, professional reputation)?
- What credibility do your referral sources have?
- Do referral sources have a sufficient client base to satisfy your income requirements?
- Are potential clients in a position to afford your services?

Although professionals employ a wide range of marketing strategies, many commonalities exist across standard approaches. It is common, for example, to consider marketing in terms of four factors: Product, Promotion, Place, and Price (Drucker, 1985; American Psychological Association, 1986).

Product. What is the "product" of the service? Is the practitioner to be a generalist or a specialist? Many factors will have an impact on this decision. Professional expertise must, of course, be a paramount consideration. Furthermore, a comprehensive study of the competitive environment should yield valuable data. The psychologist must research which services are available and at what cost, which are not available, and what needs remain unmet within the community to be served. The service offered must be fully and carefully developed. While the service must be sufficiently adjustable to meet a fluctuating demand (remaining within areas of expertise), the specific service provided must be clearly defined in the over all plan.

All business persons must remain current regarding new trends, strategies, and legislation that may have an impact on their service. Legislation mandating the provision of service to handicapped preschoolers, for example, represents an area which will affect many school psychologists regardless of their work setting.

Promotion. After the service to be provided is clearly defined, methods of promotion must be considered. How will the appropriate sectors of the public learn of the availability of the service? What referral sources are to be targeted? Loavenbrook (1980) mentioned the following:

- physicians
- dentists
- social service agencies
- school nurses
- lawyers
- insurance companies
- nursery schools
- unions
- school teachers

We would add drug treatment facilities, juvenile justice programs, and school-based psychologists.

How can referral sources be approached most productively? Mass mailings are usually ineffective since they are often discarded with little or no consideration. Personalized letters with follow-up phone calls may have more impact. Notices in the *Yellow Pages Directory* beyond the obligatory name and phone number should be carefully considered due to the cost involved. As the number of providers listed in the *Yellow Pages* has proliferated, the expense involved in this form of advertisement may not be commensurate with the resulting yield, especially for new and fragile businesses. Meetings with the appropriate administrators of agencies serving the targeted clientele are apt to be more effective.

Association with large health care providers can also be of great benefit. As insurance reimbursements become more difficult to obtain, the psychologist who is able to contract with a hospital or health maintenance organization is likely to be better secured than others. The importance of an alignment with physicians, however, cannot be overstated. Internists, pediatricians, allergists, neurologists, and family practitioners can be a reliable and constant source of referrals. Building a personal relationship with the physician is a necessary ingredient. The psychologist's own physician may represent the best entry point into the medical establishment. Personal letters to others with

follow-up phone calls can be effective. In the final analysis, as with all referral sources, the key is to provide high quality and efficient service which meets the needs of both the client and the referring professional.

Psychologists who are intent on building reputations as competent independent practitioners must find ways to increase their exposure to the public. Well-prepared presentations on topics within one's areas of expertise are low-cost but potentially highly productive methods of gaining appropriate recognition. Presentations to local schools, churches, and other public service groups can be easily arranged. Local radio and television (e.g., cable) stations are often looking for articulate and knowledgeable guests. Hospital and philanthropic associations (e.g., Kiwanis and Lion's Club) often have speakers' bureaus that may be receptive to presentations concerning child development and education.

Sophisticated marketing (or promotion) is more than informing the public or referral sources that a service is available. It also entails an analysis of the barriers that may preclude success. Why are targeted physicians, for example, not referring patients? Why do referred clients not call for an appointment? The practitioner must determine the causes for the resistance and formulate ways to overcome it. Resistance to referral may be due to a wide range of causes:

- Do sources of referral understand the services that are to be provided? Was the medium (telephone, brochures, letters) used to inform them effective?
- Is the provider a trusted and well regarded practitioner?
- Are referral patterns so established that targeted sources believe there is no reason to change providers?
- Do costs or geographic factors contribute to the low utilization of the service?

Place. The physical location of the service can be of crucial importance. In many urban centers, professionals gather in certain geographic sections — perhaps leaving other areas inadequately served. With the proper research, the would-be practitioner can determine the geographic regions that may reap the best results. While status and convenience may be sacrificed, the benefits of success should outweigh the disadvantages.

Price. The prevalence of third party insurance minimizes the importance of price to those engaged in a traditional fee-for-service approach. However, in less conventional types of independent practice (e.g., contractual models), the price of the service can be a critical factor. Costs incurred and the revenue needed to continue in operation are vital considerations. One must decide if it is wiser to keep the price of the service low (presumably to limit competition), or to charge a larger fee on the premise that consumers believe that high cost reflects quality. (It is easier to raise the price of a service than to lower it!) The volume of work available also influences price factors. The greater the volume of work, the lower the price can drop without undue hardship.

Fees. The collection of fees is a delicate but obviously essential element. If a viable method of fee collection is not established, all previous efforts — no matter how competent and comprehensive — will be for naught.

Best practices require that the practitioner insure that clients are fully informed of all fees associated with services before they are delivered. Acceptable methods of payment should be discussed so that neither the psychologist nor the client is surprised.

A variety of decisions concerning fees must be made. Should the client be charged by the session, hour, or by the service provided (e.g., separate charges for each test administered)? If the hourly option is selected, how will time provided beyond 60 minutes be billed? Will the client be charged for each fraction of the next hour? Many clinicians assess fees for each fraction of an hour consumed. This is, however, a sensitive issue. Its possible ramifications include increased short-term revenue at the cost of dissatisfied clients.

Another decision concerns the extent of pro bono work that will be provided.

Which clients will be seen and what kind of service will be offered without charge? More delicate is the decision to terminate treatment of clients who do not pay for services rendered. What is the clinician's responsibility to these clients? Should they be transferred to a social agency? Should service be continued without payment for those clients who are especially disturbed? Each clinician must answer these difficult questions to his or her own satisfaction.

Certain types of service run the risk of non-payment more than others. By definition, half the clients undergoing custodial evaluation, for example, will be disappointed with the clinician's recommendations. Psychologists are often unable to collect all the fees charged in such cases. Therefore, it is becoming increasingly common to collect either a retainer for services to be rendered (Gardner, 1982, p. 55) prior to the implementation of custodial evaluations, or withhold release of the report until all accounts are settled. Such actions may seem distasteful. Yet, any clinician who is providing a fee for service model must come to terms with these financial considerations.

Those clinicians who are eligible to collect insurance payments — a criterion that varies from state to state — must be very careful to follow insurance procedures correctly. Familiarity with the latest version of the *Diagnostic and Statistical Manual* is essential if accurate diagnostic categories are to be reported. If the clinician is unsure in billing methods, it is appropriate to contact the insurance carrier directly and candidly ask the necessary questions. It is more efficient to require full payment by the client, and to provide them with a "superbill" to submit to the insurance company. The client is then paid directly by the carrier, thus eliminating the clinician's risk of refusal of payment by the insurance company.

Uncollected fees can be an independent practitioner's nemesis. While some psychologists resort to Small Claims Court or to the services of collection agencies, such actions can have serious repercussions with referral sources. In fact, it is

344

...inicians to accept ...der to keep referral

...greatest factor affecting ...ny service is simply the cost ...siness. In psychological ven- tu... ...n other commercial enterprises, indivi... ...als often minimize expected costs and overestimate anticipated revenue. A thorough and realistic list of projected costs is an important component of any business plan. Costs can usually be divided between fixed and variable expenses. These will vary widely depending upon the model of independent practice elected. Examples of costs which are typically considered fixed are as follows:

- *Payroll Taxes:* Programs with em- ployees must pay a wide range of taxes. These include Social Security taxes, Workers' Compensation, state and federal unemployment insurance, and local, state, and federal income tax. It is most important to receive the advice of a competent accountant to under- stand fully the importance and costs of these assessments. Self-employed psychologists (especially those on a full- time basis) must also be fully conver- sant with Workers' Compensation and unemployment coverage, particularly if they choose not to contribute to these funds.

- *Rent:* The office lease may be the single most expensive cost of doing business, especially for a fledgling practice. No lease should be signed without the advice of a competent attorney. Know the rights of the lessee and the lessor (e.g., can the lessee sublet?). Under- stand how (and if) the lease may be broken. Be aware of the total cost of the lease (to consider its impact upon your financial resources should the worst scenario occur). New businesses are usually better served with short leases. Rather than open a new office, the practitioner may wish to join an ongoing practice, to open an office only several evenings a week, or to utilize an "incubator" office, paying only for the hours used.

- *Utilities:* Unless included with each lease payment, be aware of all utility charges that will be assessed. Ask to see receipts of a fair representation of past utility bills before executing the lease contract.

- *Telephone:* The costs of telephone service and *Yellow Pages Directory* listings are often minimized. Yet these services can be very expensive. Tele- phone companies are usually willing to help in the estimation of expected costs.

- *Consultants:* While the need for ac- counting and legal assistance will vary depending upon the independent prac- tice model chosen and on the size of the operation, all practitioners will require the services of these consul- tants. Tax and liability issues must be taken into account. Should the practice be organized as a sole proprietorship, a partnership, a general (C) corpora- tion, or a subchapter (S) corporation? Organizing oneself appropriately at the start can help to avoid legal and financial difficulties. Careful planning may also help to avoid undue financial burdens (e.g., taxes, capitalization).

- *Insurance:* A knowledgeable and com- petent agent should be consulted regarding insurance needs. It is just as easy to purchase too much insurance as it is to purchase too little. Most practitioners do not need the highest categories of coverage. The cost of an insurance plan, as well as information regarding exactly what the policy covers, must be clearly understood. At least general liability, professional liability, fire and theft insurance should be considered. The practitioner may also wish to consider business interrup- tion and disability insurance, although the need for these policies may be less critical than first thought.

- *Professional Membership:* Membership in professional associations provides a wide range of benefits, including the opportunity to be kept aware of new knowledge, and of remaining in contact with fellow professionals. The cost of such memberships should be included in the estimated budget.

- *Salaries:* The real cost of any employee (staff psychologists, secretaries, janitors) must be carefully estimated in advance. Such calculations must include payroll taxes and benefit programs. Consultation with a well-trained accountant is invaluable in this regard.

- *Health and Life Insurance:* This can be a very expensive commodity, especially if employees are involved in the enterprise. Check with a variety of providers (private and public carriers, health organizations, etc.) to determine the most appropriate instruments. Insurance policies offered by professional associations are usually the least expensive. Government regulations regarding equal protection for classes of employees must also be followed.

- *Retirement:* Unlike publicly-employed school psychologists, independent practitioners do not automatically receive retirement benefits. The cost of any such program (e.g., 401(k), Keogh) must be included in the business plan. Consultation with well-trained actuaries can help in accurately predicting the cost of installing and maintaining a retirement program.

- *Postage:* It is most important to estimate postage costs in advance. Start-up expenses, such as mailing marketing brochures will probably differ from the routine costs, depending upon the marketing activities utilized. However, any active business makes a surprisingly heavy use of the postal service.

- *Printing:* Almost all practices will have printing expenses. Most of these costs, such as that for marketing brochures, can be predicted, since they will be a function of the marketing strategy outlined in the Business Plan. Several printers should be contacted in order to compare costs, as well as to ascertain the printer's interest in helping to design the material.

- *Travel:* While some travel is probably necessary, it should represent a relatively small cost. Unless the delivery model is unusually complicated, travel expenses should be minimal. (Be aware that government regulations dictate travel allowances for both owners and employees.)

- *Interest:* The time value of the money involved in most independent practices may be small, but it is rarely inconsequential. Consult a banker or accountant to determine the best approach to financing your business. This is somewhat complicated if the practice has a regular payroll. Interest charges assessed may be significant and must be considered. These calculations should include a factor for late or absent payments. Few businesses are fortunate enough to collect all the funds owed. Independent professional practices are notorious for failing to collect assessed fees.

- *Furniture and Equipment:* The wise entrepreneur will only incur costs which are essential until the enterprise is secure. Using one's own home as an office and utilizing an answering and secretarial service during the early years may save enough capital to consolidate and expand the practice, helping to secure its future. Powerful computers and expensive software programs may not be necessary for young practices. One way to minimize the costs is to purchase second hand items such as copy machines, computers, and office desks. Specialists who broker second-hand equipment (including telephones) can offer significant savings.

- *Office Supplies:* Consultation with more established colleagues may help in ascertaining the types of office supplies that are necessary. Of course, this will depend largely upon the type of enterprise that has been chosen. These should be carefully purchased on an as needed basis only. Most office supply stores will offer a discount to business customers.

A wide variety of other costs will fluctuate periodically depending upon the model employed and the program's size. Many of these costs, however, are standard and can be predicted with reasonable accuracy.

Because of the common practice of underestimating the costs associated with a new business and to overestimate the anticipated cash flow, sufficient capital should be maintained to keep the enterprise afloat as long as such commitments as leases and employee contracts exist. Research, consultants, and careful planning will help keep these important estimates accurate. A worst-case scenario must be formulated in the event that revenues do not match expectations.

The Federal government provides opportunities to new and small businesses through the letting of contracts and grants. The Small Business Innovation Research program, for example, offers funding in a number of areas of interest to mental health specialists. These programs are designed specifically for new and small businesses. In fact, some grants can be obtained by companies that have yet to begin operation. Such arrangements may make it possible to start a commercial enterprise with a minimum of risk and capital outlay.

Independent practitioners must be prepared to blend the world of applied school psychology with financial and business considerations. Unfortunately, a business orientation may conflict with altruistic values (e.g., how many clients can be seen who are unable to afford the service?). Yet, these issues must be confronted if a successful venture is to be realized. A wide range of legal and financial consultants are available to assist. Their help notwithstanding, it is imperative that the practitioner be prepared to cope with an entirely new set of demands. With the appropriate preparation, the combination of financial and professional skills is a powerful asset.

BEST PRACTICES

It is critical that independent practitioners possess appropriate credentials in the form of educational background and experience. Graduation from a 1-year,

60-hour graduate program, with a year or two of experience, is by no means sufficient. In many states, doctoral level programs are available, and in some states a school psychologist with M.A. level training may be licensed after meeting fairly rigorous requirements. In no instance is independent practice appropriate either without a license, or when practicing under inadequate supervision. Unless only a psychometric function is being provided, one must be well-trained in personality assessment, counseling, theoretical foundations, and the practical implications of major psychological positions. Sufficient experience under qualified supervision is of the greatest importance. As rules and regulations vary widely from state to state, those considering a private practice should obtain and become familiar with the laws and procedures of the appropriate governing body.

Independent practice may allow for a greater utilization of professional skills and talents than traditional school-based programs. Role diversity is largely a function of the particular model chosen and the background and experience of the psychologist. Individual counseling; consultation with family members, teachers, and administrators; staff development; assessment; group counseling; and primary preventive programming can be integral aspects of an appropriately designed independent practice.

Most school-based psychologists are prepared to offer their client schools more services than are normally rendered. Time limitations, budgetary constraints, district policies, and government regulations all combine to restrict activities. An independent practice is not so bound. The only criterion is that the services be offered within appropriate boundaries of propriety and perceived as worthy of purchase. Consumers may be individuals or agencies such as school districts, health organizations, preschool programs, or various government agencies. Independent practice, therefore, can provide the opportunity to develop and implement a wide range of alternative programs.

In addition to consulting books and periodicals concerning independent practice, information and support are available from several divisions of the American Psychological Association. Most notable is Division 42; Psychologists in Independent Practice. Their meetings and periodicals can be very useful.

Professional Issues

Ethical issues are obviously of prime importance. As many psychologists in private practice also work in school settings, there are innumerable opportunities for the misuse of publicly held positions. Appropriate use of school owned equipment, recognition of school priorities, and many other factors, some — but not all — of which are spelled out in licensing board, NASP, and APA documents, must be taken into account. Unless extremely unusual circumstances prevail, it is unethical for psychologists to refer clients from their school system to their own independent practice, since school psychological services are provided without cost by most public as well as non-public schools. It is similarly inappropriate for private practitioners to refer clients to colleagues who make reciprocal referrals. At best, such activities represent a misuse of the public's trust; at worst, a collusive and deceitful practice. While such referrals may not be intended to be exploitative, the appearance of impropriety can be as damaging as substantive abuse.

One situation arises toward the end of each school year when special children seem to be in need of continuous care and may, in fact, be best served if they receive psychological service throughout the summer. While such actions may be based on the noblest of intentions, and while they may be in the best interest of the children served, the practice is subject to so much potential abuse that it is wiser to refer such cases to other psychologists.

In some circumstances, when no other psychologist is available (e.g., in a small rural "one psychologist" town, or where the psychologist has special linguistic or other pertinent skills), such arrangements may be appropriate. In these instances, signed permission forms, a letter to the state ethics board explaining the circumstances, and/or other form of clarification represent minimum safeguards. It is at best, however, a dubious practice, and in some states may be considered a specific rule violation. Publicly-employed school psychologists working part-time as independent practitioners must be especially careful in these regards.

Independent practitioners are more apt to see clients outside their areas of expertise than are publicly employed school psychologists. Therefore, each case must be carefully screened to ensure that it falls within appropriate areas of competence. Those cases that do not should be referred to other professionals. In addition, the independent practitioner of school psychology must always be certain that the reason for treatment stems from problems associated with the client. Treatment of adults under the guise of treating their childrens' school-related difficulties compromises the profession as well as the ethical integrity of the practitioner.

Any procedure delivered on a fairly routine basis risks the loss of individualization. The administration of the WISC-R, the Bender-Gestalt, Woodcock-Johnson, etc., cannot be justified in all cases. Not every child needs to be administered a thorough battery of instruments regardless of the nature of the problem being treated. Tests, as well as counseling techniques, should be geared toward the idiosyncratic needs of each individual. Furthermore, ipsative, as well as normative, interpretations of standardized instruments should be considered. Although the private practitioner may have to put a child through many seemingly repetitive tests where some question is raised about the validity of an earlier interpretation, caution must be taken that a "test mill" is not created.

Independent practice affords the psychologist the opportunity to provide services beyond the traditional psychometric approach (PSI Associates, Inc., 1989). Programs can be developed and implemented that closely conform to the needs of the population served. The extent of these programs is limited only by the skill, innovation, and initiative of the provider.

Private practitioners working in school settings, for example, can, in many instances, offer a wide range of group counseling programs that directly address common childhood problems. Counseling groups for children of divorced (or divorcing) parents can help children cope more effectively, resulting in improved school performance. Programs for the identification, treatment, and follow-up of chemically dependent students can be developed. Study skills modules (Wonderly, 1985) can help low achievers approach their academic work more effectively. Counseling groups designed to improve self-esteem and encourage appropriate behavior can also provide high impact programs. Support groups for children suffering from the separation or death of a parent, programs designed to provide opportunities for withdrawn children to contribute more meaningfully (e.g., working on a school newspaper), and coordinating peer counseling and tutoring programs for appropriately screened children represent examples of valuable services the psychologist in private practice can provide.

The private practitioner serving as a consultant can also be involved in many primary prevention programs. Conducting inservice and systems analysis functions can help school systems operate more efficiently. Parent education classes and programs that foster community involvement help schools garner the support of their constituents. These functions, described elsewhere (Wonderly, 1984), represent opportunities not always available to school-based colleagues because of factors such as time and budgetary constraints.

The proliferation of employee assistance programs (EAPs) provides another opportunity for psychological services. EAPs are vehicles through which employees may be assisted in dealing with personal problems under the auspices of their employer. About 30% of those cases identified by in-house services are referred to outside clinicians for follow-up.

Traditional (clinical) model. Private practitioners must avoid a number of potential problems. There is always a temptation for psychologists to represent themselves as "hired guns" in litigation cases and to use in-school opportunities as a source of clients. Where such services include consultancies, as in pre-employment evaluations, the training level and background experience of the school psychologist must be clearly evident. The independent practitioner must also guard against producing questionable findings for clients who wish, for example, to challenge the results of a school assessment. Since there is considerable room for disagreement regarding test interpretation, professionals in public or private practice should pursue disputed issues diligently. All pertinent data should, of course, be examined before a decision is reached. *To ignore data collected by school-based professionals is itself an unethical practice.*

The presentation of credentials to the public is a vital ethical factor. Inaccurate advertisement, ambiguous presentation of credentials (e.g., implying that the individual holds a general license rather than school psychology certification), and delivering services outside areas of expertise, represent issues to which all independent practitioners must be sensitive.

The private practitioner's tasks are occasionally unusual and exceptionally complicated. Independent practitioners are, therefore, more vulnerable to attack by innuendo and accusation than their school-based colleagues. Rules of confidentiality and the lack of an appropriate forum prevent private practitioners from explaining the rationale for many of their procedures. It is essential, therefore, that great effort be expended to ensure that ethical guidelines are adhered to in substance as well as in form. Only in this way can private practicing school psychologists come to be positively regarded and their work properly valued. A practice guided by respect for professional regulations should increase the opportunity for success as well.

Contractual models. Contractual models are of essentially two types. One emphasizes the provision of services on an as-needed basis, often of the hit-and-run variety. The other represents a comprehensive program — an arrangement by which a third party agency provides psychological personnel to schools and other institutions on a daily, weekly, or other regular basis. In school settings such a program may duplicate that of board-hired psychologists quite precisely. Unless special circumstances prevail, the "test and tell" model is often less desirable as it does not provide for appropriate follow-up and treatment options. In both situations, however, the independent practice model is attractive where an institution prefers the autonomy that such an approach provides. Regardless of the type of model employed, certain factors should be carefully considered:

- *Supervision:* If staff members are not licensed to practice privately, adequate supervision must be provided. While legal requirements vary widely from state to state, supervisory arrangements must be made to ensure that adequate training and experiential opportunities are available to provide competent treatment. This training function may include course work, participation in appropriate practical situations, and frequent case review meetings.

- *Support staff:* Because of the relative lack of immediate professional support systems, employees of a contract agency should have available to them such specialists as nurses, speech pathologists, physicians, and other qualified professionals. Independent practice arrangements do not preclude standard special education guidelines and procedures (e.g., multifactored evaluation). In fact, it is of vital importance to adhere to all policies, rules, and laws. The independent practitioner must make every effort to be part of the multifactored team, drawing upon the skills and expertise of all concerned.

- *Competitive benefits:* Since many school systems provide extensive benefit packages, contract agencies must strive to offer as many benefits as possible. Retirement plans, sick leave, personal days, health insurance programs, bonus opportunities, and support for professional development must be part of any comprehensive package. Only in this way can contract firms maintain the high quality staff necessary to perform satisfactorily.

- *Adequate accounting practices:* To protect employees from possible legal difficulties, employers should agree to handle all tax and related fiscal issues, such as Unemployment Compensation, Workers' Compensation, FICA, state and city withholding tax, etc. Employees should be kept aware of their employment status and be protected with properly drawn contracts. Both the public and the provider are best protected when the provider is hired by the contracting agency as an employee rather than as an independent contractor. Clients are better protected since the provider who acts as an employee functions under the direction and with the support of the employer. The employee is also better protected as Federal regulations are very specific about the type of work that qualifies individuals to operate as independent contractors. Furthermore, as an employee, the school psychologist receives far more benefits and services (and pays less Social Security tax) than independent contractors who receive no "extras" (e.g., Workers' Compensation, Unemployment Insurance) beyond their fees.

- *Autonomy:* Every effort should be made to assure appropriately qualified employees the opportunity to practice as free of professional constraint as possible. Yet it is the agency's obligation to monitor all practices it provides to ensure client protection and the responsible implementation of standard psychological practice.

• *Accountability:* An employer may well be considered to bear legal and ethical responsibility for the performance of its psychological staff. While it is obviously impossible to monitor every act of every employee, attorneys may attack the employer as the responsible party in any litigation on the principle of the "deepest pocket." For this reason, the parent organization should have a sufficient number of supervisory personnel to provide a continuing monitoring of the performance of its professional staff.

A wide array of other factors will have an impact on independent practitioners regardless of the model employed. Limiting liability is, of course, a primary consideration. In addition to holding adequate insurance coverage, all practitioners should be aware of the signals that may indicate which potential clients are apt to be litigious — clients who do not have (or utilize) health insurance, short-term clients, clients who express undue concern regarding fees, service "shoppers," and individuals who profess to know about particular techniques and insist on receiving those services. In such cases a determination must be made regarding whether the service is needed, and if it can be offered at minimum risk to both the client and the psychologist.

A clear explanation of expected costs and of the service to be provided (including expected outcome) may help to reduce the probability of client unhappiness and any eventual litigation. Clearly documented records are essential. Practitioners must adhere to all rules and regulations regarding the management of records, always following established procedures for the release and gathering of information. Scrutinizing the content of each psychological report (for accuracy, propriety, and limited legal exposure) will also help reduce potential problem areas.

SUMMARY

There are many reasons for considering independent practice. Potential financial reward, image enhancement, freedom from the constraints of public service, and the desire to broaden the scope of one's professional activities are among the most common. For each advantage there are risks, both of a financial and professional nature. Hard-earned capital can be quickly lost. Reputations built upon years of public service can be damaged. The clinical problems associated with independent practice can be quite different than those faced by publicly-employed school psychologists. A clear understanding of professional and legal rules and a specific professional focus can help practitioners minimize risks and best serve their clients.

Entering the field of independent practice calls for careful attention to many factors that are not encountered in the public sector. Before embarking on such a practice, it behooves the individual to study all issues involved and to recognize the difference between minimal performance and adherence to the best practices available. Competency dictates a full review of all available options before making commitments which may have far reaching implications. The acquisition of appropriate training and supervised experience, as well as the willingness to limit one's practice to those areas which are clearly appropriate, are essential. In some instances, practice models are so new that appropriate procedures have yet to be established. However, legal and ethical regulations are as binding as they are on those employed in public institutions.

Many school-based psychologists are unfamiliar with issues facing private entrepreneurs. These factors can provide exciting rewards and devastating failures. Considering the high rate of business failure, the importance of financial planning and business knowledge cannot be overemphasized. Over 40% of all new commercial enterprises fail within their first 3 years. Another 40% of those that survive the first few years fail between the 4th and 10th year of operation. Even well-established enterprises falter. (At least 20% of those in business for more than 10 years fail.)

Anyone who wishes to depend on more than good fortune to be successful is well advised to develop a thorough business plan before engaging in practice. Business considerations, financial principles, available resources, and a wide variety of competitive factors must be fully evaluated. Unless practitioners are familiar with these important considerations, they are entering a potentially glamorous, but dangerous arena. Financial resources, reputation, and time are all jeopardized. Consultation with established colleagues, familiarity with pertinent professional and financial literature, and plans which limit legal and financial exposure are among the methods that may increase the probability of developing a successful independent practice.

REFERENCES

American Psychological Association. (1986). *Marketing psychological services: A practitioner's guide.* Washington, DC: Author.

Drucker, P. F. (1985). *Innovation and entrepreneurship: Practice and principles.* New York: Harper and Row.

Gardner, R. (1982). Family evaluation in client custody litigation. *Creative Therapeutics.* Cresskill, NJ.

Loavenbrook, A. (1980). Marketing strategies from an audiological perspective. In K. G. Butler (Ed.), *Prospering in private practice: A handbook for speech-language pathology and audiology* (pp. 223-236). Rockville, MD: Aspen.

Pollan, S., & Levine, M. (1989, January). The small business guide to survival and growth. *The Atlantic,* 75-103.

PSI Associates, Inc. (1989). *Psychological Services Handbook.* Twinsburg, OH: Author.

Wonderly, D. M., & Mcloughlin, C. S. (1984). Contractual services. A viable alternative? *School Psychology International, 5,* 107-114.

Wonderly, E. (1985). *Effects of study skills on school attitude, academic aptitude, and listening skills of third grade students.* Unpublished doctoral dissertation, Kent State University, Kent, Ohio.

ANNOTATED BIBLIOGRAPHY

Bernay, T. (1983). Making a practice: Overcoming passivity and masochism. *Psychotherapy in Private Practice, 1*(1), 25-29.
The author utilized results of a survey of membership of the Division of Clinical and Professional Psychology of the California State Psychological Association regarding the current state of their professional practice. She describes setting up her own practice and integrating personal satisfaction with success.

Cantor, D. W. (1983). Independent practice: Minding your own business. *Psychotherapy in Private Practice, 1*(1), 19-24.
Anyone who decides to enter private practice and wants to do it successfully has to be able to integrate the self-image of an entrepreneur as both acceptable and ego-gratifying. This article deals with the results of a study of psychological masculinity and femininity and its relationship to striving and self-concept in achievement and interpersonal domains. Few sex differences emerged. Only with respect to subject's expected and ideal financial responsibility were there marked overall gender differences.

Hochhauser, M. (1984). Marketing for the psychologist in independent practice. *Psychotherapy in Private Practice, 2*(2), 61-74.
This paper focuses on the issue of how psychologists in independent practice can use fundamental marketing strategies to compete successfully with other professional groups. Basic marketing concepts are explained, and their applicability to independent practice are discussed. Both the psychology of selling and the selling of psychology are explored.

Psychotherapy Finances. (1988). P.O.B. 509, Ridgewood, NJ 05450.
This newsletter is a convenient (if somewhat brash) resource for practitioners. It provides current information on such topics as insurance and legislative changes, marketing strategies, methods to broaden ongoing practices, etc.

Tryon, G. S. (1983). Full-time private practice in the United States: Results of a national survey. *Professional Psychology: Research and Practice, 14*(5), 685-696.
The results obtained from a 34-item questionnaire sent to 300 practitioners across the nation. The questionnaires yielded a wealth of information concerning practitioners' professional backgrounds and orientation, financial arrangements organizational structure, and involvement in professional activities.

24

Best Practices in Evaluating Educational Programs

Scott R. McConnell
University of Minnesota

OVERVIEW

Consider three situations in which school psychologists might be asked to conduct evaluations of educational programs:

- Alexandro, a third-grade special education student, has been moved into a reading group in his regular education classroom. His parents want to know if he is making better progress now, compared with his previous performance during resource instruction.

- Ms. Johnson, a seventh-grade English teacher, is trying to decide if her students would benefit from a peer-tutoring approach to vocabulary instruction.

- Dr. Williams, a principal of a local elementary school, wants to know if a new mathematics curriculum will improve average student achievement in her school.

In cases such as all three of the above, and in many other instances, school psychologists may be asked to design and implement the evaluation of an educational program. While evaluation activities may not be typical for many psychologists practicing in the schools today, the competencies required for these tasks are well known to many in our profession. The purpose of this chapter is to describe the basic elements of educational evaluation and how school psychologists may be involved in this process.

For the purpose of this chapter, educational evaluation is defined as the systematic appraisal of one or more academic interventions, the goal being to assess the effects of intervention for an individual or a group of students. While academic interventions are the primary interest here, evaluations may include information on academic achievement, student and teacher behavior, cost, or social judgments of quality of outcomes.

Educational evaluation is quite similar to, and shares many methods with, school-based research. In both instances, investigators and their audiences are interested in careful assessment of the effects of intervention and in the comparison of these intervention effects with some standard. The major difference is that whereas research activities address issues of broad generality and importance, evaluation is more specifically directed at providing information about a single program or groups of students. Rather than generalizing to all students or programs of a certain type, evaluation activities give school psychologists and others specific information about effects of a *single* intervention for a *single* student or group. (Readers interested in more detail on school-based research are referred to T. Keith's chapter elsewhere in this volume.)

BACKGROUND INFORMATION

The 1980s witnessed a dramatic increase in attention provided to educational evaluation, and this trend is likely to continue into the 1990s. Public and professional audiences are increasingly concerned about the overall effectiveness of education in the United States: Parents want to know if schools are teaching essential skills to their children and if their school is doing as well as schools in other neighborhoods, states, or countries. School boards and legislators want to know if educational funds are being well spent and whether increased expenditures are justified. Administrators and teachers want to know if their programs are achieving the intended results and if these results can be demonstrated to parents and policy makers.

Similar attention is being directed to the effectiveness of special educational practices, both for individuals and for groups of students with handicaps. Although Public Law 94-142 and its associated amendments and regulations do not create explicit standards for demonstrating effectiveness, these laws and regulations have at least indirectly increased the need for educators to document the effects of special educational interventions. On the individual level, parents often want to know if the objectives on their child's individual education program (IEP) are being achieved and if their child is making progress relative to his or her age-mates. Similarly, parents, advocates, and courts often want to know if children are making adequate progress to justify placement in either specialized or restrictive placement settings.

At the same time, there has been an expansion in methodology and techniques that make evaluation easier to conduct. A variety of single-case or small-group designs have been developed in recent years that allow for direct comparison of two or more treatments without need for statistical analysis. Furthermore, a number of new measurement tools are now available that directly contribute to the evaluation of educational programs. Finally, rapid development of microcomputer technologies has increased the access many individuals now have to sophisticated data management and analysis programs.

School psychologists may be in a unique position to respond to this growing interest in documenting the effectiveness of educational programs. As will be seen, school psychologists have training in many, if not all, of the areas necessary to conduct most educational evaluations. Additionally, school psychologists have access to, and are available to, the building-level staff who will most often identify specific needs for evaluation studies. Finally, educational evaluation fits nicely with many school psychologists' interests in expanding their own professional roles and accounting for the outcome of alternative service delivery systems.

This chapter will provide specific attention to five steps for completing an educational evaluation: (a) specifying the evaluation question, (b) seeking an evaluation design, (c) collecting evaluation data, (d) analyzing evaluation data, and (e) reporting evaluation results.

BASIC CONSIDERATIONS

Educational evaluation requires four major sets of skills. First a design must be selected or developed for the question under consideration. This requires some working knowledge of research and evaluation design, and of the best tenets of quasi-experimental and experimental methods. Second, evaluation requires an assessment procedure that describes critical aspects of student (and perhaps teacher) performance. This requires not only an awareness of tests and measures already available through commercial publication or other sources, but also the expertise to develop new measures should this be necessary. Third, evaluation requires that data be collected in standardized, reliable ways. Here, experience in direct assessment and supervision of others conducting testing (as well as the demands of scoring, storing, and aggregating data) is especially relevant. Finally, educational evaluation requires that results be analyzed and interpreted in ways that will be meaningful to a wide variety of audiences. Prior experience in providing cogent, easy-to-comprehend summaries of complex findings can certainly be helpful here.

In most school districts, school psychologists are the only building-level professionals who have training and experience in each of these areas. Developing expertise in the selection, administration, and interpretation of assessment devices is central to all school psychology training programs, and it is generally a continuing part of most psychologists' work. Also most school psychology training programs require a basic sequence in experimental design and statistics. Although this may not be a competency that is used frequently after training, the amount of training that school psychologists receive in this area far surpasses that of other professionals in most school buildings. Finally, through both training and work experience most school psychologists develop special skills at describing complex assessment results in easy-to-understand ways.

It would appear, then, that many school psychologists have competencies in all areas required for educational evaluation, and that few of their professional colleagues in local buildings would likely have similar skills. While it certainly may be necessary to brush up on specific skills in each of these domains, school psychologists may be uniquely qualified to coordinate educational evaluations, especially those initiated and conducted at the building level.

BEST PRACTICES

Levels of Evaluation

Evaluation of educational programs can be conducted at two different levels, each of which corresponds roughly to a different overall purpose. *Formative evaluation* guides or shapes an ongoing intervention, and is characterized by concurrent evaluation and intervention efforts. Formative evaluation is most typically conducted when one is interested in program development and is useful when teachers or others are interested in developing interventions that produce maximum effects possible.

By contrast, *summative evaluation* offers an overall appraisal of the effects of intervention, and usually is characterized by assessment conducted after (or near the end of) intervention. Summative evaluation is conducted when one is interested in assessing program outcomes; it is one means of determining whether a program produced desired effects or exceeded some criterion standard.

Both formative and summative evaluation can be conducted with individual students or group of students. Formative evaluation is often used with individual students to guarantee that current instructional programs are producing optimal educational gains (Deno, 1986); it may be used with groups of students when an investigator is interested in developing a new program (such as the peer-tutoring approach to vocabulary instruction) that is maximally effective for all individuals in a class (Barlow & Hersen, 1984). Summative evaluations, on the other hand, are used with individuals when one is interested in assessing performance after some long period in intervention; and group summative evaluations are the mainstay of many non-experimental and quasi-experimental evaluation designs that assess overall outcomes of a single program or compare outcomes of two or more intervention approaches (Keith, 1988).

While formative and summative evaluation differ, to some extent, in their basic assumptions and the types of procedures employed, each approach follows the same basic steps to completion: specification of an evaluation question, selection of an evaluation design, selection of assessment procedures, data collection, data analysis, and reporting of results. These basic steps are described next, with specific information provided for both formative and summative approaches to the evaluation task.

Specifying the Evaluation Question

The first, and perhaps most often overlooked, step in evaluating an educational program is to carefully specify what information will be sought and what questions will be answered. Specification of the evaluation question provides an important opportunity to frame the evaluation activity, to decide what exactly needs to be learned, to decide which audiences are interested in evaluation information, to determine what resources are available for conducting an evaluation, and to decide what exactly is going to be done, by whom, and on what time schedule.

School psychologists interested in evaluating an educational program should prepare a written evaluation plan before initiating other activities. This plan should declare the purposes for which the evaluation will be completed, the primary audiences for this evaluation, information that will need to be collected, and the standards against which this information will be judged.

Specify the purpose of evaluation. An important first step in evaluating educational programs is to clearly specify the major questions that need to be answered and any additional information that may be needed. This is especially important when others (e.g., teachers, administrators) are requesting evaluation. By preparing a written plan, the school psychologist can guarantee that implicit or ambiguous goals are identified, clarified, and included in the final evaluation plan.

Specify target audiences. Next, it is often useful to specify the constituencies, or potential audiences, for results of an evaluation. Determining likely audiences will often suggest additional questions to be considered, for it is assumed that the various interested persons will want different information. To determine likely audiences for an evaluation, one might consider several questions: Who is requesting the evaluation? For what purposes will the results of the evaluation be used? What other audiences may be interested in information derived through this evaluation?

Determine the information needed. After primary questions are specified and the main audiences are identified, the next task is to determine what information will be needed. At this stage, the evaluator should consider all possible areas in which information regarding an educational program might be gathered, including academic achievement, child and teacher behavior, and the costs and resources required for program operation. Academic achievement measures may include direct assessment of students' performance in the curriculum (e.g., words read correctly per minute, number of comprehension questions answered, number of word problems analyzed and solved correctly) or normative measures of overall performance (e.g., percentile scores for words read correctly per minute, standard scores on Iowa Test of Basic Skills). Child and teacher behavior measures will likely be related to ways in which the academic program is actually implemented, including observation measures of students' academic engagement or teachers' use of curricular materials. Measures of costs and resources are becoming increasingly important aspects of many evaluations and may range from detailed accounting of time and effort to be expended by different professionals calculated as real-dollar costs, to more general estimates of teacher, aide, or other staff time required for implementation of the program.

Selecting standards for evaluation. In all evaluation efforts, the performance of one student or group of students at one point in time must be compared to *something;* the task here is to decide what the standard will be. Standards of comparison include (a) behavior of the same student or groups of students at a different time, (b) behavior of a different group of students, or (c) an externally established, *a priori* performance goal. Not surprisingly, the overall outcome of an evaluation effort can be influenced greatly by the standard of comparison used. Thus, it is critical that, to the maximum extent possible, the evaluator and likely audiences come to agreement about standards of comparison *before* an evaluation begins.

Examples. The three evaluation requests presented at the beginning of this chapter would be expected to lead to very different plans for actual evaluation. Sample evaluation plans for each of these requests are presented in Table 1.

Selecting and Evaluation Design

Good evaluation requires careful selection of an appropriate design. Evaluation designs can vary greatly: They vary in the extent to which causal effects can be inferred, in the numbers of students needed, and in the types of data that must be gathered and the types of analyses that must be conducted, and they vary in their complexity and costs. While this range of variation greatly expands the possibilities available to school psychologists interested in evaluating educational programs, it also requires that the design be best suited to the question under consideration.

Complete coverage of the range of possible evaluation designs is far beyond the scope of this chapter. Readers interested in more information on evaluation designs are referred to Keith (1988) for a detailed discussion of research and evaluation in school psychology, to Tawney and Gast (1984) for treatment of single-case evaluation designs in which students serve as their own controls and comparisons are made over time, and to Cronbach (1982) for descriptions of group evaluation designs that, unlike single-case approaches, use statistical procedures to compare groups of students at one or more points in time.

For the purposes of this chapter, we will focus on four basic evaluation designs: (a) Pre–post comparisons, (b) baseline-intervention evaluations, (c) nonequivalent control group designs, and (d) alternating treatment designs. These four designs were selected because they address many of the problems faced in the evaluation of educational programs and because they serve as a foundation for the development of more elaborate evaluation designs.

Two of these designs, the baseline-intervention comparison and the alternating treatments design, are based on single-case experimental (or applied behavior analysis) approaches. Both baseline-intervention and alternating treatments designs use subjects as their own controls; that is, all comparisons are made within subject rather than between subjects by collecting information under two or more conditions and directly comparing observed performance under these varying conditions. Intrasubject comparison requires frequent repeated measures of the subject's performance under each evaluation condition. These data are graphed as time series for each condition, and the graphs of the subject's performance under various conditions are then compared. Most typically, data analysis is conducted by visual inspection of time-series graphs; however, some inferential statistical procedures have been developed for these evaluation designs (Tawney & Gast, 1984).

Baseline-intervention and alternating treatments designs are appropriate for both formative and summative evaluation. Because measures of student performance are collected concurrently with intervention, teachers and psychologists have clear and continuous information regarding the effects of intervention. Rather than waiting for some preselected, perhaps distant evaluation point, they can assess the effects of intervention often. These ongoing evaluations can serve as a basis for ongoing revision of educational programs (Deno, 1986). Similarly, evaluation can be continued for some period and the overall program effect can be assessed at the end of evaluation. In this way, within-subject comparisons also produce summative evaluations of educational programs.

The remaining two designs, pre–post comparisons and nonequivalent control group designs, are based on more traditional group evaluation and experimental methods. Typically, these designs require assessment at fewer points in time and for larger numbers of students than do the baseline-intervention and alternating treatments designs. The measures are typically aggregated across students, and these estimates of mean group performance are compared across time or evaluation conditions by parametric or nonparametric statistical procedures. The

TABLE 1
Sample Evaluation Plans

Alexandro

Evaluation question: Has Alexandro's progress in daily reading performance changed since instruction began in his regular education classroom?

Audience: Alexandro's parents; Alexandro's regular and special education teachers; mainstream coordinator responsible for planning Alexandro's educational placements.

Information needed: The same information will be needed from both special and regular education teachers: Semiweekly probes on words read correctly per minute from text, correct responses to comprehension questions; time scheduled for reading instruction; curriculum materials covered. The special education teacher will be asked to provide data for 2 months prior to change in placement; regular education teacher will be asked for all data since change.

Standard of comparison: Alexandro's rate of progress in his special education placement will be compared directly with progress in regular education by means of a graph of semiweekly probes. Additionally, Alexandro's rate of progress in both settings will be compared to year-end goal of 80 words per minute, established at last IEP conference.

Ms. Johnson

Evaluation question: Do students correctly define more words on a weekly vocabulary quiz, and are there fewer classroom disruptions, when instruction is presented in peer-tutoring or lecture-and-worksheet format? Also, do students and teacher prefer the more effective of these two approaches?

Audience: Ms. Johnson; other teachers of middle-school English in her building.

Information needed: Percentage of weekly words defined correctly on Friday quiz; frequency count of disruptions during daily 15 minute vocabulary lesson; student and teacher ratings of satisfaction with peer-tutoring and lecture-and-worksheet instructional formats.

Standard of comparison: Ms. Johnson's students will be compared with themselves to identify the relative benefit of two instructional strategies. Average weekly quiz scores and frequency counts of disruptions during instruction in Ms. Johnson's third-, fifth-, and sixth-period English classes will be evaluated following 4 days of lecture-and-worksheet instruction, and 4 days of peer-tutoring instruction.

Dr. Williams

Evaluation question: Will introduction of the XYZ Mathematics Program increase average student achievement in Grades 1 through 3, and can this program be implemented with existing building resources?

Audience: Dr. Williams; teachers in Dr. Williams' building; parents of students in Dr. Williams' building; district administration.

Information needed: Year-end achievement scores for students in ABC and XYZ curriculum classrooms; quarterly description of instructional activities in each participating classroom.

Standard of comparison: Classes using each of the mathematics programs will be compared, with at least one class from each grade level in each of the mathematics programs. Comparisons will be made using district's own year-end achievement test.

---

results of comparisons of this type provide information for the *group;* information for individual students usually cannot be inferred.

Pre–post comparisons and nonequivalent control group designs are generally most appropriate for summative evaluations. These designs often employ more molar measures of student performance collected over relatively long time intervals. The result is a more static or global measure of student performance that is best suited for identifying long-standing, rather than short-term, changes in students' performance.

It should be noted that some disagreement exists on the relative power or appropriateness of group versus single-case evaluation and experimental designs in their purest form. Some observers argue that group comparisons, which allow for random assignment and sophisticated statistical analysis, provide maximum power for the analysis of causal effects in educational evaluation and research (see, for example, Keith, 1988). Others argue that single-case approaches, which permit direct analysis of variables controlling the behavior of individual subjects and highlight variability or consistency across subjects through direct and systematic replication, are most appropriate for understanding the behavior of humans and effects of intervention (Baer, Wolf, & Risley, 1988). Discussion of the relative merits or weaknesses of approaches to experimentation and evaluation is very important to the field of education and school psychology generally (Barlow & Hersen, 1984; Bijou, 1970), but it has relatively less importance for this discussion of evaluation. The task here is to select an approach to systematic evaluation that most directly, clearly, and simply answers questions that are important to students, parents, teachers, or other professionals working in the schools. The designs described here vary to some extent in their flexibility and the types of information they yield, and these features are generally more important in selecting one design over another to evaluate educational programs.

Descriptions of the four basic evaluation designs follow. Each description includes (a) an overview, (b) a summary of procedures for implementation, (c) subject requirements, (d) procedures for analyzing results from the evaluation, (e) the relative strengths and weaknesses for educational evaluation, and (f) the range of applications.

Pre-post comparison design. In many respects, pre-post comparison offers the most simple, straightforward approach to evaluating an educational program. The specifics of this evaluation design can be inferred readily from its name: Student performance is measured at one point in time, intervention is then provided, and performance is assessed again for the same group of students by an identical or highly similar measure.

Typically, pre-post comparisons are conducted for *groups* of students, such as an entire reading group, or a classroom, or a school building, or all special education students. The size of a group may vary widely (e.g., from as few as 6 to as many as 10,000), but it often will be determined by the number of students in an existing group and the types of statistical or other comparisons that are planned. It is critical, however, that the "group" included in any pre-post comparison be homogeneous with respect to the intervention received. The purpose of evaluation is to assess the effects of a program, curriculum, or other intervention. For this reason, the evaluator should have some degree of confidence that all students receive similar levels of intervention and that confounding variables are not present.

The results are analyzed by direct comparison of preintervention and postintervention assessments of student performance. Analyses may include application of appropriate parametric (e.g., correlated-groups t-test) or nonparametric (e.g., signs test) statistical tests for matched samples, or the use of any number of graphic analysis procedures such as bar charts of means or stem-and-leaf plots of means and ranges for the two assessment occasions (see Tukey, 1977, for more information on visual analysis of group data).

Perhaps the greatest strength of the pre-post comparison is its simplicity. The evaluation of an educational program's effect is very direct and easy to interpret. As a result, this design can be used in a wide range of situations, and its results can be described clearly to a wide variety of audiences.

Unfortunately, the pre-post comparison also has a number of weaknesses that must be considered carefully. First, and perhaps most importantly, it may be difficult to assess the significance of any observed changes, especially when a developmental measure of student performance is used. Often in educational evaluations we are interested in changes in students' *rate of progress:* For instance, we may want to know if students are reading more words correctly per minute, or are learning key concepts faster, or are increasing standard scores more quickly under one condition than they were under another. Measures of this type are expected to change in almost *any* condition. It is therefore impossible for an evaluator to determine if a change in scores for a single group of students from one time to another is faster, slower, or at the same rate as what would have been observed under another set of conditions. As a result, pre–post comparisons typically are not appropriate when evaluators (or their audiences) are interested in developmental measures of student performance, unless some other standard of comparison (i.e., an *a priori* criterion for rate of progress) is available.

Similarly, pre–post comparisons offer little information regarding change that would be expected without introduction of a new intervention. Thus, whether an absolute or developmental measure of student progress is available, it is difficult to assess whether change noted from preintervention assessment to postintervention assessment would have been greater, smaller, or equivalent under different intervention conditions.

Considering the basic requirements, strengths, and weaknesses of pre–post comparisons, one can identify several situations in which this design may be most appropriate for evaluating educational programs. Pre–post comparisons are especially appropriate (and may indeed be quite powerful) when student performance can be compared to some external standard. In many instances, parents and school administrators are interested in raising average student performance to a point where it is equal to or above a grade-level median on some nationally standardized test. In this instance, pre–post comparison of average percentile ranking for some group of students in a given area of academic performance may be especially appropriate. This evaluation may document that students were on average below the 50th percentile before a change in intervention and that they exceeded this standard one year after the change. This evaluation would offer information directly related to the original question and would do so in a way that is easy to interpret. Similarly, pre–post comparisons may be appropriate when the purpose is to evaluate changes in students' achievement of set numbers of competencies, or to reduce retentions or discipline referrals, or to promote placement in less restrictive settings.

Baseline-intervention evaluation. The baseline-intervention design is, in many ways, a direct expansion of the pre–post comparison design. Based on case-study (or A-B design) methods of single-case research, this approach requires the repeated and frequent measurement of students' behavior prior to and following some change in an educational program of intervention. Evaluation is conducted by comparing performance observed before and after the change in educational programs; differences in levels or trends of performance are interpreted as effects of the new intervention.

Procedurally, the baseline-intervention design requires standardized and repeated assessment of student progress across two or more intervention conditions. Assessment is initiated in the baseline (or original intervention) condition and is continued on a set schedule until at least five data points have been collected. Intervention is then changed and data collection is continued, with the same instrument and on the same schedule. Following collection of at least five data points in the new condition, evaluation can be terminated or another change in intervention can be introduced.

The use of repeated measures highlights variabilty and trends in individual students' performance, and serves as the basis for all comparisons. As a result, measures must be sensitive to small changes in student performance. At least five data points must be collected in each evaluation condition. However, if any trends or high levels of variability are noted for subjects within a given condition, assessment must be continued until performance stabilizes or trends and variability are adequately represented in the time-series data. With developmental measures of student performance, such as number of words read correctly in a standardized passage, it is not uncommon to need ten or more data points before a student's performance in a given evaluation condition can be described adequately (Deno, 1986).

Baseline-intervention comparisons can be implemented with a single student or with groups of students; in the latter case, data can be treated separately for each individual or aggregated to group means or medians. Historically, the demands of direct and repeated measurement of student performance have kept group sizes for baseline-intervention comparisons quite small. However, with the increased efficiency of various data collection and management procedures (e.g., Fuchs & Fuchs, 1988), larger numbers of students can now reasonably be included in evaluations of this type.

Baseline-intervention comparisons are analyzed through visual inspection of graphs of the time-series data. Data from baseline and intervention phases are depicted as two or more series on one graph, with time along the horizontal axis and dependent measures against the vertical axis (see Tawney & Gast, 1984, for guidelines on graphing time-series data). Student performance can then be evaluated by comparing levels, trends, or variability in data series across adjacent evaluation phases. Visual analysis can be aided by the addition of lines showing phase means or slopes. Tawney and Gast (1984) provide detailed instructions for calculating and graphing lines of slope for time-series data, and for applying systematic rules of comparison for data from adjacent phases. Additionally, student performance in any single evaluation phase can be evaluated against a standard of desired performance. In this instance, an aim line is calculated to describe the rate at which a student must progress to achieve some long-term goal (e.g., grade-level reading). Actual student performance then can be compared with this aim line to determine whether the observed rate of progress is sufficient to achieve a student's long-term goal (Deno, 1986).

The greatest strength of baseline-intervention comparisons, especially when contrasted with more simple pre-post comparisons, is the improved description of student performance. The direct and repeated measurement employed by these designs produces a rich, detailed, and narrow bandwidth description of *each* student's performance under two or more evaluation conditions. These data describe time-by-time variation (or lack of variation) in students' performance, the rate at which students are developing specific skills, or the progress students are making toward accomplishment of long-term objectives *during* any single phase of intervention. By comparing data *across* phases, the evaluator is able to assess for several possible changes: Is student performance less or more variable? Is the rate of progress accelerating or decelerating? Is the absolute level of performance in one phase better than that observed in another? These comparisons, which can be critical to the evaluation of many educational programs, are possible only because data are collected repeatedly in two or more evaluation phases.

Baseline-intervention comparisons also permit idiographic analysis, or attention to effects for individual subjects. These analyses, which are not possible when data are aggregated to group means, are often necessary in evaluation of special education programs. Students in these programs frequently respond somewhat idiosyncratically to different interventions, and teachers and parents generally want information that pertains to each student. For instance, a special education teacher might implement a parent-tutoring intervention, in which children read aloud to their parents for 15 minutes each day. The effects of this intervention might be evaluated by collecting curriculum-based measures of reading performance three times each week. While the teacher might find that this intervention increases the *average* reading performance across all students, an idiographic assessment would add other information. By examining data series for individual students, the teacher might identify two members of the class who are demonstrating little progress; further assessment might indicate that tutoring is not being completed for these students, or that remedial decoding instruction is needed. In this example, the teacher implements an intervention and conducts evaluation for a group, but also can analyze data for individuals. In this way, the evaluation helps tailor intervention for individual students.

In their simplest form, baseline-intervention comparisons share several possible weaknesses with pre-post comparisons which were discussed earlier. Fortunately, these weaknesses generally can be avoided through expansion of the basic evaluation design. First, it is sometimes difficult to assess changes in developmental measures using these designs. However, as described briefly above, data analysis procedures like the quarter-intersect estimate of slope and the use of aim lines are making clearer evaluation of these measures possible (Deno, 1986). Second, simple baseline-intervention comparisons, where one baseline phase is compared with one new treatment phase, may not offer much confidence for attributing observed changes in student performance to changes in educational programs. To increase confidence in this relationship, however, the evaluator need only replicate any effect originally observed. This can be accomplished by reverting to baseline conditions and then reinstating the new intervention (a *return to baseline* design), or by adding other students or groups of students that move from baseline to intervention at a different time (a *multiple baseline* design). If change in student performance follows each change in evaluation conditions, the evaluator and any audiences should have confidence that intervention is causally related to change in student achievement.

Another potential weakness is the perceived response demand of conducting evaluations of this type. Psychologists, students, teachers, and/or administrators (especially those not accustomed to frequent assessment of student perfor-

mance) may be put off by the seeming demands of repeated measurement required here. However, this can be conceptualized as a problem in the design or selection of data collection instruments as much as a problem of the evaluation design itself. To prevent this problem the evaluator must select an instrument that produces useful data but can be used efficiently with the resources available for the evaluation effort. Hopefully, if the task of collecting and managing data can be made more acceptable or less burdensome, resistance to these useful designs will be reduced.

Nonequivalent control group design. The nonequivalent control group design represents another extension of pre-post comparison, this time accomplished with groups of subjects. In the simplest case, the evaluator identifies two groups of students but provides some specific intervention to only one. The evaluation is accomplished by postintervention assessments for the two groups; significant differences between groups are presumed to be a result of differences in educational intervention. The addition of a control group, which is not exposed to the educational program being evaluated, increases the confidence that can be placed in the results of evaluation.

Procedurally, nonequivalent control group designs are completed in several steps. First, the evaluator forms or selects two or more comparison groups. The evaluator must make every effort to identify groups that are similar as possible before any intervention is implemented. One way to guarantee equivalence is to randomly assign students, teachers, or classrooms to "new treatment" or "no new treatment" conditions. However, because random assignment is often not possible in schools, other efforts to form similar groups, including matching on the basis of demographic factors (grade, gender, school, socioeconomic status) or pretreatment assessments, may be necessary. The more confident one can be that groups are similar before intervention, the more powerful this design will be.

Many evaluators will complete a preintervention assessment for all subjects to help describe, and perhaps control for, any differences between groups. This intervention can be used to evaluate empirically the similarity between groups, or it can be used as a covariate for subsequent statistical analyses of postintervention measures.

Next, the educational program being evaluated is provided to only one of the two groups. In educational settings, it is unlikely that students in the control group will receive "no treatment"; rather, existing programs in the area of study are typically continued.

Finally, at or near the end of treatment, students in both groups are assessed with the same instrument. This postintervention measure serves as the basis for evaluation of the intervention.

Nonequivalent control group designs typically require more subjects than any of the other three evaluation designs discussed here. In part, this is due to the use of a control group; approximately half of the participating students are not receiving the targeted intervention. Additionally, statistical procedures are often used to assess effects in nonequivalent control group designs. As in any statistical analysis, larger numbers of subjects in both groups make it easier to identify actual differences that result from the intervention.

Results are analyzed by comparison of postintervention means for treatment and control group students. As with the simpler group evaluation approach, parametric, nonparametric, and graphic analyses may all be appropriate. Furthermore, the addition of a preintervention assessment allows evaluators to use analysis of covariance (ANCOVA) or other statistical tests that offer some control for initial differences between groups. (For more information on statistical tests appropriate for nonequivalent control group designs, the reader can consult Cronbach, 1982).

The most obvious strength of the nonequivalent control group design is its relative power, or ability to yield information that will be accurate and compelling.

To the extent that treatment and control groups are known or thought to be equivalent, any differences in student performance on the post-intervention test likely can be attributed to the differences in the interventions applied. Depending on the size of between-group differences, this type of evidence can be interpreted easily and considered meaningful by a wide range of audiences.

However, two significant weaknesses should be considered before employing designs of this type. First, in spite of an evaluator's best efforts, some degree of question may always remain about whether treatment and control groups were in fact similar before intervention. Demographic and pretest matching, as well as the use of *post hoc* statistical controls, will often control for this weakness; so too will replications of the initial difference across successive groups of subjects (Cronbach, 1982). However, in some instances more complete experimental control (i.e., random assignment or use of single-case experimental procedures) will be necessary to address concerns of this type.

Second, the necessary inclusion of a control group in this evaluation design may be logistically difficult, and at times unethical. In educational settings, evaluations of this sort may mean that some students in a given building (or classroom) receive a new and promising intervention, while some of their peers do not. Teachers, parents, students, and administrators sometimes find arrangements of this sort uncomfortable or inappropriate; at other times, the evaluator may find it difficult to keep control students from being exposed to the new program. Additionally, in some circumstances denying students access to a promising intervention may be unethical or illegal. These issues must be explored before control group designs of any sort are used in applied settings, and alternative designs (e.g., multiple baseline) must be considered.

Alternating treatments design. Alternating treatments designs offer a way to directly assess the relative effectiveness of two or more interventions for a single group of students. Although logically and logistically similar to baseline-intervention comparisons, alternating treatment designs are more complex. Rather than implementing a single intervention over an extended period of time, two or more interventions are implemented on an alternating basis. Identical measures of student performance are collected in each intervention condition. By monitoring student performance under each of the alternating conditions, the evaluator can identify the specific intervention (or set of interventions) that produce the most favorable results for participating students.

Alternating treatments evaluations begin typically with a baseline phase, or a minimum of 5 days during which subjects' performance is assessed but no new intervention is provided; as with the baseline-intervention comparison, assessment must be continued until stable performance is observed or trends and variability are adequately described. Following baseline, two or more interventions are implemented in random, alternating fashion. These interventions may be alternated over classroom periods, days, or weeks, depending on the nature of the intervention. Students' performance continues to be assessed frequently, with at least one datum collected each time a different intervention is in place. Periods of alternating treatment continue until a clear difference is noted in the students' performance under one of the intervention conditions. Then, this single, most effective intervention is implemented alone.

Like the baseline-intervention comparison, alternating treatments designs are best suited for one subject or one group of subjects. When used with groups, all subjects receive the same intervention at the same time. While the logistical demands of varying types of intervention provided and collecting repeated measures of student performance typically preclude the use of this design with large groups or many small groups, there are no requirements for student selection.

Analysis is based on visual inspection of time-series data, with separate data paths graphed for student performance in each intervention condition (see Figure 2). As described earlier, the evaluator first compares each treatment with baseline and identifies the conditions that are associated with improved student performance. Next, the evaluator examines data paths within the alternating treatments phase to identify the single intervention or group of interventions that is consistently associated with superior student performance. Typically, this is represented by consistent lack of overlap between one intervention and all others. This "most effective intervention" is then implemented on all treatment occasions, and any replication of the initial effect is determined.

The most obvious strength of alternating treatments designs is that an intervention that is best suited for an individual student or group of students can be identified directly and efficiently. As noted earlier, students with handicaps are sometimes characterized by idiosyncratic responses to educational programs. Thus, a systematic evaluation design that enables school psychologists and teachers to select optimal program arrangements for individual students can be seen as central to providing effective education to these students. Furthermore, like the other approaches described in this chapter, alternating treatments designs produce results that can be easily understood and interpreted by many different persons. Teachers, parents, administrators, and many students can easily understand the basic foundations of this evaluation design, and can develop independent and informed decisions regarding its results.

The relatively complex logistical arrangements required to implement these designs represent probably their greatest single weakness. First, alternating treatment evaluation cannot be used with all educational programs; it is appropriate only for relatively fast-acting interventions that produce little carryover, or long-lasting effects. Second, teachers and students must sometimes be made explicitly aware of which intervention components are implemented at any time. Teachers often require assistance in remembering which specific procedures are to be used on any given day and which procedures are to not be used. Similarly, students may not successfully discriminate which program is in effect, and their relative performance across two or more conditions may be affected. This condition, called *multiple treatment interference*, represents a serious threat to the validity of any alternating treatments evaluation (MacGonigle, Rojahn, Dixon, & Strain, 1987).

Examples of Educational Evaluations

The three case studies described at the beginning of this chapter serve as useful illustrations of possible applications of different evaluation designs. In this section we will describe one possible solution to each evaluation request; other solutions may also be appropriate.

Alexandro. Alexandro's parents and teachers want to determine whether he is making adequate progress in his relatively new reading placement, or whether another change in program or placement should be considered. The evaluation question itself is relatively straightforward — has Alexandro's rate of progress been maintained? To answer this question, Alexandro must be compared with himself. Other comparisons (e.g., has his performance changed relative to other third graders, or has he acquired a certain new set of decoding skills?) may be important for other purposes but are not central to the question being asked here. The audience for this evaluation, Alexandro and his parents and teachers and the Mainstream Coordinator, represent the core group of providers and consumers of Alexandro's special education program. If this evaluation suggests that Alexandro's rate of progress is not being maintained, it is this group that will be most directly responsible for changing his educational program.

A baseline-intervention comparison is suited ideally to this evaluation request. Because Alexandro is still receiving services under his original IEP, an instructional aide assesses Alexandro's oral reading rate twice each week, using district-developed curriculum-based measurement procedures (Deno, 1986). A review of Alexandro's file yields semiweekly reading samples for several months prior to, and all weeks following, his placement in the regulation education reading group. These data will serve as the basis for the evaluation.

For purposes of evaluation, the school psychologist graphs oral reading rates for a 4-month period covering the last 2 months of resource room instruction and the first 2 months of instruction in Alexandro's current placement. To highlight Alexandro's progress, the school psychologist then draws slope lines (using the quarter-intersect method) for each 2-month phase.

The school psychologist can then meet with Alexandro's parents and both regular and special education teachers to review this graph (see Figure 1). After a brief explanation of the evaluation design, all members agree that Alexandro's current progress is quite similar to that observed during the final 2 months of resource room instruction. However, Alexandro's current rate of progress does not appear adequate to obtain his year-end goal of reading 80 words per minute correctly. For this reason, Alexandro's parents and teachers developed a home tutoring program that would augment regular classroom instruction and was expected to increase his overall rate of progress.

Ms. Johnson. Ms. Johnson wants to know if a peer-tutoring program will produce greater gains on weekly vocabulary tests without dramatically increasing the amount of disruption occurring in her class. At first, it would appear that the scope of this evaluation is quite narrow: Ms. Johnson wants to know if a different instructional approach will be better for students in her class. As with the previous case, students in Ms. Johnson's seventh-grade class will be compared with themselves under two different conditions. This direct comparison provides the simplest answer to Ms. Johnson's basic question.

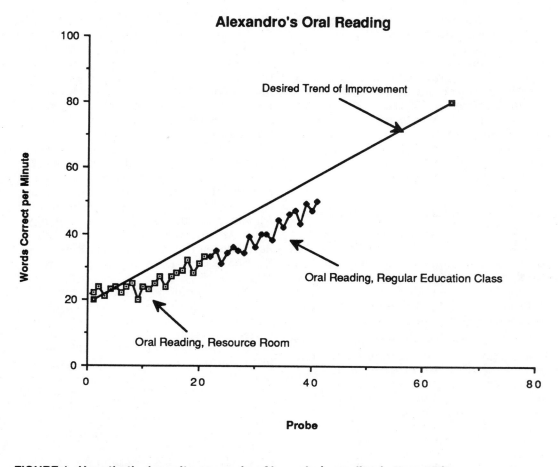

FIGURE 1. Hypothetical results comparing Alexandro's reading in two settings.

However, the scope of this evaluation can be extended in two important ways. First, Ms. Johnson is concerned that a peer-tutoring program may make classroom management more difficult and that the number of classroom disruptions may increase as a result. For this reason, evaluation has been expanded to include measures of both academic performance (i.e., mastery of vocabulary) and classroom behavior (i.e., disruptions observed during vocabulary instruction). Second, while Ms. Johnson is primarily interested in decided what instruction to use in her classes, we can also assume that information gained here will be of benefit to her coworkers in this building. For this reason, the audience of this evaluation has been extended to include other teachers in the English department.

An alternating treatments design is most appropriate for this evaluation project. Before the evaluation, Ms. Johnson introduced 10 new words each Monday, provided lecture review and worksheet practice on their definitions for 15 minutes Tuesday through Thursday, and then tested students on those 10 words on Friday. During five weeks of baseline, the school psychologist graphed the mean number of words defined correctly on the Friday test by students in Ms. Johnson's class; she also graphed the total number of disruptions counted by Ms. Johnson, using a golf counter,

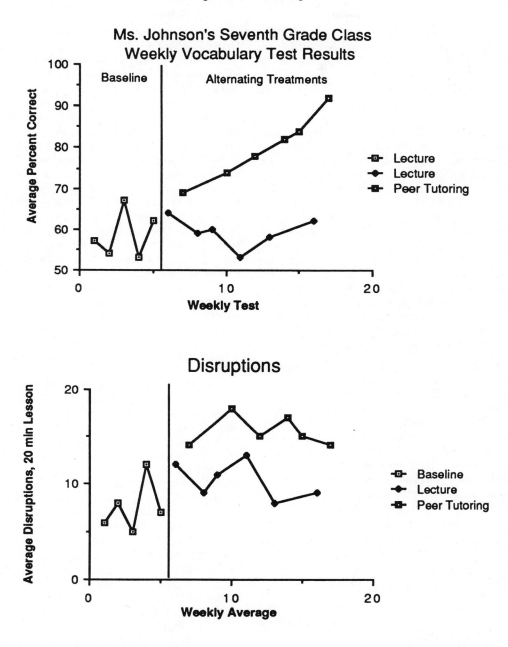

FIGURE 2. Hypothetical results of Ms. Johnson's alternating treatments evaluation.

during daily vocabulary lessons throughout each week (Figure 2).

Ms. Johnson then initiated a peer-tutoring procedure by which pairs of students worked together, drilling each other verbally on definitions for the week's 10 words. However, this peer-tutoring procedure was not used every week; instead, each Monday Ms. Johnson randomly selected either peer-tutoring or her more traditional lecture and worksheet lesson to use for the entire week.

The school psychologist continued to graph mean Friday test scores and total disruptions, creating a separate data series for the lecture-and-worksheet and peer-tutoring interventions. At the end of 12 weeks, it was clear that average student test scores were higher when the peer-tutoring procedure was used. It was also noted, however, that slightly more student disruptions were observed during peer-tutoring weeks. After reviewing the results of this evaluation, Ms. Johnson decided that the additional student disruptions were tolerable, given the dramatic increase in vocabulary test scores with peer-tutoring. On this basis, she began using peer tutoring exclusively for vocabulary instruction in all three of her seventh-grade classes. Two of her coworkers agreed, and began using a similar procedure with their students, but two other faculty members preferred to continue using lecture and worksheet practice.

Dr. Williams. In this example, a building principal wants information to help her decide if she should adopt a new mathematics curriculum. Clearly, a number of constituencies will be interested in the results of this evaluation: Parents will want to know if the change will benefit their children, teachers will want to know if the curriculum is relatively easy to implement, other administrators will want to know if costs can be maintained, and the school board may be interested in seeing if Dr. Williams' building changes its relative standing in mathematics achievement compared with other district schools. Given the nature of this request, and the wide variety of audiences that will be interested in any results, this evaluation is the broadest in scope of these three examples.

Additionally, Dr. Williams' evaluation is the only one of these three examples in which two groups of students are compared. Most academic curriculum packages are typically implemented over long periods of time, and few persons would expect to see rapid changes in student achievement. Instead, a more productive approach would be to compare students who have been exposed to old and new curricula over an entire year. Given that Dr. Williams is specifically interested in comparing this new program with the one in place in her building, a between-groups comparison is most appropriate.

While it would not be feasible to randomly assign students and teachers to curriculum groups, two quite similar groups probably can be obtained. There are at least two classrooms of students in each of the three primary grade levels in Dr. Williams' building. One teacher at each grade level can be selected to implement the new curriculum, the other teachers at that level continuing to use the existing program. Unless some bias exists in the ways students are assigned to classes (e.g., all "high-risk" students assigned to a single teacher) or the ways teachers are selected for the either group (e.g., all experienced teachers continue with the old curriculum), this procedure would likely yield somewhat similar groups.

Following group assignment, teachers are asked to implement their assigned curricula as described by the program's developers. Teachers are free to use any consulting or other ancillary services that are typically available, but are asked specifically to avoid using parts of the curriculum *not* assigned in their classroom. To check on the fidelity with which these curricula are implemented, Dr. Williams will complete three observations throughout the year in each class. During this observation, she will note the amount of time devoted to mathematics instruction, the number of adults present providing instruction, and the extent to which components of each curriculum package are implemented in the classroom.

In May, all students in each participating classroom will complete the district's regularly scheduled norm-referenced achievement test, and mean Mathematics Computation and Mathematics Comprehension scale scores will be calculated for each group. These scores will then be compared by means of t tests, and any differences between curriculum groups will be identified. Additionally, Dr. Williams' observations will be scored and aggregated for each group. Achievement test differences will be considered along with data from these observations when Dr. Williams selects the single mathematics curriculum to be used by all teachers next year, and these results will then be shared with parents, teachers, and district-level administrators to justify this program decision.

SUMMARY

This chapter has presented general considerations and four specific designs for evaluating programs. It has been suggested that school psychologists have most, if not all, of the skill necessary to implement educational evaluations and that school psychologists may be uniquely qualified for involvement in this process. Four approaches to evaluating progress of individuals or groups of students have been described and some strengths and weaknesses of each have been highlighted. These basic designs can serve as a foundation for a wide variety of educational evaluations that school psychologists will find professionally fulfilling, and that will be of benefit to students, parents, teachers, and others interested in the effects of educational programs.

ACKNOWLEDGMENTS

This chapter was prepared with support from Grant No. G00873052 (Social Interaction Training for Young Children with Handicaps: Analysis of Program Features) from the U.S. Department of Education to Vanderbilt University and the University of Minnesota. However, the opinions expressed here are not the official policy of the funding agency and no endorsement should be inferred.

REFERENCES

Baer, D. M., Wolf, M. M., & Risley, T. R. (1988). Some still-current dimensions of applied behavior analysis. *Journal of Applied Behavior Analysis, 20*, 313-328.

Barlow, D. H., & Hersen, M. (1984). *Single-case experimental designs: Strategies for studying behavior change (2nd ed.).* New York: Pergamon.

Bijou, S. (1970). What psychology has to offer education — now! *Journal of Applied Behavior Analysis, 3*, 65-71.

Cronbach, L. J. (1982). *Designing evaluations of educational and social programs.* San Francisco: Jossey-Bass.

Deno, S. L. (1986). Formative evaluation of individual student programs: A new role for school psychologists. *School Psychology Review, 15*, 358-374.

Keith, T. Z. (1988). Research methods in school psychology: An overview. *School Psychology Review, 17*, 502-520.

McGonigle, J. J., Rojahn, J., Dixon, J., & Strain, P. S. (1987). Multiple treatment interference in the alternating treatment design as a function of intercomponent interval length. *Journal of Applied Behavior Analysis, 20*, 171-178.

Tawney, J. W., & Gast, D. L. (1984). *Single subject research in special education.* Columbus, OH: Merrill.

Tukey, J. W. (1977). *Exploratory data analysis.* Reading, MA: Addison-Wesley.

ANNOTATED BIBLIOGRAPHY

Cook, T. D., & Campbell, D. T. (1979). *Quasi-experimentation: Design and analysis issues for field settings.* Chicago: Rand McNally.
This volume updates Campbell and Stanley's evaluation classic, *Experimental and quasi-experimental designs for research*, offering a detailed guide to the design and analysis of large-sample evaluations. Information is provided on a variety of specific designs for different evaluation tasks, as well as information on the interpretation and generalization of evaluation results.

Cronbach, L. J. (1982). *Designing evaluations of educational and social programs.* San Francisco: Jossey-Bass.
In this volume, Lee J. Cronbach articulates *his* approach to program evaluation. Rather than a summative, post hoc comparison of two or more treatments, Cronbach conceptualizes evaluation as a broad-based, somewhat synthetic process that incorporates features of both summative and formative analyses. As he notes, "Questions posed to get [an evaluation] under way prove to be less interesting than the questions that emerge as observations are made and puzzled over. Not infrequently, questions arising out of these observations prove to be more important in the long run than the facts the study was designed to pin down" (p. x).
Cronbach uses examples and reflections on other evaluation texts to lead the reader through issues related to the planning, design, and implementation of program evaluation; he also provides treatment of more sophisticated topics, such as the relative importance of external vs. internal validity, and factors affecting extrapolations from statistical analyses. The results is a book

that offers a thorough, yet readable introduction to the foundations and procedures of mainstream educational evaluation.

Hawkins, R. P. (1979). The functions of assessment: Implications for selection and development of devices for assessing repertoires in clinical, educational, and other settings. *Journal of Applied Behavior Analysis, 12,* 501–516.

While not an article on evaluation per se, Hawkins' analysis of assessment practices in educational settings should prove invaluable to any person trying to select an assessment device. In this article, Hawkins reviews the major functions of assessment (i.e., screening problem definition, intervention planning, progress monitoring, and follow-up) and describes what characteristics are needed in assessment devices used at these different levels. In the latter section of this article, Hawkins reviews the assessment concerns specifically related to evaluation, nicely integrating and building on information offered in the earlier section. This article presents an excellent overview of factors to consider in the selection of assessment devices for educational evaluations.

Tawney, J. W., & Gast, D. L. (1984). *Single subject research in special education.* Columbus, OH: Merrill.

This book is an excellent reference for individuals interested in designing single-case evaluations for use in educational settings. Tawney and Gast review the history of behavioral research in educational settings, provide an overview of measurement and data analysis to be considered in research and evaluation, and then provide detailed descriptions of both simple and complex single-subject (or behavior analysis) designs. Examples are used throughout the book to illustrate the application of specific techniques and designs in educational settings. This book is an excellent introduction and reference for those interested in intraindividual evaluations of educational programs.

25

Best Practices in Family–School Relationships

Marian C. Fish
Queens College of the City University of New York

OVERVIEW

There has been wide recognition in recent years of the positive effect on children of family involvement with the school. When there is collaboration between schools and families, each party benefits as do the children. Indeed, it is now generally accepted that families and schools cannot operate in isolation without detrimental effects to children (Conoley, 1987). Several recent reports on the nation's schools including *A Nation At Risk* (1983) and *Making the Grade* (1983), have addressed the necessity and importance of involving parents in their children's learning. The recommendations from these reports are consistent with the results of research indicating that children have an added advantage in school when parents encourage and support schooling (Epstein, 1984). There is considerable evidence that ongoing communication between parents and schools can improve both home and school performance in such areas as attendance, grade point averages, preventing dropouts and improving discipline; the academic and social behaviors of disabled children have also been shown to benefit from parent involvement. Looking specifically at school psychologists, Conoley (1987) makes a persuasive argument that a school psychologist-parent partnership has enormous potential for facilitating children's learning and behavior. She points out that everyone's behavior influences and is influenced by the behaviors of others,

necessitating collaboration between home and school. Of course, there are times when excessive or inappropriate parent-school involvement might be detrimental. For example, interference with the independence of the child or the relationship between the child and the teacher would not be beneficial, and it would be necessary to reassess the involvement (Swap, 1987). Generally, however, it is the lack of a relationship between schools and parents that is cause for concern and needs to be addressed by the school psychologist. The purpose of this chapter is to provide those strategies and approaches that school psychologists can use to encourage positive family-school relationships. Two goals for school psychologists to consider are (a) to improve the quality of the relationships between the parents and schools, and (b) to increase the number of parents who become involved with the school (Swap, 1987).

Historical Perspective

Despite the evidence supporting the importance of family-school collaboration, there have been only limited efforts to systematically encourage parents to become partners in education (Simpson, 1982). Parent involvement is enthusiastically supported, but not implemented. In fact, often parents are discouraged from being active participants for reasons described below. Much of the impetus toward involvement has resulted from judicial and legislative mandates. Historically, before 1935 most families lived and worked in a rural environment where the home was the center of children's lives. By 1950, however, most families lived in an urban environment with their workplace (e.g., factory) outside of the home and increasingly distant from it. School became more influential as the school day was lengthened, and parents were not as available. The momentum for parent participation in the schools began with the political advocacy of parents of exceptional children. For example, in the 1950s parent groups such as the National Association for Retarded Citizens (NARC) applied pressure in judicial and legislative areas to have active involvement of parents supported by law (Turnbull & Winton, 1984). In the 1960s compensatory education programs for economically disadvantaged children incorporated parent involvement. Turnbull and Winton (1984) suggest that parents were viewed in two ways, either as needing knowledge and skills because of deficits and/or as disenfranchised and without the opportunity to participate in decision making. During the 1970s the role of parents as decision-makers was emphasized; this can be seen in the passage of the Family Educational Rights and Privacy Act (Buckley-Pell amendment, 1974) giving parents access to student records and, of course, PL 94-142 (1975) the Education for All Handicapped Children Act providing informed consent and due process for parents. Independent parent advocacy groups were formed as well to keep parents involved with such issues as contracts and budgets. The result of these laws and court rulings " . . . has created expectancies for parents to assume tremendous education roles, to make informed decisions, to increase skills, and to participate actively in the administration and delivery of education programs" (Turnbull & Winton, 1984, p. 383). Yet, this potential has not been fully realized even with special education populations because of a number of barriers that interfere with the goal of enhanced collaboration. Let us look next at the difficulties which arise and often prevent successful family–school relationships. Then, once these have been identified, strategies and best practices for school psychologists will be presented to address these obstacles as well as to suggest additional approaches to facilitate family–school relationships.

Barriers to Family–School Relationships

While some differences and dissonance between families and schools are inevitable and perhaps functional to child growth and social change, there are significant barriers to family–school relationships that may stem from philosophical, attitudinal, or logistical factors and/or skill deficits on the part of those involved (see Figure 1). The school psychologist must carefully consider the difficulties that are standing in the way of collaboration before acting.

First, while most schools and families support the notion of family–school collaboration, there are those who believe that the role of the school and educational decision-making falls exclusively within the professional domain of the educator. This philosophy of family–school relations suggests that the two are inherently incompatible and should be separated (Epstein, 1986). Indeed, there are a number of professionals, though in the minority, who do not agree with the assumption that parents should be active participants in the school (Swick & Duff, 1979; Turnbull & Winton, 1984). Some parents support this position as well; for example, there is evidence that poor Latin American parents generally do not recognize the value of home–school interaction, believing instead that school personnel are the education authorities and know what is best for their children (Vazquez-Nuttall, Avila-Vivas, & Morales-Barreto, 1984). The school psychologist must be aware of this philosophical position in order to respond appropriately.

A second barrier to family–school collaborative relationships is the highly competitive relationship between parents (particularly mothers) and teachers (Lightfoot, 1978; Power, 1985). As de-

I. Philosophical position (e.g., educational decision-making is the exclusive domain of the educator)

II. Attitudes of parents

Feelings of competitiveness with schools/teachers
Blaming of school for child's problems
Lack of understanding of school system and how it works
Feelings of inferiority, helplessness and powerlessness
Feelings that schools lack understanding of their traditions and values

III. Attitudes of school personnel

Feelings of competitiveness with parents
Blaming of parents for child's problems
Feeling threatened by parents because of doubts about their own competence

IV. Logistical Issues

Limited time for communication (Swap, 1987)
Ineffectiveness of typical occasions such as brief twice yearly meetings for parent–school contact (Swap, 1987)
Difficulties arranging transportation, babysitting, and time off from work

V. Skill deficits (e.g., lack of knowledge and/or skills in effective communication techniques)

FIGURE 1. Barriers to family–school relationships.

scribed by Lightfoot, competitiveness involves territoriality, that is, who should be in charge of the child's life. Parents' fears grow as they lose control of the child's life, and teachers are threatened and become defensive. It is not uncommon to hear teachers blaming parents for a child's problems, and parents blaming the school (Vernberg & Medway, 1981). The issue of competency seems to play a major role in this competition. Of greatest importance to both parents and teachers in the home–school relationship were concerns about their own and other's competence (Power, 1985). Each viewed their own group as more competent than they were viewed by the other. Lightfoot reports that teachers who believed they were competent and performing an important function tended to view parents as less threatening and were open to them, while teachers who doubted their competence tended to be threatened by parents who questioned them.

Parents' attitudes toward the school evolve through their continuing interactions with school personnel. When asked to identify barriers to fuller participation, low income parents of special education children cited communication problems such as the use of unfamiliar language by the school (Foster & Culp, 1973), and the

unmanageable presentation of information (Yoshida, 1982). How confusing it must be to parents to hear school personnel talking about WISC-R, IEP, least restrictive environment and the like. Frequently much information is presented to them in a short period of time, and they have poor recall of what happened at meetings. They also reported a lack of understanding of the school system in general, feelings of inferiority, and uncertainty about ways the school could help (Lynch & Stein, 1982; Turnbull & Turnbull, 1986). Parents spoke of feeling helpless, powerless, ignored, and fearful that teachers would retaliate against their children if they complained (Lombana, 1983). Of particular concern is that parents felt there was a lack of understanding of their traditions and values (e.g., childrearing). Lightfoot (1978) suggested that positive relationships between parents and schools are dependent on the degree to which teachers have respect for the culture of the parents. Thus, attitudes of school professionals and parents toward themselves and each other seem to play a role in their degree of collaboration.

Logistical problems often arise that can serve as obstacles to parent–school relationships. For example, getting babysitters, transportation, or time off from work prevented parents from participating more actively. These barriers are of particular concern when working with nontraditional families including single-parent households where parents have enormous responsibilities and other pressing priorities. In some cases parents may view schools as a break for them (Blacher, 1984) and a welcome relief from decision-making. Swap (1987) suggests that school traditions play a role in keeping parents and teachers apart. She sees the limited time available for communication, the ineffectiveness of the typical occasions for parent-school contact, and the problems inherent in communicating during a crisis as significant obstacles to collaboration that must be understood before they can be removed. For example, the typical 15 minute parent-teacher conferences twice a year are ritualized events that are not satisfactory to parents or teachers and certainly don't permit the development of relationships or effective problem-solving.

Finally, there is evidence that special education as well as regular teachers find communications with parents a major source of job anxiety (Bensky et al., 1980). It has been suggested that these feelings may be due to a lack of knowledge and/or skills in effective communication techniques (Simpson, 1982; Swick & Duff, 1979). Rarely, in either preservice or inservice coursework are teachers given training on how to communicate (e.g., give and receive information) or work effectively with parents. Although there are books and articles available, formal and field-based training is lacking. This may result in avoidance of parent interaction, making the school a less than inviting place for parents.

Thus, philosophical, attitudinal, and logistical factors, and/or skill deficits may all have a role in undermining the development of family-school relationships.

It should be pointed out that, in general, the involvement of all families does lessen with grade and becomes less relevant to the child's academic success and social adjustment each successive year (Hansen, 1986). It seems that parents feel progressively less competent in relation to school curriculum as children grow older. They devote the most time to the home-school relationships in the early elementary grades. Further, the influence of a family may, at times, increase in some areas of schooling while decreasing in others, with increases most marked at times of heightened complexity of either academic demands or peer interaction (Hansen, 1986).

BASIC CONSIDERATIONS

There is general agreement that the impetus for family-school relationships must come from the school rather than the parents. A major issue has been who in the school should assume responsibility for leadership in this relationship. Principals, social workers, counselors, and teachers have all undertaken this role at various times, but only recently have school psychologists actively asserted themselves in this area. This has occurred because of the growing interest in families and family systems theory throughout the profession and the recognition of its importance to insure comprehensive services to children (e.g., Conoley, 1987). It seems appropriate for school psychologists to assume leadership in facilitating family-school relationships. First, we are highly qualified to take on this role with the knowledge and skills necessary to implement the strategies and interventions that enhance family-school partnerships. Second, since the purpose of home-school relationships is to foster the education and healthy development of children, then this role is an inherent part of our job; by accepting this responsibility we are fulfilling our role through the incorporation of an ecological perspective into our practice. Third, such a role is an excellent way to enhance our public image and improve public relations. The acceptance of such a leadership role by no means excludes others from participation. In fact, the skill of the school psychologist in encouraging the active participation of others is critical.

The facilitation of family-school relationships is not directly taught to school psychologists. In reviewing some of the commonly used texts in school psychology, there are no chapters directly addressing this topic. As was discussed, most of the literature in this area is focused on *teacher*-parent interactions (Lombana, 1983; Losen & Diament, 1978; Swap, 1987). Until the advent of interest in family systems theory, there was limited discussion of the role of the school psychologist in this context (e.g., Gilmore, 1974; Loven, 1978). Currently, in some of the family systems courses being taken by school psychology students, the family-school relationship is addressed; generally, however, the focus is more on systems theory and/or therapy than on the practical considerations important in developing family-school relationships. Thus, the knowledge and skills necessary for school psychologists to meet the needs of a leadership role in family-school relationships are currently acquired throughout their training, both through didactic coursework, and especially, through field experiences.

Required Knowledge and Skills.

There is a wide range of knowledge and skills necessary to effectively fulfill the role of facilitator of family-school relationships. The general knowledge base of the school psychologist should include principles of human learning and development, principles of adult learning (to permit staff training), an understanding of the school as an organization and the systemic regularities within which it operates, and certainly, group processes. Of importance is insight into the special needs of nontraditional families (e.g., single-parent, foster, adoptive, stepparent, and those with an exceptional child), as well as familiarity with the cultural traditions and values of the families within their school setting. On a more concrete and practical level, the school psychologists should be aware of community resources to facilitate social supports, volunteer opportunities, and audiovisual and bibliographic resources to share with both parents and school personnel.

Finally, a very solid understanding of parents' legal rights is essential.

The skills that follow from this knowledge base are effectiveness in interpersonal communication, conferencing, consultation, and managing group interaction. The school psychologist should be able to direct a needs assessment, design and implement programs and strategies, facilitate problem-solving and evaluate progress. The dissemination of information in varied ways is also most useful. Probably most important is flexibility in thought and action. Now, with our armamentarium of knowledge and skills we look at the Best Practices in family-school relationships.

BEST PRACTICES

There is no one type of parent-school relationship; it has been suggested that some parents prefer involvement in passive activities as opposed to active decision-making. At other times, parents may need to be decision-makers. The nature of the relationship must remain flexible and be able to change according to the needs of those involved. Best practices in family-school relationships should create an environment which encourages two-way communication between home and school. We wish to reverse the trend of communication that occurs only during formal parent-teacher conferences twice a year or involvement only when there is a crisis or a child is in trouble.

A number of different classifications or taxonomies of levels and types of family-school collaboration have been suggested. For example, Anderson (1983) used an ecological model and categorized types of involvement at four levels: micro-, meso-, exo-, and macrosystem levels. Conoley (1987) detailed four levels of interventions and presents examples of each; these are (a) information provision and sharing with parents, (b) collaborative home/school programs, (c) active involvement of parents at the school, and (d) reciprocal education of parents and teachers by each other.

Lombana (1983) presents a model of

home–school partnerships (see Figure 2) that depicts the different kinds of parent involvement with the school and the amount of educator time and expertise required.

She sees parent participation as reflecting a wide range of varied activities such as information sharing, volunteer work and fundraising. Conferences are more structured opportunities for parent-school personnel meetings with goals of shared decision-making and problem-solving. Parent education would be directed at a smaller number of parents who would like assistance, and parent counseling occurs when both parties have serious concerns about a child. Swap (1987) provides a very practical list of Options for Parent Involvement (see Figure 3). Most important, however, is her emphasis on giving parents and school personnel an opportunity to choose how and if they would like to be involved, There must be a wide enough variety of options so that there will be some option that appeals to everyone.

The Best Practices discussed below are a compilation from a wide variety of sources. They address the goals of improving the quality of home–school contacts and increasing the number of parents involved with the school. Best practices are categorized into (a) those used when working with individual parents, emphasizing the qualitative aspects of the relationship, and (b) those used when working with groups of parents, emphasizing the number of parents reached.

WORKING WITH INDIVIDUAL PARENTS/FAMILIES

To improve communication, increase understanding of school systems and how they work and to decrease feelings of parent powerlessness, the school psychologist should:

- *Prepare handouts for parents.* These can include information such as school abbreviations and acronyms (e.g., IEP, CSE, WPPSI), positions and phone numbers of relevant personnel, and best times to reach school staff.

- *Make your own phone calls to parents.* Whenever possible, call and introduce yourself to parents directly. Make good news phone calls and follow-up phone calls to report progress as well. Accessibility of the school psychologist to parents is essential to improve communication.

- *Write personal notes and/or progress reports.* It is important to maintain ongoing communication with parents.

- *Prepare parents for meetings by having a preview meeting or sending them questions to be addressed and information prior to the meeting.* As discussed above, parents are often overwhelmed by the information presented at meetings or conferences. By providing advance preparation including who will be present, what issues will be addressed, what decisions need to be made, and what options they have, parents can be more active and informed participants.

- *Limit number of school staff participants at conferences.* It can be very intimidating to parents to enter a room filled with school personnel sitting around a table. Perhaps the school psychologist can summarize the findings of other professionals, thus limiting the number of persons who need to be present. Those not in attendance should be available if questions arise. Provide a listing of those present at the meeting for parents as well.

- *Provide an advocate or support person for parents at meetings.* It is helpful for parents to have someone they can turn to, if necessary, at conferences or meetings. This may be the school psychologist or other school personnel. This person can help the parent move through the school bureaucracy as well. If this is not possible, suggest to the parents that they are welcome to bring a supportive person to the meeting.

- *Serve as translator of jargon.* Though jargon should be avoided whenever possible, it occurs often at meetings and conferences and in reports. This intim-

FIGURE 2. Lombana's model of Home–School Partnerships

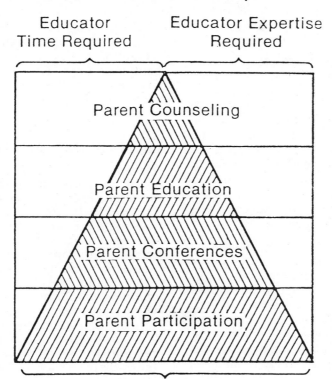

Reprinted with permission from Lombana, J. H. (1983). *Home–school partnerships.* New York: Grune & Stratton.

FIGURE 3. Options for parent involvement.

1. Parents as audience (e.g., music, drama, sports events, science or curriculum fairs).

2. Parents as advocates (attending parent/teacher conferences; participating in the development of their child's Individual Educational Plan).

3. Parents as helpers (chaperones, fund-raisers, library or classroom volunteers).

4. Parents as learners (attending parent seminars, lecture/discussion groups, joint activities for parents and educators).

5. Parents as partners (advisory board members, participants in problem-solving groups or task forces, committee members).

6. Parents as experts (leading workshops or other activities for educators in an area of expertise; consulting to schools in areas of skill such as computer software, energy efficiency, children's literature, playground construction).

7. Parents as "just people" (participating in breakfasts, pot luck dinners, hobby groups, Saturday morning activities).

Reprinted by permission of the publisher from Swap, Susan McAllister, *Enhancing Parent Involvement in School: A Manual for Parents & Educators.* New York: Teachers College Press, © 1987 by Teachers College, Columbia University. All rights reserved. (p. 31) idates parents and can be remedied by providing someone to interpret and/or explain it in clearer language.

- *Provide written summaries and/or reports following meetings.* A brief review of conference results with a list of recommendations or a plan of action after a meeting is helpful to parents. A written summary of possible home activities or relevant bibliographic materials might also be useful. A novel idea suggested by McConkey (1985) is to provide this information on an audio-recording. This may be used for less literate parents or parents who speak a different language.

- *Encourage and help parents to keep records.* When parents need special services for their children, they generally meet with numerous professionals both in and out of the school as well as contact community agencies and organizations. The school psychologist should help parents to maintain listings of who they meet with (name, address, phone, date of meeting, title), and the content of the meeting to facilitate later retrieval of information.

- *Consider special needs of nontraditional families.* When working, for example, with single parents, dual working parents, or foster parents, flexible office hours and appointments, early, late, or weekend meetings or assistance with babysitting and/or transportation may be needed (see also Carlson chapter).

- *Make home visits when appropriate.* This might be necessary when parent(s) are unable to work out a school visit due to some of the reasons discussed above (e.g., babysitting, transportation, illness). This is useful also to get a "fuller" picture of the family and allows you to include extended family members in your meetings.

- *Always recognize and comment on the strengths of the child.* Something nice can be said about all children. Say it!

WORKING WITH GROUPS OF PARENTS

A number of strategies initiated by the school psychologist can help foster partnerships between families and schools and increase participation of parents and school personnel. They fall into three areas: (a) strategies directed at school personnel, (b) strategies directed at parents, and (c) strategies for joint activities.

Strategies Directed at School Personnel

- *Provide teacher training/staff development programs for communicating with parents, involving parents in children's education and in how to hold successful conferences.* A lack of knowledge and skills in these areas accompanied by the anxiety this produces in teachers is a significant barrier to collaboration. Training in these areas will probably have the widest impact of any strategy and so should be a primary goal of the school psychologist. The school psychologist possesses the requisite knowledge about communication skills to develop and/or initiate this strategy.

- *Encourage written communication between teachers and parents.* Ongoing communication lets parents know of activities in the classroom which they can then discuss with their children. It develops relationships during non-stressful periods. If there is then a difficulty, a positive relationship is already in place.

- *Become an integral part of the school–family community.* The school psychologist should serve as a model for other school personnel by actively pursuing activities such as:
  a. writing a regular column for the school newspaper or PTA newsletter.
  b. attending school activities such as evening events and sports to mingle with parents and teachers.
  c. coaching a sport or advising a club.
  d. joining the PTA.

These activities increase communication with parents in a more relaxed, social atmosphere.

- *Encourage district level policies that reward school personnel who facilitate parent involvement.* Recognition from administration of faculty efforts in enhancing family–school relationships provides needed acknowledgment of its importance.

Strategies Directed At Parents

- *Organize a needs survey of what parents want to know and the best way to convey information to them.* There is no better way to find out about parents' interests, perceptions, and wishes than to ask them. Let parents be involved in the development of the survey as well as in the eventual implementation of the results.

- *Identify and develop neighborhood leaders.* Many parents are committed to working actively with school personnel. They are visible in their communities and can bring others along with them. Encourage and reward their participation through recognition and support.

- *Organize a program where parents share their expertise with children and/or other parents and teachers.* Parents are a valuable resource. Initially, it may be helpful to develop a catalog of parent abilities and areas of expertise, for example, finance, real estate, art. Then this can be shared and parents called upon when their specialty is needed.

- *Make presentations to parent groups on relevant topics.* These might include "Living With Your Teenager" or "The Middle School Years."

Strategies for Joint School–Parent Activities

- *Initiate the joint planning of a parent room by parents and staff.* Parents need to feel welcome in the school. A room where staff and parents can mingle helps communication.

- *Organize, provide, or facilitate the joint planning of Parent and/or Staff Education Programs.* (*See Chapter 35, this volume.*) While some workshops might be directed specifically at parenting issues, others might be broader based such as stress reduction, dealing with illness in the family, or weight loss. A family math anxiety workshop was successfully implemented in California.

- *Initiate fundraising activities.* Some novel approaches might include, for example, starting a school fund for child care during parent conferences so fathers can attend. Or, use the money to have high school or college students help out single parents in the home so they can have more time with their children.

- *Help establish and maintain the school as a neighborhood center.* For example, use the school as a community center for senior citizens and/or foster grandparent programs. Have school buses carry parents to and from school events and/or community functions.

- *Involve parents in the planning stages of all innovative programs and new curriculum.* When parents participate from the start, their support is much more likely for the product.

- *Initiate the joint planning of a social activity.* This will help build relationships that are not threatening.

- *Initiate the joint planning of a program to welcome new parents to the school.* Good relationships between families and schools start early. Arrange for a program early in the year where parents and school personnel can meet informally and share information.

- *Initiate the joint planning of effective parent conferences.* Rather than brief back-to-back conferences, help develop a structure that is more conducive to the development of good relationships and the sharing of meaningful information.

It is essential that school psychologists actively seek a leadership role in the facilitation of family–school partnerships.

It will be necessary to rearrange priorities requiring time and effort on the part of the school psychologist. The justification for the time spent, of course, is that it is preventative; enhanced parent-school relationships prevent or lessen potential conflicts and have system-wide implications.

SUMMARY

Family-school relationships that are collaborative rather than adversarial benefit children. While the importance of parent participation in schools is widely recognized, there have been only limited efforts to facilitate the family-school relationship in a systematic manner. Barriers to collaboration include philosophical, attitudinal, and logistical factors as well as skill deficits on the part of school personnel.

School psychologists are uniquely qualified to assume a leadership role in facilitating home-school partnerships. They possess skills in areas such as interpersonal communication and group processes as well as an awareness of cultural diversity and the special needs of nontraditional families.

Strategies to improve the quality of the family-school relationships and to increase the number of parents participating are presented. They include practices for working with individual families as well as groups of parents and are directed at each group (families and school personnel) alone as well as jointly. While always encouraging and making schools available to parents, care must be taken not to force parents to participate. Families should have a choice in the level of involvement they wish to have. What is important is that children see parents, teachers, and school psychologists working together on their behalf.

REFERENCES

Anderson, C. (1983). An ecological developmental model for a family orientation in school psychology. *Journal of School Psychology, 21*, 179-189.

Bensky, J. M., Shaw, S. F., Gouse, A. S., Bates, H., Dixon, B., & Beane, W. E. (1980). Public law 94-142 and stress: A problem for educators. *Exceptional Children, 47*, 24-29.

Blacher, J. (Ed.). (1984). *Severely handicapped young children and their families.* Orlando, FL: Academic Press.

Conoley, J. C. (1987). Schools and families: Theoretical and practical bridges. *Professional School Psychology, 2*, 191-203.

Epstein, J. L. (1984). School policy and parent involvement: Research results. *Educational Horizons, 62*, 70-72.

Epstein, J. L. (1986). Parents' reactions to teacher practices of parent involvement. *The Elementary School Journal, 86*, 277-293.

Foster, A. H., & Culp, W. W. (1973). School guidance with parents. In R. Friedman (Ed.), *Family roots of school learning and behavior disorders* (pp. 284-320). Springfield, IL: Charles C Thomas.

Gilmore, G. E. (1974). School psychologist-parent contact: An alternative model. *Psychology in the Schools, 11*, 170-174.

Hansen, D. A. (1986). Family-school articulations: The effects of interaction role mismatch. *American Educational Research Journal, 23*, 643-659.

Lightfoot, S. L. (1978). *Worlds apart: Relationships between families and schools.* New York: Basic Books.

Lombana, J. H. (1983). *Home-school partnerships.* New York: Grune & Stratton.

Losen, S., & Diament, B. (1978). *Parent conferences in the schools.* New York: Allyn & Bacon.

Loven, M. (1978). Four alternative approaches to the family/school liaison role. *Psychology in the Schools, 15*, 553-559.

Lynch, E. W., & Stein, R. (1982). Perspectives on parent participation in special education. *Exceptional Education Quarterly, 3*, 56-63.

McConkey, R. (1985). *Working with parents.* Cambridge, MA: Brookline Books.

National Commission on Excellence in Education. (1983). *A nation at risk.* Washington, DC: U.S. Government Printing Office.

Power, T. J. (1985). Perceptions of competence: How parents and teachers view each other. *Psychology in the Schools, 22*, 68-78.

Simpson, R. (1982). Future training issues. *Exceptional Education Quarterly, 3*, 81-88.

Swap, S. M. (1987). *Enhancing parent involvement in schools.* New York: Teachers College Press.

Swick, K. J., & Duff, R. E. (1979). *Parenting.* Washington, DC: National Education Association.

Turnbull, A. P., & Turnbull, H. R. (1986). *Families, professionals, and exceptionality: A special partnership.* Columbus, OH: Merrill.

Turnbull, A. P., & Winton, P. J. (1984). Parent involvement policy and practice: Current research and implications for families of young severely handicapped children. In J. Blacher (Ed.), *Severely handicapped young children and their families* (pp. 377–397). Orlando, FL: Academic Press.

Twentieth Century Fund Task Force on Federal Elementary and Secondary Education Policy. (1983). *Making the grade.* New York: Twentieth Century Fund.

Vazquez-Nuttall, E., Avila-Vivas, Z., & Morales-Barreto, G. (1984). Working with Latin American families. In F. Okun (Ed.), *Family therapy with school related problems* (pp. 74–90). Rockville, MD: Aspen Systems Corp.

Vernberg, E. M., & Medway, F. J. (1981). Teacher and parent causal perceptions of school problems. *American Educational Research Journal, 18,* 29–37.

Yoshida, R. (1982). Research agenda: Finding ways to create more options for parent involvement. *Exceptional Education Quarterly, 3,* 74–80.

ANNOTATED BIBLIOGRAPHY

Conoley, J. C. (1987). Schools and families: Theoretical and practical bridges. *Professional School Psychology, 2,* 191–203.
This is a seminal article that presents a comprehensive review and justification for the collaboration of families and schools with emphasis on the role of the school psychologist. It is essential reading for all school psychologists.

Lombana, J. H. (1983). *Home–school partnerships: Guidelines and strategies for educators.* New York: Grune & Stratton.
This book provides a model for collaboration between parents and schools that is directed at educators. First, an overview of home–school relationships with an historical perspective is presented. Second, it focuses on communication between home and school including facilitators and barriers. Finally, it provides examples of ways that parents can participate in schools.

Swap, S. M. (1987). *Enhancing parent involvement in schools: A manual for parents and teachers.* New York: Teachers College Press.
This is a practical manual presenting strategies that enhance family–school relationships. The examples come from real-life situations making the book relevant and meaningful. It is easy to read and well-organized. The book is directed at both parents and educators.

Turnbull, A. P., & Turnbull, H. R. (1986). *Families, professionals, and exceptionality: A special partnership.* Columbus, OH: Merrill.
This is a very comprehensive book that incorporates a systems viewpoint into the discussion of family–school relationships. The topics are wide ranging (e.g., family resources, communication skills, referral, and evaluation) and places emphasis on the families of exceptional children and the schools; legal and ethical issues are explored as well. This volume can be used along with Turnbull, H. R., & Turnbull, A. P. (Eds.). (1985). *Parents speak out: Then and now.* Columbus, OH: Merrill.

26

Best Practices in Individualized Education Programs

Nancy A. McKellar
Wichita State University

OVERVIEW

The Education for All Handicapped Children Act of 1975 (Public Law 94-142) requires that an individualized education program (IEP) be developed and implemented for each handicapped student. School psychologists are aware of this legal requirement and often encounter only perfunctory compliance with it. However, the importance of the IEP is as a format for planning and monitoring students' educational improvement, just as are state-mandated prereferral processes and individualized family service plans. The care and concern given to planning and providing education for handicapped students affect the quality of their entire lives and also the place that these students assume as adults in our communities.

Several decades ago, prior to the enactment of PL 94-142, a guiding assumption in special education was that the same educational program was needed by all students in a given handicapped category (MacMillan, Keogh, & Jones, 1986). Unfortunately, educational interventions that help one student to improve do not necessarily help another student with the same handicapped label to make the same degree of progress, if any (Deno, 1986).

This reality was recognized in PL 94-142 by the requirement that students' educational programs be individualized. The IEP is intended to be a link between the student's needs and the educational services that the student receives.

IEPs are consistent with current beliefs about how to provide quality psychological and educational services for handicapped students. They are the mandated means for providing education based on the student's own identified needs and then adjusting instruction in response to the student's progress. Once formulated, the IEP assumes great practical significance because it contains the services that the school has obligated itself to provide for the handicapped student. An important answer to whether a school must provide interventions for a student, such as counseling, computer-assisted instruction, or physical therapy, is determined when the intervention is stated on the student's IEP.

BASIC CONSIDERATIONS

The rules and regulations governing the implementation of PL 94-142 (U.S. Office of Education, 1977) contain descriptions of the content of the IEP document; the placement of IEP development and review within the chronology of the special education process; the participants in the IEP meeting; the responsibilities of the school to insure parent participation; and the parameters of accountability for the program. Yoshida (1984) has argued that although the legal description of the IEP appears to be specific, local schools were given much latitude to interpret provisions and develop procedures for IEP implementation.

Although the IEP might appear from PL 94-142 to be just a document, Kaye and Aserlind (1979) concluded after many interviews with educators, parents, and administrators that the IEP should be conceptualized as both a process and a written product. The process involves interactions among key persons in a student's instructional program and results in decisions that become the basis of the IEP document, or product. The process continues as implementation of the IEP is monitored. It is from both of these perspectives, of product and process, that IEPs must be examined as a concept and as specific plans enhancing students' education.

IEPs have both administrative and instructional purposes (Morgan, 1981). The administrative function of an IEP is to serve as a contract between the educational agency and the handicapped students and their parents for special education and related services. The IEP document itself is considered an educational record subject to the standard confidentiality safeguards (Shore, 1986). Accountability is enhanced because the IEP can be used to monitor and evaluate the delivery of these services. The school must legally provide the services specified in the IEP document, make a reasonable effort to help a student achieve the goals and objectives, and review and revise the program as needed (Shore, 1986). The law does not require that the school ensure that a student actually attains the goals and objectives, since many noneducational factors can affect a student's educational progress.

The instructional function of the IEP is as a tool to plan and monitor instruction (Morgan, 1981). It is this use of the IEP in the provision of instruction that directly influences the handicapped student's education. Failure to use the IEP to plan, deliver, and evaluate instruction violates both the intent and the requirements of PL 94-142.

The quality of the IEP is limited by the skill levels of the persons developing and implementing it. Important skills needed by IEP team members include measuring the pertinent aspects of students' performance relative to their learning environments; conveying information to others in understandable ways; generating task analyses; and writing behavioral objectives.

Assessment preceding the development of IEPs should be influenced by questions about students' interactions in the learning environment as they relate to planning instruction and questions about the most appropriate format in which to present the data to maximize their use in planning. The helpfulness of assessment data is increased to the extent that they pinpoint what students can do and where they are with respect to the hierarchy of skills represented in the school's curriculum. Criterion-referenced, as well as curriculum-based, assessment (Deno, 1986) produces data that are quite relevant in this respect. Once such information is gathered, it must be communicated clearly to all team members so that they can use it to evaluate the student's educational needs.

An important skill in planning how students will progress from their current proficiency to greater mastery is the ability to generate task analyses. This involves specification and sequencing of the skills that are prerequisite to the targeted skill (Wehman & McLaughlin, 1981). IEPs are typically based on multiple task analyses, one for each identified need and resultant goal.

There is general agreement in the literature on IEP development that the short-term objectives should be written as behavioral objectives (Wehman & McLaughlin, 1981). The essential components of such objectives are an observable and measurable behavior, the conditions under which the behavior is to be performed, and the criterion for measuring the behavior. The following objective contains all three essential elements: "The student will write the main idea (behavior) of a paragraph read silently (conditions) for at least 8 of 10 paragraphs on 4 successive occasions (criterion)."

In a survey of special education directors (Poland, Thurlow, Ysseldyke, & Mirkin, 1982), school psychologists were reported to participate in teams that make screening and placement decisions far more often than in instructional planning teams. However, school psychologists can use their expertise in measurement and learning to make valuable contributions to the IEP phase of the special education process. Maher and Yoshida (1985) have suggested that school psychologists can develop IEP goals, assess program alternatives, supervise IEP implementation, and evaluate IEP effectiveness. These types of tasks can be assigned to other IEP team members, though, since it is more important that these tasks be clearly delineated and assigned than they be assigned to specific team members.

BEST PRACTICES IN INDIVIDUALIZED EDUCATION PROGRAMS

The IEP as a Document

The goals set for the handicapped student and the interventions planned to meet those goals are legally required to be described in the IEP in terms of the student's present levels of educational performance; annual goals and short-term instructional objectives; specific special education and related services plus the extent of the student's participation in regular education programs; initial dates and duration of services; and criteria, procedures, and schedules for evaluating achievement of short-term objectives (U.S. Office of Education, 1977).

The goals and objectives are related statements of what the handicapped student is expected to achieve in school. Goals are broad, general statements of outcomes that derive from the general areas of the student's educational needs and cover the student's anticipated growth during the period of a school year. Objectives are the short-term components of goals that are written in the sequence required for specific goal attainment (Tymitz-Wolf, 1982) and are appropriate to the indicated ability level of the student (Tymitz, 1980). Objectives should always be directly observable and measurable descriptions of student behavior.

It is through the annual goals that the IEP links assessment with intervention. The student's individual needs should be evident from the assessment results, and goals to address these needs are written. The goals then determine the specific interventions that should be implemented. The percentage of diagnostic recommendations that are translated into IEP goals has been found to range from 0% to 25% (Fiedler & Knight, 1986). Unless there is a strong correspondence between assessment results and IEP goals, the IEP does not link assessment with intervention.

The IEP should contain goals and objectives for all the areas in which the student cannot substantially benefit from the regular education program (Shore, 1986). All special education and related services to be provided are described, even when these specialized services are to take place in a regular education setting. An IEP should indicate in which subject areas the student will participate in the regular education program without modification.

The IEP document should be specific enough to serve as a basis for developing a detailed instructional plan, but not to be the actual lesson plan (Morgan, 1981). Inclusion of the instructional procedures and materials is not mandated and can serve to make the document excessively long. An average of 4 short-term objectives for each of 4 to 10 annual goals is a recommended standard (Tymitz, 1980; Weisenfeld, 1986). The dangers of overly lengthy and/or specific IEPs are that implementers of the IEP will lose too much instructional decision autonomy and can become overwhelmed by paperwork.

Selecting and prioritizing the annual goals require consideration of the educational relevance of the goal and the expectations that exist for the student. Some goals are more central to overall educational achievement and generalization (Deno, 1986). Parents and students themselves have expectations that may be judged by school personnel as more or less realistic but need to be considered when selecting and prioritizing IEP goals.

Tymitz-Wolf (1982) provided an extensive checklist for evaluating the quality of goals and objectives. She also explained several errors that can exist in objectives that satisfy the behavior–condition–criterion format but are not subordinate to the goals. A faulty objective might be a restatement of the goal with a lowered performance criterion. A second pitfall is an objective that describes a specific activity rather than a skill. Morgan (1981) warned of the error of writing objectives that are not observable and measurable, inappropriately containing phrases such as "will know" or "develop confidence."

Since the passage of PL 94-142, skill sequences from which IEP objectives can be selected have been commercially available (Harrison, 1978). Such skill sequences are also embedded in many curriculum guides, developmental inventories, and adaptive behavior instruments. The sophistication of these materials has increased to the present, computer programs now being available that select objectives, based on assessment data, from large skill sequences stored in the computer's memory (McDermott & Watkins, 1985). The user of computer-generated objectives should not forget that the task analyses underlying these objectives need to be compared with the task analyses underlying the classroom curriculum and the individual student's needs. School psychologists who use such computer programs remain responsible for IEP-planning decisions based on them (National Association of School Psychologists, 1984).

The primary question answered in the IEP document, or product, is what services that modify and/or supplement the regular education program will be provided for the handicapped student. Three basic considerations in selecting services for a student are the student's current skill level, the teacher's skills and resources, and the probability that the intervention will be implemented.

The quality of assessment by all members of the multidisciplinary team determines the accuracy of the team's knowledge of the student's current skill level. Neither labels, nor ambiguous generalizations, nor statements of what the student cannot do are particularly helpful in describing current proficiencies (Morgan, 1981). Each person contributing assessment information has the responsibility for transforming those data into clear statements of the student's accuracy and rate on acquired and emerging skills. Presenting the assessment data in this manner enhances the likelihood that the goals and objectives will truly link assessment and intervention.

Intervention alternatives are constrained by the skills and resources of the teacher. Evaluation of the teachers' skills has become more objective since the advent of research on effective teaching (Levin & Long, 1981). Resources available to the teacher include not only materials, equipment, and other personnel, but also instructional options. In order to enable students to achieve their goals, some teachers may need training in specific skills as well as consultation regarding their allocations of instruction time and selection of instructional sequencing, methods, and activities.

The best intervention will not help a student unless it is utilized and properly implemented. The acceptability of treatments by teachers is influenced by factors that include their effectiveness, the length of time and skill required for implementation, their orientation of increasing adaptive versus decreasing maladaptive behavior, the problem severity, the role of the teacher in implementation, and the theoretical connotations of language used to describe the intervention (Witt & Elliott, 1985). It can be assumed that the more acceptable a treatment is to a given teacher for use with a specified student, the higher the probability that the teacher will use it and will implement it as intended. Also, the probability of implementation of the treatment as planned decreases as the treatment becomes more complex (Gresham, 1989).

An abbreviated IEP dealing with two areas of need, reading and social skills, for a fourth grader named Kelly is presented in Table 1.

TABLE 1
Abbreviated Sample IEP

Individualized Education Program for 1988–1989

Student: Kelly   Date: 9-3-88

Present Levels of Performance

A. Kelly's oral reading is fluent and comprehension accuracy is above 90% on ending second-grade text. Reading of third-grade text contains many errors on multisyllable words.

B. Kelly can state correct social behavior and expresses a desire to have more friends. Kelly rarely initiates conversation with classmates.

Annual Goals and Short-Term Objectives

Goal/Objective	Evaluation	Review
A. Kelly will increase use of syllabication rules in reading.		5/89
1. Reads compound words orally at 80% accuracy.	Word lists Paragraphs	10/1/88 11/1/88
2. Reads words with prefixes and suffixes orally at 80% accuracy.	Word lists Paragraphs	12/1/88 1/3/89
3. Reads words with closed syllables orally at 80% accuracy.	Word lists Paragraphs	2/1/89 3/1/89
4. Reads words with open syllables orally at 80% accuracy.	Word lists Paragraphs	4/1/89 5/1/89
B. Kelly will improve her peer interaction skills.		5/89
1. Approaches peers to 3 ft. two times per daily free period.	Systematic observation	9/30/88
2. Establishes eye contact for 5 sec. on 90% of approaches.	Systematic observation	10/30/88
3. Speaks first to peers on 70% of approaches.	Systematic observation	11/30/88
4. Maintains conversation with peer for 2 min two times per daily free period.	Systematic observation	1/14/89

Goal	Services	Amount	Initiate	Duration
A, B	Regular education	4¾ to 5¼ hr/day	9/4/88	1 yr
A	Special education: LD resource	45 min/day	9/4/88	1 yr
B	Related services: Psychological direct service monitoring	30 min/wk 10 min/wk	9/10/88 1/15/89	3 mo 4 mo

---

The two areas were selected as representative of services in which the primary service providers might be a special education teacher and a school psychologist. Omitted from the IEP are a rationale for the plan, materials, methods, activities, persons responsible for each objective, and a plan for coordinating regular and special education services. Such information is not mandated as part of the IEP, but does represent important decisions that must be made in order to implement the IEP. A separate instructional plan can be developed with this information.

The Process of IEP Development

The IEP goals are to be developed by a team following determination of the student's needs but prior to any placement decision (Wehman & McLaughlin, 1981). Incorrect reversal of the IEP development and placement decision steps is reported to be commonplace (Poland et al., 1982). The sequencing of events is crucial if students' needs and goals are to determine the special education and related services that they receive, rather than determination of the needs and goals by placement.

The rules and regulations governing implementation of PL 94-142 (U.S. Office of Education, 1977) require that all IEP meetings include (a) a representative of the public agency, other than the teacher, with authority to commit the agency resources required to implement the IEP, (b) the student's teacher, (c) one or both parents, (d) the child, where appropriate, and (e) other persons at the parental or agency discretion. If this is the first time that the handicapped student has been evaluated, the participants must also include an evaluation team member or someone knowledgeable about the evaluation and familiar with the results. The other persons that might be in attendance include school psychologists, counselors, social workers, speech therapists, reading specialists, physical therapists, medical personnel, and special education aides. Decisions about the number of participants at the IEP meeting are left to the discretion of local schools. The advantages of improved coordination and increased commitment among those who will implement the IEP when there are large numbers of participants need to be weighed against the difficulty of getting meaningful participation from all persons, particularly parents, in large groups (Safer & Hobbs, 1980).

Scanlon, Arick, and Phelps (1981) found that at least in one state there was not even nominal compliance at many IEP meetings with the legal requirements for participants. The mother and the special education teacher were the most typical participants, but attendance by the regular classroom teacher was infrequent, lowering the probability that an IEP would contain well-coordinated services. It is important that all persons who will be implementing the IEP participate in its development. People are more likely to carry out decisions that they make themselves than ones made for them (Maher & Yoshida, 1985), and goals that are written by persons for subjects outside their areas of specialty, such as vocational education, are often unrealistic and reflect limited knowledge of the writer (Albright & Hux, 1981).

The inclusion of parents in the IEP process, as required by PL 94-142, has been welcomed by some educators as means for sharing information about students' achievements and learning preferences and for increasing the coordination of interventions at school and home. Apprehension about the involvement of parents has been based on concerns about their inadequate background knowledge, lack of objectivity, and lack of cooperation or inappropriate interference (Morgan & Rhode, 1983).

Parents who have been actively involved in their children's education have reported the desire for increased involvement in the IEP process (Albright & Hux, 1981). Training materials exist for preparing professionals for working with parents in educational decision making (Turnbull, Strickland, & Goldstein, 1978). Likewise, guides for providing background information and teaching parents skills are available in books addressed to parents (Shore, 1986) and in training modules (Parker, Katz, Borten, Brasile, & Meisner, 1980).

The dominant task of the IEP team is to make decisions. The necessary knowledge and skills for all IEP team members are largely consistent with those needed by parents, and it has been suggested that joint training of professionals and parents would provide both groups with the opportunity to become aware of the perspectives of the other (Turnbull et al., 1978). Unfortunately, few teams receive training in decision-making skills (Poland et al., 1982). Techniques such as brainstorming, force field analysis, and nominal group technique could facilitate the IEP process.

The Process of IEP Implementation

Important questions related to implementation of the IEP are issues basic to the monitoring of student improvement: In what ways, with what criteria of change, and how often should student performance be measured? The most appropriate way to measure improvement is by having the student perform the behavior as it is described in the instructional objective. Such assessment is both criterion-referenced because the current skill level is measured relative to desired mastery level and also curriculum-based because what is measured is performance on tasks the student has been taught.

The criterion, which is part of the statement of the objective, should be of a type and level appropriate to the behavior that is being learned. Criteria can be stated in terms of the accuracy, rate, or quality of performance. The competency standard at which the criterion is set should not be complete mastery, or perfect performance, since few students would reach this level in a reasonable time or need to reach it, except for behaviors related to safety. The typical level at which similar students perform the skill and the student's own learning history need to be considered. If the objectives subordinate to a goal are sequenced by a task analysis, a crucial factor in establishing the competency standard will be the level of skill needed to move on to the next objective (Maher & Bennett, 1984).

Measurement of specific skill attainment should occur at least each time the teacher believes the student has achieved an objective. The maintenance of skills should be checked by periodic assessment of previously attained objectives. Frequent measurement of a student's improvement helps to maintain a close link between the IEP objectives and the instruction delivered. If measurement is too frequent, such as daily, there is the risk that the instructional activities used by the teacher will

be limited to the conditions specified in the objective (Fuchs & Fuchs, 1986).

Logically, the best IEP document cannot affect a handicapped student's education unless it is implemented. However, there is need for research examining the degree of correspondence between student's IEP objectives and the actual instruction they receive, both in their regular and special education classrooms. In surveys of special education teachers (Dudley-Marling, 1985; Morgan & Rhode, 1983), major complaints included insufficient time and lack of involvement by parents and regular education teachers in developing the IEP document. Apparently, the IEP does not function as a working document because it is not referred to frequently and is often not even readily accessible to teachers.

Implementation of IEPs can be improved by developing a clear, relevant IEP document and by monitoring and evaluating the implementation. Team members should ask themselves at the time that the IEP is written whether the IEP is explicit enough to evaluate later. A plan for monitoring implementation should be made when the IEP is developed, so that monitoring is expected by all team members (Yeaton & Sechrest, 1981). School psychologists can monitor early implementation by ascertaining through classroom observation or telephone contacts with teachers the specifics of how the interventions are being carried out in the classroom and by confirming that evaluation data are being collected (Rosenfield, 1987). Gresham (1989) described the design of a direct observation system for assessing implementation.

An important guideline in monitoring student performance is what Morgan (1981) called the Do Something Rule: If the intervention is not resulting in improvement, the instructional method, materials, reinforcement, setting, or even the objective should be altered. Examination of the data record and interviews with the student suggest the type of change to make. If objectives and goals are to be changed, the IEP team needs to approve such an amendment. However, the teacher may realize that substeps need to be added between objectives and can independently decide to structure instruction in this manner. It is important for school psychologists to realize that modifications may be needed and to help teachers with these adjustments until the child is making acceptable progress (Rosenfield, 1987).

Models and suggestions for facilitating IEP implementation emphasize enhancement of participation of all IEP implementers in its development; establishment of clear procedures, role assignments, and standards; and frequent IEP review by team members (Maher & Illback, 1984; Yoshida, 1984).

Evaluating and Improving IEPs

Evaluating attainment of the IEP goals must occur at least once a year and consist of judging the degree to which the objectives making up the goal are achieved. Maher and Bennett (1984) pointed out the importance of using evaluation content that validly reflects the objective being measured. Assessment should be conducted on two occasions with different samples of items and different examiners and the results should be pooled in order to increase the reliability of the evaluation. When students attain their IEP goals, team members need to develop new goals and to decide the extent to which special education services will be required to enable the student to meet these new goals.

The implementation of IEPs in a school district can be evaluated on several levels. The presence of the required contents in a sampling of IEPs can be checked. The assignment and completion of IEP-related tasks can be ascertained by a questionnaire (Maher & Yoshida, 1985). Evidence that the district is complying with the intent of the mandate can be found in a comparison of the IEPs within and between disability areas. When Nutter, Algozzine, and Lue (1982) performed this analysis, they found that IEPs were not significantly different within disability areas, suggesting that IEPs were not truly individualized.

Morgan (1981) proposed that the three factors that determine the quality of an IEP are the assessment used to establish the student's current skill levels; the specificity of the objectives; and use of the IEP for planning daily instruction. Formulation of short-term objectives is the most difficult instructional aspect of IEP planning for teachers and is a skill on which in-service training is strongly needed (Tymitz, 1980).

SUMMARY

The individualized education program, as required by PL 94-142 for handicapped students, is a format for planning and monitoring educational improvement. Assessment is linked with interventions in the chronological process of determining present performance levels, goals and objectives, and services. In the IEP document, the school commits itself to provide specified special education and related services to a given student.

The IEP is both a product and a process. The assessment, task analyses, and instructional objectives are crucial contributors to the quality of the IEP document. The IEP process involves a team of persons, whose continuous, effective communication increases the likelihood that all participants will contribute to the IEP development and that the IEP will be implemented in the student's daily instruction. Both the IEP product and process must be effective if the education of handicapped students is to be relevant to their individual needs.

ACKNOWLEDGEMENT

The author wishes to thank Judy Picard for her assistance on the sample IEP.

REFERENCES

Albright, L., & Hux, T. (1981). Concerns of educators and parents in developing IEPs for handicapped students in vocational education. *Journal for Vocational Special Needs Education, 3*, 15-20.

Deno, S. L. (1986). Formative evaluation of individual student programs: A new role for school psychologists. *School Psychology Review, 15*, 358-374.

Dudley-Marling, C. (1985). Perceptions of the usefulness of the IEP by teachers of learning disabled and emotionally disturbed children. *Psychology in the Schools, 22,* 65-67.

Fiedler, J. F., & Knight, R. R. (1986). Congruence between assessed needs and IEP goals of identified behaviorally disabled students. *Behavioral Disorders, 12,* 22-27.

Fuchs, L. S., & Fuchs, D. (1986). Curriculum-based assessment of progress toward long-term and short-term goals. *Journal of Special Education, 20,* 69-82.

Gresham, F. M. (1989). Assessment of treatment integrity in school consultation and prereferral intervention. *School Psychology Review, 18,* 37-50.

Harrison, B. D. (1978). *Dial-a-skill: A manual of procedures for team members of special education and related services.* Provo, Utah: Brigham Young University Press.

Kaye, N. L., & Aserlind, R. (1979). The IEP: The ultimate process. *Journal of Special Education, 13,* 137-143.

Levin, T., & Long, R. (1981). *Effective instruction.* Alexandra, VA: Association for Supervision and Curriculum Development.

MacMillan, D. L., Keogh, B. K., & Jones, R. L. (1986). Special education research on mildly handicapped learners. In M. C. Wittrock (Ed.), *Handbook of research on teaching* (3rd ed.; pp. 686-695). NY: Macmillan.

Maher, C. A., & Bennett, R. E. (1984). *Planning and evaluating special education services.* Englewood Cliffs, NJ: Prentice-Hall.

Maher, C. A., & Illback, R. J. (1984). An approach to implementing IEP evaluation in public schools. *School Psychology Review, 13,* 519-525.

Maher, C. A., & Yoshida, R. K. (1985). Multidisciplinary teams in the schools: Current status and future possibilities. In T. R. Kratochwill (Ed.), *Advances in school psychology* (Vol. 4; pp. 13-44). Hillsdale, NJ: Erlbaum.

McDermott, P. A., & Watkins, M. W. (1985). *McDermott Multidimensional Assessment of Children: Microcomputer systems manual.* San Antonio, TX: Harcourt Brace Jovanovich.

Morgan, D. (1981). Characteristics of a quality IEP. *Education Unlimited, 3,* 12-17.

Morgan, D. P., & Rhode, G. (1983). Teachers' attitudes toward IEPs: A two-year follow-up. *Exceptional Children, 50,* 64-67.

National Association of School Psychologists. (1984). *Principles for professional ethics.* Washington, DC: Author.

Nutter, R. E., Algozzine, B., & Lue, M. S. (1982). An evaluation model of the implementation of individualized education programs. *Planning & Changing, 13,* 172-180.

Parker, C., Katz, S., Borten, J., Brasile, D., & Meisner, M. (1980). The IEP process. *The Pointer, 25,* 35-45.

Poland, S. F., Thurlow, M. L., Ysseldyke, J. E., & Mirkin, P. K. (1982). Current psychoeducational assessment and decision-making practices as reported by directors of special education. *Journal of School Psychology, 20,* 171-179.

Rosenfield, S. A. (1987). *Instructional consultation.* Hillsdale, NJ: Erlbaum.

Safer, N., & Hobbs, B. (1980). Developing, implementing, and evaluating individualized education programs. *School Psychology Review, 9,* 212-220.

Scanlon, C. A., Arick, J., & Phelps, N. (1981). Participation in the development of the IEP: Parents' perspective. *Exceptional Children, 47,* 373-374.

Shore, K. (1986). *The special education handbook: A comprehensive guide for parents and educators.* NY: Teachers College Press.

Turnbull, A. P., Strickland, B., & Goldstein, S. (1978). Training professionals and parents in developing and implementing the IEP. *Education & Training of the Mentally Retarded, 13,* 414-423.

Tymitz, B. L. (1980). Instructional aspects of the IEP: An analysis of teachers' skills and needs. *Educational Technology, 20,* 13-20.

Tymitz-Wolf, B. (1982). Guidelines for assessing IEP goals and objectives. *Teaching Exceptional Children, 14,* 198-201.

U.S. Office of Education. (1977). Education of handicapped children: Implementation of Part B of the Education of the Handicapped Act. *Federal Register, 42,* 42474-42518.

Wehman, P., & McLaughlin, P. G. (1981). *Program development in special education: Designing individualized education programs.* New York: McGraw-Hill.

Weisenfeld, R. B. (1986). The IEPs of Down Syndrome children: A content analysis. *Education and Training of the Mentally Retarded, 21,* 211-219.

Witt, J. C., & Elliott, S. N. (1985). Acceptability of classroom intervention strategies. In T. R. Kratochwill (Ed.), *Advances in school psychology* (Vol. 4; pp. 251-288). Hillsdale, NJ: Erlbaum.

Yeaton, W. H., & Sechrest, L. (1981). Critical dimensions in the choice and maintenance of successful treatments: Strength, integrity, and effectiveness. *Journal of Consulting and Clinical Psychology, 49,* 156-167.

Yoshida, R. (1984). Planning for change in pupil evaluation practices. In C. A. Maher, R. J. Illback, & J. E. Zins (Eds.), *Organizational psychology in the schools: A handbook for professionals* (pp. 83–100). Springfield, IL: Thomas.

ANNOTATED BIBLIOGRAPHY

Maher, C. A., & Bennett, R. E. (1984). *Planning and evaluating special education services.* Englewood Cliffs, NJ: Prentice-Hall.
The chapter on individualized programs discusses issues related to designing, implementing, and evaluating any individualized program of instruction, including determination of student needs, selection of services, program implementation, and assessment of implementation and outcomes.

Shore, K. (1986). *The special education handbook: A comprehensive guide for parents and educators.* New York: Teachers College Press.
The special education process, including the IEP document and its development, is explained by a school psychologist in a clear and well-organized manner. Specific suggestions are offered to enable parents to become more active contributors to their child's individualized education program.

Wehman, P., & McLaughlin, P. J. (1981). *Program development in special education: Designing individualized education programs.* New York: McGraw-Hill.
This is one of several books that are useful guides to the pragmatics of IEP development.

27

Best Practices in Increasing Academic Learning Time

Maribeth Gettinger
University of Wisconsin-Madison

OVERVIEW

The proportion of time during which students are actively and productively engaged in learning is a strong determinant of academic achievement. Recent effective-teaching research suggests that if students' academic learning time is increased, a concomitant increase in achievement will likely occur, especially for low-achieving or at-risk students (Berliner, 1988). This linkage between time and achievement has promulgated a number of studies designed to measure and subsequently increase the amount of time students are engaged in learning. What is surprising for many educators is the variability in learning time that exists among students and across classrooms. For example, observational studies have documented that the percentage of classroom time during which students are engaged in learning may vary as much as 45% to 90% in the same classroom (Fisher, Berliner, Filby, Marliave, Cahen, & Dishaw, 1980). Average engagement rates also vary dramatically from one classroom to another, again ranging from 45% to 90%, depending on several factors including teachers' managerial competencies, mode of instruction, or composition of the class. Because of these findings, academic learning time has been accorded special significance by educators and researchers. Time is considered by many to be a manipulable facet of classrooms, one resource that teachers may be able to control. Best practices for increasing

academic learning time are ways in which teachers and school psychologists can work collaboratively to manage time in classrooms for improving students' overall performance in school.

Time has played a critical role in the development of several theoretical models of classroom learning (see Gettinger, 1984). The implication of time in most recent conceptualizations of school learning can be traced to Carroll's (1963) original model. Carroll theorized that school achievement is determined jointly by time spent and time needed for learning. According to this model, the degree of learning is a function of the ratio of amount of time spent in learning to amount of time needed for learning. Carroll's model has been influential in focusing researchers' attention on the use of time in classrooms. The most extensive study of learning time was conducted by researchers at the Far West Laboratory for Educational Research (Fisher et al., 1980). This project, the Beginning Teacher Evaluation Study, documented that only a small percentage of the time allocated for instruction is actually spent in learning. Although allocated time and engaged time are clearly essential for learning, they are not sufficient. The nature and quality of time use also affect the amount of learning that actually occurs (Walberg, 1988). In fact, the most important link to achievement lies in what has been termed productive time, active time, or academic learning time. This time variable represents the amount of time during which students are learning or gaining information from group lessons or individual study. Productive or active learning time is typically only a fraction of engaged time. For example, productive time is minimized when lessons are not suited to individual-difference characteristics, such as a student's ability level, success rate, or amount of time needed for learning. Whereas efforts to increase allocated time or engaged time may be effective in improving student achievement, increasing academic learning time has been shown to be even more effective and efficient because the nature and quality of instruction and students' abilities are taken into consideration. Thus, the time factor teachers and school psychologists should strive to affect is students' overall productive or academic learning time.

BASIC CONSIDERATIONS

When teachers are concerned with increasing the level of academic learning time among students in their classrooms, school psychologists may play an important role in helping them modify their instructional practices to achieve maximized learning time. Given the complexity of achievement-related time variables, there are two basic issues school psychologists must consider prior to working with teachers: (a) an understanding of the components of academic learning time, and (b) an assessment of time use and identification of areas in need of change. Specifically, to plan strategies for increasing active learning time, it is necessary to analyze the constituent parts and then evaluate how time is used or lost within each component. Such a time-profile assessment enables schools and teachers to focus their efforts directly on time factors that need improvement. Figure 1 depicts the time variables that contribute to academic learning time and student achievement. As the figure suggests, the process by which allocated time is ultimately converted to productive time may depend on school policies, classroom or instructional practices, and individual differences among students.

An understanding of these time variables can be facilitated by considering the following example. In a fourth-grade class, a teacher presents a mathematics unit on division. A certain portion of the academic year and each school day is allocated for this unit on division, based on instructional objectives, curriculum choices, and other district decisions. Thus, there is an upper limit on the time available during school hours for each student to work on division. In Figure 1, this quantity of time is referred to as *allocated time*. For this particular classroom, the amount of time allocated to division is structured as five, 10-minute segments, or 300 total minutes.

A consistent finding emerging from studies of time use in schools is that a limited portion of allocated time is actually used for instruction. Research indicates that only 50% to 60% of the total school day may be used for instruction (Strother, 1984). This is referred to as *instructional time* in Figure 1. A variety of events typically occur in classrooms that may reduce the number of scheduled or allocated minutes used for instruction. These include interruptions, transitions, disruptiveness among students, teachers' disciplinary actions, late starts, and early closings. In this classroom example, only 45% of the allocated time is actually used for instruction in mathematics, or 135 total minutes of instructional time.

For some of this instructional time, students will be actively engaged in work on division; they will be paying attention to the lessons and assigned tasks. Likewise, for some of this time, students will be unengaged. We know that students must attend to material in some way in order to learn it. Thus, an appropriate gauge of learning time should reflect only the time during which the students are on task. This is referred to as *engaged time* in Figure 1. Engaged time represents a more refined measure of classroom learning time than either allocated or instructional time. In this fourth-grade class, students are engaged in the mathematics lessons approximately 85% of the time, or 115 minutes.

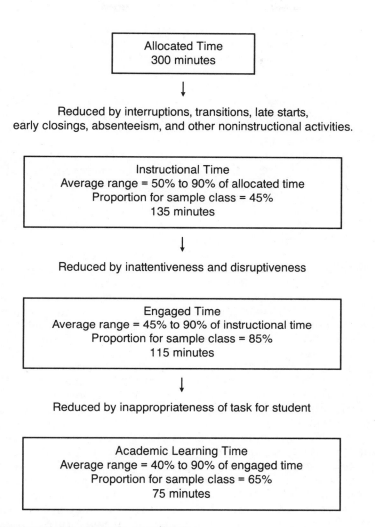

FIGURE 1. Components of academic learning time.

Finally, the degree of match between the task and individual student characteristics, such as current knowledge, ability level, and interest, influence what portion of engaged time is actually productive or academic learning time. For example, if the division lessons are too difficult and students produce few correct responses when working on problems (low success), the task will not yield much productive learning time. Conversely, high success describes situations in which students have a good grasp of the task and make only occasional, careless errors. Medium success reflects partial understanding of the material, with students producing some correct responses but also committing errors due to limitations in their understanding. According to Marliave and Filby (1985), *academic learning time* is the amount of time during which students are engaged in some balance between high and medium success tasks, with somewhat more activities at a high success level. Returning to the fourth-grade class example, the portion of engaged time that is productive learning time is about 65% or 75 minutes.

Although the amount of time that schools and teachers allocate to and use for instruction and the proportion of instructional time that students are engaged in lessons are all positively associated with learning, it is the proportion of time that is productive, active, academic learning time that relates most strongly to achievement. In sum, the more productive time that students accumulate, the more they are learning, and the higher their achievement.

This analysis of academic learning time provides a framework within which school psychologists can assist teachers in targeting areas for improvement. To help teachers become more aware of class time use, they might be encouraged to keep personal logs or diaries of how class time is allocated, both across and within content areas, and how much of this scheduled time is actually used during a school day. Paine, Radicchi, Rosellini, Deutchman, and Darch (1983) have developed a structured schedule analysis form and a step-by-step procedure to help teachers examine how they are currently using instructional time. Following these procedures, the total amount of time allocated for each daily or weekly scheduled activity (curriculum areas, lunch, recess, organizational tasks) is entered on the analysis form. Teachers then subtract the amount of time devoted to noninstructional activities to arrive at an estimate of the percentage of available time devoted to each activity. Paine et al.'s detailed procedures for this and other time management strategies are explained in their book, *Structuring Your Classroom for Academic Success* (see annotated bibliography). Using this method, school psychologists can assist teachers in computing the amount of time available for teaching and the percentage of time used for each curriculum area on their weekly schedule. Teachers may also rank order content areas according to the amount of time they allocate and use for instruction and record overall achievement in each area. By doing so, it is possible to determine whether there is a relationship between achievement and time used for instruction and whether the time allocated for particular activities reflects students' needs. For example, if spelling performance is lower than expected or desired, school psychologists

can help teachers examine instructional time in spelling relative to other subject areas and determine whether instructional time matches students' instructional needs.

It is also possible for teachers or school psychologists to collect data on the engagement rates and success levels among students through observation and questioning. Steere (1988) describes one method for determining engagement rates among groups of students. In his book, *Becoming an Effective Classroom Manager: A Resource for Teachers* (see annotated bibliography), he also provides a standard engagement rate form and detailed procedures for observing and calculating engagement rates in classrooms. His coding system allows observers to analyze further the various sources of unengagement time, including management or transitions, socializing, discipline, being unoccupied, or being out of the room.

When determining amounts and rates of allocated, instructional, or engaged time, it is important to remember that there is no specific criterion level that separates effectiveness from ineffectiveness. The objective of any time-profile assessment device is to analyze instructional time relative to desired student outcomes. Simply equating more time with more learning is ineffective in that different types of classes and students determine what constitute appropriate uses of time. Karweit (1988), nonetheless, suggests that comparing actual time use with typical or normative ranges for each time component is one way school psychologists can identify potential areas for improvement. The average ranges presented in Figure 1 for each time component are based on observational studies of time use in typical classrooms. By identifying areas where actual performance deviates from expected or desired performance and then locating time components that deviate from average ranges, school psychologists can help teachers determine where they can make instructional changes to maximize academic learning time. Returning to the example of the fourth-grade class, standardized achievement test scores and teacher evaluations identified mathematics as a problem area for many students. The time-profile assessment in Figure 1 shows that the greatest discrepancy between the teacher's time components and average values lies in converting allocated time into actual instructional time. The school psychologist, therefore, can help the teacher target strategies for increasing instructional time.

Based on the disaggregation of learning time in Figure 1 and an assessment of time use within each component, there are three general ways to increase academic learning time. First, teachers can increase the proportion of allocated time that is actually used for instruction or learning. This may be achieved primarily through organizational and managerial efforts. Second, teachers can work to increase engaged time among students. Engaged time is influenced primarily by a teacher's effectiveness in interacting with students and directing or guiding classroom learning tasks. Third, teachers can enhance the overall productivity of learning time by matching instruction to meet individual skills and needs and monitoring student performance. Specific procedures to increase instructional time, maximize engaged time, and enhance productivity of learning time are described below. Collectively these methods represent best practices for increasing academic learning time.

BEST PRACTICES

Descriptive research on effective teaching indicates that specific teacher behaviors and instructional procedures may have an impact on student achievement by influencing the components of academic learning time (Rosenshine, 1979). Intervention studies, subsequently, have demonstrated that through teacher consultation and inservice training, classroom consultants can assist teachers in implementing these procedures effectively in their classrooms. As a result of effective teaching techniques, students not only engage themselves more actively in learn-

ing, but also attain higher levels of achievement and exhibit less disruptive classroom behavior. This section of the chapter is organized around the instructional procedures listed in Table 1 that have been shown to maximize academic learning time and achievement among students.

Working from classroom observations and teachers' time-use logs, school psychologists can provide individual consultation and inservice training to assist teachers who are interested in increasing their students' academic learning time. Not every type of procedure may be effective or efficient for all classrooms and all teachers. Individual teaching approaches and classroom arrangements dictate that school psychologists should work collaboratively with teachers to analyze time use, target areas in which learning time can be increased, identify students whose academic learning time is below average, and develop strategies that are tailored to teachers' particular styles and needs. The best practices described below are effective in increasing academic learning time when used in isolation or in combination with other procedures. A critical role for school psychologists is to facilitate teachers' utilization and, when necessary, modification of these procedures in classrooms.

Increasing Instructional Time

Teachers who are task-oriented and who carefully plan and organize teaching activities use more of their available time for actual instruction than teachers who are not as planful (Goss, 1985). Thus, one way to increase instructional time is to help teachers develop effective methods for organizing their classrooms and maintaining a strong academic focus during instruction. One strategy for school psychologists is to hold workshops prior to the beginning of school to equip teachers with procedures for establishing a controlled and orderly classroom environment early in the school year. To ensure that teachers maximize the proportion of allocated time that is actually

TABLE 1
Best Practices to Increase Academic Learning Time

Increase Time Used for Instruction:
    Establish contingencies for school attendance and punctuality.
    Minimize interruptions.
    Program for smooth transitions.
    Maintain an academic focus.

Increase Engaged Time:
    Clarify instructions and expectations regarding performance.
    Keep instruction fast-paced.
    Maintain an interactive teaching style and frequent student responding.
    Adopt seating arrangements to maximize attending.

Increase Productive Learning Time:
    Use seatwork effectively.
    Provide immediate, appropriate feedback.
    Diagnose, prescribe, and monitor performance accurately.

devoted to instruction, school psychologists may encourage and monitor several time-management activities described below.

Establish contingencies for school attendance and punctuality. Student absenteeism and tardiness may lead to a significant loss of critical instruction time. Teachers usually find it necessary to review instruction or repeat directions for activities to allow absent or late students to catch up. One way to prevent this time loss is to reinforce high rates of attendance and punctuality on a consistent basis, through the use of positive procedures such as praise, points, monthly certificates, or within-class competition. In addition, teachers can be encouraged to structure their classroom routines so that being present and on time are expected. For example, instructions for daily activities should be given only once at the start of a class session and not repeated for students who are not present. Similarly, strict adherence to a daily schedule, including starting and stopping classes and lessons exactly on time, communicates to students that punctuality is expected and that maximizing instructional time is important.

Minimize interruptions. The amount of time students spend in instruction depends, in part, on what other activities occur in the classroom. Organizational activities such as listening to announcements, sharpening pencils, cleaning up, putting on coats, collecting money for lunch, or lining up for recess account for much of the noninstructional time. Even these brief disruptions of instructional time, when added up over the course of a school year, can significantly decrease the total amount of instructional time. Such disruptions of ongoing instruction can be minimized by planning and scheduling beforehand specific times during the day or week for noninstructional, managerial activities. To minimize interruptions from other teachers, Paine et al. (1983) suggest that teachers post a sign on their doors indicating they cannot be interrupted and leave a pad and pencil for messages.

To avoid excessive instructional time loss, teachers and administrators should routinely reevaluate school-wide schedules and policies with regard to activities such as announcements on the intercom, timing of recess and lunch breaks, school assemblies, and handling attendance, money collection, and other management tasks. Through team planning, activities that are not essential might be eliminated from a teacher's schedule, handled by parent volunteers or secretaries, or at least streamlined as much as possible.

Related to minimizing interruptions is an emphasis on limiting students' disruption of others and, in turn, limiting the number of teacher reprimands of misbehaving students. High levels of misbehavior and disruptiveness among students are related to lowered instructional and engaged time (Jones & Jones, 1986). In that disruptiveness typically occurs because students do not understand a task, are not engaged in a learning activity, or are unable to obtain assistance when it is needed, best practices for increasing academic learning time often simultaneously prevent the occurrence of misbehavior. Nonetheless, when disruptions do occur, it is necessary to use warnings and mild reductive procedures, such as reprimands, consistently and immediately to eliminate or reduce a potential source of lost instructional time.

Program for smooth transitions. A typical school day has many activity shifts that require movement from one location in the classroom or building to another. Observations in elementary school classrooms indicate that, on the average, 5 to 10 minutes are spent changing from one activity to another (Kuergeleis, Deutchman, & Paine, 1980). With approximately 10 activity shifts each day, transitions alone may account for more than one hour of lost instructional time. Although these transitions are necessary, the less time spent in transition, the more time available for instruction. Making smooth transitions can be facilitated by formulating, teaching, and practicing step-by-step rules and procedures for activity shifts. Brief verbal cues or teacher signals, rather than lengthy instructions, can also shorten the time between activities. For example, a teacher can signal a transition time by simply stating, "It's transition time. Get ready for spelling. You need your spelling books and pencils."

Having prepared all the materials for each lesson and activity before the school day begins and placing materials in the room where they are to be used also enable teachers to monitor and praise students' appropriate behavior during transition time. Similarly, using student assistants to distribute and collect materials frees up the teacher's time to monitor and facilitate smooth transitions. As an added incentive for minimizing the amount of time required for transitions, students can be timed during activity shifts and possibly compete with one another or against a pre-established criterion.

Maintain an academic focus. The effective-teaching research recommends that teachers maintain a strong academic, business-like focus in their classrooms to maximize learning time (Evertson, Emmer, Clements, Sanford, Worsham, & Williams, 1981). One way to maximize an academic focus is for teachers to select classroom activities primarily on the basis of their teaching potential. For example, a film may be a good use of allocated time if students are prepared for the film with advanced organizers, pay attention while they are viewing it, and are held accountable for certain information in the film. If, on the other hand, students are not prepared for what they will see, become disruptive and inattentive, and cannot relate what they have learned, then viewing a film is not a productive use of available time. Another way to maintain an academic focus for all students is to allocate time to various activities as much as possible on the basis of students' needs, abilities, and performance. Teachers may allocate time to academic subjects for groups of students and then schedule short time blocks of each day for individualized practice of concepts or skills that students failed to grasp during regularly scheduled lessons. This extra daily practice is important for low-achieving students, in particular, who may need more than the average amount of learning time to master academic material. The use of peer tutors or parent volunteers can also help students to receive the additional learning time they require. Such procedures allow teachers to maintain an appropriate academic focus to meet the instructional time needs of individual students within the structure of whole-class or group instruction. Finally, to gain the greatest benefit from instructional activities, teachers might consider scheduling activities such that a preferred activity immediately follows a less preferred one, and important activities occur when most students in a class have been observed to be at peak levels of attending and functioning.

Increasing Engaged Time

The majority of teachers agree that one of the most difficult tasks associated with teaching is maintaining student attention during whole-group instruction as well as during independent seatwork. Research shows that teachers who are structured, interactive, fast-paced, and directive in their teaching styles have students who are more highly engaged in learning (Gettinger, 1986). One goal of school psychologists should be to help teachers increase the extent to which they exhibit the types of behaviors described below. Independently, these variables may have only slight positive effects on academic learning time; however, when used in combination as part of a teacher's overall teaching style, they are likely to affect learning time and achievement in noticeable ways.

Clarify instructions and expectations regarding performance. Students are more likely to remain on task if teachers have clear and specific rules, consistent consequences for compliance and non-compliance with these rules, and routine classroom procedures with which all students are familiar. Students may become inattentive and even disruptive during instruction when they receive instructions for an activity that are inadequate or unclear. To help reduce students' uncertainty about instructions, teachers should have students write down, repeat, or paraphrase task directions after they have been given. Posting instructions where all students can easily see them, breaking tasks down into smaller segments when students are having difficulty with particular directions, and responding positively to questions about task instructions can also help eliminate students' lack of understanding of task directions, a common reason for not attending.

For independent seatwork activities, task instructions are most effective when they include precise statements about what students are expected to do, how students can request assistance, where they should hand in completed work, and what they may select as alternative activities when they finish the assigned work. Teachers can further maximize the effectiveness of task instructions when directions are worded simply and are few in number. Research indicates that students are less likely to be unengaged when teachers present directions both orally and in writing, give directions only when all students are attending, demonstrate the steps that students should follow to complete academic tasks, and direct students to begin work only after all instructions have been given. Finally, teachers should attempt to move throughout the classroom monitoring children, praising students who follow directions, and administering consequences for those who do not comply.

Keep instruction fast-paced. Student engagement is influenced significantly by the overall pacing of instruction. Better pacing of lessons is one way teachers can increase the total amount of learning time within an instructional period. Research indicates that the smoother the instructional pace, the more content that is covered, the more students are engaged in learning, and the more likely they are to achieve. Teachers tend to underestimate the amount of content that can be covered and the pace they can follow without instruction being too rapid, particularly with low-achieving students (Berliner, 1988). Shavelson (1983), for example, found that teachers tended to pace high-ability groups as much as 15 times faster than low-ability groups. Thus, school psychologists might encourage teachers to attempt to set an instructional pace that is slightly faster than normally used.

Maintain an interactive teaching style and frequent student responding. Different teaching styles and modes of instruction produce characteristic variations in engagement rates and opportunities for responding among students (Berliner, 1988). Teaching styles that are

TABLE 2
Teacher Behaviors Comprising an Interactive Teaching Style

Teacher-directed, oral presentation of new material.
Verbal interaction with teacher discussion and review of students' work.
Drill and controlled practice.
Questions to observe and assess students' performance and understanding of material.
Frequent opportunities for student responding.
Reinforcement and acknowledgement of correct responses.
Supportive correction of wrong responses.
Optimal difficulty level of instruction to ensure feedback is maximally positive.

interactive in nature and incorporate as much as possible small-group or whole-class instruction have the greatest potential for enhancing overall engagement and responding. An interactive teaching style includes the basic components presented in Table 2. The teacher behaviors listed in this table have all been shown to be positively related to active learning time and achievement.

One area of investigation emerging from the Beginning Teacher Evaluation Study is the relationship between interactive teaching behaviors and student engagement (Fisher et al., 1980). The results of this analysis indicate that students are more actively engaged in learning when they spend time in group lessons that allow frequent responding among all students. Similarly, during independent seatwork, students are more highly engaged when they have frequent contact with the teacher. Given these conclusions for group-based and individual learning, teachers may benefit from having the following guidelines to structure their teaching to provide frequent opportunities for substantive interaction.

First, it is important for teachers to include all students in classroom discussions. For example, calling upon students at random rather than relying on volunteers as well as incorporating choral responding whenever possible enable all students to take part in discussions. When teachers call on a student before asking a question, other students may not attend to or think about the question. Thus, by asking the question, looking around the room, allowing students to consider the question, and then calling on a student to answer, teachers may create greater interest, anticipation, and consequently, higher levels of attending during group instruction. Asking students occasionally to comment on an answer provided by a classmate has also been shown to maintain students' engagement, even when they are not actively responding. Second, questions are most effective in engaging all students when the difficulty level of the question is such that the student being called on is most likely to be successful. Finally, when an incorrect response is given, an interactive style involves staying with the student and prompting or rephrasing the question so that the student can succeed. An incorrect answer may also provide an opportunity for the teacher to clarify and reteach.

This interactive type of instruction is important for maintaining high engagement rates for low-functioning students in particular. In a study of math classes in 11 schools, Stallings (1976) found that the same teachers were interactive with their advanced classes, but not interactive with their lower ability classes. Low-achieving students tended to receive less instruction directly from teachers, were given more workbook assignments, and were off-task significantly more often than high-achieving students, who received explanations, review, and feedback from teachers more frequently.

Adopt seating arrangements to maximize attending. Teachers can also be guided to increase engagement rates among their students by adopting seating arrangements that permit visual contact with all students. Teachers should make conscious efforts to move around the room continuously, going to students rather than having students come to them. Teacher's movement allows all students to be actively involved in interactions with teachers, minimizes the amount of wait time spent at the teacher's desk, and limits distracting and potentially disruptive student movement throughout the classroom.

Increasing Productive Learning Time

As noted earlier, students who attain high levels of productive or academic learning time are likely to achieve more than students who accumulate less academic learning time. Increasing the overall amount of instructional time and finding ways to keep students engaged are certainly important considerations for teachers and school psychologists. Maximizing productive learning time, however, extends beyond increasing instructional or engaged time. What occurs during instructional or engaged time and the appropriateness of instruction for individual students affect the amount of academic learning time that actually occurs. The following guidelines suggest ways to enhance the appropriateness and quality of instruction and, as such, reflect best practices for increasing the overall productivity of learning time in classrooms.

Use seatwork effectively. A good deal of work in classrooms is done by students on their own. In fact, research shows that elementary school students spend more than half their time working privately at seatwork (Anderson, 1985). One finding emerging from time-on-task studies is that during seatwork, students display lower engagement rates and have less productive learning time because they are not interacting directly with the teacher. Seatwork, however, remains a necessary component of small-group practices. With small-group instruction, a teacher spends more time directly involved with one group of students while other groups are working independently. If seatwork is carefully designed and appropriately matched to the level of individual students, it is not intrinsically a bad alternative to listening to the teacher. Productive learning time can result from independent work if teachers are encouraged to consider the following guidelines:

1. Teachers should monitor seatwork by moving around the room systematically. Contacts with individual students should be relatively short in duration (30 seconds) in that longer contacts can minimize teachers' ability to scan the room. When teachers are involved with a small group, they may assign the group a task and leave briefly to monitor students involved in seatwork.

2. Clear procedures should be established about what students should do when their seatwork is completed, such as self-correcting, recording, and filing their work. Also, alternative activities should be available for students once seatwork tasks are completed.

3. A procedure should be developed for requesting and obtaining assistance during seatwork that is not disruptive and allows students to continue to work while they wait. Classroom observations suggest that when students raise their hands or leave their seats to request assistance, they stop working on assigned tasks and lose valuable learning time. Paine et al. (1983) developed a three-part solution for handling seatworkers' requests for assistance. This procedure is designed to maintain high levels of on-task behavior during seatwork without interrupting the teacher's other small-group instruction. Their procedure incorporates (a) an assistance card attached to each desk that students raise up to signal when they need help, (b) a folder of "sure-fire" work that can be done without assistance which students complete when they cannot continue on assigned tasks without help, and (c) teacher praise only for students who use their assistance cards and continue to work paired with ignoring of students who fail to use the procedures. Peer tutoring is also an effective strategy for providing help to students who need it without interrupting the teacher.

Provide immediate, appropriate feedback. Individualized feedback is a critical component of productive, academic learning time. Feedback to students characterized by specificity and academic relevance has been found to be highly associated with academic learning time (Rosenshine, 1979). The information given to students about their performance should indicate whether their responses are correct or incorrect, provide specific suggestions for reworking the problems, and make reference to the task that generated the student's responses. A related characteristic of feedback is its frequency. Teachers can be advised to increase the frequency of their feedback by (a) collecting frequent, small samples of student work, (b) providing repeated practice and assessment of knowledge of new materials, and (c) holding students responsible for maintaining records of their performance in each subject area and regularly comparing student records with teacher records. In sum, greater frequency, specificity, and academic relevance of feedback can have a significant effect on academic learning time.

Unfortunately, correcting students' daily work and providing them with immediate and specific feedback may require a great deal of a teacher's available instructional time. There are several strategies that enable teachers to offer immediate and appropriate feedback for maximizing students' productive learning while minimizing loss of instructional time. One procedure is for teachers to correct students' work as they circulate during seatwork periods. This method is particularly effective in that students are alerted to problems and have errors corrected before practicing a skill the wrong way. In other words, this procedure prevents low success learning time, which has been shown to be negatively related to achievement. Student self-correction is another method for encouraging students to become more independent and responsible for their own work as well as providing them with immediate feedback to prevent repetition of errors. Research has shown that productive learning time can result from work in which students correct and learn from their mistakes. Paine at al. (1983) suggest that teachers might develop and use a checking station in their classrooms to facilitate self-correction. Checking pens and answer keys should be available at these stations along with posted rules and procedures for correcting completed work.

Diagnose, prescribe, and monitor performance accurately. Diagnosis and prescription for maximizing productive learning time involve assessing the current knowledge, skill level, and strengths and weaknesses of students to decide on appropriate instructional goals and activities, task difficulty, grouping, and scheduling. Diagnosis may be accomplished through several assessment procedures available to school psychologists, including listening to children read, talking about their interests, watching the way they work during independent seatwork, using curriculum-based measures of performance, or giving formal tests. The monitoring of students' performance occurs during actual instruction. Teachers monitor students' responses during engaged learning time to determine whether the instructional goals are appropriate and are being met.

Accuracy in diagnosing student skill levels, prescribing appropriate tasks, and monitoring student performance during instruction are all related to academic learning time and student achievement. In effect, students are more productively engaged in learning and learn more when teachers are aware of what their students can and cannot do and adapt their instruction accordingly.

Integrating Best Practices in Classroom Instruction

In the fourth-grade class for which a time-use assessment was described earlier, the school psychologist worked with the teacher during math instruction to attempt to increase academic learning time among students. This was achieved primarily by implementing procedures to increase overall instructional time. The following scenario depicts this classroom in which students' productive learning time has been maximized.

Mrs. Jones has adopted a small-group instructional approach for introducing new concepts in math. While she directs a small instructional group, the other children work independently or in pairs on assignments. Directions for seatwork are written on the board. In accordance with Paine et al.'s (1983) procedure, children use a card on their desk to indicate they need assistance from Mrs. Jones or a designated peer helper. Students continue to work on "sure-fire" multiplication problems available in a folder at their desks while they wait for help. Occasionally, Mrs. Jones looks up from her small-group teaching and praises individual children who are engaged in their work. When the group of children with whom Mrs. Jones is working have been assigned their seatwork, they quietly pick up their work and return to their desks. The teacher takes 5 minutes to circulate among students and respond to requests for assistance. She then signals for another small group to pick up their work and go to the corner for their math instruction.

At the end of the day, Mrs. Jones uses the remaining 10 minutes to practice some division problems with which children had difficulty during the regular math lesson. She reviews how to do the problems, divides the class into three teams, and gives each team several problems to complete. When the students have completed their problems, Mrs. Jones shows the answers on the overhead projector and students grade their own work. The day's student assistant collects the papers so Mrs. Jones can record the results on each student's individual progress chart.

SUMMARY

Academic learning time is related to student achievement. Furthermore, components of academic learning time may be controlled directly by classroom teachers. These two conclusions have emerged from recent research on effective teaching and have important implications for school psychologists. First, an awareness of the concept of academic learning time and its relationship to achievement

outcomes is important for school psychologists to emphasize for educators. Second, school psychologists can assist teachers in conducting an assessment of time use in their classrooms followed by an identification of areas to target for improvement. For example, allocating more time alone does not ensure that more learning will occur. If there is low engagement or inattentiveness among students during the allocated instructional time, then providing more time in itself will not be an effective strategy for enhancing achievement.

Finally, through consultation, modeling, or inservice training addressing the best practices presented in this chapter, school psychologists can be instrumental in helping teachers acquire and implement more effective classroom practices to increase their students' academic learning time. To maximize productive learning time, teachers must be able to increase instructional time by carefully planning their academic program, managing their classrooms effectively, and structuring classroom activities. Teachers may also need to increase or maintain student engagement, and teach in a manner that is both time-efficient and matched to individual needs. In sum, how well teachers can be helped by school psychologists to manage time effectively in their classrooms is a key factor in increasing academic learning time and achievement among students.

REFERENCES

Anderson, L. M. (1985). What are students doing when they do all that seatwork? In C. W. Fisher & D. C. Berliner (Eds.), *Perspectives on instructional time* (pp. 198-202). New York: Longman.

Berliner, D. C. (1988). The half-full glass: A review of research on teaching. In E. L. Meyen, G. V. Vergason, & R. J. Whelan (Eds.), *Effective instructional strategies for exceptional children* (pp. 7-31). Denver, CO: Love.

Carroll, J. B. (1963). A model of school learning. *Teachers College Record, 64,* 723-733.

Evertson, C. M., Emmer, E. T., Clements, B. S., Sanford, J. P., Worsham, M. E., & Williams, E. L. (1981). *Organizing and managing the elementary school room*. Austin, TX: Research and Development Center for Teacher Education, University of Texas.

Fisher, C. W., Berliner, D. C., Filby, N. N., Marliave, R. S., Cahen, L. S., & Dishaw, M. M. (1980). Teaching behaviors, academic learning time, and student achievement: An overview. In C. Denham & A. Liberman (Eds.), *Time and learning* (pp. 7-32). Washington, DC: National Institute of Education.

Gettinger, M. (1984). Individual differences in time needed for learning. *Educational Psychologist, 19*, 15-29.

Gettinger, M. (1986). Issues and trends in academic engaged time of students. *Special Services in the Schools, 2*(4), 1-17.

Goss, S. S. (1983). Keeping students on task. *Schools and Teaching, 1*(1), 1-4.

Jones, V. F., & Jones, L. S. (1986). *Comprehensive classroom management: Creating positive learning environments* (2nd ed.). Boston: Allyn & Bacon.

Karweit, N. (1988). Time-on-task: The second time around. *NASSP Bulletin, 71*, 31-39.

Kuergeleis, B., Deutchman, L., & Paine, S. C. (1980). *Effects of explicit timings on students' transitions*. Eugene, OR: Direct Instruction Follow Through Project, University of Oregon.

Marliave, R., & Filby, N. N. (1985). Success rate: A measure of task appropriateness. In C. W. Fisher & D. C. Berliner (Eds.), *Perspectives on instructional time* (pp. 217-235). Hillsdale, NJ: Erlbaum.

Paine, S. C., Radicchi, J., Rosellini, L. C., Deutchman, L., & Darch, C. B. (1983). *Structuring your classroom for academic success*. Champaign, IL: Research Press.

Rosenshine, B. V. (1979). Content, time, and direct instruction. In P. L. Peterson & H. J. Walberg (Eds.), *Research on teaching, concepts, findings, and implications* (pp. 28-56). Berkeley, CA: McCutchan.

Shavelson, R. J. (1983). Review of research on teachers' pedagogical judgments, plans, and decisions. *Elementary School Journal, 83*, 392-414.

Stallings, J. (1976). How instructional processes relate to child outcomes in a national study of follow-through. *Journal of Teacher Education, 37*, 37-43.

Steere, B. F. (1988). *Becoming an effective classroom manager: A resource for teachers*. Albany, NY: SUNY Press.

Strother, D. B. (1984). Another look at time-on-task. *Phi Delta Kappan, 66*, 714-717.

Walberg, H. J. (1988). Synthesis of research on time and learning. *Educational Researcher, 17*(3), 76-85.

ANNOTATED BIBLIOGRAPHY

American Association of School Administrators. (1982). *Time on task: Using instructional time more effectively*. Arlington, VA: Author.
This book contains 77 pages of information and tips for increasing students' time on task. The detailed appendix provides a step-by-step approach that schools can use to develop a program to improve time management and increase learning time. This book is available from the American Association of School Administrators, 1801 North Moore Street, Arlington, VA 22209.

Gettinger, M. (1986). Issues and trends in academic engaged time of students. *Special Services in the Schools, 2*(4), 1-17.
This article, first, describes theoretical views of time and learning, including Carroll's model. Next, it provides a review of major empirical time-and-learning studies that document a relationship between academic learning time and achievement. Third, it addresses the implications of this research for increasing learning time among students.

Paine, S. C., Radicchi, J., Rosellini, L. C., Deutchman, L., & Darch, C. B. (1983). *Structuring your classroom for academic success*. Champaign, IL: Research Press.
The procedures presented in this book will help teachers keep students actively engaged in learning and make the most efficient use of class time. A unique feature of the book's highly practical approach is the use of step-by-step descriptions of techniques and actual scripts teachers may follow in implementing these techniques in their classroom.

Steere, B. F. (1988). *Becoming an effective classroom manager: A resource for teachers*. Albany, NY: SUNY Press.
Although the focus of this book is on overall classroom management procedures, Steere includes a chapter addressing academic engaged time. In this chapter, and throughout the book, he reviews a large body of teacher effectiveness research and presents practical suggestions for teachers that emerge from the research findings.

Strother, D. B. (Ed.). (1985). *Time and learning*. Bloomington, IN: Phi Delta Kappa.
This volume is part of Phi Delta Kappa's "Hot Topics" series. It contains a selection of reports, articles, and monographs that present both research and practical suggestions dealing with the relation of time to learning. The volume is available from Phi Delta Kappa, Box 789, Bloomington, IN 47402.

28

Best Practices in Individual Counseling with Elementary Students

Deborah Tharinger
Margaret Koranek
The University of Texas at Austin

School psychologists who work in elementary schools are key personnel for offering direct services to children. The focus of this chapter is on the process and issues involved in providing *individual counseling* to children in elementary schools. Other important direct services, such as group and crisis counseling, are not discussed here because of space limitations. The target children are those whose behavioral, cognitive, emotional, and/or interpersonal functioning causes them or others distress and interferes with their development and learning. School psychologists, provided that they possess the necessary education, training, and supervised experience, are in an excellent position to help identify these children and, if appropriate, to offer them counseling services.

This chapter is divided into three sections. The first, an overview, describes the process and goals of counseling with children and examines basic concerns in the identification and assessment of children in need of counseling, key issues in service delivery, and important features of school-based case management. The second section addresses basic considerations and discusses the essential knowledge, skills, and awarenesses necessary for engaging in counseling with children. The final section provides an eight-stage generic model designed to guide practitioners in constructing their own *best practices* in counseling elementary children.

OVERVIEW

Counseling with children can be described as the process of ongoing interactions between a mental health professional and a child who has sought, or for whom someone serving as his or her representative has sought, help for a particular problem or set of problems. The professional provides conditions to alleviate such children's distress (and the referring adults' distress) and to improve the psychological functioning of these children by directly facilitating change in them and by promoting change in their environment, possibly the family system and the school system. Psychological functioning includes the children's cognitions, perceptions, emotions, behavior, and relationship capacity. The *goals* of counseling include alleviating these children's emotional and cognitive distress, changing their behavior, assisting in their self-understanding, getting them back on track developmentally (in terms of meeting the challenges of upcoming developmental tasks successfully), promoting needed environmental changes, and ultimately, facilitating a more positive fit between them and their home and school environments. The *means* by which the goals of counseling are reached are primarily interpersonal contact (Kazdin, 1988), and they may include, with children, verbal interactions, play interactions, and interactions with other modalities, such as art or music. A variety of therapeutic aids such as puppets, games, and stories also may be used as a means of reaching therapeutic goals. Interpersonal contact with the children's parents and teachers may be an adjunct.

A developmental perspective is useful in conceptualizing, choosing, and evaluating specific and appropriate counseling goals for each child and the means by which the goals are to be met (Tharinger & Lambert, in press). By understanding normal developmental progressions and age and culturally designated developmental tasks, the practitioner can match the means to the child's developmental levels and can set, as the goals for counseling, progression to higher, more advanced and mature levels of psychological functioning and preparation for upcoming developmental tasks. The progress of counseling can be evaluated in terms of the child's reaching higher levels of psychological functioning and being able to accomplish developmental tasks successfully. Research on the effectiveness of child counseling or psychotherapy, although still lacking in rigor, is supportive. For an excellent review of this topic, see Kazdin (1988).

Unique Aspects of Counseling with Children

Unique aspects of counseling children have been described by Clarizio and McCoy (1983). First, children are unlikely to seek help voluntarily or to initiate entry into counseling. The decision typically is made by an adult in the child's environment and is met with varying degrees of acceptance, compliance, or resistance from the child. The "involuntary" nature of children's entry into counseling may result in little or no motivation on their part to engage in the process. However, with sensitive preparation of the children and awareness of techniques for handling resistance, most elementary children referred for counseling are responsive and engage in

the process. Techniques for dealing with the involuntary and possibly resistant child include acknowledging the resistance, attempting to understand the basis for the resistance, being flexible and yet enforcing limits, and using humor. Second, most children lack an explicit understanding of counseling, the purpose and goals of treatment, and the role they are to assume. It is the psychologist's responsibility to educate these children in an age-appropriate manner about the process of counseling, making sure that they understand the nature of the counseling process and related issues, such as confidentiality.

Third, children's verbal and cognitive abilities, as well as the organization of their personalities, are in the process of development. Practitioners working with children must be keenly aware of the developmental levels of each individual child and need to match the intervention to the capabilities of the child. Hughes (1988) is an excellent source on the cognitive and language capacities of children in relation to counseling. Finally, children are extremely dependent on and influenced by their immediate environments, most specifically their families and their schools. They have relatively little power to create marked change or to eliminate stressors in their environments. Although children can be assisted in developing a healthier or more adaptive perspective or attitude about their environment, it is essential whenever possible to involve significant adults in a child's life as part of a counseling intervention.

School-Based Counseling with Children

There does not appear to be a systematic model of school-based counseling. Most scholarly discussions of counseling, psychotherapy, or behavioral or cognitive therapy with children do not emphasize or even include a school-based model for practice (see Gumaer, 1984; Hensen & Van Hasselt, 1987; Kendall & Braswell, 1985; Lord, 1985; Morris & Kratochwill, 1983; Prout & Brown, 1983; Reisman, 1973; Schaefer & Millman, 1979; Schaefer, Millman, Sichel, & Zwilling, 1986). That is, they do not interrelate the basics of providing counseling or psychotherapy to children with the particulars of functioning within a school setting. A book by Dodds (1985) addresses issues in working with schools, but it is designed to assist private or clinical practitioners in their conjoint work with teachers and schools. In practice, it appears that mental health professionals conducting counseling in the schools acquire generic theoretical and research knowledge and generic counseling skills. They then attempt to integrate these models and skills into the particular school system in which they are working. Training programs in school psychology, through school-based practicum and internship experiences, have the responsibility of assisting future school psychologists in integrating their knowledge and counseling skills into practice in the school. Extensive supervision by school psychologists experienced in providing child counseling in schools is required for the school psychology trainee. In addition, psychological service departments in school districts have the responsibility of providing ongoing training and supervision for their school psychologists in the unique aspects of counseling with children and school-based counseling. Peer supervision in the schools can be an excellent method of sharing expertise and offering support within a group of school psychology professionals who are providing counseling for children.

It is important for the practitioner to remember that the educational system and the mental health system (which has provided much of the generic education and training in providing counseling), although similarly invested in promoting growth in children, have somewhat different perspectives. These differences have the potential of raising conflicts between a counselor, especially a school-based counselor, teachers, and school administrators. The primary goal of the school system is to educate all children, with a focus on academics and group socialization. The primary goal of the mental health system is to assist individuals in solving emotional, behavioral, and interpersonal problems. The school-based counselor, being employed within the school system, must engage in a delicate balance between individual child and group school goals as well as academic versus personal and interpersonal growth goals. Although this balance is very difficult, the school-based counseling practitioner must be cautioned *not* to be pulled into the trap of "changing the child's behavior quickly," talking *at* rather than *with* children, and "straightening children out" rather than trying to understand them. In addition, the school-based counselor must work hard at obtaining school district support for the activity of child counseling by educating teachers and administrators about its value and demonstrating its effectiveness. Furthermore, the school-based counselor must seek clarification of the school district's philosophy on the involvement of parents in school-based counseling. In other words, does the district see counseling as a child–school process or a child–school–family process? The latter, although more time- and resource-demanding, has the potential of promoting children's growth and development much more effectively, from both an educational and a mental health viewpoint.

Identification, Assessment, Service Delivery, and Case Management Issues

Issues of identification, assessment, service delivery, and case management need to be considered by the school psychologist who is engaged in counseling elementary school students. The processes that lead to identification and referral of children for counseling in the schools and the methods used to evaluate the appropriateness of school counseling as an intervention for individual children need to be examined. Issues of service delivery, related to such considerations as the limits of the school's responsibility for providing services and the prudent allocation of the school's resources, and case management issues, such as the interface between school counseling services and other areas of the child's life, are other areas that must be considered in providing individual counseling services to students in elementary school.

Identification of children in need of counseling. An understanding of currently accepted educational, research, and psychiatric frameworks for conceptualizing and organizing the emotional and behavioral problems of childhood is useful in developing an understanding of the referral process, in assessing the appropriateness of referrals, and in communicating with other professionals. In many schools a sharp division of labor exists in that the counseling of students classified as handicapped is relegated to special education personnel, such as school psychologists, whereas counseling students who have not been classified as handicapped is the job of regular education counselors, who also may be school psychologists. Within special education departments, Public Law 94-142, the Education of All Handicapped Children's Act of 1975, provides a system for organizing childhood handicapping conditions. In special education, children classified as seriously emotionally disturbed and as learning-disabled are likely to constitute the bulk of counseling referrals. However, children classified as mentally retarded or as physically handicapped also may be referred for counseling owing to difficulties in adjusting to their handicapping conditions or because of other emotional or behavior difficulties. Decisions about the provision of counseling for regular education students are often made by regular education counselors, whereas decisions about providing counseling for special education students are often made by teams composed of parents, administrators, teachers, and other school personnel who meet to formulate the child's individual education plan (IEP). Schools have a legal obligation to provide counseling to special education students when counseling is a part of the individual education plan.

A widely accepted method for conceptualizing childhood emotional and behavioral problems is to view these difficulties in terms of a continuum that sets externalizing difficulties at one extreme and internalizing difficulties at the other (Achenbach, 1982). This continuum describes styles of emotional expression that result in very different presenting problems for children. The typical internalizing child presents as shy, overcontrolled, and withdrawn, whereas an externalizing child is more prone to act out and present difficulties in behavior control. Children exhibiting emotional–behavioral difficulties typical of either end of this continuum, as well as children who exhibit behaviors typical of both extremes, are apt to be referred for school counseling services. However, in many settings, children who fall on the externalizing end of the continuum are most likely to be referred for special services because they exhibit disruptive behavior in the classroom that is disturbing to others (Achenbach, 1982).

The system most widely used by mental health professionals for classifying mental disorders is the system devised by the American Psychiatric Association. This system is outlined in the *Diagnostic and Statistical Manual of Mental Disorders*, Third Edition–Revised (DSM III-R) (American Psychiatric Association, 1987). Some school districts routinely apply DSM III-R diagnoses to special education students who are classified as seriously emotionally disturbed. Although acceptable validity and reliability have yet to be demonstrated for several of the diagnostic categories applied to children and adolescents, familiarity with this system is recommended because of its wide use. (For a more detailed discussion, see Quay & Werry, 1986.) Diagnostic categories specified by DSM III-R as likely to manifest themselves first in childhood or adolescence include attention deficit hyperactivity disorder, conduct and oppositional disorders, and several types of anxiety disorders. Children who exhibit symptoms of these disorders are likely candidates for counseling referrals. In addition, children referred for school counseling may be exhibiting symptoms of the various mood disorders, such as depression.

Finally, some referrals for school counseling will result more from issues related to the child's adjustment and reaction to stress than to handicapping conditions, the extremes of internalizing or externalizing behavior, or diagnosed mental disorders. Examples of children in this category include children who suffer physical, sexual, or emotional maltreatment and children who struggle to adapt to dysfunctional families. Children returning to school after placement in a hospital or residential treatment setting or young children experiencing difficulties in adjusting to school are other examples. Similarly, children struggling to adjust to the aftermath of a crisis or who are in the process of mourning a loss, such as having recently experienced a move, a divorce, or the illness or death of a family member, are likely counseling referrals. Such reactions to stress may cause difficulties for the child that are mild and short-lived or they may lead to difficulties that are more serious and long-lasting, perhaps requiring concomitant diagnosis of a mental disorder or handicapping condition.

In addition to being familiar with accepted systems for classifying the emotional and behavioral problems of childhood, professionals engaging in school counseling should be thoroughly familiar with the referral process in the school systems they serve. Thorough knowledge of both the formal and informal processes that underlie the referral, including communication with the person(s) initiating the referral, will facilitate understanding of the child and the surrounding systems and will help in evaluating the potential success of individual counseling as an intervention.

Education of those who are sources of referral as well as adjustment of the referral process toward making more appropriate referrals, is something else for the school psychologist to consider. For example, children who exhibit an excess of externalizing behavior — that is, children who act out in the classroom — are more likely to come to the attention of teachers than internalizing children who may benefit from counseling but may suffer in silence because the referral process of the school is set up to overlook

them. Educating teachers and other referral sources to be aware of the signs that children exhibit when they are in emotional distress will help prevent overlooking children who may need counseling but who may express their difficulties subtly. Conversely, the availability of consultation services and the development of classroom teachers' behavior management skills should minimize the overreferral of children whose difficulties are more appropriately handled in the classroom or with interventions other than individual counseling.

Assessment issues. After a child has been referred, an assessment usually is made to ascertain the most appropriate intervention under the circumstances. School psychologists are often in a position to make such an evaluation. In some cases, engaging in such procedures as examining existing records, observing referred children in various settings, and interviewing them and persons who know them will be sufficient to assess their needs. In other cases, formal psychological testing will be necessary. The needs of the individual child should dictate the assessment methods. Only those methods necessary to gain the needed information should be used and, when possible, only the techniques that are the least costly in terms of time and intrusiveness should be chosen.

In addition to considering whether individual counseling matches the specific needs of the child, systems issues also should be examined during the assessment, including the potential involvement of the child's family in interventions undertaken at school. Although contact with children's families has become a luxury in many school systems because of the scarcity of time that plagues both family members and school personnel, the position is taken here that contact with a child's family is essential to assessing the potential efficacy of individual counseling and to establishing an effective counseling relationship. Some assessment of the child's family situation should be made, including an estimation of the potential of family members to be involved and to either support or undermine the counseling relationship. An evaluation of the effects that individual counseling with a child will have on his or her family relationships is also important. Teaching open expression of anger, for example, to children who live in families that devalue and punish the expression of negative feelings, is not likely to be helpful to the families or the children. Assessment of the potential impact of individual counseling on a child's family relationships, as well as assessment of the family's potential for supporting progress made in counseling, is an important step before choosing individual school counseling as an intervention.

Issues in service delivery. Service delivery issues present another important set of systems issues that must be considered in choosing individual counseling as an intervention. Allocation of scarce resources is a pervasive problem in most school districts, making cost-effectiveness an important consideration in choosing interventions for the amelioration of children's problems. The question of cost-effectiveness is particularly relevant to the choice of individual counseling as an intervention because of the large amount of time involved. The school psychologist likely will be required to assess which children are most in need and which children will be most likely to profit from individual counseling and to balance the need with the availability of school resources. The ability and willingness of the child's family to provide help outside the school is another factor in this equation.

The limitations of school responsibility in relation to the multitude of problems exhibited by school children present additional issues that must be carefully considered. Public schools in the United States have come to serve functions related to the care and socialization of children that were once reserved for families and other social institutions, so that accurate delineation of school responsibility has become difficult. The Education of All Handicapped Children Act, Public Law 94-142 (1975), mandates the provision of individualized programs for handicapped children in order to maximize their ability to participate in school activities (Sarason, 1982). Maximizing a child's educational progress and ability to participate in school activities includes providing support services such as counseling when needed. However, the provision of such services is mandated only when the services are designed to ameliorate factors that interfere with children's abilities to take advantage of ordinary school activities and programs. Determination of the limitations of school responsibility in providing services for troubled children presents complex legal and ethical issues to those entrusted with planning school programs. With regard to providing individual counseling for a handicapped child, a decision must be made about whether the child's difficulties are interfering with his or her ability to take advantage of school opportunities. If not, the school is not legally mandated to provide a service. School psychologists need to consider these issues carefully in relation to the provision of individual counseling, as well as the provision of other services to school children, and they should be aware of school policies and the positions of school administrators in relation to these issues.

Case management issues. The school psychologist engaging in counseling with elementary-aged students also needs to be aware of several case management issues, including the level of intervention with the child; communication with other professionals, including making referrals; communication with the child's family, including issues of consent and confidentiality; and adjunct work with the family and in the classroom.

When beginning a counseling relationship with a child, it is important to plan the level of the intervention. This means considering how deep to go in developing the counseling relationship and in examining emotional issues. Counseling that is set up to facilitate deep emotional change is more taxing for the counselor, the child, and the child's family and takes more time than counseling planned to provide short-term support, to provide new information or skills, or to change overt behavior. In addition to considering the child's needs, availability of resources (especially the amount of time available for developing the counseling relationship) should be considered. Children should not be encouraged to uncover feelings that are difficult to manage if time and energy are not available to assist them in working through those feelings. For instance, attempts should not be made to begin a deep counseling relationship a few weeks before school adjourns for summer vacation.

Communication with school and community professionals is a necessary supplement to individual school counseling. Other professionals can often be helpful by providing information that will aid in understanding the child, and the counselor may have an opportunity to help the child indirectly by providing information to other involved professionals. As always, guidelines concerning confidentiality should be carefully considered in communicating information. An important aspect of communication among professionals is making referrals. Referrals to other professionals in the school or community are appropriate in many situations involving children in school counseling — for example, when counseling interventions that have been chosen fall outside the school psychologist's areas of expertise, when decisions have been made to recommend counseling or therapy outside the school, or when services other than counseling are needed by the children, their families, or others involved with them.

Communication with these children's parents and other family members is also important. As noted in the discussion of assessment, support from the children's families can have a great influence upon the effectiveness of the counseling relationship. Periodic evaluation of the children's family relationships and the effect of counseling on those relationships is necessary. The goal of counseling is not to provide a relationship substitute, but rather to provide a means of strengthening the children's resources for understanding and using existing relationships. Communication with the families is of vital importance in this process.

In working with children and the families, it is essential that school psychologists become knowledgeable about the issues of confidentiality and informed consent. In general, the right of parents to be approached for informed consent when interventions that are not part of the regular school program are undertaken with their children is supported by statutory and constitutional law. Similarly, our legal system tends to support parents' rights to information about their children, including information shared within counseling relationships, thus limiting the confidentiality of the counseling relationship. Although the law allows for some exceptions in the case of adolescents, legal support for parents' rights regarding these issues is relatively well established in the case of elementary-age children (Bersoff, 1982). Care should be taken to obtain informed consent from children's parents before beginning a counseling relationship. With regard to confidentiality, it is recommended that a clear agreement about this issue be negotiated with the children and their families early in the counseling relationship in order to avoid later misunderstandings.

The possibility of doing adjunct work with children in the classroom, with their families, or with individual family members presents another set of issues. Children's problems seldom occur in isolation and work with the children in other settings or with significant others in the children's lives may possibly be helpful. However, the effect of such work on the unique relationship between a child and the counselor should be considered. The relationship that evolves in individual counseling is a very special one and when the counselor changes roles or gives attention to other persons important to the child, the relationship may be affected in important ways. For example, the child's perception of the counselor as aligned with other adults may profoundly influence interactions in the counseling relationship. Teachers sometimes ask school psychologists to assist in the classroom management of their young clients. Again, the potential advantages of such involvement should be weighed against the potential effects on the counseling relationship. The counselor's acceptance of the role of disciplinarian is likely to change his or her relationship with the child. Decisions concerning such involvement should be based on the unique circumstances of each case and will depend upon the specific needs of the child and the dynamics of the relationships among the counselor, the child, and others.

BASIC CONSIDERATIONS

Obtaining Essential Knowledge, Skill, Awareness, and Experience

As described earlier, counseling with children involves the development of a relationship between the counselor and the children in which the counselor provides conditions to alleviate the children's distress and to improve their psychological functioning. The *means* by which the goals are sought are primarily interpersonal contact. In order to provide these means, the counselor working with children must obtain knowledge, skill and experience, and self-awareness.

Knowledge of developmental theories. Theory organizes and gives meaning to facts, provides a framework for them, and assigns more importance to some facts than others. In addition, a theory provides a framework for raising questions, guiding observations, and generating new information. Theory is useful to the practitioner because it provides heuristics to guide problem solving. Knowledge of developmental theories can prevent tunnel vision among practitioners working with children. A rigid perspective on children's behavior can be avoided if one incorporates several theories in an attempt to understand children's behavior. In addition, as cultural conditions change and new information about development comes to light, practitioners must select what is useful from the various

theories and research findings and ignore the aspects that no longer are applicable. For example, combining and integrating Freud's concern with underlying motivations and emotions, Erikson's concern with the mastery of psychosocial crises, Piaget's concern with cognitive structures, learning theory's concern with performance in specific situations, Bowlby's concern with the quality of attachment and the impact of separation, and Bronfenbrenner's concern with transactions between the child and multiple environmental systems produces a powerful perspective for understanding children's behavior. Extensive reviews of developmental theories are provided by Breger (1974), Langer (1969), Miller (1983), Mussen (1983), Salkind (1981), and Thomas (1985).

Knowledge of theoretical models for counseling: The need for integration in application. Models adopted to guide counseling usually correspond with the practitioner's explicit or implicit theories of developmental change. Ideally, the model or models of change adopted should fit the needs of the child and must take into account the needs and resources of significant others in the child's environment. Each of the major developmental theories proposes a model of change that can be applied to the counseling process. From the psychoanalytic perspective, the goal is to promote emotional and behavior change by interpreting the child's defenses to bring unconscious elements that have been impeding development into consciousness. From the psychosocial perspective the goal is to promote progression to higher stages of cognitive reasoning, thus allowing the child greater ego flexibility, a wider range of application of her or his new structural organization, the ability to coordinate more perspectives, and an increased capacity to handle new and previously unfamiliar problems.

From the social learning and cognitive behavioral perspectives the goal of counseling is to promote behavior change directly by reinforcing desired behavior, by providing positive models and positive vicarious experiences, and by changing children's cognitions, for example, by helping them learn cognitive mediation to control impulsive behavior or by helping them alter negative self-evaluations. From the attachment perspective the goal is to promote interpersonal change by providing a secure base for exploration by establishing a positive relationship with the children and by aiding them in understanding the quality of their earlier attachments and the significance of their losses in relation to current behavior. From the ecological and the transactional organism perspectives the goal is to promote behavioral, cognitive, emotional, and interpersonal change by effecting changes in the children (using the above methods) and in the children's environment. Environmental targets include parents (e.g., through parent consultation), family (e.g., through family therapy), teachers (e.g., through teacher consultation), and peers (e.g., through classroom interventions and group counseling).

Although each of the above models of change is applicable with children and will promote change if matched with the children's needs and developmental levels, an integrated perspective provides the most flexible and comprehensive model for change in counseling with children in schools. The practitioner cannot effect change optimally by focusing on only one domain of functioning, be it emotional, cognitive, or behavioral. A counselor needs to work simultaneously on cognitive, emotional, and behavioral change. In addition, with few exceptions, the counselor needs to work with significant adults in the child's world to effect change in the child's environment, especially parents and teachers.

Knowledge of research and clinical literatures. It is important for counselors to be knowledgeable about the clinical and research literature available on treatment guidelines for specific disorders of childhood. There are many reference materials available that specifically address prevalence, specific features, etiology, and treatment guidelines for children who have childhood mental disorders that frequently lead to a counseling referral, such as attention deficit hyperactivity disorder, conduct disorder, anxiety disorders, and mood disorders (Morris & Kratochwill, 1983; Quay & Werry, 1986). It also is important to have available literature on children's reactions, adjustment, and recovery in relation to such life stressors as loss, abuse, and handicaps. Children dealing with these issues are likely counseling candidates. Fortunately, there is a growing body of research findings on the effects of life events as stressors that negatively affect children's development (Felner, 1984; Garmezy & Rutter, 1983; Johnson, 1986). The literature on the effects of divorce of parents on children's development (Hodges, 1986; Wallerstein, 1985), as well as on the effects of death of parents (Blom, Cheney, & Snoddy, 1986) are important resources offering useful perspectives for school psychologists. As more children experience a portion of their lives in single-parent homes and with stepparents, researchers are investigating the impact of each (Canong & Coleman, 1984; Carlson, 1987). In addition, conceptual models and research are available on the effects of maltreatment on children's development, including physical abuse (Parke & Collmer, 1975), sexual abuse (Vevier & Tharinger, 1986), psychological abuse (Brassard, Germain, & Hart, 1987; Garbarino, Guttman, & Seeley, 1986), and the effects of growing up in an alcoholic family (Tharinger & Koranek, 1988).

Knowledge of children's play and the use of play therapy. Erikson (1977) has described play in a broad sense to mean the use of imagination to try out ways of mastering and adapting to the world, to express emotion, to recreate past situations or imagine future situations, and to develop new models of existence. From Erikson's view, problems that cannot be solved in reality can be resolved through doll play, dramatics, sports, art, or playing house. Similarly, Bettelheim (1987) states that if we wish to understand children, we must understand their play. Children use play to work through and master quite complex psychological difficulties of the past and the present.

From children's play we can gain an understanding of how they see and construe the world, what they would like it to be, and a sense of their concerns and problems. Through play children express what they cannot put into words. Children do not play spontaneously only to pass time, although they and the adults observing them may think so. What children choose to play at is motivated by their inner processes, desires, problems, and anxieties (Bettelheim, 1987).

Play in a counseling relationship is to the child what verbalization is to the adult. Play is the natural and comfortable medium of expression for children. It is a medium for expressing feelings, exploring relationships, describing experiences, disclosing wishes, and building solutions. Seldom do children discuss their feelings; they act them out. Thus, play is the natural medium for much of counseling or therapy with children. Play therapy does not belong to a particular theoretical orientation. It is a medium, a method of expression and communication. It has been described from a psychoanalytic perspective (Esman, 1983), a client-centered perspective (Guerney, 1983), a cognitive-behavioral perspective (Meichenbaum, 1977), and a cognitive-developmental perspective (Harter, 1983).

It is essential that a counselor working with children respect their need for expression through play. The presence and use of toys and play materials in a counselor's office indicates to children that it is a place for children, that their world is understood there, and that they can be children there. Play materials invite children to participate and establish a natural means of communication that does not require or depend upon verbal interaction. Children's play becomes the medium of exchange and is utilized by the counselor not only to understand them but also to build a therapeutic relationship and to solve problems.

Although the words *play* and *game* may seem synonymous, it is important to recognize that they in fact refer to broadly distinguishable stages of development, play relating to an earlier stage and game to a more mature stage (Bettelheim,

1987). Generally speaking, *play* refers to the activities of young children that are characterized by freedom from all but personally imposed rules that may be changed at will and by the absence of any goals outside the activity itself. Games, however, are usually competitive and are characterized by agreed-upon, often externally imposed rules, by a requirement to use the implements of the activity in the manner for which they are intended and not as fancy suggests, and frequently by a goal or purpose outside of the activity, such as winning the game (Bettelheim, 1987). Games involve performance and stress. When all is going well, children in the middle childhood usually can adhere to a game's requirements. But when things become bewildering or frustrating they may revert to spontaneous play. Although they may understand the rules governing the game and even insist that others follow them, they will be unable to obey them and may assert that the rules do not apply to them. They may ask to stop, or to start over, or to change the rules to their advantage.

The reasons for children's game behavior are not difficult to understand and are very important to the counselor's understanding of them. Children who are feeling momentarily defeated by the complex realities of the game, perhaps because they are losing and thus about to suffer damage to tenuous self-respect, are likely to revert to a play level, at which the rules no longer pertain, in order to rescue their endangered feeling of competence (Bettelheim, 1987). Some counselors may not understand and will want these children to behave more "maturely" or to not "cheat." However, insistence on mature behavior just when a child feels most threatened merely aggravates his or her sense of defeat.

It is important to examine and understand the meaning behind children's behavior in play and in games and to incorporate it into the counseling work. Excellent resources on play and game therapy with children include *Handbook of Play Therapy* by Schaefer and O'Connor (1983) and *Game Play: Therapeutic Use of Childhood Games* by Schaefer and Reid

(1986). In addition, a contribution by Landreth (1983) on providing play therapy in elementary schools addresses issues involved in providing play therapy services at school. The issues discussed are informing school personnel about what play therapy is, how it helps children, how it fits into the overall scheme of educational objectives, and what play therapy can reasonably be expected to accomplish; the cost of equipping and maintaining a playroom; dealing with noise and the reactions of others' noise coming from the playroom; limit setting; scheduling; and adjusting to school holidays and breaks.

Possession of communication, interpersonal, and interviewing skills. As discussed throughout, counseling is an interpersonal process. The counselor's ability to communicate effectively with children and to provide trust and a secure base for their psychological exploration provides the basis for the work. The humanistic or experiential, client-centered tradition in counseling has provided the best explication of these basic capacities and skills. A recent book by Benjamin (1987), although not specifically focused on counseling with children, reviews the basics of communication and facilitation, asking questions, and responding. A book on experiential therapy with children (Wright, Everett, & Roisman, 1986) discusses the core conditions of intimacy, congruence, valuing, empathy, and locus of responsibility. A chapter by Hughes (1988) provides an excellent discussion of methods of interviewing children that are developmentally sensitive, as do chapters by Harter (1983) and Bierman (1983).

Possession of office space, materials, and toys. School-based counselors need certain basic resources in order to practice with children. First, although physical office space is a luxury in the schools, it is essential for a counselor to have a space that is private and consistent. For counseling children individually, the office space does not need to be large, but it does need to be equipped in a way that welcomes children and promotes safety and security. It also is important to provide materials and toys that allow for the expression of anger and aggression, as children have few releases for these feelings. Recommended materials and toys for working with elementary-age children in counseling include paper, crayons, magic markers, scissors, clay, puppets, guns, dolls, games (of various developmental levels), stuffed animals, building blocks, plastic animals, monsters, and, if possible, a doll house and a blow-up "bobo" punching bag. In addition, a collection of books that address childhood stressors, such as divorce and death, are good to have and to use with children and their parents.

Self-awareness and self-care. The provision of counseling services to children, along with the provision of consultation to teachers and parents, is a demanding and possibly stressful role for the overburdened school psychologist. It is important to acknowledge that professionals who provide counseling may be "overgivers" or "rescuers" themselves, which can lead to overinvolvement in cases, to lack of clarity on the appropriate boundaries of involvement, or simply to taking on too much. School psychologists who are in the counseling role need to evaluate carefully any such tendencies and take necessary, appropriate, professional steps to clarify and limit their involvement. School psychologists in general need to practice self-care. That is, they need to value themselves and to realize and respect their own limits. It is not healthy to agree to provide more services to children and systems than one can responsibly deliver. Practice and support from professional peers and supervisors is necessary to enable the school psychologist to say "No, I cannot do that now," when necessary. In addition, it is essential for school psychologists in the counseling role to examine their own psychological needs and issues and to be aware of any countertransference or theme interference that may surface with a given child client. Seeking consultation on particular cases and obtaining personal counseling or therapy may be helpful in addressing these issues.

BEST PRACTICES

An eight-stage model is offered to give the school psychology practitioner a step-by-step guide to best practices in school-based counseling with elementary students, from the referral to the termination and evaluation of the counseling intervention. The counseling process has been divided into stages to facilitate understanding, but it must be recognized that the boundaries between the stages will not always be as clear in actual practice.

Stage 1: Assess Appropriateness of Referral for School-Based Counseling

When a referral for school-based counseling is received, an evaluation of the referral should be made. After reviewing the child's school records and gathering information from the referral source about the reason for the referral, the presenting problem(s), and steps that have been taken to alleviate the problem(s), a judgment should be made about the appropriateness of the referral for individual counseling in particular. Alternative interventions, such as changing the child's classroom assignment or classroom routine, consulting with the child's teachers, creating a behavior management plan, working with the child's family, or referring the child for assistance outside of the school may be chosen as more appropriate than individual school-based counseling. Two decisions typically must be made at this stage. It must be determined which intervention(s) will be most effective for the child and by whom the interventions will be provided (e.g., by the school or by outside professionals). Observations, interviews, and sometimes formal psychological testing also may be needed to inform these decisions.

Stage 2: Plan for Counseling and Prepare Goals

Information gathered at Stage 1 may be sufficient or additional assessment may be necessary in order to begin planning the counseling intervention. A theoretical framework and methods and techniques must be chosen that are appropriate for the child's difficulties and developmental level and are compatible with the personality and philosophy of the counselor. Counseling goals and interventions chosen to meet those goals should match the child's cognitive and emotional development. For example, the difficulty that young children have in taking another person's point of view or in understanding abstract concepts must be considered when formulating the plans for counseling with them.

At this stage, the child's parents must be contacted in order to obtain their permission for counseling. It also is vitally important that the parents, teachers, and other important people in the child's life be included in planning the counseling intervention. Consideration should be given to their needs, viewpoints, and relationships with the child and provisions should be made for continuing communication with them during the course of counseling. When at all possible, it is recommended that the school psychologist arrange to meet with the child's parents or, if a meeting is not possible, contact by telephone may be used to begin a relationship that is likely to be of vital importance as counseling progresses.

Stage 3: Begin Counseling

The main work at this stage involves preparing the client for the counseling intervention. This is likely to consist of eliciting the child's knowledge, feelings, and beliefs about counseling in order to discuss them and using developmentally appropriate language to share with the child the goals and expectations that the counselor and significant others have formulated for the relationship. It is desirable to give consideration to the child's needs, to involve him or her in the planning process, and to work at instilling an expectation that counseling will involve working together to remedy matters which are troubling to the child.

Guidelines concerning confidentiality should be explained to everyone involved at the beginning of the counseling relationship. Different counselors adopt different policies regarding this issue. For example, some share information with parents concerning the child's general progress while striving to keep the specific content of the counseling sessions confidential. Other counselors inform the client that the parents will have access to information from sessions, but agree to respect the confidentiality of any information the child specifically requests be kept private. Whatever policy is adopted, parents' legal rights to information about counseling with their children and the legal obligation of counselors to take appropriate action if a threat of harm to the children or others is revealed should be carefully considered.

It is also appropriate to discuss some limits and rules with the child at this time, such as time and length of sessions. However, care should be taken not to overwhelm the child with a long list of rules. Often, limits are more easily understood if they are discussed when the occasion for them arises.

Stage 4: Establish a Working Relationship

The foundation for improvement and meeting the counseling goals is laid at this stage, for the relationship is the primary tool for change in counseling. Excellent guidelines for establishing the trust necessary for an effective counseling relationship are given in the framework of the person-oriented experiential approach (see, e.g., Wright, Everett, & Roisman, 1986). Listening with empathy, making emotional connections by striving to see and feel the child's world, communicating that understanding, and offering emotional support are essential to building a relationship of trust. In order for progress to be made, a base of trust and security in the counseling relationship must be built. From such a base, threatening feelings and thoughts can be examined and new ways of thinking, behaving, and relating can be attempted. Personal characteristics, such as warmth and the counselor's ability to be comfortable with the client's and with her or his own thoughts and feelings, will help to establish

the conditions necessary to building a relationship of trust with the child. Skills, such as the ability to summarize, to reflect, and to be consistent, especially with respect to setting limits, also are pertinent to establishing a working relationship with the child.

Stage 5: Implement the Plan for Change

After a working relationship has been established, the plan for effecting change is implemented. The qualities and skills used to build the relationship in the beginning will remain relevant throughout the course of counseling. The ability to play and to communicate a sense of humor, to use self-disclosure to promote the child's growth, to use interpretation to make connections among patterns and themes in the child's life, and to use confrontation when necessary are examples of additional skills needed by counselors at this stage.

Care must be taken throughout the process to maintain communication with parents, with teachers, and with others working with the child. Environmental influences on the child need to be noted and environmental interventions made when necessary. Boundary issues must be addressed as they arise. Rather than attempting to take over the roles of others in the client's life, the counselor should encourage the caring and competence of others in relation to the child.

As the counseling relationship progresses, it also is essential for the counselor to consider his or her feelings in relation to the child and in relation to others involved with the child. Careful and consistent attention to personal feelings will help to clarify emotional reactions related to the counseling relationship, will help in understanding the client's feelings, and will help in understanding the reactions of others to the child. It is common for counselors to experience emotional reactions in their professional relationships that echo past relationships. Awareness that this is happening can help the counselor react to the present client and the present situation rather than reacting blindly to remnants of past persons and situations. The counselor should not hesitate to arrange for consultation with a colleague if difficulties in understanding and managing emotions within the counseling relationship are encountered. The value that consultation with colleagues holds for improving the practice of school-based counseling cannot be emphasized enough. The awareness that can result from meetings to discuss particular cases, to discuss theories, methods, and techniques, and to discuss personal feelings in relation to cases is a vital part of one's development as an effective counselor.

Stage 6: Continue Counseling and Adjust the Plan for Change

Ideally the counseling relationship should be continued until as much progress as possible has been made toward meeting the counseling goals. During the course of counseling, it is important to engage in a constant reevaluation of the original plan and goals. Changes in the child's environment, changes in the child, changes in the counselor's skill and knowledge, and simple mistakes in planning make constant adjustment of the goals and methods chosen for counseling essential.

Periodic feedback about the progress of the intervention (within the guidelines of confidentiality) should be given to the child, the parents, and others, such as teachers, during the course of counseling, as well as at termination. Such feedback should be honest and should be designed to maximize the potential for future improvement.

Stage 7: Plan for Termination and Terminate

In theory, it is time to end counseling when the goals have been met and the child's functioning has improved. In practice, the decision to end counseling is seldom simple or ideally planned. The child may have only partially met the goals, parents or school personnel may not cooperate; new problems may surface due to environmental stressors, the child may move, the psychologist may leave the school, or the school year may end. If all goals are met and the client is functioning well, the decision to end counseling is easier than in cases where few goals have been met and the child is not functioning well. In the latter case, it often becomes apparent that counseling that is more intensive than the school is able to provide, or perhaps an entirely different type of intervention, should be implemented. Even if the goals have been met only partially, enough progress may have been made that interactions between the child and significant others are healthier and more likely to support continued progress.

In planning for termination, it is vitally important for the counselor to be sensitive to the significance that the relationship has for the child. If a meaningful relationship has been formed, some negative feelings, such as anger and sadness, are to be expected when the relationship ends. For some children, the end of the relationship may stir up problems associated with earlier separations and losses. As much as possible, time should be taken to work through feelings associated with ending the counseling relationship. Attention should also be paid to positive feelings associated with the child's improvements and plans for the future. Reassurances that the child will be remembered, exchanging keepsakes, such as photographs or artwork, and providing the child with a telephone number or some other means of maintaining contact are examples of strategies used by counselors to help manage the feelings associated with termination. Gradually reducing the counseling time or arranging to spend some time with the child following termination of the counseling relationship may be helpful in some situations. In addition to attending to the feelings of the child and others involved with the child, school psychologists need to care for themselves by taking the steps necessary to work through their own feelings relating to terminating with their small clients.

Stage 8: Evaluate Effectiveness of the Counseling Intervention

Systematic evaluation of the effectiveness of school-based counseling interventions is essential in order to improve counseling methods and outcomes. Attention to concurrent interventions and environmental changes, to progress notes that have been kept regularly during the course of each case, to data from pre- and postassessment measures, and to measures of the child's behavior in natural contexts that correspond to the goals of the counseling intervention should prove useful in understanding the child's progress and the extent to which the counseling goals have been met. After termination, a written summary of the precounseling assessment, the counseling goals, the course of the counseling relationship, and an evaluation of the progress made by the child should be placed in the client's school record. Regular follow-up with parents and/or teachers is recommended in order to trace the child's adjustment and progress after the counseling intervention has ended.

SUMMARY

In this chapter, the process and issues involved in providing individual counseling to children in elementary schools were discussed. In the overview, counseling was defined generically as the process of ongoing interventions between a mental health professional and a client during which the child, or someone representing the child, has sought help for a particular problem or set of problems. The professional provides conditions to alleviate the distress and improve the psychological functioning of the client by directly facilitating change in the child and by promoting change in the child's environment, most centrally the family system and the school system. A developmental perspective was presented as being useful in conceptualizing the goals of counseling. Unique aspects of counseling children were discussed, as were the particular issues involved in counseling children in a school setting. The role of school psychology training programs and psychological services departments in school districts for providing initial and ongoing training and supervision in school-based counseling was addressed and possible tensions that can develop between educational goals and mental health goals in a school setting were noted. The adoption of a child–school–family philosophy, involving parents and teachers as part of a counseling intervention, was stressed throughout. In addition, extensive issues were discussed regarding the identification of children in need of counseling, service delivery, and school-based case management. The basic considerations necessary for providing school-based counseling services were reviewed and included knowledge of developmental theories; knowledge of theoretical models for counseling; knowledge of research and clinical literature; knowledge of play and the use of play therapy; possession of communication, interpersonal, and interviewing skills; possession of office space, materials, and toys; and self-awareness and self-care. Following, an eight-stage model was offered as a step-by-step guide to *best practices* in school-based counseling with elementary students. School psychologists are challenged to integrate the information presented here into their day-to-day practice with elementary children in need of counseling services.

REFERENCES

Achenbach, T. M. (1982). *Developmental psychopathology*. New York: Wiley.

American Psychiatric Association. (1987). *Diagnostic and statistical manual of mental disorders* (3rd ed.-rev.). Washington, DC: Author.

Benjamin, A. (1987). *The helping interview: With case illustrations*. Boston: Houghton Mifflin.

Bersoff, D. N. (1982). The legal regulation of school psychology. In C. R. Reynolds & T. B. Gutkin (Eds.), *Handbook of school psychology* (pp. 1043–1067). New York: Wiley.

Bettelheim, B. (1987, March). The importance of play. *Atlantic Monthly*, pp. 34–46.

Bierman, K. L. (1983). Cognitive development and clinical interviews with children. In B. B. Lahey & A. Kazdin (Eds.), *Advances in clinical child psychology* (Vol. 6, pp. 217-250). New York: Wiley.

Blom, G. E., Cheney, B. D., & Snoddy, J. E. (1986). *Stress in childhood: An intervention model for teachers and other professionals.* New York: Teachers College Press.

Brassard, M. R., Germain, R., & Hart, S. N. (1987). *Psychological maltreatment of children and youth.* New York: Pergamon.

Breger, L. (1974). *From instinct to identity: The development of personality.* Englewood Cliffs, NJ: Prentice-Hall.

Canong, L. H., & Coleman, M. (1984). The effects of remarriage on children: A review of the literature. *Family Relations, 33,* 389-406.

Carlson, C. (1987). Children and single-parent homes. In A. Thomas & J. Grimes (Eds.), *Children's needs: Psychological perspectives* (pp. 560-571). Kent, OH: NASP.

Clarizio, H. F., & McCoy, G. F. (1983). *Behavior disorders in children* (3rd ed.). New York: Harper and Row.

Dodds, J. B. (1985). *A child psychotherapy primer: Suggestions for the beginning therapist.* New York: Human Sciences Press.

Education of All Handicapped Children's Act of 1975 (PL 94-142). 20 USC Sec. 401 (Supp. 1975).

Erikson, E. H. (1977). *Toys and reasons.* New York: Norton.

Esman, A. H. (1983). Psychoanalytic play therapy. In C. E. Schaefer & K. J. O'Connor (Eds.), *Handbook of play therapy* (pp. 11-20). New York: Wiley.

Felner, R. D. (1984). Vulnerability in childhood: A preventive framework for understanding children's efforts to cope with life stress and transitions. In M. C. Roberts & L. Peterson (Eds.), *Prevention of problems in childhood.* New York: Wiley.

Garbarino, J., Guttman, E., Seeley, J. W. (1986). *The psychologically battered child.* San Francisco: Jossey-Bass.

Garmezy, N., & Rutter, M. (1983). *Stress, coping and development in children.* New York: McGraw-Hill.

Guerney, L. F. (1983). Client-centered (nondirective) play therapy. In C. E. Schaefer & K. J. O'Connor (Eds.), *Handbook of play therapy* (21-64). New York: Wiley.

Gumaer, J. (1984). *Counseling and therapy for children.* New York: Free Press.

Harter, S. (1983). Cognitive-developmental considerations in the conduct of play therapy. In C. E. Schaefer & K. J. O'Connor (Eds.), *Handbook of play therapy* (pp. 95-127). New York: Wiley.

Hensen, M., & Van Hasselt, V. B. (1987). *Behavior therapy with children and adolescents: A clinical approach.* New York: Wiley.

Hodges, W. F. (1986). *Interventions for children of divorce: Custody, access, and psychotherapy.* New York: Wiley.

Hughes, J. (1988). Interviewing children. In J. Dillard & R. Reilley (Eds.), *Interviewing and communication skills.* New York: Merrill.

Johnson, J. H. (1986). *Life events as stressors in childhood and adolescence.* Beverly Hills, CA: Sage.

Kazdin, A. E. (1988). *Child psychotherapy: Developing and identifying effective treatments.* New York: Pergamon.

Kendall, P. C., & Braswell, L. (1985). *Cognitive-behavioral therapy for impulsive children.* New York: Guilford.

Landreth, G. L. (1983). Play therapy in elementary school settings. In C. E. Schaefer & K. J. O'Connor (Eds.), *Handbook of play therapy* (pp. 200-212). New York: Wiley.

Langer, J. (1969). *Theories of development.* New York: Holt, Rinehart, Winston.

Lord, J. P. (1985). *A guide to individual psychotherapy with school-age children and adolescents.* Springfield, IL: Thomas.

Meichenbaum, D. (1977). *Cognitive-behavioral modification: An integrative approach.* New York: Plenum.

Miller, P. H. (1983). *Theories of developmental psychology.* San Francisco: Freeman.

Morris, R. J., & Kratochwill, T. P. (Eds.). (1983). *The practice of child therapy.* New York: Pergamon.

Mussen, P. (Ed.). (1983). *Handbook of child psychology* (4th ed., Vols. 1-4). New York: Wiley.

Parke, R. D., & Collmer, D. A. (1975). Child abuse: An interdisciplinary analysis. In E. M. Hetherington (Ed.), *Review of child development research* (Vol. 5). Chicago: University of Chicago Press.

Prout, H. T., & Brown, D. T. (1983). *Counseling and psychotherapy with children and adolescents: Theory and practice for school and clinic setting.* Tampa: Mariner.

Quay, H. C., & Werry, J. S. (1986). *Psychopathological disorders of childhood* (3rd ed.). New York: Wiley.

Reisman, J. M. (1973). *Principles of psychotherapy with children*. New York: Wiley.

Salkind, N. J. (1981). *Theories of human development*. New York: Van Nostrand.

Sarason, S. B. (1982). *The culture of the school and the problem of change*. Boston: Allyn and Bacon.

Schaefer, C. E., & Millman, H. L. (1979). *Therapies for children*. San Francisco: Jossey-Bass.

Schaefer, C. E., Millman, H. C., Sichel, S. M., & Zwilling, J. R. (1986). *Advances in therapies for children*. San Francisco: Jossey-Bass.

Schaefer, C. E., & O'Connor, K. J. (1983). *Handbook of play therapy*. New York: Wiley.

Schaefer, C. E., & Reid, S. E. (196). *Game play: Therapeutic use of childhood games*. New York: Wiley.

Tharinger, D., & Koranek, M. (1988). Children of alcoholics - At risk and unidentified: A review of research and the service roles of school psychologists. *School Psychology Review, 17,* 166–191.

Tharinger, D., & Lambert, N. (in press). Contributions of developmental psychology to school psychology. In T. Gutkin & C. Reynolds (Eds.), *Handbook of school psychology* (2nd ed.). New York: Wiley.

Thomas, R. M. (1985). *Comparing theories of child development* (2nd ed.). Belmont, CA: Wadsworth.

Vevier, E., & Tharinger, D. (1986). Child sexual abuse: A review and intervention framework for the school psychologist. *Journal of School Psychology, 24,* 293–311.

Wallerstein, J. S. (1985). Children of divorce: Preliminary report of a ten-year follow up of older children and adolescents. *Journal of the American Academy of Child Psychiatry, 24,* 545–553.

Wright, L., Everett, F., & Roisman, L. (1986). *Experiential psychotherapy with children*. Baltimore: John Hopkins University Press.

ANNOTATED BIBLIOGRAPHY

Dodds, J. B. (1985). *A child psychotherapy primer: Suggestions for the beginning therapist*. New York: Human Sciences Press.
An eclectic approach to practical issues encountered by beginning child therapists is presented by this book. Issues discussed include the therapy room and materials, initial evaluation, first contact, the therapeutic relationship, confidentiality, parents, potential problems, evaluation, and termination. An informative chapter on school contact, written for child therapists working outside the school, is included.

Johnson, J. H., Rasbury, W. C., & Siegel, L. J. (1986). *Approaches to child treatment: Introduction to theory, research, & practice*. New York: Pergamon.
This book reviews major approaches to the psychological problems of childhood and the conceptual models upon which they are based. General issues in child treatment and an overview of child psychopathology also are included. The authors recommend fitting the treatment to the situation of the particular child and they provide generous case studies to illustrate this approach to child treatment.

Prout, H. T., & Brown, D. T. (1983). *Counseling and psychotherapy with children and adolescents: Theory and practice for school and clinic setting*. Tampa: Mariner.
This book is a comprehensive overview of six major approaches to counseling/therapy with children. It includes coverage of behavioral approaches, rational-emotional approaches, reality therapy approaches, person-centered approaches, Adlerian approaches, and psychoanalytic approaches. This theory, view of psychopathology, and treatment guidelines for each approach are described and illustrated.

Schaefer, C. E., & O'Connor, K. J. (1983). *Handbook of play therapy*. New York: Wiley.
This book reviews the major approaches to play therapy and describes special play therapy techniques for particular settings including the elementary school. Also suggested are methods of play therapy for clients with specific childhood problems, such as victims of child abuse, children of divorced parents, aggressive children, learning-disabled children, and physically handicapped children.

Wright, L., Everett, F., & Roisman, L. (1986). *Experiential psychotherapy with children*. Baltimore: John Hopkins University Press.
This book applies the theory and methods of the humanistic, client-centered tradition to the practice of child therapy. Discussions of the historical development of this approach, of outside factors that influence the therapy, and of case studies are included, but it is the lucid and sensitive examination of the child-therapist relationship that makes this book especially useful.

29

Best Practices in Intellectual Assessment

Daniel J. Reschly
Iowa State University

Jeffrey P. Grimes
Iowa Department of Education

School psychology was born in the prison of the IQ test. This controversial thesis was advanced by a prominent American psychologist in a commentary on school psychology some years ago (Sarason, 1975). In this chapter, the appropriate role for IQ tests will be considered as school psychology emerges from the prison of the IQ test, along with fundamental considerations in intellectual assessment, appropriate and inappropriate uses of measures of intellectual functioning, and recommended best practices in intellectual assessment. This analysis will suggest a more limited role for intellectual assessment in the future practice of school psychology. Although we foresee a diminished role for IQ testing, we strongly assert that intellectual assessment should reflect best practices since use of intellectual measures is nearly always associated with significant decisions about children and youth.

The dominance of intellectual assessment in current practice and graduate education of school psychologists was apparent from the results of a recent national survey (Reschly, Genshaft, & Binder, 1987). Practicing school psychologists indicated that about two-thirds of their time was devoted to various aspects of special education eligibility determination. Intellectual assessment was nearly always a part of eligibility determination.

The typical practitioner administered 17.8 intellectual measures per month, most often the Wechsler Intelligence Scale for Children–Revised (WISC-R). Intellectual assessment appears to be a virtual daily activity for school psychologists currently. In their evaluation of the quality of graduate training, practitioners indicated that intellectual assessment was emphasized most and taught best. Similar results were obtained from a survey of graduate faculty who indicated that measures of intellectual functioning were the most frequently taught assessment procedures, most frequently supervised, and a critical component of practica and internships. If not a prison, intellectual assessment clearly represents the salient milieu of school psychology graduate education and practice. Frequent occurrence does not equate with best practices.

Professional conduct is a matter of personal choice (Grimes, 1981). We must make choices in our professional services that match client needs and enhance the likelihood of effective interventions. The following issues may complicate the exercise of appropriate choices: (a) client preferences, (b) special education rules, and (c) traditional notions of IQ tests as useful structured observations. Occasionally, consumers request IQ test results, but we have the discretion and responsibility to evaluate those requests. A patient with a headache may ask a physician to conduct a CAT scan. However, the physician must decide what diagnostic procedures are needed, and may or may not use a CAT scan. Likewise, we must carefully assess clients' needs and choose the most appropriate assessment procedures. Consumer preferences or expectations cannot be the principal basis for our professional services.

Special education rules and other legal regulations have a clear influence on our professional choices. Careful study of these regulations followed by scrutiny of current practices indicates that we sometimes overreact to the regulations. For example, the critical federal regulation regarding the content of the multifactored assessment in initial placement or reevaluations lists areas that are to be assessed *where appropriate, NOT* necessarily assessed with every student (see *Education of the Handicapped Act*, CFR 300.532). Testing in every area including the area general intelligence is often unnecessary (e.g., IQ is not critical to behavior disorder/seriously emotionally disturbed). Much IQ testing occurs now in misguided efforts to comply with legal regulations. Other special education categorical diagnoses, e.g., mental retardation or learning disability, under current state special education rules, may require IQ assessment. Alternatives are being considered in these diagnoses (Reschly, 1988a; Shinn, 1988; Siegel, 1989). Where IQ assessment is not in the best interests of clients, we can also make choices to pursue changes in the state rules. Efforts to change rules through formulating well articulated positions based on the needs of children and youth, with description of appropriate alternatives, followed by concerted action by individuals and groups, have been successful in many states. That too, is a personal choice.

One of the most frequent justifications for administering an IQ test to nearly all students with learning and/or behavioral problems is the opportunity provided for structured observations. The problem with this use is that the observations occur in an unnatural setting, on a one-to-one basis, with an adult who may have little continuing involvement, using tasks that do not directly reflect the difficulties that prompted the referral. Most important, the behavioral observations in the testing setting do not accurately predict behavior in other settings (Glutting, Oakland, & McDermott, 1989). Structured observations in natural settings are enormously useful if applied through the use of direct measures of the behavior of concern and to crucial environmental or instructional variables that can be used in interventions. The question is, in large part, whether we adapt to the client's setting or whether we require the client to adapt to our setting. Use of the IQ test for structured observations is also time consuming, usually requiring three to four hours for test administration, scoring, interpretation, and report preparation. Time is precious; our time as well as the client's. Time devoted to IQ testing inevitably reduces or eliminates the opportunity to conduct other assessment activities.

A historical perspective for the above points may provide more context. Intelligence tests are "clinical" instruments. They were developed when there were few professional service providers and clients went to clinics or clinic-like settings for evaluations. The evaluation by necessity had to use indirect samples of behavior using a structured set of tasks. These standardized measures were better than existing alternatives. Conditions have changed. School psychology by definition brings the psychologist's services to the school, the natural setting. Clinic-based procedures have become increasingly less appropriate as the number of school psychologists has increased to nationwide ratio of one to less than 2000 students (Reschly et al., 1987). Opportunities now exist, as well as the necessary technology, to conduct direct and repeated measures of the behaviors of concern in the natural setting. Practice in the 1990s needs to reflect these changes.

Dissatisfaction with the dominance of intellectual assessment has appeared in the school psychology literature for at least 30 years. These concerns relate to recognized limitations of intellectual assessment in developing educational programs or other interventions for students with learning and behavior problems. In addition to the concern about those limitations, there have been frequent allegations concerning the harm experienced by disadvantaged, minority students due to improper intellectual assessment procedures that may have penalized such students due to cultural differences. Furthermore, there is the concern about lost opportunities for the delivery of other, potentially more effective, services due to the excessive time and energy devoted to intellectual assessment. Legal challenges to intellectual assessment have been prominent over the past ten years (Reschly, Kicklighter, & McKee, 1988a, b).

Over the past five years increasing emphasis has been placed on reform of school psychology through changes in the overall special education classification/ placement system and efforts to broaden services to low-achieving at-risk students. The capstone of the reform movement is less emphasis on eligibility determination and greater emphasis on the design and delivery of interventions to students within regular education settings (Graden, Zins, & Curtis, 1988; Reschly, 1988b). Significant changes are suggested in the roles of school psychologists and the kind of assessment information needed in order to address questions of interventions rather than questions of eligibility. Assessment in the new systems suggested will involve descriptions of problems in natural settings, and information useful for designing, monitoring, and evaluating interventions. The kind of information that is useful for those purposes will necessarily involve curriculum-based measurement and behavioral assessment using techniques such as observation, direct measures of academic performance, ratings of social skills, direct and indirect measures of academic survival skills, and interviews with significant others such as teachers and parents.

As reform plans are implemented, we anticipate declining use of intellectual assessment. The current pattern of administration of an intellectual assessment measure nearly every day by school psy-

chologists will change in the direction of far greater emphasis on more functional, that is more intervention related, assessment procedures. However, intellectual assessment will continue, and in our opinion, should continue. When intellectual assessment is used, it must be carried out in ways that are consistent with theories and research on intellectual assessment and well recognized best practices. It is to these topics that the rest of the chapter is devoted.

BASIC CONSIDERATIONS

The voluminous literature pertaining to intellectual assessment cannot be reviewed in detail in this chapter. Thousands of journal articles, hundreds of book chapters, and scores of books have been written on topics related to intellectual assessment. In this section of the chapter we will review only general findings that relate directly to best practices considerations. Readers are referred to other sources such as Sternberg (1982) and Sattler (1988) for further information on theories, developmental patterns, research on various groups, research on different tests, and reviews of measures.

Nature of Current Measures

The intellectual measures used most frequently in school psychology are composed of a variety of complex tasks ranging from items requiring simple memory to abstract problem solving. Most are atheoretical in the sense that the items and scales are not derived from applications of theories of cognitive development or information processing. Analysis of their structure typically yields a general factor, not unlike the concept of Spearman's "g" with one to three group factors (Vernon, 1979). These generalizations are applicable to the most widely used intellectual measures, the Wechsler scales and the Stanford-Binet.

In recent years intellectual measures reflecting theoretical formulations of cognitive processing have begun to appear but are, as yet, used infrequently by school psychologists. For example, the Kaufman

Assessment Battery for Children (K-ABC) attempts to assess the constructs of simultaneous and successive processing. Learning potential assessment measures and other dynamic assessment procedures attempt to identify the individual's approach to problem solving and to observe the strategies applied in completing intellectual tasks. Thus far, these measures have not had substantial impact on the practice of school psychology, in part because the dynamic assessment procedures have not been well standardized and the effectiveness of interventions related to improving cognitive processing are as yet undemonstrated.

Although current measures such as the WISC-R and the Stanford-Binet Fourth Edition (SB) yield numerous scores, the most meaningful scores based on factor analytic investigations as well as concurrent validity studies are typically a composite or overall score and two to three scores reflecting group factors such as verbal comprehension and visual spatial problem solving. Scores on subtests, typically composed of items that are similar, are considerably less meaningful and substantial variation on the subtest scores is typical. The relationship of performance to important indices such as school achievement is typically best for the composite score and the primary or group factor scores. Relationships between important criteria and subtest scores tend to be highly variable and considerably weaker.

Meaning of Current Measures

Interpretation of the results of measures of intellectual functioning is highly controversial. Perhaps the most widely accepted view is that measures of general intellectual functioning reflect the results of incidental learning through exposure to the general culture. The emphasis is on incidental learning since little if anything on the test is taught directly, in a systematic fashion, in any setting. Schooling and the quality of educational experiences are reflected at least indirectly in the test results. Intellectual measures typically require a combination of facts, concepts,

problem-solving strategies, and, to a lesser extent, metacognitive operations. The results as represented in composite or group factor scores reflect the *products* of the individual's accumulation of knowledge derived over the entire developmental period. In that sense, measures of intellectual functioning are general achievement or learning measures, but they are not measures of academic achievement in a specific setting such as the school or any other precise context.

Intellectual measures are useful because of their relationship to other critical indices of human functioning. The most common use of intellectual measures is to attempt to estimate likely level of performance in educational settings or to attempt to identify causes of poor school performance. This use of intellectual measures is supported by the well known substantial correlation between intellectual functioning and school achievement. This relationship, ranging from a correlation of about .4 to about .7 depending on the criterion measure, reflects a substantial, but by no means perfect, association between intellectual functioning and school performance. Contrary to some assertions, measures of intellectual functioning and measures of school achievement do not "autocorrelate." For example, the kinds of skills measured by the WISC-R for an eight-year-old are quite different than the skills measured in a critical academic area such as reading. The results from the two measures bear a substantial, but imperfect relationship. Indeed, one of the most frequent uses of intellectual measures today involves identifying discrepancies between intellectual measures and indices of school achievement. Intellectual measures are also correlated with occupational attainment. Although there is a broad range of ability associated with each occupational category, e.g., attorney or carpenter, there is a clear relationship with the average level of ability in occupational categories. Generally, the more prestigious the occupation the higher the average level of ability. This fundamental relationship rarely has direct applicability to school psychology decision making.

Performance on intellectual measures is also related to a variety of measures of cognitive processing. Campione, Brown, and Ferrara (1982) provided an excellent discussion of these relationships. Although their review focused primarily on studies of persons with mild mental retardation, the relationships they reported in the literature reviewed were interpreted as, for the most part, applying to all ranges of ability. According to Campione et al., performance on intellectual measures is positively related to the speed and efficiency of information processing, to the individual's knowledge base, to the spontaneous use of appropriate strategies in problem solving tasks, to metacognitive operations whereby the individual exerts control over the approach to problem solving, and to transfer of problem solving skills to novel situations.

Perhaps the most salient result in the Campione et al. (1982) review was the interpretation of intellectual differences in terms of the capability of profiting from incomplete instruction. In general, the higher the level of measured ability, the greater the individual's capability of learning through indirect or incomplete instruction. The latter bears strong relationships to the concept of incidental learning, cited earlier as the process through which much of the knowledge or problem solving strategies on intellectual measures are learned. It should be noted that none of the current measures of intellectual functioning provides direct assessment of any of the cognitive processes. Rather, the complex types of items included on current measures require each of the cognitive processes to varying degrees. Furthermore, the scores on current measures whether from subtests or from composite scales cannot be directly interpreted, with few exceptions, as direct measures of any of the cognitive processes. Rather, these scores represent the products rather than the process whereby individuals recall information, explain concepts, or solve problems.

Intelligence tests work to the degree that they do because they sample essential behaviors. These behaviors relate most clearly to performance in academic settings, but the relationships are not restricted to school achievement. Other important correlates, not covered here, include various mental health criteria, social skills, adaptive behavior, and mental health adjustment. Relationships to these criteria typically are considerably weaker, but still statistically significant. The intellectual assessment instruments do not provide direct information on specific cognitive processes nor specific educational goals and objectives. Results from items, subtests, or composite scores are virtually impossible to translate directly into remediation goals or instructional objectives. Furthermore, many other individual traits are critical to effective performance in a variety of settings.

Measured Intelligence vs. Intelligent Behavior

The discrepancy between what is measured on formal instruments and effective, intelligent behavior has been recognized for many decades. In a 1921 symposium on the meaning of intelligence, E. L. Thorndike suggested three major facets of intelligence; social, mechanical (practical), and abstract thinking. He noted that the tests at that time, like most current measures, focused primarily on abstract thinking. A similar insight was offered by David Wechsler in his emphasis on intelligent behavior as the overall capacity to think rationally, act purposely, and deal effectively with the environment. Recently Sternberg (1985) has identified different components of intelligent behavior including social and practical intelligence (an aspect of which is tacit knowledge). All of these formulations, and there are many others, recognize the distinction between what is measured on current IQ tests and intelligent behavior. Clearly, intelligent behavior, defined simply as the effectiveness in dealing with one's environment, involves a variety of intellectual and nonintellectual competencies. The IQ score from a well standardized instrument such as one of the Wechsler scales represents some of these competencies, but by no means all. It is critical for users of measures of general intellectual functioning to understand this distinction and to communicate the distinction to consumers of test results, i.e., students, teachers, and parents. As Wechsler pointed out, a high level of measured intelligence, perhaps reflecting primarily abstract thinking capabilities, is rendered quite useless in the absence of goal-directedness, motivation, persistence, or sufficient mental health stability to allow concentrated effort.

Development Trends and Variations in Performance

Intellectual measures are designed to identify individual differences. Variation is therefore the hallmark of the intellectual assessment enterprise. Variations between individuals and various groups are well known, and sometimes controversial. Less well known and insufficiently appreciated are the differences within individuals across measures and variations within individuals across time.

Kaufman's (1976a, b) work with the WISC-R is particularly instructive with regard to variations within individuals. Kaufman noted, contrary to widespread belief among school psychologists and other persons involved with intellectual assessment, that considerable variation or scatter across subtests and scale scores is typical rather than unusual. Kaufman's findings concerning scatter have vast implications for the interpretation of performance on intellectual measures. First, scatter is normal rather than a sign of intellectual or social-emotional disorders. Second, scatter cannot be used as a basis for a diagnosis of exceptional or mental health categories such as disability, emotional disturbance, or brain injury. Indeed, if a high degree of scatter is normal, then nearly all of us fit into one of the categories of disorder. It is statistically impossible for scatter to be a *unique* identifying feature of any disorder. Third, the differences identified through an analysis of variations across different subtests or scales, that is profile analysis, are likely to be unreliable. Since profile analysis is based on differences in scores,

and score differences are inherently less reliable than the respective scores on which they are based, the profile patterns are correspondingly less reliable. Consider this analogy. If one is uncertain about when a vacation period begins, also uncertain about when the vacation ends, then we are even less certain about the length of the vacation. Similarly, if we are somewhat uncertain of the individual's Block Design score, also somewhat uncertain about the individual's Vocabulary score, then we are by necessity even less certain of the difference in the two scores. Norms for scatter were published by Kaufman and must be carefully considered before interpretations about intellectual abilities are rendered.

Large differences between scale scores, e.g., verbal and performance IQ, are not unusual. Kaufman reported that approximately 25% of the standardization sample had verbal-performance discrepancies of 15 points or more. Furthermore, these differences, though relatively common, are not likely to be attributable to chance phenomena or the unreliability of the measures. For example, a discrepancy of 15 points or more may occur by chance less than than one percent of the time. The 15 point discrepancy, therefore, is likely to be a real difference in pattern of intellectual performance. However, it is not unusual since 25% of the standardization sample obtained such differences. The key distinction here is the difference between statistical chance and frequency or base rates for the occurrence of a particular difference. Differences between scale scores, if they reach certain criteria, do relate to stable variations in intellectual performance. Although stable, these variations are not unusual.

A much more conservative interpretation must be attributed to variations among subtest scores. Subtest score differences must be interpreted more cautiously because the scores themselves are considerably less reliable than the scale or composite scores. Furthermore, subtest score variations are quite common as indicated by Kaufman's study of the standardization sample. Interpretations of pairs of subtest score differences in relation to cognitive processing or neurological functioning are inherently fraught with reliability problems. A high score on one subtest, accompanied by a low score on another subtest, may be interpreted by some as suggesting a particular neurological strength or weakness when, in fact, the difference is merely statistical chance, and, in any case, *not* unusual.

The performance of individuals also varies over time. IQ test results are relatively stable for many individuals after approximately age 5–7. However, the IQ scores for a significant percentage of individuals (at least 20%) change by at least 15 points or more between age 6 and maturity, and considerably larger changes of 30 or 40 points have been reported in a few cases. When large changes do occur, they tend to be associated with significant changes in the individual's environment or overall adjustment (McCall, Apelbaum, & Hogarty, 1973). The fact that IQ test results do change as a function of changes in the individual or the environment, might be seen as evidence to support the most common interpretations of test results as reflecting *current* intellectual functioning. We need to be conscious of the fact, and inform others, that scores do change, and that inferences about future intellectual status of the individual are tentative.

Controversial Issues

Allegations of bias are perhaps the most controversial issues directly related to use of intellectual measures by school psychologists. The bias concerns are related to two populations, economically disadvantaged minority students and students with sensory or motor handicaps. Issues of possible bias need to be carefully considered in selection of intellectual assessment instruments, in administration of instruments, and in interpretation of results.

The bias concerns are most often expressed with populations of minority students, particularly black, Hispanic, or native American students. Considerable research was devoted to topics of bias in the 1970s and 1980s. The voluminous results generated from this research led to complex conclusions about intellectual assessment with minority students. First, there are multiple definitions of bias with varied meanings. The results of studies of bias depend heavily on the definition used. Definitions of bias include the following conceptions: (a) Mean differences; (b) Item bias; (c) Psychometric characteristics of tests; (d) Factor analysis of underlying structure; (e) Atmosphere or examiner/examinee interaction effects; (f) Prediction; (g) Selection ratios or disproportionate classification of students; and (h) Social consequences, particularly use of test results to support racist interpretation of differences. Most conventional tests, e.g., WISC-R, are not biased according to the conventional definitions related to properties of items, psychometric characteristics, factor analysis, atmosphere effects, and prediction (Jensen, 1980; Reschly, 1979; Reynolds, 1982). Specifically, there is *no* evidence that conventional tests underpredict the actual performance of minority students. Conventional tests typically are found to be biased on the less well accepted definitions such as mean differences, selection ratios-disproportionate classification, and social consequences.

The mean differences and disproportionate classification definitions, along with several conventional definitions, were key features of extremely costly and divisive litigation over the past ten years. Four trials over these issues occurred in federal district courts between 1979 and 1986 (Reschly et al., 1988a, b). Three of the trials concluded that conventional measures of intellectual functioning were not biased, despite overrepresentation of minority students in special education programs, if a variety of other protections were included in the classification placement process, if a variety of measures of performance were used, and the referral, assessment, and placement were clearly related to well defined educational needs (Reschly et al., 1988a, b). One of the cases, in California, reached the opposite conclusion.

A slightly different concern about bias was reflected in the Education of the

Handicapped Act regulations, Protection in Evaluation Procedures Provisions section. This concern had to do with the use of measures that unfairly penalized students due to their sensory, motor, or language handicaps/differences. For example, administration of a Wechsler verbal scale to a hearing impaired or deaf student measures the effect of the handicapped to a greater extent than the underlying construct of intellectual performance. Similarly, use of highly verbal measures in the English language unduly penalizes students with mixed language capabilities (e.g., Spanish and English) or students with limited exposure to English. The population most frequently involved with the latter concern are of Hispanic origin, an increasing segment of the United States population and the school psychologist's case load. Intellectual assessment with students with sensory or motor handicaps or language differences should, to the greatest extent possible, use administration procedures and response modes that do not merely reflect the effects of the handicap or language difference. Use of special scales designed specifically for particular populations or non-language measures are preferred procedures.

Concerns about bias are intensified by the continuing debate over the relative effects of heredity and environment as influences on developed abilities. The nature-nurture debate is perhaps the quintessential issue in individual differences research. There are vast implications for social policy. Unfortunately, hereditarian interpretations of mean differences among groups have been used to diminish efforts to overcome the effects of poverty. Indeed, the term "benign neglect" arises from a social policy analysis of the worthwhileness of antipoverty programs. Resolution of the nature-nurture debate is unlikely at any time in the foreseeable future, but it is important to note that even the most ardent hereditarians acknowledge a significant role for environmental influences. Furthermore, Mercer (1979) delineated the criteria which must be met in order for a valid interpretation of an individual's score as reflecting hereditary differences. These criteria are

virtually impossible to satisfy. Nevertheless, hereditarian, sometimes racist, views of group differences in intellectual test performance are often, unconsciously, applied to individuals. School psychologists responsible for intellectual assessment must carefully guard against such interpretations in their own work and pursue assertive steps to protect children from racist interpretations by consumers of test results.

Another controversial issue concerning intellectual assessment is the usefulness of the information in important decisions about children and youth. We anticipate considerably reduced use of intellectual assessment in the future, not because the tests are biased or unfair to minorities, but because the test results are irrelevant to many important decisions. Furthermore, alternative assessment procedures provide more useful information for both classification and programming. As noted earlier, conceptions of classification criteria and assessment procedures for mental retardation (Reschly, 1988a) and learning disabilities (Shinn, 1988; Siegel, 1989) that do not include intellectual assessment were provided recently. The curriculum based measurement, adaptive behavior, social skills, and school survival skills emphasized in these conceptions would likely lead to identification of the same students as needing special services, but have the decided advantage of direct relevance to design, implementation, monitoring, and evaluation of interventions. These alternative procedures may have greater or lesser applicability to classification decisions depending on state special education rules for various categories of handicapped children. This information, regardless of state rules, does have considerable relevance for interventions and should therefore be part of the comprehensive assessment, and where appropriate, may replace the use of intellectual assessment instruments.

Appropriate Uses of Intellectual Assessment

The context within intellectual assessment measures are used must be considered before appropriate uses can be described. The typical context for school psychologists often involves determination of eligibility for possible special education programming. Federal regulations for the Education of Handicapped Act and nearly all state department of education rules require a two-pronged decision making process involving: (a) Determination of need for special education; and (b) Eligibility determination. All too often the eligibility determination, rather than the need for special education, is addressed in the multifactored assessment.

The least restrictive environment principle and other more recent changes in state rules place emphasis on attempts to resolve problems in regular education settings prior to special education eligibility considerations. Application of these principles implies that intellectual assessment and eligibility determination clearly should not be the first choice in efforts to address learning or behavior problems. The first phases of a system within which intellectual assessment can be used appropriately involves concerted efforts to resolve problems in regular education settings. Other assessment procedures and interventions must be established prior to consideration of eligibility and the use of intellectual assessment procedures. This phase must involve careful consideration of prior efforts to resolve the problem, systematic efforts to define the problem in behavioral terms, collection of baseline data, design of systematic interventions, and implementation, monitoring, and evaluation of those interventions. School psychologists have critical roles and essential contributions to each of those steps in this initial phase. If the problem behavior is pervasive and persistent, and beyond the purview of regular education, even with the interventions by support services personnel and the additional resources that can be brought to regular education, then consideration of special education eligibility is appropriate. At this stage, depending on state rules concerning classification of students as handicapped, intellectual assessment may

be part of the multifactored assessment. In fact, intellectual assessment nearly always is part of the multifactored assessment currently, often emphasized more strongly than careful assessment of other dimensions of behavior through curriculum based measures, observation, structured checklists, rating scales, and interview.

Depending on the classification criteria established by the state, intellectual assessment may be part of the multifactored assessment. Intellectual assessment should not dominate, but be a component of the comprehensive evaluation. Consideration of other aspects or dimensions of behavior should receive equal attention and the decision making about eligibility and placement should reflect a clear balance between intellectual assessment and other important information.

Intellectual assessment for classification purposes should utilize a general battery that meets relevant standards for technical adequacy (Salvia & Ysseldyke, 1988). Short forms, measures with a single item type, measures with dubious technical adequacy, particularly the quality of the norms, should be avoided in reaching inferences about current intellectual functioning. Furthermore, the test instruments must be selected, administered, and interpreted carefully so that the effects of various handicapping conditions or language differences do not unfairly penalize the student. Obviously, familiarity with a variety of instruments and knowledge of various handicapping conditions and the effects of language differences are crucial to competent assessment of current intellectual functioning.

The classification decisions must follow the state rules or other diagnostic criteria and reflect knowledge of developmental trends. For example, intellectual measures administered to infants must be interpreted cautiously due to the well known instability of such measures and the strong likelihood of significant changes in status over the preschool years when rapid growth and maturation occur.

In typical cases difficult distinctions are required. Most students who are eligible for various handicapped child classifications will be performing near the margins of the classification criteria. For example, if the IQ cutoff score for mental retardation is 75, the vast majority of students for whom intellectual assessment will be conducted and classification decisions required, will perform between roughly IQ of 70 to 79. A substantial proportion will be within one standard error of measurement, often regarded as three to four points on the composite score of the most widely used instruments, of the cutoff established by the state rules. Complex judgments are required rather than mechanical application of scores. These complex judgments should reflect application of the convergent validity principle described by Gresham (1985), i.e., the consistency of information over settings, sources, and data collection methods. Complex judgments involving students performing at the margins in regard to learning disabilities classification criteria are also the norm rather than the exception. Again, the convergent validity principle should be applied whereby the broad variety of information over different dimensions of behavior generated in the multifactored evaluation need to be considered. For students at the margins, a pattern of information consistent with the underlying diagnostic construct should lead to classifying the child as handicapped. On the other hand, one or more sources of information that are not consistent with the diagnostic construct should lead to not classifying the student as handicapped. This decision making process is relevant to the majority of the cases we encounter. Students typically are within a few points just above or just below the cutoff criteria in mental retardation or learning disabilities.

An appropriate interpretation of measures of current intellectual functioning is an estimation of current and likely future academic performance. As noted by Reschly et al. (1988, b) tests are rarely used in the sense of differential predictive validity. Rather, significant educational difficulties have been encountered *prior* to the administration of intellectual measures. The intellectual measure then, rather than being used in the sense of differential predictive validity, is used in an effort to estimate likely current and future academic performance and as one of the bases for investigating the possible causes or correlates of poor academic performance. Here the logic is admittedly somewhat confused because the test is used here both as a measure of current performance and as a basis for explaining the current performance. The logic is clarified somewhat by acknowledging that the test reflects general learning ability and the effects of prior learning experiences and developmental trends. Furthermore, since the test results reflect current performance, future academic performance may be substantially changed through the development of effective interventions. Briefly stated, the assessment of current performance and the estimation of likely future academic performance should not represent a sentence to diminished expectations or assumptions about the immutability of development trends. As noted previously, intellectual performance can vary developmentally, even after age six or seven, and substantial changes are observed for a significant proportion (20%) of students. The appropriate interpretation is that, if current developmental trends continue and in the absence of effective interventions, the likely academic and intellectual performance is estimated best by current intellectual performance. Indeed the goal is the provision of carefully designed intervention that should result in improved performance and raising expectations for academic performance. The description of current performance should never lead to the misinterpretation that the student cannot learn, nor profit from instruction.

The final appropriate use of measures of intellectual performance is to provide tentative descriptions of pattern of abilities. These tentative descriptions are empirically sound to the extent that they are related to well confirmed factor analytic results and highly reliable group factor scores. For example, the pattern of abilities for individuals is relatively stable on broad factors such as verbal comprehension and perceptual organization.

Furthermore, estimates of likely levels of academic performance should also be modified by pattern of abilities. Performance on verbal and quantitative reasoning factors typically are more closely related to academic performance than performance in nonverbal areas such as perceptual organization or visual-spatial reasoning. Assuming that the verbal scale is a valid measure of the individual's current intellectual functioning, and does not merely reflect language differences, the verbal score is a more accurate indicator of likely academic performance than the full scale or performance score if there are substantial discrepancies over the group factors, reflecting verbal and nonverbal abilities.

Inappropriate or Questionable Uses of Intellectual Assessment

An array of inappropriate or questionable uses of measures of general intellectual functioning will be described briefly in this section. One of the most common and frequent inappropriate uses is to conduct a profile analysis for the purpose of differential diagnosis, e.g., determining whether or not the student is learning disabled or emotionally disturbed. As noted previously, a considerable degree of scatter is typical. Differences between scales or subtests, because they occur frequently, simply cannot be a unique feature of any diagnostic category, nor the basis for distinguishing between diagnostic categories. We assume that a relatively small percentage of the population can be accurately diagnosed as learning disabled or emotionally disturbed. A profile characteristic that occurs frequently in the general population cannot be unique or diagnostically significant with a particular category that occurs at a low frequency. It simply does not compute.

Application of the results from studies of groups of students also need to be interpreted cautiously with individuals. For example, the WISC-R ACID profile has been reported frequently in contrasts of learning disabled and normal achieving students (Sattler, 1988). However, these findings are based on mean differences, developed from distributions of scores for normal achieving and learning disabled groups. The overall distributions overlap considerably. Therefore, a specific normal achieving child may obtain the ACID profile and a specific student accurately characterized as learning disabled may not obtain that profile. Therefore, conformance or nonconformance with the particular profile reported for groups is not an accurate indicator of the appropriate diagnosis for an individual child.

Profile analysis for the purpose of determination of neurological strengths or weaknesses or psychodynamic personality characteristics is also fraught with significant errors of logic and probable unreliability. These interpretations have a long history in applied areas of psychology including school and clinical. The empirical basis for the interpretations typically is weak or nonexistent. In virtually all instances, careful studies have *not* been done with individuals known to possess the underlying neurological or psychodynamic characteristic inferred from the test profile. Rather, analogical reasoning of the form, "what would this most likely mean," has been applied to analysis of the profile resulting in largely unsubstantial inferences about the meaning of various subtests or scale discrepancies. These interpretations in the absence of empirical support are likely to be inaccurate, unreliable, and in any case, not related to effective intervention methodology or techniques (Reschly & Gresham, 1989).

The final inappropriate use relates to the use of results on measures of general intellectual functioning to support inferences about innate abilities of individuals or groups. Although these questions are investigated, sometimes rigorously and sometimes not, the varied and controversial inferences from this research have little relationship to our day to day practice with diverse groups of students. The most popular conclusions from this research and the broad inferences to groups have varied during our careers and will likely continue to be modified as new information is generated and more sophisticated investigative techniques are developed and applied. Our concern must be with accurate interpretation for individuals which must include efforts to protect individuals from unwarranted inferences about innate abilities that may further diminish efforts to remediate problems and to intervene effectively.

A kind of "surgeon general's" warning can be formulated to protect children and youth from unwarranted inferences about their intellectual abilities and to remind all of us, especially consumers of our work, of the developmental nature of measured abilities. This "surgeon generals" warning is far from perfect. Concerned practitioners can develop appropriate modifications. However, the essential ideas are to protect students from inappropriate inferences that their intellectual abilities are determined by genetic factors, that intellectual abilities are unitary and that the IQ score reflects all of intelligent behavior, and that performance on intellectual measures is fixed, or unchanging. A statement such as the following should appear on test reports and be attached to test protocols if the latter are likely to be reviewed by other important parties such as teachers, other members of the multidisciplinary team, or parents.

IQ tests measure only a portion of the competencies involved with human intelligence. The IQ results are best seen as estimates of likely performance in school and reflections of the degree to which children have mastered the middle class cultural symbols and broad culturally rooted facts, concepts, and problem solving strategies. This information is useful but limited. IQ tests do not reflect innate genetic capacity and the scores are not fixed. Some persons do exhibit significant increases or decreases in their measured intellectual abilities.

BEST PRACTICES

Best practices considerations require careful judgments about *when* intellectual assessment instruments are used, *how* they are used, the selection, administration, and interpretation of tests, and efforts to protect children and youth from misuses and misconceptions.

1. *Appropriate use requires a context that emphasizes prevention and early intervention rather than eligibility determination as the initial phase in services to students with learning and behavior problems.*

The context within which the intellectual assessment occurs is crucial. The typical context is the investigation of the causes and correlates of learning problems. Special education eligibility may be a concern, but that concern should be investigated after, not before, the development, implementation, and evaluation of interventions within regular education settings. School psychologists should be involved in the efforts to resolve problems in regular education settings rather than merely accepting verbal reports that such interventions have been attempted and eligibility now must be considered. Intellectual assessments should be pursued only after interventions have been systematically attempted and rigorously evaluated, and then only when learning problems appear to be pervasive and persistent.

2. *Intellectual assessment should be used when the results are directly relevant to well defined referral questions, and other available information does not address those questions.*

Evaluations should be goal directed. The goal of the evaluation should be to address significant questions developed jointly between the psychologist and the referral agent. Some questions require consideration of current intellectual functioning, many do not.

3. *Mandatory use of intellectual measures for all referrals, multifactored evaluations, or reevaluations is not consistent with best practices.*

It is not uncommon for all referred students to receive IQ tests, regardless of referral questions or behavioral problems. IQ test results simply are *not* relevant to many referral questions or reevaluation issues. A critical question is, "How would the intervention, classification decision, or selection of placement option change if an IQ test is administered?" If clear alternative decisions cannot be specified, IQ testing is probably irrelevant. Some examples of cases where IQ is frequently irrelevant include: reevaluations of severely retarded students, repetition of several prior IQ tests that yielded consistent results, and use of IQ tests with many students referred due to social-emotional or behavioral problems. Where needed, efforts to modify district or state policies mandating IQ tests for all cases should be pursued by individuals through district and state professional groups.

4. *Intellectual assessment must be part of a multifactored approach, individualized to a child's characteristics and the referral problems.*

The practice of using a standard battery, often dominated by IQ tests, for all children regardless of referral questions must be avoided. The standard battery typically involves an intellectual measure such as the WISC-R, a brief screening measure of achievement such as the Wide Range Achievement Test, and a brief measure of visual motor skills such as the Bender Visual Motor Gestalt. Standard batteries provide superficial information over very limited areas of functioning. In most instances, the standard battery does not relate directly to referral problems and is not well matched to characteristics of the child. Consideration and systematic assessment of other important areas of functioning using technically adequate measures is essential in order to develop a comprehensive perspective on the child and to address significant referral questions. The development of well refined referral questions should dictate the components of the comprehensive evaluation, rather than attempts to answer all questions through a limited set of instruments.

5. *Intellectual assessment procedures must be carefully matched to characteristics of children and youth.*

A variety of instruments are available. No instrument is appropriate for all students. Special consideration needs to be devoted to choices of instrument with students exhibiting sensory or motor handicaps, language differences or significant cultural differences. Basal and ceiling problems need to be considered. For example, a low functioning youngster close to the bottom age of the test norms will not be assessed adequately by the instrument because very few items will be administered due to ceiling rules.

6. *Score reporting and interpretation must reflect the known limitations of tests, including technical adequacy, inherent error in measurement, and general categories of performance.*

Test scores should always be presented as ranges around an obtained score using confidence intervals. Furthermore, limitations in the norms for the test, in reliability or stability of scores, and questionable or undemonstrated validity, must be carefully considered and communicated to consumers of test information. Finally, the overall performance needs to be interpreted within broad categories, established by the test developer or established by other sources, e.g., state special education rules.

7. *Interpretation of performance and decisions concerning classification must reflect consideration of overall strengths and weaknesses in intellectual performance, performance on other relevant dimensions of behavior, age, family characteristics, and cultural background.*

Present behavior is described. Interpretation and description of future performance are inferred from the sample of current behavior. The sample of current behavior may need to be regarded with varying degrees of tentativeness depending on age, family characteristics, and cultural background. Furthermore, overall pattern of strengths and weaknesses in intellectual performance as well as the individual's performance on other relevant dimensions such as adaptive behavior, social skills, etc. must be incorporated in interpretations and recommendations.

8. *Users should implement assertive procedures to protect students from misconceptions and misuses of intellectual test results.*

Many consumers of test results including teachers and parents often view the findings as reflective of a predetermined characteristic, and regard the results as fixed. Many do not see the distinction between the results of measures of intellectual performance and the much broader construct of intelligent behavior. The warning suggested earlier in the chapter or some alternative means should be used by psychologists to reduce the likelihood of misuses and misconceptions.

SUMMARY

Intellectual assessment has a long, varied, and controversial status in the history of school psychology. Intellectual assessment continues as a central feature of current practice and graduate education. We anticipate intellectual assessment will continue to be an important component in school psychology services, but increasingly, will become secondary to collection of information more directly related to interventions using other instruments and procedures. Best practices for intellectual assessment currently and in the future require an appropriate context. Assessment of intelligence should be restricted to cases where precisely stated referral questions are addressed best by the results of intellectual measures. Careful choices are required concerning instruments, administration procedures, and interpretation of results. Assertive steps to protect students from misconceptions or misuses of the results of intellectual measures will continue to be an important component of best practices.

REFERENCES

Campione, J. C., Brown, A. L., & Ferrara, R. A. (1982). Mental retardation and intelligence. In R. J. Sternberg (Ed.), *Handbook of Human Intelligence* (pp. 392–490). Cambridge (England): Cambridge University Press.

Education of the Handicapped Act. 1975. PL 94-142, 20 U.S.C. 1400–1485, 34 C.F.R. Part 300 (as amended to October 8, 1986).

Glutting, J. J., Oakland, T., & McDermott, P. A. (1989). Observing child behavior during testing: Constructs, validity, and situational generality. *Journal of School Psychology, 27,* 155–164.

Graden, J. L., Zins, J. E., & Curtis, M. J. (Eds.). (1988). *Alternative educational delivery systems: Enhancing instructional options for all students.* Washington, DC: National Association of School Psychologists.

Gresham, F. (1985). Behavior disorder assessment: Conceptual, definitional, and practical considerations. *School Psychology Review, 14,* 495–509.

Grimes, J. P. (1981). Shaping the future of school psychology. In J. Ysseldyke & R. Weinberg (Eds.), The Future of Psychology in the Schools: Proceedings of the Spring Hill Symposium. *School Psychology Review, 10,* 206–231.

Jensen, A. R. (1980). *Bias in mental testing.* New York: Free Press.

Kaufman, A. (1976a). A new approach to interpretation of test scatter on the WISC-R. *Journal of Learning Disabilities, 9,* 160–168.

Kaufman, A. (1976b). Verbal-performance IQ discrepancies on the WISC-R. *Journal of Consulting and Clinical Psychology, 44,* 739–744.

McCall, R., Appelbaum, M., & Hogarty, P. (1973). Developmental changes in mental performance. *Monographs of the Society for Research in Child Development, 38,* (Whole No. 150), 1–83.

Mercer, J. (1979). *System of Multicultural Pluralistic Assessment Technical Manual.* New York: Psychological Corporation.

Reschly, D. (1979). Nonbiased assessment. In G. Phye & D. Reschly (Eds.), *School psychology: Perspectives and issues* (pp. 215–253). New York: Academic Press.

Reschly, D. J. (1988a). Assessment issues, placement litigation, and the future of mild mental retardation classification and programming. *Education and Training of the Mentally Retarded, 23,* 285–301.

Reschly, D. J. (1988b). Special education reform: School psychology revolution. *School Psychology Review, 17,* 459–574.

Reschly, D. J., Genshaft, J., & Binder, M. S. (1987). *The NASP Survey: Comparison of Practitioners, NASP Leadership, and University Faculty on Key Issues.* Washington, DC: National Association of School Psychologists.

Reschly, D. J., & Gresham, F. M. (1989). Current neuropsychological diagnosis of learning problems: A leap of faith. In C. R. Reynolds & E. Fletcher-Janzen (Eds.), *Child neuropsychology techniques of diagnosis and treatment.* New York: Plenum.

Reschly, D. J., Kicklighter, R. H., & McKee, P. (1988a). Recent placement litigation Part II, Minority EMR overrepresentation: Comparison of *Larry P.* (1979, 1984, 1986) with *Marshall* (1984, 1985) and *S-1* (1986). *School Psychology Review, 17,* 20–36.

Reschly, D. J., Kicklighter, R. H., & McKee, P. (1988b). Recent placement litigation Part III: Analysis of differences in *Larry P., Marshall,* and *S-1* and implication for future practices. *School Psychology Review, 17,* 37–48.

Reynolds, C. R. (1982). The problem of bias in psychological assessment. In C. R. Reynolds and T. B. Gutkin (Eds.), *The Handbook of School Psychology.* New York: Wiley.

Salvia, J., & Ysseldyke, J. (1988). *Assessment in special and remedial education (4th Ed.).* Boston: Houghton-Mifflin.

Sarason, S. (1975). The unfortunate fate of Alfred Binet and school psychology. *Teachers College Record, 77,* 579–592.

Sattler, J. M. (1988). *Assessment of children, (3rd Ed.).* San Diego, CA: Jerome Sattler Publisher.

Shinn, M. R. (1988). Development of curriculum-based local norms for use in special education decision-making. *School Psychology Review, 17,* 61–80.

Siegel, L. S. (1989). IQ is irrelevant to the definition of learning disabilities. *Journal of Learning Disabilities, 22,* 469–479.

Sternberg, R. J. (Ed.). (1982). *Handbook of human intelligence.* Cambridge, England: Cambridge University Press.

Sternberg, R. J. (1985). *Beyond IQ: A triarchic theory of human intelligence.* Cambridge, England: Cambridge University Press.

Vernon, P. E. (1979). *Intelligence: Heredity and environment.* San Francisco: W. H. Freeman.

ANNOTATED BIBLIOGRAPHY

Aiken, L. R. (1987). *Assessment of intellectual functioning.* Boston: Allyn & Bacon.
Aiken provides a useful overview of intellectual assessment with interesting and useful information on patterns of intellectual abilities for various groups.

Jensen, A. R. (1980). *Bias in mental testing.* New York: Free Press.
This classic work summarizes information on conventional definitions of test bias. The final chapter on uses and abuses of tests will surprise many readers who have never read Jensen's work and may be prejudiced against anything he has written due to his theories concerning level 1 and level 2 abilities and his hypothesis of a hereditarian basis for group differences. Those positions notwithstanding, and we certainly are not endorsing those positions here, this book provides a complex and thorough discussion of principles and research concerning test bias.

Kaufman, A. (1979). *Intelligent testing with the WISC-R.* New York: Wiley.
Kaufman provides excellent information on base rates of subtest scatter and scale differences, essential to appropriate explanations of variations within individuals on WISC-R performance. The latter portions of the book where various clinical interpretations are provided, involving highly inferential assertions about children's characteristics, are not recommended.

Sattler, J. M. (1988). *Assessment of children, (3 Ed.).* San Diego, CA: Jerome Sattler, Publisher.
Sattler provides an excellent text as well as an essential reference for individuals responsible for conducting intellectual assessments of children. Extensive information is provided on the most commonly used intellectual assessment measures, with guidelines suggested for interpretation.

Sternberg, R. J. (Ed.). (1982). *Handbook of human intelligence.* Cambridge, England: Cambridge University Press.
Sternberg, R. J. (1985). *Beyond IQ: A triarchic theory of human intelligence.* Cambridge, England: Cambridge University Press.
The edited volume provides complex but extremely thorough treatments of essential topics related to human intelligence including chapters on attention, perception, learning, memory, reasoning, problem solving, personality, mental retardation, education, social policy, culture, genetics, development, and theories. Collectively, these chapters provide one of the best available treatments of the meaning of intelligence.
Sternberg's paperback, *Beyond IQ,* provides an excellent treatment of his triarchic theory. Sections on social and practical intelligence and exceptional intelligence are especially useful in distinguishing between what current tests assess and the broader notion of intelligent behavior.

30

Best Practices in Internship Supervision

Roslyn P. Ross
Florence E. Sisenwein
Queens College of the City University of New York

OVERVIEW

Currently, there are about 24,000 school psychologists in the United States. Despite the diversity in their training and their roles, they have all been through an internship experience. The internship is one of the most important rites of passage. It is a crystallizing experience that helps students make the transition to professionals. Internship supervisors and experiences are long remembered with special clarity.

However, most supervisors undertake this important role with little or no formal preparation. There is limited attention paid to developing supervisory skills in graduate curricula. It is unlikely that many supervisors receive supervision themselves once they undertake this activity (Knoff, 1986; Zins, 1989). There is also little guidance to be found in the school psychology literature where the topic has received scant attention. (Several exceptions are a theme issue in *School Psychology Review* [Ross-Reynolds & Grimes, 1981], a review article by Knoff [1986], and a monograph on supervision of school psychological services in Iowa [Grimes & Happe, 1987]). For the most part, it is necessary to turn to the literature in psychotherapy, counseling, and school administration and supervision for information. Research on school psychological supervision practices is a much neglected area.

This chapter describes practices which can help school psychology supervisors provide an effective training experience for their interns. The practices are described within the context of a problem solving model which has gained considerable acceptance for providing different services within schools. Many of the practices can be applied in supervising post credentialed psychologists and other school professionals as well as interns.

The importance of providing training through supervision in school psychology was formally articulated by the participants of the Thayer conference in 1954 (Cutts, 1955). Conference participants recommended that training involve carefully supervised and meaningfully organized practica and internships. In 1977, both the National Association of School Psychologists (NASP) and the American Psychological Association (APA) published standards for the provision of services which reaffirmed the need for supervision to train school psychologists and ensure effective and accountable services. Subsequent guidelines (APA, 1981; NASP, 1984, 1986) expanded the concept of supervision to that of an ongoing and changing process throughout the school psychologist's career. It is one of the components of continuing professional development. Current professional standards for internship experiences, supervisory relationships, and supervisory responsibilities and qualifications are also included in this chapter.

BASIC CONSIDERATIONS

Goals of Supervision

Because of the broad range of services which school psychologists provide, training must prepare them for a complex role with varied functions. Trainees begin to be prepared for these functions in university programs where supervision is focused on specific knowledge and skill acquisition. In practica, trainees work with volunteer subjects or referred youngsters who have been preselected for a particular service. They are, therefore, exposed only to a limited range of situations.

Although the acquisition of additional knowledge and skills continues to be important during the internship experience, internship supervision is not as narrowly focused as it is in practica supervision. The primary goal of internship supervision is to help the intern integrate many discrete skills into one coherent, albeit complex, professional role. Interns must learn how to assess problem situations and decide which of a number of possible approaches to follow. The intern is exposed to a wide range of representative situations. A second, related, goal of supervision is to help the intern make the transition in identification from student to professional. A third goal is to facilitate both the intern's integration into the organizational structure of the school and understanding of how services are provided and change can be effected within that structure.

The Internship Site

These goals can be met only within the context of a setting which permits the supervisor and the intern to function effectively in a variety of roles. While the university bears the primary responsibility for selecting appropriate sites, we have been impressed with how often practitioners base their decisions about undertaking supervision on how wide a range of services they are able to perform in their settings. NASP standards (1986) suggest that the school setting, or the larger educational agency of which it is a part, be one that:

> Has the availability of (a) children of all school ages, (b) pupil personnel services functioning within a team framework, (c) full-range of services for handicapped children of both high and low incidences, (d) regular and special educational services at the preschool, elementary and secondary levels, and (e) at least one certified school psychologist having at least three years . . . of full-time school psychologist experience or the equivalent who serves as the internship supervisor. (p. 36)

It is also desirable that the school have working relationships with community agencies dealing with children and their families.

Further, the local educational agency should be committed to the internship as a training experience. This commitment means that services are provided only to the extent that they further the learning and training needs of the intern. The internship should not be a way of getting inexpensive services. Evidence of commitment to training can be found in the willingness of administrators to provide adequate resources in the form of space for privacy, materials, secretarial assistance, release time for attendance at professional meetings, reimbursement for job-related travel, salary commensurate with experience when financially feasible, adequate supervision, and release time for supervisors. NASP standards recommend that interns be provided with a minimum of two hours per week of direct supervision and that supervisors be granted the equivalent of one work day per week for each intern supervised. A limit of two interns per supervisor is recommended.

Qualifications of Supervisors

NASP standards (1984) define a supervising school psychologist as "a professional psychologist who has met all

NASP requirements for credentialling, has completed three years of successfully supervised experience as a school psychologist, and who has been designated by an employing agency as a supervisor responsible for school psychological services in the agency" (p. 24). At least one year of experience at the employing agency is recommended prior to undertaking intern supervision. APA Specialty Guidelines (1981) recommend that overall professional supervision be provided by doctoral level school psychologists with at least two years of experience, although supervision in specific procedures and techniques may be provided by others.

We would also recommend that the intern supervisor be employed as a full-time school psychologist in the district. School psychologists employed on a casework or consultant basis are generally not integrated sufficiently into the school organization to provide a full role model. Availability for supervision on an as-needed basis can also be problematic.

Both professional organizations stress commitment to continuing professional development as a qualification of supervisors. Included among the measures supervisors should take to preserve and enhance their professional competence are engaging in supervision themselves, engaging in peer review activities, consulting with colleagues, reading and/or preparing scientific and professional publications, attending workshops and conferences, participating in formal Continuing Professional Development programs, presenting at meetings and conventions, and actively participating in professional organizations.

NASP standards (1984) suggest that school psychologists at all levels of practice should have the opportunity to meet with supervisors, especially when they are dealing with complex cases or expanding their services into new areas. Doing supervision is certainly an expansion of service into a new area. Good practice would dictate that those who are doing supervision should be able to receive supervision of the supervision process.

Field and University Coordination: Respective Responsibilities

Supervision is a coordinated effort of both field and university personnel. For purposes of simplicity, one might say the field supervisor supervises the intern and the university supervisor supervises the internship program or process. The field supervisor bears the sole responsibility for (a) supervising the intern in his/her service delivery to clients and (b) ensuring that clients' needs are effectively met in a manner consistent with legal and ethical considerations.

University supervisors bear the responsibility for setting the stage for an effective internship experience and for resolving problems that might undermine it. They select appropriate sites and field supervisors in whom they may have confidence. They help students select appropriate sites, prepare students for interviews, and orient them to the goals of internship. They also orient field supervisors to university procedures and to special goals, if any, for particular interns. They collaborate with field supervisors to plan an individualized activity schedule for the intern, to assess the intern's progress, to assess the effectiveness of the internship program, and to work out problems that may arise.

Although evaluation is a collaborative effort, the training program and university supervisor bear the ultimate responsibility for developing an evaluation process and for assigning internship credit and grades. The evaluation process allows for ongoing evaluation with significant input from local supervisors, other school personnel, interns, and university faculty. Ultimately, evaluation involves all aspects of the internship experience, including:

(a) the experiences provided by the local educational agency, (b) the quality of local supervision, (c) the quality of university supervision, (d) the competencies of the intern, (e) the suitability of the setting for future internships, (f) the suitability of the intern's preparation for internship. (NASP, 1986, p. 22)

In order to carry out their responsibilities, university supervisors should visit internship sites at least once a semester (though this is a bare minimum), maintain phone contact with field supervisors, and meet weekly with interns either as a group or individually. NASP standards (1986) recommend that university faculty supervise no more than 12 interns, be given appropriate course-load credit, and have no more than 75% of their time assigned to practica and internship supervision combined. We would also recommend that internship supervision not be delegated primarily to adjunct faculty as a way of cutting costs or be used to fill schedules of unqualified faculty.

BEST PRACTICES

A Problem-Solving Model

The role of the school psychologist has become increasingly complex as schools have broadened their mission to educate all youngsters, even those less ready for traditional curricula. School psychologists are called upon to resolve issues for children with vastly differing needs and backgrounds. They are involved in prevention, assessment, consultation, crisis intervention, counseling, program development, training, and research. They are required to move from one role to another with ease and assurance.

Psychologists need commitment, concern, and well-formed habits of problem solving to perform these roles. It is these habits of problem solving that interns need to learn. To achieve this end, emphasis should be placed on developing critical thinking skills.

A problem solving model emphasizes critical thinking in defining problems, analyzing alternative solutions, and evaluating outcomes. It emphasizes an active approach to tackling problems and generating solutions. It is also atheoretical and can be applied with different theoretical orientations.

Problem solving approaches have been accepted in many areas of school psychology practice — in assessment, consultation, counseling, and crisis intervention. Using such a technique provides interns with a good model to follow in performing these services. It also has the advantage of developing critical thinking skills which serve as a "road map" for professional activity which interns can continue to use as they progress through their careers. In addition, it provides a good model for doing supervision itself.

Wasik and Fishbein (1982), who proposed this orientation as a model for supervision in professional psychology, suggested that its use enabled the supervisor to encourage the following important professional attitudes:

> (a) accept the fact that problematic situations constitute a normal part of professional practice and that most of these situations can be handled effectively, (b) identify problematic situations when they occur, and (c) inhibit the tendency to either respond on the first impulse or do nothing. (p. 561)

Training Interns in Problem Solving

To implement a problem solving model, supervisors need to orient interns to the concepts and rationale involved and describe the successive stages. The model proposed by Gutkin and Curtis (1982) contains the following steps: (a) define and clarify the problem, (b) analyze the forces impinging on the problem, (c) generate alternative strategies, (d) evaluate and choose among alternatives, (e) implement the chosen strategy, (f) evaluate the effectiveness of the action and recycle, if necessary.

Clarifying problems. Identifying a problem accurately is a critical first stage in finding a solution. Problems are more usefully defined when they are described in concrete, observable, behavioral terms. Supervisees often need help differentiating between observations and inferences when they analyze teacher referral statements. Are teachers describing the behavior they find problematic, or are they making inferences and generalizations about the problem? Does a referral statement represent a hidden agenda, for example, formerly classified children cannot be successfully mainstreamed? As the school psychologist and intern work with teachers to achieve clarification, teachers themselves often begin to develop more focus and precision in their referral questions.

Analyzing problems. A range of environmental and individual variables must be explored to analyze the forces impinging upon the problem. Supervisors can do much to overcome the child-as-the-problem bias that psychologists are prone to (Alessi, 1988) at this point. They should remind interns to consider curriculum, teaching practices, school administrative policies, situational determinants, and home variables as well as child factors in analyzing the forces.

Psychoeducational assessment is most often done at this stage. A problem solving model conceptualizes testing as an information gathering process, designed to aid, but not preempt, decision making (Witt, Elliott, Gresham, & Kramer, 1988). Furthermore, the primary reason for conducting a psychoeducational assessment is to improve instructional or intervention strategies. Entry level interns commonly derive comfort and security from test results. They need to be reminded that tests are simply not accurate enough and they do not sample a wide enough range of variables to be used as the sole criteria for important decisions about children. Indeed, there are many instances in which testing would not be an appropriate means to gather information needed to solve a problem.

Generating alternative strategies. After problems have been clarified and analyzed, alternative strategies are generated. Interns can have difficulty generating solutions for a number of reasons. They may think only in terms of one "best solution". They may dismiss out-of-hand potential solutions with some undesirable consequences. They may have limited knowledge about options. Supervisors may encourage brainstorming to reduce the element of evaluation in initial generation of ideas. They may also contribute their wider range of understanding of the school and community, the scope of available resources, and possible interventions. Supervisors are cautioned to guard against being critical of solutions suggested by interns in favor of a logical, respectful analysis. If supervisors are too critical of proposed solutions or too structured in suggesting solutions, interns are less likely to see the work as their own or to incorporate a problem solving approach.

Evaluating alternative strategies. Interns may have difficulty recognizing the "best" solution to a problem (D'Zurilla & Goldfried, 1971). To help interns in this process, supervisors can engage them in a review of each option. Among the perspectives to consider in reviewing options are the nature of the problem, the needs of the target child, class dynamics, teacher characteristics, administrative policies, resource support, parental concerns, etc. The potential gains for the target child must always be weighed against possible losses in a best solution model.

Implementing a strategy. Once a strategy or solution has been decided upon, the necessary steps to be taken in implementing it should be spelled out. Learning and generalization occur most effectively when interns carry out the responsibility for implementation (Caplan, 1970). However, an intern may not have acquired the necessary skill, knowledge, or confidence to carry out a particular intervention. Further guided practice may be necessary. Supervisors need to be sensitive in assessing the intern's strengths. They also have to be open and accepting so that interns are encouraged to communicate their concerns about implementation.

A note of caution has to be inserted here. In crises (e.g., potential suicide, psychotic behavior, neglect and abuse), the supervisor may set aside a teaching role and intervene directly or provide specific, structured direction. It is to be kept in mind that the supervisor retains ultimate responsibility for psychological services. With good supervision, most of these services can be provided by interns. When services cannot be provided directly by the intern, the supervisor can provide as much opportunity as possible for the intern to observe the senior psychologist at work. Client consent should be obtained for such observation.

Evaluating strategy effectiveness. Too often, a sense of closure and relief for a completed task is experienced at the end of the implementation stage and it is considered the final step in the problem solving process. However, "best solutions" should always be considered tentative until follow-up demonstrates the strategy has been effective.

The busy schedules of school psychologists rarely permit extensive data gathering to determine the overall success of interventions. Interns have to be encouraged to touch base with those who have a "hands-on" role in implementation to find out whether expected changes are beginning to take place. In the absence of any change, it is important to determine the conditions of implementation. Is there resistance to the intervention? Are conditions conducive to implementation being met by those directly responsible? Has sufficient time elapsed? Are the parameters of the plan understood, etc.? If the plan is not working as anticipated, it is important to re-cycle to earlier stages of problem solving and reassess the validity of the data, hypotheses, options, and best solutions.

The Supervisory Process

The previous section has discussed how to train interns to use a problem solving model to provide service. This section focuses on how the model can be applied to the process of providing supervision.

Broadly speaking, interns lack certain of the skills, knowledge, confidence, objectivity, or interpersonal interactions that are important to effective professional functioning (Caplan, 1970). Interns differ, of course. The supervisor has to assess the intern's level of development in each of these areas in order to (a) establish learning objectives, (b) plan the timing, progression, and complexity of the experiences provided, (c) determine supervisory focus and interventions, and

(d) provide feedback on performance. This is a process that goes on throughout the internship.

Establishing learning objectives. Depending on one's point of view, it is either fortunate or unfortunate that there are no uniform objectives for the internship experience that can be proposed. Objectives are shaped by the orientation and expertise of the supervisor, the opportunities and politics of the setting, the philosophy of the university training program, and the interests and developmental level of the intern.

It is essential that both the supervisor and the intern have a clear picture of what is to be learned. Objectives, or goals, like problems, are more usefully defined when they are described in concrete, observable, behavioral terms. They also need to be practical and relevant to good practice as a school psychologist. Effective supervisors set clear and explicit goals in open discussions with interns (Carifio & Hess, 1987). They actively engage trainees in establishing goals and sharing their concerns.

As part of establishing learning objectives, the supervisor has to assess the intern's developmental level(s). The keyword for assessment is observation. Supervisors should directly observe the intern in action in all kinds of activities. It is often helpful to use behavioral checklists (e.g., for test administrations, for conducting a meeting, etc.). Checklists have the advantage of focusing observations, clarifying expectations for interns, and guiding feedback. Checklists may be provided by the training program if it is competency based. They are also found in training guides and can be developed by supervisors. Observation includes reviewing written work and checking test protocols for accuracy of scoring.

Teaching methods. Effective supervisors use learning objectives and their assessment of the intern's development level(s) to guide them in selecting from a variety of different teaching techniques (Carifio & Hess, 1987). Among the teaching techniques with demonstrated effectiveness are direct instruction, microtraining (a skill-training approach that blends Roger's emphasis on process behaviors with a behavioral methodology), modeling, behavioral rehearsal, behavioral feedback, and self-observation/self-monitoring procedures (Forsyth & Ivey, 1980; Hosford & Barmann, 1983; Kratochwill, Bergan, & Mace, 1981; Lambert & Arnold, 1987; Leddick & Bernard, 1980).

Modeling is probably one of the most easily and often used techniques. The intern can learn more from opportunities to watch the supervisor in action if observations are guided by pre-session discussions of the supervisor's aims and what is to take place. Special foci of observation can be suggested. Post-session analyses of what has been observed are also important. Perhaps it may lessen embarrassment about identifying goofs, if supervisors keep in mind that modeling has been found to be more effective if trainees see good and poor examples of skills — as long as they are discriminated for them.

Some supervisors are quite ingenious in devising teaching techniques. In one instance, a supervisor did assertion training to help an intern develop skills for child advocacy. In another instance, this same supervisor used desensitization techniques to help a young, frightened, white intern from a parochial background become comfortable in a black urban school. The first step in making the intern comfortable with individual students was having her take the hand of an adorable kindergartener. Non-threatening younger children were seen in the guidance office, which she experienced as a safe setting, before she worked her way up to seeing adolescents. The supervisor described each student in advance to give the intern a sense of knowing the student as a person. A hierarchy of "frightening" group settings was established and imagery used to desensitize them. The intern next went to each setting with other individuals and then alone. She was instructed to monitor her anxiety level and discussed her reactions in a debriefing session after each excursion. The process took about three weeks. Though this was not a typical intervention for a supervisor to have to

make, it did prevent the termination of an internship.

Matching supervision to trainee level. Therapy supervisors who are reported to be effective by trainees match their behavior and focus of supervision to the trainee's level of development. Further, they are able to change as their trainees gain experience and skill (Worthington, 1987). Generally, they are perceived to give less instruction and structure, monitor behavior less, and be less directive as trainees advance. They also increasingly confront trainees, deal with personal issues, tackle resistance and transference issues, give negative feedback, and treat them like peers.

Developmental models of supervision, which describe supervisory behavior that optimizes growth at different stages, are currently receiving attention in the field of psychotherapy and counseling. Stoltenberg and Delworth's (1987) Integrated Developmental Model is a good example of this approach. Although the model has yet to be validated with school psychology trainees, it provides useful guidelines to consider.

Certainly, their description of Level 1 trainees sounds much like entering school psychology interns. Level 1 trainees lack an image of themselves as professionals and they are anxious. They commonly fear that they will be found wanting by themselves, their clients, and their supervisors. This causes them to focus on their own uncertainties and the techniques they are trying to learn. This makes it relatively difficult for them to understand what the client is experiencing. Their anxiety, however, is generally channeled into hard work and they exhibit a high degree of motivation to learn the correct way to provide service. They are dependent on supervisors for teaching and nurturance.

At Level 1, supervisors create an optimal environment by being supportive and providing structure to keep normal anxiety at manageable levels. The supervisor should provide information and clarify expectations. It is helpful to discuss specific fears so that the supervisor can make relevant suggestions about what to do in certain situations and reassure the trainee that such fears are common. It is also reassuring for the trainee to hear that mistakes are expected as part of the learning process. Specific techniques that are useful for providing structure and information include observations of supervisors and peers, role-playing, microtraining, and case presentations with video or audiotapes in group supervision. Skill development is emphasized during this period. The supervisor should focus on helping the trainee put into practice and refine skills that have already been developed. In supervising counseling, this focus refers to helping the trainee increase sensitivity to nuances of client statements, use appropriately expressive language, and establish an appropriate pace of responding. In supervising testing, attention can be directed toward increasing adequacy of administration, accuracy of scoring, depth of interpretation, and clarity of communication.

As trainees gain skill and confidence, there is a shift in emotional focus from the self to the client. This shift characterizes movement to Level 2. Empathic and conceptual understanding of clients and situations increase. Initial successes in activities also lessens anxiety and leads to stronger desire for autonomous functioning. However, as trainees face more difficult situations, and as they begin to appreciate complexities more fully, uncertainty regarding the efficacy of techniques in general and one's own ability leads to fluctuation in motivation.

According to Stoltenberg and Delworth, supervisors help trainees make the transition to Level 2 by increasing the range and difficulty of assigned cases, decreasing structure, and supporting more autonomous functioning. Trainees are encouraged to clarify and evaluate rationales for their actions and to evaluate alternative perspectives offered by supervisors. Unless dictated by concerns for client welfare, supervisors decrease prescriptive statements about client interventions. The focus of supervisor interventions shifts from didactic, skill oriented comments to process comments (dynamics between client and psychologist) and

cognitive interventions (ways of conceptualizing the client or the treatment process). Confrontive interventions (bringing inconsistencies to awareness) which would have been too threatening to be integrated at an earlier stage can now be introduced in a low-keyed manner. A supportive and accepting approach still remains crucial, as it does throughout the supervisory experience. Stoltenberg and Delworth claim that trainees at this level are the most difficult and challenging to supervise because of the dependency-autonomy conflicts regarding the supervisory relationship that they tend to develop.

Vascillations characteristic of the Level 2 trainee begin to subside as he/she enters Level 3. The trainee is able to maintain a balance between self and other focus, and to develop a deeper and more integrated understanding of concepts. Motivation is more consistent. Strengths and limitations of both self and professional knowledge can be acknowledged and tolerated. Opinions of others can be sought when there are doubts, but the trainee is neither overdependent nor negatively independent.

Supervision at Level 3 is characterized by increased sharing and collegiality. The trainee is engaged in careful and honest assessment of strengths and weaknesses. Although supervision becomes more reactive than proactive at this level, a major function of supervision is pointing out areas of lower level functioning and encouraging exploration and integration across domains. The supervisor has to be particularly skilled in the use of confrontation while still maintaining a supportive stance. The focus is more on helping the trainee develop his or her own idiosyncratic professional identity than on skills or knowledge. Difficulties can emerge if supervisors are not functioning at the same level as their trainees, especially if they offer an intrusive or highly structured environment.

Stoltenberg and Delworth describe an additional level of development reflecting a high degree of integration. This level is the master-level practitioner, which some may reach after about 5 or 6 years of practice. Consultation, when sought, is given at this level.

Feedback and evaluation. The purpose of the supervisory techniques that have been described in preceding sections is to help interns reach specified goals. Feedback that is closely tied to an intern's performance can be an invaluable part of the learning process. Good supervisors are generally supportive and noncritical in the way they give feedback. They create an atmosphere of trust which helps interns accurately describe their behaviors. Freeman (1985) recommends that feedback should be (a) systematic (objective, accurate, consistent, and reliable), (b) timely (delivered soon after an event), (c) clearly understood (based on explicit and specific performance criteria), and (d) reciprocal (provided in two-way interactions in which suggestions are made as only one of a number of potential ways to approach a problem).

Evaluation is an ongoing and continuous process which includes feedback given by the supervisor on a regular basis concerning strengths and weaknesses of performance and ways to improve. It also includes periodic meetings in which both the field and university supervisors meet with the intern to evaluate progress, and formal written evaluations by field supervisors (seen by the intern) in accordance with university procedures. Rating scales are useful in structuring the thinking of the supervisor and encouraging thoroughness. An example of a rating scale is provided in the Attachment. A global statement regarding progress is not sufficient. The "nice guy" approach to evaluation helps neither the student nor the profession and is a neglect of professional responsibility.

Problems in evaluation can be minimized if interns know in advance what supervisors are looking for, if evaluations deal with well-specified behaviors, if interns are made aware of problems well before final evaluations, and if interns are actively involved in the process. Interns should also have the right to submit a written reaction along with the supervisor's evaluation if they believe it is inappropriate.

Structuring a Hierarchy of Learning Experiences

The problem solving method and supervisory styles suggested in the proceeding sections are applied within the context of service delivery. Since content and method are inextricably intertwined, the intern is concurrently and systematically exposed to a sequence of increasingly complex aspects of psychological service to acquire competence in the process of service delivery.

Supervisors have to arrange a schedule to help interns learn to do increasingly complex tasks. We recommend the sequence that Alessi, Lascurettes-Alessi, and Leys (1981) provided. It is presented with minor modifications. While Alessi et al. specified a 15-week time-frame, we think it is appropriate for a nine-month period. Supervisors can move from phase to phase when they judge interns to be ready.

Phase I (generally 2 weeks): Direct modeling by supervisor. During this phase, the intern's task is to observe while the task of the supervisor is to model. The intern will: (a) learn the demographics of the community, (b) meet school personnel (administrators, secretaries, general and special education teachers, social workers, guidance counselor), (c) obtain copies of school policies, procedures, and forms used in the school, (d) observe how field supervisor handles referrals, initial contacts, assessment, consultation, IEPs and follow-up, (e) observe all alternative and support services (resource rooms, self-contained classes, reading labs, ESL classes, etc.), (f) observe mandatory procedures for classification and placement in special education, (g) learn about community agencies involved with the schools.

Phase II: Direct supervision of intern. During this phase, intern objectives and competencies are specified. There should be observations of the intern across settings: (a) administering tests used in the system prescriptively, (b) interviewing teachers, staff, parents, (c) consulting with teachers and parents, (d) performing classroom observations, (e) counseling. Time is spent reviewing written reports and discussing federal mandates and state education law, as well as professional and ethical standards.

Phase III: Indirect supervision of intern. This phase begins when the supervisor is assured of the intern's skills through observation and discussion. Independent tasks are assigned. These might include: (a) recording classroom observations, (b) taking and writing up a relevant history, (c) conducting an assessment, (d) presenting a case before a special education committee, (e) writing an Individual Education Plan, (f) developing intervention strategies, (g) consulting with a teacher.

Phase IV: Fading of direct guidance in supervision. During this phase the intern would have specified areas to work in as a school psychologist. The intern would adhere to a problem solving model and be responsible for all activities in that area, including implementation, while the supervisor acts as a consultant. At this stage, daily intern/supervisor meetings should be held to review the day's work and plan for the following day.

Phase V: Independent work by intern. During this phase the supervisor begins to withdraw all support except in emergency situations. When the intern asks for help, the supervisor focuses the intern on relevant stages of the problem solving model and encourages independent solutions and interventions.

SUMMARY

Although supervision is considered crucial in training school psychologists and ensuring effective and accountable services, little attention has been paid to it in the school psychology literature. Research is virtually nonexistent. Supervisors generally undertake this activity with little or no formal training or guidance. This chapter provides guidelines for supervision at the internship level where the goal is to help interns integrate many discrete skills, acquired in graduate training, into one coherent, complex professional role. Current NASP standards for selection of internship sites, functions and qualifications of supervisors, and the coordination of field and university supervisors in implementing an effective training program are discussed.

The guidelines for the process of doing supervision itself are based on a problem solving model which has been accepted for many areas of school psychology practice. A problem solving model emphasizes the development of critical thinking skills to define problems clearly, analyze alternative solutions, and evaluate outcomes of interventions. It also emphasizes an active approach to tackling problems and generating solutions. There are a number of supervisory techniques, which have been demonstrated to be effective, from which supervisors can choose. Supervisory style and focus also have to be matched to the intern's developmental level. A successful supervisory experience should not only aid interns in their transition to independent professionals, but develop positive attitudes toward supervision that result in a career-long commitment to continuing professional development.

REFERENCES

Alessi, G. (1988). Diagnosis diagnosed: A systemic reaction. *Professional School Psychology, 3*, 145–151.

Alessi, G. J., Lascurettes-Alessi, K. J., & Leys, W. L. (1981). Internships in school psychology: Supervision issues. *School Psychology Review, 10*, 461–469.

American Psychological Association. (1981). Specialty guidelines for the delivery of services by school psychologists. *American Psychologist, 36*, 670-681.

Caplan. G. (1970). *The theory and practice of mental health consultation.* New York: Basic Books.

Carifio, M. S., & Hess, A. K. (1987). Who is the ideal supervisor? *Professional Psychology: Research and Practice, 18*, 244-250.

Cutts, N. E. (Ed.). (1955). *School psychologists at mid-century.* Washington, DC: American Psychological Association.

D'Zurilla, T. J., & Goldfried, M. R. (1971). Problem solving and behavior modification. *Journal of Abnormal Psychology, 78*, 107-126.

Forsyth, D. R., & Ivey, A. E. (1980). Microtraining: An approach to differential supervision. In A. K. Hess (Ed.), *Psychotherapy supervision: Theory, research, and practice* (pp. 242-261). New York: Wiley.

Freeman, E. (1985). The importance of feedback in clinical supervision: Implications for direct practice. *The Clinical Supervisor, 3*, 5-26.

Grimes, J., & Happe, D. (Eds.). (1987). *Best practices in the supervision of school psychological services.* Des Moines: Iowa State Department of Education. (ERIC Document Reproduction Service No. ED 293 037)

Gutkin, T. B., & Curtis, M. J. (1982). School based consultation: Theory and techniques. In C. R. Reynolds & T. B. Gutkin (Eds.), *The handbook of school psychology* (pp. 796-828). New York: Wiley.

Hosford, R. E., & Barmann, B. (1983). A social learning approach to counselor supervision. *The Counseling Psychologist, 11*, 51-58.

Knoff, H. M. (1986). Supervision in school psychology: The forgotten or future path to effective services? *School Psychology Review, 15*, 529-545.

Kratochwill, T. R., Bergan, J. R., & Mace, F. C. (1981). Practitioner competencies needed for implementation of behavioral psychology in the schools: Issues in supervision. *School Psychology Review, 10*, 434-444.

Lambert, M. J., & Arnold, R. C. (1987). Research and the supervisory process. *Professional Psychology: Research and Practice, 18*, 217-224.

Leddick, G. R., & Bernard, J. M. (1980). The history of supervision: A critical review. *Counselor Education and Supervision, 19*, 186-196.

National Association of School Psychologists. (1984). *Professional Conduct Manual: Principles for professional ethics; Standards for the provision of school psychological services.* Washington, DC: Author.

National Association of School Psychologists. (1986). *Standards-Training programs: Field placement programs; Credentialing standards.* Washington, DC: Author.

Ross-Reynolds, G., & Grimes, J. P. (Eds.). (1981). Supervision and continuing professional development. *School Psychology Review, 10*(4).

Stoltenberg, C. D., & Delworth, U. (1987). *Supervising counselors and therapists: A developmental approach.* San Francisco: Jossey-Bass.

Wasik, B. H., & Fishbein, J. E. (1982). Problem solving: A model for supervision in professional psychology. *Professional Psychology, 13*, 559-564.

Witt, J. C., Elliott, S. N., Gresham, F. M., & Kramer, J. J. (1988). *Assessment of special children: Tests and the problem solving process.* Chicago: Scott Foresman.

Worthington, Jr., E. L. (1987). Changes in supervision as counselors and supervisors gain experience: A review. *Professional Psychology: Research and Practice, 18*, 189-208.

Zins, J. E., Murphy, J. J., & Wess, B. P. (1989). Supervision in school psychology: Current practices and congruence with professional standards. *School Psychology Review, 18*, 56-63.

ANNOTATED BIBLIOGRAPHY

Dana, R. H., & May, W. T. (Eds.). (1987). *Internship Training in Professional Psychology.* Washington, DC: Hemisphere Publishing.
This book is about the internship experience in clinical, counseling, school, clinical child, and health psychology. It includes writings on the entire process of internship from program selection to specific components of training and future agendas for cost-effective and responsible professional training. The selections on supervision and evaluation are of particular interest.

Hess, A. K. (Ed.). (1987). Special section: Advances in psychotherapy supervision. *Professional Psychology: Research and Practice, 18*(3).
Although this theme issue deals with advances in psychotherapy supervision, it deals with issues of broader concern to school psychologists as well. It contains articles on changes in supervision as both counselors and supervisors gain experience, developmental models, the ideal supervisor, and sex role and power relationships in supervision. There is also a review of research.

Illinois State Board of Education. (1984). *Manual for School Psychology internship programs.* Department of Specialized Educational Services, 100 North First St., Springfield, IL 62777.
This is a first-rate manual describing a carefully worked out internship program from initial selection of sites through evaluation of the internship process. Supervisors will be particularly interested in the section describing activities appropriate for achieving different skill and knowledge objectives.

Ross-Reynolds, G., & Grimes, J. P. (Eds.). (1981). Supervision and continuing professional development. *School Psychology Review, 10*(4).
This theme issue brings together several relevant articles on supervision in school psychology. Supervision is considered from a systems, a behavioral, and a transactional perspective. The

article by Alessi et al. provides a useful schedule of activities for the intern and lists resource material (available from the senior author) which may be of interest to supervisors.

Stoltenberg, D. D., & Delworth, U. (1987). *Supervising counselors and therapists: A developmental approach.* San Francisco: Jossey-Bass.

Developmental models of supervision are currently receiving significant attention in the field of psychotherapy and counseling supervision. This book is recommended for those who wish to learn more about how to provide optimal supervision for interns at different stages. The book also contains a list of instruments that have been used in supervision research.

Attachment

SCHOOL PSYCHOLOGY PRACTICUM STUDENT EVALUATION
Developed by Marc Cecil, University of South Carolina, and adapted to present form by School Psychology Program, University of Wisconsin-Madison

Date: _____

Name of Student: _____ Placement: _____

Evaluator: _____ Evaluator's Title: _____

Directions: The Field Practicum experience is the last practicum necessary before students seek employment as a practicing school psychologist. Ratings are intended to guide the student and the program in evaluating readiness for independent practice. Please use the following rating scale in evaluating the student on the characteristics listed below:

N/A — *Not Applicable;* Not an appropriate goal for a school psychology practicum in this setting

0 — *Not Observed*

1 — *Unsatisfactory;* Student's skills reflect insufficient mastery in this area; Student needs additional course-based instruction in this skill

2 — *Needs improvement;* Plans should be made to assure student gains extra practice in this skill prior to leaving the program

3 — *Satisfactory;* Student's skills in this area are adequate for practice in schools; Student should continue to practice this skill under professional supervision

4 — *Competent;* Student is comfortably independent in this skill

5 — *Outstanding;* Student's skills in this area are exceptionally strong; Student could be a model practitioner in this skill area

---

A. **Personal Characteristics**

1. Presents a good personal appearance	N/A	0	1	2	3	4	5
2. Demonstrates dependability	N/A	0	1	2	3	4	5
3. Meets difficult situations with self-control	N/A	0	1	2	3	4	5
4. Demonstrates good judgment and common sense	N/A	0	1	2	3	4	5
5. Communicates and listens effectively	N/A	0	1	2	3	4	5
6. Shows concern, respect, and sensitivity for the needs of staff and students	N/A	0	1	2	3	4	5
7. Works well with other staff	N/A	0	1	2	3	4	5

	N/A	0	1	2	3	4	5
8. Is able to relate well to children	N/A	0	1	2	3	4	5
9. Utilizes constructive criticism	N/A	0	1	2	3	4	5
10. Displays initiative and resourcefulness	N/A	0	1	2	3	4	5
11. Demonstrates tolerance for others' values and viewpoints	N/A	0	1	2	3	4	5
12. Accepts constructive criticism	N/A	0	1	2	3	4	5
13. Shows evidence of continued self-evaluation	N/A	0	1	2	3	4	5
14. Achieves comfortable interactions with minority students	N/A	0	1	2	3	4	5

B. Assessment Skills

	N/A	0	1	2	3	4	5
1. Clearly identifies the nature of the referral problem and the purpose of the assessment	N/A	0	1	2	3	4	5
2. Uses appropriate assessment instruments that are directly related to the identified problem	N/A	0	1	2	3	4	5
3. Analyzes and interprets test results in a meaningful and thorough fashion	N/A	0	1	2	3	4	5
4. Makes recommendations that follow logically from the assessment results and are educationally relevant	N/A	0	1	2	3	4	5
5. Displays accuracy in administering tests	N/A	0	1	2	3	4	5
6. Displays accuracy in scoring tests	N/A	0	1	2	3	4	5
7. Is sensitive to sources of bias when selecting and administering tests	N/A	0	1	2	3	4	5

C. Consultation Skills

	N/A	0	1	2	3	4	5
1. Establishes effective collaborative relationships with teachers and other school personnel	N/A	0	1	2	3	4	5
2. Conducts effective parent conferences	N/A	0	1	2	3	4	5
3. Serves effectively as a liaison for school and parents	N/A	0	1	2	3	4	5
4. Evaluates effectiveness of consultation strategies used	N/A	0	1	2	3	4	5

D. Intervention Skills

	N/A	0	1	2	3	4	5
1. Uses interventon strategies that are directly related to the assessed problem	N/A	0	1	2	3	4	5
2. Clearly delineates goals of intervention goals	N/A	0	1	2	3	4	5
3. Evaluates the effectiveness of intervention techniques used	N/A	0	1	2	3	4	5
4. Demonstrates skill in utilizing individual counseling techniques	N/A	0	1	2	3	4	5
5. Demonstrates skill in utilizing group counseling techniques	N/A	0	1	2	3	4	5
6. Demonstrates skill in utilizing behavior modification and classroom management techniques	N/A	0	1	2	3	4	5

E. **Professional Responsibilities**

1. Observes scheduled hours and appointments at assigned school(s) in a punctual manner	N/A	0	1	2	3	4	5
2. Is prompt in meeting deadlines, responding to referrals, and handing in written reports	N/A	0	1	2	3	4	5
3. Completes written reports and forms in a neat, thorough, and accurate manner	N/A	0	1	2	3	4	5
4. Writes reports in a coherent, focused, and well organized manner	N/A	0	1	2	3	4	5
5. Establishes appropriate work priorities and manages time efficiently	N/A	0	1	2	3	4	5
6. Keeps supervisors and administrators informed of unusual events and activities, as well as routine matters in their school(s)	N/A	0	1	2	3	4	5
7. Uses feedback from supervision in a productive manner	N/A	0	1	2	3	4	5
8. Consistently follows through when additional action is needed	N/A	0	1	2	3	4	5
9. Demonstrates an awareness of competency level, and doesn't accept responsibilities that exceed this level	N/A	0	1	2	3	4	5
10. Maintains visibility and accessibility within assigned school(s)	N/A	0	1	2	3	4	5
11. Considers all alternatives and implications before recommending a change in child's program	N/A	0	1	2	3	4	5
Overall Rating of Student			1	2	3	4	5

Professional Goals:

Given the above ratings of the student's current professional skills, list the three most important goals which should be established for his/her continued professional training.

1. Most important goal _____

_____

2. _____

_____

3. _____

_____

Evaluator's signture: _____   Date: _____

Student's signature: _____   Date: _____

(The student's signature indicates only that the evaluation has been discussed with student.)

31

Best Practices in Kindergarten Screening

Caven S. Mcloughlin
Kent State University

Elizabeth Rausch
PSI Associates, Inc.

The most asked question from professionals planning developmental screening programs is "which test should I use?" A more fruitful question is "what methods of observation, including parents' reports of daily behavior, professionals' observations, and formal brief test, might be used."

Lichtenstein & Ireton, 1984.

OVERVIEW

Screening for entry into kindergarten is a topic fraught with controversy, primarily because there are no accepted standards that allow for universal comparison of children's progress. There is an abundance of opinion about this practice, and a relative paucity of data. Some skeptics believe that screening is a fruitless business; others consider it to be the answer to a wide range of educational problems.

The routine screening of children prior to entering kindergarten is usually justified in several ways. A child may be screened to determine the need for schooling because the child appears to need supplemental early education or because of apparent developmental precocity. Typically, however, kindergarten screening is conducted as part of the normal matriculation process in order for school representatives to obtain data concerning each child's level of academic readiness.

It is impractical to conduct extensive testing of all children in a school district. Therefore, simple and inexpensive ways of screening children prior to their entrance into kindergarten requires effective identification procedures to maximize results. One of the most efficient ways of measuring children's abilities is to carry out a comprehensive screening process. This chapter will consider techniques and methodologies designed to determine whether entrance into the educational system is appropriate. Few academic settings can allow educators to implement all aspects of a program that is considered to represent best practices. Budgets, manpower, time, and so forth are all factors constraining educational programs. This is certainly true in the case of the "kindergarten round-up." It is the authors' fervent wish, however, that the reader of this chapter will be able to select those items which are the most relevant to a particular setting and adapt them wherever appropriate.

BASIC CONSIDERATIONS

What is Screening?

Screening is a systematic process that determines which children are most likely to develop future problems. We screen for several reasons:

1. To identify early. There is a consensus among professionals and lay people alike that the earlier a problem or need is identified, the greater is the likelihood of maximizing a child's development; similarly, early identification can minimize the effects of any existing adverse circumstances.

2. To identify those in need. Without a systematic search effort it is highly unlikely that all children with special educational needs will be fortuitously identified.

3. To ensure equal access to all children. Parents' awareness is not equal across the community; thus, we need affirmatively to compensate for circumstances in which parents might fail to call attention to their child's special requirements.

4. To document the need for special programs. Without data on prevalence, it is difficult to convince administrators that services need targeting to particular age and ability groups, geographical locations, and so forth.

5. To fulfill program goals. If a program is created to serve a particular segment of the childhood community, it must first locate sufficient children to be justified.

The basic assumption of any screening program is that it will lead to early identification of problems. However, screening techniques are of little value unless they are a part of a comprehensive system that culminates in the delivery of valued services. Thus, the usefulness of screening is related to several issues: accuracy of screening procedures; effects of labeling children; consideration for parents' rights and responsibilities; and, availability of follow-up services.

What are the Results of Screening?

There are three possible results of screening. (a) The child does not evidence discrepancy from age-expectations and thus "passes" the screening. (b) The screening results are incomplete or questionable, and rescreening is indicated. (c) The screening results suggest possible discrepancy from age-expectations or the existence of specific problems. Further assessment is recommended. The next stage, diagnosis, is more costly, for it demands extensive and definitive procedures to determine the nature of any problem.

Who is Involved in Screening?

During group screening, a child study team is constituted that ideally consists of the school principal, nurse, school psychologist, social worker, speech clinician, kindergarten teacher, and special education teacher. The most effective screening programs are products of cooperation among various professionals within a school system, collaboration among various agencies, and involvement by parents. Parental involvement can include data obtained by questionnaires and interviews. Information regarding developmental milestones, results of previous evaluations, and history of special services or treatments received, and a current description of the child, may also be included.

What are the Varieties of Screening?

Screening is not a unitary process; like all quality service models it needs tailoring to the task and population it serves. Varieties of screening, matched to particular conditions, include high-risk registers, physician referrals, and parent referrals.

High risk register. This system is being developed in many regional perinatal centers. It identifies children who are at risk for developing difficulties because of problems manifested at, or shortly after, birth. Such children are generally offered follow-up monitoring visits. Collaboration between school personnel and community personnel to coordinate screening procedures, and also to expedite transition to the educational world, will mean that fewer high-risk children will "fall between the cracks."

Physician referral. When community professionals are confident that referrals to an educational agency result in prompt, efficient, and valuable service to their pediatric patients, they will routinely screen and refer for follow-up by the schools. Efficient collaboration serves all parties well; yet this trust relationship is vulnerable to collapse wherever the linkage is less than year-round or is dependent on any particular individual's commitment.

Parent referral. When parents believe their children are developing atypically, whether delayed or precocious, they deserve to have their child's milestones compared to norms. This is an ideal role for the screen, since screening is capable only of tentatively confirming or refuting the existence of a variation for a norm. Screening cannot provide an indication of what might be done to compensate for any identified variation.

Kindergarten Screening

Kindergarten screening systematically attempts to reach all children within a school system's area of service. Typically, it is widely advertised, ongoing, and conducted at several locations, it includes formal and informal techniques, and it is cost-effective. Usually screening is offered by schools at a particular time of the year. For those who miss this screening opportunity, provisions must be made either to offer year-round screening on a small scale or to have several screenings throughout the year. These options are preferable to individual testing, with its inevitable increase in costs. The more thorough individual evaluation is better utilized at the diagnostic stage.

BEST PRACTICES

Kindergarten screening, ideally, combines several elements: It should be widely accessible; be aggressive in its goal of searching to serve children; be systematically and easily accessible across a wide spectrum; be quick and simple in administration; identify whether children's development matches age-expectations; and indicate whether further evaluation is warranted. There are several features that do not characterize the screening process. Screening is not a means for planning an intervention program, cannot be equated with an IQ evaluation, should not be a device to label children, and should never be isolated from appropriate follow-up for those who meet criteria: it is not a system for monitoring progress, and cannot substitute for comprehensive evaluation. Screening's primary purpose is to clarify the existence of a problem by discriminating a child's unique difficulties from normal fluctuations in development. Compared to comprehensive child evaluation, screening is a very limited procedure. It serves only to indicate that a child *may* have a problem worthy of further investigation.

Steps in Developing a Kindergarten Screening Program

Successful implementation of a screening program involves detailed planning, organization, coordination, and subsequent evaluation. This is typically a committee function. The overall plan requires a determination of the screening's purposes and objectives, selection of a screening's activities, an inventory of required resources, oversight of time lines, and a designation of personnel responsibilities. Also, other agencies that might be cooperatively involved in the screening need to be contacted in the early stages, particularly where medical examinations of vision and hearing acuity are to be completed by personnel from outside the school.

Initially, the population to be served requires identification (with specific attention to recognizing "pockets" of children in greatest need), with a rough estimate made of the potential number of children who will be served. This information will help determine the strategies to be employed. Next, criteria and the cutoff levels to be used for determining who will "pass" the screening must be established. The growth and development areas to be screened must be determined, and the selection of the methods to be used must be decided. It is preferable to match closely the capacity of the district to provide service with the number likely to be identified.

Since none of the instruments and screening are adequate for all conditions, age levels, or even developmental domains, the availability of more than one methodology is obviously preferable. However, each child will be administered a battery that includes only one formal screening device, which will depend on their age and apparent concerns. Screening personnel need to be identified, potentially including volunteers, paraprofessionals, professionals, and parent aides — with a careful eye to the calendar of times and days selected for the event and to the total number of children who can be seen at each mass screening. Some evening and weekend times are essential to accommodate working parents.

The decision whether to require appointments or to encourage walk-ins will have consequences on the flow and total number of children screened. The extent of the promotional activities and the location(s) selected will also have an impact on the number of children contacted. Facilities for screening have included everything from the traditional church and school building to the more exotic-leased store-fronts in malls and mobile campers. A flowchart that indicates how parents and children will move through the screening process needs to be matched to the facility floor plan and the activities to be conducted. Most mass screening models incorporate a "station" approach to aid in standardizing data collection, improving client flow, and routinizing screeners' responsibilities. The alternative, group administration, will more probably result in some children's problems being left undetected. The procedures for each station's screener needs to be identified and timed, so as to reduce the likelihood of a bottleneck at any one location.

A decision must be made regarding how parents are to be debriefed. Personnel other than station screeners need to be assigned to this role. It is most important that there be individuals who can meaningfully interpret the data to parents. One of the few reinforcers for parents to attend a screening is the prompt receipt of outcome data; they have a right to know the results of testing. While the event is fresh in their minds they should learn whether their child needs to be seen for further evaluation and what such a recommendation signifies.

Communication must be done directly rather than through an impersonal report card. If the screener is unable, or finds it difficult to interpret the screening subtests, then serious consideration should be given to evaluating the inclusion of this uncertain information in the report to parents. It is vital for parents to understand that screening procedures yield only tentative results. The strengths of their child's performance needs highlighting. Since these findings are much more significant to the parent than to any screener, debriefing is a critical responsibility.

Coordination of the total on-site screening needs to be in the hands of one person, who is responsible for the development and implementation of a system to train the screeners and later to analyze the procedures so that when next implemented appropriate revisions can be incorporated. The coordinator also has the responsibility at the end of each daily screening session to debrief the screeners, troubleshoot problems, and resolve identified problems prior to the next session.

Additional Practical Considerations for Conducting a Mass Screening

Experience suggests several guidelines that expedite an efficient screening program, among them the following. Have the facility prepared, and even tested with a mock run-through, prior to opening the doors for the first candidate; make allowance for a waiting area; make station sequencing obvious, with a clearly visible numbering system; and have sufficient file folders or alternative data recording systems ready. Utilizing a single personal computer with a user experienced in manipulating a database and spreadsheet will simplify initial data recording immensely; screeners need to have access to a fast, efficient, data-recording system to minimize their error in recording.

Toys and books should be available both for the use of station-based screeners in diverting children's attention and for children to play with while they wait their turn or while parents are completing forms. Parents should be close by, but not in the child's line of sight when items are being administered. Screeners should be sensitive to the needs of parents who require assistance in completing forms — the readability and completeness of printed material must be proofed before the event. Select child- and adult-size furniture on the basis of the likely users.

Screeners need to be identified with large-print name badges.

Screeners need to be appropriately dressed for floor activities, need a reasonable number of breaks scheduled to avert fatigue, and should be ready to assist in the central collation of general data.

A "greeter" should be assigned to meet families at the entry, orient them to the process, and sensitively recognize and deal with parents' feelings. (Of course, each station's screener, too, has a responsibility to place the parent and child at ease.) The greeter will also identify parents' expectations, correct misunderstandings, and help them be realistic about what is possible from a mass screening exercise. The greeter can also begin the data collection process by inviting the parent to begin completing any paper and pencil questionnaires.

The initial reactions of the child to the screening activities will determine the child's acquiescence to the protocol. Thus, "warming up" the child is essential. First, determine quickly whether the child would fare better working at a child-size table or on the floor. Help the child acclimate to the testing environment prior to direct involvement with test administration by selecting some "fun" initial items (typically nonverbal and motor components) to aid in building rapport. Finally, the child's comfort level when separated from the parent needs to be monitored and recorded.

Some Important Contingencies

Many professionals, including some school psychologists, equate screening of young children with the administration of formal "tests." They search for an appropriate screening instrument that is inexpensive, incorporates a group test format, and yet has the credibility of individual administration, and one that is not so simple that children's problems will be missed but not so elaborate that expensive training or many highly experienced examiners will be needed. We can confidently state that no such device exists. Consequently, time spent scanning publishers' catalogs in search of the Holy Grail of early screening instruments is likely to be time wasted. As Lichtenstein and Ireton (1984) have indicated, it is necessary to incorporate a multidimensional approach, one with multiple sources, measures, domains, and even purposes.

Prior to beginning any assessment, it is always instructive to determine exactly what the users of the information want to learn. What do educators hope to learn from the assessment and from the testing procedures? They want to gain information on what to do with young children so as to make a difference; information on the transition process from one environment to the next; and information that helps determine whether an effect resulted from treatment/education. It should be equally instructive to remember that there are no published *tests* that can provide answers to any of these needs. And with absolute assurance we can say that no *screening instrument* comes close to answering any of these important questions. Consequently, we have a professional obligation to ensure that consumers of our screening results appreciate that not all their questions will be answered nor can they be answered by the screening.

We can, however, look to what skills teachers tell us are essential for a child to be successfully integrated into the regular kindergarten. Teachers tell us that the prerequisite attributes are skill at performing independently (the number one priority); age-appropriate peer interaction skills; some functional language facility; absence of patterns of seriously disruptive behavior (either to self or to others); and a willingness by parents to offer help, as needed. Thus, reasonable objectives for our screening of a child's likely success in kindergarten should square with these considerations. We can inventory the child's degree of independent performance, peer interaction skills, and communication skills, ascertain the existence of seriously disruptive behaviors, and scan the likelihood of parental cooperation.

We also need to be sure that two further qualifications are stressed whenever we share the information that results from screening procedures: that developmental irregularities in the formative years do not universally result in problems in later years; and that exposure to the demands of the school environment will make a child's strengths and weaknesses even more apparent.

Screening's Essential Components

Screenings can include elements of norm-based, criterion-based, multidimensional, and clinical judgment assessments at the very minimum. Norm-referenced assessment compares performance with standard or peer group; yields percentages, deviations, and quotients; and often is employed for determining handicapping eligibility diagnosis (categorical placement). Examples of this type of assessment tool are the Basic School Skills Inventory and the Denver Developmental Screening Test. The Basic School Skills Inventory (1975) is a commonly used measure that evaluates self-help skills, handwriting, oral communication, reading, and a number of other readiness components. Its age range is 4–6 years.

The Denver Developmental Screening Test-Revised (DDST-R; 1975) is another popular instrument. It is designed as an aid in the identification of developmental delays in children between birth and 6 years of age. This screening instrument provides data in four domains; personal-social, fine-motor, language, and gross-motor. The personal-social items measure

a child's ability to get along with others, to play, and to initiate self-care. Fine-motor items evaluate the ability to retrieve and draw objects. Language items assess the ability to hear, understand, and utilize language skills. Gross-motor items measure bodily control, balance, and coordination. The DDST-R identifies developmental delays that signal an "abnormal" performance requiring more detailed assessment (Sattler, 1988).

Criteron-referenced assessment provides information on the direct congruence of testing, instruction, and progress evaluation; tracks individual child performance along a continuum of objectives; aids in identifying treatment objectives; and makes possible interdisciplinary communication and progress comparisons.

The Boehm Test of Basic Concepts is one criterion-referenced test that could be used. The Boehm Test of Basic Concepts-Revised (BTBC-R; 1986) is an assessment instrument that evaluates a child's knowledge of basic language concepts that are commonly encountered in teachers' directions in kindergarten or beginning primary grade classrooms, or at the beginning of instructional material. It was designed to measure knowledge of various concepts that are thought to be necessary for achievement in the first few years of school. It is a screening and teaching instrument and is not intended as a measure of mental ability.

Multidimensional batteries, which combine both criteron- and norm-referenced features, can also be used. The Battelle Developmental Inventory and the Brigance Diagnostic Inventory of Early Development are examples of multidimensional batteries implemented in screening.

The Battelle Developmental Inventory (1984) is a standardized developmental scale that is the only current example of a norm-referenced diagnostic measure that also integrates criteron-referenced features into its structure. Functional capabilities are assessed in the following domains: personal–social, adaptive, motor, communication, and cognitive. It produces norm-referenced identification of young children who are exceptional and highlights those developmental areas that require a more comprehensive appraisal (Neisworth & Bagnato, 1986).

The Brigance Diagnostic Inventory of Early Development (1978) is based on a developmental task analysis model and also combines norm- and criteron-based features, integrating assessment with curriculum goal planning. The age range is birth to 7 years old. It analyzes children's performance across 98 skill sequences in 11 major developmental domains. The instrument accommodates varied response styles so that adaptations to various handicaps is possible. However, it is not designed to provide assessments sufficiently precise for young children. Thus, it is judged to be most effective with children suffering from mild to moderate disabilities (Neisworth & Bagnato, 1986).

Clinical judgment should serve to augment the results obtained from standard tests. Such assessments measure, collect, structure, and typically quantify the impressions of professionals and caregivers concerning children's development and behavior. It relies on perceptions and can vary in structure, standardization, and reliability. It takes into account accumulated and/or immediate impressions (i.e., expert judgments) and provides a meaningful way to include input from para- and nonprofessionals; clinical judgment challenges and supplements "objective" assessment through introducing subjective "clinical" input and is useful for appraising ambiguous traits (e.g., cuteness, normalcy, clumsiness, reactivity, frustration, motivation). Most importantly, assessment by clinical judgment is easy, efficient, generally acceptable, and inexpensive.

Behavior checklists are popular because they are economical, can be easily administered and scored, survey a wide range of behaviors, and can be used to evaluate treatment effects. They identify the examinee's behavioral strengths and weaknesses, provide an objective basis for monitoring intervention efforts, permit comparison of the examinee's behavior across situations and informants, facilitate communication between and within organizations, and stimulate new intervention programs and research. However, many factors can affect informants' judgments on behavioral checklists. These may include familiarity with the child, sensitivity to and tolerance for behavior problems, personality, and expectations. While respondent bias and misconceptions may compromise the objectivity of the assessment, checklists do provide an important function in the assessment process. Numerous behavioral checklists have been published including the Child behavior Checklist, Teacher's Report Form, Conners Parent Rating Scale, Conners Teachers Rating Scale, and the Sattler (1988) Revised Behavior Problem Checklist.

The Behavior Problem Checklist (BPC; 1979) and Child Behavior Checklist (CBC; 1986) are two of the more frequently employed instruments in three primary domains (i.e., inadequacy, immaturity, and conduct and personality problems). The CBC is designed for completion by parents and teachers and contains items for both social competency and problem behaviors.

The minimal data to collect in a screening includes sensory capacities (perception and acuity); achievement history (patterns, progress, pace); primary provider observations (e.g., parents, daycare personnel, etc.); language/speech skills; physical/motor development and notation of any limiters; health/medical history; strategies used by primary providers to assist the child with any identified problems; and sociocultural/family history and variables.

Targets of Assessment

Impetus for the identification of potential problem learners has come from recent governmental initiatives, and from advances in professional knowledge, specifically in the field of learning disabilities. A major aspect of identification for school entry involves screening for cognitive development.

Cognitive screening. Cognitive screening consists of the interpretation of a child's intellectual functioning at a particular place and time. The primary purpose is twofold: to determine the nature and degree of any condition likely to limit progress and to aid in planning a program of instruction should a limiting condition be identified. Screening is designed to understand and identify the problems or characteristics of the child's cognitive functioning that may interfere with later academic learning or social development.

Nonetheless, there are major problems associated with the use of IQ as a measure of *anything* for young children. The problems exist, in part, because IQ was developed as a measure of a relatively *stable* feature, and not designed to be sensitive to growth in a dynamically developing preschooler. IQ measures are also fairly poor at discriminating among children (both with and without handicaps) whose age lies at the ends of the tests' intended age spans. Such tests typically have too few items for their steep age-range equivalents, and they are too reminiscent of "strange activities done in strange situations with a stranger." These are all major threats to the ecological validity of such tests' results. Two features remind us of the questionable utility of IQ measures for young children. Only 50% of a high school senior's *ability* can be predicted from the results of IQ tests at age 4 years — that is, at the age of 4, only half the 17-year-old's ability is predictable from skills already in place (Bloom, 1964). This fact alone should cause some hesitancy in using IQ tests with young children. Additionally, the traditional assessment batteries and low-incidence tests almost exclusively measure *fast-developing skills*, since these are the easiest qualities in which to see change over time. The abilities that develop at the fastest rate predict adult ability *least well* — another reason to shy away from IQ tests for young children.

In spite of these data, there are still professionals who will use an IQ measure as a screen. Thus, we will consider here the discrepancy model options for determining where the "screen" should be placed. There are two basic discrepancy model options, as well as permutations containing elements of each. Essentially, one may either determine eligibility by establishing a cutoff in terms of percentage deviation of developmental age (DA) from chronological age (CA) (e.g., a 4-year old whose DA is 3 years would have a 25% delay), or establish a cutoff in standard deviation units (e.g., screen for children scoring below a standard score of 75 on a test). Accordingly, a typical mix-and-match formula might be to determine that a child has "failed" the screen in the case of a single delay of >35% (or -1.5 *SD*), or two delays of >25% (or -1.0 *SD*). However, whenever one uses discrepancy analyses to provide evidence of a child's problems, one has conclusively demonstrated that whatever the test measures is fundamentally different from the problem being identified (i.e., discrepancy analyses are used only when identifying a feature for which a direct test is unavailable).

Perceptual–motor ability screening. Perceptual–motor ability screening is also an essential part of any kindergarten screening program. Perceptual–motor skills concern the ability to perceive sensory input, attach meaning to it, and to use that information in gross- and fine-motor acts. Accurate perceptions are necessary not only for adequate motor responses, but also for such cognitive abilities as conceptualization and language competence. Deficits have important social, emotional, academic, and physical consequences. Perceptual difficulties may unduly influence a child's performance on psychometric measures, rendering results inaccurate.

It is during the early years that children develop foundational perceptual motor skills that refine both gross- and fine-motor abilities. During this age span they learn to perform an increasing number of complex motor tasks. However, without appropriate and accurate sensory input and the ability to interpret stimuli, such skills are unlikely to develop normally. There are a variety of language, perceptual–motor, academic, aptitude, and achievement tests, each designed to furnish information about sensory and intersensory dysfunction.

Physical/motor development. Physical/motor development has long been considered an important component in the evaluation of children's growth and development. It is almost always one of the factors assessed when considering the overall level of maturity. It is between the ages of 2 and 6 years that most children acquire their basic repertoire of manipulative and locomotive skills, evolve goal-directed motor behaviors, and learn to combine two- and three-component motor sequences that contribute to accomplishing specific goals. All of these behavioral achievements are forerunners of important aspects of adult functioning and are themselves contingent upon the child's acquisition of an adequate base of motor development. Motor development and physical activity are integral to promoting selected aspects of the early, active learning process. Gross-motor development in the early years is characterized by the appearance and mastery of a number of fundamental skills. These include body projection (e.g., locomotor movements — running, jumping, skipping), body manipulation (e.g., nonlocomotor movements — stretching, curling, bending) and object manipulations (e.g., ball handling — throwing, catching, kicking) skills.

One of the most dramatic characteristics of gross-motor skills acquisition is its great variation across different children of the same age. Some children fall neatly into a rather traditional age-step progression, but most do not. It is for this reason that age equivalents are intentionally de-emphasized in any thoughtful discussion of developmental changes in gross-motor skills.

Socialization screening. Most children raised in the United States grow up in a two-parent household assisted by a stimulating middle-class environment. Emotional development and interactions in society may be less than optimal. Thus, it is important to analyze how a child adjusts to the social world.

The social process involves a molding of a child's attitudes, behaviors, and values to conform to standards deemed appropriate and acceptable for a current or future role in society. Socialization prescribes the child's behavior in different situations and interactions. In response to the pressures of socialization, emotional expression is the means for the child to communicate feelings, wants, and needs, so as to exert some control over the social world.

By age 2, most children display a unique personality that continues to be shaped and modified through social interactions. Children's impressions of themselves are largely formulated on the basis of how others respond to them. The way in which children relate to peers, the quality of their attachment, and their relationships with adults result from their earliest interactions with caregivers.

A child's individual temperament, physical appearance, sex, place in family birth order, and the number of children in a family all exert an influence on her or his socialization process. Economic factors and parents' social class are also influential on the child's development. Experiences with peers contribute to changes in the child's social skills and provide an incentive for attainment of skills. The wide range of factors that influence the socialization process, often in subtle ways, and the various demands placed upon children in different social settings make it difficult to draw clear distinctions between what is "normal behavior," and that which deviates from the norms. Most socialization problems are associated with children's perception of reality, their interaction with adults and with other children, and the interrelationship between their behavior and learning.

Adaptive behavior is typically defined as the manner in which a child copes with the natural and social demands of the environment. Adaptive behavior measures require that specific behavioral responses to diverse environmental demands be observed and noted. Part of the difficulty for screening this area centers around the problem of defining "necessary" and "desirable" behaviors in young children. Children learn adaptive behavior through reciprocity with others; techniques and strategies of adaptation emerge from interactions with these people. Everything a child does has an effect on the milieu and everything that happens within that milieu has an effect on the child. There is no way that these behaviors can be standardized, nor do they cluster consistently into commonly predictable patterns. Relatively little information exists concerning adaptive behaviors for otherwise nonhandicapped preschoolers.

Screening for linguistic competence. Educators frequently face children who are unready for the semiformal "linguistic code" peculiar to classrooms. While such early elementary-school-age children may be otherwise "normal," they are somewhat slow in the acquisition of language competence. They may suffer from mild to moderate hearing losses not previously detected, or they may have a learning disability. They may be youngsters who are preoccupied with fantasies and consequently have problems attending to the ongoing flow of speech. It is equally possible that they are children who are unmotivated to use their fund of linguistic knowledge for the purpose of communication.

The problems exhibited are as diverse as the causes. Children may be delayed in the acquisition of the syntactic, semantic, and articulation components of language. They may have limited vocabulary or they may require the aid of the physical context or their own actions in the comprehension and production of language. An increase in background noise may interfere with children's ability to accurately process language, or the teacher's natural rate of speech may be frustratingly fast. There are also youngsters who apparently have adequate language abilities but are otherwise not ready for language-related processes such as reading and writing. While the range of language problems manifested in the classroom is vast, screening should be considered only as a confirmatory device for determining the existence of a communicatory deficit, and not to diagnose which deficit is in evidence.

Basic concepts screening. An understanding of basic concepts used in their environment is necessary for young children to deal with the demands of everyday living, and to build upon in later learning. Basic concepts help them understand and later describe relationships among objects, locations of objects and persons, characteristics of objects (dimensions, positions, movements, quantity, and presence), and sequences of events. As children engage in readiness activities and later in the formal learning of reading and arithmetic, increasingly they need to draw upon their fund of basic concepts to follow directions and understand instructions. Screening for young children's understanding of basic concepts is particularly crucial, since it is at school entrance that the child first encounters many of the "technical" terms routinely used in instruction.

Sensory screening. The severity of a sensory limitation, for example, is a function of the cause of the impairment, the degree of loss, the child's age at the time of loss, the care or correction received, the reactions of others to the impairment, and the individual's personal strengths, weaknesses, and attitudes. Consequently, the assessment, for example, of visual impairment involves more than the measurement of the physical attribute of visual acuity. The demands and expectations of life in general, the etiology of the child's responses, and practical methods for altering the responses must also be considered. It is particularly important that assessment occur during the early years when the child is most receptive to correction and intervention.

Similarly, early assessment for hearing impairment is vital. There is increasing evidence that hearing impairment in infancy and early childhood adversely affects the acquisition of speech and language as well as intellectual, emotional, and social development.

Neuropsychological screening. Neuropsychological screening can provide information of considerable importance for the prevention of potentially handicapping conditions and for the development of optional education programs to facilitate academic readiness. Neuropsychological data can also be used to establish baseline measures for the determination of both etiology and prognosis in subsequent possible neurological impairment resulting from illness, injury, or other insults to the central nervous system.

Neuropsychological screening can provide data directly to parents concerned about their role in preparing their child for academic pursuits. Occasionally a child will be encountered who has suffered from a traumatic head injury, encephalitis, or other insult that interferes with the development of normal patterns of intellectual abilities. Neuropsychological screening for such children can provide a useful baseline for making psychoeducational plans based on prognosis for improvement. Many children experiencing mild neurological abnormalities remain undetected. Increasing recognition of the viability of neuropsychological screening and its relation to learning and behavior problems, in conjunction with increasing emphasis on the early identification of problems that can be ameliorated, combine to make neuropsychological screening a developing area of timely relevance.

Consideration of chronological age. Issues concerning maturity focus on age at school entrance. When children enter school before they are "developmentally ready to cope," their chances for failure increase dramatically. "Summer birthday children" (SBC) and "summer held-back children" (SHBC), and their standing on measures of later school success have been specifically researched. Uphoff and Gilmore (1986) summarized the findings on the importance of age at school entry as a predictor of later problems. Chronologically older children in a given class tend to receive more above-average grades from teachers than do younger children in the same grade. Older children are also much more likely to score in the above-average range on standardized achievement tests. "Thus, the less bright but older and developmentally more mature pupils were able to do more with the ability they had then were the brighter, younger

students" (Uphoff & Gilmore, 1986, p. 12). Younger children are far more likely to have failed at least one grade than are older children.

Younger children are far more likely to have been referred by teachers for learning-disabilities testing and subsequently to have been diagnosed as learning-disabled than are older peers. Perhaps the most important finding is that the academic problems of "young" children often continue throughout their school careers and into adulthood. Premature entrance into school, apparently, can cause other severe difficulties. Uphoff and Gilmore (1984) reviewed all youth suicides in one Ohio county (25 years of age and under) and found that of the male cases, at least 45% were summer children. The addition of October- and November-born males who started school even earlier elevated the statistic to 55%. In addition, 85% of the female suicides were summer children. "Birthday or chronological age, obviously, is no guarantee of readiness for school. Our position is that children's behavior age, not their birthday age, should determine the time of school entrance and of subsequent promotion" (Ames & Ilg, 1979, p. 14).

Health/medical history appraisal. Clearly, some young children are at greater risk for developmental delay than others. Formally, children are considered at-risk when they have been subjected to adverse genetic, prenatal, perinatal, postnatal, or environmental conditions that are known to cause defects or are highly correlated with the appearance of later abnormalities. Kindergarten screening programs can help determine whether a child has been subjected to these established, biological, and environmental risks.

Screening for relevant family conditions. It is clearly important to obtain information from parents and other significant individuals in the child's environment. Such information also helps focus on the parents' perception of problems, and lays the groundwork for later enlisting parents' cooperation. Where appropriate, siblings and other significant relatives or friends can be effective information sources.

SUMMARY AND CONCLUSIONS

Mass screening is the first step in the comprehensive evaluation and intervention process. It is a brief assessment procedure designed to identify children prior to school entrance. Screening tests are used only to select children who may have a discrepancy from the norm, whereas evaluation instruments are used to identify the specific deficits of those children who *have* special needs, as a prerequisite to designing an individualized educational program. If screening for entry into kindergarten is to be worthwhile, it must occur sufficiently early, while there is still opportunity to benefit and before any deficits become cumulative. The longer the lead time, the greater the prospect of providing efficient compensatory education.

The areas traditionally surveyed by screening tests include language competence, large- and small-muscle control, eye-hand coordination, adaptive and personal/social functioning, and number and reasoning skills. Screening represents one aspect of prevention, in that it contributes to minimizing the number of children requiring later special educational services. Screening programs are based on the premise that young children's growth and development are dynamic and that skills and intelligence are not fixed or immutable — thus, their development is susceptible to the efforts of early educators.

Attempts to determine children's progress across a "standard" development continuum (which itself is not universally accepted) present enormous problems. This difficulty, when combined with the task of sorting children into those who are, and those who are not, admitted into kindergarten, is further fraught with tension because of the anxiety of children, parents, and educators. Decisions are made as often on the basis of emotion and ideology as on verifiable data. Since limitations continue to exist in the technology of measuring children's devel-opmental maturity, the best we can do is adopt the compromise that produces the greatest benefits.

Remedies to some of the problems inherent in screening for school readiness include use of multiple measures, sources, and testing periods; consideration of chronological age at school entrance, and greater emphasis on measures of social and developmental maturity.

It is likely that most, if not all, the data obtained from childhood screenings are underestimates. That is because the response mode, content, and presentation of standard assessment items discriminate against children who are unsophisticated in test taking. But most devices presuppose that testees have some exposure to the items and format. Furthermore, the majority of kindergarten screening tests are heavily loaded with verbal items, and it has been known that expressive language production is under very tenuous control at this early age. The tendency to assume that nonresponding is valid evidence of skills deficiencies is potentially erroneous. There are many children who "fail" items not because they do not know the answer but because they are undermotivated to respond or because they have no relevant experience with the question's format. Others might be able to score higher if the test's response mode conformed with their preferred learning characteristics, and yet others simply do not respond optimally to adult questioning and commands.

All those involved in kindergarten screening have to be cognizant of the inherent strengths and weaknesses in available assessment procedures and tools. It is vital to stress creativity as a significant part of the screening approach in the attempt to realize an accurate assessment.

REFERENCES

Ames, L. B., & Ilg, F. L. (1979). *Your five year old.* New York: Dell.

Lichtenstein, R., & Ireton, H. (1984). *Preschool screening.* New York: Grune & Stratton.

Neisworth, J. T., & Bagnato, S. J. (1986). Curriculum-based developmental assessment: Congruence of testing and teaching. *School Psychology Review*, *15*(2), 180–199.

Uphoff, J. K., & Gilmore, J. E. (1984, July 26). Local research ties suicides to early school entry stress. *Dayton Daily News*, p. 34.

Uphoff, J. K., & Gilmore, J. (1986). Pupil age at school entrance: How many are ready for success. *Young Children*, *41*(2), 11–16.

ANNOTATED BIBLIOGRAPHY

Boehm, A. E., & Sandberg, B. (1982). Assessment of the preschool child. In C. R. Reynolds & T. B. Gutkin (Eds.), *The handbook of school psychology*. New York: Wiley.
This chapter reviews the purposes of assessment, which are identification, diagnosis, and long-term program planning for high-risk children; diagnosis of students' strengths and weaknesses; and evaluation of program effectiveness. After determining the purposes of assessment, the authors speak to the next step: selection of appropriate tests. Characteristics of pertinent evaluation instruments are reviewed.

Lichtenstein, R., & Ireton, H. (1984). *Preschool screening*. New York: Grune & Stratton.
Practical issues that must be considered for developing efficient and effective programs are addressed. Methods for selecting screening instruments and for making appropriate screening decisions, with particular emphasis on parents' participation, are also discussed. The author looks to the future of preschool screening, and how we can strive to better meet the educational needs of all children.

Martin, R. P. (1986). Assessment of the social and emotional functioning of the preschool child. *School Psychology Review*, 15(2), 216–232.
This article describes the methods and problems associated with the use of a variety of techniques and instruments to assess preschoolers' social and emotional functioning. The special challenges of assessment and design are also discussed.

Schakel, J. A. (1986). Cognitive assessment of preschool children. *School Psychology Review*, 15(2), 200–215.
The purpose, theoretical rationale, and methodology for the cognitive assessment of preschoolers are reviewed, with emphasis on the strengths and weaknesses of commonly used instruments and the implications for their utilization.

32

Best Practices in Legal and Ethical Considerations

David P. Prasse
University of Wisconsin — Milwaukee

OVERVIEW

Over the years, school psychology has been influenced in program procedure by different legal sources including legislation and judicial decision. We have witnessed an increase in that influence and experienced the inevitable accompanying professional and public scrutinization of our discipline's practices and policies. While many components of psychology and education are subject to legally defined parameters, school psychology, due in large part to its inextricable relationship with special education, has realized pervasive and significant legal impact that has modified roles, responsibilities, and the delivery of school psychological services in general.

As the programs and procedures of education have undergone radical change as a result of judicial and legislative influence, so too has the service delivery components of school psychology. Courts, in their role as mediator between the rights of the public (parent and/or student) and the rights/responsibilities of the state (schools), have moved to protect and define procedural and substantive due process rights for all children. Courts have instructed school systems to provide appropriate special education programs where there has been an absence of programs or where inappropriate programs have not met the educational needs of children. The legislative influence of PL 94-142, 99-457, and Section 504 of the Rehabilitation Act Amendment are known to us all and much of the legal influence felt by the discipline of school psychology is a direct result of this and similar legislation. Recognizing the sources of legal influence on school psychology is fundamental to a comprehensive knowledge of "best practices" with respect to school psychology and the law.

As with most applied professions, law is always changing, and therefore the school psychology/law relationship is likewise changing. The state of flux means that which is mandated or required today may not be tomorrow. A practice or process followed yesterday may be judged inappropriate or illegal in the future. As societal priorities change and individual rights are further defined, legal requirements change, and the parameters of influence expand and/or constrict. While there exist "fundamentals" of law which do, for the most part, remain stable across time, the daily practices and service delivery approaches are susceptible to legislative and judicial interpretation of those fundamentals.

What follows is a foundation for best practices. The purpose is to indicate that which we know about the influence of law on school psychology and logically therefore that which we expect all school psychologists to know and understand. The intent is not to provide great detail and the specifics of best practices. Rather it is to highlight the areas of knowledge regarding school psychology and the law that should be known to all who call themselves school psychologists.

BASIC CONSIDERATIONS

Sources of Legal Influence

There is a sequential and invariant nature to sources of law that reflect (in most cases) application of broad principles to specific situations. It is expected that specific laws, practices, and procedures be consistent with broad principles. The source of law are, for the most part, hierarchical and might be pictured as follows:

Federal Constitution

•

Federal Statute

•

State Constitution

•

State Statute

•

Administrative Rules

•

Local Policy and Procedure

Sources of law are therefore more influential (i.e., having greater impact) the higher they are in the hierarchy. Sources of law are sequentially subordinate and those sources that exist beneath others are narrower in scope and applicability. However, these same lower ordered sources may be no less important and effective than those sources situated above them in the hierarchy.

Constitution. The cornerstone for all law is the Constitution of the United States. All sources of law (federal and state statutes, state constitutions, judicial decisions, etc.) are subject to the provisions of the Constitution. Laws, practices, and procedures which are not congruent with the principles established by the Constitution are eventually judged (usually by a court) as unacceptable.

The Constitution of the United States at one level has nothing directly to say about education, yet everything to say about the manner in which education is provided to the public. There is no Federal Constitutional right of or guarantee to an education. Providing an education to the public is a matter left to the individual states by way of the Tenth Amendment which states:

> The powers not delegated to the United States by the Constitution, nor prohibited by it to the States, are reserved to the States respectively or to the people.

Therefore, states may provide a public education to its citizens but are not obligated to do so. If, however, a state chooses to guarantee to its citizens a public education, it must do so in a manner that is compatible with the principles established by the Constitution of the United States.

It is this requirement that impacts the delivery of school psychological services. As an aspect of public education, school psychological services must adhere (like education in general) to established constitutional principles. When the practices and procedures of school psychology violate those principles, they are judged (usually by a court) as unacceptable. For example, if the net result of individual assessment, or the utilization of a specific test, is to deny a certain group of students an equal educational opportunity, it is likely (and indeed has happened in *Larry P.*), that process and/or test will be judged unacceptable, as a contributor to violating individual rights guaranteed and protected by the Federal Constitution.

Legislation. Legislation, or statute, is by far the most influential source of law affecting the delivery of educational and school psychological services. Enacted by Congress or state legislatures, legislation is frequently created to provide the specifics of implementing constitutional guarantees or for purposes of specifying the details for delivering programs in a ordered and uniform manner. Federal legislation relevant to school psychology may be categorized as program legislation or civil rights legislation. Program legislation usually provides funds for service delivery, and in providing these funds mandates that agencies delivering the services do so in a manner prescribed by the legislation. The Education for All

Handicapped Children Act (PL 94-142) and PL 99-457 are certainly among the best of examples. Through this legislation federal funds are made available for educating handicapped students. The procedures by which those educational services are delivered are then specified by the legislation, and recipients are obligated to comply with those requirements. Civil rights legislation differs in that requirements are usually not tied to program funding; i.e., requirements mandated by the law must be adhered to even in the absence of funds tied directly to a program. A relevant example is Section 504 of the Rehabilitation Act of 1973 which protects the civil rights of handicapped persons.

State statutes, which must not conflict with the laws established by the Federal Government, serve to enact the principles established by a state constitution or federal mandate, and are often quite specific and detailed. For example, most states have a compulsory school attendance law and a law that provides for educating handicapped students. The later must be compatible with Constitutional principles and requirements delineated in PL 94-142 and 99-457. State laws affecting education are wide ranging (finance to suspension) and differ from state to state. Direct and indirect impact on school psychology will vary accordingly.

Administrative rules. When a law is enacted, a specific governmental agency is charged with implementing the requirements of the statute. Inasmuch as the legislation may not include all the specific details necessary for successful implementation, the appropriate governmental agency is empowered to write rules to accompany the newly enacted law. When adopted, these rules are equivalent in importance and influence as the statute itself; i.e., they carry similar weight. At the Federal level, a statute pertaining to education is usually administered by the Department of Education, which is also charged with developing the corresponding rules. At the state level, the relevant agency is frequently the Department of Public Instruction or Education which has

similar responsibilities to those found at the Federal level. These governmental agencies will usually "propose" rules, hold public hearings, and finally adopt the rules. Paying close attention to the rulemaking process as well as possessing a thorough knowledge of the final rules is a necessary and crucial component for understanding the intent and specifics of a particular statute.

Litigation. Litigation, which is an action or lawsuit in a court, forms the knowledge base for and is the source of law that we refer to as case law. The influence of judicial decision making is predicated in part on the judicial structure itself. There exists a federal court system and individual state court systems. The Federal system includes three levels: U.S. District Courts (trial courts); U.S. Court of Appeals (10 circuits) and the U.S. Supreme Court (Court of last resort). Generally, the federal judicial system is utilized when the question involves a Federal Constitution issue or a federal statute. Each state has its own judicial system and each system varies greatly. Like the federal system, there are different levels often including circuit courts ("inferior" courts), one or two levels of appellate courts, and a "supreme" court.

The impact of a judicial decision depends in part on the level of court in which the issue is adjudicated. Generally, the higher a court is in the system, the greater the impact or influence. For example, a state supreme court decision is applicable to that particular state, while a decision rendered by a U.S. Court of Appeals is applicable to that entire district which will include several states. Decisions of the Supreme Court are applicable to all states and effectively become the law of the land. So, the higher the court in the judicial hierarchy, the more authoritative its decision and accompanying opinion.

The fundamental purpose of judicial decision is to resolve conflict — conflict that arises from two different interpretations of a statute or from questions of interpretation embodied in a state or Federal Constitution. Judicial decision is based in part on determining the intention of the legislature and the compatibility of that intention and/or practices with constitutional principles. Statutes, or practices that violate constitutional principles are then overturned or modified by the court. The potential impact or influence of case law is thus twofold. First, the jurisdiction of the court (where it is in the hierarchy) determines the influence of a decision. Second is the influence established through a series of decisions which when taken together establish a clear and unequivocal historical trend, pattern, or precedent.

Professional standards and ethical codes. Professional standards or ethical codes represent an additional (albeit indirect) source of legal influence on the discipline of school psychology. The standards that directly bear on school psychology include the *National Association of School Psychologists Principles for Professional Ethics* (1984), *Ethical Principles of Psychologists*, American Psychological Association (1981), *Specialty Guidelines for the Delivery of Services by School Psychologists* (1981), and *Standards for Educational and Psychological Testing* (1984). In addition, most state school psychology associations have adopted ethical codes.

Although important to the overall process of shaping and monitoring behavior of school psychologists, professional standards are not, at least in the traditional sense, "the law" and therefore do not carry similar weight or influence as statutes and case law. Professional standards interface with the law, and in so doing, are not free to develop from disciplinary preferences alone. The existence of a standard in the NASP Principles that states, "School psychologists avoid any action that could violate or diminish civil and legal rights of clients" is clear acknowledgment of this interface. Nonetheless, they are very important to the profession (including the consumers of services) in that they represent consensual thinking with respect to "best practices." They become the standard by which

professional behavior is judged by both peers and on occasion the judiciary. Courts have and continue to refer to professional standards when "judging" the behavior of an individual psychologist and when reviewing the procedures and policies of service delivery systems. In the legal arena, the "clout" of professional standards may be described as a dynamic state of potential. That is, if a court considers professional standards during deliberations and bases decisions (even in part) on professional standards, then those standards become (at least in that particular case) like the law. The more times that occurs, the stronger is the "legal" influence of professional standards.

BEST PRACTICES — BASIC PRINCIPLES

Attempts to define or describe best practice with respect to school psychology and the law is risky for two reasons. First, as was stated earlier, law or legal influence is dynamic and therefore in a state of flux. Requirements, restrictions, and parameters respecting professional practice change, sometimes from one day to the next. Second, legal influence on practice is subject to interpretation. Professional opinions (both psychologists and lawyers) frequently differ with regard to not only basic legal principles, but also as to how specific requirements should be implemented. The "correct way" to deliver services is then open to debate both formally and informally.

What should be known by school psychologists about school psychology and the law is traced to a relatively few but important sources. They are, however, fundamental, for they serve as prerequisites for subsequent knowledge and understanding. They include an understanding of specific components of the Constitution, an understanding of the legal rights of children, an understanding of the inextricable relationship of school psychology and special education, and finally specifics of relevant legislation and litigation. We turn first to the Constitution.

The Constitutional Foundation

Frequently, a theme that permeates discussion with respect to legal requirements and mandates for school psychology is, "Can we do this?" or "Can I be held liable for this?" or "Is what we are doing wrong?" A sound and hopefully correct answer is, in large part, dependent on understanding the *intent* of the law (case or statute) which is vested in fundamental Constitutional principles. To understand these principles is to know the foundation for judicial decision, which provides a base on which questions can be answered.

The Constitutional principles relevant to judicial decisions affecting education and school psychology are relatively few in number. As indicated earlier, it is the Tenth Amendment that establishes education as a state function. Other Amendments of relevance include the First Amendment and Fourteenth Amendment. Without question, the Fourteenth Amendment has been most influential with respect to special education and school psychological services, for many court decisions that have clarified the rights of children and subsequently educational practices have in large part been based on this Amendment. The Fourteenth Amendment states, in part:

> No State shall make or enforce any law which shall abridge the privileges or immunities of citizens of the United States; nor shall any State deprive any person of life, liberty, or property without due process of law, nor deny to any person within its jurisdiction the equal protection of the laws.

The application of the Amendment to education and school psychology is better understood with a brief elaboration of the two clauses; the due process clause and the equal protection clause. Application by courts of the Fourteenth Amendment has essentially dictated that all actions respecting children in special education must guarantee procedural due process, substantive due process, and equal protection. Procedural due process guarantees a person the right and a meaningful opportunity to protest and be heard before government (in this case, schools) may take action with respect to them. Substantive due process establishes that there are certain rights and privileges that a state may not arbitrarily take from a citizen (in this case, student or parent) and that the state may not act unreasonably, arbitrarily or capriciously in dealing with a citizen. Equal protection guarantees to a person the same rights and benefits all other citizens enjoy with respect to their government (e.g., schools) unless the withholding of those rights and benefits is for a valid reason that justifies the state (the school) in singling out the person for differential treatment.

The judicial application and interpretation of the Fourteenth Amendment is a continuous and dynamic process. Court decisions, based in part on the Amendment, range from establishing an equal educational opportunity for the handicapped, to mandating assessment practices that do not result in disproportionate placement or overrepresentation of minorities. Among the procedures affecting school psychological services and supported by the Fourteenth Amendment, are written notice to parents if a school proposes to change or refuses to change, the identification, evaluation, or educational placement of the child; providing parents an opportunity to present complaints with respect to any matter relating to the identification, evaluation, or educational placement of their child; procedural requirements of informed written consent prior to assessment and special class programming; and, all requirements specific to nondiscriminatory evaluation.

Children's Rights

Inasmuch as the target population for most school psychologists is children, school psychologists must possess some fundamental understanding of the rights of children both in and out of the educational setting. Such an understanding is predicated in part on how this society views children. Generally, the status (legal and social) of children is dependent on the values, morals, and political and economic demands ascribed to children by society. The treatment of children by society shows a historical picture ranging from ignoring children, using and abusing children, to more recently viewing children as people who are afforded certain rights and privileges. The primary tenant in the "house" of children's rights is power, for power (and who has it) speaks directly to control, and the question regarding the evolution of children's rights is, "Who controls the child?"

Today, the cast of characters includes parents, child, and state. Questions, centering around the control of children involve the rights, responsibilities, and authority of each party, with the court frequently acting as mediator between these parties. Control questions often focus on parental authority and state responsibility for protecting children or enforcing laws, while the court attempts to determine parental rights and authority in a manner that protects and defends the child's interests, welfare, and legal rights. The prevailing notion (legal and social) in this nation is usually to grant complete parental authority and discretion except in specific situations involving abuse, neglect, school attendance, and matrimony. If parents are perceived as abrogating their parental responsibilities, the state, under the doctrine of *parens patriae* may assume that parental responsibility. When that occurs, however, such action by the state must proceed in a manner that affords parents certain procedural guarantees (see for example, *Stanley v. Illinois*, 1972). From a psychological perspective (if not on occasion legal) an inherent weakness of this procedure is the assumption that the interests of children are similar or identical to those of their parents. Rooted in the history of the treatment of children, this assumption is based on the professional opinion that most children by and large do not know what is best for them. The notion that children have little if any voice in the judgment of their welfare is being challenged by advocates of children's rights, particularly when actions involve the state assuming parental authority.

In 1967 the Supreme Court reached a decision that is considered by many as the most important children's' rights decision, and certainly the landmark case with respect to establishing the rights of children in the juvenile court process. Based on the Fourteenth Amendment, the decision, *In re Gault* (1967), established that children involved in juvenile court proceedings are constitutionally entitled to certain procedural due process rights. The prevailing notion prior to *Gault* was that constitutional guarantees of due process and equal protection did not apply to children involved with the juvenile court. The reasoning behind this stance was that the State was acting in the best interest of the child. Therefore, rights granted to adults, such as legal representation, confronting accusors and remaining silent were not available to children. In granting procedural protections to children involved with the juvenile court process, the Supreme Court held that children are entitled to counsel, privileged against self-incrimination, and have the right to confront and cross-examine witnesses. In the Court's words, "neither the Fourteenth Amendment or the Bill of Rights is for adults alone" (p. 13). Weighing carefully the implications and consequences of juvenile incarceration the Court stated that, "In view of this, it would be extraordinary if our Constitution did not require the procedural regularity and the exercise of care implied in the phrase 'due process' " (pp. 27–28). There is little doubt that *Gault* represents the first major acknowledgment by the Court that children, under the Constitution, are persons who are entitled to certain privileges and protections.

It was the Court's decision in *Tinker vs. Des Moines School District* (1969) that extended the constitutional rights of children, particularly those rights protected by the First and Fourteenth Amendments. The case dealt with students wearing black armbands to protest the Vietnam War. The decision affirmed that "students in school as well as out of school are 'persons' under our Constitution . . . possessed of fundamental rights which the State must respect" (p. 511). With special attention focused specifically on freedom of expression, the Court stated, "First Amendment rights are available to teachers and students. It can hardly be argued that either students or teachers shed their constitutional rights to freedom of speech or expression at the schoolhouse gate" (p. 506). The Court also reaffirmed the trend of the selective extension of certain constitutional rights to students in *Goss vs. Lopez* (1975) concluding that when schools act to remove (suspend) a student, a procedure (albeit informal) must be followed which is fundamentally fair to the student (i.e., an opportunity for a student to present his or her position).

The aforementioned decisions indicate the Court's support of viewing children as persons and thereby extending to them certain constitutional guarantees that protect their rights and interests, particularly as established by the First and Fourteenth Amendment. However, the Court clearly has not adopted an "across the board" position with respect to extending, to children, constitutional guarantees. The history of case law suggests a pattern of decision making which is selective and on occasion conservative. The definitive statement, for example, from the Court regarding corporal punishment in the public schools was made with the decision in *Ingraham vs. Wright* (1977). Two constitutionally based questions were considered by the Court: first, whether hitting a student in school in order to maintain discipline constitutes cruel and unusual punishment; and second, if it does not, whether the due process clause of the Fourteenth Amendment necessitates that some type of procedural due process be afforded the student prior to imposing corporal punishment. The court's answer to the first question was no. The Court argued that the cruel and unusual punishment clause of the Eighth Amendment, "does not apply to paddling of children as a means of maintaining discipline in the public schools" (p. 669). The Court's answer to the second question acknowledged the importance of the Fourteenth Amendment to this case by stating that, "corporal punishment in public schools implicates a constitutionally protected liberty inter-

est" (p. 672). Therefore, applicability of the due process clause relates in that there is a "strong interest in procedural safeguards that minimize the risk of wrongful punishment and provide for the resolution of disputed questions of justification" (p. 676). In spite of this the Court refused to require a procedural due process hearing before corporal punishment could be administered, in part because the Court believed such an imposition would be too costly and disruptive to school administrative procedures.

The decision in *Parham vs. J. L.* (1979), supports the notion that the Supreme Court defines the rights of children carefully and selectively. *Parham* represents well the question "Who controls the child?" and the accompanying judicial involvement in the struggle defining children's rights, parent rights, and state responsibility. The central question before the Court focused on a minor's right to be afforded a due process hearing before parents or the State could voluntarily commit the minor to a state mental health institution. Plaintiffs argued that failure to provide an adversarial hearing before a neutral fact finder violated the procedural due process clause of the Fourteenth Amendment. In many states, minors are not afforded due process rights when parents seek to have them committed to mental hospitals because the commitment is considered voluntary. The Court did acknowledge the child's "liberty interest in not being confined unnecessarily for medical treatment and that the State's involvement in the commitment decision constitutes State action under the Fourteenth Amendment" (p. 2501). Although acknowledging that commitment can produce adverse social consequences, the Court argued that failure to commit a child who exhibits abnormal behavior results in public stigma, negative public reaction and social ostracism. The Court went on to conclude that it is the parents' interests, not the child's that are most important, thereby ruling against requiring an adversarial due process hearing prior to commitment. The Court did not feel that the constitutional rights of the child were so great as to warrant subordinating parental interest and responsibility in rearing their child to the extent of requiring a hearing. The reasoning of the Court is important to thorough understanding:

> Our jurisprudence historically has reflected Western Civilization's concepts of the family as a unit with broad parental authority over minor children. The law's concept of the family rests on a presumption that parents possess what a child lacks in maturity, experience, and capacity for judgment required for making life's difficult decisions. More important, historically it is recognized that natural bonds of affection lead parents to act in the best interest of their children. (p. 2504)

In conclusion, the Court stated:

> . . . most children, even in adolescence, simply are not able to make sound judgments concerning many decisions, including their need for medical care or treatment. Parents can and must make those judgments. (p. 2505)

It is difficult to summarize the Court's "position" regarding the status of children's rights. It does appear that under certain conditions the Court will guarantee to children specific constitutional rights. In so doing however, the Court will maintain the integrity of parental control and responsibility. In the event that parental control or authority is removed, the Court will grant control not to the child, but to another party such as the State.

The Right to an Education

The legal principles established by children's rights cases are delineated through a review of education-related cases that further define the rights of children in the education arena. Courts have defined the application of the principles of equal protection and due process to educational programs. The Court's intrusion into the educational arena (*Brown vs. Board of Education*, 1954, notwithstanding) has been ambivalent and cautious. Fourteen years after *Brown* the Supreme Court cautioned that:

> . . . judicial interposition in the operation of the public school system of the nation raises problems requiring care and restraint . . . Courts do not and cannot intervene in the resolution of conflicts which arise in the daily operation of school systems and which do not directly and sharply implicate basic constitutional values. (*Epperson vs. Arkansas*, 1968, p. 104)

Five years later the Court accepted a case that challenged the widespread use of the property tax as a method for financing public education. The argument in *San Antonio Independent School District vs. Rodriguez* (1973) was that such a financing plan violated the constitutional rights of poor, low tax base districts by denying them equal educational opportunity and therefore equal protection of the law. The Court held that students did not constitute a suspect class under the Equal Protection Clause and that education was not a fundamental right under the Constitution "essential to the effective exercise of First Amendment freedoms and to the intelligent utilization of the right to vote" (p. 1298). The Court left questions of educational finance to the State. "The very complexity of the problems of financing and arranging a statewide public school system suggest that 'there will be more than one constitutionally permissible method of solving them' and that within the limits of rationality, 'the legislature's efforts to tackle the problems should be entitled to respect' " (pp. 1301–1302).

The Court is apparently hesitant to abridge the traditional rights of parents even when the child has the capacity for self-evaluation, as evidenced in *Wisconsin vs. Yoder* (1972). *Yoder* involved a challenge to a Wisconsin statute requiring parents to ensure high school attendance of their children; the failure to do so could result in criminal charges. The statute was challenged by Old Order Amish parents who insisted that it violated their religious freedom and that of their children. The majority opinion upheld the right of the Amish parents to be exempt from the statute on the basis of free exercise of religion. The dissenting opinion of Justice

Douglas is most interesting, particularly in light of the question, "whose rights and legal protection: children, parents, or state?" Dissenting from the majority only with respect to the two adolescents who did not express their own religious beliefs, the Justice expressed the following:

> I agree with the Court that the religious scruples of the Amish are opposed to the education of their children beyond the grade schools, yet I disagree with the Court's conclusion that the matter is within the dispensation of parents alone. The Court assumes that the only interests at stake in the case are those of the Amish parents on the one hand, and those of the State on the other. The difficulty with this approach is that, despite the Court's claim, the parents are seeking to vindicate not only their own free exercise claims, but also those of their high-school-age children.
> . . . On this important and vital matter of education, I think the children should be entitled to be heard. While the parents, absent dissent, normally speak for the entire family, the education of the child is a matter on which the child will often have decided views. He may want to be a pianist or an astronaut or an oceanographer. To do so, he will have to break from the Amish tradition.
> It is the future of the student, not the future of the parents, that is imperiled in today's decision. . . . It is the student's judgment, not his parent's, that is essential if we are to give full meaning to what we have said about the Bill of Rights and of the right of students to be masters of their own destiny. If he is harnessed to the Amish way of life by those in authority over him and if his education is truncated, his entire life may be stunted and deformed. The child, therefore, should be given an opportunity to be heard before the State gives the exemption which we honor today. (*Wisconsin vs. Yoder*, 1972, pp. 241–246)

The essence of Douglas' views may be applicable to different aspects of school psychological services. Decisions about children that emanate in part from psychoeducational evaluations will have a profound impact on their entire educational life and their subsequent adult life. Persons who engage in the assessment of children must consider the interests of the child. In so doing, it may be erroneous to assume that a child's best interests are being represented by the parents or the school. Therefore, if not from a legal perspective, then from a professional standard perspective, service delivery should be approached with awareness and recognition of potential benefit and detriment.

BEST PRACTICES — BASIC PROCEDURES

Notice and Consent

The implementation of federal legislation for special education services brought about numerous administrative, procedural, and substantive changes in school psychological services. The changes and emphasis on procedural activity emanates in large part from the clear intent of special education legislation that parents of handicapped persons be actively and meaningfully involved in the activities surrounding the assessment and programming of their children.

Operationalizing parental involvement requires adopting and implementing procedures; the purpose of which is to *provide notice* and *obtain consent*. These two components, notice and consent are distinct concepts as defined in the regulations implementing PL 94-142 and, in a legal context, usually treated as separate activities. Although definitions are provided in the regulations, there remains diversity between systems and states as to the procedures surrounding content of notice and consent activities. Questions about what should be said, how it should be said, and when it should be said, remain. Answers are often dependent on a systems commitment to meaningful parental involvement and subsequent interpretation given to relevant regulations. Generally, inconsistent, not consistent, procedures are the norm.

Notice. The central question is, what should constitute prior notice? The relevant regulations are:

Notice. Written notice which meets the requirements under 121a.505 must be given to the parents of a handicapped child a reasonable time before the public agency proposes or refuses to initiate or change the identification, evaluation, or educational placement of that child or the provision of a free appropriate public education to the child (121a.504).

Continuing with a definition of what is required for inclusion in the notice:

The notice . . . must include: (1) A full explanation of all the procedural safeguards available to the parents . . . ; (2) A description of the action proposed or refused by the agency, an explanation of why the agency proposes or refuses to take the action, and a description of any options the agency considered and the reasons why these options were rejected; (3) A description of each evaluation procedure, test, record, or report the agency uses as a basis for the proposal or refusal (121a.505).

Consent. The central question is what should constitute consent or the acquisition of informed (knowledgeable) written permission. The relevant regulation states:

Consent. Parental consent must be obtained before: (i) Conducting a pre-placement evaluation; and (ii) Initial placement of a handicapped child in a program providing special education and related services (121a.504). *Definition of consent.* 'Consent' means that (a) the parent has been fully informed of all information relevant to the activity for which consent is sought, in his or her native language, or other mode of communication; (b) the parent understands and agrees in writing to the carrying out of the activity for which his or her consent is sought, and the consent describes that activity and lists the records (if any) which will be released and to whom (121a.500).

The pertinent questions regarding notice and consent focus on assessment activities as opposed to placement in that school psychology is more directly involved with the former. One basic question that frequently arises deals with the listing and description of specific tests; i.e., must specific tests be identified and generally described? Given the definition of consent the answer is probably yes. Prior notice and consent requirements necessitate the disclosure that an individual comprehensive evaluation is planned, why such an evaluation is planned, and a description of the tests, records, etc. that the school proposes to use. The important terminology would be "description" and "relevant information." To simply list a test or area of assessment is not likely to *describe*. Equally important and fundamental to informed consent is that any communication (notice and/or consent) be written so as to be understandable to the consenting adult, for the cornerstone to informed consent is *knowledge;* i.e., the consenting adult must understand, and there is a clear obligation on the part of the school to determine and insure the existence of necessary knowledge (understanding) necessary to providing informed consent.

Privileged Communication and Confidentiality

Because actions and procedures respecting confidentiality and privileged communication are subject to evolving interpretation, there exists a need for some qualification. In an article on ethical issues, Trachtman states "While a paper on ethics may lean heavily on the writings of others, it inevitably represents personal opinion rather than objective fact or quantifiable data. Indeed, a culling of specific references from the voluminous literature is itself a function of selective perception, bias, or in exceptional cases exquisite discrimination of ultimate truth" (Trachtman, 1974). The caution is appropriate. Because of variation in state statute and emerging case law, the reader must seek out information beyond that presented here.

What is privileged communication, what is confidentiality, and what is the relationship, if any, between the two? We begin with privileged communication. Rooted in Supreme Court decisions with respect to a citizen's right to privacy, the doctrine of privileged communication prevents, *where expressly stated by state statute*, certain professionals from sharing information about their client gathered within the context of the professional relationship. Several features are important for clarification. Privileged communication is a doctrine that is legislated at the state level, i.e., determined by state law. Therefore differences exist between states, as to which clients are extended the privilege (e.g., attorney-client, physician-patient, psychologist-client) and if needed, a state grants such a privilege whatsoever. Second, because the principle of privileged communication is rooted in privacy rights, and without such a privilege it is claimed, professionals like those mentioned above would often be ineffective, it is a privilege that is granted to the *client* of the professional (psychologist), not to the professional. In other words, it is a privilege that belongs to the client. Often the state statute permits the client to exercise or waive the privilege of keeping communication confidential if involved with litigation. Some statutes provide exemptions such as when dangerous to self or others. Finally, meaning and intent of legislation is refined and modified through litigation. State statutes regarding privileged communication are subject to interpretation from case law. One example familiar to many is the Tarasoff decision (*Tarasoff vs. Regents of University of California* 1974) which addressed confidentiality and duty to warn. In addressing the issue of effective treatment and the client's right to privacy, the court stated, "that the public policy favoring protection of the confidential character of patient-psychotherapist communication must yield in instances in which disclosure is essential to avert danger to others. The protective privilege ends where the public peril begins" (p. 137).

The nuances of privileged communication for school psychologists are several. First, is a school psychologist legally viewed as a psychologist in your specific state? If not specifically mentioned in the statute, it is possible that you may not be viewed as such. Second, much of our work involves minors and here the waters are even muddier. Courts continue to litigate between the rights of the parent, rights of the child, and rights of the state. It does, therefore, behoove the school psychologists to review carefully state law, relevant case law, and individual school policy.

Confidentiality. The Ethical Principles of Psychologists (APA, 1981) state the following with respect to confidentiality:

> Psychologists have a primary obligation to respect the confidentiality of information obtained from persons in the course of their work as psychologists. They reveal such information to others only with the consent of the person or the person's legal representatives, except in those unusual circumstances in which not to do so would result in clear danger to the person or to others. Where appropriate, psychologists inform their clients of the legal limits of confidentiality.

The NASP Principles for Professional Ethics (NASP, 1984) do not specifically mention confidentiality, yet include at least two relevant standards. The first states,

> B2. School psychologists inform the student/client about important aspects of their relationship in a manner that is understood by the student. The explanation includes the uses to be made of information, persons who will receive specific information and possible implications of results.

> E1. School psychologists ascertain that student/client information reaches responsible and authorized persons and is adequately interpreted for their use in helping the student/client. This involves establishing procedures which safeguard the personal and confidential interests of those concerned.

To distinguish confidentiality from privileged communication one need only remember that the components of confidentiality are embodied in ethical standards, not state statute. Confidentiality is a promise made by a psychologist to a client. It is a promise to keep communication confidential and not to violate that confidence without justification and legal cause. While some courts are attending to professional standards with more interest, standards are too often vague and general to be helpful as behavior guides. Psychologists and lawyers, have demonstrated the fallibility of ethical standards when attempting to comply with professional-legal responsibilities. Too often an ethical standard is retrospective in nature, in that the psychologist's actions are deemed appropriate or inappropriate through litigation. There are limits to confidentiality and we can expect further judicial refinement. As with privileged communication, the school psychologist working with students faces a difficult situation. Psychologists need confidentiality to be effective; students say they won't "talk if you tell," parents insist on being informed and schools establish information sharing procedural priorities. The ethical standard often is left wanting.

Confidentiality and Minors

The importance of confidentiality to a therapeutic relationship is well established, and the value of trust in such a relationship encourages self-disclosure of personal and sensitive information especially when working with adolescents (Kobocow, McGuire, & Blau, 1983). In fact, many persons expect the school psychologist to ensure confidentiality, and knowing the limitations to confidentiality as well as understanding the legal basis of privileged communication is necessary. The problem is not however, a conceptual one. Rather it is one of concrete application and therein lies the rub.

The application of the confidentiality standard to children and adolescents in public schools is less clear and more difficult to implement. There are at least two dimensions that cloud the issue and both are reflected in the Ethical Principles of Psychologists (American Psychological Association, 1981), Principle 5d, (Confidentiality), that states in part, "when working with minors, or other persons who are unable to give voluntary, informed consent, psychologists take special care to protect these persons' best interest" (p. 636). One issue then is the minor's ability to give informed consent, and the other is the requirement that the psychologist

not only protect the minor's best interest, but also determine it.

Consent to Treatment

There are two dimensions to ascertaining the minor's right to consent to treatment. The first, and obvious, is the legal parameter. In many states, minors have been given consent to treatment authority, even if they are not emancipated entirely. The situations that usually grant the minor child authority to consent to treatment include pregnancy, contraception, substance abuse, sexually transmitted disease, and counseling or medical care for sexual abuse. So, at the first level, whether the minor is "able" to consent to treatment, is a question that must be answered from the legal (i.e., state law) perspective. The general rule of thumb is that the parent must give consent for the treatment of a minor unless a specific exception has been made, such as those mentioned above.

However, over the years, the law has acknowledged general exceptions in four areas to the requirement of parental consent for treating a minor (Plotkin, 1981). The first area is the situation in which the minor child is determined by state law to be an emancipated minor (i.e., married minor). A second is referred to as the mature minor. In this case the minor is considered to be sufficiently mature to understand the issues involved and able to render an independent and informed decision. The third is the emergency or crisis treatment situation, and the emergency is such that parental consent is not necessary for treatment. The final general exception is the most clear and easy to implement, and that is when treatment is court ordered.

The second dimension to ascertaining the minor's right to consent to treatment has to do not with the legal parameters, but the competence and developmental maturity of the minor. There are four basic components to assessing specific competency (Leiken, 1983; Weithorn & Campbell, 1982):

1. The person's ability to understand information that is offered regarding the consequences of the decision to be made.

2. The ability to manifest a decision.

3. The manner in which the decision is made.

4. The nature of the resulting decision (Koocher, 1987, p. 8).

When viewed for their psychological elements, these four include comprehension, autonomy, rational reasoning, anticipation, and judgments. Each of these elements of competency should be judged in the context of development, and the ability to then provide informed consent weighed accordingly. Lidz, Meisel, Zerubavel, Carter, Sestak, and Roth (1984) identify five key elements of informed consent: information, understanding, competency, voluntariness, and decision making ability (i.e., reasoning). Information means all data reasonably expected to influence a person's willingness to participate, or that which is offered or made available. Competency refers to capacity to understand (as opposed to actual understanding); i.e., weigh potential outcomes and anticipate the future consequences of the decision. Voluntariness is the person's freedom to choose to participate or to refuse, and decision making ability is standard of reasoning and choice making, and the ability to express a choice clearly (Koocher, 1987).

Judging adolescent competence for consent purposes should be done in the context of research in development. There are several principles of child development applicable to this topic, including socialization, time perspective, concept manipulation, consent versus assent, and substituted judgment (Koocher, 1987). The important aspect of socialization is the notion of choice and decision making. Although parents usually present children with requests that imply choice (e.g., Would you please make your bed?), there is usually an implied threat or imperative associated with the request. When a child reaches adolescence therefore, he/she may not be prepared to act responsibly if the implied threat has been removed.

The importance of time perspective is focused around the notion of immediate gratification and the ability to see beyond the present and conceptualize the future. The ability to conceptualize the future and express hypothetical outcomes is linked closely to stages of development and is a continuous process throughout adolescence (Lewis, 1981, 1983).

The essence of concept manipulation is closely tied to Piagetian stages of cognitive development. The fundamental point is the child's ability to take the perspective of someone else, to extrapolate and hypothesize future events and outcomes. Tied closely to the acquisition of formal operations, research in development, and particularly perspective taking, documents the developmental sequence of conceptualization and demonstrates the need to conceptualize complex events outside the realm of personal experience (Melton, 1980).

A distinction has been made in the literature between consent and assent (Lewis, 1983). The cornerstones of consent have already been presented. In essence, the idea of assent is reasoned and voluntary acquiescence. Since the developmental level of many children may not be sufficient to grant consent, the notion of permitting the equivalent of a veto is embedded in granting assent. In other words, the notion of assent is to involve the child in a decision that might allow them to say no, yet not grant them the opportunity to decide (i.e., grant consent).

The legal basis of children's rights and the extent these rights are extended to minors constitutes one of the most difficult areas associated with service delivery. The judicial decisions appear, in the aggregate, to extend greater decision making opportunity to children, yet case law is anything but consistent in this area (Melton, 1983; Prasse, 1984). The legal stance has generally been that adults make better decisions than children, and parents may make decisions for their children, and on occasion the school may make decisions for the parent (*in loco parentis*). Substituted judgment assumes the adult making a decision for a child or adolescent has the minor's best interest in mind, and is able to act in that capacity without any conflict of interest. All of this connotes the idea of subordination of needs (parental or otherwise) and that is obviously not always what occurs.

Best Interest and Privacy

The notion of privacy as applied in this country and to the individual citizen is one nested in the Constitution. In a very general sense privacy is judicially interpreted to mean that each person has a zone of privacy that is Constitutionally protected and may not be infringed on. As applied to school psychological services, privacy has to do with making decisions about sharing thoughts, feelings, events, or other personal data with others (Keith-Spiegel & Koocher, 1985).

The judicial intrusion into the minor/ privacy arena is illustrated in the major adolescent abortion case. The question of whether minors have a constitutional right to privacy in abortion decisions was answered, in part, by *Planned Parenthood of Central Missouri v. Danforth* (1976). Relying on an earlier opinion *In re Gault* (1967) the Court reaffirmed the stance that certain fundamental rights are not adults' alone. In *Danforth* the Court stated that "Constitutional rights do not mature and come into being magically only when one attains the state-defined age of majority. Minors, as well as adults, are protected by the Constitution and possess constitutional rights" (*Planned Parenthood of Central Missouri v. Danforth*, 1976, p. 74). Writing for the majority, Justice Blackmun focused the privacy issue: "Any independent interest the parent may have in the termination of the minor daughter's pregnancy is no more weighty than the right of privacy of the competent minor mature enough to have become pregnant" (p. 75).

The language sounded unequivocal. Yet, the Court left open the door for parental involvement if not by veto, by noting that it did not intend to state that "every minor, regardless of age or maturity, may give effective consent for termination of her pregnancy" (p. 75). What was to come then was the thorny issue of defining *maturity*. It is precisely that word that brings together the issue of privacy and a psychologist's determination of what is in the best interest of the student. By and large, the Court has allowed state intrusion into the minor's right to privacy on abortion decisions, only with immature minors. The Court has, in effect, avoided the issue and deferred in most instances to state/parental intrusion believing that the decision to carry a baby to term "entail(s) few — perhaps none — of the potentially grave emotional and psychological consequences of the decision to abort" (*H. L. v. Matheson*, 1981, pp. 412–413).

Many would take exception with the Court's characterization of the emotional consequences contrast set up by the Court in *Matheson*. Indeed, the long term emotional and psychological consequences of delivering and possibly keeping a baby from a unplanned pregnancy may be much greater than those involved with terminating the pregnancy. Any judgment by a psychologist as to the best interest of the minor client must be made only after thoroughly considering all these factors as applied not in the aggregate but to the specific adolescent. There is growing research base that the often presented assumption that adolescents are particularly vulnerable to psychological harm from abortion is not supported (Adler & Dolcini, 1986). The adolescent's vulnerability to a coercive environment (boyfriend, parents, etc.) is itself a potential source of emotional and psychological stress (Marecek, 1987) that can make a decision to terminate pregnancy almost impossible. What the Court has missed is the reality of the emotion of the entire situation and the import of that reality in weighing the privacy–best interest case. The psychologist must not make the same mistake.

The adolescent vulnerability to mistakes born of inexperience or feelings of helplessness and hopelessness are visible day in and day out. The reported incidence of child and adolescent depression along with increasing suicide rates are testimony enough to the struggles encountered during this time period. As practitioners we must not confuse our responsibilities associated with confidentiality and privacy with those that have become known as our "duty to warn and protect" responsibilities. School children who are a threat to themselves or others demand our immediate and comprehensive intervention, with only the short-term goal of sustaining or protecting life, guiding professional decisions.

Although arguments might be waged that challenge the notion that school professionals face greater problems today than ever before, the reality is today's professionals do encounter more complex problems and procedures. Society demands a higher degree of performance accountability, particularly when performance is reviewed by a court, and it is evident that judicial review of practice continues to increase. Children confront many threats today that are difficult for our society to handle and therefore equally as difficult for our schools. The infusion of drugs in our schools is not a minor problem and reaction to the spread of AIDS has already been played out in the public schools of our communities. A school psychologist who receives such information during a professional encounter with a student must immediately begin the process of weighing privacy rights, confidentiality responsibilities, and protection (of client or others).

In many respects children who are threats to themselves pose the most difficult challenge for practitioners, and the parameters of individual and district liability continue to expand. Today psychologists must know that there is not only a duty to warn, but a duty to protect as well. It is more evident today than ever before, that school districts must give serious effort to training and educating professionals so that they will know what to do and how to do it when the moment of crisis arrives. A careful reading of *Kelson v. Springfield* (1985) is strong support for this statement. Although the central issues of this case focused on the question of parent's constitutionally protected liberty interest in the companionship and society of their children, the facts surrounding the suicide provide another example of the importance of having experienced and knowledgeable professionals available and accessible.

Access to Records

Although several years have passed since passage of the Family Educational Rights and Privacy Act (FERPA, 1974, Buckley Amendment) there remain questions of interpretation and intent. Many of the requirements were repeated in later legislation (e.g., PL 94-142) emphasizing the requirements for handicapped children. For most school psychologists implementation of the requirements has been smooth. Indeed, many of the requirements are of little direct concern during day to day activities.

Nevertheless, questions remain with confusion and disagreement over the accessibility of certain records created by the school psychologist. Questions focus on what records are accessible, what records, if any, are exempt, and do the procedures and principles of confidentiality, privileged communication, and test security relate in any way with legal rights to access records? Frequently the questions focus specifically on accessibility of test protocols and "private notes." The answer to such questions is partially formed in the law's definition of a record *and* intent the lawmakers gave the definition. An education record is defined as follows:

A. For the purposes of this section the term "education records" means, except as may be provided otherwise in subparagraph (b), those records, files, documents, and other materials which

   i. contain information directly related to a student; and,

   ii. are maintained by an educational agency or institution, or by a person acting for such agency or institution.

B. The term "education records" does not include:

   i. records of instructional, supervisory, and administrative personnel ancillary thereto which are in the sole possession of the maker thereof and which are not accessible or revealed to any other person except a substitute.

Where psychologists have questioned the right of parents to access certain records, they have usually referred to the exemptions in Part B above. In claiming that a protocol is not an accessible record, some school psychologists have claimed that a protocol is in their sole possession and that they are the exclusive maker, or that the protocol is a private note. When the meaning of legislation is unclear, the authors' intent can be discerned by reviewing the Congressional debate and/or accompanying statements of explanation. It is here that the intent of the law is found and in this case helps clarify the issue of accessibility of protocols. It is in the Joint Statement in Explanation of Buckley/Pell Amendment (Congressional Record at S.21488, December 13, 1974) that the intent of the definition and exception is partially clarified:

> An individual should be able to know, review, and challenge all information — with certain limited exceptions — that an institution keeps on him, particularly when the institution may make important decisions affecting his future, or may transmit such personal information to parties outside the institution. This is especially true when the individual is a minor. Parents need access to such information in order to protect the interest of their child.
>
> The amendment makes certain reasonable exceptions to the access by parents and students to school records. The private notes and other materials, such as a teacher's daily record book, created by individual school personnel (such as teachers, deans, doctors, etc.) as memory aids would not be available to parents or students, provided they are not revealed to another person, other than in the case of a substitute who performs another's duties for a temporary period.

Continuing, the statement goes on to say:

> "if a child has been labeled as mentally or otherwise retarded and put aside in a special class or school, parents would be able to review materials in the record which led to this institutional decision ... to see whether these materials contain inaccurate or erroneous evaluations about their child."

The Congressional intent is affirmed in *John K. and Mary K. v. Board of Education for School District 65* (1987). This Illinois appellate court decision held that raw psychological test data was part of a student's temporary record subject to disclosure. The school psychologist who had administered the Rorschach argued that the verbatim responses were raw data and not subject to disclosure. The court was not persuaded either by professional standards or by federal regulations that the psychologist cited in support of nondisclosure.

Of relevance to the question of accessibility are the requirements of PL 94-142 that provide parents the right to inspect and review their children's records collected, maintained, and used by the school in its special education decision making. It would be difficult to argue that tests used by psychologists and test results are not used in this process and therefore inaccessible. Certainly a parental challenge to placement (either at the hearing level or judicial level) would result in a request for test protocols, that would have to be honored. To refuse would be to deny parents the right to review important records on which the school's decision was based. Finally, access does not necessarily mean obtaining a copy. With respect to test protocols, publishing companies have made it clear that such material is protected by copyright restrictions. So while parents or their legal representatives might have access, indiscriminate or wholesale copying is not condoned. Clearly, the access to records requirements necessitate a delicate balance between the public right to be informed and the psychologist's responsibilities to the student and accepted professional procedures.

The relationship between privileged communication, confidentiality, and the access provisions of the Family Educational Rights and Privacy Act is minimal. Sharing with a parent or student test results and a student record does not contradict either privileged communication or confidentiality. The dilemmas we face in this area are not matters of conflict between the provisions of privileged communication, confidentiality, or access to records. There are however, legitimate concerns about test security (protocols, etc.) and the manner in which a student record is made accessible. Our attention needs to be focused there and not confused with other principles. Readers are encouraged to determine the statutes within their own state with respect to privileged communication and confidentiality.

Special Education

Program availability. Specific professional attention and legal influence on assessment and programming is in large part a direct outgrowth of legislation involving the provision of educational services to handicapped children. It was litigation and later legislation that resulted in various mandates to provide an education to children, particularly the child with special education needs. The legal foundation for requiring educational opportunities to handicapped children is the Equal Protection Clause. Because the courts have interpreted the right to equal protection as the right to equal educational opportunity, states whose constitutions guarantee the right to a public education cannot then exclude handicapped children solely on the basis of their handicap. States that make education programs available to their citizens must therefore include the handicapped child.

The precedent-setting cases that challenged school systems and states that systematically denied a free public education to handicapped children include *PARC (Pennsylvania Association for Retarded Citizens) vs. Commonwealth of Pennsylvania* (1972) and *Mills vs. Board of Education of the District of Columbia* (1972). *PARC* challenged the exclusion from school of children who were deemed to be uneducable or unable to profit from

an education on the basis that such exclusion violated their equal protection and due process rights. Settled in favor of the children by consent decree, the case served as an impetus for similar litigation throughout the country. The children represented in *Mills* argued that they were denied an equal educational opportunity as a result of their various handicapping conditions and that the district denied them an education by utilizing procedures of suspension, exclusion, and class reassignment. In addition, they claimed their due process rights were denied when the district assigned them to special classes, thereby precluding them from access to regular education programs. In finding for the plaintiffs the court dismissed limited financial resources as a basis for the denial of educational opportunity and ordered an equal expenditure of funds so that no child would be excluded from a publicly supported education. *Mills*, unlike *PARC*, applied not only to mentally retarded children, but to other handicapped conditions as well. Together these cases served as a basis for the development of federal legislation, particularly PL 94-142, requiring educational opportunity for handicapped children.

Procedural questions arose about the manner in which the educational programs would be provided as an outgrowth of establishing equal educational opportunity for the handicapped. The answers provided by the courts were guided by the application of procedural due process to actions taken by schools involving the handicapped students. The implementation of procedural due process required that schools provide notice of any action being proposed and that an opportunity be provided for the parent (acting in the interest of the child) to be heard if the proposed action may lead to an alteration of the child's constitutionally protected interests. When a state extends the right to an education, it cannot arbitrarily withdraw that right. By extension of that right, a school may not remove a child from regular class programs unless the need to do so is clearly documented and that documentation has proceeded in a manner which is fair, impartial, and informative. That fundamental right is affirmed by a recent Supreme Court decision involving a handicapped student and the requirements of PL 94-142. The crucial issue in *Honig v. Doe* (1988) centered on the question of expelling a handicapped student from school who had emotional disabilities and aggressive behaviors and the extent that those expellable behaviors manifested as a result of the handicapping condition. Parents and grandparents of the two students argued that the school could not expel the students while the school system argued that Congress did not intend to deny a school district the opportunity to expel if student behavior warranted such action. The Court rejected the argument of the state and school district, concluding that excluding a handicapped student from school without first having parental opportunity for appeal was unacceptable. The Court did allow suspension not exceeding 10 days to continue. The Court did not directly deal with the question of disruptive behavior caused by the handicapping condition. However, earlier decisions have made it clear that the burden to establish such a link is left with the school district, not the parents (*S-1 v. Turlington*, 1981).

Assessment. The courts have addressed matters pertaining to the assessment of students, particularly minority students and those suspected of requiring special education services. Criticism of testing is not new and has been a matter for debate since massive testing programs emerged after World War I. Judicial involvement in assessment and testing matters began in earnest some 20 years ago. Judicial scrutinization of testing has included litigation in both the educational and noneducational sectors. Supported in part by the mandates of *Brown*, which precluded the separation of students on the basis of race, critics launched a judicial review of assessment and testing procedures that appeared to discriminate against minorities by disproportionately singling out minority students for educational programming in other than regular classes.

The courts have ruled on a variety of assessment related practices ranging from classification and tracking systems (*Hobson v. Hansen*, 1967) to discriminatory practices such as assessing children in a language other than their native language (*Diana v. State Board of Education*, 1970, *Guadalupe Organization, Inc. v. Tempe School District No. 3*, 1971, and *Covarrubias v. San Diego Unified School District*, 1971). These cases rightly challenged the practices being followed in assessing minority children. It was however, *Larry P. v. Riles* (1984) that focused the issues associated with assessing minority children, and forced the discipline of school psychology to redirect its efforts in developing assessment practices that related more directly to classroom performance and educational intervention. Indeed there were so many underlying issues associated with *Larry P.* (Prasse & Reschly, 1986) that it served as a catalyst for scrutinizing not only assessment practices, but special education program efficacy as well.

While the decision in *Larry P.* found the impact of assessment practices wanting, in that disproportionate placement of minorities in MMR programs was blamed on testing, these findings were followed by a mixed review of decisions with subsequent cases apparently better able to focus the litigation in ways not achieved in *Larry P.* That claim is supported by at least two important judicial decisions, both of which were rendered after *Larry P.*

In *Marshall v. Georgia* (1984, 1985) many of the same issues presented in *Larry P.* surfaced. Following a trial court finding that supported the plaintiffs, defendants appealed. The Eleventh Circuit unanimously upheld the trial court findings that had earlier ruled that overrepresentation of minorities in classes for the mildly retarded was not discriminatory practice, in that defendants had demonstrated appropriateness of placement based on educational needs. Similarly, plaintiffs in *S-1 v. Turlington* (1986) claimed violation of the Education for Handicapped Children Act with specific emphasis on test bias. Defendants argued points similar to those made in *Marshall*, and in the end the judge ruled in favor of the defendants, dismissing the claims of the plaintiffs (Reschly, Kicklighter, & McKee, 1988). These latest cases depart from the more visible findings of *Larry P.*, yet are appreciably more important in that they better focused the reality of practice and services to handicapped children. In many respects these cases have changed the assessment practices of school psychology and have helped bring forward curriculum based assessment and behavioral assessment approaches, that today are considered more relevant for meeting the educational needs of students.

Individual programming. Although not as directly important to school psychology as the assessment related cases, there have been important Supreme Court holdings that bear on service delivery. The Court has ruled on several important questions bearing on special education services, the answers to which are important to school psychology. Two cases are of importance to the IEP. The central question in *Board v. Rowley* (1982) focused on what was intended as an "appropriate" education. The issue dealt with the necessity of providing a sign language interpreter for a deaf child during classroom time. The Court ruled that in this case the interpreter was not required. The Court affirmed what might be termed a process definition of the IEP. That is, if the IEP is developed procedurally in a manner compatible with law, it will be deemed appropriate. An IEP developed by a group of professionals and parents is the basis or cornerstone for individualizing an educational program.

The importance of the IEP and the value it will be accorded by the Court was further developed in *Irving Independent School District v. Tatro* (1984). The fundamental question involved in *Tatro* was whether or not Clean Intermittent Catherization (CIC) was a necessary related service or was it excluded as a medical service as is provided under EHA. The Court held that the child was entitled to CIC as a related service. Important to the programming issue is the Court took the IEP beyond the process review it established in *Rowley*. The decision affirmed judicial review regarding the appropriateness of the IEP. Going a step beyond *Rowley*, the Court made clear its intent to judge the "appropriate education" standard not only on the basis of adherence to procedural safeguards, but on the basis of substance and content as well. Together, these decisions affirm the central role the IEP does play in providing an equal educational opportunity to handicapped children.

SUMMARY

"Always do right; this will gratify some people and astonish the rest." So said Mark Twain and the simplicity of the logic makes the notion appealing, humorous, and "truthful." If we could we would, and delivering school psychological services in our school settings would be that much easier. But the delicate legal, ethical, and professional standard balance beam we are all asked to walk somehow manages to consistently obscure the definitive answer to the, "What is right?" question. That is a reality that will in all probability not change. We must therefore learn more about those arenas that do influence the answer to the what is right question. Challenges will continue. As we look ahead to reform and begin implementation of alternative special education delivery systems, we face many hurdles that will involve important legal interpretations. In addition, our responsibilities to minor children at risk for many different reasons will undoubtedly increase. The profession is responding to the needs of students as these and other programmatic areas are addressed. Our challenge remains to continue service delivery in a manner that is effective as well as legally and ethically acceptable.

REFERENCES

Adler, N. E., & Dolcini, P. (1986). Psychological issues in abortion for adolescents. In G. B. Melton (Ed.), *Adolescent abortion: Psychological and legal issues* (pp. 74-95). Lincoln: University of Nebraska Press.

American Psychological Association. (1981). *Ethical principles of psychologists.* Washington, DC: Author.

American Psychological Association. (1981). Specialty guidelines for the delivery of services by school psychologists. Washington, DC: Author.

American Psychological Association, American Education Research Association, National Council on Measurement in Education. (1984). *Standards for educational and psychological tests.* Washington, DC: Author.

Board of Education of the Hendrick Hudson Central School v. Rowley, 102 S. Ct 3034 (1982).

Brown v. Board of Education, 347 U.S. 483 (1954).

Covarrubias v. San Diego Unified School District, Civ. No. 70-394-S (S.D. Cal., filed Feb. 1971).

Diana v. State Board of Education, C.A.N. C-70-37 R.F.P. (N.D. Cal., filed Feb. 3, 1970).

Education of All Handicapped Children Act of 1975, 20 U.S.C. S 401 (1975).

Epperson v. Arkansas, 393 U.S. 97 (1968).

Family Educational Rights and Privacy Act. Implementing Regulations, 34 C.F.R. S 99.3 (1976).

Family Educational Rights and Privacy Act. Statement of Senators Buckley and Pell, Congressional Record, p. 52, 1488 (1974).

Goss v. Lopez, 419 U.S. 565 (1975).

Guadalupe Organization, Inc. v. Tempe School District No. 3, Civ. No. 71-435. (D. Ariz. filed Aug. 9, 1971).

H. L. v. Matheson, 450 U.S. 398 (1981).

Hobson v. Hansen, 269 F Supp. 401 (D.D.C. 1967).

Honig v. Doe, 108 S. Ct. 592 (1988).

Ingraham v. Wright, 430 U.S. 651 (1977).

In re Gault, 387 U.S. 1 (1967).

Irving Independent School District v. Tatro, 104 S. Ct. 3371 (1984).

John K. v. Board of Education for School District No. 65, 504 N.E.2d. 797, (1987).

Keith-Spiegel, P., & Koocher, G. P. (1985). *Ethics in psychology.* New York: Random House.

Kelson v. City of Springfield, 767 F.2d 651 (1985).

Kobocow, B., McGuire, J., & Blau, B. (1983). The influence of confidentiality conditions on self-disclosure of early adolescents. *Professional Psychology: Research and Practice, 14,* 435-443.

Koocher, G. P. (1987). Children under law: The paradigm of consent. In G. B. Melton (Ed.), *Reforming the law* (pp. 3-26). New York: Guilford Press.

Larry P. v. Riles, 495 F. Supp. 96 (N.D. Cal. 1979) aff'd (9th cr. no. 80-427, Jan. 23, 1984).

Leikin, S. L. (1983). Minors' assent or dissent to medical treatment. *Journal of Pediatrics, 102,* 169-176.

Lewis, C. C. (1981). How adolescents approach decisions: Changes over grades seven to twelve and policy implications. *Child Development, 52,* 538-544.

Lewis, C. C. (1983). Decision making related to health: When could/should children act responsibly? In G. B. Melton & M. J. Saks (Eds.), *Children's competence to consent* (pp. 75-92). New York: Plenum.

Lidz, C. W., Meisel, A., Zerubavel, E., Carter, E., Sestak, R. M., & Roth, L. (1984). *Informed consent: A study of decision making in psychiatry.* New York: Guilford Press.

Marecek, J. (1987). Counseling adolescents with problem pregnancies. *American Psychologist, 42,* 89-93.

Marshall et al. v. Georgia. 775 F.2d. 1403 (1985).

Melton, G. B. (1980). Children's concepts of their rights. *Journal of Clinical Child Psychology, 9,* 186-190.

Mills v. Bd. of Education of the District of Columbia. 384 F. Supp. 866 (1972).

Melton, G. B. (1983). Minors and privacy: Are legal and psychological concepts compatible? *Nebraska Law Review, 62,* 455-493.

National Association of School Psychologists Principles for Professional Ethics. (1984). Washington, DC: Author.

PARC v. Commonwealth of Pennsylvania, 343 F. Supp. 279 (E.D. Pa. 1972).

Parham v. J. L., 99 S. Ct. 2493 (1979).

Planned Parenthood of Central Missouri v. Danforth, 428 U.S. 52 (1976).

Plotkin, R. (1981). When rights collide: Parents, children, and consent to treatment. *Journal of Pediatric Psychology, 6,* 121-130.

Prasse, D. P. (1984). School psychology and the law: State of the art. In J. Ysseldyke (Ed.), *School psychology: State of the art* (pp. 241-256). Minneapolis: University of Minnesota.

Prasse, D. P., & Reschly, D. J. (1986). Larry P: A case of segregation, testing, or program efficacy? *Exceptional Children, 52*, 333–346.

Rehabilitation Act of 1973 Section 504, 20 U.S.C. S 504 (1975).

Reschly, D. J., Kicklighter, R., & McKee, P. (1988). Recent placement litigation, part I, part II, part III. *School Psychology Review, 17*, 9–50.

Reschly, D. (1980). Psychological evidence in the Larry P. opinion: A case of right problem — wrong solution. *The School Psychology Review, 9*, 123–125.

S-1 v. Turlington, 635 F. 2d 342 (1981). Order on motion to dismiss no. 79-8020 — CIV — Atkins, U.S. District Court, Southern District of Florida, October 9, 1986.

San Antonio Independent School District v. Rodriguez, 93 S.Ct. 1278 (1973).

Stanley v. Illinois, 405 U.S. 645 (1972).

Tarasoff v. Regents of University of California, 13, C. 3d 177, 529 P. 2d 553, 118 Cal. Rptr. 129 (1974).

Tinker v. Des Moines School District, 393 U.S. 503 (1969).

Trachtman, G. M. (1974). Ethical issues in school psychology. *The School Psychology Digest, 3*(4), 4–15.

Weithorn, L. A., & Campbell, S. B. (1982). The competency of children and adolescents to make informed treatment decisions. *Child Development, 53*, 1589–1598.

ANNOTATED BIBLIOGRAPHY

Keith-Spiegel, P., & Koocher, G. (1985). *Ethics in psychology: Professional standards and cases.* New York: Random House.
Excellent coverage of applied practice ethical issues. Uses text and cases adjudicated before various ethics committees. Comprehensive chapters on record keeping, assessment, therapeutic intervention, dual-role relationships, and others, Each chapter begins with a definition and thorough explanation of the topic, followed by application drawing on different cases and professional standards.

Melton, G. (Ed.). (1989). *Reforming the law: Impact of child development research.* New York: Guilford.
A compilation of chapters drawing on years of child development research in a wide range of areas that assesses the impact of research on children's competence in decision making. Chapters provide coverage of the broader areas of applied psychology, scientific knowledge, and judicial decision making. Drawing from a research foundation, authors provide suggestions for influencing the legal system.

Prasse, D. (Ed.). (1986). Litigation and special education. *Exceptional Children, 52*, 311–390.
This special issue of *Exceptional Children* reviews the initial Supreme Court decision on various aspects of PL 94-142. Articles and cases reviewed cover such important topics as the relationship between assessment/diagnostic practices and placement/programming decisions, definitions of related services and an "appropriate" education, financial issues involved with special education litigation, including unilateral placement risks.

Prasse, D. (1988). Licensing, school psychology and independent private practice. In T. R. Kratochwill (Ed.), *Advances in School Psychology: Volume VI* (pp. 49–80). Hillsdale, NJ: Lawrence Erlbaum Associates.
This chapter provides an overview of regulation and licensing. Scope and authority of licensing is presented and coverage is given to professional issues in practice and legal and ethical considerations. Examples of specialty licenses in school psychology are provided along with definitions of scope of practice. Emergent problems associated with delivering school psychological services in the private sector are discussed.

33

Best Practices in Neuropsychology

Mark D. Kelly
Neuropsychology Laboratory
Ball State University

Raymond S. Dean
Neuropsychology Laboratory
Ball State University and
Indiana University School of Medicine

OVERVIEW

Rationale for School Psychology

Neuropsychology attempts to relate observable behavior to brain functioning. As such, the major objective of neuropsychological assessment is to define neurologic functioning through standardized measures (Dean, 1985a). Of increasing interest to school psychologists is the accumulating evidence that an understanding of children's neuropsychological functioning is useful in making both placement and treatment decisions (Hynd, 1981a). Indeed, the use of neuropsychological assessment has been shown to offer school psychologists a method to generate hypotheses concerning the etiology of specific school related problems and predict classroom outcomes (Gray & Dean, in press).

Because neuropsychological assessment integrates cognitive, sensori-motor, and emotional elements of behavior; it represents the most comprehensive psychological evaluation available. As such, the results of the assessment hold significant implications for understanding the child without the need to make medical, neurologic conclusions. Thus, a neuropsychological perspective, with its wide band approach to behavior, offers a framework to reconcile and integrate information (Boll, 1974). Clearly, a neuropsychological

examination with roots in both psychology and neurology provides a theoretical structure in which neurologic, behavioral, and educational data may be synthesized into a comprehensive understanding of the child.

The utility of the neuropsychological approach becomes clear when one considers that many of the measures used in neuropsychological assessment are standard elements of a psychoeducational battery (e.g., the Wechsler Intelligence Scales). Although the interpretation of psychoeducational tests may differ dramatically in medical settings, neuropsychological assessment should be seen as building upon procedures familiar to school psychologists. Whereas the school psychologist is primarily concerned with school based outcomes, the interpretation of these data in a medical setting focus more upon the correspondence between observable behavior and the intact brain. The intent of this chapter is to provide an overview of best practices in neuropsychology which may be useful and relevant to school psychologists.

Brief History of Neuropsychological Assessment

Attempts to link elements of behavior and specific brain functioning date back several centuries. However, the scientific study of neuropsychology can be traced to case studies of brain damaged patients in the late 19th century (Broca, 1861a; Wernicke, 1874). Based on these idiographic data attempts were made to localize specific functions to microstructures of the brain. Many of these early conclusions have proved to be overly ambitious and it is only within the last 40 years that a realistic picture of the relationship between behavior and cortical functioning has emerged. These recent strides have been due in large measure to advances in technology and the ability to examine the structure of the brain using noninvasive methods.

Following World War II, an expanding base of neuropsychological data became available from veterans with documented brain damage as a result of head wounds (Boll, 1974; Luria, 1963). Empirical investigations of the behavioral effects of such localized cortical lesions allowed the validation of behavioral measures in the prediction of neurologic damage. In this post war era, a good deal of emphasis was still placed on the localization of functions to particular areas of the cerebral cortex. However, at present it is generally agreed that the site, magnitude, type, and chronicity of brain lesions interact with individual neurologic differences to such a degree that localization of functions to microstructures of the brain is unsupportable (Boll, 1974; Reitan, 1955). It has also become clear that a patient's age at onset, acuteness of damage, and length of the interval between onset and neuropsychological assessment are critical to interpretation of test results (Meier, 1963; Reitan & Davison, 1974).

Neuropsychology's evolution from behavioral neurology, and elements of both clinical and experimental psychology is clearly reflected in present assessment procedures and test batteries (Reitan, 1976). In fact, the development of many neuropsychological assessment techniques are but standardized versions of neurologic procedures or adaptations from experimental psychology. For this reason, neuropsychological methods are often viewed as an extension of the neurologic examination. Most neuropsychological evaluations involve comprehensive batteries which assess intellectual, sensori-motor, perceptual, and emotional-affective characteristics shown to correspond to cortical functioning.

BASIC CONSIDERATIONS

Rationale for Neuropsychological Assessment

Neuropsychological assessment in the United States has, from its inception, focused on the identification and localization of brain dysfunction (e.g., Boll, 1974; Reitan, 1974). The choice of procedures owe more to predictive validity than any theory of brain functioning. Indeed, individual tests in most neuropsychological batteries were included on the basis of their ability to discriminate between normal controls and brain damaged patients. This empirical approach continues such that the interpretation of test data is based on actuarial standards for normal and impaired performance. Although a focus on differential diagnosis continues, increasing emphasis is being placed on functional descriptions of the patient's adaptive behavior remaining after neurologic disease or trauma. In addition, neuropsychological assessment provides an objective baseline of functioning which allows one to follow recovery or monitor a progressive disorder. These benchmarks are valuable in describing current levels of functioning and treatment planning (Lezak, 1983). In this way, a child's condition can then be empirically charted and interventions evaluated for their effectiveness. However, more frequently the neuropsychological examination offers an aid in understanding a child when equivocal results have been found from physical diagnostic techniques.

Clinical Child Neuropsychology

Many of the assessment procedures used with children are adaptations of measures which have shown utility with adults. This is true because larger numbers of adult patients with documented neurological disorders exist, and hence greater availability of subjects to validate procedures either at surgery or time of autopsy (Dean, 1985b). This relatively large research base with adults has often been generalized to children. However, children are not merely small adults and caution must be exerted in the extension of adult findings to children. Indeed, developmental and environmental variables influence children's performance on neuropsychological measures to such an extent that adult standards are often misleading with children.

Elements of Professional Training

Training in neuropsychology offers school psychologists an expanded role in more non-traditional settings. Specific guidelines for training in neuropsychology have been recommended by the Task Force of the International Neuropsychological Society (INS) and Division 40 of the American Psychological Association (APA) (Report of the Task Force on Education, Accreditation and Credentialing, 1981). These training elements include (a) a basic psychology core, (b) a generic applied core, (c) specialized training in the neurosciences, (d) specific clinical neuropsychological training, and (e) completion of a doctoral dissertation (Report of the INS — Division 40 Task Force on Education, Accreditation and Credentialing, 1987). Following appropriate practicum experiences, an additional 1800-hour internship in a neuropsychological setting is recommended.

Meier (1981) has outlined a number of training models in neuropsychology. However, neuropsychology as a subspecialty within one of the applied specialties of psychology (i.e., school, counseling, clinical), is the predominate approach in the United States (Hynd, 1981b). Within the framework of school psychology training, an emphasis would be placed on neuropsychological coursework. For example, traditional school psychology training would be concomitantly taken with medical neuroanatomy, neurophysiology, neuropsychological assessment, and cognitive rehabilitation. The overall goal of such training is to prepare school psychologists to apply neuropsychological principles in their day to day practice with referred children.

BEST PRACTICES IN NEUROPSYCHOLOGY

Theoretical Approaches

Clinical neuropsychology in the United States has traditionally been distinctly quantitative (Dean, 1982; Luria, 1966; Reitan, 1976). Emphasis has been placed on developing test batteries which reliably distinguish between groups of normals and patients with known neurological conditions. This vantage is exemplified by Ralph Reitan and reflected in the Halstead-Reitan Neuropsychological Test Batteries (Reitan, 1955, 1974). In the development of this battery specific testing procedures were included based on empirical displays of their sensitivity to brain dysfunction. Neuropsychological inferences are then made relative to correlations between scores and an independent neurological diagnosis (e.g., Reitan, 1955). In sum, the major focus of this quantitative, atheoretical, approach has been the development of standardized test batteries which allow actuarial predictions of neurologic group membership. In this way, differential diagnosis of neuropathology and localization of structural abnormalities may be inferred (Klove, 1974).

The quantitative approach to neuropsychology has been criticized for its emphasis on differential diagnosis and reduction of vast amounts of descriptive information to unitary nosological categories (Luria & Majovski, 1977). As an alternative, Luria (1966) offered a qualitative approach which stressed clinical experience in an attempt to provide a comprehensive understanding of an individual patient's functioning. Single subject observations linked with a theory of "functional systems" of the brain are the hallmarks of Luria's qualitative approach (Luria, 1963, 1966, 1973). Based on his theory, neuropsychological assessment was portrayed as a dynamic, interactive process with the patient. Rather than relying on standardized batteries or comparisons to normative populations, hypotheses of the patient's impairment followed an interview and guided the selection of specific assessment techniques. Thus, individual tests employed during evaluation varied with each patient depending upon the specific impairment in question.

The qualitative approach has often been faulted for relying on case studies and subjective clinical impressions. Similarly, the inability to systematically evaluate the reliability and validity of this approach are viewed as drawbacks. On the other hand, the quantitative method has been criticized for exclusion of observational data crucial to rehabilitation planning, and its relative narrow focus on differential diagnosis.

Neuropsychological Assessment Systems

The Halstead-Reitan Neuropsychological Test Battery (HRNB) is the most widely used and best known comprehensive battery of neuropsychological functioning (Dean, 1983). The vast majority of tests comprising the battery are adaptations of existing clinical and experimental measures. Through various processes of validation and refinement, the current battery consists of 10 measures which were shown to be the best discriminators of brain damage (Reitan, 1955, 1969). Other than an overall impairment index, comprised of a proportion of tests most sensitive to dysfunction, no summary measure exists. In general, the HRNB measures abstraction, attention and concentration, sensori-motor integration, motor speed and strength, and sensory perception. An indepth review of the HRNB is not possible due to space limitations, but can be found elsewhere (Boll, 1981; Reitan & Davison, 1974). However, Table 1 provides an overview of individual tests of the battery, constructs measured, their origins, and scores reported.

In addition to those measures in Table 1, other allied procedures are used in conjunction with the HRNB including the Wechsler Intelligence Scales, Minnesota Multiphasic Personality Inventory (MMPI), Wide Range Achievement Test (WRAT), Lateral Dominance tests, and Wechsler Memory Scale. These allied measures were included because of their specific sensitivity to particular functions and ability to discriminate between various disorders when interpreted with the HRNB.

Originally, the HRNB was designed for adults ($>$ 15 yrs.) (Reitan, 1955). However, an older children's version (age 9–14), was developed from research using successively younger children (Reitan, 1969). This version, the Halstead Neuropsychological Test Battery for Children (HNTB-C), retains basically the same measures. Other allied procedures include the age appropriate Wechsler Intelligence Scale for Children — Revised (WISC-R).

Validation studies have repeatedly shown both the HRNB and HNTB-C to be sensitive to cortical dysfunction (Boll, 1974, 1981; Klonoff & Low, 1974; Reed, Reitan, & Klove, 1965; Reitan, 1974). In the main, the battery has a high accuracy rate ($>$ 90%) in discriminating normal controls from neurological patients. However, the interpretation for children is less clear than that with adults, because greater numbers of moderating variables influence the neuropsychological functioning of younger subjects. For example, children with localized brain damage are more likely than adults to show impairment on a wide range of neuropsychological measures despite similar structural damage (Ernhart, Graham, Eichman, Marshall, & Thurston, 1963). Thus, the general depression of cognitive functioning and greater variability on neuropsychological measures seen with brain damaged children must be considered when interpreting the HNTB-C.

As mentioned above, Luria's approach to neuropsychological assessment was quite different from the quantitative approach of the Halstead-Reitan batteries (Luria, 1966). His main focus was on describing the patient's strengths and weaknesses as a prelude to treatment planning. Based on his "functional theory of the brain," neuropsychological assessment involved the investigation of "zones" of brain function (Luria, 1973). Rather than looking at the integrity of specific structural components, Luria emphasized evaluation of "systems" (e.g., speech, thought, movement).

Christensen (1975, 1980) operationalized Luria's qualitative methods into a range of objective measures. Building upon Christensen's work, the Luria-Nebraska Neuropsychological Battery for adolescents and adults (LNNB) (Golden, Hammeke, and Purisch, 1980) and the later developed Children's version (ages 8 to 12 years) (Plaisted, Gustavson, Wilkening, & Golden, 1983) were attempts to further translate Luria/Christensen's work into a standardized objective measure. The LNNB consists of 269 items, whereas the Children's LNNB has 149. Both are organized into 11 discrete scales. Each scale represents one of Luria's functional "zones" and are described in Table 2. The LNNB and Children's LNNB have the advantages of an administration time of less than 3 hours and are highly portable. Also, the Luria-Nebraska batteries have been argued by its authors to be a coherent collection of neuropsychological tests which are theory based.

Inferential Techniques

Interpretation of neuropsychological test data have traditionally relied on four inferential techniques (Reitan, 1974). The first approach focuses on the patient's "level of performance" for one or more individual measures. In this case, the obtained test score is compared with a standard or, "cut-off criterion" from normative data. Thus, the individual's performance is viewed as being "within normal limits" or in the "impaired" range. Performance in the impaired range is necessary to infer cortical impairment, but absence of poor performance does not rule out dysfunction. This is especially true for young children when being compared to adult standards because of developmental delays being misread as an impairment (Boll, 1974).

The second method of inference is the presence of pathogenic signs. Such signs are made up of a constellation of symptoms that rarely would be displayed without neurologic disorder (e.g., dyspraxia, aphasia, etc.). When these signs are present they are indicative of neuropathology and are of clear diagnostic significance. However, the absence of such signs do not rule out the presence of a specific disorder.

Another inferential method involves the lateralization of functions. Because the left and right sides of the body are served by the contralateral hemisphere of the brain, functional integrity with regard to sensory input and motor output can be compared. Comparison of the left and right sides of the body and tests shown to measure specific left and right hemispheric functions, provide information relevant to localized dysfunction within a specific hemisphere of the brain (Boll, 1972).

Pattern analysis is the last technique, which integrates level of performance, pathognomic sign, and lateralization of function techniques into an overall collage of strengths and weaknesses. This method compares a patient's pattern of strengths and deficits with documented patterns indicative of neuropathology. In other words, various configurations of scores are isolated and examined in correspondence with specific types and locations of known cortical dysfunction.

Neuropsychological Methods with Specific Populations

Learning disorders. Children's classroom learning problems represent over 25% of the referrals in pediatric neurologic settings (Dean, 1985a). Neurological assessment has shown to be of utility in both delineating cognitive processing deficits as well as ruling out various neurologic disorders. This is of interest to the school psychologist in that the Halstead Reitan Neuropsychological Test Battery has been shown to provide unique information in understanding learning disabled children over that gleaned from the traditional psychoeducational assess-

TABLE 1
Tests of the Halstead-Reitan Neuropsychological Batteries

Name	Explicit Constructs	Implicit Constructs	Format	Technical Information	Origin	Scores
Category Test	Concept Formation Abstraction Integration	Visual Acuity Attention Concentration	Semi-automated visual presentation of slides with underlying concept. Feedback provided as to correctness after depression of 1 of 4 levers. Controlled learning experience	Reitan (1955) Klove (1974)	Halstead (1947)	Total Errors
Tactual Performance Test	Tactual Discrimination, Manual Dexterity, Kinesthesis Incidental Memory, Spatial Memory	Kinesthesis Tactual-motor Integration	Shapes placed in form board without aid of vision (dominant, non-dominant, both hands). Recall of shapes & location of board.	Reitan (1974) Boll (1974)	Sequin-Goddard Form Board Halstead (1947)	1. Time 2. Memory 3. Location
Speech-Sounds Perception	Verbal and Auditory Discrimination, Auditory-Visual Integration, Phonetic Skills	Auditory acuity, Language, Attention	Select paralog presented auditorially from (3) alternatives, total of 60 items	Reitan (1974) Klove (1974)	Halstead (1974)	Total Errors
Rhythm Test	Non-verbal Auditory Discrimination, Auditory Perception	Attention Concentration	Iden. of 30 pairs of rhythmic beats as being "same" or "different"	Reitan (1955)	Seashore Tests of Musical Talent	Total Errors
Trail Making	A-Motor speed, visual scanning, B-visual-motor integration of alpha & numeric systems	Visual Acuity, Attention, Concentration	A-Connect 25 (15) numbered circles in numerical order. B-Connect 25 (15) numbered or alpha circles alter. between numerical & alpha order (i.e., 1-A, 2-B)	Reitan (1955, 1974) Boll (1974)	Army Individual Test Adjutant Generals Office (1944)	Separate Time A&B
Finger Oscilation Test	Motor Speed Dexterity	Distractibility Concentration	Measure of a foot of taps with index finger in 10 seconds for each hand. Dominant, non-dominant scores = means of 5 trials for each hand	Halstead (1974)		Mean Taps Each hand

(Table 1, continued)

Name	Explicit Constructs	Implicit Constructs	Format	Technical Information	Origin	Scores
Adjunct Measures[1]						
Reitan-Indiana Aphasia Screening Test	Wide Band Language & Non-verbal Functions	Education Occupation Concentration	32 items requiring naming, spelling, reading, writing, math, calculation, enumerating, identify body parts, pantomime actions, perform acts, draw, shapes & identify directions	Reitan (1969) Dean (1982) Klove (1974)	Halstead & Kepman (1952) Reitan (1969)	By Item Total Error Score
Reitan-Klove Sensory Perceptual Examinations	Lateralized Sensory Perc. (Visual, Auditory, & Tactile)	Distractibility	Accuracy of unilateral & bilateral simultaneous tactile, auditory, & visual imperception, finger localization from tactile stimulation without vision. Tactile & perception on fingertips. Tactile recog. of shapes without vision	Reitan (1969) Klove (1974)	Reitan (1969)	Errors Left vs. right side of body
Strength of Grip Test (Hand Dynamometer)	Motor Strength		Measure of strength of grip. Alternating measures for preferred & non-preferred hands	Reitan (1955)	Reitan (1955)	Left & Right Hand Scores

[1] In addition to the above, the age appropriate Wechsler Intelligence Scale, Minnesota Multiphasic Personality Test, Lateral Dominance Examination, the Wide Range Achievement Test, and the Wechsler Memory Scale are often incorporated.

TABLE 2
Individual Scales of the Luria-Nebraska Neuropsychological Battery

Individual Scale	Scale Description
Motor Functions	Assess a number of motor skills for left & right sides of body, unilateral & simultaneous simple & complex motor movement
Acoustico-Motor (Rhythm Scale)	Evaluate a similarity of tones; reproduce tones orally & motorically, rhythmic patterns generated from verbal description
Higher Cutaneous & Kinesthetic (Tactile Scale)	Without aid of vision, must identify where touched, head & point of pin, direction of movement, geometric & alpha numeric symbols traced on wrist, matching movements, & item identification
Spatial (Visual Functions)	Visual recognition of common objects; pictures with obscurity & disorganization; matrices tasks & complex block count
Receptive Speech Scale	Requires oral, written & motoric response to spoken speech
Expressive Speech Scale	Oral repetition of words, increasingly complex sentences; name, count, recite, offer missing words, & organize mixed-up sentence
Writing Scale	Involves basic writing skills — spelling, copying words & letters from cards & memory; writing words & letters from dictation & spontaneously
Reading Scale	Range from reading letter sounds, syllables, words, sentences, and a short story
Arithmetic Scale	Involves simple number identification, writing & reading series of numbers, simple skills to more complex skills
Memory Scale	Requires learning word list, picture memory, rhythmic pattern, hand positions, sentences, story & paired associate task
Intellectual Scales	Sequencing pictures, abstract theme of pictures, identify picture absurdities, proverbs, definitions, opposites & analogies & word problems.

ment (D'Amato, Gray, & Dean, 1988). In this study, some 90% of the variability of the HRNB was found to be non-redundant with the functions measured by the WISC-R. The overlap that did occur was attributed to "general" cognitive ability in each measure. One rationale, then, for using a broad based neuropsychological battery is that it considers a wider spectrum of cognitive-cortical functioning than accounted for in the traditional psychoeducational assessment (Dean, 1986a; Hynd & Obrzut, 1981). This utility is portrayed in a study by Strom, Gray, Dean, and Fischer (1987), who found neuropsychological data to incrementally increase a school psychologist's ability to predict academic achievement.

Challenges in diagnosis and remediation of learning disabilities continue. This is true because children with learning disorders represent a heterogeneous group, who display varying deficits result-

ing from differing etiologies (Rourke, 1975, 1983). Based upon neuropsychological methods, a number of researchers have begun to specify distinct subtypes of learning disabilities (Morris, Blashfield, & Satz, 1981; Reitan & Dean, 1987; Rourke & Strang, 1983). Not only have subtypes been shown to differ on neurologic dimensions; but also as a function of chronological age and concomitant neurologic development of the children studied (Fish & Rourke, 1979).

Hence, a number of studies suggest that reliable subtypes can be identified within a learning disordered population using neuropsychological methods (Dean, 1985a; Fisk & Rourke, 1979). Clearly then, learning disorders should not be viewed as a homogeneous diagnostic classification. Future research should be directed at understanding the types of deficiencies learning disabled children have and the treatment approaches which most clearly fit the child's strengths.

Head injuries. Traumatic head injuries are the most prevalent cause of neurologic impairment in children (Lezak, 1983); and ever increasing advances in medicine have allowed greater numbers of children with neurologic damage to survive and eventually return to the classroom. Upon return, these students are more likely to present severe behavioral deficiencies and/or psychiatric symptoms than normals (Brown, Chadwick, Shaffer, Rutter, & Traub, 1981; Rutter, Chadwick, & Shaffer, 1982). Neuropsychological research provides a structured framework in which to better understand the complex relationship between emotional disturbance and neurologic disorders. Indeed, the neuropsychological examination provides information concerning both the severity of head injury and the probability of concomitant psychiatric disturbances. Thus, psychologists can profit from knowledge in neuropsychology when confronted with head injured children in the school setting.

Recently, Dean (1986b) has postulated a two-fold risk for childhood psychiatric disorders as a result of head trauma. The first and most obvious risk factor relates psychiatric disturbance to actual aberrations in brain physiology following head injury. The second, is the child's emotional reactions to the perceived alterations in neurological functioning. These risks may lead to decreases in the child's ability to cope with stressors in the premorbid environment. From this vantage point, neuropsychological impairment interacts with psychosocial stressors as etiological factors in psychiatric disorders.

Patterns of cognitive-neuropsychological dysfunction following head injury are manifested quite differently in children and adults (Reed, Reitan, & Klove, 1965; Rutter, 1982). Whereas adult head injured patients often exhibit localized deficits, children more often show diffuse impairment with similar lesions. Head injured children are also more likely to show deficits in cognitive functions (e.g., Wechsler Intelligence Scales Vocabulary subtest) which are resistant to impairment in adults (Ernhart, Graham, Eichman, Marshall, and Thurston, 1963). Some of these neuropsychological differences between adults and children may be related to the type of head injuries suffered (Klonoff & Robinson, 1967). Indeed, children are three times more likely than adults to experience brain damage as the result of falls (Klonoff, Low, & Clark, 1977). Hence, differences in etiology of brain damage as well as the influence of developmental factors make conclusions concerning children's functioning much more tentative than for adults.

Recent research with children suggests that cognitive and behavioral disorders as the result of head injury are dependent upon the severity of the trauma (Rutter, 1982; Rutter et al., 1982). Two of the most reliable measures of the severity of cortical damage are the extent of posttraumatic amnesia and the duration of unconsciousness following injury (Russell & Smith, 1961; Smith, 1981). Therefore, at the time of initial evaluation, the length of unconsciousness and the extent of memory loss are important in both long term prognosis and extent of impairment.

Children with mild head injuries often suffer no amnesia or unconsciousness and perform within normal limits on psychoeducational measures. However, some of these children do experience school-related difficulties (e.g., reading or math deficiencies) (Chadwick, Rutter, Thompson, & Shaffer, 1981). Thus, cognitive impairment related to mild head injury may not be detected by traditional psychoeducational measures, but school psychologists trained in neuropsychology may be able to utilize other tests which are sensitive to minor dysfunctions.

Considering that most children who suffer head injuries will return to the classroom, it seems appropriate that school psychologists have a basic understanding of neuropsychological research in this area. Indeed, a psychologist with neuropsychological training may be able to offer a more comprehensive interpretation of psychometric data and specific remediation strategies for reentry into the classroom (Stone, Gray, & Dean, 1989).

Perinatal complications. Nearly 8% of all live births involve complications during the perinatal period (pregnancy, labor, delivery, and the first 28 days of life) (Behrman, 1981). Such perinatal complications have been shown to place the child at risk for cognitive, physical, and affective disorders. An understanding of these difficulties has utility for the school psychologist because children who have suffered perinatal complications are more likely than normals to exhibit neurologically related disorders during their school-age years (Gray, Dean, Strom, Wheeler, & Brockley, 1987). In addition to frank neurologic disorders (e.g., cerebral palsy, seizure disorders, etc.), less pervasive neuropsychological problems such as developmental delays, behavioral disorders, learning difficulties, and attention deficits have been linked to a history of perinatal complications (Field, Dempsey, & Shuman, 1981; Pfeiffer, Heffernan, & Pfeiffer, 1985).

Clearly, a need exists to identify infants at risk of developing handicapping conditions as the result of perinatal complications. This information is of utility not only for diagnosis, but also in an attempt at early interventions such as infant stimulation programs (Parmalee, Beckwith, Cohen, & Sigman, 1983). In light of recent legislation (PL 99-457) school psychologists will be playing an increasing role in identifying such high risk children.

The first step in the identification of children at risk from perinatal complications would be development of a screening instrument. Dean & Gray (1985) have recently designed a self report measure which queries mothers on information concerning factors their children may have been exposed to during the perinatal period. This instrument has been shown to be both economical and psychometrically sound in identifying children who have incurred perinatal complications (Gray, Dean, & Rattan, 1987; Gray, Dean, Strom, Wheeler, & Brockley, 1987). This measure offers the school psychologist a structured approach to gathering data concerning the perinatal period of life.

Seizure disorders. Although epilepsy cannot be viewed as a single disorder, as a group, patients with this diagnosis have been reported to be deficit on measures of cognitive ability. Generalization of neuropsychological aspects of functioning across various forms of epilepsy is not possible because of the great diversity of disorders. However, research of particular seizure types do have some clinical utility. For example, patients with tonic-clonic attacks show more generalized neuropsychological impairment than other seizure types (Dean, 1986b). Whereas those with petit mal (generalized absence) seizures, as a group, do not differ significantly from normals on standardized neuropsychological measures.

There exists a variety of factors which cloud the neuropsychological picture of the epileptic patient. Foremost are the neuropsychological and emotional side effects associated with anticonvulsant medication. To cite one example, high serum levels of phenytoin (Dilantin) have been shown to be related to impaired motor performance (Dodrill, 1975). Hence, it is often not clear whether neuropsychological impairment with the seizure disordered patient is due to the effects of the medication or to neurologic dysfunction.

Previous research has shown that both age at onset and frequency of seizures are related to the extent of an epileptic patient's neuropsychological impairment (Dikman, Matthews, & Harley, 1977). Dean (1985b) has reported data suggesting that the total number of lifetime seizures is a better predictor of impaired functioning in children than either of the before-mentioned factors in isolation. Moreover, he argued that a "kindling effect" associated with total lifetime seizures has neuropsychological implications.

The number of psychiatric disorders present in children who have seizure disorders is much greater than normals (Dean, 1985a). However, these emotional disturbances may be related to psychosocial stress factors. It seems clear that the embarrassment and misunderstanding often associated with epilepsy add to the patient's distress. A neuropsychological assessment utilizing measures of emotional functioning could therefore provide school psychologists with objective data useful in understanding the seizure-disordered child.

Psychiatric disorders. The major thrust of neuropsychological research of psychiatric disorders has involved differential diagnosis. Indeed, most referrals for neuropsychological assessment in psychiatric settings concern questions of the organic underpinnings of emotional disorders. However, Dean (1985a) argued that the functional and organic elements of psychiatric disorders are better understood as a continuum rather than a dichotomy. This is true because many disorders once considered to have a functional etiology (e.g., depression) have been shown to have a clear organic component.

Although the majority of research in this area is based on adult psychopathology, neuropsychological features have been reported for childhood and adolescent psychiatric disorders (Hertzig & Birch, 1968; Seidel, Chadwick, & Rutter, 1975). Recently, neuropsychological measures have been shown to have utility in the screening, diagnosis, and treatment of children's psychiatric disorders (Gray, Dean, D'Amato, & Rattan, 1968; Woods & Short, 1985).

It seems that children with psychiatric disorders can be expected to show neuropsychological impairment. Using the HRNB, Tramontana, Sherrets, and Golden (1980) reported that in a large sample of child and adolescent psychiatric patients, some 60% exhibited some form of neuropsychological impairment upon admission to the psychiatric hospital. These data were consistent with Rutter's (1977) findings that children with psychiatric disorders are likely to present neuropsychological dysfunction despite normal neurologic histories and examinations. Additionally, the extent of childhood neuropsychological impairment appears related to the chronicity of psychiatric

disorder (Tramontana, Sherrets, & Golden, 1980). Thus, children with emotional disturbances of greater than two years are far more likely to display impairment than acute cases.

Although the present state of knowledge concerning children's psychiatric disorders is limited, it seems clear that a neuropsychological perspective would aid school psychologists in better understanding the picture when called upon to assess emotionally disturbed children. Indeed, considering school psychologists' frequent role in making differential diagnoses, the need exists to define the neuropsychological aspects of a child's psychiatric disorder.

Planning for Rehabilitation

Historically, both clinical neuropsychology and school psychology have focused upon diagnosis. However, increasing numbers of psychologists are expanding their professional role to include rehabilitation and intervention (Seretny, Dean, Gray, & Hartlage, 1986). Clearly, neuropsychological data collected by school psychologists can go beyond diagnosis and may serve as the foundation for remedial strategies (Hartlage, 1975; Hartlage & Reynolds, 1981; Hartlage & Telzrow, 1983).

Cognitive rehabilitation or retraining is an attempt to use our understanding of neuropsychology in structuring programs to remediate higher order neurologic dysfunction. Gray & Dean (1989) have reviewed a number of cognitive rehabilitative techniques and theoretical approaches used with neuropsychological impaired children. They concluded that although cognitive rehabilitative programs exist, there are few studies supporting their efficacy. In fact, problems related to sample heterogeneity, lack of control groups, and failure to control for spontaneous recovery of functions allow little generalization of these techniques. Hence, the clinical utility and effectiveness of such rehabilitative approaches remains to be demonstrated.

It seems apparent that school psychologists with specialized training in neuropsychology would have the potential to implement early intervention and rehabilitation with neuropsychologically impaired children (Gray & Dean, in press). Indeed, school psychologists capable of applying neuropsychological principles may be the best prepared to treat neurologically related cognitive deficits and emotional problems seen in the educational setting. However, with the current lack of empirical support for rehabilitative techniques, the psychologist must rely upon a task analytical approach.

REFERENCES

Behrman, R. E. (1981). *Neonatal-Perinatal medicine*. St. Louis: C. V. Mosby Company.

Boll, T. J. (1972). Right and left cerebral hemisphere damage and tactile perception: Performance of the ipsilateral and contralateral sides of the body. *Neuropsychologia, 12*, 235-238.

Boll, T. J. (1974). Behavioral correlates of cerebral damage in children aged 9 through 14. In R. M. Reitan & L. A. Davison (Eds.), *Clinical neuropsychology: Current status and applications* (pp. 91-120). Washington, DC: Hemisphere.

Boll, T. J. (1981). The Halstead-Reitan neuropsychology battery. In S. B. Filskov & T. J. Boll (Eds.), *Handbook of clinical neuropsychology*. New York: Wiley.

Broca, P. (1861/1960). Remarks on the seat of the faculty of articulate language, followed by an observation of apheasis. In G. vonBonin (trans.), *Some papers on the cerebral cortex*. Springfield, IL: Charles C Thomas.

Brown, G., Chadwick, O., Shaffer, D., Rutter, M., & Traub, M. (1981). A prospective study of children with head injuries: III. Psychiatric sequelae. *Psychological Medicine, 11*, 63-78.

Chadwick, O., Rutter, M., Thompson, J., & Shaffer, D. (1981). Intellectual performance and reading skills after localized head injury in childhood. *Journal of Child Psychology and Psychiatry, 22*, 117-139.

Christensen, A. L. (1975). *Luria's neuropsychological investigation*. New York: Spectrum.

Christensen, A. L. (1980). *Luria's neuropsychological investigation* (Rev., 2nd ed.). Copenhagen: Munksgaard.

D'Amato, R. C., Gray, J. W., & Dean, R. S. (1988). A comparison between intellectual and neuropsychological functioning. *Journal of School Psychology, 26*, 283-292.

Dean, R. S. (1982). Neuropsychological assessment. In T. R. Kratochwill (Ed.), *Advances in school psychology* (Vol. II), (pp. 171-202). Hillsdale, NJ: Lawrence Erlbaum Associates.

Dean, R. S. (1983a). Neuropsychological assessment. In Staff College (Ed.), *Handbook of diagnostic and epidemiological instruments*. Washington, DC: National Institute of Mental Health.

Dean, R. S. (1985a). Neuropsychological assessment. In J. D. Cavenar, R. Michels, H. K. H. Brodie, A. M. Cooper, S. B. Guze, L. L. Judd, G. L. Klerman, & A. J. Solnit (Eds.), *Psychiatry* (pp. 1-16). Philadelphia: J. B. Lippincott Company.

Dean, R. S. (1985b). Foundation and rationale for neuropsychological bases of individual differences. In L. Hartlage & C. Telzrow (Eds.), *Neuropsychology of individual differences: A developmental perspective* (pp. 7-39). New York: Plenum Press.

Dean, R. S. (1986a). Perspectives on the future of neuropsychological assessment. In B. S. Plake & J. C. Witt (Eds.), *Buros-Nebraska series on measurement* (pp. 203-244). New York: Lawrence Erlbaum Associates.

Dean, R. S. (1986b). Neuropsychological aspects of psychiatric disorders. In J. E. Obrzut & G. Hynd (Eds.), *Child neuropsychology* (Vol. 2). New York: Academic Press, Inc.

Dean, R. S., & Gray, J. W. (1985). *Maternal Perinatal Scale*. Muncie, IN: Ball State University.

Dikman, S., Matthews, C. G., & Harley, J. P. (1977). Effect of early versus late onset of major motor epilepsy in cognitive-intellectual performance: Further considerations. *Epilepsia, 18*, 31-36.

Dodrill, D. B. (1975). Diphenylhydantoin serum levels, toxicity, and neuropsychological performance in patients with epilepsy. *Epilepsia, 16*, 593.

Ernhart, C. G., Graham, F. K., Eichman, P. L., Marshall, J. M., & Thurston, D. (1963). Brain injury in the preschool child: Some developmental considerations. *Psychological Monographs, General and Applied, 77*(11), 17-33.

Field, T. M., Dempsey, J. R., & Shuman, H. H. (1981). Developmental follow-up of pre- and postterm infants. In S. L. Friedman & M. Sigman (Eds.), *Preterm birth and psychological development* (pp. 299-312). New York: Academic Press.

Fisk, J. L., & Rourke, B. P. (1979). Identification of subtypes of learning-disabled children at three age levels: A neuropsychological, multivariate approach. *Journal of Clinical Neuropsychology, 1*, 289-310.

Gray, J. W., & Dean, R. S. (1989). Approaches to the cognitive rehabilitation of children with neuropsychological impairment. In C. R. Reynolds & E. Fletcher-Janzen (Eds.), *Handbook of clinical child neuropsychology*. New York: Plenum.

Gray, J. W., & Dean, R. S. (in press). Implications of neuropsychological research for school psychology. In T. B. Gutkin & C. R. Reynolds (Eds.), *The handbook of school psychology (2nd ed.)*. New York: John Wiley & Sons, Inc.

Gray, J. W., Dean, R. S., D'Amato, R. C., & Rattan, G. (1986). Differential diagnosis of primary affective disorder using the Halstead-Reitan Neuropsychological Test Battery. *International Journal of Neuroscience, 35*, 43–49.

Gray, J. W., Dean, R. S., & Rattan, G. (1987). Assessment of perinatal risk factors. *Psychology in the Schools, 24*, 15–21.

Gray, J. W., Dean, R. S., Strom, D. A., Wheeler, T. E., & Brockley, M. (1987). *Perinatal complications as predictors of developmental disabilities*. Manuscript submitted for publication.

Golden, C. J., Hammeke, T. A., & Purisch, A. D. (1980). *The Luria-Nebraska neuropsychological battery: Manual*. Los Angeles: Western Psychological Services.

Hartlage, L. C. (1975). Neuropsychological approaches to predicting outcome of remedial education strategies for learning disabled children. *Pediatric Psychology, 3*, 23–28.

Hartlage, L. C., & Reynolds, C. R. (1981). Neuropsychological assessment and the individualization of instruction. In G. W. Hynd & J. E. Obrzut (Eds.), *Neuropsychological assessment and the school-age child: Issues and procedures* (pp. 355–378). New York: Grune & Stratton.

Hartlage, L. C., & Telzrow, C. F. (1983). The neuropsychological basis of educational intervention. *Journal of Learning Disabilities, 16*, 521–528.

Hertzig, M. E., & Birch, H. G. (1968). Neurological organization in psychiatrically disturbed adolescents. *Archives of General Psychiatry, 19*, 528–537.

Hynd, G. W. (Ed.). (1981a). Neuropsychology in the schools [Special issue]. *School Psychology Review, 10*(3).

Hynd. G. W. (1981b). Training the school psychologist in neuropsychology: Perspectives, issues, and models. In G. W. Hynd & J. E. Obrzut (Eds.), *Neuropsychological assessment and the school-age child* (pp. 379–404). New York: Grune & Stratton.

Hynd, G. W., & Obrzut, J. E. (1981). School neuropsychology. *Journal of School Psychology, 19*, 45–50.

Klonoff, H., & Low, M. (1974). Disordered brain function in young children and early adolescents: Neuropsychological and electroencephalographic correlates. In R. M. Reitan & L. A. Davison (Eds.), *Clinical neuropsychology: Current status and applications* (pp. 121–165). New York: Wiley.

Klonoff, H., Low, M., & Clark, C. (1977). Head injuries in children, a prospective 5 year follow-up. *Journal of Neurosurgery and Psychiatry, 12*, 1211–1219.

Klonoff, H., & Robinson, G. (1967). Epidemiology of head injuries in children: A pilot study. *Canadian Medical Association Journal, 96*, 1308–1311.

Klove, H. (1974). Validation studies in adult clinical neuropsychology. In R. M. Reitan & L. A. Davison (Eds.), *Clinical neuropsychology: Current status and applications*. New York: Wiley.

Lezak, M. D. (1983). *Neuropsychological Assessment*. (2nd Ed.). New York: Oxford University Press.

Luria, A. R. (1963). *Restoration of function after brain injury*. New York: MacMillan.

Luria, A. R. (1966). *Higher cortical functions in man*. Translated by B. Haigh. New York: Basic Books.

Luria. A. R. (1973). *The working brain*. London: Penguin Press.

Luria, A. R., & Majovski, L. V. (1977). Basic approaches used in American and Soviet clinical neuropsychology. *American Psychologist, 32*, 959–968.

Meier, M. J. (1981). Education for competency assurance in human neuropsychology: Antecedents, models, and directions. In S. B. Filskov & T. J. Boll (Eds.), *Handbook of clinical neuropsychology*. New York: Wiley & Sons.

Meier, N. R. F. (1963). Selector-integrator mechanisms in behavior. In N. R. F. Meier & T. C. Schneitlar (Eds.), *Principles of animal psychology* (pp. 621–649). New York: Dover Books.

Morris, R., Blashfield, R., & Satz, P. (1981). Neuropsychology and cluster analysis: Potential problems. *Journal of Clinical Neuropsychology, 3*, 79–99.

Parmelee, A. H., Beckwith, L., Cohen, S. E., & Sigman, M. (1983). Early intervention: Experience with preterm infants. In T. B. Brazelton & B. M. Lester (Eds.), *New approaches to developmental screening of infants*. New York: Elsevier Science Publishing Co., Inc.

Pfeiffer, S. I., Heffernan, L., & Pfeiffer, J. S. (1985). The prediction of possible learning disabilities in high risk infants. *International Journal of Clinical Neuropsychology 7*, 49.

Plaisted, J., Gustavson, J., Wilkening, G., & Golden, C. (1983). The Luria-Nebraska Neuropsychological Battery — Children's Revision: Theory and current research findings. *Journal of Clinical Child Psychology, 12,* 13–21.

Rattan, G., & Dean, R. S. (1987). The neuropsychology of children's learning disorders. In J. M. Williams and C. J. Long (Eds.), *The rehabilitation of cognitive disabilities.* New York: Plenum Press.

Reed, H. B. C., Reitan, R. M., & Klove, H. (1965). The influence of cerebral lesions on psychological test performance of older children. *Journal of Consulting Psychology, 29,* 247–251.

Reitan, R. M. (1955). An investigation of the validity of Halstead's measure of biological intelligence. *Archives of Neurology and Psychiatry, 73,* 28–35.

Reitan, R. M. (1969). *Manual for administration of neuropsychological test batteries for adults and children.* Indianapolis: Author.

Reitan, R. M. (1974). Methodological problems in clinical neuropsychology. In R. M. Reitan and L. A. Davison (Eds.), *Clinical neuropsychology: Current status and applications.* New York: John Wiley and Sons, Inc.

Reitan, R. M. (1976). Neurological and physiological bases of psychopathology. *Annual Review of Psychology, 27,* 189–216.

Reitan, R. M., & Davison, L. A. (1974). *Clinical neuropsychology: Current status and applications.* New York: John Wiley and Sons, Inc.

Report of the INS — Division 40 Task Force on Education, Accreditation and Credentialing. (1987). *The Clinical Neuropsychologist, 1,* 29–34.

Report of the Task Force on Education, Accreditation and Credentialing. (1981). *The INS Bulletin,* 5–10.

Rourke, B. P. (1975). Brain-behavior relationships in children with learning disabilities: A research program. *American Psychologist, 30,* 911–920.

Rourke, B. P. (1983). Reading and spelling disabilities: A developmental neuropsychological perspective. In U. Kirk (Ed.), *Neuropsychology of language, reading, and spelling.* New York: Academic Press.

Rourke, B. P., & Strang, J. D. (1983). Subtypes of reading and arithmetic disabilities: A neuropsychological analysis. In M. Rutter (Ed.), *Developmental neuropsychiatry.* New York: Guilford Press.

Russell, W. R., & Smith, A. (1961). Post-traumatic amnesia in closed head injury. *Archives of Neurology, 5,* 4.

Rutter, M. (1977). Brain damage syndromes in childhood: Concepts and findings. *Journal of Child Psychology and Psychiatry, 18,* 1–21.

Rutter, M. (1982). Developmental neuropsychology: Concepts, issues, and prospects. *Journal of Clinical Neuropsychology, 4,* 91–115.

Rutter, M., Chadwick, O., & Shaffer, D. (1982). Head injury. In M. Rutter (Ed.), *Developmental neuropsychiatry.* New York: Guilford Press.

Seidel, U. P., Chadwick, O. F., & Rutter, M. (1975). Psychological disorders in crippled children: A comparison study of children with and without brain damage. *Developmental Medicine and Child Neurology, 17,* 563–575.

Seretny, M. L., Dean, R. S., Gray, J. W., & Hartlage, L. C. (1986). The practice of clinical neuropsychology in the United States. *Archives of Clinical Neuropsychology, 1,* 90–94.

Smith, A. (1981). Principles underlying human brain functions in neuropsychological sequelae of different neuropathological processes. In S. B. Filskov & T. J. Boll (Eds.), *Handbook of clinical neuropsychology.* New York: Wiley.

Stone, B. J., Gray, J. W., & Dean, R. S. (1989). School psychologists in neurological settings. In R. C. D'Amato & R. S. Dean (Eds.), *The school psychologist in nontraditional settings.* Hillsdale, NJ: Lawrence Erlbaum Associates.

Strom, D. A., Gray, J. W., Dean, R. S., & Fischer, W. E. (1987). The incremental validity of the Halstead-Reitan Neuropsychological Test Battery in predicting achievement for learning disabled children. *Journal of Psychoeducational Assessment, 2,* 157–165.

Tramontana, M. G., Sherrets, S. D., & Golden, C. J. (1980). Brain dysfunction in youngsters with psychiatric disorders: Application of Salz-Reitan rules for neuropsychological diagnosis. *Clinical Neuropsychology, 2,* 118–123.

Wernicke, C. (1874). *Der aphasische symptomencomplex.* Breslau, Poland: Cohn and Weigert.

Woods, B. T., & Short, M. P. (1985). Neurological dimensions of psychiatry. *Biological Psychiatry, 20,* 192–198.

ANNOTATED BIBLIOGRAPHY

D'Amato, R. C., & Dean, R. S. (Eds.). (1989). *The school psychologist in nontraditional settings.* Hillsdale, NJ: Lawrence Erlbaum Associates.
This book explores the foundation for the practice of school psychology free of the setting. It emphasizes a melding of client needs with services in neurological settings. Individual chapters address the role, function, and training necessary in applying neuropsychological principles in pediatric settings.

Hartlage, L. C. & Telzrow, C. (Eds.). (1985). *The neuropsychology of individual differences.* New York: Plenum Press.
An edited book, this volume surveys the neurologic bases of differences in human behavior. The neuropsychology of development, perception, temperament, cognitive ability, language, learning disorders, and emotion are examined in depth.

Hynd, G. W. (1988). *Neuropsychological assessment in clinical child psychology.* Newburg Park, CA: Sage Publications.
Hynd offers an introduction to the utility, rationale, and methods of a neuropsychological approach in clinical practice with children. The book stresses a dynamic interaction between neurology and psychology. Neuropsychological assessment and diagnosis is the major approach of the book.

Reynolds, C. R., & Fletcher-Janzen, E. (Eds.). (1989). *Handbook of clinical child neuropsychology.* New York: Plenum Press.
The rather large volume examines the neurological foundations, diagnosis, intervention, and future of neuropsychology with child populations. Written with both Clinical and School Psychologists in mind, it offers a reference to most current issues in the practice of neuropsychology with children.

Rourke, B. P., Fish, J. L., & Strang, J. D. (1986). *Neuropsychological assessment of children.* New York: Guilford Press.
The authors here stress how neuropsychological assessment can be used in developing intervention strategies with children. Using intensive case studies, the authors examine the most common neurological based disorders of childhood.

34

Best Practices in Observation and Ecological Assessment

Edward S. Shapiro
Lehigh University

Christopher H. Skinner
The University of Alabama

OVERVIEW

Josh's teacher reported a serious management problem. Recently, Josh, a second-grader, had begun to call out in class. The teacher noted that she couldn't ask a question to the class without Josh blurting out the answer. When she would ask him to stop, Josh began to curse and defiantly announce that if he knew the answer he was going to shout it out. Josh's teacher reported that she had tried ignoring the behavior, reprimanding it, taking away privileges, sending him to the principal, all without success.

Marna's teacher reported to the psychologist that she was doing poorly in her math. A fourth-grader, she always finished her independent seatwork but rarely had anything correct. On math tests, she consistently scored less than 50% correct. In both cases, the school psychologist was asked for help in developing strategies to solve these problems.

How did these problems develop? What maintains Josh's behavior despite his getting reprimanded? Why does Marna continue to fail? Do Josh's problems reflect problems of poor impulse control? Do Marna's failures in math suggest she has poor mathematics abilities? Where do the problems of these children reside; somewhere "inside" the child? How would the psychologist proceed to help these teachers? Hopefully, the answers to these questions reside in recognizing that the difficulties encountered by these children develop in the context of a school ecology.

There is little doubt that the instructional ecology in which children learn plays an important part in the development of a child's adaptive or maladaptive behavior. When a student is referred to a school psychologist for evaluation owing to reported classroom behavior problems, it is clear that the observed behavior problems were shaped, at least in part, by events within the student's ecology. Likewise, a student who exhibits significant academic problems may have developed these deficits because of factors in the instructional environment. Clearly, learning does not occur in a vacuum. Responses made by children in schools occur within the context of many environmental variables that can affect performance. For example, peer attention, prompting procedures, consequent events, stimulus materials, feedback procedures, and error correction procedures may all be related to student performance. Of course, these circumstances within the school ecology often interact in complex ways with student characteristics, such as cognitions and emotions, to result in the observed behaviors. Bandura (1978) conceptualized this approach to understanding human behavior as reciprocal determinism.

Questions may arise as to how best to assess those aspects of the school ecology that can clearly impact upon student performance. Typically, interviewing of teachers and/or students, use of checklists and/or rating scales, and direct observation strategies are recommended as potential methods to conduct an evaluation of the environment (e.g., Shapiro & Lentz, 1985; Ysseldyke & Christensen, 1987). Of these methods, direct observation is perhaps the method that yields the most accurate data. Indeed, direct observation is recognized by most school psychologists as a critical part of an individual student evaluation (Anderson, Kratochwill, & Cancelli, 1984). Unfortunately, the term *direct observation* can refer to a wide range of procedures, many of which are very unsystematic. Although unsystematic observation may be useful as an initial hypothesis-generating strategy, it can often lead to unsystematic and possibly erroneous conclusions.

The purpose of the present chapter is to present the best practices in strategies for conducting assessment of the school ecology by employing direct observation methods. While such observational methods are applicable equally to children with behavioral or academic problems, specific observational instruments have been developed that target these two problem areas independently.

BASIC CONSIDERATIONS

Using strategies of direct observation assumes one has a conceptual understanding of the behavioral assessment process. Nelson and Hayes (1979) define behavioral assessment as "the identification of meaningful response units and their controlling variables (both current environmental and organismic) for the purposes of understanding and altering human behavior" (p. 491). For such assessment to be used, one must recognize the significant contribution that the environment can make to the children's academic and behavioral problems and be aware of the specific environmental variables that are known to be potentially related to a student's academic or behavioral problems.

For academic problems, substantial research over many years has provided indications that academic engaged time, combined with antecedent and consequent events surrounding academic performance, can serve as critical predictors of academic success (Rosenshine, 1981; Lentz & Shapiro, 1986). Table 1 provides a listing of these variables along with the assessment method most likely to be useful in obtaining the particular information. As is evident from Table 1, direct observation can play an important role in collecting data on almost every variable.

When the problem presented is behavioral, not academic, variables similar to those identified for academic problems can also be specified. For example, various contingencies that surround behavior, such as teacher and peer attention, teachers' praise and reprimands, and rewards for performance of certain behavior, are known to have potentially strong effects on school behavior. Likewise, classroom structures such as the pattern of student's contacts with teachers and peers, grouping of students for instructional purposes, and frequency of response feedback can also affect the behavioral responses of students. It is of particular interest that the behavioral problems of students are probably best attacked by targeting academic skills rather than behavioral deficits directly (Hoge & Andrews, 1987). Additionally, behavior problems of students are likely to be related to cognitive and perceptual distortions of one's ability (e.g., self-efficacy) as well. The latter behaviors are generally not directly observable and usually are assessed through self-report only.

When a direct observation measure is chosen for assessing the environment surrounding a behavioral or academic problem, the assessment strategy employed must provide adequate data on the wide range of variables that are potentially influencing the observed problem. Thus, approaches to assessing the environment have been developed specifically to address problems in either the behavioral or academic areas.

TABLE 1
Classroom Ecological Variables and Related Assessment Methods

Variables	Behavior Interview	Direct Observation	Permanent Product
Engagement			
Scheduled time	X		
Allotted Time	X	X	
On-task		X	
Opportunities to respond	X	X	X
Response rate	X		X
Events concurrent with engagement			
Instruction	X	X	
Models	X	X	
Prompts		X	
Pacing		X	
Praise		X	
Error correction		X	
Contingencies			
Teacher attention		X	
Peer attention		X	
Accuracy feedback	X	X	
Class structure			
Grouping	X	X	
Pattern of contacts	X	X	
Competing behaviors	X	X	
Pre- or Postwork events			
Instructions	X	X	
Contingencies for completion			
Accuracy	X	X	
Performance feedback	X	X	
Teacher planning and evaluation	X	X	

BEST PRACTICES

Direct observation requires an independent observer to record overt behaviors and environmental conditions. These observations are typically conducted in the natural environment. Data are collected on behaviors that have been, or are likely to be, identified for behavior change. Because target behaviors may be elicited by specific stimuli and reinforced or maintained by events following the occurrence of the behavior, it is important to collect data on the antecedent conditions and consequent events surrounding these target behaviors.

Empirical and narrative methods of direct observation can be employed in the classroom. Empirical or quantitative methods can provide more precise data for evaluating preintervention and intervention behavior levels, but they require operational definitions of the target behaviors and the environmental conditions surrounding these target behaviors. In addition, a systematic method of recording these behaviors, conditions, and events must first be established. Narrative or descriptive methods are often useful in helping to establish these operational definitions and in choosing a recording method.

Both narrative and empirical methods of recording direct observation data require independent observers to be present. However, the presence of an observer in a classroom can cause reactive behavior change in both the teachers and the students. Johnson and Bolstad (1973) identified four factors that have shown to influence the amount of reactivity that can occur when observations are conducted in the natural setting. These factors include the conspicuousness of the observer, rationale for observation, personal attributes of the observer, and individual differences among subjects. Mechanical devices, such as one-way mirrors, and video or auditory recording devices make it possible to collect data in an unobtrusive manner, thereby reducing reactivity. Given that most schools are not equipped with such devices, the observer must enter the classroom and record data in as unobtrusive a manner as possible to reduce reactivity.

In order to reduce the conspicuousness of the observer, Saudargas and Fellers (1986) recommended that observers enter the classroom, proceed directly to the observation area, collect the data, and exit the classroom. During the observation period observers should ignore any approach by students and avoid any verbal or nonverbal response to behaviors in the classroom. Observers should move their head and eyes around occasionally to avoid staring directly at the target students for long periods of time. To reduce student reactivity that might be caused by the personal attributes of an observer Saudargas and Fellers (1986) recommended that the teacher explain the observer's presence in the classroom in a general manner (i.e., here to observe a typical class), but not introduce the observer to the class or interact with the observer after she or he enters the classroom.

Preobservation Interview

An important part of the observation process is an interview with the classroom teacher prior to collecting data. The interview helps to determine the best time to observe, where the target student(s) will be seated, where the observer will be positioned, and what the teacher will tell the students about the observer's presence in the classroom. Should the student be watched only when the target behavior is likely to occur? Should the student be observed at times when the behavior is not likely to occur as well, to provide a contrast? Should the student be observed during specific instructional activities within academic subjects (e.g., independent versus small-group activities in reading) or during similar instructional settings across different academic activities (e.g., independent seatwork in math and reading)? How many observations should be conducted? Choosing the best times to conduct observations is based primarily on the information gathered during these interviews as well as the practical limitations on one's schedule. From the teacher, it might be learned that the target student typically exhibits problems during one type of instructional setting (e.g., independent seatwork) across academic activities. In this case, it would be necessary, and helpful for interpreting the data, for observations to be conducted across two or more academic activities for which independent seatwork is assigned.

The problem of how many observations to conduct is somewhat more complex and is clearly linked to the results of the observations. For information to be useful, it must be a clear reflection of the student's behavior across time. Thus, observation obtained at a single point in time may not be very representative of the overall level of the student's behavior. Therefore, at least three observations ideally should be obtained so that a trend can be estimated. Although conducting several observations can certainly lend more confidence in the findings, it may be prohibited by practical limitations of scheduling. In completing an evaluation of a student school psychologists may be faced with opportunities to conduct direct observations during only one 45-minute period. Hence, it is important to always ask teachers after an observation has been completed whether they believe the student's responses during the direct observation period were typical of other days. If the teacher indicates that the student's behavior was indeed typical, subsequent observations, although always desirable, may not have to be obtained. It is important to recognize, however, that should the teacher indicate that the student's behavior during the observation period was not typical, additional observation data must be collected for the data to be meaningful. Over time, data that reflect stability are always desired. The possibility must be kept in mind that the problem is actually the variability of the student's behavior ("He's always different, I can never predict his behavior from day-to-day"), and that observations over time may end up showing little stability.

Narrative Recording

Narrative recording requires an independent observer to provide a written description of observable events. These descriptions can be used to identify and operationally define target behaviors, antecedents, and consequences. In addition, this information is useful for determining which quantifiable method(s) of recording behaviors will be most practical and still provide the most accurate and reliable data. Common forms of narrative data collection include daily logs, descriptive time sampling, and antecedent-behavior-consequent (A-B-C) analysis.

Teachers often use daily logs that include a general description of the subject's behavior. An independent observer can perform the same task by merely entering the classroom, observing the subject's behavior, and writing down what is observed. These observations can provide useful information about the topography of target behaviors. Making and recording such observations at predetermined intervals (e.g., every 2 minutes) is called descriptive time sampling. This more systematic method of recording behaviors provides time for the observer to record behaviors and can yield rough estimates of behavior rates. These rough estimates of behavior rates can aid in the selection of a practical and precise method for recording data quantitatively.

Antecedent-behavior-consequent analysis requires an independent observer to provide a written sequential description of the subject's behaviors and the immediate antecedent conditions and consequent events that surround them. This

information can be used to identify antecedent stimuli that may elicit specific behaviors and consequent events that may maintain these behaviors. Knowledge of these environmental conditions can lead to interventions that may alter present patterns of responding.

The above forms of narrative recordings are particularly valuable in the initial stages of assessment, in that they can aid in the development of a more empirical method of recording data. Because narrative recordings are subjective and lack operational definitions, they are difficult to empirically verify, and obtaining inter-observer agreement is nearly impossible.

Recording Behaviors Empirically

Recording behaviors empirically requires operational definitions of behaviors. Operational definitions must be clear enough that another trained observer can agree on occurrence rates or durations of these behaviors over time. The definitions must have face validity — that is, they must be broad enough to include slightly different topographies of the target student behavior(s) but still exclude untargeted behaviors. Thus, it is often useful to provide examples of behaviors that would and would not be recorded under an operational definition. Given that surrounding antecedent and consequent events may be controlling classroom behaviors, operational definitions of these events must also be provided.

Narrative recordings, checklists, rating scales, and interviews all provide data useful when developing operational definitions. Another extremely valuable source for developing operational definitions can be found in the literature. Most research that employs direct observation includes operational definitions in the reports. Furthermore, a variety of codes have been developed that include operational definitions of teacher and student behavior.

Obtaining data through direct observation once operational definitions are established requires specific methods of data collection. These methods employ strategies aimed at recording all instances of behavior as it is actually occurring or under conditions of time sampling.

Continuous recording techniques. Counting the number of times a behavior occurs (events) or the time in which the behavior is observed (duration) requires continuous observation of target behaviors and yields very precise data on behavior levels. During event recording an observer merely records the number of times operationally defined behaviors occur within a specified time period. Any device capable of tallying occurrences (paper and pencil, golf counters, grocery store counter, etc.) can be used during event recording. Event recording is most effective when behaviors have discrete beginnings and ends and low to moderate rates of occurrence, and persist for short periods of time (e.g., completing a science problem, throwing paper). Behaviors such as playing, foot tapping, and on-task are difficult to tally by event recording, since they do not have specific beginning and ending points. In some instances behaviors such as verbal aggression, which occur infrequently in response bursts, can be operationally defined as a larger set of related behaviors. Thus, *outburst* can be defined such that 15 instances of using inappropriate language and making 10 threats can be scored as a single verbal aggressive event. However, the end point of the outburst must be defined. In the above example, the verbal aggressive outburst could be said to be over when no screaming, threatening, or swearing occurs for 30 seconds.

As long as the duration of observation periods are held constant across observations, event data can be reported as total number of occurrences per observation. Rate measures, however, are a more common method of reporting event data. A rate is calculated by dividing the number of behaviors recorded by the amount of observation time. Four verbally aggressive outbursts per day or 6 problems completed per minute are examples of rate measures. Rate measures allow comparison of behavior levels when observation intervals are not equal.

Duration recording requires the use of a timing device (stopwatch) to measure the length of time from the beginning to the end of a response or the latency between the presentation of a stimulus and the occurrence of a response. Either way, duration recording is often difficult because beginnings and endings of responses must be precisely defined and monitored while the observer records behaviors and manipulates the timing device.

Although duration data are sometimes difficult to collect, they can provide critical information. For example, the duration of a verbal outburst may provide more socially significant information than the rate of such behaviors. Some students have difficulty making transitions from one task to another. For these students latency measures involving the time between the stimulus and response can be important.

Time sampling methods. Time sampling recording methods are often employed when event or duration recording is hindered by the difficulty of recording behaviors, by the occurrence of many separate student and teacher behaviors at the same time, and by the inability to observe subjects continuously in all settings. During time sampling, observation periods are divided into shorter timed intervals. Thus, the observer is not required to continuously record each behavior being measured throughout the observation period. Rather, the observer is merely required to record the presence or absence of operationally defined behaviors within each time interval. Intervals can be marked by using a stopwatch or an audiotape that has been previously prepared. The length of the interval can vary. Typically, behaviors of higher rates, or duration are recorded in shorter intervals, whereas longer intervals can be employed for lower-rate behaviors. Data are then reported by calculating the percentage of intervals in which the behavior was observed. For example, if 10 intervals were observed and the target behavior (on task) was recorded in six intervals, the report would read that the subject was on task during 60% of the observed intervals. Partial-interval, whole-interval, and momentary time sampling can all be used to record observational data.

Partial-interval recording requires the observer to score the interval positive for an operationally defined target behavior if it is observed at any time during that interval. After an interval is so scored, the observer is no longer required to monitor that behavior until the next interval begins. Partial-interval recording is most appropriate when low-rate behaviors (fighting) are observed over long intervals (hours). Using whole-interval recording requires that the target behavior be observed for the entire interval before that interval is scored positive. Whole-interval recording is practical when continuous behaviors (on task) are scored across intervals of short to moderate length. Momentary recording is tallying behaviors positive in an interval only if they are observed at the moment that an interval ends. All occurrences before or after this moment are left unscored. Both fixed and variable interval lengths can be employed when momentary time sampling is being used (Test & Heward, 1984).

Although time sampling techniques have practical advantages over continuous recording techniques (events and duration recording), the data from time sampling methods are only estimates of actual durations of target behaviors. Research has shown that partial-interval recording consistently overestimates actual behavior durations, whole-interval recording consistently underestimates behavior durations, and momentary recording both under- and overestimates true behavior durations unpredictably (Powell, Martindale, Kulp, Martindale, & Bauman, 1977). The measurement error involved with these estimates requires cautious interpretation of time sampling data. Test and Heward (1984) have shown how momentary recordings from the same series of videotapes can cause erroneous interpretation of increasing or decreasing trends when continuous observation reveals stable levels of responding.

Direct Observation Systems

Developing an empirical recording method of observation can be difficult and time-consuming. First, student behaviors and environmental events must be operationally defined. Then the variability, duration, rate, and topographies of these observable behaviors and events must be analyzed in order to choose the most efficient and precise method of recording these observations. Finally, practice is required before the observer can record the data reliably and accurately. Fortunately, several systems have been developed that provide accurate, reliable, and useful data for a wide range of academic and behavior problems in the classroom.

Classroom observation systems for behavior problems. The Western Michigan University School Psychology Program has developed a classroom observation protocol that combines narrative and time sampling recording (Alessi & Kaye, 1983). The interval length and the type of time sampling employed is left up to the observer. In addition to noting instructional descriptors, observers are required to empirically record four student behaviors (on-task, verbal off-task, motor off-task, and passive off-task) and five categories of student/teacher's response to the student in reaction to these behaviors (attention to all, positive attention to pupil, negative attention to pupil, no attention to pupil, and neutral attention to pupil). Spaces are provided for the observer to record short narrative descriptions of student behaviors. This protocol also provides columns for recording data on occurrences of target behavior by a comparison student or percentage occurrence by all students in the class.

Alessi and Kaye's (1983) system is more flexible than most in that it includes narrative recordings, choice of observation intervals, and choice of time sampling methods. Observers must have enough information about the topographies, variability, rate, and duration of the observed behaviors to select the proper interval length and time sampling. The flexibility of the system allows a variety of student behaviors to be recorded across many different environments. Additionally, because various professionals can adapt the system to meet their own needs, all service providers working with a child being observed can become familiar with the system; this allows for better communication in discussing the resulting data.

The State–Event Classroom Observation System, Research Edition (SECOS-R) (Saudargas & Fellers, 1986) is a more structured system than the Western Michigan protocol. The SECOS-R requires the observer to record occurrences of 15 student behaviors and 6 teacher behaviors that are common in most classrooms. State behaviors are recorded by momentary time sampling because they typically vary in duration and are often continuous (i.e., looking around). The recommended interval is 15 seconds. Additionally, a number of discrete behaviors that typically occur at moderate to low rates are observed (e.g., raise hand, out of seat) by event recording within each interval.

The greater number of operational definitions and the requirement to record several behaviors continuously may make the SECOS-R more difficult to learn than the Western Michigan protocol. Once learned, however, the SECOS-R may be easier to implement consistently, because the observer is not required to define interval lengths and choose the time sampling method, since they are defined by the protocol. This consistency may also reduce the number of misinterpretations of shared data that could occur when data are collected by different observers (e.g., whole-interval data compared with partial-interval data).

Both the SECOS-R and the Western Michigan observation systems can be used to identify and empirically measure levels of aberrant behaviors in the classroom. More importantly, these recordings can provide sequential data on antecedent conditions (e.g., group size, approach other child) and consequent events (e.g., attention, disapproval) that immediately surround student behaviors. By examining the data on environmental conditions that surround the target behaviors, psychologists can recommend changes in the classroom environment (e.g., ignore thumb sucking) that may alter aberrant patterns of responding.

Classroom observation systems for academic problems. Both the SECOS-R and the Western Michigan observation systems can provide data that can be used to help remediate academic problems in the classroom. The SECOS-R requires observers to record some antecedent instructional behaviors and consequent events (e.g., directions, teacher's approach for schoolwork) and student academic behaviors (e.g., schoolwork, raise hand). Similarly, the Western Michigan protocol provides information about the observed student's levels of on-task behavior and the teachers' and other students' responses to the target student's on- and off-task behaviors. By analyzing sequential data from either of these codes, it may be possible to determine which instructional variables and consequent events surround student academic and nonacademic behaviors.

Although the SECOS-R and the Western Michigan systems were developed to provide information on a variety of classroom problems, researchers at the Juniper Gardens Children's Project have developed several observation systems that focus primarily on academic responding. Research conducted with the Code for Instructional Structure and Student Academic Response (CISSAR) (Stanley & Greenwood, 1981) was successful in identifying specific ecological variables and student behaviors that correlated highly with increased achievement gains. For example, Greenwood, Delquadri, and Hall (1984) compared a classwide peer-tutoring intervention with instruction led by a teacher. The results showed that academic achievement gains were greater under the peer-tutoring intervention. By using the CISSAR these researchers were also able to identify specific student behaviors and the ecological correlates of these behaviors that covaried with achievement levels.

Using the results of various research studies, Greenwood and Carta (1987) developed an abbreviated version of the CISSAR. This version is easier to use than

	W	TP	RA	TA	RS	AT	OA	LA	D	OI
Rr										
Wb										
Ws										
Pp										
L1										
Om										
Tsd										
SSd										
Am										
NM										

School _____

Class _____

Teacher _____

Student _____

Activity _____

Primary Group _____

Date _____ Observer _____ Start _____ Stop _____

FIGURE 1. Observation data collection form from the abbreviated version of the CISSAR. From ''An ecobehavioral interaction analysis of instruction within special education; by C. R. Greenwood and J. J. Carta, May, 1987, *Focus on Exceptional Children, 19*(9). Copyright 1987 by Love Publishing Company. Reprinted by permission.

the original CISSAR because it includes only those ecological variables and student responses that were found to be significantly related to academic achievement. The abbreviated CISSAR requires observers to record two categories of ecological variables: activities and task/materials. Under activities the observer is required to code the content area being covered during the observation period (e.g., mathematics). Task/materials to be coded include eight stimuli ranging from fetch/put away to specific academic materials such as worksheets. Seven active academic response categories can be coded, including answer question, ask question, task participation, read silently, read aloud, academic task, and write. The two other student response categories scored are attention and other behavior. Figure 1 provides a copy of the data collection sheet for this code.

Passive attention is not included as an academic response, whereas it is included in the academic response category of schoolwork on the SECOS-R, and on-task on the Western Michigan protocol. This is because several research studies conducted with the code showed that high levels of student attention did not result in very significant achievement gains compared to high rates of active academic responding (Greenwood & Carta, 1987).

This observation system is relatively easy to use because the ecological variables are scored prior to the recording of students' behaviors. Given that these variables change rather slowly, the observer is free to monitor and record student behaviors. Student behaviors are recorded by momentary time sampling with 10-second intervals. In order to get an adequate sample of student behaviors, Greenwood and Carta (1987) recommend observing and recording periods of no less than 15 minutes.

The abbreviated CISSAR code is very practical and useful for recording academic responding in the classroom. By providing categories for a number of academic responses and various academic ecological variables, the data from the abbreviated CISSAR should be useful in developing instructional strategies that lead to greater achievement gains. Although little research has been conducted with the abbreviated CISSAR, this system was developed from extensive empirical research on the original CISSAR. There can be little doubt that this abbreviated version will also prove to be useful in identifying specific instructional procedures that will result in increased gains in achievement.

Assessing the academic environment. Like the SECOS-R and the CISSAR codes, a system for assessing the instructional environment that incorporates some direct observation strategies has also been developed. The Instructional Environment Scale (TIES) (Ysseldyke & Christensen, 1987) was designed to provide a method for systematically describing the events that are known to surround student academic responses and to serve as a mechanism for beginning to design instructional interventions. Although the scale primarily uses a rating scale format, it also employs teacher interviews, student interviews, and narrative recording through direct observation. The scale was based on an evaluation of 12 components of effective instruction that are supported widely through the literature: instructional presentation, classroom environment, teacher expectations, cognitive emphasis, motivational strategies, relevant practice, academic engaged time, informed feedback, adaptive instruction, progress evaluation, instructional planning, and student understanding. Semistructured interviews are conducted with both teachers and students to obtain their perceptions of the instructional process. Direct observations are conducted by having observers record in a narrative fashion information pertaining to all items except instructional planning and student understanding. Observers then assign overall ratings based on a four-point scale in each area. The data obtained are then examined for potential alterations in the instructional environment that can be made and would be likely to have significant impact on student performance.

Although the TIES provides an important conceptual framework for examining the instructional environment, it is important to recognize that the data obtained from the instrument are not based on empirically derived categories. Consequently, training in the use of the instrument is crucial to its usefulness in the classroom assessment process.

SUMMARY

What happened to Josh and Marna? After meeting with Josh's teacher, the school psychologists learned that Josh's calling out seemed to occur primarily during math. It appeared that Josh was really quite good in math and became very excited to demonstrate to his teacher that he indeed "knew his stuff." The psychologist then conducted two 30-minute observations with the SECOS-R. The results of this observation showed that Josh engaged in approximately 3 callouts every 5 minutes (compared to only one callout every 15 minutes for randomly selected peers). Interestingly, Josh was engaged in schoolwork in almost 95% of the observed intervals. He was also found to be engaged in interactions with either the teacher or other students for 45% of the observations. These data became the baseline against which reductions in callouts were to be judged after an intervention program was planned.

The psychologist decided to observe Marna during math by using the abbreviated version of the CISSAR code. The observation showed that although Marna had high levels of engaged behavior, over 70% of these observations involved passive engagement such as attention to task or reading silently. She spent only 20% of her time engaged in academic talk or writing. Additionally, most of the time in math was spent working on worksheet or workbook activities and only a small amount of time (7%) was spent in teacher–student discussion. Again, these data helped to serve as baseline levels against which the effectiveness of interventions aimed at altering the classroom ecology could be gauged.

Evaluating a classroom environment can be accomplished effectively through the use of both direct observation and interviewing strategies. Neither of these procedures alone can successfully integrate the events that occur as instruction is proceeding. It is also clear that using any system of observation requires training. Substantial caution must be raised for anyone considering the use of systematic direct observation who has not had sufficient experience and direct training in administration, interpretation, and evaluation of direct observational strategies. An investment of time and energy to learn these techniques is certainly needed. The long-term benefits, however, are the improvement of data collection procedures, which can be useful in pinpointing specific behavioral deficiencies for remediation, developing strategies for intervention, providing empirically derived data on which success or failure of an intervention program can be clearly judged, providing accountability in the consultation process, and assisting in making decisions regarding student eligibility for remedial services.

It is important to note that although direct observation can be employed through both narrative and empirical data collection methods, nonempirical data collection processes may lead to erroneous conclusions. Clearly, there are times when narrative recording is critical to the information-collecting process. However, these types of recordings should almost invariably lead to development of systematic direct observation strategies. With the use of such methods, our consultative efforts should realize accountability and observable improvements.

REFERENCES

Alessi, G., & Kaye, J. H. (1983). *Behavior assessment for school psychologists*. Kent, OH: National Association of School Psychologists.

Greenwood, C. R. & Carta, J. J. (1987). An ecobehavioral interaction analysis of instruction within special education. *Focus on Exceptional Children, 19*, 3-13.

Greenwood, C. R., Delquadri, J., & Hall, R. V. (1984). Opportunity to respond and student academic performance. In W. L. Heward, T. E. Heron, J. Trap-Porter, & D. S. Hill (Eds.), *Focus on behavior analysis in education* (pp. 55-88). Columbus, OH: Merrill.

Johnson, S. M., & Bolstad, O. D. (1973). Methodological issues in naturalistic observation: Some problems and solutions. In L. A. Hamerlynck, L. E. Handy, & E. J. Mash (Eds.), *Behavior change: Methodology, concepts, and practice* (pp. 7-68). Champaign, IL: Research Press.

Powell, J., Martindale, B., Kulp, S., Martindale, A., & Bauman, R. (1977). Taking a closer look: Time sampling measurement error. *Journal of Applied Behavior Analysis, 10*, 325-332.

Saudargas, R. A., & Fellers, G. (1986). *State–event classroom observation system Research edition.* Knoxville, TN: University of Tennessee, Department of Psychology.

Stanley, S. O., & Greenwood, C. R. (1981). *CISSAR: Code for instructional structure and student academic response: Observer's manual.* Kansas City, KS: University of Kansas, Bureau of Child Research, Juniper Gardens Children's Project.

Test, D. W., & Heward, W. L. (1984). Accuracy of momentary time sampling: A comparison of fixed-and variable-interval observation schedules. In W. L. Heward, T. E. Heron, D. H. Hill, & J. Trap-Porter (Eds.), *Focus on behavior analysis in education* (pp. 177-196).

Ysseldyke, J. E., & Christensen, S. L. (1987). *TIES: The Instructional Environmental Scale.* Austin, TX: PRO-ED.

ANNOTATED BIBLIOGRAPHY

Alessi, G. (1988). Direct observation methods for emotional/behavioral problems. In E. S. Shapiro & T. R. Kratochwill (Eds.), *Behavioral assessment in schools: Conceptual foundations and practical applications* (pp. 14-75). New York: Guilford.
This chapter provides an excellent summary of both conceptual and practical issues related to conducting direct observations. Discussions of technical and practical problems related to using direct observation are included. A case example of an actual observation on a referred child is also provided.

Greenwood, C. R., & Carta, J. J. (1987). An ecobehavioral interaction analysis of instruction within special education. *Focus on Exceptional Children, 19*(9).
This volume describes in detail the abbreviated version of the CISSAR code. The instrument described here is easy to use and very applicable as a measure to systematically and directly assess the instructional environment. Definitions of behavior categories, copies of the code, and examples on how to analyze and interpret the resulting data are provided.

Lentz, F. E., Jr., & Shapiro, E. S. (1986). Functional assessment of the academic environment. *School Psychology Review, 15*, 336-345.
This article describes the importance of assessing the instructional environment. A conceptual model for the assessment is provided as well as examples of specific methods to conduct such an assessment.

Shapiro, E. S. (1987). *Behavioral assessment in school psychology.* Hillsdale, NJ: Erlbaum.
This book contains chapters that specifically describe the use of direct observation methods for assessing school-based problems. Furthermore, the book also examines strategies for assessing academic skills, adaptive behavior, and the use of consultation as a mechanism to link the assessment with intervention strategies.

35

Best Practices in Parent Training

Jack J. Kramer
University of Nebraska–Lincoln

OVERVIEW

The relationship between parental behavior and children's skill development has been documented in both healthy and disrupted family systems (e.g., Patterson, 1986; Stinnett & DeFrain, 1985). However, schools and school psychologists have not routinely included families in the educational process (Carlson & Sincavage, 1987). Parents appear to be an underutilized resource and school psychologists may be in position to advance the academic achievement and social well-being of children by better understanding how to teach parents to teach children.

The goal of this chapter is to provide school psychologists with information on best practices in the training of parents as behavior change agents. The phrase *behavior change agents* is critical in that this chapter deals with training techniques that attempt to alter parents' behavior so that they are able to change and manage the family environment effectively. Owing to space constraints, specific strategies for evaluating the effects of training on parents' knowledge (O'Dell, Tarler-Benlolo, & Flynn, 1979), attitude (e.g., Kazdin, 1977), and behavior (e.g., Forehand & McMahon, 1981) are not reviewed. Most of the reviewed research and suggested best practice deals with parents of preadolescent children, although many of the outcomes and practices reviewed here also apply to adolescents and their parents (e.g., Robin, 1980).

The origins of parent education have been reviewed by numerous authors (e.g., Beekman, 1977; Kramer, 1985; Polster & Dangel, 1984). Although speculation about best practices in parenting has flourished, only during the past two decades has the experimental analysis of parent training received attention. As a result of this research, most professionals working with parents would agree that training can improve parents' effectiveness, although much controversy has arisen regarding the content and format of such training. Three perspectives related to the "hows" and "whats" have dominated in the parent training literature: humanistic (e.g., Ginott, 1969; Gordon, 1970), Adlerian (e.g., Dinkmeyer & McKay, 1977; Popkin, 1983), and behavioral (e.g., Becker, 1971; Blechman, 1985).

Dembo, Sweitzer, and Lauritzen (1985) examined representative parent education research in the three areas cited above. In the humanistic area, research with PET was reviewed. The majority of the research consisted of unpublished theses and dissertations. Assessment of program effectiveness has focused primarily upon changes in parental child-rearing attitudes, with mixed results. Few investigations examined changes in parents' and/or children's behaviors; however, the available evidence indicated little or no change in the behavior of those targeted (see also, Doherty & Ruder, 1980).

Mothers' study groups were the primary training format examined with Adlerian training. Parent attitude measures in these studies have indicated positive changes in child-rearing attitudes, but little evidence of change in children's behavior (Dembo et al., 1985). Recently, Wiese (1989) evaluated the effects of parent participation in a popular Adlerian-based program (Popkin, 1983). Participants perceived themselves as better parents than did persons not participating in the parenting program. Although trained parents generally indicated a more tolerant attitude, they did not improve their knowledge of child management principles following training. Neither parents' reports of children's behavior or children's reports of self-concept changed as a function of training.

Behavioral research studies dominate the parent training literature. Dembo et al. suggest that these studies appear to have fewer methodological flaws and larger numbers of outcome variables and that they more often resulted in behavior change with parents and children than either PET or Adlerian studies. The scarcity and shortcomings of research on humanistic and Adlerian approaches make the ultimate impact of these methods difficult to judge. However, the research and best practices examined in this chapter leave little question about the potential impact of the parent training methods developed from behavioral research and applications.

BASIC CONSIDERATIONS

In this section some "basic" considerations for school psychologists interested in parent training are examined. The topics discussed below may not exhaust all possible considerations for school psychologists interested in parent training. It is clear, however, that factors such as trainer qualifications, goals and objectives, and systemic family issues all influence the eventual degree of training effectiveness and deserve careful examination.

Trainer Qualifications

The assumption that differences in the level of therapist skills have an impact on therapeutic outcome is neither novel nor startling. According to Bank, Patterson, and Reid (1987), "therapists must be experienced and trained clinicians who can deal with a variety of family problems, such as marital conflict, depression, and alcoholism, which may arise as issues during the course of the parent training" (p. 79). Unfortunately, little research attention has been given to analysis of the behavior of the "parent trainer" or "therapist." Research from the more general therapist effectiveness literature provides little additional help (e.g., Garfield & Bergin, 1978).

Many commercially available parent training programs suggest only that the trainers familiarize themselves with the specific materials used in that program and/or complete a brief workshop related to the use of these particular materials. Yet the difficulties encountered by therapists in training behavior-change skills are significant. Chamberlain and Baldwin (1988) note the likelihood of resistance from as many as 30% of parents involved in a training program, particularly when the training relates to specific techniques of discipline. Both clinical (Wahler & Dumas, 1984) and experimental (Patterson & Forgatch, 1985) evidence suggest that troubled parents do not react positively to therapists who confront them or attempt to teach new skills. Unfortunately, little information is available on the specific combinations or sequencing of therapist behavior that serve to promote effective interaction and change between therapist and client. The Best Practices section of this chapter does, however, provide information on specific training techniques that are important for therapists to use and skills that are critical for parents to possess.

Establishing Goals and Objectives

It is clear that parent training programs may, and do, have many different objectives, ranging from dissemination of information to social interaction to the training of new skills. The present emphasis falls on the latter objective; however, school psychologists engage in interactions with parents for many different reasons and the analysis of the reasons for working and interacting with parents should be an important precursor to any type of training activity.

A good example of the importance of establishing goals and the impact of doing so is provided by the research on the effectiveness of verbal (oral and written) instructional methods with parents. Although I will argue that most verbal methods are not effective in making parents better behavior-change agents, these approaches have been shown to increase parents' knowledge levels, and parents often report feeling better about themselves and/or their child management skills following participation (Kramer, in press). Although knowledge does not routinely lead to behavior change and feeling good is not the ultimate goal of training, these accomplishments should not be discarded. If a goal is to improve one's knowledge of child management and behavioral technology, verbal instruction may be a cost-effective method for accomplishing this goal. Parents completing group instruction typically report the experience as positive — no small accomplishment if one is concerned about parents' perceptions of their children's school, school system, and school psychologist.

The training of parents or any other behavior-change agent is a time-consuming and expensive activity. Training is even more difficult, and positive outcomes more difficult to obtain, if trainers fail to plan or are unaware of the importance of establishing goals and objectives for their training activities.

Understanding Systemic Factors

Before and during training, school psychologists should take care in assessing family systems. Research has indicated that factors such as low socioeconomic status (SES) (e.g., Dumas & Wahler, 1983), poor parental adjustment (e.g., Griest, Wells, & Forehand, 1979), and inaccurate parental perceptions of child behavior (e.g., Lobitz & Johnson, 1975) have a negative impact on training effectiveness. The importance of social relationships in parenting is also well documented (Wahler, 1980).

Research has increased our understanding of what works and also revealed that those most in need of training are the most difficult to influence (Dumas & Wahler, 1983; Wahler, 1980). Focus on a broader understanding of parents' and children's behavior as it exists in the family ecosystem has led to a better understanding both of the importance of the setting (e.g., the family and the community) on behavior and the impact of long-term patterns of dysfunctional behavior (e.g., aggression) in the analysis and remediation of unsatisfactory parent–child functioning. Examples of assessment instruments to be used for gathering data on family systems are presented later in the chapter when strategies for school-based implementation of parent training are examined.

BEST PRACTICES — A SUMMARY OF TWO DECADES OF INVESTIGATION OF PARENTS' CONCERNS AND PARENTS' SKILLS IN PARENT TRAINING

Many authors have provided reviews of the extensive parent training literature during the recent past, which has revealed evidence of the interest generated by this research (e.g., Dangel & Polster, 1984a; Kramer, in press; Moreland, Schwebel, Beck, & Wells, 1982; O'Dell, 1985; Sanders & James, 1983). For the purpose of this chapter, best practices are derived by examining (a) the kinds of problems that parents report; (b) the skills that lead to resolution of these problems; and (c) the training techniques that promote learning and generalization of skills with parents. Later, specific strategies for implementing best practices in schools are suggested.

Parents' Concerns

To begin with, it makes sense that parent training address problems that are of concern specifically to parents. Parents refer children for a variety of reasons and parent training has been used across many different referral concerns (e.g., Bauman, Reiss, Rogers, & Bailey, 1983; Dubey, O'Leary, & Kaufman, 1983; Golub, Espinosa, Damon, & Card, 1987; Muir & Milan, 1982; Stumphauzer, 1976). When examined more closely, the research on parent training reveals some common elements to the many specific problems faced by parents. Regardless of whether one uses a number of research articles (Rogers-Wiese & Kramer, 1988) or parent-referral data (Forehand, 1977), it is evident that researchers *and* parents have defined children's noncompliance as the major problem faced by parents of young children. Furthermore, significant levels of noncompliance in young children, especially when combined with aggression, often indicate serious family conflict (Patterson, 1982). As has been stated elsewhere (Kramer, in press),

> children in homes with high rates of noncompliance and aversive control are at-risk for serious problems as adolescents and adults if the problem of childhood noncompliance is not dealt with quickly and efficiently. Failure to teach parents skills to deal with these problems in early childhood appears to have serious long-term consequences for both children and parents.

It might be felt that the focus of this chapter on parent training with parents of preadolescent children who are experiencing noncompliance and aggression with their children is too narrow. I believe, however, that the vast majority of problems experienced by troubled parents has to do with the fact that they have not been effective at teaching their children to do what they think the children need to do. That is, either the children are refusing to comply with the rules and goals established by the parents or the parents have failed to establish rules and goals in the first place. In most instances it is believed that the failure of young children to learn the importance of rules and rule following has the potential for dire consequences in subsequent adolescent

and adult development (Robins, 1981). Whether we are talking about going to bed without crying and whining, eating a balanced diet, not stealing, coming home from school on time, doing homework, not hitting other children, or all of these behaviors combined in one child, parents most often come for help when they have been unable to teach children either specific or general rules of behavior. Most often, these problems can be considered failures of compliance that have resulted from poor management practices. School psychologists and teachers must be alert to the fact that significant levels of noncompliance and aggression in young children are important signs (or signals, markers, symptoms) that should be attended to without delay.

Of course, knowing about the existence of a problem doesn't necessarily lead to its resolution. What skills do parents need and how do we teach them to use these skills?

Parents' Skills

Differences between functional and dysfunctional parents have often been studied through examination of the differences that exist between clinic-referred and nonreferred children and families. This method reveals that factors such as parents' perception of children's behavior, marital adjustment, personal adjustment, and extrafamilial relationships are among the best predictors of the severity of family distress (O'Dell, 1985). Stinnett and DeFrain (1985) have identified a number of characteristics of "strong" families, including commitment to the family, appreciation and acknowledgment of family members' contributions, communication among family members, time together, spiritual wellness or commitment to some standard of behavior, and the ability to cope with stress.

Research investigating parent–child interaction over long periods of time (e.g., weeks, months, years) in naturalistic settings has begun only recently to appear. Longitudinal data from nonclinical populations suggest that "healthier" families tend to use more positive or prosocial teaching methods than do parents of clinic-referred children (Bank, Patterson, & Reid, 1987). It is also apparent from many training studies that parents who have learned or are about to learn to attend to children, model appropriate behaviors, deliver corrective feedback, avoid or de-escalate arguments, and provide consistent consequences for behavior are able to teach more efficiently and effectively (Kramer, in press; O'Dell, 1985). The programs developed by Barkley (1987) and Forehand and McMahon (1981) for working with the parents of noncompliant and defiant children, respectively, include the training of many of the skills listed above.

In summary, research has provided information about the general characteristics that tend to define populations seeking services for noncompliant and disobedient children. Research and practice have helped to identify many different skills that when taught in clinic or home settings tend to improve parenting effectiveness in disturbed family systems. When it comes to describing optimal conditions in healthy family systems, however, considerably less is known about the occurrence of specific behaviors and their frequency, duration, and sequence.

How Should Parents Be Trained?

Specific procedures used to train parents are identified below and the relative effectiveness of each approach is evaluated. Included in this examination are bibliotherapy, verbal instruction, modeling, direct training, and group instruction. Strategies for promoting generalization of training effects are also examined.

Bibliotherapy and other verbal approaches. There is little research that indicates that self-help manuals or other self-administered instruction materials serve to promote the development of behavior change skills in parents or any other group. Although examples of training success are available (e.g., Giebenhain & O'Dell, 1984; McMahon & Forehand, 1978), verbal materials given to parents

have less effect on skill development than do most other approaches.

Talking to parents, as is done in many short-term workshops, has not been shown to promote behavior change in a consistent manner. This is true even when instruction is provided by an "expert" (Ziarnik & Bernstein, 1982). This finding has been replicated across different training formats and content (Kramer, in press). Most published materials have undergone little or no experimental testing, and published texts vary a great deal in reading level and difficulty.

Studies that have compared the instructional effects of using different training procedures have generally found verbal approaches to be among the least effective (e.g., Flanagan, Adams, & Forehand, 1979; O'Dell, Flynn, & Benlolo, 1977). The equivocal nature of much of the research on the effects of verbal instructions lead one to seriously question the exclusive use of such procedures in the training of parents as behavior-change agents.

Modeling and direct instruction. As is characteristic of other instructional tasks, procedures that require the client to be engaged in the instructional process (e.g., Greenwood, Delquadri, & Hall, 1984) do better than those that require less involvement. Both modeling (e.g., Webster-Stratton, 1981) and interactive methods such as role-playing/behavioral rehearsal (e.g., Flanagan et al., 1979) have been shown to enhance learning. In addition to the importance of having an opportunity to practice overtly or covertly, the presence of corrective feedback generally enhances training effects (Bernal, Williams, Miller, & Reagor, 1972).

The Forehand and McMahon (1981) training program for parents of noncompliant children incorporates many different training procedures, with a focus on the learning of new skills. Parents are taught to attend to and describe the behavior of their children and to eliminate commands, questions, and criticisms. Handouts are given prior to the introduction of new skills (e.g., rewards, time-out), skills are modeled and practiced, feedback is provided immediately following practice, 10-minute homework is assigned daily, and "competence" must be demonstrated before a new skill is introduced. Many successful training programs combine training techniques in a manner similar to that described above, with written materials, modeling, behavioral rehearsal, and feedback included in most packages (Azrin & Foxx, 1974; Barkley, 1987; Braukmann, Ramp, Tigner, & Wolf, 1984; Lutzker, 1984; Patterson, Reid, Jones, & Conger, 1975).

There appears to be little doubt that training methods that more directly involve the client in the training process are more likely to lead to skill development than methods that only describe the changes that need to be made.

Group versus individual training. The evidence on group training is suggestive, but not definitive. Group training can be effective (Rinn, Vernon, & Wise, 1975); however, there is little question that a group's size affects the learning of its individual members (e.g., Bloom, 1984). The precise impact of group size on training effectiveness with parents is unknown. Furthermore, the interactive effects of variables such as group size, participant's characteristics, and training content have escaped serious investigation.

Interactive group training with parents appears to have the potential to reduce the cost of delivering behavior-change training to parents (e.g., Brightman, Baker, Clark, & Ambrose, 1982). At present, the potential is unrealized. Most parents in need of learning behavior-change skills are probably best served by individual or small-group (e.g., family) training.

Maintenance and generalization. The ability of parents to generalize trained skills over time (maintenance or temporal generalization) has received more attention than any other form of generalization. Positive outcomes ranging from 6–12 months (Forehand et al., 1979) to 3–9 years (Strain, Steele, Ellis, & Timm, 1982) have been obtained; however, the failure of parents to maintain skills has been a more consistent finding.

In the attempt to promote generalization of learned skills, trainers have used many different strategies, including social reinforcement delivered by trainers, peers, spouses, and significant others; repeated discussion of the potential benefits to be accrued from training; contracting; making continuation in training dependent on successful completion of assignments; rewards such as money or books; and return of fees for attendance or completion of assignments (O'Dell, 1985). The typical outcome is that these techniques enhance generalization, if in a somewhat modest fashion.

Research on generalization across settings, such as home to school and school to community, has yielded equivocal results. As with maintenance, the addition of therapist-controlled contingencies during (e.g., Rinn et al., 1975) and following (e.g., Muir & Milan, 1982) training enhances generalization across settings. When one goes beyond case study or small-group experimental research, however, and examines attempts to provide large numbers of parents with skills that can be maintained and transferred to new settings (McMahon & Forehand, 1984; Patterson, 1982; Wahler, 1980), the evidence is less convincing.

Although much less research has been conducted on the likelihood that training effects will transfer to other behaviors and siblings not included in the training, evidence does exist that suggests that parents can apply clinic-learned skills to behaviors that were not the focus of training (Koegel, Glahn, & Nieminen, 1978; Wells, Forehand, & Griest, 1980) and children who were not the targets of the skills being trained (Eyberg & Robinson, 1982).

In summary, we can train parents to use behavior-change skills, and parents can transfer skills across settings. Verbal methods may work with some parents, but most parents may need more direct intervention. Generalization can be enhanced if contingencies (natural or imposed) for generalization are applied either during or following training. It also seems clear from the research reviewed earlier that as the number of problems beyond the parent–child conflict increase, our ability to obtain generalization of skills to the natural environment decreases.

BEST PRACTICES — TRANSLATING RESEARCH INTO PRACTICE IN THE SCHOOLS

Review of the research in parent training reveals much to be excited about. Our understanding of human behavior and the influences that individual characteristics, environmental stimuli, and systemic events have on our ability to train effective parenting skills has advanced positively. The serious consequences of long-term patterns of dysfunctional behavior in children and families, and evidence of parents' ability to learn new skills for altering children's behavior, indicate that school psychologists should find a way to be involved with parents and parent training. There would appear to be ample opportunity for school psychologists to use the information learned during the last two decades to enhance the effectiveness of psychological services provided to children and families. The best practices offered below are advanced as specific possibilities and opportunities for how school psychologists might operationalize parent training in the schools.

1. Training environment. Few data are available from investigations of the nature of an "ideal" training environment. Most training programs for parents appear to have taken place in clinic settings (e.g., Barkley, 1987; Dumas & Wahler, 1983; Forehand & McMahon, 1981; Patterson & Forgatch, 1985), although examples of successful home-based programs are available (e.g., Shearer & Loftin, 1985).

Throughout the chapter the training program described by Forehand and McMahon (1981) has been cited as exemplary for its empirical foundation and clarity of training goals. In Table 1 the training setting used in the clinical research undertaken by these scientists and their colleagues is described in detail. The materials, rooms, and equipment

described here are not available in most schools. It is important, however, that school psychologists be aware of the nature of an "optimal" training environment so that they can approximate this setting in whatever ways possible.

2. Short-term, verbal workshops. Providers of psychological services must ask themselves serious questions about the reasons for conducting short-term, didactic workshops designed to improve behavior-change skills with parents. In general these workshops don't work, if "work" is defined as changing behavior in a reliable manner. However, these types of workshops may be useful as public relations tools and have been shown to improve parents' knowledge of the specific topics discussed. The available research indicates that even in the absence of behavior change, parents report positive feelings about the group experience.

3. Published materials and training packages. School psychologists should resist the temptation to pick up popular, commercially published materials unsupported by any validity data. Although surely controversial, it is suggested that practitioners abandon the use of such materials. Unfortunately, the most popular training programs (Dinkmeyer & McKay, 1977; Gordon, 1970; Popkin, 1983) have no empirical support. Practitioners who take care to design individualized training programs based on the specific problems presented by each client are much more likely to experience success training parents as behavior-change agents than those who routinely and reflexively use the most popular training packages.

4. Assessing family systems. The attenuating effect that family dysfunction and parental stress can have on training has been highlighted throughout this chapter. School psychologists involved in parent training should take care to assess family demographics, parents' functioning (e.g., Abidin and Lloyd, 1986), parents' knowledge (e.g., O'Dell et al., 1979), marital interaction (e.g., Stuart, 1983) and family dynamics (e.g., Eyberg & Robinson, 1981)

TABLE 1
The Training Environment — One Example

The parent training program employs a controlled learning environment in which to teach the parent to change maladaptive patterns of interactions with the child. Sessions are conducted in a clinic setting with individual families rather than in groups. Treatment occurs in clinic playrooms equipped with one-way mirrors for observation, sound systems, and bug-in-the-ear (Farrell Instruments) devices by which the therapist can unobtrusively communicate with the parent. A table, chairs, and several age-appropriate toys are in each playroom. A number of discrete parenting skills are taught in a systematic manner. The skills are taught to the parent by way of didactic interaction, modeling, and role playing. The parent also practices the skills in the clinic with the child while receiving prompting and feedback from the therapist by means of the bug-in-the-ear device. Finally, the parent employs these newly acquired skills in the home setting.

From *Parent Training: Foundations of Research and Practice* (McMahon & Forehand, 1984, p. 300) by R. F. Dangel and R. A. Polster (Eds.), 1984, New York: Guilford Press. Copyright 1984 by Guilford Press. Reprinted by permission.

in as thorough a manner as possible. Some training packages include most, if not all, of the components suggested above for assessing family systems (Barkley, 1987; Forehand & McMahon, 1981). Whether a trainer gathers this information formally, as suggested in the references cited above, or informally through observation and personal interaction is not important. However it is accomplished, the collection of this information is critical and has important implications for treatment.

5. Handouts and written materials. At a minimum, all school psychologists should have access to high-quality written materials that discuss basic skills and factual information about parent–child management and parent–child interaction. For example, handouts on effective use of specific procedures (e.g., rule setting, shaping and teaching new skills, time-out) and examples of specific ways in which parents can promote school progress (e.g., attending parent-teacher conferences, having reading materials available in the home, assisting in homework completion) would all seem useful and cost-effective ways of getting information to parents. The NASP Handbook of handouts that is currently in production may be one source of these types of materials. Furthermore, well-constructed homework assignments have been shown to enhance training effects in a consistent and reliable manner.

6. Videotapes and modeling. Videotaped materials that model needed skills appear to be an effective means of teaching parents about behavior change and are certainly less expensive than direct training. For some parents, videotapes and associated instructional materials, with minimal therapist contact, may be sufficient. By using videotapes during early stages of training the therapist is in a position to monitor progress and determine if additional direct training is necessary. Although there are a number of potential sources of videotapes, many of the materials published by Research Press (Box 31779, Champaign, IL 61820) appear to be of exceptional quality and appropriate for the types of training activities discussed in this chapter.

7. Role-playing, rehearsal, and direct intervention. Direct intervention may be necessary for many parents. In most cases, direct intervention may mean not only direct instruction of parenting skills, but also some degree of "maintenance" support as parents implement the skills in the natural environment. The data continue to suggest that role-playing and rehearsal with clients is necessary in order to develop and shape the skills parents require to implement behavior change with their children. Skills must be practiced in the presence of the therapist in order to provide the opportunity for direct feedback. Clients must then be given homework assignments that necessitate the practicing of these skills in the home. As with any behavioral skill, those who are provided explicit instruction and multiple opportunities for practice and feedback are more likely to learn the skills than those who are not provided the opportunity for practice.

SUMMARY

In a perfect world, school psychologists would always use the most effective training methods for training parents in the shortest amount of time. This chapter has emphasized best practices, and it is important to know how to train parents *most* effectively. The ultimate goal of training, however, is to obtain parental competence in the areas that are the focus of training. Furthermore, we do not always have state-of-the-art equipment and parent training seldom proceeds in a paradigmatic, textbook fashion. Perhaps in our efforts to train parents as behavior-change agents the single most important step we can take towards assuring learning is to understand and operationalize the skills we want parents to learn and continue to provide training and feedback until parents achieve stipulated levels of competence. That is, it is much more important to continue to provide training to parents until they are able to consistently use the skills being trained than it is to only provide training during an 8-week workshop or to use a commercially available program because it is convenient.

There will be those who say there is not enough time for school psychologists to implement the kinds of strategies suggested above — and in many instances they may be correct. If the goal of our training efforts is to improve parental skills, however, the strategies suggested above are what it takes. Whether school psychologists provide training or whether we refer our clients in need of training to other mental health professionals is irrelevant. What is important is that practitioners understand the effort and the cost involved in effective parent training. To date, there is little evidence that shortcuts work.

REFERENCES

Abidin, R. R., & Lloyd, B. (1986). *Parenting stress index.* West Charlottesville, VA: Pediatric Psychology Press.

Azrin, N. H., & Foxx, R. M. (1974). *Toilet training in less than a day.* New York: Simon & Schuster.

Bank, L., Patterson, G. R., & Reid, J. B. (1987). Delinquency prevention through training parents in family management. *Behavior Analyst, 10,* 75-82.

Barkley, R. A. (1987). *Defiant children: A clinician's manual for parent training.* New York: Guilford.

Bauman, D. E., Reiss, M. L., Rogers, R. W., & Bailey, J. S. (1983). Dining out with children: Effectiveness of a parent advice package on pre-meal inappropriate behavior. *Journal of Applied Behavior Analysis, 16,* 55-68.

Becker, W. C. (1971). *Parents are teachers.* Champaign, IL: Research Press.

Beekman, D. (1977). *The mechanical baby: A popular history of the theory and practice of child raising.* Westport, CT: Lawrence Hill.

Bernal, M. E., Williams, D. E., Miller, W. H., & Reagor, P. A. (1972). The use of videotape feedback and operant learning principles in training parents in management of deviant children. In R. D. Rubin, H. Fernstermacher, J. D. Henderson, & L. P. Ullman (Eds.), *Advances in behavior therapy* (pp. 149-176). New York: Academic.

Blechman, E. A. (1984). Competent parents: Competent children. Behavioral objectives of parent training. In R. F. Dangel & R. A. Polster (Eds.), *Parent training: Foundations of research and practice* (pp. 34-63). New York: Guilford.

Blechman, E. A. (1985). *Solving child behavior problems at home and at school.* Champaign, IL: Research Press.

Bloom, B. (1984). The 2 sigma problem: The search for methods of group instruction as effective as one-to-one tutoring. *Educational Researcher, 13,* 4-16.

Braukmann, C. J., Ramp, K. K., Tigner, D. M., & Wolf, M. M. (1984). The teaching family approach to training group-home parents: Training procedures, validation research, and outcome findings. In R. F. Dangel & R. A. Polster (Eds.), *Parent training: Foundations of research and practice* (pp. 144-161). New York: Guilford.

Brightman, R. P., Baker, B. L., Clark, D. B., & Ambrose, S. A. (1982). Effectiveness of alternative parent training formats. *Journal of Behavior Therapy and Experimental Psychiatry, 13*, 113-117.

Burke, A. J. (1984). Students' potential for learning contrasted under tutorial and group approaches to instruction (Doctoral dissertation, University of Chicago, 1983). *Dissertation Abstracts International, 44*, 2025A.

Carlson, C. I., & Sincavage, J. (1987). Family-oriented school psychology practice: Results of a national survey of NASP members. *School Psychology Review, 16*, 519-526.

Chamberlain, P., & Baldwin, D. (1988). Client resistance to parent training. Its therapeutic management. In T. R. Kratochwill (Ed.), *Advances in school psychology* (pp. 126-143). Hillsdale, NJ: Erlbaum.

Dangel, R. F., & Polster, R. A. (Eds.). (1984). *Parent training: Foundations of research and practice.* New York: Guilford.

Dembo, M. H., Sweitzer, M., & Lauritzen, P. (1985). An evaluation of group parent education: Behavioral, PET, and Adlerian programs. *Review of Educational Research, 55*, 155-200.

Dinkmeyer, D., & McKay, G. (1977). *Systematic training for effective parenting.* Circle Pines, MN: American Guidance Service.

Doherty, W. J., & Ruder, R. G. (1980). Parent effectiveness training: Criticisms and comments. *Journal of Marital and Family Therapy, 11*, 263-270.

Dubey, D. R., O'Leary, S. G., & Kaufman, K. F. (1983). Training parents of hyperactive children in child management: A comparative outcome study. *Journal of Abnormal Child Psychology, 11*, 229-246.

Dumas, J. E., & Wahler, R. G. (1983). Predictors of treatment outcome in parent training: Mother insularity and socio-economic advantage. *Behavioral Assessment, 5*, 301-313.

Eyberg, S. M., & Robinson, E. A. (1981). *Dyadic parent–child interaction coding system: A manual.* Portland, OR: Author.

Eyberg, S. M., & Robinson, E. A. (1982). Parent-child interaction training: Effects on family functioning. *Journal of Clinical Child Psychology, 11*, 130-137.

Flanagan, S., Adams, H. E., & Forehand, R. (1979). A comparison of four instructional methods for teaching parents the use of time out. *Behavior Therapy, 10*, 94-102.

Forehand, R. (1977). Child noncompliance to parental requests: Behavioral analysis and treatment. In M. Hersen, R. M. Eisler, & P. M. Miller (Eds.), *Progress in behavior modification* (Vol. 5, pp. 111-147). New York: Academic.

Forehand, R., & McMahon, R. J. (1981). *Helping the noncompliant child: A clinician's guide to parent training.* New York: Guilford.

Forehand, R., Sturgis, E. T., McMahon, R. J., Aguar, D., Gree, K., Wells, K. C., & Breiner, J. (1979). Parent behavioral training to modify child noncompliance: Treatment generalization across time and from home to school. *Behavior Modification, 3*, 3-25.

Garfield, S. L., & Bergin, A. E. (1978). *Handbook of psychotherapy and behavior change: An empirical analysis* (2nd ed.). New York: Wiley.

Giebenhain, J. E., & O'Dell, S. L. (1984). Evaluation of a parent training manual for reducing children's fear of the dark. *Journal of Applied Behavior Analysis, 17*, 121-125.

Ginott, H. G. (1969). *Between parent and child.* New York: Avon.

Golub, J. S., Espinosa, M. A., Damon, I., & Card, J. (1987). A videotape parent education program for parent education. *Child Abuse and Neglect, 11*, 255-265.

Gordon, T. (1970). *Parent effectiveness training.* New York: McKay.

Greenwood, C. R., Delquadri, J. C., & Hall, R. V. (1984). Opportunity to respond and student academic achievement. In W. L. Heward, T. E. Heron, D. S. Hill, & J. Porter-Trap (Eds.), *Focus on behavior analysis in education* (pp. 58-88). Columbus, OH: Merrill.

Griest, D. L., Wells, K. C., & Forehand, R. (1979). An examination of predictors of maternal perceptions of maladjustment in normal and deviant children. *Journal of Abnormal Psychology, 88*, 277-281.

Kazdin, A. E. (1977). Assessing the clinical or applied importance of behavior change through social validation. *Behavior Modification, 1*, 427-452.

Koegel, R. L., Glahn, T. J., & Nieminen, G. S. (1978). Generalization of parent training results. *Journal of Applied Behavior Analysis, 11*, 95-109.

Kramer, J. J. (1985). Best practices in parent training. In A. Thomas & J. Grimes (Eds.), *Best practices in school psychology* (pp. 263-273). Kent, OH: National Association of School Psychologists.

Kramer, J. J. (in press). Training parents as behavior change agents: Successes, failures, and suggestions for school psychologists. In T. B. Gutkin & C. R. Reynolds (Eds.), *The handbook of school psychology* (2nd ed.). New York: Wiley.

Lobitz, G. K., & Johnson, S. M. (1975). Normal vs. deviant children: A multi-method comparison. *Journal of Abnormal Child Psychology, 3*, 353-374.

McMahon, R. J., & Forehand, R. (1978). Nonprescription behavior therapy: Effectiveness of a brochure in teaching mothers to correct their children's inappropriate mealtime behavior. *Behavior Therapy, 9*, 814–820.

McMahon, R. J., & Forehand, R. (1984). Parent training for the noncompliant child: Treatment outcome, generalization, and adjunctive therapy procedures. In R. F. Dangel & R. A. Polster (Eds.), *Parent training: Foundations of research and practice* (pp. 298–328). New York: Guilford.

Moreland, J. R., Schwebel, A. I., Beck, S., & Wells, R. (1982). Parents as therapists: A review of the behavior therapy parent training literature — 1975 to 1981. *Behavior Modification, 6*, 250–276.

Muir, K. A., & Milan, M. A. (1982). Parent reinforcement of child achievement: The use of a lottery to maximize parent training effects. *Journal of Applied Behavior Analysis, 15*, 455–460.

O'Dell, S. L. (1985). Progress in parent training. In M. Hersen, R. M. Eisler, & Miller (Eds.), *Progress in behavior modification* (Vol. 19, pp. 57–108). New York: Academic.

O'Dell, S. L., Flynn, J., & Benlolo, L. (1977). A comparison of parent training techniques in child behavior modification. *Journal of Behavior Therapy and Experimental Psychiatry, 8*, 261–268.

O'Dell, S. L., Tarler-Benlolo, L., & Flynn, J. M. (1979). An instrument to measure knowledge of behavioral principles as applied to children. *Journal of Behavior Therapy and Experimental Psychiatry, 10*, 29–34.

Patterson, G. R. (Ed.). (1982). *Coercive family process.* Eugene, OR: Castalia.

Patterson, G. R. (1986). Performance models for antisocial boys. *American Psychologist, 41*, 432–444.

Patterson, G. R., & Forgatch, M. S. (1985). Therapist behavior as a determinant for client noncompliance: A paradox for the behavior modifier. *Journal of Consulting and Clinical Psychology, 53*, 846–851.

Patterson, G. R., Reid, J. B., Jones, R. R., & Conger, R. E. (1975). *A social learning approach to family intervention: Families with aggressive children* (Vol. 1). Eugene, OR: Castalia.

Polster, R. A., & Dangel, R. F. (1984). Behavioral parent training: Where it comes from and where it's at. In R. F. Dangel & R. A. Polster (Eds.), *Parent training: Foundations of research and practice* (pp. 1–12). New York: Guilford.

Popkin, M. H. (1983). *Active parenting.* Atlanta, GA: Active Parenting.

Rickert, V. I., Sottolano, D. C., Parrish, J. M., Riley, A. W., Hunt, F. M., & Pelco, L. E. (1988). Training parents to become better behavior managers: The need for a competency-based approach. *Behavior Modification, 12*, 475–496.

Rinn, R. C., Vernon, J. C., & Wise, M. J. (1975). Training parents of behaviorally-disordered children in groups: A three years' program evaluation. *Behavior Therapy, 6*, 378–387.

Robin, A. L. (1980). Parent-adolescent conflict: A skills training approach. In D. P. Rathjen & J. P. Foreyt (Eds.), *Social competence: Interventions for children and adults.* Elmsford, NY: Pergamon.

Robins, L. N. (1981). Epidemiological approaches to natural history research: Antisocial disorders in children. *Journal of the American Academy of Child Psychiatry, 20*, 556–580.

Rogers-Wiese, M. R., & Kramer, J. J. (1988). Parent training research: An analysis of the empirical literature 1975–1985. *Psychology in the Schools, 25*, 325–330.

Sanders, M. R., & James, J. E. (1983). The modification of parent behavior: A review of generalization and maintenance. *Behavior Modification, 7*, 3–27.

Shearer, D. A., & Loftin, C. R. (1985). The Portage Project; Teaching parents to teach their preschool children in the home. In R. F. Dangel & R. A. Polster (Eds.), *Parent training: Foundations of research and practice* (pp. 93–126). New York: Guilford.

Stinnett, N., & DeFrain, J. (1985). *Secrets of strong families.* Boston: Little, Brown.

Strain, P. S., Steele, P., Ellis, T., & Timm, M. A. (1982). Long-term effects of oppositional child treatment with mothers as therapists and therapist trainers. *Journal of Applied Behavior Analysis, 15*, 163–169.

Stuart, R. B. (1983). *Couples pre-counseling inventory.* Champaign, IL: Research Press.

Stumphauzer, J. S. (1976). Elimination of stealing by self-reinforcement of alternative behavior and family contracting. *Journal of Behavior Therapy and Experimental Psychiatry, 7*, 265–268.

Wahler, R. G. (1980). The insular mother: Her problems in parent-child treatment. *Journal of Applied Behavior Analysis, 13*, 207–219.

Wahler, R. G., & Dumas, J. E. (1984). Changing the observational coding styles of insular and noninsular mothers: A step towards maintenance of parent training effects. In R. F. Dangel & R. A. Polster (Eds.), *Parent training: Foundations of research and practice* (pp. 379–416). New York: Guilford.

Webster-Stratton, C. (1981). Videotaped modeling. A method of parent education. *Journal of Clinical Child Psychology, 10*, 93–98.

Wells, K. C., Forehand, R., & Griest, D. L. (1980). Generality of treatment effects from treated to untreated behaviors resulting from a parent training program. *Journal of Clinical Child Psychology, 9*, 217–219.

Wiese, M. J. (1989). *Evaluation of an Adlerian parent training program with multiple outcome measures.* Unpublished doctoral dissertation. University of Nebraska–Lincoln.

Ziarnik, J. P., & Bernstein, G. S. (1982). A critical examination of the effects of in service training on staff performance. *Mental Retardation, 20*, 109–114.

ANNOTATED BIBLIOGRAPHY

Blechman, E. A. (1985). *Solving child behavior problems at home and at school.* Champaign, IL: Research Press.
An excellent, practical source for many of the most common problems experienced by parents and children. The analysis of school concerns provides material that will be especially useful to school psychologists. This text could be useful as a precursor to more direct intervention with parents, teachers, and families.

Buntman, P. H., & Saris, E. M. (1979). *How to live with your teenager: A survivor's manual for parents.* Pasadena, CA: Birch Tree Press.
An informative source of commonsense suggestions for both practitioners and parents. This book presents practical suggestions for parents who are experiencing difficulties with adolescent behavior and is also an excellent source of information for parents who are unclear about the nature of "normal" behavior for teenagers.

Dangel, R. F., & Polster, R. A. (Eds.). (1984). *Parent training: Foundations of research and practice.* New York: Guilford.
This edited text contains many excellent chapters that help to define the current state of the art and practice of parent training. Most major contributors to the parent training literature during the last decade are represented, with commentary provided by noted behavior analysts. Historical analysis, current perspectives, many examples of training programs, and future considerations are all discussed.

Forehand, R., & McMahon, R. J. (1981). *Helping the noncompliant child: A clinician's guide to parent training.* New York: Guilford.
The program described by Forehand and McMahon remains the single best source for persons interested in learning about training for parents of noncompliant children. This text provides extensive detail regarding the experimental research that serves as a foundation for the training program and provides practitioners with straightforward and concrete suggestions about best practices in developing, implementing, and evaluating parent training.

Patterson, G. R. (Ed.). (1982). *Coercive family process.* Eugene, OH: Castalia.
This volume presents a clear and convincing portrait of the effects of dysfunctional family behavior on children's behavior. The impact of coercive behavior within family systems is documented with several chapters tracing the effects of family behavior on child development. Suggestions for the implementation of training programs for these families are provided by some authors.

36

Best Practices in Peer-Influenced Learning

David W. Peterson
Janice A. Miller
LaGrange (Illinois) Area Department of Special Education

OVERVIEW

School psychologists are increasingly being called upon to serve as instructional consultants who can provide assistance to teachers, administrators, and parents in improving academic achievement for a diverse population of students with learning needs that are not being met with normally available instructional resources (Ysseldyke, 1984). The purpose of this chapter is to provide an overview of peer-influenced academic interventions, including discussions of both peer tutoring and cooperative learning, so that practitioners will be acquainted with important aspects of these powerful and efficient academic interventions and be able to serve as consultants to educators seeking to implement alternative teaching strategies.

Students helping other students learn has a long history in American education. However, there has recently been a renewed interest in ways to more effectively structure peer interactions in academic situations. The term peer-influenced academic interventions is used here to refer to a wide variety of peer tutoring and cooperative learning methods designed to facilitate student interactions for the purpose of promoting achievement (see Table 1). These interventions include a continuum of techniques and are defined as, "a variety of structured interactions between two or more students, designed or planned by a school staff member, to achieve academic (primary) and social-emotional (secondary) goals" (Miller & Peterson, 1987, p. 81). On one end of this continuum, peer and cross-age tutoring usually involves explicitly programmed learning and teaching behaviors and the individual learning of the tutee is emphasized. On the other end, cooperative learning interventions involve student-to-student instruction as a by-product of the group process and stress the simultaneous learning of students within a group, mediated by group goals or rewards.

The Need for Peer-Influenced Interventions

There are a number of related initiatives that are reshaping the face of American education. It is our belief that these forces will not only significantly change the educational delivery system, but will also change the expectations that educators hold for school psychologists. Within the special education community, Madeline Will (1986), Assistant Secretary for Special Education and Rehabilitative Services, has pointed out that the current special education service delivery system has become inappropriately segregated from regular education. She has called for the exploration of alternatives that pro-

TABLE 1
Summary Description of Peer-Influenced Academic Interventions

Peer Tutoring

Students work in pairs on academic tasks carefully prescribed by the teacher. One student is the tutor and the oher is the tutee. May involve students of the same age or grade, or the tutor may be older.

Classwide Peer Tutoring (CWPT) (Delquadri, Greenwood, Whorton, Carta, & Hall, 1986)

Within a classroom, students are assigned to dyads by the teacher and are also randomly assigned to one of two teams. Pairs take turns as tutor and tutee and follow a prescribed instructional procedure to practice basic skills content. Students earn points for their team based on the number of correct responses, for appropriate dyad behavior, and for performance on weekly individual quizzes.

Class Student Tutoring Teams (CSTT) (Maheady, Sacca, & Harper, 1988)

Combines procedures of Classwide Peer Tutoring in terms of structured teaching procedures, daily point earning and public performance display; and aspects of cooperative learning, in terms of assignment to teams by rank.

Jigsaw (Aronson, 1978)

Students are assigned to six-member teams and each team member is given one section of a five-part academic unit. Two students share a section as a precaution in case of absenteeism. Expert groups are composed of team members from different teams who share the same academic material. They meet to discuss their material before returning to teach it to their respective team members. After being taught each section by the team members, students take individual quizzes and are graded on their performance on the quiz.

Circles of Learning (Johnson, Johnson, Holubec, & Roy, 1984)

Students work in 2-6 member heterogeneous teams on a project or assignment. A single product from the group is expected and the group members may self-evaluate how well they worked together as a group at the end of the session. The teacher's role is to monitor the groups and praise the students when they demonstrate cooperative behavior. Individual tests and grades are given, but group grades/rewards may also be given.

Group-Investigation (GI) (Sharan & Sharan, 1976)

In this method, students self-select their cooperative group of 2-6 members. The group chooses a topic from a unit being studied by the class and then decides who will study and prepare informaion on subtopics of the unit for a final report. Students are encouraged to use a variety of materials, engage in discussion with each other, and seek information from many sources. The groups present their projects to the class and evaluation of the group and/or individuals is completed.

Co-op Co-op (Kagan, 1985)

Similar to Group Investigation in intent, but the procedures for implementation are more prescribed. Students may choose groups based on interest. Team building skills are taught. Student contributions to the team's efforts as well as individual papers are the basis of evaluation.

Small-Group Learning and Teaching in Mathematics (Davidsion, 1985)

The focus is on the solution of mathematics problems through group discussion. Student input into team selection is considered. Evaluation is based on many sources — individual and group performance.

Student Teams — Achievement Division (STAD) Slavin, 1978)

Four to five students are assigned to heterogeneous learning teams. The teacher introduces the material to be learned and then provides study worksheets to team members. Students study the material with their team members until everyone understands the material. Next, students take individual quizzes, but the scores are used to compute a team score. The contribution each student can make to the team score is based on improvement as compared to past quiz averages. High-scoring teams and high-performing students are recognized in a weekly class newsletter.

Teams-Games-Tournaments (TGT) (DeVries, Slavin, Fennessey, Edwards, & Lombardo, 1980)

This method of cooperative learning uses the same team structure and instructional format as in STAD. In addition, students play in weekly tournament games with students of comparable ability from other teams in the classroom. Assignments are changed every week with the high and low scores of each table moved to the next highest or lowest table respectively in order to maintain fair competition. Students can contribute to their team score based on their performance in the weekly tournaments. Again, a class newsletter is used to recognize high scoring teams and individual tournament winners.

Team Assisted Individualization (TAI) (Slavin, Madden, & Leavy, 1982)

In TAI, the focus is on mathematics instruction. Heterogeneous teams of 4-5 students are formed. Based on a diagnostic test, each student is given an individually prescribed set of materials. For each unit, students read an instruction sheet, complete skillsheets, take checkouts, and finally take a test. Working in pairs, students check each others' worksheets and checkouts. When a checkout has been passed with a score of 80% or better, the student takes te test and the results are scored by a student monitor. Teams receive certificates for exceeding preset standards on the tests and for completing units.

Jigsaw II (Slavin, 1980b)

In this modification of Jigsaw, students are formed into 4-5 member heterogeneous teams. Every student studies all of the material, but is given a section in which to become an expert. As in the original Jigsaw, students meet in expert groups, teach their fellow team members, and take individual quizzes. However, individual scores are computed based on improvements and these become a group score. A class newsletter is used to recognize high scoring teams and individuals.

Cooperative Integrated Reading and Composition (CIRC) (Slavin, Stevens, & Madden, 1988)

The focus is on teaching reading, writing, and language arts in heterogeneous intermediate classrooms using mixed-ability cooperative learning teams and same-ability reading groups. Students real aloud with their same-ability partner and practice reading comprehension and process writing skills in their mixed-ability teams. Students earn points toward their team score.

---

mote collaboration among special and regular educators and increase the effectiveness of instruction with high-risk learners within the regular classroom. Similarly, professional organizations, most notably the National Association of School Psychologists, are calling for changes that will promote prereferral intervention, minimize the need to attach negative labels to students (NCAS, 1987), and develop educational alternatives that will respond to the needs of all students (NASP, NCAS, 1985). All of these initiatives clearly indicate the need for developing instructional alternatives that can be used to meet students' academic needs without labeling them and removing them from the regular classroom.

Additionally, research associated with the school improvement movement has shown that increasing student opportunities to respond, improving student success rates, individualizing instruction, frequently assessing student progress and maximizing allocated learning time are all correlated with increased achievement (Fisher et al., 1978; Rosenshine and Berliner, 1978; Slavin & Madden, 1989).

These converging initiatives make it essential that school psychologists have a thorough knowledge of instructional alternatives that can be used within consultative relationships with teachers. Both peer tutoring and cooperative learning offer viable methods to providing additional instruction which responds to the issues outlined above. While certainly not an instructional panacea, peer-influenced academic interventions have been clearly demonstrated as effective alternatives to more traditional learning structures. The consultant with a comprehensive understanding of these interventions will be in a position to have positive impact upon the academic program of any school implementing these instructional technologies.

BASIC CONSIDERATIONS

Cooperative Learning Methods

Cooperative learning methods promote "positive interdependence" among students (Johnson & Johnson, 1978). Students are encouraged to work together, must share information to learn a task, or are rewarded based on the performance of their group or on the combined efforts of the group's members. These practices are obviously quite different from what occurs in more traditional individualistic or competitive learning situations.

In individualistic learning methods students are not encouraged, perhaps are explicitly discouraged, from working with other students. Grades or rewards are given based on whether the student has reached a preset level of performance. For example, a teacher who gives all students with 90% of math problems correct on their test an "A" has designed an individualistic learning situation.

Competitive learning methods create "negative interdependence" among students (Johnson & Johnson, 1978). Because students are competing for grades or rewards, they are not likely to help or encourage their fellow student's learning. Teachers giving special privileges to students based on the highest test performance are using competitive learning methods.

Proponents of cooperative learning have differed in terms of their emphasis on the role that student interaction in groups has on outcomes. Slavin (1988) maintains that it is the establishment of a group goal and the provision of a group reward based on the performance of individuals within the group that results in positive outcomes for cooperative learning. He suggests that the group goal motivates students to help one another and, basing the group's reward on the performance of individuals, helps insure that everyone in the group is held accountable. No single individual can do the work for the group. Simply putting students into groups and encouraging them to cooperate on a task may not produce better results than individualistic or competitive learning methods.

Other experts in cooperative learning stress the importance that the group process of student interaction has on achieving positive results (Davidson, 1985; Johnson & Johnson, 1975; Kagan, 1985; Sharan & Sharan, 1976). Although studies indicate no correlation between level of participation in groups and achievement, students do achieve more if they give and receive help in response to requests for assistance (Webb, 1982). These results might occur because students cognitively restructure their thinking as they explain a concept to another student; students may use language that other students may understand more easily; or learning from other students may be less anxiety-provoking.

There are a number of cooperative learning methods from which to choose. Understanding differences among them can be facilitated by considering the variables outlined in Table 2. Classwide Peer Tutoring (Delquadri, Greenwood, Whorton, Carta, & Hall, 1986) and Classwide Student Tutoring Teams (Maheady, Sacca, & Harper, 1988) are included as cooperative learning methods because of the assignment of students to teams and the reward/recognition given to team performance.

The variables in Table 2 include the following:

1. *cognitive complexity of the task:* low complexity refers to rote skills such as reading words or computing math facts; higher level skills would be demonstrated in social studies or math story problem discussions.

2. *group goal or product:* the group goal may be an expectation that students work cooperatively together on a specific task or may be the number of team points based on either individual or whole group performance on a task; a group product may be a completed paper or class presentation by the group.

3. *task specialization:* individual students assume responsibility for one component of an assignment and are required to teach their fellow group members their component (Slavin, 1983).

4. *intergroup competition:* competition between groups is established and group performance is rewarded or recognized.

5. *equal opportunity scoring:* students of all ability levels have an equal chance to contribute to the group's score by engaging in competition with their equals, by using improvement scores, or by working on material at their instructional level (Slavin, 1983).

6. *reward/recognition:* recognition of the group's efforts is based on either a group's final product, such as a written

TABLE 2
Characteristics and Components of Cooperative Learning Methods

Method	Cognitive Task Complexity — Low	High	Group Goal/Product	Task Specialization	Intergroup Competition	Equal Opportunity Scoring	Basis of Reward/Recognition — Group Product	Individual Evaluation	Subject Area — Reading	Math	Social Studies	Science	Varied	Explicit Peer Tutoring	Focus on Group Process?
Classwide Peer Tutoring (CWPT) (Delquadri, Greenwood, Whorton, Carta, & Hall, 1986)	X		X		X			X					X		
Classwide Student Tutoring Teams (CSTT) (Maheady, Sacca, & Harper, 1988)	X		X		X	X		X					X	X	
Student Teams—Achievement Division (STAD) (Slavin, 1978)	X		X		X	X		X					X	X	
Teams-Games-Tournaments (TGT) (DeVries, Slavin, Fennessey, Edwards, & Lombardo, 1980)	X		X		X	X		X					X	X	
Team Assisted Individualization (TAI) (Slavin, 1985)	X		X			X		X		X					
JIGSAW II (Slavin, 1980)		X	X	X	X	X		X			X	X		X	
Cooperative Integrated Reading and Composition (CIRC) (Slavin, Stevens, & Madden, 1988)	X		X	X	X	X		X	X					X	
JIGSAW (Aronson, Blaney, Stephen, Sikes, & Snapp, 1978)		X	X	X				X			X	X		X	
Circles of Learning (Johnson, Johnson, Holubec, & Roy, 1984)		X	X				X	X			X	X		X	X
Group-Investigation (GI) (Sharan & Sharan, 1976)		X	X	X			•X	X			X	X		X	X
Co-op Co-op (Kagan, 1985)		X	X	X			X	X			X	X	X		X
Small-Group Learning and Teaching in Mathematics (Davidson, 1985)		X	X				X	X		X					X

report, and/or is based on the combined total of the absolute or improvement test scores of individual students within the group.

7. *subject area:* some cooperative methods have been specifically developed for a content area such as math, while others have broad application across content areas.

8. *peer tutoring:* students are required to help one another either through task specialization or through the completion of a teacher prescribed task.

9. *group process:* some cooperative methods incorporate time for the group to decide how effectively and in what ways they have cooperated with each other on the task. For example, there may be discussion on the specific social and collaborative behaviors that were used by group members during the task.

Research on Cooperative Learning

Achievement. Studies of the effects of cooperative learning methods on student achievement are clearly positive. When compared to individualistic and competitive learning methods, they were as effective or more effective in promoting the achievement of students at various age levels, in a wide variety of subject areas and with differing characteristics (Johnson, Maruyama, Johnson, Nelson, & Skon, 1981; Sharan, 1980; and Slavin, 1983).

In terms of student characteristics, Blacks and Hispanics seem to particularly benefit from participation in cooperative groups, although Caucasian students also achieve more (Lucker, Rosenfield, Sikes, and Aronson, 1976). Studies that include student populations with handicaps also suggest the effectiveness of cooperative learning in increasing achievement (Yaeger et al., 1985). Wheeler (1977) reports that students who said they preferred to cooperate may learn best in cooperative groups, while those indicating a preference for competition may perform better in competitive situations.

There may be components of cooperative learning methods that facilitate greater achievement. Slavin (1988) reviewed cooperative learning studies to determine the effect that the stipulation of a group goal and the inclusion of individual accountability had on achievement. He found that studies incorporating both group goals and individual accountability had greater effects on achievement than studies in which neither of these components were included.

Others have hypothesized that students achieve better in cooperative groups because they have more opportunities to respond (Greenwood & Delquadri, 1982); they are engaging in review and summarization activities (Yaeger, Johnson, & Johnson, 1985); or they are more motivated to learn because working in groups is fun and there is peer pressure to achieve (Johnson & Johnson, 1986).

Student relationships. One of the often stated goals of cooperative learning groups is to increase the interaction between students of different races or ethnic groups, or between handicapped and nonhandicapped students in order to develop cross-racial and cross-handicap friendships. Research results indicate that students who work in heterogeneous cooperative groups do express greater liking for each other and maintain friendships outside their racial or ethnic group or with handicapped peers (Johnson & Johnson, 1980a, 1980b, 1984; Sharan, 1980), even in nonacademic situations such as lunch or recess time (Johnson, Waring, & Maruyama, 1986). Despite these positive findings, those implementing cooperative groups that include lower performing students should be aware of data suggesting that competition between groups may negatively affect positive cross-handicap and cross-racial interactions (Johnson & Johnson, 1984). In such situations, group members may perceive lower performing students as impediments to successful or winning group performance.

Other outcomes. In addition to academic and social effects, cooperative learning studies have examined such areas as self-esteem, attitudes toward school, relationships with classmates, and ability to understand others' perspectives. Perhaps not surprisingly, the data indicate that students participating in cooperative learning methods generally feel better about themselves, like school more, want their classmates to do better in school, and can better acknowledge another's point of view than students in control groups (Johnson & Johnson, 1986; Zahn, Kagan, & Widaman, 1986).

Peer Tutoring Methods

Peer tutoring is contrasted with cooperative learning in that instruction is almost always provided in dyads, where one student serves as a tutor and the other is the tutee. Hawryluk and Smallwood (1988) point out that peer tutoring methods incorporate a variety of instructional designs. Some programs supplement ongoing classroom instruction or provide remediation in tutoring situations outside the classroom, while other programs can involve all the students in a class and serve as primary vehicles for instruction in a particular area. The term peer tutoring implies that tutors and tutees are of similar ages while cross-age tutoring refers to dyads of different ages, the tutor most frequently being older.

Providing additional opportunities for the practice of skills introduced by the classroom teacher is a primary goal of many tutoring programs. Consequently, tutoring sessions are regularly scheduled, frequently on a daily basis, and the content and methods of the sessions are planned and supervised by the classroom teacher or some other professional staff member (e.g., school psychologist).

Most successful tutoring programs include structured tutor training and ongoing supervision to ensure that student interactions are positive and include effective instructional practices. Finally, most effective programs include frequent measurement of tutee progress to ensure that academic goals are being met (Peterson & Miller, in press).

Research on Peer Tutoring

Results of a growing body of research is clearly establishing the effectiveness of peer and cross-age tutoring as an effective instructional alternative for a wide range of students. Cohen, Kulik, and Kulik (1982) conducted a meta-analysis of 65 studies and found significant positive effects on the achievement of both tutors and tutees (the effects were somewhat stronger in mathematics) as well as the promotion of positive attitudes toward subject matter. Interestingly, this study found greater gains in tutoring programs that were more highly structured. Others also have demonstrated that more highly structured, and sequentially organized programs may well be more effective (Rosenshine & Furst, 1969; Hawryluk & Smallwood, 1988).

Peer and cross-age tutoring programs also have been shown to be effective in promoting achievement among a variety of student populations including students with handicaps labeled as learning disabled and behavior disordered (Scruggs & Richter, 1985; Maheady, Sacca, & Harper, 1988) and "high-risk" students from a variety of cultural backgrounds (Slavin & Madden, 1989). While research clearly demonstrates the success of tutoring programs with a variety of student populations, findings assessing the effect of varying tutor–tutee characteristics (e.g., skill disparities, sex differences, and age) on the effectiveness of programs appear inconclusive (Devin-Sheehan et al., 1976). Also, relatively few studies have compared the effectiveness of peer and cross-age tutoring with other instructional techniques. However, Jenkins, Mayhall, Peschka, and Jenkins (1974) reported that some tutoring programs produced greater achievement gains than did instruction provided by classroom teachers.

Hawryluk and Smallwood (1988) review some studies showing the positive effects of tutoring programs on social behavior and school attitudes. However, consistent positive effects on self-concept and other social emotional outcomes have been somewhat less than conclusive (Cohen, Kulik, & Kulik, 1982) and research on the affective outcomes of these programs is sorely needed. Hawryluk and Smallwood (1988) also appropriately caution about the possible negative effects on the self-concept of students in programs that are not carefully supervised or structured.

Commonalities and Distinctions

While peer tutoring and cooperative learning are often differentiated, they should be viewed as existing on a continuum as they frequently share specific techniques and goals. For example, some explicit peer tutoring methods like Classwide Peer Tutoring (Delquadri, Greenwood, Whorton, Carta, & Hall, 1986) reward team performance, a practice which is more frequently associated with cooperative groups. Likewise, there are also cooperative learning methods like Jigsaw (Aronson et al., 1978) that have peer tutoring as an essential component of the process.

The distinctions between peer tutoring and cooperative learning methods involve the nature of the learning task, the relationship and interaction between students and the outcomes of the student interactions. Although there is some overlap between peer tutoring and cooperative learning methods in these areas, there are also differences that define each respective method.

In terms of the kinds of learning tasks given to students both peer tutoring and cooperative learning can be used to help students acquire basic skills or knowledge (e.g., spelling words, events in history, math computation problems). However, cooperative learning methods also can be used to promote higher level thinking skills such as encouraging creative problem solving.

Positive student interaction is facilitated in both peer tutoring and cooperative learning. However, the organization of the groups significantly differs between the two methods. In peer tutoring pupils are organized into pairs, although the pairs may be nominal members of a larger team of students. The size of the cooperative learning group varies between two and six and is determined by the characteristics of the learner and the task.

The scope of peer interaction may differ in peer tutoring and cooperative learning. In typical peer tutoring situations there is usually little or no interaction between dyads. This may not be the case in cooperative learning groups as students from different cooperative groups may interact in competitive contests or may assist each other as their respective groups work on a project. In addition, there is generally more explicit focus on the development of social interaction skills in cooperative learning methods than in peer tutoring methods.

The status of the students also distinguishes peer tutoring and cooperative learning groups. In a traditional peer tutoring pair the tutor assumes the role of giver of knowledge and information and thus may be perceived as having an inherently higher status than the tutee. Within a cooperative learning group, students have been assigned equal status and equal responsibility for the attainment of the group goal. In some methods described as peer tutoring, the role of tutor and tutee changes between students within the pair and, therefore, differences in status may be minimized.

The common goal of peer tutoring and cooperative learning groups is to affect student achievement. However, in peer tutoring the focus is the achievement of the tutee. Any achievement gains made by the tutor would be considered an unintended by-product of the interaction. In contrast, the goal of cooperative learning groups is the increased achievement of all students. There are also differences in the distribution of rewards for performance between peer tutoring and cooperative learning methods. The basis for giving rewards in peer tutoring situations is the students' individual efforts. The tutor may be rewarded for faithfully and effectively delivering instruction, while the tutee may be rewarded for learning the lesson. In cooperative learning groups the basis for reward distribution is the accomplishment of the group goal or the aggregation of individual members' performance within the group.

BEST PRACTICES IN DESIGNING PEER INFLUENCED INTERVENTIONS

Implementing Cooperative Learning Programs

Changes in teacher and student roles. The implementation of cooperative learning methods requires changes in the traditional roles of both the teacher and the student. Successful implementation must acknowledge and plan for these changes.

The teacher's role changes from that of being the central source of information and instruction to that of a facilitator of learning and a mediator of the group process among students. Such changes may be difficult for some teachers (Aronson & Goode, 1980; Moskowitz, Malvin, Schaeffer, & Schaps, 1983). School psychologists who are consulting with teachers may wish to emphasize that cooperative learning methods should be implemented along with continued use of individualistic and teacher-directed lessons. Consultant effectiveness also may be enhanced by working with teachers who voluntarily participate in cooperative methods and by providing ongoing support and assistance to teachers as they experiment with cooperative groupings in their classrooms. School psychologists may also assist teachers in networking with other teachers who are using cooperative learning methods. The use of such strategies may contribute to more effective and committed use of cooperative learning.

The student's role in cooperative groupings also must change. Students are no longer responsible only for their own learning, but also become responsible for the learning of others. Students may be explicitly told to tutor their peers, or, at the very least, to assume a role in maintaining the effective functioning of the group. There are those who advocate that students be taught cooperative group skills (Aronson et al., 1978; Johnson, Johnson, Holubec, & Roy, 1984). Staff may want to initially use nonacademic tasks in cooperative groups in order to focus on the learning of group skills such as active listening, questioning, maintaining the topic, and reinforcing others. A technique called "fishbowling" can be used to model effective group interaction. The staff member sets up a cooperative group, assigns group roles and a task, and has the rest of the class circle the group to watch and record how they work together. Discussion focuses on effective or ineffective group interactions that affected the completion of the task. Another strategy that staff can use to motivate students to work together is to establish contingencies for group behavior. For example, while monitoring cooperative groups in the classroom, the staff member may award bonus points for specified cooperative behaviors.

Selection of a cooperative method. Table 2 indicates the variety of cooperative methods from which to choose. In general, those implementing cooperative methods should start small, that is, select one method to try in one curriculum area. The next aspect to consider is the goal of the cooperative lesson. Is the primary goal of the staff member to teach an academic skill, increase student self-esteem, or improve student interrelationships? While most cooperative methods have multiple outcomes, there are those that are more aptly suited for a particular goal. For example, Jigsaw may be selected as a cooperative method when the goal is to increase student self-esteem. In this method students are given information for which they are to become experts and which they must share with the group in order for the group to achieve its goal. Any success the group achieves is the result of the work of its individual members.

Another consideration in selecting a cooperative method is the subject area being studied. A cooperative method such as Group Investigation (Sharan & Sharan, 1976) is more appropriately used in the content areas of social studies, economics, history, or science. When the focus is the acquisition of basic skills or information, cooperative methods such as Classwide Student Tutoring Teams (Maheady, Sacca, & Harper, 1989) or Slavin's Student

Teams-Achievement Division (1978) are better choices.

Other factors that enter into the selection of a cooperative method include the maturity level of the student, the amount of planning time required, and the necessity of purchasing specialized materials. Cooperative learning methods in which there is more explicit peer tutoring incorporated may initially be easier to implement with less mature learners. In addition, cooperative methods such as Cooperative Integrated Reading and Composition (CIRC) (Slavin, Stevens, & Madden, 1988) require a good deal of advanced preparation and planning, as well as specially adapted materials for implementation, in contrast to a method such as Classwide Peer Tutoring (Delquadri, Greenwood, Whorton, Carta, & Hall, 1986).

Implementation issues. Staff members who implement any cooperative learning method must consider a number of variables. These include determining the size of the group, the physical lay-out of the classroom, the assignment of students to groups, the criteria for group rewards or grades, the use of intergroup competition, ways to promote individual accountability, and communication to parents.

The number of students assigned to a cooperative group should be governed by the maturity level of the students. Younger students or those less experienced in group work probably should be placed into smaller groups, or perhaps initially, pairs as larger groups require more complex social interactive skills. Other considerations involve the number of groups the teacher prefers, the availability of materials to be shared, or the amount of time available for group work since larger groups frequently require more time to accomplish a task.

Another decision that staff members must make involves the physical arrangement of the classroom. Because there will usually be a mix of goal structures used within a classroom (cooperative, individualistic, competitive), staff should consider how to physically rearrange the

room as students shift from one structure to another. In most cooperative learning methods it is important for the students to be physically close enough to see and hear their group members, while in individualistic structures it is more helpful to have students separated from one another.

The assignment of students to cooperative groups may be done randomly, according to rank order based on achievement levels, the result of student self-selection based on topic interest, or the result of teacher selection to achieve heterogeneity. Many advocates of cooperative learning stress the importance of heterogeneity in groups. Achieving heterogeneity might be difficult using random selection or student self-selection. If staff members desire that groups be heterogeneously composed in terms of ability or race, they should probably use either achievement rank ordering or select students before-hand based on personal characteristics.

Webb (1982) cautions that heterogeneity in abilities may present some difficulties. In mixed ability groups, low performing students may conform to the views of more able students. More able students may feel that they should receive greater rewards because of their greater contributions, and thus may demonstrate antagonism toward the less able group members. However, the effects of mixed abilities within a group may depend on the average level and the ability range of achievement within the group. Any negative effects of heterogeneity in ability can perhaps be eased by incorporating equal opportunity scoring within the group reward structure.

Cooperative learning methods use a variety of ways to quantify and measure the performance of the group: aggregation of individual quiz scores, daily points or tournament points; aggregation of individual improvement scores on tests; assignment of points for group cooperative behavior; random selection of one student's work to represent the group and evaluation of a group product such as a paper or presentation. It is important that staff clearly specify to students the criteria that will be used to judge group performance. These criteria may be used to assign grades or recognize and reward group effort, for example, by publicly posting the results or giving certificates of achievement.

Whether to incorporate the use of intergroup competition is another important decision that implementors of cooperative methods must face. An advantage to using competition is that it may promote group cohesiveness. Because it may create a perception of "us against them," competition can stimulate the interdependence that is crucial to the success of the group. However, intergroup competition may also encourage scapegoating of lower performing group members, particularly in losing groups. Again, equal opportunity scoring may prevent this, since it ensures that all members of a group have a fair advantage to contribute to their group's team score.

In order to affect the achievement of students in cooperative groups they must be actively engaged in the learning activity. Staff members should plan ways that will promote individual student accountability and thus guarantee active student engagement. Task specialization, as in Jigsaw, assignment of roles within the group, and the use of individual performance outcomes to determine group rewards are all strategies that can be used.

Finally, implementors of cooperative learning methods should develop a communication plan for parents. Since this method of instruction may be unknown to parents, it is likely that questions about it will arise. Especially if staff connect the assessment of the individual student to the performance of the group, parents may become concerned that their son or daughter is being unjustly evaluated. Contact through a letter or by holding a group meeting before initiating the use of cooperative groups may forestall problems.

Implementing Peer Tutoring Programs

Those designing peer and cross-age tutoring programs should carefully address a number of program issues prior to implementing a program. These include: designing an effective tutor training program; developing and structuring lessons; and monitoring, supervising, and scheduling sessions.

Effective tutor training. The overall success of a peer tutoring program may well depend upon the quality of training that has been provided to prospective tutors. Effective training programs will help to ensure that tutors display effective teaching behaviors and avoid negative interactions that inhibit progress and engender negative feelings among tutees. Analysis of the findings of a number of researchers (Deterline, 1970; Ehly, 1986; Ehly & Larsen, 1980; Jenkins & Jenkins, 1981, 1985; Lippet, 1976; Pierce, Stahlbrand, & Armstrong, 1984) suggests that tutor training programs contain instructional components assuring that tutors will be able to:

1. Locate, organize, and efficiently use all instructional materials. Actual practice in the use of tutoring materials is recommended.

2. Communicate and reinforce clear expectations for tutee learning during the session.

3. Obtain and maintain tutee attention during the session using non-punitive technique.

4. Give clear directions as to the ways in which tutees are expected to respond (e.g., "When I point to the word, you say it quietly and use it in a sentence.")

5. Effectively use and allocate time during the tutoring session (e.g., tutors move through lessons at a steady pace, and have smooth transitions between activities).

6. Consistently demonstrate teaching behaviors which avoid punishment of tutees for errors.

7. Consistently identify tutee errors and use proven error correction procedures (e.g., model, lead, test) when appropriate to lesson content.

8. Praise correct tutee responses on an intermittent schedule, and use tangible reinforcers effectively when required.

9. Use cues and prompting to shape successive approximations of correct responses.

10. Accurately measure tutee progress at the conclusion of a lesson or unit (e.g., conduct one minute timings of reading and record correct words read per minute).

11. Maintain accurate records of tutee progress (e.g., record and chart student progress on graphs).

If possible, the tutor training program should provide explicit instruction in all of these areas using modeling, role playing, and feedback. Follow-up observations during actual tutoring sessions should be conducted to ensure generalization.

Selecting tutors, tutees, and establishing dyads. The selection of tutors is best guided by common sense, and those designing programs may wish to solicit nominations from participating teachers. Research regarding any necessary tutor characteristics is equivocal, but the following guidelines may prove helpful:

1. Older students of average ability who are competent in the subject matter to be tutored may prove to be most effective when program goals emphasize academic progress (Ehly, 1986). However, documented success with tutors of varying skill suggests that this guideline need not be rigid (Scruggs & Osguthorpe, 1986).

2. When selected tutors have known skill deficits in the material to be tutored, consideration can be given to pairing with younger tutees to minimize skill deficits.

3. Interest and social characteristics may represent the most critical tutor characteristics. Attempt to recruit tutors who are sensitive, responsible, and can remain on task during sessions. However, tutors of less skill may be used if training and monitoring are very thorough.

The match between the identified instructional needs of potential tutees and the planned content of the tutoring program should be the primary consideration in the final selection of tutees. Given the success of programs with tutees with a wide range of skills and aptitudes, there are virtually no characteristics that would eliminate a potential participant. Teacher recommendations can be sought when establishing dyads and the program planner may wish to pair more competent tutors with tutees needing special attention. During implementation, dyads should be monitored for compatibility and changed if conflict becomes evident.

Developing lesson content and format. It is essential that the content of tutoring lessons be closely related to the curriculum and skills being taught within the classroom. Content selected directly from classroom materials will foster generalization of skills and increase the rate of overall classroom learning (Jenkins & Jenkins, 1985). Delquadri, Greenwood, Whorton, Carta, and Hall (1986) discuss the "functionality of key academic skill areas," recommending that tutoring program designers select the specific academic skills that teachers use in measuring a child's progress. Additionally, these authors recommend that skills taught be highly correlated with teacher determined outcomes (e.g., the tutoring program should teach actual oral reading rather than emphasizing phonetic rules).

Lesson formats should allow for efficient tutor presentations and should enable tutees to respond in a clearly specified, straightforward manner and should be relatively consistent across sessions. Younger children may be more successful with drill and practice tasks, although virtually any academic task can be adapted to a peer tutoring format.

Supervision, management, scheduling, and program maintenance. Responsibilities for the management and supervision of a tutoring program should be carefully specified and involve program maintenance activities and regular supervision of tutor dyads (Miller & Peterson, 1987). One responsibility of the consultant may be to monitor completion of responsibilities and resolve any problems in program implementation. Structured daily supervision has been associated with successful programs (Mayhall et al., 1975), and should involve specific praise, demonstration of effective teaching behaviors, and assistance in assessing and recording student progress.

Scheduling should be completed in conjunction with teachers and other relevant school staff to minimize disruptions and maximize available instructional time. Daily tutoring sessions of relatively brief duration (e.g., 30 minutes) have been found to be most effective (Mayhall & Jenkins, 1977).

Attention also should be given to providing tutors with appropriate recognition for their participation. Recognition in school newspapers, holding tutor luncheons, hosting tutoring "symposia," and conducting inservice programs for other schools or parent groups are all effective in maintaining tutor involvement over time.

Evaluating Student Progress and Assessing Program Effectiveness

Minimally, evaluation of tutee progress should include some measurement of academic gain during the program. We strongly advocate the use of daily measures of performance (Jenkins & Jenkins, 1981) or curriculum based assessment techniques that directly measure the academic skills being taught within the program. Such measures are considerably more sensitive to student growth than norm referenced measures and are better suited to formative evaluation (e.g., they can be used on a daily basis to modify instruction). Maheady, Sacca, and Harper (1988) also suggest using classroom test scores to assess student progress and the generalization of skills.

Attitudinal and affective variables also may be assessed, and some may wish to collect direct observational data to assess on-task behavior or the quality of student interactions during interventions. There are, of course, a variety of other evaluation questions that should be addressed when evaluating peer-influenced interventions. Maher (1986) provides a comprehensive evaluation format that assesses a variety of variables critical to overall program success.

SUMMARY

This chapter has provided an overview of peer-influenced academic interventions including peer and cross-age tutoring and cooperative learning. A variety of initiatives, many of which are encompassed within the Regular Education Initiative (Will, 1986), call for change in the educational delivery system serving students with special needs. One element of this change involves the provision of more effective academic instruction for students with academic skill deficits and these academic interventions offer a number of instructional alternatives that have been demonstrated to be effective, cost-efficient, and that can be implemented in a variety of settings.

Peer-influenced interventions exist on a continuum and, within specific applications, share common characteristics and techniques. Peer and cross-age tutoring involve carefully structured learning and teaching behaviors involving two students and the individual learning of the tutee is emphasized. Cooperative learning includes a variety of techniques for encouraging the simultaneous learning of students within a group of two or more students, mediated by group goals or rewards.

Research reviewed in this chapter has provided clear evidence for the efficacy of these techniques with a wide range of student populations. Specific guidelines and recommendations for implementation of these approaches have been provided and some obstacles to implementation have been discussed.

While there is evidence to suggest that the use of peer-influenced academic interventions is increasing within U.S. schools, it is ironic, given their effectiveness, that they are not more widely used. School psychologists, long associated with the introduction of innovation into educational settings, are in an ideal position to demonstrate to educational policy makers the efficacy and value of these techniques.

REFERENCES

Aronson, E. Blaney, N., Stephen, C., Sikes, J., & Snapp, M. (1978). *The jigsaw classroom*. Beverly Hills, CA: Sage.

Aronson, E., & Goode, E. (1980). Training teachers to implement jigsaw learning: A manual for teachers. In S. Sharan, P. Hare, C. D. Webb, & R. Hertz-Lazarowitz (Eds.), *Cooperation in education* (pp. 47-81). Provo, UT: Brigham Young University Press.

Cohen, P. A., Kulik, J. A., & Kulik, C. C. (1982). Educational outcomes of tutoring: A meta-analysis of findings. *American Educational Research Journal, 19,* 237-248.

Davidson, N. (1985). Small-group learning and teaching in mathematics: A selected review of the research. In R. Slavin, S. Sharan, S. Kagan, R. Hertz-Lazarowitz, C. Webb, & R. Schmuck (Eds.), *Learning to cooperate, cooperating to learn* (pp. 211-230). New York: Plenum Press.

Delquadri, J., Greenwood, C., Whorton, D., Carta, J., & Hall, R. (1986). Classwide Peer Tutoring. *Exceptional Children, 52,* 535-542.

DeVries, D., Slavin, R., Tennessey, G., Edwards, K., & Lombardo, M. (1980). *Teams-games tournaments; the team approach*. Englewood Cliffs, NJ: Educational Technology Publications.

Deno, S. L. (1985). Curriculum-based measurement: The emerging alternative. *Exceptional Children, 52,* 219-232.

Deterline, W. A. (1970). *Training and management of student tutors: Final report*. (ERIC Document Reproduction No. ED 048 133)

Devin-Sheehan, L., Feldman, R., & Allen, V. (1976). Research on children tutoring children: A critical review. *Review of Educational Research, 46,* 355-385.

Dishon, D., & O'Leary, P. (1984). *A Guidebook for Cooperative Learning*. Holmes Beach, FL: Learning Pub., Inc.

Ehly, S. (1986). *Peer tutoring: A guide for school psychologists*. Kent, OH: National Association of School Psychologists.

Ehly, S. W., & Larsen, S. C. (1980). *Peer tutoring for individualized instruction*. Boston: Allyn and Bacon, Inc.

Fischer, C., Felby, N., Marleave, R., Cohen, L., Dishaw, M., Moore, J., & Berliner, D. (1978). *Teaching and learning in the elementary school: A summary of the beginning teacher evaluation study*. San Francisco: Far West Laboratory.

Gickling, E. E., & Havertape, J. F. (1981). Curriculum-based assessment. In J. A. Tucker (Ed.), *Non-test based assessment* (pp. S1-S23). Minneapolis, MN: The National School Psychology Inservice Training Network, University of Minnesota.

Greenwood, C., & Delquadri, J. (1982, September). *The opportunity to respond and student academic performance in school*. Paper presented at the Conference on Behavior Analysis in Education, Ohio State University, Columbus, OH.

Hawryluk, M., & Smallwood, D. (1988). Using peers as instructional agents: Peer tutoring and cooperative learning. In J. Graden, J. Zins, & M. Curtis (Eds.), *Alternative educational delivery systems: Enhancing instructional options for all students* (pp. 371-390). Washington, DC: National Association of School Psychologists.

Jenkins, J. R., & Jenkins, L. M. (1981). *Cross age and peer tutoring: Help for children with learning problems*. Reston, VA: Council for Exceptional Children.

Jenkins, J., & Jenkins, L. (1985). Peer tutoring in elementary and secondary programs. *Focus on Exceptional Children, 17,* 1-12.

Jenkins, J. R., Mayhall, W. F., Peschka, C., & Jenkins, L. M. (1974). Comparing small group and tutorial instruction in resource rooms. *Exceptional Children, 40,* 245-250.

Johnson, D., & Johnson, R. (1975). *Learning together and alone*. Englewood Cliffs, NJ: Prentice-Hall.

Johnson, D., & Johnson, R. (1978). Cooperative, competitive and individualistic learning. *Journal of Research and Development in Education, 12*(1), 3-15.

Johnson, D., & Johnson, R. (1980a). Effects of intergroup cooperation and intergroup competition on ingroup and outgroup cross-handicap relationships. *Journal of Social Psychology, 124,* 85-94.

Johnson, D., & Johnson, R. (1980b). Integrating handicapped students into the mainstream. *Exceptional Children, 47,* 90-98.

Johnson, D., & Johnson, R. (1984). Effects of intergroup cooperation and intergroup competition on ingroup and outgroup cross-handicap relationships. *Journal of Social Psychology, 124,* 85-94.

Johnson, D., & Johnson, R. (1986). Mainstreaming and cooperative learning strategies. *Exceptional Children, 52,* 553-561.

Johnson, D., Johnson, R., Holubec, E., & Roy, P. (1984). *Circles of learning*. Alexandria, VA: Association for Supervision and Curriculum Development.

Johnson, D., Johnson, R., Waring, D., & Maruyama, G. (1986). Different cooperative learning procedures and cross-handicap relationships. *Exceptional Children, 53,* 247-252.

Johnson, D., Maruyama, G., Johnson, R., Nelson, D., & Skon, L. (1981). The effects of cooperative, competitive and individualistic goal structures on achievement: A meta-analysis. *Psychological Bulletin, 89,* 47-62.

Kagan, S. (1985). Co-op Co-op. A flexible cooperation learning technique. In R. Slavin, S. Sharan, S. Kagan, R. Hertz-Lazarowitz, C. Webb, & R. Schmuck (Eds.), *Learning to cooperate, cooperating to learn* (pp. 437-462). New York: Plenum Press.

Lippitt, P. (1976). Learning through cross-age helping: Why and how. In V. A. Allen (Ed.), *Children as teachers: Theory and research on tutoring* (pp. 157-168). New York: Academic Press.

Lucker, G., Rosenfield, D., Sikes, J., & Aronson, E. (1976). Performance in the interdependent classroom: A field study. *American Educational Research Journal, 13,* 115-123.

Maheady, L., Sacca, M., & Harper, G. (1988). Classwide peer tutoring with mildly handicapped high school students. *Exceptional Children, 55,* 52-59.

Maher, C. A. (1986). Direct replication of a cross age tutoring program involving handicapped adolescents and children. *School Psychology Review, 15,* 100-118.

Mayhall, W. F., & Jenkins, J. R. (1977). Scheduling daily or less-than-daily instruction: Implications for resource programs. *Journal of Learning Disabilities, 10*(3), 159-163.

Mayhall, W. R., Jenkins, J. R., Chestnut, N., Rose, F., Schroeder, K., & Jordan, B. (1975). Supervision and site of instruction as factors in tutorial programs. *Exceptional Children, 42,* 151-154.

Miller, J., & Peterson, D. (1987). Peer influenced academic interventions. In C. Maher, & J. Zins (Eds.), *Psychoeducational interventions in the schools: Methods and procedures for enhancing student competence* (pp. 81-100). New York: Pergamon.

Moskowitz, J., Malvin, J., Schaeffer, G., & Schaps, E. (1983). Evaluation of a cooperative learning strategy. *American Educational Research Journal, 20,* 687-696.

National Coalition of Advocates for Students. (1987). *Rights Without Labels.* Washington, DC: Author.

National Association of School Psychologists/ National Coalition of Advocates for Students. (1985). Advocacy for appropriate educational service for all children. Washington, DC: Author.

Peterson, D., & Miller, J. (in press). Peer-influenced academic interventions: Providing opportunities for student success through cooperative learning and peer tutoring. *Special Services in the Schools.*

Pierce, M. M., Stahlbrand, K., & Armstrong, S. B. (1984). *Increasing student productivity through peer tutoring programs.* Austin, TX: Pro-Ed.

Rosenshine, B. V., & Berliner, D. C. (1978). Academic engaged time. *British Journal of Teacher Education, 4,* 3-16.

Rosenshine, B., & Furst, N. (1969). *The effects of tutoring upon pupil achievement: A research review.* Washington, DC: Office of Education. (ERIC Document Reproduction Service No. ED 064 462)

Scruggs, T. E., & Osguthorpe, R. T. (1986). Tutoring interventions within special education settings: A comparison of cross-age and peer tutoring. *Psychology in the Schools, 23,* 187-193.

Scruggs, T. E., & Richter, L. (1985). Tutoring learning disabled students: A critical review. *Learning Disability Quarterly, 8,* 286-298.

Sharan, S. (1980). Cooperative learning in small groups: Recent methods and effects on achievement, attitudes, and ethnic relations. *Review of Educational Research, 50*(2), 241-271.

Sharan, S., & Sharan, Y. (1976). *Small-group teaching.* Englewood Cliffs, NJ: Educational Technology Publications.

Slavin, R. (1978). Student teams and achievement divisions. *Journal of Research and Development in Education, 12,* 39-49.

Slavin, R. (1980). Using student team learning: Revised edition. Baltimore, MD: Center for Social Organization of Schools, The Johns Hopkins University.

Slavin, R. (1983). *Cooperative learning.* London: Longman.

Slavin, R. (1985). Team assisted individualization: Combining cooperative learning and individualized instruction in mathematics. In R. Slavin, S. Sharan, S. Kagan, R. Hertz-Lazarowitz, C. Webb, & R. Schmuck (Eds.), *Learning to cooperate, cooperating to learn.* New York: Plenum.

Slavin, R. (1988). Cooperative learning and student achievement. *Educational Leadership, 46*(2), 31-33.

Slavin, R., & Madden, N. A. (1989). What works for students at risk: A research synthesis. *Educational Leadership, 46*(5), 4-13.

Slavin, R., Stevens, R., & Madden, N. (1988). Accommodating student diversity in reading and writing instruction: A cooperative learning approach. *Remedial & Special Education, 9*(1), 60-66.

Webb, N. (1982). Student interaction and learning in small groups. *Review of Educational Research, 52,* 421-445.

Wheeler, R. (1977). Predisposition toward cooperation and competition: Cooperative and competitive classroom effects. Paper presented at the annual convention of the American Psychological Association, San Francisco.

Will, Madeline (1986). Educating Students with Learning Problems: A Shared Responsibility. Washington, DC: U.S. Department of Education, Office of Special Education and Rehabilitation Services.

Yaeger, S., Johnson, D., & Johnson, R. (1985). Oral discussion, group to individual transfer, and achievement in cooperative learning groups. *Journal of Educational Psychology, 77,* 60–66.

Ysseldyke, J. (1984). *School psychology: A blueprint for training and practice.* Minneapolis, MN: National School Psychology Inservice Training Network.

Zahn, G., Kagan, S., & Widaman, K. (1986). Cooperative learning and classroom climate. *Journal of School Psychology, 24,* 351–362.

ANNOTATED BIBLIOGRAPHY

Aronson, E., Blaney, N., Stephen, C., Sikes, J., & Snapp, M. (1978). *The Jigsaw Classroom.* Beverly Hills, CA: Sage.
This book describes through example and explanation how to implement the Jigsaw cooperative learning technique in a classroom. Although it provides a rationale in theory and research for the use of this technique, it also anticipates problems teachers may have in implementation and suggests remedial courses of action. Appendices include a sample curriculum unit and scripts for teacher training workshops.

Dishon, D., & O'Leary, P. (1984). *A Guidebook for Cooperative Learning.* Holmes Beach, FL: Learning Pub., Inc.
The authors have provided practical suggestions for those implementing cooperative learning based on the Johnson and Johnson model. Topics include planning and implementing lessons, teaching social skills, and creating positive interdependence. The appendices include worksheets and forms for planning lessons and helping groups process their interactions.

Johnson, D., Johnson, R., Holubec, E., & Roy, P. (1984). *Circles of Learning.* Association for Supervision and Curriculum Development.
This is a text written for supervisors and administrators since it not only provides an overview of cooperative learning, but also includes a chapter on supervising teachers who implement this model of cooperative learning in their classrooms. The chapters on implementing cooperative learning and teaching cooperative skills include many practical suggestions. An additional nice feature of this slim text is the section on myths about cooperative learning which could be useful for parent presentations.

Slavin, R. (1983). *Cooperative Learning.* London: Longman Pub.
Although much of this book is devoted to the theory and research supporting the use of cooperative learning in schools, it also includes a brief overview of various cooperative learning methods. It will not help practitioners implement a specific method, but is a good reference text. It also includes a thoughtful chapter on directions for future research in cooperative learning.

Ehly, S. (1986). *Peer tutoring: A guide for school psychologists.* Washington, DC: National Association of School Psychologists.
This guidebook provides a step-by-step practical approach to establishing peer tutoring programs. Components of effective tutoring programs are reviewed and a discussion of special populations is included. The recommendations on tutor training are especially helpful. A companion videotape useful in training is available from the publisher.

Jenkins, J. R., & Jenkins, L. M. (1981). *Cross age and peer tutoring: Help for children with learning problems.* Reston, VA: Council for Exceptional Children.
This is an excellent summary of the important components of effective tutoring programs. Includes guidelines for tutor training and selection, lesson content, and measurement of student progress. This brief text (87 pages) is a must for those responsible for implementing and evaluating tutoring programs.

37

Best Practices in Personality Assessment

Howard M. Knoff
University of South Florida

OVERVIEW

The assessment of child and adolescent personality remains an important activity for the school psychologist given the mandate of the Education for All Handicapped Children's Act (EHA; Public Law 94-142, 99-457) to identify and provide services to severely emotionally disturbed (SED) students. Beyond EHA, however, the personality assessment process helps us to better understand the significant number of social-emotional and behavioral problems that *non-special education* students are manifesting in today's schools. Clearly, through personality assessment, school psychologists can provide parents and other educators with insight and direction into such problems as truancy, drug abuse, dropping out, teenage pregnancy, and suicide, and into the emotional impacts of divorce, poverty, rejection, and academic failure. But, most importantly, school psychologists can provide these individuals with recommendations and action plans that decrease or resolve current child and adolescent problems and that prevent these problems from reoccurring in the future. This is the "bottom line" of personality assessment. Personality assessment is a process of collecting valid data to explain the causes for or contingencies relevant to a child's social-emotional, behavioral, or affective status. This assessment is useless for the child having problems unless viable, acceptable, and socially valid interventions are successfully implemented with ongoing attention to treatment integrity and treatment evaluation (Knoff, 1986).

Within this context of comprehensive school psychological service delivery, an important element is the school psychologist's knowledge and understanding of normal and abnormal personality development, and his or her use of this information to create a working conceptual model that explains children's social-emotional, behavioral, and affective development. While this model must incorporate situation-specific behavior (Kenrick & Funder, 1988), it should nonetheless guide the school psychologist's thinking so that problem-solving and assessment-to-intervention procedures with referred children are integrated and wholistically organized. Indeed, it is distressing to review the literature (e.g., Prout, 1983) and find that the five most frequently used social-emotional assessment techniques are: clinical interviews, informal classroom observations, human figure drawings, the emotional indicators from the Bender Gestalt, and incomplete sentence blanks. Given the theoretical differences underlying these approaches and the diversity of data that they generate, this review suggests that school psychologists are assessing referred and other students more on a test-by-test basis than on an integrated basis where assessment and intervention are clearly linked. A personal, conceptual model of personality development helps the school psychologist to avoid this assessment diffusion. This is the first "best practice" which ensures sound personality assessment.

Beyond conceptual models, school psychologists also must identify what they want to accomplish from the personality assessment process, as well as (a) what their school districts and multidisciplinary teams want from this process and (b) the degree of congruence between these perspectives. While the ultimate personality assessment goal is to develop and implement effective intervention programs for referred students, other goals for the school psychologist might be: to determine who "owns" a specific referred problem (e.g., the referred child, a referring teacher or parent, a dysfunctional system, or a combination thereof); to validate hypotheses explaining how a referred child's behaviors are being caused, encouraged, reinforced, or supported; to create a sound baseline of data so that interventions can be evaluated from an appropriate context and so that an accurate presenting history can be documented; and to identify the referred child's behavioral assets and the home and school's resources so that they might be integrated into an intervention program.

Relative to the school district, the primary goal of personality assessment often is to determine a student's eligibility for special education services. This is a national tragedy, because it reinforces the serious misconception that the placement into special education is an intervention in and of itself. A child should be placed in special education only when that setting is clearly the optimal place to deliver the intervention program required by the referral situation. Because the personality assessment process determines the intervention program needed, a placement decision is related more to the program required than the assessment process itself. School psychologists must discourage districts from requesting personality assessment primarily as a means to qualify students for SED (or equivalent) placement. More appropriate district-related uses of personality assessment might be: to identify and analyze recurring patterns of student behavior or affect so that

effective preventive programs can be developed, to understand the severity and demands of students' social-emotional problems so that optimal staffing patterns can be organized, to investigate the relationship between unrealistic academic expectations and inappropriate student behavior so that curricular restructuring as appropriate can occur, and to address student problems that do not require formal referrals or special education placements through teacher consultation, staff development, and prereferral interventions.

Under ideal circumstances, school psychologists' professional goals for personality assessment will closely match those of their school districts. However, there are ecological and systemic realities that sometimes frustrate this matching process. One such reality helps to explain why school psychologists sometimes professionally disagree with their education colleagues when it comes to personality assessment and advocacy for referral students. This reality is that school psychologists work within a Psychology X Education interactional context, while district educators typically work only within an educational context. Thus, school psychologists independently and interdependently analyze referred students' psychological *and* educational status; other school personnel often assess the impact of students' referred behavior or affect only on their academic progress and, in many states, on the academic progress of their peers. This explains why school psychologists' assessment conclusions and program and placement recommendations for SED-referred students often differ from their colleagues on the multidisciplinary team.

The need to analyze referred students from a Psychology X Education perspective is the second "best practice" behavior for school psychologists. Children's behavior and affect are the interdependent products of the many institutions, settings, people, and contingencies with whom they interact. Personality assessment must reflect these interactions through multitrait, multisetting, and multimethod analyses which necessarily involve data collection from home, school, and community sources (Gresham, 1983). School psychologists should never yield to an education perspective that is not in the best interests of a student's educational *and psychological* needs and future. School psychologists must look at the child's entire ecology; the school setting is but one part of that ecology (Knoff, 1983).

The two "best practices" above create a foundation for sound personality assessment. Below, these two approaches are extended and operationalized by focusing on the classification systems, pragmatic beliefs, applied approaches, and fundamental procedures that translate into effective personality assessment. After reading this chapter, school psychologists not only should have an update as to the most effective ways to forge the link between personality assessment and intervention, but also should have the impetus to create or rethink the conceptual model that helps to drive this important process.

BASIC CONSIDERATIONS

Assuming a psychological and educational perspective of personality assessment, school psychologists must attend to the available classification systems that are used to categorize referred child and adolescent behavior. While a functional analysis of a students' behavior and affect will be more relevant to planning viable and effective intervention programs, the presence of these classification systems cannot be ignored given their widespread use and their determination of much of our diagnostic nomenclature. Three different classification systems, with their strengths and weaknesses briefly will be reviewed: the EHA SED definition, DSM-III-R, and empirically-based classification approaches.

The EHA Definition

Most states (approximately 75%) use the actual or an adapted EHA definition of SED despite the fact that they may or may not identify the label as "Seriously Emotionally Disturbed." Despite the apparent consensus, the fact remains that the EHA definition (a) is predominantly an educational definition that does not lend itself to psychological differentiation or analysis, (b) requires behavioral operationalization in order to be used in a consistent manner, (c) necessitates only a *yes* or *no* "diagnostic" decision, and (d) encourages a "medical-model" perspective of disturbed behavior. For example, the EHA definition focuses on conditions that "adversely affect educational performance," desensitizing our schools to children who progress educationally but still need socialization or mental health services. The definition leaves such characteristics as "inappropriate types of behaviors or feelings," "under normal circumstances," "for a long period of time," and "to a marked degree" to the state, school district, or individual multidisciplinary team to operationalize. This creates, at best, a great potential for inconsistency across referred children and, at worst, conditions allowing unchecked bias, inequity, and prejudice. Finally, the definition permits a simplistic "yes, the child qualifies as an SED child," or "no, the child does not qualify" mentally which suggests that the child owns or does not own the causal pathology and discourages an ecological perspective which focuses more on intervention and problem resolution.

While a best practices SED definition is suggested below, the school psychologist must take a leadership role at the district and individual multidisciplinary team level to operationalize and systematize the SED definition currently in use. This will require discussions with all team members as to (a) what is typical and expected behavior in the classroom and school building from both a developmental perspective and a normative or community-specific perspective; (b) what combination of child, curricular, and instructional conditions suggest a continuation of regular classroom interventions and/or necessitate special education considerations; (c) what behavioral frequencies, intensities, and durations are needed for regular versus special education classroom decisions; and (d) what types of behaviors, affects, and interactions fall under the SED definition, thereby requiring programmatic intervention. Only by having clear SED procedures and definitions can a multidisciplinary team make consistent, objective, and functional decisions, simultaneously overcoming the weaknesses of the current EHA definition. Only by operationalizing at a local level, can a multidisciplinary team make consistent, objective, and functional decisions, simultaneously overcoming the weaknesses of the current EHA definition. Only by operationalizing at a local level, can a multidisciplinary team evaluate referred children with a sensitivity to the community's individual strengths, weaknesses, history, and problems and with an understanding of what constitutes SED behavior specifically for that community.

DSM-III-R

The fourth revision of the *Diagnostic and Statistical Manual of Mental Disorders* was published in 1987 by the American Psychiatric Association. Continuing its attempts to describe its various disorders as behaviorally as possible, the DSM-III-R describes the following disorders of infancy, childhood, and adolescence; Developmental Disorders (Mental Retardation, Pervasive Developmental Disorders, and Specific Disorders), Disruptive Behavior Disorders, Anxiety Disorders of Childhood or Adolescence, Eating Disorders, Gender Identity Disorders, Tic Disorders, Elimination Disorders, Speech Disorders Not Elsewhere Classified, and Other Disorders of Infancy, Childhood, or Adolescence. While the DSM-III-R shares many of the specific disorders described by the DSM-III, a few critical changes have occurred. For example, the DSM-III *Attention Deficit Disorder* is now called *Attention-Deficit Hyperactivity Disorder (ADHD)* and criteria for mild, moderate, and severe ADHD impairments are described. And, the DSM-III *Conduct Disorder* has been reorganized into a DSM-III-R *Conduct Disorder* which discriminates between group types, solitary aggressive types, and undifferentiated types, again with criteria

for mild, moderate, and severe impairments.

Despite these changes, many of the concerns expressed for the DSM-III still exist for the DSM-III-R: (a) the DSM-III-R's reliability and validity need to be clearly demonstrated; (b) the inclusion of mental retardation and reading, arithmetic, speech, language, and other "developmental disorders" in a system of psychiatric disorders is conceptually and nosologically questionable; (c) the need for more sensitivity to the developmental manifestations of certain disorders exists, as well as the need to recognize that some childhood disorders cannot be classified using adult diagnoses and descriptors; and (d) the practical utility of the psychosocial stressors and adaptive functioning scales (and axes) needs to be established. But perhaps, the biggest concern with the DSM-III-R lies in the fact that many of its diagnoses involve composites of behaviors or symptoms with decision rules that often require that some, but not all, of the behaviors need to be present. For example, the Attention-Deficit Hyperactive Disorder (ADHD) diagnosis is made for a disturbance of at least six months duration, beginning before the age of seven, and *involving at least eight of fourteen specific manifestations. Which* eight behaviors need not be reported, and some of them (e.g., has difficulty playing quietly, often talks excessively, often does not seem to listen to what is being said to him or her) are behaviorally imprecise and dependent, at times, on situation-specific subjectivity. Thus, one ADHD diagnosis could be vastly different from another, and there would be no way for the psychologist to determine which of the fourteen ADHD behaviors were present unless they were specified in a psychological report. Without a specification of the behaviors of concern, then, the ADHD diagnosis is of limited use, especially in the development of appropriate intervention strategies and programs. With the behaviors specified, the ADHD label is basically unnecessary — school psychologists' interventions address problematic behaviors, *not* so-called "diagnostic" labels.

In summary, there are few, if any, compelling reasons why school psychologists need to use DSM-III-R. While some feel that their ability to label a referred problem means that they understand it and are ready to successfully resolve it, this has never been empirically demonstrated. What has been demonstrated is that the identification of behavioral skill deficits, performance deficits, and self-management deficits and their behavioral contingencies can be successfully addressed, and that these approaches are often parsimonious, efficient, and well-accepted by referral sources and referred individuals.

Empirically-Based Classification Approaches

An empirically-based classification system can be developed from the factor analytic results of the many researchers (e.g., Edelbrock & Achenbach, 1980; Quay, 1983) who have analyzed the characteristics of emotionally disturbed and behavioral disordered children and adolescents. At a broad-band level, two factors — Internalizing or Overcontrolled and Externalizing or Undercontrolled — have consistently been identified. These factors broadly describe children who demonstrate depressed, withdrawing, or uncommunicative behavioral styles versus hyperactive, aggressive, or delinquent behavioral styles, respectively. At a narrow-band level, many different behavioral clusters have been identified, some of which vary developmentally across age, sex, and research sample. To date, the following narrow-band factors have been most consistently identified: Aggressive, Delinquent, Hyperactive, Schizoid, Anxious, Depressed, Social Withdrawal, and Somatic Complaint (Edelbrock & Achenbach, 1980), and Conduct Disordered, Socialized Aggression, Attention Problems-Immaturity, Anxiety-Withdrawal, Psychotic Behavior, and Motor Excess (Quay, 1983).

From a psychometric perspective, the factor analytic approach, and the resulting broad-band and narrow-band factors, represent a very sophisticated approach to classifying behavior. However, this classification approach does not facilitate an accurate identification of all problems nor the development of appropriate interventions in every case. In fact, it must be emphasized that the factors derived from this approach (a) are statistical clusters of correlated behaviors or characteristics, (b) that there are numerous theoretically- and empirically-based decisions made by the researcher that influence which items appear on which factors, and (c) that the factors ultimately are named by the researcher. By way of implication, this suggests (a) that some factors may be multidimensional in nature despite the fact that a single factor is presented, (b) that the presence of an item within a factor does not imply a causal relationship relative to the diagnostic label of the factor, and (c) that there is a level of subjectivity involved in finalizing or naming any factor, especially at the narrow-band level.

While the empirically-based classification approaches have some limitations, they do provide a functional framework from which to organize a sound, school-based classification system that differentiates among referred students' primary social-emotional problems and that facilitates a link between assessment and intervention. One excellent example of an empirically-based classification system that has been adapted into a state special education definition for behaviorally disordered students exists in Iowa. There, a behaviorally disordered students is defined in this way:

1. Behaviorally disordered is the inclusive term for patterns of situationally inappropriate behavior which deviate substantially from behavior appropriate to one's age and significantly interfere with the learning process, interpersonal relationships, or personal adjustment of the pupil to such an extent as to constitute a behavioral disorder.

2. Clusters of behavior characteristics of pupils who are behaviorally disordered include: Cluster I — Significantly deviant disruptive, aggressive or impulsive behaviors; Cluster II - Significantly deviant

withdrawn or anxious behaviors; Cluster III — Significantly deviant thought processes manifested with unusual communication or behavioral patterns or both; and Cluster IV — Significantly deviant behavior patterns characterized by deficits in cognition, communication, sensory processing or social participation or a combination thereof that may be referred to as autistic behavior. A pupil's behavior pattern may fall into more than one of the above clusters.

3. The determination of significantly deviant behavior is the conclusion that the pupil's characteristic behavior is sufficiently distinct form his or her peer group to qualify the pupil as requiring special education programs or services on the basis of a behavioral disorder. The behavior of concern shall be observed in the school setting for school-age pupils. It must be determined that the behavioral disorder is not maintained by primary intellectual, sensory, cultural or health factors.

4. In addition to those data required within the comprehensive educational evaluation for each pupil requiring special education, the following areas of data collection shall be gathered when identifying a pupil as behaviorally disordered which describe the qualitative nature, frequency, intensity, and duration of the behavior of concern. If it is determined that any of the areas of data collection are not relevant in assessing the behavior of concern, documentation must be provided explaining the rationale for such a decision.

This definition emphasizes many of the critical best practices points discussed so far in this chapter. The definition (a) validates referred children's atypical behavior by comparing it to behavior that is developmentally expected at their chronological age levels and to those behaviors normatively observed in their classroom- or community-based peer group; (b) emphasizes students' behavior, affective, and interpersonal progress from a psychological perspective and their learning and instructional progress from an educational perspective; (c) acknowledges and synthesizes the empirical literature by specifying four major clusters of atypical behavior; and (d) recognizes that behavioral and emotional handicaps can be situation- and setting-specific and that referred behaviors occur within an ecological context that must be incorporated into the intervention program. While this definition is admittedly behavioral in orientation and nature, it is clear that behavioral assessment and intervention approaches are now the national norm (Grosenick, George, & George, 1987). As with any special education SED definition, this definition will need further operationalization by school psychologists within their individual school districts as part of a comprehensive approach to effective service delivery for referred and identified SED students.

Pragmatic Beliefs

Beyond the classification of SED behavior, five pragmatic beliefs assure a best practices approach to personality assessment (Knoff, 1986). These beliefs, critical both to the conceptualization and operationalization of the assessment process, will be discussed briefly below.

1. *The need for an ecological/environmental orientation to personality assessment* suggests that referred students are best understood by investigating the family, school, and community systems in which they grew up and now interact. In most cases, these systems have determined and/or influenced referred students' developmental progress, and analyses of the interdependent relationships between these systems and students may explain certain behaviors, affects, and interactions of concern. Clearly, a child's anxious or phobic behavior toward school is best understood when it is known that the child has been corporally punished and embarrassed in full view of her peer group for forgetting to bring in her homework. Similarly, a child who never attended preschool and has been in four different kindergartens and first grades due to frequent moves may never have

learned appropriate play or socialization behavior. The ecological/environmental assessment helps to efficiently explain many referred problems while decreasing the tendency to assume that the child should be the exclusive focus of the assessment process. This perspective also increases the probability that the ecological/environmental contingencies that explain referred problem are recognized and directly addressed with appropriate intervention approaches.

2. *The need for multimethod, multisource, multisetting assessments* suggests that the identification and analysis of referred problems are more accurate when the assessment procedures used involve multiple techniques and approaches from multiple informants who have interacted with the referred student in multiple situations and settings (Gresham, 1983). This process minimizes diagnostic and analytical errors and poorly developed intervention programs that have occurred because (a) only one assessment technique was used (e.g., a projective test) to the exclusion of a more comprehensive assessment battery (e.g., a projective test plus behavioral observations, plus behavior rating scales, plus home and school interviews, plus appropriate developmental scales); (b) only one assessment source (e.g., the mother) was used, when multiple sources might indicate that the mother has excessively high expectations for the child; and/or because (c) the child was evaluated in only one setting, when a multiple setting evaluation might indicate that the child experienced a traumatic event in a different setting and generalized the emotional response across settings. While some problems are legitimately related to specific individuals or settings, the multimethod, multisource, multisetting process increases assessment and intervention reliability and validity while assuring the ecological/environmental considerations described above.

3. *The need for a developmental context to assessment* suggests that school psychologists must be knowledgeable and sensitive to the typical and atypical developmental characteristics that occur for the independent variables of age, sex, multicultural status, and socioeconomic status, and that all personality assessment data be analyzed and interpreted from this perspective. For example, it makes no sense to interpret projective drawings as "psychologically significant" when a child has obvious visual–motor deficiencies or when developmental norms for certain-aged students indicate that they cannot form meaningful, interactive figures in their drawings. It is also somewhat dangerous for school psychologists to depend on their own, or others', subjective interpretations of *any* assessment method if no sound empirical base exists to guide and support those conclusions. Finally, it is important to consider referred children's cognitive-developmental status when interpreting any personality assessment data gathered directly or indirectly. Clearly, a mildly retarded child's social skills and emotional reaction to frustration may be closely related to his or her cognitive skills and developmental status.

In this context, it is important to note that much of the projective drawing literature depends on clinically-based, rather than empirically-based, studies and case examples (Knoff, in press). While projective drawings may provide insight into a student's behavioral cognitions and belief systems, their results can only be interpreted as *hypotheses* that are in need of objective and multimodal validation. In contrast, the various Achenbach behavior rating scales (e.g., Achenbach & Edelbrock, 1983) have been factor analyzed across age and sex. The narrow-band scales that exist for four-year-old boys differ from those of four-year-old girls, and the four-year-old scales for boys and girls differ from the seven-year-old scales for boys and girls, respectively.

4. *The need for a problem-solving and hypothesis testing approach to assessment* suggests that the personality assessment process should systematically involve a problem identification, problem analysis, intervention, and evaluation sequence so that problems are accurately (and ecologically) identified and then comprehen-

sively analyzed (using multimethod, multisource, multisetting assessments) *before* any intervention is attempted. This process explicitly and logically links assessment results with intervention programs, and ensures that these programs are not implemented until a full understanding of the referred problem or situation has been attained. Within the problem-solving process, it is important that conclusions drawn from individual assessment tools be considered hypotheses rather than confirmed facts until such time that they have been validated *by a confluence of indicators* and/or *by uncontestable objective and observable data.*

Most personality assessment instruments and approaches result in multiple interpretations and conclusions. Often, it is the school psychologist's comprehensive understanding of the ecological and psychoeducational characteristics of the referral situation that guides the interpretive process. Ideally, this process should entail a generation of hypotheses, behavioral predictions that operationalize the hypotheses, opportunities to test the predictions in naturalistic settings, and firm conclusions based on these empirical tests (Batsche, 1984). For example, if a diagnostic interview suggested that a referred child would verbally lash out at teachers when confronted with work at too high an academic level (the hypothesis), one would expect that this behavior would not occur when assignments were geared to the student's instructional, and not frustration, level (the prediction). If retrospective and actual classroom observations confirmed this hypothesis, then the intervention program of providing academic work at an appropriate instructional level would be obvious. Note that here, (a) the need for a classification decision is independent of an understanding of the contingencies around the referred problem, and dependent only on the seriousness of the behavior when compared developmentally and normatively; (b) a placement decision would be needed only if it was determined that the intervention program (i.e., providing

material at the student's instructional level) would be more successfully implemented in a special education setting; and (c) there is a definite link between the assessment process and the interventions recommended. This problem-solving, hypothesis-testing process allows school psychologists to strategically choose which assessment instruments and approaches are needed to confirm the hypotheses generated. In this way, the school psychologist controls the entire process; personality assessment instruments are used to "facilitate" rather than "dictate" all interpretations and conclusions.

5. *The need for objective and observable assessment strategies* emphasizes that all assessment hypotheses must be validated objectively and, ideally, through observable means. While objectivity is clearly relative, school psychologists must use instruments and techniques that have demonstrated their ability to validly and reliably generate the desired data and information. Thus, the psychometric properties of all personality assessment instruments must be investigated on an ongoing basis, and only the most sound instruments should be used among those that advertise similar assessment purposes or domains. Beyond objectivity, comprehensive behavioral observation is still the best way to assess the presence of specific social-emotional skills or deficits. Behavioral observation requires a clear operationalization of targeted skills or deficits, and the results include the frequency, intensity, and duration of a referred student's behavior and the antecedent, consequent, and ecological conditions that occur when these behaviors are exhibited. Collecting accurate and useful data through behavior observation requires training, organization, and practice; it is a learned skill. But when done effectively, behavioral observation becomes the cornerstone of any personality assessment, and the source of the objective data that can confirm or reject many important hypotheses about a referred student.

BEST PRACTICES IN
PERSONALITY ASSESSMENT

Rather than describing the various personality assessment approaches, tools, and techniques in a somewhat random, categorical form, this section will discuss the assessment process from the beginning to the end. At the root of this entire discussion, however, is the standard (a) that school psychologists have the professional training and autonomy to determine what personality assessment procedures are necessary for any SED referral; (b) that these assessments are completed within a problem-solving, hypothesis-testing process that maximizes the assessment to intervention linkage; (c) that school psychologists assess only until they have confirmed the hypotheses resulting in a comprehensive understanding of the referred student and referral situation; and (d) that school psychologists identify the intervention programs that offer the highest probability of treatment success. While some states and school districts require the completion of certain personality assessment techniques (e.g., projective tests) with any SED referral *regardless* of the circumstances around the referral, this is *not* a best practices approach. Personality assessment is an individualized process that should be fully in the hands of the professional school psychologist, and the requirement that certain techniques be used is personally and professionally appalling and potentially unwise or even damaging to the referred student.

Identifying the Referred Problem

Given the SED referral made by a classroom teacher concerning a student with problems that have not been alleviated by prereferral intervention, the school psychologist's first task is to clarify the problems of concern and then to operationally define the problems as they are perceived and as they actually exist. Using the most efficient process possible, a substantial amount of data can be collected even before the first interviews with the referring teacher and the referred

student's parents. This occurs as the school psychologist does the following:

1. Thoroughly reviews the student's cumulative folder, medical files, and other regular or special education documentation;

2. Asks the teacher to complete (a) a referral form that profiles the student's educational, social, and behavioral progress during the current year, (b) a questionnaire that behaviorally operationalizes any perceived referral problems using an antecedent–behavior–conscience paradigm, and (c) a behavior rating scale (e.g., the Burks' Behavior Rating Scale) that rates the degree to which certain behavioral or clinical descriptors of children are present in the classroom or school building over a specified period of time; and

3 Asks the parents, usually the mother, to complete (a) a background information form that provides a social, developmental, educational, behavioral, and familial history of the student, (b) the same behavior rating scale as the teacher (in order to assess the multisource or multisetting characteristics) or another behavior rating scale to assess more familial or clinical dimensions (e.g., the Achenbach Child Behavior Checklist), and (c) an objective personality scale (e.g., the Personality Inventory for Children) which provides a more multidimensional, actuarial picture of the psychological functioning of the referred student.

Behavior rating scales. Behavior rating scales are one of the most efficient, sound, and effective ways (a) to identify a referred student's behavioral strengths and weaknesses, (b) to validate a referral source's initial concerns, (c) to evaluate the severity of a wide range of specific behaviors, (d) to assess for atypical patterns of behaviors or clinical entities, and (e) to complete one facet of a multisource, multisetting evaluation. With literally hundreds of rating scales on the market, school psychologists' ability to choose the rating scales that will best accomplish their assessment goals without sacrificing psychometric quality is critical. To that end, Edelbrock (1983) noted that behavior rating scales differ dramatically across a number of critical dimensions, and he provided a number of suggestions to help school psychologists become better behavior rating scale consumers:

1. School psychologists need to match their assessment goals to the results that a particular behavior rating actually provides. Some behavior rating scales (a) assess clinical, home, and/or school concerns; (b) are descriptive, prescriptive, or diagnostic; (c) evaluate specific behaviors or simply provide a checklist indication that they exist; (d) are unidimensional or multidimensional in scope; (e) rate actual student behaviors or characteristics that correlate with certain behavioral conditions; (f) focus exclusively on behavioral deficits or problems, while others assess both behavioral deficits and assets (Wood, Smith, & Grimes, 1985). School psychologists must consider these rating scale characteristics, the referred problem, and the diagnostic and intervention questions to be answered. Clearly, behavior rating scales must be chosen in an informed manner with due consideration of their purposes and intended effects.

2. School psychologists need to recognize that behavior rating scales' technical adequacy vary greatly and need to be analyzed prior to their use. Among the variables to evaluate are: how items were selected during the development of the behavior rating scale, what response scaling approach was used (e.g., "true/false," "often/sometimes/never"), how the scale was developed and constructed, the scale's standardization and norming procedures, and the scale's validity and reliability data.

3. School psychologists need to evaluate whether behavior rating scales evaluate global or specific levels of manifested behavior, the time frames within which referred students are evaluated (e.g., one, three, or six months), and who the optimal respondent should be. To clarify this latter point, some behavior rating scales require

that the informant be the target child's mother or teacher; others are completed simply by an individual who genuinely knows the child or who has interacted with the child over a long period of time.

4. Finally, school psychologists must assess how behavior rating scales control for response bias, for example, for halo effects, leniency or severity effects, and/or central tendency or range restriction effects. Without sufficient controls for bias, a behavior rating scale's results are of extremely limited use.

From an interpretation perspective, school psychologists must strategically use all of the potential information generated by a behavior rating scale. Too often, school psychologists simply use the broad- and narrow-band results of a behavior rating scale concluding and writing in their personality assessment reports, for example, that a referred child "has significantly high externalizing or acting-out tendencies, and that he manifests hyperactive, aggressive, and delinquent behavior" by virtue of elevated scores on those scales. Unfortunately, conclusions like these are simplistic at best and downright inaccurate and damaging at worst. A best practices approach to behavior rating scale interpretation (a) begins at the individual item level to determine what specific behaviors and/or behavioral correlates are of greatest concern to the scale respondent; (b) continues at the narrow-band scale level, first to determine if the significant items are consistent with the label of the specific scale that contains them, and then to determine if the scale's scores indicate a statistical or clinical problem; and (c) ends at the broad-band scale level where the most global interpretations of a referred student's behavior are considered. Significantly, the hypotheses and interpretations at each of these three steps are continually compared with those from other personality assessment tools and approaches such that a valid profile of the student's behavior, affect, and interactions is reached based on a confluence of indicators across methods, data sources, and settings.

Objective personality scales. Objective personality assessment scales may focus on single diagnostic dimensions (e.g., self-concept, anxiety, depression) or multidimensional descriptions of referred children. At the problem identification stage, it may be best to use the latter type of objective scale so that a broad range of psychological problems or concerns can be sampled for later, more in-depth investigation. While a number of multidimensional objective scales are available, the Personality Inventory for Children (PIC; Wirt, Lachar, Klinedinst, & Seat, 1984) is one that works well in the context of best practices in personality assessment.

The PIC consists of 600 true/false items that have been normed separately for males and females from the ages of three to five, and six through 16, and that typically are answered by a referred student's mother. In total, the PIC consists of the following scales: *Factor Scales:* Undisciplined/Poor Self-Control, Social Incompetence, Internalization/Somatic Symptoms, Cognitive Development; *Validity and Screening Scales:* Lie, Frequency, Defensiveness, Adjustment; *Clinical Scales:* Achievement, Intellectual Screening, Development, Somatic Concerns, Depression, Family Relations, Delinquency, Withdrawal, Anxiety, Psychosis, Hyperactivity, Social Skills. Significantly, the PIC and many other objective personality scales have a group of validity scales that determine respondents' ability to realistically evaluate their children (the Lie Scale), their tendency to exaggerate their children's problems (the Frequency Scale), and their ability to respond in an open and forthright manner (the Defensiveness Scale). These scales allow school psychologists to assess the clinical accuracy of the rest of the PIC protocol and to predict respondents' (i.e., mothers' or fathers') generalized response styles in dealing with professionals and others working to address referred students' confirmed difficulties. For example, one might hypothesize that a mother with an extremely high PIC Defensiveness Scale would approach a school psychologist's questions either with caution and evasiveness or anger and externalized blame. Because of the advance hypothesis, however, the psychologist would be prepared with appropriate responses to the mother's defensiveness if, indeed, the PIC hypothesis was found to be true.

From an interpretive perspective and given its objective and multidimensional nature, the PIC has a distinct advantage in its ability to use actuarially-based decision rules. Based on samples of already-identified clinical and special education samples and their interactive patterns, these decision rules generate PIC hypotheses that behaviorally and affectively describe referred students and facilitate a comparison between these students' PIC profiles and those of the actuarial samples. Critically, these hypotheses are derived from an empirical base, they minimize the effects of interpretation bias or oversight, and they are easily integrated into the hypothesis-testing, problem-solving process recommended throughout this chapter. While the PIC and other objective personality scales can be used more diagnostically to classify students into clinical subgroups, this is appropriate only so far as appropriate intervention programs based on confirmed behavioral hypotheses result. Finally, given their empirical base, PIC hypotheses might be used to *confirm* behavioral and affective hypotheses. This, however, would best occur when *a priori* hypotheses have been generated and when the PIC is given specifically to confirm those hypotheses.

Overall, the PIC and objective personality scales contribute clinically useful information to the personality assessment process. When developed with sound psychometric and diagnostic properties, these scales provide low inference hypotheses, they can identify or validate the presence of specific referral problems or concerns, and their factorial nature can assess the more global aspects of personality assessment with the potential for objective and actuarial interpretation.

Problem identification synthesis. Armed with the teacher- and parent-completed referral and background information forms, behavior rating scales, and objective rating scales, the school psychologist can begin the diagnostic interview process at a much higher level of sophistication than when starting the process with a simple statement of concern. In fact, with the social, developmental, educational, behavioral, and familial history of the student already documented by both teachers and parents, a great many background questions are unnecessary, and the school psychologist need only pursue those questions that are directly or indirectly related to the referral problem. Moreover, the school psychologist now can listen to teachers' and parents' descriptions of the referral problem, match them to the behavior and objective rating scale data that has already been completed, begin to behaviorally define and operationalize the stated problems and the behavioral ecology where they exist, and identify any hypothesized behavioral contingencies again using any relevant data gleaned from the forms and scales previously completed. Or, if the teacher or parent knows that a problem exists but cannot pinpoint the specific problems or behaviors, the data can actually identify the rated areas of greatest concern.

Thus, the background, behavior rating, and objective rating data make the problem identification interview process far more efficient relative to time and behavioral specificity. Ultimately, this behavioral specificity should include (a) a definition of the behaviors, affects, or interactions of concern in such clear terms that any professional could observe the child and recognize their presence; (b) a delineation of these behaviors' frequencies, durations, intensities, and situation specificities; (c) hypothesized antecedents and consequences that precede and follow the behaviors, respectively, and that have some level of control over the behaviors; and (d) some sense as to whether the referred behaviors are skill deficits, performance deficits, or self-management deficits. In addition, the school psychologist needs to explore such issues as: the referred student's motivation to change, behavioral strengths and assets, and the

possible function of the behavioral concerns for the student; the home and school routine, settings where the referred concerns occur and do not occur most often, and what interventions have been tried in the past; the teacher's and parents' motivation to work on the problem, their preferred philosophies and approaches in solving the problem, and to what degree the concerns could continue and still be tolerable (Alessi & Kaye, 1983).

Obviously, the problem identification interview is quite complex and very dependent on the sound interviewing skills of the school psychologist. While other resources are available that discuss interviewing skills (e.g., Alessi & Kaye, 1983; Sattler, 1988), the interview must address the process of eliciting the participation, satisfaction, and commitment of the referral sources and the content of moving the personality assessment to the problem analysis phase. Typically, the personality assessment process transitions from problem identification to analysis (a) when hypotheses have been generated to explain the referral concerns and (b) when behavioral observations of the referred student and further assessments with the referred student or others are initiated to confirm or reject the hypotheses specified.

Analyzing the Identified Problem

In order to maximize any behavioral observation, the school psychologist needs (a) to have an explicit goal; (b) a valid, realistic, and acceptable observation approach to realize that goal; and (c) a way to evaluate the utility of the observation data collected. As noted above, behavioral observations will most likely occur to confirm or reject hypotheses related to already identified problems. For example, if a psychologist hypothesized that a student's tantrum behavior was being reinforced by teacher and peer attention in the classroom, one would predict that tantrum behavior would increase in frequency or duration or intensify in the presence of attention and that it would decrease or be absent in environments where no attention was available. In this example, there is a specific goal for the observation activity. The psychologist simply has to arrange a valid, realistic, and acceptable approach to observe and confirm or reject the hypothesis and behavioral prediction, and determine if the collected data was compelling, representative, and accurate.

Briefly, there are four behavioral observation approaches commonly noted in the literature (Cone, 1978; Keller, 1986): naturalistic free behavior, naturalistic role play, analogue free behavior, and analogue role play observations. *Naturalistic Observation* involves observing referred students in the actual settings where their behaviors of concern and/or the conditions that most influence those behaviors are exhibited. When used to confirm hypotheses generated to explain well-identified behaviors, naturalistic observations are both time- or cost-efficient. In addition, they are the most ecologically-sound of the behavioral approaches, and they are the least inferential relative to interpretation within the personality assessment context. *Analogue Observation* involves observing referred students in controlled situations that simulate particular environments or circumstances of behavioral concern. These situations are used to objectively evaluate *a priori* hypotheses that explain referred behaviors or situations and to provide detailed and comprehensive functional analyses of significant facets of a referred student's behavior. Significantly, analogue observations attempt to maximize the ecological accuracy of simulated situations so that interpretation requires as little inference as possible. They are also very time-efficient given their intent to elicit behaviors that test the referral-related hypotheses.

Free Behavior Observations occur when referred students are allowed to freely react and interact within environments that are either unmanipulated and naturalistic or simulated and analogue. No artificial rules or constraints are placed on the students, and they respond to situations in any way that they choose. *Role Play Observations* occur as referred students are requested to follow pre-conceived and semi-structured scripts that focus on interactions or situations relevant to particular hypotheses. These observations involve more inference than free behavior observations, because the student's roleplayed behavior is assumed to represent behavior that would be exhibited if the situation actually occurred in a real-life situation. Once again, role play observations can occur in both naturalistic or classroom-based settings and analogue or simulated settings; naturalistic observations are assumed to require less interpretive inference than analogue observations.

While behavioral observations may appear to be the easiest and most objective of all personality assessment approaches, they actually involve very complex processes. Beyond choosing which observation approach to use, school psychologists still must decide which recording method to use (e.g., narrative, interval, event, ratings), and how to best assess the antecedent conditions, environmental characteristics and interactions, overt and covert contingencies, planned and unplanned consequent conditions, and unintended effects of a referred behavior within its unique ecology. While one of the most effective ways to validate hypotheses generated during the problem identification phase of the personality assessment process, behavioral observation also can be misused or abused. School psychologists must recognize that it is a learned skill that requires training, practice, and more practice.

Other Assessment Techniques. Beyond behavioral observation, there are a number of other personality techniques that can be used during the assessment process: objective personality assessment techniques that focus on single diagnostic dimensions when needed (e.g., self-concept, anxiety, depression), family assessment techniques, thematic apperception tests, sentence completion tests, the Rorschach, projective drawing approaches (Knoff, 1986). While the objective and empirically-based approaches can only generate additional hypotheses that need subsequent validation. While projective tests, for the most part, fall in this latter category, they can provide behavioral and cognitive–behavioral data that can be critical to the personality assessment process.

From a behavioral perspective, the typical projective assessment represents an ambiguous task, completed in a face-to-face testing situation, with an unfamiliar examiner, under environmental conditions that potentially affect both interpersonal and intrapersonal functioning. In this context, the projective task allows a school psychologist to sample a child's behavior, to make numerous observations, and to hypothesize that the student's behavior is representative of how the student would act and react in similar real-life ambiguous situations. While this hypothesis would need objective validation through multi-method, multi-setting, and multi-source behavioral sampling, clearly behavioral observations noted during projective testing are no better or worse than observations taken during any other testing situation. Possible behavioral observations during projective testing, then, include the child's (a) behavior or physical reactions during the test performance or inquiry process; (b) speech and language; (c) attitude and behavior toward the examiner; (d) reaction to the examiner's style, questions, and comments; (e) reaction to the test situation and demands; (f) problem-solving and behavioral or work style in completing the task demands; and (g) comments to him or herself as a reflection of self-concept and self-confidence (Knoff, 1986). Many of these observation areas also are used to assess a referred student's general mental status (Sattler, 1988).

From a cognitive–behavioral perspective, projective tests provide information that suggest hypotheses about referred students' thoughts, beliefs, expectations, self-statements, aspirations, attributions, needs, and perceptions. These cognitions have been shown to cause, encourage, support, reinforce, change, and/or influence behavior, and thus, their identification may help to predict and explain a student's overt behavior. Unfortunately, projective tests provide a fairly unsyste-

matic and disorganized assessment of a student's cognitions. However, as in the clinical interview, the school psychologist must be able to identify potentially important information and to pursue that information so that a comprehensive and accurate picture of the student results. The school psychologist's job, then, is to integrate any cognitive hypotheses into the comprehensive personality assessment of a referred student, and to validate these and other hypotheses using additional interviews, observations, and/or objective assessment procedures such that a useful and potentially effective intervention program results.

To summarize, it should be apparent that *not all personality assessments with or for a referred student necessitate the use of projective tests.* In fact, school psychologists should use only those personality assessment approaches that are needed (a) to fully and validly identify and analyze the significant variables that are causing, supporting, maintaining, and/or encouraging the problem and (b) to fully and validly identify those interventions that will effectively and efficiently resolve these significant variables and the referred problem. In most cases, this can be accomplished by using empirically-based, objective, and behavioral approaches that are well-documented in the research literature. However, there are times when projective tests can provide a needed intrapersonal perspective for a particularly complex case. Projective tests can be important to the personality assessment process. They should be used strategically, however, and not randomly; they should be used to maximize problem understanding and treatment effectiveness, not to cloud the issues with unnecessary redundancies or irrelevancies.

SUMMARY

Once the referred problem has been comprehensively identified and analyzed from an ecological, developmental, and environmental perspective using a hypothesis-testing, problem-solving process where hypotheses are evaluated using objective, multimethod, multisource, multisetting methods, the school psychologist is ready to develop an intervention program. Intervention should be clearly linked to the assessment process, the referral concerns identified and confirmed by the personality and behavioral assessments, and the factors that interact and influence the referral concerns. As noted earlier, intervention is useless unless viable, acceptable, and socially valid approaches are successfully implemented with ongoing attention to treatment integrity an treatment evaluation. In the end, the success of the personality assessment process will be evaluated most clearly on the behavioral and treatment changes resulting from the intervention program.

To summarize, personality assessment is a process, not a product. It is simply not enough to *understand* a child's behavioral or social-emotional problems. School psychologists must move from problem analysis to interventions that resolve these problems and that facilitate children's normal development and positive mental health. This chapter has been dedicated to the ultimate best practice. Hopefully, we will soon see the day when school psychologists provide comprehensive services, when intervention success is valued over special education placement, and when social, emotional, and behavioral success is an explicit educational goal and emphasis.

REFERENCES

Achenbach, T. M., & Edelbrock, C. S. (1983). *Manual for the Child Behavior Checklist and Revised Child Behavior Profile*. Burlington, VT: University of Vermont Department of Psychiatry.

Alessi, G. J., & Kaye, J. H. (1983). *Behavior assessment for school psychologists*. Washington, DC: National Association of School Psychologists.

American Psychiatric Association (1987). *The diagnostic criteria from DSM-III-R*. Washington, DC: Author.

Batsche, G. M. (1984). *Referral-oriented consultative approach to assessment/decision-making*. Washington, DC: National Association of School Psychologists.

Cone, J. D. (1978). The behavioral assessment grid (BAG): A conceptual framework and a taxonomy. *Behavior Therapy, 9*, 882-888.

Edelbrock, C. S. (1983). Problems and issues in using rating scales to assess child personality and psychopathology. *School Psychology Review, 12*, 293-299.

Edelbrock, C. S., & Achenbach, T. M. (1980). A typology of child behavior profile patterns: Distribution and correlates for disturbed children aged 6-16. *Journal of Abnormal Child Psychology, 8*, 441-470.

Gresham, F. M. (1983). Multitrait-multimethod approach to multifaceted assessment: Theoretical rationale and practical application. *School Psychology Review, 12*, 26-34.

Grosenick, J. K., George, M. P., & George, N. L. (1987). A profile of school programs for the behaviorally disordered: Twenty years after Morse, Cutler, and Fink. *Behavior Disorders, 12*, 159-168.

Kenrick, D. T., & Funder, D. C. (1988). Profiting from controversy: Lessons from the person-situation debate. *American Psychologist, 43*, 23-34.

Keller, H. R. (1986). Behavioral observation approaches. In H. M. Knoff (Ed.)., *The assessment of child and adolescent personality* (pp. 353-397). New York: Guilford Press.

Knoff, H. M. (1983). Personality assessment in the schools: Issues and procedures for school psychologists. *School Psychology Review, 12*, 391-398.

Knoff, H. M. (Ed.) (1986). *The assessment of child and adolescent personality*. New York: Guilford Press.

Knoff, H. M. (in press). Evaluation of projective drawings. In C. R. Reynolds & R. W. Kamphaus (Eds.), *Handbook of psychological and educational assessment of children: Volume 2, Personality, behavior, and context*. New York: Guilford Press.

Prout, H. T. (1983). School psychologists and social-emotional assessment techniques: Patterns in training and use. *School Psychology Review, 12*, 377-383.

Quay, H. C. (1983). A dimensional approach to behavior disorder: The Revised Behavior Problem Checklist. *School Psychology Review, 12*, 244-249.

Sattler, J. M. (1988). *Assessment of children*. San Diego, CA: Jerome M. Sattler, Publisher.

Wirt, R. D., Lachar, D., Klinedinst, J. K., & Seat, P. D. (1984). *Multidimensional description of child personality: A manual for the Personality Inventory for Children*. Los Angeles, CA: Western Psychological Services.

Wood, F. H., Smith, C. R., & Grimes, J. (1985). *The Iowa assessment model in behavioral disorders: A training manual.* Des Moines, IA: State Department of Public Instruction.

ANNOTATED BIBLIOGRAPHY

Batsche, G. M. (1984). *Referral-oriented consultative approach to assessment/decision-making.* Washington, DC: National Association of School Psychologists. (34 pgs.)
An introductory manual to the Referral Question Consultation Process which utilizes a systematic problem-solving process to address referred problems. Using consultation processes as a foundation, this process ensures a direct link between case-related assessment and intervention by generating hypotheses that explain the referred behavior, confirming behavioral predictions based on these hypotheses, and developing interventions that address these behavioral explanations. This manual describes this decision-making process and relates it to use by support teams, team reports, and triennial re-evaluations.

Knoff, H. M. (Ed.) (1986). *The assessment of child and adolescent personality.* New York: Guilford Press. (686 pgs.)
A comprehensive volume on personality assessment specifically with children and adolescents written in four parts. Part 1 discusses the theoretical bases underlying the personality assessment process; Part 2 describes the development, administration, scoring, and interpretation of the predominant techniques now used in personality assessment from behavioral to projective to family assessment; Part 3 describes how to communicate and translate personality assessment results into effective intervention strategies; and Part 4 summarizes the issues currently in the field and presents future directions and needs. Written by leading experts in the field, this book presents a pragmatic, applied view of personality in school and community settings.

Martin, R. P. (1988). *Assessment of personality and behavior problems: Infancy through adolescence.* New York: Guilford Press. (399 pgs.)
An important book that approaches personality assessment from a developmental and integrative perspective. It is divided into four sections which discuss issues and assumptions implicit in the personality assessment process, techniques and decisions underlying the design of assessment instruments, and actual instruments and procedures used from infancy through adolescence. The book reviews specific personality assessment tools, presents case study examples, and addresses the advantages and disadvantages of different assessment and interpretation approaches.

Sattler, J. M. (1986). *Assessment of children.* San Diego, CA: Jerome M. Sattler, Publisher. (995 pgs.)
The third edition of Sattler's comprehensive volume covering all facets of the assessment process with children and adolescents has some critical chapters related to personality assessment: the assessment of adaptive behavior and behavior problems, assessment of behavior by interview methods, assessment of behavior by observational methods, assessment of ethnic minority children, and others related to consultation, conferencing, and report writing. Sattler balances theory, empirical research, and pragmatic best practices approaches in a way that facilitates appropriate assessment processes and a clear assessment to intervention linkage.

Wood, F. H., Smith, C. R., & Grimes, J. (1985). *The Iowa assessment model in behavioral disorders: A training manual.* Des Moines, IA: State Department of Public Instruction. This manual was written to train Iowa's school psychologists in how to evaluate behaviorally disordered (BD) students under the state's special education definition. It does an excellent job in reviewing characteristics of behaviorally disordered youth, special education decision-making processes, how to analyze ecological settings, how to complete behavioral observations, and how to individually assess referred BD students. A very pragmatic manual that provides numerous examples and many excellent tables and appendices.

38

Best Practices in Political Activism

Gilbert M. Trachtman
New York University

Years ago there was reason to hope that, in time, we would become a kinder and gentler nation and that ours would become a kinder and gentler profession. But the years have passed and still there are battles to be fought. Still, and perhaps increasingly, children seem to be undervalued and harshly treated. Survival for poor families and for single parent families becomes increasingly difficult. Psychology, more proactive in social policy issues than ever before, continues also to be both proactively and reactively entangled in guild issues, concerned primarily with the empowerment of clinical psychology. For school psychology there are particular battles to be fought. We join fellow psychologists, other related professionals, and the concerned public in advocacy of children's needs and rights. But school psychologists must also contend within psychology for our own empowerment, frequently challenged by the encroachment and the restrictiveness of our clinical colleagues. In the schools we constantly face the possibility of narrowed role definitions or unreasonable productivity demands, attempts to displace us with lesser trained personnel or demands and expectations of us beyond our domain of practice. At all levels, from our personal quality-of-life or work issues to the most global political and environmental issues we are all faced with conditions and circumstances which demand improvement or correction.

Yet we differ greatly among ourselves in our individual sense of power or powerlessness. Also called sense of efficacy or locus of control, this is relatively independent of current external circumstances with roots which may be traced, at least in part, to events much earlier in one's history. In even the most benign environmental circumstances where we could have great control over our own lives, there are some who passively allow the wind to take charge and never manipulate sail or rudder. In the most invasive and controlling settings, there are others who fight back and strive to maintain control over part of their lives.

Faced with inevitable dissatisfaction in some daunting aspect of our lives, the temptation for many is to "let George do it," but George may not do it and we must each bear the responsibility for our action or the consequence of our inaction.

OVERVIEW

The dictionary tells us *activism* is a "doctrine or practice that emphasizes direct vigorous action in support of or opposition to one side of a controversial issue" (Webster's New Collegiate Dictionary, 1973). Because this implies taking sides on an issue already joined, I prefer a looser definition of activism as an attempt to change something or to prevent something from changing. Thus activism may also serve to introduce controversy into a previously undisputed issue. Most dictionary definitions of *politics* refer in some way to government, but I am happier with broader definitions such as "competition between interest groups or individuals for power or leadership" or "the total complex of relations between individuals in society." By that standard, we are all involved in politics, and we all make a political statement, whether we choose to be activists or not. Even when we do nothing but "our job," we present school psychology to the public. Each of us is either helpful, neutral, or harmful. Each of us leaves behind an impression with children, parents, teachers, specialists, administrators, and others. The impressions we create generalize to attitudes which become the context within which people vote for budgets, support legislation, or communicate to colleagues and neighbors. Each consumer who experiences a school psychologist as helpful or caring becomes a potential advocate for School Psychology. Each consumer who experiences us as harmful, unhelpful, ineffective, or uncaring, may contribute to the further circumscription or rejection of our services.

Political activism occurs at many levels, including interventions beyond one's traditional job description within a single school building to attempts to influence federal legislation. The emerging themes from both the Spring Hill (Ysseldyke & Weinberg, 1981) and Olympia (Brown, Cardon, Coulter, & Myers, 1982) Conferences were the need for school psychology to be proactive rather than reactive, and to attempt to play some role in its own destiny. At the national level, we have made significant progress here. However, for one reason or another, the great majority of us are not politically active as individuals. Among a wide range of possible explanations, some of the most provocative may be found in the psychodynamic or existential literature (Becker, 1973; Fromm, 1941; May, 1950; Schachtel, 1959).

The psychological literature on activism is sparse. Although psychologists have studied activists extensively, Vanderbeek and Fodor (1988) reviewed this literature and found most recent research to be focused on college students and most results to be inconsistent and mixed. We

know little about activism among psychologists. If you are *not* politically active, consider why not. Consider whether even in your non-activist professional functioning you might not benefit from being a bit more politically aware and whether the guidelines presented in this chapter might not be useful. If you *are* an activist, or aspire to become active, the guidelines offered later should be useful and perhaps you can contribute further to the needed literature in this area.

BASIC CONSIDERATIONS

Why Activism?

Active is better than passive. This statement is made, not as a value judgment, but as a basic assumption of this chapter. A considerable body of data supports the premise that people benefit psychologically by having more control over their lives (Rappaport, 1981). Activism is seen as the natural state of the healthy human organism, striving to develop personal competency and mastery of its environment. The fetus is already an activist and the normal development of the infant is a saga of successive activist endeavors. It is only later that many of us learn not to be active.

Activism is also implied in the APA ethical expectation that psychologists "are concerned with the development of such legal and quasi-legal regulations as best serve the public interest, and they work toward changing existing regulations that are not beneficial to the public interest" (American Psychological Association, 1981). The National Association of School Psychologists is less clear. While NASP advocates "intense concern for . . . equal access to opportunity," it suggests also that "procedures and practices designed to bring about social change . . . are conducted as involved citizens and not as representatives of school psychologists" (National Association of School Psychologists, 1985).

People need to satisfy their own basic needs before they can function at social or societal levels. Similarly activism in school psychology may initially involve attempts to effect some change in those external circumstances — laws, regulations, job descriptions, people's attitudes and perceptions - which exert control over what we do as school psychologists or how we do it. Pragmatically our activism makes our working conditions or our role more personally rewarding or supports the guild interests of school psychology. Altruistically our activism is directed at effecting change that enhances the welfare of our clients, and allows us to provide more effective or valuable services. The pragmatic and the altruistic frequently coincide or, failing to do so, are at least not in conflict. In rare cases when our guild interests are detrimental to client welfare, ethical considerations must favor the interests of our clientele.

Activism can also lead the school psychologist into broader arenas of social policy. Some of us have urged for many years that we establish a political base by building alliances with parent groups, child advocacy groups, and other professional associations and by working cooperatively with these groups on political activity in the public interest (Trachtman, 1967). Teacher associations, both on the state and national level, are usually quite powerful, politically active, and share many of our interests. Primarily, political advocacy in the public interest on behalf of children benefits children, one of our major goals. As a secondary gain legislation and regulations which are beneficial to children sometimes involve constructive roles for school psychologists and, ultimately, increased recognition of the contributions school psychologists make to children, schools, and families. A tertiary benefit is that active advocacy efforts in concert with consumer groups and other professional groups, and the eventual recognitions of our shared interests, can lead to the development of support from these groups when we are involved in more narrowly defined political action of a guild nature.

Until fairly recently, school psychologists were not visible, either as individuals, or through their major professional associations, at public debate on federal education policies or the federal educa-

tion budget. Other professional groups are highly visible in the public record of these hearings. School psychologists also generally did not participate in educational policy debates at state or local levels, except for vested interest issues such as licensure and certification (Abramowitz, 1981). This has not been a failing only of *school* psychologists. Speaking of psychologists in general, APA President-elect William Bevan stated, "they either have refused to concern themselves with policy questions for fear of contamination or, when they chose to engage themselves, they have been almost *totally* preoccupied with primarily self-serving, narrowly focused guild issues" (1981).

As stated earlier, a major outcome of the Spring Hill Symposium on the Future of Psychology in the Schools (Ysseldyke & Weinberg, 1981) was the theme of proactivity. Many speakers and workshops focused on the need for a proactive stance and on the theme of social consciousness, viewing professional practice in the context of larger issues such as the state of the economy, sexism, and racism (Rosenfield, 1981). Over and over again, we reminded ourselves of the need for school psychologists to develop an internal locus of control and self-directedness, and to become politically active in public policy areas, with other professional associations, and with parent and community groups.

Where Can Activism Occur?

It has already been stated that even when we perceive ourselves as inactive, "just doing our job and nothing more," our day to day actions at work have political import, affecting people's perceptions of school psychology. Also one's daily behavior beyond the job may have unplanned or accidental political significance. When my raucous cheering for the visiting team offends a hometown spectator at a football game, the resulting altercation is often a funny footnote to the afternoon, to share with friends that evening. When it turns out on Monday that the angry football fan is chair of the state legislature's education committee with whom several of us are meeting to discuss pending legislation, my treasonable behavior at the stadium may prove costly to school psychology.

Hopefully such fortuitous events just as often prove serendipitous, and, in any case, since they are difficult to plan in advance, they are not further considered here. For purposes of this chapter, political activism refers to beyond-the-job planned behavior focused, directly or indirectly, on improving the welfare of our clientele, or ourselves, or both. Our day to day activities such as assessment, consultation and counseling are obviously conducted on behalf of clients and do have political impact, but are not considered here.

Given, then, that as working school psychologists we are motivated to become politically active and to invest energy in bringing about constructive change in the practice of school psychology, where should we contribute our efforts? The answer is "almost anywhere," as long as we get involved somewhere. Activism can begin at home. Any psychologist working in an institutional setting has a readily available list of concerns about work. Even psychologists with high job satisfaction can usually criticize something about their work situation or about the institution's impact on clients. Some of us engage actively in trying to effect change; most of us complain and do little. The reasons usually given for this passivity and the reasons which really explain it, could be explored in another chapter. Generations of school psychologists-in-training have exhibited passive behavior. There is much to complain about in even the best graduate training programs and, usually, some small group of students fights actively for change while most remain passive. Because the training context differs some from the subsequent job context, the expressed reasons for passivity may differ, but it is probable that the real reasons are similar in both contexts, and it is likely that the activist trainee has been active before and will be an activist professional later.

To be an activist in changing some broader aspect of school psychology re-

quires only that we identify an agency or a force impacting upon school psychology negatively. The complexity of these forces leaves us numerous choices for activism. A small hint of this complexity is evident when one considers the many forces impinging on accreditation and credentialing in school psychology. Fagan (1986) portrays this visually and vividly when he diagrams sources of power and authority affecting school psychology. At the state level he alerts us to the influence of professional associations, certification boards, and licensing boards, and at the national level to the influence of psychological associations, trainer organizations, and accrediting agencies. His chart only scratches the surface, however, when we consider all the additional forces which affect our day to day practice. At the local, county, or municipal level, practice is additionally regulated by educational agencies, legislatures, or courts. At the state and federal level educational agencies, legislatures, and courts also further enhance or inhibit our functioning either by regulatory action or by providing or withholding funding. Impacting on all these governmental agencies are our own psychological associations, other professional associations, and various parent and citizens groups. All are concerned about the same issues and attempt to influence who delivers what services to whom. Additionally, competing interests direct the attention of the legislature to other issues presented as more important than ours. Futurists, predicting how school psychologists will function tomorrow, find it necessary to consider the impact of disparate forces such as economic, geopolitical, and ideological factors (Ogilvy, 1981). Activists, attempting to affect how school psychologists will function tomorrow might aim their efforts at any of these contributing factors.

Were we to decide that the time had come for us to be politically active, the problem is not to locate an outlet for our energy, but rather to select the proper channels for our investment of effort. Individual efforts at political action are always possible. Getting a letter to the editor published in a newspaper, testifying before a legislative committee, speaking directly or writing to one's congressman, or questioning a board of education or an education official about certain regulations always leaves one with a sense of accomplishment. A California state senator has acknowledged voting a particular way on certain legislation because of a single letter of support or opposition (Carpenter, 1983).

Generally, however, political activism is usually more effective as a group endeavor over time, and activist effort is probably more effectively expended by contributing to selective group activity. Most organizations deal with multiple issues. Most issues are attended to by many groups. Upon becoming an organization activist, one could commit time fully to one organization, thereby supporting that organization's efforts on many issues. Alternatively, one might be so committed to a single issue that one becomes active in several organizations, focusing in each organization on activity devoted to the particular issue. Thus, a feminist psychologist might be actively involved with gender bias issues in three or four different organizations while a colleague in the same organizations might be actively involved in committees seeking to modify state or federal definitions of learning disabilities.

The machinery for political action by psychologists already exists. In recent years psychology has become active politically and quite recently, school psychology has begun to be more active. However, there is insufficient money and person-power available to do what needs to be done, unless many more of us become involved. Psychology in general is represented by the American Psychological Association, by affiliated state associations, and by many local associations affiliated with the state groups. In 1974 APA organized the Association for the Advancement of Psychology. AAP was incorporated as a national lobbying organization to advance the science and profession of psychology and has been quite active on the national scene.

The National Association of School Psychologists was organized as an alternative national organization to APA when APA established a doctoral entry level for the definition of a practicing psychologist and for full membership. NASP has grown rapidly and has become a strong and articulate voice for school psychology. Child advocacy is facilitated by the NASP Children's Fund. NASP is supported by affiliated state associations and by many local associations of school psychologists.

Organized psychology and organized school psychology now maintain parallel political structures. Many school psychologists join their local, state, and national school psychology organizations, although a distressing number of school psychologists fail to join anything. Some school psychologists also join psychology associations and most of those organizations contain school psychology divisions or sections. Often these organizations work cooperatively and are able to take similar stands on political issues involving consumer welfare. Even on some guild issues involving professional self-interest, it has been possible to work cooperatively. However, APA, AAP, and most state psychology associations are committed to the doctoral entry level and to the primary interests of clinical psychology vis-a-vis medicine. When these interests conflict with those of school psychology, clinical psychology interests usually take precedence, even in organizations where school psychology is also represented.

The individual school psychologist needs first to make a financial commitment by joining several appropriate organizations. At the organizational level political activism begins by joining these organizations. Adding funds to their operating budget and numbers to their membership rolls increases their political clout. Too many school psychologists never take this first step, but remain all too ready to complain about their lot. However, having joined an organization, many assume that responsibility ends with payment of dues and occasional participation at a convention. As a result, our professional organizations may be insufficiently monitored by and insufficiently responsive to their membership. Most professional organizations are run by a small group of hard working individuals who frequently make and implement policy. Although most are responsible and serve their membership well, it is easy to lose touch with the priorities and needs of a silent constituency. In many organizations an attempt is made to communicate regularly with the membership via bulletins, newsletters, minutes of board meetings, drafts of policy statements, and so forth, but, typically, membership response or commentary is virtually nonexistent. Most organizations report few members participating in the nomination and election process. So, the second stage of organizational activism is to be a *responsible* member. Read your newsletters, attend membership meetings when possible, express opinions, send notes to officers or committee chairs, and participate in referendums or elections.

Having taken these baby steps toward activism, we are now ready for real action. Now that we are informed about the organization(s) we have joined, about their structure, and focus, and activities, we are ready to become active in a particular arena. We may either join an existing committee or suggest the establishment of a new one. In most organizations the door is wide open for anyone interested in working. An expression of interest is enough to get involved. In some organizations it proves difficult to join an existing committee or to get a new one started. While there is occasionally a reasonable explanation for this, this should be of grave concern to the membership.

There is no shortage of relevant battles to be joined and worthy causes to be advocated. If our organization is not already involved in activities to which we feel a strong commitment, public policy advocacy might be the place to start. There is much that psychology can contribute to shaping public policy in areas of child mental health, early intervention and prevention, compensatory education, or support and assistance for young children and their families (Garbarino, 1988; Hobbs & Robinson, 1982; Inouye, 1988; Saxe, Cross, & Silverman, 1988; Takanishi, 1983). If these broad policy issues, primarily

consumer oriented and relating to federal legislation, are too broad or too abstract to catch our immediate interest, consider instead the need for systematic organization and advocacy at the state level, more often related to guild issues. For an excellent overview of these issues, primarily as they relate to state psychological associations and doctoral licensing and practice, but with great potential relevance to school psychology's political issues, see Ginsburg, Kilburg, and Buklad (1983) and the articles which follow in the same journal issue.

Most of the above discussion has focused on activism within professional organizations. The suggestion has been made that our psychology associations should more regularly join with consumer groups and other professional groups in public policy advocacy. For school psychologists who enjoy writing, a further contribution in this vein is publishing articles in the magazines or journals which consumers and other professionals read. Doing this often enough establishes school psychology in the consciousness of those whose support we seek. I did some of this years ago, and the positive feedback was most rewarding (Salten, Elkin, & Trachtman, 1956; Trachtman, 1960a; 1961a; 1961b; 1962; 1967–68; 1970).

BEST PRACTICES

This section should cite a number of case histories or detailed published accounts of political activism leading to attainment of political goals. Based on extensive experience with the California legislature, Dorken provides a generalized account of successful political process. He defines 21 key steps for getting a bill through the legislature. Although his narrative reflects some of the parochial interests of clinical psychology vis-a-vis professional psychology, it serves also as a valuable primer for school psychologists (Dorken, 1981). In a subsequent article he describes legislative activism as a systems problem and documents the need for ongoing and sustained advocacy efforts (Dorken, 1983). Forman and O'Malley (1984) describe an innovative field experience in the state legislature for school psychology graduate students which seems quite promising for the promotion of activism. Generally, however, detailed accounts of psychologist activism in the political process are rare. Therefore, borrowing freely from Dorken's suggested steps, Bevan's (1981) precepts and Alinsky's (1971) rules and mixing them all with a dash of personal experience, here are suggestions for effective political practice:

Gil's Guidelines for Political Activists

1. *Listen to others.* We are supposed to be skilled listeners, yet we often fail to take these skills with us into the political arena. Manifest content is not always what it seems to be; people do not always mean what they seem to mean. Ask them to elaborate. Be alert to the hidden agenda which others may be hiding from you or the unconscious motivations of which others may be unaware. Be sensitive to previous history, to unpaid debts, to covert alliances, to secret enmities, to unobtrusive opinion molders and leaders, and to shifting alliances.

2. *Know yourself.* Keep in touch with your own need systems, unconscious motivations, values, and attitudes which could lead to perceptual distortion. Knowing your real goals can enhance your effectiveness and increase your flexibility to consider other paths to the basic goal. An intimate and open relationship with peers who provide honest feedback is invaluable. Learn how you appear to others.

3. *Reach your audience.* At times your audience may be professional colleagues whom you are recruiting or rousing to action. Other times it may be skeptics, opponents, or strangers whom you are attempting to proselytize. The name of the game is effective communication, and speaking loudly and clearly is not enough. It is vital that you speak to others in both their linguistic and affective language. This refers, in part, to elemental components of empathy. Sensing the experience background of another, speaking from some body of shared experience, and seeking out a shared value or interest serve to establish some level of rapport. This is one of the most complex and difficult of all the ground rules to observe, and is hardly attainable by cognitive means alone. It encompasses rules 1 and 2 above, and includes also such elements as basic respect for others and establishment of trust. Cognitively it requires that you communicate psychological concepts in plain English and that you know who your audience is and how it functions. Learn to use the media effectively. If you want your voice to be heard, you need to know who the key politicians or bureaucrats are, who has their ear, which staff members are vital links to which officials, how the legislature or bureaucracy functions, how budgetary factors affect policymaking, and what the timetables are.

4. *Establish credibility.* Most people will respond not only to your agenda, but to you as a person. Although circumstances may not always permit, getting to know people, person to person, establishing rapport, and earning trust will enhance your subsequent ability to be heard. Another prior contribution to effective communication is the respect you have already earned by advocating actively on behalf of children, educational programs, and the psychological welfare of families or by providing consultation where your advice is perceived as educational, knowledgeable and nonpartisan, and where you have no guild interest.

5. *Be prepared for the vagaries of decision-making.* While all your efforts are directed toward logical and persuasive support for your cause, do not expect policy decisions to always be made on rational bases. Remember the angry football fan who turns out to be chair of the legislature's education committee. Recall the state senator whose vote was based on a single letter (Carpenter, 1983). A state licensing bill for psychologists, laboriously shepherded through both houses of the legislature was vetoed by a governor responding to personal advice from his family physician. Budding or broken romances at high levels can have more influence on a policy decision than all the logic and persuasion we can muster,

and yet we must continue to provide the logic and persuasion.

6. *Be patient and persistent.* Change comes slowly, and the work is tedious. Two childhood memories keep me going. Before the days of refrigeration, an ice man with horse and wagon came to sell us a nickel's worth of ice. He scratched a line in his huge cake of ice and then pecked along that line with his ice pick, seemingly to no avail for several moments. Suddenly, from the cumulative effect of all his previous picks, the ice cleaved cleanly at the line he had drawn. Another image which serves me well is sitting in the bleachers watching my heroes, on the New York Giants baseball club (pre-San Francisco). I realize now that even the greatest of the great failed to hit safely more often than not, and that a lifetime record of three successes in every ten tries is considered superlative. And so I have learned to keep swinging for the fences, to be undismayed when I strike out, and to be rewarded by an occasional home run and a respectable batting average. Successful politicking demands extensive spade work, preparation and organization. It requires frustration tolerance, delay of gratification, and a *realistic* level of aspiration.

7. *Maintain a sense of humor.* Receptively, humor is vital for maintaining one's balance and avoiding despair. Expressively, humor can convey truths which might not otherwise be accepted. At appropriate times in political battle, it can be used to great effect against the opposition, who may be more vulnerable to satire and ridicule than to direct confrontation.

8. *Maintain flexibility.* Today's tactics do not work tomorrow, today's alliances dissolve tomorrow, today's major issues are preempted tomorrow. Consider alternate routes to the expressed goal or other attainable goals of equivalent value.

9. *Know your bottom line.* Some issues are matters of such profound principle that no compromise is morally feasible and we must live or die by the stand we have taken. Most issues are not of such philosophical import and the art of compromise is a cornerstone of a dem-

ocratic system in which many needs and many interests compete for recognition. This guideline for political activism is quite consistent with an affirmative but flexible professional style where you know the ideal recommendation for a particular child, but the administration, your team members, or the parents disagree. You must enter the situation willing to find some balance between what you want and what others want, but also knowing your bottom line, not imposing your views unilaterally, but also not selling out your position without expressing it clearly.

10. *Acknowledge and understand power issues.* Power is a key component of all political action. It is a factor in the assumption of leadership within a group and in that group's political program. Yet we find little open discussion about power issues, power strategies, or power needs. Our psychology textbooks devote little attention to power as a motivating force. Carpenter (1983) suggests that power is not a socially acceptable human motive, and even more pointedly, that those with power tend not to talk about it. Yet, to understand your opponent's vulnerability it is vital to understand his power base. A key tactic in certain martial arts is the sudden switch from an attack mode to total passivity or relaxation which, properly timed, throws your opponent completely off balance. A metaphoric equivalent of this can be effective therapeutically in dealing with resistance, and political activists need to understand the various uses of power.

11. *Embrace conflict appropriately.* The idea of conflict or controversy, although frowned upon in polite society, is vital to the democratic process. Conflict leads to victory or defeat or compromise and is therefore an essential component of change. Without conflict we would have status-quo, obviously favorable to the "ins." The "in" group naturally finds confrontation distasteful or uncouth, and, when its power is sufficient, often prefers to remain aloof and distant from the "outs." When their power is not sufficiently absolute, the "ins" are delighted to avoid conflict by negotiating endlessly, by establishing joint task forces or study groups, by co-opting

"out" leaders into the slow moving deliberative process, by clouding the issues or by introducing less salient issues. Conflict for the sake of conflict is not desirable. Energetic but polite activism or negotiation in the true spirit of mutual accommodation is preferable, but confrontation and direct conflict is sometimes necessary to bring an issue to the surface. At times an issue has become so blurred that it needs to be dramatized, exaggerated, even polarized to the point of no imminent compromise. In the words of an early activist, "He that is not with me is against me." (Luke 11:23)

12. *Acknowledge self-interest.* We like to surround ourselves with the cloak of altruism when it is frequently obvious that our concern is not so much for the welfare of the child as for the comfort of the psychologist (Trachtman, 1960b); not so much for the protection of the public as for the protection of psychology (Trachtman, 1972). Pure altruism is quite rare and even when we are truly active on behalf of the public, we may have secondary self-interest (see #4). Sometimes self-interest and the public interest coincide. What's good for school psychology is good for the people and our political activism is still supported on the highest moral grounds. However, most administrators and legislators are pragmatists, and are more ready than we are to acknowledge the role of self-interest in policy-making. They consider our cause seriously if it is not inimical to the public interest, if we have established credibility, and if we have demonstrated power. They respect us more if we deal with the self-interest openly.

13. *Establish networks.* Networks have always existed in society, have often evolved naturally and served the purposes of support or communication, and have sometimes been used intuitively and productively by community organizers. It remained for Sarason (1976) to pioneer the formal concept of networking as a planned professional activity and to elaborate it further to cope with scarcity of human resources (Sarason, 1977; 1979). At Spring Hill and Olympia, with the focus on school psychology's need for a proactive stance, the importance of networking for political purposes was repeatedly affirmed. Networking with other groups is important for establishing a broader power base and credibility. A legislative network of psychologists (Dorken, 1981) is a vital mobilization tool at moments of political crisis. In many areas of common interest, school psychologists might work cooperatively with teacher associations or other pupil personnel organizations.

14. *Work on several issues.* Individuals may choose to focus on a single issue as their prime passion even to the extent of finding several organizations within which to carry the same issue forward. Organizations and groups are well advised to develop an agenda of several issues. A single issue agenda is likely to attract a narrow constituency, cathected to the issue rather than the organization. An organization with a multi-issue agenda attracts a wider spectrum of members which provides more power and leverage for each of its campaigns. Membership remains stable as particular issues flare up or die, but the general thrust of the group continues.

15. *Learn from your experiences.* Feuerstein's (1979) concept of mediated learning, while initially applied to interactional processes between developing children and intentional adults, is equally applicable to all of us. Feuerstein describes the adult who "mediates the world to the child by framing, selecting, focusing and feeding back environmental experiences" so as to produce the appropriate learning. This is also how a good supervisor works with an intern, and how we need to mediate our own life experience if we expect to grow from experience instead of merely living through a series of events. Political activism is a constant learning experience. No two situations are ever alike, no successful tactic is guaranteed to succeed again, and unsuccessful strategies may work next time around if we do not abandon them precipitously. It is therefore necessary to accompany each experience with reflection, analysis, and interpretation if it is to become a learning experience.

SUMMARY

This chapter defines political activism and reviews the need for activism in the field of school psychology. It was noted that many psychologists are not actively involved, but no attempt was made here to explain this inactivity. However, a major premise of this chapter is that activism is the natural style of healthy individuals.

Our developing awareness of the need for proactive behavior was described, followed by a review of possible arenas for action, from on-the-job behavior to more formal activism at all political levels. Further discussion considered individual activism versus organizational involvement, participation in psychological organizations, the monitoring of these organizations, and the range of possible issues with which to become involved. Finally, 15 ground rules for political activism were presented and discussed, borrowing heavily from the work of Saul Alinsky and several others.

ACKNOWLEDGMENTS

I acknowledge, with appreciation, the thoughtful comments of three anonymous reviewers.

REFERENCES

Abramowitz, E. A. (1981). School psychology: A historical perspective. *School Psychology Review, 10*, 121-126.

American Psychological Association. (1981). *Ethical principles of psychologists* (rev. ed.). Washington, DC: Author.

Becker, E. (1973). *Denial of Death.* New York: Free Press.

Bevan, W. (1982). On coming of age among the professions. *School Psychology Review, 10*, 127-137.

Brown, D. T., Cardon, B. W., Coulter, W. A., & Myers, J. (1982). The Olympia Proceedings. *School Psychology Review, 11*(2).

Cardon, B. W. (1982). Synthesis of the scenarios. The future: A context for present planning. *School Psychology Review, 11*, 151-160.

Carpenter, P. B. (1983). The personal insights of a legislator/psychologist. *American Psychologist, 38*, 1216-1219.

Dorken, H. (1983). Advocacy and the legislative process. *American Psychologist, 38*, 1210-1215.

Dorken, H. (1981). Coming of age legislatively: In 21 steps. *American Psychologist, 36*, 165-173.

Fagan, T. (1986). School psychology's dilemma. *American Psychologist, 41*, 851-861.

Feuerstein, R. (1979). *The dynamic assessment of retarded performers.* Baltimore: University Park Press.

Fromm, E. (1941). *Escape from freedom.* New York: Holt, Rhinehart, and Winston.

Garbarino, J. (1988). Can our nation's economy endure if we fail to educate our children? Newsletter, Division of Children, Youth and Family Services. American Psychological Association, Division 37, *VII*(1), 5.

Ginsburg, M. R., Kilburg, R. R., & Buklad, W. (1983). State-level legislative and public advocacy. *American Psychologist, 38*, 1206-1209.

Hobbs, N., & Robinson, S. (1982). Adolescent development and public policy. *American Psychologist, 37*, 212-223.

Inouye, D. K. (1988). Children's mental health issues. *American Psychologist, 43*, 813-816.

May, R. (1950). *The meaning of anxiety.* New York: Ronald Press.

National Association of School Psychologists. (1985). *Principles for professional ethics.* Washington, DC: Author.

Ogilvy, J. (1982). The forces shaping the 1980s. *School Psychology Review, 11*, 112-126.

Rappaport, J. (1981). In praise of paradox: A social policy of empowerment over protection. *American Journal of Community Psychology, 9*, 1-25.

Rosenfield, S. (1981). Small group synthesis, group A. *School Psychology Review, 10*, 285-289.

Salten, D. G., Elkin, V. B., & Trachtman, G. M. (1956). Public school psychological services: Recent growth and further potential, parts I & II. *Educational Administration and Supervision, 42*, 100-107 and 162-169.

Sarason, S. B. (1976). Community psychology, networks and Mr. Everyman. *American Psychologist, 31*, 317-328.

Sarason, S. B., Carroll, C., Maton, K., Cohen, S., & Lorentz, E. (1977). *Human services and resource networks.* San Francisco: Jossey Bass.

Sarason, S. B., & Lorentz, E. (1979). *The challenge of the resource exchange network.* San Francisco: Jossey Bass.

Saxe, L., Cross, T., & Silverman, N. (1988). Children's mental health: The gap between what we know and what we do. *American Psychologist, 43,* 800-807.

Schachtel, E. G. (1959). *Metamorphosis.* New York: Basic Books.

Takanishi, R., DeLeon, P. H., & Pallak, M. S. (1983). Psychology and public policy affecting children, youth and families. *American Psychologist, 38,* 67-69.

Trachtman, G. M. (1972). Protection for whom? *New York State Psychologist, 24,* 2, 4, 5.

Trachtman, G. M. (1970). Evils of educational research. *Phi Delta Kappan, L11,* 123-235.

Trachtman, G. M. (1967-68). Educational innovation and the school psychologist. *Education Synopsis, 13,* 1.

Trachtman, G. M. (November, 1967). The school psychologist and legislation: A position paper. *New York State Psychological Association, School Psychologists Division Newsletter,* 3-5.

Trachtman, G. M. (1962). Should parents know the results of intelligence tests? *PTA Magazine, 56,* 4-6.

Trachtman, G. M. (1961a). Role of an in-service program in establishing a new plan of elementary school organization. *Journal of Educational Sociology, 34,* 349-354.

Trachtman, G. M. (1961b). New directions for school psychology. *Exceptional Children, 28,* 159-163.

Trachtman, G. M. (1960a). The K-3 school evaluated by the K-3 principal. *American School Board Journal, 140,* 55.

Trachtman, G. M. (1960b). From the pen of the president. *Nassau County Psychological Association Newsletter, 8,* 4-5.

Vanderbeek, A., & Fodor, I. G. (1988). Psychology and activism: Who and how psychologists study activists and social change agents. (PC Reports 7-88-6). New York University, Psychoeducational Center.

Webster's New Collegiate Dictionary. (1973). Springfield, MA: G & C Merriam Company.

Ysseldyke, J., & Weinberg, R. (Eds.). (1981). The future of psychology in the schools: Proceedings of the Spring Hill Symposium. *School Psychology Review, 10*(2).

ANNOTATED BIBLIOGRAPHY

Alinsky, S. (1971). *Rules for Radicals.* New York: Random House.
Alinsky is our foremost purveyor of organizational know-how, and much of this chapter comes from Alinsky's thinking. I read Alinsky's earlier works 40 years ago and last read this book, which he subtitles "a pragmatic primer for realistic radicals" 15 years ago. In reviewing it for this chapter, I was stunned to see how much of his writing I had absorbed as my own thinking.

Bevan, W. (1981). On coming of age among professionals. *School Psychology Review, 10,* 127-137.
This was the keynote address at the Spring Hill Symposium, by the then President-Elect of APA. Bevan paints a lucid portrait of our complex society, issues of public policy, the role of professionals in this society with particular reference to school psychology issues, and closes with some simple rules of thumb about advocacy roles for professionals.

DeLeon, P. H., O'Keefe, A. M., Vanden Bos, G. R., & Kraut, A. G. (1982). How to influence public policy: A blue print for activism. *American Psychologist, 37,* 476-485.
Reviews the importance of public interest advocacy and political activism for the guild interests of psychology, with particular focus on national health policy.

Melton, G. B. (1987). The clashing of symbols: Prelude to child and family policy. *American Psychologist, 42,* 345-354.
A thoughtful analysis of mythological views of childhood and family life often held not only by the general public, but by the legislature and judiciary as well. This paper points to the potential role of psychologists as advocates in diminishing confusion in child and family policy-making because of conflicts between myth and fact.

39

Best Practices in Preparing and Presenting In-service Training

Greg A. Robinson
Iowa Department of Education, Des Moines

OVERVIEW

Due to the ever-changing roles of our schools and the students who attend them, there continues to be a need to convey information that assists educators and families in realizing goals set forth on behalf of students. No professional working in the field of education for a period of years can keep abreast of all the changes and recommendations for improvements without participating in staff development activities. These activities must be designed to disseminate information in a fashion that is meaningful, applicable, and useful over the long term.

School psychologists looking to this chapter as a guide for in-service education should realize that a workshop presentation is just one method that can be used as part of an overall staff development program. The National Education Association's Research Division lists 19 methods including classes and courses, institutes, committee work, professional readings, research, and visitations as alternatives in providing staff development (Rebore, 1987). Deciding which method is most appropriate to meet the needs of personnel is an elaborate process that, when done correctly, enables local districts and intermediate education agencies to meet current and anticipated staff development challenges.

In-service education activities frequently are selected for a number of situations. The rationale for these activities should not be just the availability of in-service days on the district's calendar; rather they should meet the specific needs of district personnel in working with students, families, or colleagues. In-service education can be a most effective strategy when done properly. This chapter will provide school psychologists with guidelines for the preparation and delivery of in-service presentations. There is no single best way to provide in-service education, yet certain elements appear to be present in all innovative and well-received presentations.

BASIC CONSIDERATIONS

School psychologists need to be cognizant of certain factors that can increase the likelihood of successful in-service presentations. These factors range from models of adult learning to the availability of specific resources.

Adult Learning

Adult learning has been described as a process involving two components: education and training (Robbins, 1982). *Education* is the acquisition of a knowledge base and the reasoning skills necessary to apply knowledge in various situations. *Training* is described as the process of acquiring a set of sequenced behaviors designed to achieve a specific goal (Robbins, 1982; Rebore, 1987).

In-service trainers can use this model of adult learning as a basic guide for the preparation and delivery of presentations.

Content activities, and other outcome measures can be developed to address one or both facets of adult learning. The topic of the in-service and the needs of the audience will dictate the extent to which both education and training should be addressed. For example, if an in-service is designed to present a new instructional procedure to classroom teachers, the presenter should provide both the basic knowledge base necessary to understand the procedure and a behavior sequence that can be followed to use the procedure effectively. Presenters are advised to include training activities when application of a specific skill or procedure is the point of the presentation.

Trainers also need to understand the process of change and how others react in the change process. At times participants may voice disagreement with what is being presented. Good trainers who understand change will look at this particular situation differently than those who are unfamiliar with dealing with individuals in the change process. Knowledgeable trainers will not view the participant who raises questions as being totally in disagreement with what is being said, but will try to assess the concerns being voiced.

To assist trainers in this area the Concerns-Based Adoption Model (CBAM) was developed through a project at the Research and Development Center for Teacher Education at the University of Texas at Austin. CBAM looks at change as a process that is personal and developmental, and it is aimed at individuals first. In the CBAM way of dealing with change, interventions must be related to people first and the innovation second. To assist trainers in understanding change, CBAM characterizes seven stages of concern that may typically be expressed about innovations, as well as eight levels of use that illustrate how individuals may implement changes. For more information on the CBAM Project, the reader is referred to the works of Gene E. Hall, Susan F. Loucks, and Shirley M. Hord.

Outcomes

If training is to be successful, it must be directed toward some specific eventual outcome ("If you don't know where you're going, how will you know when you get there?"). Outcomes have implications for both the design and evaluation of training. In-service activities usually have one of four goals: increased knowledge of educational theories and practices, new curriculums or content; changes in attitudes toward self, children, or academic content; development of a skill; and transfer of training and executive control (Joyce & Showers, 1988). The key is to first specifically define a desired outcome and then design the presentation and evaluation components to reach the goal as defined.

Training Techniques

When staff development opportunities arise, to guarantee the learning of the personnel involved four basic conditions of learning must be provided: stimulus, response, reinforcement, and motivation. Rebore (1987) gives a simple explanation that is an easy way to remember these conditions as they apply to staff development. Questioning by the trainer provides learners a stimulus. Their answers are the required responses. Feedback from the trainer to the response constitutes reinforcement. Since staff development activity is usually intended to render the staff more apt to meet a need which they currently face, the prospect of acquiring the new information that is needed should supply the learner the appropriate motivation. School psychologists who provide in-service training will want to highlight conditions of learning throughout their presentations.

Strategies and techniques (Baird, Schneier, & Laird, 1983; Eitington, 1984) are available that should enable school psychologists to broaden their repertoire of techniques for use in staff development training. Successful staff development involves the participants throughout the in-service program. Trainers must have good facilitation skills and feel comfortable in developing activities for small groups, dyads, or triads as a way to implement problem solving initiatives to address situations that participants must deal with daily. This activity could include role-playing or sharing previous experience in resolving classroom problem situations among participants in small combinations as with the trainers serving as observers and providing immediate feedback. Although some of these areas are discussed briefly in the next section, the reader is referred to the annotated bibliography.

Transfer Difficulties

Nothing is as disheartening as seeing educators leave a presentation enthusiastic about innovative techniques only to observe, upon visiting their classrooms, no subsequent implementation of the new ideas. One of the major problems with traditional "one-shot" in-service is the number of ideas presented during the training that are forgotten by participants within the first hour of the drive home. School psychologists involved in training must make sure that the new ideas presented during an in-service transfer to the classroom or worksite. Eitington (1984) and McNamara (1983) suggested that transfer is more likely if trainers include activities that demonstrate application of information, develop contracts or agreements that insure commitment on the part of participants after the initial training, and create follow-up opportunities. Understanding the commitment to follow-up separates good trainers from mediocre ones. Participants must have resources available if questions arise as they attempt to implement new ideas.

It is vital that school psychologists involved in in-service activities consider the follow-up component *before* the initial activities take place rather than after the fact. Without sound follow-up activities the ideas presented become incomplete notes, which then become unexplainable back home in the classroom and are eventually shelved. A way around this is

for school psychologists to think not only about how the information will be presented initially but also about what activities will occur later to insure that the methods or strategies trained will be incorporated into the daily routines of the participants. A significant element to making in-service activities work is planned and detailed follow-up components that are established and approved by administrators and participants prior to the training.

Speaking to Groups

Not everyone feels comfortable talking with groups of colleagues. Even when the content to be presented has been mastered, the words do not always come out smoothly. For school psychologists who struggle with this difficulty there are avenues of assistance. Public speaking organizations are available such as Dale Carnegie or Toastmaster's International groups, that provide assistance in a nonthreatening manner to persons who want to improve their public speaking skills. Another consideration may be to have a friend videotape a presentation and review the tape, noting possible phrases that are repeated or gaps in content where participants lose interest.

Computers

With the technology and software now available for presentations, computers can be used to facilitate the development of presentations. Learning one of the in-service presentation software programs now can save many hours later as additional presentations are developed. Most programs come with guides to assist the novice.

BEST PRACTICES

This section is intended to offer school psychologists a number of suggestions that constitute best practices in conducting in-service activities. Specific areas to be addressed will deal with preparation, presentation, and evaluation of in-service programs by school psychologists in the familiar situations of serving the personnel with whom they regularly work, as well as situations in which they are brought in for presentations as outside professionals with expertise in a given area.

Clarifying What, Who, and How

Before beginning preparatory activities school psychologists may wish to gain further information about the enrolled participants. Relevant information might include current practices and training needs, participant descriptions, and plans for ways in which the information presented will be used or supported in the future. Information can be obtained through a simple needs assessment form sent to potential participants. If a specific topic has been identified, a needs assessment can request participants to identify the three major points that they would like covered on the topic, areas they would like to avoid, and needs related to follow-up and information application.

When the in-service is to be presented at a familiar location, this information can be gathered directly by the school psychologist who will be involved with the in-service activities. If it is to be presented at a distant or unfamiliar location, this information can be gathered by local personnel.

Once the content areas that the in-service will address are more particularly defined, the focus then shifts to who specifically will be attending, the number of participants, and the outcomes that are expected to result from participation in the in-service activities. Who will attend depends on the needs that are to be addressed. If the need is to provide better interventions for students with hearing impairments, the participants will mostly be teachers of the hearing-impaired. Such a need calls for specific nuts and bolts, practical ideas presented in a straightforward, "This is how you do it" manner. If the skills to be trained have to do with behavioral consultation provided by support service personnel, participants could then consist of representatives from several disciplines, including school psychologists, social workers, and educa-

tional curriculum consultants. Activities could include role-playing the different components of the behavioral consultation process. Finally, if the focus is to be on skills that pertain to instructional, support, and administrative realms, for example, the development of teacher assistance teams with good decision-making skills, the in-service may be most useful if the group trained consists of a building principal, a support service person, and a teacher from general education as well as special education. The training activities must not only promote the ideas being presented but also develop appropriate communication skills among the group team members.

Selecting the participants may well depend on the trainer's ability to provide technical assistance after the initial in-service activities. If there will be ample opportunity to provide a great deal of one-to-one follow-up with participants, the trainer may wish to keep the focus narrow and group size small, so as not to later complicate the process of providing technical assistance to participants. If follow-up by the trainer will be limited or difficult because of time or distance, it may be better to train more personnel in a given discipline and designate a local contact person or learning facilitator through whom questions and answers can be funneled to the school psychologists who provided the training. The latter arrangement may also be preferred if teams are to be the focus of training. In these situations more personnel could be trained initially, since follow-up activities on the part of the school psychologist trainer will consist of dealing with a limited number of learning facilitators in addition to being available to others on an as-needed basis.

It is up to school psychologists involved in the training to consider which approach is best to use. In some programs, attention has been given to training smaller numbers first, the purpose being to render professionals proficient with the newly acquired skills so as to become trainers themselves, thus beginning a network. A weakness of this approach is that too much emphasis may be directed at too few people. If only two professionals are trained from one building as part of a larger district initiative and one of the professionals should leave the next year, the capacity for further training within the building will have been cut in half.

Likewise, there is also a problem with regard to training larger groups of professionals in given strategies or techniques. It is true that initial implementation is broader, but should variation in the application of the new techniques or strategies develop, the result might be less favorable circumstances for guaranteeing consistency through follow-up activities to reduce the variation.

Establishing an In-service Plan

Once knowledge of the specific areas to be covered, participant descriptions, and the extent of possible follow-up activities are at hand, the school psychologist can turn to the development of an in-service plan. This plan should include stated goals and objectives for the entire project, the development of a content outline, technical assistance agreements, pre- and posttest measures, and an in-service evaluation instrument.

Stating in a written format the goals and objectives for a project can make a difference in their realization. Goals and objectives that are written can be made specific, operational, and measurable, like those that instructional staff are required to develop for students in their programs.

Formation of goals and objectives is neither an easy task nor one that should be avoided because of its complexity. Goals and objectives should reflect the different stages of learning theory, which should be applied throughout the in-service project. Participants will be expecting to *acquire* new ideas/skills/strategies. All to often this component is the sole factor that is given advance consideration in the goal development process. Of equal importance are goals and objectives that will enable participants to become *proficient* at these new skills during the training, to *maintain* the newly acquired skills, and to *generalize*

them to other areas or settings once they are back in their job. As with an effective individual educational plan (IEP), the quality of the presentation is not related to the number of goals. The specific content, number of participants and the length of the in-service will enter into the presenter's determination of an appropriate number of goals and objectives.

The outline of the program content should indicate the areas to be covered during the in-service. This outline should adhere to learning theory principles not only by outlining the periods of time during which new information will be presented, but also by including time periods in which activities for practice, group discussion, and trainer feedback on the practice and discussion can occur.

Technical assistance agreements are often used in staff development, especially during in-service training. These arrangements are in a printed format and consist of a list of items or activities that can be performed in the work environment. The participants choose an activity from the list at the end of the presentation, and agree to complete it by a given date. An example item for teachers who have attended an in-service on task analysis during the first week of September would be "By October 15, develop 4 task analyses, each dealing with skills needed in recreational or domestic environments." The completed technical assistance agreements are then copied. The participants retain the originals, and copies are given to the trainers to use during the follow-up stage of the project. Technical assistance agreements may vary in length; however, the number of items required should be consonant with the amount of time and energy the presenter will devote to follow-up. Trainers cannot expect participants to engage in these activities if little or no follow-up actually is provided. As a general rule of thumb, it is appropriate to list a dozen items and require the selection of four of the activities to be completed by participants when the group size is ten participants for every trainer.

Participants should set reasonable timelines and sign off on their agreements.

It may be difficult to ensure that participants complete the activities; however, sending participants copies of letters that have been sent to supervisors complimenting the participants for the quality of their completed items will increase the likelihood of future task completion.

The verification of permanent products or observations that result from the completion of items selected on the agreement may cause trainers to feel that all goals have been realized as a result of the training. This may not be the case, however, if the level of competency of the participants was such that the information presented was already known to the participants and was simply a review. Thus pretest measures can be used to ascertain the knowledge of participants prior to the dissemination of information. The questions asked as part of the pretest can again be used upon completion of the initial in-service activity as a posttest measure, and at a later point during the follow-up stage to assess maintenance of the acquired skills. Questions can take the form of a short answer, or multiple choice or true–false questions can be employed; in any case they should assess the participant's knowledge in the major areas addressed. To reduce the anxiety level and grant anonymity, participants may substitute symbols or numbers for their names when completing the pre- and posttest measures.

In exchange for assessing the degree of learning of the participants, presenters should give the participants an opportunity to evaluate the in-service presentation. When developing an in-service evaluation instrument, trainers should check with colleagues for any existing instruments they may have used in similar circumstances. Although the content may vary from instrument to instrument, participants should have the opportunity to rate an in-service on areas dealing with overall organization, objectives, trainers, ideas presented, and activities conducted. Space should be provided for written comments pertaining to individual likes and dislikes of the in-service.

Preparation of the In-service Presentation

Content. School psychologists who conduct in-service presentations must keep in mind that although it is important to present effectively, it is the *information* that the participants will use after the in-service is over. Therefore it is important to have the most current information to share with the participants. Research for the presentation may require a visit to the local or to the nearest university library and a search through the ERIC or INFORMS databases for relevant articles. It may be appropriate to contact colleagues who have expertise in the given area including other practitioners, preservice trainers, state department consultants, or consultants from the regional resource centers throughout the United States.

As the content to be covered starts to take shape, trainers need to consider the mood or atmosphere they want to create during the in-service. Whether the in-service will have an underlying sense of seriousness, humor, or a mixture of the two will depend on the topic, audience, and length of time together. It is imperative that the mood to be established should be compatible with the personalities of the trainers. Trainers should not attempt to be something they are not. If in doubt, consider the topic. A presentation on suicide prevention and one on putting the magic back into instruction for elementary-age students call for different approaches not only in preparation but also in how the information is presented. School psychologists as trainers may also want to consider what they have enjoyed in past presentations when they were participants.

Another factor to be considered in setting the appropriate mood or atmosphere for the presentation is having some knowledge of the audience. It helps to know their job roles and responsibilities and how they get along as a group. Projecting a day's agenda that calls for a number of "tell me how you feel" group activities and then finding out that the audience participants are a joint group of administrative personnel and of instruction staff who have recently ended an embittered teachers' strike is not a situation trainers want to find themselves in *twice*! Once, maybe, for experiences or stores to tell later; twice never!

A final note deals with the art of being honest, sincere, and believable. School psychologists providing training should concentrate on being themselves and not try to endear themselves with embellishments. All the comments a trainer makes and the questions that they answer are part of the overall presentation. Telling parents of children with disabilities as part of an in-service message "I know how you feel" is a poor choice of sentiments for trainers who are not parents of children with disabilities themselves. Similar experience and vicarious or hearsay experiences are not "same" experiences. Trainers need to keep that notion in mind and choose their comments and answers to questions wisely. There is nothing wrong with saying "I don't know," or saying: "I personally can't imagine the situation, but what other parents have told me who sound like they have encountered similar situations is . . ."

Determining methods for presentations. Having determined the content to be covered and the general tone of the in-service, trainers must determine how the information will be delivered. There are numerous ways to present information and none may be construed as best practice over another. Many trainers will use a combination of techniques to provide variety to the presentation. Trainers should strive for fresh, creative presentations that are different from past in-services that participants have attended. Participants remember information presented in a novel way. The following are a few possible strategies.

Overhead projector slides. Often slides used with overhead projectors are used as a crutch and become the focal point of the presentation. The use of overhead slides or other audiovisual aides is meant to enhance a presentation, not replace it. Overhead slides should illustrate the high points of the verbal information being presented. Care should be

taken that the slides do not become the script of the presentation. If the presentation consists of the trainer reading the slides, providing a handout could save everyone time.

Use of overhead slides *must* take into consideration the size of the group. After taking numerous college courses and attending presentations given by preservice faculty, the author began to believe that preservice faculty were required to restrict the print of their overheads to less than an eighth of an inch! Overhead slides must be more than transparencies of the trainers' notes. Overhead slides that consist of typed material should have printed characters no smaller than 18 point, the majority of the typed characters being 24 point. Having print of the latter size will allow adequate viewing by an audience of 50–60 persons.

In addition, software programs for computer presentations are now available, such as Microsoft's *Power Point*, Cricket Software's *Cricket Presents*, and Letraset's *StandOut!*, for the Macintosh or IBM; they allow for the creation of magnificent overhead slides consisting of text and graphics that can be made in color. For those unable to use programs such as these, consideration can be given to creating overhead slides by using transparencies that allow for color print on a clear background, rather than black print on a colored background. The latter are a positive change from traditional clear overheads, but they are more difficult to read as group size increases. The clarity of the slide decreases when the image projected on the wall increases in size.

Videotapes. This is an excellent method for illustrating case studies or examples. Video can be used in several different ways that provide enhancement and innovation to the presentation. The development of a professional videotape can cost $750–1,000 per minute; however, if the purpose is to show a technique as it is being used in a classroom, a steady hand and a video camera are the basic requirements. Although most professional videotape is recorded on three-quarter-inch tape, most schools have half-inch VHS format machines. Trainers should carry a second copy of the tapes they plan to use in case problems arise with the first copy.

Slides. If the group is large, slides may be a better choice than an overhead projector for presenting information. Once a costly and professional procedure, the development of camera slides has now become more practitioner-friendly.

Professional color slides can be developed for 25¢ to 50¢ each. This requires photoready copy of printed text or graphics pages, which look very nice when produced by a laserwriter. Computer software presentation programs also are able to create slide format originals, which can then be photographed through the processes explained previously. These pages are then shot at the lab and developed into slides.

Slides can also be created by the trainers themselves through a rather inexpensive process that reduces their production costs yet make possible a more professional-looking presentation. A set of close-up lenses must be obtained that fit the 35-mm camera that will be used to shoot the slides. These close-up lens kits usually consist of 3 close-up lenses marked by their characteristic diopter +1, +2, +3. These lenses are then used individually or in combination with the camera lens by screwing the close-up lenses onto the threaded front mount of the camera lens. To turn photographs into color slides the easiest method is to use daylight film and place the photograph on a flat surface outside. The person making the slides should position the camera over the picture and try to make the photo image as large as possible through the use of the close-up lenses in the viewfinder of the camera. It is important to try to shoot the slides with no shadows cast on the photograph. This method can be used for photographs or print copy.

A step up from the previous process is to use a copy stand with tungsten lights. A copy stand is a board with an adapter to which a camera can be attached so that it is positioned directly above the board.

The camera can then be moved in such a way as to create the largest image possible in the camera viewfinder. Two tungsten lights are located on the left and right sides of the board, which allows for images to be photographed with no shadows. These lights create intense levels of heat and should be turned off between shots. Tungsten film (35mm), available at local camera stores, must also be used.

To add color backgrounds to the slide, colored gels or filters can also be used. Gels are nothing more than different-colored pieces of transparencies that can be mounted with a gel holder on the end of the camera lens. Filters are more expensive and screw directly onto the lens. Gels and filters come in different colors and degrees of filtration and are available at any local photography store.

Handouts. Handouts can be a nice "gift" to participants. School psychologists who spend a great deal of time developing overhead or camera slides want participants to benefit from the content of the slide. It is difficult to check for understanding when participants are scribbling madly, trying to copy the contents of the slides into their notes. One of the nicest statements that can be made by trainers to participants at the start of an in-service is "To insure that you don't get writer's cramp, I have prepared a handout of all the overheads that will be used during the presentation; therefore relax, listen, and ask questions if something isn't clear." This move will guarantee higher than usual evaluation scores. Remember, educators like to take things home for use in their jobs. Handouts can be a way to extend the presentation to another environment and provide future reference material for participants. Care should be taken in deciding what information should be included as handout material. It is a good idea to provide a cover sheet with the handout package that states the title of the presentation, where it is being presented, for whom, the date, and the names of the trainers. The computer presentation programs previously mentioned have the ability to provide handouts that have miniature images of the overhead or camera slides at the top of the page with room for notes below.

Almost as important as the content of the handouts is the time of distribution to the participants. If the in-service is one of many concurrent sessions going on at a conference, participants may step into the session to see what is going on and check for handouts. Once the handouts are in their grasp, these people often are gone. If this is not bothersome to the trainers, they should give the handouts out at the beginning of the session. This will allow those who remain to take notes during the session on the handout sheets. If losing handouts to visitors is a concern, trainers should keep the handouts at the front of the room and given them out at the end of the session. A compromise would be to give the handouts out after the first break of a longer session. For in-service presentations that are a day or more in length, the trainers should provide the handouts whenever it helps facilitate the presentation.

Articles. If repeated references are made during the presentation to journal articles or book chapters, it may be appropriate to provide a listing of the references or copies of the articles and chapters to the participants. This, of course, will depend on the numbers of participants and overall budget of the in-service project.

Prior assignments. If part of the presentation will deal with actual cases, assignments may have to be made prior to the in-service presentation to insure that the appropriate data are collected and brought to the presentation. Assignments may also include the reading of selected articles or viewing of videotapes. When this technique is used, it should be made clear to the participants why this request is being made and how they will benefit during the in-service by completing these activities prior to the presentation.

Final preparations. *Determining the materials needed.* Materials needed for the in-service could include overhead pens, blank transparencies, chalk, erasers, masking tape, and newsprint. Participants may need folders in which to keep their handouts, tablets, pencils, rubber bands, name tags or name tents. Other materials might be needed during small-group activities if participants are to be recorders or facilitators.

Determining equipment needs. Trainers also must determine their equipment needs in advance. If someone is hosting the in-service, the trainers should try to provide their equipment needs to the host as soon as possible.

If overhead projectors are to be used, trainers may wish to consider the use of two overhead projectors if they will be using a great number of overhead slides. This will enable them to expedite their presentations by placing upcoming slides on the second projector while leaving sufficient time for participants to take notes form the previous slide on the first projector. Negative feedback from participants often results when overhead slides are displayed and removed too quickly. When using video, consider the size of the audience. If the group is numerous and spread out, more than one monitor will be needed to insure that everyone will be able to see clearly.

Trainers must remember not to let the use of audiovisual equipment overshadow the presentation. Too many machines, cords, and screens can interrupt the flow of a presentation when trainers switch back and forth to present information.

Room arrangements. The physical arrangement will control the communication flow of the presentation (Grimes, Malmberg, Dublinske, & Caster, 1975). There appears to be four basic arrangements that are used for in-service presentations.

When participants are seated theater-style or in rows trainers may lose participants seated in the back, unless the trainers move about the room along the perimeter or up the center aisle if one is present. This arrangement is geared for lecturing, and trainers can expect limited discussion as participants will soon tire of bobbing their heads as they try to see who is asking questions.

If participants are arranged around a table, there will be a better chance for interaction, although the people at the corners tend to be lost from view. This is a good arrangement when the total number of participants is small (8–10); large numbers make this arrangement impossible.

A better format for presenter–participant interactions is the U-shaped arrangement, which can be used with or without tables; however, participants seem to be more at ease with tables. This arrangement allows for trainers to move around freely and is an appropriate arrangement for groups of 15–20 people.

The final arrangement is small-group clusters, which can also be used with or without tables. When in-service is being provided to participants in teams, this arrangements is preferable.

Settling on a single arrangement is not always best practice. The longer the presentation, the more the trainers might want to consider a combination of arrangements. This is especially true if different types of audiovisual equipment are being used, or if role-playing or other small-group techniques are being combined with lecture sessions.

Developing in-service schedules. If the trainers have followed this outline up to this point they will be ready to finalize their in-service schedule. The schedule should include the starting time, the times of each session, breaks, meal breaks, group activities, and the proposed ending time. If the presentation is to take place for more than one day, the presentation for the additional days should also be blocked out, although times may need to be adjusted based on the amount of information covered during the previous day.

Included in the in-service schedule should be sufficient time to discuss the content and answer questions. Many times participants respond on evaluation sheets that the presentation was meaningful but there was not enough time for questions. During this time important points can be solidified or debated.

In-service schedules must also include time for pretests, posttests, and completion of evaluation sheets. These activities are meaningful ways for the participants to measure their learning. For trainers, these activities provide important feedback on the presentation itself and may give specific recommendations on certain aspects of the in-service that the trainers may wish to expand or delete in the future.

After finalizing the in-service schedule, trainers should focus on the actual script of the inservice. Some trainers feel most comfortable when they develop verbatim scripts which they can use during the presentation. Others prefer note cards which highlight major points on specific topics. A third option for trainers who have given previous in-services on the topic may be a listing of the titles of their overhead or camera slides in the order in which they will be used. As with other areas discussed previously, a combination of these ideas may be in order. For example, the major points of the presentation could be listed down the left side of the trainers' guide and the corresponding slides listed down the right side. The important point is to know not only what will be discussed next, but what comes after that as well.

Conducting the In-service Presentation

Before the in-service. Trainers should be at the site of the presentation early. If school psychologists are serving as their own hosts, this is not as important as when they are guest trainers for someone else. Hosts have enough to do at the last minute without worrying about the location of trainers. If the presentation is to be at an unfamiliar location, it is wise to find directions and drive to the location the night before an early morning session.

Once at the location, trainers should identify the number of participants and determine if there are sufficient handouts. The arrangements of the room also should be checked. Trainers should be aware of the location of the thermostat in the room and how the thermostat functions. Participants do not fall asleep in cooler rooms.

This is especially true for a session that begins after a big lunch, when people have already been sitting for a long period of time. Trainers should locate the light switches and try different lighting schemes. If the room has dimmer switches, trainers may wish to experiment by lowering the level of lighting over the participants just enough to enable them to see their notes but make the room dark enough to allow better viewing of overhead or camera slides being projected at the front of the room.

Checking equipment and organizing the materials is the most time-consuming activity that comes before the start of the in-service. It is imperative that all of the equipment be checked. Hosts should make sure additional bulbs are available for overheads and slide projectors. The use of extension cords helps to space out equipment if more than one piece of audiovisual equipment is being used. In such a case, the trainers should think through the process of how they will change and move equipment during the presentation so that these transitions occur smoothly.

If the trainers are guests, they should check with the host of the in-service to see if there have been any changes in the schedule as a result of last-minute difficulties. If no problems are apparent, the trainers should mingle with the participants as they arrive. As introductions take place, trainers should make a mental note of each person's name and job role, which they may wish to work in during the presentation (e.g., "As a school psychologist working with preschool kids with behaviors problems, Marsha may be more apt to use . . .").

During the in-service. Giving the in-service is usually the easiest part of the process. After all, the trainers have planned their activities and are knowledgeable about the subject areas, and the participants are hoping to learn. Trainers should relax, follow their script or notes, and provide the information to the audience.

The opening segment is important, for the participants want to know as much about the trainers as the trainers do about the participants. During this time, trainers should provide the ground rules for the in-service, an overview of presentation goals, the in-service schedule, and the trainer's expectations of the participants. Trainers may wish to ask participants if there are other specific needs that must be addressed during the in-service. Trainers should attempt to increase the comfort level for the participants by making the in-service as applicable as possible.

Trainers should explain how questions will be handled. Options include holding questions until the end of a segment and then asking participants to raise their hands, or allowing questions at any time. Participants should be made aware of which option the trainers prefer. If trainers are standing in front of large stacks of handouts, participants will want to know what they are, when they get them, and if they will have to take notes. Trainers should try to anticipate and answer questions of this type.

After the introduction participants should be given pretest materials. As the participants complete the pretest materials, trainers need to evaluate initial audience reaction. Trainers should consider how the participants have reacted during the opening segment, observing verbal and nonverbal cues to see if the participants are responding to the mood the trainers are hoping to set. It is important to recognize and focus on these factors early in the process so that adjustments can be made.

Before proceeding, there are a few strategies which trainers may want to use which have been very helpful to the author in dealing with certain situations. Decisions to use these strategies are usually considered after the completion of the opening segment.

Trainers should begin by looking to one side of the room for participants who are smiling and nodding when a point is being made, and then look back at those persons when additional points are made to reinforce the participants' agreement. Once this behavior is established, trainers need to focus on participants on the other side of the room and attempt to repeat the process. Targeting participants may sound manipulative, but it establishes a foundation for agreement that will be built upon throughout the in-service.

A set of strategies also exists for participants who are not paying attention or question every statement made by the trainers. Trainers need to find out as soon as possible the names of these persons, where they work, and what they do. Then, while looking at *other* participants the trainers can pick a time when a comment or dilemma can be illustrated by using a particular person's name. If Tim is the target of this exercise and he is sitting in the back of the room, the trainer speaking can look at Jaime in the front of the room while gesturing with an outstretched hand towards Tim saying, "We have to come to grips with the fact that when that little multihandicapped nonverbal 7-year-old boy is wheeled into Tim's room over at Northwest school, Tim doesn't want to give an IQ test, but is not sure what else to do!" Please be assured that Tim will be paying attention for the next few minutes. Part of the time, he will be wondering how he became the target, but the remainder of the time will be spent attending to what is being discussed. Trainers should try to go back to Tim as soon as possible in a nonthreatening way and ask for input on the issue.

For persons who continue to ask questions that tend to become more and more picayune and irrelevant, trainers initially should try to answer the questions as best they can. The next step is to focus on another part of the room and pretend not to see the raised hand before moving on to other content areas. The third step is to respond with a comment that refers the question back to the person, for example, by asking, "Based on what we have talked about so far, what could you do in that situation?" or to ask other participants, "Does anyone have any ideas for Frank that he could use in that situation?" Finally, trainers can cite the schedule and explain that they would be glad to meet at break or at the end of the day to try to answer the questions more clearly.

As the participants complete their pretest materials, dissemination of the substantive information of the in-service begins. Maintaining an even pace during transition from one activity to another helps to keep the attention of the participants. If trainers need to make a critical point in the presentation, they should shut off the overhead or carousel projector to focus the attention of the participants on the presenters rather than the screen. Pace, flow, and direction of participants' attention are important keys to remember during the presentation.

Breaks usually are scheduled, but trainers should be flexible. If the participants seem happy, maintain the break schedule. If the information is difficult to understand, consider shifting the schedule from one fifteen-minute break midway through a three-hour session to two ten-minute breaks, one after each hour. Audiences tend to like more breaks, regardless of their length.

If the in-service is to be more than one day, upon the completion of each day's activities, trainers need to review what has been covered. They may want the participants to identify the most meaningful points of the day's presentation. Trainers should outline the next day's agenda and ask if anything has been left out that the participants want covered. If assignments are to be done during the evening, trainers need to make sure everyone understands the expectations.

After bidding everyone a good evening, it is important for the trainers to collect their thoughts and plan specifics for the next day. Consideration should be given to the amount of information covered during the day, the identification of activities that did or did not work, questions that remain unanswered, and remaining content.

The next day should begin with a review of the agenda. Trainers may wish to share some new thoughts germane to the in-service presentation that can serve as a transition into the first information segment.

Before the conclusion of the in-service, three critical steps must be performed. First, if technical assistance

TABLE 1
Best Practices in Preparing and Presenting In-service Training Checklist

○ **Clarifying what, who, and how**
- ☐ Conduct further needs assessment
- ☐ Who will be attending
- ☐ Number of participants in attendance
- ☐ Expected outcomes
- ☐ Consider follow-up activities

○ **Establishing an in-service plan**
- ☐ Written goals and objectives
- ☐ Draft content outline
- ☐ Technical assistance agreements
- ☐ Pre/posttest measures
- ☐ In-service evaluation instrument

○ **In-service preparation**
- ☐ *Content*
  - ☐ Research topic
  - ☐ Mood/atmosphere
  - ☐ Knowledge of audience
  - ☐ Being honest, sincere, and believable
- ☐ *Determining methods for presentations*
  - ☐ Overhead projector slides
  - ☐ Videotapes
  - ☐ Slides
  - ☐ Handouts
  - ☐ Articles
  - ☐ Prior assignments
- ☐ *Final preparations*
  - ☐ Determining material needs
  - ☐ Determining equipment needs
  - ☐ Room arrangements
  - ☐ Developing in-service schedules and scripts

○ **Conducting the in-service presentation**
- ☐ *Before*
  - ☐ Check with host — finalize schedule
  - ☐ Check number registered and handouts
  - ☐ Check temperature
  - ☐ Check lights
  - ☐ Check equipment
  - ☐ Meet participants
- ☐ *During*
  - ☐ Opening
  - ☐ Pretest
  - ☐ Handling questions
  - ☐ Difficulties
  - ☐ Pace
  - ☐ Review
  - ☐ Technical assistance agreements
  - ☐ Posttest
  - ☐ In-service evaluation
  - ☐ Closing
- ☐ *After*
  - ☐ Analyze in-service evaluations
  - ☐ Analyze pre/posttest data
  - ☐ Review technical assistance agreements
  - ☐ Schedule follow-up teleconferences and visits

agreements are to be used, they must be disseminated and explained. If dates have been set for teleconferences or follow-up visits, share them with the participants so they can record the dates on their calendars. Second, the participants should complete the posttest materials. The third and final task is completion of the in-service evaluation form. When all three items have been completed, trainers should collect them and explain to the participants they will receive a copy of their technical assistance agreements in the next few days.

In closing, trainers may want to consider thanking the participants for their attention and the host organization or representative for their hospitality. A statement that summarizes the goals or desired outcomes should be made, followed by a comment that some participants hopefully will want to try some of the ideas but it is understandable that some may not. This type of statement conveys to the participants that the trainers are there to assist them and not force them to do procedures against their will. Once said, tell the participants to drive safely and say good-bye. Standing by the door and shaking hands is a nice touch that participants remember. After all, ministers have been doing it for years!

After the in-service. When reviewing in-service evaluations, trainers should focus not only on what participants liked, but what they did not care for and why. Written comments are usually quite helpful in providing information on whether the presentation was organized and met the goals set at the beginning of the presentation. Feedback on the quality and amount of materials as well as the use of audiovisual equipment is also helpful for future presentations.

Checking the pre- and posttest measures will provide important data on individual learning. If trainers feel that certain parts of the in-service did not go well, the posttest measures should assist in determining whether the participants gained the information presented during

those parts of the presentation. Documentation of knowledge gains by the participants is a good body of information to leave with the host if the trainers are guests. This will assist the host in validating to their supervisors the effectiveness of the in-service.

A few days after the presentation, follow-up activities should be conducted. The technical assistance agreements should be summarized quickly to aid in the follow-up plan. If additional articles or handouts need to be distributed to participants, trainers may want to include them in a thank-you letter to the host or organization. If the trainers are from the area, arrangements to provide additional information can be made directly with the participants.

Future teleconferences or scheduled on-site visits should be scheduled within the first week following the in-service. With these tasks planned and others completed, trainers can look forward to the next opportunity to share information with other colleagues.

CONCLUSIONS

Conducting in-service presentations is just one of many staff development opportunities that school psychologists may be called upon to provide. Although in-service education is but one method of staff development, it is used a great deal in today's schools.

The intent of this chapter was to highlight certain practices that school psychologists may wish to consider as they develop in-service presentations. Understanding certain components that influence in-service development, such as adult learning and transfer of learning, were discussed as basic considerations. The best practices section examined elements of planning and delivering presentations to be considered by school psychologists who will be training others. Points discussed in this section are summarized in a checklist format in Table 1.

REFERENCES

Baird, L. S., Schneier, C. E., & Laird, D. (Eds.). (1983). *The training and development sourcebook.* Amherst, MA: Human Resource Development Press.

Eitington, J. E. (1984). *The winning trainer.* Houston, TX: Gulf Publishing Company.

Grimes, J., Malmberg, P., Dublinske, S., & Caster, J. (1975). *In-service: A how-to book.* Des Moines, IA: Iowa Department of Public Instruction.

Joyce, B., & Showers, B. (1988). *Student achievement through staff development.* New York: Longman.

McNamara, J. R. (1983). Why aren't they doing what we trained them to do? In L. S. Baird, C. E. Schneier, & D. Laird (Eds.), *The training and development sourcebook.* Amherst, MA: Human Resource Development Press.

Perry, R. H. (1980). The organizational/environmental variables in staff development. *Theory Into Practice,* (3), 256–261.

Rebore, R. W. (1987). *Personnel administration in education* (2nd ed.). Englewood Cliffs, NJ: Prentice-Hall.

Robbins, S. P. (1982). *Personnel: The management of human resources* (2nd ed.). Englewood Cliffs, NJ: Prentice-Hall.

ANNOTATED BIBLIOGRAPHY

Baird, L. S., Schneier, C. E., & Laird, D. (Eds.). (1983). *The training and development sourcebook.* Amherst, MA: Human Resource Development Press.
This excellent sourcebook for trainers includes readings, training materials, instruments, guides, and checklists, as well as strong sections dealing with the learning and training process and techniques for implementing training and development programs, and for transferring learning.

Eitington, J. E. (1984). *The winning trainer.* Houston, TX: Gulf Publishing Company.
Good resource for working with groups, this volume provides examples of techniques to use, such as role-playing, games, simulations, video, and case studies. The section on team building is well worth reading as are the sections dealing with problem solving.

Grimes, J., Malmberg, P., Dublinske, S., & Caster, J. (1975). *In-service: A how-to book.* Des Moines, IA: Iowa Department of Public Instruction.
Although somewhat dated, many good examples throughout the book have stood the test of time, and trainers may wish to incorporate them into their presentations. This is a very functional and usable document.

Joyce, B., & Showers, B. (1988). *Student achievement through staff development.* New York: Longman.
Builds on current staff development practices as the authors look towards the future. This resource would give an excellent overview to would-be trainers on broader topics of staff development.

Rebore, R. W. (1987). *Personnel administration in education* (2nd ed.). Englewood Cliffs, NJ: Prentice-Hall.
Focuses on the concept of staff development from the administrative perspective. A process is detailed on how districts and buildings can arrive at meeting needs through the staff development process.

40

Best Practices in Preschool Social Skills Training

Stephen N. Elliott
Joan Ershler
University of Wisconsin–Madison

Developing the skills for successful relationships with one's peers, parents, and teachers is one of the most important accomplishments of childhood. This interpersonal, social process, although not fully understood, begins soon after birth and is influenced by organismic variables such as one's own physical abilities, language, and communication skills, and environmental variables such as family members' and peers' involvements and interactions. Unfortunately, not all children acquire adequate social skills and consequently often experience negative child–adult or child–child relationships. Thus, the identification and treatment of socially delayed or deficient preschool children warrant the attention of teachers, parents, and psychologists. This call for attention is congruent with recent research where a number of investigators have documented that young mildly handicapped (i.e., learning disabled, behavior disordered, mildly mentally retarded) students exhibit significant deficits in social skills (Guralnick, 1986; Strain, Odom, & McConnell, 1984). Briefly, this literature suggests that mildly handicapped students display fewer positive social and cooperative behaviors, show less initiative in peer interactions, and exhibit lower rates of peer reinforcement than their nonhandicapped peers. If untreated, these social skills deficits have been shown to be relatively stable over time, related to poor academic performance, and may be predictive of social

adjustment problems in adolescence and adulthood (Parker & Asher, 1987). Given these concerns, it is assumed that psychologists and educators will increasingly need to include methods of assessing and treating social skills in their daily activities.

The purposes of this chapter are to (a) provide an overview of normal social development during the preschool years and the behavior expectations of adults; (b) briefly review the process of assessing social skills and identifying children in need of treatment; and then (c) focus on practical assumptions and effective methods of promoting social skills in preschoolers. Readers interested in more information on these topics are referred to the Annotated Bibliography at the end of the chapter.

BASIC CONSIDERATIONS

Identification of Socially Important Behaviors and Their Development

What are social skills? Behaviors such as sharing, helping, initiating relationships, requesting help from others, giving compliments, and saying "please" and "thank you" are socially desirable behaviors that most everyone would agree are examples of social skills. In general then, social skills may be defined as socially acceptable learned behaviors that enable a person to interact with others in ways that elicit positive responses and assist in avoiding negative responses (Gresham & Elliott, 1984). The acronym of CARES has been offered by Gresham and Elliott (in press) to facilitate memory for and the identification of five major clusters of social skills. The clusters are *C*ooperation, *A*ssertion, *R*esponsibility, *E*mpathy, and *S*elf-Control. These skills are all measured by the *Social Skills Rating System* and taught in the *Social Skills for the Mainstream* curriculum (Gresham & Elliott, in press). Briefly, these clusters of social behaviors can be characterized for preschoolers as follows:

1. Cooperation — behaviors such as helping others, sharing materials with a peer, and complying with rules.
2. Assertion — initiating behaviors such as asking others for information and behaviors that are responses to others' actions such as responding to peer pressure.
3. Responsibility — behaviors that demonstrate ability to communicate with adults and concern about one's property.
4. Empathy — behaviors that show concern for a peer's or significant adult's feelings.
5. Self-Control — behaviors that emerge in conflict situations such as responding appropriately to teasing or to corrective feedback from an adult.

The term social competence often has been considered synonymous with social skills. Social competence, however, is a summary term which reflects social judgment about the general quality of an individual's performance in a given situation. The concept of social skills, from a behavioral perspective, is based on the assumption that specific identifiable skills form the basis for socially competent behavior (Hops, 1983).

What is the normal course of the development of social skills in young children? In general, normative studies may be conceptualized in one of two ways: (a) those investigations whose purpose is the description of increasing sociability with increasing age; and (b) studies which identify the cognitive, linguistic, and behavioral components of successful sociability.

Parten's (1932) classic observational investigation of preschool children's free play established the early assumption that, developmentally, there is a progression from solitary (2 to 2½ years) to parallel (2½ to 3 years) to cooperative (4½ years) play. More recent research, however, has cast doubt on that sequence of development. For example, in an effort to correct Parten's cross-sectional design with a longitudinal study, Smith (1978) found that parallel play was characteristic of the youngest children, while older children (three- to four-year-olds) alternated between solitary and interactive play. Smith's findings reflect a current reevaluation of the developmental status of solitary and parallel play. There is a growing trend that supports parallel and not solitary play as the least mature form (Rubin, Maioni, & Hornung, 1976), and suggests that, while solitary play may be well represented among very young preschoolers, it is also frequent among older preschoolers who interact cooperatively, as well. As such, it represents an option that more socially mature children may choose to exercise (Moore, Evertson, & Brophy, 1974), especially when the cognitive demands of a task are challenging (e.g., Rubin, 1982).

In spite of these disagreements concerning the course of social play, there is general agreement as to the greater frequency of older preschool children engaging in socially cooperative activities relative to younger children. Attention has turned, however, to investigating the possibility that social interaction may be found in children younger than preschool age. While the absolute frequency of cooperative peer interaction may be lower in toddlers than in preschoolers, researchers have been interested in describing interactions that do occur. The intent of this research has been to look beyond the generally accepted notions of prerequisite communication skills, which, for example, enable very young children to direct their attention and that of another jointly (e.g., Bloom, Rocissano, & Hood, 1976; Brownell, 1986). Rather, the purpose has been to determine whether growth in social skills is the result of objects mediating interactions among peers (Mueller & Lucas, 1975), or is the outcome of social experience per se (Lewis, Young, Brooks, & Michalson, 1975; Mueller & Brenner, 1977). Proponents of the latter view have emphasized the positive role of parallel play in providing an entry mechanism into the interaction, a position strongly supported by Smith (1978) and by Eckerman, Davis, and Didow's (1989) finding that during the toddler years, growth in socially coordinated acts can be accounted for by the increase in the imitation of a peer's actions.

Having established the general agreement that social interaction does indeed increase ontogenetically, with interactive behavior occurring earlier developmentally than at first imagined, other empirical work has directed its attention to the behavioral components of successful interaction. Findings from these studies are especially relevant to efforts to remediate social skill deficits in children having difficulty interacting effectively (cf. Eisenberg & Harris, 1984).

One area of interest concerns social initiation, that is, the manner in which a child attempts to initiate social interaction. Leiter (1977) has found that requests to play that were accompanied by whining, crying, begging, or coercion were more likely to be denied, while friendly, smiling initiations with suggestions for an activity were more likely to be accepted. This is not to say, however, that children who are ingratiating have success at social initiation. Rather, a judicious balance between assertiveness and accommodation to others' interests constitutes a successful strategy (Lamb & Baumrind, 1978). Similarly, Hazen, Black, and Fleming-Johnson (1984) found that popular children who were successful at entering others' play situations were able to flexibly alter their entry communications to fit the demands of ongoing play situations, reflecting not only the knowledge of a wide array of social initiation strategies, but the adaptability to use them appropriately. In addition, in contrast to less successful children, popular children clearly indicated to whom they were addressing their entry statements, and they communicated to *all* children in the play situation they were trying to enter. In all, it is apparent that successful social initiations is characterized by specific nonverbal and verbal communication behaviors that clearly transmit the entering child's desire as well as his/her awareness of the contextual accommodations that must be made.

A second area of relevant developmental research is concerned with those skills that enhance the maintenance of social interaction. Asher (1978) described the characteristics of these maintenance skills frequently employed by children. These include complex perspective-taking abilities, such as adjusting the effectiveness of one's communications to other children's needs. In addition, more straightforward reinforcement strategies may be employed, such as offering other children praise and approval, as well as going along with another child's plan or wishes. Related to these maintenance skills is the manner in which interpersonal conflict is managed by children who exhibit successful interaction styles. In their study of preschool children's friendships, Hartup, Laursen, Stewart, and Eastenson (1988) found that conflicts among friends did not differ from those among nonfriends in situational inducement, frequency or duration. What did make them distinct was the effort to maintain the interaction in spite of the disagreement. This was accomplished by the children disengaging from each other temporarily, which served to reduce the intensity of the conflict, and endeavoring to have parity in outcome. This study exemplifies the recent effort to understand social skills within the context of perspective-taking. That is, behaviors that comprise successful peer interactions may be conceptualized as reflective of a maturing social–cognitive system in which children are developing the abilities to consider theirs and others' points of view and to coordinate them (Fensen & Ramsay, 1980; LeMare & Rubin, 1987).

While the above brief review illustrates the course of normative development of social skills, it does not address an additional issue of interest in the remediation of social skills deficits in preschool children, that is, the behaviors that are considered to be important to parents and teachers of young children. It is important to consider this issue, since an intervention program that addresses socially valid target behaviors and has socially valid goals has a greater chance of being used and maintained (Wolf, 1978). In a recent investigation of the social skills of preschoolers, Elliott and Barnard (1989) asked the preschool teachers and parents of a heterogeneous group of 212 children ranging in age from 3 to 5 years to rate the frequency and importance of over 50 discrete social behaviors from the *Social Skills Rating System* (SSRS). The collective ratings of parents indicated the five most important social skills for their preschool children at home were: (a) requests permission before leaving the house, (b) reports accidents or minor emergencies to an adult, (c) shows concern for friends' and siblings' feelings, (d) pays attention to parent verbal instructions, and (e) communicates problems to a parent. Thus, parents of preschoolers seem to place a high value on basic communication skills and behaviors that indicate respect for others. The teachers of these same children indicated that the social skills of greatest importance for functioning in their classrooms were: (a) attends to teacher's instructions, (b) complies with teacher's directions, (c) appropriately asks questions of the teacher when unsure of what to do in school work, (d) finishes class assignments within time limits, and (e) cooperates with peers without prompting from the teacher. These teachers valued social behaviors that are indicative of compliance, cooperation, and orderliness.

Assessment of Social Skills and Identification of Children in Need of Social Skills Training

A number of methods, including rating scales, checklists, and sociometric nomination techniques, have been designed to identify children at risk for behavior problems. In general, the social skills assessment technology for preschoolers is not well developed. Specific assessment procedures are not reviewed here due to space constraints. Reviews of social skills assessment methods have been published recently by Gresham and Elliott (1984, 1989) and Strain, Guralnick, and Walker (1986). Methods for assessing social skills vary along three primary dimensions: source, specificity, and temporal proximity of report to behavior performance (Gresham & Reschly, 1988). Thus, methods can rely on different *sources*, such as parents, teachers, peers, trained observers, or the child him/herself. From these sources, information is provided that varies in *specificity*, that is, ranging from global or molar descriptions to molecular behaviors. Finally, these methods of assessment may differ with respect to *temporal proximity to behavior performance*. For example, direct observations occur concurrently with the target behavior, whereas the completion of a behavior rating scale or analogue role-play can be quite removed in time and space from the actual occurrence of a target behavior. Table 1 characterizes social skills assessment methods along the dimensions of source, specificity, and temporal proximity of report. The combination of these dimensions plus the content focus of the method influence the utility of an assessment.

In general, the purposes of social skills assessments concern either identification/classification or intervention/program planing. From a behavioral perspective, the critical characteristic that differentiates assessment methods is the extent to which a method allows for a functional analysis of behavior (i.e., the extent to which an assessment procedure provides data on the antecedent, sequential, and consequent conditions surrounding a molecular behavior).

Process of assessment. As with the psychological assessment of any problem, the process of social skills assessment can be characterized by a series of hypothesis-testing sequences. Hypotheses are generated in an attempt to answer questions regarding identification, intervention, and evaluation of treatment effects.

TABLE 1
Overview of Social Skills Assessment Methods and Their Characteristics

1. Teacher Ratings of Social Skills
   A. Estimation of Frequency of Behaviors
   B. Estimation of Behavior's Importance to Teacher
   C. Tentative Estimation of Skill and Performance Deficits
   D. Guideline for Teacher Interview and Direct Observations

2. Parent Ratings of Social Skills
   A. Estimation of Cross-setting Generality of Deficits
   B. Parent's Perceived Importance of Social Behaviors
   C. Guideline for Parent Interview

3. Teacher Interview
   A. Further Delineation of Target Behaviors
   B. Functional Analysis of Behavior in Specific Situations
   C. Selection of Target Behaviors Based Upon Importance Ratings and Teacher's Rankings

4. Parent Interview
   A. Further Delineation of Target Behaviors
   B. Functional Analysis of Behavior in Specific Situations
   C. Selection of Target Behaviors Based Upon Importance Ratings and Teacher's Rankings

5. Direct Observations of Classroom Behavior
   A. Functional Analysis of Behavior
   B. Direct Measurement of Behavior in Applied Setting
   C. Observation of Peer Reactions to Target Child's Behavior

6. Sociometrics Using Liked Most and Liked Least Nominations
   A. Measurement of Social Preference and Social Impact
   B. Classification of Sociometric Status (Rejected, Neglected, Controversial)

7. Self-Report of Social Skills — Obtain Child's Perception of Social Behavior

8. Child Interview

A *standard* battery of tests or methods for assessing social skills does not exist. Rather, hypotheses generated dictate the direction of assessment, the questions to be answered, and the methods to be used. Assessment should proceed from global to specific to allow appropriate planning of interventions. In contrast, evaluation of intervention success typically proceeds in the opposite direction, moving from behavior specific outcomes to more global analyses of important social outcomes.

Ideally, practitioners should use assessment methods possessing the attributes of reliability (i.e., consistency of measurement), validity (i.e., capability of answering a given assessment question), and practicality (i.e., costs of collecting information) (Gresham & Cavell, 1986). Unfortunately, few social skill assessment methods meet all of these criteria. Easily administered instruments that are useful for screening purposes (e.g., self-report scales) are of little help in designing interventions. Other methods requiring considerably more effort from assessors and clients (e.g., naturalistic observations and self-monitoring) often have equivocal or unknown psychometric properties (Dodge, Murphy, & Buchsbaum, 1984; Gresham & Elliott, 1984). Moreover, there is a tendency for assessment data obtained from different sources to correlate moderately at best, and more often, to correlate quite low (Achenbach,

TABLE 2
Summary of Purposes and Procedures for Systematic Assessment Sequence of Social Skills

Method	Info Source	Info Specificity	Proximity to Target Behavior
Sociometrics	Peers	Molar (social status)	Removed in Time
Direct Observations	Third Party (psychologist/teacher)	Molecular (discrete social behaviors)	Close in Time
Ratings	Teacher Parent Self	Molar-Molecular (Domain specific behavior)	Removed in Time
Role-Plays	Third Party (psychologist/teacher)	Molecular	Removed in Time and Situation
Behavioral Interviews	Child Teacher Parent	Molecular	Removed in Time

McConaughy, & Howell, 1987). As a safeguard, multiple sources of information are required when assessing social skills.

To increase the likelihood of accurate identification/classification decisions, we recommend the use of direct observations of the target child and nontarget peers in multiple settings; behavioral interviews with the referral source and possibly the target child; rating scale data, preferably norm-referenced, from both a social skills scale and a problem behavior scale completed by the referral source; and sociometric data from the target child's classmates. Regarding intervention decisions, data contributing to a functional analysis of important social behaviors is imperative. This type of data usually results from multiple direct observations across settings; behavioral role-plays with the target child; and teacher and parent ratings of socially valid molecular behaviors. Behavioral interviews with the treatment agent(s) also will be important to assess the treatment setting, the acceptability of the final treatment plan, and the integrity with which the plan is implemented. Table 2 (from Elliott, Sheridan, & Gresham, 1989) provides a summary of an heuristic sequence for the assessment of social skills.

Basic Assumptions and Procedures for Promoting Social Skills

The characteristics of social skills interventions for children experiencing behavior problems and poor relationships with others are highly compatible with features that teachers and parents report they look for in interventions (Elliott, 1988). That is, social skills interventions focus on positive behaviors and use nonaversive methods (e.g., modeling, coaching, and reinforcement) to improve children's behavior. In addition, these programs can be built into the existing structure of a preschool classroom or home environment, thus minimizing the time required for successful implementation. Finally, social skills interventions can be used with individual or groups of students, and because they primarily concern increasing prosocial behaviors, all students can participate and benefit from the interventions.

Teaching children social skills involves many of the same methods as teaching academic concepts. Effective teachers of both academic and social skills model correct behavior, elicit an imitative response, provide corrective feedback, and arrange for opportunities to practice the new skill (Cartledge & Milburn, 1986).

A large number of intervention procedures have been identified as effective for training social skills in preschool children. These procedures can be classified into three approaches that highlight common treatment features and assumptions about how social behavior is learned. These approaches are: operant, social learning, and cognitive-behavioral.

In practice, many researchers and practitioners have used procedures that represent combinations of two or more of these basic approaches. However, we will use the three groups of interventions to describe the basic procedures and to organize a review of their effectiveness. First, however, we believe it is instructive to review five assumptions proposed by Michelson, Sugai, Wood, and Kazdin (1983, p. 3) which are fundamental to the conceptualization of social skills assessment and intervention plans:

Assumption #1: Social skills are primarily acquired through learning which involves observations, modeling, rehearsal, and feedback.

Assumption #2: Social skills comprise specific and discrete verbal and nonverbal behaviors.

Assumption #3: Social skills entail both effective and appropriate initiations and responses.

Assumption #4: Social skills are interactive by nature and entail effective and appropriate responsiveness.

Assumption #5: Social skill performance is influenced by the characteristics of an environment.

Collectively, these pragmatic assumptions provide direction to both assessment and intervention activities by stressing the multidimensional (verbal–nonverbal and initiating–responding), interactive, situation specific nature of social skills. Thus, regardless of intervention approach, effective interventions most likely will need to address target behaviors which involve both verbal and nonverbal communications used to initiate or respond to other people. With this in mind, we now examine the procedures that are germane to the operant, social learning, and cognitive-behavioral approaches to social skills interventions.

Operant intervention procedures. Operant conditioning procedures focus on overt, observable behavior and the antecedent and consequent events that surround the behavior. Control of a behavior is most often achieved through the application of reinforcement or punishment contingent on the observance of the behavior. However, many social behaviors can also be modified through the control of antecedent conditions, such as the appearance of a friend at your door or a teacher's prompting of students to observe a playground conduct rule before leaving for recess. Thus, the manipulation of both antecedents and consequences are valuable procedures for interventions in a wide variety of settings and with almost any performance deficits.

Some children experience difficulties in interpersonal relationships because the social environment is not structured such that positive social exchanges are likely. Antecedent control of social behavior can set the occasion for positive social interactions and has the advantage of requiring less teacher time and monitoring than other procedures (e.g., reinforcement-based procedures). Antecedent control procedures, however, implicitly assume the child possesses the requisite social skills but is not performing them at acceptable levels.

Strain and his colleagues (Strain, 1977; Strain, Shores, & Timm, 1977; Strain & Timm, 1974) used an antecedent control procedure termed *peer social initiations* to increase social interaction rates of socially withdrawn children. The general procedure involved having a trained peer confederate initiate positive social interactions with the withdrawn child in a free-play environment. Peer confederates were coached, prior to the intervention, to appropriately initiate and maintain social interactions. This procedure was effective in increasing the rates of social interactions in withdrawn children. Strain and Fox (1981) provide a comprehensive review of these procedures for preschoolers as well as older children.

Cooperative learning is another method which focuses upon manipulating antecedent conditions to set the occasion for positive social interactions. Cooperative learning has been used frequently in promoting academic achievement in mildly handicapped children, as well as increasing positive social interactions between nonhandicapped and mildly handicapped students (Madden & Slavin, 1983). Basically, cooperative learning requires students work together in completing an academic task. The group, rather than the individual, receives a grade on the completed academic product. This procedure requires that students cooperate, share, and assist each other in completing the task and, as such, represents an effective technique for increasing the likelihood of positive social behaviors. Thus, this procedure assumes children know how to cooperate, but are not doing so at desired levels.

A number of operant-learning procedures (i.e., manipulation of antecedent and consequences) have been used to increase the frequency of positive social behaviors and decrease the frequency of negative social behaviors. All of these procedures are based on the assumption that low rates of positive social interaction and high rates of negative social interaction result from the reinforcement contingencies (positive or negative) occurring subsequent to behavior. As such, the implicit assumption in using these procedures is that the child knows how to perform the social behavior in question but is not doing so because of the lack of reinforcement for appropriate social behavior. Due to the sheer number of studies in this area only two of the most frequently used techniques will be reviewed: (a) contingent social reinforcement and (b) differential reinforcement. Group contingencies (Litow & Pumroy, 1975) also are used frequently, but since they have much in common with cooperative learning we do not review them.

Contingent social reinforcement involves having a teacher, parent, or other significant person to a child publicly reinforce appropriate social behaviors. For example, Allen, Hart, Buell, Harris, and Wolf (1964) had a teacher socially reinforce a 4-year old socially isolated girl whenever she interacted with other children. This procedure led to a sixfold increase in social interaction rates over baseline levels. Variations of this basic procedure have been successful with elective mutes and severely and profoundly mentally retarded populations (Mayhew, Enyart, & Anderson, 1978). Although contingent social reinforcement effectively increases rates of positive social interaction, it requires a great deal of teacher/parent involvement on a consistent basis to be effective. It is therefore perhaps best used to maintain social interaction rates once they have been established using other social skills intervention procedures.

Differential reinforcement of other behavior (DRO) and differential reinforcement of low rate of responding (DRL) also have been used to modify social skills. DRO involves presenting reinforcement after any behavior except the target behavior. Thus, the individual is reinforced only when he/she does not perform the target behavior after a certain amount of time has elapsed. For example, if one wishes to decrease aggressive behavior and increase positive social interactions, any behavior that is exhibited by the child except aggressive behavior, is reinforced. This procedure has the effect of increasing all other responses and extinguishing aggressive behavior. Pinkston, Reese, LeBlanc, and Baer (1973) used a DRO procedure to decrease the aggressive behavior of a preschool boy and contingent social reinforcement to increase positive social interaction. The DRO procedure consisted of the teacher differentially reinforcing positive peer interaction and ignoring aggressive behavior. Differential reinforcement of low rates of behavior (DRL) involves the delivery of a reinforcer for reductions in performance of a target behavior. Reinforcers may be delivered for reduction in the overall frequency of a response within a particular time period, or for an increase of the amount of time that elapses between responses (interresponse time). For example, if one wanted to decrease the frequency of talking-out behavior in a classroom, a reinforcement contingency could be specified such that reinforcement would only occur if the frequency of behavior was at or below a given criterion level. Dietz and Repp (1973) used a DRL schedule to reduce the inappropriate talking of an entire EMR classroom. During the DRL contingency, students could earn reinforcement if the entire class made five or fewer "talk outs" in a 50-minute period. This also was an interdependent group contingency because reinforcement was based upon the behavior of the class.

The beforementioned studies illustrate that DRO and DRL are effective in decreasing the frequency of negative social behaviors. These procedures, however, are perhaps best used as adjuncts in social skills interventions as a means of decreasing negative social behaviors while, at the same time, teaching positive social behaviors.

Social learning intervention procedures. Social learning procedures have their roots in the social learning theory of Bandura and Walters (1963) and Bandura (1977), which suggests that social behavior is acquired through two types of learning: observational learning and reinforced learning. Social learning theorists differentiate the learning of a response and the performance of that learning. This enables social learning theorists to develop the role of modeling influences apart from their use in the acquisition of new behavior. Modeling also affects the performance of previously learned responses through its disinhibitory of cueing effects. That is, the presence of a person modeling a particular socially acceptable behavior can elicit that behavior in another person. Thus, if one student volunteers to help the teacher, he or she will often elicit similar volunteering behaviors in other students in the class. The consequences for a modeled behavior are hypothesized to influence the future occurrence of the same behavior. Observers tend to inhibit responses which they see punished in others, whereas they

are likely to perform the behavior if it is rewarded. This process of observing the consequence for a modeled behavior is referred to as vicarious punishment or vicarious reinforcement, depending on the effect of the consequence.

Modeling has a broad base of empirical support for teaching new social skills to children and youth (Gresham, 1985; Wandless & Prinz, 1982). In social skills training, modeling can be divided into two types: (a) *live modeling*, in which the target child observes the social behaviors of models in naturalistic settings (e.g., the classroom), and (b) *symbolic modeling*, in which a target child observes the social behaviors of a model via film or videotape. Both types of modeling have been effective in teaching social skills, although the majority of empirical studies have used symbolic modeling because of the experimental control afforded by filmed modeling. Live modeling, however, may be a more flexible technique for classroom settings because of the opportunity to modify the modeling sequences based upon behavioral performance.

Gresham and Nagle (1980) conducted the only published study to date in which modeling has been compared to coaching (a cognitive-behavioral procedure discussed in detail in the next section). Students were exposed to one of four conditions: (a) modeling, (b) coaching, (c) modeling and coaching, and (d) attention controls. The three treatment conditions were equally effective in increasing sociometric status and increasing the frequency of positive social interactions, although the treatments containing a coaching component were more effective than modeling in decreasing rates of negative social interactions. Given these results, let's examine the other cognitive-behavioral procedures.

Cognitive-behavioral intervention procedures. A cognitive-behavioral approach to intervention is a loosely defined group of procedures which place significant emphasis on an individual's internal regulation of his/her behavior. In particular, cognitive-behavioral approaches to social skills training emphasize a person's ability to problem solve and to self-regulate behavior. Thus, two of the most frequently used cognitive-behavioral social skills procedures are coaching and social problem solving.

Coaching is a direct verbal instruction technique that involves a "coach" (most often a teacher or psychologist, but occasionally a peer) knowledgeable as to how to enact a desired behavior, and the student in need of acquiring the desired behavior. Most coaching interventions require three steps. First, the child is presented with rules for or standards of behavior. Second, the selected social skills are rehearsed with the coach. Third, the coach provides specific feedback during the behavior rehearsal and offers suggestions for future performance. In some rehearsal situations modeling procedures may also become part of the coach's training, and if the coach praises the accurate performance of a behavior by the student, reinforcement will also be evidenced. Thus coaching, although conceptualized as a verbal instruction procedure that requires cognitive skills of the student to translate the instruction into desired behaviors, can easily be supplemented with behavioral and/or social learning procedures.

Coaching has received empirical support as a social skills training procedure. Oden and Asher (1977) used coaching to teach the social skills of participation, communication, cooperation, and peer reinforcement to students. The coaching procedure involved the three steps of verbal instructions, opportunity for skill rehearsal, and feedback on skill performance. This procedure also was effective in increasing the sociometric status of the students who successfully acquired the new social skills. Ladd (1981) obtained similar results using a coaching procedure, as did Gottman, Gonso, and Schuler (1976).

Several applied researchers have developed interventions that stress teaching children the process of solving social or interpersonal problems. As Weissburg (1985) pointed out, some of these intervention programs, which are largely classroom-based, have been called social

problem solving (SPS) whereas others have been called interpersonal cognitive problem-solving (ICPS) programs. Although the ICPS approach places more emphasis on the cognitions that accompany social problem situations and employs a narrower training procedure than does the SPS approach, both employ a similar sequence of steps in training students to identify and to react to social problems. Briefly, the steps can be characterized as: (a) identify and define the problem, (b) determine alternative ways of reacting to the problem, (c) predict the consequences for each alternative reaction, and (d) select the reaction that is "best" or most adaptive. Social problem solving methods of social skills training can be used with individual children or entire classrooms and have become common parts of several classroom social skills curriculums. It should be noted, however, that such an approach does not focus on discrete social skills training and that learning such skills generally requires more skill-focused, externally-reinforced procedures than offered by this cognitively oriented approach.

Effectiveness of Social Skills Interventions and Suggestions for Practice

The popularity of widespread use of social skills training procedures have resulted in several major reviews of the effectiveness of these procedures with children (see Cartledge & Milburn, 1986; Gresham, 1981, 1985; Ladd & Mize, 1983; Schneider & Byrne, 1985). With regard to child characteristics, Schneider and Byrne, who conducted a large meta-analysis of social skills training studies, indicated that social skills interventions were more effective for preschoolers and adolescents than elementary children. No gender differences in the effect sizes were noted, although few studies have treated gender as an independent variable. In addition, social skills training was found to be more effective for withdrawn and learning disabled students than for aggressive students. Converse to what often is expected, the duration of interventions was related negatively to the outcome. That is, interventions of fewer than 5 days were, on the average, more effective than interventions lasting more than 50 days. This result was interpreted as consistent with the overall finding that modeling and operant procedures were more effective than social–cognitive procedures, since the former procedures are usually much briefer and are likely to involve a smaller number of students.

Based on the reviews of research by Gresham (1981, 1985), Schneider and Byrne (1985), and Mastropieri and Scruggs (1985–86), there appears to be substantial support for the effectiveness of social skills training procedures in general, and in particular for operant and modeling procedures. Social cognitive procedures were found to be less effective, especially with young children. The focus of most social cognitive procedures on generalizable problem-solving strategies as opposed to more discrete, observable behavioral skills makes it difficult to measure post-intervention improvements in social performance accurately.

Practical suggestions from the research literature for teachers, parents, and other individuals interested in facilitating the development of social skills in children include the extensive use of operant methods to reinforce existing social skills. The basic operant tactics would include (a) the manipulation of environmental conditions to create opportunities for social interactions which prompt/cue socially desired behavior in a target child and (b) the manipulation of consequences so that socially appropriate behavior is reinforced and socially inappropriate behavior, whenever possible, is ignored rather than punished. In addition, the modeling of appropriate social behavior supplemented with some coaching, feedback, and reinforcement should be a primary tactic in developing new social behaviors in children.

Facilitating Generalization of Social Skills

Berler, Gross, and Drabman (1982) recommended that social skill interven-

tions not be considered valid unless generalization to the natural environment could be demonstrated. Stokes and Baer (1977) and Michelson et al. (1983) discussed several procedures, referred to as generalization facilitators, which enhance generalization beyond the specific aspects of an intervention. Examples of generalization facilitators include: (a) teaching behaviors that are likely to be maintained by naturally occurring contingencies; (b) training across stimuli (e.g., persons, setting) common to the natural environment; (c) fading response contingencies to approximate naturally occurring consequences; (d) reinforcing application of skills to new and appropriate situations; and (e) including peers in training. By incorporating as many of these facilitators as possible into social skill interventions, and by offering intervention "booster" sessions at regular intervals, maintenance and generalization of skills will be enhanced.

Classifying Social Skill Difficulties and Selecting Interventions

Most authors agree that social incompetencies observed in children can result from difficulties in response acquisition *or* response performance (Bandura, 1977). Kratochwill and French (1984), for example, remarked that response acquisition (i.e., skill) deficits "occur when the individual has not learned skills that are necessary to exhibit a socially competent response," whereas performance deficits "arise when the child fails to successfully perform behaviors he or she is capable of" (p. 332). Gresham and Elliott (1984) extended this two-way classification scheme to include four general areas of social skills problems. As shown in Figure 1, this scheme of social skill difficulties distinguishes between whether or not a child knows how to perform the target skill and the presence of interfering behaviors (e.g., anxiety, aggressiveness).

The components of this classification scheme are:

1. *Social skills acquisition deficits:* This social skill problem characterizes

	Acquisition Deficit	Performance Deficit
Interfering Problem Behaviors Absent	Social Skills Acquisition Deficit	Social Skills Performance Deficit
Interfering Problem Behaviors Present	Social Skills Acquisition Deficit with Interfering Problem Behaviors	Social Skills Performance Deficit with Interfering Problem Behaviors

FIGURE 1. A classification schema for conceptualizing social behavior problems.

children who have not acquired the necessary social skills to interact appropriately with others or to those who have failed to learn a critical step in the performance of the skill. Direct instruction, modeling, behavioral rehearsal, and coaching frequently are used to remediate these social skill acquisition deficits.

2. *Social skills performance deficits:* Children with social skills performance deficits have appropriate social skills in their behavior repertoires, but fail to perform them at acceptable levels or at appropriate times. Typically, social skills performance deficits have been modified by manipulating antecedents and consequences. Interventions have included peer initiations, contingent social reinforcement, and group contingencies.

3. *Social skills acquisition deficits with interfering problem behaviors:* This social skills problem describes a child for whom an emotional (e.g., anxiety, sadness) and/or behavioral (e.g., verbal aggression, excessive movement) response(s) prevents skill acquisition. Anxiety is one such emotional arousal response shown to prevent acquisition of appropriate coping behaviors, particularly with respect to fears and phobias (Bandura, 1977). Hence, a child may not learn to interact effectively with others because social anxiety inhibits social approach behavior. Impulsivity (a

tendency toward short response latencies) is another emotional arousal response that can hinder social skill acquisition (Kendall & Braswell, 1985). Interventions designed to remediate anxiety that interferes with social skills primarily involve emotion-arousal reduction techniques, such as desensitization or flooding, paired with self-control strategies, such as self-talk, self-monitoring, and self-reinforcement (Kendall & Braswell, 1985; Meichenbaum, 1977). Interventions that can help reduce overt behaviors such as physical or verbal aggression, inattentiveness, or excess movements are often referred to as reductive procedures (Lentz, 1988). These include the use of reinforcement techniques (e.g., DRO and DRL), group contingencies, and mild aversive techniques (e.g., reprimands, time out, response cost, overcorrection). Thus, with social skills acquisitions deficits that are accompanied by significant interfering behaviors, the intervention objectives are to teach and increase the frequency of a prosocial behavior and concurrently to decrease or eliminate the interfering problem behavior.

4. *Social skills performance deficits with interfering problem behaviors:* Children with social skill performance deficits accompanied by interfering problem behaviors have a given social skill in

their behavior repertories, but performance of the skill is hindered by an emotional or overt problem behavior response *and* by problems in antecedent or consequent control. Self-control strategies to teach inhibition of inappropriate behavior, stimulus control training to teach discrimination skills, and contingent reinforcement to increase display of appropriate social behavior are often used to ameliorate this social skill problem. Occasionally, when the interfering behaviors persist, reductive methods may also be necessary.

Summary: An Implementation Framework for Social Skills Assessment and Intervention

A general framework for social skills training can be described by the acronym DATE. First, behaviors are *defined* and stated in observable terms. In addition, the conditions (antecedent and consequent) surrounding the behavior are also defined. Second, behaviors are *assessed* preferably via multiple methods, including rating scales, direct observations of the child, interviews with teachers and/or parents, and occasionally a structured role-play to confirm deficits and to refine intervention plans. Third, *teaching* strategies are prescribed to fit the student's needs as determined by the assessment results and the classification that best characterizes social skills deficits. Fourth, the effects of the teaching procedures are *evaluated* empirically using the assessment methods upon which students were selected for training. This Define-Assess-Teach-Evaluate (DATE) model is applied continuously to each deficient social behavior that the student exhibits.

The DATE model can be implemented by a teacher, psychologist, or other specialist through five steps: (a) establishing the need for performing the behavior, (b) identifying the specific behavioral components of the skill or task analysis, (c) modeling the behavior using either live or filmed procedures (symbolic modeling or coaching the behavior), (d) behavior rehearsal and response feedback, and (e) generalization training. These five steps represent an easily implemented and generic approach to teaching social behavior using the intervention procedures which consistently have been found to be most effective. The intervention options available for young children with social skills deficits are numerous, but the majority of effective interventions combine the manipulation of antecedents or consequences with modeling/coaching procedures. When a child's social difficulty results from a lack of knowledge of a particular skill, it is generally necessary to use a direct intervention that involves modeling, coaching, and role playing techniques. On the other hand, when a child fails to perform a social behavior he/she is capable of, it is likely that interventions involving the manipulation of antecedents and/or consequences will be successful.

REFERENCES

Achenbach, T. M., McConaughy, S. H., & Howell, C. T. (1987). Child/adolescent behavioral and emotional problems: Implications of cross-informant correlations for situational specificity. *Psychological Bulletin, 101*, 213-232.

Allen, K. E., Hart, B. M., Buell, J. S., Harris, F. R., & Wolf, M. M. (1964). Effects of social reinforcement on isolate behavior of a nursery school child. *Child Development, 35*, 7-9.

Asher, S. R. (1978). Children's peer relations. In M. E. Lamb (Ed.), *Social and personality development* (pp. 91-113). New York: Holt, Rinehart, and Winston.

Bandura, A. (1977). *Social learning theory*. Englewood Cliffs, NJ: Prentice-Hall.

Bandura, A., & Walters, R. H. (1963). *Social learning and personality development*. New York: Holt, Rhinehart, & Winston.

Berler, E. S., Gross, A. M., & Drabman, R. S. (1982). Social skills training with children: Proceed with caution. *Journal of Applied Behavior Analysis, 15*, 41-53.

Bloom, L., Rocissano, L., & Hood, L. (1976). Adult-child discourse: Developmental interaction between information processing and linguistic knowledge. *Cognitive Psychology, 8*, 521-552.

Brownell, C. A. (1986). Convergent developments: Cognitive-developmental correlates of growth in infant/toddler peer skills. *Child Development, 57*, 275-286.

Cartledge, G., & Milburn, J. F. (1986). *Teaching social skills to children: Innovative approaches* (2nd ed.). New York: Pergamon.

Dietz, S., & Repp, A. (1973). Decreasing classroom misbehavior through the use of DRL schedules of reinforcement. *Journal of Applied Behavior Analysis, 6,* 457-463.

Dodge, K., Murphy, R., & Buchsbaum, D. (1984). The assessment of intention-cue detection skills in children: Implications for developmental psychopathology. *Child Development, 55,* 163-173.

Eckerman, C. O., Davis, C. O., & Didow, S. M. (1989). Toddlers' emerging ways of achieving social coordinations with a peer. *Child Development, 57,* 275-286.

Eisenberg, N., & Harris, J. D. (1984). Social competence: A developmental perspective. *School Psychology Review, 13,* 267-277.

Elliott, S. N. (1988). Acceptability of behavioral treatments in educational settings. In J. C. Witt, S. N. Elliott, & F. M. Gresham (Eds.), *Handbook of behavior therapy in education* (pp. 121-150). New York: Plenum.

Elliott, S. N., & Barnard, J. (1989). *Preschoolers' social behavior: Teachers' and parents' expectations and assessments.* Presented at annual convention of the National Association of School Psychologists, Boston.

Elliott, S. N., Sheridan, S. M., & Gresham, F. M. (1989). Assessing and treating social skills deficits: A case study for the scientist-practitioner. *Journal of School Psychology, 27,* 197-222.

Fensen, L., & Ramsay, D. S. (1980). Decentration and integration of the child's play in the second year. *Child Development, 51,* 171-178.

Gottman, J. M., Gonso, J., & Schuler, P. (1976). Teaching social skills to isolated children. *Journal of Abnormal Child Psychology, 4,* 179-197.

Gresham, F. M. (1981). Social skills training with handicapped children: A review. *Review of Educational Research, 51,* 139-176.

Gresham, F. M. (1985). Utility of cognitive-behavioral procedures for social skills training with children: A review. *Journal of Abnormal Child Psychology, 13,* 411-423.

Gresham, F. M., & Cavell, T. A. (1986). Assessing adolescent social skills. In R. G. Harrington (Ed.), *Testing adolescents: A reference guide for comprehensive psychological assessments* (pp. 93-122). Kansas City, MO: Test Corporation of America.

Gresham, F. M., & Elliott, S. N. (1984). Assessment and classification of children's social skills: A review of methods and issues. *School Psychology Review, 13,* 292-301.

Gresham, F. M., & Elliott, S. N. (1989). Social skills deficits as a primary learning disability? *Journal of Learning Disabilities, 22,* 120-124.

Gresham, F. M., & Elliott, S. N. (in press). *Social Skills Rating System.* Circle Pines, MN: American Guidance Service.

Gresham, F. M., & Nagle, R. J. (1980). Social skills training with children: Responsiveness to modeling and coaching as a function of peer orientation. *Journal of Consulting and Clinical Psychology, 48,* 718-729.

Gresham, F. M., & Reschly, D. J. (1988). Issues in the conceptualization, classification, and assessment of social skills in the mildly handicapped. In T. R. Kratochwill (Ed.), *Advances in School Psychology* (Vol. VI) (pp. 203-247). Hillsdale, NJ: Erlbaum.

Guralnick, M. J. (1986). The peer relations of young handicapped and nonhandicapped children. In P. S. Strain, M. J. Guralnick, & H. M. Walker (Eds.), *Children's social behavior: Development, assessment, and modification* (pp. 93-142). Orlando, FL: Academic Press.

Hartup, W. W., Laursen, B., Stewart, M. I., & Eastenson, A. (1988). Conflict and friendship relations of young children. *Child Development, 59,* 1590-1600.

Hazen, N., Black, B., & Fleming-Johnson, F. (1984). Social acceptance: Strategies children use and how teachers can help children learn them. *Young Children, 39,* 26-36.

Hops, H. (1983). Children's social competence and skill: Current research practices and future directions. *Behavior Therapy, 14,* 3-18.

Kendall, P. C., & Braswell, L. (1985). *Cognitive-behavioral therapy for impulsive children.* New York: Guilford.

Kratochwill, T. R., & French, D. C. (1984). Social skills training for withdrawn children. *School Psychology Review, 13,* 331-338.

Ladd, G. W. (1981). Effectiveness of a social learning method for enhancing children's social interaction and peer acceptance. *Child Development, 52,* 171-178.

Ladd, G. W., & Mize, J. (1983). A cognitive-social learning model of social skill training. *Psychological Review, 90,* 127-157.

Lamb, M. E., & Baumrind, D. (1978). Socialization and personality development in the preschool years. In M. E. Lamb (Ed.), *Social and personality development* (pp. 50-69). New York: Holt, Rinehart & Winston.

Leiter, M. P. (1977). A study of reciprocity in preschool play groups. *Child Development, 48,* 1288-1295.

LeMare, L. J., & Rubin, K. H. (1987). Perspective taking and peer interaction: Structural and developmental analyses. *Child Development, 58,* 306-315.

Lentz, F. (1988). Reductive techniques. In J. C. Witt, S. N. Elliott, & F. M. Gresham (Eds.), *The handbook of behavior therapy in education* (pp. 439-468). New York: Plenum.

Lewis, M., Young, G., Brooks, J., & Michalson, L. (1975). The beginning of friendship. In M. Lewis & L. Rosenblum (Eds.), *Friendship and peer relations* (pp. 27-66). New York: Wiley.

Litow, L., & Pumroy, D. K. (1975). A brief review of classroom troup-oriented contingencies. *Journal of Applied Behavior Analysis, 8,* 341-347.

Madden, N. M., & Slavin, R. E. (1983). Mainstreaming students with mild handicaps. Academic and social outcomes. *Review of Educational Research, 53,* 519-569.

Mastropieri, M. A., & Scruggs, T. E. (1985-86). Early intervention for socially withdrawn children. *Journal of Special Education, 19,* 429-441.

Mayhew, G., Enyart, P., & Anderson, J. (1978). Social reinforcement and the naturally occurring social responses of severely and profoundly retarded adolescents. *American Journal of Mental Deficiency, 83,* 164-170.

Meichenbaum, D. (1977). *Cognitive-behavior modification: An integrative approach.* New York: Plenum.

Michelson, L., Sugai, D. P., Wood, R. P., & Kazdin, A. E. (1983). *Social skills assessment and training with children: An empirically based approach.* New York: Plenum.

Moore, N. V., Evertson, C. M., & Brophy, J. E. (1974). Solitary play: Some functional reconsiderations. *Developmental Psychology, 10,* 830-834.

Mueller, E., & Brenner, J. (1977). The origins of social skills and interaction among preschool toddlers. *Child Development, 48,* 854-861.

Mueller, E., & Lucas, T. (1975). A developmental analysis of peer interaction among toddlers. In M. Lewis & L. Rosenblum (Eds.), *Friendship and peer relations* (pp. 223-258). New York: John Wiley & Sons.

Oden, S. L., & Asher, S. R. (1977). Coaching children in social skills for friendship making. *Child Development, 48,* 495-506.

Parker, J. G., & Asher, S. R. (1987). Peer relations and later personal adjustment: Are low-accepted children at risk? *Psychological Bulletin, 102,* 357-389.

Parten, M. B. (1932). Social participation among preschool children. *Abnormal and Social Psychology, 27,* 243-269.

Pinkston, E. M., Reese, N. M., LeBlanc, J. M., & Baer, D. M. (1973). Independent control of a preschool child's aggression and peer interaction by contingent teacher attention. *Journal of Applied Behavior Analysis, 6,* 223-224.

Rubin, K. H. (1982). Nonsocial play in preschoolers: Necessary evil? *Child Development, 53,* 651-657.

Rubin, K. H., Maioni, T. L., & Hornung, M. (1976). Free play behaviors in middle- and lower-class preschoolers: Parten and Piaget revisited. *Child Development, 47,* 414-419.

Schneider, B. H., & Byrne, B. H. (1985). Children's social skills: A meta-analysis. In B. H. Schneider, K. H. Rubin, & J. E. Ledingham (Eds.), *Children's peer relations: Issues in assessment and intervention* (pp. 175-192). New York: Springer-Verlag.

Smith, P. K. (1978). A longitudinal study of social participation in preschool children: Solitary and parallel play reexamined. *Developmental Psychology, 14,* 517-523.

Stokes, T. F., & Baer, D. M. (1977). An implicit technology of generalization. *Journal of Applied Behavior Analysis, 10,* 349-367.

Strain, P. S. (1977). An experimental analysis of peer social initiations on the behavior of withdrawn preschool children: Some training and generalization effects. *Journal of Abnormal Child Psychology, 5,* 445-455.

Strain, P. S., & Fox, J. (1981). Peers as behavior change agents for withdrawn classmates. In B. B. Lahey & A. E. Kazdin (Eds.), *Advances in clinical child psychology* (Vol. 4) (pp. 167-198). New York: Plenum.

Strain, P. S., Guralnick, M. J., & Walker, H. M. (Eds.). (1986). *Children's social behavior: Development, assessment, and modification.* Orlando, FL: Academic Press.

Strain, P. S., Odom, S., & McConnell, S. (1984). Promoting social reciprocity of exceptional children: Identification, target behavior selections, and intervention. *Remedial and Special Education, 5,* 21-28.

Strain, P. S. Shores, R. E., & Timm, M. A. (1977). Effects of peer social initiations on the behavior of withdrawn preschool children. *Journal of Applied Behavior Analysis, 10,* 289-298.

Strain, P., & Timm, M. (1974). An experimental analysis of social interaction between a behaviorally disordered preschool child and her classroom peers. *Journal of Applied Behavior Analysis, 7,* 583-590.

Wandless, R. L., & Prinz, R. J. (1982). Methodological issues in conceptualizing and treating childhood social isolation. *Psychological Bulletin, 92,* 39-55.

Weissberg, R. P. (1985). Designing effective social problem-solving programs for the classroom. In B. H. Schneider, K. H. Rubin, & J. E. Ledingham (Eds.), *Children's peer relations: Issues in assessment and intervention* (pp. 225-242). New York: Springer-Verlag.

Wolf, M. M. (1978). Social validity: The case for subjective measurement or how applied behavior analysis is finding its heart. *Journal of Applied Behavior Analysis, 11,* 203-214.

ANNOTATED BIBLIOGRAPHY

Cartledge, G., & Milburn, J. (Eds.). (1986). *Teaching social skills to children: Innovative approaches.* Elmsford, NY: Pergamon.
Oriented toward social skills training as a part of school curriculum. Part I sets out general assessment and teaching procedures. Part II focuses on specific populations: behavior disordered, young children, and adolescents.

Michelson, L., Sugai, D. P., Wood, R. P., & Kazdin, A. (1983). *Social skills assessment and training with children: An empirically based handbook.* New York: Pergamon.
Emphasis is on assessment and program-implementation details for social skills training with aggressive or withdrawn children. Reviews relevant findings on social development and of empirical studies of interventions. Details 16 training modules for discrete skills and provides assessment materials.

Strain, P. S., Guralnick, M. J., & Walker, H. M. (Eds.). (1986). *Children's social behavior: Development, assessment, and modification.* Orlando, FL: Academic Press.
This volume is divided into three sections and provides up-to-date reviews and conceptual discussions of the development, assessment, and treatment of children's social skills problems. Chapters on peer relationships of young children, naturalistic observation, and sociometrics are the best available.

41

Best Practices in Reducing Error in Identifying Specific Learning Disabilities

Cathy F. Telzrow
Cuyahoga Special Education Service Center,
Cleveland, Ohio

OVERVIEW

Since the early to middle 1980s, attention has been focused on "de-handicapping" categories of mild handicaps such as specific learning disabilities (SLD). Examples of this trend are evident in the National Association of School Psychologists' (NASP) position statement Advocacy for Appropriate Educational Services for All Children (*Position Statement*, 1988), the Office of Special Education and Rehabilitative Services "regular education initiative" (Will, 1986), and numerous other professional publications (Gartner & Lipsky, 1987; Graden, Zins, & Curtis, 1988; Reschly, 1988).

The viewpoint espoused in these publications is that the process of labeling and providing specialized, sometimes segregated instruction to students with mild handicaps is expensive and yields negative results in terms of both academic and personal growth. However, contrasting opinions have been expressed by others (Heller & Schilit, 1987; Kauffman, 1988; Kauffman, Gerber, & Semmel, 1988), who have argued that "de-handicapping" conditions such as specific learning disabilities is problematic for several reasons. First, the evidence that special education is no longer a viable system for children with mild handicaps is open to dispute. In addition, the concept of the "regular education initiative" and much of its impetus derive from *special* educators, yet it is regular educators who have been

selected to implement this idea. To date, no groundswell of commitment to the concept by the latter group has been forthcoming. Still another objection to abolishing categorical special education for the mildly handicapped is that effective alternative mechanisms for providing appropriate instruction for handicapped children are not generally operational in the public schools. Finally, failure to identify and provide appropriate special education for students who are in fact handicapped would appear to be a violation of current federal regulations (e.g., Education of the Handicapped Act, EHA). Thus, although it might be argued that de-handicapping learning disabilities may be viable in the future, for the present, school psychologists must work within the constraints of professional practice and legal structures that are operational currently. Reducing error in identifying learning disabilities is therefore an important professional issue for school psychologists.

BASIC CONSIDERATION

Learning Disabilities as a Political Entity

Unlike most other handicapping conditions, for which objective validating criteria are available (e.g., vision and hearing handicaps), learning disabilities are to a large degree defined politically (e.g., Keogh, 1988; Swanson, 1988). Although this should not be interpreted to mean that such conditions do not exist, it does mean that validation is established by politically determined criteria rather than by physical data.

Several factors influence a sociopolitical definition such as that of specific learning disabilities. The posture of governmental authorities at the federal level provides one type of sociopolitical influence (Keogh, 1988). Between 1969 and 1987, the number of children receiving special education because of a specific learning disability increased from 120,000 to 1,872,399 (Landers, 1987), resulting in considerable federal scrutiny of this condition and its remarkable growth. One response to this concern about the disproportionate increase in the SLD population was the formation of a federal task force mandated by the Health Research Extension Act "to review and assess Federal research priorities, activities, and findings regarding learning disabilities" (*Learning Disabilities*, 1987, p. 1). Ironically, the resulting report by the Interagency Committee on Learning Disabilities to Congress may serve to increase rather than decrease the escalation of the SLD population, since the report incorporated a new definition that added social skills deficits to what previously had been exclusively academic deficits. When it came time to endorse this definition, the Department of Education was the sole dissenter among the task force's 12 federal agencies. Since the responsibility for implementing EHA rests with the Department of Education, this would seem to be a very important nay vote. As Hynd (1988a) pointed out, the confusion at the federal level reflected in a vote by 11 agencies to expand the definition and an attempt by one key agency to put on the brakes, does not instill confidence. However, such happenings underscore the political nature of specific learning disabilities.

A second influence on sociopolitical definitions is brought to bear by special interest groups such as professional associations and parent and child advocates. Activities such as the National Joint Committee for Learning Disabilities (NJCLD) "new" definition of specific learning disabilities (Hammill, Leigh, McNutt, & Larsen, 1987); the Council for Learning Disabilities' (CLD) position statements (Council for Learning Disabilities, 1987); and the efforts of the Association for Children and Adults With Learning Disabilities (ACLD) to develop "Model Eligibility Criteria for Persons With Learning Disabilities" (Cannon, 1988) all represent potentially powerful, albeit sometimes contradictory, sociopolitical influences on the conceptualization of specific learning disabilities.

Finally, political influences of a more immediate nature are experienced regularly by school psychologists and other members of multifactored evaluation teams. State departments of education that impose arbitrary "caps" on numbers of children served regardless of demographic variability, local school district administrators who require unwavering allegiance to unreliable data, and parents who desperately desire some type of special intervention for their children all are examples of routine political influences on the ways in which SLD is defined (Keogh, 1988).

Clinical Versus Educational Definition of LD

Every social or health care system operates under a set of definitional rules or decision-making guidelines. Sometimes these are characterized by considerable structure and apparent precision, such as are typical of state special education rules or the specifications of the *Diagnostic and Statistical Manual of Mental Disorders* (DSM-III; American Psychiatric Association, 1980). In other instances, the principles of decision making are more individually determined and loosely defined, as in the case of clinical judgments (Barnett, 1988).

With regard to conditions such as learning disabilities, problems occur when definitional systems employed in one setting (e.g., a hospital-associated clinic) are brought to bear on another (e.g., a public school district) (Keogh, 1988). School psychologists frequently express frustration and puzzlement when they are asked to equate another agency's clinical diagnosis with definitions in use in an educational context. While there may be justification for a clinical definition of learning disabilities consisting exclusively of attentional deficits in a hospital LD clinic, such a definition does not automatically translate to a *specific* learning disability as conceptualized in EHA. School psychologists working in public schools employ educational definitions, such as those contained in federal and state educational policies.

LD Subtypes and Overlapping Conditions

One issue that has complicated the identification of specific learning disabilities is the absence of a specific "syndrome" or constellation of unvarying traits characteristic of SLD (Keogh, 1986). Our inability to clearly and consistently describe specific learning disabilities has caused some researchers to conclude that no such condition exists. However, the problem appears to lie in the multivariate nature of the umbrella condition we have come to know as specific learning disabilities. As Kavale and Nye (1985–1986) noted in a meta-analysis of over 1,000 studies of students with learning disabilities, "learning disability is a complex and multivariate phenomenon which involves a number of component deficits that all make an important contribution. Consequently, a multiple-syndrome paradigm is necessary to provide a comprehensive description of learning disability" (p. 443).

Associated with the problem of LD subtypes is the growing number of overlapping conditions that have been "patched onto" specific learning disabilities, ostensibly for the purpose of accessing special education services. Examples of such conditions are hyperactivity, attention deficit disorder (ADD), and central auditory processing disorder. While such conditions may be of diagnostic and educational significance, it is argued these conditions are not synonymous with *specific* learning disabilities as defined in EHA. For example, a youngster may have

both an attention deficit disorder and a specific learning disability, but ADD alone does not constitute a specific learning disability under EHA (e.g., Slenkovich, 1988a).

Actuarial Versus Clinical Modes of Decision Making

In the social sciences, two modes of decision making have been critiqued (e.g., Meehl, 1954; Sawyer, 1966; Willis, 1986), and compelling evidence suggests that actuarial types of decisions are superior to clinical ones. In the identification of specific learning disabilities, the use of discrepancy formulas is an example of an actuarial type of decision-making aid. Although the federal government has prohibited the *sole* use of discrepancy formulas in determining the presence of specific learning disabilities, the inclusion of such a procedure in the decision-making process is in wide use across the states (Frankenberger & Harper, 1987). There is some evidence to suggest, as has been demonstrated with other comparisons of actuarial and clinical decision modes in the behavioral sciences (e.g., Sawyer, 1966), that the inclusion of an actuarial technique such as a discrepancy formula in the decision-making process may reduce error in LD identification (Wilson, 1985).

It would be erroneous to conclude, however, that an actuarial procedure such as a discrepancy formula is free of error. Several statistical artifacts are associated with discrepancy formulas in current use in various states. As discussed in numerous sources and summarized in Telzrow (1985), the most serious of these statistical artifacts are (a) poor reliability of individual test instruments, which compounds reliability error when comparisons are made; (b) high correlations between ability and achievement measures, which results in low reliability of discrepancy scores; (c) regression toward the mean, which may result in overidentification of high-ability youngsters and underidentification of low-ability youngsters; and (d) increased error associated with multiple pairwise ability–achievement comparisons.

The Council for Learning Disabilities has adopted a position statement opposing "the use of discrepancy formulas to determine eligibility for learning disability services" (Council for Learning Disabilities, Board of Trustees, 1987, p. 349). A review of the rationale for this stance is instructive in recounting some artifacts and errors that may occur with the use of discrepancy formulas. However, there are two problems with this position. First is the assumption that abandonment of this statistical procedure will improve one's accuracy in identifying specific learning disabilities. As Faust (1986) has reminded us, "prediction contains a certain element of chance, sometimes much more than people recognize. Errors are unavoidable" (p. 428). A second concern is that the phrasing of the CLD position does not recognize the utility of discrepancy analysis as a decision-making aid in the diagnostic process (Reynolds, 1984–1985). As Slenkovich (1986) stated, "Because eligibility formulas cannot be used to *determine eligibility* does not mean that eligibility formulas cannot be used as *guidelines* for eligibility" (p. 44). The use of *both* statistical and clinical modes of decision making is recommended (e.g., Willis, 1986).

BEST PRACTICES IN REDUCING ERROR IN SLD IDENTIFICATION

The identification of specific learning disabilities, as for any handicapping condition, is viewed as one of a series of ongoing procedures designed to provide appropriate educational interventions for all students. The process is viewed as comprehensive and ongoing, with alternatives incorporated for students who have been determined not to be handicapped. Figure 1 illustrates the steps involved in a systematic identification process. A full appreciation of the process requires elaboration of the issues and considerations associated with each phase.

Step 1. Provide a Broad Range of Instructional Options

One of the most commonly cited reasons for overplacement of mildly handicapped students into special education is "overburdened regular education teachers," that is, an absence of alternative educational options (Weiner, 1985). NASP took to task this rationale for overplacement in its 1985 position statement, Advocacy for Appropriate Educational Services for All Children (*Position Statement*, 1988), reminding school psychologists that the identification of students as handicapped because of a paucity of alternative programming was not defensible.

It is the responsibility of school districts to provide a range of instructional options for all students (Heller, Holtzman, & Messick, 1982). Failure to do so results in a denial of the genuine variability and diversity inherent in the U.S. culture. Examples of educational options and ways in which school psychologists can work toward their development and implementation are included in Graden et al. (1988).

Step 2. Establishing a Differentiated Referral Procedure

Some youngsters continue to experience significant school adjustment problems despite the provision of a wide range of instructional options. When a variety of non-special-education interventions have been found to be ineffective for a particular student, investigation of the need for a multifactored evaluation (MFE) is called for.

This is best accomplished by a differentiated referral procedure, by which key variables pertaining to the student (e.g., pattern of group test scores, attendance data) are examined to determine the need for a multifactored evaluation. A differentiated referral procedure is designed to utilize a decision tree approach, such that only students for whom MFE is required for decision-making purposes receive this time-consuming and costly service. A differentiated referral proce-dure may

FIGURE 1. Steps in the SLD identification process.

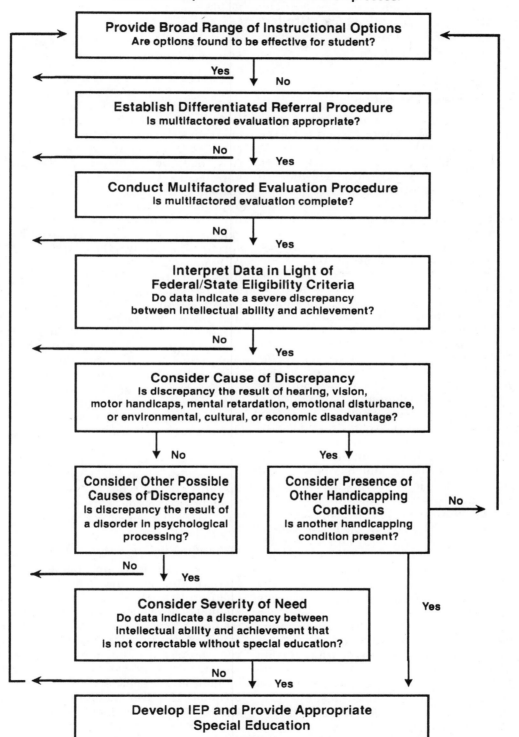

dure may incorporate building-level problem-solving teams, as described by Graden and her colleagues (Graden, Casey, & Bonstrom, 1985; Graden, Casey, & Christenson, 1985).

Step 3. Conduct a Multifactored Evaluation

Traditionally, school psychologists have been most closely aligned with the assessment role in practice (Goldwasser, Meyers, Christenson, & Graden, 1983). Despite the percentage of time devoted to assessment activities, however, there is evidence that these are not always conducted with the degree of care and thoroughness most professional school psychologists would advocate in theory. Review of MFEs for suspected handicapped students reveals common problems, including inappropriate test selection and use; missing data in required assessment areas, such as oral and written expression; and poorly conducted classroom observations (PREP Partnership, 1985). In some school districts, representatives of other disciplines (e.g., speech pathologists, LD teachers) are not routinely involved in conducting multifactored evaluations, leaving the entire assessment up to the school psychologist. This would certainly appear to compromise the multifactored intent of the MFE.

One procedure that has been found to be effective in improving the thoroughness and precision of the MFE is a summary form for assessment data (for example, see Figure 2). Each assessment area required by federal and state rules is included on the form, and sections for summarizing, integrating, and interpreting data are incorporated. Through the use of this system, school psychologists and other members of the MFE team are more likely to fulfill all assessment requirements. In addition, the form provides a bridge between data reporting and data interpretation by directing the MFE team to critical questions such as those relating to qualitative test interpretation, medical data, and the influence of the child's age. Readers may wish to customize this illustrative form to be consistent with state and local requirements.

Step 4. Interpret Data in Light of State and Federal Eligibility Criteria

Following the completion of the MFE, members of the assessment team must interpret the data in the light of federal and state eligibility criteria. The first question to be answered is whether there is a severe discrepancy between intellectual ability and achievement. Two major approaches to data interpretation are recommended (e.g., Willis, 1986). The first approach, which utilizes an actuarial decision-making aid, is illustrated by the calculation of discrepancy formulas as specified in many states' requirements. Although over half the states prescribe the use of a discrepancy formula in identifying specific learning disabilities (Frankenberger & Harper, 1987), both statistical and procedural limitations to their application have been described in the literature (Telzrow, 1985). As a result, MFE teams must employ other, nonactuarial approaches to data interpretation. These approaches also are intended to determine whether a severe discrepancy between ability and achievement is present, but they do so through the use of qualitative rather than quantitative analysis.

A systematic qualitative interpretation requires thorough knowledge of the literature on subtypes of specific learning disabilities and the ways in which these can be expressed at various ages. Five examples of qualitative interpretation of assessment data are provided below.

Central effects on measured intellectual ability. Some learning-disabled children (e.g., those who have pervasive language disorders) perform poorly on traditional measures of intelligence because of the disability itself. For such youngsters, a discrepancy between ability and achievement would not be revealed by quantitative analysis (i.e., a discrepancy formula). However, qualitative interpretation may reveal a marked discrepancy between performance on language and nonlanguage cognitive tasks. By supple-

FIGURE 2. Sample form for SLD data summary and interpretation.

Documentation of Learning Disability Qualification

Name _____ Sex ____ DOB _____ Grade _____
CA _____ Teacher(s) _____
Test/Observation Dates _____ Examiners/Observers _____
_____ _____
_____ _____

| Part I: Summary and Interpretation of Test Results | (include attachments as appropriate)

Area	Test/Method Used	Scores	
General Intelligence	_____	_____	
	_____	_____	
	_____	_____	
Academic Performance	_____	_____	**Discrepancy Score**
	_____	_____	
Basic Reading Skills	_____	_____	_____
Reading Comprehension	_____	_____	_____
Mathematics Calculation	_____	_____	_____
Mathematics Reasoning	_____	_____	_____
Oral Expression	_____	_____	_____
Written Expression	_____	_____	_____
Listening Comprehension	_____	_____	_____
Vision Abilities	_____	_____	
Motor Abilities	_____	_____	
Hearing Abilities	_____	_____	
Social & Emotional Status	_____	_____	
Educational, Family & Medical . . . History	_____	_____	
Other Information	_____	_____	
	_____	_____	
	_____	_____	

Part II: Exclusionary Criteria

Consider the following possible counter-indicators of specific learning disabilities:

1. Vision, hearing, or motor handicaps:
   _____

2. Mental retardation:
   _____

3. Emotional disturbance:
   _____

4. Environmental, cultural, or economic disadvantage:
   _____
   _____

Part III: Educationally Relevant Medical Findings

_____
_____
_____

Part IV: Relevant Behavior Noted During Observation and Relationship to Academic Functioning

_____
_____
_____
_____

Part V: Multiple Academic Deficiencies

This section considers the possible compounding effect of deficiencies in more than one of the seven academic areas.

_____
_____
_____

Part VI: Recommendations & Information from Regular Class Teacher(s) & Parents

Teacher(s) _____
_____
_____

Parents _____
_____
_____

Part VII: Evidence of Performance in the Regular Classroom

A. Group Tests Scores_____

_____

B. Work Samples (describe & attach) _____

_____

C. School Grades _____

_____

Part VIII: Additional Supportive Data

This section might include qualitative indicators of specific learning disabilities (e.g., information processing patterns, neuropsychological test results, health factors, results of classroom observation, etc.)

_____

_____

_____

_____

Part IX: Consideration of Child's Age

The child's age (_____) was a consideration in the team's judgment for the following reasons:

_____

_____

_____

_____

• • • • • • • • • • • • •

Is there a severe discrepancy between ability and achievement which is not correctable without special education?   Yes ☐   No ☐

The evaluation team concludes that the child   ☐ does   ☐ does not   have a specific learning disability. The basis for making the determination is:

_____

_____

_____

_____

_____

Signature	**Title**	**Agree or Disagree**	
_____	_____	Agree	Disagree
_____	_____	Agree	Disagree
_____	_____	Agree	Disagree
_____	_____	Agree	Disagree
_____	_____	Agree	Disagree

Date: _____

menting the cognitive assessment with other measures where the child's weakness is factored out, evidence of central effects on measured intellectual ability can be provided.

Cognitive processing strengths and weaknesses. Qualitative test interpretation involves applying many of the "intelligent testing" principles described by Kaufman (1979) and Sattler (1988). In this process, school psychologists examine not only statistical variability, but meaningfulness of identified differences in the context of base rates in the standardization population. Qualitative test interpretation might suggest a processing deficit that is masked by quantitative interpretation alone. Thus, the school psychologist might argue that even though the discrepancy formula does not reveal a severe discrepancy between ability and achievement, further analysis of the WISC-R profile reveals a significant difference between Verbal and Performance IQ that occurs in fewer than 5% of same-age children in the standardization sample. Such a pattern of scores, when interpreted in the context of other data, may indicate a nonverbal central processing disorder characterized by difficulty in arithmetic, reading comprehension, and various social behavioral weaknesses (Strang & Rourke, 1985; Weintraub & Mesulam, 1983).

Evidence of deficits in attention or executive functions. The verbal comprehension versus perceptual organization dichotomy in cognitive processing, as well as the more recent sequential versus simultaneous model, are familiar to school psychologists. A complete model of cognitive processing incorporates two additional elements. The first of these, which has been called attention or arousal (Naglieri & Das, 1988), might be revealed through observation of the student in the classroom or by the manner in which he or she performs on certain types of tasks (Naglieri, 1988). Executive functions, the second element that is important to a complete model of cognitive processing, are a planning, integrating, problem-solving ability that might be identifiable

on the Wechsler "third factor" (Ownby & Matthews, 1985) or on specialized neuropsychological tasks (Naglieri & Das, 1987). Evidence of deficiencies in attention or executive functions should alert the school psychologist to consider the effects of these constructs on test and classroom performance in determining whether a severe discrepancy between ability and achievement is indicated.

Age effects on performance profiles. Specific learning disabilities display marked age effects, in that the expression of these disorders varies over time (Rourke, 1979). This reality sometimes compromises the use of a statistical discrepancy model, as the following example illustrates. Some young children who have pervasive language disorders may have preserved ability to identify written symbols such as letters and numbers (e.g., McClure & Hynd, 1983). This produces the contradictory profile of superior "reading" and "math" scores in the early grades relative to a borderline intelligence test score. When one is knowledgeable about the patterns of test performance of such "hyperlexic" children over time, the data can be interpreted qualitatively to support the presence of a specific learning disability even though a contradictory achievement > ability discrepancy is revealed on isolated ability–achievement comparisons.

Masking effects of limited task demands. Occasionally, test data might not indicate a discrepancy between ability and achievement, although the classroom teacher and classroom work products provide contradictory evidence. In such cases, the school psychologist should consider the potential masking effect of the limited task demands that are required during most formal testing. The behavioral sampling that occurs during a typical assessment is characterized by considerable adult direction, untimed work conditions, and a small number of items within any one content area. Such conditions may not be representative of the classroom experience, resulting in a discrepancy between performance levels in these two settings. One example of this situation is provided by a dysgraphic child, who may perform much better in a controlled, untimed assessment situation than in the classroom when the volume of written work is greater and stricter time limits are imposed. Sustaining an acceptable level of performance over time in the classroom for such children may not be possible. Hence data from the teacher and from classroom work samples might override performance information from the assessment situation in suggesting the presence of a discrepancy between ability and achievement.

Step 5. Consider the Cause of Discrepancy

Students may exhibit severe discrepancies between intellectual ability and achievement for numerous reasons, both personal and pedagogical. When a severe discrepancy between ability and achievement has been identified, the cause of the discrepancy must be determined (Slenkovich, 1986). Exclusionary criteria included in the federal definition of specific learning disabilities provide one systematic way of examining the possible causes of an identified discrepancy. A discrepancy that is determined to be the result of hearing, vision, or motor deficits, mental retardation, emotional disturbance, or environmental, cultural, or economic disadvantage is by definition not due to a specific learning disability. While SLD is ruled out in such cases, the possibility of another handicapping condition may exist.

Step 6. Consider Other Possible Causes of Discrepancy

The EHA definition of specific learning disability refers to "a disorder in one or more of the basic psychological processes in understanding or in using language, spoken or written" (Procedures, 1977, p. 65083). When a severe discrepancy between intellectual ability and achievement is identified, the evaluation team must consider whether that discrepancy is the result of a specific learning disability, that is, a disorder in psychological processes. *Both* elements — severe

discrepancy and a psychological processing etiology — are necessary (Slenkovich, 1986).

More recent recognition of the central processing variable in specific learning disabilities is reflected in definitions offered by both the NJCLD (Hammill et al., 1987) and the Interagency Committee on Learning Disabilities (Interagency Committee, 1987). Swanson (1988) argued that information processing should constitute the major organizing principle in consolidating research in the LD field. Hynd (1988b) pointed out that students with specific learning disabilities have demonstrable performance profiles on neuropsychological tasks, and further asserted, "If one was truly interested in reducing the LD population to a manageable size it could be accomplished by requiring the traditional IQ/achievement discrepancy and concurrent evidence of neuropsychological impairment based on agreed upon standards" (Hynd, 1988a, p. 487).

In determining whether an identified discrepancy arises from a processing deficit, school psychologists must be familiar with and apply research findings relating to the behavioral expression of specific learning disabilities. This requires knowledge of profile analyses on various measures (e.g., Kaufman, 1981); subtypes of learning disabilities and their expression (e.g., Rourke, 1985; Vellutino, 1987); and demographic influences such as age and ethnic variability on the psychometric measurement of specific learning disabilities (e.g., Rourke, 1979). In the author's judgment, the best sources for such information are the special education, school psychology, and the pediatric neuropsychology literature.

Step 7. Consider Severity of Need

By design, special education is intended for youngsters with the most extreme conditions. In considering the discrepancy between intellectual ability and achievement, members of an evaluation team should consider whether or not the discrepancy is correctable without special education. This consideration underscores an important premise of EHA: Special education is intended for students who are unable to make academic progress without modifications in instructional techniques and procedures. As Slenkovich (1988b) put it, "The law excludes any student who is succeeding in regular education classes" (p. 166).

Step 8. Develop an Individualized Education Program (IEP) and Provide Appropriate Special Education

Special education is intended to be driven by identified pupil needs, not by district program availability. Occasionally, school personnel respond to an IEP team's judgment that a pupil requires an intensive special education intervention with comments such as "We only have tutoring" or "All LD students at the high school are mainstreamed." Such statements and the attitudes they convey are inconsistent with the individual planning intent of EHA.

SUMMARY

Although vague and ill-defined, SLD is nevertheless a legitimate and recognized category of handicap, and youngsters who are suspected of being learning-disabled are entitled to the provisions of EHA to the same degree as those in other areas of special education. Numerous issues complicate the identification of SLD. These include definitional problems, sociopolitical influences, overlapping conditions, and limitations to statistical and clinical decision aids. Despite these problems, implementation of best practices can minimize errors commonly associated with the identification of specific learning disabilities.

In this chapter, SLD identification is conceptualized as one component of a comprehensive and ongoing process of pupil assessment and service delivery. Only when a student's needs cannot be met by a broad range of instructional options is consideration given to a multifactored evaluation within the context of a differentiated referral procedure. Both quantitative (i.e., discrepancy for-mula) and qualitative (i.e., clinical) approaches to data interpretation are advocated to identify these essential components of SLD: (a) a severe discrepancy between intellectual ability and achievement, (b) resulting from a disorder in psychological processing, (c) that is not correctable without special education.

REFERENCES

American Psychiatric Association. (1980). *Diagnostic and statistical manual of mental disorders* (3rd ed.). Washington, DC: Author.

Barnett, D. W. (1988). Professional judgment: A critical appraisal. *School Psychology Review, 17,* 658-672.

Cannon, L. (1988, September/October). Eligibility criteria for LD persons discussed. *ACLD Newsbriefs*, No. 176, pp. 1, 21.

Council for Learning Disabilities, Board of Trustees. (1987). The CLD position statements. *Journal of Learning Disabilities, 20,* 349-350.

Faust, D. (1986). Research on human judgment and its application to clinical practice. *Professional Psychology: Research and Practice, 17,* 420-430.

Frankenberger, W., & Harper, J. (1987). States' criteria and procedures for identifying learning disabled children: A comparison of 1981/82 and 1985/86 guidelines. *Journal of Learning Disabilities, 20,* 118-121.

Gartner, A., & Lipsky, D. K. (1987). Beyond special education: Toward a quality system for all students. *Harvard Educational Review, 57,* 367-395.

Goldwasser, E., Meyers, J., Christenson, S., & Graden, J. (1983). The impact of PL 94-142 on the practice of school psychology: A national survey. *Psychology in the Schools, 20,* 153-165.

Graden, J. L., Casey, A., & Bonstrom, O. (1985). Implementing a prereferral intervention system: Part II. The data. *Exceptional Children, 51,* 487-496.

Graden, J. L., Casey, A., & Christenson, S. L. (1985). Implementing a prereferral intervention system. Part I. The model. *Exceptional Children, 51,* 377-384.

Graden, J. L., Zins, J. E., & Curtis, M. J. (Eds.). (1988). *Alternative educational delivery systems: Enhancing instructional options for all students.* Washington, DC: National Association of School Psychologists.

Hammill, D. D., Leigh, J. E., McNutt, G., & Larsen, S. C. (1987). A new definition of learning disabilities. *Journal of Learning Disabilities, 20*, 109-113.

Heller, H. W., & Schilit, J. (1987). The regular education initiative: A concerned response. *Focus on Exceptional Children, 20*(3), 1-6.

Heller, K., Holtzman, W., & Messick, S. (Eds.). (1982). *Placing children in special education: A strategy for equity.* Washington, DC: National Academy Press.

Hynd, G. W. (1988a). Blowing on the sails: Yes, but . . . *School Psychology Review, 17*, 485-489.

Hynd, G. W. (1988b). *Neuropsychological assessment in clinical child psychology.* Newbury Park, CA: Sage.

Kauffman, J. M. (1988). A revolution can also mean returning to the starting point: Will school psychology help special education complete the circuit? *School Psychology Review, 17*, 490-494.

Kauffman, J. M., Gerber, M. M., & Semmel, M. I. (1988). Arguable assumptions underlying the regular education initiative. *Journal of Learning Disabilities, 21*, 6-11.

Kaufman, A. S. (1979). *Intelligent testing with the WISC-R.* New York: Wiley.

Kaufman, A. S. (1981). The WISC-R and learning disabilities assessment: State of the art. *Journal of Learning Disabilities, 14*, 520-526.

Kavale, K. A., & Nye, C. (1985-1986). Parameters of learning disabilities in achievement, linguistic, neuropsychological, and social/behavioral domains. *Journal of Special Education, 19*, 443-458.

Keogh, B. K. (1986). A marker system for describing learning-disability samples. In S. J. Ceci (Ed.), *Handbook of cognitive, social, and neuropsychological aspects of learning disabilities* (Vol. 1, pp. 81-94). Hillsdale, NJ: Erlbaum.

Keogh, B. K. (1988). Learning disability: Diversity in search of order. In M. C. Wang, M. C. Reynolds, & H. J. Walberg (Eds.), *Handbook of special education: Research and practice* (Vol. 2, pp. 225-251). Oxford, England: Pergamon.

Landers, S. (1987, December). LD definition disputed. *APA Monitor*, p. 35.

Learning disabilities: A report to the U.S. Congress. Prepared by the Interagency Committee on Learning Disabilities, 1987.

McClure, P. H., & Hynd, G. W. (1983). Is hyperlexia a severe reading disorder or a symptom of psychiatric disturbance? Nosological considerations. *Clinical Neuropsychology, 5*, 145-149.

Meehl, P. E. (1954). *Clinical versus statistical prediction: A theoretical analysis and a review of the evidence.* Minneapolis: University of Minnesota Press.

Naglieri, J. A. (1988, August). *Overview of the planning, attention, simultaneous and successive models of information processing.* Paper presented at the meeting of the American Psychological Association, Atlanta.

Naglieri, J. A., & Das, J. P. (1987). Construct and criterion-related validity of planning, simultaneous, and successive cognitive processing tasks. *Journal of Psychoeducational Assessment, 4*, 353-363.

Naglieri, J. A., & Das, J. P. (1988). Planning-arousal-simultaneous-successive (PASS): A model for assessment. *Journal of School Psychology, 26*, 35-48.

Ownby, R. L., & Matthews, C. G. (1988). On the meaning of the WISC-R third factor: Relations to selected neuropsychological measures. *Journal of Consulting and Clinical Psychology, 53*, 531-534.

Position statement: Advocacy for appropriate educational services for all children. (1988). In J. L. Graden, J. E. Zins, & M. J. Curtis (Eds.), *Alternative educational delivery systems: Enhancing instructional options for all students* (pp. xiii-xv). Washington, DC: National Association of School Psychologists.

PREP Partnership. (1985). *Ohio School Psychologist, 31*(1), 16-17.

Procedures for evaluating specific learning disabilities. *Federal Register*, December 29, 1977, Part III.

Reschly, D. J. (1988). Special education reform: School psychology revolution. *School Psychology Review, 17*, 447-458.

Reynolds, C. R., Berk, R. A., Boodoo, G. M., Cox, J., Gutkin, T. B., Mann, L., Page, E. B., & Willson, V. C. (1984-1985). *Critical measurement issues in learning disabilities.* Report of the Work Group on Measurement Issues in the Assessment of Learning Disabilities. Washington, DC: U.S. Department of Education, Program in Special Education.

Rourke, B. P. (1979). Neuropsychological research in reading retardation: A review. In A. L. Benton & D. Pearl (Eds.), *Dyslexia: An appraisal of current knowledge* (pp. 139-171). New York: Oxford University Press.

Rourke, B. P. (Ed.). (1985). *Neuropsychology of learning disabilities: Essentials of subtype analysis.* New York: Guilford.

Sattler, J. M. (1988). *Assessment of children* (3rd ed.). San Diego: Author.

Sawyer, J. (1966). Measurement *and* prediction, clinical *and* statistical. *Psychological Bulletin, 66,* 178-200.

Slenkovich, J. E. (1986). The specific learning disability - A review of the legal requirements. *The Schools' Advocate, 1*(6), 41-42, 44-47.

Slenkovich, J. E. (1988a). Legal briefs: ADD not a handicapping condition . . . *The Schools' Advocate, 3*(1), 152.

Slenkovich, J. E. (1988b). Students succeeding in regular education do not qualify as learning disabled. *The Schools' Advocate, 3*(3), 166.

Strang, J. D., & Rourke, B. P. (1985). Adaptive behavior of children who exhibit specific arithmetic disabilities and associated neuropsychological abilities and deficits. In B. P. Rourke (Ed.), *Neuropsychology of learning disabilities: Essentials of subtype analysis* (pp. 302-328). New York: Guilford.

Swanson, H. L. (1988). Toward a metatheory of learning disabilities. *Journal of Learning Disabilities, 21,* 196-209.

Telzrow, C. F. (1985). Best practices in reducing error in learning disability qualification. In A. Thomas & J. Grimes (Eds.), *Best practices in school psychology* (pp. 431-446). Washington, DC: National Association of School Psychologists.

Vellutino, F. R. (1987). Dyslexia. *Scientific American, 256*(3), 34-41.

Weiner, R. (1985). *P.L. 94-142: Impact on the schools.* Arlington, VA: Capital Publications.

Weintraub, S., & Mesulam, M. M. (1983). Developmental learning disabilities of the right hemisphere. *Archives of Neurology, 40,* 463-468.

Will, M. (1986). *Educating students with learning problems: A shared responsibility.* Washington, DC: U.S. Department of Education.

Willis, W. G. (1986). Actuarial and clinical approaches to neuropsychological diagnosis: Applied considerations. In J. E. Obrzut & G. W. Hynd (Eds.), *Child neuropsychology: Vol. 2. Clinical practice* (pp. 245-262). Orlando: Academic.

Wilson, L. (1985). Large-scale learning disability identification: The reprieve of a concept. *Exceptional Children, 52,* 44-51.

ANNOTATED BIBLIOGRAPHY

Kaufman, A. S. (1981). The WISC-R and learning disabilities assessment: State of the art. *Journal of Learning Disabilities, 14,* 520-526.
This article summarizes WISC-R research data relevant to the assessment of children with SLD. Three major categories of findings are emphasized: (a) results of factor analysis studies, (b) data regarding Bannatyne recategorization, and (c) subtest scatter.

Keogh, B. K. (1988). Learning disability: Diversity in search of order. In M. C. Wang, M. C. Reynolds, & H. J. Walberg (Eds.), *Handbook of special education: Research and practice* (Vol. 2, pp. 223-251). Oxford, England: Pergamon.
The chapter provides a comprehensive data-based synthesis and discussion of issues relating to the conceptualization and identification of learning disabilities. Keogh argues for a broad classification system that can encompass the diversity in the field and guide research.

Rourke, B. P. (Ed.) (1985). *Neuropsychology of learning disabilities: Essentials of subtype analysis.* New York: Guilford.
This edited volume is a well-integrated collection of chapters focusing on LD subtypes. Major sections are devoted to theory and methodology; reading, spelling, and arithmetic disability subtypes; validity studies of LD subtypes; and personal and socioemotional dimensions of LD.

Vellutino, F. R. (1987). Dyslexia. *Scientific American, 256*(3), 34-41.
This article presents a thorough discussion of dyslexia designed for the sophisticated layperson. The author summarizes research concluding that dyslexia is a linguistics-based disorder rather than one founded in visual perceptual disturbances. Numerous writing samples of both normal and dyslexic children are included.

42

Best Practices in Report Writing

Gary Ross-Reynolds
Nicholls State University

OVERVIEW

Although reports are criticized for their irrelevance in making programming decisions or designing intervention strategies (Zins & Barnett, 1983), there has been little change in their form and substance through the years (Grimes & Ross-Reynolds, 1983). Nevertheless, psychologists consider report writing to be an essential task that consumes more time than any other component of the psychoeducational evaluation except for direct examination of the child (Kicklighter & Bailey-Richardson, 1984).

In spite of their recognized shortcomings, reports serve varied purposes which include: (a) explicitly answering referral questions; (b) documenting that a child client is handicapped and in need of special services; (c) serving as a basis for intervention, program development, and evaluation; (d) providing assistance for the child and referring agent; (e) serving as a baseline for future assessment; (f) providing documentation of services and accountability, and (g) supplying a research database (Ownby, 1987; Ross-Reynolds, 1985; Teglasi, 1983). However, the fundamental purpose of reports is *to communicate information to the referring person in such a way that the latter's beliefs, feelings, and/or behaviors relative to the child are changed* (Ownby, 1987; Teglasi, 1983). This is accomplished, according to Ownby, by including statements in the report that are credible (change beliefs) and persuasive (change behaviors). The extent to which a report clearly communicates useful information about a child is the extent to which the purpose of the report is being realized. If the information in the report either is not useful or does not result in a positive change for the child, then the report fails to fulfill its intended mission, psychologists waste their time, and children are ill-served.

Communication, by definition, necessitates an interchange between the sender (in this case the psychologist) and the recipient. School psychologists' reports typically have many recipients, including the file, the director of special education, teachers, parents, other professionals, and the child. Most psychologists, recognizing the multiple uses reports serve and the diverse audiences they reach, burden their reports with the impossible task of fulfilling all purposes for all possible audiences. Yet in trying to satisfy many consumers, psychologists risk having their efforts judged unsatisfactory by all. The consensus among experts is that reports should be written foremost to address the needs of the referring person in an idiom that this person can understand (Ownby, 1987). Since the person referring the child is generally not a psychologist, psychological terms are best used sparingly (if at all) in a report.

The problem of communication has been documented by Cuadra and Albaugh (1956), who provided various professionals with copies of psychological reports and a multiple-choice questionnaire. Raters were asked to answer each question on the basis of information in the written report. For all professional groups, the correspondence between their ratings and those of the report authors was only 53%. Shively and Smith (1969) investigated teachers', counselors', and student teachers' understanding of 30 terms commonly used in psychological reports and found that their subjects could identify only 54% of them.

Communication is the primary function of a report, and while it is problematic, it is not correct to assume that poorly written reports do not communicate. All reports communicate; some just do so better than others. "Better" is a function of the degree of concordance between the information the writer intends to relay and the information the reader receives. If in reading the report the consumer's interpretation or understanding of the content is consistent with the writer's intent, then the report has served its communicative function. On the other hand, if the reader's understanding differs from the psychologist's communicative intent, the report does a poor job of communicating.

The dimension of communication is not the only one considered in psychological report writing; value is a second critical component. Reports may communicate clearly but be of little perceived value. Conversely, reports that communicate poorly may be assigned high value by the reader.

Several research studies provide clues both to consumers' perceived valuation of psychological reports and to the variables that contribute to a report's being valued. Ownby, Wallbrown, and Brown (1982) asked special education teachers to rate the frequency with which certain types of information appeared in reports and to indicate how useful the reports were to them. Content that had a high probability of inclusion consisted of descriptions of the referral problem, lists of tests administered, IQ measures, achievement in grade equivalents, and statements concerning special education availability. Content that had a low probability of inclusion consisted of lists of specific referral questions, playground behavior, prior classroom interventions, observations of antecedent behaviors, and estimates of expected progress. Teachers generally rated reports as only somewhat important in helping them manage classroom behavior and develop specific instructional strategies. In contrast parents reported a high degree of satisfaction with the psychoeducational evaluation reports generated at a university clinic, 66% being extremely satisfied with the report and 55% indicating they would make no changes in the report (Tidwell & Wetter, 1978). Parents' reported satisfaction, in contrast to that of teachers, may be the result of differing expectations about the kinds of information that should be included in a report, as well as differing needs for information.

Numerous variables enhance or detract from the value of a report. Speed enhances a report's value (Rogers, 1977). Teachers prefer an immediate brief report to a delayed formal and comprehensive report (though they would like both) (Mussman, 1964). Reports that were too brief and lacked form and organization, and whose recommendations were either vague, short, unrealistic, or unrelated to referral concerns, were least valued (Brandt & Giebink, 1968; Noble & Dickinson, 1988; Rucker, 1967). Consumers placed highest value on recommendations and lowest value on IQ scores and projective test data (Isett & Roszkowski, 1979; Tidwell & Wetter, 1978).

BASIC CONSIDERATIONS

It is sometimes difficult to see habitual, accepted, and ingrained practices from a new viewpoint. In an effort to begin to examine common reporting conventions and pitfalls, quotations from psychological reports are presented below with commentary. Each contains one or more basic flaws that have the effect of interfering with communication or decreasing the value of the report. Further examples can be found in Ross-Reynolds (1985) and Sattler (1988).

"Doug is an attractive, well-groomed, blond-haired, blue-eyed nine-year-old who accompanied the examiner willingly to the testing room." This sentence suffers from being hackneyed and irrelevant. It is likely that the primary reader of the report (the referral agent) already knows what Doug looks like, and rarely is the purpose of the report to provide descriptive data so that someone will recognize the subject on sight. Additionally, few students fail to "accompany the examiner willingly to the testing room." Statements of that which is generally taken for granted are best avoided.

"During a 15-minute observation period Allyson was found to be on task 100% of the intervals observed compared with 86% for a peer. However, she is highly distractible." This statement is handicapped by a flaw of logic. The interpretation "she is highly distractible" is not consistent with the data reported. The psychologist needs to either change the interpretation to conform with the data presented, or present additional data supporting this interpretation. "Using the Fox–Burdette method 30 minutes per day, David learned only two new sight words in two weeks. . . . It is recommended that David receive individual instruction in reading using the Fox–Burdette method." In another lapse of logic the psychologist recommends a teaching strategy that for David clearly has proven ineffective. This problem of logic is more starkly apparent in this example than would be the case in a report in which the two sentences are separated by several paragraphs.

"Dwayne claims he has a good appetite and likes white beans, fruit, and spaghetti." Unless Dwayne's food preferences are to be used as reinforcers in a behavioral program, or he was referred for an eating disorder, the information is irrelevant and is better deleted from a report.

"On his drawing of the female figure, Jason drew breasts and genitals, suggesting deviant or inappropriate sexual interest." In this instance Jason suffers more from a problem of the misapplication of psychological science and interpretation than he likely does from deviant sexual interest. In the absence of any other corroborating data, such as high frequency of lewd comments, obsessive sexual thoughts, or compulsive sexual acts, Jason's HFD production is probably best left as an unreported curiosity in light of the poor reliability and validity of the procedure.

"Nathan approaches new situations with a paranoid ego structure that on balance is preponderantly self-defeating. However, his preferential approach to novel environments is gradually tempered as trust and confidence builds at which point he begins to amuse himself and gain control of situations through Machiavellian tactics." In this example Nathan gets lost in jargon and ponderous writing. The information is both ambiguous and inappropriately technical, leaving the reader confused or with the illusion of understanding. Better treatment would be, "Nathan approaches new situations cautiously and suspiciously. However, once he becomes comfortable he actively attempts to exercise control over his environment by manipulating those around him."

The above examples illustrate some of the specific pitfalls to be avoided in report writing. Below is a brief review of what, on the positive side, should be included in reports to make them more effective.

Ownby (1987), Ross-Reynolds (1985), Sattler (1988), Shellenberger (1982), and Tallent (1983) have clearly articulated the basic characteristics of effective psychological reports. Shellenberger's comprehensive literature review suggested that effective reports are those that (a) specifically answer referral questions; (b) describe behavior rather than present abstractions or psychological constructs; (c) describe the uniqueness of the individual; (d) are written clearly and precisely; (e) integrate, synthesize, and interpret information; (f) provide explicit, specific, and implementable recommendations; and (g) are timely.

Ross-Reynolds (1985) and Tallent (1983) summarized the fundamentals of effective report writing in quality checklists against which writers can evaluate their reports. The Ross-Reynolds checklist is presented in Table 1. In addition to citing the characteristics noted by Shellenberger, Tallent characterizes effective psychological reports as those that (a) do not unnecessarily duplicate the content of other reports; (b) provide illustrative material on which interpretations are based; (c) contain relevant and significant content; (d) contain data-based conclusions with limited and clearly identified speculations; (e) are client-oriented rather than test-oriented; (f) avoid theoretical or abstract concepts; (g) are logically and effectively organized; and (h) are adequately persuasive.

As noted earlier, the fundamental purpose of a report is to change the referring agent's beliefs, feelings, and/or behaviors relative to the child. Thus the art of persuasion becomes critical; yet the persuasive function of a report may often be overlooked or even eschewed by the psychologist. Several factors contribute to the persuasiveness of a report (Ownby, 1987). First, Ownby noted, on the basis of a review of research on persuasion, that statements moderately discrepant from one's beliefs are likely to result in the greatest attitude change. This implies the need to obtain some sense of the existing views of the child that are held by the referrer, who is the eventual consumer of the report and the one whose perceptions are to be altered. The challenge for the psychologist, then, becomes one of presenting the information in an interpretative context that accurately represents the data but also is designed to achieve the desired attitude change by being only moderately discrepant from the reader's original views.

Ownby also pointed out that the social influence variables of expertness, attractiveness, and trustworthiness can be used to the writer's advantage to persuade the reader to accept another viewpoint. Expertness cannot be communicated by the use of jargon (which, as previously noted, is inimical to effective report writing), but rather by the use of statements that demonstrate that the writer, after careful consideration of the data, has arrived at reasoned interpretations of the facts. Attractiveness in this context means the degree of perceived similarity between the writer and the reader. Such similarity

can be highlighted by noting the concordance of beliefs about the child between the referrer and the writer (e.g., "Ms. Taylor's statement that Bob is extremely disruptive was confirmed by his behavior during a 30-minute observation in spelling when he wandered about the room talking to other students for 10 minutes, talked out of turn 16 times, and hit 4 children who were working independently at their desks"). Here again the importance of acquainting oneself with the views of the referrer is evident. Both expertness and attractiveness are enhanced to the degree one is successful in tailoring the discrepancy of the message to the intended reader. Trustworthiness is communicated by conscientiously addressing the specific concerns of the referring agent and providing clear recommendations for appropriate action that the referring party can implement to help the child.

The above considerations notwithstanding, persuasion is primarily dependent upon the report's including statements that, themselves, are readily understood, credible, and persuasive (Ownby, 1987). Ownby has proposed the expository process model (EPM) to guide the psychologist in persuasive, expert report construction. He has found that material written according to this model is judged by readers to be more credible and persuasive than similar material not employing the model.

In essence the EPM is a mechanism for "clarifying the relation between the assessment data and the psychologist's *(sic)* interpretation of them" that thereby enables psychologists "to use their theories more effectively in reporting assessments" (Ownby, 1987, p. 36). At the heart of the model is the middle-level construct, which permits psychologists to cogently and logically link data with their theoretical concepts. The conceptual bridges thereby built lend a high degree of credibility to the resulting conclusions. Ownby (1987) provides detailed instruction in the use of this extremely useful approach, which can be applied to most reporting formats.

TABLE 1
Self-assessment Checklist for the Psychological Report
(Ross-Reynolds, 1985)

Yes	No	
_____	_____	1. Is the report completed promptly?
_____	_____	2. Is the client the central focus of the report rather than the assessment technique?
_____	_____	3. Are data gathered from multiple sources all illuminating the same issue integrated into a coherent whole rather than reported by procedure?
_____	_____	4. Are theoretical and abstract concepts avoided?
_____	_____	5. Is the tone professional without being dogmatic or authoritarian?
_____	_____	6. Are qualifiers avoided when there is no need to qualify?
_____	_____	7. Are qualifiers included when certainty is unwarranted?
_____	_____	8. Does the report describe the client's behavior?
_____	_____	9. Are positive outcomes predicted?
_____	_____	10. Is the report as brief as possible while relaying the necessary information?
_____	_____	11. Does the report clearly convey the current functioning and needs of the client?
_____	_____	12. Would the reader be convinced that the diagnosis and proposed interventions are appropriate and warranted?
_____	_____	13. Are specific referral issues identified and directly addressed?
_____	_____	14. Does the content differ from that of other reports on file?
_____	_____	15. Are raw data interpreted or used to illustrate a point?
_____	_____	16. Does illustrative information enhance salient points without overkill?
_____	_____	17. Does each sentence directly relate to the specific referral concerns and contribute to the total significance of the report?
_____	_____	18. Is the report tightly and logically organized?
_____	_____	19. Is language of logic used?
_____	_____	20. Are interpretations and generalizations validated by data?
_____	_____	21. Do interpretations and generalizations arise logically from the information presented?
_____	_____	22. Do conclusions emerge logically from the data?
_____	_____	23. Are speculations identified as such?
_____	_____	24. Is information distilled and synthesized rather than merely reported?
_____	_____	25. Are recommendations specific and explicit?
_____	_____	26. Are recommendatons reasonably implementable?

(Table 1, continued)

Yes	No	
_____	_____	27. Are recommendations related to the referral concerns?
_____	_____	28. Is language definite, specific, and concrete?
_____	_____	29. Are fancy words and technical language avoided?
_____	_____	30. Are needless words eliminated?
_____	_____	31. Is writing parallel?
_____	_____	32. Are awkward sentence constructions avoided?

BEST PRACTICES

The purpose of psychological reports as well as the characteristics of effective reports, briefly reviewed above, provide the basis from which best practices in report writing emerge. A variety of practices, ranging from traditional to innovative, are available, but adopting any of the approaches presented here without carefully integrating them with the basic principles of effective reporting will result in a product that falls short of fulfilling its fundamental purpose.

Traditional Report

Sattler (1988) and Shellenberger (1982) address report writing from a traditional point of view with respect to content and organization. Both the organization and the content of the traditional report (Identifying Information, Reason for Referral, Background Information, Observations, Assessment Results and Interpretations, Summary, and Recommendations) are by now too familiar to practicing school psychologists. Nevertheless, a careful review of the Shellenberger and Sattler chapters is recommended for practitioners who wish to hone their report-writing effectiveness. Practitioners who are dissatisfied with the traditional reporting format and the testing role it often reflects could still benefit from the sound review of general reporting principles both authors provide.

Psychological Reports–Revised Format

Ross-Reynolds and Grimes (1983) proposed an alternative to the traditional psychological report epitomized by Shellenberger (1982) and Sattler (1988). Called the Psychological Report-Revised Format (PRRF), it is structured to provide a document that reflects a consultative, intervention-oriented assessment approach rather than the norm-referenced test-based approach that is associated with the traditional model. In the PRRF, assessment and intervention data are organized under the following headings: Summary of Request for Conference, Purpose and Scope of the Psychologist's Investigation, Relevant History and Current Data, Discussion, Actions and Outcomes, and Follow-up.

Differences between the PRRF and the traditional report format are more than cosmetic. Whereas the PRRF's Summary of Request for Conference is similar to Reason for Referral, the former reflects the fact that a psychologist's involvement with a client begins with a conference with a concerned person who has referred the child. By doing so, psychologists more easily avoid the problems inherent in assessing clients in the absence of knowledge about the variables that need to be addressed (Hartlage, Freeman, Horine, & Walton, 1968).

Whereas the "Summary of Request for Conference" presents a brief statement of the salient concerns of the person requesting the assistance of the school psychologist, the "Purpose and Scope of the Psychologist's Investigation" explicitly narrows and defines the behaviors and critical variables that constitute the focus of the investigation. Since the focus is collaboratively developed with the referring party, the risk that psychologists' reports fail to relevantly address referral concerns is minimized. In contrast, assessment reports that convey the same information (WISC-R, WRAT, Bender, DAP), regardless of referral reason, run a risk of being viewed as irrelevant.

The section of the report called "Relevant History and Current Data" addresses each of the identified issues in turn, generally with a paragraph devoted to each area investigated. Psychologists commonly report different types of data in different sections of the report, test data being separated from observational data, and both being distinct from historical data and interview data. In the PRRF, data from interviews, observations, rating scales, diagnostic teaching, curriculum-based assessment, intervention strategies, norm-referenced and criterion-referenced testing, work samples, environmental analysis, and review of records, all of which bear upon the specified concern, are integrated and synthesized into a coherent whole. Data not directly relevant to the defined scope and purpose are not reported.

In the "Discussion" section of PRRF, the problems targeted for investigation are again mentioned to maintain the reader's focus. For each area of concern, a priority for action and an accompanying rationale are presented that are based on an interpretation of the results synthesized in the previous section. For each problem listed in "Purpose and Scope," the psychologist outlines a plan of action to remediate it. This is included in the section under "Proposed Actions and Outcomes," along with a statement of the anticipated effects of each intervention. The PRRF is concluded with specific information concerning follow-up, including when, how, and under what circumstances the psychologist should be contacted, and when the case will be reviewed by the psychologist

failing any prior request for case follow-up by concerned parties.

While the PRRF may appear cumbersome, with a little practice it can be completed in 2–4 pages. It is one way to write a concise, relevant report that highlights outcomes and changes that will make a difference in students' school functioning.

Letter and Memo Formats

Since the primary purpose of the psychological report is communication, letter and memo report formats were designed to enhance the contact between the psychologist and the referring person (McBeath, 1976; Ross-Reynolds & Grimes, 1983). The content of the letter format report is similar to that found in the PRRF, except that it is more personal and less formal though still professional in style. Copies of the letter addressed to the referring person are sent to other concerned parties and to the file for documentation purposes. Psychologists who feel that a letter or memo is too informal a substitute for a formal initial evaluation report may choose to reserve these formats to document and communicate the outcomes of other kinds of involvement, such as curriculum or class management consultation, counseling, and confirmations and reminders of agreed-upon actions developed in case conferences. The memo format is an especially effective method for recording, communicating, and confirming an ongoing consultation interaction. While research findings are not available, teachers' reaction to letters and memos has been positive both for communicating initial evaluation data and for follow-up of single or ongoing consultation.

Referral-Oriented, Consultative Assessment Report

Recognizing the need to develop reports that improve communication between psychologists and other professionals, Batsche (1983) developed a report-writing model designed both to increase the value of the report as a relevant document and to enhance the collaborative and communicative process between the psychologist and referring person. Called the Referral-Oriented, Consultative Assessment Report (ROCAR), it is based on four principles articulated by Hudgins and Shultz (1978). First, the psychologist clarifies the referral concern and emerges with a common understanding of the referral question(s). Evaluation procedures are then individualized to answer referral questions. Next, the report focuses on the child's behavior. Finally, referral questions are addressed.

The ROCAR reflects a six-step assessment process. First, upon receiving a referral, the school psychologist reviews all existing data available on the student in order to be an informed and intelligent participant in the initial interview with the referral agent. Second, an interview with the referring agent is conducted to explicitly articulate and pinpoint the concern(s) to be addressed in the report. In addition the interview is designed to increase the referral agent's ownership and involvement in the evaluation process.

The third step, developing specific referral questions, is critical to this model. Referral questions are typically formulated during the interview with the referral agent, but questions from others such as parents or the principal may be included as well. Batsche (1983) notes that questions must be definable and measurable, and they must be agreed upon by the psychologist and referring agent. Questions that simply cue assessment procedures ("What are the results of intellectual assessment?" "What was learned from the behavioral observation?") are avoided in favor of those that target a specific problem area ("What behaviors are interfering with Mike's response to the instruction in the class?" "How can these behaviors be decreased or eliminated?). "How" and "what" questions are preferable to "why" questions, since the latter are less likely to result in problem remediation. For example, "What reading skills has Mary mastered?" is a better question than "Why can't Mary read?" The former question leads the psychologist to pinpoint specific skills and skill deficits

that Mary possesses. The latter question leads to what Julie Vargas calls an explanatory fiction, such as Mary has a learning disability, which ultimately explains nothing and is useless in developing appropriate intervention strategies.

Once specific assessment questions are formulated, assessment procedures designed to answer each question are selected. Typically the procedures are listed in the report under the referral question. Information gathered from a single procedure may be used to answer more than one question. As in the PRRF, the data are then integrated under the appropriate referral question with observation, test, interview, and review data blended to answer each question. The final step is to develop specific and realistic recommendations that address each problem reflected in the referral questions with the interventions arising logically from the assessment data collected.

Translated Report

Handler, Gerston, and Handler (1965) observed that the value of psychological reports would be enhanced "if the results were translated into possible problems in educational planning and particular problems in academic functioning" (p. 77). Bagnato (1980) developed a "translated" report that focuses on children's performance relative to the specific objectives of their preschool curriculum. Bagnato found that teachers who were given translated reports "were significantly more accurate, productive, and homogeneous in linking developmental diagnostic results to curriculum goals than teachers making judgments on the basis of traditional psychoeducational reports" (p. 555). To facilitate individualized educational plan (IEP) development, Bagnato recommended that reports (a) be organized by developmental or functional domains rather than by tests given; (b) describe strengths and skill deficits in behavioral terms, with strengths and weaknesses linked to specific curriculum objectives, not norm-referenced test items; (c) emphasize data that are relevant to the child's learning strategy, such as attention, learning rate, problem-solving strategies, and reward preferences; (d) list functional levels, skill sequences, and instructional needs so as to facilitate assessment–curriculum linkages and construction of the IEP; and (e) detail specific recommendations for behavioral and instructional management.

To this point several general approaches to the assessment/reporting process have been reviewed. Two somewhat more specific reporting innovations related to the ever-increasing impact of personal computers are worth mention.

Graphs in Reports

Given that the purpose of any psychological report is to communicate data about a child and that the discipline of psychology prefers to market itself as a science, it is curious that the time-honored method of scientific data presentation, the graph, is rarely included in a report. This may change with the increasing availability of technology. A well-chosen graph vividly and concisely provides information concerning a child's performance that is only communicated tediously and fuzzily in writing. For example: "Tim's Iowa Test of Basic Skills scores in reading increased slightly from the 1.5 grade level in second grade to the 3.7 grade level in eighth grade. Math scores increased from the 2.3 grade level to the 9.0 grade level, while spelling and language scores increased from 1.5 to 5.0 and from 1.7 to 3.2, respectively."

Although the above sentences give the reader the salient data concerning Tim's ITBS progress, they are more forcefully communicated by Figure 1. The choice of a particular graph depends upon the nature of the data to be presented and the point the psychologist wishes to highlight. Whereas Figure 1 depicts Tim's progress over time, Figure 2 highlights the discrepancy between ITBS scores and grade placement. It more cogently makes the point that in the area of language arts and reading Tim has fallen progressively further behind. When using graphs in a report, the psychologist is cautioned against simply presenting a graph and describing what is presented. The referral agent is better served when the psychologist interprets the data presented in the graph by highlighting trends and focusing on its implications (Grimes, 1984). To learn more about the use and construction of graphs refer to Thomas (1985).

Computer-Assisted Reports

Use of the computer or word processor in generating psychological reports has met with mixed results. At the most rudimentary level is the form report characterized by standard, repetitive, and consistent text with no attempt to individualize the information to a specific reader (McCullough & Wenck, 1984). Individual differences in the student are addressed by a simple fill-in-the-blank format. The narrative of every form-formatted report is identical to the narrative of every other form-formatted report, the children's test scores being the only variation. Since specific interpretation is impossible, the report content is preponderantly descriptive and general, focusing primarily on what various tests are thought to measure. Readers draw their own conclusions about the child from the specific scores presented and the information concerning the general meaning, content, and purpose of the test. Relevance is sacrificed for efficiency.

"Customized insert standardized text" represents a slight improvement over the form format. It is possible to customize the report by inserting specific data such as the child's name, teacher's name, referral concern, and test scores at specific points in the standard text. This is a familiar practice to anyone receiving mailed sweepstakes notices or computer-generated narratives of MMPI results. The extent of customization varies from the insertion of a name or selection of a phrase within a standard block of test to the selection of entire blocks of standard text contingent upon assessment results, as is done with computer-generated MMPI or Rorschach reports. The greater the extent of customization, the more individualized and relevant the report is; however, test data more easily lend themselves to

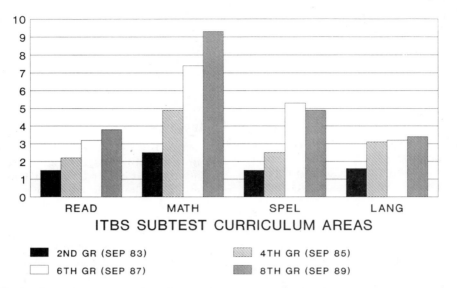

FIGURE 1. **Tim's grade equivalent scores on the Iowa Test of Basic Skills over 6 years.**

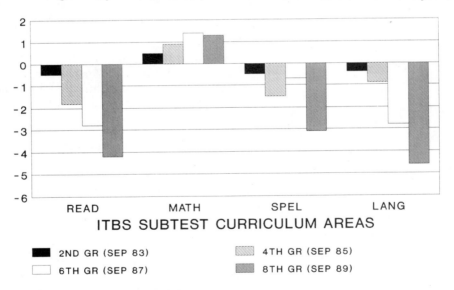

FIGURE 2. **Tim's grade level discrepancy scores on the Iowa Test of Basic Skills over 6 years.**

prepackaged interpretive paragraphs than do the data which the school psychologist synthesizes and integrates into a report. Therefore, applicability is limited.

Grimes (1983) developed a more professional and valuable alternative to computer-assisted report writing than that possible with either the form report or the standard text report. Called "starter text," it permits a degree of individualization by providing initial paragraph stems to which the psychologist can attach individually relevant data. Starter text consists of a series of frequently used blocks of text that can be included, as appropriate, in the report. The quality of the report is dependent upon the kind of information cued by the starter text.

Starter text that cues descriptive data only results in a less valuable report than one that includes both descriptive and interpretive stems.

Grimes developed representative starter text for referral concerns, background information, educational history, achievement, personal–social functioning, vocational considerations, cognitive processes and learning styles, medical and health concerns, behavior, diagnostic conclusions, and interventions. An example of starter text for diagnostic conclusions illustrates this approach.

"In considering all the information available I consider the most important areas for improvement to be ??" "With reference to special education programming, the data available support the conclusion that this student ??" "The information that most readily supports this position is ??" (Grimes, 1983).

Having selected a given stem for inclusion in a report, the psychologist enters the relevant data at the locations cued by the double question marks. An example of a report employing starter text is presented in Ross-Reynolds (1985). While starter text sacrifices the ease of the form report or standard-text format by requiring more input from the psychologist, it has the advantage of increased flexibility, thereby permitting the inclusion of relevant and highly individualized data. Computer-assisted reports are a relatively new software product and further developments and refinements in the area can be expected in the future.

SUMMARY

Psychological reports represent the permanent product of a school psychologist's assessments, and nowhere is the dictum "garbage in, garbage out" more applicable. For if the assessment on which the report is predicated is poorly planned and executed, no report, regardless of how well written, is adequate. Unfortunately the converse is not necessarily true. Thoughtful, thorough, and brilliantly conducted assessments do not ensure good reports. If the report is poorly organized or written it will be harshly judged and of little use.

There is strong consensus among writers regarding the characteristics of effective reports. Referral questions are specific and explicit, and reports are tailored to clearly and concisely answer these questions. The writer discusses the individual in behavioral terms, avoids abstractions, and highlights that which makes the individual unique. Writing is clear, fluid, precise, and straightforward. Information is synthesized and integrated rather than reported by test or other assessment technique. Recommendations that relate to the referral concerns are explicit, specific, and realistic.

Although the place of the traditional psychological report is well established in psychological practice by custom and training, consumer reaction has been mixed. Numerous alternatives to the traditional report have been proposed, including brief written reports, letters and memos, outlines, and consultation-based reports. Most of these alternatives were designed to increase communication between the psychologist and the consumer, to save time, or to increase the utility of the report. Their effectiveness has yet to be evaluated. The expository process model, which can be used with a variety of reporting formats, holds promise as a persuasive and valued reporting vehicle. A variety of computer-assisted reports are appearing. Some are quite primitive, presenting only test scores; others are highly sophisticated and provide starter text that lends structure, form, and organization to the report while allowing the entry of individualized data.

Anyone writing reports should periodically review their effectiveness. Regardless of the reporting format or the means of developing the report, the goal of the evaluation and report must always be to catalyze a positive change in the child's life. This may occur because others come to view the child in a new light, utilize new or different approaches in working with the child, or render additional services. Reports long stand as documentation of psychologists' expertise or ineptitude, of sensitivity and caring or narrow subservience to the generation of test data. It is hoped that this chapter will assist in this review process by providing useful alternative procedures and techniques from which psychologists may choose in making their report writing maximally effective.

REFERENCES

Bagnato, S. J. (1980). The efficacy of diagnostic reports as individualized guides to prescriptive goal planning. *Exceptional Children, 46,* 554-557.

Batsche, G. M. (1983). The referral oriented, consultative assessment report writing model. In J. Grimes (Ed.), *Communicating psychological information in writing* (pp. 29-43). Des Moines, IA: Iowa Department of Public Instruction.

Brandt, H. M., & Giebink, J. W. (1968). Concreteness and congruence in psychologists' reports to teachers. *Psychology in the Schools, 5,* 87-89.

Cuadra, C. A., & Albaugh, W. P. (1956). Sources of ambiguity in psychological reports. *Journal of Clinical Psychology, 12,* 109-115.

Grimes, J. (1983, October). *Micro uses in the macro world of school psychology.* Paper presented at the meeting of the Colorado Society of School Psychologists, Denver.

Grimes, J. (1984, April). *Graphically speaking.* Paper presented at the meeting of the National Association of School Psychologists, Philadelphia.

Grimes, J., & Ross-Reynolds, G. (1983). On skinning cats, choking dogs, and leaving lovers. In J. Grimes (Ed.), *Communicating psychological information in writing* (pp. 3-7). Des Moines, IA: Iowa Department of Public Instruction.

Handler, L., Gerston, A., & Handler, B. (1965). Suggestions for improved psychologist-teacher communication. *Psychology in the Schools, 2,* 77-81.

Hartlage, L., Freeman, W., Horine, L., & Walton, C. (1968). Decision utility of psychological reports. *Journal of Clinical Psychology, 24,* 481-483.

Hudgins, A. L., & Shultz, J. L. (1978). On observing: The use of the Carkhuff HRD model in writing psychological reports. *Journal of School Psychology, 16,* 56-63.

Isett, R., & Roszkowski, M. (1979). Consumer preferences for psychological report contents in a residential school and center for the mentally retarded. *Psychology in the Schools, 16,* 402-407.

Kicklighter, R. H., & Bailey-Richardson, B. (1984). Psychological assessment: Tasks and time. *School Psychology Review, 13,* 499-502.

McBeath, M. (1976). Memos to a teacher. In J. D. Krumboltz & C. E. Thorensen (Eds.), *Counseling methods* (pp. 445-451). New York: Holt, Rinehart & Winston.

McCullough, C. S., & Wenck, L. S. (1984). Current microcomputer applications in school psychology. *School Psychology Review, 13,* 429-439.

Mussman, M. C. (1964). Teachers' evaluations of psychological reports. *Journal of School Psychology, 3,* 35-37.

Noble, B., & Dickinson, D. J. (1988). Utility of school psychologists' recommendations: Perception of elementary teachers. *Psychology in the Schools, 25,* 412-418.

Ownby, R. L. (1987). *Psychological reports.* Brandon, VT: Clinical Psychology Publishing Co.

Ownby, R. L., Wallbrown, F. H., & Brown, D. Y. (1982). Special education teachers' perceptions of reports written by school psychologists. *Perceptual and Motor Skills, 55,* 955-961.

Rogers, G. W., Jr. (1977). Maximizing the practical contributions of psychological reports. *Journal of School Health, 47,* 104-105.

Ross-Reynolds, G. (1985). Psychological report writing. In J. Grimes (Ed.), *School psychology innovations: Resources for in-service training.* Washington, DC: National Association of School Psychologists.

Ross-Reynolds, G., & Grimes, J. (1983). Three counterproposals to the traditional psychological report. In J. Grimes (Ed.), *Communicating psychological information in writing* (pp. 11-25). Des Moines, IA: Iowa Department of Public Instruction.

Rucker, C. N. (1967). Report writing in school psychology: A critical investigation. *Journal of School Psychology, 5,* 101-108.

Sattler, J. (1988). *Assessment of children* (3rd ed.). San Diego: Jerome M. Sattler.

Shellenberger, S. (1982). Presentation and interpretation of psychological data in educational settings. In C. R. Reynolds & T. B. Gutkin (Eds.), *The handbook of school psychology* (pp. 51-81). New York: Wiley.

Shively, J. J., & Smith, A. E. (1969). Understanding the psychological report. *Psychology in the Schools, 6,* 272-273.

Tallent, N. (1983). *Psychological report writing* (2nd ed.). Englewood Cliffs, NJ: Prentice-Hall.

Teglasi, H. (1983). Report of a psychological assessment in a school setting. *Psychology in the Schools, 20,* 466-478.

Thomas, A. (1985). Graphing. In J. Grimes (Ed.), *School psychology innovations: Resources for in-service training*. Washington, DC: National Association of School Psychologists.

Tidwell, R., & Wetter, J. (1978). Parental evaluations of psychoeducational reports: A case study. *Psychology in the Schools, 15*, 209–215.

Zins, J. E., & Barnett, D. W. (1983). Report writing: Legislative, ethical, and professional challenges. *Journal of School Psychology, 21*, 219–227.

ANNOTATED BIBLIOGRAPHY

Ownby, R. L. (1987). *Psychological reports*. Brandon, VT: Clinical Psychology Publishing Co.
Provides an overview of research on report writing and articulates a structured model (the expository process model) with examples for writing persuasive reports bridging data and theory. An excellent model for clear, cogent report writing. Especially appropriate for the experienced practitioner and of definite benefit to the psychologist-in-training. If you plan to read only one work on report writing, this is it.

Ross-Reynolds, G. (1985). Psychological report writing. In J. Grimes (Ed.), *School psychology innovations: Resources for in-service training*. Washington, DC: National Association of School Psychologists.
A computer-assisted instructional module on report writing for the Apple, the unit provides an interactive tutorial on sound reporting practices. In addition, hard copy examples of most of the various report formats described in this chapter are included with the commentary.

Sattler, J. (1988). *Assessment of children* (3rd ed.), Chapter 23. San Diego: Jerome M. Sattler.
Delineates a traditional approach to report writing and includes many examples of correct and incorrect practice. Describes a suggested report outline and highlights common pitfalls and major considerations. A good introduction for beginners and worthwhile review for experienced psychologists.

Shellenberger, S. (1982). Presentation and interpretation of psychological data in educational settings. In C. R. Reynolds & T. B. Gutkin (Eds.), *The handbook of school psychology* (pp. 51–81). New York: Wiley.
Presents a complete and well-written literature review on report writing that highlights the characteristics of effective reports, consumer preferences and criticisms, and alternative approaches to traditional content and formats. Considerations for gathering and presenting psychological assessment data are presented, as well as an example of a traditional psychological report.

Tallent, N. (1983). *Psychological report writing* (2nd ed.). Englewood Cliffs, NJ: Prentice-Hall.
Contains a thorough treatment of report writing. Although slanted to practice in clinical settings, Tallent's insights into problems, purposes, and effective practice in report writing make this an excellent reference.

43

Best Practices in Rural School Psychology

A. Jerry Benson
James Madison University
Sharon Z. Petty
Ferndale (Michigan) School District

OVERVIEW

In recent years, issues in rural education and rural mental health have generated a surge of scholarly attention and have emphasized that serving children in the rural United States is a special challenge for human service providers. Many readers will recognize this statement to be true. They are the readers who are currently practicing or have practiced in the rural area and will likely read on looking for vindication, confirmation, and support for their beliefs and ideas. Hopefully readers who have little knowledge of what rural practice may be like will delve further to satisfy their curiosity about practice in a rural area.

The present account should generate discussion and ideas among persons currently practicing in rural areas, educators preparing practitioners for rural areas, and those persons contemplating practice or newly engaged in practice in rural areas, but it likely will provide more questions and thought than solutions to specific problems. The reasoning behind this lack of specificity will become apparent as the chapter progresses; the information presented is intended to serve as a framework to aid practitioners in formulating approaches or solutions specific to their own needs, resources, and settings.

BASIC CONSIDERATIONS

The 1980 U.S. Census defines *rural* as all persons living outside urbanized areas in the open country or in communities with less than 2,500 inhabitants. It also includes all those living in areas of extended cities with a population density of less than 1,000 inhabitants per square mile. (Worthington, 1983, p. 10)

While this definition provides some functional discrimination for the Census Bureau, it is not particularly pragmatic for defining rural in an educational context. The National Rural Small Schools Task Force (1988) notes that nationally, for all 50 states, 74% of all school districts are small (fewer than 2,500 students) or very small (fewer than 1,000 students). Fifty-nine percent (59%) of all school districts are rural (at least three-fourths of the students enrolled live in a town with less than 2,500 population or in an unincorporated area). Finally, 51% of all school districts are both small and rural. Two-thirds of all schools in the United States are in rural areas and these schools serve 32% of U.S. school children (Helge, 1981).

In a thorough review of rural education and school psychology services, Helge (1985) delineated a number of issues differentiating rural and nonrural settings (see Table 1), which may aid the reader

TABLE 1
Issues Differentiating Rural and Nonrural School Systems

Issues	Rural	Nonrural
Percentage of school population served	Two-thirds of all school districts are classified as rural.	One-third of school districts are classified as metropolitan.
Personnel turnover	Turnover occurs in all personnel. Turnover is commonly 30–50% among specialized personnel such as school psychologists and speech, physical, and occupational therapists. Turnover is especially serious among itinerant personnel serving low-incidence populations.	Turnover more commonly involves superintendents and special education directors (i.e., management personnel).
Transportation	Long distances involved in transporting services, students, and staff. Long distances problematic in planning and implementing interagency collaboration. High costs associated with transportation. Climatic and geographic barriers to travel: mountains, deserts, icy and muddy roads, flooding seasons, blizzards, snow storms, etc.	Logistics of transportation problems primarily evolve around desegregation issues of which agency or bureaucratic structure is to pay for transportation.
Community structure	Sense of community spirit prevalent. Personalized environment prevails.	Depersonalized environment except in inner-city pockets of distinctive ethnic groups, several of which may be incorporated into any one school system.
Geography	Problems posed by remote areas include social and professional isolation, long distances from services, and geographic barriers (e.g., mountains, deserts, and islands).	Logistics of city itself often pose problems (e.g., negotiating transportation transfers, particularly for wheelchairs; crossing lines for one agency versus another to pay, traffic, etc.).
Backlog of children for testing and placement	Result of lack of available services (school psychologists, agency programs, funds, etc.) or lack of parent understanding and permission for testing.	Result of bureaucratic and organizational barriers.
Communication	Communication mainly person-to-person.	Written memo frequently used.
Student body composition	Small numbers of handicapped students and diverse ethnic and linguistic groups pose difficulties for establishing "programs" for bilingual or multicultural students. Difficulties serving migrant handicapped students because of low numbers of students and few appropriate resources available.	Wide variety of ethnic and racial ethnic groups.

(Table 1, continued)

Issues	Rural	Nonrural
(student body composition, continued)	Qualified bilingual and multicultural personnel difficult to recruit to rural areas.	
	Appropriate materials and other resources typically unavailable or inappropriate for rural communities.	
	Religious minorities are frequently strong subcultures in rural U.S.	
Approach of educators	Generalists expected to be "all things to all people."	Specialists must be an expert on one topic area or with one age group or disability.
Cooperation among agencies	Cooperation is an inherent attribute of most rural communities	Bureaucratic mazes and policies make interagency collaboration difficult.
	Interagency collaboration is inhibited by long distances to travel, few staff hours available for planning, and isolation or nonexistence of many types of service agencies.	
Enrollment of school-aged children	5.3% (nearly twice that of urban figures).	Almost one-half that of rural.
Population density	Sparce populations ranging from low-density (scattered) to small (clustered) towns.	High population density.
Management	"Management by tradition."	"Management by crisis."

Note. From "The school psychologist in the rural education context" by D. Helge, 1985, *School Psychology Review, 14*(4), pp. 404–406. Copyright 1985 by the National Association of School Psychologists. Reprinted by permission.

in understanding the rural context. Rural settings present the practitioner with challenges such as lack of alternative programs and services for special needs children, heavy caseloads, limited access to fellow school psychologists for informal consultations, limited community services, limited availability of continuing education programs, lack of administrative and consumer understanding of the school psychologist's role, and difficult work conditions such as extensive travel and space problems (Benson, Bischoff, & Boland, 1983; Kramer & Peters, 1985).

Although these shared characteristics do reflect some commonality for defining *rural*, they also tend to obscure the diversity that is inherent in rural schooling. This diversity is more pronounced today than at any point in the post–World War II period because of variations in the size of the populations, in the proximity to metropolitan areas, and in the primary economic activities of rural areas (Stephens, 1988). Hobbs (1983) provides a useful perspective on this issue:

Rural communities and regions tend to reflect their individual natural environments and resources. Rural communities vary widely across the country, frequently deriving their distinctive characters from the prominence of a single local industry. There are rural farming, fishing, mining, ranching and resort communities. There are river towns, desert towns, and bedroom towns. Some rural communities are racially mixed, while others are ethnic enclaves. Some have dominant religion, while others have no particular unifying heritage or institution. In short, rural America exemplifies the diversity of the national culture. (pp. 14–15)

Since a rural school reflects the community it serves, the diversity among rural school districts is as great as or greater than the differences that commonly distinguish urban and rural systems (DeYoung, 1987; Gjetlen, 1982; Nachtigal, 1982; Sher, 1977). Thus, the specific roles for school psychologists, the problems encountered, and specific approaches to these problems must be individualized and developed in the context of a particular community.

As an alternative to the common mistake of lumping all rural districts into one universal category and prescribing one best method to ameliorate their difficulties, the practicing rural school psychologist is encouraged to formulate a typology that differentiates among the rural areas and provides a framework from which to discern appropriate interventions (from the system to the individual level). Two examples of such typologies will be reviewed.

Nachtigal (1982) suggested a typology of rural America that delineates three categories: the rural poor; traditional Middle America; and communities in transition. Rural poor communities are characterized by lower median incomes, lower levels of educational development, and lower levels of political power. Rural poverty continues to be concentrated in the South (Bender et al., 1985), but other rural areas are experiencing economic difficulties with the long-term, continuous shift in the U.S. economy from goods-producing industries to service industries (Pulver, 1986). McCormick (1988) labeled the large number of rural poor as "America's Third World" and noted that "one-fourth of all rural children now live in poverty . . . , infant mortality in America's 320 poorest rural counties tops the national rate by a chilling 45 percent

. . . [and] America's rural poverty rate now slightly exceeds the rate of our blighted big cities" (p. 21). The economic and political power of these areas tends to be concentrated outside of the community, making community-based interventions and programs difficult to implement.

Middle America is best characterized by the Midwest farm community, in which solid family lifestyle, the Puritan work ethic, and commitment to education are evident. Nachtigal (1982) observed that power structures in these communities are relatively open and political participation is broad-based.

Finally, the communities in transition are localities undergoing a demographic shift from "old-timers" to "newcomers." The social structure of these communities often is in a state of flux and may reflect conflict between the old, established inhabitants and the outsiders who bring new and different ideas.

Gjetlen (1982), based on his work with the National Rural Center of the U.S. Department of Education, proposed a typology consisting of the following five categories.

1. Stable. These communities tend to be white, homogeneous, agricultural, and located primarily in the West and Middle West. Always having been able and willing to pay for good programs, stable communities tend to have the best education in rural schools. Since the economic base of these communities is changing and school enrollments have declined, reorganization interventions (e.g., consolidation, regional programs) may be options for interventions in these districts.

2. Depressed. Similar to Nachtigal's rural poor communities, these communities have an underdeveloped economy, marginal sources of income, and an overall out-migration. There are fewer community resources for human service programs, such as parent volunteers. The educational dilemma is one of educating the young to move out of the depressed environment or to come back and intervene within the home environment.

3. High-Growth. These communities, and their schools, have new opportunities both in dollar resources and in people. Forecasting future needs and management are likely to be major issues for schools of these communities.

4. Reborn. These are communities in scenic or recreational areas that are characterized by in-migration of people freely choosing to do so. The conflicts over values and changes noted in Nachtigal's transition category are apparent here.

5. Isolated. These are truly unique communities. Because of enrollment-based funding formulas, the schools of these communities lack sufficient funding, which further isolates them from the mainstream of U.S. culture. "It is very difficult to teach about the outside world because students have such little contact with it" (Gjetlen, 1982, p. 13).

Two major economic and social trends of the recent decade should be factored into the typologies and observations offered. First, the unprecedented rural renaissance of the 1970s has not continued in the 1980s, net out-migration from nonmetropolitan areas having accelerated in recent years. The second trend, is directly related to the first: The population of nonmetropolitan areas continues to be older than that found in metropolitan areas (Brown & Deavers, 1987).

Given some perspective on the various realities of rural communities, let us turn our attention to the rural educational system. A frequently held notion about rural education, the myth that students from smaller rural schools receive an education that is inferior to that of students from large urban or suburban schools, has been debunked. Research has failed to demonstrate significant differences in performance on standardized achievement tests between students from small, usually rural, schools and those from larger, often urban institutions (Edington & Koehler, 1987). In fact, Barker (1986) noted that the small country school of yesteryear was the impetus from which many of today's better-known educational "innovations" originated: students learned independently and progressed at their own rate; older students helped the younger ones; the teacher was able to take time to individualize lessons; personal contact with each student was provided; and younger students were better prepared for what the next grade would bring because they could see and hear older children working on advanced lessons.

Additionally, there are profound developments accruing from the nationwide educational reform movement. One might consider the publication of *A Nation at Risk* (National Commission on Excellence in Education, 1983) as the benchmark of the first wave of the reform movement. In looking at the direct impact of reform initiatives on rural schools, researchers such as Forbes (1985) and Stephens (1987) have noted that while the movement is designed to improve education for all children regardless of place of residency (a positive impact on rural districts), many of the initiatives exacerbate a number of traditional rural education problems. Several trends — increased entrance or certification standards for teachers which limits multiple endorsements, the concept of family choice or a voucher system, new demands on schools to provide expanded early childhood education and daycare services, the continuing focus on enriching instructional programs (especially science, math, foreign languages, and technology), and the concept of statewide comparison of school district's performance which can lead to state receivership of poorly performing districts — are likely to disproportionately add to the burdens of rural schools.

However, future themes of the reform movement may make rural districts the "big winners" (Stephens, 1988). First, a move to restructure schools so that individual schools and school faculties are given substantial autonomy to establish priorities and decide how best to achieve them is predicted to be a centerpiece of continued reform. Such a trend would be contrary to the first wave of reform, which was largely driven by state mandates. The autonomy afforded local districts by the restructuring trend might prompt new governance alliances for decision making, increased local district contractual arrangements, and new program options and pilots encouraged by securing waivers from state or local policies. A second predicted trend, tied closely to restructuring, is the concept of integration of community services. Stephens notes that while this clearly is not a new concept, factors such as an emphasis on parental involvement, the at-risk student, and the greater use of schools to meet the growing national interest in providing adequate early childhood education and daycare services will prompt the political community to revisit this concept. Edelman (1988) points out the growing realization of the interrelatedness of many of the problems of children and youths (e.g., dropout, delinquency, teenage pregnancy, substance abuse, etc.) and the existing fragmentation of governmental structures in dealing with these problems. Together, these two future reform trends may play upon the strengths of rural communities providing an impetus for the integration of community services, the acquisition of new resources, and the improvement of human services programs. The rural school district is the greatest resource of professional expertise and physical facilities in most rural communities. "It would seem logical that the financial and programming merits of expanding the mission of this rich resource — the rural school - to include many functions now assumed by other governmental agencies will be increasingly recognized" (Stephens, 1988, p. 66).

In summary, rural school initiatives must be diverse and must reflect the different values and socioeconomic characteristics of the rural community served. The "old rural deficit model," which for decades has led external entities to tell rural schools how to improve, must be rethought. The application of any "best practice" or "best system" approach for all educational programs serves to remove control from the local community, thus inherently promoting conflicts between the educational and psychological programs and local resources and values.

BEST PRACTICES

Armed with an enhanced awareness of the multiple realities of rural communities and the impact of economic, social, political, and educational trends on these communities and their schools, the reader should better appreciate the authors' reluctance to designate specific "best practices" in this topic area. Instead, we offer considerations in the following areas which are identified as important to rural practice: service delivery, recruitment and retention, training, and technology.

Provision of Services

Many of the unique issues of rural school psychology practice can be included under the rubric of service delivery. Unique challenges to school psychologists working in rural areas include cultural factors, geographic factors, and socioeconomic factors. Yet many of the characteristics of rural settings often perceived as difficulties may also serve as opportunities.

Consider two ideas offered by Fagan and Hughes (1985) in their review of lessons learned and future directions for rural school psychology. The first idea, *reframing*, suggests that it is easy for the rural practitioner to become focused on issues of rural practice as obstacles and lose sight of the potential for change. This myopic view may in turn lead to burnout and professional disillusionment. The recitation of problems in rural areas is helpful in providing vindication and confirmation to the rural practitioner, but its helpfulness is limited if it is not coupled with actions to address the issues.

For example, rural areas are often characterized by close family ties and a personalized community structure. This community closeness may create a mistrust of outsiders that exacerbates the difficulty of obtaining acceptance both for the professional and the programs that one would like to implement; yet correspondingly, a support system exists for the school system and the individual student that extends to the family and the community. This, in turn, provides a potential resource for interventions by the school psychologist. Likewise, Barker and Gump (1964) noted that small schools typically serve as a community nucleus. This invites strong support from parents and community members as well as closer working relationships with other school staff. The close personal relationships may lead to easy acceptance of new ideas because of friendship and a strong sense of identification and belonging on the part of the professional group.

Students tend to be the center of the school; thus a potential for student participation and expression is enhanced. As a result, students are more likely to have positive attitudes towards school and are less likely to create discipline problems. Teachers are more likely to know their students as individuals and become familiar with their family backgrounds. This enables teachers to make special provisions for students' individual needs or talents and receive greater cooperation from the parents in resolving problems. The scarcity of community services, noted extensively as a problem, may also promote interagency collaboration, an inherent attribute of most rural communities.

The second idea the rural practitioner may utilize in regarding characteristics of the rural setting as opportunities rather than problems is to view the school, like the family, as a *system*. General systems theory and many of the aspects of family therapy can be applied in the conceptualization and implementation of rural services. Fagan and Hughes (1985) suggest that family therapy techniques of accommodation and joining are relevant to intervention efforts in rural communities. Accommodation in family therapy speaks of the interventionist's ability to enter the system in ways that are syntonic to it. This syntonic accommodation to a family or a school system requires adaptation. The rural school psychologist adapts to the rural school system by adopting the system's tempo, style of communication, and interpersonal style. As Fagan and

Hughes note, accommodation also involves encouraging, accepting, validating, supporting, and designing changes that build on the existing strengths of the system.

The joining aspect reflects the importance of person-to-person communication and the promotion of referent over expert power. It is not unusual for the school psychologist in a rural setting to be the expert in assessment, socioemotional development, research, and other areas. Thus, expert power is inherent in the role. The consultation literature (e.g., see Zinn's chapter in this edition) suggests that building rapport and joining with the client maximizes referent power. When a person admires a school psychologist and identifies with the school psychologist's values, attitudes, and behaviors, the resulting professional relationship is more conducive to cooperation, problem solving, and planned change. With the importance given personal relationships in rural communities, the rural school psychologist who establishes a high level of referent power is more likely to be a successful change agent.

The consultation literature also offers the rural practitioner a rich source of ideas regarding service delivery. The practice of mental health or human service program consultation grew out of the same set of problems as those facing rural practitioners today, namely, manpower needs. As the rural practitioner may visit certain schools or intervention sites infrequently owing to distance, time, and other factors, it is important to establish a network of professionals or paraprofessionals that will maintain the day-by-day intervention. Parsons and Meyers (1984) provide a framework delineating levels of consultation that may serve as a basis for the rural practitioner in designing service programs.

The use of interagency collaborative models (Benson, Hanson, & Canfield, 1982; Hughes & Clark, 1981) is another consideration in providing services in rural areas. As noted earlier, the interrelatedness of problems facing children and youth today has forced our attention to the need for interrelated service programs. Regional approaches to hiring specialized personnel that also cut across traditional agency boundaries may provide necessary financial resources. For example, a physical therapist or bilingual counselor or psychologist may serve numerous human services agencies of a community or region. Currently, the senior author is involved in the state of Virginia's response to the services mandated by Public Law 99-457. The initial step in building a service continuum for children from birth through 5 years of age involves the establishment of interagency early intervention councils within each community mental health district. These councils are to promote the sharing of existing resources, the collaborative seeking of additional needed resources, and the communication needed to avoid an overlap of services.

A final consideration in service delivery is the use of volunteers (Latham & Burnham, 1985). Volunteerism is a valued activity among rural citizens. Latham and Burnham note that the spirit of volunteerism can be harnessed in two ways: (a) as a therapy for the volunteer engaged in the activity; and (b) as a solution for manpower deficits in the service delivery systems. A model volunteer network for serving the needs of handicapped children, called the community independent living delivery system, has been developed by the National Rural Project (Latham & Burnham, 1985). This program, a computerized matching service, links the interests of volunteers to the activities or service needs of the requesting agency.

In designing a volunteer system, the school psychologist might be actively involved in delineating the tasks or responsibilities of the volunteer, which will lead to formulating specifications for recruitment and training. The psychologist is again reminded of the effective application of consultation methods and skills to such a program. Two particular pools of volunteers may warrant special consideration: (a) As noted previously, the population in rural areas is growing older, thus retired persons may be a source of additional manpower; (b) Programs utilizing school-age volunteers (e.g., peer tutoring, peer counseling, high school home economics classes running day-care programs, etc.) also fit Latham and Burnham's dual-purpose idea. One caveat: As paid professional mental health workers move onto the scene, oftentimes natural helpers move off the scene assuming the professional can fulfill all the needs.

Recruitment and Retention

Difficulty in recruiting and retaining mental health professionals is a pervasive problem in rural areas (Helge & Marrs, 1981; MITRE Corporation, 1979). Factors such as professional and social isolation, extreme weather conditions, low salaries, inadequate housing, and vast distances to travel all contribute to the difficulty in employing school psychologists in rural areas (Benson, 1985; Helge, 1985).

Inadequate funding often casts small districts in the role of training grounds for larger districts. In fact, the "experience curve" in small districts is often U-shaped; some educators with little experience, some teachers with many years' experience, and few, if any, in between (Helge, 1981; Swift, 1987). For many educators in rural schools, longevity is more dependent upon their spouse's occupation or a desire for rural lifestyle than on the school system and job satisfaction.

There are recruiting and retention incentives that could be implemented to enhance the professional preparation and development of personnel for small rural schools. Swift (1987) notes that incentives found effective in recruiting and retaining teaching personnel include salary increments for multiple endorsements and/or teaching assignments, professional leave and tuition reimbursement for professional development activities leading to additional endorsements, and reimbursement of professional dues. These incentives, however, are of little value unless they are offered in addition to pay benefits comparable to those provided in larger districts. State agencies can assist in the recruitment of personnel for small and rural schools through adequate funding to districts for these additional incentives.

Twenty-eight states provide additional funding to small districts, to districts with small and/or isolated schools, or to districts with sparse population (Wright, 1981). State funding agencies can also assist by increasing funds available to training institutions that develop and make available to educators in small rural schools alternative and nontraditional professional development opportunities.

The stages of professional development that have been outlined in the literature (Cruickshank & Callahan, 1983; Fuller & Brown, 1975; Presbury & Cobb, 1985) offer considerations for the rural districts in retaining personnel. Briefly, such a developmental perspective shows that Stage 1 professionals bring freshness, enthusiasm, and new ideas from their recent training to their job. Stage 1 professionals, however, need support in the area of control over their professional assignment, inclusion within the system, and affection and support from their peers. What they need most is concrete solutions to immediate problems. Stage 2 professionals are characterized by their increasing comfort in the area of control, that is, feelings of adequacy because strategies have been developed that ease work demands. As these strategies become ingrained, however, these professionals may become complacent and easily bored with their duties, thus needing to be stretched by new challenges. Stage 3 professionals are at a level of mastery. The paradox of Stage 3, as noted by Presbury and Cobb, is that the professional who has achieved mastery often experiences control needs because the system lacks the capability to fully tap its resources. Thus, the master professional may have a sense of isolation in which belonging needs again arise.

Viewed in this developmental framework, rural districts will need to recognize Stage 1 needs and will need to support the Stage 1 professional, both with financial and with time resources, providing the needed supervision, professional development activities, and an adequate information base (e.g., journals, books, etc.). At this stage, regional, district, or statewide conferences may serve as a system of peer consultation and support. The practitioner at this level should make a special effort to reach out and become involved in professional groups at both the state and national levels.

The Stage 2 professional should be challenged with new responsibilities and/or new approaches to the needs within the system. Stage 2 professionals will also require new ideas and feedback to keep them going. Rural districts in coalition might seek to provide personnel with continuing professional development opportunities by assigning professionals to address problems in other districts based on the expertise developed within their own districts. Stage 3 professionals might be paired with Stage 1 professionals across school districts in mentor relationships. Local education agencies may find that expenditure of time and personnel resources would be more than offset by the ideas shared across districts and the energizing of both Stage 1 and Stage 3 professionals.

Presbury and Cobb (1985) also advocate the development of professional and peer support groups. These groups are networks of people within an organizational hierarchy, or in the case of rural areas across organizations, that perceive themselves as meeting common needs and goals, working together to solve problems, affirming each other, and improving their skills. Within the school system, these may be groups of school psychologists, supervisors, principals, teachers, or other pupil services workers. There may be two roles for the school psychologist in this area: (a) growth and development by participation in an appropriate professional peer support group; and (b) facilitation of the development and implementation of professional peer support groups for other professionals.

Training

When the question of training for school psychologists to work in rural areas arises, there is the inevitable discussion of whether this is a unique subspecialty. The roles of rural and urban psychologists are often comparable. Rural and urban psychologists will provide assessment, case conferences, and consultations. Cummings, Huebner, and McLeskey (1985) point out that one's theoretical perspective is not setting-dependent and that the greatest differences between rural and urban practice are the wide variety of problems faced, the lack of sufficient resources, professional isolation, and the demand for generalist services in the rural setting.

Hughes and Clark (1981) recommend that the preservice training of school psychologists for rural areas should be at the generalist level, introducing counseling, clinical, community, and organizational psychology skills and theory in addition to educational and developmental psychology. Since rural schools frequently lack the diverse array of professionals available in suburban and urban areas, the school psychologist may be called upon to fill a variety of traditional and nontraditional functions (DeVore & Fagan, 1979). The effective rural school psychologist must then be a creative problem solver able to intervene from a variety of service delivery standpoints to help provide children with appropriate services under less than optimal conditions (Cummings et al., 1985).

Preservice training through field experiences in rural schools fosters an understanding of the given subculture and an appreciation of its unique mores and folkways. An evaluation of one's own ethnocentric attitudes and beliefs is important to the future practitioner's sensitivity to and respect for cultural pluralism (Cummings et al., 1985). This perspective is necessary for the psychologist's entry and acceptance into the local rural community.

Helge (1981), Hughes (1982), and Huebner and Huberty (1985) have all elaborated on the problems of service delivery in rural settings, which may lead to burnout. Cummings et al. (1985) offer a preservice perspective on dealing with retention issues and burnout. They suggest that the school psychologist be instructed about environmental factors that cause or exacerbate problems of burnout and be armed with appropriate strategies to cope with burnout. One such strategy would have preservice school psychologists be aware of the boundaries of their competencies and ready to seek out peer professionals for consultation as an alternative to the frustration or insecurity that might lead to burnout. If on-site contact is not available, phone consultation may be an effective alternative.

Technology

Hobbs (1984) noted that the possible substitution of communication for transportation in providing services stimulates consideration of a variety of alternative forms of service delivery. Because of recent advances in technology, the negative implications and complications created by long distances and sparse populations in rural areas can be substantially reduced.

Latham and Burnham (1985) note that the major barrier to improving rural services through technology is not in finding, tailoring, and implementing technology to meet the need; rather it is getting people to use the technologies and gain confidence so that the benefits can be realized. Tawney, Aeschleman, Deaton, and Donaldson (1979) described one example of the application of technology in a system that uses telecommunications technology to instruct rural handicapped children at home. They note that the system has the general capacity to supply an unlimited array of mental health services directly into the homes of rural families and is easily adapted to any home with a telephone. The interaction of staff personnel with parents as a component of home training increases the families' acceptance of the technology in their homes and strengthens the cooperation of the parents with staff.

Much of the technology and logistics of a telecommunications approach has been tested through projects involving the provision of higher education to professionals in remote areas and providing professional development for school psychologists (Hagstrom, 1983; S. O'Keefe, personal communication, October 28, 1988). The use of microcomputers, video equipment, and telephone services have enhanced the capabilities of teleconferencing and interactive technology based instruction, thus addressing the supervision, consultation, and continuing professional needs of rural practitioners. Likewise, Heath (1983) has made us aware of information resources such as bulletin boards and databases. This allows the school psychologist in even the remotest area access to the latest research literature.

Helge (1983) noted that equipment cost, rental of telecommunication lines, and long distance charges are still problematic to rural districts in the use of advanced technology. Barnhardt and Barnhardt (1983) have suggested making local legislators aware of this technology and its application to their needs and then piggybacking on their investments in the acquisition of hardware. Audio computer teleconferencing systems designed to facilitate legislators' interactions with their constituents during the legislative sessions can also serve the needs of children, teachers, and school psychologists in rural schools. Others have capitalized upon the wave of high technology that is being introduced into public school programs to obtain state funding for computer hardware and software. Such programs not only introduce computers into the instructional and management areas of education but also offer opportunities for use by the individual rural practitioner.

Finally, the effective use of time is a constant problem faced by rural practitioners that can be lessened by the use of existing technology. Most practitioners probably already use dictation as a way of keeping up with report writing and other paperwork during waiting or travel time. Likewise, the increased marketing of professional development materials offered on audiocassettes provides an opportunity for the rural practitioner to be engaged in continuing professional development while driving among school sites.

SUMMARY

The fact that the practice of school psychology in rural areas is perceived as being different by those practicing in rural schools seems supported by the professional literature. The differences, however, are more attributable to the characteristics of the setting than to differences in the specific skills of the practitioner (e.g., administering standardized tests), or in the content of the educational system (i.e., the curriculum).

The understanding of the rural *culture* is a prime component of effective rural school psychology practice. This requires a greater sensitivity to and respect for the cultural pluralism and traditional values of rural areas. The potential influence of the rural school psychologist on a variety of institutions beyond the boundary of the school system validates the need for a community psychology and systems orientation in rural practice and preservice preparation. The rural practitioner must rely more on referent power, person-to-person communication, and being approachable. Fagan and Hughes (1985) summarize this point well by noting that the school psychologist in the rural setting must possess the "ability to design change strategies that maximize rural strength, are congruent with the particular rural culture and are consistent with the community's perception of needs" (p. 446).

Finally, the successful practice and continued active service of the school psychologist in the rural context requires networking. Reaching out and connecting with others through phone consultation networks, peer support groups, conferences, mentoring relationships, and other activities is necessary. There are many existing structures for such networking: the NASP Rural School Psychology Special Interest Group; the American Council on Rural Special Education; and the network of Regional Educational Laboratories operated under the auspices of the U.S. Department of Education Office of Educational Research and Improvement.

REFERENCES

Barker, B. O. (1986). *The advantages of small schools.* Las Cruces, NM: ERIC Clearinghouse on Rural Education and Small Schools.

Barker, R., & Gump, P. (1964). *Big school, small school: High school size and student behavior.* Stanford, CA: Stanford University Press.

Barnhardt, R., & Barnhardt, C. (1983). Chipping away at rural school problems: The Alaskan experience with educational technology. *Phi Delta Kappan, 64*(4), 274-278.

Bender, L. D., Green, B. L., Hady, T. F., Kuehn, J. A., Nelson, M. K., Perkinson, L. B., & Ross, P. J. (1985). *The diverse social and economic structure of nonmetropolitan America* (Rural Development Research Report No. 49). Washington, DC: Department of Agriculture, Economic Research Service.

Benson, A. J. (1985). Best practices in rural school psychology. In A. Thomas & J. Grimes (Eds.), *Best practices in school psychology* (pp. 17-29). Kent, OH: National Association of School Psychologists.

Benson, A. J., Bischoff, H., & Boland, P. (1983). *Issues in rural school psychology: A survey report.* Washington, DC: National Association of School Psychologists, Assistance to States Committee.

Benson, A. J., Hanson, D. P., & Canfield, J. (1982). Rural school psychology: A practitioner's view. *NASP Communique, 10*(7), 1-2, 10.

Brown, D. L., & Deavers, K. L. (1987). Rural change and the rural economic policy agenda for the 1980s. In *Rural economic development in the 1980s: Preparing for the future.* Washington, DC: Department of Agriculture.

Cruickshank, D. R., & Callahan, R. (1983). The other side of the desk: Stages and problems of teacher development. *Elementary School Journal, 83*(3), 251-258.

Cummings, J. A., Huebner, E. S., & McLeskey, J. (1985). Issues in the preservice preparation of school psychologists for rural settings. *School Psychology Review, 14*(4), 429-437.

DeVore, J. E., & Fagan, T. (1979). Availability of professional, non-teaching pupil services in rural and urban Tennessee school districts. *Educational Quest, 23*, 9-12.

DeYoung, A. J. (1987). The status of American rural education research: An integrated review and commentary. *Review of Educational Research, 57*(2), 123-148.

Edelman, M. W. (1988). Suffer the children: Nurturing America's primary assets. *Educational Record, 68*(4), 24-30.

Edington, E., & Koehler, L. (1987). *Rural student achievement: Elements for consideration.* Las Cruces, NM: ERIC Clearinghouse on Rural and Small Schools.

Fagan, T. K., & Hughes, J. (1985). Rural school psychology: Perspectives on lessons learned and future directions. *School Psychology Review, 14*(4), 444-451.

Forbes, R. H. (1985). *State policy trends and impacts on rural school districts.* Paper presented at the National Rural Education Forum, Kansas City, MO.

Fuller, F. F., & Brown, O. H. (1975). Becoming a teacher. In K. Ryan (Ed.), *Teacher education: The seventy-fourth yearbook of the National Society for the Study of Education, Part 1*, Chicago: University of Chicago Press.

Gjetlen, T. (1982). *Ensuring excellence in rural education.* Arlington, VA: American Association of School Administrators.

Hagstrom, D. A. (1983). Teaching in Alaska. *Phi Delta Kappan, 65*(4), 276-277.

Heath, C. (1983, September), Research for the school psychologist or find in seconds what you couldn't find in weeks. *NASP CTASP Newsletter.* (Available from National Association of School Psychologists, Washington, DC.)

Helge, D. I. (1981). Problems in implementing comprehensive special education programming in rural areas. *Exceptional Children, 47*, 514-520.

Helge, D. I. (1983, August). *Technologies as rural special education problem solvers — A status report of successful strategies.* Murray, KY: National Rural Research Project.

Helge, D. I. (1985). The school psychologist in the rural education context. *School Psychology Review, 14*(4), 402-420.

Helge, D. I., & Marrs, L. W. (1981). *Personnel recruitment and retention and rural America.* Murray, KY: Murray State University, Center for Innovation and Development.

Hobbs, D. J. (1983). *Economic and social change in rural communities: Implications for rural schools* (AASA Small Schools Series #3). Arlington, VA: American Association of School Administrators.

Hobbs, D. J. (1984). Rural America in the 1980s: Problems and perspectives. *Rural Sociologist, 3*, 62-66.

Huebner, E. S., & Huberty, T. J. (1985). Burnout among rural school psychologists. *Research in Rural Education, 3*, 9-13.

Hughes, J. N. (1982, Fall). Manpower needs in rural school psychology. *Virginia Association of School Psychologists Newsletter*, pp. 4-5.

Hughes, J. N., & Clark, R. D. (1981). Differences between urban and rural school psychology: Training implications. *Psychology in the Schools, 18*, 191–196.

Kramer, J. J., & Peters, G. J. (1985). What we know about rural school psychology: A brief review and analysis. *School Psychology Review, 14*(4), 452–456.

Latham, G., & Burnham, J. (1985). Innovative methods for serving rural handicapped children. *School Psychology Review, 14*(4), 438–443.

McCormick, J. (1988, August 8). America's third world. *Newsweek, pp. 20–24.*

MITRE Corporation. (1979). *Research directions for rural mental health.* Published in collaboration with NIMH. (Available from MITRE Corp., Metrek Division, 1820 Dolly Madison Blvd., McLean, VA).

Nachtigal, P. M. (1982). *Rural education: In search of a better way.* Boulder, CO: Westview.

National Commission on Excellence in Education. (1983). *A nation at risk.* Washington, DC: Department of Education.

Parsons, R. D., & Meyers, J. (1984). *Developing consultation skills.* San Francisco: Jossey-Bass.

Presbury, J., & Cobb, H. (1985). Best practices in organizing professional support groups. In A. Thomas & J. Grimes (Eds.), *Best practices in school psychology* (pp. 341–352). Kent, OH: National Association of School Psychologists.

Pulver, G. C. (1986). *Community economic development strategies.* Madison, WI: University of Wisconsin–Madison, Cooperative Extension Service.

Sher, J. P. (Ed.). (1977). *Education in rural America: A reassessment of conventional wisdom.* Boulder, CO: Westview.

Stephens, E. R. (1987). Resisting the obvious: State policy initiatives for rural school improvement should not mean just another round of massive school reorganization. *Research in Rural Education, 4*(1), 29–34.

Stephens, E. R. (1988). *The changing context of education in a rural setting* (Occasional Paper #26). Charleston, WV: Appalachia Educational Laboratory.

Swift, D. (1987). *Facilitating certification and professional development for small schools.* Las Cruces, NM: ERIC Clearinghouse on Rural Education and Small Schools.

Tawney, J. W., Aeschleman, S. R., Deaton, S. L., & Donaldson, R. M. (1979). Using technology to instruct rural severely handicapped children. *Exceptional Child, 46*, 118–125.

Worthington, R. M. (1983, October). *A rural education policy for the 80's.* Paper presented at the conference of the Rural Education Association, Manhattan, KS.

Wright, L. O. (1981). *Special funding for small and/or isolated rural schools.* Las Cruces, NM: ERIC Clearinghouse on rural Education and Small Schools.

ANNOTATED BIBLIOGRAPHY

As networking has been emphasized as vital to the practice of school psychologists in rural settings, the following groups and addresses are offered to the reader as sources of information and support:

American Council of Rural Special Education (ACRES), Western Washington University, Bellingham, WA 98225.

Educational Laboratories, Office of Educational Research and Improvement, U.S. Department of Education, Washington, DC 20202. There are eleven regional educational laboratories. Materials are often free or provided at cost. Some laboratories offer small research grants.

Interest Group — Rural School Psychology, National Association of School Psychologists. Contact Scott Huebner, Department of Psychology, Western Illinois University, Macomb, IL 61455.

National Rural Development Institute, Miller Hall 359, Western Washington University, Bellingham, WA 98225.

National Rural Education Association, 230 Humanities Building, Colorado State University, Fort Collins, CO 80521.

Special Interest Group on Rural Education, American Education Research Association (AERA). Contact Jerry Horn, College of Education, Kansas State University, Manhattan, KS 66502.

44

Best Practices in School Discipline

George G. Bear
University of Delaware

OVERVIEW

According to the American public, lack of discipline is the biggest problem facing public schools. From 1969 to 1986, 16 of 17 annual Gallup education polls found discipline to be the public's primary educational concern (Gallup & Elam, 1988). Since 1986 lack of discipline has been rated the second biggest school problem (use of drugs has been rated first). Teachers, too, view discipline as a serious problem, although they are more likely than parents to blame school disciplinary problems on the lack of discipline in the home (Gallup, 1984). Regardless who is to blame, research substantiates the educational importance of discipline: Students show greater gains in academic achievement, and have more favorable perceptions of the classroom, in classes where little time is spent in disciplinary encounters (Good & Grouws, 1977).

Many terms are used, often interchangeably, to denote behaviors commonly associated with disciplinary referrals. These terms include misbehavior, social maladjustment, antisocial behavior, acting out, externalizing behavior, uncontrolled behavior, and conduct disorder or conduct problems. Each refers to behaviors that are socially inappropriate and violate classroom rules and/or social norms, such as fighting, swearing, noncompliance, talking without permission, stealing, lying, teasing, tardiness, and truancy. Over the course of normal de-velopment these behaviors are exhibited by most children, although seldom to the extent that they warrant a referral to a school psychologist. As reported by Feldman, Caplinger, and Wodarski (1987), over 60% of adolescents admit to exhibiting serious antisocial behaviors such as drug abuse, arson, vandalism, and aggressive acts at some point during development.

Because antisocial behaviors are not uncommon among children and adolescents, Kazdin (1987) points out that it is useful to distinguish *antisocial behavior* from a *conduct disorder*. Kazdin uses antisocial behavior to refer to behaviors exhibited by most children, and reserves conduct disorder to refer to a more serious pattern of antisocial behavior that significantly impairs functioning at school and home. Knoff (1985) makes a similar distinction between misbehavior, or "disturbing" behavior, and emotional disturbance, but considers both antisocial behavior and conduct disordered behavior as forms of misbehavior. Making these distinctions is important not only when diagnosis of a behavior disorder or emotional disturbance is necessary, but also when dealing with many discipline referrals.

For purposes of this chapter, *discipline* is used to refer to (a) instruction designed to teach appropriate conduct or to prevent disciplinary problems, and (b) actions used to correct, punish, or control disciplinary problems when they occur. This conceptualization reflects the need for school psychologists to perceive disciplinary problems as falling along a continuum of severity and requiring a comprehensive model of service delivery. Included in a comprehensive model should be a prevention-oriented program for all students, interventions designed to deal with common disciplinary encounters, and an intensive treatment-oriented program. The treatment component would be for students who exhibit serious disciplinary problems (tertiary prevention interventions) and for students with characteristics highly predictive of delinquent behavior in adolescence and adulthood (secondary prevention interventions).

BASIC CONSIDERATIONS

As noted by Hyman, Flanagan, and Smith (1982) the topic of discipline is "extremely complicated because it encompasses almost all aspects of human endeavor." Indeed, the study of discipline cuts across multiple literatures, including child development (primarily under the rubrics of socialization, child-rearing, aggression, juvenile delinquency, self-regulation, moral development, and prosocial behavior), education (under classroom management, school climate, and character education), guidance and counseling (counseling techniques, affective education, crisis intervention), and school psychology (personality assessment, consultation, intervention techniques, intervention acceptability). Although no simple task, school psychologists should keep abreast of theory and research in these areas.

An awareness of current legal and ethical issues pertaining to preventive, corrective, and treatment components of discipline is also critical. For example, conservative groups have recently used the Hatch Amendment to challenge the required participation of students in any school program or curricular activity that is "psychological" or "affective." Regulations pertaining to the Hatch Amendment, which apply to all federally funded programs and to some state-funded programs, have been interpreted by some

groups as forbidding the use of role playing, moral discussions, values clarification, behavior modification, writing in a diary, and other techniques that might influence a child's interpersonal relationships, values, attitudes, and decision making (see Kaplan & Geoffroy, 1987). The Hatch Amendment requires written parental permission before students take any psychological test or become involved in "psychological treatment." Treatment is broadly defined as "an activity involving planned systematic use of methods or techniques that are not directly related to academic instruction and are designed to affect behavioral, emotional, or attitudinal characteristics of an individual or group" (Federal Register, 1984). In the absence of any clear guidelines, perhaps every discipline technique can be included in this definition.

The use of corporal punishment in the schools is another sensitive issue. Corporal punishment is defined as "intentional infliction of physical pain, physical restraint, and/or discomfort upon a student as a disciplinary technique" (NASP, 1988). Although widely used and viewed favorably by half of the public (Gallup & Elam, 1988), corporal punishment and other punitive techniques have many shortcomings. Clearly, a best practice in dealing with discipline problems is to first become familiar with the disadvantages of punitive approaches (see Hyman et al., 1982), NASP's position on the use of corporal punishment, and school policies related to the use of suspension, expulsion, and other disciplinary procedures.

BEST PRACTICES

Models of Discipline

For heuristic purposes, discipline can best be organized according to either (a) the model's underlying theoretical perspective, or (b) the processes, strategies, and techniques emphasized in the model. Hyman et al. (1982) used a theoretical framework to group discipline models into five basic categories: psychodynamic-interpersonal model, behavioral model, sociological model, eclectic-ecological model, and human-potential model. However, as noted by Hyman et al., many popular models are not derived from a particular theory, but instead are atheoretical or multitheoretical in origin and largely based on the practical experiences and concerns of their developers. For this reason, they suggested that a better way to organize various discipline models is according to the processes or strategies emphasized in each model. However, such an organizational framework is as risky as the theoretical one because models frequently share strategies and techniques (although different terms are often used to describe them). Rarely is a technique unique to one model. For example, nearly every model uses positive reinforcement techniques and some form of time-out. Nevertheless, a process-oriented framework developed by Wolfgang and Glickman (1986) provides a useful categorization of discipline models into three major categories: Relationship-Listening, Confronting-Contracting, and Rules/Rewards-Punishment.

Relationship-Listening models emphasize the importance of a supportive environment where students can freely express feelings and attempt to solve problems with a minimum of teacher direction and control. Effective communications and the building of interpersonal relationships are stressed. Techniques commonly used in these models are silently looking on, nondirective statements, and questioning. Models grouped into this category tend to be psychodynamic or human-potential in theoretical perspective, and include Teacher Effectiveness Training (Gordon, 1974), Transactional Analysis (e.g., Harris, 1969), and Values Clarification (Simon, Howe, & Kerschenbaum, 1978).

Confronting-Contracting models emphasize the constant and reciprocal interaction of multiple elements of behavior, including cognitions, feelings, environmental factors, and overt behavior. They are primarily derived from social-learning and cognitive-developmental theories. Strategies used are questioning, directive and nondirective statements, modeling, reinforcement, and physical intervention

or isolation. The most popular confronting-contracting model is William Glasser's Reality Therapy (Glasser, 1969, 1975). Dreikurs' model of discipline (Dreikurs, Grunwald, & Pepper, 1982) is also included in this category.

Rules/Rewards-Punishment models emphasize environmental control and conditioning of behavior. Little, if any, recognition is made of the child's feelings, reasoning, and cognitive problem-solving abilities. Models in this category rely heavily on a variety of behavior modification techniques, including directive statements, modeling, reinforcement, punishment, physical intervention and isolation. In this category Wolfgang and Glickman include Assertive Discipline (Canter & Canter, 1976).

An attractive feature of Wolfgang and Glickman's categorization is that it is presented within a decision-making framework consistent with the consultation model of service delivery practiced by many school psychologists. Wolfgang and Glickman believe that instructing teachers to rely on only one model in dealing with discipline problems is "doomed to failure." This is because what works with one child might not be effective with another. And it is the teacher, rather than the consultant, who is in the best position to decide which alternative is best for a specific student. Accordingly, the role of the school psychologist is to assist, but not direct, teachers in the selection of a model or intervention technique(s) most appropriate for a given disciplinary problem or student. Wolfgang and Glickman also endorse a "professional team approach" in dealing with discipline and suggest ways in which selection among models can be guided by the evaluation of the seriousness of the misbehavior and the student's present level of moral and social development.

Another functional way to conceptualize the multiple models of discipline is to focus on each model's goal(s) and related strategies and techniques: Is the model primarily intended to prevent misbehavior and develop self-discipline, correct misbehavior during discipline encounters, or treat chronically disruptive

TABLE 1
Popular Models and Techniques for Dealing with Discipline Referrals

Models and Techniques that Focus on Prevention

Model	Techniques Emphasized
Preventive Classroom Management	Effective teaching practices, including frequent monitoring, clear rules and procedures, social praise, etc.
Prosocial Behavior	Systematic reinforcement, modeling of prosocial behavior, verbal instruction, role-playing.
Moral Education	Classroom moral discussions of real-life dilemmas, hypothetical situations, and literature; role-playing; student participaton in school government.
Social Problem-Solving	Direct teaching of SPS skills such as alternative thinking, means-ends thinking, etc.; self-instruction training; dialoguing.
Affective and Communication Models	Values clarification activities, active listening, communication and interpersonal skills training for students and teachers.

Models and Techniques that Focus on Correction and Control of Misbehavior

Model	Techniques Emphasized
Behavior Modification	Direct instruction; reinforcement techniques including social praise, material reinforcers, tokens; punishment-oriented techniques including verbal reprimand, response cost, time-out; group contingency techniques such as Good Behavior Game; behavioral contracting.
Assertive Discipline	Teacher assertion, systematic use of behavior modification techniques, continuous monitoring.
Reality Therapy	Confrontational questioning, classroom meetings, classroom moral discussions, social problem-solving, behavioral contracting, logical consequences, time-out, preventive techniques such as democratic governance.

Models and Techniques that Focus on Treatment

Model	Techniques Emphasized
Social Skills Training	Direct instruction, modeling and rehearsal, coaching, self-instruction, manipulation of antecedents and consequences.
Aggression Replacement Training	Social skills training techniques, self-instruction (Anger Control Training), moral discussions.

(Table 1 — treatment techniques, continued)

Model	Techniques Emphasized
Parent Management Training	Parent training in application of behavioral techniques.
Family Therapy	Variety of therapeutic and educational techniques, depending on particular model.
Behavior Therapy	Variety of cognitive-behavioral and operant techniques.

or "at-risk" students? Such a framework, as used in this chapter, incorporates all three major dimensions of discipline in the schools: (a) Preventive Discipline (i.e., preventing misbehavior and developing self-discipline), (b) Corrective Discipline (i.e., dealing with acts of misbehavior), and (c) Treatment Discipline (i.e., treating students with chronic behavior problems or providing extensive services to those "at-risk" for developing a conduct disorder). Table 1 presents an overview of the major models of discipline and corresponding techniques.

Preventive models. If one's primary concern is the prevention of misbehavior and the development of self-discipline, then strategies and techniques commonly associated with the preventive classroom management, prosocial behavior, moral education, social problem-solving, and affective and communication models of discipline should be considered. These models share a common purpose: To teach children prosocial behaviors and beliefs that characterize democratic ideals, such as self-discipline, respect of self and others, social and moral responsibility, empathy, and caring. They differ, however, in goals and strategies emphasized.

Preventive classroom management model. Effective teachers realize that the best way to curtail misbehavior is to keep students actively involved in appropriate academic activities, especially teacher-directed activities presented at the correct pace and instructional level. Research on effective classroom management has led to the identification of characteristics of teachers, classrooms, and schools that are correlated with successful academic learning and few disciplinary problems.

Successful classroom managers create orderly environments early in the school year (Doyle, 1986). They present clear rules and procedures, and predictable routines. Such teachers frequently monitor classroom behavior, consistently enforce classroom rules, and anticipate behavior problems and respond to them immediately whenever they occur. Interventions do not last long. Effective classroom managers insure that more public attention is directed to academic work than to misbehavior and they use praise effectively (see Brophy, 1981). They also recognize that certain physical arrangements and activities tend to invite misbehavior, such as transitional periods, long student presentations, and activities in which students frequently move about. In short, classroom management research shows that teachers can prevent frequent misbehavior by maintaining an orderly climate in which students are sustained in work-related behavior.

It is important to note that although consistency, rule-clarity, an immediate response to misbehavior, and other management skills are important, their use should not be taken to the extreme. In investigating the effectiveness of eight classroom management models of discipline and on-task behavior (authoritarianism, behavior modification, common sense or cookbook, group process, instructional, permissive, socio-emotional climate, and intimidation) Goldstein and Weber (1981) concluded that an authoritarian approach was detrimental to on-task behavior. Of the eight models examined, only the group process and socioemotional climate approaches (similar to the Confronting/

Contracting models) were positively related to appropriate classroom behavior.

Prosocial behavior model. Classroom management and prosocial behavior models share many strategies. However, rather than focusing on the ecology of the classroom and managerial procedures, the prosocial model emphasizes the use of specific behavioral techniques to teach and reinforce appropriate social behaviors. According to this model, which is largely derived from social learning theory, behavior problems can be prevented by teaching and maintaining such prosocial behaviors as sharing, helping, caring, and cooperating. The ultimate goal is to teach students to behave prosocially in the absence of external rewards (i.e., for children to become self-disciplined). Three types of behavioral techniques are most commonly employed, typically in combination with one another: (a) systematic reinforcement of desirable behaviors (using either social-, material-, or self-reinforcement), (b) exposure to prosocial models, and (c) strategic use of verbal instruction. Perhaps because serious practical and ethical concerns about the systematic use of behavior modification techniques with nondisruptive students in regular classrooms have been voiced by teachers and researchers (see Doyle, 1986), very few studies in the literature report the systematic school-wide application of the prosocial behavior model. Nevertheless, the model clearly provides effective classroom techniques for preventing and correcting discipline problems.

Moral education models. Moral education is "whatever schools do to influence how students think, feel, and act regarding issues of right and wrong" (Association for Supervision and Curriculum Development, 1988). It includes nearly all aspects of discipline: The moral and social climate of the classroom, self-control, values and goals, moral reasoning and social decision making, and prosocial behavior. Although most preventive models of discipline can also be considered moral education

models (Richards & Bear, in press), the study of moral development and education has been dominated by the cognitive-developmental approach during the past two decades. Piaget spoke little about moral education per se, but his theory has had a substantial influence on disciplinary practices, as well as many other areas of education (Murray, 1979). The greatest influence of cognitive-developmental theory on moral education, however, has been the extensive theoretical and applied work of Kohlberg and his colleagues (see Bear, 1987, for a review and references). Like Piaget, Kohlberg believed that children do not simply acquire normative behavior via reinforcement, punishment, and modeling, but do so by acting on their environments. That is, self-discipline evolves from within the individual, not simply as a consequence of external control: Although clearly influenced by one's environment, children think and reason for themselves.

The aim of the cognitive-developmental model of moral education is to facilitate children's development through Kohlberg's stages of moral reasoning. Moral discussion and role-playing are the major strategies used to achieve this aim. Recent research related to school discipline has focused on the relationship of moral reasoning to conduct problems in the regular classroom (Bear, 1989), the application of moral discussions to the treatment of serious behavior problems (Arbuthnot & Gordon, 1986; Gibbs, Arnold, Cheesman, & Ahlborn, 1984; Goldstein & Glick, 1987), and the development of "Just Community" schools in which favorable moral climates are developed to promote moral and social development (Power, Higgins, & Kohlberg, 1989).

Perhaps the most exemplary project that incorporates major elements of the cognitive-developmental model is the Child Development Project (Watson, Solomon, Battistich, Schaps, & Solomon, 1989), a longitudinal program being implemented in three elementary schools in Northern California. This comprehensive values education program uses a combination of traditional and cognitive-developmental strategies at school and home to develop children's prosocial reasoning, values, and behaviors. Strategies and techniques include modeling of prosocial behavior, cooperative learning, moral discussion, and experiences that promote perspective-taking and prosocial behavior. Building and maintaining positive teacher–child relationships and a sense of community is emphasized. The use of external rewards and punishers is minimal.

Social problem-solving model. The social problem-solving model targets specific thinking skills for instruction. These cognitive skills mediate interpersonal behavior. They also are assumed to be more generalizable than a collection of targeted prosocial behaviors typically taught in a limited classroom context. Social problem-solving skills most commonly taught are alternative thinking, consequential thinking, social-causal thinking, means-ends thinking, and sensitivity to problems (Spivack & Shure, 1982). In some preventive programs, such as *Think Aloud* (Camp & Bash, 1978), these skills are taught in combination with self-instruction training for the purpose of facilitating the development of self-control of aggressive behavior.

The social problem-solving model employs behavior modification and cognitive modeling techniques to directly teach students sequential problem solving steps. For example, in Gesten and Weissberg's curriculum (Gesten et al., 1987), students learn to apply the following eight steps when faced with interpersonal problems: (a) Look for signs of upset feelings, (b) Know exactly what the problem is, (c) Decide on your goal, (d) Stop and think before you act, (e) Think of as many solutions as you can, (f) Think ahead to what will probably happen next after each solution, (g) When you think you have a really good solution, try it!, and (h) If your first solution doesn't work, try again! An attractive feature of this eight-step process, and others like it, is that it integrates affective, cognitive, and behavioral dimensions of social problem-solving. An additional technique used in social problem-solving programs is *dialoguing.*

Dialoguing is an intervention process in which the instructor teaches self-discipline by having students apply social problem-solving skills during actual situations of interpersonal conflict.

Affective and communication models. Affective and communication models (referred to as Relationship/Communication models by Wolfgang and Glickman) are typically atheoretical or humanistic in orientation, and focus on feelings, self-concept, interpersonal communication, and values. In addition, these models emphasize the importance of a classroom climate in which teachers effectively communicate with students by demonstrating empathy, understanding, warmth, and acceptance. Values are addressed in a non-indoctrinative and non-judgmental fashion. The teacher functions as a therapist-like facilitator who wisely uses active listening skills that promote communication, expression of feelings, and clarification of values.

Affective and communication models have generated a wealth of curriculum materials and programs. Examples include *Developing Understanding of Self and Others* (Dinkmeyer & Dinkmeyer, 1982) and *Teacher Effectiveness Training* (Gordon, 1974). These programs generally rely on the use of role-playing, classroom discussions, games, and activity worksheets. They vary greatly in terms of scope, comprehensiveness, and primary focus. Given their comprehensiveness and the methodological difficulties in measuring affective goals, it is not too surprising that only a few studies have demonstrated the effectiveness of these models (see Leming, 1981; Strein, 1988 for reviews).

Models for dealing with discipline encounters. Disciplinary encounters are most likely to occur whenever a teacher perceives misbehavior as disrupting or threatening the order of a classroom activity, especially if the behavior is highly visible and contagious (Doyle, 1986). It is at this point, or whenever disciplinary encounters become intolerable, that the school psychologist typically becomes involved in the process of discipline. In such instances both correction and prevention are of primary concern. Techniques employed should communicate to students that misbehavior is inappropriate and must be corrected, but also provide a means by which future problems can be prevented.

What follows is an overview of intervention techniques designed to handle disciplinary encounters. Many of the preventive techniques cited previously can, and *should*, be used when dealing directly with discipline-related problems. This would include social problem-solving, dialoguing, active-listening, modeling, role-playing, moral discussion, and preventive classroom management techniques. However, many disciplinary encounters call for additional measures, used alone or preferably in combination with preventive-oriented techniques. Thus, added here are those techniques that focus on the correction and control of misbehavior, rather than its prevention. Because of limited space, only three models representing popular practices in direct intervention during disciplinary encounters are highlighted.

Behavior modification model. For years teachers have effectively responded to classroom misbehavior by employing behavioral techniques such as verbal reprimands, response cost (e.g., loss of earned recess time or privileges), time-out (e.g., making the student sit alone or sending the student to the principal), and other punishment-oriented procedures (e.g., extra homework, writing 100 times "I will not tease Susie," etc.). Teachers are less likely to rely on positive reinforcement techniques (Kazdin, 1982). When reinforcement techniques are used, they typically consist of privileges, material reinforcers, or exchangeable tokens rewarded contingent upon the presence of appropriate behavior (or as more commonly practiced — the absence of misbehavior).

Several studies have found an interdependent group contingency technique called the "Good Behavior Game" (Barrish, Saunders, & Wolf, 1969) to be effective in controlling classroom disruptions. Although different variations of the "game"

have been used, most share common features: (a) specific classroom rules are listed, (b) the class is divided into two or more "teams," (c) each team receives a mark on the board whenever a member of that team violates a rule, and (d) the team(s) receiving points below a predetermined criterion number are offered reinforcement (extra recess, less homework, other privileges, and rewards). In addition to being simple to use and effective, the Good Behavior Game is liked by teachers. However, school psychologists should be aware of its negative features, including the potential for undue and harmful peer pressure and ridicule of those students who cause their team to lose, and its emphasis on the reduction of inappropriate behavior. Unfortunately, the latter negative feature applies to most other punishment- or control-oriented contingency procedures in which students are not taught prosocial behaviors (see Graham-Clay & Reschly, 1987, for a review of legal and ethical issues). However, many of these problems can be avoided by basing points in the game on the presence of positive behaviors, as opposed to the absence of negative behaviors (Darveaux, 1984).

Assertive Discipline (Canter & Canter, 1976) is a popular behavior modification model of discipline framed within an argument for teachers' rights. Based primarily on principles of Assertion Training, Canter and Canter argue that teachers have the right to maintain classroom order, to demand and insure that students behave according to needs of teachers, and to obtain assistance in disciplinary matters from parents, principals, and others. In protecting these rights, teachers must be assertive. And the best way to assert themselves in the classroom is to correct or control student misbehavior by means of the systematic use of an amalgamation of behavior modification techniques. Such techniques include the continuous monitoring of behavior (a mark is put on the board when a child violates a classroom rule), behavioral contracting, response cost, verbal reprimands, sending the student to the principal, and suspending the student from school. Positive "assertions" (privileges, rewards, positive parent contacts, token reinforcement) also are employed contingent upon the absence of misbehavior.

Reality therapy model. Perhaps Glasser's (1965, 1969) comprehensive model of school discipline may best be categorized as a preventive model because it emphasizes the importance of democratic school governance, student values and responsibility, avoiding student failure, and the use of classroom meetings in which social problem-solving skills and moral reasoning are developed. It is presented here under corrective models, however, because Reality Therapy is one of the few models that offers specific and sequential steps for dealing with actual cases of discipline problems. One appealing feature of Reality Therapy is its integration of a variety of strategies and techniques commonly associated with other models of discipline. For example, as shown in Table 2, Glasser's ten-step procedure for dealing with discipline problems provides a broad-based model for the development of responsible goal-directed behavior.

Treatment. The general use of preventive and corrective discipline techniques is insufficient for dealing with students who exhibit a consistent and marked pattern of antisocial behavior, or those "at-risk" for developing such a pattern. "At-risk" indicators include: (a) poor parental management; (b) early onset of antisocial behavior; (c) reports of stealing, lying, or truancy; (d) antisocial behavior within the family; (e) poor educational achievement; and (f) rejection by peers (Loeber & Dishion, 1983; Parker & Asher, 1987). Both at-risk and conduct-disordered students require programs that are more intensive, broadly-based, and lasting than what can appropriately be provided in the regular classroom. Such programs, commonly associated with tertiary and secondary levels of mental health prevention and intervention, are often based on models of preventive and corrective discipline pre-

sented earlier. Likewise, they often employ the same techniques given previously, but use them in a more extensive fashion. For example, researchers have shown that students with conduct disorders can benefit from programs based on the social problem-solving model (e.g., Kazdin, Esveldt-Dawson, French, & Unis, 1987), cognitive-developmental model of moral education (e.g., Arbuthnot & Gordon, 1986), and behavior modification model (Kazdin, 1982). Likewise, combinations of these models have been shown to be effective. Goldstein and Glick (1987) demonstrated that their multimethod Aggression Replacement Training program enhances prosocial behaviors and decreases antisocial behaviors among incarcerated juvenile delinquents. This new and promising program consists of a combination of Structured Learning Therapy (similar to social skills training), Anger Control Training, and cognitive-developmental moral education.

Additional models and techniques are also available for treating conduct disorders, including individual and group psychotherapy, behavior therapy, pharmacotherapy, residential treatments, family therapy, and parent training. In a comprehensive review of treatments for antisocial behaviors of children and adolescents, Kazdin (1987) concluded that the most promising treatments are parent management training, functional family therapy, cognitive problem-solving skills training (including social problem-solving and cognitive-developmental moral discussion techniques), and community-based treatment. Although behavior therapies such as behavior modification and social skills training were found to effectively control or decrease isolated antisocial behaviors, Kazdin noted that there is very little evidence that their effects are lasting or that the skills learned transfer beyond the training setting and to other domains. Therefore, he recommends broad-based programs in which alternative techniques are combined to address the multiple factors influencing antisocial behavior. Kazdin also warns that these techniques should not be chosen haphazardly, but rather, on the

TABLE 2
Glasser's 10-Step Approach in Reality Therapy

1. The student's misbehavior is identified. Teacher asks "What are you doing?" (problem identification)

2. The student evaluates the misbehavior and makes a commitment to stop it. (consequential thinking and moral reasoning)

3. The student plans for student success. (preventive classroom management, reinforcement of prosocial behavior)

4. When the problem reoccurs, the teacher directs the student to stop the misbehavior. (verbal direction and cue)

5. If step #4 is unsuccessful, the teacher questions the student about the misbehavior and describes appropriate behaviors. (problem solving, possibly moral reasoning and role-playing)

6. If step #5 is unsuccessful, the teacher briefly repeats the questions in #5 and firmly tells the student that the misbehavior has to be stopped and a corrective plan developed. The plan is developed by the student, and is approved and enforced by the teacher. (problem solving, behavioral contracting, behavior modification)

7. If misbehavior continues, in-class time-out is used.

8. If misbehavior continues, in-school (outside of the classroom) time-out is used.

9. If misbehavior continues, out-of-school suspension is used. The student is not allowed to return until an acceptable plan has been made.

10. If #9 continues to be unsuccessful, student is referred for homebound instructions and/or treatment.

---

basis of theoretical and conceptual justifications.

Selecting and Implementing Models and Techniques

Knowledge of discipline models and techniques is necessary, but not sufficient, in the prevention, correction, and treatment of discipline problems. Also necessary is a practical process to help guide their selection and application (Knoff, 1984). Various models of school-based consultation provide such a process, particularly mental health consultation, system consultation (see Curtis this volume), behavioral consultation, and collaborative consultation (see Brown, Pryzwansky, & Schulte, 1987, for a review of consultation models). The choice of model, or combination of models, is likely to be influenced by many factors, including the appropriate level of consultation (direct service to student or consultee, or indirect to consultee or organization),

pervasiveness and nature of the problem, and the training and expected role of the school psychologist. Knoff (1985) suggests that the behavioral model is most appropriate when examining environmental causes of misbehavior and selecting among behavior modification techniques. The mental health model is used when the teachers are unable to deal effectively with student misbehavior due to lack of knowledge, experience, confidence, or objectivity. It would also appear that the system consultation model would be applicable when assessing, developing, and implementing school-wide preventive policies and programs. And, when functioning as a member of a child study or intervention team, the collaborative consultation model should provide additional direction.

Regardless which consultation model is used, some form of John Dewey's "scientific model," involving sequential problem-solving steps, should guide the consultation process. Knoff (1984) proposed a four-step problem solving process for dealing with discipline referrals, consisting of problem identification, problem analysis, intervention, and evaluation. Ways in which preventive and corrective components might be addressed at each step are suggested below. Note that the "consultee" referred to in this process is likely to be the classroom teacher, but depending on the case and level of consultation it also might be the student's parent(s), an administrator, or groups thereof. In most cases a best practice would be to involve as many parties as possible, particularly the teacher and parents.

Problem identification. Primary objectives for problem identification are to determine: (a) the severity of the misbehavior, and (b) who "owns" the problem. Both determinations are likely to be tentative at this point and subject to later validation. In determining severity of the problem, initial interviews with the student and consultee may indicate a need of formal assessment procedures, such as behavioral observations, teacher rating scales, role-playing, and other measures of behavior and personality (see chapter by Knoff). Informal and formal assessment should be based on both normative and developmental perspectives in order to determine whether the misbehavior reflects "normal" antisocial behavior or a more serious conduct disorder. Whereas the former should be dealt with in the regular classroom, with or without related services, the latter is likely to require placement in a special class (Braaten, Kauffman, Braaten, Polsgrove, & Nelson, 1988). Related to this concern is deciding who "owns" the problem. To what extent does the misbehavior reflect one or more of the following: The student's lack of self-discipline? The teacher's inadequate classroom management? Intolerance of normal antisocial behaviors? Lack of preventive and developmental programs? An absence of discipline-related policies, curriculum, and inservice teacher education?

Problem analysis. During this phase, problems tentatively identified during problem identification are now examined in greater depth in order to prepare an appropriate intervention. Who "owns" the problem becomes clearer upon analysis of environmental factors (including situational antecedents and consequences), and the cognitions and behaviors of the student and consultee. In many cases this analysis would include informal assessments of the student's social problem-solving skills, moral reasoning, values, and self-perceptions. Peer and family relationships also should be explored. Guiding questions at this step, in addition to questions posed earlier, include the following: Does the primary problem lie in the student not having appropriate prosocial skills and inhibitory controls, or in the student possessing but not exhibiting them? Are the consultee's discipline-related expectations, self-efficacy beliefs, lack of knowledge and skills contributing to the misbehavior? In what ways might the above factors be reciprocally related? Bandura's (1978) model of reciprocal determinism provides a framework that is useful during problem analysis since it focuses on the continuous reciprocal interaction between a person's cognitions, behaviors, and environmental factors.

Knoff (1985) briefly reviews four analytical procedures, used separately or in combination, that also might be helpful: ecological/systems, group process/social psychological, developmental/psychoeducational, and theoretical/psychological. Knoff notes that a developmental/psychoeducational analysis can direct the overall assessment of the student and is necessary when distinguishing normal antisocial behavior from a conduct disorder. A developmental analysis is particularly useful when the focus is on prevention techniques. The ecological/systems analysis is most appropriate in assessing the ecology of the classroom, school, and community, and interactions among family members, peers, teachers, and policies that might explain or contribute to the misbehavior. The group process/social psychological analysis provides a more focused ecological view of the classroom and school. Finally, the theoretical/psychological analysis can be used to assess the student's misbehavior in relation to one or more of the various models of discipline.

Planning and implementing the intervention. Whether primarily concerned about prevention or correction, the ultimate choice of model(s) and techniques rests with the consultee. The primary role of the school psychologist during this collaborative endeavor is to facilitate the decision-making process and to offer information and advice that might influence the consultee's decision. Knowledge of the various discipline models and techniques is critical at this step. In addition to basing the selection decision on information gathered in the previous steps, factors related to classroom effectiveness of various interventions should be considered. For example, Greenwood, Carta, and Vance (1987) give five major reasons why many interventions often fail: (a) research has not shown that the intervention works, (b) the intervention is not comprehensive, integrated, or systematic enough to solve the problem, (c) procedures are too ambiguous, (d) procedures are too demanding in terms of effort, time, and cost, and (e) procedures are not acceptable to school personnel. Research on acceptance of interventions by teachers (see Reimers, Wacker, & Koeppl, 1987) and students (see 1989; Witt, Galvin, & Moe, 1986) might also provide guidance on which interventions are viewed favorably. Unfortunately, there is little empirical research indicating certain discipline models and techniques are more effective than others for individual students. Nevertheless, Spaulding (1983a, 1983b) outlines procedures for tailoring models and techniques to the individual characteristics of students. These procedures are designed to provide differentiated interventions for individual students and to teach classroom responsibility, prosocial behavior, and self-discipline to all students in the classroom.

Lepper's (1983) "minimal sufficiency principle" also provides some guidance for selecting techniques. According to this principle, the internalization of social and moral norms is fostered by disciplinary procedures that exert the least amount of pressure on a student to conform. Techniques that emphasize external control encourage children to attribute their behavior to external factors and not internally. When external controls are clearly absent, students have no reason to follow social norms. In contrast, techniques with little external pressure facilitate internal attributions for behavior. When given opportunities to misbehave with little risk of getting caught, students are more likely to refrain from misbehaving, because to misbehave would violate their self-perceptions of being good students. Thus, if this principle were followed in the classroom, the use of external controls would be minimal and used only when necessary.

Evaluation. This step can be more challenging and difficult than deciding among discipline models and techniques. Not only do many evaluation models and designs exist, but there are many more instruments for measuring the objectives of each model (e.g., measures of classroom management, self-concept, values, attitudes, moral reasoning, self-efficacy, antisocial behavior, etc.). The complexity of evaluation largely depends on the purpose of the evaluation and the level at which consultation services are provided. Whereas sophisticated experimental and quasi-experimental group research designs are necessary for most system-level projects, simpler case study designs are appropriate when the focus is on an individual student or a small group of students. Regardless of the level of complexity, however, both the process of planning and decision-making (i.e., formative evaluation) and the outcomes of interventions (i.e., summative evaluation) should be evaluated. "If" and "how" an intervention succeeds or fails are equally important (Scriven, 1967). Likewise, evaluation should be ongoing so that interventions can be revised when necessary. Moreover, evaluation should include both objective and subjective data, examine intended and unintended effects, and allow for a follow-up period (Brown, Pryzwansky, & Schulte, 1987; Knoff, 1982).

SUMMARY

Responding to discipline problems requires knowledge and skills in many areas, especially child development, behavior management, assessment, and consultation. To be effective, school-based discipline programs must be broad-based, incorporating different models and techniques designed to prevent, correct, and treat varying degrees of misbehavior. The ultimate aim of a discipline program should be the development of socially and morally responsible self-directed behavior. Because discipline is a multifaceted concept, no one model or technique is sufficient for achieving this aim. Therefore, multiple models and techniques are necessary. Whether intervening at the individual, class, or system level, the process of selecting and implementing interventions can best be guided by a consultative problem solving model of service delivery.

REFERENCES

Arbuthnot, J., & Gordon, D. A. (1986). Behavioral and cognitive effects of a moral reasoning development intervention for high-risk behavior-disordered adolescents. *Journal of Consulting and Clinical Psychology, 54,* 206-216.

Association for Supervision and Curriculum Development. (1988). *Moral education in the life of the school.* Alexandria, VA: Author.

Bandura, A. (1978). The self system in reciprocal determinism. *American Psychologist, 33,* 344-358.

Barrish, A. H., Saunders, M., & Wolf, M. M. (1969). Good behavior game: Effects on individual contingencies for group consequences on disruptive behavior in a classroom. *Journal of Applied Behavior Analysis, 2,* 119-124.

Bear, G. G. (1987). Children and moral responsibility. In A. Thomas & J. Grimes (Eds.), *Children's needs: Psychological perspectives* (pp. 365-371). Washington, DC: National Association of School Psychologists.

Bear, G. G. (1989). Sociomoral reasoning and antisocial behaviors among normal sixth graders. *Merrill-Palmer Quarterly, 35,* 181-196.

Braaten, S., Kauffman, J. M., Braaten, B., Polsgrove, L., & Nelson, C. M. (1988). The regular education initiative: Patent medicine for behavioral disorders. *Exceptional Children, 55,* 21-27.

Brophy, J. (1981). Teacher praise: A functional analysis. *Review of Educational Research, 51,* 5-32.

Brown, D., Pryzwansky, W. B., & Schulte, A. C. (1987). *Psychological consultation: Introduction to theory and practice.* Boston: Allyn & Bacon.

Camp, B. W., & Bash, M. A. S. (1985). *Think Aloud: Increasing social cognitive skills — A problem-solving program for children.* Champaign, IL: Research Press.

Canter, L., & Canter, M. (1976). *Assertive discipline: A take-charge approach for today's educators.* Seal Beach, CA: Canter & Associates.

Darveaux, D. X. (1984). The Good Behavior Game plus Merit: Controlling disruptive behavior and improving student motivation. *School Psychology Review, 13,* 510-514.

Dinkmeyer, D., & Dinkmeyer, D., Jr. (1982). *Developing understanding of self and others: (DUSO) 1 and 2* (rev. ed.). Circle Pines, MN: American Guidance Service.

Doyle, W. (1986). Classroom organization and management. In M. C. Wittrock (Ed.), *Handbook of research on teaching* (3rd ed.) (pp. 392-431). New York: Macmillan.

Dreikurs, R., Grunwald, B. B., & Pepper, F. C. (1982). *Maintaining sanity in the classroom: Classroom management techniques* (2nd ed.). New York: Harper & Row.

Elliott, S. N., Witt, J. C., Galvin, G. A., & Moe, G. L. (1986). Children's involvement in intervention selection: Acceptability of interventions for misbehaving peers. *Professional Psychology: Research and Practice, 17,* 235-241.

Federal Register, Part IV, Department of Education, 34 CFR, Pts. 75, 76, and 98, *49,* 35317-35322.

Feldman, R. A., Caplinger, T. E., & Wodarski, J. S. (1983). *The St. Louis conundrum: The effective treatment of antisocial youths.* Englewood Cliffs, NJ: Prentice-Hall.

Gallup, A. (1984). The Gallup poll of teachers' attitudes toward the public schools. *Phi Delta Kappan, 66,* 97-107.

Gallup, A., & Elam, S. M. (1988). The 20th annual Gallup poll of the public's attitudes toward the public schools. *Phi Delta Kappan, 70,* 33-46.

Gesten, E. L., Weissberg, R. P., Amish, P. L., & Smith, J. K. (1987). Social problem-solving training: A skills-based approach to prevention and treatment. In C. A. Maher & J. E. Zins (Eds.), *Psychoeducational interventions in the schools: Methods and procedures for enhancing competence* (pp. 118-140). New York: Pergamon.

Gibbs, J. C., Arnold, K. D., Cheesman, F. L., & Ahlborn, H. H. (1984). Facilitation of sociomoral reasoning in delinquents. *Journal of Consulting and Clinical Psychology, 52,* 37-45.

Glasser, W. (1969). *Schools without failure.* New York: Harper & Row.

Glasser, W. (1975). *Reality therapy: A new approach to psychiatry.* New York: Harper & Row.

Goldstein, A. P., & Glick, B. (1987). *Aggression replacement training: A comprehensive intervention for aggressive youth.* Champaign, IL: Research Press.

Good, T., & Grouws, D. (1977). Teaching effects: A process-product study in fourth grade mathematics classrooms. *Journal of Teacher Education, 28,* 49-54.

Gordon, T. (1974). *TET: Teacher effectiveness training.* New York: McKay.

Graham-Clay, S. L., & Reschly, D. J. (1987). Legal and ethical issues. In C. A. Maher & S. G. Forman, *A behavioral approach to education of children and youth* (pp. 289-309). Hillsdale, NJ: Erlbaum.

Greenwood, C. R., Carta, J. J., & Hall, R. V. (1987). The use of peer tutoring strategies in classroom management and educational instruction. *School Psychology Review, 17,* 258-275.

Harris, T. A. (1969). *I'm OK — you're OK: A practical guide to transactional analysis.* New York: Harper & Row.

Hyman, I., Flanagan, D., & Smith, K. (1982). Discipline in the schools. In C. R. Reynolds & T. B. Gutkin (Eds.), *The handbook of school psychology* (pp. 454-480). New York: Wiley.

Kaplan, L. S., & Geoffroy, K. (1987). The Hatch amendment: A primer for counselors. Part I. Development and implementation of the amendment by conservative parent groups. *The School Counselor, 35,* 9-16.

Kazdin, A. E. (1982). Applying behavioral principles in the schools. In C. R. Reynolds & T. B. Gutkin (Eds.), *The handbook of school psychology* (pp. 501-529). New York: Wiley.

Kazdin, A. E. (1987). Treatment of antisocial behavior in children: Current status and future directions. *Psychological Bulletin, 102,* 187-203.

Kazdin, A. E., Esveldt-Dawson, K., French, N. H., & Unis, A. S. (1987). Problem-solving skills training and relationship therapy in the treatment of antisocial child behavior. *Journal of Consulting and Clinical Psychology, 55,* 76-85.

Knoff, H. M. (1982). The independent psychodiagnostic clinic: Maintaining accountability through program evaluation. *Psychology in the Schools, 19,* 346-353.

Knoff, H. M. (1984). A conceptual review of discipline in the schools: A consultation service model. *Journal of School Psychology, 22,* 335-345.

Knoff, H. M. (1985). Best practices in dealing with discipline referrals. In A. Thomas & J. Grimes (Eds.), *Best practices in school psychology* (pp. 251-262). Washington, DC: National Association of School Psychologists.

Knoff, H. M. (1987). School-based interventions for discipline problems. In C. A. Maher & J. E. Zins (Eds.), *Psychoeducational interventions in the schools: Methods and procedures for enhancing competence* (pp. 118-140). New York: Pergamon.

Knoff, H. M. (in press). Preventing classroom discipline problems: Promoting student success through effective schools and schooling. *Special Services in the Schools.*

Leming, J. S. (1981). Curricular effectiveness in moral/values education: A review of research. *Journal of Moral Education, 10,* 147-164.

Lepper, M. (1983). Social-control processes and the internalization of social values: An attributional perspective. In E. T. Higgins, D. Ruble, & W. Hartup (Eds.), *Social cognition and social development: A socio-cultural perspective.* New York: Cambridge University Press.

Loeber, R., & Dision, T. J. (1983). Early predictors of male delinquency: A review. *Psychological Bulletin, 94,* 68-99.

Murray, G. B. (Ed.). (1979). *The impact of Piagetian theory on education, philosophy, psychiatry and psychology.* Baltimore: University Park Press.

National Association of School Psychologists. (1986). *Supporting paper on corporal punishment position statement.* Washington, DC: Author.

Parker, J. G., & Asher, S. R. (1987). Peer relations and later personal adjustment: Are low-accepted children at risk? *Psychological Bulletin, 102,* 357-389.

Power, C., Higgins, A., & Kohlberg, L. (1989). The habit of the common life: Building character through democratic community schools. In L. P. Nucci (Ed.), *Moral development and character education: A dialogue* (pp. 125-143). Berkeley, CA: McCutchan.

Reimers, T. M., Wacker, D. P., & Koeppel, G. (1987). Acceptability of behavioral interventions: A review of the literature. *School Psychology Review, 16,* 212-227.

Richards, H. C., & Bear, G. G. (in press). *Developing moral and social responsibility.* Belmont, CA: Wadsworth.

Scriven, M. (1967). The methodology of evaluation. In R. Tyler, R. Gagne, & M. Scriven (Eds.), *Perspectives of curriculum evaluations,* (AERA

Monograph Series on Curriculum Evaluation) (pp. 39–83). Chicago: Rand McNally.

Simon, S. B., Howe, L. W., & Kerschenbaum, H. (1978). *Values clarification: A handbook of practical strategies for teachers and students* (rev. ed.). New York: Hart Publishing.

Spaulding, R. L. (1983a). A systematic approach to classroom discipline, Part 1. *Phi Delta Kappan, 65*, 48–51.

Spaulding, R. L. (1983b). A systematic approach to classroom discipline, Part 2. *Phi Delta Kappan, 65*, 132–136.

Spivack, G., & Shure, M. B. (1982). The cognition of social adjustment: Interpersonal cognitive problem-solving thinking. In B. B. Lahey & A. E. Kazdin (Eds.), *Advances in clinical child psychology, Vol. 5.* New York: Plenum.

Strein, W. (1988). Classroom-based elementary school affective education programs: A critical review. *Psychology in the Schools, 25*, 288–296.

Watson, M., Solomon, D., Battistich, V., Schaps, E., & Solomon, J. (1989). The Child Development Project: Combining traditional and developmental approaches to values education. In L. P. Nucci (Ed.), *Moral development and character education: A dialogue* (pp. 51–92). Berkeley, CA: McCutchan.

Wolfgang, C. H., & Glickman, C. D. (1986). *Solving discipline problems: Strategies for classroom teachers* (2nd ed.). Boston: Allyn & Bacon.

ANNOTATED BIBLIOGRAPHY

Glasser, W. (1969). *Schools without failure.* New York: Harper & Row.
In this classic book Glasser applies Reality Therapy to education and addresses school practices contributing to children's failure in school. Three types of classroom meetings designed to promote self-discipline are described (social-problem-solving, open-ended, and educational-diagnostic).

Maher, C. A., & Zins, J. E. (Eds.). (1987). *Psychoeducational interventions in the schools: Methods and procedures for enhancing student competence.* New York: Pergamon.
Only one chapter in this book focuses specifically on school discipline, but nearly all chapters present interventions appropriate for dealing with discipline-related problems. Included are chapters on prereferral intervention programs, social problem-solving training, study-skills training, peer-influenced interventions, counseling, social-skills training, and behavioral self-management.

Nucci, L. P. (Ed.). (1989). *Moral development and character education: A dialogue.* Berkeley, CA: McCutchan.
Chapters address important issues and practices in developing children's moral values and character. Perspectives are limited to those of developmentalists and proponents of character education. Although practical guidelines and techniques are not emphasized, the book should be of value in the development and implementation of comprehensive programs designed to prevent discipline programs and promote prosocial behavior.

Sulzer-Azaroff, B., & Mayer, G. R. (1986). *Achieving educational excellence: Using behavioral strategies.* New York: Holt, Rinehart & Winston.
Presents the major principles and techniques of behavior modification used in schools. Practical examples of their application are given and issues related to their use are discussed.

Wolfgang, C. H., & Glickman, C. D. (1986). *Solving discipline problems: Strategies for classroom teachers* (2nd ed.). Boston: Allyn & Bacon.
Presents the major models of discipline and their classroom applications. Helpful guidelines for choosing among various discipline models and techniques are suggested.

45

Best Practices in
School Reintegration

Robert W. Colegrove, Jr.
Childrens Hospital of Los Angeles

OVERVIEW

Successful adjustment to the school setting can be difficult for students who have the best of all possible support, intelligence, and social skills. When adjustment to school is affected by a prolonged absence from school due to illness, incarceration, or hospitalization, the chances for a successful adjustment to school are substantially diminished (Kagen-Goodheart, 1977). Currently, approximately 7.2 to 10.8 million American children (10% to 15% of all American children) have some type of chronic illness which results in above average absenteeism rates (Levenson & Cooper, 1984). The marked increase in survival rates of pediatric cancer patients over the past 10 years (up to 70% for some leukemia patients) has meant that thousands of these students are returning to school after missing an average of 41 days of instruction for initial treatments (Cairns, Klopovich, Hearne, & Lansky, 1982). Students with asthma will have absence rates 24% higher than average attendance rates (Cook, Schaller, & Krischer, 1985). According to the National Institute of Mental Health, over 100,000 adolescents aged 12-19 were hospitalized in psychiatric settings in 1986 alone. Thousands of other students will come back into the regular school system after being incarcerated by the juvenile courts. These students will find it difficult to reintegrate academically, socially, and psychologically to the regular school setting without specific interventions aimed at preventing potential problems.

It is difficult to measure the far reaching impact of school adjustment on the overall academic, social, and psychological welfare of students. School is the "workplace of children," a major part of the weekday for children and adolescents, and a significant factor in their development and socialization (Ross & Scarvalone, 1982). For children and adolescents who struggle academically and/or socially in the school setting, school can quickly become a place of dread. When a student must be removed from the school setting for a significant period of time due to illness or incarceration, the chances for success at school quickly decrease.

Students who are absent frequently are likely to perform poorly in school and to drop out of school prematurely (Weitzman, 1986). Weitzman has defined criteria for problem absence, that is, absence which has a marked negative effect upon academic performance, social adjustment, and ultimate ability to function in society. These criteria include missing six or more consecutive days of school, missing 10 or more days in a school quarter, and an increase of five or more days absent in a school quarter above the child's previously established pattern of absence. For students who meet these criteria, success in school is seriously jeopardized. Also,

Weitzman notes that the negative effects of absence from school seem to increase as age increases.

It is often difficult for students to return to their pre-illness level of functioning once they have been away from school for an extended period, and school problems are exacerbated upon return when the pre-illness level of functioning was already poor. Students returning to school experience considerable anxiety as they face relating to peers and resuming academic work. Thus, the challenge of reintegrating students who return to school following a prolonged absence is considerable, requiring special interventions and support.

This chapter will focus on the basic issues and concerns facing students who must return to school after prolonged absences. While most of the research related to school reintegration has primarily been concerned with chronically ill children, this discussion will emphasize the common problems shared among students who miss school for reasons other than chronic illness, such as psychiatric hospitalization and incarceration. First, the social and psychological implications of school absence will be explored, highlighting the issues critical to school adjustment. After this, interventions will be reviewed which can be adapted to individual students who return to school after prolonged absences.

Case Histories

The following are examples of students who face reintegration to the school setting following a prolonged absence and would benefit from the interventions to be described. Consider these individual cases in light of the information to be presented in this chapter.

Tim, a first-grader, returns to school after having surgery for a malignant tumor found in his kidney. During his course of chemotherapy, Tim lost all his hair. Already a shy child, Tim has become even more withdrawn, rarely initiating conversation and barely speaking above a whisper. Now, he is returning to first grade in a regular classroom of 28 children after missing three months of school.

Kate is a 15-year-old adolescent who recently spent six weeks on an inpatient unit to treat an eating disorder. After some initial weight gain, Kate returns home with a treatment plan of individual and family therapy. She has always been a high achiever in school, however, her distorted body image makes her extremely shy and withdrawn around peers. She has begged her parents to let her stay home. However, her parents and her therapist are insisting that she return to school.

Ms. Murphy, an elementary school teacher calls the district nurse for help with Amanda, a fifth-grader with chronic anemia who recently missed several weeks of school due to an infection. According to Ms. Murphy, Amanda is disruptive in the classroom, leaving her seat without permission and constantly talking. Ms. Murphy wants to know if it is O.K. to discipline Amanda like her other healthy students.

Wayne is a 14-year-old with a history of school failure. He recently has been placed in a foster home following three months in a local detention facility. Wayne has a probation officer and a social worker mandated by the Court. He does not want to return to school, but maintaining academic progress in school is a requirement of his probation and insisted upon by his foster parents.

BASIC CONSIDERATIONS

Once a student has missed school for a prolonged amount of time, there are several factors which may impact the ability of the student to reintegrate into the school setting. These factors affect not only the student, but family members and school personnel.

Physical Factors

Physical changes are a particular problem for children who have experienced acute/chronic illness or a disfiguring injury. Of special concern to students are the visible changes that can take place. For instance, students with cancer may lose their hair during chemotherapy or have a limb amputated. Some students may have growth deficiencies which result from illnesses such as kidney disease. Others may have problems with mobility.

For those with neurological complications, such as head injuries, a disruption of one or more cognitive processes may result in various forms of academic or behavioral difficulties. Pediatric cancer patients who undergo cranial radiation and certain types of chemotherapy may have delayed effects resulting in cognitive deficits. Cognitive deficits produced by radiation are often not seen until a year after treatment, often affecting short term memory, specifically mathematics calculation. Unfortunately, these deficits may not be detected or apparent when the student initially returns to school.

Psychological Factors

The student. A variety of psychological factors will influence the student who returns to school after a prolonged absence. For students who have experienced visible changes due to illness, medical treatment or injury, the fear and reality of teasing can create considerable anxiety. For older students who are entering adolescence, visible changes take on new meaning. The fear of being different from peers (e.g., having lost hair) becomes a major concern, and these students may go to great lengths to avoid peers. For students with visible differences, the experience of being ostracized by peers or staff members who do not understand the circumstances will have a devastating effect on the self esteem of the student.

Students who have been incarcerated or hospitalized for emotional problems, or have diseases with societal stigmas such as AIDS or cancer, may be particularly concerned about the stigma attached to their problems. They may anticipate, sometimes realistically, the negative reactions and judgments of peers and teaching staff. Again, these concerns may be accentuated in adolescents, who attach a great deal of importance to and find their personal identity in peer relation-

ships. Peers of younger children, who operate at a much more concrete cognitive level than adolescents, may make erroneous assumptions, such as they could "catch" the illness. The student may be shunned by peers, resulting in emotional and physical isolation from others.

Students returning to school may have lost confidence in their ability to perform academically in the school setting. For students who have had a history of poor performance before their absence, their fear and anxiety about returning to school may be quite pronounced. This may be seen in behavioral disturbances such as acting out or withdrawal. Students with chronic illness may be more shy and withdrawn than their peers, and less likely to initiate contact with peers.

The anxiety associated with returning to school may manifest itself in school phobia. Students may exaggerate somatic complaints in order to miss school. Older students may simply refuse to attend, dropping out of school, or in extreme cases may run away. For students with a history of conduct disordered behavior, impulsive reactions to the first sign of negativity in the school setting may spark an angry outburst or sudden flight.

For some students, a marked dependency may have developed between the student and one of the parents, usually the mother. The parent now views their child as vulnerable, and may actually interfere with the child's return to school. This will contribute to the student's fear of the school setting and view of the school as unfriendly and potentially dangerous. The more extreme this mutual dependency between the patient and caretaker is and the longer the student remains away from school, the more likely a phobic response to school will occur.

The family. The attitude and coping mechanisms of the family play an important role in school reintegration. If the parents see return to school as a positive and natural step towards normality in the family, the student is less likely to resist the return to school. For families dealing with a member who has an unpredictable illness or has a history of emotional disturbance or criminal behavior, constant anxiety may exist for the family whenever the student is away from their direct supervision. This anxiety within the family will have a negative impact on the student's thoughts and feelings about returning to school.

Siblings. The brothers and sisters of students with special medical, mental, or criminal problems often find it difficult to cope within the family. For instance, siblings may feel rejected because of the time their parents must spend with their troubled brother or sister. Younger children especially may become jealous of an older chronically ill sibling, who receives special attention and gifts from relatives and friends. Older siblings may feel neglected and forgotten by their parents and other caretakers as they take on more responsibility at home and receive less attention from their parents.

At school, the siblings of a troubled student may feel overwhelmed or embarrassed by the questions and comments of peers and school staff. If a sibling's brother or sister has an emotional problem or a criminal record, the sibling may feel particular embarrassment, especially if they attend the same school. Some siblings may feel a particular responsibility for their brother or sister, following them on the playground and walking them to school. Parents may purposely or inadvertently, out of their own anxiety, put pressure on the sibling to protect and care for the brother or sister at school.

School staff. Each staff person in the school setting has his or her own particular values, views, and perceptions of students who present various problems. For instance, when school staff members discover that a student has cancer, they may relate their own experience with cancer to the experience of the student. If a staff member has lost a loved one to cancer, he or she may conjure up a "death sentence" for the student, even when the student has an extremely good prognosis. In the same way, a staff person who has been victimized by a crime may view the student who has been incarcerated with similar feelings as felt toward the perpetrator of the crime. In either case, the student is not viewed as a unique person with a unique history and circumstances. Attributions by school staff based on personal values and experiences may seriously impede the reintegration of students with special problems.

The attitude of the staff is crucial in normalizing the school experience of a returning student. Some school staff members may respond to a student with deference out of pity for the condition of the student. This may be manifested by an inconsistent application or lack of classroom discipline. Thus, the student may take advantage of the teacher and/or may become isolated from peers who notice the differential treatment. In either case, the result is damaging to the overall school adjustment of the returning student.

BEST PRACTICES

The school psychologist can play an important role in the reintegration of students with significant absences. The best practices that will be described are not necessarily to be carried out by the school psychologist. However, the school psychologist may be in the best position to recommend who the most appropriate person to carry out school reintegration activities will be.

The specific interventions that will follow can be carried out by a variety of school and agency staff, such as counselors, special education teachers, nurses, and hospital social workers. However, the school psychologist may be in the best position, at least as far as school resources, to know which staff person would be best suited to meet a particular need of the student. This is a crucial aspect in helping a student reintegrate into the school setting; that is, to determine the unique needs of the student and then to find resources for those needs.

Accurate Information

The first part of any intervention for a student who is absent due to illness, incarceration, or hospitalization is to obtain the most reliable, accurate information on the student's present condition and past history. Initially, it is extremely helpful to have someone in the school serve as a liaison between the sending institution and the school. For the chronically ill student, the school nurse is often the most appropriate. The best liaison for an emotionally disturbed or incarcerated student may be the school counselor, school psychologist, or the special education teacher. As schools vary greatly as to the specific roles of different staff positions, each school must determine for itself the most appropriate person to fill the liaison role for each student. The important aspect is that someone be responsible to obtain up-to-date and useful information to provide an ongoing assessment of a student's unique needs.

School Conferences and IEP Meetings

Once a liaison between the school and the agency, institution, or hospital has been chosen, a meeting should be held with the parents, potential teachers, and other school staff, and, ideally, a representative of the sending agency such as a probation officer, nurse, or psychologist. Adolescent students should be invited to the school conference in most cases, as this will foster a collaborative relationship between the student and school staff. Again, with accurate and up-to-date information about the student, potential problems can be anticipated more accurately and planned for, and the best school placements and interventions planned.

One of the purposes of a meeting is to deal directly with staff attitudes and perceptions towards the student's presenting problem. As mentioned earlier, staff people who have lost a parent or loved one to cancer may perceive cancer as a death sentence. Therefore, a straight forward, honest discussion of the student's prognosis may help staff to develop a more accurate perception of this student's illness. The emphasis of the meeting should be the normalization of the school experience for the student.

Another purpose of the school conference is to help the parents develop a positive attitude toward the school, alleviating their anxiety about their child returning to school, and demonstrating the support of school staff for the student. It is helpful to identify a school staff member as liaison for the parents to provide regular communication between home and school. The classroom teacher who has the most regular contact with the student would probably be the best contact person. A positive and open communication between parents and staff will help the parents to feel more comfortable about their child returning to school, which in turn will reduce anxiety for the student.

For a student who has been incarcerated, the conditions of probation, the student's progress while incarcerated, family circumstances, and other relevant facts will help the staff to form an accurate view of the student. Staff should be encouraged to express concerns, even if the student is present. By airing all concerns, a more effective decision regarding placement, support services, and overall goals can be achieved.

Once accurate information has been given and the staff and family have been able to air their concerns, goals and objectives can be realistically developed. This meeting may be a formal IEP meeting, or may precede the actual IEP meeting, as students with prolonged absences are often served under some special education category such as "other health impaired" and "severely emotionally disturbed." A timetable and plan for follow-up will need to be established at this meeting as some unanticipated problems may arise during the course of reintegration.

Classroom Presentations

For the student who returns to school with visible changes, such as medical treatment related side effects (e.g., hair loss, amputation), it may be helpful to inform the peers of elementary-age classmates of the circumstances surrounding the illness. Adolescents usually do not want the extra attention from peers that a classroom presentation would bring, feeling satisfied and comfortable that only the teachers be informed and aware of their condition. As well, the logistical problems of speaking in multiple classrooms in the junior or senior high setting makes classroom presentations impractical. For younger students, however, the classroom presentation can be an important vehicle to create greater support and understanding for the student with special needs (Katz, 1985; Katz, Rubinstein, & Blew, 1988). Also, students at earlier levels of cognitive development tend to have misconceptions about illness, thinking, for instance, that they may also loose their hair if they are touched by a student with leukemia. A developmentally appropriate classroom presentation can resolve potential misunderstanding and also sharply curb incidents of teasing and ridicule.

A model for classroom presentations has been developed by Katz (Katz, Kellerman, Rigler, Williams, & Siegel, 1977; Katz, 1985; Katz et al., 1988) which has been used effectively for three major pediatric cancer centers in the Los Angeles area. The components of this model can be adapted for all types of chronic diseases and other special problems students may encounter. The components of Katz' program include: (a) a general discussion of the medical and hospital experiences of classmates, allowing students to see the commonality of their experiences; (b) a developmentally appropriate presentation of the student's illness and treatment; (c) a review of common side effects; (d) dispelling myths (e.g., cancer is contagious); (e) a discussion about the need of social support, contrasting the negative effects of teasing with the positive effects of support and friendship; and (f) giving the patient an opportunity to act as "resident expert" of his/her illness.

Classroom presentations can be conducted either by a member of the school staff or someone outside the school (e.g., from the hospital). It is important that the presentor be able to explain the components of the presentation in developmentally appropriate terms and that they themselves are familiar with the situation being discussed. The presentation is most effective if it is made within a few days of the return of the student, before major problems such as teasing have developed.

A classroom presentation may also be appropriate when a student dies from an illness or an accident. In these situations, a classroom presentation will provide accurate information to the students, as well as an opportunity for students to express their own feelings related to the loss of a classmate.

Other Interventions

Counseling. For school staff members who find they have a primary role in helping a student reintegrate into the school setting, there are some guidelines that may help in counseling. First, it is important for counselors to be aware of their own issues in reaction to the illness, emotional or behavioral problem of the student. It may be necessary for counselors to talk with colleagues to determine if they can work effectively with the student.

The counselor should be informed of the details concerning the student's absence and problems. If the information is unclear, steps should be taken to get adequate and accurate information. When the counselor is not familiar with a particular illness or condition, materials should be reviewed to learn more about the particular situation the student is experiencing.

The counselor should be willing to be open with students about their condition. It is most likely that students have particular concerns related to their situation which they themselves may be hesitant to address. By establishing a clear understanding between the student and the counselor of the issues affecting school reintegration, mutual problem solving is more likely to take place and the critical issues can be addressed.

One caution, however, when working with students who have life-threatening illnesses, is to find out how much the student knows about his/her illness. This issue should be raised in the initial conference before the student returns to school. The provision of medical information should be done by the parents and/or medical personnel.

Peer support. Peer support can be a deciding factor in successful school reintegration. Any intervention that aims at reducing isolation from other students and developing supportive peer relationships can be helpful. In some cases, a student(s) may be assigned to help the reintegrating student find their way around campus and answer questions. This can be a positive experience both for the student who is the helper and the returning student. Creative ideas which enable the student to interact with peers should be implemented.

Ongoing staff support. It is important to realize that teachers and other school personnel may need extra support and not deliberately seek it. It is helpful to check in with teachers and staff to monitor their concerns and help them to solve problems as they arise.

Sibling support. Siblings who attend the same school or within the same district can benefit from the support of school staff members. It is helpful to check in with siblings to see how their brother's or sister's problems are affecting them. The designated liaison for the returning student should inform the teacher of siblings regarding any significant changes or developments which may impact them. School staff should be told to check with the teacher or designated liaison if they have questions about the returning students, instead of directing questions to the siblings. It is tremendous pressure for siblings to be expected to explain details about the condition of their brother or sister to school staff members.

Warning signs. The progress of the student should be monitored by key school staff members to head off potential problems. For instance, excessive absences should be investigated immediately. Establishing initial communication with the family is crucial in monitoring the warning signs of a difficult school adjust-ment. Other warning signs include behavioral disturbances such as isolation, withdrawal, and acting out. As well, grades may drop and homework may be missing or incomplete. The student may also verbalize concerns and fears. These warning signs should be taken seriously and explored with a problem solving approach to help the student find solutions.

Referrals. To provide the most comprehensive reintegration plan, a variety of services outside the school setting may be useful, such as mental health clinics and other community services. For instance, a family may need counseling to learn new ways to cope with their child's handicap, indicating a referral to the local community mental health center of other agency. Parent groups, special training programs, and peer counseling are a few of many possible referral options. Referrals can provide important resources to enhance and support the overall reintegration plan.

SUMMARY

Students who are absent from school for a significant amount of time face particular difficulties reintegrating into the school setting. The prospect of returning to school can produce marked anxiety for students which may adversely affect their academic, social, and psychological performance. In order to help students successfully reintegrate into the school setting, specific interventions must be made. A model of interventions originally used for children with chronic diseases has been discussed, which includes such interventions as school conferences, classroom presentations, and counseling. The principles of this model can be used to aid students who have prolonged absences other than chronic illnesses.

REFERENCES

Cairns, N. U., Klopovich, P., Hearne, E., & Lansky, S. B. (1982). School attendance of children with cancer. *Journal of School Health, 52*(3), 152-155.

Cook, B. A., Schaller, K., & Krischer, J. (1985). School absence among children with chronic illness. *Journal of School Health, 55,* 265-267.

Kagen-Goodheart, L. (1977). Reentry: Living with childhood cancer. *American Journal of Orthopsychiatry, 47,* 651-658.

Katz, E. R., Kellerman, J., Rigler, D., Williams, D., & Siegel, S. E. (1977). School intervention with pediatric cancer patients. *Journal of Pediatric Psychology, 2,* 72.

Katz, E. R. (1985). School and Social Reintegration of Children with Cancer. Final Report of ACS-California, Contract #PBR-12.

Katz, E. R., Rubinstein, C. L., Hubert, N. C., & Blew, A. (1988). The school and social reintegration of children with cancer. *Journal of Psycho-social Oncology, 6*(3/4), 123-140.

Levenson, P. M., & Cooper, M. A. (1984). School health education for the chronically impaired individual. *Journal of School Health, 54,* 446-450.

Ross, J. W., & Scarvalone, S. A. (1982). Facilitating the cancer patient's return to school. *Social Work, 27,* 256-261.

Spinetta, J. J., & Deasy-Spinetta, P. (1981). *Living with Childhood Cancer.* St. Louis: C. V. Mosby.

Weitzman, M. (1986). School absence rates as outcome measures in studies of children with chronic illness. *Journal of Chronic Illness, 39,* 799-808.

ANNOTATED BIBLIOGRAPHY

American Cancer Society, California Division. (1987). *Back to School: A Handbook for Parents of Children with Cancer.* Oakland, CA: American Cancer Society of California.
This handbook is an excellent resource for parents. Several issues of concern to parents are discussed such as home tutoring, setting up a school conference, special education rights for medically impaired children, and how to guard against infections such as chicken pox.

American Cancer Society of California. (1987). *Back to School: A Handbook for Teachers of Children with Cancer.* Oakland, CA: American Cancer Society of California.
This handbook deals with issues of special concern to teachers. Basic information is given on the types of childhood cancer, treatment and side effects. Arterial catheters and other special needs are discussed, as well as the effect of serious illness on the family. The role of the teacher as an advocate for the student is discussed.

Morrow, G. (1985). *Helping Chronically Ill Children in School.* New York: Parker Publishing Company.
This book is designed for teachers, counselors, and administrators, written by a school psychologist with many years' experience. The subject areas include: helping prepare and plan for special needs; how children cope with chronic illness; how to help chronically ill children adjust socially and emotionally; facilitating learning; and helping parents. Numerous references are included with each chapter.

Kleinberg, S. B. (1982). *Educating the Chronically Ill Child.* Rockville, MD: Aspen Systems Corporation.
This book deals with the policy and procedural issues which impact the provision of services to chronically ill children. The impact of chronic illness is described from several perspectives. Specific educational strategies are described, as well as descriptions of the major types of chronic illnesses which may be encountered in the school setting.

Greenwood, P. W. (Ed.). (1986). *Intervention Strategies for Chronic Juvenile Offenders.* New York: Greenwood Press.
This book gives a broad perspective on juvenile offenders. Chapters are included on the etiology of juvenile delinquency and current perspectives on the problem. School-based strategies for the prevention of juvenile delinquency are discussed, including recent research and evaluations of such strategies.

46

Best Practices in School-Based Consultation

Joseph E. Zins
University of Cincinnati

Charlene R. Ponti
Hamilton County (Ohio) Office of Education

OVERVIEW

The popularity of consultation as a service provided by school psychologists has increased with such rapidity in the past two decades that it has now become one of the primary job functions of many practitioners. This trend in practice is supported by a mounting body of empirical evidence demonstrating the efficacy of consultative services (e.g., Medway & Updyke, 1985), although there remains a substantial need for further research on all aspects of the process.

Our goal in this chapter is a very practical one. We intend to present essential information about what it is necessary to know to effectively engage in school-based consultation. While much of the theoretical and empirical literature is cited, we have not hoped to provide a thorough and complete review of it. Furthermore, the assumption has been made that most readers already have at least an introductory-level understanding of consultation. Those who do not are encouraged to review the Curtis and Meyers (1985) chapter in the first edition of this book. And for those who wish more detail than can be provided in this brief chapter, a number of primary references that contain additional explanatory information are included in the bibliography at the end of the chapter.

The chapter begins with discussion of the foundations of consultation and of the prerequisite competencies and assumptions underlying practice. Next, guidelines for best practices in consultation are presented, including a description of consultative problem-solving, and of the individual and organizational factors that may exert influence on the process. Finally, a detailed outline of procedures for systems-level implementation are presented.

BASIC CONSIDERATIONS

Most readers are familiar with the three approaches to consultation most frequently employed in the schools: the behavioral, mental health, and organizational. These models have a number of parameters in common. For instance, each stresses the use of problem solving as the mechanism through which interventions are developed, they focus on work-related problems, they have long- and short-term goals, and they view participation in the process as voluntary. However, they differ in aspects such as the roles and relationships of the consultant and consultee(s), the focus of consultative interventions, and the organizational level at which they are implemented. It also is important to note that there are not universally accepted definitions of any of these approaches, and none of them were specifically developed for practice in the schools.

These issues form the context and the rationale for the definition and approach to consultation presented in this chapter. As noted above, there is significant overlap among the various models of consultation, and the approach described herein borrows heavily from each of them. We have extracted the most salient aspects of these prior works, added some new ideas, and synthesized all of this information into a coherent framework *specific to practice in the schools*. Schools are different from other settings such as hospitals, correctional facilities, and business organizations, and because the systems context is such an important aspect of consultation, it is desirable to limit consideration to school-based consultation. Such an approach also provides the freedom to discuss various types of consultation that occur within schools, including consultation with individual teachers and parents and with groups of consultees, as well as systemwide consultation directed toward changing entire school organizations.

Definition of School-Based Consultation

In this chapter, school-based consultation is defined as *a method of providing preventively oriented psychological and educational services in which a consultant and consultee(s) form a collaborative partnership in a systems context to engage in a reciprocal and systematic problem-solving process to empower consultee systems, thereby enhancing students' well-being and performance.*

A brief explanation of the essential components and underlying assumptions of this definition follows. We should note at this point, as did Gutkin and Curtis (1990), that vast numbers of ideas have been integrated in this discussion. It is difficult to attribute initial responsibility for many of the concepts as they have been so widely discussed that they now form the basic assumptions typically made about consultation (although not all have been empirically validated).

Preventive orientation. Consultation has a dual focus. It provides a mechanism through which the presenting problem is remediated, and it attempts to increase the consultee's skills and alter the envi-

ronmental variables that elicit and maintain the problematic behaviors. These procedures prevent existing problems from becoming more severe and additional ones from arising. The first goal is met by developing specific, empirically tested interventions to deal with the presenting problem. The second is accomplished in a less direct manner by (a) ensuring that the consultant's expertise is readily available to the client system through the encouragement of frequent interactions with consultees so as to facilitate the prevention and early identification of problem behaviors; (b) improving consultees' skills and knowledge so that they can more effectively address similar problems in the future; and (c) maintaining a systems perspective so that a broad array of conditions that might contribute to problem development and maintenance can be addressed. In most cases, it is necessary for consultees to address several problem situations successfully in collaboration with the consultant before they attack problems independently, as the literature suggests that training to a single exemplar is ineffective as a means of promoting generalization (Stokes & Baer, 1977; Witt & Martens, 1988). Even when consultation is applied in a clearly rehabilitative fashion, a primary intent is to prevent more serious problems from arising. In practice, this preventive goal is not accomplished as often or as easily as the first; nevertheless, it should be pursued to enhance the overall value of the consultation process.

The increasingly preventive nature of consultation gradually is shifting the focus of these efforts from individual children to entire systems — schools, school districts, the larger community — and even to state and federal policies, regulations, and legislation (Swift & Cooper, 1986). Practitioners, who often have been frustrated by the limits of individual child-focused interventions, now are recognizing the potential efficacy and long-term benefits of more widescale interventions.

Provision of services. Consultation is not a service in itself but rather a means by which services are provided, or what

Miller (1969) might call another way of "giving psychology away" to nonpsychologists. Indeed, consultation is the foundation or overarching framework from which all psychological and educational services are provided and around which all services are organized. The goal is to help the client and the consultee system. Clients (most often students) are assisted indirectly through the process, in contrast to the direct method of providing services that is traditionally associated with assessment or counseling. However, we usually do not use the term *indirect* in discussions with educational decision makers owing to concern that for some people it carries negative connotations. These persons mistakenly believe that students benefit best from "direct" forms of help, and may not understand how consultation actually facilitates the provision of such assistance. Even when a direct service is provided to a child, consultation with primary caregivers is crucial to ensure good assessment and effective treatment.

Participants. A consultant and one or more consultees participate in the consultation process. In this chapter, the school psychologist is referred to as the consultant (although this person could also be another special services staff member) and consultees as teachers, but they also could be administrators, parents, or even students. The third party sometimes considered to be involved is the client or student, who is the ultimate beneficiary despite not being actually engaged in the consultation process.

Collaborative partnership. Consultants and consultees work together to solve problems, and it is highly desirable for them to do so in the context of a partnership that emphasizes trust, openness, and cooperation. *Collaborative* implies that they work jointly on as equal a basis as possible (realizing that their level of need is unequal), and *partnership* suggests that they have specified, mutually agreed-upon responsibilities. Tyler, Pargament, and Gatz (1983) provide an excellent discussion of the "resource–collaborator" relationship that should exist

between consultants and consultees to maximize the effectiveness of consultation. From this relationship model come "people and systems that are more self-help oriented, more self-sustaining, and more pro-social" (Tyler et al., p. 396), and it helps to increase confidence regarding ability to solve problems, or sense of self-efficacy.

Participants in consultation have different contributions to make based upon their expertise and varying responsibilities to uphold to maximize consultation effectiveness; they work together in a complementary and interdependent fashion. Consultees must provide contextual, ecological information to help in developing interventions. They must also assist in determining what interventions can be implemented in their setting and within their repertoire of skills. The two participants share responsibility for defining and analyzing problems, for establishing and maintaining the collaborative partnership, and for follow-up. While the consultant and consultee both contribute to the problem solving, the consultant directs and controls the overall process (Erchul & Chewning, in press). However, since consultees (a) retain responsibility for the client, (b) can best judge treatment acceptability, and (c) usually implement most interventions and thus can ensure treatment integrity, they make the final decisions regarding intervention implementation. Because this final point is also a potential problem, it is incumbent upon consultants to work with consultees to ensure that the process by which these decisions are made is of an informed nature and carefully thought-out.

The consultant also has primary responsibility for ensuring that the atmosphere remains non-evaluative, and is in charge of identifying and presenting interventions for possible implementation. Further, it is the responsibility of the consultant to develop the evaluation plan. In sum, as consultants and consultees mutually share their expertise and knowledge within a collaborative partnership, the chances are improved that more creative solutions to problems will emerge, consultee ownership and commitment to carrying out these plans will be enhanced, and consultee self-efficacy will be increased.

Reciprocal interaction. The principles regarding the reciprocal nature of consultative interactions are derived from Bandura's (1977) social learning theory and philosophy of reciprocal determinism. Indeed, these paradigms serve as an overarching "metatheory" underlying consultation practice (Zins, 1988). Unidirectional influence approaches have usually dominated the interactions between psychologists and those they seek to assist (Tyler et al., 1983), but they do not adequately reflect the complexity of the consultation process. According to Bandura's model, consultant, consultee, and client functioning result from the interactions of behavioral, personal, and environmental factors. During the interpersonal exchanges that constitute consultation, both participants exert influence on each other, and their personal perspectives and behaviors usually are altered as a result (Reardon, 1981). The challenge is to maintain a cooperative partnership even while exerting this interpersonal influence. This goal is accomplished primarily through establishment of an atmosphere of mutual respect and trust. The client (student) likewise influences the consultant and consultee, as well as the entire system. "Therefore, understanding and changing the functioning of a consultee or clients must focus on the interlocking relationship of these three [behavioral, personal, and environmental] factors, not on a single dimension" (Brown & Schulte, 1987, p. 283).

Systematic problem-solving process. Problem solving proceeds through an orderly, systematic sequence of steps as discussed in detail later in the chapter (see Table 1), and "this process is dynamic, evolving, flexible, and cyclical in nature" (Kurpius & Lewis, 1988, p. 145). The consultant directs the overall process, but the involvement of both participants is essential to maximize the likelihood that successful solutions will be developed and implemented. Moreover, formal written documentation is kept regarding intervention development and outcomes in order to foster follow-up efforts and to increase accountability.

Systems context. Consultation increasingly has embraced not only preventive goals, but also a sensitivity to the organizational context in which it occurs and an orientation to systems change strategies. This expansion in perspective represents a major shift in consultation thought in recent years as it broadens the goals of traditional case-centered consultation approaches. The connection between a problem and the system variables that may be contributing to it or preventing its resolution must be identified and dealt with as necessary. Furthermore, problems cannot be assumed to be only internal to the child. An attributional system that appropriately identifies the variables maintaining problem behaviors or academic difficulties and places responsibility for consultation outcomes must be part of the consultation process.

Empowerment. The empowerment philosophy in consultation "requires different assumptions and behaviors on the part of the consultant than does traditional case-centered problem solving" (Witt & Martens, 1988, p. 213). This ideology more explicitly recognizes that consultees and consultee systems already *possess or readily can develop* most competencies necessary to deal with student-related problems, given the right opportunities and knowledge of available resources (Rappaport, 1981). Thus, consultees' failure to demonstrate competence can be a reflection of the system's failure to create opportunities for them to exhibit existing skills or to provide support for them to develop needed skills to resolve a specific problem, rather than solely an indication of their lack of knowledge about how to deal with the difficulty. The implications for consultants are significant. From this perspective, their role becomes one of helping consultees to clarify needs and locate resources, and of ensuring that opportunities are available so that consultees can engage in self-sustaining behaviors to resolve problems.

Enhancement of student well-being and performance. Although consultation focuses on improving consultees' skills and performance, the ultimate beneficiary is always intended to be the client. In most instances, the client is one or more students, but it is appropriate for the entire school district to be the client as in an organization development program.

Other characteristics implicit in definition. The problems that are dealt with are always *work- or caretaking-related* rather than personal. In addition, the material discussed is considered *confidential* by the consultant, consultation is entered into *voluntarily* by consultees and the relationship is temporary. Gutkin and Curtis (1990) provide an excellent, detailed discussion of these issues as well as the other core characteristics of consultation.

Prerequisite Competencies and Assumptions of Consultation Practice

In addition to a knowledge of psychological principles and techniques (e.g., human learning, ethics, social bases of behavior, research methodologies), there are a number of other prerequisites to consultation practice.

Competencies and prerequisites. *Self-awareness* with respect to feelings, beliefs, thoughts, impact on others, and a personal clarity regarding one's values and theoretical biases, is helpful to the consultant (e.g., Gallessich, 1982; O'Neill & Trickett, 1982). Because a large aspect of the consultation process involves interpersonal interaction and influence, consultants must be cognizant of their own interpersonal styles and values, and of how these can impact upon consultees and influence their problem-solving procedures.

Similarly, *good interpersonal and communication skills* are also highly desirable because consultation relies heavily upon interpersonal influence to accomplish its goals. Consultants need, for instance, to be active listeners and to utilize effective questioning techniques to extract the necessary information from consultees to develop clear conceptualizations of problems. Furthermore, establishment of warm, caring, and understanding relationships are just as important in consultation as they are in counseling.

Knowledge of intervention technology, both individual and organization-focused, is an essential competency, but one that often has not been emphasized in the consultation literature. Gutkin (1981) found that over two-thirds of the reasons consultees sought assistance were related to their lack of knowledge and skill in resolving their problems, although he did not use an empowerment framework for categorizing these reasons. Yet the implication is that process skills are important but not sufficient for resolving most issues in consultation. Problem-solving and applied behavior analysis skills are equally essential. There is an extensive body of validated intervention techniques (Martens & Meller, 1990), and the goal of consultation is to promote its application by consultees. Unless consultants are successful in this endeavor, schools will be less likely to use this technology, no matter how potentially effective it is (Wolfe, 1978).

An *understanding and knowledge of organizations and of organizational functioning* is necessary in order to take an ecological, systems perspective. Too often, school psychology training and daily practice tend to focus on the assessment and remediation of individual student-related problems, and we consequently do not attend to more global, or macro-level, variables that exert significant influence. Thus, "consultants need an understanding of the workplace [school] not only as a technological system but also as a complex social organization" (Gallessich, 1982, p. 5). School norms, values, philosophy, and organizational climate, for instance, can facilitate or impede the consultation process occurring between a school psychologist and a teacher.

An *awareness of and sensitivity to cultural, racial, ethnic, and gender issues* is necessary as they are important social dynamics of the consultative relationship. These various sociocultural factors, while not often discussed in consultation, can exert considerable influence on the communication process, on the development of trust and mutual understanding, and on the overall establishment of the relationship. In addition, they have been found to affect help-seeking patterns and utilization of services, attitudes toward self-disclosure, and the duration and outcome of treatment (Gibbs, 1985; Lorion, 1978). Further, the power–authority dimension of consultation can be affected by these issues, especially when one participant is a member of a minority and the other of a majority group.

Assumptions. In addition to the above competencies, there are several assumptions that underlie consultation. First is a belief that most parents, teachers, and other school personnel usually *want to be involved in the problem-solving process*. We recognize that there is a subset of people who (a) want to be told what to do rather than being cooperative partners in intervention development; (b) do not want to personally deal with the presenting problem for some reason, but rather desire and expect someone else to do it (e.g., have a child placed in another classroom); (c) fail or refuse to recognize the existence of a problem situation and thus do not desire consultative assistance; (d) do not have the skills or interests necessary to implement various interventions; or (e) face organizational restraints that prohibit or minimize their participation in the process. In addition to these groups, there are potential consumers who expect the school psychologist–consultant to "tell them what to do" because of their previous experiences with helping professionals, when in fact they actually would like to be involved in the problem-solving process. This group can best be dealt with through an educative process about consultation.

A second assumption is that *prevention and early intervention are advantageous* for most children. There is a growing, convincing body of literature that

supports this assumption (e.g., Price, Cowen, Lorion, & Ramos-McKay, 1988), although there is a clear need for additional research regarding the preventive aspects of consultation. Third, as noted earlier, *a vast intervention technology exists* that can be applied to address the problems experienced by children. The challenge is how to apply it within the constraints of the setting to address student-related problems.

Finally, all services to children and schools are *best provided through a consultative framework*. That is, all requests for assistance in dealing with a problem begin with consultation, and services such as psychoeducational assessment and counseling occur as part of the problem clarification process or as interventions that are developed to solve the problem.

BEST PRACTICES

Consultative Problem-Solving Process

Problem-solving is the essence of consultation. It includes a number of steps from initial designation of the problem to development and implementation of a plan to resolve it, to evaluation of goal attainment and plan effectiveness, and it concludes with planning for generalization, maintenance, and follow-up (e.g., Bergan, 1977). As described in the following pages, it is necessary to engage in many levels of analysis of problems and intervention development during this process. Because consultation is an indirect service, it requires that changes be brought about on more than just the client level. Student-related difficulties often result, at least in part, from ineffective instructional or behavior management strategies. Consequently, it is essential to remain aware of the link between changes in the environment or in consultees' behavior, and changes in the target student(s) (Hawryluk & Smallwood, 1986). Furthermore, under these conditions consultative interventions may occur at several organizational levels.

A systems perspective provides consultants and consultees with a framework for developing a broad conceptualization of problems and for examining the wide range of factors that could be contributing to a problem. This prevents the development of simplistic explanations for problems that are encountered. As stated above, problem analysis should include a thorough assessment of consultee variables as well as other factors affecting student behavior. For example, inaccurate perceptions or expectations of student behavior on the part of the consultee may contribute to a problem. Research in the area of attributions has found that teachers generally perceive problems to be caused by factors internal to the child or due to home variables (Christenson, Ysseldyke, Wang, & Algozzine, 1983; Medway, 1979). While child or home issues may contribute to students' problems, they should not automatically be considered the sole cause. Students' problems usually result from a complex and reciprocal interaction between the child's behavior and the environmental and/or instructional conditions that regularly exist in a particular classroom. Therefore, as participants in the consultation process define and analyze problems, information should be gathered not only about the child and the immediate contingencies affecting his or her behavior, but also about the ecology of the classroom or the home environment itself. Obtaining a broader conceptualization of the problem and reconceptualizing important variables as within the teacher's or parent's power to change will impact on their causal attributions and expectations for problem resolution, as well as on the type of intervention strategies considered.

The overall consultation process begins by establishing a collaborative partnership. Relationship building is an ongoing process that begins with the consultant's initial entry into the school and continues throughout the proceedings. Consultative problem solving is initiated the moment the consultee requests assistance. The various steps in the process are described below separately, but they often overlap and thus may not be pursued in this exact sequence. Because of space limitations, we purposefully limited the examples in this section primarily to one-to-one consultation occurring between a school psychologist and a teacher, but we hope readers will be able to apply the principles to other situations.

Clarifying the problem. As shown in Table 1, the first step is to clearly define the presenting problem(s) once the relationship has been established. Since there is a level of interdependence between the problem definition and the proposed intervention (Gutkin & Curtis, 1990), the following objectives should be kept in mind during this phase. First, help the consultee describe concerns, goals, and expectations in a behaviorally-specific manner. Consultees often do not have clear conceptualizations of problems when they request assistance, and they consequently present information in vague, global terms. Through skillful questioning, paraphrasing, and summarizing, a broad array of variables associated with the problem can be brought to their attention and then described in specific terms (see suggestions for questions in Table 2; also, see Bergan & Kratochwill, in press). The collection of baseline data is an essential component of this step. Often it is expedient to divide a complex problem into its component parts, thereby helping to ensure that neither consultant nor consultee is overwhelmed and that both can work toward a useful problem analysis.

At times, more than one problem may be designated, and they then must be prioritized according to the perceived level of concern. Once the main concerns have been clarified and prioritized, target behaviors are identified for intervention. These can include (a) behaviors considered to be physically dangerous to self or others; (b) positive low-frequency behaviors in need of strengthening; (c) behaviors that can be naturally reinforced in the environment; (d) behaviors viewed as essential for development; and (e) behaviors that maximize functioning in a variety of settings. All target behaviors chosen should be consistent with developmental norms (see Kratochwill, 1985, for an

TABLE 1
Consultative Problem-Solving Process

Establishment of Consultative Relationship

Problem Identification
1. Define problem in behavioral terms and obtain agreement with consultee.
2. Collect baseline data regarding problem frequency, duration, and/or intensity and conduct task analysis as needed.
3. Identify antecedent determinants of the problem behavior.
4. Identify consequences that may maintain the behavior.
5. Assess other relevant environmental factors.
6. Identify all available resources.

Intervention Development and Selection
1. Brainstorm range of possible interventions.
2. Evaluate the positive and negative aspects of the interventions.
3. Select intervention(s) from the alternatives generated.

Intervention Implementation, Evaluation, and Follow-up
1. Clarify implementation procedures and responsibilities.
2. Implement the chosen strategy.
3. Evaluate intended outcomes and any side effects.
4. Program generalization, plan maintenance, and develop fading procedures as appropriate.
5. Recycle and follow-up as necessary.

---

excellent summary of issues in target selection). Although the behaviors that are targeted are often some aspect of the child's behavior or performance, this does not imply that the child should be the sole focus of the intervention. As a rule, consultees' perceptions or environmental and instructional variables are often what is changed. For example, use of teacher praise and feedback, or opportunities for students to respond in the classroom, may be altered. However, the effects of these changes often are measured in terms of student outcomes.

Questions may be raised during the problem identification interview that need to be answered by additional methods of assessment. Direct classroom observations, utilization of curriculum-based probes, or analysis of student permanent products are among the procedures that may be considered to help answer these questions (Zins, Curtis, Graden, & Ponti, 1988).

Target behaviors must be defined in concise measureable terms. Consultant and consultee should agree about the definitions, which should be worded in such a way that both parties can reliably record the occurrence of targeted behaviors. For instance, if lack of motivation is identified as a problem, it could be operationally defined in terms of "number of spelling assignments completed on time each day in school, and percentage of correct responses." This definition is specific, easily measurable, and understandable to all.

Problem analysis. Once the target behaviors are identified, a comprehensive functional analysis of the interaction between the child's behavior and the environment is conducted. The baseline data and results of the direct observations are key components of this step, as they provide a first-hand look at the complex interactions that occur between clients, consultees, and their daily environments. Temporal and situational antecedents that appear to contribute to the problematic behavior should be identified. In addition, situations during which the behavior of concern does not occur can

TABLE 2
Guidelines for Behaviorally-Oriented Problem Identification Interview

I. Define the Problem

- Specify vague general statements regarding the consultee's concerns. ("You say that Rob is aggressive toward other children. Can you give me some specific examples of his aggressive behavior?")

- Develop an operational definition of the problem. Define the problem in measureable terms. Make it specific enough that others will be able to recognize it when they see it.

- Collect information about the frequency and duration of the problem. ("How many times per day does Mary shout out in class? How long does each episode of behavior last and for what length of time has the problem been occurring?") Actual baseline data should be collected.

- Assess intensity or severity of behavior. ("Describe what types of things Brian does when he throws a temper tantrum.")

- If more than one problem is presented, prioritize and select one target behavior on which to work initially.

II. Identify Antecedent Determinants of the Problem Behavior

- Identify temporal and situational antecedents. ("Are there times of the day when the behavior occurs most frequently? In which settings does the behavior occur?")

- Identify the behavior of others that may trigger or maintain the problem behavior. ("It seems that whenever you are paying attention to other children John's disruptive behavior intensifies.")

- Identify and analyze conditions that alleviate the problem. ("Does Sue seem to work better when you have structured her independent seatwork time through the use of goal setting and a timer?")

III. Identify Consequences That May Maintain the Behavior

- Explore positive consequences that currently are provided or could be instituted to improve behavior or performance. ("What do you do when Joe does complete all of his homework?" "What types of things does Cindy really like to do?")

- Explore forms of inappropriate reinforcement or attention operating.

IV. Assess Other Relevant Environmental Variables

- Identify significant others in the child's environment and assess their attitudes, attributions, and expectations regarding the problem and the child in general.

- Assess the discrepancy between the child's behavior and expected behavior. ("Howard is out of his seat on an average of 15 times per half-hour period. How many times would it be acceptable for him to be out of his seat within this time period in your classroom?")

- Assess relevant instructional variables and classroom or home routines.

V. Identify All Available Resources

- Identify the strengths of the child. ("What types of things does Lisa do well?" "In what subject areas is William succeeding?")

- Identify materials and human resources available for intervention (e.g., peer tutors, parent volunteers, special instructional or curricular materials).

Note. Adapted from Peterson (1968).

be noted, and consequences operating to maintain the behavior also can be recorded. When identifying consequences, the consultant should obtain information on (a) the appropriate positive reinforcement that the child is given, (b) the forms of inappropriate reinforcement or attention the child gains by exhibiting the behavior, (c) the schedules of reinforcement in operation, and (d) the child's reinforcement history.

Environmental and instructional variables relevant to targeted problem behaviors that operate regularly in the child's classroom must also be identified and analyzed. For instance, the consultant could determine whether the teacher has developed a set of rules establishing consequences for particular behaviors, how consistently the rules are enforced, the amount of reinforcement available to the child from sources other than the teacher, opportunities the student is given to respond (both oral and written), method and delay in providing instructional and behavioral feedback, and appropriateness of curriculum (Martens & Witt, 1988). For academic problems, a task analysis of the students' skills in a particular subject may be necessary through methods such as curriculum-based assessment/measurement, examination of permanent products, and think-aloud techniques. Teachers' and/or parents' perceptions and expectations also should be explored at this point to help them understand the broad array of factors that could be influencing the child's behavior or performance. As a result, they may be more open to making needed changes in behavior management or instructional strategies.

The instructional practices of the teacher and daily classroom, school, and home routines also need to be clarified to obtain a broad ecological perspective. Many problems that appear to be specific to individual students upon closer examination may also be seen to require systems-level intervention. Traditionally, however, not much attention has been given to the students' environments and the adults who function in their environments. Nevertheless, it is the adults, not the child, who primarily control the environment in which the child functions (Saxe, Cross, & Silverman, 1988). In addition, the teacher requires help in operationalizing what is acceptable behavior or performance in the classroom so that reasonable goals for the child can be developed.

Finally, all resources that potentially could be utilized in the development and implementation of interventions must be identified. These include student strengths, aspects of the system that are promoting success for the child in other situations, and materials and human resources (teachers, time, peer and volunteer tutors) available for intervention.

Brainstorming and exploring intervention options. Once the problem is clearly defined and analyzed, the level of intervention must be determined. For example, a program could be developed for an individual student, the focus could be on helping a teacher change instructional practices or behavior management strategies used for an entire class, or the districtwide curriculum for reading could be altered to address the problem of concern. When the participants have agreed regarding the level of intervention, they then generate as many intervention options as possible. The cardinal rule of this phase is to avoid evaluating ideas until the brainstorming process is completed. There often is more than one way to resolve a problem, and by generating a number of possible solutions, the probability is maximized of identifying an intervention that is both effective and acceptable to the consultee.

Interventions usually consist of some form of environmental manipulation, since (a) there is substantial research specifying what types of environments lead to effective teaching, parenting, and behavioral change; (b) all consultees routinely manipulate meaningful school and home environment variables; and (c) most consultees do not have the skills to engage in nonenvironmental manipulations such as counseling. Examples of variables that can be considered for manipulation are reward and punishment contingencies, curriculum content, instructional techniques, teacher behavior, peer and sibling behavior, and the physical arrangement of the home and classroom (Gutkin & Curtis, 1990).

Selecting an intervention. After a number of intervention ideas have been generated, each should be evaluated to determine potential benefits and risks for the child, unintended side effects, and feasibility of implementation. Remember that there generally are no "packaged" solutions to problems. A taxonomy of interventions related to a corresponding taxonomy of diagnoses does not exist (Gutkin & Curtis, 1990); therefore, treatments selected during consultation are simply high-probability hypotheses. After a careful analysis of the problem is conducted, hypotheses are formulated regarding what is eliciting and maintaining the behavior or situation, and intervention strategies are developed from this information. Although the consultant guides this problem-solving process and maintains responsibility for providing adequate information about the various intervention procedures identified, the ultimate selection of strategies rests with the consultee. The following guidelines are useful in generating and selecting interventions.

1. Positive intervention approaches should be implemented before resorting to behavior suppression or reduction techniques in all but extreme cases.

2. Choose the least complex and intrusive intervention approach possible. To the extent possible and appropriate, the focus should be on helping the consultee to modify instructional variables or general behavior management strategies. Alterations in existing techniques usually are less intrusive or aversive to the teacher than is learning a new procedure (Martens & Witt, 1988).

3. When a new skill must be developed by the consultee, it should be designed to fit into the present classroom structure and routines as much as possible (Martens & Witt, 1988).

4. Develop a pool of resources such as peer and volunteer tutors that can be utilized when changes in the classroom are not possible or sufficient to resolve the presenting problem.

5. Provide support and reinforcement to consultees for implementing the intervention. Since a behavior change on their part often is required, consultant support will encourage their continued enthusiasm and integrity in treatment implementation.

6. Interventions that require less time, are not ecologically intrusive, and are perceived by consultees to be effective tend to be more acceptable (Witt & Elliott, 1985).

Clarifying implementation procedures and responsibilities. Once the intervention is selected, clarify the pragmatic aspects of implementation. First, the roles and responsibilities of all participants with regard to the intervention must be delineated and agreed upon. The specific techniques to be used should be set out in a step-by-step outline and potential reinforcers identified. The time(s) of the day and the settings or subject areas in which the intervention will be implemented must be decided. At this time, consideration should be given to programming for generalization. Specific suggestions for maximizing the probability that behavior change will generalize across time, persons, and settings are provided later in the chapter. All aspects of the plan should be put in writing at least in outline form so that each person involved has a clear idea of his or her responsibilities. This written plan also serves as a record for accountability purposes.

Implementing the strategy. Once the intervention plan is developed, the consultant should keep in close touch with the consultee to aid in implementation, to provide other technical assistance, and to reinforce consultee efforts. Consultees often have questions about the details of the plan, unanticipated behaviors may arise, or there may be unintended reactions from other children. The consultant can enhance the consultee's motivation by involving them in goal setting, establishing a trusting and warm relationship, and demonstrating personal competence (Brown & Schulte, 1987). Further, if the intervention requires the consultee to learn a new skill or to make substantial changes in current practices, it often is helpful for consultants to model the procedure, observe the consultee implementing it, and provide constructive, supportive feedback. All of these elements — ongoing contact, adequate training, and support — are crucial for increasing and ensuring treatment integrity and success.

Consultee resistance to the planned intervention may occur, although it can be minimized through establishment of a cooperative, supportive partnership. However, consultants must remember that the consultation process may (a) require considerable consultee effort and time, (b) focus on consultee failure, (c) involve differing perspectives of desirable outcomes, and (d) not result in immediate problem resolution (Piersel & Gutkin, 1983). Since each of these possibilities is non-reinforcing for consultees at least on a short term basis, it is not surprising that resistance often is encountered. By being aware of the potentially negative aspects of consultation, consultants may be better prepared to deal with any resistance that may arise. Relatedly, it must be kept in mind that there are many legitimate problems faced by consultees that may prevent them from being able to carry out intervention plans.

Evaluating intervention effectiveness and follow-up. There are several interrelated elements in this stage of the problem-solving process, among them evaluation of intervention effectiveness, generalization, fading, and follow-up.

Evaluation of intervention effectiveness. Once the plan has been implemented, it should be systematically and regularly monitored to ensure treatment integrity and to identify any unintended side effects. Of course, the evaluation plan should be agreed upon before implementation begins. Generally, the same data collection procedures as those used to obtain baseline information can be applied again as a means of evaluation. These methods should be as simple and time-efficient as possible so that a teacher, parent, or peer can easily use the system. Single-subject methodologies such as single-phase, reversal, or multiple-baseline designs are often used to evaluate intervention effectiveness. These evaluation procedures may suggest that (a) the intervention resulted in attainment of the desired goals, thereby indicating that follow-up monitoring and/or generalization and fading procedures are needed; or (b) the intended outcomes were not reached entirely, suggesting the need to recycle through the problem-solving process.

Generalization, fading, and follow-up. The data will indicate the degree to which the intervention is producing the desired outcome. Once an effective and reliable procedure has been identified, the intervention can be extended to other settings or systematically faded.

Although there are many well-developed, validated techniques for bringing about behavior change, we know substantially less about how to maintain these gains. A number of suggestions, however, have been offered in the literature on how to program *generalization* while interventions are being developed and as they are being implemented (Meichenbaum, 1985; Stokes & Baer, 1977). Chosen reinforcers, for instance, should be naturally occurring events when possible, and techniques should be implemented in such a manner that they lead to fading or to greater transfer of control to the student (i.e., self-management approaches). Students should take an active role in development of the intervention when possible, and efforts should be made to help them understand the usefulness and relevance of the intervention to their lives. Training should take place in a number of settings so as to use multiple tasks and several trainers. Finally, opportunities to confront and deal positively with failure or mistakes also should be built into the intervention procedures.

Interventions that include specific prompts or reinforcement contingencies need to be *faded* systematically once the child is performing at desired levels. It is important to withdraw prompts or reinforcement in small steps rather than all at once to ensure maintenance of treatment gains. Fading can consist of increasing the amount of time before a child can earn a reinforcer, increasing task demands to be completed to earn a reinforcer, or decreasing the number of prompts given to children to elicit performance. If at any step in the fading process the student's behavior begins to deteriorate, reinforcement or prompting should revert to the previous level. Once the child's behavior stabilizes again for a period of time, fading can be continued.

The importance of *follow-up* by the consultant during this stage is critical. However, this aspect of the problem-solving process is often neglected. Follow-up helps ensure that intervention, generalization, and fading procedures are being implemented correctly, and it can address the issue of unintended outcomes. When interventions provide ineffective or unreliable outcomes, the consultant should observe them in operation and conduct a functional analysis of the current situation to determine what conditions might be contributing to the nonattainment of the desired goals. Oftentimes, modifications in the existing plan suggested through corrective feedback are all that are necessary to increase ease of implementation, improve intervention effectiveness, or counteract unanticipated responses by the client. If the alterations do not yield better results, a new strategy should be sought, once again through the problem-solving process.

Influences on the consultation process. Central to the success of the consultation process are the issues of treatment acceptability, adherence, and integrity. Consideration of these issues, along with establishment of a collaborative partnership, can be major factors in decreasing or avoiding resistance. *Acceptability* refers to judgments or beliefs of consultees and clients about whether a treatment is "appropriate, fair, and reasonable for the problem or client" (Kazdin, 1981, p. 493). As Wolfe (1978)

noted, if participants like the intervention (i.e., find it acceptable), they may be more likely to use it or to carry it out correctly. *Adherence* involves the willingness (a) of the consultee to carry out the intervention to its completion, and (b) of the client to engage in certain behavior changes indicated in the intervention plan (Meichenbaum & Turk, 1987). *Treatment integrity*, on the other hand, refers to the extent to which the consultee implements the intervention plan as intended (Gresham, 1989). Witt and Elliott (1985) proposed that the elements of acceptability, adherence, and integrity are mutually dependent, that is, influence and are influenced by one another. Adherence and integrity are the two elements that link intervention use with effectiveness.

Because consultation is an indirect service and the intervention is almost always implemented by the consultee, there are two levels of acceptability and adherence related to the process. The first involves the extent to which the consultee is actively and cooperatively involved in carrying out an agreed-upon course of action to produce a desired behavior change in a client. The second level involves the extent to which the child or client is involved in the process and cooperates with the treatment plan to be implemented by the consultee (Meichenbaum & Turk, 1987). Further, there are certain factors related to treatment integrity, including the complexity of the intervention, time required to implement the plan, materials or resources needed, number of treatment agents involved, perceived and actual effectiveness of the intervention, and motivation of the consultee(s), that affect implementation (Gresham, 1989).

When interventions are not followed or result in failure, consultants most often cite consultee variables such as motivation or skill as the cause (Martin & Curtis, 1981). Although consultee motivation may play a role in the success or failure of consultation outcome in some cases, it is not the predominant variable nor is it within the consultant's sphere of control. As indicated in Table 3, numerous factors influence both adherence and treatment

Table 3
Examples of Factors Affecting Treatment Adherence and Integrity

Client Variables
    Belief that a problem exists
    Belief that the problem could have a negative impact on the client
    Belief that participating in the intervention will help the client
    Perceptions regarding not having a choice about being treated

Consultee Variables
    Beliefs about potential efficacy of the intervention
    Understanding of the consultative process
    Satisfaction with the relationship with the consultant
    Misconceptions held
    Cultural beliefs
    Opportunities available to exhibit skills
    Beliefs about ability to carry out the intervention
    Personal motivation to resolve the problem
    Skills in describing problem situations and carrying out interventions
    Perceptions of consultant's expertise and competence

Consultant Variables
    Theoretical orientation and values
    Skills in problem solving
    Technical competence in intervention development and evaluation
    Understanding of organizational functioning and change
    Motivation and enthusiasm
    Self-awareness and understanding

Relationship Variables
    Interpersonal and communication factors
    Discrepancies between consultant and consultee attributions
    Participant sensitivity to cultural, racial, ethnic, and gender issues
    Extent of collaboration or mutual participation in process
    Continuity of involvement
    Extent of support and follow-up provided

Treatment Variables
    Complexity of the intervention
    Time and resources required to carry out the interventions
    Intrusiveness of intervention to established regularities
    Duration of intervention
    Number of behavior changes that are made at once
    Number of treatment agents involved
    How soon behavior change is observed

Organizational Variables
    Openness of social/organizational climate
    Opportunities and support provided for change
    Length of time until assistance is provided
    Perception of organizational support
    Time and resource availability
    Principal's leadership behavior

Note. Adapted from Gresham (1989), Gutkin (1986), and Meichenbaum and Turk (1987).

integrity. Although of a correlational nature, these factors can provide useful guidelines for consultants interested in enhancing both adherence and treatment integrity of both the consultee and the client. It is evident from the literature that relationship variables are of crucial importance. For example, adherence can be improved and resistance decreased through the establishment of a caring, collaborative relationship characterized by open communication. Within the problem-solving process, efforts should be made to clarify the consultee's beliefs and expectations about the consultation process and about intervention options and outcomes. In addition, discrepancies between consultant and consultee causal attributions for the problem need to be resolved as they clarify the problem (Zins, 1985).

Other factors that affect treatment adherence include the characteristics of the intervention procedures chosen and the extent to which the client is involved in the process. A related issue is that of consultant adherence (Meichenbaum & Turk, 1987). Consultants must be aware of their own beliefs regarding their ability to improve consultee and client adherence, make special efforts to monitor their own interactions with consultees, and develop the type of consultative relationship that maximizes the probability of adherence. Finally, since consultation often results in short-term negative outcomes for consultees (e.g., they have to devote significant effort toward resolving the problem before behavioral changes occur) (Piersel & Gutkin, 1983), providing support and encouragement is especially important.

Organizational consultation. School-based consultation is not limited to a focus on individual students. At times it is expanded to include the entire school or even the school district. Consultants increasingly are focusing on larger organizational issues in order to maximize their influence and expand their range, and to deal with problems that truly are systemic in origin. The same problem-solving procedures as those described earlier are followed in this instance, but, of course, different types of interventions are developed. However, procedures based on behavior analysis and social learning interventions continue to be relevant. Examples of organizational consultation include involvement in the evaluation of a districtwide program for gifted and talented students; establishment of a smoking prevention program at the junior high level; development of a seat-belt safety program for senior high students; and involvement in the implementation of a tutoring program utilizing the services of volunteer senior citizens. Indeed, developing an intervention assistance program as described in the next section is another example.

Implementation of Consultation: The Intervention Assistance Process

Not only have the skills of school psychologists been underutilized in general (i.e., they spend an inordinate amount of time in traditional assessment and placement activities that result in dubious outcomes for children), but the intervention techniques that have been developed for use in schools have also been underutilized. Consequently, new approaches must be developed that will expand our opportunities to apply these interventions to help students. To accomplish this goal most efficiently, a broad-scale systems-level approach is essential.

Various terms have been used in the literature to refer to the general process by which programs are developed that enable teachers to help students with special needs (e.g., prereferral intervention, teacher support teams). At this time, there is not widespread agreement regarding the meaning of these terms, few have been thoroughly developed in the literature, and there are major pitfalls in most descriptions that have been published. For these reasons, we use the term *intervention assistance programs* (IAP) to refer to these efforts. The term describes

> a system-wide consultation-based model of services delivery intended to meet the special needs of individual students

through the systematic and collaborative provision, evaluation, and documentation of problem solving strategies in the least restrictive setting prior to referral for consideration of a more restrictive placement. (Zins et al., 1988, p. 6)

We believe that this definition overcomes some of the significant shortcomings of other conceptualizations of this process.

While it is not possible to discuss the IAP in great detail within the confines of this chapter, it is described here briefly as it is the best developed method of implementing consultation on a systemic basis that is currently available. The discussion is based upon our previous works (e.g., Ponti, Zins, & Graden, 1988; Zins et al., 1988), which contain a thorough presentation of the IAP process.

Participants. Persons typically involved in the IAP process are the school psychologist, school counselor, special education teacher(s), and principal. In addition, a regular education representative, speech and language therapist, and parents frequently participate, depending upon the nature of the problem and their availability. Those involved in the IAP can rotate to varying degrees or they may remain the same. As described below, these persons may function as individual consultants or together as a problem-solving team.

Steps in the IAP process. The steps involved in the IAP process are as follows:

Personal problem solving. Teachers always engage in some form of personal problem solving before seeking consultative assistance. Typically, they may try various interventions in the classroom, confer with colleagues, or meet with parents. The majority of classroom problems are solved in this manner (Figure 1).

Request for assistance. If the personal problem solving proves ineffective, teachers may request assistance from an individual member of the IAP team or from the entire team. They follow this procedure for receiving assistance instead of the more traditional method, that is, making a referral for a psychoeducational assessment. The request for assistance initiates the IAP process.

Methods of providing assistance: Individual consultation. Any member of the IAP team can provide one-to-one consultation and it is usually arranged on an informal basis. The consultee selects the individual consultant because of his or her (a) expertise with regard to the presenting problem, or (b) prior relationship with the consultee. However, if they are unable to resolve the problem, a different consultant can become involved or a meeting with the entire team can be held.

Methods of providing assistance: Group consultation. Meetings with the IAP team can be requested by teachers, and they usually are arranged more formally because of the number of individuals involved. Team meetings are most appropriate with complex cases or when it is important to facilitate communication among a number of persons. As shown in Figure 1, far fewer problems reach the entire team than are resolved through personal problem solving or individual consultation.

Although personal problem solving is always the first step in the IAP process, individual consultation does not always follow when personal efforts are not effective. Particularly complex cases may necessitate more immediate consultation with the IAP team as a second step. In addition, all stages of consultation are not always completed in either individual or team consultation. The team may decide, for example, that it is more efficient to have an individual consultant work with the consultee to thoroughly develop the specifics of a particular intervention rather than involve the entire team in the process. Similarly, an individual consultant may help with problem identification but then suggest a team meeting for the problem solution phase.

Overview of the IAP implementation steps. An IAP can be initiated through the efforts of the school psychologist, but it usually is desirable to involve the administration at an early stage or, ideally,

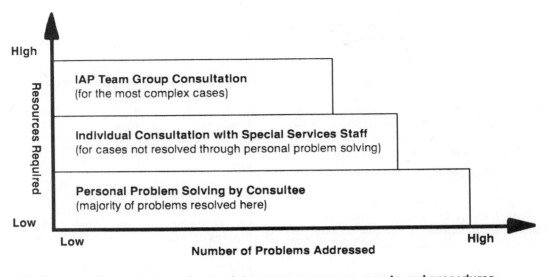

FIGURE 1. Outline of intervention assistance program components and procedures.

to proceed through the entire implementation process with them. The following steps should be taken, toward the goal of producing durable, lasting organizational change.

1. *Clarify the need for the IAP program through an organizational assessment.* This systematic and ongoing planning process (a) clarifies the need for the program, (b) describes program goals, (c) provides a clear rationale for the program, (d) determines required resources, and (e) identifies evaluation procedures (Maher & Bennett, 1984). Representative groups of administrators, staff, and parents should be involved in this process.

Operationally, the consultant (and perhaps others who are involved in the process) would examine district referral and testing data, interview (and possibly survey) staff and parents regarding their satisfaction with current practices, explore interest in altering the manner in which assistance is provided to students who need it, and observe current procedures in operation. At the end of this step, the need for the IAP should be clarified, and it should be determined whether the school is prepared to consider the new program.

2. *Gain sanction and support from representatives at all levels of the educational hierarchy,* including teachers and building and district administrators, as well as special services staff and parents. This step is a prerequisite to adoption of the IAP. Completion of the planning process described above, and particularly involving representative groups who will be affected by the program, helps to ensure the success of this step. If sanction from these groups is gained, then specific implementation activities can begin with the entire organization.

3. *Introducing the IAP program to staff and parents.* A formal presentation or in-service should be held to inform staff and parents of the availability of the IAP and of its procedures. However, even before IAP operational procedures have been finalized, the process should be introduced on an informal basis and the staff should be given an opportunity to provide input. Thereafter, they should be kept informed regarding the status of the program.

4. *Alter district/school philosophies and policies to be consistent with the program.* This step represents attainment of formal organizational sanction for

program operation, and it is important as a means of making the IAP an integral part of the overall educational program. As part of this step, it is desirable to develop a specific policy regarding the intervention assistance program that describes and provides support for its operation. Identification of incentives for participation can also be included in this step. Again, the staff should be involved and have an opportunity for input.

5. *Define the roles and responsibilities of the various professionals involved in the program.* These activities should be made part of the job descriptions of the entire staff, and to a certain extent they should have been identified in the policies developed in the previous step. In most instances, it is necessary to provide training in consultation and teaming strategies for those who serve as part of the IAP team so that they are prepared to carry out these responsibilities.

6. *Clarify the operational procedures of the program for all who will be involved,* including parents, so that they will understand it and use it effectively. This goal is accomplished most effectively through the presentations and in-service training mentioned above. Moreover, such an approach is an important means of changing consumer expectations and perceptions, particularly with regard to the consultant's role and how assistance can be obtained. As in previous steps, misconceptions about the process or potential problems should be dealt with, and a structure should be put in place by which decision makers routinely are informed of progress in program development and operation.

7. *Market the availability and the potential advantages of the program on an ongoing basis.* The goal of this step is (a) to stimulate appropriate utilization and demand for psychological services, and (b) to increase consumer and decision-maker levels of understanding and knowledge of the IAP process.

8. *Evaluate the effectiveness of the program and publicize its identified benefits.* To maximize programmatic

support, data should be collected and users of the IAP should be kept informed regarding its effectiveness. We might expect to find a decrease in referrals for psychoeducational assessment, but an increase in the percentage of students who are assessed and ultimately placed in special education, and in the number of requests for consultation. An evaluation could be made of (a) the number of requests for consultation, (b) the range of problems for which assistance is sought, (c) whether consultees seek help for the same or for different problems, (d) the time devoted to consultation relative to other professional activities, (e) the outcomes of interventions ($N = 1$ designs), and (f) the range of consumers participating in consultation. Finally, consumer satisfaction could be assessed.

Maximizing Opportunities to Consult

Although the IAP is an effective means of implementing consultation, we still need to expand our opportunities to consult and capitalize upon every opportunity that arises. Integrating consultation with other services or, as stated earlier, making consultation the foundation from which all services emanate, is the primary way of expanding our role. Consultation should occur prior to and following every psychoeducational assessment that is performed. The goal is to encourage teachers and other consumers to perceive consultation as an integral component of school psychological services. It also may be desirable to identify motivated consultees and to carefully select cases for initial consultative endeavors to increase the likelihood of success. Word of its effectiveness will thereby spread to other staff.

Another potentially effective strategy is to train consultees in consultative problem solving. There is some preliminary evidence that their ability to use problem-solving processes can be enhanced through direct training and modeling (e.g., Anderson, Kratochwill, & Bergan, 1986; Cleven & Gutkin, 1988). Such an approach may also increase consultees' preferences for consultation by enhancing their sense of self-efficacy and control in the relationship (Gutkin & Hickman, 1988).

SUMMARY

As consultation rapidly becomes a major job function for many school psychologists, it is critical for them to keep abreast of the latest theoretical and empirical knowledge of this emerging field. Understanding of effective consultative interactions, systems-level implementation, and evaluation techniques is quickly expanding, and this chapter represents an integrative summary of the most important of these recent developments. Included was a review of many essential aspects of consultation practice. The chapter began with a discussion of the major dimensions of the consultation process, including its emphasis upon a preventive and empowering ideology, consideration of systems issues and of the reciprocal nature of the interactions, and a review of the most important dimensions of the problem-solving process. It concluded with an overview of the intervention assistance process that is designed to help incorporate consultation into the routine organizational functioning of schools so that additional numbers of students can perform successfully in the least restrictive setting. The intent of this discussion is to provide the essential information needed to effectively engage in consultation. Ultimately, it is hoped that such efforts will result in school psychologists being identified with consultation-related services rather than with traditional IQ testing, so that greater numbers of effective interventions can be developed to meet the needs of our children.

ACKNOWLEDGMENTS

We gratefully acknowledge Stephen N. Elliott, William P. Erchul, and Susan M. Sheridan who stimulated and challenged our thinking with their thought-provoking comments on an earlier draft of the chapter.

REFERENCES

Anderson, T., Kratochwill, T. R., & Bergan, J. R. (1986). Training teachers in behavioral consultation and therapy: An analysis of verbal behaviors. *Journal of School Psychology, 24,* 229–241.

Bandura, A. (1977). *Social learning theory.* Englewood Cliffs, NJ: Prentice-Hall.

Bergan, J. R. (1977). *Behavioral consultation.* Columbus, OH: Merrill.

Bergan, J. R., & Kratochwill, T. R. (in press). *Behavioral consultation in applied settings.* New York: Plenum.

Brown, D., & Schulte, A. (1987). A social learning model of consultation. *Professional Psychology: Research and Practice, 16,* 283–287.

Christenson, S., Ysseldyke, J., Wang, J., & Algozzine, R. (1983). Teachers' attributions for problems that result in referral for psychoeducational evaluation. *Journal of Educational Research, 76,* 174–180.

Cleven, C., & Gutkin, T. B. (1988). Cognitive modeling of consultation processes: A means for improving consultee's problem definition skills. *Journal of School Psychology, 26,* 379–389.

Curtis, M. J., & Meyers, J. (1985). Best practices in consultation. In A. Thomas & J. Grimes (Eds.), *Best practices in school psychology* (pp. 79–94). Washington, DC: National Association of School Psychologists.

Erchul, W. P., & Chewning, T. (in press). Behavioral consultation from a request-centered relational communication perspective. *Professional School Psychology.*

Gallessich, J. (1982). *The practice and profession of consultation.* San Francisco: Jossey-Bass.

Gibbs, J. (1985). Can we continue to be color-blind and class bound? *Counseling Psychologist, 13,* 426–435.

Gresham, F. M. (1989). Assessment of treatment integrity in school consultation and prereferral intervention. *School Psychology Review, 18,* 37–50.

Gresham, F. M., & Kendall, G. (1989). School consultation research: Methodological critique and future research directions. *School Psychology Review, 16,* 306–316.

Gutkin, T. B. (1981). Relative frequency of consultee lack of knowledge, skill, confidence, and objectivity in school settings. *Journal of School Psychology, 19,* 57–61.

Gutkin, T. B. (1986). Consultees' perceptions of variables relating to the outcomes of school-based consultation interactions. *School Psychology Review, 15,* 375–382.

Gutkin, T. B., & Curtis, M. J. (1990). School-based consultation: Theory, techniques, and research. In T. B. Gutkin & C. R. Reynolds (Eds.), *The handbook of school psychology* (2nd ed.). New York: Wiley.

Gutkin, T. B., & Hickman, J. (1988). Teachers' perceptions of control over presenting problems and resulting preferences for consultation versus referral services. *Journal of School Psychology, 26,* 395-398.

Hawryluk, M. K., & Smallwood, D. (1986). Assessing and addressing consultee variables in school-based behavioral consultation. *School Psychology Review, 15,* 519-528.

Kazdin, A. (1981). Acceptability of child treatment techniques: The influence of treatment efficacy and adverse side effects. *Behavior Therapy, 12,* 493-506.

Kratochwill, T. R. (Ed.). (1985). Mini-series on target behavior selection. *Behavioral Assessment, 7,* 1-78.

Kurpins, D. J., & Lewis, J. E. (1988). Assumptions and operating principles for preparing professionals to function as consultants. In J. F. West (Ed.), *School consultation* (pp. 143-154). Austin, TX: Association for Educational and Psychological Consultants.

Lorion, R. (1978). Research on psychotherapy and behavior change with the disadvantaged: Past, present, and future directions. In L. S. Garfield & A. E. Bergin (Eds.), *Handbook of psychotherapy and behavior change* (pp. 367-381). New York: Wiley.

Maher, C. A., & Bennett, R. E. (1984). *Planning and evaluating special education programs.* Englewood Cliffs, NJ: Prentice-Hall.

Martens, B. K., & Meller, P. J. (1990). The application of behavioral principles to educational settings. In T. B. Gutkin & C. R. Reynolds (Eds.), *The handbook of school psychology* (2nd ed.). New York: Wiley.

Martens, B. K., & Witt, J. C. (1988). Expanding the scope of behavioral consultation: A systems approach to classroom behavior change. *Professional School Psychology, 3,* 271-281.

Martin, R. P., & Curtis, M. (1981). Consultants' perceptions of causality for success and failure in consultation. *Professional Psychology, 12,* 670-676.

Medway, F. (1979). Causal attributions for school-related problems: Teacher perceptions and teacher feedback. *Journal of Educational Psychology, 71,* 809-818.

Medway, F., & Updyke, J. (1985). Meta-analysis of consultation outcome studies. *American Journal of Community Psychology, 13,* 489-504.

Meichenbaum, D. (1985). *Stress inoculation training.* Elmsford, NY: Pergamon.

Meichenbaum, D., & Turk, D. (1987). *Facilitating treatment adherence.* New York: Plenum.

Miller, G. A. (1969). Psychology as a means of promoting human welfare. *American Psychologist, 24,* 1063-1075.

O'Neill, P., & Trickett, E. (1982). *Community consultation.* San Francisco: Jossey-Bass.

Piersel, W., & Gutkin, T. B. (1983). Resistance to school-based consultation: A behavioral analysis of the problem. *Psychology in the Schools, 20,* 311-320.

Ponti, C. R., Zins, J. E., & Graden, J. (1988). Implementing a consultation-based service delivery system to decrease referrals for special education: A case study of organizational considerations. *School Psychology Review, 17,* 89-100.

Price, R., Cowen, E., Lorion, R., & Ramos-McKay, J. (Eds.). (1988). *14 ounces of prevention.* Washington, DC: American Psychological Association.

Rappaport, J. (1981). In praise of paradox: A social policy of empowerment over prevention. *American Journal of Community Psychology, 9,* 1-25.

Reardon, K. (1981). *Persuasion: Theory and context.* Beverly Hills, CA: Sage.

Saxe, L., Cross, T., & Silverman, N. (1988). Children's mental health: The gap between what we know and what we do. *American Psychologist, 43,* 800-807.

Stokes, T. F., & Baer, D. M. (1977). An implicit technology of generalization. *Journal of Applied Behavior Analysis, 10,* 349-368.

Swift, C., & Cooper, S. (1986). Settings, consultees, and clients. In F. Mannino, E. Trickett, M. Shore, M. Kidder, & G. Levin (Eds.), *The handbook of mental health consultation* (pp. 347-392). Washington, DC: U.S. Government Printing Office.

Tyler, F., Pargament, K., & Gatz, M. (1983). The resource-collaborator role: A model for interactions involving psychologists. *American Psychologist, 38,* 388-398.

Witt, J. C., & Elliott, S. N. (1985). Acceptability of classroom intervention strategies. In T. R. Kratochwill (Ed.), *Advances in school psychology* (Vol. 4, pp. 251-288). Hillsdale, NJ: Erlbaum.

Witt, J. C., & Martens, B. K. (1988). Problems with problem solving consultation: A re-analysis of assumptions, methods, and goals. *School Psychology Review, 17,* 212-226.

Wolfe, M. M. (1978). Social validity: The case for subjective measurement or how applied behavior analysis is finding its heart. *Journal of Applied Behavior Analysis, 11*, 203–214.

Zins, J. E. (1985). Work-relations management. In C. A. Maher (Ed.), *Professional self-management* (pp. 105–127). Baltimore: Brookes.

Zins, J. E. (1988). Examination of the conceptual foundations of school consultation practice. In J. F. West (Ed.), *School consultation: Perspectives on theory, research, training, and practice* (pp. 17–34). Austin, TX: Association for Educational and Psychological Consultants.

Zins, J. E., Curtis, M. J., Graden, J., & Ponti, C. R. (1988). *Helping students succeed in the regular classroom: A guide for developing intervention assistance programs.* San Francisco: Jossey-Bass.

ANNOTATED BIBLIOGRAPHY

Brown, D., Pryzwansky, W., & Schulte, A. (1987). *Psychological consultation.* Boston: Allyn & Bacon. The authors present an overview of the growth and current status of consultation. The book includes a comprehensive look at various consultation models and of the processes involved in practice, with the goal of helping readers develop essential knowledge and skills.

Gutkin, T. B., & Curtis, M. J. (1990). School-based consultation: Theory, techniques, and research. In T. B. Gutkin & C. R. Reynolds (Eds.), *The handbook of school psychology* (2nd ed.). New York: Wiley. This chapter discusses in detail the various approaches to consultation as well as their core characteristics and assumptions. It also contains an extensive set of references, particularly with regard to research on consultation processes.

Rosenfield, S. (1987). *Instructional consultation.* Hillsdale, NJ: Erlbaum. The purpose of the book is to present a comprehensive overview of consultation and to integrate it with the knowledge base in instructional techniques. The goal is to improve consultants' skills in working with teachers regarding instructional issues.

Zins, J. E., Curtis, M. J., Graden, J., & Ponti, C. R. (1988). *Helping students succeed in the regular classroom: A guide for developing intervention assistance programs.* San Francisco: Jossey-Bass. In this book the authors describe a systems-level process to develop, implement, and evaluate consultation-based intervention assistance programs. The goal of these procedures is to help students with learning and/or behavioral problems function effectively in regular classrooms.

47

Best Practices in Social Skills Training

Frank M. Gresham
Hofstra University

Historically, school psychologists have devoted almost exclusive attention to the assessment of and intervention recommendations for cognitive, perceptual–motor, and academic achievement difficulties of students. A major reason for this emphasis on so-called cognitive abilities is due to the fact that federal and state classification criteria for most handicapping conditions require that the handicap adversely affect academic performance. Despite the reality that schooling, by definition, takes place in a social context, school psychological practice ignores the sometimes dramatic effects students' and teacher's social behavior have upon the educational process.

The purposes of this chapter are to highlight the importance of social behavior in school settings, to provide a definition and conceptualization of social competence, to discuss approaches to social skills training based on a social learning theory model. Information provided in this chapter should provide readers with a clear conceptualization of social skills and general strategies for social skills assessment and training based on recent empirical and theoretical treatments of the topic.

OVERVIEW

Why are social skills an important focus in school settings? There are several strong arguments for developing socially competent behaviors in students. First, social skills and peer acceptance have been related to long-term adjustment outcomes for children and youth. Parker and Asher (1987) comprehensively reviewed the literature that used longitudinal and follow-back studies and found that peer relationship difficulties in elementary school predicted long-term maladjusted outcomes such as dropping out of school, juvenile delinquency, adult criminal behavior, and psychopathology in adulthood. Based on the best available evidence, interpersonal relationship problems in childhood predict serious negative outcomes as children develop into adulthood.

Second, social skills deficits differentiate mildly handicapped (learning disabled, behavior disordered, mildly mentally retarded) from nonhandicapped students. Comprehensive reviews of the literature concerning the social skills and peer acceptance deficits of learning disabled students show that these students are between 1 and 2 standard deviations below nonhandicapped students on these variables (Gresham, 1988; Hazel, Schumaker, & Pederson, 1988). This magnitude of difference holds across raters (teachers and parents) direct observations in classrooms, behavioral analogue role play measures, and sociometric procedures (Gresham & Reschly, 1988; Hazel et al., 1988). Differences of similar magnitude have been shown between nonhandicapped students and students classified as behavior disordered (Stumme, Gresham, & Scott, 1982) and mildly mentally retarded students (Gresham, Elliott, & Black, 1987).

Third, teachers consider certain social skills to be critical for success in their classrooms. Hersh and Walker (1983) suggested that teachers consider a behavioral repertoire to be indicative of successful adjustment if it: (a) facilitates academic performance and (b) is marked by the absence of behaviors that challenge the teacher's authority and disturb the classroom ecology. Students who show such a behavior pattern could be considered to have a *model behavior profile.*

Table 1 presents the 10 most important and 10 least important social skills as rated by a nationally representative sample of teachers using the teacher version of the *Social Skills Rating System* (Gresham & Elliott, 1990). Teachers rated each social skill according to how important it was for classroom success (Critical, Important, or Unimportant). The "Top 10" constitutes what Hersh and Walker (1983) called the model behavior profile in that these behaviors are associated with a quiet and manageable classroom relatively free from disruption. These same kinds of behaviors have been labeled as *teacher-preferred social skills* by Walker and McConnell (1988). In addition, many, if not most, school psychologists will recognize that the absence of or low frequencies of these behaviors often constitute the basis for referrals to special education.

The "Bottom 10" listed in Table 1 deal primarily with peer-to-peer social interactions and these types of behaviors have been referred to as *peer preferred social skills* (Walker & McConnell, 1988). Teachers may consider these behaviors least important because the occurrence of these behaviors in classrooms may interfere with effective instruction. A closer look at the least important behaviors reveals that the majority of these behaviors are incompatible with effective teaching (e.g., invites peers to play, expresses anger or annoyance, makes positive statements to other children). Obviously, the occurrence of these behaviors would be considered by teachers to be socially inappropriate if they occurred during instructional periods.

Definition of Social Skill

Social skills have been defined various ways by different authors in the field. Some definitions view social skills as a subdomain or component of adaptive behavior. For example, the definition of adaptive behavior given by the American Association on Mental Deficiency implies that social skills are part of the adaptive behavior construct (Grossman, 1983). Leland (1978) suggests that *personal responsibility* is related to social skill in that individuals perform adaptive behaviors in terms of societal expectations. Persons are considered socially skilled or unskilled in relation to the behavioral expectations of others in specific social situations.

Research investigating the relationship between adaptive behavior and social skills has shown low to moderate correlations between the two constructs depending on how each is measured (Gresham & Reschly, 1987; Reschly & Gresham, 1988). Some research has demonstrated that the *method* used to measure adaptive behavior and social skills is more important than the *content* of what is being measured (i.e., adaptive behavior or social skills) (Gresham & Reschly, 1987).

Some view social skills as being merely positive alternatives to problem or inappropriate social behaviors. For example, the behavior of "Argues with others" might be rephrased as "Talks nicely to others" to capture a social skill alternative. The work of Achenbach and Edelbrock (1983) using the Child Behavior Checklist and Quay (1983) using the Revised Behavior Problem Checklist conceptualize social skills in this fashion, at least by inference.

Social skills, however, do not appear to be merely mirror opposites of problem behaviors given the moderate negative correlations between social skills and problem behaviors (Clark, Gresham, & Elliott, 1985; Walker & McConnell, 1988). Thus, social skills and problem behaviors are *not* opposite ends of the same continuum, but rather two different but related constructs. Logically, it is entirely possible for an individual to manifest both

TABLE 1
**Ten Most Important Social Skills and Ten Least Important Social Skills as Rated
by Classroom Teachers on the Social Skills Rating Scales (SSRS)** [a]

The Top 10: SSRS Importance Dimension (Classroom Survival Skills)

1. Completes classroom assignments in required time (1.82)
2. Looks at teacher when instructed (1.72)
3. Follows the teacher's verbal directions (1.70)
4. Requests assistance, explanations, or instructions from teacher (1.65)
5. Uses time productively while waiting for teacher assistance (1.62)
6. Asks questions of teacher when unsure of what to do in school work at appropriate times and in an appropriate manner (1.61)
7. Produces correct academic work (1.60)
8. Controls temper in conflict situations (1.58)
9. Attends to class speakers (1.59)
10. Ignores peer distractions when doing class work (1.56)

The Bottom 10: SSRS Importance Dimension (Peer Interaction Skills)

1. Invites peers to play (.86)
2. Introduces self to new people on own initiative (.85)
3. Praises peers (.82)
4. Makes positive statements of other children (.76)
5. Presents academic work before class (.75)
6. Cooperates with peers without being told (.74)
7. Appropriately expresses opinions or beliefs on some issue by giving reasons for expressed opinion or belief (.72)
8. Appropriately expresses anger or annoyance when a classmate takes a belonging without asking (.71)
9. Attempts classroom tasks before asking for teacher assistance (.70)
10. Tolerates peers whose characteristics are different from one's own (i.e., ethnic group, handicapped, etc.) (.60)

[a] Means in parentheses.

socially skilled and problem behaviors depending on the setting and situation.

The definition of social skills that seems to make the most sense has been termed the *social validity definition* (Gresham, 1983). According to this definition:

> Social skills are situationally specific behaviors that predict important social outcomes for children and youth. In school settings, important social outcomes for children and youth. In school settings, important social outcomes include, but are not limited to: (a) peer acceptance, (b) significant other's judgments of social skill, (c) academic achievement, (d) self-concept, and (e) school adjustment.

This definition has the advantage of identifying specific social behaviors in specific social situations in which an individual may be deficient and can relate these deficiencies to empirically-established social outcomes. A social validity definition uses both a social validity and criterion-related validity approach to defining social skill.

Social validation represents an important type of validity for practical purposes. Wolf (1978) indicated that social validity occurs on three levels: (a) establishing the social significance of behaviors targeted for intervention, (b) establishing the social acceptability of interventions to treatment consumers, and (c) assessing the social importance of the effects of interventions. The current definition of social skills seeks to relate specific social behaviors to outcomes valued by society thus establishing the social validity of the definition.

Although many classes of behavior could be defined as "socially skilled," Gresham and Elliott (1990) have established five classes or clusters of social skills based on the relationship between these clusters and socially important outcomes (e.g., academic achievement, sociometric status, self-concept, etc.). Using a nationally representative sample of 4,107 students between the ages of 3–18 years, Gresham and Elliott (1990) found that *C*ooperation, *A*ssertion, *R*esponsibility, *E*mpathy, and *S*elf-Control represented major clusters of social skills using the *Social Skills Rating System*. Table 2 presents examples of specific behaviors under each social skill cluster.

Several basic considerations must be dealt with before adequate social skills training programs can be designed and implemented. These considerations include: (a) assessment strategies, (b) classification of social skills deficits, and (c) selection of target behaviors for intervention. Each of these considerations will be discussed in the following sections.

Assessment Strategies

Assessment of social skills can vary along the dimensions of *source, temporal and physical proximity to performance, purpose,* and *specificity*. These dimensions also influence the reliability, validity, accuracy, and practicality of social skills assessment procedures.

Assessment information can come from different sources such as teachers, parents, peers, students, or direct observations. Social skill functioning varies across situations and settings and, as such, one usually finds relatively low agreement between information sources (Achenbach, McConaughy, & Howell, 1987). Low agreements among information sources do not necessarily imply invalidity. It is possible that assessment information obtained from each source contributes unique information regarding social skill functioning. Achenbach et al. (1987) suggest that low agreements among information sources primarily reflect the situational specificity of behavior rather than error.

Social skills assessment information also can vary according to the temporal and physical proximity of the assessment to behavioral performance. Methods can be *direct* or *indirect*. Direct assessment methods measure behavior at the time and place of its actual occurrence. Thus, direct observations of behavior in naturalistic settings (e.g., classrooms, playgrounds, etc.) and self-monitoring of ongoing behavior represent direct assessment because they measure behavior at the time and place it occurs. Indirect assessment methods are removed in time and place from the occurrence of behavior and, by definition, represent measurement of behavior that has already occurred in other settings. Informant behavior ratings, interviews, and self-reports of behavior represent indirect assessment methods.

Social skills assessment methods can also vary according to the purpose of assessment: identification/classification or intervention. Assessment procedures are classified as identification/classification or intervention techniques based on the extent to which these procedures yield a *functional analysis of behavior*. In this view, if the assessment procedure identifies the antecedent, sequential, and consequent conditions surrounding social behavior, then the procedure is primarily useful for intervention purposes. If the procedure does not yield functional analysis information, then it is useful primarily for identification/classification purposes.

Finally, social skills assessment methods can vary according to the specificity of information the method provides. Some assessment information may yield global information reminicient of personality traits (e.g., friendly, cooperative, likable). This information is not particularly useful in identifying specific social skills for intervention. Other assessment information provides a moderate level of specificity (e.g., initiates conversations with peers, joins ongoing play activities, helps others). This information is more useful in identifying target behaviors in which the

TABLE 2
Sample Items from Social Skills Rating System

Cooperation

Complies with directions
Attends to instructions
Cooperates with peers
Requests help appropriately

Assertion

Invites others to play
Initiates conversations with peers
Joins ongoing activity or group
Introduces self to new people

Responsibility

Answers phone appropriately
Appropriately questions rules that may be unfair
Asks permission before using another person's property
Requests permission to leave the house

Empathy

Feels sorry for others when bad things happen to them
Lets friends know he/she likes them by telling or showing them
Listens to friends when they talk about problems they are having
Says nice things to others when they have done something well

Self Control

Responds appropriately to physical aggression
Receives criticism well
Controls temper in conflict situations
Responds appropriately to teasing

---

child may be deficient. Finally, some assessment procedures yield very molecular information regarding social behavior. This type of assessment can be characterized as a task analysis of a moderate level of specificity. For example, the skill of initiating a conversation with peers might have 8–10 subtasks that must be identified for each social skill.

Table 3 presents an outline of the dimensions along which the assessment of social skills can vary. Table 4 provides an assessment sequence for social skills and lists the types of information obtained from each method.

Questions to Be Answered from Assessment

Table 5 presents a series of assessment questions that should be answered

in a comprehensive social skills assessment. Perhaps the most basic distinction to be made in social skills assessment is the distinction between *acquisition* and *performance deficits*. In other words, one must separate social behaviors that are "can't do" problems from those that are "won't do" problems. Intervention strategies differ for acquisition and performance deficits and, as such, this basic distinction is essential. Social skills training strategies for acquisition deficits must involve teaching the skill using procedures such as modeling and/or coaching. In contrast, social skills training strategies for performance deficits should focus on increasing the **frequencies** of behavior rather than teaching the skill.

Another important issue is the presence of interfering behaviors. Problem behaviors such as anxiety, aggression,

TABLE 3
Classification of Social Skills Assessment Procedures

I. **Different Sources of Information**
   A. Teacher Ratings
   B. Parent Ratings
   C. Trained Observers
   D. Peer Sociometrics
   E. Self-Reports/Role Plays

II. **Temporal and Physical Proximity to Performance**
   A. Direct Methods
      1. Naturalistic observations of ongoing behavior
      2. Self-monitoring of ongoing behavior
   B. Indirect Methods
      1. Ratings by others (Teacher and Parent)
      2. Self-reports
      3. Interviews with significant others
      4. Interview with child
      5. Analogue role play

III. **Specificity of Behavior**
   A. Global — Molar descriptions of characteristics
      Example: Friendly, Outgoing, Assertive, etc.
   B. Moderate Specificity — Specification of behavior in terms of behavioral events
      Example: Invites peers to play; Praises peers; Cooperates with peers
   C. Molecular Level of Specificity — Specification of behavior in terms of discrete and
      sequenced behavioral units that makeup a behavioral event
      Example: Invites Peers to Play
      1. Stops ongoing play activity
      2. Looks at peer(s) in close proximity
      3. Asks peer(s) to join activity
      4. Plays game or activity with invited peer

IV. **Purpose of Assessment**
   A. Classification/Diagnosis
      1. Sociometrics
      2. Ratings by others
      3. Self-report
      4. Behavioral role play
   B. Intervention/Therapy
      1. Behavioral interviews
      2. Direct observations
      3. Self-monitoring

Key Distinction: The degree to which each assessment yields information useful for a functional
analysis of behavior.

impulsivity, excessive motor movement, and noncompliance can either prevent the acquisition or performance of socially skilled behaviors. If these types of behaviors are present, then social skills training strategies must necessarily target these behaviors for reduction and elimination in addition to teaching or increasing the *frequencies* of social skilled behaviors.

Assessing the cross-situational generality or situational specificity of socially skilled and interfering behaviors is crucial to an adequate social skills assessment. This information helps in not only a functional analysis of behavior, but also yields information than may be useful in assessing the generalization of social skills training effects.

TABLE 4
Assessment Sequence for Social Skills and Types of Information Obtained

1. **Teacher Ratings of Social Skills**
   A. Estimation of frequency of behaviors
   B. Estimation of behavior's importance to teacher
   C. Tentative estimation of skill and performance deficits
   D. Guidelines for teacher interview and direct observations

2. **Parent Ratings of Social Skills**
   A. Estimation of cross-setting generality of deficits
   B. Parent's perceived importance of social behaviors
   C. Guideline for parent interview

3. **Teacher Interview**
   A. Further delineation of target behaviors
   B. Functional analysis of behavior in specific situations
   C. Selection of target behaviors based upon importance ratings and teacher's rankings
   D. Guideline for development of observation code

4. **Parent Interview**
   (SAME AS TEACHER INTERVIEW ABOVE)

5. **Direct observation of classroom behavior**
   A. Functional analysis of behavior
   B. Direct measurement of behavior in applied setting
   C. Observation of peer reactions to target child's behavior

6. **Sociometrics using liked most and liked least nominations**
   A. Measurement of social preference and social impact
   B. Classification of sociometric status (rejected, neglected, controversial)

7. **Self-report of social skills — obtain child's perception of social behavior**

8. **Child interview**

Perhaps the most crucial information from any assessment procedure for intervention purposes is **functional analysis information.** A functional analysis of behavior reveals the antecedent, sequential, and consequent events surrounding the behavior or behaviors in question. Knowing which events surrounding the behavior or behaviors in question. Knowing which events precede and follow behavior allows one to design interventions based on manipulating antecedent and/or consequent events to increase or decrease frequencies of behaviors. Assessments without functional analysis information are not useful for intervention purposes. Most traditional psychoeducational reports are not particularly useful for academic interventions because they lack functional analysis information.

Another important piece of information is the student's sociometric status in the classroom. Using the system developed by Coie, Dodge, and Coppotelli (1982), sociometric status is important because it provides a measure of how a child's peers feel about the target student. In addition, various sociometric statuses have known behavioral correlates (Coie, et al., 1982) and are good long-term predictors of maladjusted outcomes (Parker & Asher, 1987). For example, children who are *rejected* by peers typically have low frequencies of socially skilled behaviors and high frequencies of externalizing behaviors such as aggressive behavior, disruptive behavior, and noncompliant behavior (Coie et al., 1982; Gresham & Elliott, 1989). In contrast, socially *neglected* children usually have low rates of socially skilled behaviors, particularly assertion and social initiation, and high rates of internalizing behaviors such as anxiety, social withdrawal, and depressive behaviors.

The remainder of questions in Table 5 relate to socially valid ways of selecting target behaviors using teachers' importance ratings and deciding potential interventions and settings in which interventions can be implemented. Once an adequate assessment has been conducted, you are ready to decide what interventions will be used in social skills training.

Classification of Social Skills Deficits

Most authors agree that social incompetencies observed in children can result from difficulties in response acquisition or response performance (Bandura, 1977). Kratochwill and French (1984), for example, remarked that response acquisition (i.e., skill deficits) "occur when the individual has not learned skills that are necessary to exhibit a socially competent response", whereas performance deficits "arise when the child fails to successfully perform behaviors he or she is capable of" (p. 332). Gresham and Elliott (1984) extended this two-way classification scheme to include four general areas of social skills problems. As shown in Figure 1, this scheme of social skill difficulties distinguishes between whether or not a child knows how to perform the target skill and whether interfering behaviors are present (e.g., anxiety, impulsivity, aggressiveness).

Social skills acquisition deficits. This type of social skill problem characterizes children who have not acquired the necessary social skills to interact appropriately with others or to those who have failed to learn a critical step in the performance of the skill sequence. Social skill acquisition deficits describe a "can't do" rather than a "won't do" problem. Differentiation of acquisition from performance deficits is crucial because intervention strategies differ for these two types of problems.

Social skill acquisition deficits with interfering problem behaviors. This social skill problem describes a child for whom emotional (e.g., anxiety, sadness) and/or behavioral (e.g., verbal aggression, excessive motor movement) responses prevent or interfere with social skill acquisition. Anxiety is one such emotional arousal response shown to prevent acquisition of appropriate coping behaviors, particularly with respect to fears and phobias (Bandura, 1977). Thus, a child may not learn to interact effectively with others because social anxiety inhibits social approach behaviors. Impulsivity, a tendency toward short response latencies, is another interfering behavior that can block social skill acquisition (Kendall & Braswell, 1985). Other interfering problem behaviors that may be classified as *internalizing* (e.g., depression, phobias) and/or *externalizing* (e.g., disruptiveness, aggression) problems (Achenbach & Edelbrock, 1983) can block acquisition of socially skilled behaviors.

Social skills performance deficits. Children with social skills performance deficits have appropriate social skills in their repertoires, but fail to perform these behaviors at an acceptable level or at appropriate times. Performance deficits represent "Won't do" as opposed to "Can't do" problems. Usually, social skills performance deficits are best remediated by manipulating antecedents and/or consequences of behavior to facilitate increased frequencies of desired target behaviors.

Social skills performance deficits with interfering problem behaviors. Children with social skill performance deficits accompanied by interfering problem behaviors have a given social skill in their behavioral repertoires, but performance of the skill is hindered by an emotional or overt problem behavior response and by problems in antecedent and/or consequent control. These types of social skills deficits are best understood from the perspective of *concurrent schedules of reinforcement*. A concurrent schedule or reinforcement refers to the reinforcement of two or more behaviors according to two or more schedules of reinforcement at the same time. Based on the **Matching Law,** response rate will

TABLE 5
Questions to Be Answered from Assessment Results

1. Which behaviors are skill deficits and which behaviors are performance deficits?

2. Are interfering behaviors present?

3. Does the behavior(s) occur cross-situationally?

4. What is the functional analysis of the behaviors?
    A. What events precede the occurrence of interfering behaviors?
    B. What events follow the occurrence of interfering behaviors?
    C. Does the classroom environment set the occasion for social skills to occur?
    D. Do peers or teachers reinforce, ignore, or punish socially skilled behaviors?

5. Do classroom observations agree with teacher ratings and teacher interview?

6. What is the child's sociometric status in the classroom?
    Rejected: Interfering behaviors likely to be aggressive, disruptive behaviors
    Neglected: Interfering behaviors likely to be social withdrawal, anxiety, etc.
    Controversial: Child likely to have combination of socially skilled behaviors and
        externalizing behaviors (disruption, aggressive behavior, etc.).

7. What behaviors are not occurring that teacher considers critical for classroom success?

8. What behaviors are not occurring that teacher does not consider critical or important for classroom success?

9. What is the child's perception of his/her own social behavior and sociometric status?

10. What interventions are likely to be successful with this child?

11. Can these interventions be implemented in the classroom?

12. If classroom-based interventions are not feasible, can these interventions be implemented through other means?

match reinforcement rate (McDowell, 1982). Thus, if interfering problem behaviors are reinforced more frequently relative to socially skilled behaviors, the problem behaviors will occur more frequently (i.e., they will match the reinforcement rate).

Interventions for these types of deficits include reductive procedures for problem behaviors as well as antecedent and/or consequent control procedures to increase frequencies of socially skilled behaviors. Interventions must therefore focus on two general classes of behavior; (a) interfering problem behavior and (b) socially skilled behavior. In many cases, it may be necessary to intervene first on problem behaviors before effective social skills intervention can occur.

BEST PRACTICES

Social skills intervention strategies can be conceptualized as impacting on different dimensions of student's social environments. A popular model that captures these dimensions is known as the **SORC Model** (Kanfer & Phillips, 1970). In this model, social behavior can be changed by manipulating *S*timulus events (i.e., people, antecedent environmental events, etc.) that precede behavior in order to make certain social behaviors more probable. *O*rganismic events (mediational processes such as thoughts, emotions, etc.) can also be a focus of intervention. *R*esponses (overt behaviors in relation to a stimulus event) can serve as a third focus of intervention. Finally, *C*onsequences can be manipulated to increase socially skilled behaviors and to decrease frequencies of interfering problem behaviors. Figure 2 presents the SORC Model as an example of how behavior has different **treatment impact points** depending upon the focus of intervention.

	Acquisition Deficit	**Performance Deficit**
Interfering Problem Behaviors Absent	Social Skills Acquistion Deficit ("Can't Do")	Social Skills Performance Deficit ("Won't Do")
Interfering Problem Behaviors Present	Social Skills Acquisition Deficit with Interfering Problem Behaviors	Social Skills Performance Deficit with Interfering Problem Behaviors

FIGURE 1. Classification of social skills problems.

Figure 3 presents an alternative model that captures the same basic ideas as the SORC Model with several elaborations. This is labeled the **Social Skills Flowchart** and is intended to depict a sequence of events that can affect social behavior in specific situations. Social skill deficiencies can result from problems at any one of the steps in the Social Skills Flowchart. Note that Figure 3 denotes treatment impact points similar to the SORC model.

First, as in the SORC Model, **all** behavior occurs in a Context. The **Context** is defined as the setting within which a social behavior occurs. For example, a classroom or playground can be a context in which certain social behaviors are more probable than others. Manipulation of contexts can result in changes in social behaviors and thus serve as a treatment impact point.

Second, **Past Learning History,** represents the skills, abilities, and past experiences a child brings to the context. An individual's past learning history has an effect on how that individual might act within a given context. Learning history, however, does not represent a treatment impact point because it cannot be manipulated or changed. Past Learning History can explain, in part, why individuals act as they do, but it is not a variable that receives emphasis in this particular model.

The Cue refers to specific antecedent events that prompts or sets the occasion for persons to act in specific ways. Cues are equivalent to *discriminative stimuli* in operant learning theory which are defined as antecedent events that signal or cue that certain behaviors will be reinforced. Cues can be rather easily manipulated to prompt social behaviors already in children's behavioral repertoires.

The Menu refers to all of the available behaviors an individual has in his/her repertoire with respect to the Cue. That

Once the analysis of the SSRS ratings has been completed, it is possible to develop general intervention strategies. A rather extensive social skills treatment literature exists and is reviewed in the accompanying manual. Four basic treatment approaches emerge from this literature: (1) modification of antecedents, (2) modification of consequences, (3) modeling of desired behaviors, and (4) cognitive coaching and problem-solving. Each of these is briefly defined as follows:

Modification of Antecedents —

Modification of Consequences —

Modeling of Desired Behavior —

Coaching & Problem-Solving —

The application of any treatment procedure requires specialized training. Individuals knowledgeable of these four basic treatment strategies will recognize that their use will be dependent on (1) the severity of the social skills deficits, (2) the existence of interfering behaviors, and (3) the resources available to facilitate treatment implementation.

The figure below highlights that for any behavior, prosocial or antisocial, there are 4 main treatment impact points.

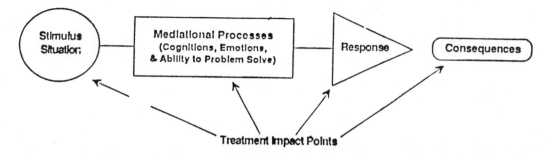

In general, it is easiest to manipulate the stimulus (antecedent) and consequences. However, in many cases of acquisition deficits it will be necessary to use modeling and/or coaching procedures to change mediational process and the target child's overt response.

FIGURE 2. Linking Assessment to Interventions.

---

is, persons usually have a number of behavioral *choices* within particular contexts and in response to certain cues. Persons with rather limited behavioral menus will have few socially skilled choices in given situations.

The Read refers to selection from a behavioral menu in a given social situation. Some social skills problems result from making the wrong read from an otherwise large menu of socially skilled behaviors. The difficult thing about socially skilled behavior is that correct and incorrect choices change as a function of nuances in social situations. Some interventions must focus on having children make the correct read in given social situations.

The Behavior represents the actual behavior a child demonstrates. Problems in social skills can occur because behavioral enactments of a social skill are not functional in obtaining reinforcement from the environment. For example, a behavioral enactment may be technically correct in the sense of inclusion of requisite subskills of a social skill, however, the *form* or *quality* of the behavioral enactment may be ineffective.

Finally, **The Outcome** represents the consequences that ensue from the action or behavioral enactment of social skill. Outcomes may be short term or long term. For example, a short term outcome for a problem behavior (e.g., verbal aggression toward a teacher) may be peer reinforce-

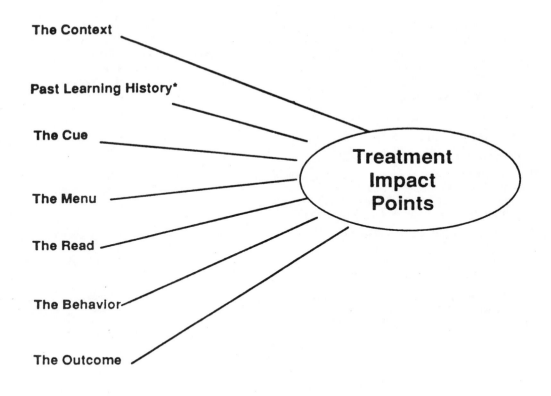

*Because an individual's learning history cannot be changed, this does not represent a treatment impact point. Learning history, however, does influence behavior.

FIGURE 3. Social skills flowchart.

ment. However, a long-term outcome of such behavior may be referral to special education or school suspension. Both of these outcomes may have the effect of removing the child from the peer group and subsequent adverse consequences for a child's social development.

Interventions for social skills problems can be focused on one or more of the treatment impact points represented in the Social Skills Flowchart. With the exception of past learning history, all components in the flowchart represent a treatment impact point. The key in designing social skills interventions is to decide for an individual where in the flowchart the problem exists. This requires comprehensive assessment of the child's social skills and an adequate functional analysis of behavior.

Figure 4 depicts another way of conceptualizing social skills interventions. This conceptualization views social skills intervention as consisting of four steps or stages: (a) facilitation of skill acquisition, (b) enhancement of skill performance, (c) removal of interfering problem behaviors, and (d) generalization of trained social skills. This view of social skills training is based on the model developed by Ladd and Mize (1983) and represents a useful heuristic for designing social skills interventions.

Page constraints of the present volume prevent a detailed discussion of social skills training strategies, however, the general principles of social skills intervention presented here should lead to better practices. Readers are referred to the chapter by Elliott and Ershler (this

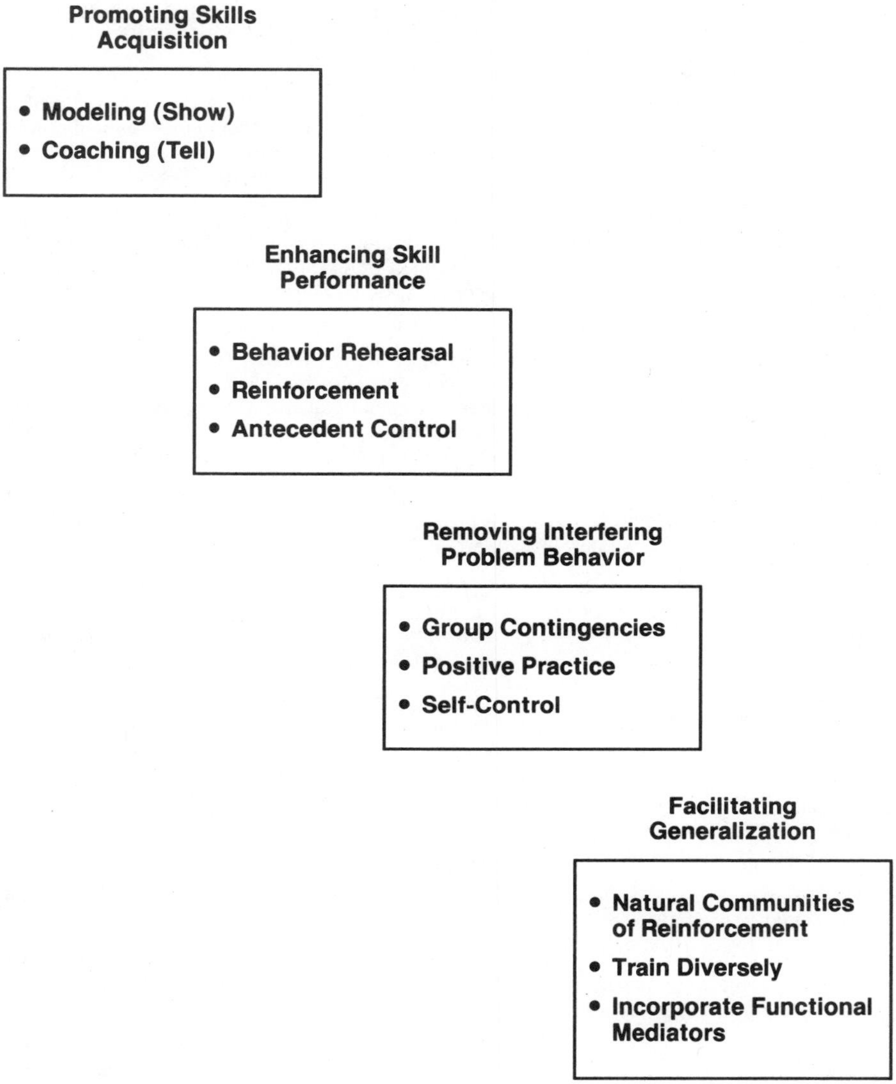

**Promoting Skills
Acquisition**

- **Modeling (Show)**
- **Coaching (Tell)**

**Enhancing Skill
Performance**

- **Behavior Rehearsal**
- **Reinforcement**
- **Antecedent Control**

**Removing Interfering
Problem Behavior**

- **Group Contingencies**
- **Positive Practice**
- **Self-Control**

**Facilitating
Generalization**

- **Natural Communities
  of Reinforcement**
- **Train Diversely**
- **Incorporate Functional
  Mediators**

FIGURE 4. Stages and conceptualization of social skills training.

volume) for additional information on this topic as well as the Annotated Bibliography at the end of this chapter.

Summary. Social skills represent an important domain of behavior in school settings because students showing social skill and peer acceptance problems tend to have long-term maladjusted outcomes such as dropping out of school, delinquency, adult criminal behavior, and adult psychopathology. Social skills and peer acceptance status differentiate mildly handicapped from nonhandicapped students. On the average, mildly handicapped students are between the 2nd and 16th percentile in social skill functioning and peer acceptance status of nonhandicapped students. Finally, teacher-preferred social skills are considered to be critical for classroom success. Deviations from the model behavior profile often result in students being referred to an subsequently placed in special education (Hersh & Walker, 1983; Gresham & Reschly, 1988; Walker & Rankin, 1983).

Social skills training strategies can be conceptualized as targeting different treatment impact points depending on the functional analysis of the social skill deficit. The SORC model and the Social Skills Flow Chart (Content, Learning History, Cue, Menu, Read, Behavior, and Outcome) were discussed as conceptual heuristics for designing social skills interventions.

REFERENCES

Achenbach, T., & Edelbrook, C. (1983). *Child Behavior Checklist and Profile.* Burlington, VT: University of Vermont.

Achenbach, T., McConaughy, S., & Howell, C. (1987). Child/adolescent behavioral and emotional problems: Implications of cross-informant correlations for situational specificity. *Psychological Bulletin, 101,* 213-232.

Bandura, A. (1977). *Social learning theory.* Englewood Cliffs, NJ: Prentice-Hall.

Clark, L., Gresham, F. M., & Elliott, S. N. (1985). Development and validation of a social skills assessment measure: The TROSS-C. *Journal of Psychoeducational Assessment, 4,* 347-356.

Coie, J., Dodge, K., & Coppotelli, H. (1982). Dimensions and types of social status: A cross-age perspective. *Developmental Psychology, 18,* 557-570.

Goldstein, A. C. (1980). *Skillstreaming the adolescent.* Champaign, IL: Research Press.

Gresham, F. M. (1981). Social skills training with handicapped children. *Review of Educational Research, 51,* 139-176.

Gresham, F. M. (1983). Social validity in the assessment of children's social skills: Establishing standards for social competency. *Journal of Psychoeducational Assessment, 1,* 297-307.

Gresham, F. M. (1985). Utility of cognitive-behavioral procedures for social skills training with children: A review. *Journal of Abnormal Child Psychology, 13,* 411-433.

Gresham, F. M. (1988). Social competence and motivational characteristics of learning disabled students. In M. Wang, M. Reynolds, & H. Walberg (Eds.), *Handbook of special education: Research and practice* (Vol. 2) (pp. 283-302). Oxford, England: Pergamon Press.

Gresham, F. M., & Elliott, S. N. (1990). *Social Skills Rating System.* Circle Pines, MN: American Guidance Service.

Gresham, F. M., Elliott, S. N., & Black, F. L. (1987). Teacher-rated social skills of mainstreamed mildly handicapped and nonhandicapped children. *School Psychology Review, 16,* 78-88.

Gresham, F. M., & Reschly, D. J. (1987). Dimensions of social competence: Method factors in the assessment of adaptive behavior, social skills, and peer acceptance. *Journal of School Psychology, 25,* 367-387.

Gresham, F. M., & Reschly, D. J. (1988). Issues in the conceptualization, classification, and assessment of social skills in the mildly handicapped. In T. Kratochwill (Ed.), *Advances in School Psychology* (pp. 203-248). Hillsdale, NJ: Erlbaum.

Grossman, H. (Ed.) (1983). *Classification in mental retardation.* Washington, DC: American Association on Mental Deficiency.

Hazel, S., & Schumaker, J. (1988). Social skills deficits. In J. Kavanagh & T. Truss (Eds.), *Learning disabilities: Proceedings of the National Conference* (pp. 293-366). Parkton, MD: York Press.

Hersh, R., & Walker, H. (1983). Great expectations: Making schools effective for all students. *Policy Studies Review, 2,* 147-188.

Kanfer, F., & Phillips, J. (1970). *Learning foundations of behavioral therapy.* New York: Wiley.

Kendall, P., & Braswell, L. (1985). *Cognitive-behavioral therapy for impulsive children.* New York: Guilford Press.

Kratochwill, T., & French, D. (1984). Social skills training for withdrawn children. *School Psychology Review, 13,* 331-338.

Ladd, G., & Mize, J. (1983). A cognitive-social learning model of social skill training. *Psychological Review, 82,* 127-157.

Leland, H. (1978). Theoretical considerations of adaptive behavior. In A. Coulter & H. Morrow (Eds.), *Adaptive behavior: Concepts and measurements.* New York: Grune & Stratton.

Litow, L., & Pumroy, D. (1975). A review of classroom group-oriented contingencies. *Journal of Applied Behavior Analysis, 8,* 341-347.

McDowell, J. J. (1982). The importance of Hernstein's mathematical statement of the Law of Effect for behavior therapy. *American Psychologist, 37,* 771-779.

Parker, J., & Asher, S. (1987). Peer relations and later personal adjustment: Are low-accepted children at risk? *Psychological Bulletin, 102,* 357-389.

Schneider, B., & Bryne, B. (1985). Children's social skills: A meta-analysis. In B. Schneider, K. Rubin, & J. Ledingham (Eds.), *Children's peer relations: Issues in assessment and intervention* (pp. 175–192). New York: Springer-Verlag.

Schumaker, J., Hazel, S., & Pederson, C. (1988). *Social skills for daily living: A curriculum.* Circle Pines, MN: American Guidance Service.

Stephens, T. (1978). *Social skills in the classroom.* Columbus, OH: Cedars Press.

Stokes, T., & Baer, D. (1977). An implicit technology of generalization. *Journal of Applied Behavior Analysis, 19,* 349–367.

Stokes, T., & Osnes, P. (1986). Programming the generalization of children's social behavior. In P. Strain, M. Guralnick, & H. Walker (Eds.). *Children's social behavior: Development, assessment, and modification.* (pp. 407–443). New York: Academic Press.

Strain, P., & Fox, J. (1981). Peers as behavior change agents for withdrawn classmates. In B. Lahey & A. Kazdin (Eds.), *Advances in clinical child psychology* (pp. 167–198). New York: Plenum Press.

Stumme, V., Gresham, F. M. & Scott, N. (1982). Validity of Social Behavior Assessment in discriminating emotionally disabled from nonhandicapped students. *Journal of Behavioral Assessment, 4,* 327–342.

Walker, H., & McConnell, S. (1988). *Walker–McConnell Scale of Social Competence and School Adjustment.* Austin, TX: Pro-Ed.

Walker, H. M. & Rankin, R. (1983). Assessing the behavioral expectations and demands of less restrictive settings. *School Psychology Review, 12,* 274–284.

Wolf, M. M. (1978). Social validity: The case for subjective measurement or how applied behavior analysis is finding its heart. *Journal of Applied Behavior Analysis, 11,* 203–214.

ANNOTATED BIBLIOGRAPHY

Strain, P., Guralnick, M., & Walker, H. (Eds.) (1986). *Children's social behavior: Development, assessment, and modification.* Orlando, FL: Academic Press.

This edited book represents one of the best and up-to-date volumes on children's social skills. Chapters that are particularly good are those on sociometric assessment, naturalistic observation of social behavior, and programming generalization of children's social behavior.

Schneider, B., Rubin, K., & Ledingham, J. (Eds.) (1985). *Children's peer relations: Issues in assessment and intervention.* New York: Springer-Verlag.

This edited volume contains 15 chapters by leading experts in children's social behavior. Excellent chapters include selecting treatment objectives, influence of evaluator on social skill assessment, fitting social skills intervention to the target group, meta-analysis of social skills training effects, and program evaluation of social skills training.

Schumaker, J., Hazel, S., & Pederson, C. (1988). *Social skills for daily living.* Circle Pines, MN: American Guidance Service.

This is a curriculum for adolescents and young adults aged 12-21. It is designed primarily for individuals with mild handicaps (e.g., learning disabilities, behavior disorders, mild mental retardation) although it can be used with general student populations. Major curricular components include: (a) Conversation and Friendship Skills, (b) Getting Along with Others, and (c) Problem-Solving Skills.

Walker, H., Todis, B., Holmes, D., & Horton, G. (1988). *The Walker Social Skills Curriculum: The ASSESS Program.* Austin, TX: PRO-ED.

This curriculum is designed for adolescents with mild handicaps and is based on principles of direct instruction. The ASSESS teaches 31 social skills distributed across three broad social skill domains: (a) Peer-Related Social Skills, (b) Adult-Related Social Skills, and (c) Self-Related Social Skills. The curriculum is designed for small group (5 or fewer) instruction and uses scripted lessons.

Gresham, F. M., & Elliott, S. N. (1990). *Social Skills Rating System.* Circle Pines, MN: American Guidance Service.

The Social Skills Rating System (SSRS) is a nationally standardized series of rating scales using multiple raters (teacher, parent, and student) for students ages 3-18. The SSRS has three forms (preschool, elementary and secondary) and measures two broad domains for social competence: Social Skills and Problem Behaviors. Within the Social Skills domain, subscales include Cooperation, Assertion, Responsibility Empathy, and Self Control. Within the Problem Behavior domain, subscales include Externalizing, Internalizing, and Hyperactivity problems. The teacher scale also includes an Academic Competence Measure, which is a rating scale of reading, mathematics, language, and achievement motivation.

48

Best Practices in Teaching Study Skills

Joan Eklund Kuepper
J. Kuepper Enterprises
Burlington, Iowa

OVERVIEW

Underlying a majority of everyday issues or questions directed to the school psychologist is academic underachievement. Relatively independent of intellectual results or even of formal achievement results are the factors of study and organizational skills. For students suspected of lacking such skills, assessment of daily functioning in respect to various classroom survival techniques will generate information needed to make meaningful recommendations for remediation. Observing and comparing students at work yields a wealth of insights into the sources of the apparent deficit, which may be further validated by records review, teacher interviews, student interviews, and analysis of work samples.

Intervention with practical, short-term training in study and organizational skills, to be provided directly by the school psychologist or others trained through in-services, frequently eliminates the need for more extensive programming. The choices of training methods are extensive, thus allowing individualized selection. Improvement in academic achievement can be dramatic. Additional benefits are less frustration at home as well as at school with improvement of morale and confidence for students and parents.

"If one thinks of education itself as a mixture of content which is the subject matter and process which is the means by which content is acquired, the reasons for a study skills program become clear" (La Voie, 1980). Setting realistic and specific study skills goals is highly valued by all those who have an investment in increasing achievement including students, teachers, parents, counselors, administrators, and society as a whole.

The skills discussed in this chapter were selected for the basic nature of their application. References cited are most often practitioner-oriented interventions. The reader will detect many openings for teaching to assessed weaknesses. A choice is made at staffing level whether training is to be directly assumed by the school psychologist or planned for collaboration or others to complete. Many citations are authored by teachers of specific content areas who have researched study skills. Most strategies are integrated into curriculum and readily transferable. The goal of this chapter is to aid in the determination of who is best suited to direct an intervention, what skills to teach, and in what manner.

DEFINITION AND DESCRIPTION OF STUDY SKILLS TEACHING

"Studying is effective when students process the 'right' information in the 'right' way" (Armbruster & Anderson, 1981). On the basis of this belief, the teaching of study skills began in the mid-1940s with primary emphasis on instruction in a highly specific set of behaviors that were targeted towards particular skills areas (Marshak & Burkle, 1981). Skills such as general organization, efficient use of time, effective note-taking, test-taking tactics, organizers for reading comprehension or writing formats were included as teaching units. The gradual awareness that many such isolated techniques did not transfer well to everyday performance, however, resulted in a changed focus.

At present, most researchers and teachers place primary emphasis on relating skills teaching to daily tasks. Ample time must be allowed to practice new study skills once they have been taught, the most recommended procedure being use of daily homework with present curriculum assignments. Emphasis must be given to directly facilitating transfer and generalization to other, similar learning and studying tasks (Herber & Herber, 1987).

In teaching study skills various techniques can be employed, but pacing and purpose must be planned with the stages of cognitive development in mind. A general plan for teaching study skills by Loene (1983) includes the following steps: (a) pinpoint and define the area to be taught; (b) describe the entire procedure including assessment, monitoring, and reinforcement; (c) model or teach the technique; (d) gradually increase students' independence while continuing to lead through the procedure with less emphasis on guidance and more on monitoring; (e) practice for full transfer to other settings or mainstreamed settings; (f) provide feedback on a regular basis and reteach or use alternative strategies if setbacks are encountered; and (g) evaluate the entire process before terminating the effort.

BASIC CONSIDERATIONS

When contemplating interventions to improve study skills, there are several parameters to consider before developing a plan.

Assessment

Whether planning direct individual or small-group work or indirect consultation with a parent, teacher, or counselor, time must be devoted to becoming acquainted with the students' present level of performance and school attitude; rapport building is essential. In order to determine whether a student truly has a study skill deficit as opposed to basic motivational problems, low intelligence, or poor self-confidence, it is necessary to briefly assess current study strategies and not just study habits. Following a folder review, there are several techniques that lend themselves well to this effort. Observing students while they work followed by an interview to document their perception of what has occurred can be most helpful. Observations can be made in class or privately depending upon the referral questions. When working one-to-one a talk-aloud system can also be added to clarify each step in a student's study reasoning. If a more standardized approach is desired, a checklist or structured interview can be used with results compared to data collected from a teacher or parent. Examination of work samples can provide some direction prior to a meeting with the student or teacher in order to answer questions. Requesting samples from peers who have been given the same assignment may help establish criteria for evaluating quality of effort and organization. Questions can then be discussed as explanations clarify ambiguities or add new information to "complete the picture."

Consumers of Information

Although every study skills intervention is ultimately designed to enhance an individual student's skills, several other consumers may be highly involved in using assessment information. Counselors, teachers, and parents are often given responsibilities in study skills training or monitoring under the direction of the school psychologist. When implementation is to be the major responsibility of others, clearly stated recommendations based on research are invaluable. Care must be taken to speak at appropriate educational levels when parents or teacher associates are involved. One wants to give expert advise without using jargon or sounding judgmental. Encouragement to continue an intervention is essential for extended plans. The school psychologist must remain available to follow up and modify procedures, if necessary.

Counselors can be helpful in monitoring and communication. Their in-depth knowledge of the staff and student schedules contributes to making realistic plans. In collaborative efforts, counselors play strong roles in preliminary screening and post-training follow-up. Linking parent concerns to skill building needs is another area of counselor expertise to be utilized in interventions.

Enlisting parents' support for study skills practice is often the most important factor in successful implementation because many study issues involve homework. Among the several factors to consider when interviewing parents are (a) the expectations of *each* parent; (b) the characteristics of the setting in which homework is done; (c) the use made of the students' study time; (d) the availability of proper materials for completing projects; and (e) evidence of long-range planning (Kuepper, 1987). If students are given recommendations at school that are contrary to expectations at home, little will be accomplished in most cases.

Task-analyzing broad referral comments such as "missing work," "incomplete work," or "low test scores" into smaller interview or observation questions can help avoid wasting students' energies or parents' time in practicing unneeded or inappropriate methods. Either overestimating or underestimating time for completion of assignments can lead to poor results as a result of procrastination or rushing. Timing a student on a "one-page reading" or a "five-minute effort on a worksheet" can help establish meaningful time guidelines when the unit time is multiplied by number of pages. Parents value such specific suggestions paired with demonstrations using an assignment notebook, storing materials in color-coded folders, and properly handing in work in

required format. Helping both the student who is to practice the method and the parent who is involved in encouraging consistency frequently more than doubles the pace of learning.

The "ultimate" study assignment for many students who are underachieving is a major test. When they are taught to begin at least 2–3 days ahead to organize all information sources, to divide their total study time into several shorter study units for better concentration, and to "chunk" information into meaningful categories before starting to memorize, the approach of test day may no longer be so frightening for students nor frustrating for parents who "want to help but do not know how" (Kuepper, 1987b).

Most teachers welcome helpful information from the school psychologist regarding what study skills are being taught and by what method. Reinforcement in classroom practice increases learning pace and motivation. When advance organizers are offered by teachers before reading or oral instruction, many students recognize the general listening pattern for improved note-taking and comprehension.

Following observation in a classroom, a school psychologist can better assess to what degree a teacher is using best teaching practices and may choose to offer suggestions during consultation on a one-to-one basis. In reviewing best practices for teaching and studying, Burton and Meyers (1987) listed several factors that contribute to improved learning in class: (a) frequent teaching contact; (b) giving many examples, up to 50% of total teaching time; (c) requiring high response rates from student; (d) providing well-spaced and clear worksheets; (e) routinely correcting errors following practice or homework; (f) assigning homework only after successful classroom practice; (g) requiring organized work in folders; and (h) testing by means that avoid a high-anxiety atmosphere, time pressure, and overemphasis on neatness or spelling. Specially focused teaching for all students needing improvement at any step would be time well spent in the classroom.

Combining in-class study with homework and paying attention to correcting homework regularly and promptly will increase the likelihood that students will practice as needed (Nadler, 1987). Expecting students to share answers and procedures during homework discussions also helps students benefit from paraphrasing in everyday English. Indeed, a vocabulary list of key terms is seen as a priority by Birken (1986), as is outlining the lesson and referring to the page number in text for each question. The creation of student self-test items is also advocated. Encouraging students to discuss procedures with other students while working through assignments also leads to gains in achievement for students at middle to upper achievement levels.

Flexible Planning

When study skills projects are piloted in a school system, greater demand for such services commonly is created. To meet such demands, multiple strategies are necessary. Moving from individual to group efforts is one option, once procedures are well defined. A time line must be projected that from the beginning allows quality time for monitoring the transition to independence. If independence is not attained, a building-based staff member must eventually assume direct contact with the group. Well-defined goals should be agreed to by all participants. A communication plan is needed. One valuable outcome of such planning is the gradual accumulation of sample plans readily available for adapting to later referrals.

A school psychologist also helps extend the availability of services by serving, for various efforts, in several roles, such as facilitator, planner, team leader, consultant, co-teacher, peer tutor trainer, staff or parent in-service provider, parent counselor, and materials developer.

The degree of responsibility in carrying out a plan shifts as one moves from consultation, in which the total work of implementation will fall on others, to collaboration, in which the school psychologist will team with at least one other professional in supplying direct services. Rarely does a full schedule allow for extended collaboration or even more intensive services such as several sessions of one-to-one counseling. Increasing knowledge of curriculum and educational systems will be required as the variety of roles expands. Choices beyond format planning also include classroom versus nonclassroom settings, school versus home settings, curriculum content versus materials created by the school psychologist, mixing or not mixing achievement levels of participants in small-group work, regular education exclusively versus a blending with special education or special education exclusively, and single-disability versus mixed-disability groupings. The advantage to the student of choosing from a broad variety of techniques creates a need for reading and observing by the school psychologist.

Adjusting Expectations

Altering expectations and content to accommodate different grade or cognitive levels of students is imperative. Major ways of accomplishing this are to teach new procedures one at a time in content area already understood, to offer more examples of each technique while using daily coursework, to avoid overly complicated methods, and to reduce the number of techniques taught. Suggestions should not be made that conflict with ongoing classroom teaching unless a conference with the teacher has resolved the issue. Respect for individual style must be shown and included as a meaningful portion of any plan. When secondary students become involved in such projects, more time flexibility is needed by the school psychologist to accommodate the more rigid school schedules.

BEST PRACTICES

Motivation

One of the factors most critical to teaching study skills successfully is adequate motivation from the student. Factors that help build motivation are relevance, timely material, and a variety of approaches to meet individual needs. In nearly all cases, the school psychologist will need to work with or work through building-based staff in order to monitor a motivational approach. Stressing the need for student success is important. Recognizing effort as well as quality is a forgotten factor that grading teachers often forget. Prompt feedback that is honest but falls somewhere between "good" and "needs improvement" can help keep students on task without discouragement. Giving examples of how to task-analyze long assignments into shorter, more manageable ones can prove beneficial also.

Contracting for grades or other reinforcers can be effective if they are limited in scope and are fair, frequently reviewed, and actively adhered to by all parties including adult providers of the reinforcers. School psychologists have much to offer in writing clear behavioral objectives that are then evaluated for further planning. Appropriately using reinforcers to shift motivation from an external to a more internal basis allows gradual fading of formal programs in most cases.

School psychologists who regularly share research information on motivation with teachers can be, in turn, motivators for teachers to utilize new classroom techniques. Ammann and Mittelstadt (1987) identified four reactions to curriculum materials that damage motivation: (a) the cop-out attitude of doing only minimum requirements; (b) peer status concerns towards such help; (c) past negative experiences with "special help and special materials"; and (d) out-of-date materials. Even last year's fads hold little interest compared to this year's celebrities and topics. A reading project for high school students using the daily newspaper can be tailored to provide relief from standardized remedial material that students consider boring or "baby stuff." Breaking word-by-word reading habits and teaching note-taking skills are recommended as areas of emphasis.

The use of contests between students to become miniexperts on one small topic also enliven sessions. Prediction skills and use of tables can be practiced through reading schedules and graphs. Paraphrasing into more colloquial student language can also be taught as a summary skill. The challenge of "Prove It" adds personal interest and forces students to organize details to support a main idea.

Stone, 1984, emphasizing the problem of motivation for frustrated readers, found that an assignment of intermediate difficulty is the most motivating for students. Students are more committed if they clearly understand the goals of a lesson and the steps toward achievement are small and concise. Allowing students to help set goals and choose reinforcers helps continue motivation throughout the assignment. Stressing evaluation of performance more than grades is encouraging both in study skills teaching and in formal classwork.

A middle school approach that addressed motivation and self-concept in small groups was reported by Thompson (1987). Cleverly named the "Yegottawanna Group" (you have to want to), the class focussed in weekly sessions on the following subsets of problems and opportunities: (a) realizing potential; (b) starting from where each student is; (c) goal setting; (d) being teachable; (e) wanting to learn; (f) doing the work; (g) having self-discipline; (h) preparing for tests; and (i) self-responsibility.

Advance Organizers

The use of advance organizers by teachers and recognition of these techniques by students can greatly facilitate skills of reading, listening, and note-taking, thus helping comprehension. Improved comprehension often leads to improved daily achievement and test scores. School psychologists have a major contribution to offer in this important area by pairing teaching of student skills with monitoring of progress by teachers or counselors. Many teachers become more conscious of their own lecture and lesson presentations when made aware that students are being specifically counseled in practicing the skills of following directions and note-taking. What is heard in their classroom, what is written on their boards, what samples are provided for guidance, and what outlines are extended before listening or reading is expected, as well as the quality of review provided before each test, will become "content" for student awareness and use. If little teacher guidance is evident, a timely opportunity exists for school psychologists to offer informal inservice on the advisability of these previewing techniques.

Various systems of previewing reading assignments have been developed that stress the need to relate new material and concepts to what is already known. Sanacore (1982) advised utilizing Pauk's PQ4R reading organizer throughout all content areas. The six steps of previewing, questioning, reading, reflecting, reciting, and reviewing ensure student involvement with reading material. The fourth step, reflecting, is considered the most critical because it encourages students to utilize previously learned "background information" or images related to the textbook topic. The entire procedure can be taught and reviewed in small groups in two or three sessions with follow-up by a trainer who scans written evidence that questions were recorded and then answered. Session 1 utilizes more verbal prompting and examples; for Session 2 it is recommended that the unit be partially completed by the trainer and partially by the students. By Session 3 the students independently complete the entire study approach in the presence of the trainer, who is available to offer encouragement and answer questions.

Another system that allows time for discussion and reflection is the listen-read–discuss heuristic advanced by Manzo and Casale (1985). Here a teacher's oral presentation precedes the reading assignment, which is followed by whole-class discussion. Such methods build on the group effort of teacher, student, and textbook author as each contributes to the total knowledge base.

In order to take full advantage of oral advance organizers, a student must be cued to listen effectively. Occasional oral reading of a lesson, followed by pauses for questions and paraphrasing, has been recommended by Maring and Furman (1985) as a good method of building listening skills. As an advance organizer, they also recommend a visual study guide to help students anticipate what they will hear. Gleason, Herr, and Archer (1988) recommended stressing proximity of speaker to listener, use of chalkboard and diagrams, and direct instruction to listen such as "Be sure you listen for the five major points." Preteaching important vocabulary is also beneficial, as is cuing students to notice use of verbal inflections and organizational vocabulary such as, "finally" and "in summary." The use of pause procedures during presentation for listening and note-taking comparison is recommended by McAndrew (1983), who also reminded teachers that some students need additional time following listening to make notes. Seldom is such time allotted in classrooms even at middle school level.

Lectures that are presented in a logical order also greatly aid in note-taking. Inserting key questions to break the listening–writing routine draws attention to main elements, as does writing on the board. Announcing what type of test will be given also helps students organize their thinking and note-taking. Handouts to augment students' notes are also valuable study tools if the students use them for review. Note-takers can then add notes to these handouts for more complete preparation.

Helpful notes can be taken only at the level of a student's present understanding of the subject matter. Therefore, advance organizers are vitally important to emerging skills in this study area. Practice in any note-taking system selected will add to improvement. Jones (1983) suggested the utilization of picture-vocabulary presentations as an advance organizer to reading material, along with study guides written at mastery reading level for the student. Also suggested are pre-highlighting text, student summaries of lessons, tape recording of text, graphic organizers, and an overall reading survey method.

Linking the use of advance organizers that preview what will be taught and preteaching key vocabulary or terminology makes reading and listening comprehension stronger.

Listening Skills

Listening underlies several other study skills and can only occur after attention is given. Keeping one's eye on either the speaker or the material to which the speaker is referring, such as a diagram, filmstrip, or overhead material, helps maintain a listening focus. When writing notes is added to both looking and listening, the filtering of material can be strengthened even more. Research has shown that information written during listening will be remembered more powerfully because of both the visual factor of seeing the written image and the cognitive work of paraphrasing in order to decide what information is worthy of recording. Students who are cued to listen for various patterns of oral presentation can function with an auditory "outline" in mind (Kuepper, 1987a). Common patterns are cause and effect, compare and contrast, sequential principles or laws followed by examples, descriptions, pro and con statements, flow chart style, and visual examples followed by possible variations.

Following Directions

Despite its importance, little time is devoted in most classrooms to explicitly teaching the skills of following written or oral directions well. An easy-to-model system can be employed with very young elementary students by teaching them to use these steps when reading directions: (a) circle each action word; (b) number in order each action; and (c) cross out each number as that portion of the directions has been completed. For oral directions, the same actions in the same sequence are needed, but the student now has to begin by writing each action word as heard before ordering by number and starting to work (Kuepper, 1987a).

A four-step direct-instruction format is proposed by Henk and Helfeldt (1987): awareness, modeling, guided practice, and independent practice. Within each step there are specific practice suggestions and a recommendation to code the written directions before beginning. If students cannot read and understand directions, a demonstration or example is useful. For students who have spatial weaknesses pictorial representations or diagrams are often even more difficult to decipher than written instructions. Monitoring readiness to begin is, itself, a skill to be learned by practice. Visualizing one's way through a detailed procedure will often reveal where confusion may still exist. Such techniques may not occur to students unless specifically suggested and modeled aloud by the instructor.

Note-taking Skills

Making notes while reading or listening in order to highlight the key elements of an exposition is seen as a valuable learning aid. Researchers believe that a complex set of subskills, as yet not thoroughly delineated, contribute to the note-taking process. Various writers differentiate between note-taking and note-making, emphasizing that making notes is a higher-order skill. Note-making implies creating a new product that incorporates the learner's past knowledge.

Elementary efforts in note-taking most often follow one of these three formats: pictorial, topical, or critical (Giordano, 1982). Pictorial outlines can stress any aspect of content whether read or heard. Topical outlines generally answer one question per paragraph of text under study, which can be posed on a special teaching sheet. The right-hand side is used for questions associated with a copied column of print on the left. This system allows reading and writing on the same sheet. Critical outlining typically involves posing an oral question before reading or listening, thus setting out a specific purpose for the notes taken.

Outlining was taught at the middle school level by Schilling (1984), who used concepts and facts with which students were already familiar. The random list of statements was then organized into categories and sequence, thus creating an outline. Outlining is considered to be a far more complex skill than note-taking by several researchers, who concluded that some students may never outline well but all can learn some degree of proficiency in note-taking.

Clary (1986) offered a review of the Cornell Notetaking System in which a paper is divided into columns by drawing lines. Running notes are placed in the widest section (approximately 6 in.), and key terms and concepts are summarized in the narrower column after class presentation. Review is conducted by first scanning the narrow column, the wider column being unfolded only for answers not remembered. Reading students also use a 5W+H notebook to record information by answering questions as to who, what, where, when, why, and how. Styles of note-taking appear to be highly individualistic, however, and this is one area in which various approaches should perhaps be tried before selecting the most appropriate.

Eidson (1984) suggested that teachers be trained on separate note-taking systems for oral and written sources. For oral information, the following suggestions are made: (a) inviting a reporter from a newspaper to emphasize the importance of notes; (b) watching a drama and taking notes of the incident; and (c) taking notes on a brief paper presentation with pauses to discuss and review before proceeding. A further exploration of notes from varied sources is strongly recommended, including sound filmstrips, computer software, personal interviews, and audio recordings.

For training in notetaking from written sources, it is prudent to stress the use of main idea and key supporting factors. Brief reading of selections from current assignments are excellent materials to use in practice sessions. Other suggestions that may prove useful are (a) creating a notebook of different and equally helpful note-taking formats; (b) providing completed notes and asking students to write a summary from such material; (c) using peer tutors for comparison notes; (d) rewarding note-taking efforts with an open-notes test occasionally; and (e) giving academic credit for notes.

Comparing the results of note-taking efforts with others is a commonly used technique to bring some agreement as to what topics should be covered; it also allows for a demonstration that there are many "right" ways to cover the information. School psychologists can attend a brief presentation and then compare their notes with students' efforts. Use of the evening television news for the hearing-impaired is also recommended to provide students with a ready comparison of their notes with those of the caption writer (Saint-Amand, 1980). Use of overhead transparancies to share group agreement can be beneficial and they would remain available for later review.

Specifically addressing the study skills needs of learning-disabled students, Towle (1982) gave a thorough listing of strategies needed to organize materials and of all phases of note-taking and the related skills of underlining, listening, and outlining. Listing separate competencies for visual and auditory materials, Towle's proposals include reworking notes to force "handling" of information, writing sample exam questions, writing summaries, discussing with peers, and listing major parts.

Underlining is a simpler mode of "taking note" of information. Underlined materials covering appropriate concepts focus students' attention and test studying selection. Restricting students' underlining to one sentence per average paragraph forces judgment and involvement from students and requires a more active role. The time saved by underlining in lieu of note-taking or outlining can best be invested in reviewing the material underlined.

A process of gradual fading from total dependence upon teachers' or peers' notes to independent note-taking or underlining is provided by Saski (1983). Initially, teachers provide a full outline from which students copy while listening. Throughout later steps, however, more information is left blank and teachers give fewer cues and shorter pauses as the process continues.

Writing Skills

A return to a heavy emphasis on written expression is fully under way in most of today's curricula. More students are writing earlier, with generally encouraging results. For students who encounter difficulties in writing, however, the various tasks it entails can prove frustrating. Avoidance, with little opportunity for growth, can be the result. Writing skills are required from earliest primary grades to show evidence of learning by completing worksheets, answering test items, and summarizing reading or personally presented materials. The overall organization of written work helps direct teachers' attention to the quality of the concepts expressed. Gleason et al. (1988) referred to a system using the acronym HOW as a reminder system for paperwork format beginning in elementary grades. The *H* symbolizes heading requirements, the *O* refers to organization, and the *W* signifies writing neatly. Another acronym strategy, COPS, reminds students to check for the following main factors in error monitoring: Capitalize, Overall appearance, Punctuation, and Spelling (Wiens, 1983).

A spelling recheck procedure suggested by Gleason et al. (1988) is to look for the word in the assignment first, next search the text material, then search the glossary, and finally underline it for later dictionary reference or help from someone else. A final suggestion pending failure of other methods is to choose a different word. Giving students time, feedback, and praise for making such efforts can build motivation and comfort with such procedures.

Moran (1983) pointed out that structured, formula writing is helpful in organizing writing skills. Model paragraphs showing the main idea, followed by supporting statements and conclusions, can be examined as a student is interviewed and guided in clearly utilizing such elements in their assignments. Different strategies include enumerative, sequential, and compare-and-contrast. The enumerative pattern, by which information is organized along the lines of a list, is an approach that is appropriate when factors can be considered nonsequential and equal in value. The sequential pattern organizes a presentation along the lines of a flow chart with factors discussed in logical order, starting at the first step or earliest date, for example. A compare-and-contrast pattern is organized around a few key factors that are then individually discussed for similarities and differences. The benefit of such models is that time is spent on actual writing practice rather than just copying. Additional advice includes focusing on only one writing feature at a time with each proofreading pass. Students with significant writing skills problems cope best with comparison only with their own past efforts. Keeping feedback as positive as possible also helps self-confidence.

Group writing instruction and cooperative project writing can offer benefits of confidence and orderly procedure for students who avoid writing as an individual task. Davey (1987) presented a model of five steps that lead to a group-produced research paper: topic selection, planning, researching, organizing, and writing. Each step involves several study and interpersonal subskills, the end result being a sample product that can serve as a model for individually produced papers on a second effort. Likewise, a three-assignment design incorporating a readers/writers workshop approach that evolves from full class to individually completed reports is described by Schumm and Radencich (1984). Long-term efforts can be started by a school psychologist and then carried to completion through a team effort with the content area teacher.

SUMMARY

This chapter has described the evolution in the teaching of study skills from focusing primarily on isolated techniques to a more content-integrated and curriculum-relevant approach. Planning deliberately for motivation and transfer was stressed. Examples were given for a multitude of school psychologist roles, and general guidelines for implementation were suggested. A variety of examples were cited with priority placed on practical direct and indirect approaches in the study skills areas of motivation, advance organizers, listening, following directions, writing, and note-taking. The school psychologist who is knowledgeable about study skills can have important input into all phases of response to individual referrals as well as to system interventions.

REFERENCES

Ammann, T., & Mittelstadt, S. (1987). Turning on turned off students: Using newspapers with senior high remedial readers. *Journal of Reading, 8*(30), 708-715.

Armbruster, B., & Anderson, T. (1981). Research synthesis on study skills. *Research Information Service,* (November), 154-156.

Beck, I., & McKeown, M. (1985). Teaching vocabulary: Making instruction fit the goal. *Educational Perspectives, 23*(1), 11-15.

Birken, M. (9186). Teaching students how to study mathematics: A classroom approach. *Mathematics Teacher, 79*(6), 410-413.

Burton, G., & Meyers, M. (1987). Teaching mathematics to learning disabled students in the secondary classroom. *Mathematics Teacher, 80*(9), 702-709.

Clary, L. (1986). Six study techniques for reading/learning disabled adolescents. *Journal of Reading, 29*(5), 448-451.

Davey, B. (1987). Teams for success: Guiding practice in study skills through cooperative research reports. *Journal of Reading, 30*(8), 701-705.

Eidson, B. (1984). Make a note of it. *Clearing House, 57*(6), 266-268.

Ellis, E., & Lenz, B. (1987). A component analysis of effective learning strategies for learning disabled students. *Learning Disabilities Focus, 2*(2), 94-107.

Frager, A. (1984). An "intelligence" approach to vocabulary teaching. *Journal of Reading, 28*(2), 160-164.

Giordano, G. (1982). Outlining techniques that help disabled readers. *Academic Therapy, 17*(5), 517-522.

Gleason, M., Herr, C., & Archer, A. (1988). Study skills: Teaching study strategies. *Teaching Exceptional Children,* (Spring), 52-57.

Graves, M., & Prenn, M. (1986). Costs of benefits of various methods of teaching vocabulary. *Journal of Reading, 29*(7), 596-602.

Henk, W., & Helfedt, J. (1987). How to develop independence in following written directions. *Journal of Reading,* (April), 602-607.

Herber, H., & Herber, J. (1987). Developing independent learners. *Journal of Reading, 30*(7), 584-588.

Jones, M. (1983). Providing reading success for academically disadvantaged students. *Clearing House, 57*(4), 167-170.

Kuepper, J. (1987a). Assessment and remediation of study skill deficits. In *Psychological approaches to problems of children and adolescents* (Vol. 3, pp. 1-101). Des Moines, IA: Iowa Department of Education School Psychological Services.

Kuepper, J. (9187b). *Homework helpers: A guide for parents offering assistance.* Minneapolis, MN: Educational Media Corporation.

La Voie, R. (1980). *Program overview: The Cherry Hill Study Skills Program.* Cherry Hills, NJ.

Lenz, K. (1987). Activating the inactive learner: Advance organizers in the secondary content classroom. *Learning Disabilities Quarterly, 10*(1), 53-67.

Leone, P. (1983). Teaching learning disabled adolescents to monitor their behavior. *Pointer, 27*(2), 14-17.

Manzo, A., & Casale, U. (1985). Listen-read-discuss: A content reading heuristic. *Journal of Reading, 28*(8), 732-734.

Maring, G., & Furman, G. (1985). Seven "whole class" strategies to help mainstreamed young people read and listen better in content area classes. *Journal of Reading, 28*(8), 694-699.

Marshak, D., & Burkle, C. (1981). Learning to study: A basic skill. *Principal, 61*(2), 38-40.

McAndrew, D. (1983). Underlining and notetaking: Some suggestions from research. *Journal of Reading, 27*(2), 103-108.

Moran, M. (1983). Learning disabled adolescents' responses to a paragraph-organization strategy. *Pointer, 27*(2), 28-31.

Nadler, M. (1987). Homework reviews — a better way of communicating. *Mathematics Teacher, 80*(9), 726-732.

Saint-Amand, P. (1980). TV news and note-taking. *Journal of Reading, 23*(8), 678.

Sanacore, J. (1982). Transferring the PQR4 study procedure: Administrative concerns. *Clearing House, 55*(5), 234-236.

Saski, J. (1983). Notetaking formats for learning disabled adolescents. *Learning Disability Quarterly, 6*(3), 265-272.

Schilling, F. (1984). Teaching study skills in the intermediate grades — we can do more. *Journal of Reading, 27*(7), 620–623.

Schumm, J., & Radencich, M. (1984). Readers/writers workshops: An antidote to term paper terror. *Journal of Reading, 28*(1), 13–19.

Stone, N. (1984). Accentuate the positive: Motivation and reading for secondary students. *Journal of Reading, 27*(8), 684–690.

Suid, M. (1984). Look it up in the dogtionary . . . and other advice that will get kids interested in words. *Instructor, 93*(8), 52–54.

Thompson III, E. (1987). The "Yagottawanna" group: Improving student self-perceptions through motivational teaching of study skills. *School Counselor, 35*(2), 134–142.

Towle, M. (1982). Learning how to be a student when you have a learning disability. *Journal of Learning Disabilities, 15*(2), 90–93.

Wiens, W. (1983). Why teach cognitive strategies to adolescents? *Pointer, 27*(2), 5–7.

ANNOTATED BIBLIOGRAPHY

Gleason, M., Herr, C., & Archer, A. (1988). Study skills: Teaching study strategies. *Teaching Exceptional Children,* (Spring), 52–57.
A well-organized overview provides the purpose and content for teaching study strategies across all grade levels. A division of differences between gaining information and responding to information is offered.

Kuepper, J. (1987). *Homework helpers: A guide for parents offering assistance.* Minneapolis, MN: Educational Media Corporation.
Practical ideas for parental involvement in study skills encouragement and homework organization are given in this workbook written at a jargon-free reading level. Common referral problems are addressed through a task analysis approach. Material equally encompasses elementary and secondary needs and provides examples preceding blank formats that are ready to use.

Schumm, J., & Radencich, M. (1984). Readers/writers workshops: An antidote to term paper terror. *Journal of Reading, 28*(1), 13–19.
A clear model is provided for the teaching of integrated study skills through a cooperative learning approach. Task analysis of a complex assignment is well illustrated. An example of transfer from group to individual efforts is included.

Thompson III, E. (1987). The "Yagottawanna" group: Improving student self-perceptions through motivational teaching of study skills. *School Counselor, 35*(2), 134–142.
A detailed example is offered of a small-group counseling and teaching approach to study skills. The content for each of nine sessions developed for middle-school ages is suggested along with materials' choices. The goals of confidence and self-esteem are noted along with study skills gains.

Towle, M. (1982). Learning how to be a student when you have a learning disability. *Journal of Learning Disabilities, 15*(2), 90–93.
Organizing, rehearsing, recalling, and applying course content information is the focus of this article. Although directed specifically to needs of learning-disabled students, suggestions are excellent for any student at academic risk.

49

Best Practices in the Training of School Psychologists: Considerations for Trainers, Prospective Entry-Level and Advanced Students

Thomas K. Fagan
Memphis State University

OVERVIEW

This chapter is an introduction to training programs in the United States and the relationships among training, accreditation, and credentialing agencies. This information may facilitate the understanding of potential training and credentialing barriers encountered when moving from one state to another and the general relationship between basic and advanced preparation. It is useful to practicing school psychologists, persons seeking initial preparation in school psychology, and those with entry-level training who are considering advanced graduate work. It is also intended to be useful to trainers establishing school psychology programs and advising students on career decisions.

BACKGROUND

School psychological services were inaugurated in the late nineteenth and early twentieth centuries. Early practitioners held various titles and their formal training was often limited; typically a bachelor's or master's degree with few having a doctorate. In part due to acute gaps in supply and demand, practitioner training ranged from advanced graduate degrees in psychology to persons with teacher training and a "crash course" in intelligence testing. Training was usually in a psychology department (often in the education college), emphasized experimental studies with few applied courses except for those in clinical psychology (a method of individual examination and intervention emanating largely from the work of Lightner Witmer). Training emphasized the use of newly developed tests of intelligence, school achievement, and motor skill. Few test instruments and theories were available. Owing to the diversity of children and problems in the schools, most practitioners operated as "generalists" who responded to a large variety of situations. Practice largely involved individual psychometric evaluation of children and adolescents suspected of being "mentally, physically or morally defective." The purpose of psychological services in most settings was to assist school personnel in sorting children into more appropriate classroom placements including the relatively few but increasing number of special education classes.

The rapid growth of psychological science and public education in the first half of the twentieth century required the services of persons broadly trained in psychology and education with an orientation to the problems of education and school children. While the extent to which this orientation has become implemented in daily practice is debatable, the dualism of psychology and education has strongly influenced the training and practice of school psychologists. Efforts to formalize quality control through training programs and credentialing procedures were not successful for several decades. University course sequences appropriate for students planning to work in the schools were available in the 1920s. However, the first programs of preparation actually labeled "school psychology" were in the undergraduate and graduate programs at New York University in the late 1920s (Fagan, 1986b). The program at Pennsylvania State University was founded in the late 1930s and by the time of the Thayer Conference in 1954 there were 28 program institutions, with ten offering the doctoral degree. Leadership roles in training were taken by New York University, Penn State, Columbia University, University of Michigan, and the University of Illinois. Growth in the number of training programs has been dramatic in the past three decades. The 1989 NASP *Directory of Training* identified 203 institutions which provided information on their programs and 28 which did not respond (McMaster, Reschly, & Peters, 1989). A discussion of historical and future growth in training programs and related areas appears in Fagan (1986b, 1989) and Brown and Minke (1986).

Many persons contributed to the early growth of programs: H. H. Goddard, Gertrude Hildreth, Leta Hollingworth, Francis Maxfield, Boyd McCandless, T. E. Newland, Percival Symonds, J. E. W. Wallin, Lightner Witmer and countless more recent figures. Contemporary trainers owe much to the planning and thinking of these persons. With the inauguration of the University of Illinois doctoral program in 1951 and the impetus of the Thayer Conference, the need for more masters and doctoral programs became apparent. While the Illinois program established by T. E. Newland was not the first doctoral program in school psychology, it was among the first well organized programs. Early descriptions of the Illinois program reveal its sensitivity to both educational and psychological foundations, the need for broad, generalist preparation, and other aspects still included in professional training standards.

The issue of whether practitioners should hold doctoral or nondoctoral preparation has existed throughout this period of development with increasing interest since the reorganization of the American Psychological Association (APA) in 1945. The intensity of the issue

has been greatest since the APA Council of Representatives in 1977 approved the doctoral level as required for the title "professional psychologist." The doctoral--nondoctoral issue is too complex for coverage here. A summary of positions and their implications appears in *School Psychology Review*, *16*(1) and *18*(1). However, it is worth noting that the percentage of school psychologists holding doctoral degrees has climbed from about 3% in 1970 to 20% or more in the 1980s. Even though the majority of school psychologists have been trained at the nondoctoral level, the demand for doctoral level personnel can be seen in the growth of such programs in the past 20 years. This trend will continue with gradual increases in the doctoral force relative to the nondoctoral force. The trend can also be observed in the growth of APA accredited doctoral programs since 1971 (Zins & Curtis, 1988).

Without significant changes in the areas of service provision and credentialing, the doctoral degree will continue to be the choice only for those practitioners desiring to hold employment with the least professional and legal restrictions. For persons desiring full-time employment in school districts, the forecast is for continued high demand for nondoctoral practitioners in most states, though such persons may experience restricted nonschool practice. Employment opportunities will be best for persons having specializations, a high degree of mobility, in rural and developing areas, some urban districts, many nonschool settings, and private practice. Moreover, there is a growing shortage of school-based practitioners in several states (National Association of State Consultants for School Psychological Services, 1987). Training programs are encouraged to recruit more students in order to offset the supply-demand gap and avoid its potentially negative influence on the profession (Fagan, 1988). Related supply-demand issues include minority recruitment (Zins & Halsell, 1986), increased accreditation and credentialing (Zins & Curtis, 1988), generally declining program enrollments with increasing female student represen-

TABLE 1
Percentage Distribution of Training in School Psychology

	Smith (1984)	Ramage (1979)	Farling & Hoedt (1971)
Bachelors	0	1	1
Master's (1 yr.)	17	22	28
Master's (2 yr.)	45	39	63
Master's (3 yr.) or Specialist	22	14	1
Doctorate	16	24	3

TABLE 2
Enrollment Patterns 1986–1987

Training Level	Number		Response Level		
Total	5634	(7293)	193	(211)	Institutions
Master's	750	(1466)	42	(80)	Programs
Specialist	3180	(2526)	164	(174)	Programs
Doctoral	1704	(2301)	67	(79)	Programs

Numbers in parentheses are 1981–82 data reported in Brown and Minke (1984).

tation (APA, 1986), and rural services (Cummings, Huebner, & McLeskey, 1985). Opportunities in nontraditional settings and independent practice are discussed in *School Psychology Review*, *17*(3) and in D'Amato and Dean (1989).

BASIC CONSIDERATIONS

This section is organized around four questions in order to provide basic information about training and related credentialing practices of the profession.

1. *What is the typical level of training of the school psychologist?*

Smith (1984) provides a representative picture of the levels of training common to practitioners. Table 1 summarizes degrees held by respondents to his and earlier surveys.

Despite methodological problems and differences in these surveys, clearly most school psychologists hold nondoctoral degrees. The current status of training appears to be approximately two-thirds

with the specialist degree or at least a two-year Master's level, and one-fifth with doctoral degrees in school psychology or a related field. A recent analysis of programs suggests that the specialist level is gaining in popularity, and growth at the doctoral level may be more pronounced than these figures may indicate (Brown & Minke, 1986). Smith's (1984) data are important because they represent practitioners only, whereas the other surveys include trainers, state consultants, and others. A five-year update of Smith's sample revealed similar proportions to those above as did a 1986 NASP survey which reported results separately for practitioners and leadership (Reschly, Genshaft, & Binder, 1987).

Enrollment patterns provide another view of typical training. Table 2 is a summary of student enrollment 1986–1987, adopted from McMaster, Reschly, and Peters (1989). A *proportional* enrollment shift toward advanced graduate training is observed; this is largely the result of increased enrollment at the specialist level. While direct comparisons are difficult, growth in the number of training institutions, programs, and enrollment are believed to have leveled or declined in the 1980s. Surveys will increasingly identify specialist and doctoral programs as most common, fewer two-year and practically no one-year master's programs. Relatedly, practitioners will have sixth-year, specialist, or doctoral training, with lesser trained personnel fading entirely within the next two decades. Persons seeking training in school psychology should pursue nothing less than a sixth-year program of preparation the curriculum of which is consistent with accepted nondoctoral accreditation guidelines, and culminates in the students' eligibility for the NASP National Certification System.

Another way of viewing typical training is through the content of degree programs. The 1989 NASP *Directory of Training* indicates that the average number of semester hours required for Master's, Specialist, and Doctoral Degrees in 1986–1987 were 41, 66, and 100 respectively. Hourly requirements for each training institution are listed along with other program specific information. The annual publication by the APA, *Graduate Programs in Psychology*, also provides information related to school psychology programs and complements the NASP directory. Since doctoral and nondoctoral graduate programs are increasingly complying with the standards advocated by NASP and APA, their program standards are also useful references. More information about course requirements at each degree level is discussed in a later section of this chapter.

In summary, school psychologist training is typically at the specialist degree level as reflected in practitioner and training surveys. While doctoral level training is becoming more common, specialist level preparation will continue to be more common for the foreseeable future.

2. *What resources are available to assist in the selection of a training program and level of preparation?*

Students should answer the following questions before exploring specific training institutions:

1. Do you desire to work with school-age children, many of whom have handicapping conditions?

2. Do you desire to work primarily in public school settings?

3. Will you be comfortable employed in the public school environment?

4. Do you desire a nondoctoral or doctoral degree?

5. Do you desire generalist or specialized training?

6. Are your long-term interests in a practice or academic setting?

7. In what state or region do you intend to seek employment?

The answers to these questions help focus the program selection process. The previously mentioned *Directory of School Psychology Training Programs* and *Graduate Programs in Psychology* can then be used to gather basic information on several institutions under consideration. It is best to seek answers to program questions from the program administrator. With the rapid growth of training in the past 10 years, even recently published directories cannot keep pace with policy and curriculum changes. University bulletins often lag 1 or 2 years on these matters. The program administrator is the most reliable source of information. Inquiries to these institutions will provide sufficient program data to allow the student to make more specific decisions regarding the appropriateness of the program for his/her needs and interests. These resources are useful in decision making for doctoral programs as well. Information on the historical development and philosophy of selected doctoral programs can be found in recent issues of *Professional School Psychology*.

In addition to the NASP and APA program standards and the directories mentioned above, certain other documents are helpful. Gerner and Genshaft (1981) serves as a guide to selecting a program, assisting the student with such issues as degrees, field experiences, credentialing requirements, program orientations, and interviewing questions.

TABLE 3
Academic Unit Location of Programs

Academic Unit (N = 203)	Number	Percent
Psychology	76	37
Education	117	58
Unable to Determine	10	5

It also refers to the relationship between a training program and the credentialing requirements of the state in which the program is located. This is a major consideration at the nondoctoral level. Since most programs are organized to meet requirements of a particular state department of education (SDE) or other regulatory authority such as a psychology licensing board, the nondoctoral program often conforms closely to the state agency requirements. Thus, *The Handbook of Certification/Licensure Requirements for School Psychologists* (Prus, White, & Pendleton, 1987) is helpful in the process of choosing a program (see Appendix to this textbook for a summary of state requirements).

3. *Why are many school psychology programs operated from within a college of education or other apparently nonpsychology academic unit?*

School psychology has experienced a confusing history of credentialing, accreditation and locus of training. Throughout this history, training programs were located in psychology and nonpsychology departments in both colleges of education and colleges of arts and sciences. Anyone who reviews current program data will be surprised by the diversity of department and college titles in which training occurs. The diversity is related to historical trends in the development of school psychology. These trends include the admission of students from diverse backgrounds in education and psychology, conflicts between psychology and education departments, accreditation influences from different agencies, and until recent years, lack of clear professional identity. Thus, departmental diversity is the norm, not the exception, in school psychology

training, and is expected to continue. There are more than a dozen different departmental titles housing school psychology programs in the United States. An analysis of the 1989 NASP *Directory of Training* resulted in the distribution shown in Table 3. Since 18 of the psychology departments were also judged to be in education units, at least 67 percent of programs are in education based units. The above distribution is consistent with Brown and Lindstrom (1977) and Goh (1977). The diversity can also be observed in the 12 different degree titles granted, with the most common being MS, MA, EdS, PhD, and EdD.

Frequently, programs are in a department of educational psychology, counseling and guidance, or similarly titled unit which can legitimately claim to be psychological in nature. Thus, being "housed" in an education unit does not necessarily mean the program is not psychological. There are both education and psychology department programs accredited at the doctoral and nondoctoral level. As of December, 1989, all but five APA accredited doctoral programs were in education unit departments (N = 38). Accredited programs in psychology departments are more frequent at the nondoctoral level, though the majority are in education units. In 1984, the APA proposed a project on Program Designation which would have provided another avenue to evaluate programs. Designation would have facilitated assurance that a participating school psychology (or other) program was basically psychological in nature as defined by APA, and met certain criteria for administration and curriculum regardless of departmental location. It was not proposed as an accreditation process and would not have assured the quality control that accreditation procedures seek. However, APA has not implemented the program designation proposal. From the standpoint of those seeking training, the question then becomes, "Does academic location of the program make a difference in the quality of preparation?" There are no studies directly bearing on this question and, on the basis of accreditation, there is no reason to judge programs in one academic unit as consistently superior to others. Additional data come from faculty ratings which strongly suggest that the importance of content areas does not differ significantly as a function of program departmental location (Goh, 1977).

It has been the author's impression that programs located within education units are often more flexible in admissions criteria and scheduling classes. Thus, in an education-based program a student may be more likely to be admitted on a part-time basis with a selection of daytime and evening courses. Some psychology-based school psychology programs are actually located in a college of education where a "spread effect" has probably influenced greater flexibility than is the case in psychology units in arts and sciences. Urban programs may also be more flexible in these respects than rural programs. There are also pragmatic concerns related to licensure or certification that encourage persons to seek one unit or another. For example, the licensing board may only recognize courses completed in a psychology unit; state departments of education usually grant approvals through mechanisms coordinated with colleges of education.

Thus, students should feel confident that training programs in either education or traditional psychology administrative units will provide appropriate preparation. Applications should be directed only to those programs holding appropriate state and national approval and accreditation.

4. What is the relationship among training, accreditation, and credential-
ing? Why are these relationships important?

Levels of training and types of degrees have complex relationships to the procedures and outcomes of both accreditation and credentialing. The relationships dictate the type of title and practice one is eventually permitted. The complexity of these relationships is suggested by Figure 1. Practitioners and trainers understanding the organizations, committees, agencies, and programs represented in the chart should have little difficulty in recognizing the complex nature of accrediting and credentialing in school psychology (see Fagan, 1986a). However, they may feel powerless to change it. An introductory understanding of these relationships is obtained by reviewing the summary analysis in Figure 2. Imagine that Figure 2 is superimposed on Figure 1. What emerges are two major areas of quality control in the profession: (a) accreditation, the procedure for evaluating the preparation of persons desiring to function as and call themselves school psychologists, and (b) credentialing, the procedure for granting titles and functions to persons after professional preparation.

A few guidelines will assist understanding the relationships of Figures 1 and 2.

1. Organization, committee, and agency relationships in the top portion of the chart relate to accreditation; those at the bottom relate to credentialing.

2. Relationships in the top portion of the chart are typically conducted at the national level; those in the bottom portion at the state level.

3. Relationships in the left portion of the chart relate to established structures and policies of education; those on the right relate to psychology.

4. Dotted lines represent power relationships and solid lines represent authority regardless of the extent of power that may coexist.

5. It should be obvious that there is considerably greater power than authority relationships involved in these aspects of quality control. In fact, decisions to get involved in accreditation or credentialing

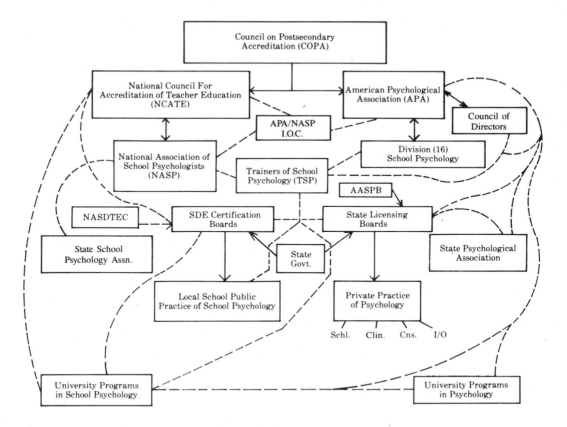

FIGURE 1. Power and authority for accreditation and credentialing in school psychology. Reprinted from Fagan (1986a). Copyright 1986 by the American Psychological Association. Reprinted (or adapted) by permission of the publisher.

are strictly voluntary for most training programs, agencies, associations, and individuals.

It is as important to understand these relationships as it is to grasp other areas of professional preparation. Since most of the relationships in the education sector lead to SDE certification (some SDEs now give a license) while those in the psychology sector lead to nonschool based and private licensure, and since these credentialing mechanisms are authoritatively regulated at the state level, applicants should be knowledgeable about the state(s) in which they would eventually like to practice. While commonalities exist among state certification and state licensing authorities, reciprocity of credentials and/or equivalence of credentialing requirements in school psychology is the

exception, not the norm. Two examples demonstrate the importance of the decisions involved and the relationships in Figure 1.

1. Student "A" is interested only in employment as a school psychologist in his home state, has no interest in nonschool setting practice and feels uncommitted at this time to pursuing a lengthy program of graduate preparation leading to a doctoral degree. "A", familiar with the nondoctoral nature of SDE certification in his home state and the fact that SDE closely scrutinizes the programs of preparation, selects an institution which holds both NCATE(NASP) accreditation at the specialist level and SDE program approval, a state-level mechanism of quality control not unlike accreditation in some ways but available in only certain states.

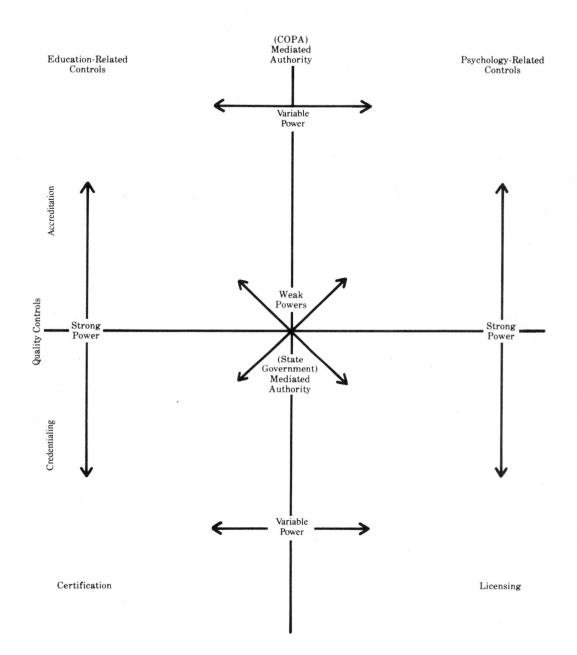

FIGURE 2. Power and authority relationships among the four major areas of control in the accreditation and credentialing process. Reprinted from Fagan (1986a). Copyright 1986 by the American Psychological Association. Reprinted (or adapted) by permission of the publisher.

Upon completion of the program, "A" is automatically endorsed for certification by his institution and the SDE subsequently grants the certificate. "A" is now authorized to practice as a school psychologist in the public school systems of that state. Depending on the similarity of the home state's requirements to those of other states, "A" may or may not achieve similar certification elsewhere. Nor is "A" authorized, or perhaps even eligible, for nonschool practice as a school psychologist because licensing requirements in his state do not specify a nondoctoral credential. Should "A" move to another state with different certification requirements, no reciprocity with his SDE, and a doctoral-level-only licensure requirement, "A" could be without any credential to continue practicing school psychology.

2. Student "B" is interested in maximizing flexibility in the marketplace and seeks preparation for school and nonschool based practice, while retaining the title "school psychologist" in both sectors. "B" wants to practice in the same state as "A" but is interested in subspecializing in a particular area of school psychology. "B" selects an out-of-state institution that holds NCATE accreditation at the nondoctoral and doctoral levels, APA accreditation in school psychology at the doctoral level, and an advanced graduate concentration in the desired subspecialty. "B" also notes that the program requirements readily match those for certification of her home SDE. Upon completion of the doctoral degree which included a year internship, "B" returns to her home state and makes application for both certification via the SDE and licensure as a school psychologist via the State Board of Examiners in Psychology. After completing additional written and oral examination requirements, "B" is both certified and licensed to practice as a school psychologist in school and nonschool settings, and privately. Should "B" choose to move to another state, it is very likely that additional credentials for both school and nonschool practice could be obtained with a minimum of additional examination or other requirements. Certification to practice in the schools would be virtually guaranteed in every state.

The examples above are not meant to suggest any preference. They serve only to demonstrate the manner in which two persons, defining their goals differently, achieve appropriate training. Many variations of these patterns could be employed to show the intricate relationships among training, accreditation, and credentialing. For example, had the home state provided nondoctoral licensure for school psychologists to practice in the nonschool sector, or had all credentialing of school psychologists been under the control of the State Board of Examiners in Psychology, each person may have made substantially different choices for training. Thus, it is important for prospective entry-level and advanced students to consider the credentialing requirements of their chosen state(s) and the accreditation status of the training program. For a discussion of the types of credentials offered in professional psychology see Pryzwansky and Wendt (1987).

In 1988, NASP initiated a program of national certification premised on its standards for training and credentialing. Among the long-term objectives of the program is to establish the conditions under which improved reciprocity would emerge. The Educational Testing Service's National School Psychology Examination, one part of the NASP National Certification System (NCS), has already been adopted by several states as part of their credentialing requirements. Ideally, reciprocity would improve to a point where holding a NASP certificate would be sufficient to reestablish one's state-level credentials when moving. The NCS provides the framework within which NASP guidelines for training and credentialing, APA and NCATE(NASP) accrediting guidelines, and the diverse state credentialing requirements could evolve into greater homogeneity. For a comprehensive discussion of credentialing, see the chapter by Batsche.

Thus, in selecting a training program, close attention should be given the national professional standards for accreditation and credentialing and the requirements of the SDE and state licensing board of the state in which the program is offered and/or the trainee desires to practice.

TRAINING LEVELS AND SUBSPECIALTIES[1]

Generalists versus Specialists

Throughout the history of school psychology, most practitioners have performed a variety of functions while adapting to the range of problems presented them. The necessity for practitioners to have broad training to meet these conditions has long been recognized. Thus, most training programs have espoused a generalist orientation which drew upon knowledge and skills from education, psychology, special education, and other related fields. The generalist model has prevailed in training despite the common reference to school psychologists as "specialists" or members of "specialized services teams." This is true even for those practitioners holding the Educational Specialist Degree.

The issue of whether practitioners should be trained as generalists or specialists has been discussed frequently although little has been published on the subject. With the rapid development of professional identity in the past two decades, the issue gained attention in both training and practice. Studies suggest that rural or urban practitioners benefit from specialized training experiences related to the sociocultural characteristics of their settings; that subspecialty training is more likely to occur in doctoral programs than in nondoctoral programs; and that there is need for, and growing interest in, several areas of specialization, including consultation, early childhood, vocational school psychology, and neuropsychology.

The research by Goh (1977) and Brown and Minke (1986) suggest greater similarity of training emphases at the nondoctoral level with areas of subspecialization generally occurring at the doctoral level. Students can anticipate considerable commonality of training in the two-year master's and specialist level programs. Considering the interrelationship of training and credentialing, the commonality may be greatest within states where credentialing requirements are anchored to course or competency areas. Accreditation standards encourage commonality at the entry level while encouraging advanced generalist training or subspecializations at the doctoral level. Thus, greater diversity at the doctoral level can be anticipated and often doctoral programs in the same state have different areas of specialization despite commonalities in their nondoctoral programs.

Of course, through experience, continuing education, and personal interests, many school psychologists specialize without obtaining a doctoral degree. For example, recognizing need in their district, they may obtain additional expertise in the assessment of low-incidence handicaps. Areas of special expertise are common among practitioners, but differ from concentrated subspecializations obtained through advanced graduate courses or programs. The growth of special interest groups in NASP is another vehicle for promoting communication among persons sharing expertise in selected areas. A list of these groups can be obtained from NASP.

Additional future prospects on the generalist–specialist issue include:

1. With increasing numbers of students selecting doctoral programs and the continuing education requirement of the NASP National Certification System, greater specialization throughout the profession is anticipated.

2. There is a trend in the direction of practitioners moving into nonschool practice in hospitals, clinics, professional groups, and self employment. With generalist level services common to most communities through school-based practitioners, nonschool based school psychologists may compete on the basis of specializations. Generalists often seek the assistance of specialists and the exchange of referrals from one school psychologist to another school psychologist is becoming more common. In the past, such referrals were commonly exchanged across groups

TABLE 4
Average Number of Semester Hours by Areas and Degree

Areas	Master's	Specialist	Doctorate
Core Psychology	15	18	31
Assessment	10	12	13
Intervention	9	12	13
Educational Foundations	6	8	8
Professional School Psychology	9	16	20

usually from school psychologist to clinical psychologist.

3. A strong employment market for doctoral generalists and specialists both in and out of school settings should persist, though at a lesser level than for nondoctoral generalists. That is, a stronger nondoctoral practitioner market will persist.

4. Observing the developments in related professions, we can anticipate that school psychologists in nonschool settings will first seek employment in other agencies or self-employment, and may later seek collective employment with other health services providers, the latter encouraging specialization.

5. The implementation of state and federal requirements will encourage greater specialization. For example, PL 99-457 will foster specialized training at the infant–toddler and preschool levels. The potential impact of the "highest qualified provider" standard in the personnel requirements of PL 99-457 could hasten advanced training and specialization generally. This impact will vary according to state interpretations of the standard. As the impact of PL 94-142 moves to the secondary school level, there will be increased need for practitioners specializing in vocational school psychology, secondary, and post-secondary services.

Prospective doctoral students should consider their desire and need for advanced generalist or subspecialty training. In addition to deciding upon advanced generalist or subspecialty training, choosing a particular subspecialization helps to focus the process of program selection.

The Content of Programs

Despite the growth and diversity of training, the complexity of relationships in accreditation and credentialing, and the generalist–specialist issue, the content of entry-level programs has considerable similarity. This similarity reflects the influences of professional and political forces in our history and the realities of daily practice. With the recent development of program accreditation in school psychology, more comprehensive training has emerged at the entry level. Table 4 is a summary of content emphases at each program level taken from the 1989 NASP *Directory of Training:*

What follows is a discussion of program content for entry-level and doctoral programs with the latter including a listing of available subspecializations.

Entry-Level Programs

Because NASP program guidelines have gained widespread acceptance, they provide one of the best means of anticipating entry-level program content. The NASP curriculum guidelines are by areas of competency, rather than courses and are divided into the following broad areas:

Psychological Foundations
1. Biological Bases of Behavior
2. Cultural Diversity
3. Child & Adolescent Development (Normal and Abnormal)
4. Human Exceptionalities
5. Human Learning
6. Social Bases of Behavior

Educational Foundations
1. Education of Exceptional Learners
2. Instruction & Remedial Techniques
3. Organization & Operation of Schools

Assessment
Interventions (Direct and Indirect)
1. Consultation
2. Counseling
3. Behavior Modification

Statistics & Research Design
Professional School Psychology
1. History and Foundations of School Psychology
2. Legal and Ethical Issues
3. Professional Issues and Standards
4. Roles and Functions of the School Psychologist

The guidelines also specify practica and internship experiences. Accreditable programs are expected to demonstrate in both policy and practice that they have sixty semester hours or more credit embracing the academic and field experiences. The terms "specialist" and "sixth year" programs represent similar levels of graduate training, but the specialist level typically involves a degree awarded at the termination of work while the sixth year level indicates at least one year beyond the master's but not necessarily a separate degree. Specialist degree programs often have more requirements, such as terminal exams and research papers, than a sixth-year program entails. As a general rule, students pursuing specialist level training on a full-time basis can expect a minimum of 3 years of study, including the internship. The internship is full-time for 1 academic year or part-time over 2 years. Guidelines for the internship and its supervision are incorporated into the revised training guidelines (NASP, 1984).

The above program content guidelines are consistent with trainers' program emphases ratings in the Goh (1977) study. In that study, nine areas of emphasis were found to account for 73% of the total variance: (a) school-based consultation, (b) educational assessment and remediation, (c) behavior modification technology, (d) psychological evaluation, (e)

psychotherapeutic procedures, (f) quantitative methods, (g) community involvement and consultation, (h) professional roles and issues, and (i) psychological foundations including child development and learning. These factors were present in both doctoral and nondoctoral programs with factors a, b, and c accounting for 49% of the variance at all levels!

Since areas of emphasis and accreditation guidelines are met through courses/experiences with varying titles, it is impossible to provide a listing of the common courses in all nondoctoral programs. However, from surveys of course content and an earlier NASP *Directory of Training* (Brown & Lindstrom, 1977) it appears that the following courses are present in most specialist level programs:

Advanced Statistics
Research Methods/Design
Child and Adolescent Development
Psychology of Learning
Intellectual Assessment
Personality Assessment
Educational Assessment
Educational Foundations (e.g.,
    administration, curriculum)
Child Study Practicum
Seminar on School Psychology
Counseling/Psychotherapy
Consultation
Educational Remediation
Characteristics of Exceptional Children
Behavior Management
Internship

Specific topics within most of these courses are described in Knoff (1986).

Doctoral Programs

Most doctoral programs are offered in departments that also offer nondoctoral school psychology programs. Usually the doctoral degree is more than an extension of the nondoctoral level although a career ladder approach may be available. Even in the first few years of training, doctoral students often pursue a different curriculum than nondoctoral students. In some instances, the differences are minimal in the first few years and doctoral students may even be drawn from applicants who are already credentialed. It is important for prospective doctoral students to explore these differences since considerably more time may be required to complete doctoral work if a nondoctoral track is followed in the early years of graduate study. As a general rule, full-time students pursuing doctoral degrees can expect a minimum of 4 years of study which may or may not include the academic year of internship.

Goh (1977) reported factor results on combined doctoral–subdoctoral programs and analyzed emphases that trainers rated significant to the doctoral level. The only areas consistently cited at the doctoral level were "school-based consultation" and "quantitative methods." These results are supported by a more recent analysis (Brown & Minke, 1986) that advanced graduate training in school psychology differs most from previous training levels in providing specializations and additional research information/skills. This reflects traditional conceptualizations of the doctoral degree and the significance placed on the scientist-practitioner model in professional psychology (Martens & Keller, 1987). A precise grasp of doctoral program content is not readily available from NCATE-(NASP) or APA (1980) accreditation guidelines. The NCATE(NASP) guidelines are the same for both doctoral and nondoctoral levels, insuring that practicing school psychologists emerging from either level of preparation have the same basic skills and competencies. The APA standards apply only to doctoral programs and are generic to professional psychology programs. Comparisons of the NCATE(NASP) and APA Standards by the APA/NASP Joint Task Force found them to be highly similar in curricular expectations. As a general rule, the doctoral student can expect to encounter additional statistics and research courses; a major research requirement such as a dissertation; related requirements such as major area papers; additional written and oral examinations; and an internship experience. Some institutions accept previous internships completed at the entry level. Dana and May (1987) provide

information on professional psychology internships, and APA (1987) has developed a guide to full-time and half-time internship sites in school psychology.

Doctoral courses in psychology and education are used to create an advanced generalist concentration, and subspecializations elected by the student in consultation with an advisor. Subspecializations are emphasized by several doctoral programs. Table 5 is a list of doctoral programs and associated areas of subspecialization reported for the 1988–1989 year. In some instances, subspecialization is provided at the nondoctoral level. For example, Gallaudet College offers nondoctoral subspecialization with the hearing impaired. Such instances are rare and therefore no listings are provided for nondoctoral programs.

A final note about subspecializations: Many subspecializations are related to faculty expertise more than to orientation of the administrative unit and may wax or wane as a function of faculty mobility and interests. For example, rural subspecialization is not always related to the geographic location of the program. Some students attend urban universities but obtain rural specialization as a function of selected courses, faculty expertise, and field experiences. In short, when the faculty leave, the subspecializations usually go with them!

In recent years, professional degrees such as the Doctor of Psychology (PsyD) have emerged and made advanced training in nontraditional formats available to school psychologists. A recent study of the acceptability of the PsyD suggests it is not as widely accepted for academic employment as the traditional PhD or EdD though greater acceptability may occur in the future (Prout, Meyers, & Greggo, 1989). However, the PsyD seems to have appeal for persons seeking nonacademic positions, and it may be that programs seeking doctoral status but unable to get authorization for the PhD will opt for the PsyD. The 1989 NASP *Directory of Training* identified only four programs offering the PsyD. Holding the PsyD degree does not appear to be a hindrance in seeking

TABLE 5
Subspecializations in Doctoral School Psychology Programs[1]

Code No.	Name of Institution	Code No.	Name of Institution
1.	Arizona State University	36.	University of Arizona
2.	Ball State University	37.	University of California at Berkeley
3.	Central Michigan University	38.	University of Cincinnati
4.	East Texas State University	39.	University of Colorado
5.	Fordham University	40.	University of Connecticut
6.	Georgia State University	41.	University of Denver
7.	Howard University	42.	University of Detroit
8.	Illinois State University	43.	University of Florida
9.	Indiana State University	44.	University of Georgia
10.	Indiana University	45.	University of Kentucky
11.	Indiana University of Pennsylvania	46.	University of Maryland
12.	Kent State University	47.	University of Massachusetts
13.	Louisiana State University	48.	University of Minnesota
14.	Loyola University of Chicago	49.	University of Mississippi
15.	Michigan State University	50.	University of Missouri
16.	Mississippi State University	51.	University of Nebraska
17.	National College of Education (Illinois)	52.	University of North Carolina
18.	New York University	53.	University of North Texas
19.	North Carolina State University	54.	University of Northern Colorado
20.	Northeastern University (Boston)	55.	University of Northern Iowa
21.	Northern Arizona University	56.	University of Oregon
22.	Northern Illinois University	57.	University of the Pacific
23.	Ohio State University	58.	University of Pittsburgh
24.	Oklahoma State University	59.	University of South Carolina
25.	Pace University (New York City)	60.	University of South Florida
26.	Pennsylvania State University	61.	University of Southern Mississippi
27.	Rutgers University (New Jersey)	62.	University of Tennessee
28.	State University of New York at Albany	63.	University of Texas
		64.	University of Toledo
29.	Syracuse University	65.	University of Utah
30.	Teachers College, Columbia University	66.	University of Washington
31.	Tennessee State University	67.	University of Wisconsin–Madison
32.	Texas A & M University	68.	University of Wisconsin–Milwaukee
33.	Texas Woman's University	69.	Virginia Polytechnic Institute and State University
34.	Tulane University		
35.	University of Alabama	70.	Yeshiva University

Subspecialization Areas[2]	Institutions
1. Applied Behavior Analysis	13, 27, 44, 65
2. Behavioral Assessment/Intervention	13, 27, 51, 60, 65
3. Behavioral Consultation	13, 51, 61, 62
4. Behavioral Medicine	None Identified
5. Bilingual/Multicultural	None Identified
6. Child Pediatric	None Identified
7. Childhood Psychopathology	32, 65
8. Clinical and Clinical Child Psychology	13, 42
9. Cognition/Instructional Psychology	14, 22, 40, 61, 66

10. Computers in Education	None Identified
11. Consultation, School-Based Consultation	3, 12, 13, 14, 19, 27, 28, 30, 32, 43, 45, 48, 60
12. Counseling	12, 27, 57, 60, 64, 66
13. Developmental Psychology	6, 12, 22, 34, 36, 48
14. Discipline	None Identified
15. Educational Psychology	4, 30, 32, 66
16. Experimental	None Identified
17. Family–School Relations*	11
18. Family Systems	6, 9, 51, 64, 69
19. Generalist Orientation with selected course emphases, minors, or concentrations	1, 5, 7, 8, 10, 15, 17, 18, 20, 23, 24, 25, 26, 29, 31, 33, 35, 37, 38, 39, 41, 46, 47, 49, 50, 52, 53, 54, 55, 56, 58, 59, 63, 67, 68, 70
20. Gifted	9, 45
21. Hispanic Handicapped	32, 40
22. Learning Assessment/Intervention	28, 40
23. Measurement/Statistics	36, 43, 44
24. Organizational Development	27
25. Neuropsychology	2, 6, 9, 11, 16, 44, 64, 65
26. Pediatric Psychology	None Identified
27. Preschool/Early Childhood	9, 12, 21, 22, 30, 44, 45, 48, 61
28. Prevention*	12, 62
29. Program Evaluation	3, 27
30. Psychoeducational Assessment	3, 6, 9, 16, 19, 30, 40, 43, 44, 45, 60, 62, 66
31. Research/Field Experimental	2, 13, 14, 19, 36, 48, 51, 69
32. Special Education	4, 9, 28, 48
33. Therapeutic Interventon	14, 16, 27, 28, 32
34. University Teaching/Training	16, 61
35. Vocational School Psychology	11, 69

[1]Responses are based on a survey of the 74 institutions offering doctoral programs listed in the *Directory of School Psychology Graduate Programs* (McMaster, Reschly, & Peters, 1989). Data were gathered from January through May, 1989. The survey was also sent to institutions thought to have a doctoral level program from among those institutions which were named but did not participate in the *Directory* data gathering. A total of 72 responses were received, two of which indicated they did not have a doctoral degree program specifically in school psychology (University of California at Santa Barbara and University of Michigan).

[2]All areas identified in the 1984 survey are herein listed even though some were not specified by institutions in the 1989 survey. The (*) indicates an area not listed in the 1984 survey. If an institution specified a "generalist orientation" no other areas were listed in the table even if the institution listed others. Some of these institutions appear to offer concentrations or minors in certain areas but not subspecializations. Institutions were not required to provide documentation of the subspecializations they listed. Persons inquiring about training at any institution should request specific informaton about subspecializations.

credentialing from state departments of education or licensing boards.

Since the doctoral degree is seldom required for practice in the schools, and schools will continue to be the major practice setting, the issue of cost is important to the consideration of advanced graduate training. In 1986–87, the average tuition for resident students was $2016 and the average cost per credit hour was $107 (McMaster, Reschly, & Peters, 1989). Cost issues are related to when one seeks doctoral training. Assuming one already holds the specialist degree and is credentialed for school practice, pursuing doctoral work on a full-time basis would involve giving up one's salary for perhaps 3 years before returning to employment.

For example, the salary loss for 3 years might total $75,000 and tuition might cost at least $6000. The conservative estimated cost ($81,000) will not be matched by graduate student stipends, tuition waivers, and a paid internship, the total of which might be only $40,000. Add to this example the costs for living, transportation, out-of-state tuition, books, and materials and it is obvious that under any circumstances doctoral preparation is a long-term investment and not a short-term financial advantage! Unless the practitioner anticipates returning to a better salary level in his/her former employment and/or additional sources of revenue such as from private practice, or an administrative position, there may be no financial advantage to pursuing formal advanced training. Nor does pursuing the doctorate in order to enter a university position offer much financial advantage; many academic positions do not pay as well as doctoral practitioner positions. Financially, it is better for the student to pursue a doctoral program initially than to return for such training because the total length of preparation is often 1 or more years greater and the internship may have to be repeated. Of course, other issues than money are involved including greater knowledge, competence, and status. Prospective doctoral students should weigh the advantages and disadvantages of advanced training against their long-term career goals. While doctoral programs often prefer full-time students, many offer part-time studies in order that students can maintain employment and defray the cost of their education. Graduate student stipends and tuition waivers are seldom available to part-time students.

Noncurricular Characteristics and Accreditation

There are many aspects of a program's overall quality that are not necessarily expressed in its curricular offerings. Gerner and Genshaft (1981) advise students to look for several factors when making program selections and even include hints on interviewing. The APA

and the NCATE(NASP) Guidelines specify many areas in addition to program content. Such aspects as the qualifications of the faculty, physical facilities, research interests, student production, admissions criteria, continuing education, and field supervision are important. Since the accreditation of school psychology programs is based upon comprehensive reviews, the accrediting bodies' decisions provide an excellent source of information. School psychology accreditation is conducted by both APA and by the National Council for Accreditation of Teacher Education (NCATE). The 1989 NASP *Directory of Training* indicated that NCATE accredited 62% of the 287 reporting programs; NCATE accredited 25 (54%) of the 46 Master's programs and 107 (63%) of the 171 Specialist programs. At the doctoral level, NCATE accredited 46 (66%) of the 70 programs and APA accredited 36 (51%); 25 (36%) of the 70 doctoral programs held both NCATE and APA accreditation, 21 (30%) NCATE only, and 11 (16%) APA only. Apparently, 13 (18%) were not nationally accredited. The most commonly reported "accreditation" at all degree levels was from a State Department of Education (91% Master's, 92% Specialist, and 81% Doctoral). These data are consistent with those of a 1987 summary of program accreditation by the APA-NASP Interorganizational Committee. In the past 10 years, there has been rapid growth in specialist and doctoral programs that meet the NCATE(NASP) and/or APA accreditation. Such growth was partially responsible for the joint accreditation project (1983–1984) between NCATE and APA. The continuation of that project is uncertain though procedures for parallel accreditation visits and minimum reciprocity have been implemented.

The APA publishes an annual list of accredited doctoral programs in the December issue of *American Psychologist*. NCATE publishes an *Annual List* which includes a listing of programs in school psychology at the doctoral and nondoctoral levels in the accredited education units. Listings of accredited programs and accreditation standards may be obtained by writing to the following organizations:

Accreditation Office
American Psychological Association
1200 17th St., NW
Washington, DC 20036

NCATE
2029 K St., NW, Suite 500
Washington, DC 20006

In the NCATE accreditation process, doctoral and nondoctoral program folios are reviewed by NASP as a complement to the NCATE's unit accreditation model. Since NCATE officially accredits the education unit and not specific programs, a school psychology program listing in NCATE's *Annual List* does not in itself guarantee that the program adequately met NASP guidelines. A list of those favorably reviewed by NASP in the folio process will be made available by NASP. Several states have a program approval process whereby the State Department of Education reviews school psychology programs either independently or concurrently with other reviews. For a list of these states contact: National Association of State Consultants in School Psychology, c/o NASP. In some instances a program participates in regional accreditation activities. Names and addresses of the six regional accrediting bodies are available through most libraries or from NCATE.

SUMMARY

Responses have been given to several commonly asked questions of prospective entry-level and advanced students in school psychology. The complex relationships of training, accreditation, and credentialing were discussed in the context of program selection and related precautions. Typical program content at both doctoral and nondoctoral levels as well as sources for additional information were presented. Accrediting agencies and program directors are considered the most reliable sources of information about program content and organization. Opinions about future training directions and the employment of school psychologists are also presented. Upgraded certification and licensure standards, gradual increases in the proportion of school psychologists holding doctoral degrees, increased specialization of practitioners, and a trend toward practice in nonschool settings all suggest continued positive growth in school psychology and expanding employment opportunities.

REFERENCES

American Psychological Association, Joint Committee Council of Directors of School Psychology Programs and the Division of School Psychology. (1987). *Directory of predoctoral internships for students in school psychology.* Washington, DC: Author. (Available from School Psychology, 104 CEDAR, Penn State U., University Park, PA 16802).

American Psychological Association, Committee on Employment and Human Resources. (1986). The changing face of American psychology. *American Psychologist, 41*, 1311-1327.

American Psychological Association. (1980). *Accreditation Criteria.* Washington, DC: Author.

Brown, D. T., & Lindstrom, J. P. (1977). *Directory of school psychology programs in the United States and Canada.* Washington, DC: National Association of School Psychologists.

Brown, D. T., & Minke, K. M. (1984). *Directory of school psychology training programs.* Washington, DC: National Association of School Psychologists.

Brown, D. T., & Minke, K. M. (1986). School psychology graduate training: A comprehensive analysis. *American Psychologist, 41*, 1328-1338.

Cummings, J. A., Huebner, E. S., & McLeskey, J. (1985). Issues in the preservice preparation of school psychologists for rural settings. *School Psychology Review, 14*, 429-437.

Dana, R. H., & May, W. T. (Eds.). (1987). *Internship training in professional psychology.* Washington, DC: Hemisphere Publishing Corp.

D'Amato, R. C., & Dean, R. S. (1989). *The school psychologist in nontraditional settings: Integrating clients, services, and settings.* Hillsdale, NJ: Erlbaum.

Fagan, T. K. (1986a). School psychology's dilemma: Reappraising solutions and directing attention to the future. *American Psychologist, 41*, 851-861.

Fagan, T. K. (1986b). The historical origins and growth of programs to prepare school psychologists in the United States. *Journal of School Psychology, 24*, 9-22.

Fagan, T. K. (1988). The historical improvement of the school psychology service ratio: Implications for future employment. *School Psychology Review, 17*, 447-458.

Fagan, T. K. (1989). School Psychology: Where next? *Canadian Journal of School Psychology.*

Farling, W. H., & Hoedt, K. C. (1971). *National survey of school psychologists.* Washington, DC: National Association of School Psychologists.

Gerner, M., & Genshaft, J. (1981). *Selecting a school psychology training program.* Washington, DC: National Association of School Psychologists.

Goh, D. S. (1977). Graduate training in school psychology. *Journal of School Psychology, 15*, 207-218.

Knoff, H. M. (1986). *Graduate training in school psychology: A national survey of professional coursework.* Washington, DC: National Association of School Psychologists.

Martens, B. K., & Keller, H. R. (1987). Training school psychologists in the scientific tradition. *School Psychology Review, 16*, 329-337.

McMaster, M., Reschly, D. J., & Peters, J. M. (1989). *Directory of school psychology graduate programs.* Washington, DC: National Association of School Psychologists.

National Association of School Psychologists. (1984, April). *Standards for training and field placement programs in school psychology.* Washington, DC: Author.

National Association of State Consultants for School Psychological Services. (1987, August). Committee report on personnel shortages in school psychology. Available from NASP, Washington, DC.

Prout, H. T., Meyers, J., & Greggo, S. P. (1989). The acceptability of PsyD graduates in the academic job market. Available from authors at ED 233, SUNY-Albany, Albany, NY 12222.

Prus, J. S., White, G. W., & Pendleton, A. (1987). *The handbook of certification and licensure requirements for school psychologists.* Washington, DC: National Association of School Psychologists.

Pryzwansky, W. B., & Wendt, R. N. (1987). *Psychology as a profession: Foundations of practice.* New York: Pergamon.

Ramage, J. C. (1979). National survey of school psychologists: Update. *School Psychology Review, 8*, 153-161.

Reschly, D. J., Genshaft, J., & Binder, M. S. (1987, April). *The 1986 NASP survey: Comparison of practitioners, NASP leadership, and university faculty on key issues.* Washington, DC: National Association of School Psychologists.

Smith, D. K. (1984). Practicing school psychologists: Their characteristics, activities, and populations served. *Professional Psychology: Research and Practice, 15*, 798-810.

Zins, J. E., & Curtis, M. J. (1988). Current status of professional training and practice: Implications for future directions. In T. R. Kratochwill (Ed.), *Advances in school psychology Vol. VI* (pp. 7-48). Hillsdale, NJ: Erlbaum.

Zins, J. E., & Halsell, A. (1986). Status of ethnic minority group members in school psychology training programs. *School Psychology Review, 15*, 76-83.

ANNOTATED BIBLIOGRAPHY

Brown, D. T., & Minke, K. M. (1986). School psychology graduate training: A comprehensive analysis. *American Psychologist, 41*, 1328-1338.
From both historical and contemporary perspective, the authors describe the decline in master's level programs with attendant increases in specialist and doctoral programs. It is estimated that half the graduate students in school psychology will be enrolled in doctoral programs by 1990. The content analyses of specialist and doctoral programs suggest the practical proximity of the specialist to the doctorate and the need for greater opportunities for some programs to acquire the doctoral status. Implications for the issues of entry-level titles and credentials are presented.

McMaster, M., Reschly, D. J., & Peters, J. M. (1989). *Directory of School Psychology Graduate Programs.* Washington, DC: National Association of School Psychologists.
This revision of the previous NASP Directory includes detailed information of every responding training program and a listing of others known to exist (a total of 231 programs). Each program entry provides information on degrees offered, accreditation status, faculty, enrollment and graduates (1986-87), admission criteria, tuition, financial support, field experiences, program philosophy, and development. Summary tables are also presented.

Zins, J. E., & Curtis, M. J. (1988). Current status of professional training and practice: Implications for future directions. In T. R. Kratochwill (Ed.), *Advances in school psychology Vol. VI* (pp. 7-48). Hillsdale, NJ: Erlbaum.
A comprehensive analysis of the development and implementation of the training and practice standards of APA and NASP described within the context of program and practice growth over the past 30 years. The authors have integrated information from numerous sources to provide discussion of many issues including practice titles,

accreditation, program levels, school and non-school practice, APA-NASP differences and the future ways in which these organizations can work together. The authors present the most understandable overview of organizational positions and standards available.

FOOTNOTE

[1]The term subspecialty refers to any area of special proficiency or competency within the specialty of school psychology. As used herein, the terms specialization and subspecialty are synonymous.

50

Best Practices in Transitional Services

Edward M. Levinson
Lynne M. McKee
Indiana University of Pennsylvania

OVERVIEW

It is early Monday morning as you enter Testa U. Child High School, fully prepared for the multidisciplinary staffing to come. You have completed a comprehensive psychological evaluation on Tom, a 16-year-old special education student who was due for his triennial re-evaluation. As you enter the staffing room, you reflect on your evaluation results and recommendations: intelligence test scores and adaptive behavior suggest functioning within the range of educable mental retardation; no evidence of social or emotional adjustment difficulties; recommendation for continued placement in the current special education class. As the staffing begins and other team members begin presenting their evaluation results, it becomes clear to you that this will be a fairly standard, routine re-evaluation staffing. When the time comes to present the results of your evaluation, you do so clearly and eloquently. A few team members have questions, and you answer the questions with no difficulty. You are clearly a well respected and highly valued member of the multidisciplinary team. The team relies heavily on you in formulating recommendations for program planning. The team accepts your recommendation for Tom, and the meeting ends. As you are leaving the staffing, you are joined by another member of the multidisciplinary team. You and she are talking about Tom, when she asks, "What do you think will

happen to him once he leaves school?" "I don't know," you reply. There is a bit of silence, and then your colleague bids you farewell. As you leave the school, your mind begins to wander and your stomach feels empty. Suddenly, you don't feel as good as you did earlier. "What *will* happen to Tom when he leaves school?" you wonder.

Unfortunately, studies which have investigated the extent to which handicapped students like Tom successfully adjust to post-school life have not yielded positive findings. The President's Committee on the Employment of the Handicapped reports that only 21% of handicapped persons will become fully employed, 40% will be underemployed and at the poverty level, and 26% will be on welfare (Pennsylvania Transition from School to Work, 1986). Similarly, Rusch and Phelps (1987) have reported that 67% of handicapped Americans between the ages of 16 and 64 are not working. Of those handicapped persons who are working, 75% are employed on a part time basis, and of those who are not employed, 67% indicated that they would like to be employed. Similarly, statewide surveys in Florida (Fardig, 1985), Washington (Edgar, 1987), Colorado (Mithaug, Horiuchi, and Fanning, 1985), Vermont (Haszadi, Gordon, and Roe, 1985), and Nebraska (Schalock and Lilley, 1986) have indicated that the employment rate for handicapped individuals ranges between 45% and 70% depending upon disability and geographical location. Between 64% and 82% of this population report living at home with a parent or guardian. According to Edgar (1987), 42% of learning disabled and behaviorally disturbed students leave school before graduating and 18% of mentally retarded students do the same.

There is little doubt that given the high unemployment and underemployment rates which exist among the handicapped population, the high percentage of individuals who are handicapped and continue to live at home, and the elevated drop-out rate that exists among the handicapped population, efforts in the area of special education have not resulted in successful integration of these individuals into society. The economic cost of this to society is staggering. In 1984, the U.S. Department of Education, Office of Special Education and Rehabilitative Services, reported that 15 million of the 16 million unemployed, noninstitutionalized handicapped persons of working age were employable at a potential cost savings of 114 billion dollars per year. Poplin (1982) and Batsche (1982) have offered similar statistics with the latter indicating that the cost of maintaining an individual in an institution in Illinois exceeded the cost of educating a person at Harvard! Although most of the money going to handicapped persons in recent years has been to support dependency rather than to facilitate independence, recent efforts at both the state and federal levels to develop transition programs are an attempt to reverse this trend.

In an effort to facilitate successful transition from school to work and community living, federal and state governments are making the issue of school-to-work transition a priority for all handicapped individuals. Wehman, Kregel, and Barcus (1985) offer the following definition of vocational transition:

> Vocational transition is a carefully planned process, which may be initiated either by school personnel or by adult service providers, to establish and implement a plan for either employment or additional vocational training of a handicapped student who will graduate or leave school in three to five years; such a process must involve special educators, parents and/or the student, an adult service system representative, and possibly an employer.

This definition clearly suggests that transitioning efforts must involve a variety of school and community personnel (thus being multidisciplinary in nature), must include the parent of the handicapped student or the student themselves, is a planned and systematic process, and is a process that occurs well before the student is eligible to leave school. Although the definition provided by Wehman et al. (1985) emphasizes school-to-work transition, many transition specialists argue that transition programs must focus upon community adjustment as well. Madeline Will, of the Office of Special Education and Rehabilitative Services, in the landmark document, "OSERS Programming for the Transition of Youth with Disabilities: Bridges from School to Working Life" defined transition as follows:

> The transition from school to working life is an outcome oriented process encompassing a broad array of services and experiences that lead to employment. Transition is a period that includes high school, the point of graduation, additional postsecondary education or adult services, and the initial years of employment. Transition is a bridge between the security and structure offered by the school and the opportunities and risks of adult life. Any bridge requires both a solid span and a secure foundation at either end. The transition from school to work and adult life requires sound preparation in the secondary school, adequate support at the point of school leaving, and secure opportunities and services, if needed, in adult situations. (Will, 1986; p. 10)

Will's document has essentially become the generic roots from which transitional programs have developed. Consequently, a comprehensive transition program will provide handicapped individuals with the services they need in order to develop interpersonal and social skills, independent and home living skills, and skills necessary for employment.

The social, physical, and emotional benefits to be derived by the handicapped individual as a result of successful implementation of transition programs is not to be slighted by the economic benefits to be derived by society. Research has indicated that successful adjustment to work is associated with increased feelings of self worth (Dore & Meachum, 1973; Kalanidi & Deivasenapathy, 1980), improved physical and mental health (O'Toole, 1973; Portigal, 1976), and overall life satisfaction (Bedian & Marbert, 1979; Schmitt & Mellon, 1980). Consequently, should a transition plan be developed and implemented for a handicapped student, and should this plan be successful in allowing this student to make a successful adjustment to employment and community living, not only will society benefit economically, but that individual will, in all likelihood, experience a higher overall quality of life.

It is for these reasons that federal and state governments are providing funding for the development and implementation of programs designed to assist in the transition of handicapped youth from school to work and community. Legislation such as The Education for All Handicapped Children Act of 1975 (PL 94-142) and its amendment (PL 98-199), the Rehabilitation Act of 1973 (PL 93-112) and its amendment (PL 95-602), the Vocational Education Act of 1963 and its amendment in 1968 (PL 90-576) and 1976 (PL 94-482), and, most recently, the Carl D. Perkins Act (PL 98-524) have all combined to encourage the development of school and community based services designed to facilitate transition of handicapped youth. The remainder of this chapter will: (a) explore the knowledge and training school psychologists and other school-based professionals need in developing and implementing transition programs for handicapped youth, (b) provide an overview of transition models and the steps involved in establishing transition programs, and (c) discuss specific actions school psychologists and other school-based professionals can take when developing an individual transition plan for a referred student.

BASIC CONSIDERATIONS IN TRANSITIONAL PROGRAMMING

When one considers the knowledge and information needed by a school psychologist or other school-based professional when facilitating transitioning of handicapped youth, one must first consider what skills the handicapped youth needs to adjust to community living and to obtain and maintain employment successfully. Generally, these skills can be broken down into three major areas: daily living skills, personal-social skills, and occupational/vocational skills (Wehman, Moon, Everson, Wood, & Barcus, 1988). Daily living skills necessary for independent living include managing finances, maintaining a home, caring for personal needs, buying and preparing food, buying and caring for clothing, engaging in recreation and leisure pursuits, and being mobile within the community. Personal/social skills include maintaining hygiene and appearance, accepting praise and criticism, exhibiting situationally appropriate behavior, exhibiting appropriate interpersonal skills, exhibiting adequate problem solving skills, and exhibiting adequate communication skills. Occupational/vocational skills include understanding and exploring occupational and vocational alternatives, exhibiting appropriate work habits and behaviors, possessing marketable vocational skills, and exhibiting appropriate job seeking skills.

In order to develop an appropriate transition plan for a particular student, the aforementioned information about the student must first be obtained. This can be done easily via assessment. Comprehensive assessment of a student's intellectual, academic, and social skills can be combined with measures of adaptive behavior, vocational interests and aptitudes, and work habits to identify individual needs and preferences which must be addressed in the transition plan. Anderson, Hohenshil, Heer, and Levinson (1989) describe this assessment process elsewhere in this volume. School psychologists interested in assisting in the development of transition plans for handicapped youth must become familiar with the means by which vocational assessment data can be gathered. It is most appropriate to integrate this vocational assessment process with the triennial special education re-evaluation process mandated by law for handicapped children in public school programs. Readers are referred to Levinson and Capps (1985) and Hohenshil, Levinson, and Buckland-Heer (1985) for more information on how the two processes can be integrated.

Having identified the individual needs of a particular student and having determined the particular skills which this student needs to learn to facilitate successful transition, school personnel must then structure the educational curriculum accordingly. Generally, this will involve the development of a "functional curriculum." A functional curriculum is one in which the goals and objectives of the curriculum are based upon the demands of adult life across a variety of settings (Wehman et al., 1988). In such a curriculum, the particular skills a student lacks across the domains cited previously (daily living, personal/social, occupational/vocational) are taught in a way that enables the student to utilize the skills in the workplace, leisure and residential settings, and community facilities. Given the difficulty that severely handicapped individuals have in generalizing skills taught in one setting to another setting, it is sometimes necessary to conduct instruction in the setting itself. Consequently, professionals involved in transitional services must be familiar with residential and community-based educational programs. For more information on Life-Centered Career Education, Functional Community Based Special Education, Work Adjustment Training Programs, and other organized programs designed to accomplish the goals listed above, the reader is referred to Levinson, Peterson, and Elston (in press).

Knowledge of local vocational employment options available for handicapped individuals is also necessary for those developing transition plans for students. Generally, options include competitive employment, supported employment, and sheltered employment. The appropriateness of each of these employment options for a particular student depends upon that student's individual skills. Competitive employment options are those in which individuals are placed in competitively salaried community jobs without the provision of ongoing support services. Supported employment options are those in which individuals are placed in jobs with special assistance from "job coaches" who provide continual, ongoing support (including training, retraining, problem resolution, etc.). Sheltered employment options are those in which individuals are placed in businesses operated by human service agencies (typically termed sheltered workshops or work activity centers). The various residential options which are available for handicapped individuals in the local community must also be considered by transition personnel when planning for students. Residential options may include independent living in single family or shared group homes and apartments, living with family or friends, foster homes, nursing homes, and other private and public residential facilities. Again, the appropriateness of each of these alternatives will be determined by the unique needs and circumstances of each student.

Finally, school psychologists and other professionals involved in transitional services must be knowledgeable about the support service agencies which exist in the local community, and must understand the nature of the services provided by these agencies and the extent to which these agencies can assist in the transition process. As will be discussed shortly, the transition process involves a variety of school and community-based professionals working together as a team to provide for the needs of handicapped individuals. To the extent that various team members understand, respect, and utilize the expertise and services provided by one another, the transition process will be greatly facilitated. Figure 1 summarizes the various assessment, training, and

FIGURE 1. Components of Transitional Programming.

Assess			Plan		Train			Place			Follow-up
Needs in:	**Utilizing:**	**By:**	**Objectives in:**	**By:**	**Skills in:**	**In:**	**By:**	**Vocationally in:**	**Residentially in:**	**By:**	
Cognitive Area	Tests	School Psychologists	Employment Area	School Personnel	Cognitive Area	School Setting	Teachers	Competitive Employment	Independent Living in:	School Personnel	
Academic Area	Interviews	Teachers	Residential Living Area	Vocational Rehabilitation Personnel	Academic Area	Residential Setting	School Psychologists	Supported Employment	• Single Family Home	Vocational Rehabilitation Personnel	Provide Needed Support Services
Personal-Social Area	Observations	Counselors	Community Functioning Area	Mental Health/Mental Retardation Personnel	Personal-Social Area	Community Setting	Vocational Rehabilitation Counselors	Sheltered Employment	• Group Home	Mental Health/Mental Retardation Personnel	Evaluate Adequacy of Services Provided
Occupational-Vocational Area	Rating Scales	Vocational Evaluators		Social Service Agency Personnel	Occupational-Vocational Area		Social Workers		Supported Living in:	Social Service Agency Personnel	
Independent Living Area	Work Samples			Employers	Independent Living Area		Job Coaches		• Family's Home		
	Situational Assessment			Parents			Employers		• Group Home		
							Parents		Institutional Living in:		
									• Nursing Home		
									• Hospital		

placement components involved in transitional programming.

BEST PRACTICES IN TRANSITIONAL PROGRAMMING

Transition Models

Within the last five years, a variety of transitional models have been developed which can provide a philosophical foundation for the development of local transitional initiatives. The model developed by the Office of Special Education and Related Services (OSERS) (Will, 1984) provides for three "bridges" from high school to employment: (a) transition without special services — individuals use their own resources to find gainful employment or to continue their education at the postsecondary level; (b) transition with time-limited services — individuals use vocational rehabilitation services and job training programs to obtain employment; once employment is obtained, the individual ceases to need services; and (c) transition with ongoing services — individuals use continuing adult services to obtain and maintain employment as an alternative to custodial or sheltered employment. This model emphasizes the development of a secondary school educational curriculum conducive to the development of job-related skills, advocates community-based job training and incorporates involvement of local employers.

Paul Wehman (1986) of Virginia Commonwealth University has developed a plan which expands upon many of the concepts outlined by Will (1984). Wehman advocates the development of a functional curriculum, specifically designed to prepare students for vocational placement. The model advocates community-based instruction in which students over the age of 12 spend decreasing amounts of time in the classroom and increasing amounts of time at job sites learning both interpersonal and vocational skills. Wehman advocates the development of an Individualized Transition Plan for students, which specifically identifies the competencies to be acquired by the student and

the transitional support services to be provided by school and community agencies, both during and following the school years. This plan incorporates functional skills required on the job, at home, and in the community, and involves both interagency cooperation and involvement of the parent or guardian of the handicapped student.

The use of a functional curriculum designed to facilitate acquisition of life skills is a component of most transition models. Brolin (1986) has developed a "Life-Centered Career Education Model for the Transition from School to Work" which emphasizes the inclusion of career-oriented education even at the preschool level. Among the propositions inherent in Brolin's model are the following: (a) career education is integrated in all aspects of instruction; (b) "hands on" learning experiences are a part of the educational process wherever possible; (c) an active partnership among schools, parents/guardians, business/industry, and community agencies must be developed; and (d) a professional responsible for all aspects of transition must be identified. Brolin's model is one which can be considered to be a total-person approach which emphasizes all aspects of an individual's development equally.

Development of Transitional Programs

As has been suggested earlier, transitional programming of handicapped individuals involves a variety of school and community-based professionals. Consequently, the initial step in developing a transition program at the local level is to identify, organize, and mobilize these various professionals and agencies. Wehman et al. (1988) advocate the establishment of a local core transition team to include such professionals as a special education administrator, a vocational education administrator, a vocational rehabilitation administrator, the director of mental health/mental retardation, a developmental disabilities planning council member, and a parent and/or client advocate. Other professionals who could serve on this team might be a university representative, a private industry council representative, and a Social Security Administration representative. According to Wehman et al. (1988), this local core team has the following responsibilities:

1. *Conducting a needs assessment or gathering existing needs assessment information.* The purpose of the needs assessment is to determine the adequacy of existing school, employment, and adult programs. School programs must be evaluated to determine the relationship between educational/vocational programs and employment opportunities available in the local community, the number of students who have successfully been placed in jobs and residential facilities following graduation, the functional nature of the educational program, and the extent to which students have access to community-based vocational training. Employment programs must be evaluated to determine the number of individuals placed in employment, the retention rate of placed clients, wages earned by employees, and the nature and type of follow-along services provided. Adult service programs must be evaluated to determine the type of vocational assessment and postsecondary training services provided and the availability of supported and sheltered employment opportunities. The quality of community living arrangements, transportation, recreational and leisure programs, and medical and psychological services available in the local area must also be evaluated.

2. *Establishing guidelines for interagency programming.* Based upon the needs assessment data gathered, the team recommends improvements in school and community services and begins developing transition planning procedures. Decisions such as the age at which to begin formal transitional planning, the types of students to receive transitional services, the format and components of the individual transition plans to be developed for students, the professionals to be involved in developing individual transition plans, and the roles of these professionals, etc. are made by this local core team.

3. *Developing a local interagency agreement and action plan.* The team verifies the procedural decisions made with formal written agreements, which have the purpose of further defining the various school and community agency roles and responsibilities in transition programming. Because many states have developed similar interagency agreements at the state levels, these should be reviewed and considered when developing local agreements. According to Wehman et al. (1988), the core team identifies and verifies participation of key agencies and organizations, establishes flow patterns of handicapped students across local agencies and organizations (i.e., when a particular student is likely to be serviced by a particular agency and the nature of the services likely to be provided) and identifies the means by which services will be evaluated.

Individual Transitional Programming

Having established interagency agreements which specify the kinds of transitional services to be provided by the various agencies (school and community) involved and the population to whom these services are provided, individual transitional programming can be initiated. According to Wehman et al. (1988), the first step in implementing this programming is the establishment of Individual Transition Planning Teams (ITPTs) for all students for whom plans are to be developed. Both school and community agency personnel participate on these teams. Appropriate school personnel include teachers (regular, special education, and vocational education), counselors, psychologists, and administrators. Representatives from community agencies such as Mental Health/Mental Retardation, Vocational Rehabilitation, and Social Services also participate on the ITPT. Parents need to be involved in these meetings since research has indicated that parental participation increases the effectiveness of transitional services (Hasazi et al., 1985; Schalock & Lilley, 1986).

Since an overlap obviously exists between those school-based professionals involved in development of the student's Individual Education Plan (IEP) and those who are to be involved in development of the student's Individual Transition Plan (ITP), it makes sense to hold initial ITP meetings as part of annual IEP meetings for handicapped students. That is, at a certain designated point during a student's educational career (the point at which transition planning is to be initiated), the IEP team is expanded to include relevant community agency personnel. Although the age at which this transition planning should begin is debatable, it is the authors' opinion that planning should be initiated at least four years prior to the student leaving school. With more severely handicapped individuals, transition planning should probably be initiated earlier in the student's educational career.

The purpose of the ITPT meeting is to identify realistic and desirable employment and community living outcomes for the student and the school and community agency services which will be necessary to generate these outcomes. Clearly, these outcomes emanate from assessment of the student's skills in the various areas identified earlier. Much like an IEP, the ITP lists these outcomes as long term goals and for each long term goal, cites sequential actions to be taken to accomplish these goals. The implemented ITP is reviewed, revised, and updated annually. Figure 2 provides a sample Individual Transition Plan format.

Roles for School Psychologists

It is likely that school psychologists will become increasingly involved in transitional programming as a result of their extensive involvement in the assessment and programming of handicapped students. Although the specific role that school psychologists will play in the process is yet undefined, it is clear that the skills possessed by school psychologists are critical to the development and implementation of successful transitional plans. The remainder of this chapter will discuss the various roles school psychologists may assume in transitional programming.

Currently, a variety of professionals may assume major responsibility for the development and implementation of transitional programs. Although no agreement currently exists as to whom should assume this major responsibility, a number of "transition specialist" training programs for professionals with such titles as job coach, individual living specialist, supported employment specialist, rehabilitation counselor, and special education teacher do exist. The competencies acquired in these programs clearly overlap with the knowledge and skills possessed by school psychologists. In their study of the competencies taught in 13 university "transition specialist" training programs across the country, Baker, Geiger, and deFur (1988) found that general knowledge of learning theory (particularly behavioral theory) and assessment were areas in which an extensive amount of training was concentrated. Both Baker, Geiger, and deFur (1988) and Marinelli, Tunic, and LeConte (1988) agree that adolescent psychology is a frequently omitted, but important, area in the training of transition specialists. Clearly, the school psychologist's expertise in assessment, learning and behavior theory, and adolescent psychology may be most critical to their involvement in transitioning and will most assuredly render them an important member of the transition planning team. The roles of the various professionals on this team, however, will vary depending upon interest and expertise.

From an assessment perspective, school psychologists have much to contribute to transition planning. As mentioned previously, particularly important in transitional planning will be evaluation of interpersonal and social skills, independent living skills, and vocational skills. School psychologists working at the secondary school level may wish to alter their assessment strategies somewhat in order to emphasize these areas. For example, school psychologists might choose to incorporate measures of vocational interests and aptitudes and social skills (via interviews, observations, and paper-pencil tests) into their assessments. A number of time and cost-efficient procedures for gathering this information are available to school psychologists and are discussed elsewhere in this volume. Likewise, school psychologists might also wish to incorporate an evaluation of functional living skills into their assessments. An instrument such as the Social and Prevocational Information Battery (Halpern, Raffeld, Irvin, & Link, 1975) would provide functional skills assessment data which could be utilized in transitional programming.

The school psychologists' knowledge of learning and behavior theory and of adolescent psychology allows them to serve as effective consultants to teachers (regular, special education, vocational education), rehabilitation counselors, job coaches, and employers relative to the conditions under which optimum learning and performance might be facilitated. As a member of the Individual Transition Planning Team, this knowledge can assist in the development of specific actions designed to accomplish identified learning objectives. Because a large amount of training may occur outside of the school in job, community, or residential settings, school psychologists will have to prepare themselves to provide consultation services in settings other than the office or classroom. As a consultant, the school psychologist may also function as a liaison among parents, the Individual Transition Planning Team, community service agencies, and employers or, in some cases, actually initiate the development of transitional programming. School psychologists who plan to function as behavioral consultants within transition programs are referred to Kratochwill's (1989) chapter on behavioral consultation.

Other roles for school psychologists in the transition process encompass the areas of direct intervention, inservice, and research. From a direct intervention perspective, the school psychologist may facilitate transition by initiating development of social skills training programs. Such programs might be most effective when implemented within residential, community, or employment settings. Readers are referred to Gresham (1989), who discussed social skills training. Similarly, school psychologists will probably find themselves working directly with parents of handicapped students as a function of their role in transition programs and are referred to Murray's (1989) chapter on counseling parents of handicapped children. School psychologists might conduct inservice workshops on the use of assessment data in transitional programming with those involved in the development of ITPs, and on basic issues in adolescent psychology or learning for those professionals involved in direct training of skills necessary for successful transition. Finally, a need exists to evaluate the effectiveness of the various programs designed to facilitate acquisition of the skills needed for successful transition. The degree to which local school and community-based services are successful in facilitating the successful transition of students from school to work and community must be evaluated. School psychologists interested in evaluating the effectiveness of transitional programming are referred to Keith's (1989) chapter on conducting school based research.

SUMMARY

As the full impact of recent federal legislation aimed at facilitating the transitioning of handicapped youth between school and adult living is realized, it is likely that an increased number of school psychologists will become involved in transitioning efforts. The success of these efforts may ultimately influence the overall quality of life experienced by the handicapped students with whom school psychologists work. School psychologists, working as part of a transitioning team comprised of both school and community-based professionals, will need to upgrade their knowledge of vocational and independent living skills assessment, functional curricula and community-based education, and the various employment and residential options available in their

FIGURE 2. Individual Transition Plan.

Student's Name: _____ Home School: _____

Last _____ First _____ Middle

Address: _____ Date of Birth: _____ Age: _____

_____

Parents' Names: _____ Telephone: _____

Date of Meeting: _____ Proposed Graduation Date: _____

Participants	Agency	Position	Telephone
_____	_____	_____	_____
_____	_____	_____	_____
_____	_____	_____	_____
_____	_____	_____	_____
_____	_____	_____	_____

Major Goal:

Employment: _____

Residential Living: _____

Community Functioning: _____

ACTION PLAN:

	Employment				Residential Living				Community Functioning			
	Action	Timeline	Person	Pos.	Action	Timeline	Person	Pos.	Action	Timeline	Person	Pos.
School	1.											
	2.											
	3.											
Vocational Rehabilitation	1.											
	2.											
	3.											
Mental Health/ Mental Retardation	1.											
	2.											
	3.											
Other: _____	1.											
	2.											
	3.											
Other: _____	1.											
	2.											
	3.											

local community. Although the exact role school psychologists will assume in transitioning efforts is yet undefined, the school psychologist's assessment, counseling, consultation, and research skills will prove to be valuable assets to the development, implementation, and evaluation of Individual Transition Plans, and overall transition programs. It is hoped that this chapter has provided an initial base of information pertinent to the school psychologist's involvement in transitioning efforts.

REFERENCES

Anderson, W. T., Hohenshil, T. H., Heer, K., & Levinson, E. M. (1990). In A. Thomas & J. Grimes (Eds.), *Best practices in school psychology* (pp. 787-797). Washington, DC: National Association of School Psychologists.

Baker, B. C., Geiger, W. L., & deFur, S. (November, 1988). *Competencies for transition personnel.* Paper presented at the Mid-East Regional Conference of the Career Development Division of the Council for Exceptional Children, White Sulphur Springs, WVA.

Batsche, C. (1982). *Handbook for vocational school psychology.* Des Moines, IA: Iowa Department of Public Instruction.

Bedian, A. G., & Marbert, L. D. (1979). Individual differences in self perception and the job-life satisfaction relationship. *Journal of Social Psychology, 109,* 111-118.

Brolin, D. E. (1986). A model for providing comprehensive transitional services: The role of special education. In J. Chadsey-Rusch & C. Hanley-Maxwell (Eds.), *Enhancing transition from school to the workplace for handicapped youth: Personnel preparation implications* (pp. 116-128). Champaign, IL: National Network for Professional Development in Vocational Special Education.

Dore, R., & Meachum, M. (1973). Self concept and interests related to job satisfaction of managers. *Personnel Psychology, 26,* 49-59.

Edgar, E. (1987). Secondary programs in special education: Are many of them justifiable? *Exceptional Children, 53*(6), 555-561.

Fardig, D. B., Algozzine, R. F., Schwartz, S. E., Hensel, J. E., & Westling, D. L. (1985). Postsecondary vocational adjustment of rural, mildly handicapped students. *Exceptional Children, 52*(2), 115-121.

Gresham, F. (1990). Best practices in social skills training. In A. Thomas & J. Grimes (Eds.), *Best practices in school psychology* (pp. 695-709). Washington, DC: National Association of School Psychologists.

Hasazi, S. B., Gordon, L. R., & Roe, C. A. (1985). Factors associated with the employment status of handicapped youth exiting high school from 1979 to 1983. *Exceptional Children, 51*(6), 455-469.

Halpern, A. S., Raffeld, P., Irvin, L. K., & Link, R. (1975). *Social and prevocational information battery.* Monterey, CA: Publishers Test Service.

Hohenshil, T. H., Levinson, E. M., & Buckland-Heer, K. (1985). Vocational assessment practices for school psychologists. In A. Thomas and J. Grimes (Eds.), *Best practices in school psychology* (pp. 215-228). Kent, OH: National Association of School Psychologists.

Kalanidi, M. S., & Deivasenapathy, P. (1980). Self concept and job satisfaction among the self employed. *Psychological Studies, 25,* 39-41.

Keith, T. (1990). Best practices in conducting school based research. In A. Thomas & J. Grimes (Eds.), *Best practices in school psychology,* (pp. 207-218). Washington, DC: National Association of School Psychologists.

Kratochwill, T. (1990). Best practices in behavioral consultation. In A. Thomas & J. Grimes (Eds.), *Best practices in school psychology* (pp. 147-169). Washington, DC: National Association of School Psychologists.

Levinson, E. M., & Capps, C. F. (1985). Vocational assessment and special education triennial reevaluations at the secondary school level. *Psychology in the Schools, 22*(3), 283-292.

Levinson, E. M., Peterson, M., & Elston, R. (in press). Vocational counseling with the mentally retarded. In D. C. Strohmer & H. T. Prout (Eds.), *Counseling and psychotherapy with mentally retarded persons.* Clinical Psychology Publishing.

Marinelli, R. P., Tunic, R. H., & Leconte, P. (November, 1988). *Vocational evaluation education: Regional programs.* Paper presented at the Mid-East Regional Conference of the Career Development Division of the Council for Exceptional Children, White Sulphur Springs, WVA.

Mithaug, D. E., Horiuchi, C. N., & Fanning, P. H. (1985). A report on the Colorado statewide follow-up survey of special education students. *Exceptional Children, 51*(5), 397-404.

Murray, J. (1990). Best practices in counseling parents of handicapped children. In A. Thomas & J. Grimes (Eds.), *Best practices in school psychology* (pp. 823-836). Washington, DC: National Association of School Psychologists.

O'Toole, J. (Ed.). (1973). *Work in America: Report of a special task force to the Secretary of Health, Education, and Welfare.* Cambridge, MA: MIT Press.

Pennsylvania Transition from School to the Workplace. (1986). (pp. 3, 7, 83). Pennsylvania Departments of Education & Labor and Industry.

Portigal, A. H. (1976). *Towards the measurement of work satisfaction.* Paris: Organization for Economic Cooperation and Development.

Poplin, P. (1981). The development and execution of the IEP: Who does what, when, to whom? In T. H. Hohenshil & W. T. Anderson (Eds.), *School psychological services in secondary vocational education: Roles in programs for handicapped students.* Blacksburg, VA: Virginia Tech. (ERIC Document Reproduction Service, No. 215 245)

Rusch, F. R., & Phelps, L. A. (1987). Secondary special education and transition from school to work: A national priority. *Exceptional Children, 53*(6), 487–492.

Schalock, R. L., & Lilley, M. A. (1986). Placement from community-based mental retardation programs: How well do clients do after 8 to 10 years? *American Journal of Mental Deficiency, 90*(6), 669–676.

Schmitt, N., & Mellon, P. M. (1980). Life and job satisfaction: Is the job central? *Journal of Vocational Behavior, 16*(1), 51–58.

Wehman, P., Moon, M. S., Everson, J. M., Wood, W., & Barcus, J. M. (1988). *Transition from school to work: New challenges for youth with severe disabilities.* Baltimore, MD: Paul H. Brooks Publishing Co.

Wehman, P. (1986). Transition for handicapped youth from school to work. In J. Chadsey-Rusch & C. Hanley-Maxwell (Eds.), *Enhancing transition from school to the workplace for handicapped youth: Personnel preparation implications* (pp. 26–43). Champaign, IL: National Network for Professional Development in Vocational Special Education.

Wehman, P., Kregel, J., & Barcus, J. M. (1985). From school to work: A vocational transition model for handicapped students. *Exceptional Children, 52*(1), 25–37.

Will, M. (1986). OSERS programming for the transition of youth with disabilities: Bridges from school to working life. In J. Chadsey-Rusch & C. Hanley-Maxwell (Eds.), *Enhancing transition from school to the workplace for handicapped youth: Personnel preparation implications* (pp. 9–

24). Champaign, IL: National Network for Professional Development in Vocational Special Education.

ANNOTATED BIBLIOGRAPHY

Brolin, D. (Ed.). (1986). *Transition from school to work and adult life.* Columbia, MO: Division on Career Development, Council for Exceptional Children.
This volume, which contains abstracts on more than 80 projects, curricula, teaching methods, and transition models, is a useful reference guide for professionals and parents interested in the development of transition programs.

Wehman, P., Moon, M. S., Everson, J. M., Wood, W., & Barcus, J. M. (1988). *Transition from school to work: New challenges for youth with severe disabilities.* Baltimore, MD: Paul H. Brooks Publishing Co.
This text provides a comprehensive overview of transitional services, including a discussion of the initial planning process and development of interagency agreements, professional and parent roles in the transition process, and individualized transitional planning.

McCarthy, P., Everson, J. M., Moon, S., & Barcus, J. M. (Eds.). (1985). *School-to-work transition for youth with severe disabilities.* Richmond, VA: Virginia Commonwealth University, Project Transition Into Employment.
This compendium of articles by various authors describes step-by-step procedures for the development and implementation of transitional programs for severely handicapped students.

Technical Assistance for Special Populations Program (TASPP). The National Center for Research in Vocational Education, Department of Vocational and Technical Education, The University of Illinois — 345 Education Building, 1310 South Sixth St., Champaign, IL 61820. Dr. Carolyn Maddy-Bernstein, Director, 217-333-0807.
TASPP is a resource center specifically designed to assist in the transition of special needs learners to workplaces and continuing education programs, and can provide professionals with information on model programs, project materials, etc.

Horton, B., Maddox, M., & Edgar, E. (1984). *Adult transition model: Planning for postschool services.* Bellevue, WA: Edmark Corporation.
This handbook contains strategies and methods in the areas of administration, parent education, staff education, and student training which can be used to facilitate the transition process. Sample questionnaires, proposed meeting agendas, evaluation forms, etc. are included. Materials can be duplicated.

51

Best Practices in Urban School Psychology

John H. Jackson
Milwaukee Board of School Directors, retired

OVERVIEW

Best practices in urban school psychology need to be identified and utilized for several reasons. First, large numbers of students are referred for psychological services and the best practices in the field ought to be available to reduce these numbers. Second, many teachers and other urban school personnel are stymied in trying to educate vast numbers of students whose multicultural backgrounds condition learning. Some of the frustration of these educators may be relieved if the psychological insights of best professional practices are made available from knowledgeable and empathic school psychologists. Third, many of our urban schools operate as if under siege both from within and without. These schools may be assisted through best practices to get in touch with the communities they are intended to serve. Fourth, specific behavioral problems of students and staff in urban schools, such as violence and gang activities, are deep-seated and potentially life-threatening and demand the best of practices in school psychology.

If our best practices can be identified and effected generally in school psychology, school psychology practitioners and their school clients should experience a degree of success not heretofore generally realized. Best practices could modify the perceptions among some school people, as well as some parents and students, that white psychologists all too often cannot or will not relate directly to and work effectively with minority urban adolescent students. Best practices could increase trust by school people in the validity and reliability of psychological assessment/diagnostic procedures. Best practices certainly could help school people understand and use the types of therapeutic interventions that school psychologists can provide both to troubled urban students and to school staffs.

School psychology and urban school psychology can be defined in a number of ways. The definitions selected for this chapter are those that are intended to be useful in discussing psychological services in urban schools. From this vantage point, school psychology is that specialty area that is composed of constructs, principles, instruments, methods, and procedures designed to assist learning and learners singly or in groups, families, and institutions with developmental or pathological problems. Urban school psychology is the adaptation of school psychology, as defined here, to the needs of learning and learners in large cities or similar geographic areas by practitioners who have skills, sensitivities, attitudes, and values appropriate to working with variegated urban populations.

The parameters of urban school psychology overlap the parameters of school psychology as it is practiced in other geographic settings. The definition of urban school psychology, therefore, cannot naively assert that urban school psychology in its every aspect is found only in an urban school setting. Some aspects of school psychology may be observed in schools that are located *everywhere*, but in the urban school setting they have distinguishing nuances.

A related, alternative set of terms has been defined by Jackson (1986) as a basis for discussing urban school psychology. The reader might find these terms helpful for a slightly varying view of urban school psychology. Included are definitions of schools, urban schools, school psychological service delivery, as well as conceptual and logistical hurdles to services delivery.

School psychology began its first applications outside the university in the urban setting of the Chicago School System (Mullen, 1967). However, it was only about 20 years ago that urban school psychology began to depart from the testing and reporting model of its origin. Bernauer and Jackson (1974) have documented this trend from the perspective of their positions as administrators in a large Midwest urban school system. The process of change has been slow, with greatest broadening of service delivery coming in recent years. Therefore, what we conceptualize as best practices in urban school psychology are in continual transition. In fact, continual change as a function of the interplay of urban factors is the basic characteristic of best practices in urban school psychology.

From the perspective of the foregoing *overview* to urban school psychology, the reader will be presented *basic considerations* for the practice of urban school psychology and specified *best practices* in urban school psychology followed by a *summary statement*. The *annotated bibliography* will provide indepth glimpses of specific aspects of best practices in urban school psychology.

BASIC CONSIDERATIONS FOR PRACTICE OF URBAN SCHOOL PSYCHOLOGY

The immediate context for the practice of urban school psychology shapes and directs the specific nature and quality of practice. This context lies both outside and within the practitioner. Perhaps the most relevant factors, those with the greatest impact upon the nature and quality of practice, are factors external to the urban school psychologist, which may include characteristics of the urban student population, type of school organization and operation, philosophy and policies of the school or school system, and public laws, statutes, ordinances, and administrative codes. Other external factors that exert significant influence upon practice are the university training programs from which a given school or system recruits the majority of its psychological services staff and the availability of services in the larger community outside the school or school system. Factors internal to the urban school psychologist include personal attitudes, opinions, sensitivities, and values, as well as skills and techniques involved in testing, consultation, program building, and therapy. These internal factors constitute the driving forces that shape the image and identity of the specialty.

Characteristics of the Current Urban School Student Population

The characteristics of the urban student population are perhaps the single factor external to the school psychologist that has the most influence upon how the specialty is practiced. Therefore, the characteristics of urban school students should be well understood, appreciated, and used as signposts in service delivery. The following annotated list is in no particular order.

1. A large number of students from economically poor families. These students have missed out on so much of the schooling and development required to successfully meet the academic demands and other school pressures for certain social behaviors that they must have special assistance merely to fulfill the more surface roles of students. These missing social behaviors include *giving the appearance* of paying attention to what the teacher is saying, which the school

psychologist may help the students accomplish as a means of producing teacher reinforcement and general approval.

2. Great number of minorities. In many, if not most, of the nation's large urban schools, minorities comprise the majority of the student population, presenting many teachers with various and relatively unknown cultures, the black social caste background, and varied learning styles, which require adaptation of instructional approaches and some psychological procedures. The range of values, perceptions, motivations, and so forth that issue from caste status and the varied cultures and learning styles may require more concrete classroom lessons and culture-specific interpretation of individual psychological test results.

3. Discontinuities between home and school and academic underachievement. Many students come from homes characterized by values generally at variance with what is taught in the schools, and school learning can seem meaningless. Specific variances such as that between the insistence of teachers that students value learning and the indifference of students and parents to the school's academic subjects can be reduced through parent–teacher conferences conducted by school psychologists to discuss the integration of culture-related content. Some variances are reduced through the participation of school psychologists on curriculum committees.

4. Racism. Social distance and rejection are daily experiences, which trouble the self-concept and engender strong negative emotions that interfere with learning. Racial self-hate, for example, may require psychological therapy, carefully guided personal experiences, and human relations skills training to unblock the learning process.

5. Socialized delinquency. Formal and informal gangs exist and support their members in opposition to organized society, including the school. To substitute the influence of the teacher for that of the gang often requires that school psychologists utilize the services of specialists in gang processes.

6. Need for special education. There is continuing confrontation over who needs and who does not need special education classes. Decision making involving school psychologists and others on placement teams regarding recommendations for special education can be facilitated by the promulgation of explicit criteria.

7. "Gray area" students. Large numbers of troubled students don't qualify for special education placement, receive no other help, and burden the school with considerable disruptiveness. These are the students whose needs are documented by psychological test data, which school psychologists use to argue their case for services and needed programs in the regular education program before the school administration and school board.

8. At-risk students. At-risk students sometimes are defined so broadly as to include practically every child in a particular building. Students who truly are at risk experience a shortage of services under nondiscriminatory definitions, which school psychologists and others need to work to have appropriately delimited.

Features of the Urban School Organization and Operation

The characteristics of schools, as urban institutions, impact heavily on the practice of school psychology in numerous ways, some of which are detrimental to the provision of services. The school may be organized and administered democratically or autocratically or somewhere between these polarities. The administration may be relatively insensitive to the needs of students and staff and try to use the services of the school psychologist to rid the school of referred students. In an effort to maintain firm control, formal lines of communication may be the modus operandi in the building, thus slowing the interchange of ideas and messages to the point where timeliness in supplying services is no longer honored.

In the author's experience, the greater the number of poor, minority, and central city students in a school, the more challenge there is for the administrator. As a result, the administration may tend to be more autocratic, bureaucratic, and rigidly formal in its procedures and relationships. There often is considerable lack of understanding by the school administrator and staff of the functions of the school psychologist and of ways to utilize the school psychologist's services to the greatest benefit of the students and the entire school. The school psychologist will need to provide information formally and informally to help the administration and staff to understand, appreciate, and use psychological services under urban conditions effectively.

In the complex urban school organization the relationship of school psychology with the special education establishment may be anything but facilitating. In the more highly organized and bureaucratic school systems in big cities, one is likely to encounter school psychology programs that are administered separately from the special education programs rather than being *jointly* administered with the special education program or subsumed by the special education program. Potentially, within this structure, a certain paranoia may be generated such that special education personnel attempt to control school psychology decisions even when apparently there is no need for self-protection in reality. There may be special education efforts to dictate which tests are to be administered with different suspected disabilities, how they are to be interpreted, and whether the findings satisfy their understanding of the criteria for the respective programs. All too frequently time-consuming efforts are needed to search for even a temporary reapproachment between special education and school psychology in the urban school, and those efforts may be deeply embittering. *The urban school psychologist's attitude has to be harmony with, but professional independence from, special education personnel.*

Legal Content

It is important for urban school psychologists to familiarize themselves with the interpretations that their respective school systems place upon the laws and statutes that affect school psychology practice, and to follow the expected practices pursuant to the interpretations. This practice within the particular limits of the system can help to assure the psychologist of legal defense from the system in the event of a lawsuit or a hearing subsequent to an appeal from the assessment team results.

A variety of legislation and court decisions, at the federal, state, and local school board levels, help to shape the practice of school psychology. School board legislation or regulations will be discussed in the next section.

At the current time, perhaps the most intrusive *federal legislation* into school psychology practice is The Education of All Handicapped Children Act of 1975 (Public Law 94-142), together with its preschool amendment PL 99-457, and the Family Education Rights and Privacy Act (PL 93-112, or FERPA). As Prasse (1978) has illustrated, there are many sections of PL 94-142 that have implications for school psychology. Given these implications, the school psychologist needs to fully understand which types of tests the school system accepts for placement purposes, which procedures the system considers to be racially discriminatory, whether consultation with the teacher as the treatment of choice for an assessed student requires a psychological component in the individualized education program (IEP), and so on. With regard to FERPA and its provisions granting to parents the right of access to their children's records, the right to obtain copies of the records, and the right to challenge content in the record, the school psychologist needs to understand which records the school or system has decided are to be created and how soon they are to be destroyed; if raw data are to be destroyed immediately, only the report is available for parent access and use.

Overcast and Sales (1980) have observed that the majority of all of the state legislatures have left implementation of state statutes on special education under the direction of administrative agencies and agency rules and regulations that have the force of law. Specifically, this means that at the state level it is the rules and regulations of the department of education or public instruction that are most relevant to school psychology practice. These rules and regulations, in the experience of the writer, tend to be strictly enforced in the large cities especially because of racial politics and organized advocacy groups. Thus, urban school psychologists often, and I think correctly, feel the pressure of being held to the highest levels of accountability.

Philosophies and Policies of Schools and School Systems

The philosophy and policies of various schools and school systems offer students and others different programs of psychological services that place differing demands upon practicing school psychologists. Some systems choose to offer the narrowest possible program: testing, reporting, and referring cases to help outside the school system. Some provide a limited range of services: testing, reporting, consulting, and referring out of students who need psychotherapeutic interventions. Other schools or systems offer the full range of school psychological services: advising, testing, reporting, consulting, program building, counseling, and a variety of other interventions such as behavioral therapy, psychoeducational therapy, and psychotherapy. In this type of program, referrals to services outside the school ordinarily are for students determined to be in need of 24-hour residential care. Legal vulnerabilities inhere in each type of program; the more comprehensive the program, the more vulnerable is the school psychologist and the more professional liability insurance he or she needs. Even though the schools ordinarily carry liability insurance to cover staff, many urban school psychologists carry their own professional liability insurance as a precautionary measure in what has been called a litigious world.

Not only are there legal abilities for school psychologists in the *types* of services provided, but there also are legal liabilities associated with the *place* where services are delivered. If the schools do not allow services delivery in the home, psychologists who insist upon going to the home, especially in some urban settings, may be exposing themselves to a high probability of personal mishaps not covered by school board insurance. Thus, one must understand board policy thoroughly.

The philosophy and policies of the urban school or school system are likely to be highly political and closely monitored by competing community groups. In such a politically charged setting, a serious prospect is that the practitioner will be caught in a dilemma posed by contradiction between mandates of the profession and directives from the schools. In an authoritarian or rigid school, in a hostile school environment, or in a school in which special education personnel try to control school psychology practice, this dilemma may arise fairly often. In these instances, the school psychologist needs to (a) inform the school or system administrator of the dilemma and of the strength of professional guidelines and ethical principles, and of the intention of not abrogating these; (b) if necessary, seek clarification from a national professional membership organization, such as the American Psychological Association and the National Association of School Psychologists; (c) seek support from the state school psychologist consultant; and (d) finalize a decision that is communicated clearly to the persons concerned and be prepared for whatever consequences may result.

Appropriate Background of Personhood and Training for School Psychology Services Practice in the Urban Setting

The backgrounds of developed personhood and of professional training that the most successful school psychologists bring to urban practice should enable them to do the following: First, they should have the skills to minister, with objectivity, validity, and reliability, to all students and, as appropriate, to all school staff and parents. This has been especially problematic with regard to the assessment of minority children (Oakland, 1973). In addition to assessment, the requirements of the modern urban school might include skills in consulting, counseling, and giving individual, group, and family therapy, as well as providing psychoeducational therapy (Jackson, 1970; Jackson & Bernauer, 1975a), promoting program building; serving on school or systemwide committees, and managing special projects (Jackson & Bernauer, 1975b). Currently, much training does not respond to the needs of students. Green (1981) has pointed out the failure of traditional training programs to provide psychologists with the type of therapeutic skills required to keep minority clients in therapy.

Second, they should have the self-awareness to know, understand, and accept their own limitations and biases. Third, they should have knowledge and understanding of a variety of ethnic and racial groups (Rosenfield & Esquivel, 1985; Rosado, 1986). Fourth, they should have the qualities of respecting, accepting, and caring for others who are different from themselves in culture, race, and language. Self-evaluations in respect to these qualities and continuing education are important.

Because of the rapidity with which problematic events can develop and the large number of students in urban schools who are referred for services as a result of these events, the most successful school psychologists in this setting are adaptable to a very rapid pace in conducting various evaluation procedures with students and engaging in quick decision making, hurried reporting, and timely and creative follow-up.

Due to the administrative complexity of the urban school, the most successful urban school psychologist is prepared to manage, with a degree of patience, the simultaneity of many demands and requests from all directions. These come from the school, from colleagues, from the community, and from the psychological services unit itself. The condition is further aggravated by the professional demands that the psychologist places upon himself or herself for professional quality in the face of external demands and repeated requests.

Toleration of frustration and severe personal stress, and the use of specific techniques to control them likely are the urban school psychologist's trustiest sidearms. Pressures, failures, lack of openly expressed appreciation by clients, and sometimes unjustified criticism are visited upon the psychological services practitioner in the urban school.

The urban school psychologist ordinarily moves freely among assigned schools, community social agencies, hospitals, and clinics. This requires careful management of time and dutiful documentation of local travel. Related to the business of time management is the habit of avoiding the appearance of too frequent and too long habitation of the lounge or dungeon or whatever the coffeeroom is called. Time-wasting and failure to shoulder a fair share of responsibility are easy accusations by those who are engaged in classrooms with 25–30 or more students against those who work one-on-one or with small groups in schedules that are perceived to be unilaterally arranged.

Availability of Community Psychological Services

In the urban setting a goodly number of individual psychological practitioners, agencies, clinics, and hospitals are available for students of all ages and they do have an impact on services provided within the schools. These agencies need to be recognized and employed to the best advantage of school clients. Briggs (1973) has discussed referring out to the community mental health center all problems needing long-term attention.

Most of these community resources are available upon request, but some follow different procedures. For example, community service providers may aggressively enter the building without prior communication and planning with the school psychologist and other school providers. In the building, they independently seek out and screen student clients and refer them to their own agencies, evidently ignoring the conflict of interest represented in such procedures, as well as the possible violation of bargaining contracts. To prevent this, service providers, including the school psychologist, need to monitor closely personnel from other agencies.

Some school administrators play school personal services providers against community providers, thereby causing direct confrontation between these two groups. School psychologists need to guard against this divisive practice.

BEST PRACTICES IN URBAN SCHOOL PSYCHOLOGY

Best practices acknowledge the basic considerations delineated above and build upon their positive aspects while trying to avoid or trying to manage the negative aspects. These best practices are the efforts of qualified professionals who are developing and integrating structures and organizations to provide sound service and professional practice to urban school clients in accordance with high standards and guidelines. In this context, best practices are incorporated in the overall features of the psychological services unit, services to individuals and groups (clinical services), and special projects (programmatic services), systemic services, and evaluation.

The practices that have gained the status of "best practices" are those that formally or informally have been evaluated and found to be successful. Jackson and Pryzwansky (1987) have detailed the planning and implementation stages of a formal evaluation of one urban school psychology services unit, utilizing professional standards. This study, the only one of its kind in the current professional literature, provides a useful model for helping to identify effective and best school psychology practices. In identifying best practices, it is important to observe and evaluate what is actually done on the job instead of assuming the transfer of training from the university to the field. The actual services provided define the specialty and its practitioners, despite what is (or it not) taught in university training programs as school psychology.

The Overall Program of the School Psychology Services Unit

A number of specific overall program components constitute best practices, although ordinarily they are not thought of as *practices:* determining the program model, student advocacy, supervision, staffing, development of special projects, and in-service training.

Determining the model of service delivery. School psychologists ethically are obligated to provide appropriate professional services to a needful referred student. When they do not or cannot provide the needed services, it is incumbent upon them to assist the student in obtaining the needed help from elsewhere. The student may be referred to other in-school providers or to community providers. In either case, the referring school psychologist, as appropriate, needs to maintain a linkage with the other service or services in order to collaborate in meeting the student's broad needs regardless of the limitations of their respective programs.

Figure 1 depicts the concept of potential relative size of the student population that might need to be referred out from the three types of programs mentioned earlier. The narrow-range programs potentially refer out the most students and, assuming proper follow-up, have a large task of monitoring services received from the outside programs. Broad-range programs refer the fewest students and have fewest outside services to monitor.

Given urban students' characteristics and the difficulties that poor and minority families have in accessing agencies, clients quite frequently don't follow up referral into the community. Thus, a program that comprehensively serves students at school

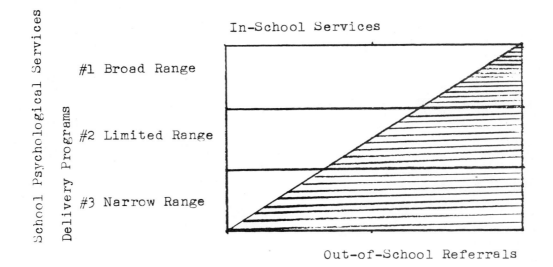

FIGURE 1. **School psychological services strategies for provision of services.**

may be the most serviceable in the urban setting.

Some school psychology services units may find it preferable to seek and obtain community psychological services for students *at the time they are needed.* However, if these services are to be used, there are very effective alternatives to this ad hoc arrangement. A within-school psychological services program can be strengthened considerably through proactive planning, before need arises, with community agencies, institutions, and individual practitioners. Pro bono or paid prior-to-service agreements can ease and quicken access to community services. Prearranged psychological services may be most effective if provided at school under the supervision of the school psychology services unit.

It is important to recognize not only that community professionals can be helpful in some ways, but also that their services often may be a waste at best and

deleterious at worst. They may view clients as sick when they are not, or as sicker than they are, if their usual practice is only with seriously ill youths. Teachers often complain that students who return from community therapy services evidence more disturbed and disturbing behavior than before they left. The novice urban school psychologist is eager to use community services, only to be frequently disillusioned. To avoid such disillusionment, it is important that consultants and outside providers be carefully judged, for example, through extensive and intensive interviews, for what they truly can offer to the urban school psychologist serving a multiracial student population.

Student advocacy. When the urban student characteristics cited above are reviewed vis-a-vis the actual program of the ordinary urban school psychology services unit, needs for additional services or programs become fairly obvious to the urban practitioner. Regardless of the type of program of psychological services authorized by the school board, the psychological services unit and its staff are obligated to advocate for appropriate and sufficient services and programs. In urban schools it is the *absence* of programs and services for regular education students, who make up approximately 90% of a school system and many of whom are hurting, that is most obvious.

Thus, in the urban schools advocacy on behalf of disabled and hurting students in the regular education program is a major task to be carried out. Advocacy needs to be perceived by everyone as a role function of the psychological services unit and staff. Advocacy for additional psychological services can be conducted through advising community groups, by appealing directly to the school administration, by documenting unserved regular education cases by means of proposed annual service projects and increased staff, and though a variety of other approaches.

Advocacy may be for short-term or long-term goals. The specific nature of advocacy activities is shaped largely by these goals.

Professional supervision for professional people. There have been and continue to be efforts by urban school personnel to control school psychologists and other support services personnel. Special education administrators often assume this stance. Building principals, wanting complete control over all that goes on within their buildings, have been very active in attempting to supervise school psychologists, especially where urban decentralization is occurring. The general compromise on this matter has resulted in the assignment of some administrative supervision to special education administrators and principals, and both professional supervision and general administration to the head of the psychological services unit.

The concept of cross-categorical supervision has come to special education. Here supervision is exercised across several special education disability programs by a supervisor in one of the programs. Some special educators view cross-categorical supervision as subsuming school psychology, and herein lies the threat of nonprofessional supervision. The antidote to this view can be the firm reminder by the school psychologist and psychological services unit that special education and school psychology are separate professions, with different content, methods, and procedures, and they therefore require different types of supervision.

Multicultural staffing. Given the great mix of races and ethnic groups in the urban schools and the overrepresentation of minorities in special education programs (Jennings, Mendelsohn, May, & Brown, 1988), a major consideration of the psychological services unit is that staff represent the student mix. This makes available the racially variegated staff necessary to understand, respect, and appreciate the backgrounds and cultural contexts of at least the major student groups, but without implying that practitioners should work only with students from their respective racial and ethnic groups.

Despite the great need for racial and ethnic variety in urban school psychology staffing, such staffing is not available. Psychologists likely to fill these positions are white. They need to be the best alternatives possible. Special knowledge, skills, sensitivities, and other resources need to be obtained through continuing education, self-education, and especially associations and direct experience in the community where the students live.

In-service training. Continuing education in the profession is necessary to stay abreast of changing roles (Mowder, 1979), to understand new developments, and to systematically develop unmastered or advanced proficiencies. With large staffs in urban schools, it can be economical to plan some on-site in-service education programs; they can be tailored to the identified needs of the staff. Specially tailored in-service series can move a staff in different directions, as desired. Therefore, it is important that urban school psychologists take all actions necessary to ensure that these programs serve their professional needs.

In-School Services Provided to Individuals and Groups: Clinical Services

Clinical services provided at school by the psychological services units are of three types. These include practices under PL 94-142, practices with regular education students not qualified under PL 94-142, and services directly to the staff, administration, and parents.

Practices under PL 94-142. In the typical urban school today, the majority of school psychology services and time are related to due process, the multidisciplinary team (M-Team), case staffing, reporting, the individual educational plan (IEP), follow-up mandated intervention, and reevaluation, all under PL 94-142. This requires continuous *teaming* with special education staff and staff from other disciplines, where there are myriad problems (Maher & Pfeiffer, 1983).

Provisions for specific services, for example, reevaluations every 3 years or oftener, bear so heavily upon school psychologists that, as a group, they are stressed greatly in the effort to adapt professional services to the law's provisions. The demands are too great for the time and energy that school psychologists have to give. They are distressed over having to cut corners, over having to modify standard procedures, over having to meet arbitrary time lines established primarily to suit the purposes of other in-school practitioners, and over continual efforts to avoid transgressing professional practice guidelines and ethical principles. Some have taken *stress leaves* from their positions.

In order to manage this process positively, to adapt, many urban school psychologists have taken a number of specific steps, which include the following: (a) In many cases informing the schools, with minimal assessment, that the referred students have no *psychological* problems, but indicating the types of problems it is believed they really have;

(b) conducting less testing, overall; (c) recommending brief consultation that can be discharged in one or two short visits with the teacher instead of recommending ongoing therapy, which requires a commitment of greater time; and (d) adapting shorter reevaluation reports. Gutkin and Tieger (1970) have observed that under current funding statutes, psychologists are able to use only a small percentage of their actual skills.

The process of *teaming*, itself, with special education personnel has been stressful for many school psychologists in the urban school. Difficult problems need to be overcome in the relationship in order to best serve handicapped students. Problems may vary from system to system, but the following are some of the problems and viable correctives.

1. Asserting the right to decide if one's specialty is needed on the M-team, instead of having this decided by someone else. This may be resolved through the creation of vehicles that involve the school psychologist in decision making from the start.

2. Deciding which tests to employ in the evaluation and reevaluation process, instead of being forced to select specific tests desired by special education members on the M-Team.

3. Interpreting independently their own test data, without having other interpretations imposed upon them by special education personnel in staffing sessions. Clarification of the type of diagnostic data that the special education program criteria call for can do much to help eliminate the confrontations that result.

4. Exercising the right to follow the dictates of case data in reaching diagnostic conclusions and recommending needed programming, without being pressured by special education personnel on the M-team to agree with their preferred conclusions and recommendations. Using the disagreement report as often as necessary in order to remain consistent with the data, and being willing to go to legal hearings, if necessary, enable the school psychologist to maintain the

independence of a professional psychologist.

5. Insisting upon the prerogative of providing to the special education student the type of psychological intervention that one's professional insights dictate as proper, rather than allowing the M-Team to decide. This prerogative may be guarded by means of guidelines that enable the M-Team to refer to the school psychologist for "psychological services," the individual psychologist deciding upon the treatment of choice.

Services for regular education students not covered by PL 94-142. Many students in the regular education program of an urban school system are more in need of psychological help than are many students in the special education program. The reason for this incongruity is that the former do not satisfy the relatively narrow criteria of the special education programs and receive no special services.

In the wake of the funded service mandates of PL 94-142, poorly funded to unfunded services to regular education students in urban schools were reduced to practically zero in some locations. One method subsequently developed for providing services to regular education students is the prereferral service program, suburban and semirural versions of which have been described by Gutkin, Henning-Stout, and Piersel (1988) and Ponti, Zins, and Graden (1988), respectively. In the Milwaukee Public Schools, this method is referred to as the Student Services Process and is the model referred to in this description. This program is a means both of getting services to regular education students and of reducing the number of cases that might be referred to the M-Team only to be found ineligible for a special education service. The prereferral process may be described as assistance to teachers by the school psychologist or other support staff on the basis of a teacher's carefully reviewed description of problematic student behavior. No further referral is necessary when this process is efficacious. When the problem continues or worsens despite the process, referral is necessary for additional help through the Student Services Process or from the M-Team if the student is suspected of having a special education need.

Because of the large numbers of students referred for services in the urban school system, it continues to be difficult to provide adequate services, despite well-designed prereferral plans. Nevertheless, it is important to recognize that urban school psychologists are dedicated to providing, to the extent possible, the full range of psychological services to referred students. Pryzwansky, Harris & Jackson (1984) found that although pressed for time even to do assessments, 66% of a random sample of urban doctoral practitioners and 55% of sampled subdoctoral practitioners provided counseling/therapy services. These writers indicated that such services were evaluated by the psychologists, in some cases employing as many as three criterion measures, and that such services were desired by both school personnel and the school psychologists. Urban school psychologists would do well to continue to find time to include counseling/therapy among their best practices.

Direct services to school personnel and parents. The urban school psychologist provides clinical services not only to students but also to school staff members and parents for presenting behaviors that negatively impact on the teaching–learning process or the parenting–learning process. These services include both consultation and psychodynamic interventions (Jackson, 1969). Additionally, urban school psychologists may assist in helping school staff members to obtain outside services provided through the Employee Assistance Program (EAP) and other resources.

Services to school personnel are a very sensitive area because of the potential danger in admitting to having mental health problems. Nevertheless, because of the intensity and constancy of daily pressures, this is an area that the urban school psychologist may give much attention in the future.

Special Projects Within the Urban Psychological Services Unit: Programmatic Services

In some urban school systems, the psychological service units have developed beyond providing only clinical services to individuals and groups. In response to epidemiological data, they have begun to provide programs of services organized and administered from within the unit but involving, as needed and appropriate, other instructional and service personnel.

From time to time one or another student characteristic may exacerbate negative student behaviors, reaching to epidemic proportions. When this occurs and, for example, violent or suicidal behaviors become a special problem, the urban school system's psychological services staff, utilizing available community professionals, may find it necessary to develop and pilot intervention projects appropriate to the problematic behavior. The size of the urban psychological services unit ordinarily is large enough to assign a small cadre of skilled and interested staff members to the project.

The practical reality and success of such projects in urban schools depend heavily upon assessing the problem area in relation to the student populations most involved and shaping a project to fit the needs of these groups. Once again the great need to thoroughly understand racial minorities served is paramount.

Systemic Services

The urban school psychologist is responsible for services beyond the levels of clinical and programmatic services. Here, the services are focused upon broad problems or system concerns, whether the psychologist is working with the school administrator, staff and/or parents.

Perhaps the major advantage the school psychology practitioners have over other psychological specialists is their knowledge, understanding, and appreciation of the school as a socializing institution and multicultural teaching-learning as a process. The urban school psychologist, in most instances, is an itinerant staff member, who travels to two or more schools that sometimes have different grade levels and that most often are in different geographic locations with varied subcultures. The itinerant nature of the position provides the urban school psychologist with a broad view of the system, its operations, and its needs. Thus, other than providing direct student services or student case-centered consultation, school psychologists first of all may serve as valued members of school or systemwide committees, task forces, and other bodies that plan, regulate, or exercise oversight of major aspects of the school or system. These committees and task force groups address such topics as supply of services to identified subpopulations, the grading system, promotions and retention, health problems and the curriculum, and the middle school organization. Psychologists' input into such important areas of school decision making can have a pervasive psychological impact upon school behavior and the teaching-learning process.

Second, urban school psychologists may routinely offer in-service training or continuing education to school staffs. These are based upon expressed needs, such as self-understanding and skills in motivating learners. In-service training may be credited for salary increases or not. Such offerings ordinarily are developed by school psychologists wishing to teach them usually outside of work hours for extra financial remuneration or credit toward future salary increments.

Third, parenting skills are frequently in need of improvement among urban parents, regardless of the level of their formal education. Parent, parent-teacher, or parent-teacher–student meetings in the evenings are easy to reach without distant travel; therefore, invitations from these groups are good opportunities for one-time presentations on any number of topics, *if parents will attend.*

Fourth, in the urban school, the quality of interpersonal relations often is problematic at best and downright negative at worst. School psychologists may organize and conduct or participate in human relations programs. These most often are conducted outside of school hours in order to enable all staff in a given building to participate.

Fifth, another major activity of urban school psychologists outside of direct clinical services and case-centered consultation is that of consulting with school staff on problems that psychological input might ameliorate.

Sixth, with the many stresses that are experienced by school personnel in the urban setting, there is frequent need for individual and/or group counseling or therapy for school staff members in the school. The school psychologist may be requested to provide the counseling or therapy because of the availability of the service and because of the in-depth understanding of the problems that motivate staff to seek the help. Where counseling and therapy are not needed, stress management training can be helpful and seems to be a form of help that school administrators can request and accept without embarrassment.

Evaluation of Practices to Find the Best Practices in School Psychology

Practitioners who make requests for additional programs and staff pursuant to the ever increasing number of cases and situations calling for psychological services have begun to face demands from the ultimate shapers of school and system budgets for databases of support for each request. Without hard data it appears that it will be difficult to obtain requests. Without the documentation of hard data, it is likely to be impossible to have requests even considered. Urban school psychologists are learning to include an evaluation component in proposals and pilot efforts consistently as a means of identifying and documenting best psychological practices in their schools and systems.

SUMMARY

It is imperative that best practices in urban school psychology be identified and employed widely and consistently for both the effectiveness of services and the

perception of the specialty as a major helping resource.

Urban school psychology is the application of the content, instruments, methods, and procedures of psychology to learners singly or in groups, to families, and to institutions. The application may be developmental or rehabilitative and may be practiced in the large cities or metropolitan areas, as well as in smaller cities with characteristics very similar to those of the bigger areas. *Any one or two individual practices do not characterize urban school psychology, since urban school psychology is the totality of a set of attitudes, sensitivities, appreciations, and practices of service delivery to learners, school staffs, and parents in the urban setting. This totality with its own nuances defines urban school psychology.*

The Chicago Public Schools undertook the original practice of specialized urban school psychology. The practice was long focused upon testing for special education placement, its original purpose. The Milwaukee Public School System has been a pioneer in broadening the practice of urban school psychology.

Many parameters shape the needs and context of the practice of urban school psychology. The most salient of these include the unique values and problems of students from many cultural and ethnic backgrounds, great numbers of whom are poor. Other parameters are the organization and operation of the school or system, legislation, and school board philosophy, policies, and procedures, as well as the type of training received by the school psychologists and the availability of community psychological services.

Specific school psychological services may be viewed as clinical, programmatic, or systemic. Clinical services subsume direct help to students, school staff members, and parents. Pragmatic services comprise projects and programs that are developed and administered by the school psychology services unit for students engaged in epidemic outbreaks of negative behaviors. Systemic services constitute psychological help for institution-level organization and process problems.

REFERENCES

Bernauer, M., & Jackson, J. H. (1974). Review of school psychology for 1973. *Professional Psychology, 5*, 155-165.

Briggs, C. H. (1973). Transition in school psychological services: A case study. *Journal of School Psychology, 11*, 88-91.

Green, L. (1981). Training psychologists to work with minority clients: A prototypic model with black clients. *Professional Psychology, 12*, 732-739.

Gutkin, T., Henning-Stout, M., & Piersel, W. C. (1988). Impact of a districtwide behavioral consultation prereferral intervention service on patterns of school psychological service delivery. *Professional School Psychology, 3*, 301-308.

Gutkin, T., & Tieger, A. G. (1970). Funding patterns for exceptional children: Current approaches and suggested alternatives. *Professional Psychology, 10*, 670-676.

Jackson, J. H. (1969, September). *The school psychologist as therapist for teachers and parents.* Paper presented at the 77th annual convention of the American Psychological Association, Washington, DC.

Jackson, J. H. (1970). Psychoeducational therapy as the primary activity of school psychologists. *Journal of School Psychology, 8*, 186-189.

Jackson, J. H. (1986). Conceptual and logistical hurdles: Service delivery to urban schools. In S. N. Elliott & J. C. Witt (Eds.), *The delivery of psychological services in schools: Concepts, processes, and issues* (pp. 171-202). Hillsdale, NJ: Erlbaum.

Jackson, J. H., & Bernauer, M. (1975a). A responsibility model for the practice of professional school psychology: Psychoeducational therapy. *Journal of School Psychology, 13*, 76-81.

Jackson, J. H., & Bernauer, M. (1975b). *Skills for comprehensive and effective psychological services in large urban school districts.* Summary report of the Division of School Psychology, Division 16, American Psychological Association, Preconvention Workshop. Washington, DC: American Psychological Association.

Jackson, J. H., & Pryzwansky, W. B. (1987). An audit-evaluation of a school psychological services unit utilizing professional standards: An example. *Professional School Psychology, 2*, 125-134.

Jennings, K. D., Mendelsohn, S. R., May, K., & Brown, G. M. (1988). Elementary students in classes for the emotionally disturbed: Characteristics and classroom behavior. *American Journal of Orthopsychiatry, 58*, 65-76.

Maher, C. A., & Pfeiffer, S. I. (Eds.). (1983). Multidisciplinary teams in the schools: Perspective, practices, possibilities [Special issue]. *School Psychology Review, 12*(2).

Mowder, B. (1979). Legislative mandates: Implications for changes in school psychology training programs. *Professional Psychology, 10*, 681-686.

Mullen, F. A. (1967). The role of the school psychologist in the urban school system. In J. F. Magary (Ed.), *School psychological services in theory and practice: A handbook* (pp. 30-67). Englewood Cliffs, NJ: Prentice-Hall.

Oakland, T. (Ed.). (1973). Assessing minority group children [Special issue]. *Journal of School Psychology, 11*(4).

Overcast, T. D., & Sales, B. D. (1980). Psychologists in state special education legislation. *Professional Psychology, 11*, 774-783.

Ponti, C. R., Zins, J. E., & Graden, J. L. (1988). Implementing a consultation-based service delivery system to decrease referrals for special education: A case study of organizational consideration. *School Psychology Review, 17*, 89-100.

Prasse, D. (1978). Federal legislation and school psychology: Impact and implication. *Professional Psychology, 10*, 592-601.

Pryzwansky, W. B., Harris, J. F., & Jackson, J. H. (1984). Therapy/counseling practices of urban school psychologists. *Professional Psychology: Research and Practice, 15*, 396-404.

Rosado, J. W. (1986). Toward an interfacing of hispanic cultural variables with school psychological services delivery systems. *Professional Psychology: Research and Practice, 17*, 191-199.

Rosenfield, S., & Esquivel, G. B. (1985). Educating school psychologists to work with bilingual/bicultural populations. *Professional Psychology: Research and Practice, 16*, 199-208.

ANNOTATED BIBLIOGRAPHY

Jackson, J. H. (1986). Conceptual and logistical hurdles: Service delivery to urban schools. In S. N. Elliott & J. C. Witt (Eds.), *The delivery of psychological services in schools: Concepts, processes, and issues* (pp. 171-202). Hillsdale, NJ: Erlbaum.
Describes the delivery of school psychology services from the perspective of conceptual and logistical hurdles, which originate both within and outside the schools. Addresses future service delivery and potential hurdles.

Jackson, J. H., & Pryzwansky, W. B. (1987). An audit-evaluation of a school psychological services unit utilizing professional standards: An example. *Professional School Psychology, 2*, 125-134.

Details the planning and implementation stages of an audit-evaluation review of a school psychological services unit in a major urban school district.

Mullen, F. A. (1967). The role of the school psychologist in the urban school system. In J. F. Magary (Ed.), *School psychological services in theory and practice: A handbook* (pp. 30-67). Englewood Cliffs, NJ: Prentice-Hall.
As the title suggests, focus is upon the *role* of the urban school psychologist.

Pryzwansky, W. B., Harris, J. F., & Jackson, J. H. (1984). Therapy/counseling practices of urban school psychologists. *Professional Psychology: Research and Practice, 15,* 396-404.
Presents the results of a survey of therapy/counseling practices of school psychologists in 18 school systems.

52

Best Practices for Utilizing Technology

C. Sue McCullough
Texas Woman's University

OVERVIEW

Best practices for school psychologists utilizing technology in the Information Age include both traditional and innovative practices. Following a traditional scientific-practitioner approach, school psychologists utilize a wide variety of sources of information — observations, interviews, standardized and nonstandardized tests, and existing records. This information is then analyzed, synthesized, integrated, and promulgated in a usable form through the use of technology — typewriters, audio or video tape recorders, telephones, calculators, or computers.

Information Age school psychological best practices involve a three-step *input–process–output* process. *Input* is the retrieval of information, gathering the information needed to answer the referral questions. *Process* is the analysis, synthesis, and evaluation of the information gathered, and the determination of whether the referral question has been adequately answered. *Output* is the application and dissemination of the information in a usable form for those who are entitled to have access to it. This model is recursive, as the output may become input for another component in the scientific-practitioner problem-solving process, as in the evaluation of student progress or psychological services.

This Information Age definition of school psychology practices departs from the traditional NASP definition found in the *Standards for Service Providers* (National Association of School Psychologists, 1985), which lists six primary functions: consultation, assessment, intervention, supervision, research, and program planning and evaluation. Each of these six functions can be reconceptualized by the three-step model above. For instance, consultation requires input of information, processing of that information, and output in a variety of forms.

This chapter will explore this three-step model in detail, particularly addressing best practices in the use of technology in each component. First, competencies required to utilize technological best practices will be presented, followed by best practices in input, process, and output components. Then ethical and professional issues will be addressed.

BASIC CONSIDERATIONS

Every school district in the country has computers available to certain staff and students. Increasingly, school psychologists are expected to utilize computer technology whether dictating a report for clerical word processing, accessing a data bank for student information, preparing an individualized educational plan (IEP), or scoring a standardized test. Minimum competencies at four levels have been identified (Deupree, 1988):

1. The awareness level includes basic computer literacy skills and recognition

of the capabilities of the technology for assisting handicapped individuals;

2. The knowledge level includes knowledge of specific software and hardware applications, sources of information, and evaluation standards;

3. The utilization level includes implementing technology in case management duties, and in intervention and remediation strategies;

4. The proficiency level includes developing innovative practices with technology and being a resource for information on uses and evaluation of technology applications.

These four levels of basic competencies are detailed in Table 1. For the best practice in utilizing technology, school psychologists should be trained at least through Level 3, the utilization level. This training must include not only case management applications, but also knowledge and practice in applying technology in instructional, remediation, and behavioral intervention strategies. The school psychologist should be able to evaluate instructional software for its appropriateness and usefulness in teaching or remediating basic skills in order to include this information in recommendations and consultation activities. School psychologists should also evaluate and implement technological innovations that assist handicapped persons. As an educational consultant, the school psychologist should not only enter the field with practice in these skills, but should also take the responsibility for keeping current on technological changes.

An actual case study illustrates some possibilities for integrating the skills at the proficiency level. In this case, after receiving a referral of a child with a reading problem, the school psychologist first checked the computer data bank to see the child's school records. These carefully controlled records included group achievement test scores administered annually, monthly criterion test scores in reading, spelling, and arithmetic, and other personal and behavioral information. The data provided specific information regarding core academic skills

achieved to date. The psychologist electronically copied and transferred the data into a graph to see changes over time, setting, and instructional method. With printouts in hand, the psychologist consulted with the teacher, the parents, and the child. With the specific skill strengths and deficits identified, and with information about instructional or behavioral handicaps obtained, the psychologist consulted a database that matched specific skills with specific technology (software and/or hardware) designed to remediate or teach that skill. The psychologist included this information in the recommendations made to address the referral question and followed up to evaluate the child's progress in using the technology. The school psychologist in this case had served on the district committee that devised this database, which linked core academic skills with the technology designed to remediate or teach them, and had reaped the rewards of these efforts many times over.

This case study emphasizes the strong dependence that school psychologists have on collecting and synthesizing information. Technology assists greatly in the organization and accessibility of this information. Without electronic databases, information about group achievement tests or classroom academic tests would likely be located not just in separate file drawers, but more likely in separate buildings miles apart! And gathering information across settings would mean chasing down teachers who may or may not have maintained accurate and needed records, or more likely it would mean conducting an assessment to obtain needed information. This case study was in a school district that had centrally organized information on each student in an electronic database. More and more school districts are centralizing records on special education students, on IEPs, and on regular education students' core skills. Teachers are using central databanks to record not only semester grades, but regular academic test grades as well. Security of these databanks is essential, but school psychologists should make sure they are on the list of approved users. In

TABLE 1
Technological Competencies for School Psychologists

Awareness level

Introduction to technology for individuals who know little about it, especially as an educational tool, and who may need to acquire a positive attitude about the use of technology in special and general education. At this level, the school psychologist will:

1. Recognize component parts, functions, and appropriate care.
2. Use and understand terms.
3. Recognize need to utilize technology to assist handicapped persons to compensate, remediate, communicate, and control environments.
4. Recognize need to integrate technology into instructional curriculum of handicapped.
5. Identify general uses of storage and manipulation of data.
6. Be aware of questions for and sources of external evaluation of technology.
7. Recognize need for planning and cost effectiveness.
8. Understand purchasing guidelines and sources.
9. Recognize need for telecommunications and networks.
10. Identify present uses of technology in the workplace and for effective living for the handicapped.
11. Recognize need to be familiar with documentation for hardware, software, and adaptive devices.
12. Understand input–output information-processing model, including impact that sensory deficits have on learners and how technology can be used to compensate for these deficits.

Knowledge level

At this level, the goal is to provide a personal orientation so that the school psychologist can approach the computer with relative comfort and have a broad understanding of its capacity. The school psychologist will have knowledge of:

1. Appropriate uses of:
   a. CAI (computer-assisted instruction).
   b. CMI (computer-managed instruction).
   c. applications software, e.g., word processing, spreadsheet, data base management.
   d. emerging technologies, e.g., videodisk, telecommunication networks, adaptive devices.
2. Integrating computers/technology into curriculum.
3. Research on special education applications.
4. Implications of FERPA, copyright laws, and licensing on school setting applications.
5. Basic operations of computers.
6. Funding sources for special education technology.
7. Evaluation components of instructional and administrative software.
8. Special education applications information and assistance resources.
9. Professional development resources.
10. Technology used to compensate in:
    a. environmental control.
    b. communication.
    c. mobility.
    d. skills in learning, leisure activities, vocational activities, and basic living skills.
11. Software evaluation components:
    a. instructional information.
    b. educational adequacy.
    c. technical adequacy.
    d. hardware/adaptive device compatibility.
    e. appropriateness in meeting special needs.
12. Purchasing questions to ask for adaptive devices.
13. Adaptive devices evaluation components:
    a. alternative switches.
    b. touch-sensitive input devices.
    c. speech output.

(Table 1 — Knowledge level, continued)

     d. modified displays.
     e. tactile output.
     f. special needs software.
14. Developing a team approach and the available resources for information and assistance with uses and evaluation of adaptive devices.
15. Resources for information and assistance with the uses of technology with the handicapped through user groups, and other human resources, banks, data bases, etc.

Utilization level

At this level, the school psychologist will develop the skills needed to implement computer applications for case management and to understand the computer's instructional value. The school psychologist will:

1. Organize and manage technology for effective educational use in the classroom and/or lab situation.
2. Select software for specific uses and needs in case management and assessment.
3. Communicate effectively with others using appropriate technological/computer terminology.
4. Identify and remedy common problems with hardware, software, and adaptive devices.
5. Use hardware and appropriate software for basic computer operations, including "booting" a program, formatting a disk, backing up (copying) a disk, and copying selected files to another disk.
6. Access and use software for:
     a. CAI (computer-assisted instruction):
        (1) drill and practice.
        (2) tutorial.
        (3) simulation.
        (4) problem solving.
        (5) utilities.
     b. shell programs adaptable to individualized content material.
     c. CMI (computer managed instruction).
     d. word processing, database management, telecommunications and networks, adaptive devices.

Proficiency level

At this level, skills will be developed that are necessary for the school psychologist to be more innovative in the delivery of professional and special education services. The technology proficient school psychologist will:

1. Use application software to complete case management and assessment tasks.
2. Be a resource to instructional staff in the selection, use, and evaluation of appropriate hardware and software.
3. Write goals and objectives that integrate technology into teaching specific skills to handicapped students.
4. Evaluate the appropriateness of hardware, software, and adaptive devices.
5. Evaluate hardware, software, and adaptive devices for instructional, educational, and technical adequacy.
6. Develop evaluation plans for hardware, software, adaptive devices, etc. that are applicable to specific populations and specific situations and/or educational systems.
7. Have a directed experience utilizing adaptive devices that compensate for specific student deficits.

addition, it would be wise to serve on the committee that determines which data get stored and in what form, so that information needed for psychological services will be included with appropriate support technology, such as graphing programs, and the capability to import data into a report writing system.

BEST PRACTICES IN UTILIZING TECHNOLOGY

Information Retrieval — Input

After identifying the referral questions, it is necessary to collect information to answer the questions. The individual may be consulted directly, of course. Additionally, other personnel or school records may be consulted. Technology provides several means to efficiently gather information, including school district databases or commercial databases on CD ROMs (Compact Disk Read Only Memory), Information Services, Computer Assisted Instruction (CAI), Computer Managed Instruction (CMI), Intelligent Computer Managed Instruction (ICAI), and Computer Adapted Testing (CAT). Information retrieval may also involve direct assessment on the computer, such as measuring perceptual speed or eye-hand coordination.

Databases. Databases are of two primary types: straight-line and relational. Straight-line databases contain files of information in much the same format as if the information were being filed in a paper file. Each piece of information stands alone, such as an address file containing names, addresses, and telephone numbers. A relational database also contains distinct pieces of information but some of those items are related in some way to other database items, or there may be an overlap in information needed for two different purposes. As one piece of information changes, it may alter other pieces of information also contained in the database. For instance, unpaid library fines may prevent the release of a report card, but when the fine is paid, the report card will be sent. There is a relationship between the paying of library fines and

the release of a report card. A relational database makes these kinds of connections, and as one piece of information is altered, all related pieces of information are altered as well.

Databases may be developed and used on any computer. Extremely large databases requiring megabytes of memory may be found on CD ROMs (compact disk read only memory) or in information services on telecommunication networks. A CD ROM looks like the CD that plays such high-quality music on a stereo. However, instead of music, the CD ROM contains information that is accessed with key words. For instance, the entire *Psychological Abstracts* is contained on two CD ROM disks. The ERIC database and the entire *Encyclopedia Britannica* are on CD ROMs. Ask the CD ROM for information on a topic (for instance, autism in preschoolers), and the screen will show not only reference information but the abstract as well. Looking up the latest research on autism in preschoolers takes just a few minutes, and a printout of desired references and abstracts is ready immediately. CD ROM databases make researching information fun, and very efficient. With the technology not only to read from a CD but also to write to one (WORM drives do this task — Write Once Read Many), school psychologists may soon find school districts beginning to choose this technology for record keeping over banks and banks of file cabinets.

Information services also maintain huge databases. These are accessed over telecommunications networks. Accessing these databases requires a modem attached to a computer and to a telephone line. (A modem is a device that allows the transmission of information between different kinds of computers over telephone lines.) There are many general as well as specialized databases that make it possible not only to retrieve information, but to ask questions and share information with other psychologists or educators. Charges are levied that are based on the long distance telephone charges, time of day, and length of access. However, there are many local networks that are free of charge and are a good place to begin exploring telecommunication functions. Local computer clubs and computer dealers will usually have information on local networks. Professional publications often list professional telecommunication links.

Other databases accessible to school psychologists include computer-assisted instructional programs. These are known as CAI, CMI, and ICAI. Many of these programs teach and test, storing test information on each user as well as on the group of users as a whole. Statistics on what the users know and don't know, and which questions were answered correctly and which incorrectly, are readily available in either individual or group format. ICAI utilizes artificial intelligence programming to do error analysis, to reteach in weak areas, or to branch to different instructional options as the user progresses. If these programs are being used in a school district, the school psychologist should be familiar with them and know how to access and interpret the information. Teachers may need assistance in interpreting the statistical output, which can be produced in copious amounts.

With curriculum-based assessment increasing in use, these computer-assisted learning programs offer an opportunity to collect ongoing academic information. In addition, computer-adapted testing (CAT) databases also provide individualized assessment of basic academic skills with tests randomly generated at the student's level of knowledge (Weiss, 1979). Some CAT databases generate the questions or problems, then produce a paper copy for the student to use. The results must then be input by the student, an aide, or the teacher. Other CAT databases allow the student to take the test on the computer, and automatically score and analyze the results. Then a statistical report can be accessed as needed by the psychologist or teacher (Plake, Witt, & Mitchell, 1986).

Best practices dictate that school psychologists utilize the many databases already available to them to retrieve information either about an individual student or as background information (for research, or for classroom, building, or district group means). Furthermore, best practice also involves the school psychologist in developing the skills necessary to organize and manage the information considered most important for daily practice, and to provide input into the formation of centralized databases. If the school psychologist doesn't have input into the storage and retrieval of this information, someone else will, and the outcome may not meet the needs of psychological services.

Direct assessment. Videotape recordings of classroom behavior have been used to help the student see herself or himself, to analyze student–teacher or student–student interactions, or as feedback in learning a new skill. Video is a powerful medium because it is hard to deny what is recorded, and often behavior or circumstances are noticed that either the observer or the participant were unaware of during the filming. Often the student(s) will want to see the video more than once.

Eye–hand coordination, motor response time, and visual tracking are a few of the skills that can be measured directly on the computer with simple game programs or with specialized programs designed to record the data directly into the computer. Simulations of visual–motor skills required for certain tasks, such as tracking a radar scope, have been found a more effective means of assessing perceptual–motor skills than paper–pencil tests. Computer problem-solving tasks have been used to assess higher-order thinking skills.

Many tests are available for direct administration on the computer, though research on the correlation of computer results with paper–pencil results remains contradictory (Plake et al., 1986). For some personality tests, such as the MMPI or the Millon, computer results appear to be more accurate than paper–pencil results, or even direct interviews. Research has found that people appear to be more honest when reporting personal information to a computer than to a human, even a trained human (Lucas, 1977). Psychologists should check that norms used for computer administrations have been obtained from computer versions and not from paper–pencil versions of the test. Research does not support the assumption that the norms will be identical across the two versions.

Information Analysis and Synthesis — Process

Given that the necessary data have been collected, it now falls to the psychologist to analyze the information for trends; support for hypotheses; strengths and weaknesses; and clues to appropriate remediation or intervention strategies. The information must be synthesized into an understandable product, usually a written report, consultative plan, or treatment strategy. This was the area of the earliest computer assistance in the psychological profession and there is much technology from which to choose, including scoring and analysis programs, report writing programs and procedures, intervention analysis and recommendations, systems analysis for counseling, research design planning, and statistical analysis.

Test scoring and analysis. Few new tests are released without an accompanying computer scoring program, and many older tests have "official" scoring programs and many "unofficial" ones. For instance, the Weschler tests have many scoring and analysis programs available that represent many different viewpoints about appropriate analysis of the test results. Best practice demands that the psychologist learn to evaluate each scoring program along several dimensions: ease of data entry, clarity of the manual and the output, consistency and research support of the interpretations given, upgrade policy as research adds to the interpretive databank, technical and statistical accuracy, compliance with ethics standards, limitations of the program and the output, identification of decision-making rules or algorithms, and reliability and validity of the results. The statistical rule that reliability is not sufficient justification for validity should

be kept foremost in mind. Computer programs are very reliable, that is, they will do the calculations the same way each time. It is the validity of the results that must be carefully scrutinized. The judgment of the validity of the results may vary depending upon the theoretical orientation of the judge. Difficulties may be evident in interpretive results that may make no sense, that do not vary across individuals or protocols, or that do not take important variables into account. To test a program's validity, psychologists can input data from recently completed cases, then compare the computer output with their own judgments.

Another dimension to consider when evaluating test scoring and analysis programs is that some programs follow an actuarial decision-making orientation but others use a clinical decision-making orientation. Actuarial programs adhere strictly to statistical tests of the results, using multiple regression formulas to judge whether results are significant deviations. Interpretive results of these programs contain tables or graphs showing which comparisons were significant and at what level. It is left to the practitioner to attach interpretive significance to these numerical results. These programs do the complex calculations that practitioners often do not have the time or motivation to do. Clinically oriented programs usually have more text in their output, offering several possible interpretations of the data, and using simple comparison, clinical "rules of thumb," research results, or "expert" clinical practice to judge significant deviations. These clinically oriented programs usually reflect the interpretive opinions of individuals claiming "expertise" with that particular test. Research results may or may not support the opinions.

Actuarial programs are criticized for being too number-oriented and for not being able to take into account variables that cannot be translated into numbers, such as motivation, environmental support, or attitude. Clinical programs are criticized for often providing conflicting interpretations to the same data, both across and within programs, and for lack of statistical and research support for some interpretations. Best practice and ethical behavior dictate that neither actuarial nor clinical programs should be used as the "last word" on the interpretation of test results, nor should a computerized interpretive report be used without alteration as the psychological report. The responsibility for interpretive judgments rests on the practitioner. It is the practitioner who may have to support the judgment in a court or a due process hearing, not the computer programmer. Actuarial and clinical programs can provide important and useful information for the psychologist to consider and may even suggest ideas that would not otherwise have been considered. Best practice entails the use of these programs as valuable tools that may save time and provide important input into the interpretive process, while retaining the final decision-making responsibility. These programs may be called "expert systems" but the practitioner is the most expert judge of all the variables in the case.

Given the wide variety of programs available, the psychologist must take the time to investigate and evaluate the programs. Several sources of information are available to aid in this endeavor. In this chapter's references are descriptions of sources of information, one of which contains sample printouts of many programs (Krug, 1988). Some school psychology and special education journals also have software review sections that may be consulted. Both NASP and APA have computer special interest groups that publish newsletters with software reviews and other helpful information.

Report writing. Who has the perfect report writer? That question is not yet answered, though dedicated report-writing programs (that only write reports and do nothing else) and adaptations of generic word processors abound. In the previous edition of this book, the different kinds of report writing programs were described (McCullough, 1985); that information will not be repeated here, since those basic types remain on the market. The choice of a report-writing system

depends in large part on the choice of computer and software, and the preferred, or imposed, means of producing reports (dictating, typing by author, or filling in blanks on a form). Data from one school district indicated that instituting a report-writing system cut report preparation time by 75% and increased the length and quality of the reports. In this district the school psychologists worked together with the clerical staff to devise a system that worked for them.

Planning and evaluation are the key to selecting and setting up an effective report-writing system. What is the preferred mode of report preparation by the psychologists and by the clerical staff? What are the limits of the word-processing software? How much individuality and flexibility can be built into the system? What are the duplicative parts of the report that could be automated or limited to a few relevant choices? Can a databank, set of template files, paper form, or notebook be devised with the choices available, but still leave room for individuation of the report? Are the dedicated report-writing programs flexible enough to meet the needs of both the psychologists and the clerical staff? Do the reports all sound alike, only the names and numbers being changed? What means are provided for security, for saving the report, for transfer of the report to other computer files or software? Can information from other computer files, such as databases, graphs, or spreadsheets, be transported into the report-writing system?

Since reports tend to take on a life of their own and are a permanent representation of the school psychologist's expertise, it is best practice that the content display the uniqueness, strengths, and weaknesses of the individual about whom it is written and that it be grammatically correct and have perfect spelling and punctuation. Word-processing programs with spelling and grammar checkers built in are readily available. Though we may not like to admit it, there are parts of our reports that are repetitive across evaluations, such as test descriptions or reasons for referral. Most word processors have a means of storing the repeated items as text files, allowing them to be copied and inserted into the text of the report as needed. Some multifunction or integrated programs have databases that can be set up for data entry of demographic information, test results, and other idiographic information. This information may then be merged or copied into a word-processing format that has been stored as a master template while at the same time providing a database of important information. Multifunction programs with spreadsheets and graphing components have also been used in much the same way, entering information in the spreadsheet in order to perform calculations, such as learning disability formulas, or graphing the spreadsheet information and inserting it into the report.

Multifunction programs that contain word-processing, databases, spreadsheet, and sometimes graphing components appear to provide the most flexible base for developing a report-writing system. It will take planning and development time to individualize the system to meet the needs of the school psychologists using it. This time investment will be paid back many times over in increased satisfaction with the outcome and eventually in reduced time for the clerical chore of report writing. Information on systems that have been devised is available from professional computer interest groups through their regular newsletters, annual meetings, and presentations.

Intervention and remediation. Information analysis and synthesis includes the planning of intervention or remediation strategies. School psychologists should be aware of research results that have demonstrated the effectiveness of using computer software in remediating learning deficiencies and in effectively intervening in a variety of behavior and social problems (Chen & Paisley, 1985). Research has shown that computer programs excel at reteaching or providing repeated practice in deficient academic skills. The computer provides immediate corrective feedback, infinite patience in waiting for a response, infinite numbers of repetitions without a grumble, and even customized

branching to test and teach weak steps in the problem-solving process. Software reviews are available in a number of computer and education journals.

Best practice dictates that the school psychologist be familiar with and evaluate instructional programs so that judgments can be made about their appropriateness for each individual. Some programs flash too much or move too quickly for some children. The amount and kind of corrective feedback is important to note. The reading level of text on the screen, the amount and size of text, and the use and placement of graphics should be evaluated. The content should be evaluated to determine which skills are being assumed, and which are being taught and practiced. The amount of control that the user has over timing of presentations, movement through the program and correction of errors should be noted. If color is used to discriminate certain concepts, it should be clearly differentiated. The amount and ease of data or text entry, the record-keeping capabilities, and the kind of hard copy produced should also be evaluated. Practical considerations such as amount of time the computer is available for remediation, the amount and kind of supervision needed and available, and the child's response set and experiences with computers must be taken into account.

Numerous software programs are available to teach psychological, behavioral, and social skills concepts, such as drug and alcohol abuse, safe sex, assertiveness skills, child development milestones, or weight control. Computer programs will walk teachers or practitioners through the planning of a behavioral intervention. Computer simulations will simulate the psychological decision-making process, demonstrate split-brain functioning, let the user run a rat through a maze, or measure the saliva of Pavlov's dogs. Access to the computer and computer games have been used successfully as behavioral intervention contingencies. Research has shown that communication skills actually increase among students who use computers as they compare notes, ask each other questions, and assist each other in solving problems that arise.

The use of computer software can be structured to promote cooperation and communication and the development and practice of appropriate social skills.

Computer programs are available to collect and to analyze behavioral data (Fitzpatrick, 1977). Graphs of the behavior are produced as well. These programs may be used on small laptop computers or any convenient computer in the environment in which the observation is occurring. If school psychologists are ignoring the computer, they are ignoring a very powerful medium for instructional remediation and behavioral intervention (Chen & Paisley, 1985).

Counseling systems. Analysis and synthesis of information may include an analysis of the family or environmental system that surrounds the child in order to plan an appropriate intervention or counseling strategy. Computer programs are available that assist in mapping out the system, analyzing patterns of interaction, and suggesting strategic interventions (Atkinson, McKenzie, & Keeney, 1985).

Specialized programs have also been developed to assist in maintaining case notes and case management information. Generic database programs can also be used for this purpose.

Research design and statistics. Computer programs assist in selecting the appropriate research design and statistical tests for a research project. The program asks questions about the independent and dependent variables, then offers suggestions for appropriate design and statistical tests. Many statistical programs, from simple to complex, are available for statistical data analysis. School psychologists should look for statistical programs that will allow them to import data from databases or spreadsheets that may have been developed in conjunction with their report-writing and data management systems. Then data would have to be entered only one time to serve many purposes. Again, planning ahead to determine what uses the infor-

mation may need to serve is the most important step in planning for the utilization of computer technology.

Evaluation. As computers generate and maintain enormous amounts of data, information analysis and synthesis becomes a critical skill for Information Age school psychologists. A unique part of the training of a school psychologist is in evaluation: problem solving by the scientific method. Computers assist in the organization of information, but human judgment is still needed to decide what information is important enough to keep, and to make sense of it all, to interpret the information in light of the particular circumstances and individuals affected by it. As already noted, evaluation is a key component in identifying appropriate software for instructional and remediation uses, for planning and developing a report-writing and data management system, and for selecting test scoring and analysis software.

Evaluation can be at the individual level, as in the tasks outlined above or as used in the evaluation of performance. Information maintained on databases is readily available for inclusion or summation in quarterly or annual reports. Evaluation can be at the group or program level also: Database information in CAI or CAT programs may show group means and standard deviations; a pattern may emerge on LD referrals. Database information from many psychological service providers can be analyzed for service demands and projections. The evaluation may be continuous, momentary, or cumulative. A caveat that is appropriate here is not to let the collecting and evaluation of information become tyrannical or overwhelming. It is the meaning to be attached to the data that is relevant. It is evaluating the information with certain goals in mind that will make it meaningful. It is deciding ahead of time what is important, and what is not, that will streamline the data collection, analysis, and synthesis processes and help make the evaluation of the information less threatening and more meaningful.

Information Dissemination — Output

When the information has been retrieved, analyzed, and synthesized, then it must be disseminated. The information, usually in a report form of some kind, can be transmitted through the electronic interoffice mail, parked in a secure storage device such as a disk or tape, or printed as paper copy. Computers have not, as predicted, cut down on paper production. In fact, some studies suggest that there is more printed copy produced than ever before. We must feel a need for something substantial in our hands to show for all our work instead of keeping it hidden away in the magical never-never land of computer memory storage devices. Nevertheless, it is possible to disseminate information without resorting to paper copy.

Telecommunication is increasing in use among school psychologists. In a 1982 survey (McCullough, Andre, & Olson, 1982) of school psychology computer users, none used modems to telecommunicate. By the time of a 1988 survey (McCullough, 1988), more than one-third of the correspondents were using modems regularly to access state, national, and professional telecommunication networks or to access mainframe computers in their workplace. Electronic mail is appearing in larger school districts and in universities. Electronic mail (also known as "E-mail") consists of messages sent from one computer to another. The messages wait in the computer's memory ("electronic mailbox") until the receiver calls for it. An answer can be returned electronically without ever being printed on paper. Electronic mail supposedly eliminates playing "telephone tag." However, the users do have to check their electronic mailbox regularly or communication breaks down. Electronic mail is used for scheduling computer labs or testing schedules, following up on cases with memos to teachers or other professionals, and exchanging ideas or gaining answers to professional questions from others across the country. Electronic bulletin boards are used to get the most recent information about computer hardware or software, employment information, special education innovations, or convention programs. The NASP Executive Board communicates via electronic mail.

Fax machines provide a means to transmit actual copies of documents over telecommunication lines. The fax machine is a computer device that uses a visual scanner to electronically digitize documents for transmission over telephone lines. The receiving fax machine recomposes and prints out the document. Fax machines are increasingly used in school districts for the transfer of documents to other school districts. For instance, school records have a hard time keeping up with some itinerant students who change schools frequently. With a fax machine, the student's records can arrive the same day he or she does, transferred with only a telephone call.

BEST PRACTICE ISSUES

Several professional and ethical issues surround the increasing utilization of technology in the school psychology profession including failure of schools to make data-based decisions, control of information, nonstandardization of computer stimuli used in assessment, effects of the response set of the computer user, cognitive-processing differences and practicality considerations.

In spite of the presence of enormous amounts of information in school systems, there is a tradition of making decisions based on a teachers', psychologists', or principals' "best judgment," which may or may not have any basis in fact or be supported by available data. This tradition may have evolved because the necessary information was likely spread out from a teacher's desk drawers to the central office filing room, located in a basement guarded by rats with one unshaded lightbulb swinging above (usually burned out). As centralized databases and telecommunication networks become more prevalent, will this tradition fade? Will "Don't confuse me with the facts" be replaced by "What do the data show?" A lot depends upon how well organized that database is, how cogently and clearly the data are presented, how easily accessible the system is to all users, how much support the administration gives to building and maintaining an accurate system, how much support and training is given to all users and how strongly enforced is the expectation that all staff use the system appropriately. Refusal of one person or department to use the system weakens the system for all.

A related issue is the control of information, which has to do with the determination not only of what information is included in the database, but who has access to that information. Most sophisticated databases have security codes that can be applied on different levels. A Level 1 access code would allow only input of demographic information, for instance. A Level 6 of a six-level code would allow unlimited access to all information for both reading and writing of information. The privacy of confidential information must be protected by limited access. The legal obligation also exists to inform parents of what information is contained in the database and to notify parents or students of legal age when information in the database is being eliminated. The length of time to keep information in the database is another often unresolved issue but one that needs a consistent policy. Best practice dictates that school psychologists should participate in these decisions, following ethical and professional practice guidelines.

As computers are used more frequently for assessment purposes, the nonstandardization of the computer stimuli raises serious questions. Computer screens display various colors, sizes, and types of text in a variety of sizes of monitors and keyboards. Input can be accomplished by typing on a keyboard, pointing and clicking with a mouse, touching the screen, or talking slowly to the computer. Technical difficulties may arise during the assessment, causing loss of data or interruption of the testing session. How comparable are the results of assessment given under these different conditions? How valid are the norms developed under one set of conditions when utilized under totally different circumstances?

A related assessment issue is the response set of the individual who is facing assessment on a computer. Research indicates that individuals who have experiences with computers generally have more favorable attitudes towards them. However, research also shows that many girls may perceive a computer or a computer lab to be the equivalent of a pool table or pool hall — that is, it is the "boys" domain. They are intimidated by the prospect of using a computer. Sex equity research has shown that significantly fewer girls take computer courses, utilize computer labs, or indicate interest in a career in a computer field (Anderson, Welch, & Harris, 1984). The majority of girls are introduced to computers in business career courses, such as typing classes. Another common perception among school-age students, and some teachers, is that computers belong in the math department, again raising fear and intimidation as a possible response set. Before using a computer to do assessment, the school psychologist should assess a student's response set towards the computer and judge whether that attitude would be conducive to obtaining the student's optimal performance (Lee, 1986).

Not only will a student's attitudes and response sets toward technology affect outcomes, but cognitive processing differences influence outcomes as well. Just as attention is paid to learning styles and cognitive strengths in traditional assessment practices, so it must be considered when utilizing technology. A computer program may rely on perceptual–motor skills for success, as in some math programs in which objects containing arithmetic problems or answers must be shot down with accurate firing from a joy stick. Another program may demand higher-order thinking skills, or problem-solving skills in order to solve problems, as in computer programming tasks. Technology tends to be highly visually oriented, audio tapes, and CDs being exceptions. For the student who needs auditory input in addition to visual, the choices of software decrease. However, there are some very good programs that do use multiple input and output of information. The school psychologist needs to be aware of the wide range of software and hardware that exists in order to make the most appropriate recommendations.

How practical are all these ideas and recommended best practices? Costs, school system inertia, professional resistance to change, and traditions loom as inhibitors. The other side of the picture, however, is the tremendous impact of technology on the schools since the beginning of the 1980s. Extremely few students or educators had access to personal computers at the beginning of the decade; now it would be difficult to find a school or school district that does not own a substantial inventory of high-tech equipment, including computers, video cameras, video recorders and playback equipment, fax machines, calculators, or dedicated word-processing units. Having the technology available is the first step towards implementing its use. As noted before, the support of the administration for the training of staff, its clear expectations regarding utilization, and the provision of ongoing technical support personnel is critical to the most effective utilization of the technology. Bridging the gap between having the technology and utilizing it effectively requires strong administrative support and commitment. Best practice also requires professional pride in achieving the highest level of service possible, willingness to learn new skills, and commitment to leadership in working with others to achieve goals related to the implementation of effective uses of technology.

SUMMARY

Best practice for Information Age school psychology follows the traditional scientific problem-solving model represented as information input, processing, and output. Effective utilization of technology demands planning and evaluation skills, adherence to high ethical and professional standards, and leadership in implementing technological goals. Best practice demands that school psychologists have training and practice in utilizing technology for case management, remediation, and intervention and knowledge of technology that assists the handicapped. The result will be more effective services to students, educators, and parents, and a sense of professional pride in learning to control the technology for the benefit of others and ourselves.

REFERENCES

Anderson, R. E., Welch, W. W., & Harris, L. J. (1984). Inequities in opportunities for computer literacy. *Computing Teacher, 11*(8), 10-12.

Atkinson, B. J., McKenzie, P. N., & Keeney, B. P. (1985). The Multiple Vantage Profile: A computerized assessment of social organization in family therapy. *Journal of Psychotherapy and the Family, 1*(1-2), 133-152.

Chen, M., & Paisley, W. (1985). *Children and microcomputers: Research on the newest medium.* Beverly Hills, CA: Sage.

Deupree, C. (1988). Basic technological competencies for school psychologists. *CTASP Newsletter, 7*(1), 6-7.

Fitzpatrick, L. J. (1977). Automated data collection for observed events. *Behavior Research Methods and Instrumentation, 9*, 447-451.

Lee, J. A. (1986). Effects of past computer experience on computerized aptitude test performance. *Educational and Psychological Measurement, 46*(3), 727-733.

Lucas, R. W. (1977). Psychiatrists and a computer as interrogators of patients with alcohol-related illnesses: A comparison. *British Journal of Psychiatry, 131*, 160-167.

McCullough, C. S. (1985). Best practices in computer applications. In A. Thomas & J. Grimes (Eds.), *Best practices in school psychology.* Kent, OH: National Association of School Psychologists.

McCullough, C. S. (1988). Computer utilization survey. *NASP CTASP Newsletter, 7*(2), 4-5.

McCullough, C. S., Andre, M., & Olson, K. (1982). *Computer Applications in School Psychology: Survey Report.* Report prepared for Assistance to the States Committee of the National Association of School Psychologists. Kent OH: National Association of School Psychologists.

National Association of School Psychologists. (1985). *Standards for service providers*. Washington, DC: Author.

Plake, B. S., Witt, J. C., & Mitchell, Jr., J. V. (Eds.). (1986). *The future of testing*. Hillsdale, NJ: Erlbaum.

Romanczyk, R. G. (1986). *Clinical utilization of microcomputer technology*. New York: Pergamon.

Torrance, E. P. (1981). Implications of whole-brained theories of learning and thinking for computer-based instruction. *Journal of Computer Based Instruction, 7*(4), 99–105.

Weiss, D. J. (1979). Computerized adaptive achievement testing. In H. F. O'Neil, Jr. (Ed.). *Procedures for instructional systems development*. New York: Academic.

ANNOTATED BIBLIOGRAPHY

Brand, S. (1987). *The media lab: Inventing the future at M.I.T.* New York: Viking.
A look into the future, describing the Media Lab at M.I.T., which has the latest and most far-reaching technology available anywhere. To read it is to imagine a technological future unlike anything we know today and to dream of the possibilities for school psychology. Must reading for anyone involved in planning for the future.

Krug, S. E. (Ed.). (1988). *Psychware sourcebook, 1988–89* (3rd ed.). Kansas City, MO: Test Corporation of America. (1-800-822-8485).
A reference guide to computer-based products for assessment in psychology, education, and business. The book is descriptive, not evaluative. It provides information useful for making initial decisions about the appropriateness of products for a specific setting and purpose, including categories of intended use, areas of application, types of delivery systems, price, supplier, and (especially useful), sample output or screens from many of the programs. Look for the most recent edition.

NASP.CTASP Newsletter. Washington, DC: National Association of School Psychologists.
A quarterly newsletter, free to members of NASP, that contains articles of interest on computer applications in school psychology. The newsletter is the product of the Computer and Technological Applications in School Psychology Special Interest Group of NASP.

Schwartz, M. D. (Ed.). (1984). *Using computers in clinical practice, psychotherapy, and mental health applications*. New York: Haworth.
Dr. Schwartz has reprinted in this book many articles that were originally published in the newsletter *Computers in Psychiatry/Psychology*, which he edits, as well as new pieces. Some of the topics addressed are choosing a computer system, data management systems for effective case management and clinical record keeping, clinical assessment and interview programs, psychological assessment, computer-based diagnosis, therapeutic applications, issues and research, word processing, and effects on office and clinical procedures, staff, and clients.

53

Best Practices in Vocational Assessment of Students with Disabilities

W. T. Anderson
Division of Youth Services,
Commonwealth of Virginia

T. H. Hohenshil
Virginia Tech

K. Buckland-Heer
Fairfax County (Virginia) Schools

E. M. Levinson
Indiana University of Pennsylvania

OVERVIEW

The evolution of the school psychologist's role in helping special needs students make career and vocational decisions has been well documented (Hohenshil, Levinson, & Buckland-Heer, 1985). As these students progress in the educational system, school psychologists are increasingly involved in the assessment and planning phases of vocational programs for students with disabilities.

The implementation of the vocational assessment role in day-to-day school psychology practice has been problematic. Although numerous articles and publications and more than 30 state and national presentations have featured the topic, many school psychologists do not have specific knowledge of specialized vocational assessment procedures or the foundations necessary to translate traditional psychological results into vocational terms. Part of the problem stems from the lack of recognition accorded the assessment role of school psychologists in planning educational programs for handicapped students. A cursory review of vocational educational and vocational rehabilitation publications reveals that few references are made to the school

psychologist's contribution. The maintenance of essentially separate literature bases further impedes the understanding of the school psychologist's role, as few resources articulate roles and functions in a common vocabulary. Given that vocational practices have been incorporated into the training standards of school psychologists, it can be expected that future graduates will be prepared to assume the role. Current practitioners, however, are also expected to be knowledgeable in regard to standards for practice.

BASIC CONSIDERATIONS

Vocational assessment is a broad term that encompasses an array of models and procedures. At times this variety is confusing, since different professions conduct assessments for different reasons and use different techniques. Traditional vocational assessment in the schools was conducted by guidance counselors for the purpose of helping students select among vocational training programs or for postsecondary planning. Students considering vocational programs typically participated in a sequence of vocational exploration activities designed to acquaint them with vocational programs offered at the high school level. They were also given aptitude tests and interest inventories to help select a program. This approach combined both curriculum-based assessment and formal testing. In the field of vocational rehabilitation vocational assessment relied on a similar trait–factor matching model but used different procedures to evaluate the vocational potential of persons who could not participate in mainstream vocational programs or provide reliable and valid results with more familiar paper-and-pencil tests. Performance tests and work samples were often available only in rehabilitation settings. Rehabilitation facilities also placed more emphasis on adaptive accommodations, daily living skills, and work adjustment outcomes than did the schools.

Currently many school systems are developing intermediate assessment sites that lie conceptually between traditional school-based assessment and vocational rehabilitation. These may be local or regional assessment centers that combine curriculum-based awareness and exploration activities with performance tests and work samples. This expanded assessment continuum provides placement committees with an additional option for assessment while freeing up time in rehabilitation facilities for intensive training and placement functions not available in schools.

To school psychologists, vocational assessment is a relative term applied to the process of collecting data to be used by decision makers involved in the placement of adolescents. The process itself is guided by the students' current educational levels and their ability to proceed unassisted through the career development hierarchy. For example, a student (or their placement committee) preparing to enter an exploration program in the middle school needs information that differs significantly from that needed by the student preparing to enter the workforce. Because career development is a process that begins in childhood and continues throughout a student's educa-

tional career, it has been the position of the NASP Vocational School Psychology Interest Group that vocational considerations should be part of every evaluation. This does not imply, however, that the psychologist must administer a standardized vocational test to each student. During the elementary years it is often sufficient to monitor a student's progress through career development milestones in informal ways and ensure that students with disabilities participate equally in career awareness activities. It is not necessary that school psychologists always administer interest inventories at the secondary level. What is important is that they understand the nature of career development and appropriate assessment procedures — not all of which are necessary for all students.

Vocational assessments in which school psychologists are involved can encompass either prevocational or vocational factors. *Prevocational assessment* highlights a student's progress toward attainment of career developmental competencies, and the acquisition of behavioral, psychological, and motor skills necessary for success in vocational programs (Sabatino, Goh, & Jenson, 1982). Prevocational assessments sensitize the students and decision makers to factors that might interfere with the student's *access* to a vocational program or content. *Vocational assessments* examine factors related to expected vocational levels (e.g., skilled or unskilled) and the specification of a vocational program.

Presently vocational assessment in the schools is concentrated at the ninth- and tenth-grade levels. The Carl D. Perkins Vocational Education Act (Public Law 98-524) mandated that all handicapped students be assessed for vocational interests and aptitudes at least 1 year prior to the grade in which vocational programs are available and in no event later than ninth grade. Compliance with the Perkins Act strained both resources and technology, because few reliable instruments had been published for use with exceptional students that could be given on a large scale in the public schools.

Career Development

Implicit in traditional vocational assessment is the assumption that students are willing and able to use occupational information with little help. And in vocational rehabilitation centers the clients have typically been older, displaced workers who needed help adapting to a previous job setting or retraining for new jobs. Because of these emphases career development and its implications for assessment and planning were not highlighted, since most clients had attained the prerequisite decision-making skills and career orientation before entering a program. It is generally acknowledged that the selection of a career culminates a developmental sequence involving a series of age-related tasks. The process is both cognitive (e.g., involved with decision making) and affective (e.g., dealing with valuing and interests). As students mature, they are expected to gather and process increasingly complex types of information about themselves and about possible occupations. An analysis of current theories reveals that career development closely parallels cognitive development and the self-concept. In fact, Super and his colleagues hypothesized that the selection of a career is an implementation of the vocational self-concept (Osipow, 1983). The vocational self-concept develops in three phases:

1. Fantasy. This substage, between the ages of 4 and 11 permits an individual to attain an orientation to the world of work and to internalize stereotypic job functions. A child may, for example, express an interest in various careers such as firefighting, teaching, or even the Presidency. Fantasy elements are observable in various role-playing activities. Appropriate educational activities include role-plays, field trips, and career games.

2. Interest. As children acquire more complex cognitive functions, their ability to perform comparisons and self-appraisals increases. Between the ages of 12 and 14 youngsters typically begin to crystallize preferences for various activities and school subjects. Activities include hands-on vocational and avocational exploratory activities.

3. Ability. The integration of interests with a realistic appraisal of ability culminates the formation of the vocational self-concept. It is expected that by ninth grade most students can actively participate in planning for the remainder of their education. Exploratory activities and realistic feedback (including grades) are important to the development of a realistic picture of ability.

Most persons proceed through the process of career development with little assistance. Students with disabilities, depending on the nature and severity of the condition, may require help in gathering information and making decisions. Since career development is highly dependent on cognitive and affective factors, impairments in these functions are critical indicators for intervention and for the selection of assessment techniques. Generalizations about the specific needs of a population are often misleading. However, there is sufficient information available to highlight some common problems faced by different populations that need to be addressed in the assessment process.

Mentally impaired individuals have faced stereotypic placement in the past despite the fact that research has not supported a higher tolerance for repetitive activities. Particular attention should be given to self-care and independent living skills, since these relate to functional autonomy in the postsecondary world (Alcorn & Nicholson, 1975).

Learning-disabled students often have limited knowledge of the world of work. Because of specific difficulties, whether related to comprehending written information or organizing for efficient decision making, this population typically encounters problems in seeking and retaining jobs (Anderson, 1986).

Emotionally disabled students frequently have trouble with authority figures. In order for these students to compete in the job market it is important to assess their reaction to supervision and plan a behavioral program to enhance their interpersonal skills, since this is the reason given most often by employers for termination.

Levels of Vocational Assessment

Levels of assessment are determined by the type of information needed to make decisions and may involve a variety of techniques.

Level 1 of vocational assessment begins during the elementary school years and focuses on the work personality (Brolin, 1985). *Work personality* was defined by Dawis and Lofquist (1984) as an individual's vocational needs (values and interests) and abilities (aptitudes and competencies). Assessment of the work personality provides important information to decision makers when planning programs. With a Level 1 assessment, the process of giving students information necessary for refining interests and shaping work-related competencies is more precise and focused.

Level 2 vocational assessments, while continuing to examine work personality and career development information, extend the process to a formal evaluation of interests and aptitudes (Brolin, 1985; Hohenshil et al., 1985). A Level 2 evaluation generally is given during the eighth, ninth, or tenth grade and is geared toward providing specific recommendations regarding vocational programs for intensive exploration and projected training levels. It is apparent that the requirements of the Perkins Act primarily describe a Level 2 assessment.

Level 3 assessment signals the transition from school to work by focusing on training opportunities and specific transitional needs such as job coaches to accompany students, arrangements for independent living, and periodic follow-ups.

Assessment Techniques

Several techniques are used to gather information needed by decision makers (whether students themselves or placement teams). A battery of assessment tools based on a particular student's disability and developmental needs can be drawn up from the following techniques: (a) interviewing, (b) paper-and-pencil tests; (c) performance tests, (d) work samples, (e) simulated work experiences, and (f) work experience.

Interviewing is a standard vocational assessment technique. Evaluators gauge self-concepts, interests, aptitudes, and aspirations during a vocationally-oriented interview. Teachers, parents, and other professionals, in addition to the student, can provide information regarding attention, reaction to criticism, motivation, and work habits — all of which are vocationally relevant. Interviews also provide the evaluator with information about a student's manipulative skills, attention span, vocational interests, training needs, work habits, and aspirations.

Paper-and-pencil tests are the easiest vocational assessment technique to use for sampling occupational interests, vocational aptitudes, work personality, and job-related values. Paper-and-pencil tests are also economical, since many are group-administered and can be scored by various personnel. Specific disabilities may compromise prerequisite test-taking skills, however, and so limit the use of paper-and-pencil tests with special needs populations (Alcorn & Nicholson, 1975).

Performance tests are manipulative tasks that typically minimize the use of paper and pencil and of language (Anastasi, 1982). Performance tests are often abstractions of job tasks (e.g., testing dexterity by having the student assemble a series of nuts and bolts). Performance tests are sold as single-trait samples or may be grouped into multiple-trait batteries.

Work samples encompass a variety of techniques. Work or job samples use the tools, materials, and machines found in particular occupations. Here students actually "try out" selected job functions associated with a job or group of jobs while being observed by a trained "work evaluator." The evaluator rates student interests and obtains ability estimates during work sampling, in addition to observing the work personality, work speed, and product quality.

Simulated work experiences resemble work samples, but are even more realistic in the simulation of work. Simulated work experience is an exploratory technique usually offered as short courses (2–6 weeks) in middle schools or early high school. Here the major goal is to provide students with exploratory vocational experiences, rather than teaching specific occupational skills. Vocational education courses are another, more intensive type of experience.

Work experience or work history is a standard component of assessment in the rehabilitation field, because it provides insight into vocational skills and the work personalities. Since most special needs students have little or no employment history (Hohenshil et al., 1985) the technique has limited usefulness in the schools.

BEST PRACTICES IN VOCATIONAL ASSESSMENT

School Psychologists Role in Vocational Assessment

From the preceding discussion it is apparent that school psychologists might be involved in vocational assessment at different levels of the career development process and might be called on to provide interest and ability information in cases where other methods have not produced concise results. While few school psychologists will work directly in specialized assessment centers, practitioners gather a large amount of vocationally relevant information during a psychological evaluation. The proposed assessment battery outlined in Table 1 overlaps to a considerable degree with traditional psychoeducational test batteries. A specific examination of each component will not be necessary during an evaluation, but it is important for school psychologists to be familiar with the areas to enhance the quality of services to special needs students. In most areas an array of techniques is available to sample information and the actual selection is based on test-taking skills of the student.

Vocational Assessment Techniques

Mental ability. Mental ability, achievement, and interests together yield the most accurate prediction of success in a vocational training program (Hohenshil et al., 1985). Each provides important information to decision makers relating to level of training (cognitive), training needs and accommodations (achievement), and motivation (interests). Mental ability serves a second purpose by sensitizing decision makers to factors, that are likely to interfere with a student's career development.

Achievement. Achievement also serves a dual purpose in vocational assessment. By examining a student's past academic accomplishments and interventions, the decision makers gain insights into factors to consider in the vocational training program in much the same way that an employment history serves to guide rehabilitation goals. In addition, achievement results can highlight the need for specific vocational reading and math requirements rather than general concepts.

Small/large motor coordination. Some degree of motor coordination is required for every job. From a vocational standpoint, however, the emphasis is on functional motor skills rather than pure psychomotor performance. There exists a substantial resource base of equipment to help individuals adapt to many work and training environments. Motor skills can be assessed by observational methods as well as with more specialized instruments.

Personality/social maturity. Personality and social factors are the most common reason given for failures to get or retain jobs (Hohenshil et al., 1985). These include grooming habits, communication skills, and reactions to supervision. Brolin (1985) suggested that decision makers should carefully consider interpersonal skills, independence, self-awareness, self-confidence, and problem solving.

Vocational interest. Vocational interests are correlates of motivation (Anastasi, 1982). For example, a student may

TABLE 1
Vocational Assessment Techniques

Component	Technique
Mental ability/vocational aptitudes	Intelligence tests Aptitude tests (single and multiple) Work samples Work simulations
Achievement	Achievement tests Curriculum based assessment
Small/large motor coordination	Observations Performance tests Work samples Work simulations Curriculum based assessment
Personality/social maturity	Observations Personality tests Rating scales
Interests	Observations Interviews Inventories
Adaptive behaviors	Interviews Observations Rating scales
Career maturity	Observations Interviews Inventories

Note: Adapted with permission from W. T. Anderson and T. H. Hohenshil, in press.

have clearly defined interest in a particular job, but little or no aptitude. Interest assessment is based on an analysis of likes and dislikes for various activities or academic subjects.

Vocational interests are closely related to aptitudes but are poor predictors of skill attainment. The assessment of interests is critical because they represent motivational aspects of behavior. It is important to recognize that interests change over time as students acquire more information about themselves and the world of work. A good indication of this is the student who produces a flat interest profile; with inadequate knowledge of various occupations, such students cannot choose reliably among various options.

Many of the more familiar interest inventories are inappropriate for handicapped students because of reading and comprehension requirements and occupational coverage (Anderson, 1986). For selecting interest inventories, several considerations should be kept in mind. The first is to consider the student's educational level and degree of occupational knowledge. Students who need to begin exploration benefit more from information provided by an inventory that surveys broad categories of jobs, but a student preparing to select a training program needs more differential information (Spitzer & Levinson, 1988).

A second consideration is the level of training required for occupations that are targeted by the inventory. For example, the Reading-Free Interest Inventory

TABLE 2
General Characteristics of Selected Print-Oriented Interest Inventories

Title	Publisher or Distributor	Grade/Age Range	Reading Level
California Occupational Preference Survey	Educational and Industrial Testing Service (EDITS)	High School and College	Eighth Grade
Strong Campbell Interest Inventory	National Computer Systems	High School, College, and Adult	Eighth Grade
Self-Directed Search	Psychological Assessment Resources	Ages 15–70	Eighth Grade (Form E–4th)
Ohio Vocational Interest Survey	Psychological Corporation	Grades 8–12	Eighth Grade

Occupational Levels	Standardization Groups
Skilled and Professional	Grades 7–12 and College
Professional and Technical	Representative
Varied	Keyed to Three-digit Code
Varied	High School Students

Note: Adapted from Anderson (1982) and Spitzer and Levinson 1988).

targets unskilled and semiskilled jobs, whereas the Strong Campbell looks at more technical and professional occupations (Anderson, 1982).

Paper-and-pencil or nonreading inventories may be used with handicapped students depending on their test-taking abilities. Tables 2 and 3 summarize characteristics of both types for comparison.

Vocational aptitude. Aptitude tests are designed to sample fairly narrow skills related to vocational training and performance in the same way that intelligence tests are designed to sample skills related to classroom success. Multiple aptitude batteries typically sample both general ability and specific skills. The number of empirically valid aptitude tests is small and includes scholastic (verbal, numerical, and perceptual–performance), clerical (perceptual speed and accuracy), manual dexterity, mechanical reasoning, and spatial visualization abilities (Anderson, 1986).

The manner in which aptitude tests are constructed enables users to set precise cutoffs for matching abilities to job requirements. The General Aptitude Test Battery (GATB), for example, is used in conjunction with a multiple cutoff system keyed to specific jobs. These profile subsets or Special Aptitude Tests Batteries (SATB) purport to be representative of job functions or occupational aptitude patterns (OAP). For example, the OAP for a bank teller includes the Numerical, Form Perception, and Clerical subtests.

Vocational aptitude tests were developed to supplement tests of general cognitive ability (Anastasi, 1982). Intelligence tests are useful for predicting

TABLE 3
General Characteristics of Selected Picture Interest Inventories

Title	Publisher or Distributor	Grade/Age Levels	Occupational Levels	Standardization Groups
Reading-Free Vocational Interest Inventory	Psychological Corporation	Age 13–Adult MR and LD	Unskilled and Semi-skilled	6,400 EMR Students
Wide Range Interest and Opinion Test	Slossen Educational Publications	Grades 8–12 and Adults	Varied	Grades 8–12 and Adults
Geist Picture Interest Inventory[a]	Western Psychological Services	Grades 8–12 and Adults	Unskilled to Technical	Varied
Vocational Research Interest Inventory	Vocational Research Institute	Junior High to Adult	Varied	Prevocational and Vocational

[a]Requires some reading to answer questions.

Note: Adapted from Anderson (1982) and Spitzer and Levinson (1988).

training potential and aptitude tests are more useful for predicting skills proficiencies (Herr & Cramer, 1979). Since the focus of a Level 2 aptitude assessment is on the specification of probable training levels and areas for exploration, both intelligence and aptitude tests provide important information to decision makers. Because few aptitude techniques are designed specifically for exceptional students, they are often referred to specialized assessment centers.

Recently researchers have examined the utility of intelligence tests for aptitude assessment. Initial studies of the factor structures of the GATB and Wechsler scales revealed that the tests overlapped to a considerable degree in the prediction of training potential. The results of these students have been encouraging. Miller (cited in Heinlein, 1987) examined Wechsler Intelligence Scale for Children (WISC) profiles and GATB aptitude profiles produced by educable mentally retarded (EMR) students and reported significant correlations. Miller also constructed a table by which examiners could

extrapolate GATB scores from WISC subtest standard scores.

Heinlein (1987) examined the relationship between Wechsler Adult Intelligence Scale–Revised (WAIS-R) scores and GATB scores for learning-disabled adults. While the tests overlapped considerably in global constructs, the author deemed the error variance too high to recommend the use of regression equations of WAIS-R scores to estimate GATB aptitudes. Inspection of the reported beta weights revealed that there were some similarities between Heinlein's and Miller's findings, but the range of standard errors was greater in the former. Heinlein reported that the GATB cognitive factor (General, Verbal, and Numerical aptitudes) was best accounted for by Information, Comprehension, and Block Design. The GATB Spacial/Perceptual factor (Spacial, Form Perception, and Clerical Perception aptitudes) was estimated by Picture Arrangement and Object Assembly. The GATB Psychomotor factor (Motor Coordination, Finger Dexterity, and Manual Dexterity aptitudes) was estimated by Digit Symbol,

Block Design, and (inversely) Arithmetic.

The lack of specific regression equations should not deter the school psychologist from using Wechsler scores in a Level 1 assessment, since it is a monitoring function, or a Level 2 evaluation as a preliminary step for developing hypotheses, estimating training levels, and designing exploration programs for handicapped students. Intelligence scores are useful supplements to aptitude tests and are reasonable estimates when no other aptitude information is available.

Thus far the discussion of aptitude testing has concentrated on the use of the Wechsler scales. Since the passage of the Perkins Act, evaluators have reexamined the use of more traditional paper-and-pencil instruments, such as the Differential Aptitude Test. These tests typically are well-researched, because they are group-administered and easily machine-scored. It is important for school psychologists to familiarize themselves with group tests in order to function as effective members of interdisciplinary assessment teams. Many of the same considerations that apply to interest inventories also apply to selecting aptitude tests. An additional consideration is to select tests that have documented concurrent validity with the GATB, since most occupational information is related to it. Several of the common paper-and-pencil aptitude tests are reviewed in Table 4.

Vocational adaptive behaviors. Adaptive behavior covers a broad range of competencies. Brolin (1985) groups these competencies into two broad categories: daily living skills (managing finances, food preparation, clothing care, transportation use, and leisure pursuits and occupational skills (work habits, specific occupational skills, and job seeking and retention). Munger, Seiler, and Altman (1983) articulated one of the most frustrating aspects of vocational assessment — determining the freedom a student has in seeking jobs and their willingness to relocate. In addition to formal scales, observations of students in exploratory and simulated environments are excellent sources of information on interpersonal functioning.

Career maturity. The developmental nature of the cognitive and affective components of career maturity provide school psychologists with an opportunity to monitor student progress and estimate independent decision-making skills. This assessment also provides information about a student's developmental limits and need for interventions.

SUMMARY

Students with disabilities have long faced obstacles in obtaining appropriate educational services despite federal initiatives to enhance their participation in vocational programs that date from 1963. Recent mandates have completed the continuum of programs and services beginning in preschool and following an individual throughout life. Central to the process is the slow but inevitable change occurring in special education from a time-limited academic focus to a pragmatic life span perspective.

In order to serve students more appropriately, school psychologists must also adopt a life span approach to assessment. Cognitive ability is the cornerstone of evaluation because of its prediction of training needs in educational settings. As educators refocus their attention on student's postsecondary adjustment, concern will move from where individual students will be in the years they spend in school to where they will be when they leave the educational system. Vocational assessment provides one way to gain a broader perspective of the educational process. The interest and aptitude tests described in this chapter are one part of a larger developmental process. In order to understand the uses of these instruments, it is first necessary to develop an idea of when they become useful in planning vocational goals. It is for this reason that the NASP Vocational School Psychology Interest Group recommends that vocational considerations become part of every evaluation.

TABLE 4
General Characteristics of Selected Multidimensional Aptitude Batteries

Title	Publisher or Distributor	Grade/Age Range	Aptitudes Assessed
Armed Services Vocational Aptitude Battery	U.S. Military Enlistment Processing Command	Grades 10–12	10 subtests yield composite scores in: Academic Ability, Verbal, Math, Mechanical and Crafts, Business and Clerical, Health, Social, and Technology, Electronics and Electrical
Differential Aptitude Tests	Psychological Corporation	Grades 8–12	Verbal Reasoning, Numerical Ability, Total, Abstract Reasoning, Clerical Speed and Accuracy, Mechanical Reasoning, Space Relations, Spelling, Language Usage
Occupational Aptitude Survey and Interest Schedule	Pro-Ed	Grades 8–12 and Adults	General Ability, Verbal Ability, Numerical Aptitude, Spatial Aptitude, Perceptual Aptitude, Manual Dexterity
General Aptitude Test Battery (GATB)	U.S. Employment Service	Ages 16 years and over	Intelligence, Verbal, Numerical, Spatial, Form Perception, Clerical Perception, Motor Coordination, Finger Dexterity, Manual Dexterity
Non-Reading Aptitude Test Battery	U.S. Employment Service	Disadvantaged individuals, Grades 9–12, and Adults	Intelligence, Verbal, Numerical, Spatial, Form Perception, Clerical Perception, Motor Coordination, Finger Dexterity, Manual Dexterity

Administration/Scoring						Technical Characteristics		
Time	Hand	Machine	Individual	Group	Computer	Reliability	Validity	Standardization
2¾ hr.	No	Yes	No	Yes	No	Good	Good	National sample of 12,000 youths aged 16–23
3 hr.	Yes	Yes	Yes	Yes	Yes	Good	Good	64 school districts in 32 states incorporating males and females, Grades 8–12
45 min.	Yes	No	Yes	Yes	No	Good	Good	1,398 students in Grades 8–12 from 11 states
2½ hr.	Yes	No	No	Yes	No	Good	Fair	National sample of 4,000 workers from the "general working population"
3 hr.	Yes	No	No	Yes	No	No data	No data	None (uses GATB norms)

REFERENCES

Alcorn, C. L., & Nicholson, C. L. (1975). A vocational assessment battery for the educable mentally retarded and low literate. *Education and Training of the Mentally Retarded, 10,* 78-83.

Anastasi, A. (1982). *Psychological testing* (5th ed.). New York: Macmillan.

Anderson, W. T. (1982). Vocational interest assessment procedures. In T. H. Hohenshil, W. T. Anderson, & J. F. Salwan, (Eds.), *Secondary school psychological services: Focus on vocational assessment procedures for handicapped students.* Blacksburg, VA: Virginia Tech in cooperation with the Virginia State Department of Education. (ERIC Document Reproduction Service No. ED 229704).

Anderson, W. T. (1986). Prevocational and vocational assessment of handicapped students. In P. J. Lazarus & S. S. Strichart (Eds.), *Psychoeducational evaluation of children and adolescents with low-incidence handicaps.* New York: Grune and Stratton.

Anderson, W. T., & Hohenshil, T. H. (in press). Vocational assessment in the United States: School psychology's evolving roles. *School Psychology International.*

Brolin, D. E. (1985). Vocational assessment in the public schools. In R. Fry (Ed.), *The issues papers: Second national forum on the issues in vocational assessment.* Menomonie, WI: University of Wisconsin.

Dawis, R. V., & Lofquist, L. H. (1984). *A psychological theory of work adjustment.* Minneapolis: University of Minnesota.

Heinlein, W. E. (1987). *Clinical utility of the Wechsler Scales in psychological evaluations to estimate vocational aptitude.* Unpublished doctoral dissertation, Virginia Polytechnic Institute and State University, Blacksburg, VA.

Herr, E. L., & Cramer, S. H. (1979). *Career guidance through the lifespan.* Boston: Little, Brown.

Hohenshil, T. H., Levinson, E. M., & Buckland-Heer, K. (1985). Best practices in vocational assessment for handicapped students. In A. Thomas & J. Grimes (Eds.), *Best practices in school psychology.* Washington, DC: National Association of School Psychologists.

Munger, S. J., Seiler, E. L., & Altman, J. W. (1983). *Vocational diagnosis and job placement of the mentally handicapped.* Verndale, MN: RPM Press.

Osipow, S. H. (1983). *Theories of career development.* Englewood Cliffs, NJ: Prentice-Hall.

Sabatino, D. A., Goh, D. S., & Jenson, G. (1982). Psychological assessment of handicapped adolescents. *School Psychology Review, 1,* 377-383.

Spitzer, D., & Levinson, E. M. (1988). A review of selected vocational interest inventories for use by school psychologists. *School Psychology Review, 17,* 673-392.

ANNOTATED BIBLIOGRAPHY

Bolton, B. (1987). *Handbook of measurement and evaluation in rehabilitation,* Second Edition. Baltimore, MD: Paul H. Brooks Co.
This edited text discusses vocational assessment from a rehabilitation perspective, provides reviews of various assessment instruments, and includes separate chapters on the assessment of mentally retarded, deaf, and visually impaired individuals.

Kapes, J. T., & Mastie, M. M. (1988). *A counselor's guide to career assessment instruments,* Second Edition. Alexandria, VA: National Career Development Association.
This volume summarizes uses and technical characteristics of numerous frequently used vocational assessment instruments. Measures of interests, aptitudes, work values, and career maturity are all included. Sections on test selection and instruments for special populations are also included.

Levinson, E. M. (1987). Children and career development. In A. Thomas & J. Grimes (Eds.), *Children's needs: Psychological perspectives.* Washington, DC: National Association of School Psychologists.
This chapter summarizes the career development stages through which school-age children progress, identifies a career planning model which incorporates assessment as a means of gathering information necessary for effective decision-making, and briefly discusses the major actions which can be taken to facilitate vocational decision-making based upon the assessment data gathered.

Seligman, L. (1980). *Assessment in developmental career counseling.* Cranston, RI: Cranston Press.
This classic text summarizes the career development needs of individuals at different stages of life, and discusses the various assessment approaches and techniques which can be utilized at these different life stages. Case studies and descriptions of assessment tools are included.

54

Best Practices in Working with Children with Motor Impairments

Barbara Christensen
Central Michigan University

OVERVIEW

School psychologists are more frequently being asked to assess children with motor impairments because there are more such children in the general population. Recent medical and technological advances have increased the number of children who survive prenatal, perinatal, or postnatal traumas, life-threatening accidents, or the results of congenital anomalies.

This chapter will familiarize school psychologists with issues involved in the assessment of motorically impaired children and provide a guide for designing an individualized assessment. It will assist the school psychologist who has little experience with motorically impaired children in conducting a comprehensive assessment and generating programming recommendations; the more experienced practitioner will be exposed to current research and instruments appropriate for use with this population.

Primary emphasis will be placed on cerebral palsy and spina bifida, because these conditions are the most frequently occurring motor impairments, but it is important to recognize that motor impairments seldom occur in isolation from other disabilities. Concurrent visual and auditory dysfunction, communication problems, cognitive differences, convulsive disorders, and other difficulties must also be addressed so that testing is "consistent with the individual's ability to perceive stimulation and respond" (Lazarus & Strichart, 1986, p. 271).

BASIC CONSIDERATIONS

The school psychologist will need to communicate with other specialists as well as understand information encountered in school files or medical reports. Knowledge of the following terms will facilitate this process.

Cerebral palsy (CP) is a diverse disorder resulting from generally nonprogressive central nervous system pathology. It frequently causes impaired movement and may include varying degrees of sensory, psychological, speech, language, and learning handicaps. CP tends to be a very broad label used for a group of handicapping conditions. The following terms are frequently used in describing CP.

Ataxic CP: Uncoordinated gross motor movements and poor balance or equilibrium, particularly evident in walking or standing, with tremors during intentional movement.

Athetoid CP: Involuntary, purposeless movements of the hands, fingers, and eyes, with tremors occurring at rest and during intentional movement.

Spastic CP: Muscles stiff or contracted due to increased muscle tone, resistant to passive movement.

Mixed CP: Both spasticity and athetosis.

Paraplegia: Involvement of both lower extremities.

Hemiplegia: An upper and lower limb on the same side of the body are affected.

Diplegia: Both arms or both legs affected.

Quadriplegia: All four limbs affected.

Hypotonic: Diminished muscle tone; child appears "floppy."

Hypertonic. Opposite of hypotonic; greater than normal muscle tension; appears "tight." (Adapted from Thomas, 1981; Hurley & Sovner, 1987; and Barnett, 1982.)

Spina bifida is a nonprogressive congenital condition in which closure of the spinal column is incomplete. The continuum from mild to severe spina bifida includes the following common labels.

Spina bifida occulta: There is an opening in one or more of the vertebrae of the spinal column, but the spinal cord remains undamaged.

Meningocele: The meninges, or protective covering around the spinal cord, have pushed out through the opening in the vertebrae in a sac called the "meningocele," with the spinal cord still intact. Surgical repair results in little or no damage to the nerve pathways or effect on functioning.

Myelomeningocele: Not only are there openings in the vertebrae, but the spinal cord itself does not close, usually protruding from the back and requiring surgical repair(s). Children with this form of spina bifida may experience muscle weakness, paralysis, and loss of sensation below the cleft. Hydrocephalus may also develop. Difficulties in attending, expressive and receptive language, or reading and math may be experienced. (Adapted from the newsletter of the National Information Center of Handicapped Children and Youth, undated.)

Muscular dystrophy (MD) is a progressive, degenerative condition in which muscles atrophy, or waste away. (Cerebral palsy and spina bifida are not progressive per se.)

Hydrocephalus is the accumulation of fluid in the cerebral ventricles or outside the brain. Although it may occur without spina bifida, the two defects often occur together. (Adapted from Thomas, 1981, and National Information Center for Handicapped Children and Youth, undated.)

BEST PRACTICES

The assessment of a motorically impaired child is one of the most multidimensional assessments that a school psychologist is likely to perform, with each of four phases being crucial to understanding the child's overall functioning.

Phase 1. Information Gathering and Assessment Planning

Records review. In addition to school records, hospital records and doctors' reports frequently include information about a child's medical history that may facilitate understanding of development and current functioning. The etiology and progressiveness of the condition may be relevant to program planning. Restructive surgery as well as medications the child is receiving or has been given might affect the child's performance during evaluation. For example, medications for seizures, such as many of the anticonvulsant drugs, "have the side effects of lethargy and drowsiness which can interfere with the child's ability to concentrate, speak coherently, and/or perform smooth, well-coordinated motions" (Stephens, 1982, p. 66).

Planning the assessment. Before test selection can begin, the school psychologist must determine the areas that are to be addressed for the individual child. In addition to cognitive functioning, academic achievement, and adaptive behavior, there are several other important areas to consider.

Because of the increased likelihood of child abuse in motorically impaired children (Diamond & Jaudes, 1983), the school psychologist must be keenly aware of the possibility that the child being assessed may be in an abusive situation. Abuse may actually be a causal factor in the motor impairment or it may be secondary, perhaps the result of parental frustration.

Maladaptive as well as adaptive behavior should be assessed. Even though a child may be showing normal cognitive development, consideration should be given to how the child is functioning outside the school as well as within it, since there may be discrepancies between the situations. According to Hosokawa, Kitahara, and Nakamura (1985), behavior problems and delayed social skills development are frequently observed in this population. These authors suggest that acquisition of social skills is not contingent on improving motor or cognitive skills, but rather on "special intervention programs . . . [that] . . . facilitate the interpersonal aspect of social skills" (p. 79). Programs such as Skill-Streaming (McGinnis & Goldstein, 1984) include training for basic prosocial skills, such as listening and asking for help, as well as more complex skills such as decision making and dealing with failure.

Vocational assessment should not be perfunctorily addressed with motorically impaired children, particularly older school-age students, since the degree of independence possible in their future daily living may be affected by their opportunities for gainful employment. It is crucial to assess vocational interests as well as vocational capabilities. Lazarus & Strichart (1986) suggested that decision making for career development be based on intraindividual factors including mental ability, academic achievement, perceptual skills, motor skills, and personal and social behavior, as well as aptitudes and interests (p. 289).

A frequently unvoiced concern of the motorically impaired student is his or her developing sexuality, particularly when puberty is entered: "Physical maturation and pubertal development occur for those with spina bifida prior to that seen in age-matched controls" (Blum, 1983, p. 331). Although not in a position to provide the specific kind of information a doctor can, the psychologist may be called upon to help the child obtain answers and deal with information. Perry and Flanagan (1986) found that emotional impairment in adolescence may be related to knowledge of the sexual impotence that occurs in some (not all) motorically impaired individuals.

Test selection. Designing an assessment to meet the needs of a motorically impaired child is a challenging task whether the child is verbal or nonverbal. Several issues must be considered. The school psychologist must recognize the "penalizing nature of power or timed standardized tests" (Lazarus & Strichart, 1986, p. 272) for this population. The effect of motor impairment on performance of timed tasks may take the form of awkward or slow responding or it may show up as latency between the presentation of the stimulus and the beginning of a response. In either case, responding is compromised and the child's disability, rather than ability, is being assessed.

Many tests require visual–motor responses: the psychologist must be sensitive to the degree of motor loading present and select those that do not make excessive demands. The motor components of some tasks may initially seem minimal but with further examination be found to seriously bias test results. For example, the Picture Arrangement subtest of the Wechsler Intelligence Scales for Children–Revised (WISC-R) (Wechsler, 1974) differs from Photo Series on the Kaufman Assessment Battery for Children (K-ABC) (Kaufman & Kaufman, 1983) in the motor skills required. On the WISC-R the student rearranges the picture cards, but on the K-ABC only one card at a time is selected, which can be done by pointing only.

Testing-the-limits may give insight into a motor-impaired child's performance of timed tasks when time constraints are removed, but it should not be the primary basis for understanding the child's overall functioning or making eligibility decisions.

Use of tests that include teaching items, such as the K-ABC, are advantageous because the psychologist can ascertain that the child understands the task before testing begins. Spina bifida children are particularly likely to indicate that they comprehend test directions even when errors on practice items show the need for further instruction.

Test items inappropriate for use with a motorically impaired child must sometimes be scored as failures, according to the administration procedure given for the particular test. Some tests, such as the Uniform Performance Assessment System (Haring, White, Edgar, Afflect, & Hayden, 1981) provide scoring options for indicating that the item was adapted, required the use of prosthetic devices for completion, or was omitted as inappropriate for the child.

The motorically impaired child may require adaptive devices for completion of test tasks: penalties should not be imposed for their use, but rather the item should be scored as successfully completed, unless the particular test procedure dictates otherwise. For example, if the child uses a device for assistance in zipping a zipper, the very ability to zip should be of primary importance.

When selecting tests for use with verbal motorically impaired children, the school psychologist has a variety of instruments from which to choose. Intellectual and achievement tests that require only vocal responding or can be modified for it (as is discussed below) are commonly available. It is more challenging to design a battery for use with the nonverbal motorically impaired student, since fewer tests are available that require little or no motor or verbal responding yet reflect ability and not disability.

Cognitive assessment. Tests that should be considered for use in cognitive assessment include the following:

Test of Nonverbal Intelligence (Brown, Sherbenou, & Dallor, 1982) (ages 5-0 to 85-11; administration time about 10 minutes) Instructions pantomimed, pointing response (or adaptation) required. Percentiles and quotients above 55 given. Untimed tasks assess problem solving. Give both forms A and B to increase reliability, but use along with other measures in eligibility decisions.

Pictorial Test of Intelligence (French, 1964) (ages 2-6 to 8-0; administration time about 45 minutes; short form for children under 5) Pointing response required, easily adapted to eye pointing owing to large item cards with ample space separating choices. Deviation IQs and percentiles given. Assesses verbal comprehension, matching and differentiation, range of knowledge and general understanding, conceptual grouping, early math skills, and short-term visual memory.

Leiter International Performance Scale (Leiter & Arthur, 1950) (ages 2 to 18; administration time approximately 60 minutes) Selection and positioning of tiles required for responding are easily adapted. Ratio IQ generated. Assesses general reasoning ability. Yields supplemental information for eligibility decisions.

Kaufman Assessment Battery for Children (Kaufman & Kaufman, 1983) (ages vary with subtest; administration time varies with subtests selected). Pointing response or adapted responding required. Scaled scores, standard scores, and percentiles generated, but no overall quotients possible. Use Matrix Analogies (ages 5 to 12-5), Spatial Memory (5 to 12-5), Photo Series (6 to 12-5), and Face Recognition (ages 2-6 to 4-11), to assess reasoning in determining relationships, short-term visual recall, sequential logic, and attending with short-term visual memory respectively. Provides supplemental information for eligibility decisions.

Detroit Test of Learning Aptitude–2 (Hammill, 1985) (ages 6 to 17-11; administration time about 30 minutes) Pointing response or adapted responding required. Percentiles and standard scores produced, but no overall quotient. Use Object Sequences, Symbolic Relations, and Conceptual Matching subtests, to assess short-term visual memory, nonverbal reasoning, and categorization respectively. Provides supplemental information for eligibility decisions.

Battelle Developmental Inventory (Newborg, Stock, Wnek, Guidubaldi, &

Svinivki, 1984) (ages birth to 8; administration time approximately 20 minutes) Use Cognitive Domain items. Gives adaptations of items for the handicapped, but when adaptations are not possible a zero must be scored, penalizing the child. Can be scored by direct testing, interview, or observation. Percentiles and standard scores given. Assesses concept development, reasoning, early academic skills, auditory memory, and perceptual discrimination. Necessary toys and materials not provided in test kit. Provides supplemental information for eligibility decisions.

Columbia Mental Maturity Scale (Burgemeister, Blum, & Lorge, 1972) (ages 3-6 to 9-11; administration time about 20 minutes) Pointing response or adapted responding. Gives age deviation score and maturity index. Assesses concept development from concrete to more abstract, usually by having child select the figure that does not belong with the others. Use for supplemental information only.

Academic assessment. Tests that should be considered for use in academic assessment include the following:

Peabody Individual Achievement Test (Dunn & Markwardt, 1970) (ages K to 12, norm-referenced; administration time about 20 minutes) Requires pointing or adapted responding for multiple-choice items. Use Mathematics, Reading Comprehension, and Spelling subtests. Gives percentiles and standard scores. Note: This test is currently being revised.

Test of Reading Comprehension (Brown, Hammill, & Wiederholt, 1978) (Grades 1-8, norm-referenced; administration time about 30 minutes) Requires pointing or adapted responding. Use General Vocabulary, Syntactic Similarities, Paragraph Reading, and Sentence Sequencing. Gives scaled scores, Reading Comprehension Quotient.

Peabody Picture Vocabulary Test–Revised (Dunn, 1981) (ages 2-6 to 40, norm-referenced, administration time about 15 minutes) Pointing response required, easily adaptable to eye pointing. Gives standard scores and percentiles. Use

overall score as a measure of receptive language only.

Test of Language Development–Primary (Newcomer & Hammill, 1982) (ages 4-0 to 8-11, norm-referenced; administration time about 20 minutes) Requires pointing or adapted responding. Use Picture Vocabulary and Grammatic Understanding subtests to assess receptive language. Percentiles and standard scores given; no overall quotient based on only two subtests should be calculated.

Test of Language Development–Intermediate (Hammill & Newcomer, 1982) (ages 8-6 to 12-11, norm-referenced; administration time about 20 minutes) Adapted responding required to indicate whether item is true or false on Characteristics subtest and whether correct or incorrect on Grammatic Comprehension. Percentiles and standard scores available, but no overall quotient.

Brigance Diagnostic Comprehensive Inventory of Basic Skills (Brigance, 1983) (elementary and middle school age, criterion-referenced; administration time depends on number of skills assessed) *Significant* adaptations of many items will be necessary for use of this criterion-referenced measure, since vocal or motor responses are frequently required. Skills tested include Reading, Listening, Spelling, Writing, Reference Skills, and Math. Grade placement tests should not be used as norm-referenced measures for making eligibility decisions.

Brigance Diagnostic Inventory of Essential Skills (Brigance, 1981) (secondary school age, criteron-referenced; administration time depends on number of skills assessed) *Significant* adaptations of many items will be necessary. Skills tested include Reading, Essential Word Recognition, Reference Skills, Writing, Spelling, and Math.

Clinical Evaluation of Language Functions, Diagnostic Battery (Semel & Wiig, 1980) (Grades K to 12; administration time approximately 30 minutes; best used as a criterion-referenced measure, but norms are available) Pointing and yes/

no responses required; adaptive responding also possible. Use Processing Word and Sentence Structure, Processing Word Classes, Processing Linguistic Concepts, and Processing Relationships and Ambiguities subtests to assess receptive language development.

Assessment of adaptive behavior. Tests that should be considered for use in assessment of adaptive behavior include the following:

Uniform Performance Assessment System (Haring, et al., 1981) (birth to 6 years, criteron-referenced; administration time varies with functioning level of individual) Use to assess Communication and Social/Self-help Skills, with sections on inappropriate behaviors and wheelchair use. Special codes are used to indicate adapted and nonadapted items, as well as those that are omitted as inappropriate. Items can be scored by observation, prior knowledge, or direct testing. This test is particularly sensitive to small changes in performance. Materials for testing must be gathered by the examiner.

Vineland Adaptive Behavior Scales–Expanded Form (Sparrow, Balla, & Cicchetti, 1984) (birth to 18 years; norm-referenced; administration time varies with functioning level of individual) Standard scores and percentiles produced. Information is obtained in interview with caregiver. Items inappropriate for motorically impaired students must be scored as failures. Expanded form provides more information but Survey form can also be used.

Phase 2. Observations

The time spent observing a student prior to direct assessment is valuable in three ways: it allows the psychologist to become more familiar with the child, it permits gathering information about the child's functioning, and it provides opportunities for getting ideas about how to adapt the testing situation. Multiple observations in a variety of settings are desirable for a more global picture of how the child functions.

When particular areas of concern have surfaced during interviews with teachers, specialists, or parents, it is appropriate to use structured observation techniques (Hersen & Bellack, 1981; Thomas & Grimes, 1985). For example, if a child tends to be withdrawn, recording the frequency of social initiations will quantify a somewhat vague descriptor.

Phase 3. Individualized Testing

Environment. Providing an environment in which optimal performance can be elicited is particularly crucial because the setting for assessment may greatly impact performance. The difficulty in concentrating and attending experienced by spina bifida children (Horn, Lorch, Lordh, & Culatta, 1985) demands that both visual and auditory distractors be minimized. Children with cerebral palsy "perform significantly poorer than normal individuals when the stimulus is accompanied by noise" (Laraway, 1985, p. 260).

Just knowing about being tested may make a motorically impaired child tense; stress may interfere with responding and muscular control. Allowing the child time to become comfortable with the setting and the examiner results in improved rapport and contributes to best performance.

Motorically impaired students require as much structure in the testing situation as their nonimpaired peers. Some children, particularly those with spina bifida, have learned to use manipulation to avoid tasks that may be less than exciting or actually difficult. Conversations with teachers or parents prior to testing may provide information about reinforcers that can be used to promote positive interactions with the student. Caution in the use of food reinforcers is indicated if a child has any difficulty with swallowing or is prone to choking.

Positioning. The child's position and muscle tone may seriously impact on performance: upper extremity function, hyperactive reflexes, and even breathing

(Nwaobi & Smith, 1986) may be compromised. The effects of residual reflexes may impair responding by pointing or eye movement.

Arranging to assess motorically impaired children with an occupational or physical therapist present is desirable, but if it is not possible, these specialists may provide information about how best to position and normalize muscle tone. Frequent checks for proper positioning during testing will also be required, since many children have difficulty maintaining a posture for any length of time.

Optimal responding in hypotonic children may be obtained if the psychologist can help them to "tense" muscles a bit, perhaps by gently bouncing them on a large ball or an adult's lap. Support must be provided such that this gentle bouncing will not be injurious. In some conditions involving low muscle tone, notably Down Syndrome, atlantoxial instability leaves a child vulnerable to dislocation of this joint in the top of the spine (Cooke, 1984). Children with high muscle tone, or spasticity, must be helped to relax: this can be accomplished by rocking them, speaking quietly, avoiding sudden movements, and especially through proper positioning.

For very motorically impaired children, positioning in their custom-fitted wheelchair is likely to be helpful in achieving an upright posture. Floor chairs, such as the commercially available Tumbleform chairs, which curve to fit the body into C shape, provide comfortable seating and free the child's arms for responding. Some children can be positioned in devices that allow them to assume a standing position for testing. Straddling a bolster or small bench is sometimes more comfortable than using a regular chair. Although it would be possible to position a child on a parent's or teacher's lap for testing, it is not recommended, because cues for responding may inadvertently be given.

Using a wedge on the floor with the child positioned on the tummy so that the arms are freed for responding is another good position; weighted sandbags or even the psychologist's hand on the child's bottom may be necessary to keep it from popping up. Side-lying positions, generally on a mat or some soft surface, make it possible to free up a better functioning limb if it is placed uppermost. When floor sitting is feasible, side sitting is a good choice; the child's bottom is positioned on the floor to the left or right of his or her bent legs. A lap table, which fits over the lap and is supported by the floor, provides a good working surface for a floor-seated child.

Impaired sensation is of particular concern in spina bifida children who lack feeling below the level of the lesion. If they are improperly positioned, circulation to the legs may be compromised and they will not be alerted to this by discomfort. Proper support for the legs and feet must be provided at all times.

Use of more than one position during testing serves to optimize performance as well as delay the fatiguing effects of testing. The child's position should be changed a minimum of every 20–30 minutes (Dupont & Tucker, 1985, p. 116). Multiple testing sessions, over the course of several days, are desirable.

Modified responding. While verbal responding is likely to give the examiner more of a sample of verbal skills and cognition, it is possible to achieve valid test results with alternative responding methods. "Careful examination of expressive modality functioning is essential in order to select and present the testing materials in a manner that affords the child a feasible opportunity for responding at an optimal level" (Barnett, 1982).

Tests standardized by pointing responses should be selected whenever possible. Adaptation of tests by presenting open-ended questions as multiple-choice items is also a possibility, but the use of a test that requires the least amount of modification would be expected to provide the most reliable results. Pecyna and Sommers (1985) have pointed out the need to look at the motivational value of the tasks — several hours of selecting from four choices on test cards could get boring!

Someone who is familiar with a child's speech may interpret for the psychologist during testing, but such verbal responses should be viewed in light of other test results. If the child is able to point with either hand or head and visually scan several pictures, then simple pointing responses can be used, making it possible to emphasize tests standardized with this response format.

For children whose repertoire includes a simple yes/no response, the examiner can point to each possible response in turn so that they can indicate which one is being selected. Their response might take the form of squeezing the psychologist's hand, blinking their eyes, or any other logical responding pattern that is physically possible and consistently available. If their repertoire does not include the yes/no response, teaching such a response is possible, but it may not provide reliable results.

The technique of eye pointing can also be used. The psychologist assumes a position that makes it possible to see the eyes of the student, who is asked to fixate on the correct response. In this situation, the psychologist should be particularly conscious of whether the child is actually scanning all possible responses before making a selection, since limited visual functioning may make it difficult or impossible for the child to do so. If such is the case, it may be necessary to reposition materials to take advantage of the child's existent field of vision or to cue the child to look at all items before selection.

Simple modifications of the testing procedure may improve a motorically impaired child's chances of responding to tasks. For example, using large sheets of paper and easily grasped, mushroom-shaped markers or using tape to attach the response sheet to the desktop may greatly facilitate performance. A rubber mat on the table or desktop may help the student to keep materials from sliding. Using a desk or lap table with raised edges is also helpful in keeping materials within reach.

If adaptive devices such as a symbol board or voice synthesizer are used for communication, such equipment should be available during testing. The psychologist should become familiar with such devices and comfortable in interpreting the communication produced.

Student interview. Motorically impaired children should be interviewed during this phase of the assessment to determine areas of concern, such as drooling or incontinence, as well as areas in which particular interest or success is felt. Hurley and Sovner (1987) have suggested that psychological problems associated with CP include docility, frustration and depression, low self-esteem, and guilt feelings. Lazarus and Strichart (1986, p. 215) presented sample clinical interview questions in the areas of family dynamics, emotional functioning, academic and school competence, physical health, peer relations, and self; these questions can be adapted by school psychologists to fit their own particular interviewing styles while providing a comprehensive framework for the interview.

Test results. Some patterns emerge in the test results of motorically impaired children, with higher scores on verbal scales than on performance scales being frequently noted, even when time constraints do not depress performance scores. Caution should be used in interpretation of high verbal scores, particularly in spina bifida students, since deficits have been found in their comprehension of written and spoken language in spite of normal or nearly normal "development of syntax . . . acquisition of vocabulary skills, rote memory and short-term memory" (Knowlton, Peterson, & Putbrese, 1985). For example, high scores on the Similarities subtest of the WISC-R may be misleading, particularly in light of lower scores on subtests tapping "memory, speed of response, acquired knowledge, integrated functioning and coordination" (Shaffer, Friedrich, Shurtleff, & Wolf, 1985, p. 334). Spina bifida children, particularly those with hydrocephalus, may also evidence hyperverbal behavior, commonly called "cocktail party syndrome," that is characterized by excessive verbalization uttered out of context or inappropriately (Knowlton et al., 1985). Discussing responses and probing for further information will give the psychologist insight into the child's language development.

The predictive validity of intelligence tests may not be as good for motorically impaired students because unstable physical conditions may effect cognitive functioning, although Tew and Laurence (1983) found that "very reliable predictions regarding intellectual status [of spina bifida students] at 16 years of age can be made upon entry to school" (p. 13).

Test scores may be observed to decline with age, even in students whose condition is not progressive, as a function of limited learning experiences. Performance may be depressed by the inability to increase in speed as nonhandicapped students do with age. Even verbal tasks, such as naming as many members of a certain classification as possible within a time limit, may be affected in this way.

Other generalizations in terms of response patterns are difficult to make and probably less than useful to the psychologist who wishes to understand a particular child's functioning without bias. Berninger and Gans (1986) summed up by saying that "verbal intelligence may be relatively superior to nonverbal intelligence in many nonspeaking individuals of normal intelligence with severe cerebral palsy and . . . unqualified generalizations about language abilities in this patient population should be avoided" (p. 45).

Generating recommendations. Criterion-referenced tests and adaptive behavior measures that are used with nonhandicapped children can also be consulted for assistance in generating recommendations for the motorically impaired. Additional skills related to the area of disability may be required, such as wheelchair mobility. The way in which tasks are accomplished may be different, too, for example, if a severely motorically involved child is ready to learn about cause and effect relationships, the common task of pulling a string to attain a toy will not be appropriate. In such a situation

> special switching devices that can allow children to activate different types of toys are often used. A young child may become very motivated to be more involved in his environment if he feels he has some control and can act on this environment. Children with spina bifida [as well as other motorically impaired children] may be discouraged more easily and need the extra incentive that such specialized switches and adaptive toys can provide. (Knowlton et al., 1985, p. 260)

Frequently, occupational therapists who know a child may assist in adapting the tasks to be mastered to meet the individual child's needs.

Phase 4. Postassessment

When testing has been completed, it is the school psychologist's responsibility to accurately report and interpret test results to the school and the parent. Such communication is crucial in facilitating ongoing, integrated learning at school and in the home, particularly in light of the number of specialists frequently involved in such a child's care.

The school psychologist may be in a position to facilitate and maintain interdisciplinary communication, particularly between the school and the medical community. For example, if the parent or guardian gives permission, it would be very appropriate to send regular reports from the school to the child's pediatrician, giving information about the observed effects of current medication levels.

As a motorically impaired child grows and changes, the demands upon the family are likely to change. For example, young children may ambulate with crutches, but older children may not be able to because of their increased body weight: the adjustment to this change may not be easy for child or family. At the very least, the school psychologist should be willing to listen to parental frustration and facilitate a problem-solving approach to such difficulties, perhaps implementing a parent training program (Feldman & Varni, 1982).

Criterion-referenced tests frequently provide perspective on motorically impaired children's strengths — what has been accomplished and what growth may have occurred. They are especially useful in helping parents to see the *progress* their child has made rather than focusing on the limitations, because more detailed analyses of component skills is possible. Tests of adaptive behavior may also be useful in helping parents see their child's growth, particularly when academic performance is slowly changing.

The status of the motorically impaired child, even when it is the product of a static condition, may not remain the same for a period as long as the 3 years that commonly elapse between evaluations. The psychologist must be alert to the child's changing needs and schedule reevaluations as needed, not just as required: ongoing communication with teachers and parents will facilitate the psychologist's awareness of the child's functioning.

SUMMARY

Working with motorically impaired children necessitates multidimensional assessment procedures, particularly in light of the fact that motor impairments seldom occur in isolation from other conditions, such as visual or mental impairments. Information must be gathered through records review, including medical reports. Observations in structured and unstructured settings provide insight into the child's functioning as well as possible adaptations to the testing situation. The assessment is planned to optimize perception of the stimuli and encourage responding, with tests and tasks selected to meet these needs. Power or timed tasks should be avoided, since they are likely to penalize responding. Adaptive equipment used in daily living should be utilized in the testing situation. Provision of an optimal environment potentiates responding: proper positioning, relaxed but structured atmosphere, and elimination of distractors are crucial. Test results frequently show greater verbal ability than performance, even with time constraints removed, but this may be misleading and caution should be used in interpreting these results. Recommendations may require individual modification as a particular child's capacity for inter-

action with the environment is considered. In addition to reporting and interpreting test results, the psychologist may facilitate interdisciplinary communication of the specialists involved. Reevaluation may be needed more frequently than every 3 years because of a changing physical condition.

REFERENCES

Barnett, A. J. (1982). Designing an assessment of children with cerebral palsy. *Psychology in the Schools, 19*, 160-165.

Berninger, V. W., & Gans, B. M. (1986). Language profiles in nonspeaking individuals of normal intelligence with severe cerebral palsy. *AAC Augmentative and Alternative Communication, 2*(2), 45-50.

Blum, R. W. (1983). The adolescent with spina bifida. *Clinical Pediatrics, 22*(5), 331-335.

Brigance, A. (1981). *Brigance Diagnostic Inventory of Essential Skills.* North Billerica, MA: Curriculum Associates.

Brigance, A. (1983). *Brigance Diagnostic Comprehensive Inventory of Basic Skills.* North Billerica, MA: Curriculum Associates.

Brown, L., Sherbenou, R., & Dallor, S. (1982). *Test of Nonverbal Intelligence.* Austin, TX: PRO-ED.

Brown, V., Hammill, D., & Wiederholt, J. L. (1978). *Test of Reading Comprehension.* Austin, TX: PRO-ED.

Burgemeister, B., Blum, L. H., & Lorge, I. (1972). *Columbia Mental Maturity Scale.* New York: Harcourt, Brace & Jovanovich.

Cook, R. E. (1984). Atlantoaxial instability in individuals with Down's syndrome. *Adapted Physical Activity Quarterly, 1*, 194-196.

Diamond, L. J., & Jaudes, P. K. (1983). Child abuse in a cerebral-palsied population. *Developmental Medicine and Child Neurology, 25*(2), 169-174.

Dunn, L. M. (1981). *Peabody Picture Vocabulary Test, Revised.* Circle Pines, MN: American Guidance Service.

Dunn, L., & Markwardt, F. (1970). *Peabody Individual Achievement Test.* Circle Pines, MN: American Guidance Service.

Dupont, B. B., & Tucker, S. L. (1985). Reading, "righting," and arithmetic for the cerebral palsied child: A therapeutic approach for the classroom teacher. *Exceptional Child, 32*(2), 115-120.

Feldman, W. S., & Varni, J. W. (1982). A parent training program for the child with spina bifida. *Spina Bifida Therapy, 4*(2), 77–89.

French, J. (1964). *Pictorial Test of Intelligence.* Geneva, IL: Houghton Mifflin.

Hammill, D. D. (1985). *Detroit Test of Learning Aptitude–2.* Austin, TX: PRO-ED.

Hammill, D., & Newcomer, P. (1982). *Test of Language Development — Intermediate.* Austin, TX: PRO-ED.

Haring, N., White, O., Edgar, E., Afflect, J., & Hayden, A. (1981). *Uniform Performance Assessment System.* Columbus, OH: Merrill.

Hersen, M., & Bellack, A. S. (Eds.). (1981). *Behavioral assessment.* New York: Pergamon.

Horn, D. G., Lorch, E. P., Lorch, R. F., & Culatta, B. (1985). Distractibility and vocabulary deficits in children with spina bifida and hydrocephalus. *Developmental Medicine and Child Neurology, 27*(6), 713–720.

Hosokawa, T., Kitahara, T., & Nakamura, R. (1985). Social skills of children with cerebral palsy. *Journal of Human Ergology, 14*(2), 79–88.

Hurley, A. D., & Sovner, R. (1987). Psychiatric aspects of cerebral palsy. *Psychiatric Aspects of Mental Retardation Reviews, 6*(1), 1–5.

Kaufman, A. S., & Kaufman, N. L. (1983). *Kaufman Assessment Battery for Children.* Circle Pines, MN: American Guidance Service.

Knowlton, D. D., Peterson, K., & Putbrese, A. (1985). Team management of cognitive dysfunction in children with spina bifida. *Rehabilitation Literature, 46,*(9–10), 259–263.

Laraway, L. A. (1985). Auditory selective attention in cerebral-palsied individuals. *Language, Speech, and Hearing Services in Schools, 16*(4), 260–266.

Lazarus, P. J., & Strichart, S. S. (1986). *Psychoeducational evaluation of children and adolescents with low incidence handicaps.* New York: Grune & Stratton.

Leiter, R. G., & Arthur, G. (1950). *Leiter International Performance Scale.* Chicago: Stoelting.

McGinnis, E., & Goldstein, A. P. (1984). *Skillstreaming the elementary school child.* Champaign, IL: Research Press.

National Information Center for Handicapped Children and Youth. (Undated.) *Cerebral Palsy.* Washington, DC.

Newborg, J., Stock, J. R., Wnek, L., Guidubaldi, J., & Svinivki, J. (1984). *Battelle Developmental Inventory.* Allen, TX: DLM Teaching Resources.

Newcomer, P., & Hammill, D. (1982). *Test of Language Development–Primary.* Austin, TX: PRO-ED.

Nwaobi, O. M., & Smith, P. D. (1986). Effect of adaptive seating on pulmonary function of children with cerebral palsy. *Developmental Medicine and Child Neurology, 28*(3), 351–354.

Pecyna, P. M., & Sommers, R. K. (1985). Testing the receptive language skills of severely handicapped preschool children. *Language, Speech, and Hearing Services in Schools, 16*(1), 41–52.

Perry, J. D., & Flanagan, W. K. (1986). Pediatric psychology: Applications to the school needs of children with health disorders. *Techniques, 2*(4), 333–340.

Semel, E., & Wiig, E. (1980). *Clinical evaluation of language functions.* Columbus: Merrill.

Shaffer, J., Friedrich, W. N., Shurtleff, D. B., & Wolf, L. (1985). Cognitive and achievement status of children with myelomeningocele. *Journal of Pediatric Psychology, 10*(3), 325–336.

Sparrow, S. S., Balla, D. A., & Cicchetti, D. V. (1984). *Vineland Adaptive Behavior Scales.* Circle Pines, MN: American Guidance Service.

Stephens, S. (1982). Learning difficulties and children born with neural tube defect. *Spina-Bifida Therapy, 4*(2), 63–76.

Tew, B. J., & Lawrence, K. M. (1983). The relationship between spina bifida children's intelligence test scores on school entry and at school leaving: A preliminary report. *Child Care, Health, and Development, 9*(1), 13–17.

Thomas, A., & Grimes, J. (Eds.) (1985). *Best practices in school psychology.* Washington, DC: National Association of School Psychologists.

Thomas, C. L. (Ed.). (1981). *Taber's cyclopedic medical dictionary.* Philadelphia: F. A. Davis.

Wechsler, D. (1974). *Wechsler Intelligence Scale for Children–Revised.* New York: Psychological Corporation.

ANNOTATED BIBLIOGRAPHY

Barnett, A. J. (1982). Designing an assessment of children with cerebral palsy. *Psychology in the Schools, 19,* 160–165.
Examines approaches to conceptualization of assessment design, and supplies cross-referencing of basic psychological processes with expressive modality used to systematize individual evaluation.

Lazarus, P. J., & Strichart, S. S. (1986). *Psychoeducational evaluation of children and adolescents with low incidence handicaps.* New York: Grune & Stratton.
Comprehensive resource that is useful in designing assessment of the motorically impaired child with

other handicaps as well. Includes chapters on evaluation of infants with low-incidence handicaps and on cerebral palsy.

National Information Center for Handicapped Children and Youth. (undated). *Cerebral palsy*. Washington, DC.
Newsletters published on various handicapping conditions, with references and extensive resource list (agencies, associations, etc.).

Schleichkorn, J. (1983). Coping with cerebral palsy. Austin, TX: PRO-ED.
A parent resource covering areas of common concern, such as causality, development, medical problems, and psychological concerns.

Thomas, C. L. (Ed.). (1981). *Taber's cyclopedic medical dictionary*. Philadelphia: F. A. Davis.
Comprehensive dictionary that covers medical terms and concepts found in hospital records or medical reports.

55

Best Practices in Working with Gifted Children

Betty E. Gridley
Ball State University

OVERVIEW

General Background/History

Gradually, many educators are adopting a philosophy that all children have the right to an education designed specifically for them. Optimists see a future in which school environments will be challenging, stimulating, and adapted to the needs of individual learners. Pessimists point to past practices and public education's history of being unable or perhaps unwilling to deal effectively with the needs of especially capable youngsters, and they are much less sure that the future will be brighter.

The well-known experiences of Thomas Edison and Albert Einstein and their frustrations with the school system, certify that for many such people, the existing educational structures not only have failed to provide for development of their capabilities, but have actually been punitive. Many people who have gone on in later life to make significant contributions to society have actually been labeled "retarded" or "emotionally disturbed" by our public schools. David Elkind (1987) highlighted our failures with the comment that "for the gifted and talented, formal instruction is miseducation at all age levels" (p. 155).

Our experiences with differentiated programs for various learners have been merely moderately successful, at best, and in the future it is possible that the individual needs of all children will be better met within the mainstream. Until that time, however, we must acknowledge the potential contribution to society of particularly capable learners and provide nourishment for development of that potential.

Even in earliest times, outstanding individuals were rewarded for their prowess in demonstrating important skills that were closely tied to societal needs and norms. Early societies rewarded outstanding warriors and hunters because these skills were essential to the survival of the tribe (Albert, 1975). Galton, in his early studies of genius, looked for physical correlates and hereditary contributions. However, Terman (1925) initiated the first modern studies, almost certainly the most scientific up to that point, of intellectually capable individuals. His longitudinal work helped to dispel many of the myths that until that time had been accepted as factual information concerning those with especially high levels of intelligence. These myths included the idea that highly intelligent persons had a much greater likelihood of displaying both emotional and social problems.

As the twentieth century progressed, the conviction that giftedness was primarily a function of intellect was expanded. Guilford, Getzels and Jackson, and Torrance urged that giftedness be viewed as a multidimensional construct and that intelligence be seen not as a singular entity, but as a composite that includes many individual aspects. For example, Guilford

(1967) identified a number of facets of intelligence and suggested that some were not tapped by traditional IQ tests. Getzels and Jackson (1958) and Torrance (1962) insisted that any definition of giftedness include divergent thinking or creativity in addition to convergent abilities. Modern writers have sought to broaden our definition even more. Joseph Renzulli (1979), one of the most prolific writers and researchers in the field, suggested a three-element definition of giftedness which includes above-average (although not necessarily very superior) ability, high levels of creativity, and high levels of task commitment.

Throughout its history, the movement for gifted education has been plagued by variability in support, by misunderstanding, and by an elitist attitude. Support has been in times of extreme competition from outside challenges, such as the launch of Sputnik by the Russians in midcentury and, more recently the introduction of economic competition by Japan. However, at the present time, there is no federal mandate for gifted programs such as those for other exceptional learners. In spite of the lack of federal support, some states have developed fairly good programs, but others provide no formal recognition or programming. Furthermore, funds are often limited and distributed according to somewhat arbitrary policies. Is it any wonder that in this circumstance school psychologists and other professionals who are called upon to lend their expertise feel stymied and more than a little confused? A further complication is that professionals who are asked to provide guidance often have very little formal training or experience with the gifted.

The following discussion is designed to provide insight into working effectively with gifted learners. Major roles for which school psychologists and other professionals may need to be prepared include identification, programming, and involvement with social and emotional needs. Although school psychologists occasionally are asked to provide direct service to gifted students, more often they are called on to provide information in consultation with others.

BASIC CONSIDERATIONS

Definition

Definitions of the term *gifted* range from a rather limited notion of anyone who scores above a particular cutoff score on a single individual IQ test to more inclusive definitions such as the "official" federal definition of giftedness from the Gifted and Talented Children's Act of 1978 (PL 95-561, Section 902):

> Gifted and talented children are those identified by professionally qualified persons who by virtue of outstanding abilities are capable of high performance. *These are children who require differentiated programs and/or services beyond those provided by the regular school programs in order to realize their contributions to self and society* [italics added].
>
> Children capable of high performance include those with demonstrated achievement and/or potential ability in any of the following areas, singly or in combinations: (1) general intellectual ability, (2) specific academic aptitude, (3) creative thinking, (4) leadership ability, (5) visual and performing arts, (6) psychomotor ability. (Marland, 1971, p. 2)

It is important to note that the federal definition specifically states that differentiated programming is needed for gifted students. On the basis of this definition, the estimated incidence of gifted at a particular time would range from 3% to 5%. Certainly a minority, but a group whose talents must be called upon to provide direction for the future. Other definitions project incidences ranging from 2% if a stringent IQ-only criterion is established, to 20% for more liberal definitions (Freeman, 1985). A number of factors must be considered both in identification and programming.

Dealing with Biases and Prejudices

One fundamental difficulty in providing services for gifted students remains that of attitudes. School psychologists and other personnel often need to examine not only the biases of others but also their own.

There is a danger of allowing our attitudes to influence our approach to the needs of these capable students. I have lost count of the number of times colleagues have reminded me that *their* children never qualified for Gifted and Talented programming, so what was the big deal? Unsurprisingly, not a single person has lamented the fact that his or her child did not qualify for mentally handicapped placement. It is often difficult for us to see that these children who already seem to have so many advantages actually have great unfilled needs as those whose abilities lie at the lower end of the continuum.

Students Often Overlooked

There are categories of students who are systematically overlooked in identification of gifted youngsters. These include the very young, the handicapped, the culturally different, youngsters with behavioral problems, and underachievers. There are many good sources available that deal specifically with the problems encountered by subpopulations of gifted students, (e.g., Fox, Brody, & Toby, 1983; Hansford, 1987; Karnes, 1983; Masten, 1985; Whitmore & Maker, 1985; Yewchuck, 1986). This field of study is a growing one, but the fact remains that the students who are often overlooked by traditional identification methods are those who might best profit from special programming designed especially for their unique needs. Because of this danger, we need to know as much as possible about gifted students with various characteristics and the steps that can be taken to guard against their being denied appropriate experiences.

Learning disabled. The term *learning disabled gifted student* has been widely discussed. The combination seems to be an oxymoron, or contradiction in terms. Learning-disabled gifted learners are characterized by the same perceptual problems, poor motor skills, poor memory, and other specific disabilities that are found in the more typical learning-disabled. The question often becomes How do we know they are gifted? Many times the answer is that we don't.

We might look for two unique types of learning-disabled gifted. The first type is students who score extremely high on individual tests of intelligence or on some subtests, although a wide range of scatter may lower the overall score. Unfortunately, many of these students never actually get individual evaluations. Instead, their progress is charted by group achievement tests and classroom performance where they compensate for their difficulties by succeeding to some extent, albeit not as well as could be predicted from their abilities in certain areas. Indeed, because they are functioning at or about grade level, they are rarely identified as having any difficulty. Even those who have been referred may be denied special education services because *chronic failure* is interpreted to mean students who fail in the traditional sense of getting F's or D's. Because they are not outstanding achievers, they would also not be identified for gifted programs.

The second group of learners are those who have learning disabilities severe enough to fail in the traditional sense. For these children, placement in classes for the learning-disabled may result in greater frustration and isolation, as they are required to participate in programming that stresses drill and repetition rather than development of their stronger problem-solving and conceptual abilities. They don't fit into the traditional LD class, yet they are usually not even considered for gifted programs.

Physical, neurological, and communication problems. Physically, neurologically, or communication-impaired youngsters may be hampered by the masking of their abilities by their problems. The risk of this oversight comes from assessing the disability rather than the ability. For example, Matt, a first-grader, was referred by his teacher because she was seriously considering retention. He was currently having a very difficult time in school, and he had had problems in kindergarten. Matt scored in the mildly mentally handicapped range (EMR) on the Stanford-Binet LM. There were many indications, however, of both neurological and emotional problems. On review of Matt's history, it was evident that he had been abused physically and had been hospitalized with head injuries on several occasions. His home life was chaotic at best, with an alcoholic father who came and went. Matt was his father's "target" and his mother was struggling just to cope with financing basic needs for Matt and his brothers and sisters. Many indicators showed more potential than was measurable on the formal testing. My suggestion was that maybe retention would be helpful for this child. Usually I oppose retention, but I really wanted to see this child kept with his age peers instead of being sent to a special education classroom in another school. At the end of his second year in first grade, Matt was reevaluated. He scored well above average on measures of intelligence, but qualified for learning disabilities resource services on the basis of achievement. This year, Matt is in fourth grade. He will soon be mainstreamed for all classes with support services from the learning disabilities teacher. Figure 1 is just a sample, in his own handwriting, of the poetry he writes regularly.

Minorities and females. Many similar problems exist in identification of minorities and females. Because of cultural and/ or societal expectations and values, superior intellect is not dealt with in the same way for these groups. Young females sometimes receive mixed messages about the value of developing their intellectual abilities and pursuing their career goals in respect to the price that must be paid in terms of relationships and personal goals (Fox & Zimmerman, 1985; Whitmore, 1985). As to ethnic minorities, many of the faculties valued in these cultures are not conducive to traditional western definitions of success. In fact, U.S. educators seem to have been particularly backward in recognition of many legitimate forms of intelligence, especially those that are difficult to measure. For example, Gardner (1983) has suggested that these are many intelligences, including linguistic, musical, logical–mathematical, spatial, body–kinesthetic, and personal.

Young children. While early identification of gifted students is often recommended and even urged, there are very real limitations to identification of gifted performance at young ages. For this age group it may be wise to ignore or at the very least minimize standardized testing and rely on a number of informal measures such as parent recommendations and rating scales. Gridley (1987) provided a list of characteristics of gifted children that may help identify gifted potential even in young children.

Children with behavioral problems. Children with behavioral problems often get overlooked in identification for gifted programming. This is especially interesting in light of earlier work (Gridley & Treloar, 1984), that indicated that teachers do associate certain behaviors with gifted students. For example, behaviors might be labeled nonconformist were found to be *more* rather than less often identified with students whom teachers rated as having "gifted" characteristics (Gridley & Treloar, 1984). These include such problems as boredom, frustration, egocentricism, laziness, omission of detail, etc.

Limitations of a Narrow View of Giftedness and Psychometric Limitations of Instrumentation

The aspects of evaluation that are most commonly ignored in identification of and programming for gifted youngsters have to do with errors in measurement, psychometric inadequacies for certain tests, nonacademic aspects of intelligence, and nonintellective factors, such as motivation and anxiety, that influence test scores. Any identification primarily or solely using a single cutoff score on an individual IQ test ignores the limitations of the measurement process. Although we formally recognize the deficiencies of IQ tests, many of us continue to subscribe to the notion that the "really gifted" individual will score at least two standard deviations above the mean on an individual intelligence test.

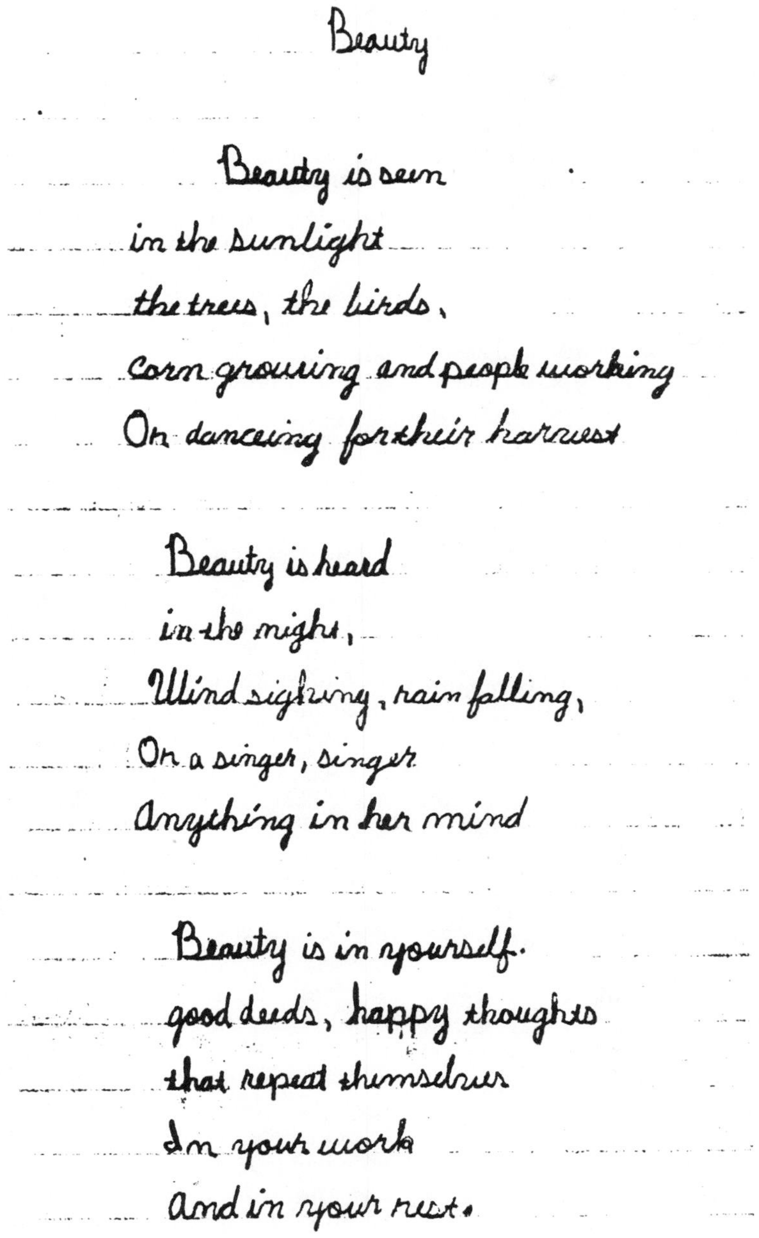

Beauty

Beauty is seen
in the sunlight
the trees, the birds,
corn growing and people working
Or danceing for their harvest

Beauty is heard
in the night,
Wind sighing, rain falling,
Or a singer, singer
Anything in her mind

Beauty is in yourself.
good deeds, happy thoughts
that repeat themselves
In your work
And in your rest.

FIGURE 1. Matt's poem about beauty.

In spite of our most enlightened view of the weaknesses of a single test score, Tammy might not qualify for gifted programs in some school districts. On the Wechsler Intelligence Scale for Children-Revised, she had a Full Scale IQ score of 129. It is still possible for a child to score 129 and not be eligible for programming. This, of course, would be the result of a procedure that ignores the idea of standard error of measurement. The psychologist who tested Tammy noted that her

Verbal IQ score (139) was in the superior range, with Performance IQ (114) *only* above average [my emphasis]. However, the Verbal IQ score was high enough to elevate the overall IQ to the superior range, yielding the conclusion that "this may be sufficient for enrichment within the AG [gifted] program." No mention was made of the fact that the performance scores actually ranged from 7 in Coding to 19 on Block Design. Verbal scores ranged from 11 in Arithmetic to 19 in Vocabulary. In this case, two characteristics of individual IQ tests are subject to possibly being overlooked. First, the IQ was reported as a single score, which negates the import of the standard error of measurement; consequently, Tammy could have been denied entrance into the program regardless of the qualitative interpretation made by the psychologist. Second, there is wide variation in the abilities of very intelligent children; contrary to popular belief, "truly gifted" children do not necessarily have evenly developed abilities in all areas. While most educators of the gifted stress the need to avoid a simple one-sided view of the construct as illustrated above, inclusion of a number of different aspects produces identification, based on many criteria, that tends to be unwieldy and often confusing. The more information we are forced to consider, the greater the chance for misinterpretation.

Common measurement problems encountered in identification of the gifted include the unreliability of certain types of information, such as parent and teacher ratings and tests of creativity, task commitment, and critical thinking. Group tests are problematic for various subgroups of learners and sometimes have inadequate ceilings for measuring gifted performance. Although the individual IQ test remains one of the best predictors of school achievement, many other facets of intelligence are not measured. Furthermore, differences in scores among different individual IQ tests have been found for gifted students (McCallum, Karnes, & Edwards, 1984; Sattler, 1988). For example, verbally adroit children were found to score very well on the Stanford Binet-LM, which had become *the* standard in identification of gifted students. However, although scores were found to be generally lower on the K-ABC, it was predicted that the chances of gifted placement of minority students would be increased with the use of the K-ABC, since they scored higher on it than on the WISC-R and the Stanford Binet-LM (McCallum et al., 1984). Use of the Stanford Binet-IV has not been adequately established for gifted students. However, studies reported in the Technical Manual (Thorndike, Hagen, & Sattler, 1986) indicated that gifted persons scored significantly lower (13.7 points on the average) on the SB-IV than on Form LM.

BEST PRACTICES

Identification

As mentioned previously reliance on a single IQ score for identification is very unsound. To avoid the problem attendant in such a process, identification with multiple criteria has been urged. However, many of the alternative sources of information available have not proven to be especially reliable or valid.

Nearly every source dealing with identification of gifted individuals stresses the importance of the match between assessment and programming. This warning is intended to focus attention on the fact that given the variety of possible program goals, the professional must be able to effectively match the characteristics of the learner to the program so as to avoid programs that are disjointed and disorganized. In my experience, many educators have no idea of the objectives involved in the programs they are carrying out and often describe the curriculum in terms of the activities accomplished. While teaching creative thinking and problem solving may be legitimate and desired activities for gifted programs, we know little about the types of students who profit most from such instruction nor, more importantly, how to identify them. This is one important reason for a school psychologist with expertise in instructional design and learning to be included on any team that is developing programming. This involvement must continue throughout the entire process from identification to evaluation.

Ideally, identification consists of at least three phases: initial screening, more comprehensive evaluation of various sources of information, and individual evaluation and case study (e.g., Alexander & Muia, 1982; Martinson, 1977). Our track record in screening of students for handicapping conditions is not great. However, the process of screening, the first step in identification of gifted students, is even more complicated. Most educators agree as to what constitutes poor or failing performance, but outstanding performance seems to be another matter entirely. The screening process should take into consideration a number of variables, including examination of scores on group ability; creativity and achievement tests; nomination by teachers, parents, peers, and students themselves; rating scales of various characteristics thought to be associated with outstanding potential; and evaluations of past accomplishments, such as poems, paintings, performance, and so forth. At the screening stage, the danger of making false negative decisions is greater than that of false positives: Processes that included more students as potentially gifted, even if they later are not outstanding producers, are to be preferred over excluding some who might make substantial contributions. The label of "giftedness" scarcely carries the stigma attached to handicapped labels. While some emotional problems (to be addressed later) may be associated with this population, they do not usually arise from providing programming that really is not warranted.

Group tests are useful when administered in combination with other sources, but their use is not suggested for final identification. Typically, lower cutoff scores (e.g., 120 on group IQ tests) may need to be used in order to guard against elimination of good candidates.

Although individual evaluation is often recommended, the realities of life may militate against thorough case study. In fact, in many districts, individual evaluations are not part of the identifi-cation process, and personnel must be content with decisions made during the first two steps mentioned above. Unfortunately, cost is often the most important factor in the process and few school systems are able to use the suggested three-step process as outlined above. Because of limited resources individual evaluation may be provided *only* for those individuals who can be reasonably expected to qualify for programming. In any case this individual evaluation needs to be multifaceted and complete. Again, the necessity of multiple sources of information cannot be stressed too highly.

Today a number of alternatives to traditional assessment methods are being noted in the school psychology literature. For example, McCluskey & Walker (1986) suggested avoiding traditional testing instruments such as individual IQ tests altogether and instead proposed utilizing the test–teach–test paradigm in identification. For this procedure, youngsters are tested on tasks included in the curriculum, the concepts are then taught, and the children are retested to measure the amount of learning that has taken place. This process promises not only a good method of identification, but also a way to directly link assessment with intervention.

Programming

Specialized programming options for gifted children can generally be categorized on two separate dimensions. The first, might be described as time spent with their peers, and conceived of as a continuum of service modalities that has as one of its poles complete segregation from the mainstream, the peer group being defined according to intellectual and other capabilities. At the opposite end of the continuum would be placement in the regular classroom with peers of similar chronological age and no special programming. Most services take various forms along this continuum. Two commonly used programs are full-time self-contained classes, and various integrated approaches (often called "pull-out" programs). In integrated approaches, the learner has an opportunity to interact with children of all ability levels, but acknowledgment is made of the gifted student's unique needs in regard to appropriate programming. Many observers argue against segregation as pulling children away from their peers, but it is not clear what constitutes the peer group for these learners. Other observers have suggested that the appropriate peer group is one based on mental rather than chronological age. However, the latter perspective ignores the wide variability found among gifted learners in development of social and emotional skills.

A second continuum of services can be described as qualitatively versus quantitatively different programming. The types of experiences that can be provided in quantitatively different programming include early school entrance, and acceleration in one or more areas. Acceleration recognizes the advanced pace at which many gifted persons are able to assimilate new information. Qualitatively different programming, on the other hand, involves enriching or broadening the curriculum beyond the ordinary scope by providing additional information, not just the same information at a faster pace. The most useful programs include both quantitative and qualitative aspects. Colangelo and Zaffran (1979) suggested that this dichotomy actually parallels the different learning styles of gifted youngsters and that differentiated programs should be based on their individual needs. For example, they declared accelerated learners to be interested in mastering increasingly complex material and to be highly efficient at processing information. These students generally do well in school but are sometimes frustrated by teaching situations in which they are forced into routine skills requiring a lot of repetition and drill. They have a need to master a great amount of material and register high achievement. On the other hand, enriched learners are seen as those who become totally engrossed in a particular problem. Being highly emotional, internally motivated, and curious, they often tend to follow their interests. Their need for achievement is less than their need for a

wide range of knowledge in a particular area. These learners are often described as daydreamers or are thought to be bright, but not working up to potential.

To combine the two modes of programming, then, a school may decide on a pull-out program in which gifted students from fourth, fifth, and sixth grades spend one hour per day together doing advanced math such as algebra (acceleration). Another group might spend one hour per day together learning about the history of mathematics (enrichment). In contrast, separate academies or the popular "magnet" schools would place all gifted learners together for the complete academic program.

A good source of information about specific systems and models for gifted education is Joseph Renzulli (1986), which is described in the Annotated Bibliography. All of the above options have advantages and disadvantages that need to be explored before any one is chosen. Many school systems have found flexible integrated programming for gifted students to be the superior option.

What about schools in which formal programming is not available? What can professionals do to help provide appropriate education for gifted learners? Elkind (1987) introduced the idea of a structural imperative, a kind of intrinsic motivation, that derives from children's need to realize intellectual potential or mental structures. In order to strengthen this imperative for all children, they must develop a sense of confidence in themselves and their abilities. To accomplish this end, we need to provide programs rich in materials, ample time for reflection, and thoughtful guidance. Elkind emphasizes not so much providing earlier formal instruction, but rather answering questions and providing stimulation for language development. The teaching should grow from the child's own interests.

While many see gifted children as being able to profit from early formal instruction, Elkind recommends a prolongation of the types of activities he endorses for all preschoolers. These include ample opportunity for youngsters to explore and investigate on their own. In other words, he would delay instruction in the conventional sense and do what good early childhood educators do, only at a higher level. Included in such programming would be provision of the right science materials, right literature, and right math materials, along with thoughtful guidance. Drill and instruction in skill areas would be de-emphasized. Process rather than content would be taught in order that bright students be challenged to take things further. This does not mean a completely unstructured environment; indeed, structure and organization are essential for program planning — too often gifted programs become playgrounds. The purpose of acknowledging the needs of these exceptional learners is to provide differentiated experiences to expand the talents they bring to the situation.

Socioemotional Considerations

With all of the identification, labeling, and programming for gifted youngsters, it is easy to lose sight of some of the fundamental insecurities of childhood. The problems that gifted learners have are similar to those other children face, but there are some special emotional needs that arise because of their gifts. Often, their view of the world separates them from their families and peers. Many younger children are not aware of what their special abilities mean in a positive light. They instead are apt to focus on being different and to translate different to mean strange or weird. Their advanced interests and vocabulary set them apart from others their age. Hence it is up to the adults who work with gifted children to provide for appropriate attention without contributing to the social isolation often felt by capable learners.

Gifted children also may be faced with parental or self-imposed standards that are unrealistically high in many areas. They may become frustrated when some of their abilities such as fine motor control do not keep pace with others and they are unable to put their plans into action.

Later in middle childhood, just when most youngsters are developing a real need for conformity, the gifted find themselves pulled between the need to belong to the group and the inner drive for self-attainment and perfection. More intense individual interests in science or history may also contribute to their sense of alienation. When they learn material easily, it is difficult to realize that their age mates may not.

Many gifted youngsters have extremely well-developed moral or emotional sensitivity. These children may have trouble dealing with hypocrisy, double standards, and other forms of logical and ethical contradictions. They are labeled as trouble-makers by adults who are unable to deal effectively with the challenges these students raise.

Adults who work with the gifted must be secure enough themselves to recognize the special attributes of these students without becoming envious or resentful. Those characteristics essential to working effectively with gifted children also include intelligence (although not necessarily in the gifted range), a sense of humor, patience, tolerance of individual differences, excellent communication skills, flexibility, firmness, and organization.

Although the gifted do not seem to have a greater number of problems than other children, the nature of their difficulties is often related to their gifts. Clark (1983) provides a comprehensive list of the cognitive and affective characteristics of gifted children, examples of related needs, and possible concomitant problems.

SUMMARY

Working with gifted learners calls for professionals who have an understanding of the construct of intelligence as well as an understanding of the heterogeneous nature of this population. Recognition of the profound qualitative differences that exist among and within these children is essential. Professionals who are truly adept at dealing with all children acknowledge their individual differences and the need for appropriate programming. Typically, different kinds of gifts emerge in all children at different ages. In addition, different abilities may not develop at similar rates. Individual students' needs depend to a great deal on maturity level, type of intelligence, culture, environment, etc. Unfortunately few professionals realize the nature of these individual differences, nor are they fully aware of their own beliefs and attitudes toward these children. In addition, national efforts to improve education for the gifted are fragmented and discontinuous at best. Every individual involved in programming for the gifted must make an effort to see that the potential of these children is not buried or dissipated.

No single magical technique exists to maximize the potential of our finest learners, nor is there any barrier that can guard against miseducation. Perhaps the single most important thing to remember is that, with all of the emphasis placed on the superior abilities of these children, it is easy to lose sight of the fact that gifted children are *children first*. Although they often require special help to develop their gifts, they, like all human beings, need the love and understanding of the significant others in their lives.

REFERENCES

Albert, R. S. (1975). Toward a behavioral definition of genius. *American Psychologist, 30,* 140-151.

Alexander, P. A., & Muia, J. A. (1982). *Gifted education, A comprehensive roundup.* Rockville, MD: Aspen Systems.

Clark, B. (1983). *Growing up gifted.* Columbus, OH: Merrill.

Colangelo, N., & Zaffran, R. T. (1979). *Counseling the gifted.* Dubuque, IA: Kendall/Hunt.

Elkind, D. (1987). *Miseducation: Preschoolers at risk.* New York: Knopf.

Fox, L., Brody, L., & Toby, D. (1983). *Learning disabled/gifted children: Identification and programming.* Baltimore: University Park Press.

Fox, L. H., & Zimmerman, W. Z. (1985). Gifted women. In J. Freeman (Ed.), *The psychology of gifted children* (pp. 219-243). New York: Wiley.

Freeman, J. (Ed.). (1985). *The psychology of gifted children.* New York: Wiley.

Gardner, H. (1983). *Frames of Mind.* New York: Basic Books.

Getzels, J. W., & Jackson, P. W. (1958). The meaning of "giftedness" — An examination of an expanding concept. *Phi Delta Kappan, 40,* 275-277.

Gridley, B. E. (1987). Children and giftedness. In J. Grimes & A. Thomas (Eds.), *Children's needs: Psychological perspectives* (pp. 234-241). Kent, OH: National Association of School Psychologists.

Gridley, B. E., & Treloar, J. H. (1984). The validity of the Scales for Rating the Behavioral Characteristics of Superior Students for the identification of gifted students. *Journal of Psychoeducational assessment, 2,* 65-71.

Guilford, J. P. (1967). *The nature of human intelligence.* New York: McGraw-Hill.

Hansford, S. J. (1987). *Intellectually gifted learning disabled students: A special study.* Reston, VA: Council for Exceptional Children. ERIC Document Reproduction Service No. ED287242.

Karnes, M. B. (Ed.). (1983). *The underserved: Our young gifted children.* Reston, VA: Council for Exceptional Children.

Marland, S. P., Jr. (1971). *Education of the gifted and talented,* Vol. 1 (Report to the Congress of the United States by the U.S. Commissioner of Education). Washington, DC: U.S. Government Printing Office.

Martinson, R. (1977). *The identification of the gifted and talented.* Ventura, CA: Ventura County Schools.

Masten, W. G. (1985). Identification of gifted minority students: Past research, future directions. *Roeper Review, 8*(2), 83-85.

McCallum, R. S., Karnes, F. A., & Edwards, R. P. (1984). The test of choice for assessment of gifted children: A comparison of the K-ABC, WISC-R, and Stanford-Binet. *Journal of Psychoeducational Assessment, 2,* 57-63.

McCluskey, K. W., & Walker, K. D. (1986) *The doubtful gift: Strategies for educating gifted children in the regular classroom.* Kingston, Ont.: R. P. Frye.

Renzulli, J. (1979). *What makes giftedness: A reexamination of the definition of the gifted and talented.* Ventura, CA: Ventura County Superintendent of Schools.

Renzulli, J. S. (Ed.) (1986). *Systems and models for developing programs for the gifted and talented.* Mansfield Center, CT: Creative Learning Press.

Sattler, J. (1988). *Assessment of children* (3rd ed.). San Diego, CA: Jerome Sattler.

Terman, L. M. (1925). *Genetic studies of genius: Vol. 1: Mental and physical traits of a thousand gifted children.* Stanford, CA: Stanford University Press.

Thorndike, R. L., Hagen, E. P., & Sattler, J. M. (1986). *Technical manual: Stanford Binet Intelligence Scale: Fourth Edition.* Chicago: Riverside.

Torrance, E. P. (1962). *Guiding creative talent.* Englewood Cliffs, NJ: Prentice-Hall.

Whitmore, J. (1985). New challenges to common identification practices. In J. Freeman (Ed.), *The psychology of gifted children* (pp. 93-113). New York: Wiley.

Whitmore, J. R., & Maker, C. J. (1985). *Intellectual giftedness in disabled persons.* Rockville, MD: Aspen Systems.

Yewchuck, C. (1986). Issues in identification of gifted/learning disabled children. *B. C. Journal of Special Education, 10*(3), 201-209.

BIBLIOGRAPHY

Elkind, D. (1987). *Miseducation: Preschoolers at risk.* New York: Knopf.
Must reading for all educators, psychologists, and parents alike. This book points out the dangers of trying to teach academic skills such as math and reading at too early an age. Elkind urges a return to child-centered, age-appropriate curricula. Primarily aimed at parents, this a well-written, common-sense approach to early childhood education.

Gridley, B. E. (1987). Children and giftedness. In J. Grimes & A. Thomas (Eds.), *Children's needs: Psychological perspectives* (pp. 234-241). Kent, OH: National Association of School Psychologists.
Two practical summary sources for information about gifted children. The *Communique* handout is in a form that can easily be duplicated to give to parents and teachers. The "Needs" handbook article includes a handy table of characteristics to look for as an aid to identification of potentially gifted persons.

McCluskey, K. W., & Walker, K. D. (1986). *The doubtful gift: Strategies for educating the gifted child in the regular classroom.* Kingston, Canada: Ronald P. Frye.
A comprehensive book that includes definitions, identification, and programming. Very readable and concise in covering a wide range of aspects of giftedness. If you can only read one source, read this one.

Freeman, J. (1985). *The psychology of gifted children,* New York: Wiley.
Edited book that deals with many of the issues and concerns of the gifted. Several chapters explore the most overlooked gifted, including sensory handicapped, culturally different, and females.

Renzulli, J. S. (Ed.). (1986). *Systems and models for developing programs for the gifted and talented.* Mansfield Center, CT: Creative Learning Press.
Edited book that includes descriptions of 15 different models of programming for gifted students. Each program is described by its developer(s). Rationale, practical applications, and research and evaluation have been included for all models.

56

Best Practices in Working with Parents of Handicapped Children

Joseph Murray
Kent State University

School psychologists today are working with a more sophisticated type of family than they were prior to the coming of special education legislation. Legislation has created an awareness in our society of parents' rights, and school psychologists must know the law when working with parents of handicapped children. In addition to being more aware of legal provisions, parents of handicapped children have undergone some rather profound changes in attitude toward handicapped children as a result of the change in our *society's* views toward the handicapped. School psychologists working with parents today will probably have to deal less with the sense of stigma in relation to having a handicapped child. This, in turn, could impact upon the way in which psychologists and their ideas are received by parents of handicapped children. Turnbull, Summers, and Brotherson, 1983, commented on another attitudinal change in our society that relates to families of handicapped when they wrote, "As social attitudes toward sex roles have changed, the burden of caring for a handicapped child becomes more evenly shared between fathers and mothers, brothers and sisters." This, too, will affect school psychologists as they work with handicapped children and their parents. Along with legislation and societal attitudes impinging on the family, the last decade has also witnessed a substantial improvement in services to families with handicapped members. School psychologists have a significantly larger number of resources to keep in mind when trying to help families.

School psychologists of the eighties have to deal with a myriad of factors that simply were not present 10 years ago. The opportunity to be an effective change agent rather than a psychometrician is available. The laws, the knowledge and sophistication, the attitudes, and the resources have changed and are dictating change on the part of school psychologists who want to carry out the best practice possible.

The purpose of this chapter is to impress on school psychologists the need to involve the family as a part of any plan to help a handicapped child. The theme suggests that, as professionals, we all too often focus on the observable, behavioral aspects of a disability while ignoring or minimizing the dynamics of the family as they relate to the handicapped child. School psychologists need to assess and intervene with respect to the whole family, not just the handicapped child within the family.

BASIC CONSIDERATIONS

School psychologists working with families that have handicapped children should be sensitized to numerous factors that may be, in varying degrees, unique to these families.

The Issue of Homogeneity

It cannot be assumed that families of handicapped children are all similar in their reactions to the handicap or in their method of coping with circumstances surrounding the condition. The nature of the child's handicap plus a variety of psychosocial and familial factors will create quite different dynamics within such families. A child with profound retardation and significant motoric involvement will pose different challenges to parents than one who is simply mildly retarded. The literature on handicapped families is often too simplistic and tends to suggest stereotypic tenets when discussing handicapped families. Superficial thinkers may be prone to accept without question the following generalizations about families having a handicapped child: (a) More stress exists, which leads to numerous daily and long-term adjustment problems; (b) specific adaptive behaviors can be predicted among mothers, fathers, and siblings; (c) intrafamily dynamics are different in families of handicapped children. There is, of course, a varying amount of truth to each of these descriptors. Because of the many situation-specific variables that can occur, however, best-practice-minded psychologists need to evaluate each concept as they attempt to help handicapped children and their families.

Unusually high stress often will be noted among parents who have a handicapped child. Friedrich and Friedrich (1981), in a study of 34 handicapped and 34 nonhandicapped children, found that families with handicapped children experience more stress and less marital satisfaction, enjoy less psychological well-being, show more need for support, and tend to be slightly less religious than do families without a handicapped child.

Some observers feel that ambiguity of diagnosis, and the consequently unclear expectations may be a source of stress. An identifiable condition and a distinctive diagnosis such as Down's Syndrome allow for more specific information about expectations and limitations (Beavers, Hampson, Hulgus, & Beavers, 1986).

The purportedly higher divorce rate in families having handicapped children, estimated to be twice that of the general population, may serve as a gauge of stress. Conflicting thoughts surround this issue, some researchers feeling that the most important factor influencing marital quality in "handicapped" families is the degree of integration prior to the child's birth. Others suggest that lower rates of family interaction and ongoing stress, both because of the handicapped child, are responsible for the higher divorce rate (Kazak, 1986).

Another perspective related to stress that is of possible use to practitioners looks at stress as being periodic, surfacing more at critical developmental points. It is suggested that, well after the traumatic period when parents first learn of the handicap, other stress points seem to arise quite commonly (Beavers et al., 1986). A survey of the literature suggests that critical transition points for families occur when the handicapped child is of preschool age (3-5 years), entering school (6-8 years), beginning adolescence (12-14 years), and reaching chronological adulthood (19-21 years). Some researchers have observed that family disruption increases with the age of the child in view of the fact that the older the child, the more obvious the discrepancies between the child's age and capabilities. The family that has made a successful adjustment to the child's handicap should, however, not be as affected by these discrepancies and should be capable of mollifying potential stress.

Research has frequently attempted to find common characteristics among mothers, fathers, and siblings of handicapped children. There do appear to be predictable feelings and behaviors inherent in specific family members and there often appears to be a direct causal relationship for these feelings and behaviors. Caution, however, must be exercised lest forced diagnoses and consequent remedial plans result from possible stereotyping. One mother, referred to a psychiatrist because of her *lack* of grief at giving birth to a son with Down's Syndrome said "He asked me how I got on with my Down's child and when I said 'Terrific,' he told me there was no need to be defensive!" Psychologists working with families of handicapped children need to guard against this overly generalizing type of thinking.

Mothers of Handicapped

Mothers of handicapped children have common characteristics that are manifested in varying degrees depending upon such factors as the amount of support they have, their resources, their individual strength, and the number and degree of additional stressors with which they have to deal. Featherstone (1980) emphasized that our entire culture "supports a mother in the opinion that her children are what she has made them.... Whether from upbringing, Freud, or Family Circle, most women learn this lesson thoroughly by the time they are grown." Failure to produce the desired child may produce feelings of guilt and inadequacy that carry with them numerous behavioral manifestations.

While not universally accepted, many persons feel that mothers often have a high probability of greatly exaggerated intensity of feelings across all emotions. This heightened intensity is not necessarily a negative characteristic and may often be channeled in a positive direction. One mother wrote of her doctors' perceived callous treatment of her, "If they had been kind, I never would have fought so hard to prove them wrong" (Murphy, 1981). Professional child study specialists, being aware of the intensity concept, allow for parental venting and learn to handle statements containing excessive emotionality to the exclusion of objective realistic thought.

For mothers of handicapped children major portions of each day are consumed by their handicapped offspring. Driven by guilt and other feelings related to the sense of having produced in the eyes of the society something less than "perfect," the mother may try to sustain a level of activity beyond her capacities. Mothers function as teachers, wives, therapists, trainers, transporters, and psychologists, and as

such they may diffuse their energies too much to adequately perform in some or all of those areas. Consider an already overextended mother who is approached by a school psychologist with several suggestions on how she might work with her handicapped child at home. What might be perceived by the psychologist as helping may be seen differently by the mother.

A mother who does not make a satisfactory adjustment to her handicapped child may establish a depressed attachment to the child. She may fail to adequately relate to other members of the family because of feeling compelled to give over her life to the care of the "damaged" child. Such a mother's everyday task-orientation may create a myopia that may be effectively corrected by an alert psychologist trained to look for that particular possibility.

Fathers of Handicapped

Fathers appear to assume different feelings and behaviors than do mothers of handicapped children. Societal expectations inculcate certain beliefs and expectations in fathers, just as in mothers, and as they fail to materialize, many fairly predictable outcomes may result. The father of a handicapped child once said, "I suffer for myself in terms of what I expected — what I hoped for in a son. But that's the suffering that goes with a loss like this. I suffer because he's got to, but also because I myself have had a loss. Yet, what have we lost? Only something I imagined" (Murphy, 1981). The last phrase of this quote, "only something I imagined," is especially meaningful as we look at the father's part in the dynamics of the family having a handicapped child. It refers to the father's extension of himself or, from another perspective, the male ego.

A common behavior among many fathers of handicapped youngsters is to remove themselves from the scene. This removal, it can be speculated, is often directly related to the hurt that the father experiences as he realizes the improbability of his child serving adequately as the extension of his ego. Not only do some fathers bow out of their handicapped child's life as a pain avoidance behavior; there is also a very practical reason that fathers play less of a role in their son's or daughter's life. Traditionally, the man has served as the breadwinner in our society. The father's having to work has permitted him to focus for large periods of time on things other than the handicapped child. Mothers, by contrast, have stayed at home, often being consumed daily by requirements of the handicapped child. In essence, our social system has created a coping mechanism for fathers by providing a respite from the negative and mundane world with which mothers of handicapped children often have to cope. Because increasing numbers of women have recently begun working outside the home, the issue of mothers at home has lessened, but it remains a significant factor, particularly with mothers of handicapped children.

Absence from the scene may cause a number of characteristics to emerge in fathers of the handicapped. Not being with the child causes the father to have far less knowledge of the handicapping condition than the mother, who quite naturally becomes an "expert" on cerebral palsy, epilepsy, or whatever condition exists. Over time, realization of this brings about the father's removal from the scene simply because he is something of a stranger to it. The phenomenon of *denial*, a term frequently used in describing the behavior of fathers of handicapped youngsters, is perhaps related to the fact that fathers necessarily spend much time away from home, with the result that they may tend not to develop a frame of reference that would lead them to compare their child with nonhandicapped children. Mothers, by contrast, more consistently see their handicapped son or daughter in relation to other, "normal" children and are constantly reminded of developmental differences between their child and others not victimized by a handicapping condition. Because of this lack of time with the child, fathers can and often do avoid reality on two bases: They deny the extent of the actual handicap, and they do not

reach the level of emotional intensity, particularly profound sorrow, that mothers do. In essence, the wider nature of the father's world is directly responsible for modifying his perceptions and feelings toward the handicapped child.

Fathers of handicapped children, more so than mothers, may receive gratification and recognition from their jobs. In our society, mothers are typically given the responsibility for successful child rearing; as a consequence, particularly for mothers of a handicapped child, the place for them is seen to be in the home. This denies mothers the possibilities for enhancement of self-esteem from job-related activities. Increasing this interference with attaining self-esteem is the mother's lack of opportunity to see her child measure up to either society's standards or her own, thus providing a constant threat to her self-image. Men, more career-oriented, in the best circumstance have an opportunity for enhancement of self-esteem on the job and under the worst are often able to remove themselves from the home scene for a socially encouraged and acceptable reason: to work.

Numerous beliefs exist suggesting that fathers of handicapped children have difficulty accepting their children (Widerstrom & Dudley-Marling, 1986). Not all of the possible explanations proposed can be applied in all cases, but they should be considered when assessing family dynamics. Some observers feel that fathers may react more negatively to their handicapped child if mothers are the first to be told by professionals that the child is handicapped. Others feel that fathers may have a stronger tendency to withdraw if the child is a boy. Level of occupational stress and the nature of the handicap may also be factors in fathers' reactions. Fathers seem best able to cope with handicaps other than retardation, and they are more effective with their retarded sons than with their retarded daughters.

The literature frequently provides ideas for promoting fathers' acceptance of their children's handicaps. Among these are involvement of the father as much as possible in the child's daily care, acceptance of the handicapped child by the father's parents, and provision of informal support from friends and family.

The essential generalization about fathers of the handicapped is that there appear to be commonalities in their behavior, in differing degrees, and school psychologists need to be sensitized to them.

Siblings of Handicapped

Are there specific behaviors and feelings among the siblings of handicapped children? After talking to several hundred mothers and fathers, one researcher concluded that brothers and sisters of the cerebral palsied, retarded, deaf, and blind accept their handicapped sibling and present few significant continuing problems to their parents (Barsch, 1968).

Variables such as religion, relative age, sex, income, family size, degree of handicap, and parental attitudes all contribute to the siblings' adjustment. In a review of the research Simeonsson and McHale (1981) isolated a number of factors related to sibling adjustment. The nature of the evidence was such that identification of a factor that was associated with good adjustment did not imply that its reciprocal was associated with poor adjustment. Additional research on siblings of handicapped children permits us to view both positive and negative reactions of siblings living with a handicapped child.

On the positive side, siblings were reported to be generally more supportive of their handicapped sibling and less hostile than siblings in so-called normal families. Many siblings of handicapped were found to be teachers/trainers and many expressed satisfaction in their roles as teachers for mentally retarded and handicapped children. Numerous children reported delight and satisfaction at having developed the ability to apply behavioral procedures effectively and at having learned to become behavior change agents.

However, living as a sibling of a handicapped child may have negative consequences that school psychologists need to be mindful of. Negative reactions stem from such things as having less time with parents, feeling left out, being subject to greater demands, and being "bribed." There is some evidence that having handicapped brothers or sisters may produce social withdrawal, more conflict with parents, poorer self-concept, and heightened anger over damage to personal belongings and to greater restrictions of family activities.

The overall effect of sibling relationships in families of handicapped children does not appear, however, to conform to a consistent pattern. Certain factors apparently contribute more than others to sibling adjustment to handicapped children (Simeonsson & Bailey, 1981). Young siblings of chronically ill children have been reported to show higher degrees of psychopathology. Closeness in age of sibling to handicapped child may contribute to poorer adjustment of the "normal" child. Male gender is also frequently associated with poorer adjustment. An important point to consider is that the traits, temperament, and functional behavior of the handicapped child, more than the handicapping condition, will probably influence most the adjustment or maladjustment of siblings. This, in tandem with the parents' acceptance or nonacceptance of the handicap and their consequent reaction, should be evaluated as one assesses the family dynamics.

The Issue of Intrafamily Dynamics

Intrafamily dynamics may have a high degree of commonality in families of a handicapped child, although once again one cannot assume sameness across all families. School psychologists are typically not well trained in the area of analyzing family dynamics. The payoff, however, from focusing on the interactions of family members living with the child may well contribute more to effective change and family–child well-being than any of the psychologist's assessment approaches.

Several potential breakdowns in a family system may occur with the presence of a handicapped child. Consider the following points as significant in analyzing

TABLE 1
Factors Associated with Adjustment of Siblings of Handicapped Children

Positive Adjustment	Negative Adjustment
Small family	Large family
Sibling younger than handicapped child	Sibling older than handicapped child
Male handicapped child	Female handicapped child
Sibling and handicapped child same gender	Sibling and handicapped child different gender
Handicapped child older than sibling	Handicapped child younger than sibling
Severe level of impairment	Mild level of impairment
Impairment of undefined, ambiguous nature (e.g., mental retardation)	Impairment visible, clearly defined (e.g., blind)

the intrafamily efficiency when a handicapped child is present:

1. The relative power of the handicapped child in the family

2. The issue of rigidity versus flexibility in the family

3. Parental equality

4. Family nuclearity and extended family

5. Relationship with the outside world

"The relative power of the handicapped child in the family system proves to be a useful indicator of the family's overall adaptation" (Beavers et al., 1986). In less healthy families handicapped children can significantly modify the roles of other family members to the point that the overall growth of the handicapped child as well as the family is adversely affected. In many families a coalescence of the primary caretaker and the handicapped child may form that can further exacerbate the situation. Because of multiple, consistent demands of many handicapped children, parents may often understandably focus on a task maintenance–efficiency concept in order to "survive." A possible rigidity may set in that will interfere with creativity within the family and lessen the opportunity for individuation among family members.

Our present society finds both mother and father increasingly working outside the home. This contributes to the identity of each, benefits the family financially, and generally creates what some refer to as a "coequal structure or symmetrical rapport" (Cirillo & Sorrentino, 1986). The mother and father share equally in decision making and derive satisfaction from their contributory roles. The presence of a handicapped child often fractures this, causing an imbalance. Now, one spouse, often the mother, becomes restricted, has less financial and social freedom, and often has to deal with an inordinately negative, mundane world on a daily basis. The corresponding adjustment of each spouse to this situation should be noted in the assessment of the family with an eye to remediating any breakdown that may have resulted from the inequality.

Family nuclearity may realize modification as a result of the existence of a handicapped child. The child, or the adjustment of the parent(s) to the child, may serve to keep the extended family at a distance. Potential support will be reduced, which could increase the family burden. Conversely, of course, the opposite could occur, the extended family rallying around the nuclear family. In either case, the assessor of this family must be sensitive to the nuclear issue and how the coping mechanism of the family is being affected by it.

A family's relationship with the outside world beyond the extended family is often cut off by the presence of a handicapped child. Sensitivity of family members toward the handicapped child plus the pragmatic issues that may restrict social interaction can cause a distancing phenomenon that may create feelings of unacceptance or hostility to the outside world. Again, the perceptive psychologist looking for this possibility may modify these dynamics in a positive way and improve the overall attitude and health of the family.

The Issue of
Parent-Professional Relationships

The relationship between professionals and parents has gradually changed over the years owing in large part to special education legislation. Today school psychologists and other human service providers tend to work more as consultants to parents and children and serve as architects of programs. This has tended to involve parents more in such roles as educational decision makers, advocates, teachers, case managers, and program evaluators. The involvement of parents working in various capacities with their handicapped children has reduced the boundaries between home and school and has caused parents to be less dependent and more active in the education of their handicapped child. School psychologists working with parents should be mindful that while many parents want to assume more responsibility and involvement with their handicapped child, others do not and cannot afford the investment. The emerging trend of increasing the number of roles played by parents and their degree of involvement should be carefully considered by school psychologists.

Psychologists who have worked with handicapped children and their parents are aware of the high level of emotional intensity that is often found. Parents have been known to nearly come to blows with school officials over appropriate education for their child. Illustrating this point is a statement made by a parent (Murphy, 1981). "I'm sure the school authorities and hospitals think I'm a damned nuisance. I don't mean to be mean. I think they all liked me better when I was a shrinking violet. Well, I'm hardly that any longer, and we're all better for it." Psychologists who are aware of the possibility of intense emotionality can develop a mind set of objectivity prior to interacting with parents, which should do much to create a better working relationship.

The literature has made generalizations suggesting that parent-professional partnerships are not feasible. Parents have been found to be overprotective, to be unable to accept the child, to experience marriage breakdowns, and to focus irrational hostility on the professional. While undoubtedly these descriptors are accurate in some instances, professionals who expect parents to behave in the above ways will find it difficult to establish the necessary rapport to insure a good intervention.

The authority figure concept suggesting that parents have great faith in and expect inordinate help from the psychologist can have a plus-minus effect. As to its positive aspects, the strength enjoyed by the psychologist permits a directive type of behavior that allows for the utilization of resources that will permit psychologists to act as change agents. On the negative side, psychologists often have to deal with excessive parental expectations and must help parents to develop a congruency between their expectations and reality.

BEST PRACTICES

School psychologists can improve their skills in working with families of handicapped children by being mindful of the numerous concepts discussed above in the Basic Considerations. In addition to understanding issues related to homogeneity, intrafamily dynamics, and parent-professional relationships, there are specific best practices that school psychologists should consider when trying to help handicapped children and their families.

The Partnership Concept

School psychologists need to develop their own set of criteria to be used in determining the degree of "partnership" with families that might be possible in any given situation. Brynelsen (1984) listed the following obstacles that professionals and parents have to overcome to create a good working relationship and gave solutions for both professionals and parents to use in overcoming these obstacles. These solutions can be used by psychologists to formulate the criteria that will allow them both to establish partnerships and to evaluate their effectiveness in working with families of handicapped children.

Obstacles Faced by Professionals

- No preparation or previous experience in working with parents

- Anxiety and/or resistance to the prospect of parent involvement

- A tendency to adopt an authoritarian approach to parents

- Uncertainty about admitting limitations in knowledge or skills, and/or not referring to others

- Limited understanding of the range of differences from one family to another in respect to life skills, abilities, priorities, or restraints

- Expecting too much or too little from parents

- Not taking parents' concerns seriously; adopting a wait-and-see attitude

- Withholding information, or refusing access to information

- Using professional jargon

- Emphasizing weaknesses in child and family and not acknowledging their strengths

Obstacles Faced by Parents

- Lack of confidence in themselves as parents

- Negative past experiences with professionals

- Problems in balancing the demands of the child with special needs and the needs of other family members

- Under or overestimating their child's potential

- Under or overestimating the contribution professionals can make

- Coping with the demands placed on them by professionals

Solutions to Obstacles Faced by Professionals

- Give parents recognition for their strengths and successes

- Tell parents they are experts, too, through specific and accurate comments

- Do not patronize

- Believe the parent; children do act differently in different settings

- Show respect for children and value them as persons

- Accept people's right to be different; avoid generalizing and stereotyping

- Listen to parents' opinions; then show you value them

- Do not pressure parents to participate

Solutions to Obstacles Faced by Parents

- Don't be afraid to ask for help

- Ask for clarification if information given is not clear to you

- Challenge professionals if you disagree

- Be honest about home happenings; explain practical restrictions on time and energy

- Seek other kinds of help if you need it

- If you are not pleased with professionals' advice or treatment, tell them

- Show your appreciation for good service and attitude

Unless good rapport is developed in the psychologist-parent partnership, other best practices in working with families of handicapped children have less of a chance to be realized.

What do parents need from school psychologists? Knowing what parents need and want from school psychologists, and often do not get, should help professionals better determine the direction and the boundaries to be developed in working with families. Families at all points along the developmental continuum appear to have common needs, one of which is *information*. Looking to professionals for information carries with it numerous residual ideas and problems. Parents associate absolute knowledge and definitive solutions with authority figures (professionals). When the reality hits parents that the professional does not have all the answers, disappointment, disillusionment, anger, and frustration may arise. Not getting the desired information, incidentally, creates a frequently observed type of parental behavior called "shopping around." Consider a mother who had taken her child to nine different places in 5 years. She obtained a different diagnosis each time: "Retarded," the first one said; "aphasic," the second one said; then she got "autistic," "hard of hearing," and "minimally brain damaged." For parents wanting definitive information, this type of experience generates frustration and anger. Further complicating the interaction between parent and professional is the frustrated reaction of the psychologist when forced to acknowledge that desperately sought answers are unavailable. Psychologists' frustrations might well distort their perception of parents, thus introducing another complication to the interaction process.

At times psychologists have substantial information but do not share it with the parents. Psychologists may not want to deal with the pain of the parents' reaction, may want to spare parents pain.

But parents, for the most part, want the truth, and in withholding information or evading questions psychologists may implicitly criticize parents' good sense. When psychologists discuss a child's problems candidly with the family, they convey respect for their intelligence and judgment.

Parents' inability to get information may result from improper training of professionals in low-incidence disabilities. Unfortunately, people have an amazing tendency to assume that an authority is knowledgeable in all areas of his specialization. Recent legislation has put demands on school psychologists to know more about developmental disabilities and disorders of young children. School psychologists often have not had good training in these areas, and many universities have failed to adapt their curricula to meet the new role needs of school psychologists. Until changes are made, many school psychologists will find themselves lacking information sought by parents.

To be effective in helping parents, school psychologists not only need to be as knowledgeable as possible about handicapping conditions, but they should be able to direct parents to reading material that will further their understanding of any given condition. School psychologists may want to use a resource by Mullens (1987) to establish for themselves a list of readings on a wide variety of handicaps. Sixty books authored by articulate parents of handicapped children are listed by Mullens and broken down into the following themes: Realistic appraisal of disability, extraordinary demands on the family, extraordinary emotional stress, and resolutions. This resource may provide a starting point for developing a library of readings for parents. Table 2 reveals the content areas of Mullens' survey.

Another way in which school psychologists can serve as a source of information is by being familiar with community resources. This pragmatic knowledge combined with a strong theoretical base can do much toward making psychologists effective change agents.

TABLE 2
Disabilities in Families as Portrayed in 60 Books by Parents

Disability	Number of Books
Sensory problems	
Blind	1
Deaf	4
Emotional problems	
Autism	3
Cognitive problems	
Brain injury	2
Down's Syndrome	4
Mental retardation	3
Schizophrenia	1
Speech & language disorders	
Aphasia	2
Dyslexia	1
Speech problems	1
Health problems	
Brain tumor	1
Colitis	1
Cystic fibrosis	2
Degenerative brain disorder	1
Heart disease	1
Hemophilia	1
Hodgkin's disease	1
Leukemia	3
Lymphhemangioma	1
Organ transplant	2
Neuromuscular problems	
Cerebral palsy	1
Epilepsy	2
Hydrocephalus	1
Muscular dystrophy	1
Orthopedic deformity	1
Osteogenesis imperfecta	1
Scoliosis	1
Spina bifida	1
Multiple/severe	7
Various	8

The second helpful quality of professionals desired by parents is a multidimensional characteristic, *support.* Listening heads the list of characteristics subsumed under support. Listening conveys respect. Parents desperately need to be heard and may well benefit most from a nondirective approach by the psychologist.

Understanding on the part of the professional provides support to parents. Complete understanding of the parents' thoughts and feelings is not possible for the professional. The professional who unthinkingly says "I understand" may indeed create a sense of falseness and reduce credibility. Perhaps the best one can do is try to understand and respond realistically. Often it may be necessary to rely on support groups, be they specifically related to a handicapping condition or generally directed toward parents of handicapped children, to provide the understanding sought by parents. Credibility is assured; each parent knows that the other understands.

Parents beset by unrelenting problems frequently develop a lack of confidence in themselves. This is brought about because of accentuated emotions, the lack of a frame of reference, and the need to "survive" from day to day. Emotions temporarily distort judgment. Several negative occurrences resulting from poor judgment can lessen a parent's confidence. The handicapping condition is often unique, disallowing the parent an opportunity to make decisions based on well-established knowledge. Often the sheer mechanics of caring for a handicapped child create chronic fatigue, depression, and a sense of hopelessness. At some point, parents may either refrain from making decisions on their own as their confidence level wanes or require approval or advice from others. Professionals need to steer parents away from this dependency level with reassurance, and move them in a direction that stresses independence and confidence. Helping in this way allows professionals to indeed be meaningful support persons.

Encouragement is also desired by parents. One of the biggest mistakes, however, in working with parents of special children is giving false encouragement. There is a natural tendency to want to say something to console. Parents, however, quickly learn to view platitudes at best as an act of kindness and at worst as a serious credibility weakness, especially when delivered by professionals. Parents don't want to hear "Everything is going to be all right" when their common sense tells them it won't be.

Encouraging parents to provide some time for themselves is one of the most therapeutic things professionals can do. Parents of special children often withdraw from the world and consequently need to be encouraged to continue contacts outside the immediate family.

Many handicapped people and their parents do not want sympathy, praise, or pity; properly related encouragement stresses realistic thoughts of how parents might improve a situation. Parents want reassurance, but back away from praise given on an emotional basis.

On the other hand, parents want psychologists to *care*. To care is to go beyond oneself into the life of another; and to realize that the meaning one has to fulfill in life is beyond oneself; it is never merely oneself. Albert Schweitzer's message to a group of aspiring physicians suggested that only those who had sought and found how to serve would really attain happiness in their careers. In addition to developing a sound technical knowledge base, successful professionals must either learn or be endowed with this caring characteristic. An understanding of the components of this quality is important: Frankness on the part of the professional to the parent, respect for the child, and careful listening and responding to the parents' ideas and concerns are all major characteristics of caring. Nevertheless, frankness is a difficult attribute to learn and to use. It takes courage and confidence on the part of the professional, and psychological insight into others. The accomplished professional finds a way, however, to honestly share the most unpalatable information with parents.

Showing respect to the child through listening and by making realistic conversation gives a message to the parents. "My child is an individual, a person." Parents desire normality in their child and a professional's relating in an unaffected way toward the child brings that goal closer. Personalizing of the handicapped child, while not a highly technical skill, is an essential part of showing care to both child and parent. Legitimate responding and listening is probably interferred with most by the pressure of time. School psychologists, reacting to time pressures, often do not offer an opportunity for parents to work through their concerns. In an ideal setting, psychologists agree or disagree with parents, thus demonstrating meaningful listening. They do not expect passive acquiescence from parents and do not assume the omnipotent role of an arbiter rather than advisor. Caring is all of these things, which, when synthesized, suggests the need for authenticity.

Parents may need help in *decision making*. Help is a key word. The effective psychologist does not necessarily tell parents what to do, but undertakes to help them decide. Again, school psychologists may have the technical information, but of prime importance is their ability to prepare parents for decision making — to properly address certain requisites that facilitate decision making. What are the characteristics that permit effective decision making? What do psychologists need to be aware of in readying parents for decision making? The following criteria are offered.

- Parents should be able to verbalize and accept their feelings. In tandem with this concept, of course, is the need for a person to whom they can relate meaningfully.

- Often helpful, but not always, is a mutual support group, which can provide information for decision making as well as allow for emotional support and confidence building.

- Parents with decision-making capability will have remembered to satisfy their own needs and will have developed interests beyond the world of their handicapped child. They will have not allowed the child to dominate their lives.

- Parents must have developed a belief in something to live for. This belief may be a religious faith, it often is represented by giving and sharing with other parents, and it may be something quite unrelated to the handicapping situation. Whatever that something is, it often represents a removal of the parent from the immobility created by being caught up in the constraining life that can be imposed by a handicapped child.

- To accept that life is not fair and that one's sense of justice will be constantly outraged will help persons to attain objectivity and reduce sorrow and self-pity, thus permitting more capable decision making.

Individual Assessment

The school psychologist must be skillful in the use of normative, criterion-referenced, and developmental assessment materials, and diagnostic data gained from these instruments should be integrated with information gained from assessing the family. This combination will do much to help insure best practice in working with handicapped children and their families.

Hopefully the days are gone in which school psychologists simply give normative tests to handicapped children while ignoring the need to functionally and developmentally describe the child. A good assessment now includes an analysis of the following domains: self-help, personal-social, cognitive, emotional, visual, auditory, academic, motor, language, and prevocational/vocational. Legislation has had an enormous impact on the role of school psychologists, requiring them to learn much more about diagnosis and remediation of children aged 0-5 years. Additionally, school psychologists striving for best practice have had to develop a prevocational–vocational orientation permitting them to work effectively at the upper end of the age continuum. School psychologists must have a thorough knowledge of both normative and criterion-referenced instrumentation and they must be prepared to discuss such things as validity, reliability, test appropriateness, and test bias with parents. Additionally, school psychologists should be able to relate test results to meaningful programming and curriculum design.

Parent interviewing is often minimized as an individual assessment component and yet it may offer more usable information than any other approach. School psychologists may want to use an instrument, such as the Vineland-R, as a format for interviewing parents, teachers, or childcare workers. The Vineland-R or similar forms may serve as the interviewing instrument per se, or they may be used to help develop an instrument that psychologists tailor to meet their own needs.

A medical consultant is a must for school psychologists desiring to complete a comprehensive individual assessment. Strong consideration should be given to establishing a good working relationship with several members of the medical community because of the frequent interplay between medical and other problems with which psychologists must deal.

The Consultant Role

Strong consideration should be given by pupil personnel leaders to creating school psychology positions that permit specialization in working with handicapped children, especially low-incidence handicapped. School psychologists can no longer work in their traditional psychometric roles and must develop a consultant or architect role — one that permits them to be directly involved in assessment, to coordinate assessment, to be involved in curriculum design and to creatively formulate prescriptive programs for children and their families. Assessment should continue to be a major responsibility of psychologists. However, it will be done differently than previously, less attention being given to describing a child quantitatively and more emphasis being placed on functional, descriptive assessment of child and family. Good school psychologists must relate their diagnostic findings to classroom operations and therefore must be familiar with curriculum. Unfortunately, school psychologists are often ill-prepared in the various areas of special education curriculum and need to consider ways to lessen this deficit.

Recent trends have suggested that psychologists working as consultants can develop cost-effective programs by working with groups of teachers and parents. One such program is to train teachers to work more effectively with parents through integration of counseling theory and special education practice (Berry, 1987). Teachers are trained in four sessions, ranging over 3–6 hours. Sessions focused on concepts such as grief response, family systems theory, parental self-esteem, and how-to information. While great logistical problems are inherent in establishing and maintaining such programs, the potential geometric gain from such an endeavor may make it worthwhile. In any case school psychologists must redesign their roles from the traditional psychometric orientation to the consultative approach in order to effectively establish such a training program.

Besides working with teachers to enhance the lives of handicapped children and their parents, school psychologists may want to create groups designed to cause parents to work with educators. A program described by Humes, (1986) addresses this project. A concept referred to as *parents-as-partners* encourages parent groups to work cooperatively with school personnel to bring about understanding of, and participation in, special education programs for their children. This peers-as-helpers idea seems to work most effectively when members of the pupil services staff are used as part of the instructional cadre. Reportedly some of the parent volunteers who were previously parent activists changed to become supporters of the special education system.

The parents-as-partners schema, like the training program for teachers, can't be developed and implemented by psychologists adhering to the traditional psychometric role. Psychologists must have the freedom to work more in a consultative capacity.

In summary, best practice school psychologists will be very skilled at assessing the family to determine the dynamics which might be operating to improve or lessen the chances of helping children and family. They will be sensitized to pitfalls that might interfere with their ability to work with parents successfully and they will be mindful of parental needs and wants. Individual assessment knowledge will cover the 0–22 age continuum and will incorporate nonnormative and normative assessment that ties in directly to the curriculum and the operation of the classroom.

Finally, best practice school psychologists will move more toward the role of a consultant and will de-emphasize strict psychometry, opting more for a role that will permit greater use of their leadership experience and training.

REFERENCES

Allen, D. A. (1987). Are we professionalizing parents? Weighing the benefits and pitfalls. *Mental Retardation, 25*(3), 133–139. Barsch, R. (1968). *The parent of the handicapped child: Study of child-rearing practices.* Springfield, IL: Thomas.

Berry, J. (1987). A program for training teachers as counselors of parents of children with disabilities. *Journal of Counseling and Development, 65*, 508–509.

Beavers, J., Hampson, R., Hulgus, Y., & Beavers, W. (1986). Coping in families with a retarded child. *Family Process, 25*, 365–378.

Brynelsen, D. (1984). *Working together: A handbook for parents and professionals.* (British Columbians for Mentally Handicapped People, Vancouver). Toronto: National Institute on Mental Retardation.

Cirillo, S., & Sorrentino, A. (1986). Handicap and rehabilitation: Two types of information upsetting family organization. *Family Process, 24*, 283–292.

Featherstone, H. (1980). *A difference in the family life.* New York: Basic Books.

Friedrich, W. N., & Friedrich, W. L. (1981). Psychosocial assets of parents of handicapped and nonhandicapped children. *American Journal of Mental Deficiency, 85*, 551–553.

Humes, C. (1986, May). Parent counseling in special education: Case description of a novel approach. *School Counselor, 5*, 345–349.

Kazak, A., (1986). Families with physically handicapped children: Social ecology and family systems. *Family Process, 25*, 265–281.

Mullens, J. (1987). Authentic voices from parents of exceptional children. *Family Relations, 36*, 30–33.

Murphy, A. (1981). *Special children, special parents.* Englewood Cliffs, NJ: Prentice Hall.

Simeonsson, R., & McHale, S. (1981). Research on handicapped children: Sibling relations. *Child: Care, Health and Development, 7*, 153–171.

Turnbull, A., Summers, J., & Brotherson, M. (1983). *The impact of young handicapped children on families: Future research directions.* Lawrence, KS: University of Kansas, Kansas Research and Training Center on Independent Living.

Widerstrom, A., & Dudley-Marling, C. (1986, May). Living with a handicapped child: Myth and reality. *Childhood Education, 62*, 359–366.

ANNOTATED BIBLIOGRAPHY

Brynelsen, D. (Ed.), (1984). *Working together: A handbook for parents and professionals,* British Columbians for Mentally Handicapped People, Vancouver: National Institute on Mental Retardation, Toronto (Ontario).
This handbook provides information on ways in which parents can work with professionals in selecting and monitoring services for their special needs child. Information is presented on parents' and professionals' attitudes and needs and on obstacles, solutions, myths, and realities regarding an effective parent–professional relationship.

Featherstone, H. (1980). *A difference in the family.* New York Basic Books.
The author of this book is an assistant professor of education at Wellesley College and the mother of a handicapped child. The book discusses how the lives of family members are affected by the presence of a handicapped child. How they cope, and the fear, anger, guilt, sense of personal inadequacy, and loneliness that are experienced is expressed. The book is well researched and represents more than one person's feelings and opinion.

Mullens, J. (1987). Authentic voices from parents of exceptional children. *Family Relations, 36*, 30–36.
This article contains a list of 60 books authored by articulate parents of handicapped children. Titles appear under the following themes: sensory problems, emotional problems, cognitive problems, speech and language disorders, health problems, and neuromuscular problems.

Murphy, A. (1981). *Special children, special parents.* Englewood Cliffs, NJ: Prentice-Hall.
This book discusses over 200 critical incidents with parents, relatives, and others who come into contact with handicapped children. Coverage includes a series of issues that are not commonly discussed, yet are important, in the lives of special families, including doubting, believing, hoping, daring, enjoying, feeling, loving, and single-parenting.

57

Best Practices in Working with Single-parent and Stepparent Family Systems

Cindy I. Carlson
University of Texas at Austin

"I just can't seem to stop thinking about killing myself. I know that I won't do it. It would hurt too many people . . . my mother, my kitten. But I just don't want to live anymore. All my friends get on my nerves. My school work is hard. I want to do well, but I am so far behind. I can't work less hours at McDonalds. I need the money to pay for gas for my car. My mother used to let me clean the house for money, but my stepfather says that I shouldn't get paid for that . . . it's a chore. My mother and I were so close. Now I have to compete for her attention all the time." Excerpt from an interview with a 15 year old girl whose mother remarried within the past two years.

"I don't know what else to do with Christy. She used to not be like this. She was a good student, and she worked hard. She has always had a lot of friends. But now she is dating the manager of the restaurant where she works. He's 22 and she's only 16. She wants to move in with him, and sometimes I get so angry with her I almost want her to. She lies to me all the time. I can't trust her. I'm afraid every time the phone rings that something else has happened. She has totalled her car, been in an accident with my van, and wrecked my boat. She says to leave her alone. She knows what she's doing." Excerpt from an interview with the single-parent father of a teen-age girl.

These cases demonstrate the negative effects that the family transitions of divorce, single-parenting and remarriage can have on school-age children. Each represents a case referred to a school psychologist in a predominantly Caucasian, middle to upper-middle class suburban school system. Both children were highly competent and successful in school prior to the stress created by living in a single-parent and stepparent home. Both had biological parents who were college educated, economically secure, and committed to the well-being of their children. The purpose of this chapter is to assist school psychologists in the assessment and intervention of single-parent and remarried child and family systems.

OVERVIEW

The living arrangements of children have dramatically changed within the past two decades. In 1960 88% of children were living with two natural parents; currently, only 56% of children live with both biological parents. For every ten Caucasian children in a classroom, it can be anticipated that at least half will have experienced life in a single-parent family, and one or two are currently living in a stepfamily. Statistical projections suggest that White children may spend, on average, as many as 6 of their first 18 years in a single-parent home. For Black children, eight or nine of every ten children will have resided in a single-parent home spending, on average, 11 of their first 18 years without two parents (Hernandez, 1988). Single parenting is most prevalent among Blacks, more prevalent among American Indians and Hispanics than among Whites, and least prevalent among Asians. The antecedents of single and stepparenting also vary by ethnic group (Laosa, 1988). Of all White children, over 75% result from marital separation or divorce. In contrast, the most frequent precursor of single-parenting for Blacks is out-of-wedlock births and for Hispanics it is marital separation, but not divorce (Laosa, 1988). These data suggest that remarriage and stepparent families are most likely to be experienced by White children and least likely to be experienced by Hispanic children (Laosa, 1988). Three demographic trends are primary in accounting for the increase in single-parent and stepfamily homes: (a) a substantial rise in the number of births occurring to unmarried mothers, (b) the continuing high rate of divorce, and (c) the associated increase in the proportion of divorced women with children who remarry (Hernandez, 1988).

The never-married single-parent home is considered to be at greatest risk. Both Black and White children living with a never-married mother are more likely to live with a younger mother (less than 25 years old), who has not graduated from high school (50% of White births, 40% of Black births), with an annual family income of less than $10,000 (77% White, 80% Black). This low annual income persists despite the fact that for both Blacks and Whites, 34% of children living with never-married mothers have at least one additional adult relative in the home.

Divorce is the second major demographic variable that affects the living arrangements of children. Although the dramatically increasing divorce rate observed from 1965 to 1979 has begun to level off, it is still predicted that 60% of all children will experience a divorce. The transition from a two-parent to a single-parent family, when caused by divorce, is usually accompanied by significant related socioenvironmental changes including lowered income, income instability, and changes in employment, residence and school (McLanahan, 1983). These changes must be considered in the context of the substantial emotional confusion and loss which accompanies the loss of a parent or spouse (Wallerstein & Kelly, 1980). Furthermore, when single-parenting is the result of divorce, the likelihood of remarriage is higher than for separated or never-married mothers. Therefore, children in post-divorce single-parent homes can be expected to continue to experience more transitions than their intact family peers.

The resources available to children in single-parent homes, regardless of antecedent, are consistently fewer than two-parent families. Without exception, across median income groups, the annual incomes of single-mothers were less than half, and more frequently one-third to one-fourth, the income of married couple families (Laosa, 1988). Economic adversity has multiple implications. Directly, family income can affect the physical health of the child and mother. In addition, socioeconomic status is related to parental behavior toward children, teacher and peer attitudes and behavior, social and educational opportunities, environmental stimulation and attention, childrearing styles and expectations. Indirectly, the social and economic support available to the biological parent in both single-parent and remarried family systems has been found to be positively related to the quality of the parent–child relationship (Hetherington, 1987; Hetherington, Cox & Cox, 1978; Kanoy, Cunningham, White, & Adams, 1985; McLanahan, 1983; Wallerstein, 1986). Contrary to the experience of custodial single-mothers, both noncustodial and custodial fathers typically maintain or improve their standard of living following divorce (Hetherington, 1989).

The availability of resources to children improve significantly with remarriage and more closely parallel intact families (Hernandez, 1988). It is estimated that 80% of divorced women and 85% of divorced men remarry (Clingempeel, Brand, & Levoli, 1984). Remarriages tend to occur relatively soon following divorce with a median interval of three years. Remarriage rates are highest and most rapid for younger women with children and lower levels of education (Norton & Glick, 1986). While remarriage typically reduces the economic stress of the single-parent family, and may increase the social support of the custodial single-parent, it again sets in motion the necessity of a reorganization of family roles, affectional ties and possible changes in residence, school, and neighborhood. Furthermore, the divorce rate for remarriages is higher than first marriages, thus children of divorce are likely to experience multiple marital transitions, household rearrangements, and geographic moves. The patterning and timing of these multiple transitions may be critical to the long-term adjustment of children (Hetherington, Stanley-Hagan, & Anderson, 1989).

The increasing numbers of children residing for some period of time per year in more than one home has caused scholars to label these families as binuclear, that is, having two parent-based centers (Ahrons & Wallisch, 1987). It is clear from the preceding discussion that binuclear families represent complex family relationships which are embedded within a socioeconomic milieu, are influenced by multiple variables, and are in continuous transformation over time. Children's responses to the loss or gain of a parent and related family members, to chronic economic strain, and to multiple transitions will be more characterized by diversity than predictability. Thus, in the subsequent section complementary theoretical frameworks are provided to organize our understanding of the complex processes associated with the multiple transitions characteristic of single-parent and stepparent family systems.

THEORETICAL FRAMEWORKS

Systems theory, family life-cycle theory, ecological–developmental theory, attachment theory, and stress and coping theory provide complementary frameworks for consideration of single-parent and remarried families.

At the core of systems theory is the concept that elements exist in a state of active communicative interrelatedness and interdependence within a bounded unit, such as the family. The interrelatedness of elements assures that the behavior or attitudes of one element or family member will have a direct or indirect influence on the other elements or person in the system. System elements are often organized by function and hierarchy. Family systems are universally hierarchically and functionally organized with parents or other adults in control of and performing the function of nurturance of children. Critical to well-functioning systems are clear boundaries between the subsystems. Clear boundaries are characterized by an adequate flow of information and resources to preserve the essential interrelatedness of elements of the system but also an adequate blockage of information such that the differentiation of system elements is protected from unnecessary intrusion which would compromise its functioning. The properties of boundary, role, and hierarchy are evident in the repeated interactional or communication sequences between members of the system. From the systems perspective, child dysfunction is reflective of a system with properties and organization that do not optimally support the development of the child. The implication of systems theory for binuclear family systems is that the adjustment of the child will be influenced by the roles, organization, and repeated patterns of transaction between all members within and between related households.

A shift in system organization is often reflective of necessary adaptation to either extrafamilial or intrafamilial growth or change. Family developmental life cycle theory provides a framework for viewing the necessity of systems change over time. Family developmental life cycle theory, like individual developmental life cycle theory, (e.g., Erikson, 1950), proposes that families face different tasks at progressive stages of development. Normative family life cycle stages are characterized by changes in the status of family members, and particularly first events for the family, e.g., marriage, birth of a child, child enters school. With each new stage of family development, a reorganization of family roles and subjective experience is required for the optimal growth of family members (Carter & McGoldrick, 1980; 1989). Failure to reorganize the family system when faced with a major developmental life cycle transition is hypothesized to result in symptomatology of a family member (Terkelsen, 1980).

Single-parent and remarried family systems have unique or paranormative family life cycle stages which are superimposed upon the universal family life cycle (Carter & McGoldrick, 1989; Beal, 1980; McGoldrick & Carter, 1980). The completion, often simultaneously, of multiple family life stages, both the normative and the paranormative, within single family life-time space increases the complexity and difficulty of family reorganization. For example, if two divorced parents remarry within two years and integrate families with children at multiple age levels, the remarried family will be challenged with simultaneously negotiating the family life cycle stages of marriage, organization of parenting roles, establishment of relations with the non-custodial parent and family and with new extended family members, the establishment of sibling relationships, and parenting at multiple child developmental stages. Developmental adjustment may additionally be compounded by a move to a larger house in a new neighborhood and city. Empirical support for the distinctiveness of the life cycles of single-parent and remarried families has been provided by Hill (1986) who found, based on survey data, that the timing and duration of stages, transitions between stages, and length of time to make transitions are increased for single-parent and remarried family systems. For the practitioner, the family life cycle framework provides a useful normative reference for the type of challenges facing single-parent and remarried families, and a means for evaluating the degree of adaptation and direction of family reorganization that is essential for restabilization of the system.

Family transitions occur within a social context which may enhance or reduce the resiliency of family members' coping. A framework for understanding the interface of family and social context is provided by ecological development theory which conceptualizes the development of children as occurring simultaneously within multiple, nested social environments or systems (Bronfenbrenner, 1979). Ecological developmental theory states that the quality of the interconnections between systems will be as critical a determinant of child functioning as within-system variables. Applied to binuclear family systems, ecological theory underscores both the impact of multiple ecological levels on the adjustment of children and the importance of well-functioning system linkages such as the relationship between family and school, family and family, family and broader social support. The role of children as the "link" in binuclear or "linked" family systems is discussed by Jacobson (1987) who claims the child is often the major channel of communication, overt and covert, between systems in single-parent and stepfamilies. Children who serve as communication links between hostile systems are likely to become symptomatic (Minuchin, 1974).

The theoretical frameworks provided to this point center on the family as an organized communicative system with roles, tasks, and boundaries that change with development over time. However, the distinguishing characteristic of family relationships is emotional ties, and family transitions most commonly involve a dramatic alteration of affectional bonds. It is this author's contention that a primary source of the distress that often accompanies family transitions is the disruption of strong emotional bonds in family dissolution, unstable or insecure emotional bonds in single-parent homes, and the insertion of more tenuous emotional bonds in remarriage. Attachment theory provides a theoretical framework for understanding the impact of disruptions of emotional bonds on the parent-child system and subsequent child developmental outcomes. Attachment is defined as, "any form of behavior that results in a person attaining or maintaining proximity to some other clearly identified individual who is conceived as better able to cope with the world" (pp. 26–27,

Bowlby, 1988). The expression of attachment behavior is most evident when the organism is under stress. Although attachment behavior is most obvious in early childhood, it can be observed throughout the life cycle in intimate relationships. The key feature of attachment behavior, present irrespective of age, is the intensity of the emotion that accompanies it and the kind of emotion that is aroused between the attached person and the attachment figure. When the relationship goes well, the attached person experiences joy and security; when the relationship is broken, anxiety, anger, and jealousy are aroused.

Attachment is viewed as being at the root of the parent–child relationship. Parents, through responsiveness to their children, provide a secure base for the child from which he/she can venture forth into the world of school, peers, and individual exploration. Children who are insecurely attached to a caregiver demonstrate consistently less well-organized developmental functioning in settings beyond the family. Furthermore, research has demonstrated that the security of parent–child attachment is vulnerable to family stress and changes in the romantic relationships of parents (Egeland & Farber, 1984). When children lack secure attachment figures, or when their secure attachments are threatened, their anxiety and anger can be expected to find expression both within the family and in the domains beyond the family toward which the child is oriented to master, such as school.

The family disruption and reorganization inherent in single-parent and stepfamily systems present children with a significant number of changes with which to cope. Rutter (1979) has reported that when children experience only a single stress, it carries no appreciable risk. When children are exposed to a series of stressors or several concurrent stresses, however, the adverse effects increase multiplicatively, not additively. Hetherington (1984) argues that a critical mediator of the adverse effects of multiple stressors is the degree of control available to the child over life events. Given that the

changes experienced by children in the transitions to single-parent and remarried family systems, are changes initiated by adults and most likely perceived by children to be primarily of benefit to the adults, a high perceived level of control over events seems unlikely for children. Stolberg and Anker (1984) lend empirical support with data which find that extent of environmental changes benefit children in intact families but have an adverse effect on post-divorce children. These researchers further found that as extent of environmental change increased for the divorced group, children perceived themselves and their parents to be less able to control their world. Thus, cognitive-behavioral strategies that permit children increasing control over their environments are likely to assist children in single-parent and stepparent families with the greater number of environmental changes to which they are likely to be required to adapt.

Five complementary theoretical frameworks have been presented which clarify our understanding of the complexity and range of child development outcomes associated with single-parent and stepparent families. In the remainder of the chapter these theoretical frameworks will guide discussion of the specific characteristics of the single-parent and stepparent family system. This will be followed by a discussion of intervention implications at the family–school interface. For each family type definitional issues, system properties, associated child outcomes, mediating variables, and family tasks will be examined.

BASIC-CONSIDERATIONS — SINGLE-PARENT HOMES

Definitional Issues

A single-parent family has been defined as one in which someone raises children alone without the household presence of a second parent or parent substitute (Weiss, 1979a). Over 90% of single-parent homes are headed by mothers (Glick, 1979). Within the definition of single-parent families, variations exist differentiated primarily by the route to single-parenthood. Divorce or marital separation is the most common antecedent (79%), followed by never married parents (25% and increasing), and death of a spouse (7%) (Weiss, 1979a). Single-parent homes created by death of a spouse demonstrate the least adverse effects upon children, never-married single-parent homes are consistently found to produce developmental risks for children, with post-divorce single-parent families falling somewhere between widowed and never-married single-parents on risk factors.

System Properties and Adaptations

Single-parent homes are notable for the necessity of accomplishing the same functions or roles as the biologically intact family but with fewer adult participants (Carlson, 1985, 1987). All families must complete the role-based survival tasks of economic support, childcare, child socialization, and housekeeping, as well as the companionship roles of recreation, leisure, emotional support, and sexual satisfaction (Rollins & Galligan, 1978). The role overload inherent in the single-parent family structure assures a degree of stress and strain on family members, particularly the single-parent. Research has found, for example, that single employed mothers when compared with other mother groups spend the least amount of time in personal care (including rest and sleep) and recreational activities (Sanik & Mauldin, 1986).

The "undermanned" structure of the single-parent family demands reorganization of the system to permit a minimal level of acceptable accomplishment of family tasks. Children in single-parent homes are often called upon to assume some of the burden. The advantage of this system reorganization is that it is convenient, biologically-based, may enhance the developmental potential of children, establishes a "cooperative" family environment, and reduces the role strain of the single-parent. Children in single-parent homes do, in fact, express greater independence and emotional sensitivity than their peers in intact homes, and they are more likely to be involved in decisions typically restricted to the parental subsystem, such as how to spend the family income (Weiss, 1979b). The potential risks of more egalitarian role-sharing within the single-parent family include excessive or developmentally inappropriate role demands on the child or the blurring of generational boundaries. If role demands are excessive for the child's developmental status or unique characteristics, the child may experience stress, anger, or depression, may lack the family support essential for development in arenas beyond the family, or may exhibit precocious or pseudo-mature development as characteristic of the "parentified child" (Glenwick & Mowrey, 1986; Minuchin, 1978). Thus, critical to the success of internal role restructuring is the establishment of the clear, consistent, and developmentally appropriate parent–child relationship boundaries and expectations.

An alternative to internal role sharing in the single-parent family, is the use of social support external to the family. Social support has been consistently found to be positively related to single-parent family health (Hanson, 1986). A variety of social support network options for single-parent families have been identified. These include use of family of origin, a spouse-equivalent, extended friendships, and organized social support, e.g., day care, paid housekeepers (McLanahan, Wedemeyer, & Adelberg, 1981; Grief, 1985). Although utilization of external social support can be considered essential to the well-being of the single-parent family, costs may also be engendered with each type of social support. Family of origin ties can undermine the authority of the single-parent (see Dell & Appelbaum, 1977). Spouse equivalent social support may lack the commitment essential for family security and may risk physical and sexual abuse of children. Extended friendship networks require considerable emotional energy and time to maintain whereas organized social support is a financial burden. Therefore, single-fathers are most likely to use organized social support. "Insular" single-parents are at high risk for child abuse (Wahler, 1980). Although social support is associated with single-parent family health, in recent research Hetherington (1989) found that social support had no positive effect on mothers who were either psychologically at risk or without stress. Thus, it would appear that moderately stressed single mothers benefit most from social support.

In summary, the undermanned structure of the single-parent family requires the adjustment of internal roles and the utilization of external social support for optimal functioning. The ability of the single-parent to organize internal and external social support is a critical key to successful functioning. Single mothers who are exhausted by full-time employment, worried by inadequate financial support, emotionally bereft of friendships and leisure time, are vulnerable to depression and less than optimal parenting of their children. However, it appears important to bear in mind that "it takes money, to make money." Single parents with the least available resources appear least able to utilize social support suggesting that differentiated intervention strategies are necessary for single parents.

Child Outcomes and Mediating Variables

The child development outcomes associated with single-parent homes have been well summarized in previous reviews and are found to be significantly different for boys and girls (Carlson, 1987; Emery, 1988; Hetherington, Stanley-Hagan, & Anderson, 1989). Briefly, rearing in a single-parent home has been associated academically with lower cognitive functioning, lower school achievement, lower achievement motivation, and a "feminine" cognitive style. Findings regarding lowered academic performance are stronger for boys than girls, and most applicable to post-divorce single-parent homes (Emery, 1988). Regarding social and personality effects, single-parent homes are associated with a less secure masculine style, greater difficulty with self-control, lower moral development and maturity, and higher rates of antisocial and delinquent

behavior in boys. For girls, negative effects of single-parent child-rearing are seldom obtained; however, a few studies have found that early maturing girls in single-parent homes may be at some risk for early sexual activity (Hetherington, 1972; Newcomer & Udry, 1987). Results regarding self-esteem have been inconsistent across studies for both boys and girls; lower self-esteem appears to be strongly associated with parental conflict regardless of family structure (Emery, 1988). As noted earlier, rearing in a single-parent home has been clinically identified with "growing up a little faster", the implications of which have not been adequately investigated empirically (Weiss, 1979b).

Although finding adverse effects associated with single-parenting, particularly for boys, is consistent across many studies, in reality the range of child adjustment is quite diverse. Multiple variables mediate the child development outcomes associated with single-parent homes. These variables include child gender, child temperament and personality, parent psychological well-being, parenting competence and style, the co-parental relationship, the child's relationship with the noncustodial parent, and social support.

Investigators concur that measures of parent–child processes relate more strongly to child outcomes than single-parent status (Hetherington, Cox & Cox, 1978). High quality single mothering can compensate for loss of the father, whereas low quality fathering can negatively influence children's development in intact homes (Biller, 1981). It has been argued, however, that when one parent is absent, the remaining parent will have a more intense effect upon the child (Hetherington, Cox & Cox, 1978). An authoritative parenting style, that includes adequate control and supervision with adequate nurturance and warmth, is associated with child competence in single-parent homes (Santrock & Warshak, 1979). Single mothers who err in the direction of an authoritarian style of childrearing are also more likely to have competent children; however, permissive single mothering is associated with behavior problems.

Authoritative parenting is emotionally demanding, that is, it produces physiological arousal in the parent (Patterson, 1982). Thus, the psychological well-being of the single-parent provides the foundation for capacity to parent competently. Empirical support has been provided by Kanoy, Cunningham, White, & Adams (1985) who found that divorced mothers' self-concept predicted the quality of mother–child interaction, father–child interaction, the ex-spouse relationship, and children's self-esteem. Unfortunately, single-parent mothers often report lower self-esteem, lower personal efficacy and control, and less optimism about the future when compared with married, never-divorced mothers (McLanahan, 1983). Long-term single mothers report higher rates of depression, psychosomatic symptoms, and loneliness than married or remarried mothers (Wallerstein, 1986).

Several child characteristics have been found to ease or exacerbate parenting in single-parent homes. Boys in single-mother homes consistently appear to be at greater risk than do girls. Boys residing in single-parent homes exhibit higher rates of behavioral, academic, and interpersonal difficulties than boys in intact or remarried homes, or girls in single-parent homes, and there is evidence that boys may adapt better in the custody of the same-sex parent (Camara & Resnick, 1988; Warshak & Santrock, 1979; Zill, 1988). Many reasons have been offered for the difficult single-parent mother–son relationship. Boys are biologically predisposed to higher rates of activity and aggressive behavior and have been found to display higher rates of acting out behaviors in the custody of both fathers and mothers than girls (Hetherington, et al., 1989). Relations among male siblings in single-mother homes have also been found to be more antagonistic than in other family structures (Hetherington, et al., 1989). Perhaps not surprisingly then, single mothers are vulnerable to child management difficulties, particularly with aggressive sons (Patterson, 1980). In addition to difficulty with authoritative parenting, however, it has been proposed that boys in single-parent homes are more likely to be exposed to parental conflict than girls, and marital conflict is consistently associated with poor child outcomes (Hetherington, et al., 1989).

Child temperament and personality are also associated with single-parent family adjustment. Children with easy temperaments, as well as other positive characteristics, such as intelligence, independence, internal locus of control, high self-esteem, and who also have adequate social support, seem to be quite adaptable to family transitions (Hetherington, et al., 1989; Rutter, 1980). Temperamentally difficult children are both more vulnerable to the stress of family transitions and more likely to be the elicitors and recipients of parental negativism. Difficult children also contribute to the social isolation of single-parents. The incidence of divorce and desertion is high among families with an exceptional or difficult child (Allen, Affleck, McGrade, & McQueeney, 1984), and remarriage rates are lower for single-parents with difficult children (Ambert, 1985).

Another critical mediator of children's adjustment in single-parent homes is the involvement of the noncustodial parent and the interparental relationship. Children typically wish to have a relationship with both parents, and, in general, involvement between the noncustodial parent and child is beneficial, particularly for boys and noncustodial fathers (Hetherington, et al., 1989). The benefits to be derived from involvement with the noncustodial parent, however, are attenuated by the degree to which the co-parental relationship is conflictual. Children show fewer social and emotional problems when divorced parents control their anger and cooperate with one another.

Socioeconomic status is frequently more strongly associated with adverse consequences for children's development in single-parent homes than is parent absence. Given the financial and physical demands characteristic of the single-parent family life, social support can be critical to the success of children. Authoritative schools and day care centers have been found to offset negative effects of family transitions (Hetherington, et al.,

1982; Guidabaldi, Cleminshaw, Peery & McGloughlin, 1983; Rutter, 1979). Relatives also can offer assistance with finances, child care and household tasks. Research has found that Black children adjust better when residing with a grandmother and mother than with a single mother, and Caucasian boys adjust better when they have an involved grandfather (Hetherington, et al., 1989). Additionally, there is some evidence that siblings, particularly female siblings, may buffer the effects of unresponsive parents in single-parent homes (Hetherington, et al., 1989). However, as noted earlier, social support networks can create stress, as well as support, for single-parents and their children.

In summary, children in single-parent homes are least likely to experience adverse effects if (a) they are female, (b) their custodial parent is confident, mentally healthy, educated, and authoritative, (c) the family is economically secure and resides in a community with resources oriented to the well-being of children, and (d) relationships between the single custodial parent and other family system members, including the noncustodial parent, are cooperative and nonconflictual.

Family Tasks

The essential family tasks that must be completed by single-parent families follow logically from the previous discussion. These tasks also serve to guide intervention with single-parents and their children. Single-parent family tasks include the establishment of the following: (a) economic stability; (b) authoritative parenting; (c) adequate support for the custodial single-parent such that optimal parenting can be established and maintained; (d) healthy and cooperative relationships with extra-familial members, including (in post-divorce) the noncustodial parent and his/her family; (e) provision of supplemental support for the growth and development of children if the single-parent's extended family or social network system is unable to provide adequate support.

Consistent with the "undermanned" nature of the single-parent family system, *support* is the key component of many of the family tasks. For the school psychologist intervening with single-parent families, support is best construed broadly with a view to all the possible sources of support for the child. Supplemental support of the child, for example, may include school and teacher selection, taking advantage of free programs, enrollment in extracurricular activities, developing a volunteer car pool such that children of employed single-parents can engage in extracurricular activities. It is important to bear in mind, however, the research findings of Hetherington, et al. (1989) regarding the inability of single-parents to benefit from social support when they were most in need of it. Therefore, the critical groundwork for single-parent social support is empowerment of the single-parent (Dunst, 1987). In summary, assessment and intervention with the single-parent family should focus on the adequacy of support across the ecological niches of the child and the capacity of the single-parent to create or utilize social support.

STEPFAMILY HOMES

Definitional Issues

The identity of stepfamilies is noteworthy for its variation and complexity. As with single-parent homes, the adjustment of children to stepfamilies will be more characterized by diversity than similarity. A stepfamily can be defined as one that is created by the marriage or committed partnership of two adults, one or both of whom have children (adapted from Crohn, Sager, Brown, Fodstein, & Walker, 1982). Many varieties of stepfamilies exist, each with unique adjustment demands. Katz & Stein (1983) identify four types based upon marital patterns: (Type 1) A previously married woman with children marries a man with no children; (Type 2) A previously married man with children marries a woman with no children; (Type 3) A remarriage where both spouses have children from previous marriages; (Type 4) A single-parent with children whose spouses remarries. The unique family adjustment demands of each stepfamily type have been outlined in Carlson (1985). The diversity of stepfamilies attenuates the clarity with which their effects on children can be ascertained.

System Properties and Adaptations

Stepfamily systems are notable for the complexity of family members' roles, for the necessity of communication links across households, and for the inclusion in households of members with varying degrees of emotional attachment. Regarding roles, stepfamilies can be considered "overmanned" family systems in that there may be two or more family members engaged in similar family roles, e.g., father, mother, sister, financial provider, social director. Although this supplement of resources may be viewed as enviable given the undermanned condition of the single-parent home, the placement of multiple persons in similar roles appears to create considerable disequilibrium and distress in stepfamilies (Visher & Visher, 1988). For children, stepparenting fuels loyalty conflicts in which obedience to the stepparent is not possible because it would evidence disloyalty to the biological parent. For adults, the social and universal expectations associated with the family roles of mother and father appear to fuel pressure for stepparent involvement in childrearing equivalent to that expected of a natural parent.

Stepfamilies are also distinct from intact families in that the attachments, or intense emotional bonds among family members, are not uniform. Both research and clinical work with stepfamilies finds that adjustment is enhanced by the *gradual* development of an attached stepparent–stepchild relationship and the acceptance by all family members of the differentiated roles that parents must play in childrearing as a result of differing emotional attachments (Hetherington, 1987; Visher & Visher, 1989).

Thirdly, stepfamilies are distinguished by the necessity of frequent and continuous coordination of the schedules, rules, and expectations of multiple households. This characteristic of the stepfamily system demands a high level of interaction within and between households, often made more difficult by the emotional injury that accompanies divorce and remarriage. Participation in multiple households also demands that each family system provide mechanisms, both emotional and physical, for the frequent absence and addition of family members.

In summary, stepfamily systems are characterized by a complexity of roles and relationships across multiple households that vary in emotional attachment. Optimal stepfamily functioning depends upon establishing clarity of relationship roles, rules, and boundaries. Furthermore, relationship roles are most likely to be successful if they conform with the level of emotional bonding between family members. This requires consistent and clear communication within and across households, a behavioral skill that may be difficult in the face of emotional injury. Stepfamilies further demand tremendous patience, faith, and commitment on the part of the adults, and particularly stepparents, that the emotional bonds and attachments that ease parenting stress will be forthcoming, given consistent, responsive, and respectful stepparenting, albeit over a considerable period of time.

Child Outcomes and Mediating Variables

Research studies on the child outcomes associated with rearing in a stepfamily have produced inconsistent findings when children in stepfamilies are compared with children in intact homes. In his review of the research, Bray (1988) cites many studies which find children in stepfamilies to be less well-adjusted, manifest more anxiety and withdrawal, exhibit more behavior problems, and have lower self-esteem than children from nondisrupted homes. In contrast, many research studies find no differences, differences only in clinical samples, or differences only in early remarriage (Ganong & Coleman, 1987). The most recent research, however, suggests a complex picture pointing to consistent sex differences in the behavioral outcomes and family relationship patterns of step versus intact families, and in stepfather versus stepmother families (see Hetherington & Arasteh, 1988; Pasley & Ihinger-Tallman, 1987).

Multiple studies have found that girls, particularly between the ages of 9 to 12, exhibit difficulties following remarriage in stepfather families, that were not evident when residing with single-parent mothers. Studies cited in Bray (1988) found girls in stepfather homes to have more problematic family and peer relationships, to be more angry with their mothers, to exhibit more behavior problems, and to perceive greater life stress and anxiety when compared with boys in stepfather families, girls in intact homes, or girls in single-parent homes. The self-reported life stress of girls in stepfather homes, not surprisingly, was related to their internalizing and externalizing problems, as well as to lowered school performance (Bray, 1988). In the most comprehensive investigation of stepfamily processes to date, Hetherington (1987, 1989) found that following remarriage, both mother–daughter and stepfather–stepdaughter conflict and hostility is high. Stepdaughters exhibit more demandingness, hostility, coercion, and less warmth toward both parents than girls in single or intact homes. Furthermore, whereas mother–daughter hostility was found to ease over a two year family transition period, stepfather–stepdaughter hostility remained high. Neither a positive marital relationship or positive behavior on the part of the stepfather toward stepdaughters eased the conflictual stepfather–stepdaughter relationship. Thus, over the course of the remarriage, stepfathers were found to dramatically increase their disengagement from stepdaughters (Hetherington, 1988). In summary, although both preadolescent boys and girls exhibit higher rates of behavior and learning problems following remarriage, boys, but not girls, demonstrate improved adjustment over a two year period (Hetherington, et al., 1989). Furthermore, in contrast with girls, multiple studies have reported the long-term beneficial impact of stepfather homes on boys including improved social competence, intellectual performance, and behavioral control (Bray, 1988).

Although the stepfather family system appears most difficult for girls, the stepmother family structure poses challenges to both girls and boys, particularly in middle childhood. In a national survey, Zill (1988) found a higher incidence of behavior and learning problems among children in stepmother homes when compared with intact homes as well with mother-headed and father-headed single-parent homes. Furthermore, contact with the biological mother in stepmother families was related to an increase in adjustment problems for children and greater conflict with stepmothers (Brand, et al., 1988; Zill, 1988).

How is one to interpret the complex gender-related child outcomes associated with stepfamilies? Bray (1988) and Hetherington (1989) note that the differences in outcomes between boys and girls in stepfamilies appear to be related to the different processes that characterize the development of males and females. In particular, the development of girls is more strongly associated with competence in relationships, whereas the development of boys is more strongly associated with competence in vocation. Thus, in single- and stepparent families, dyadic relationships involving females, (e.g., single-mother/son, stepmother/children, stepfather/stepdaughter), are consistently found to be more stressed by family transitions.

One mediator of gender-related differential child outcomes associated with remarriage is developmental status (Hetherington, et al., 1989). Younger children appear most able to form attachments with a stepparent, and thus are most likely to improve in adjustment over time with positive stepparenting. The impact of remarriage on older adolescents is inconclusive. Although the risk of sexual abuse is higher for stepfathers and stepdaughters when remarriage occurs in late childhood or adolescence, in general, older adolescents may find the entry of a stepparent to be less difficult as their developmental focus is already shifting away from the family. Early adolescents, particularly girls, appear to be at the greatest risk in remarriage. The unique developmental demands of this age with puberty, individuation, intense peer relationships, adjustments to a larger social system, intense self-consciousness with the onset of formal cognitive operations, and the intensification of the identity development process, appear to increase vulnerability to the introduction of a family member into the affective family system. In addition, the affectional displays between remarried partners may be particularly difficult for early adolescents to handle during puberty when their own sexual urges are emerging.

In summary, children in stepparent homes are least likely to experience adverse effects if (a) they are male and they reside in stepfather homes, (b) they are not early adolescents, (c) the stepparent does not attempt to become a parent too quickly, and (d) the remarried biological parent does not expect the stepparent–stepchild relationship to replicate a biological parent–child relationship.

Family Tasks

The primary tasks for stepfamilies to accomplish, based upon the previous discussion, include: (a) clarification of the roles, rules and relationship boundaries both within and across families; (b) developing attachments; (c) accepting a process view of relationships; and (d) balancing cohesion and autonomy.

With the complexity of stepfamily relationships, clarity regarding the roles in the linked family system is critical to success. For example, are stepparents responsible for establishing and monitoring rules, are they responsible for the emotional well-being and cognitive development of their stepchildren, to what degree are they financial responsible for stepchildren? These responsibilities have legal responses in the negative; however, legal decisions provided only the framework for parental roles, not the solutions to day-to-day decision-making. Based on

the reports of stepfamily members, the process of establishing and clarifying roles is difficult, even in the best of circumstances (Visher & Visher, 1989). Stepfamilies appear to be at greatest risk when role expectations vis-a-vis role enactment within the family are quite discrepant, or when there is competitive role enactment across families.

A second task of stepfamilies is the formation of attachment bonds between family members. Critical to the formation of attachment is responsive parenting; however, responsive parenting will not create quick attachments. Since attachment reflects an intense emotional bond, this must be viewed as a process that occurs over time. Thus, a third stepfamily task is the adoption by family members of a process view of relationships. A process view of relationships is one which recognizes that, although attraction may be immediate, trust, shared interests, and intimacy, develop slowly. The development of attachment bonds and the adoption of a process view of relationships may be particularly difficult for post-divorce stepfamily members who have previously experienced the anxiety and grief associated with breaches of trust and attachment. Stepfamilies are most likely to experience difficulty when adults expect the rapid formation of attachment bonds between stepparents and stepchildren or between stepsiblings. The development of attachment bonds is not only related to the characteristics of family members and their histories, but also related to developmental stage and sex. The formation of close attachments is most feasible for stepfamilies who reconstitute with young children, and between boys and stepfathers. Close emotional attachments may be inappropriate to expect in families with adolescents.

In summary, the overlapping tasks of family formation, which demands cohesion, with the task of individual development, which demands autonomy (particularly in adolescence), highlights the complexity of processes facing stepfamilies. The development of cohesion in stepfamilies is attentuated by the necessity of children maintaining associations

TABLE 1
Key Dimensions in Assessment and intervention with
Single-parent and Stepparent Families

Dimension	Key Variables	Methods	Interventions
System Organization (Minuchin, 1978)	Family Roles Family Rules Clarity of Roles & Rules	Family Observation Parent/Family Interview Kinetic Family Drawing Family Apperception Test	Family Therapy
Family Life Cycle Stage (Carter & McGoldrick, 1980, 1989; McGoldrick & Gerson, 1985)	Family Developmental Stage(s)	Genogram Parent/Family Interview	Parent Consultation Parent Education
Parent–Child Relationship (Steinhauser, 1983; Grotevant & Carlson, 1989; Sameroff & Emde, 1989)	Parenting Style Parenting Knowledge Quality of Attachment	Parent & Child Interview Self-Report Measures Kinetic Family Drawing Family Apperception Test	Parent Consultation Parent Education Family Therapy Supplemental Child Support
Family Social Support (Hartmann, 1979)	Sources of Support Sources of Strain	Ecomap Parent/Family Interview	Parent Consultation Supplemental Support Parent & Child
Coping Style (Epstein, Schlesinger, & Dryden, 1988; Garmezy & Rutter, 1983; McCubbin & Figley, 1983)	Coping Style Cognitions	Parent/Family/Child Interview Self-Report Measures	Parent, Child, or Family Cognitive-Behavioral Therapy

and affectional loyalties with multiple households, as well as by the differentiated biological and affectional bonds within stepfamilies. Encouragement of individual autonomy is attenuated to the degree that stepfamilies use as their social comparison norm the cohesiveness characteristic of harmonious intact families. Thus, a final task for stepfamilies is the balancing of cohesive family relationships with family member autonomy and mobility.

BEST PRACTICES — ASSESSMENT AND INTERVENTION

It is recommended that school psychologists evaluate the needs of single-parent and stepfamily children and their family members along the basic theoretical dimensions discussed: system organization; family developmental life cycle stage; quality of parent–child relationship and affective bonding; adequacy of social support; and adequacy of responses to stress and coping. There are multiple strategies and methods for gathering information on these dimensions. Assessment guidelines, methods, intervention implication, and key references appear on Table 1.

It is strongly recommended in completing an assessment of single-parent or stepparent children that school psychologists interview the parental figures, as well as the individual child, and preferably, conduct a whole family interview. An excellent beginner's guideline for completing a family interview can be found in Weber, McKeever & McDaniel (1985). For additional discussion of family assessment methods, the interested reader is referred to Carlson (1987) and Grotevant & Carlson (1989). Interviews specifically designed for single-parent and stepparent families are available in Carlson (1985) and Visher & Visher (1988).

The goal of assessment is differential diagnosis and the selection of a targeted intervention. School psychologists have many options from which to chose in working with children in single-parent and stepfamily homes. The choice of intervention will depend upon the nature and severity of the presenting problem, the accessibility and motivation of persons involved with the child, and the resources available to the school psychologist. For purposes of clarity, the following discussion is organized by the primary focus of intervention child, parent, or school.

Child-Centered

The goal of child-centered interventions is to increase the individual competence of the child such that the child is maximally able to utilize available resources and maintain a realistic sense of self-efficacy. Empirical studies find that school-based groups are beneficial for children of divorce (Cantor, 1977; Wilkinson & Bleck, 1977). Two intervention projects, each designed to include opportunities for children to express their feelings as well as the teaching of social problem-solving skills, have been conducted and carefully evaluated. Results found improvements in anxiety on Pedro-Carroll's Children of Divorce Project (Pedro-Carroll & Cowen, 1985; Pedro-Carroll, Cowen, Hightower, & Guare, 1986) and increased self-esteem and social skills in Stolberg's Divorce Adjustment Project (Stolberg & Anker, 1984; Stolberg, Cullen & Garrison, 1982; Stolberg & Garrison, 1985). Although these school-based group interventions were not specifically designed for the transition to remarriage or for life in a stable single-parent family, the format and content are expected to be applicable with adaptation. Helpful audiovisual resources are identified by Kimmons & Gaston (1986) and Hausslein (1983).

The technique of bibliotherapy is another child-centered intervention that may be helpful to children coping with family transitions. Bibliotherapy may be used by the school psychologist as an adjunct to individual child psychotherapy, an assignment in school-based groups, or in teacher consultation and curriculum development. Useful books for school-age children are *My other-mother, my other-father* (Sobol, 1979), and *Two homes for Lynn* (Noble, 1979). Middle-school children would be able to read on their own *The boys and girls book about one-parent families* (Gardner, 1978), and *The boys and girls book about stepfamilies* (Gardner, 1982). In addition, a list of relevant fiction references for adolescents in stepfamilies has been compiled by Coleman, Marshall, & Ganong (1986). Excellent guides for additional books include Dreyer (1977), *The bookfinder: A guide to children's literature about the needs and problems of youth aged 2–15, Children and divorce* (Hausslein, 1983), the "Reading List for Children" (Visher & Visher, 1988, p. 253–254), and the *Educational Materials Program* (Stepfamily Association of America). Bibliotherapy is expected to be well suited for the school setting as it requires minimal organizational support and is compatible with school educational/reading goals. No empirical support, however, for the effectiveness of bibliotherapy was identified.

In addition to group interventions and bibliotherapy, individual child psychotherapy is always an intervention option available to school psychologists. Wallerstein and Kelly (1980, 1983), Kelly & Wallerstein (1977) have developed a model of brief intervention for children following divorce. Robson (1982) provides a developmental model of treatment for children in remarriage. Given the time constraints of many school psychologists, it is anticipated that the more cost-beneficial school-based group approach may be preferable. School-based groups have the additional benefit of building supportive peer relationships which may be attenuated by the stress of family transitions. On the other hand, in cases of acute distress, individual psychotherapy will most likely be the intervention of choice.

In addition to child-centered interventions, which directly address difficulties associated with single-parent and stepparent homes, children in these family situations can also be expected to benefit from interventions which enhance their overall competence. Nastasi & Guidabaldi (1987) found, for example, that good social-coping skills (self-efficacy, social problem solving, and social interaction) predicted academic success, popularity, conduct, and physical health in both post-divorce and control groups of school-aged children, and predicted fewer family transition problems in post-divorce children. These results suggest that an intervention enhancing social-coping and social skills could be beneficial for children who are currently or have previously experienced a family transition. It is expected that socially competent children will be more able to access social support from peers and teachers during times of family stress than children at risk. In addition to interventions which strengthen the competence of children in single-parent and stepfamily homes, attention to adequate models and opportunities for sex-role development would appear to be appropriate, especially for boys in single-parent homes (see Carlson, 1987). In summary, any intervention that enhances the child's experience of success in school is likely to be beneficial to children who demonstrate adjustment difficulties related to the multiple transitions of separation, divorce, single-parenting, and remarriage.

Parent-Centered

The quality of the parent–child relationship is critical for children's adjustment in both single-parent and stepparent homes. Although it is not within the mandate of the school to provide treatment to parents, schools, unencumbered by the stigma and financial burden attached to seeking therapy, have the opportunity to provide critical preventive and indirect mental health services via education, support, and consultation with parents.

Group approaches with single-parents and stepparents are popular. Support groups for single-parents have been described by Johnson (1986) and by Stolberg and his associates (Garrison, Stolberg, Carpenter, Mallonee, & Atrim, no

date; Stolberg & Anker, 1984; Stolberg, et al., 1982; Stolberg & Garrison, 1985). The popular STEP (Systematic Training for Effective Parenting) program has been recently extended to address the concerns of single parents and stepfamily parents (Dinkmeyer, McKay, & McKay, 1987). Several stepparent educational programs have been developed including the following (cited in Visher & Visher, 1988): *Learning to Step Together: A course for Stepfamily Adults* (Currier, 1982); *Strengthening Stepfamilies* (Albert & Einstein, 1986); and *Banana Splits: A School-Based Program for the Survivors of the Divorce Wars* (McGonagle, 1985). In addition, parent education programs, in general, should be considered appropriate for single-parents and stepparents. In particular, single mothers with sons, single fathers with daughters, stepfathers with daughters, stepmothers with sons, and/or stepparents who have not previously had children, are the adults most likely to benefit from education regarding parenting and child development. Although there appears to be minimum risk involved in conducting parent support/education programs, the effectiveness of such groups has not been adequately evaluated.

Parent consultation offers a second intervention method for use with single-parents and remarried parents. School psychologists are frequently called upon to engage parents in discussion of their children's progress, particularly when learning or behavioral difficulties are evident. Parent consultation provides an opportunity for assessment of parent competence, support regarding the challenging parent role, education about family and child processes associated with family transitions, and a reframing of the parent's cognitive beliefs and expectancies about the child, family, and school. Parents, like children, are likely to benefit from books on single-parenting and stepparenting. Excellent book and resource lists for parents have been provided by Greenwood, 1983; Kimmons & Gaston, 1986; Visher & Visher, 1988. In addition, two national organizations compile a wealth of information for single-parents and stepparents: Parents Without Partners and Stepfamily Association of America. Most importantly, parent consultation provides the opportunity for the establishment of communication between the "linked" family and school systems of the child. As noted by Bronfenbrenner (1979), children's developing competence can be expected to be enhanced by involvement in multiple ecological niches when these environments have congruent expectations, mutual regard, and supportive communication.

School-Centered

Research studies find that schools make a difference in the adjustment of children to family instability, (e.g., Guidabaldi, Peery, & Cleminshaw, 1984; Rutter, 1979). Specifically schools that have high expectations, opportunities for success, and structure, along with supportive teacher–student relationships have been found to positively influence the development of children despite family stress. Thus, schools that are authoritative, that is, characterized by high expectations as well as responsiveness to individual children, provide the most supportive environments for children under family stress. One direction of school-centered intervention then is the provision by school psychologists of "goodness-of-fit" between child characteristics and school environment. Rather than the more traditional random placement of children with teachers in classrooms, or the more stressful reshuffling of a child following a classroom failure, it is recommended that children who are more vulnerable due to a family circumstances be thoughtfully placed in classroom environments that will provide structure and support.

Research also indicates that school personnel (as well as the population at large) hold negatively biased perceptions of children in single-parent homes (Fry & Addington, 2984; Santrock & Tracy, 1978), and children in stepfamilies (Coleman & Ganong, 1987), when compared with children in intact families. In these studies, boys were more negatively perceived than girls, although both differed significantly from children in intact homes. In addition, single-parents and stepparents, are viewed more negatively than their never-divorced counterparts (Coleman & Ganong, 1987). What are the possible effects of these negative stereotypes? Negative stereotypes predispose persons to evaluate the stereotyped group less favorably no matter what behavior is observed, i.e., the "cognitive confirmation" effect (Darley & Gross, 1983), and to influence interaction in such a way that expected behaviors are elicited, the "behavioral confirmation" effect (Snyder & Swann, 1978). Although these cognitive biases have not been investigated in school settings, the consistency of findings elsewhere suggests that the negative stereotyping of students from single-parent and stepfamily homes may be a concern. Cognitive distortions can be altered with the presentation of didactic materials (e.g., information handouts, inservice training) and with collaborative problem-solving consultation in which consultees discover the inaccuracies of their thought processes (Epstein, Schlesinger, & Dryden, 1988). The traditional school psychology roles of teacher consultation and inservice training then provide fertile ground for sensitizing school personnel to the possible influence of negative stereotypes with children from non-nuclear families.

In summary, interventions targeted to the child, parent or family, and school are all likely to be appropriate for children from single-parent and stepfamily homes. As noted on Table 1, the target of intervention should reflect the differential assessment of the source of difficulties in the family or child system.

SUMMARY

Single-parent and stepparent homes continue to be the family form in which the majority of children in the United States will reside. These family forms place unique adjustment demands upon children, parents, and schools. Understanding the dynamics of single-parent and stepparent families, and remaining conscientious about the distinctiveness, but not lesser quality, of these family types, is the first step to effective school psychological practice with the children residing in these homes.

Single-parent and stepparent families are more characterized by diversity than similarity. However, commonalities exist both across and within these family types. Both single-parent and stepparent families are characterized by transformations of family roles and affective relationships, by emotional loss, and by an intensification of the biological or custodial parent-child relationship. Single-parent and stepparent families may differ in degree of family stress associated with lowered income and parent overload.

Children's adjustment to life in single-parent and stepparent families is highly variable and appears dependent upon multiple variables including age, sex, and temperament of the child, the quality of the parent–child relationship, the quality of the parent–parent relationship, and the quality of extra-familial social support (including school environment). In particular, boys residing in single-parent, mother-headed homes, and early adolescent girls whose single-parent remarries, appear to be at greatest risk. It is important to note, however, the vast majority of children in single-parent and stepparent families do not evidence problems requiring intervention.

When children evidence adjustment difficulties associated with single-parenting or stepparenting, school psychologists have many choices available to them in assessment and intervention. A multidimensional approach to assessment has been recommended in which the key variables of family system organization, family life cycle stage, quality of parent–child attachment, adequacy of child and family social support, and adaptative quality of parent and child coping responses are evaluated and linked with appropriate interventions.

REFERENCES

Ahrons, C. R., & Wallisch, L. (987). Parenting in the binuclear family: Relationships between biological and stepparents. In E. M. Hetherington & J. D. Aratesh (Eds.), *Impact of divorce, single parent-*ing, and stepparenting on children (pp. 225-256). Hillsdale, NJ: Erlbaum.

Allen, D. A., Affleck, G., McGrade, B. J., & McQueeney, M. (1984). Effects of single-parent status on mothers and their high-risk infants. *Infant Behavior and Development, 7*, 347-359.

Ambert, A. (1985). Custodial parents: Review and a longitudinal study. In B. Schlesinger (Ed.), *The one-parent family in the 1980s: Perspectives and annotated bibliography, 1978–1984* (pp.13-34). Toronto, University of Toronto.

Anderson, J. Z., & White, G. D. (1986). An empirical investigation of interaction and relationship patterns in functional and dysfunctional nuclear families and stepfamilies. *Family Process, 25*, 407-422.

Biller, H. B. (1982). Father absence, divorce and personality development. In M. E. Lamb (Ed.), *The role of the father in child development* (2nd ed.) (pp. 489-552). New York: Wiley.

Bowlby, J. (1988). *A secure base: Parent–child attachment and healthy human development.* New York: Basic.

Brand, E., Clingempeel, W. G., & Bowen-Woodward, K. (1988). Family relationships and children's psychological adjustment in stepmother and stepfather families. *Impact of divorce, single parenting, and stepparenting on children* (pp. 299-324). Hillsdale, NJ: Erlbaum.

Brassard, M. R. (1986). Family assessment approaches and procedures. In H. Knoff (Ed.), *The assessment of child and adolescent personality* (pp. 399-449). New York: Guilford.

Bray, J. H. (1988). Children's development during early remarriage. In E. M. Hetherington & J. D. Aratesh (Eds.), *Impact of divorce, single parenting, and stepparenting on children* (pp. 279-298). Hillsdale, NJ: Erlbaum.

Bronfenbrenner, U. (1979). *The ecology of human development.* Cambridge, MA: Harvard University Press.

Burns, R. C., & Kaufman, S. H. (1970). *Kinetic Family Drawing (K-F-D): An introduction to understanding children through kinetic drawing.* New York: Brunner/Mazel.

Camara, K. A., & Resnick, G. (1988). Interparental conflict and cooperation: Factors moderating children's post-divorce adjustment. *Impact of divorce, single parenting, and stepparenting on children* (pp. 169-196). Hillsdale, NJ: Erlbaum.

Cantor, D. W. (1977). School-based groups for children of divorce. *Journal of Divorce, 1*, 183-187.

Carlson, C. I. (1985). Best practices in working with single-parent and stepfamilies. In A. Thomas & J. Grimes (Eds.), *Best practices in school psychology* (pp. 43-60). Kent, OH: The National Association of School Psychologists.

Carlson, C. I. (1987a). Single-parent homes. In A. Thomas & J. Grimes (Eds.), *Children's Needs: Psychological perspectives* (pp. 560-571). Washington, DC: The National Association of School Psychologists.

Carlson, C. I. (1987b). Family assessment and intervention in the school setting. In T. R. Kratochwill (Ed.), *Advances in school psychology* (Vol. VII.) (pp. 81-129), Hillsdale, NJ: Erlbaum.

Carter, B., & McGoldrick, M. (1989). *The changing family life cycle* (2nd ed.). New York: Allyn & Bacon.

Coleman, M. & Ganong, L. H. (1987). The cultural stereotyping of stepfamilies. In K. Pasley & M. Ihlinger-Tallman (Eds.), *Remarriage and stepparenting: Current research and theory* (pp. 19-41). New York: Guilford.

Coleman, M., Marshall, S. A., & Ganong, L. (1986). Beyond Cinderella: Relevant reading for young adolescents about stepfamilies. *Adolescence, 21*, 553-560.

Crohn, H., Sager, C. J., Brown, H., Rodstein, E., & Walker, L. (1982). A basis for understanding and treating the remarried family. In J. Hansen & L. Messinger (Eds.), *Therapy with remarried families*. Rockville, MD: Aspen.

Dell, P., & Appelbaum, A. S. (1977). Trigenerational enmeshment: Unresolved ties of single-parents to family of origin. *American Journal of Orthopsychiatry, 47*(1), 52-59.

Dinkmeyer, D., McKay, G. D., & McKay, J. L. (1987). *New beginnings: Skills for single parents and stepfamily parents*. Champaign, IL: Research Press.

Dreyer, S. S. (1977). *The bookfinder: A guide to children's literature about the needs and problems of youth aged 2-15*. Circle Pines, MN: American Guidance Service, Inc.

Emery, R. E. (1988). *Marriage, divorce, and children's adjustment*. Newberry Park, CA: Sage.

Epstein, N., Schlesinger, S. E., & Dryden, W. (1988). A mediational model for the effect of divorce on antisocial behavior in boys. In E. M. Hetherington & J. D. Aratesh (Eds.) *Impact of divorce, single parenting, and stepparenting on children* (pp. 135-154). Hillsdale, NJ: Erlbaum.

Fulmer, R. (1983). A structural approach to unresolved mourning in single-parent family systems. *Journal of Marital and Family Therapy, 9*, 259-269.

Furstenberg, Jr., F. F. (1987). The new extended family: The experience of parents and children after remarriage. In K. Pasley & M. Ihlinger-Tallman (Eds.), *Remarriage and stepparenting: Current research and theory* (pp. 42-61). New York: Guilford.

Furstenberg, Jr., F. F. (1988). Child care after divorce and remarriage. In E. M. Hetherington & J. D. Aratesh (Eds.) *Impact of divorce, single parenting, and stepparenting on children* (pp. 245-262). Hillsdale, NJ: Erlbaum.

Ganong, L. H., & Coleman, M. (1987). Effects of parental remarriage on children: An updated comparison of theories, methods, and findings from clinical and empirical research. In E. M. Hetherington & J. D. Aratesh (Eds.), *Impact of divorce, single parenting, and stepparenting on children* (pp. 94-140). Hillsdale, NJ: Erlbaum.

Gardner, R. A. (1978). *The boys and girls book about one-parent families*. New York: Bantam.

Gardner, R. A. (1982). *The boys and girls book about stepfamilies*. New York: Bantam.

Garmezy, N., & Rutter, M. (Eds.) (1983). *Stress, coping, and development in children*. New York: McGraw-Hill.

Garrison, K. M., Stolberg, A. L., Carpenter, J. G., Mallonee, D. J., & Atrim, Z. D. (no date). *Single parent support group: Leader's Manual*. (DHEW Publication No. 1 R01MH34462-02).

Gladlow, N. W., & Ray, M. P. (1986). The impact of informal support systems on the well being of low income single parents. *Family Relations, 35*, 113-123.

Glenwick, D. S., & Mowrey, J. D. (1986). When parent becomes peer: Loss of intergenerational boundaries in single parent families. *Family Relations, 35*, 57-62.

Greif, G. L. (1985). *Single fathers*. Lexington, MA: Lexington.

Greenwood, P. D. (1983). Contemporary family and human development materials. *Family Relations, 32*, 1983, 149-152.

Grotevant, H. D., & Carlson, C. I. (1989). *Family assessment: A guide to methods and measures*. New York: Guilford.

Guidabaldi, J., Cleminshaw, H. K., Peery, J. D., & McGloughlin, C. S. (1983). The impact of parental divorce on children: Report of the nationwide NASP study. *School Psychology Review, 12*, 300-323.

Guidabaldi, J., Peery, J. D., & Cleminshaw, H. K. (1984). The legacy of parental divorce: A nationwide study of family status and selected mediating variables on children's academic and social competencies. In B. B. Lahey & A. E. Kazdin (Eds.), *Advances in clinical child psychology (Vol. 7)* (pp. 109-151). New York: Plenum.

Guidabaldi, J., Cleminshaw, H. K., Peery, J. D., Nastasi, B. K., & Lightel, J. (1986). The role of selected family environment factors in children's post-divorce adjustment. *Family Relations, 35,* 141-151.

Haley, J. (1987). *Problem-solving therapy.* San Francisco, CA: Jossey-Bass.

Hanson, S. M. H. (1986). Healthy single parent families. *Family Relations, 35,* 125-132.

Hartmann, A. (1979). *Finding families: An ecological approach to family assessment in adoption.* Beverly Hills, CA: Sage.

Hausslein, E. B. (1983). *Children and divorce: An annotated bibliography and guide.* New York: Gardner.

Hernandez, D. J. (1988). Demographic trends and the living arrangements of children. In E. M. Hetherington & J. D. Aratesh (Eds.), *Impact of divorce, single parenting, and stepparenting on children* (pp. 3-20). Hillsdale, NJ: Erlbaum.

Hetherington, E. M. (1972). Effects of paternal absence on personality development in adolescent daughters. *Developmental Psychology, 7,* 313-326.

Hetherington, E. M. (1984). Stress and coping in children and families. In A. Doyle, D. Gold, & D. S. Moskowitz (Eds.), *New Directions for Child Development: No. 24, Children in families under stress* (pp. 7-34). San Francisco, CA: Jossey-Bass.

Hetherington, E. M. (1987). Family relations six years after divorce. In K. Pasley & M. Ihlinger-Tallman (Eds.), *Remarriage and stepparenting: Current research and theory* (pp. 185-205). New York: Guilford.

Hetherington, E. M. (1989). Coping with family transitions: Winners, losers, and survivors. *Child Development, 60* 114.

Hetherington, E. M. & Aratesh, J. D. (Eds.) (1988). *Impact of divorce, single parenting, and stepparenting on children.* Hillsdale, NJ: Erlbaum.

Hetherington, E. M., Cox, M., & Cox, R. (1982). Effects of divorce on parents and children. In M. Lamb (Ed.), *Nontraditional families: Parenting and child development.* Hillsdale, NJ: Erlbaum.

Hetherington, E. M., Hagan, M. S., & Anderson, E. R. (1989). Marital transitions: A child's perspective. *American Psychologist, 44*(2), 303-312.

Hill, R. (1986). Life cycle stages for types of single parent families. *Family Relations, 35,* 19-29.

Ihinger-Tallman, M., & Pasley, K. (1987). Divorce and remarriage in the American family: A historical review. In K. Pasley & M. Ihinger-Tallman (Eds.), *Remarriage and stepparenting: Current research and theory* (pp. 3-18). New York: Guilford.

Jacobson, D. S. (1987). Family type, visiting patterns, and children's behavior in the stepfamily: A linked family system. In K. Pasley & M. Ihlinger-Tallman (Eds.), *Remarriage and stepparenting: Current research and theory* (pp. 257-272). New York: Guilford.

Johnson, B. H. (1986). Single mothers following separation and divorce: Making it on your own. *Family Relations, 35,* 189-197.

Julian III, A., Sotile, W. M., Henry, S. E., & Sotile, M. (1988). Family Apperception Test. Feedback Services, Charlotte, NC [Distributor].

Kanoy, K. W., Cunningham, J. L., White, P., & Adams, S. J. (1984). Is family structure that critical? Family relationships of divorced and married parents. *Journal of Divorce, 8*(2), 97-105.

Katz, L., & Stein, S. (1983). Treating stepfamilies. In B. Wolman & G. Streicker (Eds.), *Handbook of family and marital therapy.* New York: Plenum.

Kelly, J. B., & Wallerstein, J. (1977). Brief interventions with children in divorcing families. *American Journal of Orthopsychiatry, 47*(1), 23-39.

Kimmons, L., & Gaston, J. A. (1986). Single parenting: A filmography. *Family Relations, 35,* 205-211.

Knoff, H. M. (1987). Divorce. In A. Thomas & J. Grimes (Eds.), *Children's Needs: Psychological perspectives* (pp. 173-181). Washington, DC: National Association of School Psychologists.

Laosa, L. M. (1988). Ethnicity and single parenting in the United States. In E. M. Hetherington & J. D. Aratesh (Eds.), *Impact of divorce, single parenting, and stepparenting on children* (pp. 23-52). Hillsdale, NJ: Erlbaum.

Lewis, W. (1986). Strategic interventions with children of single-parent families. *The School Counselor, 33,* 375-378.

Lindblad-Goldberg, M. (1987). The assessment of social networks in Black, low-income single-parent families. In M. Lindblad-Goldberg (Ed.), *Clinical issues in single-parent households* (pp. 39-46). Rockville, MD: Aspen.

McCubbin, H. I. & Figley, C. R. (Eds.) (1983). *Stress and the family, Vol. 1: Coping with normative transitions.* New York: Brunner/Mazel.

McGoldrick, M. & Gerson, R. (1985). *Genograms in family assessment.* New York: Norton.

McLanahan, S. S. (1983). Family structure and stress. A longitudinal comparison of two-parent and female-headed families. *Journal of Marriage and the Family, 45*(2), 347-357.

McLanahan, S. S., Wedemeyer, N., & Adelberg, T. (1981). Network structure, social support, and psychological well-being in the single parent family. *Journal of Marriage & the Family, 10*, 601-612.

Minuchin, S. (1974). *Families and family therapy.* Cambridge, MA: Harvard University Press.

Nastasi, B. K., & Guidubaldi, J. (1987). *Coping skills as mediators of children's adjustment in divorced and intact families.* Paper presented at the biennial meeting of the Society for Research in Child Development, April, Baltimore, MD.

Norton, A. J., & Glick, P. C. (1986). One parent families: A social and economic profile. *Family Relations, 35*, 9-17.

Pasley, K., & Ihinger-Tallman, M. (Eds.) (1987). *Remarriage and Stepparenting: Current research and theory.* New York: Guilford.

Patterson, G. R. (1982). *A Social Learning Approach: Vol. 3, Coercive family process.* Eugene, OR: Castalia.

Pedro-Carroll, J. L., & Cowen E. L. (1985). The Children of Divorce Intervention Program: An investigation of the efficacy of a school-based prevention program. *Journal of Consulting and Clinical Psychology, 53*, 603-611.

Pedro-Carroll, J. L., & Cowen, E. L., Hightower, A. D., & Guare, J. C. (1986). Preventive intervention with latency-aged children of divorce: A replication study. *American Journal of Community Psychology, 14*, 277-290.

Robson, B. (1982). A developmental approach to the treatment of children with divorcing parents. In J. Hansen & L. Messinger (Eds.), *Therapy with remarried families.* Rockville, MD: Aspen.

Rollins, B. C., & Galligan, R. (1978). The developing child and marital satisfaction in parents. In R. M. Lerner & G. B. Spanier (Eds.), *Child influences on marital and family interaction* (pp. 71-106). New York: Academic.

Sanik, M. M., & Maudlin, T. (1986). Single versus two parent families: A comparison of mothers' time. *Family Relations, 35*, 53-56.

Santrock, J. W., & Sitterle, K. A. (1987). Parent-child relationships in stepmother families. In K. Pasley & M. Ihlinger-Tallman (Eds.), *Remarriage and stepparenting: Current research and theory* (pp. 273-299). New York: Guilford.

Santrock, J. W., & Tracy, R. L. (1978). Effects of children's family structure status on the development of stereotypes by teachers. *Journal of Educational Psychology, 70*(5), 754-757.

Santrock, J. W., & Warshak, R. A. (1979). Father custody and social development in boys and girls. *Journal of Social Issues, 35*(4), 112-125.

Sameroff, A. J. & Emde, R. N. (Eds.) (1989). *Relationship disturbances in early childhood.* New York: Basic Books.

Steinhauer, P. D. (1983). Assessing for parenting capacity. *American Journal of Orthopsychiatry, 53*(3), (468-481).

Stolberg, A. L., & Anker, J. M. (1983). The cognitive and behavioral changes in children resulting from parental divorce and consequent environmental changes. *Journal of Divorce, 7*(2), 23-39.

Visher, E. B. & Visher, J. S. (1988). *Old loyalties, new ties: Therapeutic strategies with stepfamilies.* New York: Brunner/Mazel.

Wahler, R. G. (1980). The insular mother: Her problems in parent–child treatment. *Journal of Applied Behavior Analysis, 13*, 207-219.

Wallerstein, J. (1986). Women after divorce: Preliminary report from a ten-year follow-up. *American Journal of Orthopsychiatry, 56*(1), 65-77.

Wallerstein, J., & Blakeslee, S. (1989). *Second chances: Men women, and children a decade after divorce.* New York: Ticknor & Fields.

Wallerstein, J., & Kelly, J. B. (1980). *Surviving the breakup.* New York: Basic Books.

Wallerstein, J., & Kelly, J. B. (1983). Children of divorce: Psychological tasks of the children. *American Journal of Orthopsychiatry, 53*(2), 230-243.

Weber, T., McKeever, J. E., & McDaniel, S. H. (1985). A beginner's guide to the problem-oriented first family interview. *Family Process, 24*(3), 356-364.

Weiss, R. (1979a). *Going it alone.* New York: Basic.

Weiss, R. (1979b). Growing up a little faster: The experience of growing up in a single-parent household. *Journal of Social Issues, 35*(4), 97-111.

Wilkinson, G. S., & Bleck, R. T. (1977). Children's divorce groups. *Elementary School Guidance and Counseling, 11*, 205-213.

Zakariya, S. B. (1982). Another look at children of divorce: Summary report of the study of school needs of one-parent children. *Principal, 62*, 34-37.

Zill, N. (1988). Behavior, achievement, and health problems among children in stepfamilies: Findings from a national survey of child health. *Impact of divorce, single parenting, and stepparenting on children* (pp. 325–368). Hillsdale, NJ: Erlbaum.

BIBLIOGRAPHY: PROFESSIONALS

Hetherington, E. M. & Aratesh, J. D. (Eds.) (1988). *Impact of divorce, single parenting, and stepparenting on children.* Hillsdale, NJ: Erlbaum.
This edited volume provides the best compilation of recent research on the effects of divorce, single parenting, and remarriage on children. Available in paperback.

Lindblad-Goldberg, M. (Vol. Ed.) (1987). *Clinical issues in single-parenting households.* Rockville, MD: Aspen.
This edited volume is noteworthy for attention to ethnic variation and special problem single-parent families. Included, for example, are chapters on single parents who are (a) Black and low-income, (b) adolescents, (c) Puerto Rican, (d) fathers, or those who have (e) a handicapped child.

Patterson, G. R. (1982). *A social learning approach: Vol. 3: Coercive family process.* Eugene, OR: Castalia.
This book remains essential reading for the school psychologist who wants to understand the dynamics underlying the single parent mother and unmanageable son.

Pasley, K. & Ihlinger-Tallman, M. (Eds.) (1987). *Remarriage and stepparenting: Current research and theory.* New York: Guilford.
This edited volume provides the best compilation of recent research on the effects of remarriage and stepparenting on children. Available in paperback.

Visher, E. B. & Visher, J. S. (1988). *Old loyalties, new ties: Therapeutic strategies with stepfamilies.* New York: Brunner/Mazel.
This is the single-most authoritative and readable guide to working with stepfamilies. Clear conceptual frameworks, clearly described interventions, many case examples, and an excellent compendium of additional resources make this book a necessity for clinicians working with stepfamilies.

BIBLIOGRAPHY: PROFESSIONALS AND PARENTS

Gardner, R. A. (1978) *The boys and girls book about one parent families.* New York: Bantam Books, and Gardner, R. A. (1982). *The boys and girls book about stepfamilies.* Cresskill, NJ: Creative Therapeutics.
These books were written to help children cope with the problems likely to occur in single parent or stepparent families. The books are written at the third or fourth grade reading level and are appropriate for children to read alone, for parents to read to young children, or for parents and children to read together.

Parents Without Partners, Inc., 7910 Woodmont Avenue, Suite 1000, Bethesda, MD 20814.
This national organization provides a monthly newsletter with articles and informational materials that are informative to single parents.

Stepfamily Association of America, 602 E. Joppa Road, Baltimore, MD 21204.
This national organization publishes a quarterly newsletter, *Stepfamily Bulletin,* which contains informative articles, personal experience stories, a column for therapists, and other relevant material.

Wallerstein, J. S. & Blakeslee, S. (1989). *Second chances: Men, women, and children a decade after divorce.* New York: Ticknor & Fields.
This book, based on the only ten-year longitudinal study of divorce ever conducted, provides information on the long-term impact of divorce, single-parenting, and remarriage on parents and children. It is written in a highly compelling and readable style which dramatically brings home the fact that family transitions are life-changing events for all family members. It may be important to bear in mind that this report is based on a clinical, not random, population. The book is appropriate and would be of interest to educated parents as well as professionals.

Weiss, R. (1979). *Going it alone: The family life and social situation of the single parent.* New York: Basic Books.
This book continues to be one of the most sensitive, human, and comprehensive discussions of single parent family issues. Highly recommended for professionals and educated parents.

58

Best Practices in Working with Students with a Hearing Loss

Susan M. Vess
University of Southern Maine
Laura S. Douglas
Colorado School for the Deaf and Blind

OVERVIEW

Hearing impairment in one or both ears is frequently described as the number one handicapping condition in the United States because it affects more persons than heart disease, blindness, tuberculosis, multiple sclerosis, venereal disease, and kidney disease combined (Stein, 1988). There are as many as 15 million hearing impaired (HI) Americans who experience mild to profound difficulty registering or processing aural communication (Moores, 1987). Of these, approximately two million are deaf, i.e., individuals who are unable to understand and learn through speech and audition even when using amplification devices (Schein & Delk, 1974).

Variations in the incidence figures for hearing impairment relate to factors including the degree and kind of impairment, age of onset, communication style, survey methods, etc. However, the biggest discrepancy in incidence figures is accounted for by differences in the proportion of the population that is acoustically impaired at different age levels. The incidence of hearing impairment among adults increases with advancing age so that in the 75 years and older population, it is estimated that almost 40% experience some limitations to their hearing (Stein, 1988).

In children, hearing impairment is a low incidence handicapping condition.

According to Stein (1988), less than 2% of children from birth through 14 years of age experience impaired hearing. There are fewer than 400,000 children with educationally relevant losses in the U.S. (Sontag, Smith, & Certo, 1977) with perhaps 49,000 youngsters enrolled in programs for the severely HI during the 1984 school year (Craig & Craig, 1985).

Since PL 94-142, the trend for HI children with mild to profound losses is attendance at day classes in the public schools. Now there are fewer private residential schools for the deaf and, of the 30% of deaf attending residential schools, 40% are day students (Moores, 1987). Although few teachers of the HI are Black, Native American, Hispanic, or Asian American, approximately one third of HI children are members of minority groups (Belcastro, 1987).

Persons who lost their hearing after they had acquired some speech, language, and skill in the pragmatic aspects of communication are termed postlingually or adventitiously deaf. Those who lost their hearing after 16 years are considered deafened. Adult onset HI is attributed to presbycusis, which is loss of high frequency hearing and speech recognition associated with aging; Meniere's disease, which includes hearing loss, vertigo, and ringing in the ears; exposure to environmental noises over time or in one acoustically traumatic incident; dysfunction of the Eustachian tube and middle ear infections; and otosclerosis, a hereditary disease of the bones surrounding the inner ear.

Persons whose loss exceeds 90 decibels (dB) are classified as profoundly deaf. Among the school-aged deaf population, about 90% have a congenital hearing loss and another 5% became deaf by 2 years (Schein & Delk, 1974). These children are described as prelingually deaf. For these deaf children, hearing is non-functional for communication and learning because the children are virtually unaware of the existence of sound, have not developed listening skills, do not recognize audition's contribution to communication, and have not acquired adequate speech or language skills.

Children who lose their hearing after two years of age, the adventitiously deaf, have varying degrees of sound awareness and may even understand hearing's importance to communication. They have an ongoing struggle to maintain whatever speech and language developed prior to their hearing loss and must acquire subsequent communication skills through vision and other channels. Adventitiously deaf children also must resolve any adjustment problems arising from their new hearing impairment. Concurrently, their parents must grapple with problems in communicating with, socializing, and managing them as well as resolving their own reactions to their children's hearing loss.

Deaf children whose deaf parents are established in a HI community are often more fortunate than other HI children in adjustment, language, and educational attainment because their need for social interaction, acceptance, and learning opportunities has been satisfied from infancy (Schlesinger & Meadow, 1972). Additionally, their exposure to gesture in early childhood facilitates their acquisition of language and manual communication skills. Unfortunately, 90% of deaf children are born to hearing parents who know little about the implications of their children's auditory disability (Liben, 1978).

According to definitions used for educational placements, children whose hearing loss in their better ear exceeds 70 dB are classified as deaf. These children's hearing is so nonfunctional for communication and learning that they routinely require special speech, language, acoustical, and instructional assistance. Less than one-fourth of their speech is rated as intelligible by their teachers (Jensema, Karchmer, & Trybus, 1978) and only about 17% of these children are mainstreamed (Karchmer, Milone, & Wolk, 1979). These severely and profoundly HI children represent the largest proportion of students in classes for HI. They usually communicate through signs and become members of a deaf community in adulthood.

The terms hearing impaired or hard of hearing describe persons whose hearing loss ranges from 35 to 70 dB in the better ear. Although mildly and moderately HI children often require some amplification to acquire and process language, they use hearing for communication and learning. Children with a 40 dB or less loss are unlikely to use amplification (Karchmer, Milone, & Wolk, 1979).

According to classification criteria used in making educational placements, hard of hearing children routinely need special speech and language assistance; but may not require special class or school placement. If they need special education, these mildly and moderately HI children enter special classes at an older age and leave at a younger age than severely and profoundly HI children. While in special education, they are frequently mainstreamed. According to Jensema, Karchmer, and Trybus (1978), 60% of hard of hearing children communicate through speech alone with that speech rated as intelligible by their teachers.

Mildly to moderately HI children are often multihandicapped. Associated conditions include mental retardation, epilepsy, cerebral palsy, uncorrected visual impairment, brain damage, and behavior problems. The incidence of multiple handicapping conditions among this HI population appears to be increasing (Schildroth, 1980).

The etiology of hearing impairment, including its pathology and pathophysiology, is listed as "unknown" in about 30% of deafness (Moores, 1987). Currently, genetics contributes to about half the cases of deafness. In an individual case of HI, however, it is difficult to determine the etiology of the hearing loss. Additionally, it appears likely that some etiologies are wrongly attributed. Lack of a clearly identified etiology occurs because retrospective diagnoses of hearing impairment often obscure factors which indicate the cause of the hearing loss.

Historically, deafness occurred more often in middle childhood and resulted from infections, especially scarlet fever, measles, and meningitis. Currently, infants are more frequently at risk of hearing loss, especially from a group of infectious diseases called the TORCH complex: TO for toxoplasmosis; R for rubella; C for cytomegalic inclusion disease (CMV), a member of the herpes group of viruses; and H for herpes (Stein, 1988). On occasion, O designates other infections, including mumps and streptococcus.

Except for an unanticipated epidemic or environmental hazard, medical technology such as surgery, medication, and immunization has reduced the risk of early childhood hearing loss from environmental and infectious causes. However, the same medical technology, because it has enabled severely ill children to live, has contributed to the increase in the number of children for whom hearing impairment is one of multiple handicaps.

The etiology of a hearing loss is an important determiner of the likelihood of concomitant handicapping conditions. Maternal rubella, meningitis, complications from the Rh factor, and prematurity all increase the risk of additional handicaps. Although genetically deaf children have few additional handicapping conditions, about one-fourth to one-third of HI children have multiple physical and learning problems (Schein & Delk, 1974).

The etiology of hearing loss is an important consideration for the treatability of the loss, the potential for additional handicaps, and/or the possibility of hearing impairment among subsequent children in the family. However, while postlingual hearing impairment from trauma, illness, accident, or late onset genetic disorder determines the presence of complications or additional handicapping conditions, its etiology is somewhat irrelevant to the loss itself.

HI individuals do not always learn and communicate through lip reading because of the difficulties inherent in speech reading. Only about 40 to 60% of English sounds are distinguishable on the lips and those visible sounds may be blocked by pencils, chewing gum, mustaches, or anything else that obscures the mouth (Levine, 1981). Assuming that the speech of the speaker is distinct, the message may be lost because speech moves rapidly and leaves no permanent record. Finally, many English words are difficult to discern by someone with little opportunity to learn or practice the association among sounds, visual images, and context. The best lip readers understand one-fourth of spoken language (Sullivan & Vernon, 1979). The average deaf child accurately speech reads only about 5% of what is said (Vernon & Koh, 1970). Even for someone whose hearing loss followed acquisition of speech and language, learning to lip read is comparable to learning a foreign language from a television whose sound is turned off.

Visual acuity does not automatically become heightened in the HI. When a HI person appears to see better, it means that his/her visual skill has been carefully nurtured and trained. Indeed, visual problems are at least as common in the HI as they are among the hearing. Moreover, eye strain and fatigue often occur as a result of the sustained vision needed to help understand communication from either lip reading or signing.

A variety of mechanical devices are used by the HI to intensify their reception of sound. However, amplification equipment does not necessarily compensate for deficient hearing. Because hearing aids equally intensify all sounds including the human voice and environmental noise, hearing aids often aggravate the wearer, especially when initially worn. Additionally, training and time are needed to learn to screen out unwanted sound and derive meaning from speech and important environmental sounds. If the hearing loss affects both the volume of sounds and its transformation to neural energy, a hearing aid intensifies the sound, but may not clarify the sounds themselves. In these sensorineural losses, hearing aids may operate like a radio which is not correctly tuned in, but is quite audible.

A cochlear implant is a prosthetic device that stimulates the residual structures of the inner ear (Karmody, 1986). Rather than a transplant or a bionic ear, it consists of insulated wires that are attached to a coupling device located under the ski which, in turn, is connected to a receiver worn on the chest. The receiver processes speech signals that are selectively transmitted to the electrodes in the implant (Karmody, 1986). Rather than increasing the volume of auditory input, the cochlear implant electrically excites the auditory nerve fibers in the inner ear.

Although some persons consider it to be a miracle cure for deafness, the cochlear implant is primarily recommended for adults with a profound, postlingual hearing loss in both ears which has not been successfully remediated by traditional amplification efforts (Ross, 1986). Cochlear implants are not recommended for children with prelingual deafness because of the potential risks associated with this new, sophisticated technology. More importantly, young, profoundly hearing impaired children lack a language base that enables a sound-meaning association. Considering the intensity of auditory training involved in learning to use a cochlear implant, it would be more sensible and less risky to devote a comparable amount of time to enhancing the residual hearing of deaf children (Martin, 1986).

Although the individual child is diagnosed as hearing impaired, the entire family becomes hearing impaired because all members must accommodate the deficient auditory acuity. Parenting a HI child is more complex, rather than different from, parenting hearing children. Thus, social emotional issues such as affiliation, affection, and control are important in parenting all children; but resolution of these issues with a HI child demands more thought and care (Luterman, 1987).

Since parents often perceive the HI child as fragile, his/her needs may take priority over the satisfaction of the needs and the allocation of emotional and financial resources to other family members. Indeed, parents may become so wrapped up in not making any mistakes in compensating for their child's hearing impairment that they fail to provide for the child's developmental and psychological needs (Luterman, 1987).

Parental determination to overcome their child's hearing loss is often an outgrowth of their attempts to implement all the suggestions made by professionals, friends, and members of the extended family. In their attempt to provide the best education for their HI child, parents often sacrifice their parenting role by interacting with the HI child in controlling, directive methods which mimic the teaching style of the child's intervention program (Schlesinger & Meadow, 1972; Schlesinger, 1986; Luterman, 1987). According to Luterman (1987), professionals deify hearing impairment at the expense of parental competence and self confidence by their overemphasis on the importance of the intervention program and the necessity for carefully implemented homework.

Control and protecting the HI child from legitimate dangers while fostering independence provide major challenges in parenting the HI child. According to Luterman (1987), there is a reciprocal relationship between the HI child's performance and the parents' behavior. If the child meets parental expectations, s/he is allowed greater freedom and independence. However, if expectations are not attained, parents react by placing greater restrictions on and overprotecting the child. Parental domination and overprotection are thought to result in the HI child's passivity, reluctance to take initiative, external locus of control, and poor self esteem (Luterman, 1987).

Siblings are important in the acquisition and practice of social interaction skills, including sharing and cooperating; resolving conflict; negotiating between equals; competing; responding to winning and losing; and dealing with authority figures. The effect of a hearing loss on hearing siblings is described as both subtle and variable, dependent of the parents' ability to cope with the hearing loss, and related to the speed and sensitivity with which professional help is available to the family (Luterman, 1987). Nevertheless, the HI child and his/her hearing sibling(s) provide a reciprocal flow of effect on socialization and communication (Luterman, 1987). Since the reaction of siblings to a hearing loss reflects parental reaction, working with parents of the HI child influences the dynamics of the sibling system.

HI children are expected to attend school to master language and academic skills that are deemed necessary to succeed in mainstream hearing society. Consequently they are periodically evaluated by the school to measure their progress in achieving these goals. The question, then, is how to conduct the most effective evaluation for HI children and the schools.

The psychological evaluation of HI children shares some of the same dilemmas and frustrations of assessing bilingual/bicultural children. However, since the majority of hearing impaired children are born to hearing parents, they are neither socialized to the same culture nor share a language with their parents. Profoundly HI children are raised with the goal of living in the hearing world; but, in adolescence, often choose between the deaf community and their parents.

When parents opt for total communication for their HI children, they must learn a second language, signing. Since parents frequently stop attending signing classes before they have achieved fluency, their HI children outstrip them linguistically and cognitively. Thus, parents and the HI children become proficient performers in different languages and cultures (Luterman, 1987).

BASIC CONSIDERATIONS

Norm referenced tests have consistently indicated deficient academic progress in HI children when compared to hearing children, despite a long history of deaf education. However, deaf students enter post-secondary education at about the same rate as hearing students and 65% of the graduates of Gallaudet attend graduate schools with hearing students (Moores, 1987). Therefore, the nature and extent of the gap between academic achievement of hearing and HI students is unclear.

The curriculum of programs for the HI is heavily skewed toward developing proficiency in receptive and expressive language at the expense of instruction in academic content. This trend runs counter to the current emphasis on improving test scores on standardized tests of achievement and research indicating that time on task is an important predictor of academic acquisition. The education of HI children is caught in a "Catch 22" in which academic content and language are both significant needs, but individually require intense, organized instruction. Moores (1987) argues that HI children like their hearing counterparts benefit from exposure to books, increased time on task in academic areas, homework, and improved instructional materials.

In the fourteen years since PL 94-142 mandated appropriate assessment practices with handicapped children, school psychologists continue to struggle with ethical and legal dilemmas associated with the evaluation of HI children. Practitioners are compelled to conduct assessments with tests which lack normative information for the HI population. Additionally, assessments are sometimes conducted by good-intentioned persons with little information about the profound and far reaching effects of living in an auditorily oriented world without equal access to that environment.

The assessment of HI children requires basic competencies that begin with meeting the standards and qualifications for school psychologists that are required by training programs and credentialing bodies. Additionally, school psychologists need at least one course that considers both normal and pathological speech and language development.

School psychologists should possess the sensitivity to recognize and respond to behavioral cues and the imagination, flexibility, and theoretical grounding to modify the assessment situation for the HI child's unique needs. A sense of whimsy and creativity are important assets in adapting the environment and contents of a test kit for an acoustically impaired child. On a personal competency dimension, school psychologists who like and respect children and who are liked and respected in turn are most likely to be effective evaluators of HI children. This latter point is particularly important as HI children are very sensitive to facial and body cues which reveal genuine feelings.

School psychologists' assessments for the purpose of determining eligibility for special education services are adjuncts to audiological assessments. Therefore, the practitioners may feel relatively at ease in most states because eligibility criteria address the level of the child's hearing acuity as the key factor in determining the need for special services.

The degree to which a HI child's acuity loss and residual hearing influences the student's educational progress becomes the major question and ultimate consideration in determining the kind and extent of services which are appropriate. It is at this point that school psychologists draw on their background in the typical and atypical educational, social, and linguistic implications of hearing loss. The question then centers on the amount of educational and social progress the HI child is expected to make given factors such as age of onset and severity of the hearing loss, age of diagnosis, and the duration and benefit of aided hearing.

Although it only measures what the HI child cannot hear, it is important to review the audiogram prior to testing because substantial differences in HI children's communicative, academic, and behavioral functioning are related to the pattern of hearing loss. Additionally,

knowing the extent of the HI child's residual hearing is critical because some children with a greater magnitude of hearing loss have more access to their remaining hearing than less severely HI children. Indeed, available audition is among the best predictors of language development and academic achievement.

During an audiometric examination, both aided and unaided hearing in both ears are measured and compared. Evaluating both aided and unaided hearing is broadly comparable to measuring the differences in vision with and without corrective lens. As an example, some persons whose uncorrected functioning is handicapped by deficient vision may approach normal vision and be allowed to drive a car with correction. Because of aided and residual hearing and intensive training in the use of both, socially and academically successful deaf children are sometimes elevated to hard of hearing status despite an audiogram that suggests severe or profound hearing loss (Levine, 1981; Moores, 1987).

The configuration of volume of loss (decibels) across frequencies (pitch) tells what and how well HI children hear. HI children do not perceive sounds below their threshold (decibel) level. Additionally, sounds vary in pitch with higher pitched sounds needing greater volume to be heard. While some HI children hear consonants better than the high pitched vowels, others are more aware of low frequency environmental sounds. When contiguous sounds are unevenly perceived, one syllable words such as *is* and *if;* sounds including *sh, th, ch, p, t,* and *k;* and plurals and ending sounds can all be poorly heard.

Many HI children do not perceive key words or directions and thereby respond incorrectly when intellectually capable of supplying the desired response. Hard of hearing children who appear to hear and understand in a one-to-one situation very well and whose speech is flawless are particularly difficult to assess because of their uneven language development. HI children often respond with pleasant looks and knowing smiles that conceal their inability to derive meaning from the examiner's communication. Thus, difficulty in communicating directions to HI children results in some misunderstanding of the task demand for both hard of hearing and deaf students. This results in some deviation of performance from one test situation to the next.

Mildly and moderately HI children use speech to communicate but may experience some lapses in receiving or communicating spoken language. Most severely and profoundly HI children employ conventional communication methods, especially some variation of manual communication. However, others communicate idiosyncratically through home signs or a jumble of manual communication systems. Therefore, the examiner should not complicate already difficult communication with exaggerated mouth movements, large dramatic gestures, and screamed questions.

BEST PRACTICES

The first step in the assessment of a HI child includes a thorough review of records, screening data, and information obtained from parents. The age at which early developmental milestones were attained provides a clue about the HI child's rate of learning in the first months and years of life.

For a HI child, the presence of an aid in working condition is important for successful performance in school, in social activities, and on tests. Just as a working amplification device is important, corrective eyewear should be worn, if prescribed.

An etiology suggesting particular syndromes has implications for associated behavioral manifestations and for educational planning if the hearing loss is progressive. Thus, a child doing well with an oral/aural approach may need the addition of a manual supplement when his/her hearing deteriorates.

Before the evaluation, it is vital to review the HI child's medical status and history because s/he is reliably and validly evaluated only when at peak hearing efficiency and in good health. The HI child who displays symptoms of a respiratory illness or who is recovering from one should not be tested until those symptoms,

especially reduction in hearing acuity, abate. A HI child may experience intermittent hearing loss from infections such as otitis media, an infection of the Eustachian tube and middle ear which often includes fluid in the ear. Additionally, s/he may be at risk for further decline in hearing and the onset of additional handicapping conditions because of a variety of disorders including Usher's Syndrome, a genetic disorder of progressive auditory and visual impairments.

Conferences with the HI child's teacher(s) and parents also provide valuable information. When communication with the HI child is less than optimal, teachers and parents are vital sources of information about the child's typical behavior and response style and provide reliability checks for the assumptions and observations made by the school psychologist. Additionally, the behavioral concerns of these significant others are further explored through the observations and clinical judgment of the examiner. Behavior observed in fewer than several settings should be verified as typical or atypical by the child's parents and teacher.

Ideally, pretest observation of the HI child in the classroom and other salient environments reveals how s/he interacts with others at home and school and how his/her gestures, postures, and facial expressions contribute to the meaning of his/her messages or signal his/her understanding of incoming communication. The HI child's ability to communicate and socialize with peers in informal situations is indicative of his/her style of communication and functional use of spoken language.

Even within settings where all staff and students are bilingual in speech and sign, communication hierarchies exist. Note with whom the HI child prefers to sit when allowed open seating. Note participation in informal games and formal instructional activities. Avoidance of social interactions may have more implications than a tendency toward shyness. Rather, it may reflect the child's difficulty in conversing with others or understanding the rules of organized games and tasks.

As communication style changes by level of hearing impairment and from program to program, educational records should be reviewed prior to assessment to determine which communication mode predominated in the child's family and educational background. Whatever the method, the HI child's communication style should be used in the evaluation, as far as possible. Misdiagnosis occurs when it is assumed that a hearing impairment can be ignored or by-passed through the use of nonverbal tests and/or communicating through pantomime, writing, slowed speech, etc.

Informal play activities which allow the HI child to demonstrate inner language by imaginative play provide information about the child's cognition, reasoning, and problem solving skills. The psychologist who works with infants and young children should collect an assortment of toys that tantalize children, including the HI.

There are few psychological and educational tests specifically normed for HI children. Consequently each child becomes his/her own reference group. Test results are more reliable if they are similar to those previously obtained by the HI child using the same instrument. Differences in test performance occur because of changes in the child's rate of progress and his/her behavior. Apparent discrepancies result from alternate forms, changes in comparative structure, and/or modifications of test format, communication methods, examiners, etc. Problems in replication of test findings occur when standardization was broken, but not reported. Both hard of hearing and deaf children should be afforded the benefit of assessments that derive from more than quick and dirty information gathered with misapplied testing procedures and inadequate communication.

Several general suggestions are made for selecting and administering norm referenced tests to hard of hearing and deaf children.

1. Adhere as closely as possible to standard administration guidelines of the test. Repeat a verbatim statement or question once, but add demonstrations or visual cues as needed. If it is necessary to repeat, rephrase or modify directions to ensure they are understood, be sure to mention that accommodation in the test report.

2. Use a certified interpreter for the deaf when the student's primary language is sign. Interpreters are located through the local or state Registry for Interpreters for the Deaf. Before the assessment, it may be necessary to acquaint the interpreter with general assessment principles and the expectation that the student will not complete all tasks. The interpreter sits beside and slightly behind the examiner so as to facilitate, not supersede or subvert, the examiner-child relationship. If an interpreter is not available, the child's teacher is preferred to a family member as an aid to communication because the family's emotional investment in the HI child may be conveyed and thereby increase the child's test anxiety.

3. With a hard of hearing student in the mainstream, use a verbal test of intelligence as an indicator of language delay, not intelligence. Comparison of the HI child's performance with that of hearing peers supplements the findings of language tests administered by the speech and language clinicians and provides insight into the child's need for additional assistance in competing in the regular classroom.

4. Recognize that verbal and nonverbal tests and techniques which are invalid with hearing and/or bicultural children are invalid for the HI, even when communication is apparently facilitated. Additionally, nonverbal tests such as the Leiter which are popularly used with the HI have very outdated and even questionable norms. The Hiskey Nebraska is considered a useful tool in the assessment of HI children, but it urgently needs revision.

5. Select tests with a sufficient age range so that already tenuous test scores need not be extrapolated up or down. Deaf students often take academic tests designed for younger children because of their deficient academic skills.

6. Schedule several short evaluation sessions because fatigue and communica-

tion problems reduce reliability of test data and lengthen evaluation time. Increasing difficulty in comprehension, frequent requests for repetition of directions, and behavior suggestive of boredom and restlessness indicate the need to stop testing.

7. Investigate the variety of resources that are available for choosing assessment instruments for the HI. *Assessment of hearing-impaired people* (Zieziula, 1982) and *Mental health assessment of deaf clients: A practical manual* (Elliot, Glass, & Evans, 1987) discuss the use of a variety of tests, including projectives, with the HI.

Most currently available tests are not appropriate means of evaluating HI children, especially younger pupils. Nevertheless, understanding how and how well information is learned, processed, sequenced, conserved, and manipulated is critical to educational planning. Therefore, criterion referenced methods, including the Brigance tests, Piagetian tasks, and a test-teach-test paradigm provide relevant information for instructional planning. Moreover, if the HI child is being evaluated for an additional handicapping condition or as part of a triennial review, the use of curriculum-based assessment is suggested for determination of rate of learning. Norm referenced tests such as the old Binet are inappropriate, but contain a treasure of manipulatives.

Deaf children who perform best in technical scholastic areas such as spelling and arithmetic are often 3 to 5 years behind hearing peers academically (Levine, 1981). Children with a milder hearing loss also perform below grade placement with variable skill levels across academic areas. A learning disability in the HI is associated with etiologies that include brain damage, not only severe discrepancies in academic skills. Mentally retarded HI children are severely deficient across academic areas and are lacking in adaptive behavior skills. Gifted HI children share the zeal, enthusiasm, curiosity, and sense of humor displayed by hearing gifted children; but perform at grade level or only slightly higher.

The assessment of the psychosocial development of a HI child centers around the behavioral expectations of home and school. Even a severely HI child can meet age expectations in adaptive behavior, especially self help skills. However, family expectations are a critical variable in the HI child's psychosocial development. Unreasonable parental demands to meet the expectations of hearing society confounds some HI children. Others are inhibited from maximizing their adaptive potential because of parental restraints and overprotectiveness. Inappropriate behavior in a HI child often signifies poor management and/or inappropriate expectations unless the child is not able to establish and maintain interpersonal ties in any environment.

SUMMARY

To ensure consistency and accuracy of information, the school psychologist should conduct assessments of a HI child as part of a multidisciplinary team. Through their combined input, a variety of professionals evaluates the impact of a hearing loss on a child's receptive and expressive language and, by extension, learning. They consider the severity of hearing loss and extent of residual hearing, the age of onset of hearing loss and age at which intervention procedures were initiated, the effectiveness of acoustical and medical intervention, and a host of intangibles such as the child's intelligence, talents, and temperament; the emotional and financial resources of the family; the availability of services in the community; and the kind and intensity of intervention devices and procedures.

It should be remembered that variable test performance is the rule rather than the exception with HI children. Multiple instruments measuring the same construct, observations, review of records, and close scrutiny to the adaptive demands placed by the family and school provide a checks and balance system for evaluating current assessment findings. Behavior observation and criterion referenced testing supplement norm referenced tests and are invaluable indicators of the HI child's skills and abilities, approach to problem solving, facility in grasping task demands, need for assurance, and quality of response.

REFERENCES

Anderson, R. J., & Sisco, F. H. (1977). *Standardization of the WISC-R*. Series T, Number 1, Washington, DC: Gallaudet College, Office of Demographic Studies.

Belcastro, F. P. (1987). Hearing impairment. In V. B. Ban Hasselt & M. Hersen (Eds.), *Psychological evaluation of the developmentally and physically disabled* (pp. 93-114). New York: Plenum.

Craig, W., & Craig, H. (1985). Directory of services for the deaf: Tabulated summary. *American Annals of the Deaf, 130*(2), 132-133.

Elliot, H., Glass, L., & Evans, J. (Eds.). (1987). *Mental health assessment of deaf clients: A practical manual*. Boston: Little, Brown, & Company.

Jensema, C. J., Karchmer, M. A., & Trybus, R. J. (1978). *The rated speech intelligibility of hearing impaired children: Basic relationships and a detailed analysis*. Series R., No. 6. Washington, DC: Gallaudet College, Office of Demographic Studies.

Karchmer, M. A., Milone, M. N., Jr., & Wolk, S. (1979). Educational significance of hearing loss at three levels of severity. *American Annals of the Deaf, 124*, 97-108.

Karmody, C. S. (1986). Otology in perspective. In D. M. Luterman (Ed.), *Deafness in perspective* (pp. 1-13). San Diego: College Hill.

Levine, E. S. (1981). *The ecology of early deafness: Guides for fashioning environments and psychological assessments*. New York: Columbia University Press.

Liben, L. S. (Ed.). (1978). *Deaf children: Developmental perspectives*. New York: Academic Press.

Luterman, D. (1987). *Deafness in the family*. Boston: Little, Brown (College Hill Division).

Martin, F. N. (1986). Audiology in perspective. In D. M. Luterman (Ed.), *Deafness in perspective* (pp. 35-53). San Diego: College Hill.

Moores, D. (1987). *Educating the deaf: Psychology, principles and practices* (3rd ed.). Boston, MA: Houghton-Mifflin.

Ross, M. (1986). A perspective on amplification: Then and now. In D. M. Luterman (Ed.), *Deafness in perspective* (pp. 35-53). San Diego: College Hill.

Schein, D., & Delk, M. (1974). *The deaf population of the United States*. Silver Springs, MD: National Association of the Deaf.

Schildroth, A. (1980). Public residential schools for deaf students in the United States, 1970-1978. *American Annals of the Deaf, 125*, 80-91.

Schlesinger, H. (1986). Total communication in perspective. In D. M. Luterman (Ed.), *Deafness in perspective* (pp. 87-116). San Diego: College Hill.

Schlesinger, H., & Meadow, K. (1972). *Sound and sign: Childhood deafness and mental health*. Berkeley, CA: University of California Press.

Sontag, E., Smith, J., & Certo, N. (1977). *Educational programming for the severely and profoundly handicapped*. Reston, VA: Council for Exceptional Children.

Stein, L. (1988). Hearing impairment. In V. B. Van Hasselt, P. S. Strain, & Michel Hersen (Eds.), *Handbook of Developmental and physical disabilities* (pp. 271-294). New York: Pergamon.

Sullivan, P. U., & Vernon, M. (1979). Psychological assessment of hearing impaired children. *The School Psychology Digest, 8*, 271-290.

Vernon, M., & Koh, S. D. (1970). Effects of manual communication of deaf children's educational achievement, linguistic competence, oral skills, and psychological adjustment. *American Annals of the Deaf, 115*, 527-536.

Zieziula, F. R. (Ed.). (1982). *Assessment of hearing-impaired people*. Washington, DC: Gallaudet College Press.

ANNOTATED BIBLIOGRAPHY

Gallaudet College. (1980). *Directions: Assessment of hearing impaired youth. Update on academic, professional, career and research activities.*
This publication contains an overview of appropriate procedures for classroom assessment and audiological, vocational, medical, psychological, and educational evaluations. Additionally, it has a chapter on the use of criterion-referenced tests that are appropriate for regular education and special education settings. This is one publication in a fine quarterly series produced by Gallaudet.

Luterman, D. (1987). *Deafness in the family*. Boston: Little, Brown (College Hill Division).
Luterman's short book clearly and concisely discusses family systems theory and relates it to deafness. He uses three families to illustrate the importance of deafness to family dynamics, including parenting, sibling relationships, and the development of independence.

Schlesinger, H. S., & Meadow, K. P. (1972). *Sound and sign: Childhood deafness and mental health*. Berkeley: University of California Press.
This book discusses child development, manual communication and family and mental health issues in childhood deafness. It considers deafness in light of Erikson's developmental theory and

investigates problems of childrearing such as toilet training and safety. *Sound and Sign* is a very practical contribution to understanding the young deaf child.

Moores, D. (1987). *Educating the deaf: Psychology, principles, and practices.* (3rd ed.). Boston: Houghton-Mifflin.
This book presents a very basic overview of hearing impairments and issues related to deafness. It is a good beginning in learning about hearing impairments, etiology of deafness, historical trends in education of deaf children, family relationships, etc.

Levine, E. S. (Ed.). (1981). *The ecology of early deafness: Guide to fashioning environments and psychological assessments.* New York: Columbia University Press.
This book contains the best discussion of the impact of deafness on child development, personality, intelligence, and education. Levine's perspective is that deaf children are normal youngsters who are forced to adapt to an atypical environment. Her book includes "examination guides" for the psychological assessment of deaf persons of all ages. If you have any background in deafness and can buy only one book in the area, Levine is strongly recommended.

59

Best Practices in Working with Students with a Visual Loss

Sharon Bradley-Johnson
Shirley Harris
Central Michigan University

Many school psychologists feel uncertain about how to proceed when faced with a referral for a student with a visual loss. Obviously these students have unique needs that cannot be overlooked. The special procedures needed for each stage of the assessment process for these students are described, background issues are discussed, the students' unique needs and how to address them are noted, and appropriate norm- and criterion-referenced tests as well as informal assessment methods are presented; issues relevant to remediation are included in the discussion. It was not possible to include the following areas that may be important to consider for certain referrals: vocational assessment, assessment of visual loss, and working with infants, preschoolers, and students who are severely multiply impaired. Information on assessment of infants and preschoolers with a visual loss can be found in Bradley-Johnson (1986).

OVERVIEW

An effective educational program for an individual student with a handicapping condition necessarily must begin with a thorough and educationally important assessment. Such an assessment should allow an examiner to diagnose a student's problems, identify strengths and instructional needs, and provide a baseline for monitoring progress in special programs. Generally, the process proceeds from gathering rather general information to obtaining data on specific skills the student has learned, the next skills that are important to teach, and information on conditions under which the student learns best.

There are numerous sources from which this information can be obtained: interviews, school records, observation, and direct assessment. Especially for physically handicapped students, each of these sources can provide unique information that is critical to educational planning. Hence, each source ought to be given careful consideration. The order in which these sources are used can affect the usefulness of the information obtained.

Interviews

For many reasons, it is best to begin the assessment by carrying out the interviews first. Many school psychologists have had little or no training or experience with students who have a visual loss. Consequently, it is not uncommon to feel unsure and anxious when beginning the assessment of a student with a visual impairment. By carrying out the interviews first, it is possible to obtain a great deal of helpful information from persons who know the student well. This information is required, even for examiners experienced in working with these students, in order to plan how observation, direct assessment, and intervention will proceed.

Teachers. The interview with a student's teacher is obviously important. As with any referral, the teacher's opinion regarding a student's strengths and difficulties, and the effectiveness of various educational procedures and programs that have been tried, should be obtained. For students with a visual loss, it is also important to know what special equipment, materials, and procedures have been employed in the classroom that might be useful for the assessment and for further program planning.

Depending upon the teacher's background and experience, it may not be possible to obtain all the needed information during the interview. Information that the teacher cannot provide can often be obtained by observing the student in the classroom. Table 1 is a checklist for use during the interview and classroom observation to obtain information on factors of particular importance for students with a visual loss.

During the teacher interview it is helpful to obtain samples of the student's classroom work. These work samples can be examined for error patterns that may be useful in planning remedial programs.

If checklists or rating scales are to be used to assess classroom behavior and adaptive behavior, it is a good idea to give them to the teacher to complete at the end of the interview. Thus, the psychologist is available to clarify any questions the teacher may have about the forms. Detailed information on assessment of adaptive behavior is presented later in the chapter.

One rating scale that it is beneficial to ask the teacher to complete at this time is the Pupil Behavior Rating Scale (Swallow, Mangold, & Mangold, 1978). This scale is designed specifically to assess classroom behavior of students with a visual handicap. The areas it covers are auditory comprehension and listening, spoken language, orientation, behavior, and motor skills.

Other professionals and parents. Because the limitations of a visual handicap are likely to vary as a function of situational requirements, it is important to interview others, in addition to the teacher, who work with the student. For example, a consultant for the visually impaired, a mobility instructor, or the parents will have observed the student's performance in situations other than the classroom, when more or fewer demands were placed upon the student. Hence, they may be able to provide additional information.

Student. It is usually productive to obtain the student's opinion regarding his or her academic performance and classroom situation. The interview with the student can be carried out prior to direct assessment.

School Records

The records review needs to be completed prior to observing the student in the classroom and before direct testing, in order to obtain sufficient background information to carry out these other phases of the assessment. The records review will provide information on a student's academic and family history.

For a student with a visual loss, it is necessary to obtain information from the records about the eye examination as well. It is important to note the age of onset of the visual loss. For students who sustained the loss prior to age 5, educational progress is likely to be negatively affected (Salvia & Ysseldyke, 1981) because they must learn new concepts through senses other than vision, whereas students who enjoyed unimpaired vision to age 5 or later usually have visual memories that should assist in learning new material.

It is also useful to note whether the visual condition is stable or deteriorating, whether the condition occurred gradually or suddenly, the amount of unusable vision that exists, and any restrictions or prescriptions made by the opthalmologist.

A description of a student's visual acuity in a medical report will not provide sufficient information regarding how to work with the student. Observation is needed, as well as interview information from those who have worked with the

TABLE 1
Teacher Interview/Classroom Observation Checklist
for Visually Impaired and Blind Students

Does student	Yes	No
1. Request help when needed?	_____	_____
2. Accept help courteously?	_____	_____
3. Refuse help courteously?	_____	_____
4. Display an appropriate degree of independence?	_____	_____
5. Listen well to instructions?	_____	_____
6. Move freely about the classroom?	_____	_____
7. Avoid hazards as much as possible?	_____	_____
8. Have desk well organized and free of unnecessary materials?	_____	_____
9. Put materials back in their appropriate places so they can be easily located?	_____	_____
10. Interact with peers about as often as other students?	_____	_____
11. Interact in a positive way with peers?	_____	_____
12. Handle difficult or frustrating tasks without becoming overly upset?	_____	_____
13. Respond to corrective feedback appropriately?	_____	_____
14. Seem to appreciate praise from the teacher? Examples of effective praise statements.	_____	_____

15. What type of instructional materials are used?

_____ braille   _____ talking books   _____ large print
_____ Optacon   _____ cassettes   _____ material read to student
_____ computer   other _____

16. What low-vision aids are used? _____

17. What special writing materials are used?

_____ braille writer   _____ slate and stylus   other _____
_____ typewriter   _____ special paper (embossed or bold line)

18. What special arithmetic aids are used?

_____ abacus   _____ computer aids
_____ talking calculator   _____ braille ruler
_____ special paper (embossed or bold line)   _____ special clock (braille or raised numbers)

19. How frequently does student need breaks due to fatigue?

---

20. Approximately how much extra time does student require to complete assignments?

Source: S. Bradley-Johnson. (1986). *Psychological assessment of visually impaired and blind students.* Austin, TX: PRO-ED. Reprinted by permission of the publisher.

student, to determine how a student utilizes her or his usable vision. Two students with the same visual acuity may differ considerably in ability to employ usable vision. When observing the student in the classroom, it is beneficial to note the size of print that can be read and the distance materials are held from the eyes.

Because auditory input is so important to the functioning of students with a visual loss, more frequent assessments of hearing are needed than for sighted students. Hearing loss can fluctuate owing to problems such as colds, allergies, and infections; so hearing abilities must be monitored closely. If there is any concern about hearing abilities, they should be evaluated prior to assessment of cognitive or academic skills.

Observation

Observation of students with a visual loss in the classroom is essential, but it is also important to observe their functioning in the home. Because the home environment is more familiar to the student, and the demands are likely to be different than those in the classroom, a visually impaired student's functioning may vary considerably in the two environments. Any differences noted can provide useful information regarding the environmental circumstances and demands that are likely to result in the student's best performance and greatest independence.

When observing in the classroom and in the home, it is useful to note whether, in trying to help the student, others seem to be overprotective. A balance between safety and independence must be found and this is sometimes difficult to do. Though safety is of foremost concern, overprotection will limit learning experiences.

Classroom observation can begin with the use of the checklist presented in Table 1. As with any student, if behavior problems are mentioned during interviews, or if they are noted in classroom observation, a systematic procedure for data collection will be necessary. Alessi and Kaye (1983) have described various data collection procedures designed specifically for school psychologists. Behaviors requiring intervention, which tend to occur more often for students with a visual loss, are discussed later in this chapter.

Direct Assessment

After completion of interviews, review of school records, and observation of the student's performance in several settings (including the classroom and the home),

direct assessment may be needed to further identify strengths and difficulties and clarify eligibility concerns. Several issues in respect to test selection require careful thought.

As with any student with a physical handicap, the number of tests that are appropriate for use is limited. Tests must be selected so as to ensure that the student has the skills required to perform the tasks to be accomplished; that is, the handicap must be circumvented on norm-referenced tests so that assessment results accurately describe the student's abilities.

In order to obtain an accurate picture of the abilities of a visually handicapped student, it is likely that a combination of norm-referenced, criterion-referenced, and informal measures will be needed. Each of these measures will help to determine the validity of the results of the other measures, and each can provide unique information for educational program planning.

Furthermore, an assessment for a student with a visual loss should cover academic performance, cognitive skills, and adaptive behavior in order to obtain a comprehensive picture of the student's skills. This is particularly important with a student who has a physical handicap, given the limited measures available and the need to consider performance in various settings with different demands. Assessment of adaptive behavior often allows one to obtain data on a student's strengths, especially when academic performance is very low. Periodic reevaluation will serve as a check on the validity of results as well as provide information on a student's progress.

For students with a visual loss, tests without time limits ought to be used, if possible. Timed tests penalize a blind or visually impaired student because reading regular-sized print, enlarged print, or braille takes much longer than it does for sighted students. Also, if objects are used in testing, more time is required to locate and interpret these objects.

Finally, a decision whether to use tests with norms for sighted students or for students with a visual loss must be made. Use of tests standardized on sighted students that do not require vision for completion of the tasks (e.g., the Verbal section of the Wechsler scales), allows comparison of the student's performance with that of sighted students in regular classrooms. However, use of these norms assumes that the student with the visual loss has had a background similar to that of sighted students. This is not likely to be the case, given that the student's visual experiences have been more limited. Also, the student may have been overprotected and thus have had more limited experiences. Students who have attended, or are attending, a residential school rather than a public school program have had different educational experience than that received by sighted students. Salvia and Ysseldyke (1981) suggested that such a comparison with sighted students may be unfair. Furthermore, if tests standardized on sighted students are used, some items may require modifications to circumvent visual requirements, which makes the use of the norms questionable.

Though the task requirements on tests standardized on students with a visual loss would be more appropriate, the use of these norms is problematic also. Most tests standardized on students with a visual handicap are out-of-date and technically inadequate (i.e., poorly standardized and with inadequate reliability and validity information). Also, there are only a few published tests of this nature and some of these have been standardized only with students attending residential programs. In view of present-day efforts at mainstreaming handicapped students, this is not an appropriate comparison group. Finally, the population of students with a visual loss is very heterogeneous because academic, adaptive, and cognitive performance levels can be affected by factors such as age of onset of the visual loss, gradual or sudden onset, and the degree of loss. Hence, the norm group for these tests may not be more appropriate.

Thus, in selecting norm-referenced tests, the background of the student, the purpose of the assessment (i.e., comparison with students in regular or special classrooms), and the enabling behaviors required by the test need to be considered.

Until there are more up-to-date norm-referenced tests appropriate for use with this population of students, there is no clear-cut answer to this question and in some cases no acceptable solution. Regardless of the type of norms used, caution must be used in interpreting results in the attempt to ensure that the student is not penalized because of the handicap, and that the results are not inflated or depressed by use of an inappropriate comparison group. The problem of selecting an appropriate norm group is another reason why results from academic, cognitive, and adaptive areas should be compared as a means to enhance the accuracy of results. The use of norm-referenced, criterion-referenced, and informal measures also serves this purpose by providing a larger data base. Such information, combined with observation in several settings, data on academic and medical history from school records, interview information, and periodic reevaluation, should provide an extensive data base from which to draw conclusions regarding a student's skills and needs. Assessment of students with physical handicaps is necessarily expensive and time-consuming, but it can be very beneficial when done comprehensively and accurately. Especially for students with physical handicaps, test scores alone cannot provide sufficient information to make important educational decisions.

BASIC CONSIDERATIONS

Legal blindness is defined as maximally corrected vision in the better eye of 20/200 or less or limitation of the field of vision to a diameter of no more than 20 degrees. Thus, students who are legally blind must use senses other than vision in the educational process (Scholl, 1983).

Few persons are totally blind and the majority of blind persons have some usable vision. Many students can read regular or enlarged print. According to the Federal Quota Registration (American Printing House for the Blind, 1987), of the legally blind students registered, 33% primarily read regular or large print, 12% primarily used braille, 17% were auditory readers, and the remainder were either nonreaders or prereaders.

According to PL 94-142 121a.5 (1975), "Visually handicapped" means a visual impairment which, even with correction, adversely affects a child's educational performance. The term includes both partially seeing and blind children."

As to prevalence, the American Printing House for the Blind maintains an annual register of legally blind students eligible for federal funds. In 1987 there were 16,670 students enrolled in grades K through 12. Of these 2,061 (12%) attended residential schools, 14,365 (86%) attended state department of education programs, 19 (.1%) were enrolled in programs for the multihandicapped, and 226 (1.4%) were in rehabilitation programs. There were an additional 15,532 school-age students with additional handicaps who were enrolled in prevocational programs leading to placements such as sheltered workshops.

BEST PRACTICES IN ASSESSMENT AND REMEDIATION

When working with a student who is blind, a multidisciplinary effort is essential. If the student is a braille reader, much of the assessment must be done in braille, and an evaluation of the student's braille-reading skills is required. Hence, someone who reads braille should be involved in the assessment, in program planning, and in implementing instructional programs.

The only published reading series for teaching braille to young children is *Patterns: The Primary Braille Reading Program* (Caton, Pester, & Bradley, 1980). Word recognition is taught using tactile memory and phonological and syntactic skills. Sections of the program can be used by a regular classroom teacher, but other sections must be taught by a teacher knowledgeable in braille.

Orientation and mobility is another area in which a specialist is essential. For example, a person untrained in orientation and mobility may think a student is doing very well in moving about the classroom, considering that the student has a visual loss. A specialist in orientation

and mobility, however, may recognize that the student's mobility skills can be improved considerably. Hence, for blind students, assessment of orientation and mobility skills by a specialist (unfortunately not required in all states) should be part of any assessment.

During direct assessment, or in working with students with a visual loss in the classroom, there are a number of special practices to be considered that differ from those involved in working with sighted students.

Reducing Anxiety

Uneasiness is a common feeling for professionals who have had limited experience working with students with a visual loss. However, if uncertainty arises as to how to respond to a student, the best approach is to ask the student directly.

To be unsure of what is occurring can cause anxiety for a blind student, particularly during assessment. Thus, when carrying out activities such as getting together materials, putting them away, or recording responses, it helps if the examiner describes what is taking place. Otherwise, in the absence of auditory or tactile clues the student must guess what is happening, which can cause unnecessary anxiety.

Communication

In responding to students with handicaps, speaking in a loud voice in an effort to interact more effectively is not helpful, even with students who have a hearing loss. Loud speech distorts and interferes with communication; the use of normal conversational levels is more effective. Use of common language is also more productive, rather than trying to avoid use of terms such as "look" and "see." Blind students use these terms in their conversation and trying to avoid such terms makes conversation awkward. If other people are present, it is helpful to call on blind students by name so that they can recognize that they are being addressed.

When handing materials to students with a severe visual loss, it is helpful to verbally warn them so as to avoid a startle response when the materials touch the hand.

Verbal directions need to be specific, such as "to your left" or "at the top of the page," rather than general such as "over there" or "here." Also, when students drop things, allow them to retrieve them and assist by providing specific verbal directions. Verbal guidance is preferable to physical guidance.

Maintaining Appropriate Behavior

Because students with a visual loss may not be able to see facial expressions and gestures, or see them well, provision of feedback on performance through other senses is required. Verbal praise and tone of voice can play a significant role in helping to motivate a student to perform well. Verbal feedback will be needed more frequently with students with a visual loss than for sighted students. Some physical contact, such as a pat on the shoulder or hand, can be helpful also, as long as the student is not startled by the touch.

Discipline to maintain appropriate behavior should be used as it would be for sighted students. To use lower standards of appropriate behavior does not benefit students with a visual loss. Inappropriate behavior will interfere with learning in the classroom and yield invalid results from an assessment that will underestimate a student's abilities.

Monitoring a student's performance for signs of fatigue is critical to obtaining and maintaining the best performance possible. Fatigue and eye strain are common problems when students with a visual loss employ their usable vision. Reading takes much longer than it does for sighted students. Braille may require twice the time it takes to read print. Hence, recommendations for working with a student in the classroom must include consideration of the extra time required to complete assignments as well as the fact that activities need to be discontinued whenever a student becomes fatigued.

Scheduling extra time and several sessions will be necessary for an assessment also, if valid results are to be obtained.

Testing Environment

An assessment should be carried out in a room free from distractions. Because students with a visual loss rely heavily on auditory input, a noisy testing environment can be a serious problem. In some cases, even subtle auditory distractions can interfere with performance. Oddly enough, the room needs to be well lighted. Glare and flickering lights must be avoided. Some students will require extra illumination; others may be sensitive to light and need low illumination. It is best if the light source comes from the side of the better eye. Hence, arrangements for an appropriate testing environment will need to be made in advance. Appropriate lighting and a relatively quiet environment are important to consider in planning classroom programs as well.

Any special equipment or materials used in the classroom ought to be used during the assessment. The equipment and materials required will depend upon the way items are presented (i.e., orally, or to be read) and the type of responses requested. Examples of special materials for presenting items include enlarged print, braille materials, magnifiers (hand-held, on a stand, or special glasses), and book stands. Examples of special materials and equipment for writing responses include a braille writer, a typewriter, paper with bold or raised lines, and a felt-tip marker.

Objects to be used in testing (e.g., wooden shapes, toys, or blocks) should be presented on a tray. The tray makes objects easier to locate and less likely to be dropped. The sides of the tray need to be low (about 2 inches or less) to make it easy to use. The American Printing House for the Blind has a Work/Play Tray that works well for this purpose. This tray can be of assistance in the classroom as well as during an assessment.

Making the Student Comfortable

When taking the student from the classroom to the testing room, the examiner should offer to lead by allowing the student to hold on to the examiner's arm. The student will grasp either the elbow or upper arm and follow a step or two behind the examiner. A young child's hand can be held.

Upon arriving at the room where the assessment is to take place, the student should be encouraged to explore the room. This can be done by physically guiding the student or by providing verbal descriptions of what is in the room. This procedure can help to decrease anxiety also. It is critical that all doors be either closed or open all the way to prevent injury should the student walk into a door left partially open. Such exploration of the room is helpful when a student is entering a new classroom also.

Adequate time must be allowed to establish a good rapport. An examiner who is uneasy will miss important observations and perhaps make errors in administering the tests. Anxiety can interfere with a partially sighted student's ability to employ usable vision. In some cases, it may be necessary to schedule a short session or two, just to establish rapport. Both the examiner and student need to feel comfortable and be able to engage in easy conversation prior to any testing.

Selecting Tests

The following description of tests and procedures for assessing cognitive, academic, and adaptive skills, with the exception of the Wechsler Preschool and Primary Scale of Intelligence (Wechsler, 1967) includes no tests published more than 20 years ago because they would be out-of-date. For a detailed description of these tests and their technical adequacy, see Bradley-Johnson (1986).

Cognitive assessment. Because of the limited number of appropriate measures for students with a visual loss, and the problems with technical adequacy of several of the scales, it is necessary to use sections of several measures to obtain sufficient data on a student's cognitive abilities.

The Williams Scale for Children With Defective Vision (Williams, 1956) is not recommended because it is out-of-date and was standardized on children in England only. The Perkins-Binet Test of Intelligence for the Blind (Davis, 1980) also is not recommended, having been withdrawn from the market as it was in need of major revision and further research.

The Verbal section of the Wechsler scales — Wechsler Adult Intelligence Scale–Revised (Wechsler, 1981), Wechsler Intelligence Scale for Children–Revised (Wechsler, 1967) — can be used with students with a visual loss. In interpreting the results, it must be kept in mind that abstract concepts are difficult for young visually impaired students, so scores may somewhat underestimate ability. However, for some students, the results may overestimate ability if verbal skills are rote. Therefore, it is important to probe any questionable responses.

A number of studies investigating the pattern of performance of blind students on the Wechsler Intelligence Scale for Children (Wechsler, 1949) have found similar results (e.g., Tillman & Osborne, 1969; Gilbert & Rubin, 1965). Blind students tend to score high on Digit Span and Information and to score low on Similarities and Comprehension. In fact, such a pattern is common for blind students, rather than unusual.

It is beneficial to supplement results of a Wechsler scale with the Blind Learning Aptitude Scale (BLAT) (Newland, 1971). This test is for students 6–16 years of age and is nonverbal. Items are presented in bas relief and no knowledge of braille is needed. Various problem-solving tasks are involved, including classification, matching, and recognition of sequence. The BLAT is old and has problems in respect to technical adequacy, especially standardization and validity. However, it provides a nonverbal measure of cognitive skills and was standardized on students with a visual loss. The results may be inflated because of the age of the test and the fact that 79% of the standardization sample was from residential programs.

The results from a Wechsler scale and the BLAT can be supplemented with subtests from the Detroit Test of Learning Aptitude–2 (Hammill, 1985). This is a recent test with reasonably good technical adequacy. Though standardized on sighted students, three of the subtests do not require vision: Word Opposites, Sentence Imitation, and Word Sequences. These subtests tap mainly short-term auditory memory, vocabulary, attention, and some grammar. Use of these subtests takes little time and can provide useful information that is supplemental to the other measures.

Assessment of achievement. Adaptive materials or equipment normally used in the classroom will be needed for achievement testing. For example, in assessing mathematics, braille rulers, watches, clocks, and graphs might be used. For students who have learned to use one, an abacus can replace paper and pencil on tests that allow sighted students to write out their calculations. For a student who became blind after learning to write, raised line (embossed) paper can be used for items requiring written responses. Examples of special equipment that can be used are low-vision aids, a closed-circuit TV system, and a typewriter.

No norm-referenced achievement tests have been standardized on students with visual loss. Several individually administered tests, including the *Keymath* (Connolly, Nachtman, & Pritchett, 1976) and the Wide Range Achievement Test (Jastak & Jastak, 1984), have been transcribed into braille and large print. Unfortunately, these tests are not technically adequate, even for sighted students. Several group-administered achievement tests have been transcribed also. Eligibility decisions must be based on individually administered tests. However, the Stanford Achievement Test (SAT) (Psychological Corporation, 1988a), and its upward extension, the Test of Academic Skills (TASK) (Psychological Corporation, 1988b), are group-administered tests that merit special consideration.

These tests have unusually good technical data, and though not standardized on students with a visual loss, they have been adapted for these students. The adapted versions in both braille and large print, and the special administration manual (Duckworth, 1989), are available from the American Printing House for the Blind. The SAT is for use with students in primary through junior high grades and TASK is for students in Grades 9–12, and for entering college freshmen. Each level of the tests typically covers one grade level, from midgrade to midgrade e.g., 2.5 to 3.5. The subtests involved depend upon the level of the test that is used. However, the areas covered include reading, mathematics, written expression, listening skills, study skills, science, and social studies. A multiple-choice format is employed. The results provide a technically adequate and detailed source of data on achievement that could be supplemented with information from less technically adequate, but individually administered tests. The amount of time required to administer these tests is considerable, if the entire test is used. The regular-size-print version takes about 6 hours, the large-print version about 1½ times that long, and the braille version about 2½ times that long. However, the resulting information should be worth the time.

For students aged 5 and 6, the results of the SAT can be supplemented with information from the Basic School Skills Inventory–Diagnostic (BSSI-D) (Hammill & Leigh, 1983). This scale is designed to be completed by the classroom teacher. Though standardized on sighted children, it has 3 subtests that can be used for students with visual loss: Daily Living Skills, Spoken Language, and Classroom Behavior. Several items on each subtest may require modification, and sometimes should be scored by taking the visual loss into consideration. For example, the item "Can the child go through the normal school day without becoming overly tired and listless?" should be scored so as to not penalize a child with a visual loss because he or she is likely to become more easily tired than a sighted child. "Can the child tell time by looking at a clock?" would obviously require a braille clock or watch for a blind child. Because of problems with standardization and reliability, the results of the BSSI-D should be supplemented with results of other tests. However, the scale can provide useful information for program planning that is not provided by other tests, and it helps to quantify teacher input.

The Battelle Developmental Inventory (Newborg, Stock, Wnek, Guidubaldi, & Svinicki, 1984) might provide some limited information for students through age 8. Although this test was standardized on sighted children, adaptations are given in the manual for children with physical impairments. However, a number of items require vision and cannot be adapted for blind children. Furthermore, there are relatively few items in each section. Hence, scores for students with severe visual losses are not likely to be useful. However, some useful information may be obtained for planning programs. For students with considerable usable vision, most or all items could be given. There are five domains: Cognition, Communication, Motor, Adaptive, and Personal--Social. The Motor and Personal–Social domains have the largest number of items that do not require vision. Because the Personal--Social area is so important for visually handicapped students, this domain may be particularly useful. Reasonably good technical data are available on the scale, the limited number of items being the major problem. Results from the scale seems to correlate better with measures of adaptive behavior than other types of tests.

Fortunately, there are several quite technically adequate tests that can be used to assess oral language skills for visually handicapped students. Though all of the tests were standardized on sighted students, some subtests do not require vision. The Test of Language Development-2 Primary (Newcomer & Hammill, 1988) is for students aged 4-0 to 8-11. The subtests Oral Vocabulary, Sentence Imitation, Grammatic Completion, and Word Discrimination do not require vision. The Test of Language Development-2 Intermediate (Hammill & Newcomer,

1982) can be used with students aged 8-6 to 12-11. No vision is required for the entire test. The Diagnostic Achievement Battery (Newcomer & Curtis, 1984) was designed for students from age 6-0 to 14-11. Subtests that do not require vision are Story Comprehension, Characteristics, Synonyms, and Grammatic Completion. These subtests tap both listening and speaking skills. For students aged 12 to 18-5, the Test of Adolescent Language-2 (Hammill, Brown, Larsen, & Wiederholt, 1987) can be administered. Two of the subtests that do not require vision are Speaking Vocabulary and Speaking Grammar. For students who can write responses in braille, script, or with a typewriter, the Written Vocabulary subtest could also be used to assess this aspect of written expression.

To obtain sufficient information for planning instructional programs, measures in addition to norm-referenced tests are needed. Use of only norm-referenced tests in an assessment would result in an incomplete picture of a student's skills. Fortunately, there are several useful criterion-referenced tests and informal measures to assess achievement for students with a visual loss.

For the Brigance Comprehensive Inventory of Basic Skills (Brigance, 1983) a tactile supplement in braille is available (Duckworth, 1988) from the American Printing House for the Blind. The Brigance is a comprehensive and technically adequate measure that covers skills typically taught from kindergarten through Grade 9. The areas assessed include readiness skills, reading, mathematics, written expression, and some listening skills. If the tactile supplement is used, the examiner needs to know braille. If the regular version is administered, no special skills are required.

The Informal Assessment of Developmental Skills (Swallow, Mangold, & Mangold, 1978) is another excellent resource designed specifically for use with students with a visual loss. Skills used in kindergarten through Grade 12 are covered. The areas assessed are Visual Functioning, Unique Academic Needs (e.g., use of braille writer, typewriter, Optacon), Orientation and Mobility, Vocational Skills, and Behavior. No data on technical adequacy are provided; the checklists are intended only as informal measures of classroom skills. The checklists assess the unique classroom needs of students with a visual handicap. For some of the checklists, special skills are needed by the examiner (e.g., use of the Opticon or braille reading), but for many checklists no special skills are required.

To assess the instructional needs of braille readers, the Braille Unit Recognition Battery (Caton, Duckworth, & Rankin, 1985) can be employed. It is designed mainly for students in Grades 3–12, but can be used with braille readers who are younger or older. The battery must be administered by an examiner who has had experience with blind students and with knowledge through Grade 2 literary braille. The areas assessed are knowledge of braille alphabetic letters and numbers, phonograms, morphograms, letter words, wordlets, units for punctuation, and register. Also included is a checklist of behaviors relevant to braille reading. A considerable amount of data on field testing, reliability, and validity are provided. Results from this battery make it easy to determine specific braille skills that need to be taught.

The Tactile Test of Basic Concepts (Caton, 1976) is useful for assessing a student's knowledge of commonly used concepts. This is a tactile analog to the Boehm Test of Basic Concepts (Boehm, 1971), designed for students in Grades K, 1, or 2. The 50 concepts tested are presented on plastic cards using raised-line figures (i.e., no knowledge of braille is required). Given the limited technical adequacy of the measure, the test is best used to obtain information for instruction, though normative information is available on sighted students. Because concept development is so important for students with a visual loss, use of the Tactile Test could be very beneficial for designing instruction for students in the early elementary grades and for older students who have difficulties in this area of oral language.

To assess a student's knowledge of words typically taught as sight words, a set of braille and large-print Dolch (1955) cards is available from the American Printing House for the Blind. This set of cards was revised in 1988 to include 95 nouns (picture words) that can be used to make sentences. One side of a card is written in Grade 1 braille (i.e., with words spelled out) and the other side is in Grade 2 braille (e.g., with braille contractions). The words appear in large print on both sides of the card.

Assessment of adaptive behavior. Several unique issues are relevant to the assessment of adaptive behavior for a student with a visual loss. Because of the visual handicap, it is not unusual for social skills to be less well developed than for sighted students. Thus, social skills are important to assess and to target for instruction, if necessary.

Students with little or no vision usually have some behaviors that may negatively affect social interaction if not understood. Examiners and teachers must be sensitive to these behaviors. If they are noted during direct assessment or observation, they should be targeted for change. If they are not changed, they will make the student look different and social interactions may be problematic, especially with peers. These behaviors are listed in Table 2, along with suggestions for intervention.

Being orderly is a type of adaptive behavior that is critical for a student with a visual loss. As early as possible, it is important to begin teaching visually impaired children to have specific places for things and to habitually return materials to their places. In working with students in the classroom or during an assessment, an informal evaluation of their ability to be orderly with their things is very important. If orderliness is a problem, it will affect the efficiency of their functioning and it will limit their independence as well. Such skills are needed much more by students with a visual loss than by sighted students, and so ought to be targeted for instruction if orderliness is a problem.

TABLE 2
Behaviors Affecting Social Interaction

Behavior	Possible remedial procedures
Lack of (or infrequent) facial orientation toward speaker.	See Raver (1987) for a procedure for teaching appropriate gaze direction.
Lack of (or infrequent) use of gestures or facial expressions.	Teach common gestures using physical guidance and positive feedback.
Self-stimulation when bored or stressed, such as pressing thumbs into eye sockets (eye pressing), rocking, head rolling, and light gazing.	Teach relaxation procedures (e.g., Poppen, 1988) or use overcorrection (e.g., Kelly & Drabman, 1977; Foxx & Azrin, 1973).

Students should be allowed the use of adaptive devices when an informant is rating adaptive behavior, if they typically use the devices for self-care and other tasks. Examples of devices that can be used are adaptive measuring equipment, slicing guides, or coin organizers.

Evaluation of orientation and mobility skills by an orientation and mobility instructor should be considered part of the assessment of adaptive behavior.

Finally, it is wise to have both a parent and the classroom teacher complete an adaptive behavior scale, because students' performance is likely to be quite different at home than it is in school. Any discrepancies noted between the two environments may be useful in planning instructional programs. However, discrepancies may be due to differences in the scales or the raters (parent vs. teacher), rather than to actual performance differences. Observational data from the classroom and home can provide a reliability check on this information.

None of the norm-referenced measures of adaptive behavior that have been standardized in this country have been standardized on students with a visual loss. Hence, numerous items on scales of adaptive behavior will be inappropriate for these students. The Vineland Adaptive Behavior Scale (Sparrow, Balla, & Cicchetti, 1984) has supplementary norms for students with a visual loss. However, these norms are based on a residential population. With today's efforts at mainstreaming, the large majority of students with a visual loss attend public schools, rather than residential schools. Hence, the appropriateness of these supplemental norms is questionable, as it cannot be assumed that performance is the same for these two populations of visually handicapped students.

The most technically adequate measure of adaptive behavior, when the informant is the teacher, is the Adaptive Behavior Scale (Brown & Leigh, 1986). When the informant is a parent, the most technically adequate measure is the Vineland Adaptive Behavior Scale (Interview Edition or Expanded Form). The regular norms can be used, if appropriate. Both of these measures are appropriate for students in kindergarten through Grade 12. For a discussion of technical adequacy and other issues relevant to the assessment of adaptive behavior, see Evans & Bradley-Johnson (1988). As noted, both scales contain many items that require vision and so are likely to underestimate a student's adaptive behavior. Reported scores should be qualified by an explanation of this fact. Use of the scales is still worthwhile to obtain a comprehensive picture of a student's functioning, to check on the reliability of the results of other tests, and to provide some information that may be useful in planning instructional programs in this area.

An extremely comprehensive resource for planning instructional programs for academic skills and adaptive behavior is *Foundations of Education for*

Blind and Visually Handicapped Children and Youth (Scholl, 1986). This book also includes information on teaching social skills.

Interpretation of Results

Two issues are pertinent to the interpretation of the norm-referenced tests noted. First, any score is made up of a student's true score plus error. One way to describe the degree of error is to use the standard error of measurement and report results as a range, rather than as a single score. Because of the problems associated with norm-referenced tests for students with a visual loss noted in the Overview section (e.g., poor technical adequacy, inappropriateness of the norm group), there will probably be more error in test results for these students. Hence, whenever possible, the standard error of measurement should be employed so that results will be less likely to be interpreted as more precise than they are.

A second issue is that concept development can influence both test behavior and classroom performance of students with a visual loss. These students may use concepts correctly in speaking but not have a complete understanding of the concepts. Some words are particularly difficult to learn without vision, for example, *castle, cow, ruby*. In some cases, students with a visual handicap may be reinforced for rote learning to the point that reinforcement facilitates the development of echolalia. Hence, it is particularly important to probe questionable responses. Probing these responses should help to reduce the probability of obtaining an inflated score. In addition, the test items administered should be reviewed to determine the number of items a student has been given that involved concepts particularly difficult to learn without the use of vision. If there are many of these items, test results should be qualified by considering this problem. In the classroom, confusion or inadequate understanding of vocabulary needs to be clarified in order to prevent further interference with learning.

SUMMARY

Clearly, if assessment and intervention are to be productive, students with a visual loss have special needs requiring consideration. All phases of the assessment process (interviews, review of school records, observation in both the classroom and home environment, and direct assessment) can provide unique and worthwhile information, so none should be overlooked. Because of the special needs of students with a visual handicap, and the limitations of appropriate measures, the assessment of cognitive, academic, and adaptive areas will be needed to obtain a comprehensive picture of a student's functioning. Furthermore, to obtain sufficient data for making decisions regarding both eligibility and instructional needs, norm- and criterion-referenced tests as well as informal measures will be required. If a student is a braille reader, someone knowledgeable in braille will need to be involved in the assessment and in classroom instruction. Involvement of an orientation and mobility instructor is also of foremost importance for blind students. Working with students with a visual loss is very time-consuming and requires considerably more effort than working with most sighted students. However, despite the special needs of visually impaired students and the limitations of current measures, a surprising amount of worthwhile information can be obtained from a comprehensive assessment, and beneficial recommendations can be made for these students.

ACKNOWLEDGMENTS

We greatly appreciated the assistance of Bill Duckworth in the preparation of this material. His support, suggestions, and help with numerous questions were invaluable.

REFERENCES

Alessi, G., & Kaye, J. H. (1983). *Behavior assessment for school psychologists.* Stratford, CT: NASP Publications Office.

American Printing House for the Blind. (1987). *Federal Quota Registration.* Louisville, KY: Author.

Boehm, A. (1971). *Boehm Test of Basic Concepts*. San Antonio: Psychological Corporation.

Bradley-Johnson, S. (1986). *Psychoeducational assessment of visually impaired and blind students*. Austin, TX: PRO-ED.

Brigance, A. (1983). *Brigance Diagnostic Comprehensive Inventory of Basic Skills*. North Billerica, MA: Curriculum Associates.

Brown, L., & Leigh, J. E. (1986). *Adaptive Behavior Inventory*. Austin, TX: PRO-ED.

Caton, H. (1976). *Tactile Test of Basic Concepts*. Louisville, KY: American Printing House for the Blind.

Caton, H., Duckworth, B., & Rankin, E. (1985). *Braille Unit Recognition Battery*. Louisville, KY: American Printing House for the Blind.

Caton, H., Pester, H., & Bradley, E. J. (1980). *Patterns: The primary braille reading program*. Louisville, KY: American Printing House for the Blind.

Connolly, A., Nachtman, W., & Pritchett, E. M. (1976). *KeyMath Diagnostic Arithmetic Test*. Circle Pines, MN: American Guidance Service.

Davis, C. (1980). *Perkins-Binet Test of Intelligence for the Blind*. Watertown, MA: Perkins School for the Blind.

Dolch, E. (1955). *Methods in reading*. Champaign, IL: Garrard.

Duckworth, B. (1988). *Tactile Supplement to the Brigance Diagnostic Comprehensive Inventory of Basic Skills*. Louisville, KY: American Printing House for the Blind.

Duckworth, B. (1989). *Administration manual for the Stanford Achievement Test*. Louisville, KY: American Printing House for the Blind.

Foxx, R. M., & Azrin, N. H. (1973). The elimination of autistic self-stimulation behavior by overcorrection. *Journal of Applied Behavior Analysis, 6*, 1–14.

Gilbert, J., & Rubin, E. (1965). Evaluating the intellect of blind children. *New Outlook for the Blind, 59*, 238–240.

Hammill, D. D. (1985). *Detroit Tests of Learning Aptitude–2*. Austin, TX: PRO-ED.

Hammill, D. D., & Leigh, J. E. (1983). *Basic School Skills Inventory–Diagnostic*. Austin, TX: PRO-ED.

Hammill, D. D., & Newcomer, P. L. (1982). *Test of Language Development–2 Intermediate*. Austin, TX: PRO-ED.

Jastak, J., & Jastak, S. (1984). *Wide Range Achievement Test*. Wilmington, DE: Jastak Associates.

Kelly, J. A., & Drabman, R. S. (1977). Generalizing response suppression of self-injurious behavior through an overcorrection punishment procedure: A case study. *Behavior Therapy, 8*, 468–472.

Newborg, J., Stock, J. R., Wnek, L., Guidubaldi, J., & Svinicki, J. (1984). *Battelle Developmental Inventory*. Allen, TX: DLM/Teaching Resources.

Newcomer, P. L., & Hammill, D. D. (1988). *Test of Language Development–2 Primary*. Austin, TX: PRO-ED.

Newland, R. E. (1971). *Blind Learning Aptitude Test*. Champaign, IL: University of Illinois Press.

Poppen, R. (1988). *Behavioral relaxation training and assessment*. New York: Pergamon.

Psychological Corporation. (1988a). *Stanford Achievement Test*. San Antonio, TX: Author.

Psychological Corporation. (1986). *Test of Academic Skills*. San Antonio, TX: Author.

Public Law 94-142. (1975). Washington, DC: Educational Amendments.

Raver, S. (1987). Training blind children to employ appropriate gaze direction and sitting behavior during conversation. *Education and Treatment of Children, 10*, 237–246.

Salvia, J., & Ysseldyke, J. (1981). *Assessment in special and remedial education*. Boston: Houghton Mifflin.

Scholl, G. T. (1983). Assessing the visually impaired child. In S. Ray, M. J. O'Neill, & N. T. Morris (Eds.), *Low incidence children: A guide to psychoeducational assessment* (pp. 67–90). Natchitoches, LA: Steven Ray.

Scholl, G. T. (1986). *Foundations of education for blind and visually handicapped children and youth*. New York: American Foundation for the Blind.

Sparrow, S., Balla, D., & Cicchetti, D. V. (1984). *Vineland Adaptive Behavior Scale*. Circle Pines, MN: American Guidance Service.

Swallow, R., Mangold, S., & Mangold, P. (1978). *Informal Assessment of Developmental Skills for Visually Handicapped Students*. New York: American Foundation for the Blind.

Tillman, M. H., & Osborne, R. T. (1969). The performance of blind and sighted children on the *Wechsler Intelligence Scale for Children:* Interaction effects. *Education of the Visually Handicapped, 1*, 1–4.

Wechsler, D. (1949). *Wechsler Intelligence Scale for Children*. San Antonio, TX: Psychological Corporation.

Wechsler, D. (1967). *Wechsler Preschool and Primary Scale of Intelligence.* San Antonio: Psychological Corporation.

Wechsler, D. (1974). *Wechsler Intelligence Scale for Children–Revised.* San Antonio, TX: Psychological Corporation.

Wechsler, D. (1981). *Wechsler Adult Intelligence Scale–Revised.* San Antonio, TX: Psychological Corporation.

Williams, M. (1956). *The Williams Scale for Children With Defective Vision.* Montreal: Institute of Psychological Research.

ANNOTATED BIBLIOGRAPHY

Alessi, G., & Kaye, J. H. (1983). *Behavior assessment for school psychologists.* Stratford, CT: NASP Publications Office.
This manual describes various methods for carrying out systematic direct observation. The manual and procedures were designed to fit the needs of school psychologists. A videotape is available for use in practicing the coding systems.

American Printing House for the Blind (APH). PO Box 6085, Louisville, KY 40206. (502) 895-2405.
The Printing House has the latest in educational aids and materials. Also, APH publishes adapted and transcribed tests for use with visually impaired persons as well as braille, large type, and recorded books, and magazines. The APH is a national nonprofit organization that publishes materials solely for visually impaired persons.

Bradley-Johnson, S. (1986). *Psychological assessment of visually impaired and blind students: Infancy through high school.* Austin, TX: PRO-ED.
This book contains extensive reviews of norm- and criterion-referenced tests including technical adequacy, and a summary of each test's strengths and weaknesses for use with students with a visual loss. Information is included on assessment procedures and on developmental delays that are often found with these children during infancy and preschool age.

Caton, H., Pester, H., & Bradley, E. J. (1980). *Patterns: The primary braille reading program.* Louisville, KY: American Printing House for the Blind.
This reading program is for students who will use braille as their primary medium for reading. The program is made up of six levels from readiness through the third reader. Each level has a student's book, a set of consumable worksheets, a teacher's manual, a criterion-referenced posttest, and consumable review worksheets. Characters in the stories include a partially sighted child, and the content covers real life and fantasy.

Raver, S. (1987). Training blind children to employ appropriate gaze direction and sitting behavior during conversation. *Education and Treatment of Children, 10,* 237–246.
This study describes a procedure involving discussion, modeling, physical prompting feedback, and positive reinforcement that was successful in teaching five congenitally blind children to use appropriate gaze direction and sitting when engaged in conversation.

Scholl, G. (1986). *Foundations of education for blind and visually handicapped children and youth.* New York: The American Foundation for the Blind.
This edited text covers development of children with a visual loss from infancy to adulthood. Some areas covered are definitions, theories, resources, media, technology, communication, orientation and mobility, social skills, and curricular adaptations. Issues in implementing a quality educational program are discussed. The book is very comprehensive. Material is presented from a practical point of view so that it can be easily applied in the classroom.

60

Best Practices in Credentialing and Continuing Professional Development

George M. Batsche
University of South Florida

OVERVIEW

Basic Assumptions and Foundations

Credentialing. Although the term *school psychology* appeared as early as 1915, the credentialing of school psychologists is a much more recent occurrence. Forty years ago only seven states credentialed school psychologists. Since that time, credentialing has grown to include virtually every state in the United States and includes certification as well as licensure. The term *credentialing* in school psychology has changed throughout the period of time that school psychologists have been recognized. Its predominant use, both in the early history of school psychology and at present, reflects the requirement by state departments of education that school psychologists must be certified to practice in the public schools. More recently, however, the term has been expanded to include licensure and/or certification to practice school psychology in the private sector (Knoff & Batsche, 1987). The credentialing process for the practice of school psychology in the public schools is called *certification*. Certification statutes, most often administered by state teacher certification boards, regulate the title "school psychologist."

The credentialing process for the practice of school psychology independently (outside of the school setting, more commonly known as "private practice"), is generally known as *licensure*, and it is administered by psychology licensing boards. Although the doctoral-level practice of generic psychology is typically permitted through the use of a "license" given by state psychology licensure boards, the independent practice of school psychology is legitimated through a number of methods. Some states provide a "license" for the independent practice of school psychology (Ohio, Florida); others provide an "exemption" from the psychology licensing law (e.g., Illinois). No license or certificate is issued but school psychologists practice in the private sector while using their certificate issued by the teacher certification board. Finally, some states (e.g., Wisconsin) provide an exemption certificate. Actual certificates are issued by the state psychology licensing boards that exempts the school psychologists from the doctoral licensing requirements, as long as they practice school psychology as prescribed by state law. Licensure statutes regulate the title *and* practice of school psychology. The difference is important. In states where there is certification, only professionals certified as school psychologists may call themselves *school psychologists*. The actual practice of school psychology (e.g., administering psychoeducational tests) may be carried out by any number of professionals in the school setting. In states where there is licensure, one can engage in a particular practice (e.g., administering psychoeducational tests) only if such "practice" is delineated in the licensure statute. A number of regulated professions may have the same "practice" specified in their licensure statutes, however.

Whether credentialing reflects certification for public school practice or licensure for private practice, the major influences on credentialing in school psychology have historically been felt at the state level. Nationally, certification policy for state departments of education is influenced most directly by the National Association of State Directors of Teacher Education and Certification (NASDTEC). Individual state departments credential school psychologists to practice in their state, and the role of professional associations has been to influence the state credentialing process, not to create it (Batsche, Knoff, & Peterson, 1989). In a similar manner, the role of professional associations has been to influence the state psychology licensure boards in the area of licensure, not to create it. Nationally, licensure policy for state psychology licensing boards is influenced most directly by the American Association of State Psychology Boards (AASPB) and the American Psychological Association (APA). In school psychology, unlike other professional areas, school psychologists do not directly control their own certification at the state level. This is done by state department of education certification boards, composed primarily of teachers. This is a unique situation in which members of a given profession do not have direct control of their own credentialing process. Historically, school psychologists have most often relied on legislative and administrative rules changes in order to affect certification and licensure because direct access to the decision makers was not available. Therefore, methods of changing certification and licensure in school psychology require more creativity and more involvement with a wider range of groups, allied across two professional areas: education and psychology.

Assumptions. The situation described above leads to the following assumptions.

1. The majority of school psychologists will receive credentialing through certification by state teacher certification boards.
2. Credentialing requirement decisions, at the state level, will be made by professionals other than school psychologists (teachers, administrators, university personnel on certification boards).
3. Because certification controls only title, there will be other professionals in the school district who will engage in professional practices similar to the practices of school psychologists.
4. Changes in school psychology certification will often come about through legislative action.

Continuing professional development. Continuing professional development (CPD) requirements, unlike certification requirements, are in place in relatively few states. Although professional associations have long recognized the value of CPD, few state teacher certification boards have required CPD hours for renewal of certificates. Therefore, CPD has been viewed more as a "best practice," something that is left up to individual professionals, rather than a requirement. Many professional associations, at both the state and national levels, have methods of recognizing professionals who participate in such CPD programs. However, the number of practitioners reporting CPD hours is relatively few in such voluntary programs.

Until recently, there has been no pressure to require CPD. One of the effects of the Excellence in Education movement has been to place an emphasis on continuing education for professionals in the schools. There may be a number of reasons why educators have been slower to respond to CPD requirements than other professional groups. First, there are usually a number of "institute" days set aside each year for continuing education. As these are required and may add up to 24 contact hours a year, educators feel that this is as stringent as most CPD requirements. However, there is seldom a plan or organized way in which these institutes are delivered. As well, the topics do not necessarily meet the individual needs of teachers, and it proves even more difficult to meet the individual needs of such a diverse group of professionals (school psychologists, counselors, speech therapists, occupational therapists, etc.) as is found in the schools. Second, mandatory CPD requires some type of monitoring and documentation system. This will increase the cost of a state certification program and certainly increase the cost of certificate renewal. This increased cost is passed on to the individual professional. Third, a required CPD program in a system that has not previously required such a program implies that practitioners have not been meeting their professional obligations on their own. Professionals may resent this implication and oppose such a system. Therefore, CPD programs must be delivered in such a way that (a) educators feel that their professional growth needs are being met while no deficiency in their skills is implied, and (b) that they are documented in an easy, cost-efficient way.

Assumptions. The above considerations suggest the following assumptions.

1. Relatively few individuals will participate in a voluntary CPD program.
2. Best practices and actual practices will remain very divergent.
3. CPD programs may remain difficult to implement because of cost and documentation difficulties.
4. Resistance will arise from a number of sources: perception of little need, perception of difficulty to document, high cost, and feelings that a required CPD program violates individual professional freedoms.

Brief History and Background

Credentialing. The profession of school psychology has had an extremely short history of statutory regulation. In 1946, only seven states (Connecticut, Maine, Nebraska, New York, Ohio, Indiana, and Pennsylvania) certified school psychologists (Horrocks, 1946). Brown (1982) noted that an estimated 20 states were certifying school psychologists in 1956 and

38 states by 1967; and that virtually all states had credentialing regulations for school psychology by 1979. More recently, Prus (1987) noted that 45 states certify a position with the label *school psychology* at the nondoctoral level, four states reserved the label for doctoral level exclusively, and two states certified persons utilizing some other title (educational diagnostician, psychological examiner). Brown (1982) noted that 11 states had enacted licensure provisions for the independent practice of school psychology. Block (1985) conducted a survey composed of 35 responding state associations that indicated that 10 states were identified as having some provision for the independent practice of school psychology and three others reported that such proposals had been submitted to their respective legislatures. Most recently, Prus (1987) reported that 18 states have some type of provision (school psychology, generic psychology, psychological examiner, etc.) for nondoctoral independent practice. Of these, 7 have nondoctoral independent practice privileges in school psychology, and 4 states have independent practice privileges in school psychology at the doctoral level.

Continuing professional development. The National Association of School Psychologists (NASP) introduced an original professional development certificate program in 1975 (Walker, 1977). In the first 2 years of operation, only 3% of the NASP membership requested applications and only 1% of the NASP membership actually applied. This prompted a major revision of the system in 1977. However, the number of people participating in the CPD recognition program did not increase significantly, and NASP dropped the CPD program in 1984. Apparently, without required CPD, school psychologists felt that the CPD recognition system either was not necessary or did not provide a desirable service. The NASP CPD system utilized a "cafeteria" approach, recognizing three competency areas (assessment and evaluation, intervention and remediation, program planning, development and research). CPD activities were required in all three areas within a 3-year period. In order to earn a CPD certificate, 50 contact hours of CPD were required in *each* competency (150 contact hours total). A Special Certificate of Distinction was awarded to those who earned three CPD certificates within a 5-year period. CPD units could be earned through activities that fell into five categories: accredited college or university courses, formal workshops and seminars, attendance at professional gatherings, teaching and instruction, and documentation related to research and development (publications, presentations, program planning). The original NASP CPD program attempted to recognize major areas of practice and research utilizing a number of flexible activity categories. It was a well-conceived and "available" program. However, the lack of incentive to participate in light of the few state requirements mandating CPD activities for certificate renewal resulted in a program with very few participants.

BASIC CONSIDERATIONS

Current Practices

Credentialing. Current guidelines for credentialing in school psychology have been influenced by two sources. NASP has published the *Standards for the Credentialing of School Psychologists* (1985) and the APA has published the *Specialty Guidelines for the Delivery of Services by School Psychologists* (1981). NASP is committed to 60 semester hours of training (specialist level) and a full-year internship of at least 1,200 hours, 600 hours of which must be in a school setting. The APA *Guidelines* suggest a two-tiered system in which the professional school psychologist has earned a doctoral degree from an APA approved program or the equivalent and the (60-hour) specialist in school psychology has completed at least 2 years of school psychological training with at least 1,000 hours of experience supervised by a professional school psychologist. The APA *Guidelines* also allow for a transition period until 1995 by which an individual who has attained

the specialist degree, state certification in school psychology and "at least three additional years of training and experience in school psychological services, including a minimum of 1,200 hours in school settings" (p. 680) will be considered a professional school psychologist when practicing in elementary and secondary schools (Batsche, Knoff, & Peterson, 1989). The NASP credentialing standards specify credentialing requirements in three areas: personal characteristics, educational qualifications, and practitioner competencies. The educational qualifications specify not only the 60 semester hours and the 1200-clock-hour internship but program content as well. Specifically, the NASP standards require that school psychologists must have preparation in the areas listed in Table 1. In addition, these same standards specify two levels of practice: entry and independent. The independent level requires fulfilling all of the requirements for entry level as well as having successfully completed 3 years of supervised experience and participation in CPD activities specified in NASP's *Standards for the Provision of School Psychological Services* (1984a).

At the present time, only 15 states meet the NASP credentialing standards in respect to semester hours (60) and internship (1,200 clock hours). An additional 11 states require the 60 semester hours of credit for academic training but have internship requirements with fewer than 1,200 clock hours. All other states have requirements of less than 60 semester hours of academic preparation and 1,200-clock-hour internships. At the present time, 11 states currently offer some type of licensure/registration for the practice of school psychology at the non-doctoral level in the private sector. See Table 2 for a summary of these states.

Continuing professional development. Seventeen states currently require CPD for doctoral license renewal; 33 do not (Prus, 1987). Three of the 11 states that currently provide for some type of independent practice in school psychology require CPD. Analysis of the information

TABLE 1
Educational Requirements to Meet NASP Credentialing Standards

Psychological Foundations
    Biological Bases of Behavior
    Cultural Diversity
    Child and Adolescent Development (normal and abnormal)
    Human Exceptionalities
    Human Learning
    Social Bases of Behavior

Educational Foundations
    Education of Exceptional Learners
    Instruction and Remedial Techniques
    Organization and Operation of Schools

Assessment

Interventions (direct and indirect)
    Consultation
    Counseling
    Behavior Management

Statistics and Research Design

Professional School Psychology
    History and Foundations of School Psychology
    Legal and Ethical Issues
    Professional Issues and Standards
    Roles and Functions of the School Psychologist

in the Prus (1987) manual indicates that 24 of the 50 states require CPD for school psychology certificate renewal. Thirteen of the 24 limit CPD activities to university coursework. Clearly, there are some forces of resistance in a system in which fewer than 50% of the states require CPD.

The CPD requirements for school psychology are typically related to generic requirements for certificate renewal in all educational areas for a given state. Few, if any, state school psychology associations require CPD for membership or renewal of membership. Therefore, current practice indicates that in states where CPD is required, there is substantial documentation of such activities; but in states where there is no requirement, there is little documentation of such activities. Documentation practices in voluntary systems vary widely. The range of practices include the following: no

requirements for CPD documentation, only a statement of participation; no ceilings on the types of activities for which one can earn CPD credits (for instance, all credits might be earned by self-study); rigid rules on documentation and range of activities required for CPD credit (course work, seminars, workshops, self-study, etc.). Some state school psychology associations collate and keep records of individual members' CPD activities (Illinois), while some state departments of education offices provide a similar service for school psychology. NASP is currently conducting such research (P. Harrison, personal communication, October 1, 1989).

In summary, CPD practices vary widely. The majority of state certification offices and state school psychology associations provide no requirements or guidelines. Recently, however, such re-

TABLE 2
Type of Independent Practice in School Psychology by State

State	Type of Licensure/Certification
California	Specialty license.
Connecticut	Exemption from license law through amending school certification law to apply to public and private sector.
Florida	Specialty license within generic law. Three years of experience required.
Illinois	Exemption from clinical psychologists licensure law. Three years of experience required.
Maine	Generic law with licensing at master's level as a certified school psychological examiner. One year of experience required.
Massachusetts	1974 law allows independent practice by certified school psychologists.
North Carolina	Generic law with licensing at master's level as "psychological associate."
Ohio	Specialty licensure within generic law. Four years of experience required.
Oregon	"Psychologist Associate" at the master's level with specialty area of school psychologist identified. Four years of experience required.
Virginia	Specialty license within generic law. Four years of experience required.
Wisconsin	Specialty license within generic law. One year of experience required.

quirements and guidelines appear to be developing and are being pursued by state associations and certification offices.

BEST PRACTICES

National School Psychology Certification System

Credentialing. A major reason why the NASP credentialing standards are met by fewer than 20 states is that professional associations are limited in their ability to affect state-level credentialing. Although NASP has advocated for the specialist level credentialing standard for over a decade, there has been little change in state credentialing requirements during that time. Therefore NASP determined that a national credential, controlled by a professional association, would provide a vehicle with which to highlight and implement credentialing standards developed by school psychologists. In order to accomplish this task, NASP created the National School Psychology Certification System (NSPCS), administered by the National School Psychology Certification

Board (NSPCB) (Batsche, 1989). The purpose of the NSPCS is to (a) provide uniform credentialing standards across states, agencies, and training institutions; (b) monitor the implementation of NASP credentialing standards at the national level; (c) promote continuing professional development (CPD) for school psychologists; (d) facilitate credentialing of school psychologists across states through the use of reciprocity; (e) ensure a consistent level of training and experience in service providers who are nationally certified; (f) promote the utilization of NASP *Standards for Training and Field Placement Programs in School Psychology* by training institutions; and (g) encourage individual school psychologists to seek national certification.

In order to be eligible for national certification, the requirements cited in Table 3 must be met.

Although reciprocity is not yet automatic, those who meet the requirements for national certification meet or exceed the certification requirements in 47 of the 50 states (Texas, Hawaii, and Maine continue to require a doctoral degree in

TABLE 3
NASP Requirements for National Certification

Degree: Completion of a sixth year/specialist (master's degree plus thirty (30) graduate hour minumum) program consisting of course work, practica, internship and an appropriate graduate degree from an accredited institution of higher learning.[a]

Internship: Successful completion of a 1200 hour internship in school psychology, of which 600 hours must be in a school setting.

Certification: Applicants must hold state certification/licensure to practice school psychology.

Examination: Applicants must achieve a passing score on the National School Psychology Examination administered by Educational Testing Service.

Renewal: Triennial renewal contingent upon completion of 75 contact hours of continuing professional development.

---

[a]Graduates of NASP approved programs automatically meet this requirement. All other applicants must meet the *Standards for Training and Field Placement in School Psychology.*

Note. From *Standards for Training and Field Placement in School Psychology,* NASP (1984).

---

order to use the title *school psychologist*). National certification, therefore, is the best vehicle available to insure that certification is possible across the country. A few individual states continue to have some requirements that prevent "automatic" reciprocity (such as a state-specific examination, short-term supervision, AIDS education requirement). Obtaining national certification can be viewed as a best practice in credentialing for a number of reasons: (a) It can facilitate certification across states for practitioners who hold the nationally certified school psychologist (NCSP) certificate. The National School Psychology Certification Board publishes the *Directory of Nationally Certified School Psychologists* (1989) and disseminates this document to all state certification boards in an effort to facilitate reciprocity. (b) It can ensure a consistent, yet broad range of educational requirements within the profession. (c) It can provide consumers with professionals who hold a credential (NCSP) that is consistent, regardless of state certification titles. School psychology began with individuals providing school psychology services while using 75 different titles and credentials (Tindall, 1979). (d) The NCSP certificate requirement can be used as a blueprint for either certification or licen-

sure by state school psychology associations seeking to obtain or change certification or licensure standards in their own states.

Educational Testing Service (ETS), with technical assistance from NASP, developed the national school psychology examination. NASP wanted to ensure that a quality examination was developed (as long as states were already requiring one) and that a single, quality examination was utilized, rather than many state-specific ones. To that end, NASP included the examination as part of the NCSP credential requirement and encouraged individual states to adopt the examination if state law required one. To date, this has been very successful, with many states adopting the national examination for state use. The use of the national school psychology examination developed by ETS for NASP is to be considered a best practice for the following reasons: (a) The examination was developed by utilizing the latest principles in professional competency examination procedures (Batsche, 1987). (b) It was developed by school psychologists for school psychologists. (c) It has undergone extensive validity studies and is a psychometrically sound test. (d) It is an applied test, based upon a national job analysis survey in school psychology (DeMauro, 1989). (e) State-level passing scores can be obtained by conducting a state-based validity study. This enables individual states to set their own passing score.

As mentioned earlier, different states have utilized different methods of achieving certification of independent practice in school psychology (licensure, exemption, exemption with certificate). A major concern of state licensure boards is the provision of adequate protection for consumers in the form of complaint procedures. In some states, the jurisdiction for monitoring complaints in independent practice is unclear, particularly where there is a simple "exemption" clause (does the state board of education or the state licensing board monitor complaints?). Therefore, best practices for independent practice (through licensure or certification) in school psychology should include the following: (a) use of the NASP *Standards for the Credentialing of School Psychologists* (1985) to set training and experience requirements; (b) use of the NASP *Standards for the Provision of School Psychological Services* (1984a) to set scope of practice; (c) a policy clearly delineating which agency is responsible for the monitoring and regulatory responsibility for the license or certificate; (d) issuance of a "license" or "certificate" by the responsible agency; and (d) specific use of the NASP *Principles for Professional Ethics* (1984).

The majority of school psychologists trained at the nondoctoral level will have exposure to the NASP ethics, training, credentialing, and service provider standards. Therefore, it is logical to include in licensure laws standards that are consistent with the training and experience of those providing the services.

The best practices in credentialing can be summarized by the following recommendations to a prospective school psychology student seeking guidance in nondoctoral entry into the profession:

1. Enroll in a NASP-approved specialist-level training program in school psychology or a specialist-level program that meets the program content requirements listed above.
2. Complete a 1,200-hour, supervised internship in school psychology. At least 600 hours of the internship must be completed in a school setting.
3. Take the national school psychology examination during the spring semester of the internship year or during the summer following the internship year.
4. Apply for the Nationally Certified School Psychologist (NCSP) Certificate.
5. Obtain 3 years of supervised experience following initial certification. This will require taking a job in a setting in which supervision is possible by a school psychologist with 3 years of experience. It will meet the NASP guidelines for the "independent" level of credentialing. The 3 years of supervised experience is a requirement for *nondoctoral* licensure in many states (see Table 2).

Continuing Professional Development. The *Standards for the Provision of School Psychological Services* (NASP, 1984a) specify that all school psychologists must engage in activities designed to enhance their professional training and skills. Professionals who hold the NCSP *must* meet the CPD requirement of 75 contact hours each 3 years in order to renew the NCSP certificate. In addition, some states require documentation of CPD for state certification renewal. To date, the only system that requires participation and documentation of CPD on a national level is the NASP CPD program tied to the NCSP certificate renewal. The NASP CPD program is available to all NASP members on a voluntary basis but is a requirement for all NCSP certificate holders, both members and nonmembers (Danielson, 1989).

The NASP CPD program recognizes six skill development areas: consultation, psychological and psychoeducational assessment, intervention, supervision, research, and program planning and evaluation. There are 12 different activities or methods of meeting the CPD requirement of participation in at least three of the six skill development areas. These activities range from attendance at conferences/workshops, to self-study (see Appendix V, Attachment A, this volume).

There are a number of features of the NASP CPD program that can be regarded as best practices: (a) The program identifies a wide range of skill development areas. This recognizes the diverse settings and applications of school psychology services encountered by practicing school psychologists. (b) The program utilizes many (12) methods of building skills. This recognizes that not all school psychologists have access to the same number of workshops, courses, conventions, or other more restrictive activities. Instead, emphasis is intentionally placed on activities other than university coursework, including informal and sequenced self-study, intern supervision, professional organization leadership, and presentations. (c) Documentation is simple and easy. (d) Although there is a requirement for CPD in a minimum number of skills, the number (three of six) gives individual school psychologists flexibility in order to meet their personal and work-related needs.

The NASP credentialing standards, the National School Psychology Certification System, and the continuing professional development program all provide a "blueprint" to guide state certification officers, university-based training programs, and state school psychology associations in the credentialing, training, and postcredentialing CPD of school psychologists. The question then arises, How are these programs implemented at a state level?

Contemporary Methods of Credentialing at the State Level: Multiple Approaches to Problem Solving

Legislative. State legislatures create statutes that assign state teacher certification boards the authority to set requirements for certification in school psychology. Similarly, legislatures create statutes that provide licensure boards the authority to set requirements for independent practice. One method of influencing certification and licensure is to change the laws that such boards must adhere to in the development of certification and licensure standards. Nondoctoral licensure has been accomplished successfully in a number of states (Wisconsin, Illinois, Florida, Virginia, and others). Influencing the decisions of the legislature directly often avoids the political difficulties encountered with certification and licensure boards. State school psychology associations can, through lobbying a legislative committee, coordinate the introduction, advocacy, and passage of such laws. This has been carried out recently (1989) in Illinois, where it accomplished modification of the statute governing *certification* of school psychologists. State school psychology associations are creating legislative networks and political action committees, hiring professional lobbyists, and networking with allied professional groups in order to affect credentialing standards. The majority of laws initiated by state school psychology associations are in the area of credentialing.

Administrative. Attempts to change credentialing standards at the certification or licensure board level is often achieved through administrative changes. University training programs can often play a significant role in modifying certification standards through changes in administrative rule making (change in requirements by the board itself). NASP is a full voting member of the National Association for the Accreditation of Teacher Education (NCATE), the body that accredits teacher education programs. The NASP training standards must be met in the NASP/NCATE accreditation process. As university training programs change their requirements in order to meet NASP accreditation standards, state certification boards will note that new students graduating in that state are meeting different (usually higher) standards. The inconsistency between the state certification requirements (lower) and graduation requirements (higher) is often sufficient to lead to development of new certification standards. In order for this to occur, however, all of the universities that train school psychologists in a given state must agree to raise their training standards. This is often accomplished through interuniversity councils. This procedure has been successful in many states. Certification boards often view raising standards as a threat to providing adequate numbers of practitioners; to date, however, there is no evidence that raising standards diminishes the pool of available school psychologists. To the contrary, a state that has quality training programs will attract students from out of state and increase the number of available school psychologists for certification.

State school psychology associations can fill the role of coordinating and facilitating efforts to change credentialing requirements. State associations have the vehicles (legislative committees, liaisons with state departments and universities, political action committees and lobbyists) to achieve these goals. The goals are best achieved in a state with strong interuniversity cooperation and a belief that school psychologists should determine the credentialing standards for their own profession.

Contemporary Methods in Continuing Professional Development: Multiple Approaches to Service Delivery

The NASP CPD program is currently the only model designed for national implementation. In order for CPD programs to succeed they must adopt the following best practices and recognize multiple methods of service delivery:

1. They must recognize that school psychologists work in many service delivery settings that require a wide range of skills.
2. They must recognize that school psychologists have different opportunities available to achieve skill development. Traditional and nontraditional methods of skill development must be available.
3. They must recognize that school districts, state and national associations, and state boards of education may have existing documentation requirements for CPD. Any successful system must

recognize and accept CPD documentation from these systems. Individual school psychologists should only have to document each activity once. One system should recognize the documentation system of the other.
4. Finally they must recognize that the individual school psychologist knows his or her needs best and is in the best position to select required skill areas.

The NASP CPD system has attempted to incorporate all of the above best practices. The text of the system, with documentation sheets, is in Appendix A, this volume.

SUMMARY

Credentialing and continuing professional development in school psychology have changed significantly, the greatest changes occurring in recent years. Current trends suggest that although the greatest increase in students is in the doctoral training area (Curtis & Zins, 1989), there is no general increase in the requirement of the doctorate for credentialing in school psychology. In fact, the number of states requiring the doctoral degree for certification has dropped. Conversely, the number of states moving to the 60-semester-hour coursework program and 1,200-clock-hour internship has slowly increased. There may be a greater number of doctoral school psychologists entering the public schools, but this will not be due to an increase in the credentialing requirements. In the area of licensure, there has been little movement at the nondoctoral level. Given the increase in the number of students in doctoral training, it is only logical to assume that there will be an increase in the number of school psychologists seeking doctoral licensure in the private sector. In a recent survey (Reschly, Genshaft, & Binder, 1987) 78% of school psychologists surveyed indicated that they wished to seek licensure.

Although the number of students in doctoral training has increased, the reflection of that increase in the field has yet to be seen. The percentage of doctoral-level school psychologists continues to be approximately 23% (Reschly et al., 1987; DeMauro, 1989). Fagan (1989) speculates that it will be the year 2050 before the profession is predominantly doctoral. Given current trends in training and state certification, it appears that the specialist level will prevail as the entry level in school psychology for this and the next generation of school psychologists.

The advent of the NSPCS and the national school psychology certificate promise to facilitate a model certification/licensure and reciprocity program across states. This program clearly represents a best practice in setting standards for certification/licensure boards and for the training of prospective school psychology students. Perhaps the "sleeper" benefit of the NSPCS will be the CPD requirements for school psychologists. Because the CPD requirement is mandated for renewal of national certification, school psychologists may be able to use this requirement for additional support and release time from their place of employment in order to pursue skills development. This will translate into improved services for teachers, children, and families.

School psychology has searched for a method of implementing best practices in credentialing and continuing professional development. I suggest that the search has substantially ended, for the near future, with the blueprints provided by the National School Psychology Certification System and the NASP Continuing Professional Development Program.

REFERENCES

American Psychological Association. (1981). *Specialty guidelines for the delivery of services by school psychologists.* Washington, DC: Author.

Batsche, G. (1987). A national school psychology certification system. *Communiqué, 16*(3), 1-2.

Batsche, G. (1988). Standardization of the national school psychology examination. *Communiqué, 16*(8), 14.

Batsche, G., Knoff, H., & Peterson, D. (1989). Trends in credentialing and practice standards. *School Psychology Review, 18*, 193-202.

Block, N. (1985). NASP independent practice task force summary of December, 1984 survey. In D. Hill & N. Block (Eds.), *Independent practice of school psychology* (pp. 14-25). Stratford, CT: NASP Publications.

Brown, D. B. (1982). Issues in the development of professional school psychology. In C. R. Reynolds & T. B. Gutkin (Eds.), *Handbook of school psychology* (pp. 14-23). New York: Wiley.

Curtis, M. J., & Zins, J. (1989). Trends in training and accreditation. *School Psychology Review, 18*(2), 182-192.

Danielson, E. (1989). The NASP continuing professional development program. *Communiqué, 17*(7), 7-9.

DeMauro, G. (1989). *Knowledge areas important to the job of a school psychologist.* Unpublished manuscript. Princeton, NJ: Educational Testing Service.

Directory of Nationally Certified School Psychologists. (1989). Washington, DC: National Association of School Psychologists.

Fagan, T. (1989). Guest editor's commentary on the entry-level debate. *School Psychology Review, 18*(1), 34-36.

Hill, D., & Block, N. (1987). *Independent practice of school psychology: A handbook for action.* Stratford, CT: NASP Publications.

Horrochs, J. E. (1946). State certification requirements for school psychologists. *American Psychologist, 1*, 399-401.

Knoff, H., & Batsche, G. (1987). The revised credentialing standards of the National Association of School Psychologists: Implications for independent practice in school psychology *Professional Practice of Psychology, 8*, 7-17.

National Association of School Psychologists. (1984b). *Standards for training and field placement programs in school psychology.* Washington, DC: Author.

National Association of School Psychologists. (NASP). (1984a). *Standards for the provision of school psychological services.* Washington, DC: Author.

National Association of School Psychologists. (1985). *Standards for the credentialing of school psychologists.* Washington, DC: Author.

National Association of School Psychologists. (1988). *National School Psychology Certification System.* Washington, DC: Author.

Prus, J., White, G., & Pendleton, A. (1988). *Handbook of certification/licensure requirements for school psychologists* (4th ed.). Washington, DC: National Association of School Psychologists.

Reschly, D. J., Genshaft, J. L., & Binder, M. S. (1987). *The 1986 NASP survey: Comparisons of practitioners, NASP leadership and university faculty on key issues.* Washington, DC: National Association of School Psychologists.

Tindall, R. H. (1979). School psychology: The development of a profession. In G. D. Phye & D. J. Reschly (Eds.), *School psychology: Perspectives and issues* (pp. 3-24). New York: Academic.

Walker, W. N. (1977). The NASP certificate program for continuing professional development (CPD)- revised. *School Psychology Digest, 6,* 70-79.

ANNOTATED BIBLIOGRAPHY

Knoff, H., & Batsche, G. (1987). The revised credentialing standards of the National Association of School Psychologists: Implications for independent practice in school psychology. *Professional Practice of Psychology, 8,* 7-17.
The article compares the 1978 and 1985 *Standards for the Credentialing of School Psychologists* and specifically applies the 1985 *Standards* to the independent practice of school psychology. This article would be helpful for individuals in states that were contemplating a change in the certification standards for school psychologists. It would be particularly useful for state associations that were attempting to obtain licensure in school psychology.

Danielson, E. (1989). The NASP continuing professional development program. *Communiqué, 17*(7), 7-9.
This is the first publication that fully described the NASP CPD program. The articles contain a full program description, requirements, methods of achieving CPD credits, credit conversion tables, and documentation forms. This article is ideal for persons wishing to participate in CPD or state associations wishing to obtain a "blueprint" to utilize in a particular state.

Hill, D., & Block, N. (1987). *Independent practice of school psychology: A handbook for action.* Stratford, CT: NASP Publications.
This publication provides information with which states have achieved nondoctoral licensure in school psychology, a description of the types of licensure, copies of model licensure acts, and steps taken by individual states to obtain licensure. This is the only publication available that conducts a comparative analysis of all the states that currently have nondoctoral licensure in school psychology.

National Association of School Psychologists. (1988). *National School Psychology Certification System.* Washington, DC: Author.
This document contains a description of the National School Psychology Certification System, including criteria for application and application materials. This is the document that should be requested by those wishing to obtain national certification.

Prus, J., White, G., & Pendleton, A. (1988). *Handbook of certification/licensure requirements for school psychologists* (4th ed.). Washington, DC: National Association of School Psychologists.
This book is the most recent complilation of state-by-state requirements for both certification and licensure in school psychology. Application procedures, state contacts, and a comparative analysis of all 50 states and the District of Columbia are provided. The use of a standardized format allows an easy comparison of state standards.

61

A Summary of Certification and Licensure Requirements for School Psychologists

Joseph S. Prus
Garry W. White
Winthrop College
Rock Hill, South Carolina

Certification and licensure are crucial aspects of the credentialing process for school psychologists. In addition to ensuring minimum levels of training and experience needed for entry level professionals, certification and licensure requirements have important practical implications for students, trainers, practitioners, and administrators. Such requirements influence standards for training, level of independent professional functioning, opportunities to engage in professional practice, and geographic mobility. Thus, familiarity and compliance with such requirements are important prerequisites to school psychologists and aspiring school psychologists interested in pursuing "best practices."

Licensure and certification requirements affect the roles and functions of most educators, health care practitioners, and human service providers, including school psychologists. They are part of the mechanism by which state governments protect the health, safety, morals, and welfare of their citizens (Council of State Governments, 1952). The existence of extensive credentialing requirements for school psychologists thus reflects the perceived importance of our profession in its potential benefit, as well as harm, to members of the public.

As stated by Pryzwansky and Wendt (1987), "Credentialing is the mechanism, then, by which a profession regulates itself or is regulated. It . . . implies that a relationship exists between the credential and the competency of the practitioner within the profession" (p. 18). The degree to which this relationship exists in reality has been questioned (Gross, 1978). Nonetheless, credentialing standards are intended to insure minimum training and competency among school psychologists and are crucial requirements for those desiring entry into the field.

Interest in certification and licensure requirements for school psychologists has been consistent over at least the past four decades (Horrocks, 1946; Clayton, 1950; Hodges, 1960; Gross, Bonham, & Bluestein, 1966; Graff & Clair, 1973). Since its inception, the National Association of School Psychologists (NASP) has been the primary source of review and dissemination of such requirements (Sewall & Brown, 1976; Brown, Horn, & Lindstrom, 1980; Prus, White, & Pendleton, 1987).

This appendix presents a summary of certification and licensure requirements for school psychologists. It is based on the most recent national review of such requirements contained in NASP's *Handbook of Certification and Licensure Requirements for School Psychologists* (Prus, White, & Pendleton, 1987) and on updates and revisions made since the time that document was written. A risk inherent in any summary is that potentially important details may not be represented adequately or may be subject to misinterpretation. The highly detailed information typically contained in state certification regulations, along with frequent modifications, makes this area particularly vulnerable to these concerns. The reader interested in the requirements of a particular state should refer to the handbook on which this summary is based or to the actual state credentialing requirements (names, addresses, and phone numbers of state contacts can be found in the *Handbook*).

Data Collection and Validation

Standardized survey protocols were used to collect certification and licensure information from relevant agencies in a systematic manner for the *Handbook*. Mailing lists of state departments of education, state boards of psychology, and similar agencies related to professional practice and standards were compiled through information from the National Association of State Directors of Teacher Education (NASDTEC), the National Association of School Psychologists (NASP), and the American Psychological Association (APA). Initial surveys, along with a letter of transmittal were mailed to appropriate agencies.

Respondents were asked to complete the survey and provide copies of administrative regulations and licensing laws needed to clarify state requirements. Follow-up mailings and phone calls were used to obtain a 100% response rate from state offices and agencies related to certification and 82% response rate from state psychology boards. Additional licensure information was obtained from remaining states through personal requests for licensure applications and associated information.

Validation of certification information contained in the *Handbook* included the mailing of proofs to respective state department officials for review and corrections. Follow-up phone calls and assistance from state school psychology consultants also occurred in some cases, as did consultation with state psychology boards.

Follow-ups were also conducted in March, 1989, with states indicating antic- ipated changes in certification requirements at the time the *Handbook* was finalized in late 1986. Changes in the requirements of eight states have been incorporated into the present summary.

Every effort was made to insure the presentation of the most valid information on certification and licensure in the *Handbook*, and to update information for this summary in cases where changes were anticipated. Ultimately, however, the responsibility and authority to provide and interpret certificate and licensure requirements lie with the appropriate agencies within individual states.

Interpretation of Summary Tables

Considerable variation exists in the content and related terminology of certification and licensure laws and regulations. Most commonly, however, "licensure" refers to the process of regulation applicable to private practice in psychology or school psychology. Licenses are usually issued by state boards of psychology or psychological examiners. "Certification" is the credentialing process most frequently applicable to public school professionals, including school psychologists. This process is usually regulated by state departments of education.

Although the above descriptions of licensure and certification are those which have been adopted for this summary, they are not universally applicable. For example, some state boards of psychological examiners *certify* psychologists for private practice, while some state departments of education refer to their credentialing process as *licensure*. Other variations, including a process of "approval" (Michigan) interdependent certification/licensure (Texas and Maine), and the involvement of an independent professional standards board (Oregon), also exist.

The basic requirements for certification applicable to school psychologists are presented in Table 1. It is suggested that the reader review the notes appearing at the end of this table as these will define some of the terms and abbreviations that are used to clarify information presented in the table.

School psychologists concerned with the "mobility" of their professional credentials should be aware of the processes of certification/reciprocity that states utilize for out-of-state applicants. Reciprocity is the process by which an individual may become credentialed in one state by virtue of possessing a comparable or equivalent credential in another state. The certification/reciprocity processes or criteria that each state utilizes in evaluating the credentials of out-of-state applicants are presented in Table 2. Further information regarding the means by which the credentials of out-of-state applicants are reviewed by state departments can be found in the *Handbook of Certification and Licensure Requirements for School Psychologists* (Prus, White, & Pendleton, 1987).

In addition to the options listed in Table 2 and delineated in the table's notes, a number of state departments of education are considering adopting NASP's recently implemented national certification as a criteria or option for credentialing school psychologists. This may well become a significant trend that could bring consistency to the process of credentialing in the profession.

Table 3 presents a summary of the basic licensure requirements for psychologists in each of the fifty states and the District of Columbia. In cases where a specialty license exists specifically for school psychologists, the requirements for that license, if different from other licenses, are delineated. This could be of particular interest in states where licensure by the state board is a prerequisite to certification and practice in the public schools (Maine and Texas).

In interpreting Table 3, several additional points should be noted. First, since many statutes allow licensure boards considerable autonomy in setting requirements, the lack of an indicated requirement (a blank space on the table) may mean that there is no requirement or that the specific details are left to the board's discretion.

Secondly, where no specialty licenses were indicated in state requirements, the term "generic" was used in the table. In cases where both years and hours were cited in provisions for required experience, only years are reported in the table.

Finally, the EPPP listed under "Mandatory Exam" requirements in almost all states refers to the *Examination for the Professional Practice of Psychology*. A large number of states require an additional exam conducted on an oral or written basis. This is referred to as a "Board Exam" in the table.

ACKNOWLEDGMENTS

We gratefully acknowledge the assistance of Leigh Armistead and Anne Pendleton in the data collection and preparation of tables.

REFERENCES

Brown, D. T., Horn, A. J., & Lindstrom, J. P. (1980). *The handbook of certification/licensure requirements for school psychologists* (Third Edition). Washington, DC: National Association of School Psychologists.

Council of State Governments. (1952). *Occupational licensing legislation in the states: A study of state legislation licensing the practice of professions and other occupations.* Chicago: Author.

Graff, M. P., & Clair, T. N. (1973). Requirements for certification of school psychologists: A survey of recent trends. *American Psychologist, 8,* 704–709.

Gross, F. P., Bonham, S. J., & Bluestein, V. W. (1966). Entry requirements for state certification of school psychologists: A review of the past nineteen years. *Journal of School Psychology, 4,* 43–51.

Gross, S. J. (1978). The myth of professional licensing. *American Psychologist, 33,* 1009–1016.

Hodges, W. (1960). State certification of school psychologists. *American Psychologist, 6,* 346–349.

Horrocks, J. E. (1946). State certification requirements for school psychologists. *American Psychologist, 1,* 399–401.

Prus, J. S., White, G. W., & Pendleton, A. (1987). *Handbook of certification and licensure requirements for school psychologists.* Washington, DC: National Association of School Psychologists.

Pryzwansky, W. B., & Wendt, R. N. (1987). *Psychology as a profession.* New York: Pergamon Press.

Sewall, T. J., & Brown, D. T. (1976). *The handbook of certification/licensure requirements for school psychologists.* Washington, DC: National Association of School Psychologists.

TABLE 1
Summary of Basic Certification Requirements

State	Title Level/Type	Minimum Degree	Credit Hours	Experience Internship	Experience Field	Exam
Alabama	School Pychometrist (A)	Master's	33	10 weeks	2 years (T)	yes
	School Psychometrist (AA)	Master's	66	10 weeks	2 years (T)	yes
	School Psychologist (AA)	Master's	66	10 weeks	2 years (T)	yes
Alaska	School Psychologist	Master's		A P		no
Arizona	School Psychometrist	Master's	30	1 semester		no
	Assistant School Psychologist	Master's	50	1 year		no
	School Psychologist	Master's	70	1 year		no
Arkansas	Education Examiner	Master's	45	1 semester	1 year (T)	yes
California	Pupil Personnel Services — School Psychology	Master's	60	Required		yes
Colorado	School Psychologist Option 1/Type P	6th Year		Required		yes
	School Psychologist Option 2	Doctorate		Must be licensed by Board of Examiners		
	School Psychologist Type E	6th Year		Required	3 Years (C)	
Connecticut	Provisional	Master's	45	1 year		no
	Standard	Master's	60	1 year	3 years (C)	no
Delaware	School Psychologist	Master's	60	1200 hours		yes
District of Columbia	School Psychologist (Standard License)	Master's	45	300 hours		no
Florida	Specialist in School Psychology	Master's	42	6 semester hrs. credit		yes
Georgia	School Psychology (Nonrenewable Service Certificate NS5)	Master's		10 quarter hours credit		yes
	School Psychology (Professonal Service Certificate S-6)	Specialist		1000 hours		yes
	School Psychology (Professonal Service Certificate S-7)	Doctorate		1200 hours		yes
Hawaii	Psychological Examiner I, II, III, IV	Bachelor's			0-3 years (varies)	no
	School Psychologist	Doctorate		Required		no

(Table 1, continued)

State	Title Level/Type	Minimum Degree	Credit Hours	Experience Internship	Experience Field	Exam
Idaho	School Psychologist	Master's		300 hours		yes
Illinois	School Psychologist	Master's	60	1 year		yes
Indiana	School Psychologist I	Master's	60	3 semester hrs. credit		no
	School Psychologist II	EdD or PhD		1 year		no
Iowa	School Psychologist	Master's	60	600 hours		no
Kansas	School Psychologist	Master's		1 year		no
Kentucky	School Psychologist (Standard)	Master's	60 + intern.	1 semester		yes
Louisiana	School Psychologist Level B	Master's	60	1225 hours 1 year		no
	School Psychologist Level A	Doctorate	60	1225 hours 1 year		no
Maine	School Psychological Examiner	Master's	18	750 hours	Must be licensed by Board of Examiners	
	School Psychologist Professional Certificate	Doctorate		750 hours	Must be licensed by Board of Examiners	
Maryland	School Psychologist Level I	Master's	45 (G&U)	500 hours		no
	School Psychologist Level II	Master's	60	1000 hours		no
	Supervisor of School Psychological Services	Doctorate			3 years (C)	no
Massachusetts	School Psychologist	Bachelor's	60	600 hours		no
Michigan	School Psychologist (Temporary Approval)		30	500 hours		no
	School Psychologist (Full Approval)	Master's	45 + intern.	500 hours	1 year (C)	no
Minnesota	School Psychologist (Provisional)	Master's	45 quar. hrs.			no
	School Psychologist	Specialist	90 quar. hrs.	600 hours		no
Mississippi	School Psychologist AAA	Specialist		6 semester hrs. credit		yes
	School Psychologist AAAA	Doctorate				yes

(Table 1, continued)

State	Title Level/Type	Minimum Degree	Credit Hours	Experience Internship	Field	Exam
Missouri	School Psychological Examiner	Master's				no
Montana	School Psychologist (Class 6 Specialist)	Master's		6 quar. hrs. credit		no
Nebraska	School Psychologist	Bachelor's A P	60	1000 hours		yes
Nevada	School Psychologist (Provisional)	Master's	60	500 hours		no
	School Psychologist (Professional)	Master's	60	1000 hours		no
New Hampshire	Associate School Psychologist	Master's				yes
	School Psychologist	Master's	60	1 year	1 year (C)	yes
New Jersey	School Psychologist	Bachelor's A P	60	450 hours		no
New Mexico	Educational Diagnostician	Master's		6 semester hrs. credit	2 years (T)	no
	Psychological Counselor	Doctorate		Must be licensed by Board of Examiners		
New York	School Psychologist (Provisional)	Bachelor's	60	Required		yes
	School Psychologist (Permanent)	Master's	60	Required		yes
North Carolina	School Psychologist Level II (Initial)	6th year		Required		yes
	School Psychologist Level II (Continuing)	6th year		Required	2 years (C)	yes
	School Psychologist Level III (Initial)	Doctorate		A P		yes
	School Psychologist Level III (Continuing)	Doctorate		A P	2 years (C)	yes
North Dakota	Psychologist (Initial Certificate)	Master's		350 hours/ 10 weeks		no
	School Psychologist (5 year Certificate)	Master's		350 hours/ 10 weeks	18 months	no
Ohio	School Psychologist (Provisional)	Master's	60	9 months		yes
	School Psychologist (Professional)	Master's	60	9 months	4 years (C)	yes
	School Psychologist (Permanent)	Master's	60	9 months	8 years (C)	yes

(Table 1, continued)

State	Title Level/Type	Minimum Degree	Credit Hours	Experience Internship	Experience Field	Exam
Oklahoma	School Psychologist (Initial)	Master's	60	1 semester		yes
	School Psychologist (Standard)	Master's	60	1 semester	1 year (C)	
Oregon	School Psychologist (Basic)	Master's	75 quar. hrs.	1 quarter		yes
	School Psychologist (Standard)	Master's	75 quar. hrs. (G&U)	1 quarter	2 years (C)	yes
Pennsylvania	School Psychologist Educational Specialist I	Bachelor's A P		1000 hours		no
	School Psychologist Educational Specialist II	Bachelor's + 24 hours A P		1000 hours	3 years (C)	no
Rhode Island	School Psychologist (Provisional)	Master's	48 (G&U)	12 semester hrs. credit		yes
	School Psychologist (Professional)	Master's	48 (G&U)	12 semester hrs. credit	3 years (C)	yes
South Carolina	School Psychologist I	Master's	36	500 hours		yes
	School Psychologist II	Master's	60	1000 hours		yes
	School Psychologist III	Doctorate	90	1000 hours		yes
South Dakota	School Psychologist Examiner	Master's	30 (G&U)			no
	School Psychologist	A P		A P		no
Tennessee	School Psychologist	Master's		1 semester		yes
Texas	Associate School Psychologist			Must be licensed by Board of Examiners		
	School Psychologist			Must be licensed by Board of Examiners		
Utah	School Psychologist (Basic)	Master's		1 year		no
	School Psychologist (Standard)	Master's		1 year	2 years (C)	no
Vermont	School Psychologist (Probationary)	Master's		1 semester		no
	School Psychologist (Continuing)	Master's		1 semester	3 years (C)	no
Virginia	School Psychologist	Master's	60	1 year 12 sem. hrs.		no

(Table 1, continued)

State	Title Level/Type	Minimum Degree	Credit Hours	Experience Internship	Field	Exam
Washington	School Psychologist (Initial)	Master's		Required		no
	School Psychologist (Continuing)	Master's		Required	3 years (C)	no
West Virginia	School Psychologist (Provisional)	Master's		A P		no
	School Psychologist (Professional	Master's		A P	3 years (C)	no
	School Psychologist (Permanent)	Master's		A P	5 years (C)	no
Wisconsin	School Psychologist (Provisional)	Master's	48	600 hours		no
	School Psychologist	Specialist	60	1 year		no
Wyoming	Educational Diagnostician	Master's	45			no
	School Psychologist	Master's	60	1 year		no

Notes: Levels and types of certificates that vary in basic training or experience are presented. In some states, additional types of certificates (e.g., a temporary certificate provided to an applicant who lacks one requirement) are available.

Some states accept the equivalent to the minimum required degree.

Credit hours are given in graduate semester hours unless otherwise designated. "G & U" indicates that a combination of graduate and undergraduate credits may be applied to certification requirements.

In the "Experience" column, "Internship" refers to pre-degree field experience which may be referred to as practica, externships, or internships. Although typically consisting of post-degree experience, the experience listed under the "Field" column may at least in-part include pre-degree experience in some states.

"T" indicates experience that at least partly must be in teaching or its equivalent.

"C" indicates experience that must be attained while holding the next "lower" level or type of school psychology certification. For example, Colorado requires 3 years of experience under the Type P certificate for the Type E certificate.

"A P" designates an implied, but not explicitly stated, requirement or additional requirement inherent in the state's mandate regarding the completion of an approved program.

TABLE 2
Processes of Certification/Reciprocity for Out-of-State Applicants

State	State Approved Program[1]	NASDTEC[2]	NCATE/ NASP[3]	APA[4]	Interstate Reciprocity Agreement[5]	Course Review[6]	Equivalent Training & Certificate[7]	Other[8]	Exam[9]
Alabama		X	X		X	X			X
Alaska			X	X					
Arizona			X			X			
Arkansas								O	
California							X		X
Colorado			X					X	X
Connecticut								X	
Delaware		X	X	X		X			X
District of Columbia		X			X	X			
Florida						X			X
Georgia			X						X
Hawaii								O	
Idaho		X						X	X
Illinois	X					X	X		X
Indiana						X	X		
Iowa								X	
Kansas	X						X		
Kentucky	X	X	X						X
Louisiana			X				X		
Maine		X	X			X		X	
Maryland			X			X			
Massachusetts					X	X			
Michigan						X		O	
Minnesota	X					X			
Mississippi		X	X					X	X
Missouri						X		O	
Montana									
Nebraska	X							X	X
Nevada						X			
New Hampshire			X						X
New Jersey						X			
New Mexico						X		O	

(Table 2, continued)

State	State Approved Program[1]	NASDTEC[2]	NCATE/ NASP[3]	APA[4]	Interstate Reciprocity Agreement[5]	Course Review[6]	Equivalent Training & Certificate[7]	Other[8]	Exam[9]
New York	X				X				X
North Carolina		X	X				X		X
North Dakota		X	X			X			
Ohio						X			X
Oklahoma						X		X	X
Oregon		X				X	X		X
Pennsylvania						X			
Rhode Island		X	X		X	X			X
South Carolina	X	X	X				X		X
South Dakota						X		X	
Tennessee						X		X	X
Texas								X	
Utah		X	X		X				
Vermont		X			X				
Virginia						X			
Washington	X								
West Virginia	X				X		X		
Wisconson	X					X			
Wyoming			X			X			

[1]Completion of an approved training program in state of origin.

[2]Completion of a program approved via the standards of the National Association of State Directors of Teacher Education and Certification.

[3]Completion of a program accredited by the National Council for Accreditation of Teacher Education (utilizing standards of the National Association of School Psychologists).

[4]American Psychological Association-approved program.

[5]Formal interstate reciprocity agreement (e.g., Interstate Compact Agreement, Interstate Reciprocity Project).

[6]Course-by-course transcript review.

[7]Documentation of training and/or certification equivalent to that in the state in which certification is desired.

[8]Other method of certification review. An "O" indicates the absence of certification specifically for school psychologists. In these states an alternate certificate (e.g., "Educational Evaluator") or method of reviewing credentials (e.g., "approval") is used.

[9]Examination is required in addition to other requirements.

TABLE 3
Summary of Basic Licensure Requirements

State	Title	Minimum Degree	Specialities	Experience			Mandatory Exam	Renewal Period
				Post-Degree	Supervised	Total		
Alabama	Psychologist	Doctorate	Generic	Satisfactory to the Board			EPPP/ Board Exam	1 year
Alaska	Psychologist	Doctorate	Generic	1 yr.	1 yr.	1 yr.	EPPP/ Board Exam	4 years
	Psychological Associate	Masters	Clinical Counseling School I/O	4 yrs.	4 yrs.	4 yrs.	EPPP/ Board Exam	4 years
Arizona	Certified Psychologist	Doctorate	Generic	Internship requirements determined by training institution			EPPP	2 years
Arkansas	Psychologist	Doctorate	Generic			1 yr.	EPPP/ Board Exam	1 year
	Psychological Examiner	Masters	Generic				EPPP/ Board Exam	1 year
California	Psychologist	Doctorate	Several, including Educational	1500 hours	3000 hours	3000 hours	EPPP/ Board Exam	2 years
Colorado	Psychologist	Doctorate	Generic	2 yrs.	2 yrs.	2 yrs.	EPPP/ Board Exam	2 years

Note: Licensure by the State Board of Psychological Examiners is one option for obtaining certification as a school psychologist by the Colorado Department of Education.

State	Title	Minimum Degree	Specialities	Experience			Mandatory Exam	Renewal Period
Connecticut	Psychologist	Doctorate	Generic	35 hr/wk for 46 weeks	same	same	EPPP/ Board Exam	1 year
Delaware	Psychologist	Doctorate	Generic	2 yrs.	2 yrs.	2 yrs.	EPPP/ Board Exam	2 years
District of Columbia	Psychologist	Doctorate	Generic	2 yrs.	2 yrs.	2 yrs.	EPPP/ Board Exam	1 year
Florida	Psychologist	Doctorate	Generic	1 yr.	2 yrs.	3 yrs.	EPPP/ Board Exam	2 years
	School Psychologist	Specialist	School	2 yrs.	2 yrs.	3 yrs.	EPPP/ Board Exam	2 years
Georgia	Psychologist	Doctorate	Generic			1 yr.	EPPP/ Board Exam	2 years
Hawaii	Psychologist	Doctorate	Generic		1 yr.	1 yr.	EPPP/ Board Exam	2 years
Idaho	Psychologist	Doctorate	Generic	1000 hours	2000 hours	2000 hours	EPPP	1 year
Illinois	Registered Psychologist	Doctorate	Generic	1 yr.	2 yrs.	2 yrs.	EPPP	2 years
Indiana	Certified Psychologist	Doctorate	Generic	Proof of internship must be provided			EPPP/ Board Exam	2 years

(Table 3, continued)

State	Title	Minimum Degree	Specialities	Experience			Mandatory Exam	Renewal Period
				Post-Degree	Supervised	Total		
Iowa	Psychologist	Doctorate	Generic	1 yr.	1 yr.	1 yr.	EPPP/ Board Exam	2 years
Kansas	Licensed Psychologist	Doctorate	Generic	1 yr.	2 yrs.	2 yrs.	EPPP/ Board Exam	2 years
Kentucky	Licensed Psychologist	Doctorate	Several, including School		1 yr.	1 yr.	EPPP/ Board Exam	3 years
	Certified Psychologist	Masters	Several, including School		1 yr.	1 yr.	EPPP/ Board Exam	3 years
Louisiana	Psychologist	Doctorate	Generic	1 yr.	2 yrs.	2 yrs.	EPPP/ Board Exam	1 year
Maine	Psychologist	Doctorate	Generic		2 yrs.	2 yrs.	EPPP/ Board Exam	2 years
	Psychological Examiner	Masters	Generic		1 yr.	1 yr.	EPPP/ Board Exam	2 years
	Certified School Psychologist	Doctorate	School		2 yrs.	2 yrs.	EPPP/ Board Exam	2 years
	Certified School Psychological Examiner	Masters	School		1 yr.	1 yr.	EPPP/ Board Exam	2 years

Note: Licensure as a psychologist or psychological examiner is required for certification as a school psychologist or school psychological examiner.

State	Title	Minimum Degree	Specialities	Experience			Mandatory Exam	Renewal Period
				Post-Degree	Supervised	Total		
Maryland	Psychologist	Doctorate	Generic	1 yr.	2 yrs.	2 yrs.	EPPP/ Board Exam	1 year
Massachusetts	Psychologist	Doctorate	Generic	1600 hours	3200 hours	3200 hours	EPPP	2 years
Michigan	Psychologist	Docctorate	Generic	4000 hours	2000 hours	6000 hours	Board Exam	2 years
	Psychologist	Masters	Generic	2000 hours	500 hours	2500 hours	Board Exam	2 years
Minnesota	Licensed Consulting Psychologist	Doctorate	Generic	2 yrs.	2 yrs.	2 yrs.	EPPP/ Board Exam	2 years
	Licensed Psychologist	Masters	Generic	2 yrs.	2 yrs.	2 yrs.	EPPP/ Board Exam	2 years
Mississippi	Psychologist	Doctorate	Clinical Counseling		2000 hours	2000 hours	EPPP/ Board Exam	1 year
	Psychologist	Doctorate	School		1500 hours	1500 hours	EPPP/ Board Exam	1 year
	Psychologist	Doctorate	I/O				EPPP/ Board Exam	1 year

(Table 3, continued)

State	Title	Minimum Degree	Specialities	Experience Post-Degree	Experience Supervised	Experience Total	Mandatory Exam	Renewal Period
Missouri	Psychologist	Doctorate	Generic	1 yr.	1 yr.	1 yr.	EPFP	1 year
	Psychologist	Masters	Generic	3 yrs.	3 yrs.	3 yrs.	EPPP	1 year
Montana	Psychologist	Doctorate	Generic	1 yr.	2 yrs.	3 yrs.	EPPP/ Board Exam	1 year
Nebraska	Psychologist	Doctorate	Generic	—	—	—	EPPP	2 years
	Clinical Psychologist	Doctorate	Clinical	1 yr.		1 yr.		2 years
Nevada	Psychologist	Doctorate	Generic	1 yr.	1 yr.	1 yr.	EPPP/ Board Exam	2 years
New Hampshire	Psychologist	Doctorate	Generic	1 yr.	2 yrs.	2 yrs.	EPPP	1 year
New Jersey	Psychologist	Doctorate	Generic	1 yr.	1 yr.	1 yr.	EPPP/ Board Exam	2 years
New Mexico	Psychologist	Doctorate	Several, including Educational	1 yr.	1 yr.	1 yr.	EPPP/ Board Exam	1 year
	Psychological Associate	Masters		5 yrs.	5 yrs.	5 yrs.	EPPP/ Board Exam	1 year
New York	Psychologist	Doctorate	Generic		2 yrs.	2 yrs.	EPPP/ Board Exam	3 years
North Carolina	Practicing Psychologist	Doctorate	Generic	2 yrs.	2 yrs.	2 yrs.	EPPP/ Board Exam	1 year
	Psychological Associate	Masters	Generic				EPPP/ Board Exam	1 year
North Dakota	Psychologist	Doctorate	Generic	Applicants must present a detailed description of the supervised internship			EPPP/ Board Exam	1 year
Ohio	Psychologist	Doctorate	Generic	1 yr.	2 yrs.	2 yrs.	EPPP/ Board Exam	2 years
	School Psychologist	Masters	School	3 yrs.	4 yrs.	4 yrs.	Board Exam	2 years
Oklahoma	Psychologist	Doctorate	Generic	1 yr.	2 yrs.	2 yrs.	EPPP/ Board Exam	1 year
Oregon	Psychologist	Doctorate	Generic	1 yr.	1 yr.	1 yr.	EPPP/ Board Exam	1 year
	Psychologist Associate	Masters	Several, including School	3 yrs.	4 yrs.	4 yrs.	EPPP/ Board Exam	1 year
Pennsylvania	Practice of Psychology	Doctorate	Generic	2 yrs.	2 yrs.	2 yrs.	EPPP/ Board Exam	None indicated
	Practice of Psychology	Masters	Generic	4 yrs.	4 yrs.	4 yrs.	EPPP/ Board Exam	None indicated

(Table 3, continued)

State	Title	Minimum Degree	Specialities	Experience Post-Degree	Supervised	Total	Mandatory Exam	Renewal Period
Rhode Island	Psychologist	Doctorate	Generic	1 yr.	2 yrs.	2 yrs.	EPPP/ Board Exam	1 year
South Carolina	Psychologist	Doctorate	Several, including School	1 yr.	2 yrs.	2 yrs.	EPPP/ Board Exam	2 years
South Dakota	Psychologist	Doctorate	Generic	1 yr.	2 yrs.	2 yrs.	EPPP	2 years
Tennessee	Psychologist	Doctorate	Several, including School		1 yr.	1 yr.	EPPP/ Board Exam	1 year
Texas	Licensed Psychologist	Doctorate	Generic	1 yr.	2 yrs.	2 yrs.	EPPP/ Board Exam	1 year
	Certified Psychological Associate	Masters	Generic				EPPP/ Board Exam	1 year
Utah	Psychologist	Doctorate	Generic	2000 hours	4000 hours	4000 hours	EPPP/ Board Exam	2 years
Vermont	Psychologist	Doctorate	Generic		2 yrs.	2 yrs.	EPPP	2 years
	Psychologist	Masters	Generic		2 yrs.	2 yrs.	EPPP	2 years
Virginia	Psychologist	Doctorate	Several, including School	1 yr.	2 yrs.	2 yrs.	EPPP/ Board Exam	2 years
	Clinical Psychologist	Doctorate	Clinical	1 yr.	2 yrs.	2 yrs.	EPPP/ Board Exam	2 years
	School Psychologist	Masters	School	3 yrs.	4 yrs.	4 yrs.	EPPP/ Board Exam	2 years
Washington	Psychologist	Doctorate	Generic	1500 hours	1500 hours	1500 hours	EPPP/ Board Exam	1 year
West Virginia	Psychologist	Doctorate	Generic	1 yr.	1 yr.	1 yr.	EPPP/ Board Exam	2 years
	Psychologist	Masters	Generic	5 yrs.	5 yrs.	5 yrs.	EPPP/ Board Exam	2 years
Wisconsin	Psychologist	Doctorate	Generic		1 yr.	1 yr.	EPPP/ Board Exam	2 years
	Psychologist	Masters	Generic		3 yrs.	3 yrs.	EPPP/ Board Exam	2 years
	Private Practice of School Psychology	Masters	School	1 yr.	1 yr.	1 yr.	Board Exam	2 years
Wyoming	Psychologist	Doctorate	Generic		2000 clock hours	2000 clock hours	EPPP/ Board Exam	1 year

62

A Brief History of School Psychology in the United States

Thomas K. Fagan
Memphis State University

OVERVIEW

In the past decade, there has been growing interest in the history of school psychology. Several investigations have helped to clarify origins, trends, events, and persons significant to this development. While considerable research and writing has been done in recent years, there is still a dearth of historical information available (Fagan, in press). For all practical purposes, everything important to the history of school psychological services has occurred in the past 100 years, and most of the persons involved in school psychology's development in the past 50 years are still alive! This appendix is a synopsis of the development of school psychology. It is intended to sensitize school psychologists to their history and provide a broader perspective and appreciation of their work. Because it is a synopsis, the scope does not permit a discussion of concurrent social, economic, and political history, or the historical development of related fields. It focuses on the growth of the profession in several areas, but excludes worthy discussions of related technological developments in such areas as assessment, interventions, and research. A chronological discussion of major developments is provided, organized into several decades within the periods referred to as the Hybrid Years and the Thoroughbred Years.

The Hybrid Years and Thoroughbred Years Defined

School psychology's historical development can be divided into the Hybrid Years (1890-1969) and the Thoroughbred Years (1970-present). These are arbitrary delineations between two distinct historical periods. The first was a period when "school" psychology was a blend of many kinds of educational and psychological practitioners loosely mobilized around a dominant role of psychoeducational assessment for special class placement. The second period, while certainly not rid of the earlier theme, differs from the former period because of the growth in the number of training programs, practitioners, state associations, and the expansion of literature, NASP, and regulations, all of which have contributed to a stabilized professional entity called school psychology. Thus, school psychology in the Thoroughbred Years is no longer a mix of persons certified in various fields, many from teacher education or guidance and counseling who entered school psychology as an "add on" to their existing education credentials. Since 1970, school psychologists have been employed consistently in positions titled "school psychologist," in states offering school psychology credentials, after having completed training programs titled as school psychology, operated by school psychologists, and accredited as school psychology programs. These conditions did not generally exist during the Hybrid Years. Table 1 provides a chronology of "firsts" in school psychology, and Table 2 illustrates a decade-by-decade division of our history. Each division is labeled according to my impressions of the most salient characteristics, not necessarily accomplishments, of the decade. For example, the decade of the 1950s was an era of strong effort toward professional identity, even though that identity was not generally accomplished until the 1970s.

The Hybrid Years (1890–1969)

1890–1920. The origins of school psychological services can be traced to an era of social reform in the late 19th and early 20th centuries. The condition of American education in that era of heavy immigration, compulsory education, and child labor laws, created the need for specialized school services to work in conjunction with the small but growing services in remedial and special education. Enrollment increased dramatically, and included many children who had not been in school previously or had been unsuc-

---

TABLE 1
Landmarks in the History of School Psychology

1. First organization for psychologists, APA, 1892
2. First psychological clinic, University of Pennsylvania, 1896
3. First psychological clinic in the schools (Chicago), 1899
4. First version of the Binet-Simon Scales, 1905
5. First practitioner journal, *Psychological Clinic,* 1907
6. First internship in clinical psychology (Vineland), 1908
7. First literary usage of term, "school psychologist," 1910
8. First psychoeducational clinic (University of Pittsburgh), 1912
9. First survey of practitioner/examiners (Wallin), 1913
10. First person appointed as "school psychologist," 1915
11. First Stanford revision of the Binet Scales (Terman), 1916
12. First association of clinical psychologists (AACP), 1917
13. First journal article with "school psychology" title, 1923
14. First public school licensing exam for psychologists, 1925
15. First training program in school psychology (NYU), 1928
16. First textbook on school psychology (Hildreth), 1930
17. First state department of education certification (NY), 1935
18. First practitioner association with sections (AAAP), 1937
19. First organizational identity for school psychology, 1945
20. First recognized/organized doctoral program, 1953
21. First state approved internships (Ohio), 1954
22. First national conference on school psychology (Thayer), 1954
23. First school psychology journal (J. School Psychology), 1962
24. First NCATE reference to school psychology program, 1962
25. First national association for school psychologists (NASP), 1969
26. First accreditation of school psychology program (APA), 1971
27. First joint APA/NCATE accreditation of a program, 1983
28. First National School Psychology Examination, 1988
29. First National Certification in School Psychology, 1989

Reprinted with the permission of Lawrence Erlbaum Associates, Inc. and based on information which may change as further research is conducted.

TABLE 2
School Psychology's First Century

I. THE HYBRID YEARS (1890-1969)

1890-1909 Origins of Practice
    1890 Cattell publishes article on mental tests
    1892 Founding of American Psychological Association
    1896 Witmer establishes his psychological clinic
    1899 Chicago schools start psychological services
    1905 Binet Scales published
    1907 Journal, *Psychological Clinic,* starts publication
    1908 Clinical psychology internships at Vineland
    1909 Rochester appoints Binet examiner

1910-1929 Expansion and Acceptance
    1910 Cincinnati starts Vocational Bureau
    1911 Term, "school psychologist" appears in English literature
    1915 Terman publishes Stanford-Binet Scales
    1915 Gesell serves as first school psychologist until 1919
    1917 American Association of Clinical Psychologists founded
    1919 APA Section of Clinical Psychology founded
    1923 Hutt publishes article on the school psychologist
    1925 New York City schools establishes psychologist exam
    1928 New York University offers degrees in school psychology

1930-1939 Emerging Regulation
    1920 Hildreth publishes text on school psychology
    1932 Association of Consulting Psychologists founded
    1935 New York SDE establishes certification standards
    1937 Pennsylvania establishes certification standards
    1937 American Association of Applied Psychologists founded
    1938 Penn State University initiates PhD in school psychology

1940-1949 Organizational Identity
    1942 Special issue *Journal of Consulting Psychology* on school psychology
    1943 Ohio School Psychologists Association founded
    1945 APA reorganizes into divisional structure
    1945 Connecticut initiates psychologist licensure
    1947 Accreditation of professional psychology programs
    1948 Boulder Conference on Clinical Psychology

1950-1959 Professional Identity
    1953 University of Illinois starts PhD in school psychology
    1954 Thayer Conference on School Psychology
    1954 NCATE formed from other organizations

1960-1969 Training and Practitioner Growth
    1962 *Journal of School Psychology* founded
    1963 *Psychology in the Schools* founded
    1963 Peabody Conference on the school psychology internship
    1968 Ohio holds invitational conference
    1969 Organizational meeting for NASP held in St. Louis

II. THE THOROUGHBRED YEARS (1970-Present)

1970-1979 Trainer and Practitioner Regulation; Association Identity and Growth;
    Professional Division
    1971 Division 16, APA establishes accreditation
    1972 *School Psychology Digest* founded
    1974 PL 94-142 enacted

(Table 2, continued)

      1976 NASP affiliates with NCATE
      1977 Training, Certification Directories published
      1978 APA/NASP Task Force established
      1979 *School Psychology International* founded

1980–1989 Professional Reorganization
      1980 Spring Hill Symposium
      1981 Olympia Conference
      1983 APA/NASP Joint Accreditation Project
      1985 *Professional School Psychology* founded by Division 16
      1988 NASP starts National Certification System

This table is an expansion of a similar table appearing in *Advances in School Psychology Volume 7* and is reprinted with the permission of Lawrence Erlbaum Associates, Inc.

TABLE 3
Comparison of Attendance and Enrollment Data for 1890 and 1930

	1890	1930
Average Days in School Year	135	173
Average Days Attended Per Pupil	86	143
Public School Enrollment	12,723,000	25,678,000
Public Secondary School Enrollment	203,000	4,399,000

cessful in school, and yet whose attendance was required. Enrollment comparisons for this period (Table 3) demonstrate the rapid growth of elementary and secondary education. These conditions were particularly acute in the major city school systems which enrolled large percentages of students with "mental, physical, and moral" impairment. Each of the modern day pupil personnel services (e.g., school guidance, nursing, psychology, social work) originated in this period with the probability that truant officers (i.e., attendance services) were first.

Psychological services emerged from the activities of Lightner Witmer at the psychological clinic (the first in the United States) which he founded at the University of Pennsylvania in 1896. Considered by many as the father of both clinical and school psychology, he advocated the training of a "psychological expert who is capable of treating the many difficult cases that resist the ordinary methods of the school room" (Witmer, 1897, p. 117). Witmer is also credited with coining the term "clinical psychology" and founding *The Psychological Clinic,* an early journal related to clinical services and handicapped children. Witmer stressed an individualized approach to children which would use psychological knowledge to solve their problems.

Another major early figure was G. Stanley Hall who founded the American Psychological Association in 1892, as well as several journals. In contrast to Witmer's idiographic clinical method, Hall espoused a nomothetic approach expressed in the later work of his Clark University students, Goddard, Gesell, and Terman. Hall was the father of the child study movement which influenced the establishment and functions of the Department of Scientific Pedagogy and Child Study in the Chicago Public Schools in 1899 — the first clinic facility operated within the public schools. Wallin and Ferguson (1967) described the mix of normative and clinical casework conducted in the early years of this facility.

Thus, school psychological services evolved from at least two orientations (idiographic clinical psychology and nomothetic educational psychology). These orientations, even if not derived simply from Witmer and Hall, can be seen in the different pursuits of the emerging clinics in the United States. Some provided individualized services organized around case studies, while others were at least in part organized around research emphases, perhaps studying individuals in terms of normative bases. These orientations, singly or in combination, are observed throughout our history of training and practice. For example, school psychologists have continued to provide individualized psychological services while making categorical decisions for special education along normative lines of deviance. School psychology has also been influenced by developments in education and psychology and by the research in these fields (Fry, 1986).

School and nonschool-based clinics (sometimes called research bureaus or child study departments) spread quickly between 1900 and 1930 with most large city school systems having access to some form of what was most often called "clinical psychology." Child study services were also provided to children by clinics located in juvenile institutes, courts, universities, hospitals, vocational guidance bureaus, and other settings. These services were a mixture of educational and clinical psychology that were more akin to modern day school psychology than to either current educational or clinical psychology. The spread of psychological services was spurred by the development of psychological and educational tests and the interest of school systems in segmenting their student population, especially according to "intelligence." Developments of the late 19th century in measurement and psychological science had laid the groundwork for the study of individual differences and test standardization; these concepts fit well with the need to segment the school population into different instructional groups including special education.

The early years of the testing movement demonstrated the advantage of ability and achievement tests in segregating individuals for specialized treatment. World War I had a major influence on the development of standardized tests and their public acceptance. Interventions were influenced by many ideas including Thorndike's learning principles and educational psychology, the thinking of Dewey and James, Freudian therapeutic conceptualizations, and Watsonian behaviorism. Educational literature of this period suggests an acceptance of learning and behavioral principles decades in advance of the widespread influence of Skinnerian applications familiar to contemporary school psychologists. These and other early orientations continued to influence psychoeducational services for many decades. Yet, throughout the Hybrid Years the dominant ideology was diagnostic services for special education placement which encouraged a dominant school psychology role model of psychological assessment. Psychological testing, especially with the available adaptations of Binet's scales, was widespread by the 1920s and encouraged Hollingworth (1933) to comment that the situation "within the past 25 years has transformed Binet's name into a verb. (nearly all teachers now know what it is to 'binet' a pupil)." (p. 371). The growth of psychological and special educational services was observed mainly in urban schools, though some rural services existed; however, not until the latter decade of the Hybrid Years and the era of PL 94-142 were widespread rural services observed.

Well known "school" psychologists of the period included Arnold Gesell, Henry Goddard, Leta Stetter Hollingworth, Bertha Luckey, Clara Schmitt, Lewis Terman, John Edward Wallace Wallin, Margaret Washburn, Lightner Witmer, and Helen Thompson Wooley. Women held many early administrative positions in clinics and contributed widely to the spread of school services (French, 1988). The early representation of women in school psychology practice can be attributed to discrimination in academic settings, lack of career options for women outside of education, and the feminization of the teaching force which spread in the 19th century. In comparison to other psychology fields, women have held strong proportional representation throughout the history of school psychology (perhaps never less than 30% and currently approaching 70%). Goddard and Gesell provided early training classes on testing and special education in New York City and Goddard is credited with organizing the earliest internships at the Vineland Training School in New Jersey (Morrow, 1946). One of his assistants, Norma Cutts, was at Vineland in 1913–1914 and with Goddard's aid found employment as a psychological examiner with Gesell. That position provided the stage for her own eminent career in school psychology and special education in New Haven, CT. Arnold Gesell is believed to have held the first position titled "school psychologist," serving the Connecticut State Board of Education from 1915–1919. His position was a mix of direct and indirect services and records detail the conditions of his employment and practice. His experiences were similar in many ways to contemporary practitioners; his caseload was often too large, his administrative superiors insisted on diagnostic services over others, he traveled considerably, and mixed school and nonschool practice (Fagan, 1987).

The period 1890–1920 provided a framework for many later developments. In addition to the origination of services, the period also included the founding of several journals (e.g., *Journal of Educational Psychology*), organizations for applied/clinical psychologists, individual and group tests, and scores of special education classes. Special educational services were also emerging. Dunn (1973) reported a national special education enrollment of more than 26,000 children in 1922, most of whom were children with mental retardation. By comparison to modern times when special education enrollment represents at least 10% of the school population, Dunn's figures suggest less than 1% representation. Literary benchmarks included the first appearance of the term "school psychologist" in American literature, and several early articles and manuals that described the state of services. Wallin (1914) and Van

Sickle, Witmer, and Ayers (1911) provide the most comprehensive descriptions of school conditions, availability of special classes, psychological services, and the nature of service providers. Working for the State of Connecticut, Gesell wrote several manuals which were prototypical of materials produced by contemporary state consultants for school psychological services. There were many test manuals and compendiums of tests which appear to have enjoyed widespread popularity.

Organizational developments were also important. The APA, founded in 1892, failed to respond to the interests of applied psychologists for standards and assistance, and provoked the founding of the American Association of Clinical Psychologists in 1917. Responding to overtures from the APA, the AACP disbanded and became the Clinical Section of the APA in 1919. Many consulting psychologists, especially in New York state, continued to maintain a separate association that led to the founding of the American Association of Applied Psychologists in 1937. Throughout APA's first 50 years, scientific, as opposed to professional orientations, dominated its political structure and policy.

1920–1940. Though 1890–1920 was a formative period, school psychology lacked the characteristics of a profession: autonomy and control of training, credentialing, and practice. To a limited extent these characteristics are discernible in the period 1920–1940. Available training courses at some institutions, formal programs at New York University and Pennsylvania State University, state department of education certification in New York and Pennsylvania, an examination for employment in the New York City Schools, and national certification were developed during this period. French (1984) provides a detailed description of developments in Pennsylvania which was among the few early states actively developing school psychology. More rapid and widespread growth in training and regulation emerged in future periods. Though services were still concentrated in urban areas, by 1940 school psychology had been accepted nationwide and the number of practitioners had grown from only a few hundred to possibly a thousand persons employed under various titles. The clinic system was not widespread, with some rural areas gaining services through traveling clinics, but increasingly districts that could afford it were employing their own school psychologists.

In the absence of school psychology journals, much of our literature appeared in related psychology and education journals, particularly *The Psychological Clinic, School and Society, Journal of Educational Psychology*, and *Journal of Consulting Psychology*. Literary accomplishments also included the first text on school psychology by Hildreth (1930). Figure 1 is taken from her pioneer text and demonstrates the typical practice of the period and remarkable similarity to contemporary practice. Psychological testing continued to be the dominant characteristic of role and function for school psychologists throughout this period as well as the earlier period. The adequacy of instrumentation improved, but the basic conceptualization of the school psychologist's role did not change.

Association representation had been available in the form of the APA, a few related psychology groups, and more recently the American Association of Applied Psychologists (AAAP) founded in 1937. School psychological practitioners typically belonged to AAAP's Clinical or Educational Sections and there were several AAAP state level affiliates; but many school practitioners did not hold organizational memberships in this period. Relationships between the AAAP and the APA were generally cordial with many shared memberships and annual meetings. The two groups remained separate until encouraged by developments surrounding World War II to unite psychology groups under one organization.

1940-1970. The final three decades of the Hybrid Years are noteworthy for role confusion, shaping of organizational identity, and growth in the number of training programs and practitioners. The merger of the AAAP into a reorganized APA in 1945 gave school psychologists their first national organizational identity in the form of the Division of School Psychologists (Division 16). As a separate division, school psychology was finally a distinct entity from clinical psychology (Division 12) and educational psychology (Division 15). Membership in the Division grew from 133 in 1948, to 601 in 1956, to 1229 in 1968. Though the Division struggled for many years to gain stability, it provided an organizational identity for a growing number of trainers and practitioners, established a loose network of existing state associations, drafted guidelines for training and credentialing, and in 1963 initiated efforts at doctoral program accreditation. From 1940-1970 the number of practitioners grew from about 500 to 5000 and the number of training institutions from as few as 2 to more than 100, the latter enrolling perhaps 3000 students. The ratio of practitioners to school children improved from 1:36,000 in 1950 to 1:10,500 in 1966 (Fagan, 1988). Credentialing accomplishments included the growth of school certification from 13 states in 1946, to 23 in 1960, to perhaps 40 states by 1970; and the initiation of licensure for psychologists in 1945 with licensure in all states by 1977. During the latter part of the Hybrid Years, the Division of School Psychology (APA) was an important factor in giving school psychology national recognition and shaping the sensitivity of state departments of education to the need for credential and practice standards improvements.

Literature continued to be scattered though some concentration was provided by the *Journal of Consulting Psychology* (now *Journal of Consulting and Clinical Psychology*) and the newly founded *American Psychologist*. Until the 1960s, the Division 16 newsletter provided the only national school psychology publication. The 1960s was the most productive literary decade of the Hybrid Years and included the founding of the *Journal of School Psychology, Psychology in the Schools*, and *Professional Psychology* (now *Professional Psychology: Research and Practice*), and the presence of 14

AN ILLUSTRATION OF A PSYCHOLOGIST'S DAY

The following outline illustrates the daily activities on an ordinarily busy day of one psychologist employed in a progressive school:

MORNING

Examination with the Binet test of a child applying for admission.

The administration of group tests to a small group of absentees who missed the test during the recent testing survey.

Conference on a problem child in the high school.

Conference on a problem child in the elementary school.

Answering correspondence and making requisitions for the tests to be used in the next survey.

AFTERNOON

Completion, for the principal, of reports of a group of seventh-grade children whose achievement was found to be deficient on recent tests.

Further work on the construction of reading and arithmetic readiness tests for the primary grades.

Instructions to an assistant for making a set of flash cards for diagnostic work in reading.

Partial diagnosis of the reading difficulties of an upper elementary grade pupil.

Study of the reading progress of a French child who had recently entered the school.

Conference with a high school teacher.

This day began at 8:30 and closed at 5:45, with half an hour's recess at noon.

On another day the work consisted more largely of routine matters. Activities which occupied most of the time included summarizing data for a school survey, completing a card file of all varieties of tests, selecting from this file a list — requested by a staff member — of tests suitable for kindergarten children, assisting a college student in measuring the reactions of individual pupils with a psycho-galvanometer, conferring with parents regarding a suitable school for a child with borderline intelligence and making up a list of suitable schools for the child, conferring with a teacher concerning the construction of a new achievement test, measuring with experimental tests perceptive abilities and information possessed by kindergarten children.

The rank order of activities engaged in by the same psychologist, arranged according to the amount of time consumed in their performance during the year, is approximately as follows:

1. Conferences with school staff members, parents, visitors, psychologists in training.
2. Individual testing of pupils.
3. Group testing.
4. Test scoring.
5. Tabulation of results and the construction of graphs and charts.
6. Diagnostic work with individual pupils.
7. Research including test construction and conferences with staff members conducting research.

FIGURE 1. Illustration of a psychologist's day. (From Hildreth, 1930, pp. 246–248.)

books on school psychology. The literature reflected the role confusion and professional identity problems of the period. Still, it was the first period in which school psychologists could write books on topics of their own interest and publish in their own journals for their own audiences. Perhaps the most important were those books presenting philosophies on the training and practice of school psychologists. Gray's (1963) "data-oriented problem solver" and Reger's (1965) "educational programmer" are orientations with continuing relevance. The Gottsegens' three edited volumes were without peer until the *Advances in School Psychology* series of the 1980s. The frequency of authored, as opposed to edited, texts is a trademark of the 1960s. Only in recent years have unedited texts of significance returned to our literature. The many edited volumes of the past two decades reflect the complexity of the field, while the return of unedited books reflects a return of philosophical orientation, some espousing certain practice orientations such as consultation and behavioral applications (Reynolds, Gutkin, Elliott, & Witt, 1984).

Among the most cited accomplishments of the period 1940–1970 is the Thayer Conference conducted in 1954 (Cutts, 1955). The conference helped to shape ideas for several decades regarding levels of training, credentialing, and practice. During the 1950s and 1960s, other professional school psychology conferences were conducted in several states. For example, the Peabody Conference in 1963 was part of a series of meetings held by the Southern Regional Education Board that drew attention to the need for training programs and internships. State and regional conferences brought together practitioners which often led to the founding of a state organization. California is an excellent example of how coordinated efforts of the State Department of Education and university staff led to substantial development in a short period of time. It is difficult to determine if this flurry of meetings was stimulated by the Thayer Conference and Division 16, but there

appears to have been some connection. These conferences served to facilitate the development of a consensus on role and function and training even though this was not achieved during this period.

While the impact of the Thayer Conference is difficult to judge, its impact seems to have been less than that of the Boulder Conference on clinical psychology held in 1948. Clinical psychology shared a closer kinship nourished by an APA Division of Clinical Psychology dating to 1919, numerous state affiliates, a training and internship system supported by accreditation and the Veterans' Administration, struggles with organized medicine and psychiatry, and a rapidly growing network of state licensing boards. For its part, school psychology had little nationwide kinship at the time of the Thayer Conference and lacked such throughout the Hybrid Years. Thus, when APA reorganized, school psychology was off to the slowest start of the professional specialties. While state and local associations for psychologists dated to the 1920s, those for school psychologists were more recent. Ohio appears to have had the first separate state association for school psychologists founded in 1943 and it was probably among no more than three state groups at that time. Five more were founded in the 1950s and by 1969 there were only 17 state school psychology associations. The literature of the 1960s helped disseminate the proceedings of invitational school psychology conferences to a loose network of state and local association members, and piqued the interest of some in Ohio to call their own invitational meeting in 1968. That meeting led to the historic St. Louis convention at which the National Association of School Psychologists was officially formed.

The growth and change in school psychology during the period 1940–1970 can be gleaned from Farling and Hoedt (1971), Cutts (1955), and Symonds (1942). Education had grown enormously as a result of the post World War II "Baby Boom." Once again, the schools were expanding and in need of psychological services. Special education was serving more than two million children in 1968;

up dramatically from 310,000 in 1940, and 837,000 in 1958 (Dunn, 1973). Psychology was changing as well. Where the First World War had demonstrated the value of tests, the Second World War launched therapeutic interventions as another psychologist service domain. Prior to this time, clinical psychology services were frequently delivered to children, as well as adults. The state hospital system was largely controlled by psychiatry, and clinical psychologist services to adults were frequently restricted or supervised by psychiatrists. State education agency certification for school practice antedated licensure by at least a decade and freed school psychologists from medical supervision (French, 1989). Psychologists had been unsuccessful in gaining legislative recognition for practice in other settings. The first licensure (Connecticut, 1945) occurred when almost a dozen states already had certification for psychologists practicing in schools.

With the reorganization of APA along divisional lines, the need for psychological interventions, government interest in promoting training and interning of clinical psychologists, and a network of state association affiliates already in operation, an upward spiral of development in adult clinical psychology was launched. The full effects of that spiral are observed in contemporary licensing, accrediting, reimbursement policies, and other aspects of clinical psychology. The adult focus was so strong that only in the past decade have we observed the reemergence of a strong child clinical subspecialty. School psychologists gained only indirect benefits from the post-war, government encouragement of clinical psychology. Instead, much of school psychology's growth was tied to developments in education. Nevertheless, the post-war period of the Hybrid Years was important to school psychology even if its growth lagged significantly behind that of clinical psychology. It was the first era in which distinct lines became officially recognized between different groups of professional psychologists and drew attention to the separateness of practice specialties. Those lines would have much to do with the struggles and growth of school psychology in the Thoroughbred Years.

The accomplishments of the post-war period created an atmosphere of identity for school psychologists, even if it seemed confused in the philosophies of authors and the perplexing mix of training, credentialing, and practice titles. The period was also historically significant for the struggles in civil rights along lines of race, ethnicity, gender, and sexual preference. The unprecedented increase of federal involvement in education was observed in events surrounding the space race, school desegregation, and federally funded educational programs (including Head Start); these were a significant departure from the past. Public education had for many decades been viewed as an appropriate arena within which to seek major changes in the social fabric of society. Now, however, it was federal, instead of state and local, agendas that would be encouraged. With federal assistance (seen by some as intrusion), the schools could be called upon by the federal government to accomplish goals which state and local authorities had failed or refused to accomplish. It was under these conditions, and the perceived need to bring practitioners nationwide together in a more stable and strengthened identity, that the National Association of School Psychologists (NASP) was established in 1969. The event marked the end of the Hybrid Years and served as the first in a series of events that would characterize the Thoroughbred Years.

The Thoroughbred Years (1970–Present)

By the end of the Hybrid Years, school psychology was a *potentially* significant entity in psychology and education. Most current components of our profession had appeared in some form decades earlier, and in a miniature state of their present form by 1970. For example, in the 1930s, state education agencies informally identified universities which offered classes appropriate for school psychologists, but formal recognition via accreditation did not appear until the 1960s from the National Council for the Accreditation of Teacher Education (NCATE) and 1971 from APA; and the use of school psychology standards via NCATE did not occur until the 1980s! Thus, during the Hybrid Years program recognition emerged, but the model changed to that observed today; the earliest model was a prototype for modern day state department of education program approval. In many states today, both models of recognition exist, often interdependently. Likewise, certification procedures today are much more sophisticated than at earlier times when one seeking a credential went to the state education agency and demonstrated his/ her skill in giving the Binet. Examples for other components could be given. The point is that much of what we have accomplished in accreditation, associations, credentials, levels of training, literature, loci of practice, or role and function was discernible by the end of the Hybrid Years. Their existence and impact (i.e., our identity) were not equally distributed across the country. Many states and most rural areas still lacked viable psychological services in their schools. Variability in services, especially along rural–urban lines, has persisted throughout the history of school psychology.

Table 2 labels the decades of the Thoroughbred Years as characterized by regulation, association growth, and professional division and reorganization. A number of factors during the period 1970–1990 strengthened our identity and promoted more widespread services of school psychologists. One of these was a series of legal challenges to special education; perhaps best known was the Larry P. case which involved minority assessment and placement issues. These challenges, and subsequent court decisions, brought into sharp focus the need for more sensitive multicultural assessment, improved technical adequacy of tests, broader conceptualizations of assessment, and more adequate caseloads. Perhaps the most significant event was the enactment of landmark civil rights legislation for the handicapped (PL 94-142) which sensitized every school district

to the need for the availability and proper implementation of special education, including psychological services. The legislated right to education regardless of the nature of handicap, followed a long historical struggle of guaranteeing education to minorities including women, native and Black Americans. The implementation of PL 99-457 in the 1990s extends the educational rights of the handicapped to birth! A third event, legislation regarding the handling and confidentiality of school records (PL 93-380), drew attention to service issues in special and regular education. The due process aspects of these laws had widespread affect on the delivery of psychological services. Prior to this time, it was common practice to conduct psychological assessments and recommend special class placements without parent permission! While the legislation, and the related litigation affected education generally, they served to draw attention (albeit not always favorable) on psychological services which served as a catalyst for improved practice guidelines. The guidelines emanated from local, state, and national levels. As in the Hybrid Years, many of these guidelines were externally produced by state education agencies, or other nonpsychologist groups.

Another factor in the Thoroughbred Years was the decline in regular education enrollments with corresponding increases in special education which served 4.5 million children by the late 1980s; the increase was largely a function of PL 94-142. The impact on school psychology was observed in the growth in the number of practitioners, and national and state association activity. The number of practitioners grew from 5,000 in 1970, to at least 10,000 by 1980, and 20,000 by 1988; and the ratio of practitioners to school children improved to 1:2,000. Services were available nationwide despite continued variability in delivery systems and practitioner qualifications.

Most states now had enough practitioners to organize an association and the number of state associations for school psychologists increased from 17 in 1970 to 48 in 1989. In concert with a rapidly growing NASP, the associations fostered the development and implementation of guidelines for improved practice. One fundamental difference between this and the earlier historical period was a shift from reactive to proactive modes of operation. School psychology was no longer simply responding to what other agencies decided. Instead, they were working proactively to influence the types of decisions these other agencies might make. Thus, professional regulation was shifting from external to internal influence. This was most clearly seen in the 1980s but originated in association activities of the 1970s.

APA also took reactive and proactive positions on legislation throughout this period. Its Division of School Psychology was influential in these positions but lacked the resources to have a significant impact on the field beyond input to its parent organization. The successful growth of NASP drew attention away from Division 16, which prior to 1969 had been the only national level school psychology group. Division 16 membership remained stable during this period at between 2000–2500. Still, APA and Division 16 played an important role in recent decades. After eight years of planning by Division 16, APA accredited its first school psychology doctoral program in 1971. APA accreditation grew from three programs in the early 1970s to about a dozen by 1980 (Zins & Curtis, 1988), and spurred by growing interest in doctoral training and non-school credentials, the number grew to 38 in 1988. The 1977 APA Council resolution declaring the doctoral degree as required for the title "professional psychologist," and the growing tension between NASP and APA surrounding entry-level and title issues, led to the creation of the APA/ NASP Task Force in 1978 (currently called the Interorganizational Committee). This body influenced several interorganizational events and facilitated joint accreditation at the doctoral level. The Task Force also worked with the Division, NASP, and the University of Minnesota's National School Psychology Inservice Training Network to plan the Spring Hill Symposium in 1980 and the Olympia Conference

in 1981. NASP and the Division jointly published the proceedings of the conferences in the *School Psychology Review*. In 1981, APA published its *Specialty Guidelines for the Delivery of Services* which included school psychology guidelines. In 1986 the Division began publishing *Professional School Psychology*, the field's most recent journal.

In contrast to its first half-century, the second half-century of APA history was increasingly practice oriented. APA membership had taken a dramatic shift toward practice. Organizational changes within APA led to the creation of a Practice Directorate which in 1988 added a school psychology position. Internal political issues led to several unsuccessful attempts to reorganize the Association along lines more palatable to members with scientific interests, and in 1988 the American Psychological Society was founded as an alternative organization. Whereas practitioners established an alternative association in 1917, scientists established one in 1988. The longevity of this latest organizational lifeform, and its impact on school psychology, remain to be seen.

From the standpoint of national representation, the Thoroughbred Years have been dominated by NASP whose membership grew from 856 in 1969, to 3385 in 1978, to more than 15,000 in 1989. NASP began accepting state affiliate associations in the early 1970s. Soon, existing associations were affiliating with NASP while NASP was fostering the establishment of new associations which would later affiliate. By 1980, there were 43 state associations, 33 of which were NASP affiliates; by 1989 the number had grown to 48 affiliates in 47 states. The relationship of state associations and NASP was symbiotic. Their affiliation with NASP provided a reciprocal network for action which was not possible through Division 16. An example of the utility of the NASP–state relationship came from the 1980 Spring Hill Symposium and its follow-up Olympia Conference in 1981. The main impact of Division 16 had to be made at the conference; it lacked a network for further action. In contrast, NASP and its affiliates took the framework established at these conferences and carried it back to the state associations for further implementation. This network promoted NASP policy implementation and ideas throughout the states. The policies and ideas of Division 16 and APA had to be promoted via the state psychological association network which included few school psychologists. Almost every new state school psychology association was established apart from the existing state psychological association. Thus, the growth of differently affiliated associations served to extend the NASP-APA differences at the national level to the state level.

APA–NASP differences were greatest over policies on the appropriate entry-level and title for school psychologists. At the state level, differences were reflected in conflicts over credentialing. In several states, school psychologists challenged the authority of state level credentialing agencies to restrict their practice and title to school settings on the basis of not holding the doctoral degree. Where the struggles of clinical psychologists to obtain practice privileges had involved battles with psychiatry and medicine, the battles for nonschool practice by school psychologists were almost exclusively between school and clinical psychology groups. The efforts of state associations were assisted by NASP but this was not a nationally coordinated effort; nor was APA's general opposition coordinated. Primarily these were state-level skirmishes bolstered by national level technical and financial assistance. Several successes for school psychology were gained, though less so since the mid 1980s. The struggles and successes did much to spur the identity and morale of the profession. In most states, these struggles could not have occurred before the growth of the Thoroughbred Years.

Where Division 16 had carried the national banner for school psychology from 1945 to 1970, NASP increasingly carried it since. Both groups helped to enhance the regulation of the profession and to shift such regulation from strictly external to largely internal mechanisms. The two systems of school psychology operating in the United States — one controlled by education and the other by psychology — will continue to influence training and practice. Differences between APA and NASP will dissipate over the coming decades and the stage may already be set for a future consolidation of organizational efforts in school psychology. Such could lead to the long awaited single control system of the profession.

For many years there had been a workforce of school psychologists ready to respond to a call for professional organization. NASP and its affiliates provided the call with guidelines and activities that went beyond reactive responses to legislative and litigious events of the period. Almost from the start, NASP initiated training guidelines and accreditation inquiries to NCATE. By the end of its first decade, NASP had officially approved standards for training, field placements, credentialing, and practice, in addition to a code of ethics and several position statements on important issues (Batsche, Knoff, & Peterson, 1989; Curtis & Zins, 1989). The standards documents were revised in 1984 and those for training were promulgated through a revised NCATE unit accreditation process that allowed NASP to do program evaluations through folio review. This followed upon NASP's formal relationships with NCATE including affiliation in 1976, and constituent member status in 1978. The revised credentialing standards were prominent in the National Certification System initiated in 1988–89 which included the National School Psychology Examination developed by the Educational Testing Service. The involvement of NASP in the creation of this exam is an excellent example of reactive-proactive involvement of the 1980s.

In literary accomplishments, NASP established a newsletter in 1969 (now the *Communiqué*), the *School Psychology Digest* in 1972 (now *School Psychology Review*), and published the first directories of training programs and credentialing requirements. The second decade of NASP witnessed a shift toward also publishing books and products for the purpose of revenue generation, the most successful being *Best Practices in School Psychology* (Thomas & Grimes, 1985). For a comprehensive review of NASP history see *School Psychology Digest*, *8*(2), and *School Psychology Review*, *18*(2).

The period 1970–1990 was an extension of the literary accomplishments of the 1960s. In addition to the literary accomplishments of Division 16 and NASP, this period included the founding of *School Psychology International, Journal of Psychoeducational Assessment, Special Services in the Schools*, and more than 30 books on school psychology. Several literary shifts are discernible: (a) the proportion of edited books reflected the increased diversity of the field, (b) subspecializations were emerging in training and practice, and (c) school psychologists were not only writing for themselves but for other educational and psychological audiences. The latter is especially true in the areas of test construction, child neuropsychology, and preschool assessment. The *Handbook of School Psychology* (Reynolds & Gutkin, 1982) reflected the combination of diversity and specialization and provided a major resource for the field along lines of an earlier handbook (Magary, 1967). Content analyses of this literary period suggested emphasis on testing and assessment and role and function (Fagan, 1986).

Training programs grew from an estimated 100 to more than 200; program enrollment increased in the 1970s but decreased by perhaps 10% between 1977 and 1987. Program and enrollment growth were most notable at the specialist and doctoral levels. Program accreditation became increasingly desirable, benefiting both NCATE and APA. Credentialing in the Thoroughbred Years was notable for the growing number of school psychologists interested in licensure or other privileges for nonschool practice. In the school certification arena, much of the activity was directed at maintaining high standards in states threatening to downgrade requirements, and at raising state requirements to the NASP expectation in states undergoing long needed revisions. Much of the success in changing certification can be attributed to the efforts of the members of the National Association of State Consultants for School Psychology Services. Even though state consultant positions date to the time of Gesell's practice, only about half the states have a state consultant today. Little has been written to recognize the efforts of the persons in these state government positions and perhaps they are among the endangered species in our future.

It is more difficult to discern changes in the role and function of practitioners. The testing model of school psychological services evident in the early part of the century persisted, and probably intensified, throughout the Hybrid Years. The 1970s began with a surge of interest in school consultation and organization/systems development, but seemed to regress to traditional assessment models as a function of PL 94-142. The 1970s was a period of intense special education placement and litigation. By the 1980s, however, forces internal and external to the profession were raising concerns regarding the proliferation of special education (especially the more than 100% increase in the number of learning disabled children served). Reformers, including school psychologists, rallied around the banners of alternative services and the Regular Education Initiative in opposition to the traditional refer-test-place delivery model. The Regular Education Initiative and its opposition reflected the instability of traditional special education service models. Discussions of earlier decades about noncategorical services in special education were shifting (at least for the mildly handicapped) to discussions of services outside of special education, the possible reduction of special education enrollments, and the use of funds to prevent children from eventually needing to be placed in special education. Prereferral assessment models rapidly gained attention.

By the late 1980s, the intensity was shifting to another target group — children at risk. These were not former special education children under a new catch phrase. Instead, these were different children under new catch phrases: children of divorce, latchkey kids, substance abusers, suicide prone, teen pregnancy, and other students that required academic and psychological assistance, but not necessarily special education. Since most of these were not at risk for special education, the potential for consultation-intervention models, in regular education and special education settings, seemed greater than prior to PL 94-142. The recent clamor of direct and curriculum-based assessment may set the stage for the return of widespread remedial services between regular and special education, and the emergence of more effective teacher-assistance services. Where the first decade of the PL 94-142 era was assessment and placement intensive, the second shifted toward instruction and related services. The shifts toward prereferral assessment, interventions, and at least secondary prevention for at risk groups are important indicators of change in role and function. The coming decade will help determine if the field is truly emerging from the retrenchment of the 1970s and making its first lasting major role and function change. The 1989 Office of Education position statement on the role of school psychological services to all children is a further impetus for positive change.

One potential barrier at least to role change is the shortage of practitioners in recent years. The supply-demand gap is becoming a major training and service issue in the 1980s. With trainees seeking higher levels of required training and employment in more diverse practice settings, the supply problems are anticipated to persist for at least a decade. Other potential barriers to role and function changes are well known: high caseloads, modest salaries, role perceptions held by school administrators, and narrow conceptualizations of the nature of psychological services in schools. It is not yet clear what impact technological advancements such as computerization will have on this process of change.

The events of the Thoroughbred Years have helped the profession of school psychology realize its potential to be a significant entity in education and psychology. The first decade of the Thorough-

bred Years was characterized by association growth and division, professional identity, and increasing regulation of training and practice. It remained for the second decade to seek the means to effectively implement such regulation and to consolidate the forces in school psychology. Half or more the number of training programs, accreditations, practitioners, credentials, state associations, and literature developed in the Thoroughbred Years!

CONCLUSION

The history of school psychology is interwoven with the development of education and psychology in the latter 19th and 20th centuries. Many of the structural characteristics of contemporary education and psychology were present by 1920; and most structural characteristics of school psychology emerged by that time. This is the first century, however, in which education, psychological science, and school psychology coexisted and in which formal schooling was widely accepted, and required. Historical study in school psychology suggests different models of training, credentialing, practice, etc. as opposed to direct extrapolations or expansions of earlier models. For example, in the practice area we still observe many school psychologists functioning similar to practitioners in the 1920s; but the dominant form today is much different in terms of employer expectations, available technology, referral situations, and practitioner preferences. While testing has persisted as the dominant model, its conceptualizations have changed. In the 19th century, phrenology had many advocates but that method appears not to have been a part of school psychology. By the late 1800s Cattell had proposed a battery of psychological "tests" reflecting anthropometric and other ideas which also never "caught on." It was Binet's work in the early 1900s which brought "mental testing" to the study of higher processes and gained widespread acceptability. Stern added the notion of the ratio intelligence quotient and Terman and Merrill made the Binet

TABLE 4
**Growth of Practitioners, Training Programs, Journals,
Certification and State Associations in School Psychology**

Area	1890	1920	1940	1970	1990
Practitioners	0	200	500	5000	22,000
Training Programs	0	0	2	100	230
Certification by SDE	0	0	3	40	50
State Associations	0	0	3	17	48
Journals	0	0	0	2	5

The data are approximations based on data known for dates closest in time to the divisions presented.

a household word. Much later the concept of ratio IQ was replaced by the deviation IQ concept so familiar to the Wechsler Scales, and eventually to all major intelligence tests. More recently we observe the growing influence of less inferential assessment forms in adaptive behavior scales, behavior rating scales, and curriculum based assessment. Still, some of the items on contemporary intelligence tests are identical with items 70 years ago, and certain subtests have similarity to Cattell's 1890 list. The case records of Witmer's clinic also reveal practical approaches to the assessment of academic problems similar to approaches advocated today. Such development serves to remind us of our roots and that earlier forms may continue to influence present practice. Despite some similarities to earlier practitioners, the dominant ideology of earlier decades was directed at limited ability testing and direct services, and practically no preventive or accountability components. Current ideology, espousing consultation and nontesting functions, prevention, and accountability, could be observed in limited ways at earlier times but the testing ideology was dominant in the preferences of employers *and* school psychologists.

Over the course of our profession's history, we observe a chronology of perceived need for services, emergence of services, then training, then credentialing, followed by rapid growth in all former areas, then accreditation, external and internal regulation. The process can be observed in Table 4. We should view our history as a period of evolution and transition from various available ideologies and practice models, with one ideology and model being dominant at specified times. But we must also acknowledge that ideology and practice are not always synonymous. Current professional standards espouse an ideology of training, credentialing, and practice that is far from being widespread. Even today, in an era of ideological transition to treatment and prevention in educational settings, we continue to see some educators and practitioners insist on testing functions. What school psychology has sought for many years is a consensus of its ideology with that of its employers that would lead to practice along lines of prevention, consultation, and accountability (research and evaluation), in addition to necessary assessment and intervention functions. The advancements of the Thoroughbred Years have placed such consensus within reach for the first time. For more than a century, our society has looked at its schools and its children as the potential long-range solution to its problems. In that process, it has increasingly turned to various professionals to assist its long-term goals. The historic model of school psychology served well the limited arena of special education placement. That model, and its arena, are ready for change, and may already be in transition. The future of school psychology depends largely on being able to learn from, and improve upon, the ideologies and models of its past.

REFERENCES

Batsche, G. M., Knoff, H., & Peterson, D. (in press). Trends in credentialing and practice standards. *School Psychology Review, 18*(2).

Curtis, M. J., & Zins, J. E. (1989). Current status and future directions in school psychology training and accreditation. *School Psychology Review, 18*(2).

Cutts, N. E. (Ed.). (1955). *School psychologists at mid-century.* Washington, DC: American Psychological Association.

Dunn, L. M. (Ed.). (1973). *Exceptional children in the schools: Special education in transition.* New York: Holt, Rinehart and Winston.

Fagan, T. K. (1986). The evolving literature of school psychology. *School Psychology Review, 15,* 430–444.

Fagan, T. K. (1987). Gesell: The first school psychologist, Part II. Practice and significance. *School Psychology Review, 16,* 399–409.

Fagan, T. K. (1988). The historical improvement of the school psychology service ratio: Implications for future employment. *School Psychology Review, 17,* 453–464.

Fagan, T. K. (in press). Research on the history of school psychology: Recent developments, significance, resources, and future directions. In T. R. Kratochwill (Ed.), *Advances in school psychology, vol. 7.* Hillsdale, NJ: Erlbaum.

Farling, W. H., & Hoedt, K. C. (1971). *National survey of school psychologists.* Washington, DC: National Association of School Psychologists.

French, J. L. (1984). On the conception, birth, and early development of school psychology: With special reference to Pennsylvania. *American Psychologist, 39,* 976–987.

French, J. L. (1988). Grandmothers I wish I knew: Contributions of women to the history of school psychology. *Professional School Psychology, 3,* 51–68.

French, J. L. (in press). History of school psychology. In C. R. Reynolds & T. B. Gutkin (Eds.), *Handbook of school psychology* (Revised edition). New York: Wiley.

Fry, M. A. (1986). The connections among educational and psychological research and the practice of school psychology. In S. N. Elliott & J. C. Witt (Eds.), *The delivery of psychological services in schools: Concepts, processes and issues* (pp. 305–327). Hillsdale, NJ: Erlbaum.

Gray, S. W. (1963). *The psychologist in the schools.* New York: Holt, Rinehart and Winston.

Hildreth, G. H. (1930). *Psychological service for school problems.* Yonkers-on-Hudson, NY: World Book Co.

Hollingworth, L. S. (1933). Psychological service for public schools. *Teachers College Record, 34,* 368–379.

Magary, J. F. (Ed.). (1967). *School psychological services in theory and practice, a handbook.* Englewood Cliffs, NJ: Prentice-Hall.

Morrow, W. R. (1946). The development of psychological internship training. *Journal of Consulting Psychology, 10,* 165–183.

Reger, R. (1965). *School psychology.* Springfield, IL: Charles C Thomas.

Reynolds, C. R., & Gutkin, T. B. (Eds.). (1982). *The handbook of school psychology.* New York: Wiley.

Reynolds, C. R., & Gutkin, T. B., Elliott, S. N., & Witt, J. C. (1984). *School psychology: Essentials of theory and practice.* New York: Wiley.

Symonds, P. M. (Ed.). (1942). *Journal of Consulting Psychology, 6*(4). This issue is devoted almost entirely to school psychology.

Thomas, A., & Grimes, J. (Eds.). (1985). *Best practices in school psychology.* Washington, DC: National Association of School Psychologists.

Van Sickle, J. H., Witmer, L., & Ayres, L. P. (1911). *Provision for exceptional children in the public schools* (U.S. Bureau of Education Bulletin No. 14). Washington, DC: Government Printing Office.

Wallin, J. E. W. (1914). *The mental health of the school child.* New Haven, CT: Yale University Press.

Wallin, J. E. W., & Ferguson, D. G. (1967). The development of school psychological services. In J. F. Magary (Ed.), *School psychological services in theory and practice, a handbook* (pp. 1–29). Englewood Cliffs, NJ: Prentice-Hall.

Witmer, L. (1897). The organization of practical work in psychology. *Psychological Review, 4,* 116–117.

Zins, J. E., & Curtis, M. J. (1988). Current status of professional training and practice: Implications for future directions. In T. R. Kratochwill (Ed.), *Advances in school psychology vol. 6.* Hillsdale, NJ: Erlbaum.

NASP Principles for Professional Ethics

I. INTRODUCTION

Standards for professional conduct, usually referred to as ethics, recognize the obligation of professional persons to provide services and to conduct themselves so as to place the highest esteem on human rights and individual dignity. A code of ethics is an additional professional technique which seeks to ensure that each person served will receive the highest quality of service. Even though ethical behavior involves interactions between the professional, the person served and employing institutions, responsibility for ethical conduct must rest with the professional.

School psychologists are a specialized segment within a larger group of professional psychologists. The school psychologist works in situations where circumstances may develop which are not clearly dealt with in other ethical guidelines. This possibility is heightened by intense concern for such issues as due process, protection of individual rights, record keeping, accountability and equal access to opportunity.

The most basic ethical principle is that of the responsibility to perform only those services for which that person has acquired a recognized level of competency. Recognition must be made of the uncertainties associated with delivery of psychological services in a situation where rights of the student, the parent, the school, and society may conflict.

The intent of these guidelines is to supply clarification which will facilitate the delivery of high quality psychological services in the school or community. Thus they acknowledge the fluid and expanding functions of the school and community. In addition to these ethical standards, there is the ever present necessity to differentiate between legal mandate and ethical responsibility. The school psychologist is urged to become familiar with applicable legal requirements.

The ethical standards in this guide are organized into several sections representing the multifaceted concerns with which school psychologists must deal. The grouping arrangement is a matter of convenience, and principles discussed in one section may also apply to other areas and situations. The school psychologist should consult with other experienced psychologists and seek advice from the appropriate professional organization when a situation is encountered for which there is no clearly indicated course of action.

II. PROFESSIONAL COMPETENCY

A. General

1. The school psychologist's role mandates a mastery of skills in both education and psychology. In the interest of children and adults served

in both the public and private sector, school psychologists strive to maintain high standards of competence. School psychologists recognize the strengths, as well as limitations, of their training and experience, and provide services only in areas of competence. They must be professional in the on-going pursuit of knowledge, training and research with the welfare of children, families, and other individuals in mind.

2. School psychologists offer only those services which are within their individual area of training and experience. Competence levels, education, training, and experience are accurately represented to schools and clients in a professional manner. School psychologists do not use affiliations with other professional persons or with institutions to imply a level of professional competence which exceeds that which has actually been achieved.

3. School psychologists are aware of their limitations and enlist the assistance of other specialists in supervisory, consultative, or referral roles as appropriate in providing services competency.

4. School psychologists recognize the need for continuing professional development and pursue opportunities to learn new procedures, become current with new research and technology, and advance with changes that benefit children and families.

5. School psychologists refrain from involvement in any activity in which their personal problems or conflicts may interfere with professional effectiveness. Competent professional assistance is sought to alleviate such problems and conflicts in professional relationships.

III. PROFESSIONAL RELATIONSHIPS AND RESPONSIBILITIES.

A. General

1. School psychologists take responsibility for their actions in a multitude of areas of service, and in so doing, maintain the highest standards of their profession. They are committed to the application of professional expertise for promoting improvement in the quality of life available to the student, family, school, and community. This objective is pursued in ways that protect the dignity and rights of those served. School psychologists accept responsibility for the consequences of their acts and ensure that professional skills, position, and influence are applied only for purposes which are consistent with these values.

2. School psychologists respect each person with whom they are working and deal justly and impartially with each regardless of his/her physical, mental, emotional, political, economic, social, cultural, racial, or religious characteristics.

3. School psychologists apply influence, position, and professional skills in ways that protect the dignity and rights of those served. They promote the improvement of the quality of education and of life in general when determining assessment, counseling, and intervention.

4. School psychologists define the direction and the nature of personal loyalties, objectives, and competencies, and advise and inform all persons concerned of these commitments.

5. School psychologists working in both public schools and private settings maintain professional relationships with students, parents, the school, and community. They understand the importance of informing students/clients of all aspects of the potential professional relationship prior to beginning psychological services of any type. School psychologists recognize the need for parental involvement and the significant influence the parent has on the student/client's growth.

6. In a situation where there are divided or conflicting interests (as between parents, school, student, supervisor, trainer) school psychologists are responsible for attempting to work out a plan of action which protects the rights and encourages mutual benefit and protection of rights.

7. School psychologists do not exploit their professional relationships with students, employees, clients, or research participants sexually or otherwise. School psychologists do not engage in, nor condone, deliberate comments, gestures or physical contacts of a sexual nature.

B. Students

1. School psychologists are guided by an awareness of the intimate nature of the examination of personal aspects of an individual. School psychologists use an approach which reflects a humanistic concern for dignity and personal integrity.

2. School psychologists inform the student/client about important aspects of their relationship in a manner that is understood by the student. The explanation includes the uses to be made of information, persons who will receive specific information and possible implications of results.

3. School psychologists recognize the obligation to the student/client and respect the student's/client's right of choice to enter, or to participate, in services voluntarily.

4. School psychologists inform the student/client of the outcomes of assessment, counseling, or other services. Contemplated changes in program, plans for further services and other pertinent information are discussed with the student as a result of services. An account of alternatives available to the student/client is included.

5. The student/client is informed by the school psychologist of those who will receive information regarding the services and the type of information that they will receive. The sharing of information is formulated to fit the age and maturity of the student/client and the nature of the information.

C. Parents

1. School psychologists confer with parents regarding assessment, counseling, and intervention plans in language understandable to the parent. They strive to establish a set of alternatives and suggestions which match the values and skills of each parent.

2. School psychologists recognize the importance of parental support and seek to obtain this by assuring that there is direct parent contact prior to seeing the student/client. They secure continuing parental involvement by a frank and prompt reporting to the parent of findings and progress.

3. School psychologists continue to maintain contact with the parent even though the parent objects to having his/her child receive services. Alternatives are described which will enable the student to get needed help.

4. School psychologists discuss recommendations and plans for assisting the student/client with the parent. The discussion includes alternatives associated with each set of plans. The parents are advised as to sources of help available at school and in the community.

5. School psychologists inform parents of the nature of records made of parent conferences and evaluations of the student/client. Rights of confidentiality and content of reports are shared.

D. Service Delivery

1. School psychologists employed by school districts prepare by becoming knowledgeable of the organization, philosophy, goals, objectives, and methodology of the school.

2. School psychologists recognize that a working understanding of the goals, processes, and legal requirements of the educational system is essential for an effective relationship with the school.

3. Familiarization with organization, instructional materials, and teaching strategies of the school are basic to enable school psychologists to contribute to the common objective of fostering maximum self development opportunities for each student/client.

4. School psychologists accept the responsibility of being members of the staff of those schools. They recognize the need to establish an integral role within the school system and familiarize themselves with the system and community.

E. Community

1. Although enjoying professional identity as a school psychologist, school psychologists are also citizens, thereby accepting the same responsibilities and duties expected of all members of society. School psychologists are free to pursue individual interests, except to the degree that these may compromise fulfillment of their professional responsibilities and have negative impact on the profession. Awareness of such impact guides public behavior.

2. As citizens, school psychologists may exercise their constitutional rights as the basis for procedures and practices designed to bring about social change. Such activities are conducted as involved citizens and not as representatives of school psychologists.

3. As employees or employers, in public or private domains, school psychologists do not engage in or condone practices based on race, handicap, age, gender, sexual preference, religion, or national origin.

4. School psychologists avoid any action that could violate or diminish civil and legal rights of clients.

5. School psychologists in public and private practice have the responsibility of adhering to federal, state, and local laws and ordinances governing their practice. If such laws are in conflict with existing ethical guidelines,

school psychologists proceed toward resolution of such conflict through positive, respected and legal channels.

F. Related Professions

1. School psychologists respect and understand the areas of competence of other professions. They work in full cooperation with other professional disciplines in a relationship based on mutual respect and recognition of the multidisciplinary service needed to meet the needs of students and clients. They recognize the role and obligation of the institution or agency with which other professionals are associated.

2. School psychologists recognize the areas of competence of related professions and other professionals in the field of school psychology. They encourage and support use of all the resources that best serve the interests of their students/clients. They are obligated to have prior knowledge of the competency and qualifications of a referral source. Professional services, as well as technical and administrative resources, are sought in the effort of providing the best possible professional service.

3. School psychologists working within the school system explain their professional competencies to other professionals including role descriptions, assignment of services, and the working relationships among varied professionals within the system.

4. School psychologists cooperate with other professionals and agencies with the rights and needs of their student/client in mind. If a student/client is receiving similar services from another professional, school psychologists assure coordination of services. Private practice school psychologists do not offer their own services to those already receiving services. As school psychologists working within the school system, a need to serve a student may arise as dictated by the student's special program. In this case, consultation with another professional serving the student takes place to assure coordination of services for the welfare of the student.

5. When school psychologists suspect the existence of detrimental or unethical practices, the appropriate professional organization is contacted for assistance and procedures established for questioning ethical practice are followed.

G. Other School Psychologists

1. School psychologists who employ, supervise, and train other professionals accept the obligation of providing experiences to further their professional development. Appropriate working conditions, fair and timely evaluation and constructive consultation are provided.

2. School psychologists acting as supervisors to interns review and evaluate assessment results, conferences, counseling strategies, and documents. They assure the profession that training in the field is supervised adequately.

3. When school psychologists are aware of a possible ethical violation by another school psychologist, they attempt to resolve the issue on an informal level. If such informal efforts are not productive and a violation appears to be enacted, steps for filing an ethical complaint as outlined by the appropriate professional are followed.

IV. PROFESSIONAL PRACTICES — PUBLIC SETTINGS

A. Advocacy

1. School psychologists consider the pupils/clients to be their primary responsibility and act as advocates of their rights and welfare. Course of action takes into account the rights of the student, rights of the parent, the responsibilities of the school personnel,and the expanding self-independence and mature status of the student.

2. School psychologists outline and interpret services to be provided. Their concerns for protecting the interests and rights of students is communicated to the school administration and staff. Human advocacy is the number one priority.

B. Assessment and Intervention

1. School psychologists strive to maintain the highest standard of service by an objective collecting of appropriate data and information necessary to effectively work with students. In conducting a psychoeducational evaluation or counseling/consultation services, due consideration is given to individual integrity and individual differences. School psychologists recognize differences in age, sex, socioeconomic and ethnic backgrounds, and strive to select and use appropriate procedures, techniques, and strategies relevant to such differences.

2. School psychologists insist on collecting relevant data for an evaluation that includes the use of valid and reliable instruments and techniques that are applicable and appropriate for the student.

3. School psychologists combine observations, background information, multi-disciplinary results and other pertinent data to present the most comprehensive and valid picture possible of the student. School psychologists utilize assessment, counseling procedures, consultation techniques and other intervention methods that are consistent with responsible practice, recent research, and professional judgment.

4. School psychologists do not promote the use of psychoeducational assessment techniques by inappropriately trained or otherwise unqualified persons through teaching, sponsorship or supervision.

5. School psychologists develop interventions which are appropriate to the presenting problems of the referred student/client, and which are consistent with the data collected during the assessment of the referral situation.

6. The student/client is referred to another professional for services when a condition is identified which is outside the treatment competencies or scope of the school psychologist.

7. When transferring the intervention responsibility for a student/client to another professional, school psychologists ensure that all relevant and appropriate individuals, including the student/client when appropriate, are notified of the change and reasons for the change.

C. Use of Materials and Computers

1. School psychologists are responsible for maintaining security of

psychological tests which might be rendered useless by revealing the underlying principles or specific content. Every attempt is made by school psychologists to protect test security and copyright restrictions.

2. Copyright laws are adhered to regarding reproduction of tests or any parts thereof. Permission is obtained from authors of noncopyrighted published instruments.

3. School psychologists who utilize student/client information in lectures or publications, either obtain prior consent in writing or remove all identifying data.

4. When publishing, school psychologists acknowledge the sources of their ideas and materials. Credit is given to those who have contributed.

5. School psychologists do not promote or encourage inappropriate use of computer-generated test analysis or reports.

6. School psychologists maintain full responsibility for computerized or any other technological services used by them for diagnostic, consultative, or information management purposes. Such services, if used, should be regarded as tools to be used judiciously without abdication of any responsibility of the psychologist to the tool or to the people who make its operation possible.

7. In the utilization of technological data management services, school psychologists apply the same ethical standards for use, interpretation and maintenance of data as for any other information. They are assured that the computer programs are accurate in all areas of information produced prior to using the results.

D. School-Based Research and Evaluation

1. School psychologists continually assess the impact of any treatment/intervention/counseling plan and terminate or modify the plan when the data indicate that the plan is not achieving the desired goals.

2. In performing research, school psychologists accept responsibility for selection of topics, research methodology, subject selection, data gathering, analysis and reporting. In publishing reports of their research, they provide discussion of limitations of their data and acknowledge existence of disconfirming data, as well as alternate hypotheses and explanations of their findings.

E. Reporting Data and Conferencing Results

1. School psychologists ascertain that student/client information reaches responsible and authorized persons and is adequately interpreted for their use in helping the student/client. This involves establishing procedures which safeguard the personal and confidential interests of those concerned.

2. School psychologists communicate findings and recommendations in language readily understood by the school staff. These communications describe possible favorable and unfavorable consequences associated with the alternative proposals.

3. When reporting data which are to be representative of a student/client, school psychologists take the responsibility for preparing information that is written in terms that are understandable to all involved. It is made certain that information is in such form and style as to assure that the recipient of the report will be able to give maximum assistance to the individual. The emphasis is on the interpretations and recommendations rather than the simple passing along of test scores, and will include an appraisal of the degree of reliance and confidence which can be placed on the information.

4. School psychologists ensure the accuracy of their reports, letters, and other written documents through reviewing and signing such.

5. School psychologists comply with all laws, regulations, and policies pertaining to the adequate storage and disposal of records to maintain appropriate confidentiality of information.

V. PROFESSIONAL PRACTICES — PRIVATE SETTINGS

A. Relationship with School Districts

1. Many school psychologists are employed in both the public and private sectors, and in so doing, create a possible conflict of services if they do not adhere to standards of professional ethics. School psychologists operating in both sectors recognize the importance of separation of roles and the necessity of adherence to all ethical standards.

2. School psychologists engaged in employment in a public school setting and in private practice, may not accept a fee, or any other form of remuneration, for professional work with clients who are entitled to such service through the schools where the school psychologists are currently assigned.

3. School psychologists in private practice have an obligation to inform parents of free and/or mandated services available from the public school system before providing services for pay.

4. School psychologists engaged in employment in a public, as well as private practice setting, maintain such practice outside the hours of contracted employment in their school district.

5. School psychologists engaged in private practice do not utilize tests, materials, or services belonging to the school district without authorization.

6. School psychologists carefully evaluate the appropriateness of the use of public school facilities for part-time private practice. Such use can be confusing to the client and may be criticized as improper. Before the facility is utilized, school psychologists enter into a rental agreement with the school district and clearly define limits of use to the district and the client.

B. Service Delivery

1. School psychologists clarify financial arrangements in advance of services to ensure to the best of their ability that they are clearly understood by the client. They neither give nor receive any remuneration for referring clients for professional services.

2. School psychologists in private practice adhere to the conditions of a contract with the school district, other agency, or individual until service thereunder has been performed, the contract has been terminated by mutual consent, or the contract has otherwise been legally terminated. They have responsibility to follow-up a completed contract to assure that conclusions are understood, interpreted, and utilized effectively.

3. School psychologists in private practice guard against any misunderstanding occurring from recommendations, advice, or information given a parent or child which a school may not be prepared to carry out, or which is in conflict with what the district is doing for the child. Such conflicts are not avoided where the best interests of those served require consideration of different opinion. Direct consultation between the school psychologist in private practice and the school psychologist assigned to the case at the school level may avoid confusing parents by resolving at the professional level any difference of interpretation of clinical data.

4. School psychologists provide individual diagnostic and therapeutic services only within the context of a professional psychological relationship. Personal diagnosis and therapy are not given by means of public lectures, newspaper columns, magazine articles, radio and television programs or mail. Any information shared through such media activities is general in nature and utilizes only current and relevant data and professional judgment.

C. Announcements/Advertising

1. Considerations of appropriate announcement of services, advertising and public media statements are necessary in the role of the school psychologist in private practice. Such activities are necessary in assisting the public to make appropriate and knowledgeable decisions and choices regarding services. Accurate representation of training, experience, services provided, and affiliation are made by school psychologists. Public statements must be made on sound and accepted theory, research, and practice.

2. Individual, agency, or clinical listings in telephone directories are limited to the following: name/names, highest relevant degree, certification status, address, telephone number, brief identification of major areas of practice, office hours, appropriate fee information, foreign languages spoken, policy with regard to third party payments and license number.

3. Announcements of services by school psychologists in private practice, agency, or clinic are made in a formal, professional manner limited to the same information as is included in a telephone listing. Clear statements of purposes with clear descriptions of the experiences to be provided are given. The education, training, and experience of the staff members are appropriately specified.

4. School psychologists in private practice may utilize brochures in the announcement of services. The brochures may be sent to professional persons, schools, business firms, governmental agencies, and other similar organizations.

5. Announcements and advertisements of the availability of publications, products, and services for sale are presented in a professional, scientific, and factual manner. Information may be communicated by means of

periodical, book, list, directory, television, radio, or motion picture and must not include any false, misleading, or comparative statements.

6. School psychologists in private practice do not directly solicit clients for individual diagnosis or therapy.

7. School psychologists do not compensate in any manner a representative of the press, radio, or television in return for personal professional publicity in a news item.

8. School psychologists do not participate for personal gain in commercial announcements or advertisements recommending to the public the purchase or use of products or services.

NASP Standards for Training and Field Placement Programs in School Psychology

I. STRUCTURE OF PROGRAMS IN SCHOOL PSYCHOLOGY

Training programs in school psychology lead to a recognized degree at the doctoral level, or to a sixth-year credential granted by the university or state. Graduate credentials are customarily based upon satisfactory completion of a minimum number of course credits. In each instance there is a planned, supervised and integrated program of graduate study. Programs are titled School Psychology and are clearly identifiable as organizational units.

1. Doctoral Program Requirements

1.1 *Standard:* Doctoral programs shall consist of a minimum of four years of full-time academic study or its equivalent beyond the baccalaureate degree. The program shall include a minimum of 84 graduate semester hours or the equivalent, at least 72 hours of which are exclusive of credit for the predoctoral supervised internship experience and any terminal doctoral project (e.g., dissertation) and shall culminate in institutional documentation.

1.2 *Standard:* The program shall limit the number of credit hours acquired through courses, seminars, and other learning experiences not open exclusively to graduate students to no more than one-third of the student's program.

1.3 *Standard:* Doctoral program requirements exclude credit for undergraduate study, study which is remedial, or study which is designed to remove deficiencies in meeting requirements for program admission.

1.4 *Standard:* Doctoral programs shall include at least one academic year of predoctoral supervised internship experience consisting of a minimum of 1200 clock hours, at least 600 hours of which must be in a school setting.

1.5 *Standard:* No more than 12 graduate semester hours awarded as credit for the predoctoral supervised internship experience shall be counted toward the required minimum of 84 graduate semester hours.

1.6 *Standard:* A full-time continuous residency or an alternate planned experience is required for all doctoral candidates. Programs allowing alternate planned experiences as a substitute for full-time residency must demonstrate how those experiences are equivalent to those commonly associated with residency requirements for the doctoral degree.

2. **Sixth-Year/Specialist Program Requirements**

    2.1   *Standard:* Sixth-Year/Specialist programs shall consist of a minimum of three years of full-time academic study or the equivalent beyond the baccalaureate degree, including at least 60 graduate semester hours or the equivalent, and shall culminate in institutional documentation.

    2.2   *Standard:* The program shall limit the number of credit hours acquired through courses, seminars and other learning experiences not open exclusively to graduate students to no more than one-third of the student's program.

    2.3   *Standard:* Sixth-Year/Specialist program requirements exclude credit for undergraduate study, study which is remedial, or study which is designed to remove deficiencies in meeting requirements for program admission.

    2.4   *Standard:* Sixth-Year/Specialist programs shall include at least one academic year of supervised internship experience consisting of a minimum of 1200 clock hours, at least 600 hours of which must be in a school setting.

    2.5   *Standard:* No more than 12 graduate semester hours awarded as credit for the supervised internship experience shall be counted toward the required minimum of 60 graduate semester hours.

    2.6   *Standard:* A full-time continuous residency or an alternate planned experience is required for all Sixth-Year/Specialist candidates. Programs allowing alternate planned experiences as a substitute for full-time residency must demonstrate how those experiences are equivalent to those commonly associated with residency requirements for the Sixth-Year/Specialist degree.

3. **Content of School Psychology Program**

    3.1   *Standard:* The curriculum shall be based on explicitly specified objectives that reflect the program's conception of the professional roles for which the school psychology trainee is being prepared. There shall be a direct and obvious relationship between those objectives and the components of the curriculum. (Foundation areas in which all school psychology trainees must be prepared are presented in Standard 3.4.) The curriculum shall differentiate the level of preparation for Doctoral study as being advanced in breadth and/or beyond that for Sixth-Year/Specialist study.

    3.2   *Standard:* Through multicultural education for all school psychology trainees, the program shall promote understanding of respect for, and responsiveness to cultural diversity.

    3.3   *Standard:* The program shall promote understanding of and responsiveness to the special needs of exceptional persons in all school psychology trainees.

    3.4   *Standard:* The program shall insure the substantial preparation of all school psychology trainees in each of the following areas through courses, course content or other appropriate means:

Psychological Foundations
Biological Bases of Behavior
Cultural Diversity
Child and Adolescent Development (Normal and Abnormal)
Human Exceptionalities
Human Learning
Social Bases of Behavior

Educational Foundations
Education of Exceptional Learners
Instructional and Remedial Techniques
Organization and Operation of Schools

Assessment
Interventions (Direct and Indirect)
Consultation
Counseling
Behavior Management

Statistics and Research Design
Professional School Psychology
History and Foundations of School Psychology
Legal and Ethical Issues
Professional Issues and Standards
Roles and Functions of the School Psychologist

4. **Orientation to the Educational Process**

4.1 *Standard:* Programs shall employ a systematic and reasoned sequential plan to orient school psychology students to the educational institutions they will ultimately serve.

4.2 *Standard:* Programs shall provide students with a planned program of directed observations and participation in educational settings.

4.3 *Standard:* Programs shall acquaint students with roles, responsibilities, and functions of other pupil service personnel, including the operation of interdisciplinary teams.

4.4 *Standard:* Programs shall familiarize students with available school and community resources.

5. **Practica Experiences**
   (For a description of suggested practices, see page 948)

5.1 *Standard:* Practica experiences shall be distinct from and occur prior to the internship.

5.2 *Standard:* Practica experiences shall occur at the time(s) appropriate to the specific training objectives of the program.

5.3 *Standard:* Practica experiences shall be of sufficient length of time to be appropriate to the specific training objectives of the program.

5.4 *Standard:* There shall be a direct and obvious relationship between the practica experiences and the objectives for which the practica are intended.

5.5 *Standard:* Practica experiences shall occur under conditions of supervision appropriate to the specific training objectives of the program.

5.6 *Standard:* Practica experiences shall be provided appropriate recognition through the awarding of academic credit.

5.7 *Standard:* Practica experiences shall be provided in settings supportive of the specific training objectives of the program.

5.8 *Standard:* Practica experiences shall occur with university involvement appropriate to the specific training objectives of the program.

5.9 *Standard:* Practica experiences shall be systematically evaluated in a manner consistent with the specific training objectives of the program.

6. Internship Experiences
(For a description of suggested practices, see page 950)

6.1 *Standard:* The internship experience shall be provided at or near the end of the formal training period.

6.2 *Standard:* The internship experience shall occur on a full-time basis over a period of one academic year, or on a half-time basis over a period of two consecutive academic years.

6.3 *Standard:* The internship experience shall be consistent with a written plan and shall meet the specific training objectives of the program.

6.4 *Standard:* The internship experience shall occur in a setting appropriate to the specific training objectives of the program.

6.5 *Standard:* At least 600 clock hours of the internship experience shall occur in a school setting and shall provide a balanced exposure to regular and special educational programs.

6.6 *Standard:* The internship experience shall be provided appropriate recognition through the awarding of academic credit.

6.7 *Standard:* The internship experience shall occur under conditions of appropriate supervision. Field-based internship supervisors shall hold a valid credential as a school psychologist for that portion of the internship that is in a school setting. That portion of the internship which appropriately may be in a non-school setting shall require supervision by an appropriately credentialed psychologist.

6.8 *Standard:* Field-based internship supervisors shall be responsible for no more than two interns at any given time. University internship supervisors shall be responsible for no more than twelve interns at any given time.

6.9 *Standard:* Field-based internship supervisors shall provide at least two hours per week of direct supervision for each intern. University internship supervisors shall maintain an on-going relationship with field-based internship supervisors and shall provide at least one field-based contact per semester with each intern.

6.10 *Standard:* The internship placement agency shall provide appropriate support for the internship experience which shall include: (a) a written contractual agreement specifying the period of appointment and the terms of compensation, (b) a schedule of appointments consistent with that of agency school psychologists (e.g., calendar, participation in in-service meetings, etc.), (c) provision for participation in continuing professional development activities, (d) expense reimbursement consistent with policies pertaining to agency school psychologists, (e) an appropriate work environment including adequate supplies, materials, secretarial services, and office space, (f) release time for internship supervisors, and (g) a commitment to the internship as a training experience.

6.11 *Standard:* The internship experience shall be systematically evaluated in a manner consistent with the specific training objectives of the program.

6.12 *Standard:* The internship experiences shall be conducted in a manner consistent with the current legal-ethical standards of the profession.

7. Continuing Professional Development

7.1 *Standard:* The program shall provide an active continuing professional development program for practicing school psychologists.

8. Program Approval

8.1 *Standard:* Programs shall meet established approval standards for the state department of education in whose jurisdiction the program is located.

II. CRITERIA FOR PROGRAM FACULTY

9. Program Administrators

9.1 *Standard:* Both Doctoral and Sixth-Year/Specialist programs shall be directed/coordinated by persons who hold the doctorate with specialization in school psychology and are certificated and/or licensed for the practice of school psychology in the state in which the program is located.

9.2 *Standard:* The director/coordinator of both Doctoral and Sixth-Year/Specialist programs shall possess at least two years of experience as a school psychologist in an appropriate setting.

10. Preparation of Full-Time Faculty

10.1 *Standard:* Full-time faculty shall possess the doctoral degree in psychology, education, or a closely related discipline with a specialization supportive of their training responsibilities in school psychology.

10.2 *Standard:* Faculty with responsibilities for field supervision in school psychology and/or teaching professional courses in school psychology shall possess at least two years of experience as a school psychologist in a school setting.

10.3 *Standard:* Each full-time faculty member shall engage in ongoing learning relevant to his/her training responsibilities and shall provide evidence of continuing professional development in school psychology.

10.4 *Standard:* Each full-time faculty member shall provide evidence of ongoing contributions to the field of school psychology through professional service activities such as writing, research, consultation, involvement with professional organizations, and/or field experiences.

11. Preparation of Part-Time Faculty

11.1 *Standard:* Part-time faculty shall meet the preparation requirements for appointment to the full-time faculty (10.1, 10.2, 10.3, 10.4) and shall be selected based upon their ability to make special contributions to the school psychology program.

12. Composition of Faculty for Doctoral Degree Programs

12.1 *Standard:* The faculty for each doctoral program shall include at least three full-time positions. At least two of the positions must be filled by full-time faculty who hold the doctorate with specialization in school psychology and who possess at least two years of experience as a school psychologist in a school setting. At least one additional full-time position must be filled by a full-time faculty member who holds the doctorate in a field which directly supports the program.

12.2 *Standard:* The program shall provide a plan to recruit, maintain, and promote the professional development of faculty with minority characteristics in terms of sex, race, ethnic origin, and handicapping conditions.

12.3 *Standard:* The faculty shall be sufficient to assure an average faculty-student ratio not in excess of 1:10.

13. Composition of Faculty for Sixth-Year/Specialist Degree Programs

13.1 *Standard:* The faculty for each Sixth-Year/Specialist program shall include at least three full-time equivalent positions. At least two of the positions must be filled by full-time faculty who hold the doctorate with specialization in school psychology and who possess at least two years of experience as a school psychologist in a school setting. At least one additional full-time equivalent position must be filled by full-time faculty who hold doctorates in fields which directly support the program.

13.2 *Standard:* The program shall provide a plan to recruit, maintain, and promote the professional development of faculty with minority characteristics in terms of sex, race, ethnic origin, and handicapping conditions.

13.3 *Standard:* The faculty shall be sufficient to assure an average faculty-student ratio not in excess of 1:10.

14. Conditions for Faculty Service

14.1 *Standard:* In addition to teaching, supervision, advising, professional involvement and research or scholarly activities, faculty responsibilities may also include community service and administrative functions.

14.2 *Standard:* Institutional policies shall provide for the allotment of sufficient time for faculty to engage in each area of responsibility.

14.3 *Standard:* Institutional policy shall limit teaching and supervision of practica and internship assignments to a maximum of 75% of the total faculty workload.

14.4 *Standard:* Institutional policy shall provide for at least 25% release time from other faculty responsibilities for the program administrator.

III. CRITERIA FOR STUDENTS

15. Admission to Program

15.1 *Standard:* The program shall apply specific published criteria, both objective and subjective, for the admission of students to the program at each level.

15.2 *Standard:* Program policy and actions shall reflect a commitment to multicultural education in the recruitment and retention of students with minority characteristics in terms of sex, race, ethnic origin, and handicapping conditions.

16. Evaluation of Students in the Program

16.1 *Standard:* The program shall apply a published selective retention process which includes clearly stated evaluative criteria and a time frame for the systematic review of the progress of all students.

16.2 *Standard:* The evaluation criteria included in the selection retention process shall address the academic and professional competencies, as well as the personal characteristics appropriate for practice as a school psychologist.

IV. INSTITUTIONAL RESOURCES AND FACILITIES

17. Physical Facilities

17.1 *Standard:* The program shall insure that adequate office, clinical and laboratory facilities, data and information processing facilities, supplies and equipment are available to and appropriate for the necessary demands of faculty and students in school psychology.

17.2 *Standard:* The program shall provide reasonable accommodation for the special needs of handicapped students and faculty which is consistent with that provided for non-handicapped persons.

18. Library

18.1 *Standard:* The library shall provide resources that are adequate to support instruction, independent study, and research relevant to school psychology.

18.2 *Standard:* Through the library or a materials and instructional media center, pertinent films, videotapes, microfilms, and other media materials and equipment shall be accessible in support of the school psychology programs.

V. EVALUATION OF GRADUATES, PROGRAM, AND PLANNING

19. Evaluation of Graduates

19.1 *Standard:* The program shall engage in systematic efforts to evaluate the quality of its graduates upon completion of their programs of study and after they enter their professional roles. The evaluation shall include evidence of graduate performance in relation to stated program objectives.

20. Evaluation of Program

20.1 *Standard:* The program shall engage in systematic efforts to evaluate the quality of its instructional offerings. Evaluation shall include consideration of student input.

20.2 *Standard:* The program shall insure representative student, faculty, and consumer participation in the evaluation of the school psychology program.

20.3 *Standard:* The results of the program evaluation shall be used in the modification and improvement of the school psychology program.

21. Program Development

21.1 *Standard:* The program shall have plans for its long-range development and the enhancement of its relationship to the profession of school psychology.

PRACTICA EXPERIENCES

Suggested Practices.

Practica are viewed as integral and essential components of professional training. They provide opportunities for trainees to gather knowledge and skills most appropriately learned in the field and to refine skills and clarify knowledge learned as a part of the university training program. Practica experiences are characterized in the following manner:

1. They may be offered through on-campus agencies (e.g., Child Study Center, Psychology Clinic), community agencies (e.g., public or private schools, mental health centers) or some combination of the two.
2. Supervision and principal responsibility for the student typically rest with the faculty of the university training program.
3. The experience is offered for academic credit.
4. The experience is completed prior to an internship.
5. The experience is a requirement for credential completion.
6. The experience is more limited than the internship with regard to the range of cases, situations, etc., to which the trainee is exposed.
7. On-campus instruction is often provided concurrently or as part of the experience.
8. The experience is a direct extension of specific training activities.
9. The experience is generally part-time.

Programs provide practica experiences as integral parts of the training sequence. This is typically accomplished through the provision of separate practicum courses or practical application components of courses specifically designed for skill acquisition.

Practica experiences are provided to students at times most appropriately related to the acquisition of specific skills. They also are of sufficient time to allow for desired skill acquisition. Courses designed to develop skills in diagnostic assessment, for example, have practicum components which allow students opportunities to become thoroughly familiar with instruments being taught.

Practica, or practical application course components, are provided under conditions appropriate to the program objectives. The typically offered practicum experience in diagnostic assessment, for example, is offered in settings conducive to the appropriate skill acquisition such as in schools, clinics, or service agencies. Similarly, the tasks required of students are to be clearly related to the desired skill acquisition and the sample of subjects employed (or target population) is suitable.

Where practicum experiences and supervision are provided in the facilities of, and under the supervision of the program faculty, it may be assumed that adequate support is provided. Often, however, such experiences are provided in facilities which may be affiliated with the program in other administrative arrangements such as schools, clinics, or service agencies outside the immediate administrative control of the program faculty. In such situations, attention is given to the provision of adequate support (e.g., equipment, facilities, resource personnel, etc.).

As required by Standard 5.5, all practica supervision *must* be provided by program faculty or other supervisory personnel who possess background, training, and credentials appropriate to the practicum experiences. Supervision is available to students in sufficient amounts of time (a minimum of two hours per week is recommended in courses designated specifically as practica) to assure the acquisition of desired skills. Program faculty and other supervisory personnel receive adequate release time from normal duties to supervise practicum students. Such assigned time is consistent with the academic credit assigned to the practicum and compatible with the full-time duties of the staff member. Thus program faculty members assigned to practicum supervision are credited with an hour load which is consistent with the credit hours assigned to the practicum when the practicum is provided as a separate course. When provided in the context of practical application to existing courses, the duties are reflected in the credit hour assignment for the course. Similarly, field-based supervisors are provided load recognition of their duties as field supervisors for university practica.

The program faculty are responsible for providing appropriate orientation to non-program supervisors. This facilitates the clarification of the role and function of all parties and assists the non-program supervisors in carrying out responsibilities in a manner consistent with the program objectives. The responsibility of program faculty and non-program supervisors are clearly understood and agreed upon by both parties when both are engaged in practicum supervision of the same students.

Support is also evidenced in the number of students considered reasonable to be supervised by either program faculty or field-based supervisors. A maximum of six students per practicum, when offered as a separate course, is advised for program faculty. Where field-based supervisors provide the major supervision as a part of their full-time duties, a maximum of three students is advised. The number of students to be supervised may vary as a function of the time allowed by the university or field agency.

There is a systematic means of evaluating the practicum experience which seeks to ensure the acquisition of desired skills by students. This evaluation is appropriate to the program objectives whether accomplished via on-campus or off-campus placements or through practical application components of separate courses. The evaluation also seeks to clarify the utility of the experience in terms of setting, supervision, etc. In this manner, the evaluation process is twofold, evaluating both the students' progress and the suitability of the various characteristics of the experience. This allows for future planning in terms of student needs and practicum placements. Where practical applications are incorporated into various courses in the training sequence, evaluation is appropriate to the total course evaluation conducted by the university department or program.

INTERNSHIP EXPERIENCES

Suggested Practices

The internship has the basic characteristics of allowing the student to demonstrate skill proficiencies acquired during formal training on campus and to acquire additional knowledge and skills most appropriately gained through field placement settings. The internship experience is characterized in the following manner:

1. It is generally offered in school settings and in other agencies serving children from infancy to late adolescence.
2. Supervision and principal responsibility for the student typically rest directly with the local off-campus agency, although indirect supervision is provided by the university.
3. The experience is typically offered for academic credit.
4. The experience occurs after the successful completion of practica.
5. The experience is a requirement for credentialing.
6. The experience is far less limited than the practicum experience and allows the intern to be exposed to cases, situations, etc., that are considered representative of the role and function of the school psychologist.
7. The experience occurs on a full-time basis over a period of one academic year, or on a half-time basis over a period of two consecutive academic years.
8. The experience is primarily a training activity and provides a balance of training and service objectives and functions.
9. On-campus coursework is reduced in proportion to the demands of the internship experience.

The internship is an intense and diversified experience as compared to the practicum placement and requires the provision of close supervision.

Training programs have written guidelines which specify the academic and non-academic experiences prerequisite to the internship placement. Those guidelines are employed in determining whether or not students are adequately prepared for the internship experience.

A written plan for the internship experience is prepared and agreed upon by representatives of the local educational agency, the intern supervisor(s), training program supervisory staff and the intern, prior to the placement. Such plans identify internship objectives, describe appropriate experiences for the achievement of the objectives and outline an evaluation plan for determining the achievement of each objective. The plan also delineates the responsibilities for both the university and the local supervisory personnel.

The intern seeking credentialing as a school psychologist must have internship experiences in a school setting. Though other settings may be incorporated into the internship experience, the school setting shall constitute at least 600 clock hours of the internship experience. Where additional settings are employed, a rationale specifies its appropriate relationship to the practice of school psychology.

The school setting has the availability of:

a. children of all school ages,
b. pupil personnel services functioning within a team framework,
c. full-range services for handicapped children of both high and low incidence,
d. regular and special educational services at the preschool, elementary, and secondary levels,
e. at least one certified school psychologist having at least two years of full-time school psychologist experience or the equivalent who serves as the internship supervisor.

It is not essential that the above all be provided within the context of the local educational agency to which the intern is assigned. However, it is essential that all elements be available and integrated into the internship experience. Thus rural districts participating in joint agreements, special education districts, and other administrative arrangements for the provision of special services are considered equally appropriate as internship settings to larger educational agencies which provide all elements as part of their educational programs.

The required school-based internship experience is provided off-campus in a local educational agency. While the authority for providing internship credit and grades rests with the university faculty, primary responsibility for intern supervision usually rests with appropriately credentialed local educational agency personnel.

Local supervision is provided by a person(s) holding a valid credential as a school psychologist, who is employed full-time as a school psychologist in the local educational agency and who has held such employment in that agency for a minimum of one school year prior to undertaking supervisory responsibilities. In non-school settings, supervisory personnel hold an appropriate credential for that setting.

Program faculty are responsible for providing appropriate orientation to non-program supervisors. This facilitates the clarification of the role and function of all parties and assists the non-program supervisors in carrying out responsibilities in a manner consistent with the training objectives.

Both local and university supervisors demonstrate active involvement in the profession as evidenced through professional association memberships, scholarly pursuits, experience and professional competence, and continued professional development.

a. **Contract and salary:**
   A written contractual agreement is prepared and agreed to by both the local educational agency and the intern school psychologist. The contractual agreement specifies the time period and salary provided. When financially possible the intern is provided a salary commensurate with his or her level of training, experience, and period of appointment. Contractual agreements are not entered into which require the intern to remain in the employment of the local educational agency beyond employment during the internship. Moreover, such arrangements do not specify in advance that employment for the intern is guaranteed beyond the internship.

b. **Schedule of appointment:**
   The intern is assigned to the same schedule and calendar time as are other school psychology staff employed by the local educational agency. Experiences such as inservice meetings, conferences, etc., participated in by local educational agency school psychologists are also expected of interns. Like regularly employed psychological services personnel, the intern evidences a commitment to the provision of psychological services not necessarily reflected in hourly schedules.

c. **Awareness of the need for continued professional development:**
   It is important that continued professional development be recognized as a significant aspect of the internship. The intern is expected to participate in scheduled appropriate university, regional, and state-wide meetings for school psychologists. The opportunity to participate in national level meetings is also encouraged. The appropriation of reimbursement monies is strongly encouraged. When reimbursement or other financial support is unavailable, released time for attendance at professional meetings is provided. In instances where released time is judged to detract from the provision of the internship experiences as planned, an agreement may be reached in which the intern serves additional time beyond the contractual schedule or calendar.

d. Travel expenses:
The provision of appropriate internship experiences often requires job-related travel. When such exists, the intern is provided reimbursement consistent with policies of the local educational agency.

e. Work environment:
The provision of quality psychological services requires a supportive work environment. The local educational agency ensures that the intern is provided adequate supplies and materials to carry out the functions of the internship. In addition, adequate privacy of office facilities and access to secretarial assistance is maintained. The physical plant has available central office facilities for files, professional library, storage of supplies and material, and telephone services. Access to office equipment such as duplication devices and recording equipment is also provided. The provisions are consistent with the availability afforded regular staff members.

f. Provision of supervision:
The local educational agency ensures that supervisory personnel meet the criteria specified in Standard 6.7. Released time for personal supervisory contact with each intern in the amount specified above and the maximum number of interns to be served is afforded the supervisor. In order to provide the quality of internship supervision required, local educational agency supervisors are granted the equivalent of one work day per week of assigned time for each intern supervised, with full-time assignment of duties granted to the supervision of six interns. In no instance shall more than six interns be assigned to one supervisor.

g. Training commitment:
The local educational agency is committed to the internship as basically a training experience. The appointment of interns as a means of acquiring less expensive services is inappropriate. Interns are expected to engage in tasks appropriate to the completion of the plan of internship. The intern is not asked to serve in any capacity other than that for which he or she was appointed. Tasks requiring teaching assignment, playground or other supervision, etc., indigenous to the roles of other school personnel are included only when there is a specific rationale related to the completion of the internship objectives.

A specific plan of internship evaluation is provided. The plan includes provisions for the evaluation of all significant aspects of the internship experience, including:

a. the experiences provided by the local educational agency,
b. the quality of local supervision,
c. the quality of university supervision,
d. the competencies of the intern,
e. the suitability of the setting for future internships,
f. the suitability of the intern's preparation for internship.

Procedures are designated which recognize the importance of due process, respecting the rights and privileges of the parties involved. In most instances, the assignment of academic credit to the experience necessitates that the university personnel or specifically designated representatives have authority for the official specification of the grade. Significant input of local supervisory personnel to the internship must be indicated. Evaluation procedures indicate a process which allows for ongoing evaluation during the internship as opposed to any single evaluation occurring at the end of the experience. Evaluation is the combined responsibility of all parties involved, including local supervisors, interns and university faculty.

NASP Standards for Credentialing of School Psychologists

I. CREDENTIALING STRUCTURE

1. Legal Basis for Credentialing

1.1 Credentialing is the process whereby a state authorizes the provision of school psychologist services and the use of the title School Psychologist by professionals meeting acceptable standards of training and experience. The basis of a state's credentialing policy is found in its statutory laws, whereby all providers of such services and all users of such title must hold a current credential, and legal sanctions and sanctioning procedures are provided for violators.

2. Credentialing Body

2.1 The state legislature should empower one or more bodies to administer the credentialing process. Administrative codes and regulations adopted by such bodies should comply with these *Standards for the Credentialing of School Psychologists*, and should carry the weight of law.

3. Nature of the Credential: Entry Level and Independent Practice

3.1 The credential should be issued in writing, and should expressly authorize both the practice of school psychology and the exclusive use of the title School Psychologist in all settings, public and private.

A. The *Entry Level* credential shall allow for the practice of school psychology as defined by NASP's *Standards for the Provision of School Psychological Services* (1984) in public and private settings (e.g., school, educational, mental health-related, or university-based child study clinics) under supervision as defined by the appropriate governing body(ies) in each state. This *Entry Level* credential shall be issued for an initial period of three years and may be renewed only once (see Entry Level Credential Renewal, Section 8.1).

1. Supervision at the *Entry Level* credential status shall involve a minimum of one face-to-face contact hour per week or two consecutive face-to-face contact hours once every two weeks with a Supervising School Psychologist or a state licensed Psychologist with appropriate training and experience equivalent to that specified in NASP's *Standards for Training and Field Placement Programs in School Psychology* (1984). Such supervision will continue for the duration of the school psychologist's *Entry Level* status.

B. The *Independent Practice* credential allows school psychologists to have professional autonomy in determining the nature, scope and extent of their specific services in all settings, public and private. These services are consistent with the NASP definitions of school psychological services, and are delivered within the bounds of the school psychologist's training, supervised experience, and demonstrated expertise as specified in NASP's *Standards for the Provision of School Psychological Services* (1984) and *Principles for Professional Ethics* (1984). The *Independent Practice* credential shall be renewable and shall be issued for durations of no more than five years (see Section 8.2)

3.2 In instances where a state empowers more than one body to issue more than one type of credential, such as for the separate regulation of school psychological services in the public schools and in private practice, the lowest entry levels of all such credentials should conform to these standards, as long as this lowest level is not below the 60 semester hour level. All rights and privileges granted for school psychological practice at the lower entry level should be accepted at the higher entry level and therefore by both state empowered bodies.

4. Post-Credential Options and Criteria

4.1 Supervising School Psychologist
A school psychologist may function as a Supervising School Psychologist if he/she holds or is eligible to hold a valid Independent Practice Credential issued by the Credentialing Body. Such an individual would perform the duties of supervision of individuals holding the entry level credential, under the guidelines of supervision delineated in Section 4.4.2 of NASP's *Standards for the Provision of School Psychological Services* (1984).

II. CREDENTIALING REQUIREMENTS

5. Criteria: Entry Level

Entry level credentialing requires that criteria be met in three professional competency areas: personal characteristics, educational qualifications, and practitioner competencies.

5.1 Personal Characteristics
The applicant shall provide evidence that his/her professional work is characterized by the following behaviors as developed and evaluated through courses, course content, practica, internship, or other appropriate means:

1. Adaptability
2. Communication Skills
3. Conscientiousness
4. Cooperation
5. Independence
6. Motivation
7. Personal Stability
8. Productivity
9. Professional Ethics
10. Professional Image

5.2 Educational Qualifications

The minimum requirement for entry level credentialing shall be a sixth year/specialist (i.e., a Master's degree plus 30 graduate semester hours) program, with a 60 graduate semester hour minimum, consisting of coursework, practica, internship, and an appropriate graduate degree from an accredited institution of higher learning. Criteria for each area will be consistent with NASP's *Standards for Training and Field Placement Programs in School Psychology* (1984). The applicant shall provide evidence of his/her ability to acquire, integrate, and express factual and theoretical information and his/her ability to make inferences, interpretations, and conclusions from conceptual and experimental research or applications in the following core competency areas:

Psychological Foundations
Biological Bases of Behavior
Cultural Diversity
Child and Adolescent Development (Normal/Abnormal)
Human Exceptionalities
Human Learning
Social Bases of Behavior

Educational Foundations
Education of Exceptional Learners
Instruction and Remedial Techniques
Organization and Operation of Schools

Assessment Interventions (Direct and Indirect)
Consultation
Counseling
Behavior Management

Statistics and Research Design
Professional School Psychology
History and Foundations of School Psychology
Legal and Ethical Issues
Professional Issues and Standards
Roles and Functions of the School Psychologist

5.3 Practitioner Competencies

A. The applicant shall provide written evidence of his/her ability to perform competently as a practitioner.

B. Such evidence shall consist minimally of successful completion and documentation of a practicum experience and internship consistent with criteria outlines in NASP's *Standards for Training and Field Placement Programs in School Psychology* (1984).

1. The internship experience shall consist of a minimum of one academic year or its equivalent with a minimum of 1200 clock hours, at least 600 hours of which must be in a school setting. Other acceptable internship experiences include private, state-approved educational programs or other appropriate mental health-related programs or settings for the education of children and youth.

2. The state credentialing body may waive or give credit for up to 400 hours of the internship requirement for documented, professional experience in another related psychological or educational field as long as such experience was completed while permanently credentialed in that area. Under such conditions, 600 of the remaining 800 hours of the internship must be completed in a school setting.

C. Other practicum and internship criteria are outlined in NASP's *Standards for Training and Field Placement Programs in School Psychology* (1984).

D. Evidence of adherence to legal, ethical, and professional standards cited in NASP's *Standards for the Provision of School Psychological Services* (1984) and NASP's *Principles for Professional Ethics* (1984) as verified through the procedures outlined in Section 7.1.C.

6. **Criteria: Independent Practice Level**

Independent Practice Level credentialing utilizes the Entry Level Credential as its foundation. Therefore, the same three competency levels apply: personal characteristics, educational qualifications, and practitioner competencies.

6.1 Personal Characteristics: Same as for Entry Level, see Section II.5.1.

6.2 Educational Qualifications: Same as for Entry Level, see Section II.5.2

6.3 Practitioners Competencies:

A. Evidence of successful completion of three years (Full Time Equivalent, F.T.E.) of supervised experience in a school or other acceptable setting (see Section 3.1.A under Entry Level Criteria), after entry level credentialing in the practice of school psychology. Three years will be defined as 27 months (three 9-month academic years) of F.T.E. experience. This experience must be accumulated over a period of time not to exceed six calendar years.

B. Written evidence of adherence to legal, ethical, and professional standards cited in NASP's *Standards for the Provision of School Psychological Services* (1984) and NASP's *Principles for Professional Ethics* (1984) as verified through the procedures outlined in Section 7.1.C.

C. Written evidence of participation in Continuing Professional Development (CPD) activities consistent with NASP's *Standards for the Provisions of School Psychological Services* (1984) and evidence of maintenance of high professional standards and practice as verified through procedures outlined in Section 7.1.C.

III. CERTIFICATION REVIEW PROCEDURES

7. Applying for Certification-Evaluation of Materials

A modified "Approved Program" mechanism should form the basis for the credentialing assessment. Only graduates from NASP/NCATE Accredited programs, or from acceptable state-approved programs, or the equivalent, shall be eligible for credentialing. Each accredited program shall be responsible for assessing a program candidate's admission qualifications and for granting advanced program standing if appropriate. The responsibility for the final determination of minimum professional competencies in all credentialing areas, however, rests with the Credentialing Body. All assessment methods by both the training program and the Credentialing Body should rely on the most objective, quantifiable, and accountable procedures available.

7.1 Entry Level Credential

A. Personal Characteristics

The assessment of appropriate personal characteristics shall be verified and completed by the applicant's accredited training program. Such verification shall include, but not necessarily be limited to, a written rating document. This verification shall be provided by at least one of each of the following, each of whom has had at least one full semester of continuous contact with the applicant: a trainer, a field supervisor who has directly supervised the applicant, and a consumer of the applicant's supervised services (e.g., a superintendent, principal, teacher, or parent). A rating of satisfactory from all input sources must be obtained.

B. Educational Qualifications

Evidence for this standard shall consist of grades in coursework and practica which has been designated by the Approved Program's Director as meeting each content objective. The minimum 60 graduate-level semester hour program shall consist of at least 48 semester hours or the equivalent of academic coursework and a maximum of 12 semester hours of internship or the equivalent. This program shall be fully documented on the candidate's official transcript with evidence of satisfactory completion.

C. Practitioner Competencies

All practitioner competencies must be demonstrated in academic coursework, practica, and in supervised internships. Evidence for the attainment of minimum practitioner competencies shall be verified by the Program Director in the academic setting and by both the Program Director and the internship supervisor in the internship setting.

7.2 Independent Practice Level Credential

A. Personal Characteristics

The assessment of appropriate personal characteristics shall be based on the candidate's experience as a practicing school psychologist. Such verification shall include, but not necessarily be limited to, a written rating document. This verification shall be provided by at least one of each of the following, each of whom has had at least one half school year (i.e., not less than 90 school days) of continuous contact with the applicant: a supervising school psychologist (or the equivalent) who has directly supervised the applicant and a consumer of the applicant's supervised services (e.g., a superintendent, principal, teacher or parent). A rating of satisfactory from all input sources must be obtained.

B. Educational Qualifications: Same as 7.1.B, this document.

C. Practitioner Competencies

1. Evidence for this standard shall consist of written supervisor verification of minimum competence in each of the core

competency areas listed in Section 5.2 during the supervised experience and verification of adherence to the legal, ethical, and professional standards of the profession as specified in NASP's *Standards for the Provision of School Psychological Services* (1984) and NASP's *Principles for Professional Ethics* (1984). Such verification shall include, but not necessarily be limited to, a written rating document.

2. Evidence for this standard shall also consist of written verification of participation in Continuing Professional Development (CPD) activities as documented by NASP or an equivalent agency.

8. Certificate Renewal/Continuing Education

All school psychologists must actively participate and engage in activities designed to maintain, expand, and extend their professional training and skills, thus ensuring the continuation of quality service delivery. Such efforts are documented by participation in the NASP or affiliated Continuing Professional Development (CPD) Program or its equivalent. Regularly scheduled credential renewal affords the opportunity to document such activities.

8.1 Entry Level Credential Renewal

The *Entry Level* credential should be issued for an initial period of three years by the designated State Credentialing Body. The Entry Level credential may be renewed only once except under conditions specified in Section 8.1.D below. Therefore, three years of successful supervised experience in settings specified in Section 3.1.A must be obtained within six calendar years of the initial credentialing date. The *Entry Level* credential renewal shall be granted to applicants meeting the following criteria:

A. Verified evidence of continued competence in Personal Characteristics (see Section 7.s.A).

B. Verified evidence of continued competence in Practitioner Competencies (see Section 7.2.C).

C. Verified evidence of continued professional development consistent with NASP's *Standards for the Provision of School Psychological Services* (1984).

D. Practitioners who do not attain the necessary supervision may petition the State Credentialing Body for consideration of additional time or opportunity to meet these supervision standards while maintaining their Entry Level status. The Credentialing Body should have a documented mechanism to guide this process.

8.2 Independent Practice Level Credential Renewal

The independent practice credential should be issued for a period of five years by the designated State Credentialing Body. Renewal should be granted to applicants meeting the following criteria:

A. Verified evidence of public, private, or university-based practice for a minimum of 18 months of F.T.E. experience during the previous five years.

B. Verified evidence of continued professional development consistent with the NASP's *Standards for the Provision of School Psychological Services* (1984).

C. Practitioners who do not attain the necessary 18 months of experience may reapply to the Credentialing Body for consideration of a renewal of the Entry Level Credential. All materials for this re-evaluation must be updated from any previous application.

9. Withdrawal/Termination of the Credential

The Credentialing Body, after following a documented procedure ensuring the due process rights of the school psychologist, shall have the right to cancel, revoke, suspend, or refuse to renew the credential of any school psychologist or to reprimand any school psychologist, upon proof that the school psychologist:

1. has been convicted by any court of a felony or of a violation of the law involving moral turpitude; the conviction of a felony shall be the conviction of any offense which if committed within the state would constitute felony under the laws of that state;

2. uses drugs or intoxicating liquors to an extent that affects his/her professional competency;

3. has been guilty of fraud or deceit in connection with his/her services rendered as a school psychologist;

4. has aided or abetted a person, not a credentialed school psychologist, in representing him/herself as a school psychologist within the state;

5. has been guilty of unprofessional conduct as defined by NASP's *Principles for Professional Ethics* (1984) or *Standards for the Provision of School Psychological Services* (1984).

V. IMPLEMENTATION OF THE NASP CREDENTIALING STANDARDS

10. New Applications for Credentialing

All school psychology trainees completing an approved program on or after January 1, 1989 and all other new applicants, should be trained and credentialed in accordance with these standards. All practitioners currently credentialed shall be recredentialed according to Standards 8.1 and 8.2 in an appropriate state renewal cycle. Practitioners with three F.T.E. years of documented experience as school psychologists shall be credentialed at the *Independent Practice* Level.

DEFINITION OF TERMS

Standard 3.1.A

NASP's Standards for the Provision of School Psychological Services (1984): The current standards document from the National Association of School Psychologists (NASP) describing procedural standards supporting the comprehensive delivery of school psychological services for administrative and employing agencies.

Public setting: Any setting (e.g., school, educational, mental health-related, or university-based) which is legislated, regulated, and/or supported by public funds (i.e., is non-profit) and whose staff serve, without bias or special selection processes, individuals primarily from the public domain.

Private setting: Any setting (e.g., school, educational, mental health-related, or university-based) which is supported in whole or in part by private funding sources, which may be for profit, and whose staff can specifically select the populations that it serves.

Standard 3.1.A.1

"State licensed psychologist with appropriate training and experience equivalent to that specified in NASP's Standards for Training (1983)": an individual licensed as a psychologist given the specific criteria in one's particular State who, if required to do so, could also meet the criteria in *NASP's Standards for Training and Field Placement in School Psychology (1983)* as a school psychologist at the sixth year/ specialist level and the criteria as specified in this Credentialing Standards document as a Supervising School Psychologist.

NASP's Standards for Training and Field Placement Programs in School Psychology (1983): The current standards document from the National Association of School Psychologists (NASP) describing procedural standards supporting the comprehensive training of school psychologists at the doctoral and sixth-year/ specialist levels.

Standard 3.1.B

NASP's Principles for Professional Ethics (1984): The current document of principles from the National Association of School Psychologists (NASP) describing guidelines for ethical behavior including professional competency, professional relationships and responsibilities, and professional practices in public and private settings.

Standard 5.3.B

Practica experiences (from the NASP Standards for Training and Field Placement Programs in School Psychology 1983): Practica experiences shall be distinct from and occur prior to the internship; shall occur at the time(s) appropriate to the specific training objectives of the program; shall be of sufficient length of time to be appropriate to the specific training objectives of the program; shall occur under conditions of supervision appropriate to the specific training objectives of the program; shall be provided appropriate recognition through the awarding of academic credit; shall be systematically evaluated in a manner consistent with the specific training objectives of the program.

Internship experiences (from the NASP Standards for Training and Field Placement Programs in School Psychology, 1983): Internship experiences shall be provided at or near the end of the formal training period; shall occur on a full-time basis over a period of one academic year, or on a half-time basis over a period of two consecutive academic years; shall be consistent with a written plan and meet the specific training objectives of the program; shall occur in a setting appropriate to these training objectives; shall involve at least 600 clock hours in a school setting and a balanced exposure to regular and special educational programs; shall be provided appropriate recognition through the awarding of academic credit; shall occur under the conditions of appropriate supervision; shall be systematically evaluated in a manner consistent with the specific training objectives of the program.

School setting (from Appendix B of the NASP Standards for Training and Field Placement Programs in School Psychology, 1983): Has the availability of (a) children of all school ages, (b) pupil personnel services functioning within a team framework, (c) full-range of services for handicapped children of both high and low incidences, (d) regular and special educational services at the preschool, elementary and secondary levels, and (e) at least one certified school psychologist having at least three years (now extended from two years by these *Credentialing Standards)* of full-time school psychologist experience of the equivalent who serves as the internship supervisor . . . It is not essential that the above all be provided within the context of the local educational agency to which the intern is assigned. However, it is essential that all elements be available and integrated into the internship experience.

Standard 5.3.B.2

"Another related psychological or educational field": any field of psychology that is directly related to the delivery of direct psychological or educational services to school-aged children and adolescents, or any field of education that is credentialed by the authorized State credentialing body and that is directly related to the delivery of direct psychological or educational services to school-aged children and adolescents.

Standard 7

A modified "Approved program" mechanism: Process whereby a training program is accredited by the National Council for the Accreditation of Teacher Education (NCATE) which currently accepts the *NASP Standards for Training and Field Placement Programs in School Psychology (1983)* for the training of school psychologists, or is approved by an authorized State credentialing body *and* would meet the criteria stated in the *NASP Training Standards* if the State criteria differ in any way from those specified, or would meet these *Training Standards* if evaluated independently.

Standard 7.2.C.2

Continuing Professional Development activity: activities designed to continue, enhance, and upgrade school psychologists' professional training and skills which help to ensure quality service provisions. Such activities include, but are not limited to, participation in formal Continuing Professional Development Programs, memberships in professional organizations, readings of professional journals and books, discussions of professional issues with colleagues.

NASP Standards for the Provision of School Psychological Services

1.0 Definitions

1.1 A *School Psychologist* is a professional psychologist who has met all requirements for credentialing as stipulated in the appropriate NASP standards. The credential is based upon the completion of a school psychology training program which meets the criteria specified in the NASP *Standards for Training and Field Placement Programs in School Psychology.*

1.2 A *Supervising School Psychologist* is a professional psychologist who has met all NASP requirements for credentialing, has completed three years of successful supervised experience as a school psychologist, and who has been designated by an employing agency as a supervisor responsible for school psychological services in the agency.

1.3 *Parent(s)*, as used in these *Standards*, includes both biological parent(s) and/or legal guardian(s).

2.0 Standards for Administrative Agencies

The purpose of this section of the standards is to provide guidance to federal and state administrative agencies in regard to administrative organization, laws, and regulations as they pertain to the provision of school psychological services.

2.1 Federal Level Administrative Agency

2.1.1 Organization

The federal education agency should employ a supervising school psychologist in order to accomplish the following objectives:

2.1.1.1 To provide professional leadership and assistance to the federal education agency, state education agencies, and the school psychology profession in regard to standards, policies, and procedures for program delivery, and for utilization, funding, education and training, and inservice education of school psychological services personnel.

2.1.1.2 To participate in the administration of federal programs providing funding for school psychological services in state, intermediate, and local education agencies, and for the education and training of school psychologists.

2.1.1.3 To encourage and assist in evaluation, research, and dissemination activities; to determine the effectiveness of school psychological education, training, and service programs; to determine needed changes; and to identify and communicate exemplary practices to training and service units.

2.1.1.4 To assure that consistent communication is established and maintained among professional organizations, federal, state, and local education agencies, and university training programs involved in providing and developing school psychological services.

2.1.2. Laws

2.1.2.1 The Congress of the United States should ensure that the rights of all parents and children are protected by the creation and modification of laws which provide for the services of school psychologists. These services include, but are not limited to, consultation, assessment, and intervention for individuals, groups, and systems. These services are available to all children, their families, and school personnel.

2.1.2.2 The Congress should ensure that school psychological services are provided in a free and appropriate manner to all children, their families, and school personnel in need of such services.

2.1.2.3 The Congress should ensure that federal laws recognize the appropriate involvement of school psychologists in educational programs and that adequate federal funding is made available for the education, training, services, and continuing professional development of school psychologists in order to guarantee appropriate and effective services.

2.1.2.4 The Congress should create no laws which effectively prohibit the credentialed school psychologist from the ethical and legal practice of his/her profession in the public or private sector, or which would be in violation of these standards.

2.1.3 Regulations

2.1.3.1 All federal agencies should utilize the services of the federal educational agency school psychologist in developing and implementing regulations pursuant to all relevant federal laws.

2.1.3.2 All federal agencies should seek the advice and consultation of the National Association of School Psychologists prior to the adoption of regulations pursuant to any federal law which involves or should reasonably involve the profession of school psychology.

2.1.3.3 Federal agencies should promulgate regulations consistent with the principles set forth in these *Standards* and the NASP *Principles for Professional Ethics.*

2.2 State Level Administrative Agencies

2.2.1. Organization

Each state educational agency (SEA) should employ at least one full-time supervising school psychologist for each 500 (or fewer) school psychologists within the state. An equivalent ratio should be maintained if there are more than 500 school psychologists. It is recognized that this ratio may vary based upon administrative structures, available resources, and types of programs served. Appropriate objectives to be accomplished by the SEA school psychologist(s) include the following:

2.2.1.1 To provide professional leadership assistance to the SEA, local educational agencies, and the profession with regard to standards, policies, and procedures for school psychology program delivery.

2.2.1.2 To support the utilization, funding, education, training, and inservice education of school psychologists.

2.2.1.3 To participate in the administration of state and federal programs providing funding for school psychological services in intermediate and local educational agencies, and for the education and training of school psychologists.

2.2.1.4 To encourage and assist in evaluation, research, and dissemination activities to determine the effectiveness of school psychological education, training, and service programs; to determine needed changes; and to identify and communicate exemplary practices to training and service units.

2.2.1.5 To maintain communication with and assure the input of state school psychological associations into the policy making of the SEA.

2.2.1.6 To communicate with the federal education agency school psychologist to ensure recognition of state issues and to facilitate input into federal policy.

2.2.2 Laws

2.2.2.1 All state legislative bodies should ensure that the rights of parents and children are protected by the creation and modification of laws which provide for the services of school psychologists. These services include, but are not limited to, consultation for individuals, groups, and systems, assessment, and intervention. These services are available to all children, their families, and school personnel.

2.2.2.2 The state legislature should ensure that school psychological services are provided in a free and appropriate way to all children, their families, and school personnel in need of such services.

2.2.2.3 The state legislature should ensure that state laws recognize the appropriate involvement of school psychologists in educational programs.

2.2.2.4 The state legislature should ensure that adequate funding is made available for the education, training, services, and continuing professional development of school psychologists in order to guarantee appropriate and effective services.

2.2.2.5 The state legislature should ensure that state laws provide for the credentialing of school psychologists consistent with NASP standards.

2.2.2.6 The state legislature should create no laws which prohibit the school psychologist from the ethical and legal practice of his/her profession in the public or private sector, or that prevent the school psychologist from practicing in a manner consistent with these *Standards*.

2.2.2.7 The state legislature should ensure that there are sufficient numbers of adequately prepared and credentialed school psychologists to provide services consistent with these *Standards*. In most settings, this will require at least one full-time school psychologist for each 1,000 children served by the LEA, with a maximum of four schools served by one school psychologist. It is recognized that this ratio may vary based upon the needs of children served, the type of program served, available resources, distance between schools, and other unique characteristics.

2.3.3 Regulations

2.2.3.1 All state agencies should utilize the services of the SEA school psychologist(s) in developing and implementing administrative rules pursuant to all relevant state laws, federal laws, and regulations.

2.2.3.2 All state agencies should seek the advice and consultation of the state school psychologist's professional association prior to the adoption of rules pursuant to any state law, federal law, or regulation which involves or should reasonably involve the profession of school psychology.

2.2.3.3 All state education agencies should utilize the services of the SEA school psychologist(s) in the SEA review and approval of school psychology training programs.

2.2.3.4 All state education agencies should utilize the services of the SEA school psychologist(s) in developing and implementing administrative rules for credentialing school psychologists. Such rules shall be consistent with NASP *Standards for the Credentialing of School Psychologists*.

2.2.3.5 State education agencies should promulgate regulations consistent with the principles set forth in these *Standards* and the NASP *Principles for Professional Ethics*.

3.0 Standards for Employing Agencies

The purpose of these standards is to provide employing agencies with specific guidance regarding the organization, policies, and practices needed to assure the provision of adequate school psychological services.

3.1 Comprehensive Continuum of Services.

Employing agencies assure that school psychological services are provided in a coordinated, organized fashion, and are deployed in a manner which ensures the provision of a comprehensive continuum of services as outlined in Section 4.0 of these *Standards*. Such services are available to all students served by the agency and are available to an extent sufficient to meet the needs of the populations served.

3.2 Professional Evaluation, Supervision, and Development

3.2.1 Supervision

Employing agencies assure that an effective program of supervision and evaluation of school psychological services exists. School psychologists are responsible for the overall development, implementation, and professional supervision of school psychological service programs, and are responsible for articulating those programs to others in the employing agency and to that agency's constituent groups.

3.2.2 Supervisor(s)

The school psychological services program is supervised by a designated school psychologist who meets the requirements for a supervising school psychologist (Section 1.2) and who demonstrates competencies needed for effective supervision.

3.2.3 Availability of Supervision

Supervision is available to all school psychologists to an extent sufficient to ensure the provision of effective and accountable services (see Section 4.6 for specific requirements). In most cases, one supervising school psychologist should be employed for every ten school psychologists to be supervised (an equivalent ratio should be maintained for part-time supervisors). It is recognized that this ratio may vary based upon the type of program served, staff needs, and other unique characteristics.

3.2.4 Intern Supervision

A credentialed school psychologist meeting the requirements of a supervising school psychologist, with at least one year or experience at the employing agency, supervises no more than two school psychology interns at any given time (consistent with the NASP *Standards for Training and Field Placement Programs in School Psychology*).

3.2.5 Peer Review

After attaining independent practice status (see Section 4.5), school psychologists continue to receive appropriate supervision. The independent practitioner should also engage in peer review with other school psychologists. Peer review involves mutual assistance with self-examination of services and the development of plans to continue professional growth and development. Employing agencies assure that school psychologists are given appropriate time and support for peer review activities.

3.2.6 Accountability and Program Evaluation

Employing agencies assure that school psychologists develop a coordinated plan for accountability and evaluation of all services provided in order to maintain and improve the effectiveness of services. Such plans include specific, measurable objectives pertaining to the planned effects of services on all relevant elements of the system. Evaluation and revision of these plans occurs on a regular basis.

3.2.7 Continuing Professional Development

Employing agencies recognize that school psychologists are obligated to continue their professional training and development through participation in a recognized Continuing Professional Development (CPD) program (see Section 4.6). Employing agencies provide release time and financial support for such activities. They recognize documented continuing professional development activities in the evaluation and advancement of school psychologists. Private practitioners who contract to provide services are responsible for their own CPD program, and these activities should also be encouraged by employing agencies.

3.3 Conditions for Effective Service Delivery

In order to assure that employment conditions enable school psychologists to provide effective services, employing agencies adopt policies and practices ensuring that Sections 3.3.1 through 3.3.4 are met.

3.3.1 School psychologists are not subjected to administrative constraints which prevent them from providing services in full accordance with these *Standards* and the NASP *Principles for Professional Ethics.* When administrative policies conflict with these *Standards* or the NASP *Ethics,* the principles outlined in the *Standards* or *Ethics* take precedence in determining appropriate practices of the school psychologist.

3.3.2 School psychologists have appropriate input into the general policy making of the employing agency and the development of programs affecting the staff, students, and families they serve.

3.3.3 School psychologists have appropriate professional autonomy in determining the nature, extent, and duration of services they provide. Specific activities are defined within the profession, although school psychologists frequently collaborate and seek input from others in determining appropriate service delivery. Legal, ethical, and professional standards and guidelines are considered by the practitioner in making decisions regarding practice (see Section 4.4).

3.3.4 School psychologists have access to adequate clerical assistance, appropriate professional work materials, sufficient office and work space, and general working conditions that enhance the delivery of effective services. Included are test materials, access to a private telephone and office, secretarial services, therapeutic aids, professional literature (books, journals), and so forth.

3.4 Contractual Services

It is recognized that employing agencies may obtain school psychological services on a contractual basis in order to ensure the provision of adequate services to all children. However, each student within the educational system must be assured the full range of school psychological services necessary to maximize his/her success and adjustment in school. When an employing agency utilizes contractual services, the following standards are observed.

3.4.1 Contractual school psychological services encompass the same comprehensive continuum of services as that provided by regularly employed school psychologists. Overall, psychological services are not limited to any specific type of service and include opportunities for follow-up and continuing consultation appropriate to the needs of the student. Individual contracts for services may be limited as long as comprehensive services are provided overall.

3.4.2 Persons providing contractual psychological services are fully credentialed school psychologists as defined by these *Standards.* In specific instances, however, services by psychologists in other specialty areas (e.g., clinical, industrial/organizational) might be used to supplement school psychological services.

3.4.3 Contractual school psychological services are not to be utilized as a means to decrease the amount and quality of school psychological services provided by an employing agency. They may be used to augment programs but not to supplant them.

3.4.4 School psychologists providing contractual services are given appropriate access and information. They are familiar with the instructional resources of the employing agency to ensure that students they serve have the same opportunities as those served by regularly employed school psychologists.

3.4.5 Contractual school psychological services are provided in a manner which protects the due process rights of students and their parents as defined by state and federal laws and regulations.

3.4.6 Contracting for services is not to be used as a means to avoid legitimate employee rights, wages, or fringe benefits.

3.4.7 Psychologists providing contractual school psychological services provide those services in a manner consistent with these *Standards*, NASP *Principles for Professional Ethics*, and other relevant professional guidelines and standards.

3.5 Non-Biased Assessment and Program Planning

Employing agencies should adopt policies and practices in accordance with the following standards:

3.5.1 General Principles

3.5.1.1 School psychologists use assessment techniques to provide information which is helpful in maximizing student achievement and educational success.

3.5.1.2 School psychologists have autonomous decision-making responsibility (as defined in Section 4.4) to determine the type, nature, and extent of assessment techniques they use in student evaluation.

3.5.1.3 School psychologists have autonomy (as defined in Section 4.4) in determining the content and nature of reports.

3.5.1.4 School psychologists use assessment techniques and instruments which have established validity and reliability for the purposes and populations for which they are intended.

3.5.1.5 School psychologists use, develop, and encourage assessment practices which increase the likelihood of the development of effective educational interventions and follow-up.

3.5.2 Professional Involvement

3.5.2.1 A multidisciplinary team is involved in assessment, program decision-making and evaluation. The team conducts periodic evaluations of its performance to ensure continued effectiveness.

3.5.2.2 The multidisciplinary team includes a fully trained and certified school psychologist.

3.5.2.3 The school psychologist communicates a minority position to all involved when in disagreement with the multidisciplinary team position.

3.5.3 Non-Biased Assessment Techniques

3.5.3.1 Assessment procedures and program recommendations are chosen to maximize the student's opportunities to be successful in the general culture, while respecting the student's ethnic background.

3.5.3.2 Multifaceted assessment batteries are used which include a focus on the student's strengths.

3.5.3.3 Communications are held in the client's dominant spoken language or alternative communication system. All student information is interpreted in the context of the student's socio-cultural background and the setting in which she/he is functioning.

3.5.3.4 Assessment techniques (including computerized techniques) are used only by personnel professionally trained in their use and in a manner consistent with these *Standards*.

3.5.3.5 School psychologists promote the development of objective, valid, and reliable assessment techniques.

3.5.3.6 Interpretation of assessment results is based upon empirically validated research.

3.5.4 Parent/Student Involvement

3.5.4.1 Informed written consent of parent(s) and/or student (if the student has reached the age of majority) is obtained before assessment and special program implementation.

3.5.4.2 The parent(s) and/or student is fully informed of all essential information considered and its relevancy to decision-making.

3.5.4.3 The parent(s) and/or student is invited to participate in decision-making meetings.

3.5.4.4 The parent(s) and/or student is routinely notified that an advocate can participate in conferences focusing on assessment results and program recommendations.

3.5.4.5 A record of meetings regarding assessment results and program recommendations is available to all directly concerned.

3.5.5 Educational Programming and Follow-Through

3.5.5.1 School psychologists are involved in determining options and revisions of educational programs to ensure that they are adaptive to the needs of students.

3.5.5.2 The contributions of diverse cultural backgrounds should be emphasized in educational programs.

3.5.5.3 School psychologists follow-up on the efficacy of their recommendations.

3.5.5.4 Student needs are given priority in determining educational programs.

3.5.5.5 Specific educational prescriptions result from the assessment team's actions.

3.5.5.6 Where a clear determination of the student's needs does not result from initial assessment, a diagnostic teaching program is offered as part of additional assessment procedures.

3.5.5.7 Regular, systematic review of the student's program is conducted and includes program modifications as necessary.

3.6 School Psychological Records

3.6.1 The employing agency's policy on student records is consistent with state and federal rules and laws, and ensures the protection of the confidentiality of the student and his/her family. The policy specifies the types of data developed by the school psychologist which are classified as school or pupil records.

3.6.2 Parents may inspect and review any personally identifiable data relating to their child which were collected, maintained, or used in his/her evaluation. Although test protocols are part of the student's record, school psychologists protect test security and observe copyright restrictions.

3.6.3 Access to psychological records is restricted to those permitted by law who have legitimate educational interest in the records.

3.6.4 School psychologists interpret school psychological records to non-psychologists who qualify for access.

3.6.5 School psychological records are only created and maintained when the information is necessary and relevant to legitimate educational program needs and when parents (or student if age of majority has been attained) have given their informed consent for the creation of such a record. This consent is based upon full knowledge of the purposes for which information is sought, and the personnel who will have access to it. The school psychologist assumes responsibility for assuring the accuracy and relevancy of the information recorded.

3.6.6 School psychological records are systematically reviewed, and when necessary purged, in keeping with relevant federal and state laws in order to protect children from decisions based on incorrect, misleading, or out-of-date information.

4.0 Standards for the Delivery of Comprehensive School Psychological Services

The purpose of these standards is to ensure the delivery of comprehensive services by school psychologists.

4.1 Organization of School Psychological Services

4.1.1 School psychological services are planned, organized, directed, and reviewed by school psychologists.

4.1.2 School psychologists participate in determining the recipients and the type of school psychological services offered.

4.1.3 The goals and objectives of school psychological services are available in written form.

4.1.4 A written set of procedural guidelines for the delivery of school psychological services is followed and made available upon request.

4.1.5 A clearly stated referral system is in writing and is communicated to parents, staff members, students, and other referral agents.

4.1.6 The organization of school psychological services is in written form and includes lines of responsibility, supervisory, and administrative relationships.

4.1.7 Where two or more school psychologists are employed, a coordinated system of school psychological services is in effect within that unit.

4.1.8 Units providing school psychological services include sufficient professional and support personnel to achieve their goals and objectives.

4.2 Relationship to Other Units and Professionals

4.2.1 The school psychological services unit is responsive to the needs of the population that it serves. Psychological services are periodically and systematically reviewed to ensure their conformity with the needs of the population served.

4.2.2 School psychologists establish and maintain relationships with other professionals (e.g., pediatricians, bilingual specialists, audiologists) who provide services to children and families. They collaborate with these professionals in prevention assessment, and intervention efforts as necessary. They also cooperate with advocates representing children and their families.

4.2.3 Providers of school psychological services maintain a cooperative relationship with colleagues and co-workers in the best mutual interests of clients, in a manner consistent with the goals of the employing agency. Conflicts should be resolved in a professional manner.

4.2.4 School psychologists develop plans for the delivery of services in accordance with best professional practices.

4.2.5 School psychologists employed within a school setting coordinate the services of mental health providers from other agencies (such as community mental health centers, child guidance clinics, or private practitioners) to ensure a continuum of services.

4.2.6 School psychologists are knowledgeable about community agencies and resources. They provide liaison and consulting services to the community and agencies regarding psychological, mental health, and educational issues.

   4.2.1.6 School psychologists communicate as needed with state and community agencies and professionals (e.g., child guidance clinics, community mental health centers, private practitioners) regarding services for children, families, and school personnel. They refer clients to these agencies and professionals as appropriate.

   4.2.6.2 School psychologists are informed of and have the opportunity to participate in community agency staffings of cases involving their clients.

   4.2.6.3 Community agency personnel are invited to participate in school system conferences concerning their clients (with written parental permission).

4.3 Comprehensive School Psychological Services Delivery

School psychologists provide a range of services to their clients. These consist of direct and indirect services which require involvement with the entire educational system: (a) the students, teachers, administrators, and other school personnel; (b) the families, surrogate caretakers, and other community and regional agencies, and resources which support the educational process; (c) the organizational, physical, temporal, and curricular variables which play major roles within the system; and (d) a variety of other factors which may be important on an individual basis.

The intent of these services is to promote mental health and facilitate learning. Comprehensive school psychological services are comprised of diverse activities. These activities complement one another and therefore are most accurately viewed as being integrated and coordinated rather than discrete services. However, for descriptive purposes, they will be listed and described separately. The following are the services that comprise the delivery system.

4.3.1 Consultation

4.3.1.1 School psychologists consult and collaborate with parents, school, and outside personnel regarding mental health, behavioral, and educational concerns.

4.3.1.2 School psychologists design and develop procedures for preventing disorders, promoting mental health and learning, and improving educational systems.

4.3.1.3 School psychologists provide inservice and other skill enhancement activities to school personnel, parents, and others in the community, regarding issues of human learning, development, and behavior.

4.3.1.4 School psychologists develop collaborative relationships with their clients and involve them in the assessment, intervention, and program evaluation procedures.

4.3.2 Psychological and Psychoeducational Assessment

4.3.2.1 School psychologists conduct multifactored psychological and psychoeducational assessments of children and youth as appropriate.

4.3.2.2 Psychological and psychoeducational assessments include consideration as appropriate of the areas of personal-social adjustment, intelligence-scholastic aptitude, adaptive behavior, language and communication skills, academic achievement, sensory and perceptual-motor functioning, environmental-cultural influences, and vocational development, aptitude, and interests.

4.3.2.3 School psychologists utilize formal instruments, procedures, and techniques. Interviews, observations, and behavioral evaluations are included in these procedures.

4.3.2.4 When conducting psychological and psychoeducational assessments, school psychologists have explicit regard for the context and setting in which their assessments take place and will be used.

4.3.2.5 School psychologists adhere to the NASP resolutions regarding non-biased assessment and programming for all students (see Section 3.5.3). They also are familiar with and consider the *Standards for Educational and Psychological Tests* (developed by APA, AERA, and NCME) in the use of assessment techniques.

4.3.3 Interventions

4.3.3.1 School psychologists provide direct and indirect interventions to facilitate the functioning of individuals, groups, and/or organizations.

4.3.3.2 School psychologists design programs to enhance cognitive, affective, social and vocational development.

4.3.3.3 School psychologists facilitate the delivery of services by assisting those who play major roles in the educational system (i.e., parents, school personnel, community agencies). Such interventions consist of but are not limited to: inservice training, organization development, parent counseling, program planning and evaluation, vocational development, and parent education programs.

4.3.4 Supervision

School psychologists provide and/or engage in supervision and continuing professional development as specified in Sections 3.2 and 4.6.

4.3.5 Research

4.3.5.1 School psychologists design, conduct, report, and utilize the results of research of a psychological and educational nature. All research conducted is in accordance with relevant ethical guidelines of the profession (e.g., APA *Ethical Principles in the Conduct of Research with Human Participants*).
Applied and/or basic research should be pursued, focusing on:
(a) psychological functioning of human beings;
(b) Psychoeducational assessment tools and procedures;
(c) Educational programs and techniques applied to individual cases and groups of various sizes;
(d) Educational processes;
(e) Social system interactions and organizational factors associated with school communities; and
(f) Psychological treatments and techniques applied to individual cases or groups.

4.3.5.2 School psychologists' involvement in research can range from support or advisory services to having direct responsibility for one or more major components of a research project. These components may include planning, data collecting, data analyzing, disseminating, and translating research into practical applications within the school community.

4.3.6 Program Planning and Evaluation

4.3.6.1 School psychologists provide program planning and evaluation services to assist in decision-making activities.

4.3.6.2 School psychologists serve on committees responsible for developing and planning educational and educationally-related activities.

4.4 Autonomous Functioning

School psychologists have professional autonomy in determining the nature, scope, and extent of their specific services. These activities are defined within the profession although school psychologists frequently collaborate with and seek input from others in determining appropriate services delivery. Legal, ethical, and professional standards and guidelines are considered by the practitioner in making decisions regarding practice. All practice is restricted to those areas in which the school psychologist has received formal training and supervised experience.

4.4.1. Professional Responsibility and Best Practices

Professional autonomy is associated with professional responsibility. The ultimate responsibility for providing appropriate comprehensive school psychological services rests with the individual practitioner.

While being cognizant of the fact that there often are not explicit guidelines to follow in providing comprehensive school psychological services, the individual practitioner has a responsibility to adhere to the best available and most appropriate standards of practice. There is no substitute for sensitive, sound, professional judgment in the determination of what constitutes best practice. Active involvement in supervision and other continuing professional development activities will assist the practitioner in adhering to best professional practices.

4.5 Independent Practice.

A credentialed school psychologist who has completed a school psychology training program which meets the criteria specified in the NASP *Standards for Training and Field Placement Programs in School Psychology* and three years of satisfactory supervised experience is considered qualified for independent practice, regardless of work setting.

4.6 Continuing Professional Development

The practice of school psychology has and will continue to undergo significant changes as new knowledge and technological advances are introduced. The development of new intervention techniques, assessment procedures, computerized assistance, and so forth, will require that practitioners keep abreast of these innovations as well as obtain appropriate professional education and training in these areas. All school psychologists actively participate and engage in activities designed to continue, enhance, and upgrade their professional training and skills and to help ensure quality service provision. These efforts are documented by participation in the NASP or other formal Continuing Professional Development (CPD) programs, although they are not limited to such activities. Memberships in professional organizations, reading of professional journals and books, discussions of professional issues with colleagues, and so forth, are also an integral component of a school psychologist's overall CPD activities.

4.6.1 Participation in CPD activities and the maintenance of high professional standards and practice are continuing obligations of the school psychologist. These obligations are assumed when one initially engages in the practice of school psychology and should be required for continued credentialing.

4.6.2 School psychologists receive supervision by a supervising school psychologist for the first three years of full-time employment (or the equivalent) as a school psychologist. The supervisor shares professional responsibility and accountability for the services provided. While the level and extent of supervision may vary, the supervisor maintains a sufficiently close relationship to meet this standard. Individual face-to-face supervision is engaged in for a minimum of one hour per week or the equivalent (e.g., two hours bi-weekly). Standards for intern supervision are contained in the NASP *Standards for Training and Field Placement Programs in School Psychology.*

4.6.3 After completion of the first three years of supervision, all school psychologists continue to engage in supervision and/or peer review on a regular basis, and further their professional development by actively participating in CPD activities. The level and extent of these activities may vary depending on the needs, interests, and goals of the school psychologist, with more comprehensive service delivery requiring more extensive related professional exchanges. At a minimum, however, these activities are at the level required for successful participation in an appropriate CPD program.

4.6.4 School psychologists, who after three years no longer have supervision available, engage in peer review activities. These may include discussions of cases and professional issues designed to assist with problem solving, decision-making, and appropriate practice.

4.6.5 School psychologists readily seek additional consultation with supervisors, peers, or colleagues with particularly complex or difficult cases, and/or when expanding their services into new areas or those in which they infrequently practice (e.g., low incidence assessment).

4.7 Accountability

4.7.1 School psychologists perform their duties in an accountable manner by keeping records of these efforts, evaluating their effectiveness, and modifying their practices and/or expanding their services as needed.

4.7.2 School psychologists devise systems of accountability and outcome evaluation which aid in documenting the effectiveness of intervention efforts and other services they provide.

4.7.3 Within their service delivery plan, school psychologists include a regular evaluation of their progress in achieving goals. This evaluation should include consideration of the cost effectiveness of school psychological services in terms of time, money, and resources, as well as the availability of professional and support personnel. Evaluation of the school psychological delivery system is conducted internally, and when possible, externally as well (e.g., through state educational agency review, peer review). This evaluation includes an assessment of effectiveness, efficiency, continuity, availability, and adequacy of services.

4.7.4 School psychologists are accountable for their services. They should make information available about their services, and provide consumers with the opportunity to participate in decision-making concerning such issues as initiation, termination, continuation, modification, and evaluation of their services. Rights of the consumer should be taken into account when performing these activities.

4.8 Private Practice

4.8.1 School psychologists practicing in the private sector provide comprehensive services and adhere to the same standards and guidelines as those providing services in the public sector.

4.8.2 School psychologists document that they have formal training, supervised experience, licensure and/or certification, and demonstrated competence, in any areas of service they intend to deliver to clients within the private sector. They also have a responsibility to actively engage in CPD activities.

4.8.3 School psychologists in private practice adhere to the NASP *Principles for Professional Ethics*, and practice only within their areas of competence. If the services needed by clients fall outside the school psychologist's areas of competence, they are referred elsewhere for assistance.

4.8.4 It is the responsibility of the school psychologist engaging in private practice to inform the client that school psychological services are available without charge from the client's local school district.

4.8.5 School psychologists do not provide services on a private basis to students residing within their employing district who would be eligible to receive the services without charge. This includes students who are attending non-public schools located in the district.

4.8.6 School psychologists offering school psychological services in the private sector ensure that, prior to the commencement of treatment/services, the client fully understands any and all fees associated with the services, and any potential financial assistance that may be available (i.e., third-party reimbursement).

4.8.7 Parents must be informed by the school psychologist that if a private school psychological evaluation is to be completed, this evaluation constitutes only one portion of a multidisciplinary team evaluation. Private services must be equally comprehensive to those described in Section 4.3

4.8.8 School psychologists in private practice provide and maintain written records in a manner consistent with Section 3.6

4.9 Professional Ethics and Guidelines

Each school psychologist practices in full accordance with the NASP *Principles for Professional Ethics*, and these *Standards*.

NASP Continuing Professional Development Program

1.0 PHILOSOPHY AND INTENT

With the inception of the National Certification System for School Psychologists, NASP has, for the first time, a mechanism for advocating its long established position regarding appropriate standards for the provision of school psychological services as it pertains to Continuing Professional Development:

> The practice of school psychology has and will continue to undergo significant changes as new knowledge and technological advances are introduced. The development of new intervention techniques, assessment procedures, computerized assistance, and so forth, will require that practitioners keep abreast of these innovations as well as obtain appropriate professional education and training in these areas. **All school psychologists actively participate and engage in activities designed to continue, enhance, and upgrade their professional training and skills and to help ensure quality service provision** [emphasis added]. These efforts are documented by participation in NASP or other formal Continuing Professional Development (CPD) programs, although they are not limited to such activities. Memberships in professional organizations, reading of professional journals and books, discussions of professional issues with colleagues, and so forth, are also an integral component of a school psychologist's overall CPD activities. ["Standards for the Provision of School Psychological Services," *Professional Conduct Manual, NASP, 1984, Section 4.6*]

It is assumed that all school psychologists, and particularly those participating in the National School Psychology Certification System, have a common ethic and goal to grow professionally by keeping abreast of trends and new research in order to enhance their services. Because the knowledge base of the field is broad, training and skill levels are varied, and the professional role has many dimensions, individuals will want to have a personal plan for professional development. The plan should be designed to include a broad range of experiences and should be unique to the needs of the individual. Meeting the requirements of the NASP CPD program (which is part of the National School Psychology Certification System) provides an opportunity to reach this goal.

Inasmuch as school psychologists function in a variety of job assignments in a number of diverse locations, it is important to recognize the variables in availability of formal and informal inservice opportunities. **The intent of the CPD requirement, therefore, is not to limit the school psychologist's continuing professional development by approving only specific activities, but rather to acknowledge and encourage participation in the variety of activities that are available to each individual.**

2.0 PROCESS

Consistent with the *NASP Standards for the Provision of School Psychological Services* (1984), participation in activities designed to maintain and expand skills to insure quality service provision is the continuing obligation of school psychologists. For renewal of National Certification, it is expected that school psychologists will enhance their skills in the following areas as defined in the *Standards* (see Attachment A):

CONSULTATION
PSYCHOLOGICAL AND PSYCHOEDUCATIONAL ASSESSMENT
INTERVENTION
SUPERVISION
RESEARCH
PROGRAM PLANNING AND EVALUATION

The emphasis of Continuing Professional Development (CPD) is upon recency and regularity of participation in skill development activities. It is also expected that the effective practice of school psychology reflects, as its most basic level, a broad knowledge base and that, for continued effective service delivery, school psychologists enhance their skills in a variety of areas.

2.1 Professional Development Activities

2.1.1　For school psychologists who are Nationally Certified, certification renewal will require participation in CPD activities during the initial period from January 1988 to the NCSP renewal date.

2.1.2　Subsequent NCSP renewals will occur on a three-year cycle. Credit for NCSP renewal must be accrued within that three-year cycle.

2.1.3　CPD activities include (see Appendix B for specific explanations):

2.1.3.1　National, state, and local school psychology association conferences and workshops

2.1.3.2　Related professional conferences and workshops

2.1.3.3　Completion of college and university courses beyond those required for entry-level certification as a school psychologist

2.1.3.4　Teaching courses and provision of in-service when not an ordinary aspect of employment

2.1.3.5　Research

2.1.3.6　Publication

2.1.3.7　Presentations

2.1.3.8　Supervision

2.1.3.9　Program planning/evaluation when not an employment requirement

2.1.3.10 Sequenced programs of self-study

2.1.3.11 Informal programs of self-study

2.1.3.12 Professional organization leadership

2.1.4　Activities should be chosen as part of an overall professional development plan devised by the participant to enhance knowledge in several foundation areas. While submission of a formal plan is not required, participants are encouraged to devise such a plan for their own use.

2.1.5 Participation time must be accrued **in at least three of the six specific skill areas** (see Section 2.0)

2.1.6 The individual will participate in a variety of activities which emphasize learning, including both coursework or workshop experiences and instruction, presentations, program development or research. These activities go beyond the ordinary aspects of employment.

2.2 Continuing Education Units

2.2.1 Participation in CPD activities may be represented through the use of Continuing Education Units (CEUs).

2.2.2 One CEU is equivalent to 10 *contact hours.*

2.2.3 A contact hour is defined as an actual clock hour (60 minutes) spent in direct participation in a structured educational format as a learner.

2.2.4 When college or university courses are taken to fulfill the CPD requirement, the following equivalencies shall be used: 1 semester hour = 1.5 CEUs or 15 contact hours; 1 quarter hour = 1.0 CEUs or 10 contact hours.

2.2.5 When CPD activities cannot be represented by contact hours, equivalencies may be established (see Attachment B)

2.2.6 Maintenance of National School Psychology Certification requires the completion of 75 contact hours of professional development activity or the accumulation of 7.5 CEUs every three years.

3.0 PROCEDURES

3.1 Documentation

3.1.1 Participation in CPD activities must be documented.

3.1.2 For purposes of NCSP renewal, contact hours/CEUs will be listed on a CEU summary sheet provided (see Attachment C).

3.1.3 Verification for each activity listed must be submitted with the Summary Sheet(s). Several forms of verification will be acceptable.

3.1.3.1 In cases where state school psychology associations collect validation forms or other proof of CPD participation and provide summary sheets to members of reports of credits, these may be submitted as verification.

3.1.3.2 In states where professional development is required for maintenance of certification or licensure, summary reports or activity validation forms generated by the state board of education or credentialing agency may be submitted as verification of participation.

3.1.3.3 When CPD involves college or university coursework, a copy of the course transcript will serve as verification.

3.1.3.4 Certificates of participation or receipts of course or workshop fees may be submitted as verification.

3.1.3.5 Any activity not otherwise documented per above instructions is to be documented through completion of an Individual Activity Sheet (see Attachment D). A separate activity sheet is to be submitted for each activity claimed.

3.2 Submission of Documentation for National Certification Renewal

If CPD activities are used to renew status as a Nationally Certified School Psychologist, the following procedures must be followed:

3.2.1 Prior to each third anniversary of the individual's National Certification, the NSPCB will notify the participant of renewal procedures.

3.2.2 Documentation of CPD activity will be submitted as part of the renewal procedure.

3.2.3 Documentation to be submitted will include the CEU Summary Sheet(s), verification of participation in formal CPD activities, and Individual Activity Sheets for each informal CPD activity.

3.2.4 Questions regarding the acceptability of a specific activity should be directed to the NASP Professional Development Committee *prior* to application for renewal.

3.2.5 The documentation will be reviewed and approved by the Professional Development Committee.

3.2.6 The Professional Development Committee will submit approved summary sheets to the NSPCB.

3.2.7 Documentation will not be returned to the NCSP. Therefore, copies, rather than original documents, are acceptable.

ATTACHMENT A
Continuing Professional Development Skill Area Definitions

The areas of skill development cited in Section 2.0 of the NASP Continuing Professional Development Program document are those defined in the NASP *Standards for the Provision of School Psychological Services* (1984) Section 4.3. The salient points of that section of the document are reprinted here to assist the participant in determining the skill area under which a specific CPD activity might fall.

CONSULTATION

1. Activities which enhance the school psychologist's skills in:
   a. mental health consultation
   b. behavioral consultation
   c. educational consultation
   with parents, school personnel or outside agencies

2. Training in the promotion of
   a. mental health and learning
   b. prevention of disorders
   c. improving educational systems

3. Provision of inservice in the areas of:
   a. human learning
   b. human development
   c. behavior
   to parents, school personnel and others in the community

4. Development of skills to enhance collaborative relationships with clients, including:
   a. students
   b. school personnel
   c. parents
   d. outside agencies

PSYCHOLOGICAL AND PSYCHOEDUCATIONAL ASSESSMENT

1. Development of skills in multifactored assessment

2. Enhancement of skills in specific assessment areas, including:
   a. personal-social adjustment
   b. intelligence
   c. scholastic aptitude
   d. adaptive behavior
   e. language and communication skills
   f. academic achievement
   g. sensory and perceptual-motor functioning
   h. environmental-cultural influences
   i. vocational development, aptitude, and interests

3. Development of skills in non-test based measurement, including:
   a. observation
   b. behavioral measurement

4. Development of skill in non-biased assessment

5. Activities that promote ethical considerations and conduct regarding evaluation of students

INTERVENTIONS

1. Skill development in both direct and indirect intervention strategies that will enhance or facilitate the functioning of:
   a. individuals
   b. groups
   c. systems

2. Enhancement of theory and practice in designing programs to enhance:
   a. cognitive development
   b. affective development
   c. social development
   d. vocational development

3. Assisting others within the community to enhance service delivery skills through such avenues as:
   a. inservice
   b. organizational development
   c. parent counseling
   d. parent education

SUPERVISION

1. Participation in specific activities which enhance the school psychologist's supervisory and administrative skills

2. Provision of practicum and/or internship experiences to school psychology graduate students

RESEARCH

1. Designing or conducting research of a psychological and educational nature, including:
   a. psychological functioning of human beings
   b. psychoeducational assessment tools and procedures
   c. educational programs and techniques applied to individual cases and groups of various sizes
   d. educational processes
   e. social system interactions and organizational factors associated with school communities
   f. psychological treatments and techniques applied to individual cases or groups

PROGRAM PLANNING AND EVALUATION

1. Development of skills in the area of program planning and evaluation

2. Provision of program planning and evaluation services that assist in decision-making

3. Serving on committees responsible for developing and planning educational and educationally-related activities

ATTACHMENT B

Credit Equivalencies and Credit Ceilings

The NASP Continuing Professional Development Program lists a variety of activities which have potential for enhancing a school psychologist's knowledge and the quality of service provision. These activities are listed in the *CPD Program* document in Section 2.1.3. Hour and CEU conversions for all listed activities are provided here. CPD hours may be transformed into CEUs by dividing by 10 (for example: one hour of participation equals .1 CEU).

Group A: Hour-for-Hour Activities

All workshop and conference activities earn one hour of CPD credit (.1 CEU) for each actual hour of participation:

2.1.3.1   National, state, and local school psychology association conferences and workshops.

2.1.3.2   Related Professional conferences and workshops.

> *An Example:* Two hours of attendance at a NASP Convention miniskills workshop = 2 hours of participation time = .2 CEU.

Group B: Standard Conversions

Taking or teaching college/university courses and inservice workshops are credited on a standard basis as follows:

2.1.3.3   Completion of college courses and university courses beyond those required for entry level certification.

a. The participant earns 10 CPD hours (1 CEU) for each hour of course credit if the course is for *one quarter*.

> *An Example:*   a 3-quarter credit course in consultation earns 30 CPD hours or 3 CEUs.

b. If the course is for *one semester*, then one hour of credit is worth 15 CPD hours (1.5 CEUs).

> *An Example:*   A course in advanced research earns 3-semester hours = 45 CPD hours or 4.5 CEUs.

2.1.3.4   Teaching courses and provision of inservice when not an ordinary aspect of employment.

CPD credit should not be claimed for activities which are a part of the school psychologist's regular job requirements. However, credit may be claimed for those teaching/presenting activities which go beyond the normal demands of that psychologist's job setting. Additionally, although the course or inservice may be repeated, credit may only be claimed once. Credit claimed is equal to the number of hours or CEUs obtained by those attending the course or workshop, as described in items 1–3 above.

> *Examples:* A university trainer presents a workshop on curriculum-based assessment at a state conference. The workshop is 4 hours long. Participants obtain 4 CPD hours of credit or .4 CEUs. The presenter may also claim 4 hours or .4 CEUs. However, credit may only be claimed *once* for workshops on this subject.
>
> A school psychologist teaches one course as a guest lecturer at a local university. Students taking the course earn 3 semester hour credits. The lecturer can earn 45 CPD hours or 4.5 CEUs for teaching the course. However, the psychologist may only obtain those credits the *first* time the course is taught.

Group C: Conversions and Limitations

Other types of activities are also valuable in professional development. However, participation in these activities is *not counted on a per hour basis alone.* These activities might:

1. require more actual time than the credit that may be earned.
2. be limited in the credit they offer.

Limited activities include the following:

2.1.3.8   Supervision of interns in field placements by school psychologists

> For purposes of claiming CPD credit, field supervisors should consider the extent to which this role leads to professional growth on the part of the supervisor. Up to 10 CPD hours or 1 CEU may be obtained for supervising one or two students for one academic year. Credit for supervision may be claimed *no more than twice* (two years) during a three-year renewal period.
>
> *An Example:* A school psychologist supervised an intern for 1 academic year. They decided to run a group at one of the elementary schools for children whose parents were divorced. This and several other activities involved new learning for both the supervisor and intern. The supervisor may claim 10 CPD hours or 1 CEU.

2.1.3.5   Research

2.1.3.6   Publication

2.1.3.7   Presentation

> To claim credit in these categories, it is necessary for the participant to reasonably examine the amount of time spent and claim those actual hours up to the maximums specified. Also, the participant should claim credit *only once for any topic.*
>
> • Unpublished research — up to 10 hours or 1 CEU
>
> • Research *and* publication or presentation on a topic — up to 25 hours or 2.5 CEUs
>
> • Non-research based published articles with references *or* poster presentation at a state or national convention — up to 10 hours or 1 CEU
>
> • Published theoretical or editorial articles — up to 5 hours or .5 CEUs

2.1.3.9 Program planning/evaluation, when not an ordinary aspect of employment.

As with the research/publication categories above, actual hours should be claimed, but *no more than* 25 hours or 2.5 CEUs may be obtained in this area.

An Example: A school psychologist promotes the development of teacher assistance teams in the district. Considerable time is spent planning for the program, training staff, developing procedures, etc. The psychologist estimates 80 actual hours of work. 25 hours or 2.5 CEUs are claimed.

2.1.3.10 Sequenced programs of self-study

Programs developed and published to provide training in a specific knowledge or skill area are valid for obtaining CPD credit. *No more than two topics may earn credit in this category during a three-year renewal period.* ("Refer to informal programs of self-study.") Credit may be determined by:

- obtaining the CPD or CEU credit designated by program developers.

    An Example: A course on non-biased assessment is developed by NASP for Continuing Professional Development. It involves purchasing a course manual and video tapes. The credit offered is 20 hours or 2 CEUs.

- estimation of credit based on time spent mastering the material. Credit obtained in this manner is limited to 15 hours or 1.5 CEUs.

    An Example: A course on Counseling Techniques with Children involved 20 hours of reading, 3 hours of audio tapes and 3 written exercises. 15 hours or 1.5 CEUs may be claimed.

2.1.3.11 Informal programs of self-study

When a school psychologist pursues a topic of interest by systematically reviewing the literature, developing a comprehensive list of resources and studying these resources, CPD credit may be obtained. Included in this category would be book, journal and manual reading. To obtain credit, the psychologist must provide the reading list with the required validation form (see Appendix D). At least 4 resources should be included on any 1 topic. Actual hours claimed in this activity are not to exceed 15 hours or 1.5 CEUs per topic. *No more than two topics may earn credit in this category during a three-year renewal period.*

An Example: A school psychologist decides to study "collaborative consultation." A review of the literature reveals 5 well-known authors on this topic. Additionally, the *School Psychology Review* lists four recent articles. The psychologist spends 20 hours reading these and earns 15 hours of credit or 1.5 CEUs.

2.1.3.12 Professional organization leadership

A school psychologist who holds a position in a state or national school psychology organization may earn:

- 10 hours/1 CEU as president

- 5 hours/.5CEU as other officer
- 5 hours/.5 CEU as committee chair or NASP delegate or regional director

Credit may be obtained for no more than *one position, per year, per organization.* No more than 20 hours or 2.0 CEUs may be obtained in this category during a three-year renewal period.

An Example: A school psychologist serves as treasurer of the state school psychology association one year and holds a NASP delegate position for all three years of a renewal period. She may claim 5 hours of credit for the treasurer's position and 15 hours for the delegate's position (5 CPD credits for each of three years) for a total of 20 hours. This activity should be claimed under the area of Program Planning and Evaluation.

CREDIT EQUIVALENCIES AND CREDIT CEILINGS SUMMARY TABLE

CATEGORY	CONVERSION	CEILING LIMITS	DOCUMENTATION REQUIRED
2.1.3.1 School psychology workshops/conferences	Each hour = 1 CPD	None	Certificate of attendance or Activity Documentation Form and receipt.
2.1.3.2 Other professional workshops/conferences	Each hour = 1 CPD	None	Certificate of attendance or Activity Documentation Form and receipt.
2.1.3.3 College/university courses	One quarter hour = 10 CPD One semester hour = 15 CPD	None	Transcript
2.1.3.4 Teaching/workshop presentation	Hour-for-hour or university credits as defined in 2.1.3.1-3 above.	Credit may be claimed only first time content is taught.	Copy of syllabus for course or copy of program flyer or Activity Documentation Form.
2.1.3.5 Research 2.1.3.6 Publication 2.1.3.7 Presentations	Actual hours, up to ceilings established	Unpublished research = 10 CPD Research & publication or presentation = 25 CPD. Article published or poster presented = 10 CPD. Theoretical/editorial article = 5 CPD Each project may only be claimed once.	Activity Documentation Form and Abstract of Program, if possible.
2.1.3.8 Intern supervision	1 year of supervision = 10 CPD	Only one intern claimed per year. No more than 2 interns in three years.	Activity Documentation Form
2.1.3.9 Program planning/evaluation	Actual hours, up to ceiling	1 project = 25 CPD	Activity Documentation Form
2.1.3.10 Sequenced self-study	Actual hours, up to ceiling	1 project = 15 CPD (or other as established). No more than 2 topics in 3 years.	Activity Documentation Form
2.1.3.11 Informal self-study	Actual hours, up to ceiling	1 topic = 15 CPD. No more than 2 topics in 3 years.	Activity Documentation Form
2.1.3.12 Professional organization leadership	President = 10 CPD Other officer = 5 CPD Committee Chair / delegate / regional director = 5 CPD	No more than one activity per organization per year. No more than 20 CPD in this category in 3 years.	Activity Documentation Form

ATTACHMENT C

National Association of School Psychologists
Continuing Professional Development Summary Sheet

NATIONAL ASSOCIATION OF SCHOOL PSYCHOLOGISTS

CONTINUING PROFESSIONAL DEVELOPMENT SUMMARY SHEET

INSTRUCTIONS: This form is to be completed and submitted to the NASP Professional Development Committee when the required 75 hours (7.5 CEUs) of continuing professional development activity have been completed. Documentation for each activity claimed on this CPD Summary Sheet must be attached. Use the Summary Sheet as the cover sheet for the individual documentation forms. If more space is needed, attach additional sheets. Activities must be listed for at least three of the six skill areas on this form.

NAME: _____   NCSP NUMBER: _____

ADDRESS: _____   DAYTIME PHONE NO.: _____

_____   ACTIVITIES LISTED ON THIS FORM WERE
                                          COMPLETED BETWEEN _____
                                                              (starting date)

_____   AND _____
                                                          (ending date)

PRIMARY ROLE (check only one):

_____ School psychologist   _____ University trainer

_____ Administrator/supervisor   _____ Other (specify): _____

Skill Area	Activity Title	Date	Clock Hours/ Equivalent	Skill Area Subtotal
Consultation				
Assessment				

Skill Area	Activity Title	Date	Clock Hours/ Equivalent	Skill Area Subtotal
Intervention				
Supervision				
Research				
Program Planning/ Evaluation				

I attest that the activities reported on this form reflect actual activities in which I participated. I understand that falsification of this information is an ethical violation and may result in my being ineligible for future certification and/or legal action may be taken against me.

_____
(signature)

TOTAL CPD
HOURS
EARNED

ATTACHMENT D

National Association of School Psychologists
Activity Documentation Form

NATIONAL
ASSOCIATION OF
SCHOOL
PSYCHOLOGISTS

ACTIVITY DOCUMENTATION FORM

INSTRUCTIONS: This documentation form is to be used to report activities for which no other standard documentation form exists. A separate form must be used for each activity.

NAME: _____   NCSP Number: _____

ADDRESS: _____   Daytime Phone No.: _____

_____

_____

Title of Activity: _____

Description of Activity:

Date(s) of Activity _____ Location: _____

Skill Area Addressed Through This Activity:

_____ Consultation   _____ Supervision
_____ Assessment   _____ Research
_____ Intervention   _____ Program Planning/Evaluation

Actual Number of Clock Hours of Participation: _____

CPD Credits Claimed (See allowed equivalencies/caps in Appendix B): _____

I certify that this activity merits CPD credit in that it meets the following criteria:

1. This activity enhanced or upgraded my professional skills or added to my knowledge base.
2. This activity was relevant to the professional practice of school psychology.
3. This activity fits into my personal plan for continuing professional development.

_____
(signature)

Medications Commonly Used with School Children

Susan M. Vess
University of Southern Maine

School psychologists encounter many children with emotional and health problems which hinder the students' abilities to profit from instruction and social interaction. In addition, through their contact with parents and their review of school and health records, practitioners are often confronted with the names of medications with which they are unfamiliar.

The following is a listing, which is by no means complete, of drugs used to control disturbances in behavior or to reduce the discomfort of arthritis and respiratory illnesses. None of the medications eliminate the behavior or health problem, but all are expected to provide the child with sufficient relief of symptons that s/he is able to learn.

The medications are listed in chart form for convenient access, with specific information about a particular drug listed under the Treatment Comments column and information about a group of drugs appearing as a footnote. More complete information about a disorder and its medication should be sought from professionals such as physicians, pharmacists, school nurses, and from reference books including the Annual Physicians Desk Reference (PDR).

PSYCHOTROPIC DRUGS

Psychotropic drugs such as major and minor tranquilizers, stimulants, and antidepressants are medications prescribed by a doctor to alter the behavior or emotions of children with severe childhood disturbances (Martin & Agran, 1988). These drugs change the children's behavior in both positive and negative directions. Although psychotropic drugs have been used in the treatment of many childhood disorders, relatively few children with these disturbances are treated with psychotropic medication.

Which particular drug is chosen for use with a given patient relates to the doctor's evaluation of information about how and how well a drug works to treat a particular disorder and what side effects accompany its use. The physician also considers the usual dosage of the drug, its schedule of administration, and its interaction with other drugs.

DISTURBANCES IN BEHAVIOR

Anxiety and Psychosis
"Tranquilizers (Psychotropic Drugs)"

Trade Name	Generic Name	Treatment Comments
Thorazine[4]	chlorpromazine[1]	aggressive, very agitated behavior; often associated with weight increase (Martin & Agran, 1988); because of sedative effects, may be used with severely or profoundly mentally retarded (Thomas, 1988)
Mellaril[4]	thioridozine[1]	hyperkinesis; least extrapyramidal side effects of major tranquilizers (Martin & Agran, 1988); among most commonly used neuroleptics with children (Gittelman & Kanner, 1986); may be used to control aggression and hostile and self-injurious behavior in the mentally retarded (Martin & Agran, 1988); because of sedative effects, may be used with severely or profoundly mentally retarded (Thomas, 1988)
Stelazine	trifluoperazine[1]	may cause extrapyramidal side effects (Martin & Agran, 1988); may control head banging, self-injury, hyperactivity, & assaultiveness in the mentally retarded (Thomas, 1988)
Phenergan	promethazine[1]	
Compazine	prochlorperazine[1]	may cause extrapyramidal side effects (Martin & Agran, 1988)
Haldol[4]	haloperidol[2]	childhood schizophrenia; Tourette Syndrome and emotional tics; autism with hyperactivity or alternating hyperactivity with hypoactivity; autistic children with serious management problems to decrease maladaptive behavior and to increase discrimination learning (Perry & Meislas, 1988); reduces high levels of stereotypies and increases orienting reaction in children who previously showed little orientation (Perry & Meislas, 1988); may cause extrapyramidal side effects (Martin & Agran, 1988)
Valium	diazepam[3]	ulcers; status epilepticus, reduce spasticity of cerebral palsy; used along with psychological treatment to treat adolescents and young adults with anxiety disorders (Martin & Agran, 1988); antiepileptic properties
Librium	chlordiazepoxide[3]	used along with psychological treatment to treat adolescents and young adults with anxiety disorders (Martin & Agran, 1988); antiepileptic properties
Dalmane	flurazepam	may be used with adolescents for night time sedation (Thomas, 1988)
Equanil, Miltown	meprobamate[3]	among the propanediols; a group of drugs which are used with caution because of their association with accidental poisoning & suicide (Martin & Agran, 1988)

Trade Name	Generic Name	Treatment Comments
Lithane, Lithotabs	lithium[2]	bipolar affective disorders and mania; psychotic symptoms
Tofranil	imipramine[3]	anti-depressant; used to treat enuresis and severe, chronic childhood depression

Tranquilizers: produce sedation; decrease motor activity including hyperactivity and restlessness; reduce anxiety, aggression, combativeness.

[1]phenothiazines: major tranquilizers; used to control aggressive and self-destructive behavior in psychotic children; major tranquilizers used most often in the treatment of children (Martin & Agran, 1988); most of the children are students in special classes for emotionally disturbed and mentally retarded children (Martin & Agran, 1988).

[2]strong (major) tranquilizers: antipsychotics and neuroleptics; historically used to treat almost all childhood disorders; treat perceptual alterations such as hallucinations, altered mood, disturbed thinking, and unusual interpersonal behavior including hyperactivity, aggression, self-injurious and self-stimulatory behavior; side effects include sedation, dyskinesias, and somatic symptoms; not useful in treating most cases of autism (Martin & Agran, 1988); used in early and middle childhood for behavior management of severe conduct problems and in adolescence for schizophrenia and severe affective disorders (Martin & Agran, 1988); little is known about these drugs' affect on learning (Martin & Agran, 1988).

[3]mild (minor) tranquilizers: anxiolytics; control anxiety; produce sedation, the drugs' most common side effect; when withdrawn, symptoms return because anxiolytics remove tension, fears, and anxiety rather than improve the patient's coping skills; little information about the use of mild tranquilizers with children under thirteen years; used to treat problems of childhood other than anxiety (Martin & Agran, 1988); appear to limit responsiveness to stimuli and depress learning (Martin & Agran, 1988).

[4]Thorazine, Mellaril, and Haldol: prescribed to assist in the management of children's aggression, destructiveness, and antisocial behavior and to treat self-injurious behavior (Martin & Agran, 1988).

Affective Disorders
(Depression and manic depressive disorder)

Trade Name	Generic Name	Treatment Comments
Tofranil	imipramine	first antidepressant found (Gittelman & Kanner, 1986); soothes adult panic attacks (Gittelman & Kanner, 1986); used to treat enuresis and severe, chronic depression in children who are not mentally retarded; since its efficacy in treating childhood depression has not been demonstrated, it is not endorsed for use in children under 12 years (Carlson, 1988); yet, most studied TCA in the treatment of childhood depression; sometimes used to treat hyperactivity, ADD, school phobia, & separation anxiety disorders (Thomas, 1988; Gittelman & Kanner, 1986)
Elavil	amitriptyline	used in the treatment of severe, chronic childhood depression in children with normal intelligence; may be used to treat hyperactivity (Martin & Agran, 1988)
Aventyl Pamelor	nortriptyline	used to treat childhood depression
Norpramine Pertofrane	desipramine	used to treat childhood depression
Eskalith Lithobid	lithium carbonate	most effective treatment of manic depressive disorders; may be used to treat children with ADD, conduct disorders, anorexia, and schizophrenia when family members show a history of manic depressive illness; may also be used to treat childhood behavior disorders that include emotional lability and aggression when family members show a bipolar or major depressive disorder; seldom used in the treatment of children because they rarely show a manic depressive disorder; used in mentally retarded children to treat aggression, hyperactivity, or self injurious behavior (Thomas, 1988); may result in serious medical complications when combined with electroconvulsive shock therapy (ECT) and Haldol (Kalat, 1988); drug works by regulating the permeability of the cellular membrane which seems to smooth out the individual's mood; the therapeutic dosage of lithium is very close to the toxic dosage (Kalat, 1988), but the safety and adequacy of dosage is readily monitored by measuring the serum lithium levels in the blood (Carlson, 1988; Gittelman & Kanner, 1986); side effects include nausea, vomiting, tremor, weight gain, & stomach aches

Tricyclics: tricyclic antidepressants (TCAs); used for about 30 years in the treatment of depression in adults and children (Carlson, 1988); takes days to weeks to work; treatment lasts for 3 to 6 months (Martin & Agran, 1988); necessary to measure plasma levels to maximize treatment effectiveness (Carlson, 1988); few controlled studies of their effectiveness with children and even fewer about their usefulness with adolescents (Carlson, 1988; Gittelman & Kanner, 1986); may rarely precipitate seizures in seizure-prone persons (Carlson, 1988); children demonstrate variable tolerance of side effects and withdrawal symptoms

(Carlson, 1988); side effects include: nausea, blurred vision, drowsiness, and dry mouth; divided dosages, although not administered at school, most effective in children (Carlson, 1988); clomipramine, a TCA not marketed in the U.S., used to treat phobic and compulsive disorders of children (Gittelman & Kanner, 1986).

Monoamine oxidase inhibitors (MAOIs): no drug of this group of anti-depressants included in the chart; their use is restricted to adults because these drugs combine modest effectiveness with toxicity; no controlled studies of their use with children (Carlson, 1988); raise blood pressure when the person eats fermented foods such as hard cheese, pickles, and alcoholic beverages (Gittelman & Kanner, 1986).

**Attention-Deficit Hyperactivity Disorder
(ADD, ADHD, MBD, Hyperacivity)
"Stimulants"**

Trade Name	Generic Name	Treatment Comments
Ritalin Dexedrine Cylert	methylphenidate dextroamphetamine pemoline	Ritalin, Dexedrine and Cylert most commonly used drugs to treat ADD in the past 25 years (Pelham & Murphy, 1986); control overt symptoms but not the sole treatment of ADD; learning may improve as a consequence of increased attention span; stimulants insufficient to produce normal academic and social functioning; sometimes used to treat drowsiness associated with anticonvulsants and narcolepsy; stimulants best researched psychotropic drugs (Martin & Agran, 1988); used to treat learning and behavior problems in 1 to 2% of children in elementary schools (Martin & Agran, 1988); 80 to 90% of children with ADD treated with Ritalin, Dexedrine or Cylert at some time (Pelham & Murphy, 1986); estimated that 30% of children with ADD do not show significant improvement (Pelham & Murphy, 1986); contraindicated in children with motor tics and Tourette Syndrome or a family history of either (Gadow, 1988)
Pondimin	fenfluramine	promising drug in the treatment of autism to improve behavior of child without severe management problems; along with haloperidol, best studied medication for autism; does not alter history or course of autism; chemically related to amphetamines but produces CNS depression rather than stimulation; mechanism of action involves the serotonergic nervous system; also prescription diet drug (Perry & Meislas, 1988)

Stimulants: strengthen selective attention; reduce impulsivity, hyperactivity and restlessness in children of normal ability with ADD; suppress aggression, noncompliance and other non-social behavior (Martin & Agran, 1988); most common psychotropic drugs for children with mild and moderate mental retardation (Gadow, 1988).

Side Effects: insomnia and anorexia, diminished weight gain, increased heart rate; with proper moderate dose, few and rarely serious side effects; in beginning of treatment, may find moodiness, headaches, irritability, difference in sleep patterns, and loss of appetite; if dosage is too high, detrimental effect on cognitive performance because attention over-focused (Martin & Agran, 1988).

MEDICAL CONDITIONS

Seizure Disorders (Epilepsy)
"Anticonvulsants (Antiepileptics)" *

Trade Name	Generic Name	*GM	*PM	*PM(TL)	Treatment Comments
Luminal	phenobarbital	X		X	safest overall, first tried, also used with febrile seizures
Dilantin	phenytoin	X		X	little sedative effect
Mysoline	primidone	X		X	often combined with other medication, may act as sedative, converted to phenobarbital in the body
Zarontin	ethosuximide		X		choice drug for petit mal
Tegretol	carbamazine	X		X	best for psychomotor seizures
Clonopin	clonazepam		X		for seizures resistant to other drugs, including myclonic seizures
Depakene	valproic acid	X	X	X	also for febrile convulsions
Mesantoin	mephenytoin	X		X	especially psychomotor seizures; often reserved for resistant cases
Mebaral	mephobarbital	X		X	barbituate; sedative effect
Tridione	trimethadione		X		effective but may be toxic
Paradione	paramethadione		X		effective but may be toxic
Celontin	methsuximide		X		mixed seizure types
Diamox	acetazolamide		X		supplemental in petit mal; diuretic for women several days before menstrual cycle with epilepsy associated with menstruation

Anticonvulsants reduce or control seizure activity; but may have multiple side effects that affect different tissues of the bodies. These side effects include: gastrointestinal distress such as nausea and vomiting; drowsiness; irritability; malaise; rashes; headache; dizziness; sedation; and more serious diseases, including severe blood anomalies and liver damage. According to Spunt, Hermann, and Rousseau (1986), side effects to the use of anticonvulsants could be expected because of their long-term use, their relatively high dosages, and combinations with other antiepileptics.

[* drug chosen by seizure type]   * GM = Grand Mal seizures
                                      * PM = Petit Mal (Absence) seizures
                                      * PM(TL) = Psychomotor (Temporal Lobe) seizures

Status epilepticus: Valium (diazepam) — used as an adjunct to other anticonvulsants to treat anxiety related to epilepsy and anxiety absence seizures
         Dilantin (phenytoin)
         Sodium phenobarbital
         Paraldehyde

Juvenile Rheumatoid Arthritis
"Analgesics and anti-inflammatories"

Trade Name	Generic Name	Treatment Comments
Aspirin	acetylsalicylic acid	reduce fever and relieve pain in order to restore and maintain joint motion
Ascriptin	acetylsalicylic acid, buffered	
Tylenol	acetaminophen	
Tolectin	tolmetin	
Anaprox	naproxen	approved for children?
Butazolidin*	phenylbutazone	
Indocin*	indomethacin	
Motrin*	ibuprofen fenoprofen	
Corticosteroids	prednisone	intermittent symptomatic treatment of inflammatory symptoms; may require stepwise discontinuation of therapy to prevent dangerous withdrawal symptom

* NOT FDA approved for JRA, but may be used by physicians.

Goal: enable normal physical and emotional functioning so that the child is sufficiently comfortable to attend school and learn.

Respiratory Illnesses
Allergies, Rhinitis, and "Colds"
"Antihistamines, nasal decongestants, cough suppresants"

Trade Name	Generic Name	Treatment Comments
Actidil	triprolidine[1]	All antihistamines listed below used to neutralize the effects of histamines (chemical mediators responsible for causing many of the typical symptoms of allergies); work best if treatment begun before histamines released into the blood and symptoms appear; may be used for symptoms of hay fever, allergies, allergic rhinitis, allergic conjunctivitis
Chlor-Trimetron Histaspan Teldrin	chlorpheniramine[1]	
Dimetane Veltane Symptom[3]	brompheniramine[1]	
Benadryl	diphenhydramine	above plus frequently used for acute allergic reactions, skin rash, etc., sedative effect

(Respiratory Illnesses — allergies, rhinitis, and "colds" continued)

Trade Name	Generic Name	Treatment Comments
PBZ (Pyribenzamine)	tripelennamine[1]	also used for allergic skin reactions
Decapryn	doxylamine[1]	
Temaril	trimeprazine[1]	used primarily for itching, related to major tranquilizers structurally
Tacaryl	methdilazine[1]	same as Temaril
Atarax Vistaril	hydroxyzine[1]	mild tranquilizer with antihistaminic effects; used frequently for itching and allergic rash, hives; used to manage hyperactivity & induce sleep (Martin & Agran, 1988)
Periactin	cyproheptadine[1]	itching, rash, hives; rarely used as "antihistamine"; may increase appetite and occasionally used for this purpose
Dramamine	dimenhydrinate[1]	antihistaminic used for nausea, vomiting and dizziness; motion sickness
Bonine Antivert	meclizine[1]	as above
Marezine	cyclizine[1]	as above
Sudafed Novafed Afrinol Neosynephrol	pseudoephedrine[2]	nasal decongestant, stimulant side effects in some cases
Neosynephrine drops Alconefrin drops Isophrin	phenylephrine[2]	topical nasal decongestant
Afrin drops	oxymetazoline[2]	long acting product
Otrivin drops	xylometazoline[2]	long acting product
Dimetapp	brompheniramine[1] phenylephrine[2] phenylpropanolamine[2]	antihistamine nasal decongestant combination for head cold and allergy
Rondec	carbinoxamine[1] pseudoephedrine[2]	
Actifed	triprolidine[1] pseudoephedrine[2]	
Co-Tylenol	chlorpheniramine[1] pseudoephedrine[2] dextromethorphan[3] acetaminophen	as above with Tylenol for fever, aches, pains, etc.

Trade Name	Generic Name	Treatment Comments
Novahistine products	chlorpheniramine[1] phenylpro-panolamine[2] or pseudoephedrine[2] dextromethor-phan[3] or codeine[3]	cough and cold combination of antihistamine with nasal decongestant, cough suppressant, and/or expectorant; consult specific product for specific combination
Sudafed products	codeine[3] guaifensin[4]	label of specific product should be consulted for specific combination
Robitussin products	same as above without antihistamine	
Triaminic products	pyrilamine[1] and pheniramine[1] or chlorpheniramine[1] phenylpropanolamine[2] dextromethorphan[3] or codeine[3] guaifensin[4]	
Actifed-C	triprolidine[1] pseudoephedrine[2] codeine[3] quaifensin[4]	cough and cold combination
Phenergan products	promethazine[1] ipecac fluidext[4] pot. guaicolsulfonate[4] citric acid[4] sodium citrate[4] dextromethorphan[3] or codeine	
Naldecon products	phenyltoloxamine[1] chlorpheniramine[1] phenylephrine[2] phenylpropanolamine[2] dextromethorphan[3] or codeine[3] guaifensin[4]	

Treatment goal: relief of symptoms with minimum or no side-effects.

[1] antihistamines: control itching and runny nose and sneezing of allergy, unknown potency, variable side effects including drowsiness and drying of mouth, nose, and throat.

[2] adrenergic agents, decongestants: improve airflow by causing constricted air passages to relax, reduce congestion by constriction of vessels of the nasal mucosa.

[3] cough suppressants: suppress the cough reflex, for non-productive dry cough.

[4] expectorants: liquefy phlegm and secretions to make easier to cough up.

Asthma
"Adrenergic agents, bronchodilators, steroids"

Trade Name	Generic Name	Treatment Comments
Theodur Slo-Phyllin Elixophyllin Aerolate Sustaire Theolair Theobid Theovent Somophyllin Slo-bid	theophylline[1]	oral bronchodilator; long-acting products; used for prophylactic treatment of severe recurrent asthma; early signs of excessive blood levels of theophylline include nervousness, tremulousness, gastrointestinal upset (nausea & vomiting), fast heart beat; reduces frequency & severity of bronchospasms (Creer, Marion, & Harm, 1988)
Aminodur Aminophylline (var. mfg.)	aminophylline[1]	chemically related to and converted to theophylline in the body
Lufyllin Dilor Neothylline	diphylline[1]	theophylline analog
Choledyl	oxtriphylline[1]	theophylline analog
	theophylline with:	
Bronkaid tablets Tedral tablets Primatene tablets Marax Brondecon Quibron Isuprel compd.	ephedrine[2], guaifensin[3] ephedrine[2], phenobarbital[4] ephedrine[2], phenobarbital[4] ephedrine[2], hydroxyzine[4] guaifensin[3] guaifensin[3] ephedrine[2], isoproterenol[2] phenobarbital[4] pot. iodide[3]	combination products used for asthma
Adrenalin Asthma Meter Medihaler-Epi Primatene Mist Bronkaid Mist AsthmaNefrin Vaponefrin AsthmaHaler	epinephrine[2]	inhalation for acute asthma attacks, adrenergic bronchodilator with short activity, used by inhalation
Bronkosol	isoetharine[2]	adrenergic bronchodilator with longer duration of effect
Medihaler-Iso Isuprel Mistometer Norisodrine Inhaler	isoproterenol[2]	short-acting adrenergic bronchodilator used by inhalation
Proventil	albuterol[2]	longest acting (4-6 hrs.) inhalation bronchodilating adrenergics; may be used for prophylactic treatment by inhalation or as oral tablets
Alupent Metarprel	metaproterenol[2]	adrenergic bronchodilator used either by inhalation or oral tablets; inhalation may be used for acute attacks

Trade Name	Generic Name	Treatment Comments
Bricanyl Bretnine	terbutaline[2]	primarily used to prevent asthma attacks, oral preparation
Intal Aarane	cromolyn[5]	used to de-trigger or prevent acute attacks of asthma caused by cold or exercise; takes two weeks for full effect; requires complicated technique for inhaling powder contents of capsule; will worsen an acute attack due to irritation of airways, if used then; prevents release of chemical mediators induced by allergen and nonallergen stimuli (Creer, Marion, & Harm, 1988); used when theophylline or Beta-adrenergics are ineffective or result in significant side effects (Creer, Marion, & Harm, 1988)
Beconase Vanceril	beclomethasone[6]	inhalation steroid used to decrease frequency of asthma attacks if used regularly; may be used for allergic rhinitis occasionally

Asthma attacks are induced by multiple irritants and vary widely in severity, frequency, and timing of episodes within the individual and from person to person. Environmental and air pollution, including exposure to passive smoking, are potent triggers of asthma attacks (Creer, Harm, & Marion, 1988). Because of asthma's extreme variability, methods of asthma prevention are tailored to the individual (Creer, Harm, & Marion, 1988). The first step in the treatment of asthma involves preventing asthma attacks by avoiding contact with the irritant(s) triggering an episode.

[1]theophylline: non-adrenergic bronchodilator; use with adrenergic bronchodilators may give additive effects. Relaxes smooth muscle lining of the airways in bronchioles of lungs to reduce obstruction of the lungs and to keep the respiratory system free of excess secretions and cellular debris.

[2]adrenergic bronchodilators: same activity as theophylline but by a different mechanism or action; fastest growing area of asthma pharmacology; frequent side effects include muscle tremors and nervousness, sometimes seen even at normal dosages; in children, muscle tremors may be manifested by trembling hands and deterioration of penmanship; may be stimulant in some patients.

[3]expectorants: used to liquefy thick mucus secretions present in an acute asthma attack or bronchitis.

[4]sedatives: thought to "calm" asthmatics and decrease the possibility of attacks triggered by nervous excitement; their value in treating asthma is questionable.

[5]cromolyn: product is thought to "stabilize" cells in the airway surface which might initiate an asthma atack in response to allergic stimulation.

[6]steroids: anti-inflammatory agents felt to decrease the frequency and severity of asthma attacks due to allergic inflammatory stimuli; used only when all other treatment forms were unsuccessful; may produce serious side effects from adrenal suppression (Creer, Marion, & Harm, 1988).

COMPLIANCE

Compliance or treatment adherence is defined as the ability and willingness to subscribe to recommended medication or treatment (Feist & Brannon, 1988). La Greca (1988) concludes from her review of the literature that a significant, substantial percentage of children and their care givers fail to comply with treatments of both acute ailments such as otitis media and upper respiratory infections and chronic disorders, including diabetes and asthma. The overall predicted rate of compliance approximates 50% for both adult and pediatric populations (La Greca, 1988; Feist & Brannon, 1988). Indeed, mothers are about as compliant with their children's treatment as they are with their own (Feist & Brannon, 1988). It must be noted, however, that compliance with prescribed treatment does not assure relief from symptoms or recovery; especially when the condition requires complex treatment (La Greca, 1988).

Generally, patients adhere to treatment when there is an immediate, positive reduction in symptoms or relief from pain. With acute illnesses, patients discontinue treatment when symptoms have abated. Regardless of the illness, chronicity of an illness is associated with poorer compliance (La Greca, 1988). Compliance with treatment for chronic disorders is complicated when that treatment alters the patient's lifestyle or personal habits, is prescribed for an extended period, includes multiple medications, involves different schedules for administration of medication, and/or works by preventing the appearance of symptoms (La Greca, 1988; Feist & Brannon, 1988).

Little is known about the relationship between a patient's coping skills and behavior style with his/her compliance with medical treatments. Thus, it is impossible to predict who will and who will not comply with prescribed medical advice and treatment. Nevertheless, there are some indicators of the likelihood of noncompliance. The severity of an illness predicts the compliance rate only as far as the patient perceives the illness to be severe and/or painful. The cost of treatment is not significantly related to the compliance rate while the presence or severity of side effects is a secondary explanation for noncompliance. The doctor-patient relationship, however, is an important variable in compliance rates. Noncompliance is associated with physicians who are unfriendly, arrogant, and poor communicators and with a delay in scheduling an appointment or extensive periods spent in the doctor's waiting room (Feist & Brannon, 1988).

Parents are responsible for their child's treatment and must also cope with the impact of the child's illness on the family. Many parents fail to subscribe to the child's medical treatment by adjusting dosages of medication. They administer extra medication or terminate its use on their own initiative and give medication irregularly (Feist & Brannon, 1988).

The family and the child participate in decision making about medical treatment that balances the child's health needs and well being with the family's functioning. Noncompliance occurs when the treatment restricts or disrupts the family's lifestyle or routine. Additionally, noncompliance is more common in dysfunctional families while a supportive family is associated with the best compliance. There is new interest in adaptive noncompliance in which less extreme treatments are undertaken (La Greca, 1988).

A child's cognitive and developmental status influences his/her knowledge and understanding of disease and affects his/her reaction to and participation in treatment. The child's socioemotional development level affects his/her position relative to dependency on parents versus preference for personal independence and peer acceptance and consequently, influences his/her compliance with medical regimens.

Compliance with treatment is related to the child's adjustment and coping styles with more severe emotional problems and poorer self esteem and adaptation associated with noncompliance. Conversely, it should be noted that poor control of an illness may contribute to a child's emotional and behavior problems.

Compliance is also influenced by biological factors of childhood including growth and changes in metabolism. Additionally, although medications are prescribed on the basis of their typical effects on groups of patients, the individual may vary in physiological functioning and responsiveness to medical interventions. When the patient's response to treatment is neither as expected nor optimal, compliance is reduced.

Because there are no uniform causes of noncompliance, the reasons for failure of a particular child to adhere to prescribed treatment must be systematically investigated. Treatments that address noncompliance must focus on the needs and perceptions of the individual patient and his/her family. These treatment plans may include education about the disease, teaching self-monitoring strategies to the child, and instituting reinforcement procedures and cues.

SIDE EFFECTS

Drug-induced side effects are the result of exaggerated pharmalogical action of the drug in which the patient is drug toxic either from an acute overdose of the medication or from accumulation of the drug in the patient's body (Spunt, Hermann, & Rousseau, 1986). Side effects that are related to the central nervous system (CNS) are generally manifested by disturbances in adaptive behavior such as irritability and restlessness and/or in physical symptoms including drowsiness, ataxia, nystagmus, and dizziness (Martin & Agran, 1988; Spunt, Hermann, & Rousseau, 1986). Drug-induced side effects are managed by adjusting dosage of the medication.

Non-dose dependent side effects are abnormal or peculiar reactions such as increased susceptibility or unresponsiveness to the drug, abnormal tolerance, or a qualitatively different effect such as excitation with a sedative (Spunt, Hermann, & Rousseau, 1986). Non-dose dependent side effects include drug allergies in which histamines produce allergic symptoms from skin rashes to fatal toxicities. Symptoms of non-dose dependent side effects range from mild to severe, show local to widespread reactions, and appear immediately to days after administration of the drug. Non-dose dependent side effects are treated by removal of the drug from treatment of the particular patient.

Polypharmacy or multiple drug treatment is the concurrent administration of 2 or more drugs (Martin & Agran, 1988). Concurrent administration of multiple drugs to one patient can result in side effects in which the action of one drug influences or negates the action of another drug.

SUMMARY

The information contained in the charts and narrative portions of this appendix provides a very quick summary of medications used in the treatment of children with behavior problems and health concerns. It is expected that the reader will consult appropriate professionals and literature, including PDR and the books in the annotated bibliography, about the use of a drug in the treatment of a particular individual, dosage levels, means of administration, and desirable and undesirable behaviors associated with use of a specific drug.

REFERENCES

Carlson, G. A. (1988). Depression: Pharmacotherapies. In J. L. Matson (Ed.), *Handbook of treatment approaches in childhood psychopathology.* New York: Plenum.

Creer, T. L., Harm, D. L., & Marion, R. J. (1988). Childhood asthma. In D. K. Routh (Ed.), *Handbook of pediatric psychology.* New York: Guilford.

Creer, T. L., Marion, R. J., & Harm, D. L. (1988). Childhood asthma. In V. B. VanHasselt, P. S. Strain, & M. Hersen (Eds.), *Handbook of developmental and physical disabilities.* New York: Pergamon.

Feist, J., & Brannon, L. (1988). *Health psychology: An introduction to behavior and health.* Belmont, CA: Wadsworth.

Gadow, K. D. (1988). Attention deficit disorder and hyperactivity: Pharmacotherapies. In J. L. Matson (Ed.), *Handbook of treatment approaches in childhood psychopathology*. New York: Plenun.

Gittelman, R., & Kanner, A. (1986). Psychopharmacotherapy. In H. C. Quay & J. S. Werry (Eds.), *Psychopathological disorders of childhood*. 3rd edition. New York: Wiley.

Kalat, J. W. (1988). *Biological psychology*. 3rd edition. Belmont, CA: Worth.

La Greca, A. (1988). Adherence to prescribed medical regimens. In D. K. Routh (Ed.), *Handbook of pediatric psychology*. New York: Guilford.

Martin, J. E., & Agran, M. (1988). Pharmacotherapy. In J. L. Matson (Ed.), *Handbook of treatment approaches in childhood psychopathology*. New York: Plenum.

Pelham, W. E., & Murphy, H. A. (1986). Attention deficit and conduct disorders. In M. Hersen (Ed.), *Pharmacological and behavioral treatment: An integrative approach*. New York: Wiley.

Perry, R., & Meislas, K. (1988). Infantile autism and childhood schizophrenia. In J. L. Matson (Ed.), *Handbook of treatment approaches in childhood psychopathology*. New York: Plenum.

Spunt, A. L., Hermann, B. P., & Rousseau, A. M. (1986). Epilepsy. In M. Hersen (Ed.), *Pharmacological and behavioral treatment: An integrative approach*. New York: Wiley.

Thomas, M. (1988). Mental retardation and learning disability: Pharmacotherapies. In J. L. Matson (Ed.), *Handbook of treatment approaches in childhood psychopathology*. New York: Plenum.

ANNOTATED BIBLIOGRAPHY

Routh, D. K. (Ed.). (1988). *Handbook of pediatric psychology*. New York: Guilford.
According to the author, this handbook is designed for professionals interested in the delivery of psychological services in pediatric settings. It deals with topics related to child health psychology including life threatening and chronic diseases, medically related and lifestyle issues, and the management of pain from medical treatment, dentistry, and burns. The handbook includes an excellent chapter on the legal and ethical issues of child health and health care.

Matson J. L. (Ed.). (1988). *Handbook of treatment approaches in childhood psychopathology*. New York: Plenum.
This handbook considers the major psychological and pharmacological treatment approaches for childhood psychopathology. It includes an overview of treatment methods for conduct and anxiety disorders, severe mental disorders, and physical and learning disabilities. Its audience consists of students and practitioners in school psychology, clinical psychology, and related fields.

Van Hasselt, V. B., Strain, P. S., & Hersen, M. (Eds.). (1988). *Handbook of developmental and physical disabilities*. New York: Pergamon.
This handbook considers lifespan issues of the disabled; their psychological evaluation; family adjustment; and review of specific disabilities, such as asthma, cerebral palsy, hearing and visual impairments, and learning disabilities. The chapters are clearly written, concise, and contain a wealth of information about disabilities, their evaluation and treatment, and their impact on the individual's functioning and their significant others.

Best Practices in Identifying Community Resources

David Happe
Western Hills (Iowa) Area Education Agency

To address the needs of children it is important to draw upon resources both within and outside the school. The utilization of outside resources shifts the focus of the school psychologist's role from one of doing (administering tests, counseling, consulting) to roles of finding (seeking information, answers, and assistance) and linking — bringing those in need together with appropriate resources. To fill these roles basic information and an expansive sense of service delivery is necessary. This appendix presents a variety of specific resources for the school psychologist and tips on how to locate other resources.

BASIC CONSIDERATIONS IN SEEKING ASSISTANCE

General Considerations

Seek starting points. It is more important to have a few reliable means of entering systems that provide information, expertise and assistance than it is to try to be knowledgeable about the single best source for all possible situations. Government agencies; private, state, and national organizations/ and information and referral services are good starting points.

Anticipate a long search. Expect to make a number of calls and inquiries in your search for assistance. Your pleasant requests can easily turn into unpleasant demands as the frustrations of being transferred here, referred there, and put on hold accumulate.

Information becomes dated. Names, addresses, and phone numbers change frequently. Small organizations, in particular, do not usually maintain a permanent headquarters, and the address and phone you may find is typically that of an officer of the organization. This person may move or the responsibility for being a contact person may shift annually. The most efficient search method may be to contact the national office of an organization and to ask if there is a chapter in your state or area.

Telephone Contacts

Most initial contacts will be made by telephone. The following suggestions are adapted from Lesko's 1988 *Information USA Workbook* (see Print Resources, below). These are commonsense guidelines but they are easily forgotten, especially as a search drags on and patience wears thin.

1. Introduce yourself cheerfully. Your opening sets the tone of the phone call and may determine whether you are successful in getting what you need.

2. Be open and candid. Explain your need clearly and in as much detail as is needed. If making a contact for a parent or child, it is better to explain the need for confidentiality than to appear evasive in your conversation.

3. Be optimistic. By conveying a sense of confidence you encourage the person

you have reached to exert some effort on your behalf.

4. Be humble and courteous. Never question the authority or expertise of the individual you have reached.

5. Be concise. You may be seeking assistance from this person in addressing a single aspect of a complex situation. Don't confound efforts to help by overwhelming your contact.

6. Don't be a "gimme." Even if your contact represents a public agency that is required by law to provide some information or service, your chances of success — especially timely success - are increased by consideration for your contact.

7. Be complimentary. A compliment or two will express your appreciation for the assistance you received and respect for the individual who provided it.

8. Be conversational. A little time spent on topics that are not strictly business — news, weather, sports — may get your source to open up to you.

9. Return the favor. When you are seeking information or assistance, you have an area of shared interest with your potential source. Be willing to share your own knowledge and expertise with those you contact.

10. Send thank you notes. If you are tapping a source you may wish to utilize again, a thank you note helps ensure future cooperation.

11. Explain your need to whomever answers your call. If the specific person you seek is not in, the message you leave can allow your potential source to be prepared to respond or will allow a secretary or receptionist to provide important information.

Record of telephone contact. Sometimes it is helpful to have a form to jot some notes on, to organize your thoughts, and to help you make sure that you include all necessary topics in making a contact. Figure 1 provides an example. Each item on this form guides you to collect potentially valuable information, and it is important that you have an understanding of the need for each piece of information.

Agency/office contacted. Be precise. Many organizations, bureaus, offices, and divisions have similar names. A recipient of the information you collect should know whether you have called the Developmental Disabilities Division of the State Department of Health, Disabilities Services at County Social Services, or some other place. Check the information that you already have (names, addresses, titles, etc.) for accuracy when making a contact.

Individual reached. Space is provided for two names. Often you will explain your need to one person, a secretary or receptionist, who will put you in contact with someone else. Record both names so that you, or someone else, can recontact the appropriate person. If you are searching for assistance for reluctant parents, not knowing whom to ask may be enough to discourage them from calling.

Situation/questions/concerns. Fill this section out before calling. Jot down any pertinent information, special circumstances, and specific questions that you want answered. Doing this ahead of time accomplishes two things: You make sure that you have included information that the person you have contacted will need to be able to answer your question, and you make sure that you don't forget to ask all of your questions. Check off each point as it is covered in your call.

Answers/services/assistance available. Record what is actually being offered carefully and in as much detail as necessary. Ask follow-up questions to your original queries. Many organizations have better names than services and mere availability does not guarantee any particular level of quality.

Eligibility/fees/timelines/other information. Be specific in asking about eligibility, fee, and timeline issues. Other information could include meeting sites and times, specific forms a parent should

CONTACT RECORD

Agency/office contacted _____

Address _____

_____

Phone # _____ Date _____

Individual reached _____ Position _____

Individual reached _____ Position _____

Question/concern:

Answers/services/assistance available:

Eligibility:

Fees: Fixed   Sliding

Timelines:

Other information:

_____

Referred to _____

Address _____

_____

Phone _____

FIGURE 1. Record of telephone contact.

ask for, names of other contacts you might consider, and so forth.

Referred to. The individual or organization you contact may be incorrect for your need or may be able to refer you to a source of further assistance. Use this space to record these new resources.

GENERAL RESOURCES

Your Workplace

The people you work with can be the greatest resource you have available. Ask lots of questions and don't be afraid of asking dumb ones. Your employer may have formal agreements with outside agencies for the provision of services to students. These may include agreements for the provision of mental health services, evaluative services, or educational services for preschoolers or children with low-incidence handicaps. Make sure you are aware of these arrangements and the services that can be obtained through them. Also, acquaint yourself with the print and media resources of your employer.

State and Local Resources

Telephone directories. Most telephone directories include a listing of public and private service providers under the title Community Resources or Community Services. The Yellow Pages will provide listings of professional service providers and the White Pages or Government section will help guide you to public resources. Look for an Information and Referral listing either in the Community Services Section or in the Yellow or White Pages. Information and referral services are available in many cities, often funded by United Way or similar organizations.

Local resource directories. Many information and referral services publish directories of community resources that are available for a nominal fee. Your library may have such a directory and your employer may have one available or may be willing to obtain one.

Your local library. The public library is an often overlooked resource. A good reference librarian can be a most valued ally in your search for information and assistance. In addition to knowing what resources are available in the library collection, the reference librarian knows how to use these resources, saving you the time needed to decipher each source's way of organizing information.

Government agencies. The agencies responsible for education, health, and human services possess different names, structures, and missions from state to state, and no attempt will be made here to direct you through your own state's bureaucratic structure. Government agencies publish many informational materials such as directories to the many offices and personnel within the government or guides to public and private service providers within the state. For example, Public Law 99-457 mandates that each state develop a central directory of experts, resources, and services for handicapped infants and toddlers. Your employer may possess state directories or resource materials, or you may be able to obtain copies by asking the appropriate office or individual.

SPECIFIC RESOURCES

NICHCY. The National Information Center for Handicapped Children and Youth (NICHCY) is a national clearinghouse that provides personal responses to specific questions through its databases; referrals to other organizations or sources of help; prepared information packets; two publications, *News Digest* and *Transition Summary;* and technical assistance to parent and professional groups. NICHCY's informational materials are written at a level appropriate for professionals and most parents and contain references to further print materials and organizations. NICHCY can be contacted at:

NICHCY
PO Box 1492
Washington, DC 20013
(703) 893-6061 (voice and TDD)
(800) 999-5599 toll-free (recorded message)

NICHCY is also accessible to SpecialNet and SCAN users under the name NICHCY.

HEATH. HEATH (Higher Education and Training for People with Handicaps) provides services regarding postsecondary education for the handicapped. A newsletter, factsheets, a resource directory, and technical assistance are among HEATH's services. HEATH can be contacted at:

HEATH Resource Center
One Dupont Circle, NW
Washington, DC 20036-1193
(202) 939-9320 (voice and TDD)
(800) 544-3284

HEATH is accessible to SpecialNet users under the name HEATH.ACE.

National Clearinghouse for Professionals in Special Education. This clearinghouse provides information regarding the supply, demand, recruitment, and retention of professionals in the field of special education. You can contact:

National Clearinghouse for Professionals
   in Special Education
2021 K Street, NW, Suite 315
Washington, DC 20006
(202) 296-1800

National Referral Center. This service, maintained by the Library of Congress, will attempt to locate providers of free informaion on any subject anywhere in the world. Contact:

National Referral Center
Library of Congress
Washington, DC 20540
(202) 287-5670

Print Resources

There are several particularly noteworthy print resources that may be available from your local library or your employer's professional collection. *Exceptional Parent* magazine is one excellent source of information. Each issue is organized around a particular theme and contains a directory of providers of information and services regarding that theme. Directories appearing in past issues have included recreational organizations, model supported work programs, state maternal and child health programs, pediatric health care, computer resource information regarding communication devices, and technology resources. Annually, the September issue of *Exceptional Parent* carries a comprehensive directory of organizations that serve children and adults with disabilities and their families, including information and advocacy agencies, parent groups, and government and professional agencies.

Another service to subscribers of *Exceptional Parent* is the monthly Family Forum column. Through this column parents can seek to establish contacts with families with similar interests and concerns. *Exceptional Parent* can be contacted for subscription information at:

Exceptional Parent
PO Box 3000, Dept. EP
Denville, NJ 07834

Subscription rates at this writing are $16.00 per year for individuals and $24.00 per year for libraries, schools, and agencies. An additional $5.00 is charged for foreign orders.

The following are other important print resources worthy of mention.

Koek, K., Martin, S., & Novallo, A. (Eds.). (1989). *Encyclopedia of associations.* Detroit: Gale Research.
This set of three volumes (an index volume and two volumes of entries) lists over 25,000 national and international organizations. Examples of organizations of potential interest to school psychologists in the 1989 edition are groups concerned with cerebral palsy (seven), autism (three), and anorexia (five). The entries include (a) the organization's name, address, and phone number, (b) the number of members and staff size, (c) budget and organization (state, local chapters, etc.), (d) publications and affiliations and other groups, and (e) a description

of the organization, its purposes, and services.

Lesko, M. (1986). *Information USA*. New York: Viking–Penguin Books.
Lesko, M. (1988). *Information USA workbook* (2nd ed.). Chevy Chase, MD: Information USA.
These two works by Matthew Lesko describe the means that individuals can use to tap available sources of information and expertise, often at little or no cost. Information on government departments, free information and assistance and available hotlines and recorded messages, and utilizing your rights under the Freedom of Information Act are among the topics on information-seeking covered in these works.

Plas, J. M. (1981). The psychologist in the school community: A liaison role. *School Psychology Review, 10*(1), 72–81.
Plas, J. M., & Williams, B. (1985). Best practices in working with community agencies. In A. Thomas and J. Grimes (Eds.), *Best practices in school psychology*. Kent, OH: National Association of School Psychologists.
Locating information and enlisting assistance can be precursors to the orchestrating of resources. Theoretical and philosophical bases for the "liaison" role of school psychologists are discussed in these resources.

PARENT TRAINING AND INFORMATION CENTERS

Services of PTIs

Many states are served by a parent training and information center (PTI). PTIs provide a variety of beneficial services for parents of handicapped children, such as workshops, informational materials, and referral to other agencies. In addition to centers that serve individual states, several centers serve regionally or nationally. The following listing of parent training and information centers was provided by the National Information Center for Handicapped Children and Youth (NICHCY).

State Centers

Alabama

Special Education Action
   Committee, Inc.
PO Box 161274
Mobile, AL 36616
(205) 478-1208
(1-800) 222-7322 (AL)
Director: Carol Blades

Arizona

Pilot Parents, Inc.
2005 North Central Avenue
Suite 100
Phoenix, AZ 85004
(602) 271-4012
Director: Mary Slaughter

Arkansas

Arkansas Coalition for the
   Handicapped
519 East Fifth Street
Little Rock, AR 72202
(501) 376-3420
Director: Paul Kelly

California

Team of Advocates for Special
   Kids (TASK)
18685 Santa Ynez
Fountain Valley, CA 92708
(714) 962-6332
Director: Joan Tellefsen

Colorado

Parents Education and Assistance
   for Kids (PEAK)
6055 Lehman Drive, Suite 101
Colorado Springs, CO 80918
(719) 531-9400
Directors: Judy Manz & Barbara Buswell

Connecticut

Connecticut Parent Advocacy Center
c/o Mohegan Community College
Mahan Drive
Norwich, CT 06360
(203) 886-5250
(1-800) 445-CPAC (CT)
Director: Nancy Prescott

Delaware

PIC of Delaware, Inc.
700 Barksdale Rd. #6
Newark, DE 19711
(302) 366-0152
Director: Patricia Frunzi

Florida

Parent Education Network/Florida, Inc.
2215 East Henry Avenue
Tampa, FL 33610
(813) 238-6100
Director: Nadine Johnson

Georgia

Parents Educating Parents
Georgia/ARC
1851 Ram Runway, Suite 104
College Park, GA 30337
(404) 761-2745
Director: Mildred Hill

Illinois

Coordinating Council for Handicapped
    Children
20 East Jackson Boulevard, Room 900
Chicago, IL 60604
(312) 939-3513
Director: Charlotte Des Jardins

Designs for Change
220 South State Street, Room 1900
Chicago, IL 60604
(312) 922-0317
Director: Donald Moore

Indiana

Task Force on Education for the
    Handicapped, Inc.
833 Northside Boulevard, Bldg. 1-Rear
South Bend, IN 46617-2993
(219) 234-7101
Director: Richard Burden

Iowa

Iowa Exceptional Parent Center
33 North 12th Street
PO Box 1151
Ft. Dodge, IA 50501
(515) 576-5870
Director: Carla Lawson

Kansas

Families Together, Inc.
4125 Southwest Gage Center Drive
Topeka, KS 66604
(913) 267-6343
Mailing Address:
    PO Box 86153
    Topeka, KS 66686
Director: Patricia Gerdel

Louisiana

Project PROMPT
United Cerebral Palsy of
    Greater New Orleans
1500 Edwards Avenue, Suite O
Harahan, LA 70123
(504) 734-7736
Director: Sharon Duda

Maine

Special-Needs Parent Information
    Network (SPIN)
PO Box 2067
Augusta, ME 04330
(207) 582-2504
(1-800) 325-0220 (ME)
Director: Virginia Steele

Massachusetts

Statewide Parent Information
    Network (SPIN)
Federation for Children with
    Special Needs
312 Stuart Street, 2nd Floor
Boston, MA 02116
(617) 482-2915
(1-800) 331-0688 (MA)
Director: Artie Higgins

Michigan

Parents Training Parents Project
United Cerebral Palsy Assn. of
    Metropolitan Detroit
17000 West 8 Mile Road, Suite 380
Southfield, MI 48075
(313) 557-5070
Training Coordinator: Edith Sharp

(Michigan, continued)

Citizens Alliance to Uphold Special
  Education (CAUSE)
313 South Washington Square
Suite 040
Lansing, MI 48933
(517) 485-4084
Director: Eileen Cassidy

Minnesota

Parent Advocacy Coalition for
  Educational Rights (PACER)
4826 Chicago Avenue, South
Minneapolis, MN 55417-1055
(612) 827-2966
(1-800) 53-PACER (MN)
Directors: Marge Goldberg &
  Paula Goldberg

Mississippi

Association of Developmental
  Organizations of Mississippi
6055 Highway 18 South, Suite A
Jackson, MS 39209
(601) 922-3210
(1-800) 231-3721 (MS)
Director: Anne Presley

Montana

Parents, Let's Unite For Kids
Eastern Montana College
Montana Center for Handicapped
  Children
1500 North 30th Street
Billings, MT 59101-0298
(406) 657-2055
(1-800) 222-PLUK (MT)
Director: Katherine Kelker

Nevada

Nevada Specially Trained Effective
  Parents (N-STEP)
Nevada Association for the
  Handicapped
6200 West Oakey Boulevard
Las Vegas, NV 89102
(702) 870-7050
Coordinator: Charlene Rogerson

New Hampshire

New Hampshire Parent Information
  Center (PIC)
155 Manchester Street
PO Box 1422
Concord, NH 03301
(603) 224-6299
Director: Judith Raskin

New Jersey

Involve New Jersey, Inc.
26C 2 East Second Street
Moorestown, NJ 08057
(609) 778-0599
Director: Mary Callahan

Puerto Rican Congress of New Jersey
515 South Broad Street
Trenton, NJ 08611
(609) 989-8888
Director: Jose Morales

New Mexico

PL 94-142 Parent Training and
  Support Program
Protection and Advocacy System
2201 San Pedro, NE
Building 4, #140
Albuquerque, NM 87110
(505) 888-0111
Director: Beatriz Mitchell

Education for Indian Children with
  Special Needs (EPICS Project)
PO Box 788
Bernalillo, MN 87107
(505) 867-3396
Director: Randi Malach

New York

Advocates for Children of New York, Inc.
24-16 Bridge Plaza South
Long Island, NY 11101
(718) 729-8866
Director: Norma Rollins

Parents' Information Group/
  Parent Training Project
215 Bassett Street
Syracuse, NY 13210
(315) 478-0040
Director: Deborah Olson

Parent Network Center
1443 Main Street
Buffalo, NY 14209
(716) 885-1004
Director: Joan Watkins

North Carolina

Exceptional Children's Advocacy
  Council
PO Box 16
Davidson, NC 28036
(704) 892-1321
Director: Connie Hawkins

PARENTS Project
300 Enola Road
Morganton, NC 28655
(704) 433-2864
Director: Anita Hodges

Ohio

Tri-State Organized Coalition for
  Persons with Disabilities
SOC Information Center
3333 Vine Street, Suite 604
Cincinnati, OH 45220
(513) 861-2475
Director: Cathy Heizman

Ohio Coalition for the Education
  of Handicapped Children
933 High Street, Suite 220-H
Worthington, OH 43085
(614) 431-1307
Director: Margaret Burley

Oklahoma

Parents Reaching Out in Oklahoma
  (PRO-Oklahoma)
United Cerebral Palsy of Oklahoma, Inc.
2701 North Portland
Oklahoma City, OK 73107
(405) 948-1618
(1-800) PL 9-4142
Director: Connie Motsinger

Oregon

Oregon COPE Project
(Coalition in Oregon for Parent
  Education)
999 Locust Street, NE, #42
Salem, OR 97303
(503) 373-7477
Director: Cheron Mayhall

Pennsylvania

Parents Union for Public Schools
401 North Broad Street, Room 916
Philadelphia, PA 19108
(215) 574-0337
Director: Christine Davis

Parent Education Network
240 Haymeadow Drive
York, PA 17402
(717) 845-9722
Director: Louise Thieme

Puerto Rico

Associacion de Padres ProBienestar
de Ninos Impedios de PR, Inc.
Box 21301
Rio Piedras, PR 00928
(809) 765-0345
(809) 763-4665
Director: Carmen Selles Vila

South Dakota

South Dakota Parent Connection
4200 South Louise, Suite 205
Sioux Falls, SD 57106
(605) 361-0952
Director: Judie Roberts

Texas

Partnerships for Assisting Texans
  with Handicaps (PATH)
Parents Resource Network, Inc.
6465 Calder Avenue, Suite 202
Beaumont, TX 77707
(409) 866-4726
Director: Janice Foreman

Utah

Utah Parent Information Center (PIC)
4984 South 300 West
Murray, UT 84107
(801) 265-9883
Director: Jean Nash

Vermont

Vermont Information and Training
  Network (VITN)
Vermont/ARC
Champlain Mill, #37
Winooski, VT 05404
(802) 655-4016
Director: Connie Curtin

Virginia

Parent Education Advocacy Training
  Center
228 South Pitt Street, Room 300
Alexandria, VA 22314
(703) 836-2953
Director: Winifred Anderson

Washington

Parents Advocating Vocational
  Education (PAVE)
6316 South 12th Street
Tacoma, WA 98645
(206) 565-2266
(1-800) 5-PARENT (WA)
Director: Martha Gentili

Wisconsin

Parent Education Project
United Cerebral Palsy of SE Wisconsin
230 West Wells Street
Milwaukee, WI 53203
(414) 272-4500
Director: Liz Irwin

National Centers

NaDSAP

National DIRECTION Service Assistant
  Project (NaDSAP)
The National Parent CHAIN
90 East Wilson Bridge Road, Suite 297
Worthington, OH 43085
(614) 431-1911
Director: Donna Owens

NaDSAP is a technical assistance project
aimed at helping states design, develop,
and implement statewide systems of
DIRECTION services.

STOMP

Specialized Training of Military Parents
  (STOMP)
Georgia/ARC
1851 Ram Runway, Suite 104
College Park, GA 30337
(404) 767-2258
Coordinator: Kathy Mitten

Specialized Training of Military Parents
  (STOMP)
12208 Pacific Highway, SW
Tacoma, WA 98499
(206) 588-1741
Program Manager: Heather Hebdon

STOMP provides information and training
to military families with children who have
special educational needs. The project
assists parents in networking within the
military and civilian community. Services
are provided to families both in the United
States and overseas.

TAPP

Technical Assistance for Parent
  Programs (TAPP)
312 Stuart Street, 2nd Floor
Boston, MA 02116
(617) 482-2915
Director: Martha Ziegler

TAPP provides technical assistance for
programs that work with parents of
children with disabilities. Technical assistance is provided through the following
four regional centers:

New Hampshire Parent Information
  Center (PIC)
155 Manchester Street
PO Box 1422
Concord, NH 03301
(603) 224-6299
Director: Judith Raskin

Parent Advocacy Coalition for
  Educational Rights (PACER)
4826 Chicago Avenue, South
Minneapolis, MN 55417-1055
(612) 827-2966
(1-800) 53-PACER (MN)
Directors: Marge Goldberg &
  Paula Goldberg

Parents Educating Parents
Georgia/ARC
1851 Ram Runway, Suite 104
College Park, GA 30337
(404) 761-2745
Director: Mildred Hill

Parents Advocating Vocational
Education (PAVE)
6316 South 12th Street
Tacoma, WA 98645
(206) 565-2266
(1-800) 5-PARENT (WA)
Director: Martha Gentili

For information regarding these programs
contact:

U.S. Department of Education
Office of Special Education and
Rehabilitative Services (OSERS)
Office of Special Education Programs
Division of Personnel Preparation
Switzer Building, Room 4620
400 Maryland Avenue, SW
Washington, DC 20202
(202) 732-1032
Contact: Jack Tringo, Project Officer

PROTECTION AND ADVOCACY SERVICES

Each state has at least one agency
whose charge it is to advocate in behalf
of and provide legal services for handicapped persons. These agencies are
publicly funded but are, by law, independent of other government agencies. While
the services of protection and advocacy
agencies are most frequently sought by
handicapped individuals or by their
parents or guardians, these services are
also available to schools and professionals
working with handicapped children.
Protection and advocacy providers are
listed below.

Alabama

Suellen Galbraith, Program Dir.
Alabama DD Advocacy Program
PO Drawer 2847
The University of Alabama
Tuscaloosa, AL 35487-2847
(205) 348-4928 (E-Mail: PA.AL)

Alaska

David Maltman, Director
Advocacy Service of Alaska, 2nd Floor
325 East Third Avenue
Anchorage, AK 99501
(907) 274-3658 (E-Mail: PA.AK)

American Samoa

Minareta Thompson, Director
Client Assistance and Protection
and Advocacy Program
PO Box 3407
Pago Pago, AS 96799
9/011-684-633-2418

Arizona

Amy Gittler, Executive Director
Arizona Center for Law in the
Public Interest
363 North First Avenue
Suite 100
Phoenix, AZ 85003
(602) 252-4904 (E-Mail: PA.AZ)

Arkansas

Nan Ellen East, Exec. Director
Advocacy Services, Inc., Suite 504
12th & Marshall Streets
Little Rock, AK 72202
(501) 371-2171 (E-Mail: PA.AR)

California

Albert Zonca, Exec. Director
California Protection & Advocacy, Inc.
2131 Capitol Avenue
Sacramento, CA 95816
(916) 447-3324 or (800) 952-5746
(213) 481-7431
(E-Mail: PA.CA)

Colorado

Mary Anne Harvey, Executive Dir.
The Legal Center
455 Sherman Street, Suite 130
Dennver, CO 80203
(303) 722-0300 (E-Mail: PA.CO)

Connecticut

Eliot J. Dober, Exec. Director
Office of P&A for Handicapped
DD Persons
60 Weston Street
Hartford, CT 06120-1551
(203) 287-4300 or (800) 842-7303
(E-Mail: PA.CT)

Delaware

Christine Long, Administrator
Disabilities Law Program
144 East Market Street
Georgetown, DE 19947
(302) 856-0038
(E-Mail: PA.DE)

District of Columbia

Yetta W. Galiber, Exec. Director
Info. P&A Center for Handicapped
Individuals
300 I Street, NE, Suite 202
Washington, DC 20002
(202) 547-8081 (E-Mail: PA.DC)

Florida

Jonathan P. Rossman, Director
Governor's Commission on Advocacy for
Persons with Disabilities
Office of the Governor, Capitol
Tallahassee, FL 32301
(904) 488-9070 (E-Mail: PA.FL)

Georgia

Pat Powell, Exec. Director
Georgia Advocacy Office, Inc.
Suite 811
1447 Peachtree Street, NE
Atlanta, GA 30309
(404) 885-1447 or (800) 282-4538
(E-Mail: PA.GA)

Guam

Edward del Rosario
The Advocacy Office
PO Box 8830
Tamuning, GU 96911
10288-011-671/646-9026

Hawaii

Patty Henderson, Exec. Director
P&A Agency, Suite 1060
1580 Makaloa Street
Honolulu, HI 96814
(808) 949-2922 (E-Mail: PA. HI)

Idaho

Brent Marchbanks, Director
Idaho's Coalition of Advocates
for the Disabled, Inc.
1409 West Washington
Boise, ID 83702
(208) 336-5353 (E-Mail: PA.ID)

Illinois

Zena Naiditch, Director
P&A, Inc.
175 W. Jackson , Suite A-2103
Chicago, IL 60604
(312) 341-0022 (E-Mail: PA.IL)

Indiana

Ramesh K. Joshi, Director
Indiana Advocacy Services
850 North Meridian St., Suite 2-C
Indianapolis, IN 46204
(317) 232-1150 or (800) 622-4845
(E-Mail: PA.IN)

Iowa

Mervin L. Roth, Director
Iowa P&A Service, Inc.
3015 Merle Hay Rd., Suite 6
Des Moines, IA 50310
(515) 278-2502 (E-Mail: PA.IA)

Kansas

Joan Strickler, Executive Dir.
Kansas Advocacy & Protection Svs.
513 Leavenworth Street, Suite 2
Manhattan, KS 66502
(913) 776-1541 or (800) 432-8276
(E-Mail: PA.KS)

Kentucky

Gayla O. Peach, Director
Office for Public Advocacy
Division for P&A
151 Elkhorn Court
Frankfort, KY 40601
(502) 564-2967 or (800) 372-2988
(E-Mail: PA.KY)

Louisiana

Lois V. Simpson, Executive Dir.
Advocacy Center for the Elderly
    & Disabled, Suite 300A
1001 Howard Avenue
New Orleans, LA 70113
(504) 522-2337 or (800) 662-7705
(E-Mail: PA.LA)

Maine

Director
Advocates for the DD
2 Mullikan Court
PO Box 5341
Augusta, ME 04330
(207) 289-5755 or (800) 452-1948

Maryland

Steve Ney, Director
Maryland Disability Law Center
2510 St. Paul Street
Baltimore, MD 21218
(301) 333-7600

Massachusetts

Richard Howard, Project Director
DD Law Center for Massachusetts
Suite 925, 11 Beacon Street
Boston, MA 02108
(617) 723-8455 (E-Mail: PA.MA)

Michigan

Elizabeth W. Bauer, Exec. Dir.
Michigan P&A Service
109 W. Michigan
Suite 900
Lansing, MI 48933
(517) 487-1755 (E-Mail: PA.MI)

Minnesota

Steve Scott, Director
Legal Aid Society of Minneapolis
222 Grain Exchange Building
323 Fourth Avenue, South
Minneapolis, MN 55415
(612) 332-7301 (E-Mail: PA.MN)

Mississippi

Rebecca Floyd, Exec. Director
Mississippi P&A System for DD, Inc.
4793B McWillie Drive
Jackson, MS 39206
(601) 981-8207 (E-Mail: PA.MS)

Missouri

Carol D. Larkin, Director
Missouri P&A Services
211 B Metro Drive
Jefferson City, MO 65101
(314) 893-3333 or (800) 392-8667
(E-Mail: PA.MO)

Montana

Kris Bakula, Executive Director
Montana Advocacy Program
1410 8th Avenue
Helena, MT 59601
(406) 444-3889 or (1-800) 245-4743
(E-Mail: PA.MT)

Nebraska

Timothy Shaw, Executive Director
Nebraska Advocacy Services
522 Lincoln Center Building
215 Centennial Mall South
Lincoln, NE 68508
(402) 474-3183 (E-Mail: PA.NE)

Nevada

Holli Elder, Project Director
DD Advocate's Office, Suite B
2105 Capurro Way
Sparks, NV 89431
(702) 789-0233 or (800) 992-5715
(E-Mail: PA.NV)

New Hampshire

Donna Woodfin, Director
Disabilities Rights Center
94 Washington St.
Concord, NH 03301
(603) 228-0432 (E-Mail: PA.NH)

New Jersey

Sara Wiggins-Mitchell, Director
NJ Dept. of Public Advocate
Office of Advocacy for the DD
Hughes Justice Complex CN850
Trenton, NJ 08625
(609) 292-9742 or (800) 792-8600
(E-Mail: PA.NJ)

New Mexico

James Jackson, Director
P&A System, Inc.
2201 San Pedro, NE
Bldg. 4, Suite 140
Albuquerque, NM 87110
(505) 888-0111 or (800) 432-4682
(E-Mail: PA.NM)

New York

Clarence J. Sundram, Commissioner
NY Commission on Quality of Care for
   the Mentally Disabled
99 Washington Avenue
Albany, NY 12210
(518) 473-4057 (E-Mail: PA.NY)

North Carolina

Lockhart Follin-Mace, Director
Governor's Advocacy Council for
   Persons with Disabilities
1318 Dale Street, Suite 100
Raleigh, NC 27605
(919) 733-9250 (E-Mail: PA.NC)

North Dakota

Barbara D. Braun, Director
P&A Project for the DD
Governor's Council on Human
   Resources
State Capitol, 13th Floor
Bismarck, ND 58505
(701) 224-2972 or (800) 472-2670
(E-Mail: PA.ND)

Northern Mariana Islands

Felicaded Ogamuro, Exec. Director
Catholic Social Services, Box 745
Saipan, Commonwealth of the Northern
   Mariana Islands, 96950
10288-9-011-670-234-6981

Ohio

Carolyn Knight, Exec. Dir.
Ohio Legal Rights Svc., 6th Fl.
8 East Long Street
Columbus, OH 43215
(614) 466-7264 or (800) 282-9181
(E-Mail: PA.OH)

Oklahoma

Dr. Bob M. VanOsdol, Director
Protection & Advocacy Agency for DD
Osage Building, Room 133
9726 East 42nd
Tulsa, OK 74126
(918) 664-5883 (E-Mail: PA.OK)

Oregon

Elam Lantz, Jr. Executive Dir.
Oregon Advocacy Center
625 Board Trade Building
310 SW Fourth Avenue
Portland, OR 97204-2309
(503) 243-2081 (E-Mail: PA.OR)

Pennsylvania

Elmer Cerano, Executive Director
PA Protection and Advocacy, Inc.
116 Pine Street
Harrisburg, PA 17101
(717) 236-8110 or (800) 692-7443 or
   (800) 238-6222 (E-Mail: PA.PA)

Puerto Rico

Helga E. Santiago, Director
Planning Res. and Spec. Projects
Ombudsman for the Disabled,
   Governor's Office
Chardon Avenue, #916
Hato Rey, PR 00936
(809) 766-2333 or 766-2388

Rhode Island

Elizabeth Morancy, Exec. Director
Rhode Island P&A System, Inc.
55 Bradford St., 2nd Floor
Providence, RI 02903
(401) 831-3150 (E-Mail: PA.RI)

South Carolina

Louise Ravenel, Exec. Director
SC P&A System for the Handicapped,
Inc.
3710 Landmark Dr., Suite 208
Columbia, SC 29204
(803) 782-0634 or (1-800) 922-5225
(E-Mail: PA.SC)

South Dakota

Robert J. Kean, Executive Director
South Dakota Advocacy Project, Inc.
221 So. Central Avenue
Pierre, SD 57501
(605) 224-8294 or (800) 742-8108
(E-Mail: PA.SD)

Tennessee

Harriette J. Derryberry, Dir.
EACH, Inc.
PO Box 121257
Nashville, TN 37212
(615) 298-1080 or (800) 342-1660
(E-Mail: PA.TN)

Texas

Dayle Bebee, Executive Director
Advocacy, Inc.
7800 Shoal Creek Blvd., Suite 171-E
Austin, TX 78757
(512) 454-4816 or
(800) 252-9108 (special ed. calls)
(1-800) 223-4206 (all others)
(E-Mail: PA.TX)

Utah

Phyllis Geldzahler, Exec. Dir.
Legal Center for the Handicapped
455 East 400 South, Suite 201
Salt Lake City, UT 84111
(801) 363-1347 or (800) 662-9080
(E-Mail: PA.UT)

Vermont

William J. Reedy, Esq., Director
Vermont DD P&A, Inc.
12 North Street
Burlington, VT 05401
(802) 863-2881 (E-Mail: PA.VT)

Virginia

Carolyn White Hodgins, Director
Dept. of Rights for the Disabled
James Monroe Building, 17th Flr.
101 North 14th Street
Richmond, VA 23219
(804) 225-2042 (E-Mail: PA.VA)
(800) 552-3962 (TDD & Voice)

Virgin Islands

Russell Richards, Director
Center on Advocacy for the DD, Inc.
Apartment No. 2, 31A New Street
Fredericksted, St. Croix, VI 00840
(809) 772-1200 (E-Mail: PA.VI)

Washington

Barbara Oswald, Acting Director
1550 West Armory Way, Suite 204
Seattle, WA 98119
(206) 284-1037 (E-Mail: PA.WA)

West Virginia

Nancy Mattox, Executive Director
WV Advocates for the DD, Inc.
1200 Brooks Medical Bldg.
Quarrier Street, Suite 27
Charleston, WV 25301
(304) 346-0847 or (800) 642-9205
(E-Mail: PA.WV)

Wisconsin

Lynn Breedlove, Exec. Director
Wisconsin Coalition for Advocacy, Inc.
Suite 400
16 North Carroll St.
Madison, WI 53703
(608) 251-9600 or (800) 328-1110
(E-Mail: PA.WI)

Wyoming

Jeanne A. Kawcak, Executive Director
Wyoming P&A System, Inc.
2424 Pioneer Avenue, #101
Cheyenne, WY 82001
(307) 632-3496 or (800) 328-1110
(E-Mail: PA.WY)

National

Curtis L. Decker, Executive Director
National Association of Protection
and Advocacy Systems, Inc.
220 I Street, NE, Suite 150
Washington, DC 20201
(202) 546-8202 (E-Mail: PA.NAPAS)

EDUCATIONAL RESOURCES INFORMATION CENTER

The Educational Resources Information Center (EIRC) is a national information network that collects, organizes, and disseminates information on education-related topics. A monthly abstract journal, *Resources in Education*, is published by ERIC to report recently acquired reports. ERIC's database, the largest in the field of education in the world, can be accessed through many libraries and schools. ERIC can be contacted at:

Educational Resources Information
Center
National Institute of Education
1200 19th Street, NW
Brown Building
Washington, DC 20208
(202) 254-7934

ERIC operates 16 clearinghouses located at universities or professional organizations throughout the country. Each clearinghouse is responsible for a different area of education. These are listed below.

Adult and career vocation

ERIC Clearinghouse on Adult Career
and Vocational Education
Ohio State University
1960 Kenny Road
Columbus, OH 43210
(614) 486-3655

Counseling and personal services

ERIC Clearinghouse on Counseling and
Personal Services
University of Michigan
School of Education Building
Room 2108
Ann Arbor, MI 48109
(313) 764-9492

Early childhood education

ERIC Clearinghouse on Elementary and
Early Childhood Education
University of Illinois
805 W. Pennsylvania Avenue
Urbana, IL 61801
(217) 333-1386

Educational management

ERIC Clearinghouse on Educational
Management
University of Oregon
Library, Room 108
Eugene, OR 97403
(503) 686-5043

Handicapped and gifted children

ERIC Clearinghouse on the
Handicapped and Gifted Children
Council for Exceptional Children
1920 Association Drive
Reston, VA 22091
(703) 620-3660

Higher education

ERIC Clearinghouse on Higher
Education
One Dupont Circle
Suite #630
Washington, DC 20036
(202) 296-2597

Information resources

ERIC Clearinghouse on
Information Resources
Syracuse University
School of Education, Area of
Instructional Technology
130 Huntington Hall
Syracuse, NY 13210
(315) 423-3640

Junior colleges

ERIC Clearinghouse on Junior
Colleges
Powell Library, Room 96
405 Hilgard Avenue
Los Angeles, CA 90024
(213) 825-3931

Language and linguistics

ERIC Clearinghouse on Language
and Linguistics
Center for Applied Linguistics
3520 Prospect Street, NW
Washington, DC 20007
(202) 298-9292

Reading and communication skills

ERIC Clearinghouse on Reading and
Communication Skills
National Council of Teachers of English
1111 Kenyon Road
Urbana, IL 61801
(217) 328-3870

Rural education

Rural Education and Small School
ERIC Clearinghouse
New Mexico State University
Box 3AP
Las Cruces, NM 88003
(505) 646-2623

Science, mathematics, and environmental education

Clearinghouse for Science, Mathematics,
and Environmental Education
Ohio State University
1200 Chambers Road, Third Floor
Columbus, OH 43212
(614) 422-6717

Social science

ERIC Clearinghouse for Social Studies
University of Colorado
Social Science Education
855 Broadway
Boulder, CO 80302
(303) 492-8434

Teacher education

Clearinghouse on Teacher Education
American Association of Colleges
for Teacher Education
One Dupont Circle NW, Suite 610
Washington, DC 20036
(202) 293-2450

Tests, measurement and evaluation

ERIC Clearinghouse on Tests,
Measurements, and Evaluation
Educational Testing Service
Princeton, NJ 08540
(609) 921-9000, Ext. 5181

Urban education

ERIC Clearinghouse on Urban
Education
Box 40, Teachers College
Columbia University
525 W. 120th Street
New York, NY 10027
(212) 678-3433

HOTLINES AND TOLL-FREE NUMBERS

The following listing of hotlines and
toll-free numbers was provided by the
National Information Center for Handicapped Children and Youth (NICHCY). As
these numbers are subject to change, you
may wish to periodically contact NICHCY
for an updated list.

Adoption

National Adoption Center
1-800-TO-ADOPT

AIDS

National Gay Task Force AIDS
Information Hotline
1-800-221-7044

National Sexually Transmitted Diseases
Hotline
1-800-227-8922

Public Health Service AIDS Hotline
1-800-342-AIDS

Alcoholism

Alcoholism Hotline at AD Care Hospital
1-800-ALCOHOL
(if calling from New Jersey)
1-800-322-5525

National Clearinghouse for Alcohol and
Drug Information
1-800-662-HELP

Blindness/Vision

American Council for the Blind
1-800-424-8666

American Foundation for the Blind
1-800-AFBLIND

Job Opportunities for the Blind (JOB)
1-800-638-7518

National Association for Parents of the
Visually Impaired
1-800-561-6265

National Eye Care Project Hotline
1-800-222-EYES

National Library Services for the Blind
and Physically Handicapped
1-800-424-8567

National Retinitis Pigmentosa
Foundation
1-800-638-2300

Burn Victims

International Shriners Headquarters
1-800-237-5055
(if calling from Florida)
1-800-282-9161
(if calling from Canada)
1-800-361-7256

Cancer

AMC Cancer Information Line
1-800-525-3777

National Cancer Institute
Information Service
1-800-4-CANCER

Career Counseling

ERIC Clearinghouse on Adult Career
and Vocational Education
1-800-848-4815

Higher Education and Adult Training of
People with Handicaps
(HEATH Resource Center)
1-800-54-HEATH

Job Accommodation Network (JAN)
1-800-526-7234
(if calling from West Virginia)
1-800-526-4698

Job Opportunities for the Blind (JOB)
1-800-638-7518

National Committee for Citizens in
Education
1-800-NETWORK

Cerebral Palsy

United Cerebral Palsy Associations, Inc.
(UCPA) National Headquarters
(New York, NY)
1-800-USA-1UCP

UCPA Affiliate Relations Division
(Washington, DC)
1-800-USA-2UCP

UCPA Community Services Division
(Washington, DC)
1-800-USA-5UCP

Child Abuse

National Child Abuse Hotline
1-800-422-4453

Parents Anonymous Hotline
1-800-421-0353
(if calling from California)
1-800-352-0386

Cleft Palate

American Cleft Palate Educational
Foundation
1-800-24-CLEFT
(if calling from Pennsylvania)
1-800-23-CLEFT

Computers

Apple Office of Special Education
1-800-732-3131 (ext. 275)

AT&T Computers (General Sales)
1-800-247-1212

Center for Special Education
Technology
c/o Council for Exceptional Children
1-800-345-TECH

IBM National Support Center for
Persons with Disabilities
1-800-IBM-2133

Communication Disorders

American Speech–Language–
Hearing Association
(V/TDD) 1-800-638-8255

National Center for Stuttering
1-800-221-2483

Deaf–Blindness

National Information Center on
Deaf–Blindness
1-800-672-6720
(V/TDD) Extension 5289
(if calling from Washington, DC)
(V/TDD) 651-5289

Deafness/Hearing Impairments

Better Hearing Institute Hearing
HelpLine
(Voice) 1-800-424-8576

Captioned Films for the Deaf
(V/TDD) 1-800-237-6213

John Tracy Clinic on Deafness
(V/TDD) 1-800-522-4582

National Hearing Aid Society
Hearing Aid Helpline
(Voice) 1-800-521-5247

Occupational Hearing Services
(Dial A Hearing Screening Test)
(Voice) 1-800-222-EARS
(if calling from Pennsylvania)
(Voice) 1-800-345-3277

TRIPOD GRAPEVINE, Service for
Hearing Impaired
(V/TDD) 1-800-352-8888
(if calling from California)
(V/TDD) 1-800-346-8888

Diabetes

Juvenile Diabetes Foundation Hotline
1-800-223-1138

Diseases

Alzheimer's Disease and Related
Disorders Association
1-800-621-0379
(if calling from Illinois)
1-800-572-6037

American Leprosy Missions
(Hansen's Disease)
1-800-543-3131

Huntington's Disease Society of America
1-800-345-4372

Lupus Foundation of America
1-800-558-0121

National Association for Sickle Cell
Disease, Inc.
1-800-421-8453

National Cystic Fibrosis Foundation
1-800-344-4823

National Health Information Center
(NHIC)
1-800-336-4797

National Information Center for
Orphan Drugs and Rare Diseases
(NICODARD)
1-800-336-4797

National Organization for Rare
Disorders (NORD)
1-800-477-NORD

National Parkinson Foundation
1-800-327-4545
(if calling from Florida)
1-800-433-7022

Parkinson's Education Program
1-800-344-7877

Down Syndrome

National Down Syndrome Congress
1-800-232-NDSC

National Down Syndrome Society
1-800-221-4602

Drug Information

Drug Abuse
1-800-544-KIDS
(if calling from New Jersey)
1-800-225-0196

National Clearinghouse for Alcohol
and Drug Information
1-800-662-HELP

Parents Resource Institute for Drug
Education (PRIDE)
1-800-221-9746

Education

    Educators Publishing Service, Inc.
    (Specific Learning Disabilities)
    1-800-225-5750

    National Committee for Citizens in
    Education
    1-800-NETWORK

Employment

    Job Accommodation Network (JAN)
    1-800-526-7234
    (if calling from West Virginia)
    1-800-526-4698

    Job Opportunities for the Blind (JOB)
    1-800-638-7518

Equipment

    AT&T National Special Needs Center
    1-800-833-3232

Epilepsy

    Epilepsy Foundation of America
    1-800-EFA-1000

Financial Aid

    Federal Hill–Burton Free Care Program
    1-800-492-0359
    (if calling from Maryland)
    1-800-638-0742

    Financial Aid for Education Available
    from the Federal Government
    1-800-333-INFO

    Health Care Financing Administration
    1-800-638-6833
    (if calling from Maryland)
    1-800-492-6603

Growth Disorders

    Human Growth Foundation
    1-800-451-6434

Head Injury

    National Head Injury Foundation
    (for use by patients & their families
    only)
    1-800-444-NHIF

Health Information

    National Information System for
    Health Related Services
    1-800-922-9234

    National Health Information Center
    1-800-336-4797

Heart Disorders

    Association of Heart Patients
    HeartLine
    1-800-241-6993

Immunology

    National Jewish Center for Immunology
    and Respiratory Medicine
    1-800-222-5864

Kidney Disorders

    American Kidney Foundation
    1-800-638-8299
    (if calling from Maryland)
    1-800-492-8361

Learning Disabilities (dyslexia)

    Educators Publishing Service, Inc.
    Specific Language Disabilities
    (Dyslexia)
    1-800-225-5750
    (if calling from Maryland)
    1-800-792-5166

    Orton Dyslexia Society
    1-800-222-3123

Liver Disorders

    American Liver Foundation
    1-800-223-0179

Mainstreaming into the Community

    National Organization on Disability
    1-800-248-ABLE

Media

    Handicapped Media, Inc.
    1-800-321-8708

    Information Center for Special
    Education Media and Materials
    1-800-772-7372

Medical Devices

Practitioners' Reporting System
1-800-638-6725
(if calling from Maryland, call collect)
301-881-0256

Mental Retardation

American Association on Mental
Retardation
1-800-424-3088
(if calling from Washington, DC)
387-1968

Association for Retarded Citizens of
the United States (ARC)
1-800-433-5255

Missing Children

National Center for Missing and
Exploited Children
1-800-843-5678

Neurological Impairment/Paralysis

American Paralysis Association
1-800-225-0292

National Head Injury Foundation
(for use by patients & their
families only)
1-800-444-NHIF

National Headache Foundation
1-800-843-2256
(if calling from Illinois)
1-800-523-8858

National Spinal Cord Injury Hotline
1-800-526-3456
(if calling from Maryland)
1-800-638-1733

Nutrition

Beech-Nut Nutrition Hotline
1-800-523-6633

Gerber Products Co.
1-800-443-7237

Johnson & Johnson Baby Products
Information
1-800-526-3967

Organ Donors

The Living Bank
1-800-528-2971

Orthopedic Problems

International Shriners Headquarters
1-800-237-5055
(if calling from Florida)
1-800-282-9161

Rare Disorders

Cornelia deLange Syndrome
Foundation
1-800-223-8355

National Information Center for
Orphan Drugs and Rare Diseases
(NICODARD)
1-800-336-4797

National Organization for Rare
Disorders (NORD)
1-800-477-NORD

National Reye's Syndrome Foundation
1-800-233-7393
(if calling from Ohio)
1-800-231-7393

National Tuberous Sclerosis Association
1-800-CAL-NTSA

Rehabilitation

D. T. Watson Rehabilitation Hospital
1-800-233-8806

National Rehabilitation Information
Center (NARIC)
1-800-34-NARIC

Respiratory Disease

National Jewish Center for Immunology
and Respiratory Medicine Lung Line
1-800-222-LUNG

Spina Bifida

Spina Bifida Hotline
1-800-621-3141

Sudden Infant Death Syndrome (SIDS)

National Sudden Infant Death
Syndrome Foundation
1-800-221-SIDS

Suicide Prevention

National Adolescent Suicide Hotline
1-800-621-4000

Surgery

National Second Surgical Opinion
Program
1-800-638-6833

Telephone Usage for Persons with Disabilities

Tele-Consumer Hotline
1-800-332-1124
(if calling from Washington, DC)
223-4371

Toys (safe)

Consumer Product Safety Commission
1-800-638-2772

Trauma

American Trauma Society
1-800-556-7890

ORGANIZATIONS

The organizations and agencies listed below provide a wide variety of services to professionals, parents, and their children. The primary source of this listing is *Exceptional Parent* and the annual September issue should be consulted to ensure correct, up-to-date information.

National Organizations: Information and Advocacy

American Bar Association,
  Child Advocacy Center
1800 M St., NW
Suite 200
Washington, DC 20036

Canadian Association for Community
  Living
Kinsmen National Institute for
  Community Living
York University
4700 Keele St.
Downsview, Ontario
Canada M3J 1P3

Canadian Rehabilitation Council
  for the Disabled
One Yonge St.
Suite 2110
Toronto, Ontario
Canada M5E 1E5
(416) 862-0340

Challenge International
6719 Lowell Ave.
McLean, VA 22101
(703) 790-1616

Children's Defense Fund
122 C St. NW
Suite 400
Washington, DC 20001
(202) 628-8787

Coalition on Sexuality and
  Disability, Inc.
380 2nd Ave.
4th Floor
New York, NY 10010
(212) 242-3900

Congress of Organizations of the
  Physically Handicapped
16630 Beverly Ave.
Tinley Park, IL 60477-1904
(312) 532-3566

Digestive Diseases Clearinghouse
Box NDOIC
Bethesda, MD 20892
(202) 296-1138

Disability Rights Education and
  Defense Fund, Inc.
1616 P St. NW, Suite 100
Washington, DC 20036
(202) 328-5185

Disability Rights Education and
  Defense Fund, Inc.
2212 Sixth St.
Berkeley, CA 94710
(415) 644-2555

Especially Grandparents Newsletter
ARC of King County
2230 Eighth Ave.
Seattle, WA 98121
(206) 461-7800

International Shriners Headquarters
2900 Rocky Point
Tampa, FL 33607
(813) 885-2575

Kinsmen Rehabilitation Foundation of
British Columbia
2256 W. 12th Ave.
Vancouver, BC
Canada V6K 2N5
(604) 736-8841 (Voice)
(604) 738-0603 (TDD)

Learning How, Inc.
(formerly: Organization for Handicapped
Women)
P.O. Box 35481
Charlotte, NC 28235
(704) 376-4735

National Catholic Office for Persons
with Disabilities
P.O. Box 29113
Washington, DC 20017

National Center for Education in
Maternal and Child Care
38th & R Streets NW
Georgetown University
Washington, DC 20057
(202) 625-8400

National Center for Youth with
Disabilities
Adolescent Health Program
University of Minnesota
Box 721 — UMHC
Harvard Street/East River Road
Minneapolis, MN 55455
(612) 626-2825

National Easter Seal Society
2023 W. Ogden Ave.
Chicago, IL 60612
(312) 243-8400 (Voice)
(312) 243-8880 (TDD)

National Organization on Disability
910 16th St. NW
Washington, DC 20006
(202) 293-5960

National Self-Help Clearinghouse
33 W. 42nd St.
New York, NY 10036
(212) 840-1259

National Organizations: Specific Disability or Condition

Albinism/Hypopigmentation

National Organization for Albinism and
Hypopigmentation (NOAH)
4721 Pine St.
Philadelphia, PA 19143
(215) 471-2278

Allergies and Asthma

Asthma and Allergy Foundation of
America
1717 Mass. Ave. NW
Suite 305
Washington, DC 20036
(202) 265-0265

National Foundation for Asthma, Inc.
PO Box 30069
Tucson, AZ 85751-0069
(602) 323-6046

Amputation

National Amputation Foundation, Inc.
12–45 150th St.
Whitestone, NY 11357
(718) 767-0596

Arthritis

American Juvenile Arthritis
Organization (AJAO)
Arthritis Foundation, National Office
1314 Spring St. NW
Atlanta, GA 30309
(404) 872-7100

Ataxia

National Ataxia Foundation
600 Twelve Oaks Center
15500 Wayzata Blvd.
Wayzata, MN 55391
(612) 473-7666

(Ataxia, continued)

Friedreich's Ataxia Group in
   America, Inc.
PO Box 11116
Oakland, CA 94611
(415) 655-0833

Attention Deficit Disorders

Children with Attention Deficit
   Disorders (CHADD)
1859 N. Pine Island Road
Suite 185
Plantation, FL 33322
(305) 384-6869
(305) 792-8900

Autism

National Autism Hotline
Autism Services Center
Douglas Education Bldg.
10th Avenue & Bruce
Huntington, WV 25701
(304) 525-8014

National Society for Children and
   Adults with Autism
1234 Mass. Ave. NW
Suite 1017
Washington, DC 20005
(202) 783-0125

Birth Defects

Association of Birth Defect Children
3526 Emerywood Lane
Orlando, FL 32812
(407) 859-2821

March of Dimes Birth Defects
   Foundation
303 S. Broadway
Tarrytown, NY 10591
(914) 428-7100

National Birth Defects Center
30 Warren St.
Brighton, MA 02135
(617) 787-5958

National Network to Prevent
   Birth Defects
PO Box 15309
Washington, DC 20003
(202) 543-5450

Brain Diseases

Children's Brain Diseases Foundation
   for Research
350 Parnassus
Suite 900
San Francisco, CA 94117
(415) 566-5402
(415) 566-6259

Cancer

AMC Center
Information Center
1600 Pierce St.
Lakewood, CO 80214
(800) 525-3777

American Cancer Society
Tower Place
3340 Peach Tree Road, NE
Atlanta, GA 30026
(404) 320-3333

Cancer Information Clearinghouse
National Cancer Institute
9000 Rockefeller Pike
Bldg. 31, Room 10A21
Bethesda, MD 20205
(800) 638-6694

Candlelighters Childhood
   Cancer Foundation
1901 Pennsylvania Ave. NW
Suite 1001
Washington, DC 20006
(202) 659-5136

Cerebral Palsy

Canadian Cerebral Palsy Association
40 Dundas St. W
Suite 222, PO Box 110
Toronto, Ontario
Canada M5G 2C2
(416) 979-7923

United Cerebral Palsy Association
66 E. 34th St.
New York, NY 10016
(212) 481-6300
(800) USA-IUCP

Charcot–Marie–Tooth Disease

CMT International
(Charcot-Marie-Tooth Disease)
34 Bayview Drive
St. Catharines, Ontario
Canada L2N 4Y6
(416) 937-3851

Children Who Have Died

Compassionate Friends, Inc.
Box 3696
Oak Brook, IL 60522-3696
(312) 323-5010

Cleft Palate

Prescription Parents, Inc.
PO Box 426
Quincy, MA 02269
(617) 479-2463

Cornelia de Lange Syndrome

Cornelia de Lange Syndrome Foundation
60 Dyer Ave.
Collinsville, CT 06022
(203) 693-0159
(800) 223-8355

Cri du Chat (Cat Cry Syndrome)

The 5p-Society
11609 Oakmont
Overland, Park, KS 66210
(913) 469-8900

Cystic Fibrosis

Cystic Fibrosis Foundation
6931 Arlington Road,
Second Floor
Bethesda, MD 20814-5205
(301) 951-4422
(800) FIGHT CF

Diabetes

American Diabetes Association
National Service Center
PO Box 25757
1660 Duke St.
Alexandria, VA 22314
(703) 549-1500
(800) 232-3472

Canadian Diabetes Association
78 Bond St.
Toronto, Ontario
Canada M5B 2J8
(416) 362-4440

Juvenile Diabetes Foundation
  International
423 Park Ave. S
New York, NY 10016
(212) 889-7575
(800) 223-1138

Down Syndrome

Association for Children with
  Down Syndrome
2616 Martin Ave.
Bellmore, NY 11710
(516) 221-4700

Caring Inc.
PO Box 400
Milton, WA 98354
(206) 922-5680

National Down Syndrome Congress
1800 Dempster St.
Park Ridge, IL 60068-1146
(312) 823-7550
(800) 2232-6372

National Down Syndrome Society
141 Fifth Ave., Seventh Floor
New York, NY 10010
(212) 460-9330
(800) 221-4602

Dysauntonomia

Dysauntonomia Foundation, Inc.
20 E. 46th St.
Room 302
New York, NY 10017
(212) 949-6644

Dyslexia

National Institute of Dyslexia
3200 Woodbine St.
Chevy Chase, MD 20815
(301) 652-0942

Orton Dyslexia Society
724 York Road
Baltimore, MD 21204
(301) 296-0232
(800) 222-3123

Dystonia

Dystonia Medical Research Foundation
First City Bldg.
Suite 1800
777 Hornby St.
Vancouver, BC
Canada V6Z 1S4
(604) 661-4886

Dystonia Medical Research Foundation
8383 Wilshire Blvd.
Suite 800
Beverly Hills, CA 90211
(213) 852-1630

Dystrophic Epidermolysis Bullosa

Dystrophic Epidermolysis Bullosa
Research Association of America, Inc.
Kings County Medical Center
451 Clarkson Ave.
Building E, 6th Floor, E6101
Brooklyn, NY 11203
(718) 774-8700

Epilepsy

Epilepsy Foundation of America (EFA)
4351 Garden City Drive
Landover, MD 20785
(301) 459-3700
(804) EFA-1000

Facial Reconstruction

National Foundation for Facial
  Reconstruction
550 First Ave.
New York, NY 10016
(212) 340-6656

Fragile X Syndrome

National Fragile X Foundation
PO Box 300233
Denver, CO 80203
(800) 835-2246 ext. 58

Head Injuries

National Head Injury Foundation
333 Turnpike Road
Southboro, MA 01772
(617) 485-9950

Hearing Impaired

Alexander Graham Bell Association
  for the Deaf
3417 Volta Place, NW
Washington, DC 20007
(202) 337-5220

American Society for Deaf
  Children (ASDC)
814 Thayer Ave.
Silver Spring, MD 20910
(301) 585-5400

Better Hearing Institute
PO Box 1840
Washington, DC 20013
(800) 424-8576

Canadian Hearing Society
271 Spadina Road
Toronto, Ontario
Canada M5R 2V3
(416) 964-9595 (Vice)
(416) 964-2066 (TDD)

Deafpride, Inc.
1350 Potomac SE
Washington, DC 20003
(202) 675-6700

National Association of the
  Deaf (NAD)
814 Thayer
Silver Spring, MD 20910
(301) 587-1788

National Captioning Institute
5203 Leesburg Pike
Falls Church, VA 22041
(703) 998-2400
(800) 528-6600

National Hearing Aid Society
20361 Middlebelt
Livonia, MI 48152
(313) 478-2610
(800) 521-5247

National Information Center on
  Deafness
Gallaudet University
800 Florida Ave. NE
Washington, DC 20002
(202) 651-5051 (Voice)
(202) 651-5052 (TDD)

National Technical Institute for the
  Deaf at Rochester Institute of
  Technology
One Lomb Memorial Drive
PO Box 9887
Rochester, NY 14623
(716) 475-6400

Parents of John Tracy Clinic
806 W. Adams Blvd
Los Angeles, CA 90007
(213) 748-5481

Self-Help for Hard of Hearing
  People, Inc. (SHHH)
7800 Wisconsin Ave.
Bethesda, MD 20814
(301) 657-2249
(301) 657-2248

Signing Exact English (SEE) Center
  for the Advancement of Deaf Children
PO Box 1181
Los Alamitos, CA 90720
(213) 430-1467

Tripod Service for the Hearing Impaired
955 N. Alfred St.
Los Angeles, CA 90069
(213) 656-4904
(800) 352-8888

Heart Disorders

American Heart Association
7320 Greenville Ave.
Dallas, TX 75231
(214) 750-5300

Hemophilia

Canadian Hemophilia Society
100 King St. W, Suite 210
Hamilton, Ontario
Canada L8P 1A2
(416) 523-6214

National Hemophilia Foundation (NHF)
The Soho Bldg.
110 Greene St., Room 406
New York, NY 10012
(212) 219-8180

Hirschsprung's Disease

American Hirschsprung's Disease
  Association, Inc.
22½ Spruce St.
Brattleboro, VT 05301
(802) 257-0603

Hydrocephalus

Guardians of Hydrocephalus
  Research Foundation
2618 Avenue Z
Brooklyn, NY 11235
(718) 743-4473

Hydrocephalus Support Group
225 Dickinson St., H-893
San Diego, CA 92103
(619) 695-3139
(619) 726-0507

National Hydrocephalus Foundation
Route 1, River Road
Box 210A
Joliet, IL 60436
(815) 467-6548

Ileitis and Colitis

National Foundation for Ileitis and Colitis
444 Park Ave. S
New York, NY 10016
(212) 685-3440

Immune Deficiencies

Immune Deficiency Foundation (IDF)
PO Box 586
Columbia, MD 21045
(301) 461-3127

Incontinence

Help for Incontinent People (HIP)
PO Box 544
Union, SC 29379
(803) 585-8789

Intraventricular Hemorrhage

I.V.H. Parents
PO Box 56-1111
Miami, FL 33156
(305) 232-0381

Kidney Disorders

American Kidney Fund
6110 Executive Blvd.
Suite 1010
Rockville, MD 20852
(800) 638-8299

National Kidney Foundation, Inc.
432 Park Ave. S
New York, NY 10016
(212) 683-8018

Laurence-Moon-Biedl Syndrome

Laurence-Moon-Biedl Syndrome Network
122 Rolling Road
Lexington Park, MD 20653
(301) 863-5658

Learning Disabilities

Association for Children and Adults with
    Learning Disabilities
4156 Library Road
Pittsburgh, PA 15234
(412) 341-1515
(412) 341-8077

Foundation for Children with Learning
    Disabilities
99 Park Ave.
New York, NY 10016
(212) 687-7211

Leukemia

Leukemia Society of America
733 Third Ave., 14th Floor
New York, NY 10017
(212) 573-8484

Leukodystrophy

United Leukodystrophy Foundation, Inc.
2304 Highland Drive
Sycamore, IL 60178
(815) 895-3211

Little People

Little People of America, Inc.
PO Box 633
San Bruno, CA 94066
(415) 589-0695

Parents of Dwarfed Children
11524 Colt Terrace
Silver Spring, MD 20902
(301) 649-3275

Liver Disorders

Children's Liver Foundation, Inc.
76 South Orange Ave.
South Orange, NJ 07079
(201) 761-1111

Lowe's Syndrome

Lowe's Syndrome Association
222 Lincoln St.
West Lafayette, IN 47906
(317) 743-3634

Lung Diseases

American Lung Association
1740 Broadway
New York, NY 10019
(212) 315-8700

Lupus

American Lupus Society
23751 Madison St.
Torrance, CA 90505
(213) 373-1335

Lupus Foundation of America, Inc.
1717 Mass. Ave. NW, Suite 203
Washington, DC 20036
(800) 558-0121

Maple Syrup Urine Disease

Maple Syrup Urine Disease Family
   Support Group
RR 2, Box 24A
Flemingsburg, KY 41041
(606) 849-4679

Mental Retardation

Association of Retarded Citizens
   of the U.S.
2501 Avenue J
Arlington, TX 76011
(817) 640-0204
(800) 433-5255

Mucopolysaccharidoses

National Mucopolysaccharidoses
   Society
17 Kraemer St.
Hicksville, NY 11801
(516) 931-6338

Multiple Sclerosis

National Multiple Sclerosis Society
205 E. 42nd St.
New York, NY 10017
(212) 986-3240
(800) 822-3379

Muscular Dystrophy

Muscular Dystrophy Association
810 Seventh Ave.
New York, NY 10019
(212) 586-0808

Neurofibromatosis

National Neurofibromatosis
   Foundation, Inc.
141 Fifth Ave., Suite 7-S
New York, NY 10010
(212) 460-8980

Orphan Drugs/Rare Diseases

National Information Center for Orphan
   Drugs and Rare Diseases
PO Box 1133
Washington, DC 20013-1133
(800) 336-4797

National Organization for Rare Disorders
PO Box 8923
New Fairfield, CT 06812
(203) 746-6518

Osteogenesis Imperfecta

Osteogenesis Imperfecta Foundation, Inc.
PO Box 14807
Clearwater, FL 34629-4807
(813) 855-7077
(202) 872-1300

Ostomy

United Ostomy Association, Inc.
36 Executive Park, Suite 120
Irvine, CA 92714
(714) 660-8624

Parkinson's Disease

National Parkinson Foundation
1501 Ninth Ave. NW
Miami, FL 33136
(800) 327-4545

Peroneal Muscular Atrophy

National Foundation for Peroneal
   Muscular Atrophy
University City
Science Center
3624 Market St.
Philadelphia, PA 19104
(215) 387-2255

Prader-Willi Syndrome

Prader-Willi Syndrome Association
6490 Executive Blvd. E--102
St. Louis Park, MN 55436
(612) 933-0113

Rehabilitation

National Rehabilitation Association
633 S. Washington St.
Alexandria, VA 22314
(703) 836-0850/0852

(Rehabilitation, continued)

National Rehabilitation Information
  Center
4407 Eighth St. NE
The Catholic University of America
Washington, DC 20017
(202) 635-5826

World Rehabilitation Fund, Inc.
400 E. 34th St.
New York, NY 10016
(212) 340-6062

Rett Syndrome

International Rett Syndrome
  Association
8511 Rose Marie Drive
Fort Washington, MD 20744
(301) 248-7031

Reye's Syndrome

National Reye's Syndrome Foundation
462 N. Lewis
Bryan, OH 43506
(419) 636-2679

Scoliosis

National Scoliosis Foundation
PO Box 547
93 Concord Ave.
Belmont, MA 02178
(617) 489-0888/0880

Sickle Cell Disease

National Association for Sickle Cell
  Disease, Inc. (NASCD)
4221 Wilshire Blvd., Suite 360
Los Angeles, CA 90010
(213) 936-7205
(800) 421-8453

National Sickle Cell Research
  Foundation, Inc.
PO Box 8095
Houston, TX 77004
(713) 651-8071

Spina Bifida

Spina Bifida Association of America
1700 Rockville Pike #540
Rockville, MD 20852-1631
(301) 770-7222
(800) 621-3141

Spina Bifida Association of Canada
633 Wellington Crescent
Winnipeg, Manitoba
Canada R3M 0A8
(204) 452-7580

Spinal Cord Injuries

National Spinal Cord Injury
  Association
600 W. Cummings Pkwy.
Suite 2000
Woburn, MA 01801
(617)935-2722
(800) 962-9629

National Spinal Cord Injury Hotline
2201 Argonne Drive
Baltimore, MD 21218
(800) 526-3456

Spinal Muscular Atrophy

Families of Spinal Muscular
  Atrophy (SMA)
PO Box 1465
Highland Park, IL 60035
(312) 432-5551

Stress

Families of Children Under Stress
  (FOCUS)
PO Box 1058
Conyers, GA 30207
(404) 483-9845

Stuttering

National Center for Stuttering
200 E. 33rd St.
New York, NY 10016
(212) 532-1460
(800) 221-2483

National Stuttering Project
1269 Seventh Ave.
San Francisco, CA 94122
(415) 566-5324

Sudden Infant Death Syndrome

National Center for the Prevention of
  Sudden Infant Death Syndrome
330 N. Charles St.
Baltimore, MD 21201
(800) 638-7437

National Sudden Infant Death Syndrome
  (SIDS) Foundation, Inc.
8240 Professional Place
2 Metro Plaza, Suite 205
Landover, MD 20785
(301) 459-3388
(800) 221-SIDS

Tay-Sachs Disease

National Tay-Sachs and Allied
  Diseases Association
385 Elliot St.
Newton, MA 02164
(617) 964-5508

Technology-Dependent Children

Sick Kids Need Involved People
  (SKIP)
216 Newport Drive
Severna Park, MD 21146
(301) 647-0164

Terminal Illness

Children's Hospice International
1101 King St., Suite 131
Alexandria, VA 22314
(703) 684-0330

Tourette Syndrome

Tourette Syndrome Association
Park 50 Tech. Center
2001 Ford Circle, Suite G
Milford, OH 45150-2713
(513) 831-2976
(513) 543-2675

Trisomy 18, 13

Support Organization for Trisomy 18, 13
c/o Debbi Stutz
3648 W. Valley West Drive
West Jordan, UT 84088
(801) 569-1609

Tuberous Sclerosis

American Tuberous Sclerosis Association
PO Box 1305
Middleboro, MA 02346
(617) 947-8893
(800) 446-1211

National Tuberous Sclerosis
  Association, Inc.
4351 Garden City Drive
Suite 660
Landover, MD 20785
(301) 459-9888

Turner's Syndrome

Turner's Syndrome Society
Administrative Studies #006
4700 Keele St.
York University
Downsview, Ontario
Canada M3J 1P3
(416) 736-5023

Visually Impaired

American Council of the Blind
1010 Vermont Ave. NW
Suite 1100
Washington, DC 20005
(202) 393-3666
(800) 424-8666

American Foundation for the Blind
15 W. 16th St.
New York, NY 10011
(212) 620-2000

American Printing House for the Blind
1839 Frankfort Ave.
PO Box 6085
Louisville, KY 40206
(502) 895-2405

Canadian National Institute for the
  Blind
1929 Bayview Ave.
Toronto, Ontario
Canada M4G 3E8
(416) 486-2500

(Visually Impaired, continued)

Catholic Association of Persons with
   Visual Impairment
PO Box 29113
Washington, DC 20017

National Association for Parents of the
   Visually Impaired
PO Box 562
Camden, NY 13316
(315) 245-3442
(800) 562-6265

National Association for Visually
   Handicapped
22 W. 21st St., Sixth Floor
New York, NY 10010
(212) 889-3141

National Federation of the Blind
1800 Johnson St.
Baltimore, MD 21230
(301) 659-9314

National Society to Prevent Blindness
500 E. Remington Road
Schaumburg, IL 60173
(312) 843-2020

Recording for the Blind (RFB)
20 Roszel Road
Princeton, NJ 08540

Retinitis Pigmentosa (RP)
   Association International
PO Box 900
Woodland Hills, CA 91365
(818) 992-0500
(800) 344-4877

RP Foundation Fighting Blindness
1401 Mt. Royal Ave.
Fourth Floor
Baltimore, MD 21217
(301) 225-9400
(800) 638-2300

Williams Syndrome Association
PO Box 178373
San Diego, CA 92117-0910
(713) 376-7072

Parent Coalition Groups

Alabama

Special Education Action
   Committee, Inc.
2970 Cottage Hill Road
Suite 125
Mobile, AL 36606
(205) 478-1208
(800) 222-7322

Alaska

Southeast Regional Resource Center
210 Ferry Way, Suite 200
Juneau, AK 99801
(907) 586-6806

Arizona

Pilot Parents, Inc.
2005 N. Central #100
Phoenix, AZ 85004
(602) 271-4012

Arkansas

Focus Inc.
2917 King St., Suite C
Jonesboro, AR 72401
(501) 935-2750

Arkansas Coalition for the Handicapped
519 E. Fifth St.
Little Rock, AR 72202
(501) 376-0378

California

Multicultural Impact, Inc.
University Affiliated Program
Children's Hospital of L.A.
PO Box 54700
Los Angeles, CA 90054
(213) 669-2300

Parents Helping Parents
535 Race St. #220
San Jose, CA 95126
(408) 288-5010

Project COPE
9160 Monte Vista Ave.
Montclair, CA 91763
(714) 985-3116

Team of Advocates for Special
 Kids (TASK)
18685 Santa Ynez
Fountain Valley, CA 92708
(714) 962-6332

Colorado

Denver Association for Retarded
 Citizens
899 Logan
Suite 311
Denver, CO 80203
(303) 831-7733

Parent Education and Assistance for Kids
6055 Lehman Drive #101
Colorado Springs, CO 80918
(719) 531-9400

Connecticut

Connecticut Parent Advocacy Center
PO Box 579
East Lyme, CT 06333
(203) 886-5250
(800) 445-2722

Delaware

Parent Information Center of Delaware
700 Barksdale Rd. #6
Newark, DE 19711
(302) 366-0152

Florida

Broader Opportunities for the
 Learning Disabled (B.O.L.D.)
PO Box 546309
Surfside, FL 33154
(305) 866-3262

Parent Education Network/Florida
2215 E. Henry Ave.
Tampa, FL 33610
(813) 239-1179

Georgia

Parents Educating Parents (PEP)
Association for Retarded Citizens of
 Georgia
1851 Ram Runway
College Park, GA 30337
(404) 761-2745

Specialized Training of Military
 Parents (East)
1851 Ram Runway
College Park, GA 30337
(404) 767-2258

Illinois

Coordinating Council for Handicapped
 Children
20 E. Jackson, Room 900
Chicago, IL 60604
(312) 939-3513 (Voice)
(312) 939-3519 (TDD)

Designs for Change
220 South State St.
Suite 1900
Chicago, IL 60604
(312) 922-0317

Keshet
Jewish Parents of Children with
 Special Needs
PO Box 59065
Chicago, IL 60645
(312) 588-0551

Parentele
8331 Kimball Ave.
Skokie, IL 60076
(312) 677-3796

Parents of Chronically Ill Children
29 Lovell Valley Drive
Springfield, IL 62702
(217) 522-6810

Indiana

Task Force on Education for the
 Handicapped, Inc.
833 Northside Blvd.
Bldg. #1 Rear
South Bend, IN 46617-2993
(219) 234-7101

Iowa

Iowa Pilot Parents
33 No. 12th Street
PO Box 1151
Ft. Dodge, IA 50501
(515) 576-5870

(Iowa, continued)

Pilot Parents
1000 Sims
Council Bluffs, IA 51501
(712) 621-3884

Kansas

Families Together, Inc.
Box 86153
Topeka, KS 66686
(913) 273-6343

Kentucky

Kentucky Coalition for Career and
  Leisure Development
366 Waller Ave.
Suite 119
Lexington, KY 40504
(606) 278-4712

Maine

Maine Parent Federation, Inc.
PO Box 2067
Augusta, ME 04330
(207) 582-2504
(800) 325-0220

SPIN (Special-Needs Parent
  Information Network)
PO Box 2067
Augusta, ME 04330
(207) 582-2504
(800) 325-0220

Massachusetts

Federation for Children with
  Special Needs
312 Stuart St.
Second Floor
Boston, MA 02116
(617) 482-2915

Technical Assistance for Parent
  Programs (TAPP)
312 Stuart St.
Second Floor
Boston, MA 02116
(617) 482-2915

Michigan

Citizens Alliance to Uphold Special
  Education (CAUSE)
Parents Training Program
313 S. Washington Square
Suite 040
Lansing, MI 48933
(517) 485-4084

United Cerebral Palsy Association/Detroit
  Community Service Dept.
17000 W. Eight Mile Road
Suite 380
Southfield, MI 48075
(313) 557-5070

Minnesota

Parent Advocacy Coalition for
  Educational Rights
Pacer Center, Inc.
4826 Chicago Ave.
Minneapolis, MN 55417
(612) 827-2966

Mississippi

Association of Developmental
  Organizations of Mississippi
6055 Highway 18 S, Suite A
Jackson, MS 39209
(601) 922-3210

Mississippi Parent Advocacy Center
6055 Highway 18 S.
Jackson, MS 39209
(601) 922-3210

Montana

Parents, Let's Unite for Kids
1500 N. 30th Street
Billings, MT 59101
(406) 657-2055

Nevada

Nevada Association for the
  Handicapped
6200 W. Oakey Blvd.
Las Vegas, NV 89102-1142
(702) 870-7050

New Jersey

Involve New Jersey, Inc.
26 C2 East 2nd Street
Moorestown, NJ 08057
(609) 778-0599

New Hampshire

New Hampshire Coalition for
  Handicapped Citizens, Inc.
Parent Information Center
PO Box 1422
Concord, NH 03302
(603) 224-7005

Technical Assistance to Parent Programs
  Project (T.A.P.P.P.)
PO Box 1422
Concord, NH 03302
(603) 224-6299

New Mexico

Protection and Advocacy System
2201 San Pedro, NE
Bldg. 4, #140
Albuquerque, NM 87110
(505) 888-0111

Southwest Communication
  Resources, Inc.
PO Box 788
Bernalillo, NM 87004
(505) 867-3396

New York

Parent's Information Group for
  Exceptional Children, Inc.
129 Cheerwood Dr.
Baldwinsville, NY 13027
(315) 423-2735

Parents Coalition for Education
  of New York City
24-16 Bridge Plaza S
Lobby Floor
Long Island, NY 11101
(718) 729-8866

Parent Network Center
1443 Main Street
Buffalo, NY 14209
(716) 885-1004

Parents of Galactosemic Children, Inc.
1 Ash Court
New City, NY 10056

Western New York Association for the
  Learning Disabled
255 Elmwood St.
Kenmore, NY 14217
(716) 874-7200

North Carolina

Advocacy Center for Children's
  Education and Parent Training
  (A.C.C.E.P.T.)
PO Box 10565
Raleigh, NC 27605
(919) 294-5266

Exceptional Children's Advocacy Council
PO Box 16
Davidson, NC 28036
(704) 892-1321

Parents Project
300 Enola Rd.
Morganton, NC 28655
(704) 433-2864

Ohio

National Parent CHAIN, Inc.
933 High St., Suite 106
Worthington, OH 43805
(614) 431-1307 (Voice and TDD)

Ohio Coalition for the Education of
  Handicapped Chilren
933 High St.
Suite 106
Worthington, OH 43805
(614) 431-1307

Support Group for Monosomy 9P
c/o Jonathan Storr
43304 Kipton Nickle Plate Rd.
LaGrange, OH 44050
(216) 775-4255

Tri-state Organized Coalition for
  Persons with Disabilities
SOC Information Center
3333 Vine St., Suite 604
Cincinnati, OH 45220
(513) 861-2400

Oregon

Coalition in Oregon for Parent
   Education (COPE)
999 Locust St. NE #42
Salem, OR 97303
(503) 373-7477 (Voice/TDD)

Pennsylvania

Association for Retarded Citizens/
   Allegheny
1001 Brighton Road
Pittsburgh, PA 15233
(412) 322-6008

PA Association for Children and Adults
   with Learning Disabilities
Box 208
Uwchland, PA 19408
(215) 458-8193

Parent Education Network
240 Haymeadow Dr.
York, PA 17402
(717) 845-9722
(800) 522-5827

Parents Union for Public Schools
401 N. Broad St., Room 916
Philadelphia, PA 19108
(215) 574-0337

Puerto Rico

Asociacion de Padres Pro Beinstar
   de Ninos Impedidos de Puerto Rico, Inc.
   (APNI)
Box 21301
Rio Piedras, PR 00928
(809) 765-0345
(809) 763-4665

South Dakota

South Dakota Parent Connection
PO Box 84813
Sioux Falls, SC 57118-4813

Tennessee

E.A.C.H., Inc.
PO Box 121257
Nashville, TN 37212
(615) 298-1080
(800) 342-1660 (Voice/TDD)

Texas

Advocacy, Inc.
7800 Shoal Creek Blvd., 171-E
Austin TX 78757
(512) 454-4816

Association for Retarded Citizens
   of Texas, Inc.
833 Houston St.
Austin, TX 78756
(512) 454-6694

Early Parent Intervention Association
   for Retarded Citizens of Texas
910 Seventh St.
Orange, TX 77630
(409) 886-1363

PATH
6465 Calder Ave., Suite 202
Beaumont, TX 77707
(409) 866-4726

Utah

Utah Parent Information &
   Training Center
4984 S. 300 W.
Murray, UT 84107
(801) 265-9883
(800) 468-1160

Parents Involved in Education
Developmental Center for
   Handicapped Persons
Utah State University
DCHP UMC 6580
Logan, UT 84322
(801) 750-1172

Vermont

Vermont Association for
   Retarded Citizens
37 Champlain Mill
Winooski, VT 05404
(802) 655-4016

Virginia

Parent Educational Advocacy
   Training Center
228 South Pitt St.
Suite 300
Alexandria, VA 22314
(703) 836-2953

Washington

Parent to Parent Support
ARC of King County
2230 Eighth Ave.
Seattle, WA 98121
(206) 461-7800

Specialized Training of Military
  Parents (West)
12208 Pacific Hwy. SW
Tacoma, WA 98499
(206) 588-1741

Washington PAVE Parent-to-Parent
  Training Project
6316 S. 12th
Tacoma, WA 98465
(206) 565-2266 (V/TDD)

Wisconsin

Parent Education Project
United Cerebral Palsy of Southeastern
  Wisconsin
230 W. Wells St. #502
Milwaukee, WI 53203
(414) 272-4500/1007 (TTY)
(800) 472-5525

Government Agencies

Administration on Developmental
  Disabilities
Department of Health and Human
  Services
200 Independence Ave. SW
336E Humphrey Bldg.
Washington, DC 20201
(202) 245-2890

Closer Look/Parents' Campaign
  for Handicapped Children
1201 16th St., Suite 233
Washington, DC 20036
(202) 822-7900
(800) 522-3458

National Information Center for Children
  & Youth with Handicaps
PO Box 1492
Washington, DC 20013
(703) 893-6061
(800) 999-5599 (Recording)

National Institutes of Health
National Institute of Child Health
  and Human Development
Bldg. 31, Room 2A03
9000 Rockville Pike
Bethesda, MD 20892
(301) 496-3454

National Institutes of Health
National Institute of Neurological &
  Communicative Disorders
Bldg. 31, Room 8A-08
Bethesda, MD 20892
(301) 496-3454

National Library Service for the Blind
  and Physically Handicapped
Library of Congress
1291 Taylor St., NW
Washington, DC 20542
(202) 287-9286/87

National Health Information Center,
  Office of Disease Prevention and
  Health Promotion (ODPHP)
PO Box 1133
Washington, DC 20013-1133
(800) 336-4797

Office of Special Education and
  Rehabilitation Services
Clearinghouse on the Handicapped
U.S. Dept. of Education
330 E Street SW
Switzer Bldg.
Washington, DC 20202
(202) 732-1273
(202) 732-1245

President's Committee on Employment of
  the Handicapped
1111 20 St. NW
Room 636
Washington, DC 20036
(202) 653-5044
(202) 653-5050 (TDD)

Professional Organizations

American Academy for Cerebral Palsy &
  Developmental Medicine
PO Box 11086
Richmond, VA 23230-1086
(804) 282-0036

Association for the Care of
  Children's Health
3615 Wisconsin Ave. NW
Washington, DC 20016
(202) 244-1801

ACPA/CPF National Office
  (Cleft Palate)
1218 Grandview Ave.
University of Pittsburgh
Pittsburgh, PA 15261
((412) 481-1376
(800) 24-CLEFT

American Deafness and Rehabilitation
  Association
PO Box 55369
Little Rock, AR 72225
(501) 663-4617

Convention of American Instructors
  of the Deaf (CAID)
PO Box 2163
Columbia, MD 21045
(301) 461-9988

Academy of Dentistry for the
  Handicapped
211 E. Chicago Ave.
Suite 1616
Chicago, IL 60611
(312) 440-2660

National Foundation of Dentistry
  for the Handicapped
1600 Stout St.
Suite 1420
Denver, CO 80202-3132
(303) 573-0264

American Association of University
  Affiliated Programs for the
  Developmentally Disabled
8605 Cameron St.
Suite 406
Silver Spring, MD 20910
(301) 588-8252

National Association of Developmental
  Disabilities Councils
1234 Massachusetts Ave. NW
Suite 103
Washington, DC 20005
(202) 347-1234

Council for Exceptional Children
1920 Association Dr.
Reston, VA 22091
(703) 620-3660

National Education Association
1201 16 St. NW
Washington, DC 20036
(202) 833-4000

National Association for Hearing and
  Speech Action (NAHSA)
10801 Rockville Pike
Rockville, MD 20852
(301) 897-8682
(800) 638-8255

National Association for Home Care
519 C St. NE
Washington, DC 20002
(202) 547-7424

American Medical Association
535 N. Dearborn St.
Chicago, IL 60610
(312) 645-5000

National Mental Health Association
1021 Prince St.
Alexandria, VA 22314-2971
(703) 684-7722

Accreditation Council of Services for
  Persons with Mental Retardation
4435 Wisconsin Ave. NW
Washington, DC 20016
(202) 363-2811

American Association on Mental
  Retardation
1719 Kalorama Rd. NW
Washington, DCC 20009
(202) 387-1968

American Occupational Therapy
  Association, Inc.
1383 Picard Dr.
PO Box 1725
Rockville, MD 20850-4375
(301) 948-9626

American Orthotic and Prosthetic
  Association
717 Pendleton St.
Alexandria, VA 22314
(703) 836-7116

American Academy of Pediatrics
141 Northwest Point Blvd.
PO Box 927
Elk Grove Village, IL 60009-0927
(312) 228-5005

American Physical Therapy Association
1111 N. Fairfax St.
Alexandria, VA 22314
(703) 684-2782

National Association of Physical
   Therapists, Inc.
12601 Strothmore
Garden Grove, CA 92640
(213) 332-7755

American Psychiatric Association
1700 18 St. NW
Washington, DC 20009
(202) 682-6000

American Psychological Association
Office of Social and Ethical
   Responsibility
1200 17 St. NW
Washington, DC 20036
(202) 955-7727

Association of Medical Rehabilitation
Directors and Coordinators, Inc.
87 Elm St.
Framingham, MA 01701
(617) 877-0517

National Institute for Rehabilitation
   Engineering
PO Box T
Hewitt, NJ 07421
(201) 838-2500

Rehabilitation International
25 E. 21st St.
New York, NY 10010
(212) 420-1500

Council of State Administrators of
   Vocational Rehabilitation
PO Box 3776
Washington, DC 20007
(202) 638-4634

American Association for Rehabilitation
   Therapy, Inc.
PO Box 93
N. Little Rock, AR 72116

National Association of Private
   Residential Facilities for the
   Mentally Retarded
6400H Seven Corners Pl.
Falls Church, VA 22044
(703) 536-3311

American Association for
   Respiratory Care
11030 Ables Lane
Dallas, TX 75229
(214) 630-3540

National Association of Private Schools
   for Exceptional Children (NAPSEC)
1625 I Street, Suite 506
Washington, DC 20006
(202) 223-2192

Association for Persons with Severe
   Handicaps (TASH)
7010 Roosevelt Way, NE
Seattle, WA 98115
(206) 523-8446

American Council on Rural Special
   Education (ACRES)
Western Washington University
Bellingham, WA 98225
(206) 676-3576

National Association of State Directors
   of Special Education
1201 16 St. NW
Suite 404E
Washington, DC 20036
(202) 822-7933

American Speech-Language
   Hearing Association
10801 Rockville Pike
Rockville, MD 20852
(301) 897-5700

National Association of Social
   Workers
7981 Eastern Ave.
Silver Spring, MD 20910
(301) 565-0333